C.H. DENAULT

RECORDS OF
NORTH AMERICAN
BIG GAME

"THE CHADWICK RAM"

Harry Antis—1980

Donated by the artist to the Boone and Crockett Club for use in raising money for the National Collection of Heads and Horns by a limited edition print series made available to donors. Details may be obtained from the club office.

Records of North American Big Game

A BOOK OF THE BOONE AND CROCKETT CLUB
CONTAINING TABULATIONS OF OUTSTANDING NORTH AMERICAN
BIG GAME TROPHIES, COMPILED FROM DATA IN
THE CLUB'S BIG GAME RECORDS ARCHIVES.

EDITED BY WM. H. NESBITT AND
PHILIP L. WRIGHT

EIGHTH EDITION
1981
THE BOONE AND CROCKETT CLUB
ALEXANDRIA, VIRGINIA

Records of North American Big Game

Library of Congress Catalog Card Number: 81–68426
ISBN Number: 0–940864–00–2
Published July 1981

Second Printing April 1984

Published in the United States of America
by the
Boone and Crockett Club
205 South Patrick Street
Alexandria, Virginia 22314

This book is dedicated to the members
of the Club Committee that in 1949–1950
developed the Official Scoring System
for native North American big game

Samuel B. Webb, Chairman
Dr. Harold E. Anthony
Milford J. Baker
Frederick K. Barbour
Dr. James L. Clark
Grancel Fitz

Photography by Wm.H.Nesbitt

The Boone and Crockett Club medal(top), is normally awarded to trophies voted a place award at the Final Judging. In addition, an unusually outstanding specimen taken under excellent conditions of Fair Chase, may be awarded the Sagamore Hill medal(bottom), given by the Roosevelt family in memory of Theodore Roosevelt, Theodore Roosevelt, Jr., and Kermit Roosevelt.

FOREWORD

This is the eighth in the series of *Records of North American Big Game,* all of which have been published by the Boone and Crockett Club, with the exception of the seventh edition which was published jointly by the Boone and Crockett Club and the National Rifle Association. These volumes cover a span of 57 years beginning in 1932 and provide a faithful documentation of superior trophies collected on the North American Continent. The record book of 1952 was the first to incorporate the present scoring system which was adopted by the Boone and Crockett Club Records of North American Big Game Committee in 1950. While modest modifications have been made over the years to that basic system, it still stands as the essential criteria for determining the trophy value of heads and horns.

It is only appropriate that we recognize those Boone and Crockett members who have over the years provided the contributions of impetus and scientific review that has made the catalogue and scoring system of heads and horns what it is today. Men such as Prentiss Gray, Karl Frederick, James Clark, George Browne, Milford Baker, Frederick Barbour, Lt. Gen. Richard K. Mellon, Ernst von Lengerke, Robert C. Reeve, Harold Anthony and Bob Waters, all of whom have now left us, joined with Sam Webb, Don Hopkins, Duncan Hodgson, Elmer Rusten, Frank Cook and Phil Wright over time to establish and maintain the rules of scoring and the importance of fair chase as applied to the taking of North American big game.

As the native habitat of big game animals throughout North America is encroached upon by the requirements—and unfortunately sometimes the excesses—of modern society, adherence to the strict rules of Fair Chase becomes of paramount importance to all sportsmen and hunters if the many magnificent species which we are privileged to have available to us are to be maintained. Accordingly, extensive efforts are made to assure the Records of North American Big Game Committee that each trophy recorded was taken legitimately in every sense. This is not an easy task and in some instances has required lengthy and tenacious

FOREWORD

investigation by members of the committee. The work done by Harold Nesbitt over the last several years in this regard has been outstanding.

It is gratifying in the highest degree to note that the enlightened conservation and management activities of our state and federal fish and game agencies have kept the herds of North American big game in outstanding condition, despite increased hunting pressure and further encroachment on their native habitat. It is also worthy of note that very recent years have seen new world's records in black bear, mule deer, pronghorn antelope, mountain caribou, Alaska Yukon moose, and muskox. This obviously gives the lie to the frequently heard assertion that "great heads are a thing of the past". It's also a great tribute to the conservation work which has been done relative to North American big game—and the effectiveness of the big game conservation effort which has been and continues to be the primary thrust of Boone and Crockett Club activities.

Special thanks should be given to official measurers of the Boone and Crockett Club throughout the country, and to the panel of judges which served last year under Glenn St. Charles—namely William I. Crump, Glen C. Sanderson, Dean A. Murphy, Scott Showalter, Frank Cook, Phil Wright, and Bernard Fashingbauer. We extend our very special appreciation to Harold Nesbitt, Administrative Director, and Phil Wright, Chairman of the Records of North American Big Game Committee, for putting this fine new volume of the record book together. The Boone and Crockett Club is indebted to all who have contributed to this effort and to the dedicated sportsmen whose records lie herein.

J.S. Parker
President
Boone and Crockett Club

Contents

CONTENTS

Illustrations

ILLUSTRATIONS

RECORDS OF
NORTH AMERICAN
BIG GAME

8th Edition, 1981

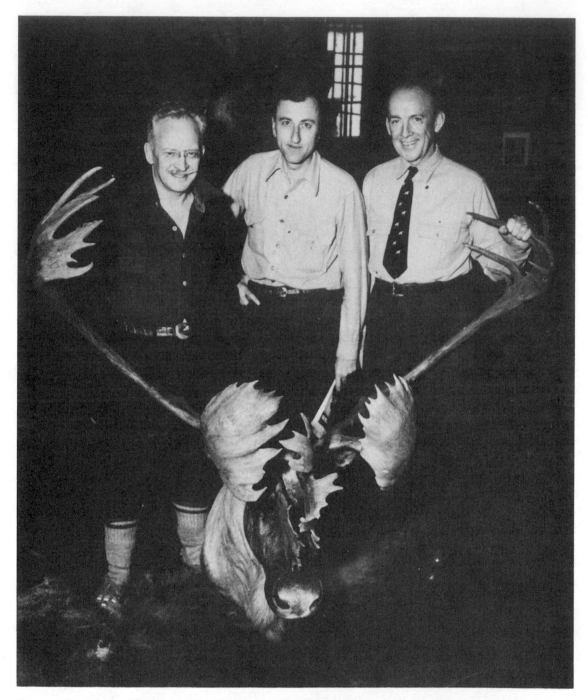

The magnificent Quebec-Labrador caribou shot by the Indian Zack Elbow in 1931. Also pictured here about 1951 are (l. to r.) Grancel Fitz, Samuel B. Webb, and Millford Baker, all members of the Boone and Crockett Club committee that developed the official scoring system.

Early History of the Boone and Crockett Records Keeping*

From time immemorial man has always been interested in comparisons. Our early ancestors had no measures or scales, but they were very interested in the size of the pre-historic animals they slew; perhaps not only because they feared large animals but also because a slain large beast brought fame and a badge of courage to the hunters. In the modern era, man's interest in records is boundless. In some fields we are statistically "slap happy."

Rowland Ward, the London firm of well-known taxidermists, has for many years published records book editions of the big game of the world. Up to and including the 1928 edition, North American big game was included in these editions. The value of these records was that they were the only lists available and recorded the owner and location where the animal was taken. The majority of these trophies were mounted by Rowland Ward and ranked by a single measurement either beam length or spread. Naturally these lists were very incomplete because many fine trophies adorned saloons and American hunters' homes. Other lists and ranking systems for European, Indian, Asiatic and African big game were devised by Kobylinski, Nadler, and Bieger; but all of these fell far short of ranking a trophy which the majority of sportsmen or guides would choose as being more desirable than another of the same species.

By and large, with a few exceptions, a single measurement of the horns, tusks or antlers of the European and Asiatic deer families suffices to give one a pretty good idea of the relative size of a trophy. However, our North American deer carry a more complex set of antlers. A European method which was never widely accepted was based on the idea that the finest specimen is one with the greatest amount of horn or antler material. Various ways were worked out for immersing the trophy in water and measuring the amount of water displaced.

---

*This article appeared in the 1977 records book and is repeated here for its unique historical perspective.

3

Aside from the fact that it would be extremely difficult to set up official checking stations, such a system would put a premium on freak trophies which are not typical or beautiful even though interesting. Pages 61 through 64 of the 1952 edition of *Records of North American Big Game* carry pictures of a palmated wapiti head, a dall sheep head with a solid left horn in the shape of a nautilus shell, and a three-tusked walrus. These are interesting freaks but cannot be considered beautiful trophies.

In 1932, under the auspices of the Boone and Crockett Club, the late Prentiss N. Gray published the first American edition of *Records of North American Big Game.* Only 500 copies of this book were printed by the Derrydale Press. High quality printing with black and white plates representing each species have made the book a collector's item. Mr. Gray ranked these trophies by a single measurement. For the first time two additional measurements plus number of points are listed—a long step forward over Rowland Ward's lists even though only the longest antler or horn is the only one listed. The trouble here is that the opposite antler or horn could be badly broken off, whereas the second ranked head might only be one half inch shorter and equally long on the opposite side. Mr. Gray recognized this fact and in the book's introduction wrote, "There is always the question of which measurements or combination of measurements should be regarded as constituting the record. We have not attempted to answer this question in this edition. . . . We recognize fully that no one dimension is the controlling factor, and we hope that eventually some fair method of scoring a head may be devised which is acceptable."

Shortly after the publication of the 1932 records book, Mr. Gray asked Dr. James L. Clark, head of the Dept. of Arts, Preparation and Installation at the American Museum of Natural History, if he would devise an equitable scoring system. Aside from Dr. Clark's professional background, he was a renowned hunter and had his own taxidermy studio, so he was extremely well qualified to do the job. He devised a system and, commencing in 1935, ran a North American big game competition annually in his studio for those trophies which he mounted. This was the initial scoring system with a total score. Great credit was accorded Dr. Clark for accomplishing this even though it had some flaws.

In 1939 the Boone and Crockett Club decided to publish a more pretentious record book called *North American Big Game.* It not only greatly expanded the 1932 record lists but contains authoritative chapters on each species, how to hunt them, and maps showing their geographical locations. It is an extremely valuable reference book. The editorial committee asked Mr. Grancel Fitz, a famous big game sportsman and an authority on North American big game, to write a chapter called Rating of Trophies for the 1939 book. Mr. Fitz gives Dr. Clark full credit for devising the first composite scoring system but does point out its flaws and makes constructive suggestions as to how to correct them.

Regrettably but perhaps understandably, Dr. Clark did not take kindly to these suggestions. Dr. Harold E. Anthony, at that time Director of the American Museum of Natural History and also a member of the editorial committee of the 1939 book, was blamed for suggesting that Mr. Fitz write the chapter instead of suggesting Dr. Clark. Owing to my consuming interest in this subject dating from the early 1920's, I knew all three of these men very well and could understand their respective differences of opinion. It became clear that unless some one could get these experts together to resolve their differences, no official standard scoring system would be established during their lifetime. I was determined to try to accomplish this, but four years in the Army Air Forces postponed my effort until after the War.

In 1949, I was able to get a committee together consisting of Drs. Anthony and Clark and Messrs. Fitz, Baker and Barbour. The last two were well-known big game sportsmen and amateur naturalists. Over a two-year period we had many meetings and finally hammered out 15 scoring charts to cover all North American big game species. These charts were duplicated and circulated to all heads of Conservation Departments in each big game state, Canadian provinces, some Zoology professors and over 100 qualified big game sportsmen asking for their comments and suggestions. We received a number of replies, some good suggestions and some impractical ones. The most impractical one came from a game biologist who insisted that the only fair way to grade the bears was by measuring the length of the femur bone. We told him politely that some of us knew where the femur bone was, but that the large majority of sportsmen did not. We also mentioned the difficulty of removing it.

All recommendations were carefully considered by the committee; some were adopted. We were constantly aware of the necessity of keeping the system as simple as possible while still having it accurately evaluate the overall excellence of a trophy. We regretted the length of the deer charts, particularly the caribou and non-typical deer charts, but found no way to simplify them further. Final proofs were mailed to all who received the initial mailing, and we turned them over to the Boone and Crockett Club with the understanding that remeasuring of all known trophies that would exceed the established minimum scores would commence; and that the Club would hold North American Big Game competitions to turn up more trophies and to promote selective hunting. (The 17th competition was held recently). The remeasuring job and that of educating official measurers here, in Canada, and in Mexico was begun. Mr. Fitz and I personally remeasured all trophies in the National Collection of Heads and Horns, the Philadelphia Academy of Natural Sciences, the Smithsonian Institution and many, many others. The results of this work, in addition to the records, charts and excellent photographs of all established world's record trophies at that time, were published in the 1952 edition of *Records of North American Big Game*. The response to the official system was virtually unanimous in favor of it. Today it is the universal standard used everywhere. Many states and Canadian provinces conduct their own competitions using this system with lower minimum scores. The acceptance of it by the hunting public and sports writers is the criterion of its success.

Since 1952 a few minor changes in the instructions for taking measurements have been made in the interest of clarification. Minimum scores have been raised from time to time in some categories. Human nature being what it is, a panel of judges is required to check measurements recorded by individuals or other official measurers located all over North America. An error may be very minor but it could substantially change a trophy's ranking, particularly in the records of bears and cats. New editions of the records book are published periodically, the complete set consists of 1932, 1939, 1952, 1958, 1964, 1971, 1977, and 1981 publications. All but the last edition are out of print. Copies of early editions can be found occasionally through sporting book dealers.

Samuel B. Webb of Shelburne, Vt., was chairman of the committee which established the Official Scoring System for the Club in the late 1940s. For many years he was a member of the Records of North American Big Game Committee, and he served as its Chairman.

A great number of the trophies shown in the early records books were measured personally by Webb and his close friend, the late Grancel Fitz. He was closely involved with the National Collection of Heads and Horns for many years and played a key role in its transfer from the New York Zoological Society to the Boone and Crockett Club.

He retired as Vice President of the Marsh-McLennan Co. of New York several years ago.

He regularly hunted big game in Alaska during the 1930s, and had both moose and caribou in several of the early record books.

The Current Records Keeping Program

PHILIP L. WRIGHT

HISTORY

The first formal recognition of outstanding North American big game by the Boone and Crockett Club was in the 1932 records book. The 1939 records book further expanded the content of the earlier book and listed many more trophies. The ranking was based on a single measurement: the length of the longer antler or horn in most categories, the greatest spread in moose and the greatest length of the skull of bears, cougar and jaguar. Samuel B. Webb was chairman of a special Club committee named after World War II to devise and to obtain approval of a broader, more comprehensive system for evaluating and ranking major North American big game trophies. Included on this committee were Dr. James L. Clark and Grancel Fitz, each of whom had devised his own system of scoring trophy heads. The successful efforts of Webb to effect a compromise between these two men and their systems, described in another chapter in this book, resulted in the Official Scoring System adopted in 1950.

In 1947, the first "competition" (as it was called) resulted in invitations to the owners of outstanding trophies to submit their specimens for evaluation by a panel of judges. This was followed in 1948 and 1949 by similar programs. These first three competitions resulted in 137 awards being made, all on the basis of a single measurement of horn, antler, or skull length.

The fourth competition in 1950 was the first based on the use of the new Official Scoring System. This new system was extensively critiqued and applied before publication of the 1952 records book. The basic score charts were circulated to more than 250 experienced sportsmen, guides, authors, taxidermists, game officials and scientists for evaluation. The more than 500 trophies of the fourth and fifth competitions of 1950 and 1951 were evaluated by the new system, with satisfactory results. Trophies listed in previous editions of the records book and those recognized in the first three competitions were reevaluated by the new system, including new minimum scores, before they were included in the 1952 edition. The third edition of the records book is then really the "first" for most considerations and uses.

It is the first records book published with trophy scores derived by use of the Official Scoring System adopted by the Boone and Crockett Club in 1950.

The real worth of the work of the special committee that established the Official Scoring System is brought out by the fact that no major changes have been made to the scoring system since its adoption. Thousands of persons applying this system on hundreds of thousands of trophies have failed to discern major faults needing correction in the system.

The first 10 competitions were conducted at the American Museum of Natural History, New York City, and the award winning trophies were displayed there. The 11th through the 14th competitions were conducted at the Carnegie Museum in Pittsburgh, each accompanied by public exhibitions of the invited trophies that lasted several weeks.

In 1973, the Boone and Crockett Club signed a formal agreement with the National Rifle Association (NRA) to cosponsor the records keeping, with the competitions being renamed "awards programs" to better indicate the goal of trophy recognition. The 15th, 16th and 17th awards programs (1974 through 1980) were conducted during this period under the cosponsorship title of the North American Big Game Awards Program (NABGAP). The 15th Awards were in Atlanta in 1974; the 16th in Denver in 1977; and the 17th in Kansas City, Mo. in 1980.

On January 1, 1981, after several months of discussion by representatives of both organizations, the Boone and Crockett Club reassumed full and complete responsibility for all aspects of the records keeping and records books, and NABGAP was officially dissolved. On reexamining their objectives and priorities, both organizations decided that the Club alone was best prepared to handle the obligations of the records keeping.

The name "Boone and Crockett" has long been synonymous with trophy North American big game. The long-time records keeping for native big game is but one of the many conservation activities of the Boone and Crockett Club. Its forefront role in conservation activities and leadership during this century is well documented in the book *An American Crusade for Wildlife,* by the late James B. Trefethen, a Boone and Crockett member.

Starting with the Competition of 1947, the supervision of the records keeping has been assigned to the Club's North American Big Game Committee. The chairmen of this committee were successively: Harold E. Anthony, Samuel B. Webb, Robert S. Waters, Elmer M. Rusten, Jack S. Parker, and Philip L. Wright. When the NRA and the Club began cooperative sponsorship in 1973, William Harold Nesbitt was hired by the NRA to conduct the records program. With the termination of the cooperative agreement at the end of 1980, the Club named Nesbitt Administrative Director, and he continues to conduct the program under the direct supervision of the Records Committee.

This edition is the first published by the Club after reassuming sole responsibility for the records keeping on January 1, 1981. Records books are generally published after completion of two Awards Programs (six years of trophy entry) or when significant changes have occurred in trophy rankings or in the categories and requirements. All accepted trophy score charts are entered in the records archives, with their data being accepted for publication in the next edition of the records book, barring unforeseen circumstances.

Over the years the records books have become valuable references for trophy hunters, wildlife managers, and serious students of big game populations. This edition adds the accepted trophies of the 17th Awards entry period (1977–1979) to the listings published in the 7th edition, bringing the total to nearly 7,000 individual trophies in 31 categories. Trophy rankings are revised by the results of the 16th and 17th Awards, and five new world's records are recognized.

MINIMUM SCORES

The minimum scores for trophy listings were raised periodically from 1950 to 1968, as more information on the maximum sizes of trophies became available (see summary on adjacent page). This resulted each time in the dropping of some trophies from the listings. Although some of the lists are now long, the committee has not raised the minimum entry scores since 1968 because in most categories these minimums are very difficult to attain. One class where the minimum entry score is likely to be raised in the future is muskox, as most trophy animals taken from Nunivak Island score above the present minimum. If minimum entry scores are raised in the future it will be done at the start of an awards entry period, with details being properly publicized. Since 1968 only one additional trophy category has been recognized, that of Roosevelt's elk, bringing the current total of categories recognized to 32. Of course, in some categories (such as walrus and jaguar) current federal regulations preclude hunting and therefore possible entry of trophies.

TROPHY BOUNDARIES

The records keeping now recognizes 32 categories of native North American big game. This is an increase of one from the 1977 book, with the new category for Roosevelt's elk added in 1980. All trophies must be taken in North America, north of the south boundary of Mexico. For records keeping, Greenland is considered part of North America.

Sometimes the boundaries used for record keeping correspond to the boundaries of zoological subspecies, but in many cases they do not. The geographical boundary of the diminutive Coues's whitetail in southwestern New Mexico, central and south Arizona, and north central Mexico, corresponds precisely to the geographical range of that single subspecies. This category has been recognized by the records program since the 1932 records book. There have been described, however, a total of 30 subspecies of whitetail deer in North America, including the Coues'. No specialist has attempted to assemble sample specimens from throughout the vast range of the whitetail deer over most of the U.S. and southern Canada to determine the extent of geographical variation, and therefore the validity of many of these forms remains in doubt. Large symmetrical antlers in the regular whitetail trophy categories, both typical and non-typical, are known from a vast area extending from Texas northward to British Columbia and east across the continent to Nova Scotia and then south to Georgia and back to Texas. At least six different subspecies names have been applied to the whitetails within this huge range, but the great uniformity in antler configuration and size suggests that some if not all of these subspecies may not be valid.

The wapiti or American elk ranges primarily in the Rocky Mountains of western Canada

Summary of Minimum Entry Scores, 1950–1981

Category	1950	1951	1953	1961	1963	1968	1980
black bear	20				19	21	
grizzly bear	23					24	
Alaska brown bear	27					28	
polar bear	20			25	26	27	
jaguar	12				14	14½	
cougar or mountain lion	12				14	15	
Atlantic walrus	100	95				95	
Pacific walrus	115	100				100	
wapiti or American elk	340	330			360	375	
Roosevelt's elk							290
mule deer (typical antlers)	165		170	175	185	195	
mule deer (non-typical antlers)	195		200		225	240	
Columbian blacktail deer	135	100			110	130	
whitetail deer (typical antlers)	140		150		160	170	
whitetail deer (non-typical antlers)	160				180	195	
Coues' whitetail deer (typical antlers)	90				105	110	
Coues' whitetail deer (non-typical antlers)						120	
Canada moose	180				185	195	
Alaska-Yukon moose	205	200			215	224	
Wyoming or Shiras moose	155	150				155	
mountain caribou	310	350			375	390	
woodland caribou	300	295				295	
barren ground caribou	330	350			375	400	
Quebec-Labrador caribou						375	
pronghorn	60	70	75		80	82	
bison	100				110	115	
Rocky Mountain goat	47				49	50	
barren ground muskox	90					90*	
Greenland muskox	90					90*	
bighorn sheep	170	175				180	
desert sheep	150				155	168	
Dall's sheep	160				168	170	
Stone's sheep	160				165	170	

*In 1977, both muskox consolidated into a single category

and the U.S. But, on the west coast of northern California, western Oregon, western Washington, and Vancouver Island, British Columbia, a distinct subspecies, Roosevelt's elk, occurs in sizable numbers. Roosevelt's elk, although larger and darker in color than its Rocky Mountain relative, has shorter, thicker and smaller antlers. No known Roosevelt's elk has antlers large enough to reach the minimum score required for the Rocky Mountain list. After repeated requests from interested sportsmen who hunt this fine animal, the Records Committee established a new class for Roosevelt's elk at the Club's 1979 meeting. Roosevelt's elk trophies scoring 290 or more points can now be entered in the records, and the panel of judges that will assemble for the 18th Awards in the spring of 1983 will score the top few submitted and name a World's Record. Roosevelt's elk have been transplanted to Afognak and Raspberry Islands in Alaska, and specimens from Alaska can also be entered in this new category. In the Riding Mountain area of western Manitoba and eastern Saskatchewan, a third subspecies, *Cervus elaphus manitobensis,* occurs. The few large trophies of this subspecies are eligible for listing in the American category.

The classification of the caribou and reindeer of the world has now been thoroughly studied by Dr. Frank Banfield, a Boone and Crockett Club member. He places all of the living forms of caribou and reindeer of northern Eurasia, as well as North America, in a single species, but recognizes a number of subspecies in different geographical regions. Caribou trophies from the southern Yukon and the Mackenzie Mountains of Northwest Territories have been assigned in previous editions of the records book to the barren ground category. But guides and trophy hunters have been aware for some time that these animals resembled caribou of northern British Columbia rather than those of Alaska and northern Yukon. On the basis of the work of Dr. Banfield, and with input from big game biologists working in the Yukon and Northwest Territories, the Records Committee voted in 1978 to move the boundary separating these two classes northward. Thus, caribou trophies taken in the southern third of the Yukon and in the Mackenzie Mountains of the Northwest Territories will be classed as mountain caribou in this and future editions (see trophy listing section for details of boundary).

The bighorn sheep which range in suitable habitat from western Alberta and eastern British Columbia southward to Sonora and the tip of the Baja Peninsula in Mexico are classified into several subspecies. For records keeping purposes trophy animals of this species are broken into two categories: Rocky Mountain and desert. Listing specimens of four subspecies together in the desert sheep category has proven satisfactory. The Rocky Mountain category consists largely of one subspecies, *Ovis canadensis canadensis;* the Audubon subspecies of eastern Montana and the western Dakotas disappeared in the early part of the century before the modern period of trophy hunting. There is presently no special class for the so-called California bighorn, actually a misnomer because the main range of this form was originally from Oregon and Washington northward into southcentral British Columbia and it occurred only in the northeastern corner of California. The original populations of this sheep in Oregon and Washington have been extirpated, but transplants of stock from southcentral British Columbia were used to restock suitable ranges in these states and in western North Dakota where Audubon's sheep once roamed. Some of these transplants have been successful, and trophy hunting on a very limited basis has been reinstituted. The

Photograph by William J. Reneau

Larry Raveling stands by his magnificent non-typical whitetail deer at the 16th Awards trophy display, held in Denver, Colorado in 1977.

Photograph by Wm. H. Nesbitt

One of the highlights of the 17th Awards trophy display (Kansas City, Missouri, 1980), was the presence of four magnificent Alaska Yukon moose racks, each entered at an entry score higher than the world record at that time.

Records Committee has been requested to establish a new category for this subspecies, *Ovis canadensis californica,* but there are very limited numbers of trophies being harvested and insufficient information available on which to take such action at this time. Some trophies of *californica* from British Columbia are listed in this record book with the Rocky Mountain animals. Probably horns of fully matured examples of *californica* are slightly smaller than those of *canadensis.*

<h2 style="text-align:center">FAIR CHASE</h2>

The concept of Fair Chase, of avoiding available but unfair advantage that would deprive the animal of using its normal escape mechanisms, took its early written form in the 1893 Boone and Crockett Club publication, *American Big Game Hunting.* In it, Theodore Roosevelt set forth that, "The term 'Fair Chase' shall not be held to include killing bear, wolf, or cougar in traps, nor 'fire hunting' nor 'crusting' moose, elk or deer in deep snow, nor killing game from a boat while it is swimming in the water, nor killing deer by any other method than fair stalking or still hunting." The foresight contained in this statement is striking when one remembers that these practices were not unlawful in the 1890's. This was a distinct step toward formation of higher standards of sportsmanship afield.

Rapid advances in the field of transportation in the 1940's and 1950's forced a further definition of the Fair Chase concept in a written form adopted in 1963. That statement, printed on the back of the score charts, reads: "Spotting or herding land game from the air, followed by landing in its vicinity for pursuit, shall be deemed UNFAIR CHASE and unsportsmanlike. Herding or pursuing ANY game from motor-powered vehicles shall likewise be deemed Unfair Chase and unsportsmanlike." Hunters entering trophies eligible for Competition were required to sign a statement specifying that the above methods were not used in taking the trophy scored on the chart. Pickups and unknown origin trophies were excluded from this requirement, for obvious reasons.

This basic statement was again revised in January 1968, to include the use of electronic communications for attracting, locating or observing game, or guiding the hunter to such game, as unfair chase, and such conditions were organized into three statements that precede the certification statement of the hunter. The hunter's statement was also expanded to include acknowledgement that all local game laws or regulations were followed in the hunt. Beginning on January 1, 1975, the hunter's signature of the Fair Chase Statement was required to be witnessed by a Notary Public. This is further verification of the serious intent of the Fair Chase requirements for entries.

A fourth statement of unfair chase conditions was approved for implementation as a requirement for the 17th Awards entry period (1977–1979). This additional statement specifies as unfair chase, "Hunting game confined by artificial barriers, including escape-proof fencing, or hunting game transplanted solely for the purpose of commercial shooting".

Thus, the Fair Chase Statement required for hunter-taken entries in the 17th Awards and later entry periods has four statements of unfair chase conditions that specifically disqualify trophies for possible awards and publication. Violation of the intent or substance of the Fair Chase concept may also disqualify trophies. Such cases are considered on an individual basis by the Records Committee, and its decision is final in such matters. The current Fair Chase Statement is reproduced in the score chart section of this book.

THE AWARDS PROGRAM

The first five competitions were held at yearly intervals from 1947 to 1951. The next seven were conducted at two-year intervals, and since 1970 they have been conducted at three-year intervals. The 15th (1974) and succeeding ones have been designated as "Awards" programs rather than "Competitions" to better state the purpose of the post-entry period activities, that of awarding recognition to fine trophies and excellent conditions of hunting.

In addition to being accepted for publication in the next edition of the records book, trophies accepted during an Awards Program entry period are also eligible to be invited to the final judging of invited trophies. The owners of the few top entries, as determined by entry scores in each category, are usually invited to send their trophies to a selected location after the close of each entry period. There, a select Panel of Judges, picked from the ranks of the 300-plus Official Measurers, remeasure each trophy carefully. When all remeasurement is completed, the Judges Panel carefully evaluates both the final score and the hunting story for each trophy before voting a possible award. Should the Judges' remeasurement change the entry score for a trophy, the Judges' scoring stands as final for both awards and future publication in the records book(s).

Awards available to invited trophies are the Boone and Crockett Club medal and/or certificate. Both the medal and certificate are normally given to trophies voted a place, while the certificate only is given for Honorable Mention and Merit. Trophies collected more than five years before the close of the entry period are eligible for a certificate only. Over the years, the 17 recognition programs have recognized only 1300 trophies, making the awards truly symbolic of trophy excellence.

It is important to remember that the awards are given in recognition of both trophy excellence and a high attainment of ethical hunting conditions. For that reason, only Fair Chase trophies are normally invited to the final judging. However, in the case of record or near-record pickups and trophies of unknown origin, these may be invited for necessary verification of their score and rank by the Judges Panel.

In addition to the Boone and Crockett Club medal and certificate, there are occasional awards of the Sagamore Hill Award to truly outstanding trophies certified by the Judges Panel. This medal is given by the Roosevelt family in memory of Theodore Roosevelt (founder and first president of the Boone and Crockett Club), and his sons, Theodore Jr., and Kermit. This award is made for truly exceptional trophies, the taking of which the Records Committee believes to have been in undisputed Fair Chase. The Sagamore Hill Award is the highest award given by the Club and only 12 have been made since the initial one in 1949. The last trophy to be recognized by this award was the new world's record mountain caribou scoring 452 points that was entered in the 16th Awards Program by Gary Beaubien. The Boone and Crockett Club has also made three awards of the Sagamore Hill Award to Club members for distinguished devotion to the objectives of the Club.

Photograph by Doug Pifer

The 17th Awards Panel of Judges and Consultants. Standing (l. to r.) are: W. Harold Nesbitt (NABGAP Coordinator), Scott M. Showalter (J.), Philip L. Wright (C.), Dean M. Murphy (J.), Frank Cook (C.), Bernard M. Fashingbauer (C.), and William I. Crump (J.). Kneeling beh nd the Ken Best new world's record moose rack are Glen C. Sanderson (J.), and Glenn St. Charles (Chairman of Judges Panel).

The Awards are presented at a banquet that is associated with the public display of trophies certified for awards. These trophy displays have proven very popular with the public, offering an unequaled opportunity to view outstanding specimens of our native big game. Usually, the public display is continued for several days after the banquet so that the public can view the trophies and their awards.

The final scores and awards given to invited trophies in an Awards Program are summarized in photo brochures prepared for each awards banquet. Photos are included of first place winners in most categories, along with useful information about the program. Copies of the 15th (1971–1973), 16th (1974–1976), and 17th (1977–1979) Awards photo brochures can be purchased from the Club's office, but previous brochures are currently out of print.

TROPHY ENTRY PROCEDURES

Trophy entry begins with an official entry measurement, taken by a currently listed Official Measurer for the Club. In order to standardize shrinkage, trophies must dry under natural atmospheric conditions for a minimum of 60 days prior to official measurement. Lists of Official Measurers are available, on request, from the Club office. As measurers volunteer their services, an appointment to have the trophy measured must be made at the measurer's convenience, and the trophy owner is responsible for transporting the trophy to and from the measurer's address.

Trophies that have been entered in a previous B & C or NABG Awards Program, or in a Boone and Crockett Club Competition, are not eligible for further entry. Trophies in the deer, wapiti, caribou, and moose categories, in which the spread measurement is part of the score, are *not* eligible for entry if their skulls have been split. Also ineligible are trophies in which the measurable material has been repaired or restored.

In 1974 the Records Committee voted to encourage the submission of a tooth with each entered trophy and to request unmounted rack weights for elk, moose and caribou and tusk weights for walrus. Teeth of most big game species develop an annulus each year in the cementum layer surrounding the root, which can be counted to determine the age in years, using a microscope. The information on rack and tusk weights was desired so that North American trophies can be better compared with their European counterparts, which are generally scored by methods differing from the Boone and Crockett Club system. Quite a number of teeth have been submitted and sectioned, but the sample is not large enough to draw valid conclusions at this time. Hunters are encouraged to be aware of the desirability of saving a lower jaw or tooth from record class animals and to record unmounted rack and/or tusk weights for submission with their entires.

After the entry measurement confirms that the trophy meets or exceeds minimum score, the following materials are forwarded with the score chart original to the records office to constitute an entry in the 18th Awards (1980–1982):
   —$20.00 entry fee
   —a notarized signature of the 1977 revised Fair Chase Statement (except pickups and unknown origin trophies)

—a completed Hunter, Guide, and Hunt Information Form

—a copy of the hunting license and/or big game tags (except pickups and unknown origin trophies)

—sharply focused photos (no slides) of the front, right side, and left side of the horns, antlers, or tusks; for cat and bear, the front, right side, left side, and top of the clean, dry skull

Trophy owners are encouraged to measure their own trophies, to see if an official entry measurement is warranted. If an owner's measurement shows the trophy to be well below the required minimum score, there is obviously no need to proceed further. All that is needed to make such a rough measurement is a quarter-inch-wide steel measuring tape and a copy of the correct score chart for the category. The score charts include instructions that will cover measurement of the most usual cases of trophy development. All necessary forms for trophy entry, including the score charts, are supplied to the Official Measurers. In addition, the score charts are available to the general public at a cost of 25¢ each to cover postage. If score charts are ordered, the number of charts for each category must be clearly specified, and payment must accompany the order.

Orders for score charts, submission of entry materials and all correspondence concerning present or past trophy records keeping and the records book(s) should be directed to:

Boone and Crockett Club
205 South Patrick Street
Alexandria, Virginia 22314

Philip L. Wright, Professor of Zoology and Wildlife Biology at the University of Montana, joined the faculty in 1939. For 14 years he was Chairman of the Zoology Department and for several years Director of the Wildlife Technology Program. In 1980 he held the Maytag Chair in Zoology at Arizona State University. He has B.S. and M.S. degrees from the University of New Hampshire and a Ph.D. in Zoology from the University of Wisconsin.

In 1950 he was appointed one of the original Official Measurers by the Boone and Crockett Club. He has served successively as judge, chairman of the judges, and consultant at the Awards Programs of 1971, 1974, 1977, and 1980. A Boone and Crockett Club member since 1971, he serves on the Conservation Committee and is Chairman of the Records of North American Big Game Committee.

The author of numerous scientific publications in mammalogy and ornithology, he is currently a Trustee of the American Society of Mammalogists, and a former Director. He is a Fellow of the American Association for the Advancement of Science, and a member of the American Ornithologists Union, the Wildlife Society, the Audubon Society, the National Rifle Association, the Explorer's Club, and the Sierra Club among others.

He has hunted extensively in Montana and British Columbia, and also in Northwest and Yukon Territories, Alaska, and Africa. He has a mule deer listed in the 1958 records book.

Stories Behind the New World's Records

WM. H. NESBITT

Five new world's records are recognized in this edition of the records book. Two of these are the result of the de-ranking of long-standing records, allowing the second-place trophy to advance to world record status. The other three are new entries accepted during the 17th Awards entry period of 1977–1979, the latest to be shown in this edition of the records book.

Two of the new world's records are pick-ups. They are included, as are all other non-hunter-taken trophies, to enhance the scientific value of the records and to complete the standard by which sportsmen can judge their best trophies.

Robert J. F. Decker, an employee of the Canadian Wildlife Service, found the new world's record muskox on the Perry River, N.W.T., on July 12, 1979. This tremendous specimen scores 122 points, far exceeding the previous world record of 115⅖. The previous record was a specimen taken by I.S. Wombath at Ellsemere Land, N.W.T. in 1900. Decker's muskox was awarded a certificate of merit at the 17th North American Big Game Awards (1980) in recognition of its outstanding trophy excellence. In addition to the new world record, there are a number of other very fine muskox specimens that are recognized in this edition, many as a result of the very successful management program established for the muskox herd of Nunivak Island, Alaska.

Merill Daniels and Alma Lund found the new world's record black bear skull about seven miles east of Ephraim, Utah, on July 1, 1975. It was an old carcass and they were unable to determine the cause of death. When the entry score chart was received for this trophy, it was greeted with skepticism since its score exceeded that of the previous world record trophy by more than an inch. With the concurrence of the trophy owners, the skull was shipped to Washington, D.C., where it was examined by experts at the Smithsonian Institution. Their assessment, after careful comparisons with type specimens and other identification criteria, was that this was indeed a bonafide black bear skull. This trophy, scoring 23¹⁰⁄₁₆, was awarded a Certificate of Merit in recognition of its outstanding trophy character at the 17th North American Big Game Awards (1980). Its score places it well ahead of the previous record trophy taken by Rex W. Peterson in 1970 in San Pete County, Utah, and scoring 22⁶⁄₁₆.

Kenneth Best, a native of Alaska, had the unusual good fortune of taking two trophies during 1978 that not only made the records book but were recognized with first place awards in their respective categories at the 17th North American Big Game Awards (1980). His barren ground caribou, from Becharof Lake, Alaska, was recognized as best in its category, while his Alaska-Yukon moose was recognized as being not only the best in its category, but also a new world's record. Best's moose was taken near McGrath, Alaska, on an early September hunt. Its final score of 255 moves it ahead of the previous world record taken by Bert Klinberger at Mt. Susitna, Alaska, in 1961 at a score of 251. Best was not really looking for a record moose when he came upon this giant; it was just hunter's luck. Best shot his moose with a 7mm magnum, using a 175 grain reload. His trophy provided a very unusual ending to a hunt that came close to never beginning.

In early September 1978, Art Beatie and Best were having a casual conversation. Beatie mentioned that a mutual friend, Brent Jones, had a raft and camp set up on the Innoko River that Jones and his party of hunters were going to abandon shortly. Best suggested that they fly there and take advantage of the camp and raft to do some moose hunting. Neither of them was very enthusiastic about the trip, as Beatie had heard that hunting was slow in the area. A couple of days before Jones was due to break camp, Best called Beatie and they decided to fly their small airplanes up the Innoko for a pleasure trip, with no real intention of hunting. Arriving on September 7, they found Jones and his party had experienced little luck and were mainly hunting the upper river. Best and Beattie decided that the excellent weather merited a float trip down the river for some fishing and perhaps a shot at a meat moose.

Most of the next day was spent loafing and saying goodbye to the Jones' party, whose trip was over. That afternoon, Best and Beattie flew their planes 40 miles downstream, leaving Beattie's to be their transportation back from the float trip. No game was spotted on the trip down or back, as weather conditions were generally foggy and rainy, with poor visibility.

The following morning, the weather had improved to a typical Alaska fall morning with everything soaked and a 12 ft. ceiling hovering over the willows. At 7:30 A.M., well-dressed in raingear, the hunters left in their 12 ft. raft.

About two hours downstream, they came to a very long sandbar, covered with willow brush. Best suggested that they get out and hunt the thicket for moose. They hunted for roughly an hour, occasionally raking the bushes with a branch to try to call in any bulls present but to no avail. Perhaps there were no bulls in the area, or perhaps it was still early for the rut. Back in the raft, they traveled downstream for another 45 minutes. As they rounded a sharp curve in the river, they saw a moose on a sandbar, feeding on the edge of a willow patch. He was about 300 yards away, hind quarters to them, and with his head in the bushes. They floated to within 150 yards, but he still didn't offer a good target. When they were within 75 yards, the moose vanished into the woods.

The hunters paddled to shore with their eyes glued to the bushes, hoping he had not been spooked. Failing to see him when they reached land, the two moved into the brush. Best raked a willow with a piece of driftwood, waiting for an answer that did not come. Working slowly, they came to a long, narrow clearing about 75 ft. wide, which branched off in two directions. Best moved eastward, while Beattie took the west fork. Best had traveled perhaps

Kenneth Best with his huge moose rack, soon after his hunt near McGrath, Alaska.

100 yds., when he spotted the moose. He was browsing about 40 ft. from Best, on the opposite side of a thick willow patch. Best watched him browse for several minutes, not clearly seeing his huge antlers. Finally, through a hole in the brush, Best took a clear shot at what he thought was the neck. At the roar of the 7mm mag., the moose ran about 60 ft. into the center of the clearing and sat down. This gave Best time for a second shot, which he placed in the neck, bringing the moose down.

Upon reaching him, Best found that his first shot had hit the moose in the shoulder, a good but not fatal hit. Best admired the six-foot antlers as he waited for his partner. He had shot many a meat moose but never a trophy such as this.

After Beattie arrived and started butchering the moose, Best went back to the raft for his camera to record the event. After butchering, the meat was loaded in game bags and hung by the riverbank. Best then carried the 78 inches and 73 pounds of skull and antlers to the raft, bulling his way several hundred yards through the thick alders and willows to the riverbank. All the way, he asked himself if it was really worth it. He was still a bit unsure until he got his trophy scored officially and realized he might just have the new world's record; then, it was all worth it.

The new world record mountain caribou, scoring 452 points, was taken on the Turnagain River, B.C., on September 15, 1976 by Garry Beaubien.

The Beaubien party, including his father, his 12-year-old son, and his 13-year-old daughter, left Dease Lake on horseback on September 8, after a week of preparations. They were outfitted with four saddle horses and two pack horses. They headed east from Dease Lake in weather that remained beautiful the entire trip. Caribou were spotted on the second day out, so they made a good camp on the third day, hunting from there for two days. At this camp, they looked at two herds numbering 20 animals and more, each. Although there were some nice bulls, there were not the large ones that they were seeking.

They broke camp after the second day's hunt, heading farther east. On the seventh day out, they left the main trail to move up a long side valley. There they spotted a herd with a huge bull, about five miles from them, up the side of the mountain. After looking the herd over with a spotting scope, they decided to make camp to try to get close enough to stalk the big bull.

Since it was still early in the afternoon, camp was quickly made and the pack horses were left in camp. They rode up the mountain, through heavy brush, until about 5:00 P.M. when they tied their horses and Beaubien and his father began their stalk.

The herd included 20 cows and 5 bulls, all feeding on the side hill. The biggest bull was very impressive. Checking the wind, Beaubien and his father worked to within 200 yards. When the bull looked directly at them, Beaubien's father, who they had already agreed would take the shot, took careful aim and squeezed the trigger. The bull took two jumps and fell dead. Then, something totally unexpected happened.

From over a little knoll 200 yards to their left, 10 bulls appeared on the horizon, with a massive bull in the lead. After a quick look at Beaubien and his father, the huge bull led the other nine back over the ridge and out of sight.

Hardly believing what he had just seen, Beaubien ran to the knoll as fast as he could and

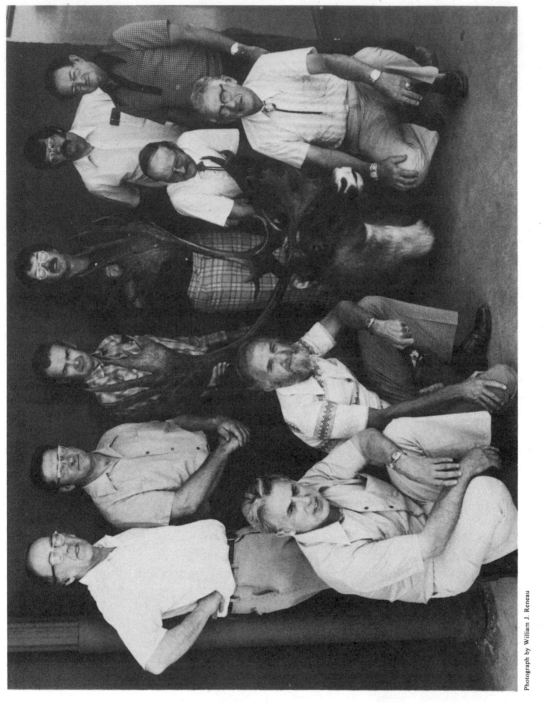

Photograph by William J. Reneau

The 16th Awards Panel of Judges and Consultants. Standing (l. to r.) are: Philip L. Wright (Chairman of Judges Panel), Frank Cook (C.), James W. Straley (J.), Scott M. Showalter (J.), W. Harold Nesbitt (NABGAP Coordinator), Dean M. Murphy (J.). Kneeling (l. to r.) are: Glenn St. Charles (J.), Bernard M. Fashingbauer (C.), John Stefox (J.), and Arnold O. Haugen (J.). Pictured with the panel is the magnificent Beaubien mountain caribou that received a first place award and also the Sagamore Hill Medal for its trophy excellence.

looked over. The bulls were several hundred yards away, running up a side hill. They had only 200 yards to go before they would go over the mountain top forever. Quickly lying down on the knoll and putting the cross hairs of his scope on the top of the bull's shoulder, Beaubien waited for him to stop. When he did, Beaubien carefully squeezed the trigger. His father, watching through binoculars, cried, "You shot way low". The bulls took off again for the top. The next time the bulls stopped they were just 100 yards from the summit. Beaubien aimed over the big bull's antlers and fired again. His father told him that he had still shot too low.

Beaubien's heart was pounding mightily as he waited, hoping for one last chance. The big bull stopped just as he reached the skyline, the nine other bulls strung out behind him. Holding about 10 feet above him and right in the middle, Beaubien squeezed off his final effort, hoping that the 180 grain bullet from his 300 Winchester magnum would do the job. As the rifle report died, his father yelled, "You got him!". The bull crumpled on the skyline, his back broken by the final shot. Beaubien and his father watched through their binoculars for several minutes to make sure that he was indeed down for keeps.

It took them three days of hard work to get the capes, meat and antlers back to Dease Lake. When they had stepped off the distance to Beaubien's trophy, it was 650 paces, a shot that in Beaubien's own words truly had some luck involved. Beaubien's father's trophy also turned out to be a very fine one, scoring 340 points.

Beaubien's caribou was recognized at the 16th North American Big Game Awards (1977) as the best in its category, and it was further honored with an award of the Sagamore Hill Medal. The Sagamore Hill Medal can only be given to one trophy in any entry period awards, and its award signifies both trophy excellence and a hunt exhibiting the finest standards of Fair Chase.

Scoring 452, Beaubien's trophy was second in the 1977 edition of the records book to the long-standing world record trophy taken by G.L. Pop in 1923. The Pop record had continued as the world record since the start of the current records keeping system in 1950.

On January 1, 1980, the Boone and Crockett Club removed the G.L. Pop caribou from the records and affirmed the Beaubien trophy as the world record for the category. The action against the Pop trophy was taken after examination of the trophy (prior to restoration activities by a taxidermist) revealed that the antlers had been cut from the skull cap base and reinserted with lag screws at the time of the original taxidermy. Additionally, the skull cap plate had been split and a wooden wedge inserted to give a wider antler spread, thus altering the score. Once these alterations to the trophy had been established beyond any doubt, there was no choice but to remove this trophy from the records since either of these alterations constitutes disqualification. It is unfortunate that these alterations were performed to this trophy, as it would have been a very high ranking specimen and probably still the world record, if it had been left unaltered.

The story behind the new world record pronghorn, scoring 93 points and taken by Edwin Wetzler in Williamson Valley, Arizona, on September 21, 1975, is very similar to the previous one. It also involves the removal from the records of the previous world record trophy.

In this case, a trophy belonging to Dr. H.M. Beck (taken by an unknown hunter prior to the turn of the century) has been in the possession of the Academy of Natural Sciences, Philadelphia, since early in the century. It has been recognized as the world record since the inception of the current records keeping system in 1950. Its score of 101⅝ exceeded by a sizeable margin the scores of the next highest ranking pronghorns, leading many to believe that it represented a genetic strain of pronghorn that had been lost forever in the early days of the country. A more simple explanation was found through a detailed examination by a taxidermist, prior to its display loan to the National Taxidermists Hall of Fame in 1979.

That examination of the horn material revealed the possibility of trophy alteration. Not wishing to destroy the possible value of this world record, the taxidermist contacted the Academy of Natural Sciences, whose official then contacted the records office. Acting as a representative of the Club's Records of North American Big Game Committee, I personally examined this trophy, along with a representative of the National Taxidermists Hall of Fame. We found that nearly two inches of horn material had been added to the bases of both horns to make them longer. This was a most skillful job, and one that involved use of such simple material as paper maché and lampblack, being done in the early part of the century before modern molding materials were available. The alteration was invisible on surface, being noticed only on the inside of the horns, when removed from the mount.

After reviewing photos and x-rays of the horns, the Records Committee approved removal of this trophy from the records listings, since altered trophies are specifically excluded from entry. As a result of this action, Wetzler's second place trophy then became the world record.

It is quite possible that if the additional material had not been added to the Beck prong-horn, it might have still been the world's record, or at least in the top few trophies. As the alteration was done *before* the start of formal records keeping, one can only surmise that it was an attempt to "gild the lily". Perhaps it was an attempt to make the horns look more "normal", since the prongs were unusually low on this specimen, even with the added material. In any case, it was a tremendous specimen, with or without the alterations.

The story of Wetzler's hunt for his record pronghorn began in June 1975 when he and his hunting partner, Jim Embry, were awaiting the drawing date for pronghorn in Arizona. Not hearing from the Game Department whether they had been drawn or rejected, Wetzler and his partner kept calling the department. Finally they discovered that their permits had been discarded with a bunch of empty envelopes. Accepting blame for the mistake, the Game Department awarded permits to Embry, Wetzler and several others involved in this mix-up. This occurred only three weeks before hunting season, leaving very little time to get ready.

After carefully looking over possibilities, Wetzler and his partner decided to hunt in an area that Wetzler had hunted several times before with his father, Art. Art agreed to go along. with them to help Embry who had not hunted pronghorn before.

Opening morning failed to produce a pronghorn for Wetzler, although Embry connected with a nice buck that required a good stalk and use of his hunting skills.

Arriving at their noon rendez-vous, the hunters talked over the morning and decided that Embry and Wetzler would pack Embry's pronghorn to camp after lunch. On their way to the buck, they found a small herd lying down, without any trophy-size bucks. A little farther on, at nearly 500 yards, they spotted a very nice buck lying in a small depression. He looked to be in the 15- to 16-inch class, and Wetzler decided to try to stalk to within 100 yards or so for a good shot.

Wetzler had worked his way to within 250 yards, when a jeep appeared over the hill to his right, spooking the herd. As they ran away from him, Wetzler took a quick shot but hit the ground in line with the buck's shoulder. In a few seconds they were out of range, leaving Wetzler disappointed and angry at the jeep driver. The remainder of the day was spent in getting Embry's pronghorn back to camp and taking care of the meat and cape.

Wetzler's father departed camp early the next morning so Embry decided to walk along with Wetzler, even though his own hunting was completed.

Just before daylight, they began walking down a small wash that ran in the general direction they wanted to go. As soon as it became light enough to see clearly, Wetzler and Embry would stop often, crawling up the side of the wash to glass the area for pronghorn. After a couple of scannings, they spotted a buck about a half mile away, all by himself and walking in the same direction they were going. They could tell that he had good-sized horns, but they could not tell how good since they had no spotting scope, only field glasses.

After they had followed him about a mile, the buck turned and went over a small hill out of their view. At this point, Wetzler and Embry broke out of the wash and walked towards the hill where the pronghorn had disappeared, hoping that he was still going in the same direction. Working their way to the top of the hill, they glassed the area but could not see the buck anywhere. They did spot a small herd lying down some 400 yards away, but it had no large bucks. Deciding to work around the hill, they had moved about 150 yards when the big buck broke out of a small wash to their left on a dead run. Wetzler knew that he would not get a better shot, because the pronghorn was running. He fired, striking the buck in the rib cage. The shot turned the buck broadside and slowed him down slightly, but by that time he was nearly 250 yards away. Taking quick aim, Wetzler fired again, hitting the ground behind him. On the third shot, Wetzler led him farther, hitting him in the left front leg and breaking it. Still the buck kept running. Taking aim with even more lead, Wetzler sent the 180 grain softpoint from his .300 Savage on its way. This time, a broken back leg brought the buck down, but he required a final finishing shot in the neck.

Wetzler and Embry had to carry the buck just over two miles to get back to their vehicle. By late afternoon, they were back in camp, savoring their success. In light of their unusual difficulty in getting permits, it was an especially memorable hunt.

Our final story deals with the taking of the world record whitetail deer. This trophy scores 206-1/8 and has long been attributed to Sandstone, Minnesota, where it first turned up in a rummage sale. Currently owned by Dr. Charles T. Arnold, this trophy has never been bested in terms of final score for the category. The date of kill and hunter remained unknown until late 1978, when the Records Committee became satisfied that there was sufficient evidence to identify the true hunter and kill date for this exceptional trophy. The uncovering of the facts for this particular trophy unfolds like a mystery novel.

Over 65 years ago James Jordan shot a whitetail buck with an exceptionally large rack

Photograph by Bernard A. Fashingbauer

James Jordan stands behind the bar he formerly operated, 17 miles east of Hinkley, Minnesota. Photo taken on April 4, 1978, when Jordan was 86 and still waiting to be recognized as the hunter for the world's record whitetail deer.

near Danbury, Wisconsin, along the Yellow River, long before 1932 when formal records keeping was begun by the Boone and Crockett Club.

Jordan was 22 years old when he and a neighbor, Egus Davis, rented a horse and wagon to go deer hunting about three miles south of Danbury, Wisconsin, in the fall of 1914. The hunt began shortly after dawn, when Jordan jumped a doe that he shot and severely wounded. Trailing it for quite a distance, he finally killed it after it had crossed the Yellow River and was scrambling up the bank on the Minnesota side. Davis agreed to stay with the meat while Jordan continued hunting. Jordan soon ran across the tracks of a big buck, which he followed.

The buck's trail soon crossed the Yellow River to the Minnesota side, heading north toward town and the Soo Line railroad. The tracks indicated the buck was browsing, and Jordan figured it would soon bed down.

The whistle of a passing freight train frightened the buck into the open, where Jordan took a quick neck shot. The buck started running and Jordan emptied his rifle at it. Jordan knew some of his .25–35 bullets had hit the deer, but they did not seem to slow it down. Jordan had only one shell left, and this, he put into the chamber before starting to trail the wounded deer.

The buck's trail followed the Yellow River for a distance before crossing the river to the Wisconsin side. As the deer paused on the riverbank, Jordan carefully placed his last shot and brought down the huge buck for keeps.

Shortly after killing his deer, Jordan accepted the offer of a part-time taxidermist, George Van Castle of Webster, Wisconsin, to mount his trophy for five dollars. Van Castle took the rack and hide to his home to work on it, but he soon moved to Hinckley, Minnesota, after the death of his wife. Before Jordan could make a trip to Hinckley to recover his trophy, he heard that Van Castle had moved to Florida. (Jordan himself moved to Hinckley in his later life.)

When Van Castle moved to Florida, he left Jordan's mounted deer head behind in Hinckley, where it gathered dust in an attic corner until it was purchased in 1964 at a rummage sale for three dollars by Robert Ludwig.

Passing through Sandstone, Minnesota, Ludwig decided that the exceptional antlers were worth the price, although the cracked and peeling mount would have to be thrown away. Ludwig kept the antlers in his home in Sandstone for several years, then sold them to Dr. Charles T. Arnold, whose hobby is collecting exceptional deer antler racks.

In 1964 Bernard A. Fashingbauer of St. Paul, Minnesota, measured this rack for Ludwig. Fashingbauer, an Official Measurer for the Boone and Crockett Club Big Game Records, determined that this trophy was a potential world's record.

Later, a select panel of judges, chosen from the ranks of the Official Measurers, certified this trophy as the world record at 206⅝ points. (Score changed to 206⅛ in 1981 when math error discovered.) At that time, the trophy still belonged to Ludwig. By the time it was first published in the records book (1971 edition), it was the property of Dr. Arnold and was shown with hunter and kill date as "unknown".

In 1964, when James Jordan first viewed the huge deer rack owned by Ludwig (a distant relative), he knew it was the same deer he had shot so many years ago. But for more than a decade, he was frustrated in his quest to be recognized as the hunter who had shot this deer.

Jordan's claim to this trophy was convincing to many who talked to him. Ron Schara, outdoor writer for the Minneapolis Tribune, featured Jordan's story on several occasions. The current trophy owner (Dr. Arnold) wrote to the records office in late 1977, suggesting that Jordan's story be fully explored and that he be designated as the hunter if the Records Committee was convinced. The Committee then asked Fashingbauer to gather all the evidence that he could about this trophy, in order that Jordan's claim could be fully considered.

Information gathered by Fashingbauer and from other sources was considered by the Records Committee at their December 1978 meeting. After careful review, the Committee was convinced. They voted to list James Jordan as the hunter with a kill date and location of 1914 on the Yellow River, near Danbury, Wisconsin.

This story, unusual for its twists and turns, ends on a rather melancholy note. James Jordan died in October 1978, at age 86, before he could be informed of the Club's decision.

These stories behind the new world's records are obviously of great interest to the serious big game hunter. Perhaps their underlying theme should be of even greater interest to the general public. Truly exceptional trophies are regularly produced as a continuing product of our highly successful programs of modern wildlife management. The large number of entries accepted each year for future publication in the records book from all over the continent points to the generally healthy status of all our big game populations. It is a success story that merits telling to the general public by all hunters and conservationists.

William Harold Nesbitt is currently Administrative Director of the Boone and Crockett Club. From 1977–1980, he was Director of the Hunter Services Division of the National Rifle Association, and Manager of the NRA Hunting Activities Department during 1973–1977. He served as Coordinator of the North American Big Game Awards Program throughout its existence (1973–1980).

He has a B.S. in Wildlife Biology from N.C. State and an M.S. from Clemson University. He has taught wildlife biology and zoology at Clemson and Southern Illinois Universities, worked with the U.S. Fish and Wildlife Service, and the Illinois Natural History Survey. His published research interests include ruffed grouse, bobwhite quail, and feral dogs.

He is an associate member of the Boone and Crockett Club, a Life Member of the NRA and the American Ornithologists Union, a member of the Wildlife Society, and other conservation and hunting organizations.

He has served as ex officio recording secretary for the Records of North American Big Game Committee since 1973, and is an Official Measurer.

He has authored a number of articles and book chapters and served as co-editor of the 1977 records book.

He has hunted whitetail, mule deer, pronghorn, elk, and black bear in several locations, and he hunts with both gun and bow.

Walking With Deer

LYNN ROGERS

This story really began 24 years ago under a big oak tree that overlooks a well-worn deer trail near my home in southwestern Michigan. I had settled against the tree in the first light of a chilly November morning, checked the safety of my 16 gauge Browning, and waited with eyes and ears at full alert. It was opening day of my second deer season.

Each stirring of leaves brought a new surge of anticipation. Deer sign had been abundant when I checked the area two weeks earlier. However, midday arrived with nothing spotted larger than a fox squirrel. Had the deer changed their travel patterns in the past two weeks? What new foods were they seeking, and what kind of cover were they using on this calm, chilly day? I realized there was a lot I wanted to know about deer.

In early afternoon a doe appeared off to the side, about 30 yards away. She was angling slowly upwind, feeding on ground plants that I couldn't quite see through the leafless brush. She passed 20 yards in front of me, not seeming to notice me until I moved slightly to see what she was eating. She bounded into denser cover, looked back, then browsed slowly off. I wished I could watch her long enough and closely enough to get answers to some of my questions.

Some 20 years later, I got the chance to do exactly that with some other deer. In 1976, I was hired as a deer biologist by the USDA Forest Service's North Central Forest Experiment Station. I was assigned to determine how foresters might better manage forests for deer in northeastern Minnesota. My job involved research funded jointly by the USDA Forest Service, the National Rifle Association, the Boone and Crockett Club, and the Minnesota State Archery Association.

Although much was already known about the winter diet of deer in northern forests, little was known of their diet during the snowfree months. Knowledge of food preferences during this period could prove important in deer habitat management because it is during those months that deer raise their fawns and store fat for winter. In northern forests, this stored fat can be critically important for survival.

I felt that an accurate picture of the year-round food and habitat choices of deer in northeastern Minnesota could only be obtained by observing their eating habits firsthand. My coworkers and I spent 125 hours a month for the next 4 years doing just that, using 8 females that were bottle-fed from birth. When they were old enough to fend for themselves, we fitted them with radiotransmitter collars and released them. The collars would enable us to find them at any time, while the hand-rearing would ensure that we could closely approach them for observations.

I hoped to find out if the fawns could make a full-time living on their own after they were released, if they would retain their wild instincts for escaping predators, raising young, and establishing home ranges, and if they would remain friendly to people after they matured. Yardsticks of success of this method would be how well the tame deer fared compared with wild deer and how well the tame deer would adapt to people observing them. The pleasant surprise was that everything went much better than anticipated. The bottleraised deer set up home ranges of about a square mile, the same size that wild does use in northeastern Minnesota. They eluded wolves and bears as successfully as wild deer. They grew as rapidly as wild deer. They joined wild deer in winter deeryards, and they mated with wild deer, successfully raising young. As far as I could tell, they retained all of their natural instincts for survival. Yet, they never forgot their human friends. They seemed to view my coworkers and me as friendly, noncompetitive members of their group. They showed neither fear nor excessive attraction to us.

Our main method of gathering data from the deer was to remain with an individual for 28 consecutive hours. When traveling with the deer, we described each habitat the deer entered, estimated the abundance of each plant species in each habitat, and counted the number of bites the deer took of each species. We also kept a minute-by-minute record of the deer's activities—how much time was spent chewing its cud, grooming, intently alert, sleeping, etc. The data we collected revealed food and habitat preferences, amounts eaten, and how all these things varied with season.

Of all the deer, my favorite was the one we named Browser. Being with her and seeing her respond to the slightest distant rustlings while ignoring my own sounds seemed like the rarest of privileges. It was this deer that first revealed to me many of the basic patterns of deer behavior-patterns we saw repeated by all the deer we studied. Detailed analyses of the data are not completed, but I can share some of the more obvious findings.

In all aspects of their lives, the deer behaved as though the major consideration was to avoid predation. They avoided cover from which flight would be difficult. In summer they circumvented areas of very dense sapling growth or excessively rough terrain. In winter, they avoided areas where deep snow hindered movement. Like all ruminants, deer rapidly fill their stomach with a minimum of chewing, then finding a good vantage point to bed down, regurgitate the food, and chew it more thoroughly. This manner of feeding minimized time spent rustling about, possibly attracting the attention of predators. In addition, most chewing, which seems to reduce their ability to hear approaching predators, is done while bedded in a good vantage point. Upon bedding, the deer usually did not immediately begin chewing their cuds. They first spent a period of full alertness with eyes wide open, ears pivoting, and nose sniffing the air. Eventually they relaxed, began chewing their cuds, and often let their eyes half close. Still, they stopped chewing, opened their eyes fully, and listened intently at any strange sound.

After chewing their cuds for a few minutes to a few hours (depending upon season and diet), the bedded deer curled up and slept for a few minutes. The Rapid Eye Movement stage of this sleep, from which arousal in most species is difficult, usually lasted only a half minute or so. This period usually lasts longer in people and large predators. Overall, the deer slept lightly, raising their heads and opening their eyes at unfamiliar sounds.

The cycle of feeding, lying alert, cud-chewing, and sleeping was repeated through the day as well as the night. This was a surprise to me. Before this study, I had seen deer mainly at dawn, dusk, and at night, so I thought they were not active during the day. However, the tame deer, and the wild deer we encountered while with the tame deer, showed us that feeding continues under forest cover through the day. One day I accompanied a deer we called Rosie into a clear-cut area with many birch and willow sprouts. She entered the clearing hesitantly. Instead of feeding efficiently, she spent more than half her time with head up and ears pivoting. She soon moved back into the forest where she fed more calmly and continuously. But, that night she moved into the clearing with seeming confidence and fed calmly and efficiently on the sprouts. Browser showed similar behavior as she fed through the day in the forest and in small forest openings. At one point she came to a highway and bounded across it to continue feeding in the forest on the other side. Then, at dusk, she returned to the same point on the highway and spent the night eating roadside vegetation. She left the roadside only to chew her cud and sleep, or to retreat briefly from passing vehicles. Shortly after dawn she switched to feeding on forest vegetation again.

In November and December, deer in northern Minnesota move from their summer ranges and gather into "deeryards". For some deer, winter and summer ranges are more than 20 miles apart. As snow depth increases through winter, the deer congregate more closely into yards that may be as large as several square miles. One of these yards was within the area explored by the tame deer during the snowfree seasons, and it was in this yard that they concentrated their activities in winter. Browser became the leader of two wild deer that moved into this yard. Browser and her group ran the gauntlet of timber wolves in the area without a loss, although several other deer in the yard were killed.

With Browser as the leader, the wild deer became somewhat accustomed to human observers. By midwinter, the wild deer routinely fed and bedded 50–60 feet away from us, and we learned that their food choices were similar to Browser's.

All the deer we watched in winter ate large amounts of old man's beard, an arboreal lichen. They visited and revisited fallen fir trees to obtain them. These trees had become covered with lichens 10–20 years earlier following a spruce budworm epidemic that had weakened or killed them. The deer also ate dead aster flower stalks that protruded above the snow, digging through snow up to a foot deep for dead aster leaves. As the snow deepened, nonwoody plants became less available and the deer turned to twigs of woody shrubs. The digestibility of these twigs is low, and deer lose weight when feeding on them, even if they

Photograph by Donna Rogers

Lynn Rogers with his favorite deer of the study, Browser, during late 1980.

are available in unlimited supply. However, in northeastern Minnesota and other regions of deep snow, this is the only food abundant enough for deer to fill up on in winter.

When patches of bare ground appeared in April, the deer ate small plants whose leaves had remained green overwinter. Commonly eaten plants were strawberry, twinflower, bunchberry, violet, and shinleafs. These were largely forsaken, as soon as the new green leaves poked through the forest floor in May. Major foods then were new aster leaves, false lily-of-the-valley, and Clinton's lily. Later in May, the expanding leaves of shrubs also became principal food. Shrub leaves & small green plants remained the main foods through the summer. Mushrooms, including some poisonous species, were major foods in September.

In fall, food supplies were reduced through leaf fall and the annual deterioration of many species of small plants. The deer then turned to the persistently green species of plants that they had fed on in early spring but had rejected during the summer. At the same time, they began feeding on old man's beard. As deepening snow covered ground vegetation, the deer turned increasingly to woody browse again, and the annual cycle of feeding had come full circle. Although cedar is a major deer food in parts of northern Minnesota, it was scarce in the study area.

When the snow melted in spring, the deer left the winter deeryard and returned to their summer ranges. There we saw a number of aggressive interactions among mature tame and wild deer. In one case I was with Browser when she discovered two wild does encroaching on an area that was usually exclusively hers. We were moving along the shore of a lake, when Browswer suddenly became stiff and alert. Following her gaze through the brush, I saw two does about 40 yards away, feeding at the edge of an opening. They seemed unaware of us. Browser stood sniffing, listening, and looking in their direction for about two minutes. Then she bounded through the brush, burst into the opening, chasing and kicking the startled deer. The wild deer tried to avoid the angered Browser, without striking back. After a few seconds of zig-zagging and running in circles, the wild deer left and Browser resumed feeding. She showed similar aggressiveness toward two tame yearling does that she found in the same area in early June, a week before she gave birth to her fawn. The two yearlings were radiocollared, which allowed us to follow their movements following this incident. After being chased, the does didn't return to that part of Browser's range for more than a month.

Browser gave birth to a single male fawn on June 3rd, in the same area where she had chased away the yearlings. Researcher Laura Mason was witness to the birth. Laura watched Browser lick her fawn clean and then pull the allantoic membranes out of her birth canal and eat them. Browser also ate or licked any plants or other objects that were touched by these membranes. This undoubtedly minimized odors that might attract predators. Browser remained in a reclining position to give her fawn his first meal. Throughout the occasion, she directed a frequent soft mewing grunt toward the fawn. She raised this fawn successfully, showing that she retained the natural instincts for motherhood even though she had been raised by people.

The major drawback of the study was that the deer, trained from birth to trust people, sometimes went up to hunters to be petted. As a result, 7 of the 8 does, including Browser, were killed by hunters. The eighth was killed by wolves. The last three study animals were killed (illegally, in a bucks only area) on November 22, 1980, ending the observations. Nevertheless, the four years of observations up to that point provided a wealth of new information about white-tailed deer in the northern portions of their range. When final analyses of the data are completed, they should help point the way to better management programs.

———————

Lynn Leroy Rogers is a wildlife biologist serving with the U.S. Forest Service Northcentral Forest Experiment Station in Ely, Minnesota. He holds a B.S. degree from Michigan State and a Ph.D. degree from the University of Minnesota.

He has published several papers resulting from his studies of black bears and whitetail deer. In 1974 he received the Anna N. Jackson Award from the American Society of Mammalogists for a paper on the social systems of black bears.

He is a member of the American Society of Mammalogists, The Wildlife Society, the American Association for the Advancement of Science, and Alpha Zeta honorary.

He has received several grants from the Boone and Crockett Club for his studies of bear and deer.

Black Bears and Humans in Michigan's Lower Peninsula

ALBERT M. MANVILLE, II

Black bears in Michigan's Lower Peninsula? Not likely, many would say. Quite the contrary, bears do indeed exist here and, in fact, are rather numerous in some areas of the northern sector. In 1977, 777 bears were legally shot in the State, of which 143 were from Lower Peninsula. But like most wildlife today, bears face an uphill battle for existence. The greatest threat to black bears is loss of habitat and related disturbances brought on by man.

The northern Lower Peninsula of Michigan has been a popular resort area for many years, and now is becoming heavily populated with permanent residents. The Higgins-Houghton Lakes Area of this region is one of Michigan's largest resorts. Adjacent to and immediately west of these two lakes lies the Dead Stream Swamp, the largest swamp and roadless tract in the Lower Peninsula. The Swamp is perhaps one of the best haunts of the black bear in the Lower Peninsula. But, private and commercial development, human encroachment, oil field expansion, and habitat destruction, all threaten the black bear population in the area. Seven oil and gas fields, with some 694 wells, are located around the lakes region. Added to this is an increasing and demanding human population. In Roscommon County, for example, the 1976 population of 15,100 people was projected to double by the end of 1980. And, recreational services are numerous around Houghton Lake: 46 motels (40 of which are open year-round), 3 trailer parks, 3 recreational areas, 14 restaurants, 8 food and beverage stores, 7 sporting goods stores, and 75 businesses and professional services. In addition to the permanent residents, the Higgins and Houghton Lakes Area receives heavy year-round use by vacationers. Sail and power boating, bow and rifle hunting, fishing, trail-biking, camping, hiking, snowmobiling, and crosscountry skiing are popular sports, all of which attract many participants and occasionally bring humans into contact with bears. With increasing people pressure on bears, and a moderately high level of bear nuisance and damage complaints, the Higgins-Houghton Lakes Area was ripe for a study of bear-human interactions.

The study was begun during the summer of 1977, with 35 bears captured and 25 radio-collared between September 1977 and January 1980. My objectives were several: to assess the effects of humans and oil development on bear habitat and the population; to evaluate hunting pressure; to establish the extent of the nuisance bear problem; and, to examine bear habitat size, home range, movements, and winter dens.

Bears were captured in barrel traps (two 55 gallon drums welded end-to-end), culvert traps, Aldrich foot snares, and in dens. In one case, a pack of bear-hunting dogs was used to tree a female which had previously eluded recapture at her den. Once immobilized, each bear was marked with numbered ear-tags, with six-inch plastic fluorescent colored streamers attached. The bright ear streamers, as well as the radio collars themselves, proved very effective for visual identification. Local residents reported sighting 23 marked bears on 63 separate occasions. While still immobile, about 30-cc of blood were extracted from each bear for parasite analysis and determination of elemental selenium levels.

In Wisconsin, bears commonly carry the larvae of a blood parasite similar to the dog heartworm—a parasite that fortunately does not appear to hurt bears—and I wanted to determine the incidence of this parasite in Lower Peninsula bears. No parasites were found. Because of a high level of periodontal disease (a serious gum infection) blood was analyzed for levels of selenium since the Lower Peninsula is a selenium-deficient belt and insufficient selenium is suspected of causing gum problems in bears. Results indicated that selenium levels were low, but apparently not enough to cause the disease. Thirteen of 35 bears had periodontal disease in varying degrees of severity, suffering tooth loss, jaw and gum atrophy. Bacterial swabs were also taken from infected gum tissues, and these were cultured in the lab. Only one type of bacteria was present in all bears that had periodontal disease; it is not known whether this organism could have caused the problem. Seven bears were also found to have tooth cavities. Bears are the only carnivores known to have problems with cavities, probably due to the high levels of sugary fruits in their diet, as well as large amounts of soft foods.

Anesthetized bears were also weighed and measured. Weights of 22 males and 13 females ranged up to 375 pounds. Males averaged 150 pounds, while females averaged 125. The largest female ever live-trapped in Michigan—affectionately named Gertrude—weighed 340 pounds in September 1977. Her denned weight was estimated at 500 pounds. The largest male weighed 320 pounds in May 1978 and also was estimated to weigh 500 pounds the following winter. When his radio-collar was finally removed in March 1980, he weighed 375 pounds. The average nose-to-tail length for 27 bears at the time of first capture was 57.5 inches; males averaged 59.4 inches, females 54.1. A small premolar tooth was extracted from each bear for aging purposes. Each permanent tooth has growth rings in its root much like a tree. Ages of bears known alive in February 1980 ranged from 0.02 to eight years. The average age of all bears in this study was 4.4 years; males averaged 4.5 years while females averaged 4.3. In studies of this nature, males tend to be younger than females, probably because they are more likely to be shot. The results of this study indicated that females were slightly younger on the average, possibly from a result of slight over-harvest or other mortality factors.

Bears are not true hibernators like ground squirrels or marmots, but rather go into a semi-deep or torporous sleep and may remain in dens for five or more months in Michigan. My study discovered some interesting information about denned bears. Bears in a deep-sleep state have depressed cardiac, respiratory, and metabolic functions. Heart rate and respiration drop slightly, but body temperature is more depressed. Rectal temperatures of bears captured in this study during the spring, summer, or fall varied from 98 to 105 F (average of 100.8). In den situations, bear rectal temperatures varied from 91.4 to 99.4 (average of 94.5). Much of the literature on bears indicates that in denned situations bears neither defecate nor urinate. I found evidence indicating that several males defecated while in the dens, and two males urinated just outside their dens. Forty-five attempts were made to immobilize bears in dens; 49% of the time the bears fled the site before I actually arrived. One bear, a large male, ran from his den in conditions as cold as −20 F, with as much as four feet of snow on the ground. Generally, the wariness of bears in cold, snow-laden conditions was much greater than expected.

Black bears have been reported using many different types of dens, including tree cavities, road culverts, stumps, underground depressions, rock caves, etc. I found several bears denned in open snow "nests" with no protection from snow or wind, and a den lining of little or no vegetation. This type of den was used by not only males but also a female with two cubs. Another female denned on top of a muskrat house for two winters.

After bears were radio-collared and released, they were tracked on the ground from automobile, truck, van, trail bike, snowmobile, and foot. A Super Cub, Callair A-2, and a Beaver aircraft were used for aerial tracking, with antennas mounted on both right and left wing struts. On one occasion aerial tracking was conducted from a helicopter. While ground tracking, signals were received from collared bears up to four miles away, but the average reception distance in thick swamps was usually no more than a mile. While flying, signals were picked up to 35 miles away with the aircraft at some 9,000 feet above ground. Without the use of a Super Cub, three far-ranging males would likely never have been located. All three moved from the Dead Stream Swamp like spokes of a wheel during the spring and summer of 1979. One bear traveled north to the Straits of Mackinac area, some 90 air miles away; the second went west to the Manistee area, some 65 miles away; and the third moved south to the Harrison area, some 31 miles away. All three, in addition to four others (three males and one female), returned in early November to a five mile square area in the Dead Stream Swamp, apparently in preparation for denning. Two of the three far-ranging males moved during the breeding season in May and June. These migrations may have resulted from competition from more dominant males, since food did not appear limiting in the Higgins-Houghton Lakes Area during the summer of 1979.

Of the 35 bears captured during this study, 25 were radio-collared for up to a 22-month period. Seventeen bears (49% of the total captured) died during the study, while 13 collared animals (52% of those collared) died. Of the latter, 8 were shot by hunters (3 illegally), 2 were shot as nuisance bears, 1 died of a drug-related problem, 1 was killed by a car, and 1 died of an apparent strangulation.

Some 4,224 radio fixes (279 aerial fixes during 44 flights; 3,945 ground fixes) were made on the 25 collared bears from September 1977 to March 1980, enabling calculations of home ranges of these animals. For males followed for six months or more by radio-location, home ranges averaged 58 square miles (ranging from 2.3 to 119) while female ranges averaged 23.2 square miles (ranging from 4.2 to 59). The home ranges of all radio-collared males averaged 49.3 square miles; for all collared females, 25.6 square miles. I also calculated the greatest lengths of home range for the collared bears followed for six months or more by radiotelemetry. Ranges varied from 3 to 87 miles in length, with males averaging 26.6 miles and females, 7.3.

Bear use of vegetation types also was monitored during this study. Swamp conifers (white cedar, tamarack, balsam fir, black spruce, etc.) were found to be most heavily used by bears, followed by lowland brush (alder, dogwood, willow, huckleberry, blueberry, etc.), lowland hardwoods, and northern hardwoods. I found differences in the use of such vegetation according to sex. Females used upland hardwoods more extensively than males, particularly during periods of mast (acorn, nut, fruit) production. Males, however, used cedar swamps more extensively, denning in them more frequently than females. Both sexes were found extensively in cedar swamps during spring when feeding on carrion, sedges, tubers, grasses, etc. was most active. From a management standpoint, lowland swamps, brush, and hardwood habitat appeared to be critical for bears. Such areas must be preserved as critical habitat for bears in Michigan's Lower Peninsula.

Since the major emphasis of this study was on the impact of humans on bears, attempts were made to categorize bear activities in relation to or as a result of human action. Impacts of humans were classified as positive, negative, questionable (impact data available but insufficient to reliably classify), or unknown (impact recorded but effect on bears unknown).

Several positive impacts of humans on bears were recorded. Evidence indicated that the bear population in the Higgins-Houghton Lakes Area increased since 1975, very possibly a result of changes in hunting regulations. Prior to implementation of a new permit system, hunts organized by the Michigan United Conservation Clubs were conducted in the Dead Stream Swamp and surrounding area. From 1946 to 1963, 33 organized, single-day hunts resulted in a reported harvest of 16 with 1 bear reported wounded. Hunting was conducted almost exclusively with the use of dogs. Prior to 1969, hunters in the Lower Peninsula could shoot a bear in September, October, or November as a bonus on their deer tag. The use of large (greater than 20) packs of dogs and large (185 or more) hunting parties was previously also permissible. Since 1969, only permit holders are allowed to hunt bear. Closure of hunting in the Dead Stream Swamp and all of Missaukee County (1965), elimination of the use of dog packs larger than six and registration of dog packs (1976), termination of non-permit bear hunting in the Lower Peninsula, and declines in hunting pressure following permit implementation, all appear to have benefited the bear population.

Track counts, scats, and radio signals from 14 bears indicated the use of oil pipeline right-of-ways, oil well service roads, and lumber roads as travel lanes. Bears, however, still used off-the-road swamp and forest trails, stream banks, and river bottoms probably 95 + % of the time. During periods of little or no human activity or presence, a travel lane into the Dead Stream Swamp was used by at least six different bears. At least five different bears frequented an old lumber road in the northeast portion of the Swamp. Another lumber road in the same vicinity was used by at least four different bears. A main gas pipeline right-of-way road was traveled by at least six different bears during the fall 1978. A service road to an oil well was used by at least four different bears. Next to this road, a plastic and fiberglass wellhead cover was chewed and clawed by bears in October 1979. After replacement later that month, bears again damaged the cover in November.

Cutting and clearing of roadsides benefited bears as fruiting and berryproducing plants increased in abundance in clear-cut areas. Bears were found to feed on cherries, raspberries, blueberries, serviceberries, hawthorne, and apples along 31 roadsides in Roscommon County and 21 roadsides in Missaukee County. Commercial lumbering, clear-cutting for deer management, controlled burns for Kirtland's warbler nest habitat improvement, and construction of new service roads to oil wells resulted in fruiting and berry-producing plants which also benefited bears.

Beekeeping provided bears with an additional, supplementary source of food. Of 46 nuisance or damage complaints reported between September 1977 and July 1980, 14 (30%) involved damage to beehives. Between May 1975 and September 1980, one beekeeper totally lost 63 hives to bears while 200 hives were knocked over and partially damaged. In the past 12 years, beekeepers in Missaukee County have totally lost 230 hives to bears ($23,000 estimated loss). Clearly, from a supplementary food standpoint, the impact of humans on bears has been positive.

The negative impacts of humans on bears were more extensive. The rapid increase in resident human population in the Higgins-Houghton Lakes Area (estimated doubling of the Roscommon County population, 1976–1980) provided perhaps the greatest direct threat to the area bear population. Between 1977 and 1980, swamps were land-filled for residential and commercial development in the Prudenville area of Roscommon County. Construction of pipe and pumping facilities for wastewater treatment around Houghton Lake resulted in the loss of hundreds of acres of swamp habitat. Construction of a 100 acre wastewater treatment facility, dug in an oak upland, eliminated a portion of a prime feeding area for bears. Another wastewater treatment facility, a gravel pit, and various recreational facilities disrupted potential denning and feeding areas.

Heavy traffic on three state highways restricted movements of four collared females; the highways marked their home range boundaries. Heavy southbound traffic of US-27 restricted movement of a then subadult female (Daisey May) in September 1978; this highway marked the eastern boundary of her home range. This same highway also marked the western boundary of the home range of another female (Rhea); heavily traveled M-55 defined the northern boundary of yet a third female (Lady) and highway M-18 marked the eastern

Photograph by A.M. Manville

A male black bear, "Dirty Harry", ready for release after tranquilization and attachment of the radio collar transmitter to allow later tracking of his movements.

Photograph by Doug Threloff

Albert Manville uses a directional receiver to track the radio-collared female black bear, Tanya, during the spring of 1979.

boundary of a fourth female (Tanya). Male movements apparently were not blocked by major highways, as they readily crossed them, with one adult male car-killed while crossing I-75. Eight unmarked bears were also reported hit by cars in the study area, with seven being killed.

Service roads to oil wells likely aided bear hunters. Hunting pressure was heavier on bears in areas that contained extensive road systems. Areas that were criss-crossed with roads improved chances of shooting a fleeing bear. The average distance from point of harvest to the nearest light-duty, all-weather improved road for nine bears was 0.29 mi; males were shot at an average of 0.37 mi. from roads while females were shot at an average of 0.29 mi. Statistical testing indicated that as the ages and weights of males (and males and females together) increased, the distance(s) from point of harvest to nearest improved road decreased, suggesting that bears had decreasing fear or intolerance of humans with increasing age and weight.

Hunters negatively impacted the marked bears in this study as 11 (39%) of 28 marked (25 radio-tagged) animals were shot. Three were shot over bait, 2 were shot as nuisances (over garbage and destroying beehives, respectively), 2 were shot by hunters using dogs; of the remaining 4, 1 was shot legally and the harvest method for the 3 shot illegally was unknown. Between 1977 and 1980, 16.7, 17.4, 18.2, and 10 percent respectively, of the marked bear population known or suspected of being alive each year were shot. A 39% harvest during the period of this study was a sizable loss to the marked population.

Hunting females with cubs is legal in Michigan, while shooting cubs of the year is not. Of four females shot during the study, two were shot in the company of cubs. Although cubs as young as 5.5 months and as small as 18 lb. were found to be self-sufficient in Michigan's Upper Peninsula, cub survival is likely greatly enhanced in the company and protection of the mother.

My own impact on denned bears often was negative, since 49% of the time bears examined in dens (45 attempts to immobilize them) fled before I actually arrived. Only four bears on five occasions were successfully approached in dens, but not drugged, without fleeing. Bears were far more wary than had been expected.

Several impacts were classified under the questionable category, including the impact of humans on denned bears. Distances of den sites from centers of human activity (areas receiving daily or near daily use) were plotted. Males on the average denned 0.78 miles from centers of human activity (range from 0.09 to 1.7) while females averaged 0.34 miles (range from 0.006 to 0.73). Females, even those with cubs, tended to den closer to areas of human activity than males, possibly due to selection of upland den sites closer to centers of human activity than the swamp sites selected by males.

The closure of most sanitary landfills, and the centralization and proper maintenance of dumps in the Higgins-Houghton Lakes Area, possibly negatively impacted bears. Before its closure in 1978, at least six bears appeared to feed at a landfill in northwest Roscommon County. Whether the closing of landfills resulted in increases in nuisance complaints or not, nuisance problems did indeed increase during the study. Six complaints were reported in the fall of 1977, 9 in 1978, 22 in 1979, and 9 in 1980 (through July only). Was the 1979 increase due to dump closure(s), or was the evidence only circumstantial? Of the 46 complaints reported during this study, 14 involved damage to beehives, 18 involved bears frightening people, 8 involved bears damaging property, and 6 involved bears harassing, injuring, or killing animals.

The effects of small game and deer (gun) hunters on bears were generally questionable. During 9 times that nearby gunshots were heard, and once when loud trail bikes were audible, 5 bears moved an average of 0.9 mile, probably due to the disturbances.

Several impacts of humans on bears were recorded but could not be reliably classified. Six adult males were located from 0.06 to 0.19 miles from active oil wells whose exhausts were clearly audible up to 1.5 or more miles away. And, an adult male denned within 0.09 mile of an active oil well, but later moved 0.6 mile into a cedar swamp. An adult female was tracked six different times near different oil wells. Whether the noise and the H_2S odor indeed bothered bears, or whether they learned to adjust to these disturbances was unknown.

Snowmobile effects on denned bears were unknown, even though two females denned extremely close to actively used trails, (0.04 and 0.06 mile). The first bear stayed in her den all winter, even though snowmobiles were actually seen passing the den. But, this female (Tanya) was indeed a sound sleeper as I was able to hand inject her with tranquilizer in the den, without waking her. No other bear slept quite this soundly. The other bear stayed in her den during periods of snowmobile activity in December, but ran from the site one night late that month when I attempted to drug her and change her radio-collar.

Contact between humans and bears (marked bears were sighted 63 times by the public) may have resulted in some bears partially losing their fear of humans. The largest nuisance complaint category involved bears frightening humans. These included: a female (Gertrude) placing her paws on a resident's picture window (after she had been hand-fed peanut butter, cookies, and suet); a female (Lucille) breaking into a dog pen and eating the dog food; and, a male (Liberty V) visiting a Bible camp for two weeks, eating garbage, frightening campers, and destroying property. Other unmarked bears were equally as troublesome. Three cabins were extensively damaged by a large male, dogs were killed on several instances by an unmarked bear in Roscommon County, and a bear extensively damaged several deer hunting blinds by tearing up the plastic, shredding the boat seat cushions, and eating the emergency foods.

The frighteningly high incidence of periodontal disease (13 of 35 bears captured) did not appear to be age-dependent, being found in bears from 1.5 to 6.5 years of age at the time of capture. How the disease affects bear behavior is unknown. I do know that the bear with the most critical infection denned six different times during two winters, and only once did I disrupt this bear in his den. The disease could create difficulties in feeding, and increase the chances of infected animals becoming nuisances. Michigan is not the only place where periodontal disease has been found in bears. I found it once in a live-trapped bear in Wisconsin, and it was evident in skulls of bears from Alaska, Arizona, Florida, Mexico, New York, and elsewhere. The cause of the disease is still unknown.

In summary, these recommendations should be made concerning bears in Michigan's

Lower Peninsula. Bears causing damage to beeyards should first be trapped and moved considerable distances from the area, say at least 75 miles. When trapping is unsuccessful, beehive depredators should be destroyed. Bears that are bold, cause property damage, or threaten human life and limb, should be eliminated. Bringing back hunting on a limited basis, carefully controlled and monitored, might make bears more wary of humans and less likely to cause problems. Most important of all, bear habitat must be protected and preserved if the animal is to survive in Michigan's Lower Peninsula.

Albert M. Manville, II is currently an ecologist, solar energy consultant, and a part-time teacher. He holds a B.S. from Allegheny College, an M.S. from University of Wisconsin, Stephens Point, and a Ph.D. in wildlife biology from Michigan State.

He has pursued his study of black bears for 14 years in several states and has also worked on the grizzly bear. He has served as an assistant game manager, a park naturalist, and an instructor in wildlife courses.

His bear research, partially described here, has been financed in part by grants from the Boone and Crockett Club and the National Rifle Association. He is the author of several publications related to his bear research.

He is a member of the American Society of Mammalogists, the Wildlife Society, the Bear Biology Association, the National Wildlife Federation, the Wilderness Society, and Alpha Zeta honorary, among others.

Balancing Civilization's Demands With Conservation's Needs

Daniel A. Poole

In 1895, less than a decade after the Boone and Crockett Club was founded, the number of white-tailed deer in the United States was estimated to be about 350,000. The animals had been extirpated from more than half of the states. Today, whitetails exceed 12 million in 48 states.

The fortunes of some other of North America's most prominent wildlife followed similar paths. The animals decreased drastically, both in number and range, because of human abuse and neglect and then, as specific conservation actions were devised and put in to effect, there followed tenuous periods of population stabilization and, ultimately, increase.

Bison, the native-born cattle of the American plains, for example, numbered about 800 in 1895. Prior to that the animals had been destroyed by the millions, shot for their meat and hides, killed as a military strategy to subdue Indian tribes, and used unthinkingly as convenient targets, a manifestation of that era's casual attitude toward the land and its resources. Today, the U.S.A. population of bison is about 6,000, with most available range well stocked.

Pronghorn antelope, down to not more than 26,000 and only in Montana and Wyoming by 1925, now exceed a half-million in all western states. In 1909, an English visitor reported to a British sports journal, "Antelope in Wyoming are comparatively scarce. The general impression seems to be that they are practically a doomed animal."

By 1907, elk south of Canada were common mainly in and around Yellowstone National Park, totaling less than 50,000 animals. The California wildlife agency, in 1914, said there were only about 400 Tule elk on two ranches there. Today, there are about 1 million elk in 16 states. And so it went with beaver, wild turkeys, wood ducks, herons and egrets, trumpeter swans, fur seals, sea otter and others. For some animals, the passenger pigeon among them, help did not come in time. But early conservationists clearly demonstrated that diminished wildlife populations could be rebuilt once it was realized the animals were in difficulty and public support could be marshaled.

From today's perspective, wildlife in early America easily separates into three categories: animals prized for food, hides, fur or sport; those believed to be a threat to man, his livestock, crops or other property; and those species offering neither apparent value nor danger to man and hence were tolerated or, more commonly, ignored. For the most part, those species that were rescued from potential extinction had sporting and/or utilitarian values, depending on individual circumstances.

Associations of hunters, particularly in the East, were among the first organized and legislatively active conservation groups in the country. The New York Sporting Association was formed in 1844. Members of such groups did not rely on wildlife for food nor did they have a commercial interest in it. Essentially, they were conservation-minded citizens, who hunted, fished and sought the out-of-doors for personal and family recreation. Bird protection societies also were at work, hence the early and much-needed protection given herons and egrets from the plume hunters. Nonetheless, sportsmen had a major role in reversing the dire outlook for wildlife.

In his 1937 book, *Adventures in Bird Protection,* T. Gilbert Pearson, one of the founders and an energetic officer of what is now the National Audubon Society, wrote: "In a word, the fight to preserve the wild life of America had been waged in large part by a class of those men who had tramped the forests and fields and marshes, gun or fishing rod in hand. . . . It is to hunters of the type I have mentioned that we must pay our homage for leading all of the effective movements that brought about legal measures for the relief of our hard-pressed wild birds and mammals, and which, in many cases, have saved species from extirpation over large regions."

A North Carolina biology instructor, Pearson became a wildlife conservation activist largely because of the wasteful and thoughtless destruction of birdlife witnessed in his home state. Illustrative of the men to whom Pearson referred was Theodore Roosevelt, a founder, in 1887, of the Boone and Crockett Club and later president of the United States, whose life-long interest in wildlife and conservation is well known.

"In order to preserve the wildlife of the wilderness at all," Roosevelt noted, "some middle ground must be found between brutal and senseless slaughter altogether and the unhealthy sentimentalism which would just as surely defeat its own end by bringing about the total extinction of game. It is impossible to preserve the larger wild animals in regions thoroughly fit for agriculture; and it is perhaps too much to hope that the larger carnivores can be preserved for merely aesthetic reasons. But throughout the country there are large regions entirely unsuited for agriculture, where if people only have the foresight, they can, through the power of the state, keep the game in perpetuity."

Theodore Roosevelt's terminology offers interesting contrast to use of the same words today. Wilderness now has a legal standing, and areas so designated by Congress must meet certain standards of defined naturalness. Roosevelt was referring to country that yet had to show much permanent and visible effect of man's activities. Farming, ranching, mining and timbering were the principal evidences of the opening and development of the West, together with the railroads, roadways, settlements and facilities that inevitably accompanied them. With today's large and rapidly expanding human population and its concomitant upward-spiraling need and demand for goods and services, the threats to wild country that provides habitat to wildlife of any kind are infinitely more formidable now than in Roosevelt's day. Then, habitat was much more plentiful than it is now. Then, some animal populations were reduced because of overuse. Today, habitat is the limiting factor.

Roosevelt mentioned both "wildlife" and "game," although it appears from his specific reference to the "larger carnivores" that he had all members of the animal kingdom in mind, not just those prized for sport, food, hides or pelts. The words continue to be used interchangeably today, although only in comparatively recent times has recognition spread that balanced and effective wildlife conservation programs must take all forms of animal life into account. This viewpoint gained further credence, in part, by a widely endorsed congressional act in 1980 that authorizes financial incentives to the states to encourage comprehensive planning and programming for native vertebrate animals. Wildlife agencies now understand that the public's interest extends to most wildlife, not just those prized for hunting.

Interestingly, and in contrast to the outlook of informed persons of Theodore Roosevelt's time, the larger carnivores, such as the grizzly bear, wolf and mountain lion, are subject to much conservation attention today precisely for "aesthetic reasons." True, the animals do not occupy anywhere near as large a part of the country as they once did, except for the coyote which has increased its range. But specific programs now are in place to learn more about the animals and to maintain or increase their ranges and numbers. While some interests, mainly ranching, still feel threatened by carnivores, this development reflects the public's new recognition and awareness of wildlife. How well civilization's demands are balanced with conservation's needs will depend, in part, on how skillfully and persuasively this growing public interest and concern can be focused in support of proper laws, policies, programs and myriad other actions that must be taken in wildlife's behalf in coming years.

No matter where a species may occur around the world, all wildlife share a common need, that being suitable, secure habitat in sufficient quantity in which to find food and shelter and to bear and safely rear their young. Habitat is the key to wildlife abundance, diversity and continuance.

In North America, as elsewhere in the world, man poses a severe threat to wildlife and increasingly will do so in the future. A constantly enlarging human population requires more of the globe's bounties—more water, more land in intensified agriculture, more forage for domestic livestock, more timber, minerals and energy, and more of all other resources. As these resources are extracted and converted for man's benefit, the capability of land to supply the needs of wildlife can be diminished or destroyed. Further, man requires space for his homes, factories, highways, airports and other conveniences, again occupying land otherwise suitable for wildlife. Then there are the spill-over effects of civilization—air and water pollution, soil erosion, acid rain, and toxic materials, some capable of killing animals directly or interfering with their physiological and reproductive processes, deforming their young or in some other way interrupting the animals' life cycles. Finally, there is the disturbance factor, whether it be backpackers in sensitive nesting or calving areas, snowmobilers in key wintering grounds when animals' energy reserves are low, legal and illegal commercialization, poaching and sport hunting.

When viewed from the standpoint of human population increase and the direct and indirect effects of civilization's spread, there is good reason to be apprehensive about the long-term future of North American wildlife, some species more than others because of their specialized habitat needs.

The danger to wildlife is much greater and more immediate in the world's developing countries that lack a concerned public and responsive laws, policies and scientific wildlife management programs than in North America. Overall, the challenges are severe, more so than in Roosevelt's day and sharper, without doubt, than only a half-century ago when the foundation for modern scientific wildlife management was laid on this continent.

Despite the realities of current and foreseen threats to wildlife, North Americans are better prepared to protect and maintain their wildlife than are most developed and developing countries.

Because of the vigorous pioneering work of Roosevelt and like-minded conservationists, succeeding generations of wildlife enthusiasts, step by step, have established policies, laws and institutions, on state, national and international levels, that give North American countries increased capability to blunt civilization's impacts on wildlife. By no means are the systems perfect, either in organization, execution or availability of financing, but they are considerably advanced over those in most of the rest of the world. Further, there exists today, and particularly in the United States, a large electorate sincerely dedicated to wildlife's maintenance and enhancement, and ready to support enactment of necessary new laws and to pay for required programs. Thus, there is substantial support in North America for the further refinement and strengthening of policies, laws and programs, as well as for increased funding to take necessary actions. In many countries, the people have yet to be alerted to the need for scientific wildlife management programs.

Second, both the United States and Canada have a considerable land base, with substantial acreages remaining in public ownership and hence susceptible to laws and policies requiring that wildlife be given equal attention with other permitted uses of the lands, such as timbering and grazing. Fortunately for wildlife in the United States, fully one-third of the land base is in public ownership, including national forests, national resource lands, national wildlife refuges, defense installations, and parks and recreation areas administered by federal agencies. State wildlife, forest and park agencies also control significant acreages.

Because these lands are publicly owned, all public interests in them—ranging from water flow, wildlife, forage for grazing, minerals, energy, timber, recreation and the rest—are to be accommodated under congressional mandates and policies. With this as a given, wildlife agencies and interests must remain vigilant to assure that wildlife receives commensurate consideration in the planning for and conduct of all other resource activities on public lands, including the appropriation of sufficient funds and the employment of sufficient adequately qualified persons to conduct necessary activities.

The enhancement and retention of wildlife habitat on the private lands making up two-thirds of the U.S. presents other challenges. Private property is managed as an owner decides, and there is little disposition in the U.S. to prescribe how individual lands may be handled. Thus, various approaches are used to induce landowners to create and retain wildlife habitat.

Some species move freely between public and private lands, while many others, which are neither migratory nor require extensive acreages to meet their life requirements, find all their needs on either private or public land.

Foremost among the approaches authorized to aid wildlife on private lands are federal programs of financial assistance to landowners who undertake certain designated practices, such as maintaining wetlands or creating shrubby fence rows or food plots, for example, to benefit wildlife. Cost sharing normally is provided under the terms of pertinent agricultural laws. Eligible landowners also may receive technical assistance, such as surveying, engineering and planning services, under federal land and water conservation programs. Extension-type educational programs and printed materials also are made available to interested landowners. State wildlife agencies frequently offer landowners free technical advice and may provide seed, planting stock, and other mateirals and services to improve wildlife habitat on farms and ranches. A popular wetlands preservation program, known as the water bank, pays landowners in designated states not to drain, fill or burn wetland areas and associated uplands that provide habitat for migratory birds and other wildlife. Federal and state forestry programs offer assistance to landowners to create or maintain wildlife habitat. That these efforts are beneficial to some degree is proven by the abundance and diversity of wildlife in largely agricultural areas. Some prominent private conservation organizations also have contributed greatly to wildlife by their acquisition, development and maintenance of habitat.

Other federal programs are aimed at lessening inducements to landowners to convert natural habitat to other purposes. Permits are required, for example, for activities that would result in the disruption of flowing streams and other waters. This provides an opportunity for examining proposed activities, determining their potential impact on fish and wildlife habitat and proposing modifications as deemed advisable. Presidential executive orders direct federal agencies not to conduct programs that would facilitate the drainage of wetlands or the development of the natural flood plains of rivers and streams. These water-associated areas are among the country's richest wildlife habitats. Still other policies require the mitigation of fish and wildlife habitat damaged or destroyed as a result of the construction of federal water resources projects.

As might be expected, these programs do not always work as well as might be hoped. The problems encountered are complex—so complex, in fact, that no single law or program is a panacea. Often there is individual, community or state resistance to program requirements. Nonetheless, in the aggregate, they constitute a substantial body of law and policy, and much good has resulted from their implementation.

Increasingly, recognition of the interdependence of resources is gaining wider acceptance in North America. Responsible agencies and the public are beginning to realize that resource programs no longer can be planned and conducted on a single-resource basis—timbering, grazing, recreation, wildlife or whatever. Maximization of the output of one resource can harm the outputs of other resources from the same area of land. Society's demands for the goods and services of land simply are too great to sacrifice or diminish the flow of other goods and services merely to enhance the production of one resource. Hence, and particularly in public land management programs, intensified effort is being made to plan for and coordinate various activities so as to avoid the serious impacts on other resources and resource values that can arise from single-resource management. Timber programs, for example, are being coordinated closely with programs for wildlife, recreation, water flow, soil erosion control and others. This kind of coordinated planning and programming, required nationally in two recent congressional acts, holds significant promise for improving the level of attention given the resources and capabilities of both public and private land.

Despite what has been done to benefit wildlife in the United States, despite the sound and useful laws, policies and programs now in place, and despite the solid framework of federal and state responsibility for caring for our wildlife resources, no sincere sportsman, such as an individual who reads this book, can divorce himself or herself from individual responsibility for wildlife. As recently as up to two decades ago, the wishes and desires of sportsmen had considerable impact on lawmakers in national and state legislatures. This no longer holds true. For several reasons, sportsmen have lost much initiative and standing. Organizations that once strongly and primarily represented sportsmen have, of necessity, become involved in broader environmental matters, such as water and air quality, human population increase, and the like. And as evidence of man's pollution and destruction of wildlife habitat has become more pronounced, major groups have given increasing attention to these threats to wildlife habitat. The effect of this has been to create an impression of lessened interest by sportsmen.

During this same period, antihunting and wildlife preservation groups have voiced increasingly bitter and often groundless criticism of scientific wildlife management, sportsmen and hunting. Too frequently, these critics argue, those responsible for wildlife management have focused attention on the species of wildlife desired by hunters and often to the disadvantage of other animals valued for aesthetic reasons. Some prominent elements of the national news and television media, ever watchful for exploitable controversy, have joined in this criticism and alarmist stance, the result of which has been to raise apprehension about the actual purposes and results of scientific wildlife management.

Criticism is the hallmark of a democratic society. Accurate, constructive criticism can result in the further broadening of federal and state wildlife programs. Thinking sportsmen, however, must take care to ensure that actions taken in response to the criticism do not get out of hand and are not harmful to wildlife or their interest. This can best be done by more sportsmen becoming supportive of and active in organizations that represent their viewpoints at state and national levels.

Every sportsman should bear in mind the four "givens" that determine whether there will be wildlife and hunting in coming years. They are: (1) to have wildlife, there must be habitat; (2) to have hunting, there must be adequate supplies of wildlife; (3) to enjoy wildlife, there must be access to private and public lands; and (4) to attempt to take wildlife, there must be public acceptance of hunting.

With respect to the first, many people frequently overlook the fact that a wild animal, the same as any domestic animal, needs food, water and shelter. Whether moose or mouse, every species of wildlife needs a specific type of habitat that will provide food, shelter from weather and enemies, and a secure place to bear and rear its young. Even animals completely protected from predation and hunting will perish if their habitat is destroyed or seriously impaired. Hence, the sportsman's interest is linked to the federal, state and private lands that constitute the habitat of America's wildlife. On-going programs and new proposals and actions must be monitored regularly to determine their impacts, if any, on the availability of land for wildlife.

The second given logically follows the first. The abundance and diversity of wildlife is related directly to the quantity, quality and distribution of suitable habitat. Under our system of wildlife management, with state and federal involvement, sport hunting is permitted only for those species of animals sufficiently plentiful to withstand regulated harvest that does not jeopardize the capability of the base population to reproduce and sustain itself. Aside from basic seasons and bag limits, special regulations—such as limited number of permits, restricted areas, prescribed methods of taking, and other special provisions—are used, as necessary, to assure that the sporting take does not exceed the biological limits determined for each hunted species or subpopulation of such species.

Most American hunters do not own private land on which to hunt. For many, their sport depends on the availability of public lands—lands administered by the U.S. Forest Service, Bureau of Land Management, Fish and Wildlife Service, Department of Defense, individual state wildlife agencies and consenting private landowners. The United States and Canada have large land bases, but growing populations and other claims for the use of land, particularly near population centers, are reducing the suitability of land as wildlife habitat and its availability for sport hunting. Continuing attention must be given to providing access to land for hunting and other wildlife-oriented recreation.

The final given—to attempt to take wildlife, there must be public acceptance of hunting —deals with a subject that deserves the utmost personal attention and consideration of sport hunters. A hunter would have to be completely out of touch with today's events not to realize that well-financed antihunting and wildlife protectionist groups are dedicated to the abolition of sport hunting. In various ways, and frequently with the unwitting assistance of the press, they seek to arouse public reaction against hunting. Unfortunately, by their anti-social and thoughtless actions while afield, some hunters assist the antihunting cause.

To the present, the critics of hunting and hunters have made little progress toward achieving their objectives. But they have succeeded, perhaps to the true sportsman's benefit, in stimulating the hunting fraternity to give more attention to the way hunting is done by a small segment of our society. In recent years, respected national polls and studies have made three points clear about public opinion on hunters and hunting, the significance of which should not be lost on sportsmen. Many Americans, (1) while not opposed to hunting, ask that hunting be done as humanely as possible, (2) do not believe that, under our system of seasons, bag limits, and other necessary restrictions, sport hunting in any way poses a threat to the continued existence of wildlife species, and (3) desire that maximum use be made of animals taken by hunters. Most persons associating themselves with this latter position apparently are unaware that state and federal laws of long standing prohibit wanton waste of wildlife.

Most significant in all the polls and studies is that the public reacts adversely to hunters, not to hunting. If there is a single area in which sportsmen can broaden public acceptance of hunting, it is in upgrading the actions of hunters in the field. Social acceptance of hunting hinges on this simple fact.

Increasingly, more and more states are requiring first-time hunters to complete success-fully a formal course of hunter education as a prerequisite to licensing. Course content has broadened in recent years and is sure to improve still further, expanding from the earlier focus solely on safe firearms handling to: animal identification, the principles, purposes and practices of wildlife management, hunters' responsibilities toward landowners and others, sportsmanship, ethics, and allied subjects. States currently lacking adequate hunter educa-tion programs and requirements are under pressure to improve them. This effort deserves high priority and should have the support of all sportsmen.

Finally—and this pertains to every hunter—everyone should strive constantly to maintain the highest levels of ethics and sportsmanship in the field. All actions should be tempered with the utmost respect for the animals hunted and for other persons, both hunters and nonhunters alike, and their property. In large degree, the future of wildlife and hunting rests, as always, on hunters themselves.

The charge of the sport hunter to conduct himself ethically in the field, to cull from his ranks those who do not and accordingly educate those who will follow in his footsteps, is not a knee-jerk reaction to the antihunting and wildlife preservation factions. It is, in fact, a necessary and logical step in the long-evolving process of assuring that wildlife has a place —both actually and figuratively—in our society, and that hunting remains as a satisfying recreational opportunity.

The term "conservation" was not coined by the sportsmen of this nation; it was coined for them. It expressed their catalytic contributions to the restoration and maintenance of wildlife, and it still characterizes their role.

Daniel A. Poole, President of the Wildlife Management Institute since 1970, holds B.S. and M.S. degrees in wildlife management from the University of Montana. He worked with wildlife agencies in Montana, California, and Utah prior to joining the Institute in Washington, D.C. in 1952.

From 1966 to 1970, he was Secretary of the Natural Resources Council of America, a service organization of nearly 50 of the country's foremost conservation organizations and professional societies. He served as Council Chairman in 1973 and 1974. Since 1978, he has been Chairman of the Boy Scouts of America's National Conservation Committee. He has also served on several National advisory committees regarding planning for conservation of our natural resources.

In 1969, he received the Jade of Chiefs Award of the Outdoor Writers Association of America for distinguished service to conservation. Drew University conferred a L.H.D. degree on him in 1974 for his conservation work.

He is a trustee of the North American Wildlife Foundation, which issues fellowships in support of wildlife studies and operates the famed Delta Waterfowl Research Station in Manitoba. From 1971 through 1978, he was Chairman of the Citizens Committee on Natural Resources, the first such natural resources lobbying organization in the United States.

He is an active hunter and has taken elk, pronghorn, mule deer, and whitetails.

The Boone and Crockett Club in Conservation

FREDERICK CHILDS PULLMAN

December 12, 1963, New York City.

It is a cold, gray day with a hint of fine snow in the air. In front of the Knickerbocker Club the taxies pull up to the curb and the men in their overcoats, greeting each other warmly, are gathering for the 76th Annual Meeting of the Boone and Crockett Club. They are, for the most part, dressed in dark suits with white shirts and striped ties, and by their looks could just as well be the Board of Directors of a bank or insurance company. They have come from near and far; from Oyster Bay and Montreal, from Fort Myers and Fifth Avenue, from Washington, D.C. and St. Louis, from Los Angeles and Boston. One is a son of Theodore Roosevelt, another is a chairman of the board of one of the country's largest industrial corporations, another is the director of a natural history museum. The earliest of Alaska's bush pilots, the founder of one of its principal airlines, is there, along with a former head of the U.S. Forest Service. The eldest brother of one of the country's most financially formidable families is there, as is the man who is to become the Secretary of the Smithsonian Institution. But almost without exception, these men have one thing in common. They have hunted with a rifle; they have sweated their way up a mountain and crawled on their bellies in the tundra; they have lived in the wilderness and relished it; and, they have an abiding respect for the wealth and diversity of North American wildlife. There were 38 of them there on that cold day in December.

The meeting was called to order at 1:30 in the afternoon and routine matters were dispensed with, the minutes of the previous meeting were approved, the secretary and the treasurer made their reports and the chairman of the Conservation Committee made his report. It was the latter report that made this apparently routine meeting so significant, as the events of the future were to develop, because it was the first time Alaska's proposed Rampart Dam was brought up for discussion. Some of you will remember the Rampart Dam as being the pet project of the late Senator Gruening of Alaska, a project for which he fought hard and defended viciously against its critics.

The Rampart Dam was to be a hydroelectric project on the upper Yukon River in central Alaska, estimated to cost more than 1.5 billion dollars of public funds. The dam's stated purpose was to provide electricity for the cities to the south and employment for Alaskan natives. The fact that Alaska did not need the power and the natives, subsistence hunters and fishermen, did not want the employment, was not discussed by the dam's proponents. It was estimated that the lake behind the dam would take 20 years to fill, by which time it would be larger than Lake Erie, and then another 100 years to silt-in. The reservoir would destroy the habitat of nesting waterfowl, which produced approximately 1.5 million ducks and geese annually, as well as the habitat of sandhill cranes with a population estimated at 20,000. It would eliminate at least 5,000 moose, an unknown number of caribou and untold numbers of small mammals and birds. The dam would have blocked the northern-most run of chinook salmon in North America as well as enormous runs of chum and silver salmon. Finally, it would have inundated four indian villages in the ancestoral territory of the 2,000 Athabascans living on the Yukon flats. The Rampart Dam was clearly an outrageous boondoggle.

The question was, what to do about it? That was the subject of the report of the Conservation Committee at that meeting in the Knickerbocker Club on December 12, 1963.

The President of the Club appointed a committee of five to study the matter. On January 7, 1964 another meeting was held in New York at which the Rampart Dam Committee made its recommendations to the Executive Committee of the Club. They recommended that funds be raised to finance an impartial study of the Rampart project that would: report upon its predictable effect upon wildlife, the economics of its potential production of energy, and the feasibility of alternative energy sources.

The financing of the study was arranged first through the Club and its members, then from other conservation organizations, among them: the Duck Hunter's Association of California, Izaac Walton League, National Audubon Society, Nature Conservancy, New York Zoological Society, Wildlife Management Institute and The Wildlife Society. Then a report committee was appointed, headed by Stephen H. Spurr, Professor of Natural Resources at the University of Michigan. Dr. Spurr's committee consisted of Gunter Schramm of the University of Michigan, who had water resource development experience in British Columbia; Robert A. August of the University of Michigan, who was experienced in Alaska natural resource development; Professor A. Starker Leopold of the University of California and Professor Justin W. Leonard of the University of Michigan, with responsibilities for fisheries and wildlife; Dr. L. Lee Eberhardt of the Battelle Northwest Memorial Institute; Professor Michael F. Brewer of the Center for Natural Resource Policy Studies, George Washington University; Professor William A. Spurr of the Graduate School of Business, Stanford University, a recognized expert on business and population forecasting for the Pacific Coast region; and, Professor Ernest F. Brater of the Department of Civil Engineering, University of Michigan.

Over the course of the next year, this distinguished committee compiled the data and wrote the report that was to be the demise of the Rampart Dam. The report was given wide distribution, particularly to outdoor writers and to members of Congress and their staffs. Then, with the support of Secretary of Interior Stewart Udall and responsible members of Congress, the biggest pork barrel ever to come to Congress was permanently pigeonholed.

That is how the Boone and Crockett Club works; quietly, behind the scenes, and without fanfare. Almost invariably with the cooperation of other conservation organizations, the Club has had an impact on the conservation of wildlife in North America far beyond its size and without the knowledge of the general public. Known to most North American big game hunters as the keeper of the records of trophy heads and horns, as well as the organization that established and supervises the measuring system and publishes this record book, it is generally known for its conservation activities only in those other conservation organizations with which it has cooperated and to wildlife biologists whose research it has financed.

For example, in the middle 1960s Maurice Hornocker (now leader of the Idaho Cooperative Wildlife Unit), who had previously worked with the Craighead brothers in Yellowstone National Park on grizzly bears, came to the Club with a request for funding for a project to study mountain lions in the Idaho primitive area. At that time, in the western states where they existed in marginally viable populations, mountain lions were either bountied or given "varmint" status which left them unprotected. Little was known about their reproductive rate, their impact upon their prey species or their territoriality. Hornocker proposed a project to gather these facts. After receiving a grant from the Boone and Crockett Club, other financing was shortly forthcoming.

To effectively conduct this research it was apparent that individual lions would have to be captured, identified and fitted with radio telemetry collars. For this task Hornocker solicited the aid of an old-time lion hunter, Wilbur Wiles, who lived with his hounds at the headwaters of Big Creek, a tributary of the Middle Fork of the Salmon River. In the dead of winter Hornocker, Wiles and the hounds went up into the back country to catch lions. They established a series of spike camps and food caches a day's walk apart and traversed the country on snow shoes looking for fresh lion tracks. If you know the country of The River of No Return, you can imagine the physical endurance it took to cross those ridges in two feet or more of snow, day after day, packing gear and leading leashed hounds. Upon finding a fresh track, the hounds would be released, the lion shortly treed, tranquilized, collared and released.

After capturing essentially all of the lions in an area approximately 60 miles long and 30 miles wide (the drainage of Big Creek), the next phase of the study was to determine the degree of their territorialty and the boundaries of their territories. This was done by radio telemetry and using the hounds, with the treed lions identified by their collars and tags without being tranquilized. The project took seven years to complete and here are some of the things that were learned from it:

Mountain lions are so highly territorial, and their territories are so large, that an area cannot become overpopulated with them.

Young mountain lions stay with their mother for three years in order to learn the hunting skills necessary to support themselves when they go off on their own. Accordingly, mountain lion litters are born at three year intervals, resulting in a low reproductive rate. Litters consist of one to three kittens.

During the course of the study the elk and deer populations of the study area were increasing. It appeared that predation by mountain lions was beneficial to the prey species in that a lion kill on a winter congregation of elk or deer caused them to move out of that valley into the next one, thereby diversifying the intensity of their browsing.

Lions invariably killed elk by breaking a cervical vertebra, a technique that can be assumed to require an impressive amount of skill, but also one that is dangerous to the lion. During the course of the study one lion was found with a broken jaw, presumably the result of an attack on an antlered elk.

Young lions, upon leaving their mothers at three years of age, could move through the territories of older lions but remained transient until they could find a vacant territory. Most young lions in the study area were not seen again after they left their mothers.

This research project received wide publicity. Among the major national publications in which it was reported were National Geographic and Natural History magazines. Upon its completion, it was published as a Wildlife Monograph of The Wildlife Society.

How did we benefit by this study? By the early 1970's every western state had given mountain lions protection by establishing them either as game animals under the state's fish and game laws, or as a fully protected species. This project was one of a number of wildlife research projects sponsored and supported by the Boone and Crockett Club over the past three decades.

Some of the others were:

A study of the wolves of Mount McKinley by Gordon Haber under the leadership of Ian McTaggart Cowan of the University of British Columbia.

Continuing support of the long-term study of the wolves of Isle Royale, Michigan by Durward Allen which is being carried on now by Rolf Peterson of Northern Michigan College.

A study of the interaction between black bears and man in the lower peninsula of Michigan by Albert Manville.

Two projects by Lynn Rogers in Minnesota; one on black bears, the other on whitetail deer.

A project by Maurice Hornocker on wolverines in northwestern Montana

A study of coyote predation by William F. Andelt at the Welder Wildlife Foundation with particular emphasis on their impact on whitetail deer.

A study by Derek Stoneroff under the leadership of Allen Stokes of Utah State University on the behavior of brown bears in Alaska.

Support of a movie produced by the Sierra Club on the damage done by feral burros to the ecosystems of our southwestern National Parks.

These are typical of the types of projects which have been supported by the Boone and Crockett Club, along with cooperating organizations which included, among many others, the Wildlife Management Institute, the National Audubon Society, the National Rifle Association and the Campfire Club of America.

In 1973 the Club began a revision of its policy with respect to supporting wildlife research. It decided that rather than simply reacting to requests for funding projects, it would initiate projects of its own. The first of these was the Workshop on the Management Biology of North American Wild Sheep, held at the University of Montana, Missoula, on June 18–20, 1974. At this workshop the prominent wild sheep biologists of Mexico, the United States and Canada were brought together to prepare a document which could be used by state, provincial and federal agencies responsible for the management of wild sheep. The sponsors of this meeting were the Boone and Crockett Club, the National Audubon Society and the Wildlife Management Institute. As John Hanes, then Secretary of the Boone and Crockett Club, said in his opening remarks to the conference:

> The sponsors of this meeting are a well selected group. These organizations are, in their diverse ways, three of the older organizations in this country that have been associated with the problems of conservation, ecology and wildlife resources. Each, with its own particular area of special interest, has a very long and continuing and, I may say, very effective record of accomplishment. Usually what they have accomplished has been done by drawing on the knowledge of those who have knowledge and then using their resources to turn that knowledge into effective action. That is the purpose of this meeting. The sponsors felt that this was a timely point to have a meeting of this sort. There is an enormous amount of data concerning our sheep populations. Obviously, there are many things that are not known; but there is much that is known. Probably a great deal more is known than anyone is doing anything with effectively. There have been, as you all know, numerous symposia. There have been two this year. There have been a good number in recent years. These have been immensely productive. They are not generally, however, productive of data in a form that is readily translatable into management action.

The participants in this conference worked intensely for three days. The net result of their efforts was the publication in 1975 of *The Wild Sheep In Modern North America.* This publication has become the source book for all people dealing with the administration and the management of wild sheep in North America. It is also widely used as a textbook by students of wildlife management.

In 1977, the Boone and Crockett Club, joined this time by the Campfire Club of America, sponsored another workshop. This Workshop on the Management Biology of the North American Black Bear was held in Kalispell, Montana between February 17 and 19, and was attended by the prominent bear biologists of the United States and Canada. The purpose, the same as that of the sheep workshop, was to prepare a management document. Again quoting John Hanes in his opening remarks to the participants of the bear workshop:

> That is one reason for the format of this meeting. It does not really aim to add to knowledge—those of you here today already possess that knowledge in most significant respects. Rather, the job is for you to take that knowledge and put it into a form that can and will be used. All of you, by your knowledge or your positions, are managers of a part of our wildlife heritage. As such, you have a responsibility to do more than simply be wise —you must also make that wisdom effective so that the administrators and the politicians,

and all the others whose actions ultimately determine the course of events, can use it. You must try to present it so that they will use it.

The result of this workshop was the publication of *The Black Bear in Modern North America*. Again, the most comprehensive book available today on the status and management of black bears on this continent.

This is the Boone and Crockett Club in action.

Epilogue:

For most of the period of which I have written, from the late 1960's to 1979, I have served as Chairman of the Conservation Committee of the Boone and Crockett Club. During that time, I have been fortunate to have made a number of deep and lasting friendships; Durward Allen of the Isle Royale wolves; Maurice Hornocker of the Idaho cougars, with whom I have fished the back country streams and shot the back country chukars; Dan Poole of the Wildlife Management Institute; C.R. "Pink" Gutermuth of about every conservation organization you can think of; Frank Cook of Anchorage with whom on the shore of a remote Alaskan lake during a storm, we watched my son and a friend in the process of drowning before a previously unseen and unknown of helicopter rescued them; Phil Wright of the University of Montana; and, especially Robert Munro "Papago" Ferguson, either the last, or the youngest of Theodore Roosevelt's godchildren and, for the past twenty years, the godfather of the Boone and Crockett Club. Finally, and perhaps most of all, the late John Rhea, of the Boone and Crockett Club. John Rhea preceded me as Chairman of the Conservation Committee and later as President. Throughout my early years working on Club activities, his counsel and guidance were enormously valuable to me. John died in November, 1980, and by dedicating this chapter to him, I express not only my own appreciation, but that of all of those who have worked with him, for both his friendship and for the enormous contribution he made during his life to the conservation of wildlife.

Frederick C. Pullman is a native of northern Illinois. After serving in the Army Air Corps during World War II, he attended Williams College, earning a B.S. in Biology. He was a commercial banker in Chicago until 1979, when he moved to northeastern Nevada to become a consultant to ranch owners.

He is a past Chairman of the Illinois Chapter of the Nature Conservancy, a Vice-Chairman of the Chicago Zoological Society, a Director of the Morton Arboretum and the International Crane Foundation. He is presently a member of the Executive Committee of the Wildlife Preservation Trust International, a Director of the Upper Humboldt Water Users Association and a member of the Bureau of Land Management Multiple Use Advisory Council. He is a past President of the Boone and Crockett Club and for most of the past decade has been Chairman of its Conservation Committee.

He has hunted throughout North America, including Alaska and Canada, as well as in Scotland and Germany.

He presently resides on a ranch in Lamoille, Nevada, at the base of the Ruby Mountains.

Books of the Boone and Crockett Club

The editors acknowledge, with grateful appreciation, the use of information from the fine chapter on the books of the Boone and Crockett Club that was prepared by the late Milford J. Baker and appeared in several of the earlier editions of this book.

As is well known, the Boone and Crockett Club was founded by Theodore Roosevelt, who also served as its first President. A well known writer of his day, he helped edit many of the early books of the Club. As his co-editor, another very famous naturalist of that era, George Bird Grinnell, added additional insight and flavor. The early books of the Boone and Crockett Club offer a unique historical perspective of hunting and conservation at a time when conservation was only a dimly perceived concept and the science of wildlife management yet to be born. The later books of the Boone and Crockett Club had similarly notable editors and authors, and all enjoy high value in the collector's market.

For convenience, the books of the Boone and Crockett Club may be divided roughly into two categories: general books on conservation and big game hunting and the well-known records books.

GENERAL HUNTING/CONSERVATION BOOKS

1. *American Big Game Hunting.* 1893. Theodore Roosevelt and George Bird Grinnell, eds. New York: Forest and Stream Publishing Company. 345 pages.

The authors of this volume, in addition to the editors, were Owen Wister, Winthrop Chanler, Archibald Rogers, W.D. Pickett, and Dean Sage. This book was the beginning of the format that soon became standard for the first six titles of the Club. It was octavo in size, dark red cloth, silver titles, a big game head on the cover, and the spine stamped in silver. It proved successful enough that a second edition was issued in 1901. It apparently was the only one of the first seven books to have more than a single edition. One of its most interesting sections was a very early attempt to catalog the literature of "American Big Game Hunting". Also included was a most interesting account of the log cabin exhibit erected and managed by the Boone and Crockett Club at the Chicago World's Fair.

2. *Hunting in Many Lands.* 1895. Theodore Roosevelt and George Bird Grinnell, eds. New York: Forest and Stream Publishing Company. 447 pages.

A wide range of hunting topics was covered in this volume. Chapters included a wolf hunt in Russia, bear hunting in the Sierras, big game of Mongolia and Tibet, a chapter on wolf coursing, and a chapter by Theodore Roosevelt on hunting in cattle country. Also included were some very informative chapters on the early stages of the developing conservation ethic, including the Yellowstone National Park Protection Act, the National Park Protective Act, and a chapter on game laws.

This volume also contains an account of what may well have been the first organized attempt in North America to display native trophies, ranking them by measured qualities. This exhibition took place at Madison Square Garden in May 1895 under a "Committee on Measurements" of Theodore Roosevelt, George Bird Grinnell, and Archibald Rogers. The article includes comments by Roosevelt on the importance of symmetry and beauty in final evaluation of a trophy.

3. *Trail and Camp Fire.* 1897. Theodore Roosevelt and George Bird Grinnell, eds. New York: Forest and Stream Publishing Company. 355 pages.

This volume contains the usual wide spread of hunting stories, covering Africa, the U.S. and Newfoundland. Additional chapters of interest include one outlining the development of the Adirondack deer law and a chapter detailing the formation of the New York Zoological Society. There is also an excellent chapter by Theodore Roosevelt on books then available on big game subjects. It includes suggestions on setting up a foundation of a collector's library in the subject matter, and lists the more desirable books to accomplish this goal. A rather impressive list of books on hunting, exploration and natural history, written by Boone and Crockett Club members, is included.

4. *American Big Game in Its Haunts.* 1904. George Bird Grinnell, ed. New York: Forest and Stream Publishing Company. 497 pages.

By the time of this publication, Theodore Roosevelt was President and Grinnell alone acted as editor. Roosevelt did contribute an interesting article on Wilderness Reserves. The range of this volume was mostly North American, with rather intensive coverage of Alaska, including chapters on bear hunting, moose, and the white sheep of Kenai Peninsula. Henry Fairfield Osborne authored a chapter outlining his concern for diminishing stocks of native game species. Several other chapters urged the creation of big game refuges and forest preserves, pointing to the growing interest in conservation activities of the sportsmen of America.

5. *Hunting at High Altitudes.* 1913. George Bird Grinnell, ed. New York: Harper and Brothers. 511 pages.

Theodore Roosevelt, founder and first president of the Boone and Crockett Club, also edited many of its early books in addition to his other well recognized accomplishments.

This volume is the first to be produced by a book publisher not associated with the Boone and Crockett Club. In binding and format, it is similar to its four predecessors. There was only one edition, and as in earlier volumes, there is no indication of the number printed. Nearly half of this book is devoted to the lengthy chapter "Memories of a Bear Hunter" by Col. W.D. Pickett. Pickett was perhaps the premiere bear hunter of his day, and the chapter is noteworthy for insight into a period of hunting opportunity that is gone forever. George Bird Grinnell authored the chapter "Notes on Memories of a Bear Hunter" that covered an additional 50 pages. Other chapters of this volume include hunting stories of Rhodesia, Alaska, Cuba, and the Thian Shan Mountains. As in the previous books, other chapters deal with the officers of the Club, the Club committees, and various reports pertinent to the Club's activities.

6. *Hunting and Conservation.* 1925. George Bird Grinnell, and Charles Sheldon, eds. New Haven: Yale University Press. 548 pages.

Much like the previous volumes in binding and format, this volume provides chapters on conservation alternating with accounts of hunting. The range covered geographically is wide, and the list of authors is impressive, including many of the better known sportsmen of the day such as J.C. Phillips, Charles Sheldon, Madison Grant, John Burnham, W.H. Osgood and Winthop Chanler. The conservation chapters include the beginnings of Glacier National Park, the establishment of Mount McKinley National Park, and a chapter on the need to save the redwoods.

7. *Hunting Trails on Three Continents.* 1933. George Bird Grinnell, Kermit Roosevelt, W. Redmond Cross, and Prentiss N. Gray, eds. New York: Derrydale Press and Windward House. 302 pages.

This volume is the seventh and last in the format established by the first book. It is notable for having two publishers' imprints, Derrydale Press and Windward House. The Derrydale edition was limited to 250 copies; there is no indication of the size of the printing by Windward House.

The Derrydale edition is in the dark red cloth of the six earlier volumes and includes the Boone and Crockett Club silver stamping. The edition by Windward House is in a rich red cloth, with gold stampings for the title and the giant sable on the cover. Both carry the bison of all previous books on the spine. The dust jacket included the table of contents as a display.

As in the previous books, the range of chapters is great, covering subjects ranging from "Days with a Beaver Trapper" to "Wild Life and Sport in Bulgaria". Among the more notable chapters of this volume are "The Vanished Game of Yesterday" by Madison Grant and "Taps for the Great Selous" by Frederick Burnham.

8. *American Game Mammals and Birds: A Catalogue of Books, 1582 to 1925.* 1930. John C. Phillips, ed. New York: Houghton Mifflin Company. 639 pages.

This book is completely different in concept and purpose from the proceeding volumes. It is a catalogue of the thousands of books published through nearly 350 years on sport, natural history, and conservation. It is basically a catalog of Charles Sheldon's magnificent library of such books which has since become part of the great library at Yale University. This volume is a very useful tool for the sportsman-bibliophile, although quite difficult to find.

9. *Crusade for Wildlife.* 1961. James B. Trefethen. Harrisburg, Pa.: Stackpole Company and the Boone and Crockett Club. 377 pages.

This book was commissioned by the Boone and Crockett Club as a history of its activities. It turned out to be a history of the conservation movement in this country, since the Club was inextricably intertwined with such developments from its inception. Carefully researched by James Trefethen, one of the premiere historians of the conservation movement, it has become a standard reference for the subject in many college courses, only recently being supplanted by the slightly larger scope of its successor, *An American Crusade for Wildlife.*

10. *An American Crusade for Wildlife.* 1975. James B. Trefethen. New York: Winchester Press and the Boone and Crockett Club. xii, 409 pages.

This expanded version of the history of the Boone and Crockett Club brings the developments in conservation up to date through 1975. Often used as a reference source by students of conservation and wildlife management, it is also a most interesting book for the average sportsman and lay person with interest in the subject.

11. *The Wild Sheep in Modern North America.* 1975. James B. Trefethen, ed. New York: Winchester Press and the Boone and Crockett Club. xv, 302 pages. (paperback)

Responding to the lack of organized information on wild sheep populations in North America needed to offset inflammatory articles that were occasionally generated in the early 1970's by anti-hunting groups, the Boone and Crockett Club joined with the Audubon Society and the Wildlife Management Institute to sponsor a workshop on the management biology of North American wild sheep in 1974. The workshop included the best known experts from the North American continent on sheep biology and management, and their recommendations for proper management of the species are included, along with summaries of knowledge of the four major categories of our North American wild sheep.

This volume was published as a high quality paperback to keep the cost down to a level that would encourage utilization by wildlife managers and other persons with a sincere interest in these animals.

12. *The Black Bear in Modern North America.* 1979. Dale L. Burk, ed. Clinton, N.J.: The Amwell Press and the Boone and Crockett Club. 301 pages. (paperback)

Following the general concept established in the sheep workshop, the Boone and Crockett Club and the Camp Fire Club of America co-sponsored a workshop on the management biology of the North American black bear in 1977. As with the sheep book, this volume details the more pertinent findings of the workshop and summarizes management recommendations of the assembled experts. Outward size and general format are identical to that of the sheep book. Both volumes are very useful additions to the sportsman's library.

THE RECORDS BOOKS

1. *Records of North American Big Game.* 1932. Prentiss N. Gray, ed. New York: Derrydale Press. 178 pages. (500 copies)

This is not only the first records book but also the rarest and most valuable. Published by Derrydale in an edition of 500 copies at $10 per copy, it soon went out of print. Copies can be found today in excellent shape, due to the high quality of materials that were used, but at a price many times the original cost. This edition is also notable for being published under the auspices of the National Collection of Heads and Horns of the New York Zoological Society. (Ed. note: The effect that this volume had on the eventual fate of the National Collection is detailed in the chapter by Lowell E. Baier of this book.)

An especially noteworthy chapter of the first records book was the one on horns and antlers by Harold E. Anthony. It provides an authoritative yet readable review of the development of these appendages in the several categories of big game trophies. Other chapters detail what was then known about the life history of the many species of big game represented in the book. The actual listings are ranked according to the length of longer antler or skull or tusk and include relatively few specimens in each category. It was, however, a start which would give life to the continuing series of records books and eventually help bring about the uniform system of trophy evaluation adopted several decades later.

2. *North American Big Game.* 1939. Alfred Ely, Harold E. Anthony, and R.R.M. Carpenter, eds. New York: Scribner's. 533 pages. (3000 copies)

This volume is considerably thicker than the first volume, although reduced in outward size. Its trophy listings are somewhat longer than the first volume, with the rankings still being derived by the very simple evaluation of length. It includes many fine chapters on the known life history of big game animals of the continent, care of big game trophies, selection of equipment, and related subjects. Perhaps its most notable chapter is the one by Grancel Fitz in which he outlined his scheme for the rating of trophies. Fitz's system made a strong case for evaluation based upon symmetry, with a penalty subtracted for its lack. Later, Fitz and his ideas would play an important role in formulation of the Boone and Crockett Club's system of trophy evaluation.

3. *Records of North American Big Game.* 1952. Samuel B. Webb, Grancel Fitz, and Milford Baker, eds. New York, Scribner's. 174 pages. (3,500 copies)

This slender volume became the prototype for the next six volumes of the records book. All are very similar in format and composition, varying only in the number of trophies published and the accompanying articles. In a practical sense this is the "first" records book, since it is the first to be based upon the copyright system of trophy evaluation adopted by

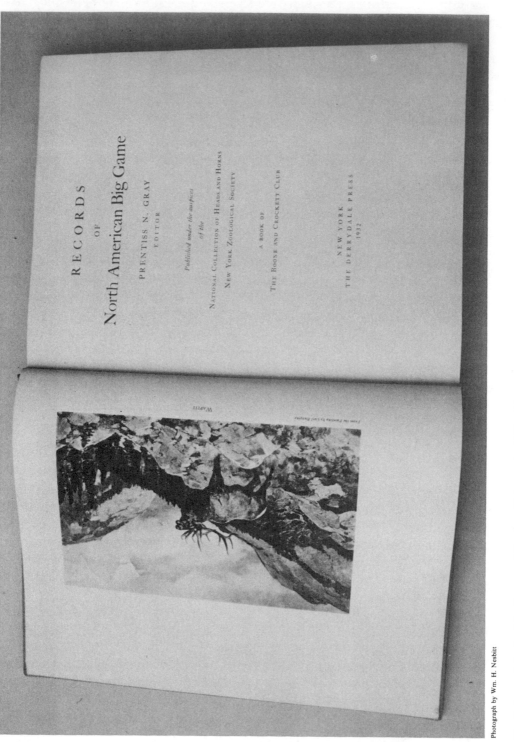

Photograph by Wm. H. Nesbitt

The first records book of the Boone and Crockett Club was the 1932 edition, published by the Derrydale Press. It enjoys considerable collector's value today.

the Boone and Crockett Club in 1950. All trophies published in it were rescored and evaluated by the new method, even if they had been published in previous editions.

One of the more interesting chapters in this edition was one in which Grancel Fitz described what had happened to former world records when they were submitted to the official scoring system. Especially in the antlered categories, some of the former world records had slipped far down from the top when evaluated by the system with its penalties for lack of symmetry. Other chapters covered diverse topics of care of mounted trophies, care of trophies in the field, and a picture section of interesting trophy rooms. A copy today will bring many times its original price of $6.

4. *Records of North American Big Game.* 1958. Samuel B. Webb, Grancel Fitz, and Milford Baker, eds. New York: Henry Holt and Company. 264 pages. (6,500 copies)

The 1958 records book was scarcely larger than the 1952, although it represented considerable refinement in many areas of trophy recordation, including the minimum score raises adopted in 1951 and 1953. Articles included in the book detail the history of the Boone and Crockett Club, the development of the official scoring system, the current objectives and requirements of the trophy program, and several additional articles dealing with stories behind the records, freak trophies, and other such subjects. A chapter on rifles for North American big game is notable for being written by Donald S. Hopkins, who along with Charlie O'Neil and Elmer Keith developed several "wildcat" cartridges that found broad popularity.

5. *Records of North American Big Game.* 1964. Milford Baker, ed. New York: Holt, Rhinehart and Winston. xvii, 398 pages. (10,500 copies)

This volume, in spite of higher minimums in several popular categories, listed more than 5,000 trophies, or approximately double the trophies shown in the 1958 book. The choice of articles that accompanied the trophy listings indicates a growing concern for emphasizing conservation and aesthetic satisfactions in big game hunting. Robert M. Ferguson contributed a chapter on Fair Chase, C.R. "Pink" Gutermuth wrote about conservation and the trophy hunter, and Arthur C. Popham, Jr. wrote on the satisfactions of trophy hunting. A chapter by Grancel and Betty Fitz detailed some of the hunting stories behind the current world records.

6. *North American Big Game.* 1971. Robert C. Alberts, ed. Pittsburg, Pa.: The Boone and Crockett Club. xvii, 403 pages. (17,300 copies)

This volume included many provocative chapters on a wide range of subjects. The records keeping program was described by Elmer M. Rusten; John E. Rhea contributed a chapter on changes in hunting practices; the classic chapter by Harold E. Anthony on horns and antlers was repeated; and, Charles F. Nadler contributed a chapter on the relationships of systematic zoology to big game records. Russell E. Train contributed a chapter on big game hunting in the environmental age and Durward Allen provided a fine summary of the role of predators in the ecosystem. Perhaps the most important chapter of this volume was the lengthy discussion of the North American wild sheep by Ian McTaggart Cowan and Valerius Geist.

7. *North American Big Game.* 1977. Wm. H. Nesbitt and Jack S. Parker, eds. Washington D.C.: The National Rifle Association and the Boone and Crockett Club. xvi, 367 pages. (10, 500 first printing, 1977; 5,650 second printing, 1978)

This edition is especially noteworthy for two things. It is a larger volume in length and width of page size than the preceding books. The larger size was chosen to more effectively display the trophy data, while avoiding an appearance of crowding. It is also the only records book not produced by the Boone and Crockett Club alone. It was produced in cooperation with the National Rifle Association of America, with whom the Boone and Crockett Club had signed an agreement of cosponsorship of the records keeping activities in June of 1973, with the relationship continuing through 1980.

This volume includes several fine chapters on subjects relating to game management. Wild sheep management was discussed by Valerius Geist; mountain lions and their prey by Maurice Hornocker; the black bear by Lynn Rogers; wolf research on Isle Royale by Durward Allen; and, the role of habitat in big game management was covered by Daniel A. Poole and James B. Trefethen. Ladd S. Gordon presented a provocative chapter on the need for hunter education, and Richard Borden discussed wildlife photography based upon his many years as a professional.

This volume is also noteworthy for the four-color section of big game trophy paintings by Robert Thom. Six world record animals (at the time the paintings were done in the early 1970's) were depicted in the actual locality where taken. The paintings provided a painstakingly accurate, vicarious adventure for the reader, by presenting essentially the same scenes that confronted the lucky hunters who took the world records.

Of all the records books, only the seventh is still in print at the time of publication of the eighth edition.

8. *Records of North American Big Game.* 1981. Wm. H. Nesbitt and Philip L. Wright, eds. Alexandria, Va.: The Boone and Crockett Club.

The first printing of the current book is for 15,000 copies. An interesting sidelight is the availability of a limited edition of 750 copies, signed and numbered by the editors. This is the first time that a limited edition of the records book has been offered and it is certain to become a collector's item. Details may be obtained by writing directly to the Club office.

This completes the review of the records books of the Boone and Crockett Club *per se.* Nevertheless, one interesting variant deserves mention. The 1932 records book was, in part, reprinted by Remington Arms Company and apparently distributed free as an advertising promotion. This paperback booklet not only listed the trophy ranking sections, but also published the score charts, which incidentally were not shown in the 1932 records book. It is some 52 pages long and includes ballistics tables for popular Remington cartridges as well as advertising for Remington firearms. It is avidly sought by records book collectors and is rather dearly priced.

Sport Hunters and Federal Laws

Lynn A. Greenwalt

Americans who travel to other countries in order to hunt big game need to know that there are federal statutes and treaties that regulate the importation of wildlife into the United States. These include the Convention on International Trade in Endangered Species of Wild Fauna and Flora (Convention), the Endangered Species Act of 1973, the Marine Mammal Protection Act of 1972, and the Lacey Act. The two primary importation requirements implemented under the authority of the Convention and the Acts are that a hunter take and export wildlife in accordance with foreign law and that he import such wildlife in accordance with United States law.

The Lacey Act is designed to help foreign nations and our individual states enforce their wildlife conservation laws. It prohibits the transportation in interstate commerce of wildlife taken, transported, possessed, or sold in violation of state law. It also makes it a violation of United States law to import into this country any wildlife that has been taken, transported, possessed, sold, or exported in violation of the law of a foreign country. Therefore, the Lacey Act places the responsibility on the hunter to comply with foreign law regarding take and export.

The hunter must also comply with United States law regarding import. A hunter should be aware that a foreign country may permit the taking and exportation of a species whose importation into this country is strictly regulated by United States law. In such cases, even though he has lawfully taken and exported a wildlife trophy from another country, the hunter may not be permitted to bring it into the United States. For example, the Marine Mammal Protection Act and the Endangered Species Act are restrictive in the purposes for which they allow designated species to be imported. These Acts regulate the importation of such species by requiring permits, which may not be issued for sport trophies.

The Marine Mammal Protection Act of 1972 allows the importation of marine mammals only for scientific research or public display purposes, in accordance with permit provisions. The Endangered Species Act of 1973 allows the importation of endangered species for scientific purposes or the enhancement of propagation or survival of the species, again in accordance with permit provisions. Regulations made under authority of the Act expand the purposes for which permits may be issued for the importation of threatened species to include zoological exhibition or educational purposes. Sport trophies do not qualify under the permit requirements of either the Marine Mammal Protection Act or the Endangered Species Act.

The Convention also regulates the importation of certain species of wildlife by means of permit requirements, imposing the most stringent restrictions on species whose continued existence in the wild is most seriously in danger. The Convention lists protected species under one of its three appendices—I, II, or III. In order to import an Appendix I species, a person is required to obtain an export permit or re-export certificate from the Management Authority of the exporting country and an import permit from the United States Management Authority, which is the U.S. Fish and Wildlife Service (USFWS). Appendix I species are considered to be threatened with extinction. Trade in such species is therefore strictly regulated.

Requirements for importing Appendix II and Appendix III species are less restrictive. In order to import an Appendix II species, a person is required to obtain an export permit or re-export certificate from the exporting country. In order to import an Appendix III species from a country that lists the species, a person is required to obtain an export permit or re-export certificate. In order to import an Appendix III species from a country that does not list the species, a person is required to obtain a certificate of origin.

When a person imports wildlife from a country that is not a party to the Convention, comparable documentation issued by the appropriate authority of that country is required in lieu of Convention permits and certificates. Canada is a party to the Convention; Mexico is not. The Canadian Management Authority is the Canadian Wildlife Service, Department of the Environment, Ottawa, Ontario, KIA OH3, Canada. The Mexican Agency authorized to issue export permits is Direccion General de Fauna Silvestre, Netzahualcoyotl #109, 1-er Piso, Mexico 1, D. F.

Although the Convention specifies an exception to the documentation requirement for Appendix II species that are brought into this country as accompanying personal baggage or as part of a shipment of household effects of a residential move, this provision does not apply to trophies. All wildlife trophies, even non-Convention species, require a foreign export permit in order to be imported into the United States. In general, then, a hunter will need a hunting license from the appropriate jurisdiction, a trophy or game tag, and a foreign export permit and/or a Convention permit in order to import wildlife he has lawfully taken in another country.

The Endangered Species Act is the most far-reaching of laws restricting commerce in wildlife. Except as the Act specifically allows by permit, it prohibits the take, import or export, and the sale, trade, or shipment in interstate or foreign commerce of any endangered or threatened species, including their parts and products. It also prohibits the possession, sale, delivery, carrying, transporting, or shipping of wildlife taken in violation of the Act.

If a species is listed under the Convention and also under the Act, importers must comply with provisions of both. The goal of both the Convention and the Act is to protect listed species. The Convention approaches such protection by regulating trade (which is defined as being import or export) through the permit requirements discussed above.

The Act approaches protection more broadly, regulating not only the import and export of listed species, but also the other activities described above. Items imported in violation of the Act will be seized, and violators are subject to civil or criminal penalties.

The Marine Mammal Protection Act of 1972 establishes a moratorium on the taking and the importation of marine mammals, except as specifically allowed in accordance with permit provisions. Since December 21, 1972, it has been unlawful under this Act to take or import marine mammals, including parts and products, except as permits provide for scientific research or public display purposes. This has ended the sport hunting of polar bears and walrus in Alaska and the importation of either from Canada. An exception to the taking prohibition is allowed for Alaskan natives, who may take marine mammals for subsistence purposes and may use the parts of animals so taken in the manufacture of native handicrafts.

On April 9, 1976, the USFWS proposed waiving the moratorium on the taking of three Alaska marine mammals—the polar bear, sea otter, and Pacific walrus—and returning their management to Alaska, following the Service's approval of the state's regulations. As yet, Alaska has not implemented such regulations, so the taking prohibition is still in effect. Violators of the Marine Mammal Protection Act are subject to civil or criminal penalties.

Under new federal regulations regarding the importation, exportation, and transportation of wildlife (50 Code of Federal Regulations 14), the USFWS has initiated a new licensing program for commercial wildlife importers and exporters. Sport hunters do not need to obtain federal licenses to import wildlife for personal use, but should be aware that the requirement exists for commercial importers.

Sport hunters who lawfully take wildlife in Canada or Mexico may import such wildlife, for non-commercial purposes, at any Customs port of entry. This applies both to shipments and to accompanying personal baggage, including even Convention species. United States residents who import game mammals or birds from Canada or Mexico are required to fill out a "Declaration for Free Entry of Game Mammals or Birds Killed by United States Residents" (Customs form 3315) or a "Declaration for Importation or Exportation of Fish or Wildlife" (USFWS form 3-177) at the port of entry.

These forms require similar information—a description of the wildlife by common name and quantity and a declaration of its country of origin. The 3315 form differs from the 3-177 form in requiring the importer's hunting license number, while not requiring the scientific name of the wildlife.

The Customs Service assists the USFWS and other agencies in enforcing their laws and regulations. In general, wildlife will only be "cleared" by Customs if USFWS inspectors or agents have inspected and approved it for entry. At ports where wildlife can lawfully enter and there are no USFWS personnel, Customs may clear the wildlife subject to post-clearance inspection and investigation by USFWS. To obtain clearance by Customs and/or the USFWS, the importer must make available for inspection all required documents (including licenses, permits, and declaration forms) as well as the wildlife itself.

In the event that an importer ships the wildlife into this country, rather than carrying it as accompanying personal baggage, he is required to mark on the exterior of all containers and packages the name of the shipper and the consignee and provide a complete description of the number and kinds of wildlife included in the package or container.

SOME NORTH AMERICAN WILDLIFE WHOSE IMPORTATION AND/OR EXPORTATION IS FEDERALLY REGULATED AS OF DECEMBER 1981

1- Marine Mammals - Importation is prohibited, except as specifically allowed by permit for scientific projects and public display purposes under the Marine Mammal Protection Act:

polar bear   walrus

2- Endangered Species - May be imported only in accordance with strict permit requirements for scientific research or propagation purposes under the Endangered Species Act:

jaguar   Mexican grizzly bear
ocelot   wood bison
margay

3- Convention Species—May be imported with appropriate Convention documentation:

cougar   Rocky Mountain bighorn sheep
brown or grizzly bear   desert bighorn sheep

USFWS DIVISION OF LAW ENFORCEMENT DISTRICT OFFICES
(DECEMBER 1980)

1. Post Office Box 42597
   Anchorage, Alaska 99509
   Telephone: (907) 276-3800

2. Lloyd 500 Building, Suite 1490
   500 North East Multnomah Street
   Portland, Oregon 97232
   Telephone: (503) 231-6125

3. 2800 Cottage Way, Room E-1924
   Sacramento, California 95825
   Telephone: (916) 484-4748

4. Post Office Box 25486 Denver Federal Center
   Denver, Colorado 80225
   Telephone: (303) 234-4612

5. Post Office Box 329
   Albuquerque, New Mexico 87103
   Telephone: (505) 766-2091

6. Post Office Box 45
   Twin Cities, Minnesota 55111
   Telephone: (612) 725-3530

7. 1010 Gause Boulevard, Building 936
   Slidell, Louisiana 70458
   Telephone: (504) 255-6471

8. Post Office Box 4839
   Atlanta, Georgia 30302
   Telephone: (404) 221-5872

9. U.S. Courthouse Annex, Room A-906
   110 Ninth Avenue South
   Nashville, Tennessee 37203
   Telephone: (615) 251-5532

10. 95 Aquahart Road
    Glen Burnie, Maryland 21061
    Telephone: (301) 761-8033

11. Century Bank Building, 2nd Floor
    700 Rockaway Turnpike
    Lawrence, New York 11559
    Telephone: (212) 995-8613

12. Post Office Box E
    Newton Corner, Massachusetts 02158
    Telephone: (617) 965-2298

If a shipment arrives with incomplete foreign documentation or permits, it may be held in Customs custody, re-exported, abandoned, or released under bond pending the receipt of the required documents. If the appropriate documents are not forthcoming in a reasonable period, the matter is turned over to a USFWS special agent for investigation.

Sport hunters should be aware that wildlife trophies, other than those taken in Canada, Mexico, or the United States, may be imported or exported only at the eight ports designated under the Endangered Species Act. These are Los Angeles, San Francisco, Miami, Honolulu, Chicago, New Orleans, New York, and Seattle. Although Dallas-Fort Worth has been proposed as a designated port, such status has not been implemented.

It is the responsibility of the importer to know the legal requirements for importing the species in which he is interested. Because listing and delisting occur at irregular intervals, the information compiled here may not be current at a future date. In addition, Canada and Mexico may have further restrictions on their native species. For more specific information, sport hunters may contact the Special Agent in Charge of the appropriate District Office shown on the accompanying list.

The United States continues to be committed to the conservation of wildlife. Our national policy reflects our recognition of the aesthetic, scientific, cultural, recreational, and economic value of these irreplaceable life forms. Toward this goal the Service enforces existing legal protection as part of our national commitment to preserving wildlife for future generations.

Lynn A. Greenwalt, a former Director of the U.S. Fish and Wildlife Service, is a native of Cache, Oklahoma and now lives in Rockville, Maryland. He holds a B.S. degree from the University of Oklahoma and a M.S. in Wildlife Management from the University of Arizona.

He began his Federal career with summer jobs on the Wichita Mountain Wildlife Refuge while attending college. In 1955 he joined the Service as Assistant Manager of the Bear River National Wildlife Refuge in Utah.

In the years since, he has worked with wildlife research units and in various assignments in wildlife refuges throughout the west. He held staff positions at the Albuquerque and Minneapolis Regional Offices and has served as Supervisor for the Service's law enforcement agencies in the northwest region.

He was transferred to the Washington office in 1971 as Chief of the Division of Wildlife Refuges, and in May 1973 was named an Assistant Director of the Service. Six months later, in October 1973, he was appointed Director. He remained in that position through the terms of offices of Presidents Ford and Carter, leaving office on January 30, 1981.

He is an associate member of the Boone and Crockett Club.

The National Collection of Heads and Horns—a Historical Perspective

LOWELL E. BAIER

The National Collection of Heads and Horns in historical perspective poses a real paradox. How could the world's finest big game trophy collection be assembled just after the turn of the century by one of the country's strongest hunting opponents while America was decrying the destruction of its vanishing wildlife? Yet, three-quarters of a century later, how could that same collection be discarded when the sporting fraternity has its largest membership, is enlightened, organized and politically active? These curious questions can only be answered by searching for clues amongst the available record woven by history.

The history of the National Collection is not as much a story about big game trophies as it is about the dominating personality and zealous imagination of its principal founder William T. Hornaday, and a century in American history when concerned sportsmen, naturalists and zoologists came to grips with the problem of vanishing game populations. It is moreover, a story about the formation, growth and evolution of the New York Zoological Society and the Bronx Zoo, created to be the finest zoological park in the world. Hornaday, the first Director of the Bronx Zoo, completed his concept of the Zoological Park with the Heads and Horns Museum. When the Museum was dedicated on May 25, 1922, "In memory of the vanishing big game of the world," Hornaday stated the National Collection of Heads and Horns "will stand for at least 200 years." It stood for less than 50 years!

The history of the National Collection starts with the beginning of the New York Zoological Society in 1895. At the Boone and Crockett Club's annual meeting in January, 1895, Club President Theodore Roosevelt appointed a committee chaired by Madison Grant to monitor legislation introduced in the State of New York relating to game preservation. The creation of a zoological park in New York City was one of the committee's objectives. As early as 1880, attempts had been made without success to establish a zoological garden in New York City.

When Madison Grant revived interest in this project in 1895, legislation was reintroduced on the condition that the Boone and Crockett Club would organize a zoological society and that some of its members would appear as incorporators. The bill passed the New York State Assembly, and the New York Zoological Society was organized May 7, 1895. Included as incorporators were club members Madison Grant, C. Grant LaFarge and Charles F. Whitehead. The New York Zoological Society's 1896 Board of Managers (now Board of Trustees) included 11 members of the Boone and Crockett Club, and 6 of the 8 executive officers were Club members, including the 2 vice presidents, both secretaries, and 6 members of the Scientific Council. In the Boone and Crockett Club's early history (written in 1913 by George Bird Grinnell) Grinnell observed that, "The New York Zoological Society has been and is a child of the Boone and Crockett Club."

The purposes of the Zoological Society were clearly defined: The establishment of a zoological park and gardens unique in its concept and design; promotion of zoological science for research and education; and preservation of the native animals of North America. Madison Grant had long dreamed that New York should have a great zoological park that permitted wild animals, particularly those of North America, to be exhibited in surroundings as nearly proximate as possible to their native habitats. This new principle of park design in 1895 was revolutionary. With a few minor exceptions, in London and Berlin, cramped pens, paddocks and cages were the traditional zoo enclosures. The main function of a zoo was the exhibition of as many kinds of animals as possible. To accomplish its goals, the Zoological Society selected 261 acres from the City's Bronx Park as the site for the new zoological gardens and immediately began to study Europe's finest zoological parks for details of design. Work commenced on the first building in 1898, and the park was opened to the public in November 1899, with 843 animals representing 157 species.

The burden of organizing and operating the New York Zoological Society fell primarily to Madison Grant, C. Grant LaFarge, Professor Henry Fairfield Osborn, Charles E. Whitehead and John L. Cadwalader, with later help from Percy R. Pyne, George Bird Grinnell, Winthrop Chanler and Philip Schuyler (all members of the Boone and Crockett Club), together with Andrew H. Green, John S. Barnes and Levi P. Morton. Immediately prior to final site selection, the principal Zoological Society organizers sought out a recognized individual with experience to aid in the final site selection, take on the expanding affairs of the Society, and head up the development of the Zoological Park.

Enter William Temple Hornaday.

Hornaday was hired in April 1896 at the age of 41 as the first Director of the Zoological Park. He made the final site selection of the South Bronx Park over three other locations for the zoo's home and continued to firmly impress his personality upon the development of the Zoological Park until his retirement in 1926.

Born prior to the Civil War in 1854 on a farm near Plainfield, Indiana, Hornaday later moved to a farm in Iowa and graduated from Iowa State Agricultural College. During college, he taught himself taxidermy and assembled a collection of native mammals and birds for the college museum. Determined to become a naturalist, he joined Ward's Natural Science Establishment in Rochester, New York, as an assistant taxidermist in 1873. Ward's supplied mounted specimens for schools and museums throughout the world. Within a year, Hornaday was off on specimen collection expeditions to Cuba and the West Indies, South America, India, Ceylon, the Malay Peninsula, and Borneo.

In 1882, Hornaday was appointed Chief Taxidermist for the U. S. National Museum in Washington, D.C., where he created artistic and lifelike displays that significantly advanced the art of natural history exhibitions. He had a strong interest in living animals and, in 1888, he advocated that Congress establish a great National Zoological Park in Washington. Congress authorized the Park and appropriated $200,000 in 1889 for its establishment. Hornaday was appointed its first Superintendent and he designed the Park's 168 acres. He was not given the full authority he felt he needed to implement his many ideas in the Park, and he resigned after one year to become Secretary of the Union Land Exchange.

Hornaday had written three books by the time he was appointed Director of the New York Zoological Park: *Two Years in the Jungle* (1885), *Taxidermy and Zoological Collecting* (1892), and *The Man Who Became a Savage* (1894). Although it was as Director of the Zoological Park that he received international recognition for creating the finest modern zoological park in the world, Hornaday's writings and personality had already begun to establish his reputation in the field of conservation.

Hornaday in his youth had been an avid hunter, a hobby that had led him into his taxidermy career. On specimen collection trips around the globe for Ward's, he killed as wide a variety of rare and endangered species as any contemporary American. Hornaday made a careful distinction between killing for sport or the market and killing for scientific study and exhibition in a natural history museum. Natural history was explained and studied in dioramas exhibiting native habitat scenes and full mounted animals, lacking access to the audio-visual equipment of today. "I have never been what you might call a sportsman," he told a reporter in an interview soon after he became Director of the Zoological Park. "While I have killed scores of species and hundreds of individuals of large game animals, I have never hunted save as a naturalist, bent on making studies and preserving in one form or another every animal killed that was worthy of a place in a museum."

Hornaday grew up in an era in which the herds of big game that once populated this continent and the world were measureably vanishing from pressures of man's increasing habitation and indiscriminate killing. Bison were slaughtered to virtual extinction; market hunting was still practiced; spring shooting of game birds was a universal practice; game management was an unknown science; and game laws were extremely liberal or non-existent. Hornaday's observations of this period evolved a simplistic, one-track theory that hunting, and only hunting, was responsible for the decline in wildlife populations and that the way to save wildlife was "to prevent its killing." His book, *Our Vanishing Wild Life,* published by the New York Zoological Society in 1913, became a hard-hitting indictment of America's casual neglect of its wildlife resources.

Hornaday was a commanding personality. A man of elegant appearance, with clipped beard and flashing eyes, he was a forceful speaker and persuasive writer, ideal as a crusader. He was a Victorian, a 19th century figure, who never learned to mask his zeal with wit or grace. His caustic statements endeared him to the press, and he received more publicity than any other conservationist of his time. In his makeup, there was no room for compromise. His image as a lone warrior resulted from his unfortunate tendency to claim personal credit for achievements that involved hard effort and sacrifice by many others. But his prolific writings and forceful presence commanded ready recognition and national attention. In zoological park affairs, his word was absolute and his enthusiasm and zeal to impress his work upon the park caused one critic of the time to describe him as the "autocrat's autocrat."

Hornaday had a private collection of 131 heads and horns that he assembled as a naturalist throughout his career, most of which were bought or donated since his own best trophies had gone into museums. His collection was assembled on a broad, systematic base to include representative species of several continents such that a scientist could recognize it as something more than a hunter's pride. In Scribner's Magazine in the Fall of 1905, he undertook to educate the general reader on how interesting a really broad collection could be, albeit not the product of one sportsman's career afield. He decried the egotistical impulse that caused sportsmen of that period to ignore the typical head of any animal they had not personally shot. During his career, he'd been called upon to inspect the hunting trophies of hundreds of men collected throughout the world; what were their families to do with them upon their demise? What about his own collection? He didn't want it broken up and sold. An all inclusive exhibition of hoofed and horned game of the world was impossible for the private collection but perhaps not for a widened range of interest with an institutional base. And, a precept of the New York Zoological Society was to foster zoological science for research and education, which to that point was largely a product of studying fully mounted animals, heads and horns in schools and museums.

All of these thoughts and considerations slowly began to crystalize in Hornaday's mind into a course of action. He wanted some central depository, some institutional trust, for his own collection and the collections of other sportsmen, where the finest trophies might find a permanent home and the systematic plan he had written about might be worked out on a grand scale! Such a depository would be, in essence and fact, "a national collection of heads and horns." Hornaday discussed his plan with Madison Grant, the Chief Executive Officer of the Zoological Society, and secured his enthusiastic support before the Society's Executive Committee.

On December 20, 1906, the Executive Committee, by formal resolution, assumed responsibility for the creation of two complete and perfect collections of all the heads, horns and tusks of the world's ungulates, one to be arranged zoologically and the other geographically. The title designated for this great collection was "The National Collection of Heads and Horns." The Secretary of the Smithsonian Institution complained that the name should be "The American Collection of Heads and Horns" leaving "National" to be applied only to collections under governmental auspices. But Hornaday and sportmen welcomed the prestige of "National Collection" as a repository for their trophies and "National" it remained.

With John M. Phillips of Pittsburgh, President of the Lewis and Clark Club, acting as a liaison with the sportsmen, Madison Grant representing the Boone and Crockett Club, and Hornaday the Camp-Fire Club, a prospectus was addressed to the sportmen of America on March 20, 1907, setting forth exactly what they wanted:

... a depository for the finest wild animal trophies which it is possible to bring together ... accessible, spacious, fireproof, well lighted, finely appointed in every detail, and managed by sportsmen ... There should be formed a zoological series and a geographical series—by continents—each as nearly complete as it can be made.

Close on the heels of that prospectus came an announcement, dated May 1, 1907, that The National Collection of Heads and Horns was an actuality. Hornaday had presented the institution with his own collection, the "Nucleus Collection" as he called it in "The National Collection of Heads and Horns," a handsome brochure that followed the prospectus. In that first brochure, Hornaday described his Nucleus Collection and the details of what the National Collection should include:

It is natural for one who is interested in a special group of animal forms to desire a collection which in one way or another will represent its members. Of groups which embrace only small-sized individuals, it is often possible for one man to possess a large assortment of species and individuals. But in the gratification of a taste involving individuals of large bulk, the limitations are many and severe. With such important forms as the large hoofed mammals of the world, it is not desirable that many men should be animated by the desire for large collections. The undue gratification of too wide-spread a desire for heads and horns, irrespective of their origin, would mean great and deplorable slaughter "for commercial purposes." A collection limited to personal trophies won by the owner is quite another matter, chiefly because of its wholesome limitations; and in these days, *no sportsman or naturalist should shoot more animals than he preserves.*

In America, museums generally are treating the Order *Ungulata* merely as an integral part of the great living world, which is not to be unduly exploited at the expense of other zoological groups of equal scientific importance. In the zoological parks and gardens, the limitations upon the collections of hoofed animals are numerous, and it is possible to procure and exhibit only a few representative species, which as far as possible must typify the whole vast series.

Nevertheless, the desire to behold complete collections of large game specimens springs eternal in the human breast. The wish for a comprehensive and all embracing exhibit of the world's horn bearing animals is both natural and legitimate. To us, the logical sequence of the situation is a national collection of heads and horns, as fine and as nearly complete as American sportsmen and travelers can make it, located in the New York Zoological Park, and owned and maintained in perpetuity by the New York Zoological Society.

A survey of the ways and means that are available for the attainment of such an end quickly leads to the conclusion that a well considered plan, properly inaugurated and diligently pursued, would lead to a successful result. There is reason for the belief that a collection founded on lines sufficiently brought and dignified to command the respect of the sportmen of America, would receive from them active support sufficient to guarantee its ultimate success. A collection so large, so rich in fine specimens, and so nearly complete in species as to command national and international respect, surely would possess sufficient zoological value to make its existence and its increase well worth while. There are few, if any, American sportsmen who will not welcome the idea of a great national collection of ungulate heads and horns which in time will rank with the best collections of Europe.

Naturally, in the founding of such a collection, the standards must be fixed high, and the conditions of admission must be reasonably severe. No specimen should be accepted without a specific reason to justify its presence. Perhaps the first great object to be sought should be zoological completeness. That once attained, mediocrity should be weeded out, and the average of excellence should constantly rise.

There should be two series of specimens, both of which eventually should be made complete. The first should be zoological, the second geographical, and each should command an abundance of space. The first should be arranged in accordance with the system of Nature, to show evolution in the relationships. Dull indeed is the imagination which cannot foresee the intense interest which would attach to certain groups, such for example as the *Cervidae,* when it is possible for the eye to comprehend at one sweep the long line of forms related to the Altai Wapiti. Imagine, also, the radiation of the Genus *Ovis* from western Mongolia southward to India, westward to Sardinia and Morocco, and northeastward by the grand loop to Kamchatka, Alaska and Mexico.

The second series naturally would be created to display the ungulate resources of the continents; and herein would maps of the geographical distribution of families, of genera, and of species be strongly in evidence. In this series would be showing the centers of distribution and the culminating points of many species popular with American sportsmen and naturalists. Here would be displayed or deposited an endless series of maps and pictures illustrating the haunts and homelife of important species. Here would naturally be gathered together such a collection of photographs of living wild animals, both in their haunts and in captivity, as never yet has been formed. The records of big game which naturally would accumulate in the national collection, soon would represent great zoological value.

There are many reasons why a National Collection of Heads and Horns should be formed and displayed in New York, rather than elsewhere. The metropolis of the western continent is the natural home of the greatest educational collections of America. Hither come, sooner or later, all American sportsmen and naturalists, and the majority of those who visit our continent from abroad. New York is truly a pan-American city. Its Zoological Society is in keen sympathy with the proposition, and offers the guarantee of space and permanency which is absolutely essential to success. The natural home of such a collection as that proposed is in the beautifully forested grounds of the Zoological Park, surrounded by the living representatives of now sixty-five—but presently a hundred-species of hoofed animals. Furthermore the Zoological Park already enjoys the support and cooperation of a large number of American sportsmen who are especially interested in the ungulates of the world.

In England practically all British sportmen pour their finest and rarest horned trophies into the South Kensington Museum. Very naturally, the result is a collection of ungulates which is at once the envy and the dispair of Americans. As yet no American museum possesses a collection which is even second to it; and we greatly fear that, for reasons only too apparent, no museum on this side of the Atlantic will ever rival that marvelous gathering of hoofed and horned rarities.

What Hornaday and Grant were undertaking was nothing less than preserving a complete and noble memorial to the vanishing big game of the world while there was yet time. To give the dream reality, Hornaday presented his personal collection of 131 heads and horns representing 108 species to the Society, a nucleus that defined many of the lines the completed collection would later develop.

A memorable early donation was by Charles T. Barney, Chairman of the Executive Committee of the Society, who presented the world's record (in length) elephant tusks, 11′ 5½″ and 11′, totaling 293 pounds in weight. They were said to have been presented by King Menelik of Abyssinia (Ethiopia) to a European political officer; their history was not well documented until they were offered for sale on the ivory market in London in 1906, where they were acquired by Rowland Ward and sold to Barney for $2,500. Hence, the National Collection began with 132 specimens.

On September 1, 1908, "The National Collection of Heads and Horns, Part II" was published by Hornaday wherein a broader outline of the Collection's objectives and purposes was stated. This companion to the original brochure called upon the sportsmen of all countries to contribute to the Collection:

> The National Collection of Heads and Horns represents an effort to build up a collection that will adequately represent the big game of the world in general, and that of America in particular. Such an undertaking is now rendered necessary by the rapid disappearance of large mammalian life, all over the world . . . The objective of this collection is to afford to the sportsman, naturalist, and every other person interested in animals, a comprehensive and satisfactory view of the big game of the world, with a wealth of detailed information and illustration. The first effort will be to bring together materials of two complete series of heads and horns, one zoological, and the other geographical. In addition to these, it is desirable to form collections of horns and antlers of specially important species, such as the moose, wapiti, mountain sheep and caribou, to show their status in widely separated localities, and under varying conditions of food and climate . . . Such special collections surely will be of real value to everyone who is interested in the species thus represented; and they will form an important feature of the National Collection as a whole.

> While it is quite essential that every specimen accepted for the National Collection shall serve some specific purpose, and serve it well, it is not to be expected that each object shown shall be of an extraordinary character. Of the rare species we must accept small specimens and make much of them until large ones are offered. The tape measure is not to be the sole arbiter, but of common species it is necessary that a high standard should be maintained.

> Although this collection will be located in America, we hope that all sportsmen and naturalists from abroad will enjoy it with us. The brotherhood to true sportsmanship is universal. While we do not seek to impose upon foreign sportsmen any burdens in connection with this undertaking, we do not hesitate to say that world-wide cooperation in the up building of a world-wide collection will be welcomed as cordially as we would welcome any brother-sportsman to a seat at our camp-fire in a land of big game.

The response of the sporting fraternity was overwhelming, as described by Hornaday. "The record of the first year is profoundly gratifying. It shows, beyond the possibility of doubt, that the idea meets the hearty approval of American sportsmen and that they will work it out to a splendid consummation".

Individual gifts and entire collections came from British Columbia, China, California, London and Philadelphia. New York contributed what was by far the most outstanding accession of the first year, the Reed-McMillin collection of heads, horns and skins of Alaskan big game. A. S. Reed was an Englishman who between 1896 and 1902 lived in Victoria, British Columbia. On his frequent hunting expeditions to Alaska and Northern British Columbia, he made it a practice to hunt very late in the fall or early in the winter, and go after only the best and most magnificent specimens. The result was, of course, an unparalleled collection of Alaskan big game that included 6 moose, 6 caribou, 10 sheep, 10 bear skins, 2 mounted walrus heads and 7 pairs of tusks. Mr. Emersom McMillin of New York, a member of the Camp-Fire Club of America, donated $5,000 to purchase the entire collection.

Madison Grant donated an extraordinarily large pair of walrus tusks and a family group of white mountain sheep heads, from the extreme northern end of the Rocky Mountain chain, within 50 miles of the Artic Ocean. He later presented two Rocky Mountain bighorns and a Columbia mountain goat. John Roger Bradley sent heads of a Coke Hartebeest, an impala, a common waterbuck, the fine head of a Siberian argali and the mounted head of an Atlantic walrus. George L. Harrison, Jr., of Philadelphia, sent three shipments of African heads, representing about 60 species. The African groups were further enriched by an extensive gift from John W. Norton of New York and Cazenovia, including a greater kudu, an eland, a Baker roan antelope and a Crawshay waterbuck.

Caspar Whitney donated a fine mounted head of a wood bison. Warburton Pike, probably the first sportsman to penetrate the Barren Grounds north of Great Slave Lake, offered a tremendous muskox head that still stands high among the record heads. From George H. Gould of Santa Barbara, California, came a mountain sheep head that Hornaday described as ". . . not only one of the finest heads ever taken on the American continent, but . . . probably the greatest trophy of *Ovis canadensis* that ever fell to the rifle of a gentleman sportsman."

Even China contributed in that first year. Mason Mitchell, the American Counsel at Chungking, forwarded what was then the rarest specimen in the young collection: the entire skin, skull and horns of a takin from Szechuan. That form had only recently been discovered and it was named *Budorcas texicolor mitchelli* in honor of its discoverer. Mr. Mitchell had himself shot the specimen and it arrived safely after five months' transit, swathed in many layers of cloths impregnated by ". . . the most pungent powders that are dealt in by the Chinese apothecary to keep off bugs, mice and rats of all sorts."

Out of a special interest in the wapiti group, Ferdinand Kaegebehn presented a fine pair of antlers of the Arizona wapiti from the Santa Catalina Mountains, of which only three pairs were known to exist. The species apparently became extinct about 1901. The fabulous F. H. Barber South African Collection of 63 species, presented by Messrs. Frederick A. Schermerhorn, Lispenard Stewart, Frederick G. Bourne, Charles F. Dieterich and William D. Sloane, contained many records, with the most important being Cape buffalo, greater kudu, waterbuck, lechee antelope, white-tailed gnu, wart-hog, springbuck and steinbuck. Mr. H. Casimir de Rham contributed the monsterous 89″ horns of an Indian buffalo for the Asiatic section, the head of an Astor markhor for the Zoological Series and two fine sheep heads, *Ovis karelini* and *O. nigrimontana,* that were collected in eastern Turkestan by Douglas Carruthers.

A big prize in another sense was the magnificently mounted head of a gigantic African elephant shot in British East Africa (Kenya) in 1906 by Richard Tjader. It was presented to the museum in 1910 by his son, Richard Thorne Tjader. It was said to have stood 10′ 4″ high and carried 6′ 9″ tusks weighing 160 pounds. A white rhinoceros head, presented by Colonel Theodore Roosevelt early in 1911, was then regarded as the most rare and valuable single specimen of that year. It was the second finest specimen obtained by the Roosevelt expedition, with the best one donated to the National Museum at Washington. Roosevelt shot the rhino in the Lado District, west bank of the Nile, on January 28, 1910. It was mounted by James L. Clark of New York. The length of the front horn was 25″ and the rear 27⅛″.

ZOOLOGICAL SOCIETY BULLETIN   821

THE ENTIRE MACKAY COLLECTION OF ELK, BISON AND MOOSE HEADS.

One of the most significant early donations to the National Collection of Heads and Horns was this magnificent group of moose and elk trophies collected by C.H. Mackay. The donation was described in this issue of The Zoological Society Bulletin.

Perhaps the largest collection to be presented was the Clarence H. Mackay Collection of 26 elk, bison and moose heads, collected in 1902. The moose were collected on the Kenai Peninsula of Alaska and measured 76", 74⅝", 74⅞", 69⅛", 66⅝" and 64⅛". The 10 wapiti heads from Wyoming were equal in size and variation to the moose. The four bison were the first plains bison received in the collection. The 1912 Zoological Bulletin regarded this great collection as ". . . almost impossible to duplicate at any price."

A "Combat Collection" of locked antlers was assembled including locked moose, caribou, and mule deer antlers. Other than these, and a "Collection to Illustrate Horn Development and Anatomy", all other specimens fell into either the Zoological or Geographical divisions of the Collection. No collection of freaks was accepted; a few freak heads were used to fill gaps in the two primary divisions, but they were few in number. Notwithstanding the many heads offered in the formative years, Hornaday was persistent in not accepting a specimen without a specific place for its presence in the collection's two divisions, zoologic or geographic.

By the end of 1910, four years after it was formed, 695 specimens were contained in the National Collection. The stories behind many of the trophies are themselves separate and often fascinating histories of trophy hunts. The names of a few of the early well known collectors are enough for the reader to mentally conjur up long, exhausting and dangerous shikars, safaris and treks: Douglas Carruthers, Frank Buck, Sir Edmund Giles Loder, Charles Sheldon, Frederick Sealous, William Morden, James L. Clark and Roy Chapman Andrews, to mention a few.

The Zoological Society's 1910 Annual Report listed 12 world's record heads and 5 number two heads contained in the Collection. While the Collection had grown substantially and provided a well organized scientific foundation, Hornaday continued to stress that ". . . In all comparisons of horns and antlers, it is both right and necessary that the tape line should play an important part in determining records and fixing comparative values . . . it is therefore quite fair to judge every important collection by the number of record or world record specimens it contains . . . It is fit and proper that New York City should possess and exhibit on a scientific basis to the world at large, one of the world's finest collections of big game trophies." Clearly the National Collection was to be more than simply a scientific collection that was a valid and valuable appendage to the Zoological Park. Hornaday also intended it to be the world collection of record big game hunting trophies.

While trophies continued in lesser numbers to be donated to Hornaday's collection, which grew to 798 specimens by the end of 1912, he complained that the offerings of record heads were few by 1914. His reasoning for this was the lack of money available for outright purchase of record heads, which became a bitter resound in his annual Director's report. With the publication of the Collection's second reference text in 1908 (Part II), a Contributors' Fund was created to fund the purchase of many specimens not otherwise available, to pay for taxidermy work and shipping costs of newly acquired heads. A $2,500 goal was established for initial working capital with annual subscriptions sought to maintain this minimum working capital level. Thirty-three sportsmen were credited with contributing to the Contributors' Fund in 1909. When the fund became exhausted, H. Casimir de Rham, a substantial benefactor of the Zoological Society and National Collection, subscribed an additional $2,500. The first published report of the Heads and Horns Fund on March 1, 1910 shows receipts of $7,610 and disbursements of $5,568.

But such funding and private support was short-lived and declined to a low of $15 contributed in 1917 against expenses of $18. Support for the National Collection was of necessity primarily by private subscription, since the Zoological Society had its own burden of meeting the operating expenses and building expansion program of the Zoological Park. From 1908 through 1917 a total of $8,729 had been raised from 66 sportsmen-benefactors toward support of the National Collection against expenses of $11,638, with the Zoological Society contributing $2,700. The broad base of sustaining financial support Hornaday and Madison Grant had hoped to generate in their 1908 appeal never materialized from the ranks of the sporting fraternity. Perhaps it was a general decline in interest in the National Collection. Or perhaps the interest initially was never sufficiently broad enough to support such an undertaking and the National Collection was Hornaday's private dream and ambition to which few subscribed. Or, perhaps it was the irritation of Hornaday's irascible, dominating, lone warrior image that stood him apart in conservation circles, matched with his often caustic, prickly personality that frequently sought singular credit for accomplishments achieved by many collectively. The apparent lack of broad-based support was, nevertheless, quickly overshadowed by Hornaday's unquestionable one-man campaign to secure erection of a special building to house the National Collection.

When the National Collection was installed in the Administration Building's picture galleries, in February 1910, it consisted of 688 specimens. By 1916 it had grown to 850 specimens, far beyond the capacity of the two picture galleries to be properly displayed in a scientifically meaningful fashion. Hornaday began harping vociferously upon New York City and the Zoological Society for a special building as early as 1909, even before the Administration Building was completed, and continued his refrain yearly in the Park's Annual Report.

Hornaday took matters into his own hands in 1916 and single-handedly raised $100,000 from 10 contributors for a new building to be built along Baird Court, thus completing the grand concourse of the park. Henry A. Whitfield was retained to prepare the building plans and specifications with a view of a building dedication on May 20, 1918.

By the time Hornaday had raised the money, the first World War had come along and construction prices were rising so rapidly that the Executive Committee of the Zoological Society advised delay. Even worse, it changed Hornaday's design and for reasons not now apparent, decided that there should be two building entrances, one on the south end and one on the north, instead of a single entrance and exit on the west side facing Baird Court. In a life time of affronts to Hornaday's wisdom, this was the worst. The ensuing debate heated and escalated as construction costs accelerated rapidly during the War, and the $100,000 proved inadequate. Even after the war ended, the Society had to wait for prices to come down, and then raise more money before the building could be erected. Time—and perhaps the attrition of Hornaday's arguments—came to his aid. The Executive Committee backed off from its insistence on two entrances, Hornaday made some slight concessions and all was harmony when the building was finally dedicated at 4:00 PM May 25, 1922. Hornaday described the event in the Zoological Bulletin as follows:

> With the dedication and opening on May 25 of the Museum of the National Collection of Heads and Horns, another dream comes true. . . . It owes its existence to the generosity and good-will-to-man of the persons whose names are as follows: Mrs. Frederick Ferris Thompson, Mrs. Russell Sage, John D. Archbold, Jacob H. Schiff, George F. Baker, Mrs. Andrew Carnegie, Andrew Carnegie, Edmund C. Converse, Samuel Thorne (In Memoriam) and George D. Pratt. . . . The National Collection of Heads and Horns was founded and formed as a duty owed to the American people and to the vanishing big game of the world. . . . It seemed necessary to get while the getting was good, and before further exterminations of species rendered it too late. . . . As wild animal extermination now is proceeding all over the world, it is saddening to think that 100 years hence many of the species now shown in our collection will have become totally extinct.

Hornaday valued the collection at $450,000 in 1922. It contained approximately 800 specimens and included 11 world record trophies and 14 seconds, plus other irreplaceable specimens of extreme rarity and value.

The building design was of classic, Romanesque architectural style, built of brick and Indiana limestone. It is two stories high and includes 10,842 square feet. Two main public exhibition halls were on the upper level and carried out to the letter the original plan of two distinct but equally complete series of heads and horns, arranged zoologically and geographically. The lower level was reserved for zoologists, educators and sportsmen, with a spacious exhibition hall and areas for duplicate specimens, reference and study. The inscription carved over the entrance reads: NATIONAL COLLECTION OF HEADS AND HORNS. The flanking exterior tablet at the left was inscribed: ERECTED BY THE NEW YORK ZOOLOGICAL SOCIETY 1922; the tablet at the right reads: IN MEMORY OF THE VANISHING BIG GAME OF THE WORLD. The building was built by the Miller-Reed Company of New York for a contract price of $114,782, which in 1981 dollars equals $1,010,008.

One historian of the period has noted, "If there is any one building in the Zoological Park that is more than another a monument to Dr. Hornaday, it is the Heads and Horns Museum. True, Madison Grant shared and abetted his enthusiasm for it, but Hornaday took the lead."

The National Collection entered the second period of its history with the completion of the Heads and Horns Building and the appointment of Martin S. Garretson as Attendant (and subsequently Curator) of the Collection in May 1924. Until then, Hornaday had maintained the tedious position of curator along with his many vigorous responsibilities as Director of the Zoological Park. Hornaday and Garretson had been friends for many years since both were instrumental in founding the American Bison Society in 1905. Hornaday was 70 when he appointed Garretson. He had been Director of the Zoological Park for 28 years and he retired in June 1926 at the age of 72 after 30 years of service.

Hornaday's concept of the Zoological Park was rounded out with the opening of the Heads and Horns Museum in 1922, the last of 12 exhibition buildings to be built in the park until much later in the century. Exhibition merely for the sake of exhibition was the purpose of the Zoological Park in Hornaday's opinion (and the Society's), and he had accomplished this

Photograph by Wm. H. Nesbitt

The National Collection of Heads and Horns Museum was of classic brick construction, specially designed to house and display the collection to best advantage.

with his capstone being the Heads and Horns Museum. The Zoological Society had two other goals, conservation of wildlife and promotion of zoological science for research and education. Hornaday was, of course, outspoken and legendary in his role as a defender of wildlife with his singular refrain "stop the killing". But he was contemptuous of the rudimentary wildlife research efforts that were developing throughout his career, although he readily accepted any findings that supported his own prejudices.

Garretson continued Hornaday's drive to complete all the gaps in the National Collection's family orders and zoologic classifications throughout his 17-year curatorship that lasted until 1940. But a parallel development introduced definite confusion in the focus and interpretation of what the National Collection stood for and eventually led to its discredit and demise under the increasingly scientifically oriented leadership of the New York Zoological Society. That development was the big game records keeping system of the early 1930's.

In 1930, the Society's President, Madison Grant, appointed a Committee on Record Heads. That Committee issued a report in 1931 entitled "Records of North American Big Game" which was signed by Prentiss N. Gray, Chairman, Kermit Roosevelt, E. Hubert Litchfield and W. Redmond Cross, Madison Grant and George Harrison. This report begins,

> The committee appointed by President Grant in 1930 to compile a record of North American Big Game trophies, is approaching the completion of its task. The idea of this record originated not through a desire to inspire hunters to indiscriminate killing in an effort to acquire a record head, nor to promote a market for heads of extraordinary size, but rather to preserve an official record of vanishing game of North America.

Subsequently in 1932 the Boone and Crockett Club's first records book, *Records of North American Big Game,* was issued under the auspices of the National Collection of Heads and Horns of the New York Zoological Society. Its Foreword outlines the impetus behind the book:

> . . . some of the best trophies which were recorded even a generation ago have entirely disappeared, relegated perhaps to attics, or the waste heap through the death of the owner who prized them for sentimental reasons. Therefore this record seems timely as preserving an authentic history of the many splendid trophies taken before some of our big game animals have been brought practically to the point of extinction . . . no museum can contain even a small percentage of the largest trophies and therefore this volume was conceived to record the finest specimens of North American Big Game in this country and abroad of which, after three years diligent search, we were able to obtain authenticated measurements.

Moreover, 1932 marked the first year a standing Heads & Horns Committee was appointed by the Zoological Society, consisting of Prentiss Gray, Chairman, Kermit Roosevelt and Charles F. Davidson. In 1933, the Zoological Society's President Madison Grant, at the request of Prentiss N. Gray, wrote to 40 people who owned record North American big game trophies listed in the 1932 Records Book and requested they place their trophies in the National Collection either by gift or on loan.

In 1939, the Boone and Crockett Club's second records book, *North American Big Game,* was published in cooperation with the National Collection of Heads and Horns of the New York Zoological Society and the American Museum of Natural History. The Foreward contains the following appeal:

> With the decimation of our game herds, we have arrived at a time when it is of utmost importance to preserve the best trophies now in existence. The National Collection of Heads and Horns of the New York Zoological Society was founded for this purpose. There, in the Bronx Zoological Park, is the finest and most comprehensive collection of heads and horns of the big game of the world, including by far the best collection of North American Big Game in existence, among which are many records. All owners of record heads are urged to make this collection the ultimate repository of their trophies in order that they may be preserved beyond peradventure from the ignominous oblivion that has been the lot of the magnificent specimens of the past and that this collection may be further established as a lasting tribute to these wonderful animals.

Throughout this decade, Hornaday's old friend and hand-picked successor as Curator of the National Collection, M.S. Garretson, consistently affirmed Hornaday's primary theme behind the National Collection, the necessity of zoological completeness and educational relevance against the historical backdrop of the world's vanishing species. Not a year passed that Garretson didn't appeal in his Annual Report for specimens to complete certain zoological family orders, and he quickly praised donors for filling certain classification gaps. Conversely, he publicly chided those offering freaks or collections that carried a proviso that they be exhibited only as a group memoralizing a particular sportsman's career field.

The Society's Editor and Curator of Publications, William Bridges, writing a history in 1935 about the National Collection, closed with the following assessment:

> Where the National Collection is still lacking is in the perfection of its exhibits. From the very beginning heads that were definitely "poor" were excluded, but perforce some had to be admitted that could only be classified as mediocre, if anything approaching completeness was to be obtained. In the course of the years, many of the mediocre heads have been replaced by better ones, and even some of the "good" heads have given way to outstandingly fine examples. To realize to the fullest the dream of the founders, the collection will be complete only when every big game species is represented and every head on its walls is the finest obtainable. Ideally the National Collection should contain nothing but heads worthy to appear in Ward's "Records of Big Game" or in the late Prentiss N. Gray's "Records of North American Big Game," the two works that stand in the same relation to the big game trophies of the world as Burke's "Peerage" does to the human nobility of the world.

In December 1936, the Heads & Horns Committee of the New York Zoological Society issued a Special Report that exhaustively classified every specimen in the National Collection by zoological family and order and meticulously detailed specimens required to complete the Collection. In describing the scope of the Collection and threshold qualifications for entry of any specimen at the beginning of the Report, the Committee stated:

> The Collection is one of trophies of big game of the world. Manifestly and properly so, this necessarily excludes educational or scientific phases which are the functions of natural history museums and like institutions, where complete specimens including skeletons, skins and so forth are preserved for study and research.

While there may be differences of opinion as to whether certain species fall within the term "Big Game", generally speaking what is "Big Game" is pretty definitely established today, as manifested by such publications as "Records of Big Game" by Roland Ward (now in its 9th edition) and "Records of North American Big Game" edited by Prentiss N. Gray, the late and much lamented chairman of this Committee.

Members of the Committee included Alfred Ely, Chairman, Charles F. Davidson, Kermit Roosevelt and Irving K. Taylor. Ely succeeded Prentiss Gray as chairman of the Boone and Crockett Club's Committee on Records of North American Big Game that subsequently published the 1939 Records Book.

The available written history of this period is unclear as to whether the apparent philosophical differences on emphasis in the National Collection's raison d'etre were real or imaginary between Hornaday's successor, M. S. Garretson, the Zoological Society's Heads & Horns Committee, and the Boone and Crockett Club. But, history is clear on several facts. Notwithstanding Garretson's regular reports of large crowds visiting the Museum from throughout the world, the Society refused to provide him funds to print a catalog or guide book of the exhibits, although he pleaded for over 10 years. Of course, the 1930's brought the Zoological Park into a hard financial period, since much of their funding was privately donated. But their budget shows the Heads and Horns Collection being the only category in which funding, once begun, was totally suspended between 1896 and 1963 (save for building renovations in 1959–60). Moreover, the only private donations to the Heads and Horns Fund after 1922 were $1,000 donated by Madison Grant in 1937 and $200 by Alfred Ely in 1936–39.

Where were the Zoological Society's monies going? Into the Wild Life Protection Fund, the Education Fund, the Tropical Research Account, The Scientific & Research Fund, the Stokes Bird Fund, the Biological Laboratory Construction Account, the Art Gallery and Library Accounts, the Aquarium Research Account, the Conservation Account, the Publications and Photography Account, Maintenance and Building Modernization Account, and the Animal Hospital, etc. The budget figures clearly signalled a shifting of emphasis in the focus of the Zoological Park.

History has also recorded a major changing of the guard within the Zoological Society and Park during this period. Between 1935 and 1940, all of the original founders and staff of the Zoological Society and Park that shepherded it into being over the previous 40 odd years died or retired, leaving no one in high command who had been molded by the past and felt an obligation to the old ways and traditions.

Dr. W. Reid Blair, Park Veterinarian since 1902 and successor to Hornaday as Director, retired in 1940. Madison Grant, the primary original founder in 1895, died in 1937 while still serving as President of the Society. Hornaday, who maintained close ties with the Park subsequent to his retirement in 1926, also died in 1937. Garretson retired in 1940 after 17 years of service. Professor Henry F. Osborn, one of the Society's principal founders in 1895 died in 1935. His son, Fairfield Osborn, left Wall Street to become Secretary of the Society in 1935 and President in 1940, immediately assuming a vigorous new leadership emphasizing conservation, research and education.

It is clear that Hornaday's primary and secondary objectives for the National Collection, zoological completeness and record class trophy quality, were dramatically reversed during the 1930's. This change in emphasis and interpretation would eventually have a catastrophic effect on the future of the Collection amidst a Zoological Society rapidly altering its own focus and direction with new leadership not beholden to the past.

Fairfield Osborn inherited a completed Zoological Park in 1935 that represented a realization of the dreams of its founders. The Zoological Society's charter however prescribed two other obligations: conservation and education, and research. Hornaday and Grant classified these as "secondary, tertiary, or of quaternary importance" in comparison with their main objectives of building a zoological park and "exhibiting fine and rare animals." *Osborn's* Zoological Society would vigorously pursue these long subordinate goals during his 33-year tenure, with Osborn's determination making him one of the most influential conservationists of his generation.

Throughout World War II and the ensuing recovery, the focus of the Zoological Society on mass education emphasized the role of the Zoological Park as one of presenting a "living textbook" and "interpreter of nature" to the public. President Osborn's intention to break with the past was rapid and dramatic during this period in expanding the education role of the Bronx Zoo. An exhibition building featuring many of the Zoo's oddities and more entertaining species was operated during the 1939–40 World's Fair and the Zoo went "on tour." The 40-year ban on cameras and amateur photography within the park was lifted; vending machines disbursing packaged animal food were installed and visitors were exhorted to "feed the animals", long prohibited by tradition. A tractor drawn tourmobile, complete with sound, was introduced to make a trip through the Zoo's 261 acres easier and more informative. A Children's Petting Zoo was created along with a Farm-In-The-Zoo, complete with an old farm lane, a fence to sit on, straws to chew on, and hay wagons for rides and tours. The farm broke the prohibition against domestic animals being allowed in the parks. Finally, as money became available, fences and bars surrounding the animal enclosures were replaced by moats, to create a closer visual relationship with the animals in their native habitat displays. The public's response was immediate and the success of the new programs dramatic. Some 3.3 million people visited the Zoo in 1940 alone, and with successive increases yearly thereafter, compared with a static 2.5 million annual attendance over the previous decade. Membership in the Zoological Society rose steadily, and the old quarterly Bulletin, sent to the Society's members since 1898, was retitled Animal Kingdom and altered in style and content to relate better to the contemporary readership.

A realization that the entire ecosystem is interdependent upon its various integral parts was developing, and the Zoological Society saw its role as one of encouraging conservation of all of the interdependent resources of nature collectively. The Society's goal of wildlife preservation and conservation was expanded to include the whole environment that made possible the survival not only of wild animals but also of human life. In 1948, the Zoological Society created the Conservation Foundation, an enterprise dedicated to the protection and wise use of life and supporting resources. The Foundation turned out books, films, and research reports on a myriad of environmental issues including pesticides, flood control, population pressures, Alaska's vast resources, fire ants, underground water resources, big horn sheep, etc. Also in 1948, a 1500-acre reserve was established as the Jackson Hole Wildlife Park to show Americans, under natural conditions, the wild animals they were being asked to conserve. In 1945, the Society created a Department of Insects and established a permanent home for the Department of Tropical Research in Venezuela and later Trinidad. Osborn's new emphasis at the Zoological Society on education, research and conservation was firmly implanted.

The National Collection seems to have been forgotten during the 1940's and the initiation of the Osborn era. Dr. John Tee-Van, then the Executive Secretary of the Zoological Society and operational chief of the Zoological Park, wrote Alfred Ely in 1950, "As far as sportsmen are concerned, the collection now is something of the past. I do not believe that many sportsmen think about it or come to see it." The South Hall containing the "Geographic Collection" was closed to the public and used for temporary exhibits. Dr. Tee-Van, in consultation with Dr. James L. Clark, proposed consolidating the two collections into one (total of 2,371 specimens in 1940) to achieve Hornaday's first objective of zoological completeness, discarding all duplicates and retaining only the best specimens of each species and subspecies. They advocated an exhibit devoted to the biology of the horns (their evolution, growth, and purpose in the scheme of life) and a reorganization that would relate the heads whenever possible to living animals in the park.

This was probably the last attempt to re-emphasize Hornaday's original goal of the Collection of zoological completeness and to reaffirm its interpretive, educational, and scientific focus and meaning. Tee-Van appealed to Ely in his dual capacity as head of the Society's Heads & Horns Committee and also Treasurer of the Boone and Crockett Club to assemble a group from the Club to aid in this reorganization.

In 1949, President Fairfield Osborn encouraged Boone and Crockett Club member Samuel B. Webb to cull the Collection and "sell" it to the American Museum of Natural History or the Smithsonian. Neither museum wanted it. Webb did, however, cull the inferior heads, reorganize the remaining Collection and arrange for a taxidermist to spend over a year at the Zoological Park to renovate the Collection. Webb also classified, measured and ranked the remaining 73 North American heads using the measurement system under development by the Big Game Records Committee of the Boone and Crockett Club. The best 11 trophies were photographed by Grancel Fitz for the 3rd edition of the Club's records book, published in 1952.

Although the Zoological Society's interest, as expressed in Dr. Tee-Van's 1950 appeal, was to achieve Hornaday's objective of a collection with zoological completeness and educational relevance, the end result was a consolidated collection that emphasized North American big game trophies ranked by the new records keeping system. Notwithstanding a fundamental precept upon which both the records keeping system and the National Collection were founded—to preserve an official record of vanishing game—the Zoological Society took a dim view of this system. The Zoological Society's attitude toward the records keeping system and their lack of response to the Club's efforts for restoration and reorganization was lamented by Webb in a letter to Alfred Ely in 1953:

My hope is that the Zoological Society or the Conservation Foundation will be willing to recognize our work in this field [of big game record's keeping] as the type that does promote sound conservation and help us with a financial contribution. Of course, you realize that the National Collection cannot benefit in future without our knowledge and leads on record trophies. It is too bad we can't get Fairfield [Osborn] to take some action to revitalize that collection which could be made into an asset to the Zoo. I believe that funds for such work are available. In its present condition, I cannot solicit world's record trophy gifts from owners known to this Committee. We are ready and willing to help guide its restoration.

Again in 1955, Webb (then a member of the Society's Heads & Horns Committee) writing to Dr. Tee-Van, candidly expressed his displeasure with the Society's lack of interest in the National Collection: "We are glad to be able to channel outstanding trophies to the National Collection. I'm confident more would come to rest there if the Park Trustees would get busy and put the exhibit in good order."

The Zoological Society finally responded to the Club's growing concern over the state of the Collection. In 1959 they expended $21,800. (the first monies spent since 1937–39) to renovate the Heads and Horns Museum, then 38 years old, and refurbish the collection. The Collection was further consolidated to show only "the most important and significant heads," reducing it to about 300 specimens, with the balance being disbursed, most without a trace. The emphasis of the Collection was now solidly on trophy character rather than zoological completeness and classification. Moreover, the Collection now contained the treasured Chadwick Ram that had been restored in 1955 at the expense of the Boone and Crockett Club and transferred from the American Museum of Natural History.

Rebirth of the National Collection with its new emphasis and orientation on the trophy character of the specimens was short lived. The Zoological Society's activities and interest under President Fairfield Osborn's vigorous leadership had become broad and diverse by the end of the 1950's: Mountain gorillas in Central Africa; wild life resources in Alaska; birds, butterflies and fiddler crabs in Trinidad; prairie dogs in the American West; land-and-sea fauna in the Bahamas; and fire ants and the urgently important problem of chemical pesticides in many parts of the United States.

Osborn and the Zoological Park were increasingly preoccupied with endangered species being perpetuated as "living treasures" in "zoo wards" and with the development of new methods through which animal life could be more sensitively and imaginatively maintained in captivity. The animals within the Zoo were referred to as "the living collection." The Zoological Society began to assume the responsibility of providing the last safe refuge to hard pressed, endangered species including the Arabian oryx, Siberian tiger, Pere David's deer, European wisent and Przewalski's horse; maintaining fewer species better became the trend at the Park. Scientific accomplishment, moreover, became the keynote of the Zoological Society's energies with the establishment of the Osborne Laboratories of Marine Sciences (1967) and The Institute for Research in Animal Behavior (1965). The plight of vanishing African wildlife and its heritage caught President Osborn's close attention. A plethora of wildlife preservation and ecological research projects in Africa were subsequently funded, along with studies throughout the world, beginning in the early 1950's and continuing into the present day.

The Osborn regime necessarily ushered in a new breed of staff at the Zoological Park to shepherd the diverse interests of the Society. Osborn himself was a businessman from Wall Street when he arrived in 1935; but he was raised in the inner and intimate circles of the Zoological Society by his father. Fascination with wild animals consumed him throughout life, and his dedication to conservation and ecology was genuine. After 1940, Osborn assumed most of the responsibilities of Park Director (albeit untitled) until 1952, along with presidency of the Zoological Society until he died in 1968. John Tee-Van was a self-trained ichthyologist (later Sc.D.) who assumed operational control over the park's affairs in 1940 and later was appointed Director of the park in 1952, where he served until retirement in 1962. Dr. James Oliver, a professional herpetologist, succeeded Tee-Van and he was succeeded by the Park's current director, William G. Conway, an ornithologist. Moreover, the heads of most of the departments came with academic, field, or research backgrounds, and advanced degrees.

In 1967, the priorities of furthering education and enhancing the welfare of captive animals caused Fairfield Osborn to call for adapting or demolishing all existing buildings within the Zoological Park to meet his new standards. Early in his career, Osborn had the Bison Range exhibit bulldozed to create a highly successful African Plains exhibit where antelopes, zebras, ostriches and cranes brought a spot of Africa to the Bronx. With Osborn's 1967 pronouncement, the Park's Department of Education formally moved into the remodeled lower level of the Heads and Horns Museum, marking the culmination of a gradual trend to utilize the Museum for multiple purposes beginning in 1943 with the creation of a basement auditorium for children's shows and exhibits.

As if writing the epitaph of the National Collection, Zoological Park Director William G. Conway's 1968 Annual Report stated:

> Even if zoos had not been established for education and recreation, they would be instituted today as sanctuaries for the growing number of species threatened with extinction. Increasingly, the potential of zoos and aquariums for research upon forms of life not readily maintained in conventional laboratories is being recognized—and it is about time. It is remarkable that museums holding collections of dead animals have always been deemed places worthy of research and study while living collections of animals have frequently been relegated to the status of mere amusement.

Thereafter, the Zoological Society's standing Heads & Horns Committee, in existence since 1932, was dropped from their Annual Report and the National Collection of Heads and Horns was quietly closed to the public, ceasing to exist as an appendage of the New York Zoological Society's Bronx Zoo. The Society's genuine concerns lay in sustaining *existing* diminishing species of wild life on an environmental level worldwide. The Center for Field Biology and Conservation (later Center for Wild Life Conservation and Research) was begun in 1971 followed by the Wild Life Survival Center program which initiates gene banks and wild life breeding reserves under its management elsewhere throughout the world. On the Zoological Park's 80th anniversary (1979), Director William G. Conway prophetically looked to the past and the future focus of the Society:

> The Society's history tells us that an institution devoted to live wild animals and to man's relationships with them must have an overwhelming concern with the future. Neither a

static warehouse of natural artifacts nor an historical collection of unchanging objects, the living breeding collections of zoos and aquariums make them museums of the here and now and, increasingly, repositories for the future. . . . It is a goal of the Society's scientific programs to provide basic information essential to understanding and to rational action and it is the mission of the conservation and captive propagation programs to act in order to save "pieces of nature" to help preserve options for the future. In sum, that is a new kind of institution.

The Zoological Society, through the eyes of its historian (Curator of Publications Emeritus) examined the National Collection's potential relevance in 1974 against the backdrop of its origins and current state-of-the-art of zoological science:

> For its era the [Heads and Horns] museum was a logical and valid appendage of a great zoological park. Hunting big game was a recognized sport, at least among men wealthy and hardy enough to penetrate the wildest and most difficult parts of the world. Books on tracking and hunting abounded—shelf after shelf in the Zoological Society's Library is filled with them—and not all are merely literary trophies recording the exploits of intrepid hunters. Many book-writing sportsmen and explorers were accurate observers of animal habits and habitats, and of the lives and customs of little-known native peoples who served them as guides. Along with the heads and horns and skins they brought back to decorate their homes, they brought a good deal of solid natural-history information. It was valuable as far as it went, but at the beginning of this century the day of the field naturalist trained to observe scientifically and record without killing had not yet dawned.

It is clear in historical retrospect why the National Collection of Heads and Horns was no longer deemed a valid appendage of the Zoological Park. The focus and concern of contemporary zoological science at the New York Zoological Society is behavioral research, endangered species, wildlife survival centers, gene banks, breeding reserves, and a myriad of arcane and exotic research projects, all highly relevant and meaningful concerns in the space age of the 20th century. Hornaday's and Grant's primary objective was the creation of the world's finest Zoological Park from a virgin 261 acre wooded tract in 1896. A mounted animal to the zoological scientist at the Park today has the same relevance that the Wright brothers' airplane has to a lunar physicist—both are manifestations of the same decade, nearly a century ago, when their sciences were beginning. The orientation of the Zoological Society today is on *living* animals; there is no place or compassion for a collection of heads and horns deemed purely sportsmen's trophies.

Hornaday, the naturalist-taxidermist, viewed the National Collection at the turn of the century as a zoological entity against the backdrop of rapidly vanishing big game populations. The sporting fraternity of the 1930's viewed it as a trophy collection of record heads and horns at a time when the decline of big game had been successfully reversed. The hunter's interest in maintaining trophies and big game records overshadowed his many conservationist accomplishments and contributions in the eyes of an enlightened Zoological Society which was itself forging a new identity within the emerging environmental community. And, the sportsman's trophy interests colored the historical purpose and value of the National Collection in the eyes of the Zoological Society as purely self-serving, without broader educational or zoologic relevance; hence, it was not deemed worthy of a place of recognition in the Zoological Park.

The story of the National Collection of Heads and Horns would perhaps have ended here but for my chance discovery of the state of the National Collection in 1977. I had gone to the Zoological Park on January 20, 1977, to talk with Dr. George Schaller about his recent expeditions through Asia. After visiting, I asked to see the National Collection and was relunctantly admitted after being told it was closed and no longer open to the public. I found the Collection in a deplorable state, boarded up from public view, dusty, dirty, unhumidified, and many of the hides badly in need of repair.

After a robbery of 13 heads in 1974 (including the world's record mule deer and Atlantic walrus, and number three pronghorn) the Zoological Society had quietly begun trying to find another home for the Collection. The Boone and Crockett Club was contacted but could offer no aid. Subsequent to my discovery, I mounted what became a year-long crusade to enlist the aid of the sporting fraternity in trying to find a suitable home for the Collection that would allow public display while satisfying the Society's requirements of potential use in education of the public and/or research.

My efforts proved fruitless, although considerable interest was generated. By late 1977, it was apparent that the American Museum of Natural History was reluctantly going to receive the Collection, but could not display it as all their space was being utilized. At this point, W. Harold Nesbitt, then Director of the Hunter Services Division at the National Rifle Association and a Boone and Crockett Club Associate Member, picked up the standard, convincing the Boone and Crockett Club to seek ownership of the Collection. Into the breech reappeared long-time club member Samuel B. Webb who agreed to present the Club's plan to the Zoological Society. He convinced them that the Collection rightfully should pass to the Boone and Crockett Club, with formal acceptance being noted by letter dated January 23, 1978 from the Club's President, Wesley M. Dixon. Nesbitt and I served as an ad hoc club committee that inventoried the collection, packed it for shipment and attended to the numerous small details of such an undertaking.

Our inventory of the Collection in February 1978 revealed only 238 specimens; 34 of North American origin and 204 from the world's five other continents. Six of the 238 specimens were retained by the Zoological Society, making the total transfered 232, of which 34 were from North America. Arrangements were made by Nesbitt with the National Rifle Association, which generously renovated one section of its Firearms Museum in Washington, D.C., to display the North American specimens. On May 5, 1978, these trophies, re-designated as the National Collection of Heads and Horns, were put on public display for the first time in a decade. The remaining non-North American specimens were re-designated the International Collection of Heads and Horns and were deeded to Safari Club International in 1978 for installation in their museum, scheduled for future construction in Tucson, Arizona.

In June 1978, the Boone and Crockett Club formed a subcommittee of its Big Game Records Committee, with Nesbitt as Chairman and myself as member, to watch over the National Collection of Heads and Horns. With strong input and help from Michigan sportsman P. Franklin Bays, Jr., an enthusiastic fund raising program has been established, offering donors a limited edition print of a handsome oil painting of the Chadwick ram that

Photograph by Wm. H. Nesbitt

A view of the special display area constructed by the National Rifle Association in its Washington, D.C. museum to house the National Collection of Heads and Horns during 1978–1981.

was donated to the club by Michigan artist Harry Antis. The funds generated by this project will be utilized to maintain and expand the Collection on a sustaining basis. Display of the Collection at the National Rifle Association Museum will continue through late 1981, with the collection then moving to a location in the West to provide Western sportsmen an opportunity to view these outstanding trophies that have never been displayed west of the Mississippi River.

The National Collection now includes these notable trophies: The world's record Chadwick Stone's sheep; The world's record Zack Elbow Quebec-Labrador caribou; The world's record De Rham woodland caribou; The world's record Witherbee Canada moose; The former world's record Scull Pacific walrus; the former world's record Pop mountain caribou; The No. two Kitto Rocky Mountain goat.

In a very real sense, the Collection is today where it was in 1907, when William T. Hornaday created a Nucleus Collection with his own private specimens. It is a foundation around which a regeneration of the Collection can occur, albeit only with native North American specimens. The Collection contains irreplaceable specimens of significant historical value and extreme rarity. Life and vitality are given to such a collection by perpetual renewal and upgrading so that the collection takes on a living existence. It is this very character that becomes self regenerating by drawing to it the finest specimens as they become available, which Hornaday himself had in mind. The "new" National Collection definitely has the potential to attract the top trophies of the 32 categories of native North American big game. Picture, if you will, the top 32 big game trophies ever taken on the North American continent all located in one collection! That mental image, coupled with the spirit and heritage of the hunt, should rekindle the necessary spark within the breast of the sporting fraternity to keep the North American Collection as valid a legacy today and tomorrow as it was at the turn of the century.

Editor's Note—The Harry Antis painting of the Chadwick ram is featured as the frontis of this book. Donors to the Boone and Crockett Club's NCHH Fund can receive a signed and numbered print of this handsome painting and a specially reproduced portion of Chadwick's hunting diary. Write directly to the club office for further details.

SELECTED REFERENCES

Gathering of Animals: An Unconventional History of the New York Zoological Society. 1974. William Bridges. New York: Harper and Row.

Records of North American Big Game. 1932. Prentiss N. Grey, ed. New York: Derrydale Press. 178 pages.

North American Big Game. 1939. Alfred Ely, Harold E. Anthony, and R. R. M. Carpenter, eds. New York: Scribners. 533 pages.

New York Zoological Society Annual Reports 1896–1980.

Zoological Society Bulletin (NYZS) 1898–1942.

Animal Kingdom (NYZS) 1942–1980.

The National Collection of Heads and Horns, Part I and II (NYZS) 1907 and 1908.

Special Report of the Committee on the National Collection of Heads and Horns (NYZS) December 29, 1936.

Brochure No. 3, List of Specimens and Guide Book to the Collection (NYZS) 1931.

A Listing of the More Desirable Game Trophies in the National Collection of Heads and Horns in the opinion of T. Donald Carter. 1956. Unpublished loose-leaf manuscript.

Lowell E. Baier of Potomac, Maryland is President and Chairman of Baier Properties, Inc., investment builders in the Metropolitan Washington D.C. area since 1968.

He is an attorney and former mortgage banker. He has a B.A. from Valpariso University and a J.D. from Indiana University.

He is a Life Member of NRA, a member of the Boone and Crockett Club, the Explorers Club, Foundation for North American Wild Sheep and other hunting organizations.

An avid hunter, he has taken all four North American wild sheep, and most other North American trophies.

Carl Rungius—an Appreciation

JOHN H. BATTEN

To the knowledgeable lover of North American art a Rungius is unmistakable. Other game artists may in due course have approached or equalled his talent for setting and background, but no one has delineated our big game with the same touch.

Rungius' animals are flesh and blood, bone, muscle and tendon, frozen immobile in an instant of time, but poised for immediate action. A taut tendon here, a relaxed muscle there, the attitude of head and body all clearly suggest whether the subject is wary and alert or calm and relaxed. One can accurately sense what the animal is about to do. Rungius possessed an uncanny ability to convey this understanding anatomically. One might compare that talent to Michelangelo's.

On the prompting of his parents, Rungius sailed from his native Germany in 1894 to visit an uncle in New York. The family's intent was to redirect the interests of the 25-year old toward a more acceptable calling than art. During the late 19th century an artist was often considered to exist on the very fringe of polite society. People of breeding, substance, and station were patrons of the arts, certainly not artists.

In our association over a period of 21 years, Carl often used to chuckle over the irony of his parents' plan. "You know, John, they wanted me to become a minister like my father; if not, then at least a respectable business man. They never thought I would discover in America more opportunity than ever before to paint animals, and in the wilds rather than in the Berlin Zoo."

What his parents had overlooked was that the uncle, Dr. Fulda, was himself a keen sportsman. He was delighted to have his young nephew on a Maine moose hunt, followed by many less ambitious outings nearer New York. They shot deer in Maine but saw no moose. The wilderness, itself, completely charmed Carl. It took little persuasion on Dr. Fulda's part to convince the young artist he should spend that year painting in New York from his new material; they would try again for moose the following fall.

Meanwhile at an exhibition Rungius met a Wyoming rancher and guide whose suggestion was readily accepted that he go to Wyoming instead to hunt, study, and paint pronghorn antelope, elk, moose, and mule deer. It was only a start. Carl loved Wyoming. After his initial trip he made quite a few more, outfitting and guiding himself and developing into a skilled outdoorsman almost completely reliant on his own resources.

During a visit home in 1896, he made a decision. He returned to the United States for good, drawn by the constant challenges found there in connection with his work and by the fact he had fallen in love with his cousin, Louise Fulda. Their marriage took place in 1907. He was then 38.

In the closing years of the century, Carl concentrated his field studies and hunting in Wyoming. Along with wildlife, his work included canvases of frontier ranch life and the western plains. Meanwhile the turn of the century saw game becoming scarcer in Wyoming. An interest in moose, which he had first taken in Wyoming, now led him to the lakes, forests, and barrens of New Brunswick, where he quickly added to his other skills those of the competent woodsman. Calling in moose with the birch bark horn proved immensely challenging to European-born Rungius, steeped in the lore of the stag during his childhood days.

Simultaneously, his path led to the Yukon when, on invitation of Charles Sheldon, he joined an expedition in 1905 to study and hunt the Dall's sheep in the far north. Companions included Wilfred Osgood of the Smithsonian Institute and Frederick C. Selous, the noted African big game hunter.

Perhaps it was in the Yukon that Rungius developed his technique for representing big game anatomy. As a student in Germany, he had dissected and sketched the anatomy of animals beginning with house cats. Hunting alone as he so often did both in Wyoming and in New Brunswick, it was perhaps not as convenient to follow the same method completely with large game. In the Yukon, however, he had well-trained scientifically oriented companions prepared to assist. Working from Sheldon's trophies as well as from his own, Rungius sketched incessantly. Sheldon often photographed Rungius seated at his drawing board, a Dall's sheep suspended in front of him by a series of cords attached to a frame work. Having studied and sketched the ram "in the white," Carl would carefully remove the skin as a scientific specimen, and next draw in all of the muscles and tendons. When the meat had been removed, he tackled the skeleton in this way literally mastering the anatomy of a sheep. Accordingly, Rungius' sheep are justly famous for the artist's faultless understanding of what lay below the skin. Few illustrators have had this same opportunity in depth, generally having to work from photographs.

In the field Rungius was an indefatigable producer of field sketches in oils. He painted and kept on file literally thousands of 9″ by 11″ sketches recording landscapes, trees, underbrush, flowering plants, rocks, soil, and sky formations. Simultaneously he studied and recorded his impressions of the wildlife in all aspects of their group behavior, such that a Rungius painting of a group of rams can be depended upon, for example, as an accurate social document. When my wife and I met with Carl Rungius every few years to plan the next addition to our growing collection, we had a first hand experience of how he worked from this collection of small field sketches.

Having produced the magnificent paintings which illustrated Charles Sheldon's *The Wilderness of the Upper Yukon* and William Beach's *In the Shadow of Mt. McKinley,* Rungius' work came to the attention of a most unusual man, Jim Simpson of Banff and Bow Lake, Alberta. The dean of Alberta sheep guides, Jim was himself an accomplished water colorist and derived a deep inner satisfaction from the work of men like Rungius. Far from affluent, Simpson decided that Rungius must see and paint the North Sasketchewan and Brazeau wildernesses, and he invited him as his guest for such an expedition in the fall of 1911. When the successful hunt had ended, Carl knew he had found more than a lifetime friend; he had found the place he wanted to live and work the rest of his days. Simpson sold him land in Banff on the Bow River and helped him build the comfortable log home which is now a museum dedicated to Rungius' memory. In turn, Simpson built up the most unique collection of Rungius' work, both on canvas and in bronze, as part payment for his outfitting services over a period of many years.

As Jim Simpson's client (and later that of his son, Jimmie) over the period 1930–1970, I literally grew up under these art treasures and achieved a long held ambition by meeting both Carl and his wife, proud to consider myself in due course one of their friends. A prized wedding present was a painting of bighorn rams Carl did for my wife, Katie, and me in 1938.

Aside from several trips north of Jasper, Rungius concentrated his work thereafter on the Brazeau and Ram River watersheds. Although Rungius frequently told me the moose was always his favorite subject, he surprisingly painted even more sheep and especially bighorns. I have always suspected this represented old Jim Simpson's lifetime enthusiasm shared. In Jim's lexicon, hunting meant ram hunting. No other game was worth much consideration, except for the grizzly. As well, the Banff outfitters were generally sought out by bighorn hunters, and Rungius had a ready market right at hand. Thus, the Rungius' spent spring, summer and fall in Banff and the winter at their studio apartment at 27 West 67th Street, New York.

When we asked Carl what in particular tied him to the east slope of the Alberta Rockies, his answer was simple. "It is the atmosphere here. The air has been washed clear of dust. Everything becomes more sharply distinct on the east slope. This is important to my technique both in painting the animals on the one hand and the foreground and landscape on the other. No where else have I ever been where the atmosphere possesses this same quality."

Here, without a doubt, is the primary reason for the apparent change in Rungius' rendition which occurred between his work in New Brunswick, even in the Yukon, and that done in Alberta. It became the style which characterized what he painted from the 1930's through his death in 1959.

When Carl came to our shores in 1894, he was steeped as an artist in the style of 19th century romanticism. His early works dramatize the subject matter by sharp distinctions between light and shadow. His first moose paintings remind one of Landseer. During the Wyoming days, a change occurred, apparently since he was painting in a drier atmosphere under normally clearer skies. The old feeling returns in a degree with some of the canvases done in the Yukon, frequently a wet and stormy land. Early portrayals in Alberta often echo the European representation. Subtly, and not all at once, Rungius began to paint the atmosphere of the east slope of the Canadian Rockies in terms of his own description—"air washed clean." He began to add depth and light to his canvases because he was painting the air as he recognized it between his animals and the landscape.

The Italians called it chiaroscuro, the pictorial representation of light and shade, without specific reference to color, based on a perception of the corpuscular quality of atmosphere. Distinct from his earlier work that was flatter and somewhat foreshortened, Rungius' developing technique added depth to his canvases as the years went on. In my view this was accomplished by a combination apparent by comparisons: a dramatic change in the use of colors, deeper pigmentation for emphasis, a broadened brush stroke, and the subordination of detail working into the background.

All of the paintings from the wonderful Rungius collection in the Shelburne Museum do represent the attributes of Rungius' later work and a few comments are certainly in order on each. Perhaps the bull elk bugling into the mist filled valley below has a little more of the feeling than the others of Rungius' European background. But, the broad brush strokes and palette are those of his fully developed style that would be thought typical of the artist's later and greatest works. The magnificent bull moose is Rungius at his best, with his favorite subject. In my opinion, no one has equaled the sculptured aspect of Rungius' animals, and especially of the moose, so often portrayed as a sort of shapeless mass of flesh. The Alaska brown bear is another outstanding example of the artist's incredible definition of meat, bone and sinew, an extremely difficult animal to depict with anatomical precision because of his long hair. I have a personal feeling the caribou may have been painted earlier in his career than the other three. They are nevertheless fully representative of his technique. The big-horns are, in my view, Rungius at his very best and suggest to me the work he was doing in the late '30's and '40's. There is little doubt that the background comes from one of the upper basins of the Ram River, Alberta, where above all he loved to camp, study, and sketch. A finer or more representative selection of his masterpieces could not have been put together than the group chosen from the Shelburne Museum collection for this book.

While as a landscapist Rungius was superb, landscapes did not interest him as such. During his Wyoming period he did paint landscapes; later, in Alberta, a number were done to qualify for the American Academy of Design. The two best known of these were of Lake McArthur and Lake O'Hara. The former won him the Carnegie prize. The latter is now in our collection. His fame might have been even greater had he turned to landscapes.

Thus, when about 1954 we asked him to paint a picture of a lone billy in the foreground with a line of goats crossing a slide in the middle distance, all set in the Rungius fork of the Ram River, he protested. "But you realize that will be a landscape, John. I really am not interested in painting more landscapes."

My wife, Katie, who seemed to be somewhat of a favorite of his, prevailed. In due course he let us know the painting had been finished and was about to be shipped. While we were waiting in anticipation of its receipt, a further letter arrived asking our indulgence, as his agents had pressed him to let it be hung in a New York gallery for three months. To Carl's surprise, the reaction was overwhelming. The public loved what he continued to regard as essentially a landscape. Under the circumstances this canvas can be considered unique.

One night after dinner the Simpsons, Rungius, my wife and I were seated in the Simpson's

Num-Ti-Jah Lodge admiring the canvases Carl had done for old Jim. "I paint much better now," he said reflectively. "I have learned so much about painting since I first came to Alberta." He followed with some relevant comments on what had gone into these changes in style. One can fairly accurately date a Rungius on representation and style. What is changeless from start to finish is his uncanny depiction of anatomy.

"You still love to paint moose the best?" I queried. He seemed to glance briefly at Old Jim before he replied. "Perhaps, I really don't know. To a European the stag comes first. In my case, it was my thrill at seeing in an exhibition in Berlin the painting of a bull moose by Richard Friese, the famous German painter. I was just an impressionable boy. To me that moose was the essence of the wilderness itself."

Unfinished at the time of his death was a wonderful painting of a moose being done for us, which we were never able to obtain.

As for the man, he never lost the courtliness of the well-born European aristocrat, nor was he ever at a loss in the company of the men of the frontier. His quietly straightforward manner, courage, resourcefulness, self-reliance, and durability endeared him to all who met him. His gift for names and faces was remarkable. We looked forward eagerly to meeting him almost every fall from the War's end until his death, whether in Banff, at his New York Studio, or on the Ram River, his favorite hunting ground. The last time our paths crossed on the trail, my wife and I were leaving the Whiterabbit to cross over the Clearwater to Forbidden Creek. We stopped to visit, asking what luck to date.

"Oh much luck, you know. I have several canvases well in mind. I will do them in New York this winter."

"And the rams? Have you shot yet?"

"No, not yet. It is time I got a 40-incher. When I see him, I shall shoot."

Later that fall we were happy to know he had indeed found the rare 40″ ram, and as usual he had not missed.

Carl Rungius was a man to remember and an artist for all time.

For the record, those among the living who knew him well are Bill Sheldon, Dick Borden, Sam Webb, and Jimmy Simpson, Jr. The definitive biography on the artist was written by William J. Shaldach and published by the Countryman Press, West Hartford, Vermont in 1945. Be prepared to discover that, long out of print in two limited editions, it is very, very hard to find and priced accordingly in today's market.

John H. Batten has been employed by Twin Disc, Incorporated, Racine, Wisconsin in various capacities since 1935. He served as President and Chief Executive Officer, 1948–1976, and Chairman and Chief Executive Officer, 1976 to date.

He graduated from Phillips Academy, Mass., cum laude; Yale University, B.A. degree, Phi Beta Kappa; and earned a Certificate in Mechanical Engineering from the University of Wisconsin Night Extension Division.

He has served as a director of many corporations, both here and abroad. He is a member of the Society of Automotive Engineers, and served ten years as a Director of National Association of Manufacturers. He is a former member of the Young President's Organization, and a member of the Chief Executives Forum.

He is a member of the Boone and Crockett Club, having served as Vice President, member of the Executive Committee, and member of the Big Game Records Committee. He is a trustee of the African Wildlife Leadership Foundation, and member of the Foundation for North American Wild Sheep and other hunting groups.

He edited *The Best of Sheep Hunting,* for Amwell Press, (1980) and is currently authoring *Skyline Pursuits,* to be published by Amwell Press.

He began his big game hunting career in the Yukon in 1928, followed by numerous mountain sheep hunts in Alberta, British Columbia, Alaska, Mexico, Iran, Afghanistan, Mongolia and Spain. Many other high altitude hunts have been in Austria, Spain, Sudan, South Africa, and New Zealand, plus three Indian shikars and nine African safaris. He has hunted on numerous occasions in Montana, Wyoming and Texas. He currently has bighorn and desert sheep in the records books and a number of others in previous books. He has been recognized with a number of hunting awards.

Jim Simpson, Dean of Alberta sheep guides, offers comments to Carl Rungius on a painting that Rungius has just completed of sheep at the Rungius fork of the Ram River in Alberta. The photograph is inscribed in pen: "The art critic, To Katy and John Batton from Carl Rungius. January 1952." Photograph courtesy of John Batton.

Carl Rungius Paintings

The six magnificent paintings reproduced in this section are provided through the courtesy of the Shelburne Museum, Shelburne, Vermont. The Shelburne Museum features one of the better collections of Rungius paintings, in addition to their many other fine exhibits.

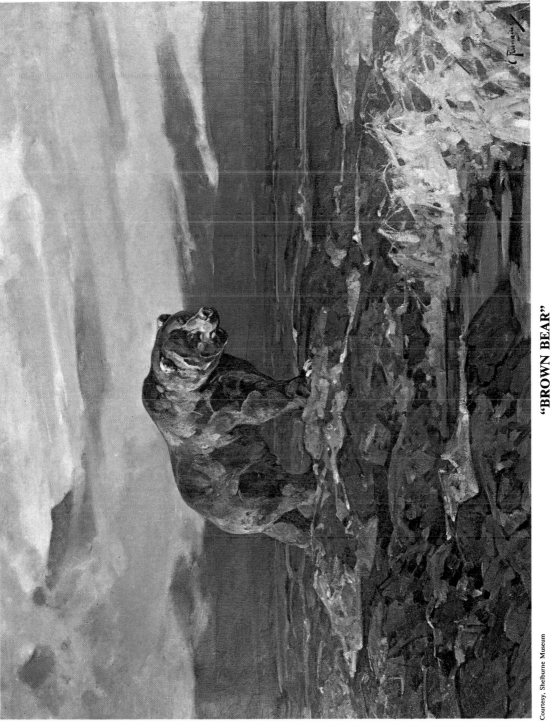

"BROWN BEAR"

Carl Rungius

105

"CARIBOU"
Carl Rungius

"MOOSE ON LANDSCAPE"
Carl Rungius

107

"SIX BIGHORN RAMS"
Carl Rungius

"THE CHALLENGE"
Carl Rungius

"CHILDREN OF THE SAGE"

Carl Rungius

Tabulations of Recorded Trophies

The trophy data shown herein have been taken from score charts in the Records Archives of the Boone and Crockett Club. Trophies listed are those that continue to meet minimum score and other requirements of the program, through the 17th Awards entry period (1977-1979). The final scores and rank shown are official, except for trophies shown with an asterick. The asterick is assigned to trophies that rank in top ten of the category, but whose final score has not been certified by an awards program panel of judges. The asterick can be removed by the submitting of two additional, independent scorings by Official Measurers. The Records Committee of the Boone and Crockett Club will review the three scorings available (original, plus two additional) and determine which, if any, will be accepted in lieu of the judges panel measurement. When the score has been accepted as final by the Records Committee, the asterick will be removed in future editions of the records book.

The scientific and vernacular names, and the sequence of presentation, follows that suggested in the Revised Checklist of North American Mammals North of Mexico, 1979 (J. Knox Jones, *et al.*; Texas Tech University, 14 December 1979)

BLACK BEAR

A U.S. Fish & Wildlife Service photograph taken in Wyoming by E.P. Haddon.

Black Bear

Ursus americanus americanus and related subspecies

Minimum Score 21

Score	Greatest Length of Skull Without Lower Jaw	Greatest Width of Skull	Sex	Locality Killed	By Whom Killed	Owner	Date Killed	Rank
23 9/16	14 12/16	8 4/16	U	San Pete Co., Utah	Picked Up	Alma R. Lund & Merrill Daniels	1975	1
22 6/16	13 11/16	8 11/16	M	San Pete Co., Utah	R. W. Peterson & R. S. Hardy	Rex W. Peterson	1970	2
22 6/16	14 6/16	8 3/16	M	Gila Co., Ariz.	Roy A. Stewart	Roy A. Stewart	1978	2
22 5/16*	13 12/16	8 9/16	M	San Carlos Indian Res., Ariz.	Joseph A. Waite	Joseph A. Waite	1975	4
22 4/16	13 9/16	8 11/16	M	Apache Co., Ariz.	R. R. Barney & Hal E. Booher	Richard R. Barney	1968	5
22 4/16	14 1/16	8 3/16	M	Ft. Apache Res., Ariz.	Jimmie C. James	Jimmie C. James	1971	5
22 2/16	13 11/16	8 6/16	M	Uintah Co., Utah	Hal Mecham	Hal Mecham	1975	7
22	13 6/16	8 10/16	M	Hahns Peak, Colo.	W. L. Cave	W. L. Cave	1964	8
22	13 8/16	8 8/16	M	Graham Co., Ariz.	Thomas E. Klepfer	Thomas E. Klepfer	1972	8
22	13 12/16	8 6/16	M	Garfield Co., Colo.	Joseph R. Maynard	Joseph R. Maynard	1977	8
21 9/16	13 6/16	8 12/16	M	Land O' Lakes, Wis.	Ed Strobel	Ed Strobel	1953	11
21 9/16	13 13/16	8 6/16	M	Swan River, Man.	Jim E. Russell	Jim E. Russell	1973	11
21 9/16	13 6/16	8 10/16	M	Lincoln Co., Wyo.	C. William Recshaw	C. William Redshaw	1976	11
21 7/16	13 11/16	8 3/16	M	Smithers, B. C.	Indian	Jack Adams	1975	14
21 3/16	13 6/16	8 6/16	M	Ft. Apache Res., Ariz.	Gib Brewer, Greg Boyd & Pete Ellsworth	Greg Boyd	1964	15
21 3/16	13 8/16	8 6/16	M	Tatlanika River, Alaska	Barry W. Campbell	Barry W. Campbell	1966	15
21 3/16	13 8/16	8 6/16	M	Ft. Apache Res., Ariz.	Gary W. Sholl	Gary W. Sholl	1969	15
21 3/16*	13 13/16	8	M	White Fox, Sask.	Picked Up	Douglas E. Miller	1974	15
21 3/16	13 6/16	8 6/16	M	Graham Co., Ariz.	Bruce Liddy	Bruce Liddy	1976	15
21 2/16	13 6/16	8 6/16	M	Delta Co., Colo.	Quincy Hines	Quincy Hines	1967	20
21 2/16	13 10/16	8 6/16	M	Bayfield Co., Wisc.	Byron Bird, Jr.	Byron Bird, Jr.	1976	20
21 1/16	13 5/16	8 6/16	U	Mendocino Co., Calif.	E. J. Vamm	Univ. Calif. Museum	1928	22
21 1/16	13 6/16	8 5/16	M	Gila Co., Ariz.	Clay Warden	Milo Warden	1975	22
21 1/16	13	8 10/16	M	Mendocino Co., Calif.	Andy Bowman	Univ. Calif. Museum	1930	24
21 1/16	13	8 10/16	M	Custer Co., Idaho	Robert L. Caskey	Robert L. Caskey	1967	24
21 1/16	13 5/16	8 6/16	M	Lake Co., Oreg.	Martin V. Pernoll	Martin V. Pernoll	1967	24
21 1/16	13 4/16	8 6/16	M	Silt, Colo.	Robert C. Maurer	Robert C. Maurer	1955	27
21 1/16	13 3/16	8 6/16	M	Collbran, Colo.	O. K. Clifton	O. K. Clifton	1957	27
21 1/16	13 6/16	8 6/16	M	Williams Fork River, Colo.	Clyde Stehle & Jan Grove	Clyde Stehle	1958	27
21 1/16	13 6/16	8 6/16	M	Vilas Co., Wis.	Wisc. Cons. Dept.	Neal Long Taxidermy	1959	27
21 3/16	13 6/16	8 5/16	M	Mesa Co., Colo.	Hartle V. Morris	Hartle V. Morris	1962	27

BLACK BEAR–*Continued*

Ursus americanus americanus and related subspecies

Score	Greatest Length of Skull Without Lower Jaw	Greatest Width of Skull	Sex	Locality Killed	By Whom Killed	Owner	Date Killed	Rank
21 9/16	13 5/16	8 5/16	M	Clinton Co., Pa.	Donald Sorgen	Donald Sorgen	1968	27
21 9/16	13 7/16	8 2/16	M	Vilas Co., Wisc.	John J. Volkmann	John J. Volkmann	1973	27
21 8/16	13 7/16	8 7/16	M	Gallatin River, Wyo.	J. P. V. Evans	U. S. Natl. Museum	1914	34
21 8/16	13 9/16	7 15/16	M	Bayfield Co., Wis.	Earl B. Johnson	Earl B. Johnson	1953	34
21 8/16	13 5/16	8 3/16	M	Forest Co., Wisc.	Richard Ruthven	Wisc. Buck & Bear Club	1968	34
21 8/16	13 5/16	8 3/16	M	Chiricuahua Butte, Ariz.	W. O. Morrison	W. O. Morrison	1969	34
21 8/16	13 6/16	8 2/16	M	Lincoln Co., Wyo.	Charles R. Nixon	Charles R. Nixon	1973	34
21 8/16	13 7/16	8 1/16	M	Augusta Co., Va.	Joseph R. Lam	Joseph R. Lam	1977	34
21 8/16	13 6/16	8 4/16	M	Ventura Co., Calif.	James B. Wade	James B. Wade	1977	34
21 8/16	13 6/16	8 7/16	M	Apache Co., Ariz.	Joseph H. Lyman	Fred Peters	1978	34
21 7/16	13 7/16	8 5/16	M	Mariposa Co., Calif.	Bert Palmberg	Bert Palmberg	1957	42
21 7/16	13 7/16	8 5/16	U	Wales Is., Alaska	Picked Up	L. R. Hall	1962	42
21 7/16	13 7/16	8 4/16	M	Megal Mt., Nfld.	Ben Hillicoss	Ben Hillicoss	1963	42
21 7/16	13 7/16	8	M	Albemarle Co., Va.	Grover F. Sites	Grover F. Sites	1964	42
21 7/16	13 5/16	8 4/16	M	Pierce Co., Wash.	Tracy Johnson & Bernie Paque	Tracy Johnson	1968	42
21 7/16	13 6/16	8 1/16	U	McKean Co., Pa.	Picked Up	Pa. Game Commission	1969	42
21 7/16	13 6/16	8 3/16	M	Douglas Co., Wisc.	Kenneth J. Burton	Kenneth J. Burton	1972	42
21 7/16	13	8 7/16	M	Nordegg, Alta.	Leo F. Hermary	Leo F. Hermary	1977	42
21 6/16	13 7/16	8 5/16	M	Prince Of Wales Is., Alaska	Picked Up	Robert Kase	PR1954	50
21 6/16	13 6/16	8 4/16	M	Walland, Tenn.	William M. Lyell	William M. Lyell	1967	50
21 6/16	13 13/16	7 9/16	M	Sandpoint, Idaho	Ronald Lee Book	Ronald Lee Book	1969	50
21 6/16	13 6/16	8 5/16	M	Walland, Tenn.	Paul Bonnett	Paul Bonnett	1969	50
21 6/16	13 5/16	8 1/16	M	Reserve, N. M.	C. J. McElroy	C. J. McElroy	1970	50
21 6/16	12 12/16	8 10/16	M	Franklin Co., N. Y.	James Donner	James Donner	1970	50
21 6/16	13 11/16	7 11/16	M	Pike Co., Pa.	Robert Loux	Robert Loux	1971	50
21 6/16	13 10/16	7 12/16	M	Carbon Co., Utah	Rex Peterson & R. S. Hardy	Rex Peterson	1975	50
21 6/16	13 6/16	8	M	Bayfield Co., Wisc.	Larry L. Frye	Larry L. Frye	1975	50
21 6/16	13	8 6/16	M	Humboldt Co., Calif.	Dean Earley	Dean Earley	1977	50
21 5/16	13 7/16	8 4/16	U	Colo.	E. T. Seton	U. S. Natl. Museum	1897	60
21 5/16	13 6/16	7 15/16	M	Yarmouth Co., N. S.	John L. Bastey	John L. Bastey	1945	60
21 5/16	12 15/16	8 6/16	U	Centre Co., Pa.	Picked Up	Wayne B. Harpster	1946	60
21 5/16	13	8 5/16	M	Buffalo Park, Colo.	John L. Howard	John L. Howard	1958	60

		M/U		Locality			Date	Rank
21 5/16	13 5/16	M	8	Coburn Lake, Calif.	Lauren A. Johnson	Lauren A. Johnson	1960	60
21 5/16	13 5/16	M	8 3/16	Olympic Pen., Wash.	Bert Klineburger	Bert Klineburger	1963	60
21 5/16	12 15/16	M	8 6/16	Cynthia, Alta.	R. LeVoir	R. LeVoir	1968	60
21 5/16	13 5/16	M	8 2/16	Mendocino Co., Calif.	Gene H. Whitney	Gene H. Whitney	1971	60
21 5/16	13 5/16	M	8	Vilas Co., Wisc.	Michael G. Duwe	Michael G. Duwe	1972	60
21 5/16	13 4/16	M	8 1/16	Lincoln Co., Wyo.	Gregg G. Fisher	Gregg G. Fisher	1975	60
21 4/16	13 5/16	M	8 1/16	Winchester Mts., Ariz.	Mexican	Univ. Calif. Museum	1928	70
21 4/16	13 5/16	U	7 14/16	Los Angeles Co., Calif.	Picked Up	Anselmo Lewis	1952	70
21 4/16	13 5/16	M	7 14/16	Shoshone River, Wyo.	Loren L. Lutz	Loren L. Lutz	1956	70
21 4/16	13 5/16	M	7 13/16	Ann Arbor, Mich.	Albert Erickson	Albert Erickson	1957	70
21 4/16	13 5/16	M	8 2/16	Ariz.	Paul B. Reynolds	Paul B. Reynolds	1965	70
21 4/16	13 5/16	M	7 11/16	Olympic Pen., Wash.	Bert Klineburger	Bert Klineburger	1967	70
21 4/16	12 12/16	M	8 8/16	Curry Co., Oreg.	Joe W. Latimer	Joe W. Latimer	1968	70
21 4/16	12 11/16	M	8 8/16	Sawyer Co., Wisc.	Ted Roberts	Ted Roberts	1968	70
21 4/16	13 1/16	M	8 3/16	Hudson Bay, Sask.	Neil Southam	Neil Southam	1969	70
21 4/16	13 3/16	M	8 3/16	Williams, Ariz	James E. Coy	James E. Coy	1970	70
21 4/16	13 5/16	M	7 14/16	Snowmass, Colo.	Ronald D. Vincent	Ronald D. Vincent	1974	70
21 3/16	13 5/16	U	7 13/16	Queen Charlotte Is., B.C.	C. de Blois Green	Univ. Calif. Museum	1911	81
21 3/16	13 6/16	M	7 11/16	Alta.	James C. Wynne	James C. Wynne	1966	81
21 3/16	13 5/16	M	8 4/16	Bayfield Co., Wisc.	G. Michaels	Gerald M. Weber	1966	81
21 3/16	12 15/16	M	8 3/16	Alta.	F. A. Stromstedt	Univ. Of Calgary	1967	81
21 3/16	13	M	13	Thurston Co., Wash.	Hugh M. Oliver	Hugh M. Oliver	1969	81
21 3/16	12 5/16	M	8 4/16	Eagle Co., Colo.	Charles T. Coffman	Charles T. Coffman	1971	81
21 3/16	13 5/16	M	7 15/16	Ashland Co., Wisc.	Herman Straubel	Herman Straubel	1972	81
21 3/16	13 3/16	M	8 2/16	Stonecliffe, Ont.	Robert M. Weir	Robert M. Weir	1974	81
21 3/16	13 3/16	M	8 2/16	Oneida Co., Wisc.	Fred C. Hageny	Fred C. Hageny	1975	81
21 3/16	13 4/16	M	7 15/16	Gila Co., Ariz	Kae L. Brockermeyer	Kae L. Brockermeyer	1977	81
21 2/16	13	M	13	Kuiu Is., Alaska	L. W. Potter	L. W. Potter	1951	91
21 2/16	12 12/16	M	8 8/16	Essex Co., N.Y.	William R. Waddell	N. Y. Cons. Dept.	1955	91
21 2/16	13 6/16	M	7 12/16	Lincoln Co., Wyo.	Ralph Langford & W. R. Ryan	Ralph Langford	1955	91
21 2/16	13 3/16	M	7 15/16	Los Angeles Co., Calif.	Leo J. Reihsen	Leo J. Reihsen	1961	91
21 2/16	13 3/16	M	8	Mammoth Mt., Calif.	Clarke Merrill	Clarke Merrill	1963	91
21 2/16	13 12/16	M	7 8/16	Chinitna Bay, Alaska	Basil C. Bradbury	Basil C. Bradbury	1964	91
21 2/16	13 5/16	M	7 13/16	Shasta Co., Calif.	Ivan L. Marx	Ivan L. Marx	1965	91
21 2/16	12 15/16	M	8 3/16	Chelan Co., Wash.	Virgil R. Bedient	Virgil R. Bedient	1965	91
21 2/16	12 12/16	M	8 8/16	Collbran, Colo.	R. R. Lyons & H. V. Morris	Raymond R. Lyons	1965	91
21 2/16	13	M	8 3/16	Mesa Co., Colo.	Waldemar R. Kuenzel, Jr.	Waldemar R. Kuenzel, Jr.	1966	91
21 2/16	12 14/16	M	8 8/16	Raven Lake, B.C.	Robert G. Wardian	Robert G. Wardian	1967	91
21 2/16	13	U	8 8/16	Trinity Co., Calif.	Pick Up	Robert E. Frost	1967	91
21 2/16	12 10/16	M	7 11/16	Montrose, Colo.	Earl L. Markley	Earl L. Markley	1970	91
21 2/16	12 10/16	U	7 8/16	Clam Lake, Wisc.	Picked Up	Mike Reynolds & Jim Olson	PR1971	91
21 2/16	14 1/16	M	8	Sublette Co., Wyo.	A. Jack Welch	A. Jack Welch	1971	91
21 2/16	14 3/16	M	8	Lake Co., Calif.	David C. Sharp	David C. Sharp	1972	91

BLACK BEAR–Continued

Ursus americanus americanus and related subspecies

Score	Greatest Length of Skull Without Lower Jaw	Greatest Width of Skull	Sex	Locality Killed	By Whom Killed	Owner	Date Killed	Rank
$21\frac{7}{16}$	$13\frac{5}{16}$	$7\frac{12}{16}$	M	Gila Co., Ariz.	Daniel J. Urban	Daniel J. Urban	1972	91
$21\frac{7}{16}$	$13\frac{3}{16}$	$7\frac{11}{16}$	M	Gunnison Co., Colo.	Dick Cooper	Dick Cooper	1977	91
$21\frac{7}{16}$	$13\frac{1}{16}$	$8\frac{1}{16}$	M	Gila Co., Ariz.	Robert E. Barnes	Robert E. Barnes	1978	91
$21\frac{7}{16}$	$13\frac{1}{16}$	$8\frac{1}{16}$	M	Lodgepole, Alta.	Jim H. Van Manen	Jim H. Van Manen	1979	91
$21\frac{7}{16}$	13	$8\frac{2}{16}$	M	Ethelbert, Man.	Paul A. Bormes	Paul A. Bormes	1979	91
$21\frac{1}{16}$	$13\frac{3}{16}$	$7\frac{14}{16}$	M	Indian Lake, La.	B. V. Lilly	U. S. Natl. Museum	1904	112
$21\frac{1}{16}$	$13\frac{3}{16}$	$7\frac{14}{16}$	M	Coahuila, Mexico	B. V. Lilly	U. S. Natl. Museum	1906	112
$21\frac{1}{16}$	$13\frac{1}{16}$	$7\frac{9}{16}$	U	Santa Barbara Co., Calif.	Charles Tant	Univ. Calif. Museum	1940	112
$21\frac{1}{16}$	$13\frac{3}{16}$	$7\frac{15}{16}$	M	Columbia Co., Wash.	Glenn Ford	Fred Van Arsdol	1954	112
$21\frac{1}{16}$	$13\frac{3}{16}$	$7\frac{15}{16}$	M	Mt. Gentry, Ariz.	Cliff Edwards	Cliff Edwards	1960	112
$21\frac{1}{16}$	$12\frac{12}{16}$	$8\frac{5}{16}$	M	Paonia, Colo.	William O. Good	William O. Good	1960	112
$21\frac{1}{16}$	$12\frac{9}{16}$	$8\frac{9}{16}$	M	Steamboat Springs, Colo.	Norman Garwood	Norman Garwood	1964	112
$21\frac{1}{16}$	$13\frac{3}{16}$	$7\frac{11}{16}$	M	Peace River, Alta.	Don Wm. Caldwell	Don Wm. Caldwell	1965	112
$21\frac{1}{16}$	13	$8\frac{1}{16}$	M	Price Co., Wisc.	Jim Hanson & Joseph Valiga	Joseph Valiga	1971	112
$21\frac{1}{16}$	$13\frac{3}{16}$	$7\frac{15}{16}$	M	Gila Co., Ariz.	George L. Massingill	George L. Massingill	1971	112
$21\frac{1}{16}$	$12\frac{13}{16}$	$7\frac{14}{16}$	M	Iron Co., Wisc.	Gerald Brauer	Gerald Brauer	1972	112
$21\frac{1}{16}$	$13\frac{3}{16}$	$8\frac{4}{16}$	M	San Carlos Indian Res., Ariz.	Michael D. Gunnett	Michael D. Gunnett	1973	112
$21\frac{1}{16}$	$12\frac{15}{16}$	$7\frac{11}{16}$	M	Hubbard Co., Minn.	Dean J. Como	Dean J. Como	1974	112
$21\frac{1}{16}$	$13\frac{3}{16}$	$8\frac{3}{16}$	M	Logan Lake, B.C.	Norman W. Dougan	Norman W. Dougan	1978	112
$21\frac{1}{16}$	$12\frac{15}{16}$	$7\frac{14}{16}$	M	Graham Island, B.C.	Roger Britton	Roger Britton	1978	112
21	$12\frac{9}{16}$	$8\frac{1}{16}$	U	Queen Charlotte Is., B. C.	Unknown	Douglas McIntyre	—	127
21	$12\frac{9}{16}$	$8\frac{8}{16}$	M	Vancouver, B. C.	Elmer E. Kurrus, Jr.	Elmer E. Kurrus, Jr.	1964	127
21	13	8	M	Hamilton Co., N. Y.	James McIntyre	N. Y. Cons. Dept.	1965	127
21	$12\frac{12}{16}$	$8\frac{4}{16}$	M	Collbran, Colo.	Cecil E. Alumbaugh, Jr.	Cecil E. Alumbaugh, Jr.	1967	127
21	$12\frac{11}{16}$	$8\frac{5}{16}$	M	Oconto Co., Wisc.	Calvin E. Schindel	Calvin E. Schindel	1968	127
21	$13\frac{3}{16}$	$7\frac{13}{16}$	M	Overflowing River, Man.	Victor Kostiniuk	Victor Kostiniuk	1971	127
21	$12\frac{15}{16}$	$8\frac{1}{16}$	M	Garfield Co., Colo.	J. D. Liles	J. D. Liles	1974	127
21	$13\frac{3}{16}$	$7\frac{14}{16}$	M	St. Louis Co., Minn.	Robert J. Manteuffel	Robert J. Manteuffel	1977	134

*Final Score subject to revision by additional verifying measurements.

116

GRIZZLY BEAR

A National Park Service photograph taken in Yellowstone National Park by William S. Keller.

BOUNDARIES OF THE ALASKA BROWN BEAR AND GRIZZLY BEAR

A line of separation between the larger growing coastal brown bear and the smaller interior grizzly has been developed such that west and south of this line (to and including Unimak Island) bear trophies are recorded as Alaska brown bear. North and east of this line, bear trophies are recorded as grizzly bear. The boundary line description is as follows: Starting at Pearse Canal and following the Canadian-Alaskan boundary northwesterly to Mt. St. Elias on the 141° meridian;thence north along the Canadian-Alaskan boundary to Mt. Natazhat; thence west along the divide of the Wrangell Range to Mt. Jarvis at the western end of the Wrangell Range; thence north along the divide of the Mentasta Range to Mentasta Pass; thence in a general westerly direction along the divide of the Alaska Range to Houston Pass; thence westerly following the 62nd parallel of latitude to the Bering Sea.

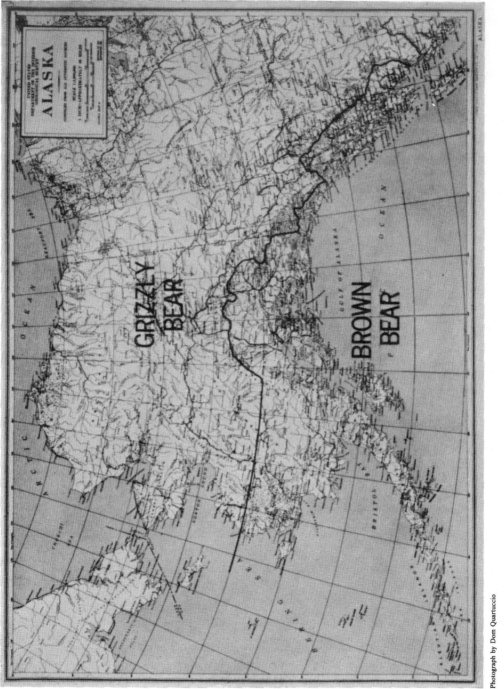

This map shows the line of demarcation between Alaska brown and grizzly bears, as drawn by the Boone and Crockett Club for records keeping purposes.

Grizzly Bear

Ursus arctos horribilis

Minimum Score 24

Score	Greatest Length of Skull Without Lower Jaw	Greatest Width of Skull	Sex	Locality Killed	By Whom Killed	Owner	Date Killed	Rank
27²/₁₆	17⁶/₁₆	9¹²/₁₆	U	Bella Coola Valley, B. C.	Picked Up	James G. Shelton	1970	1
27¹/₁₆*	17¹/₁₆	10	M	Alexis Creek, B. C.	Doug Edman	Doug Edman	1970	2
26¹⁰/₁₆	16¹⁰/₁₆	10	M	Rivers Inlet, B. C.	F. Nygaard	Univ. Of B. C.	1954	3
26¹⁰/₁₆	17	9¹⁰/₁₆	M	Lonesome Lake, B. C.	J. Turner	Douglas Kenefick	1965	3
26⁸/₁₆	16⁹/₁₆	9¹⁴/₁₆	M	Yanert Glacier, Alaska	Xavier T. Riedmiller	Xavier T. Riedmiller	1970	5
26⁶/₁₆	16⁵/₁₆	10	M	Bella Coola, B. C.	Walter C. Shutts	Walter C. Shutts	1957	6
26⁶/₁₆	16¹²/₁₆	9¹⁰/₁₆	M	Farewell Lake, Alaska	John C. Schwietert	John C. Schwietert	1968	6
26⁵/₁₆	16⁹/₁₆	9¹¹/₁₆	M	Slave Lake, Alta.	Bella Twin & Dave Auger	R. W. H. Eben-Ebenau	1953	8
26⁵/₁₆	16⁵/₁₆	10	M	Knights Inlet, B. C.	Thomas N. Bernard	Thomas N. Bernard	1967	8
26⁵/₁₆	16⁵/₁₆	9⁶/₁₆	M	Swan Hills, Alta.	Wilfred Hartfelder	Wilfred Hartfelder	1974	8
26⁴/₁₆	16⁹/₁₆	9¹⁰/₁₆	U	Elliott Hwy., Alaska	Unknown	Alaska Game Dept.	1967	11
26⁴/₁₆	16⁵/₁₆	9¹⁵/₁₆	M	Ferry, Alaska	Jamie C. Smyth	Jamie C. Smyth	1973	11
26⁴/₁₆	16⁵/₁₆	10⁶/₁₆	M	Nulato Hills, Alaska	Randy A. Tarnowski	Randy A. Tarnowski	1978	11
26⁴/₁₆	17	9⁴/₁₆	M	Kakwa River, Alta.	Klaus Wernsdorf	Klaus Wernsdorf	1979	11
26³/₁₆	17	9³/₁₆	M	Tatla Lake, B. C.	Robert Lawrence Tuma	Robert Lawrence Tuma	1971	15
26³/₁₆	16¹/₁₆	10²/₁₆	M	Buckland River, Alaska	Bill McDavid	Bill McDavid	1977	15
26²/₁₆	16⁸/₁₆	9⁸/₁₆	M	Nechako River, B. C.	R. J. Nielsen	R. J. Nielsen	1971	17
26²/₁₆	16	10⁵/₁₆	M	Kantishna River, Alaska	Theodore B. Kelly, Jr.	Theodore B. Kelly, Jr.	1972	17
26²/₁₆	16⁵/₁₆	9¹³/₁₆	U	Kwatna Bay, B. C.	J. G. Bartlett	J. G. Bartlett	1976	17
26¹/₁₆	16¹/₁₆	10	M	Smiths Inlet, B. C.	Donald M. Swarthout	Donald M. Swarthout	1963	20
26	16	10	M	Lake Minchumina, Alaska	Val J. Blackburn	Val J. Blackburn	1956	21
26	17	9	M	Bella Coola, B. C.	J. Harstad	John Lesowski	1959	21
26	16¹/₁₆	9¹⁵/₁₆	M	Tweedsmuir Park, B. C.	Michael R. Caspersen	Michael R. Caspersen	1969	21
26	16⁸/₁₆	9⁸/₁₆	M	Kobuk River, Alaska	Charlie Horner	Charlie Horner	1971	21
25¹⁵/₁₆	15¹²/₁₆	10³/₁₆	M	Rapids Roadhouse, Alaska	H. Herring	H. Herring	1964	25
25¹⁵/₁₆	16⁵/₁₆	9¹²/₁₆	M	Bella Coola, B. C.	Bernard J. Meinerz	Bernard J. Meinerz	1968	25
25¹⁵/₁₆	16⁵/₁₆	9¹²/₁₆	M	Klinaklini River, B. C.	Jerry Stubblefield	Jerry Stubblefield	1970	25
25¹⁴/₁₆	16	9¹⁴/₁₆	M	Telkwa River, B. C.	Matt Helstrom	Lowell A. Davison	1957	28
25¹⁴/₁₆	16⁸/₁₆	9⁵/₁₆	M	Owikeno Lake, B. C.	Alexander M. Peterson	Alexander M. Peterson	1959	28
25¹³/₁₆	15¹⁵/₁₆	9¹⁴/₁₆	M	Fairbanks, Alaska	Horace Black	Horace Black	1963	30
25¹³/₁₆	16⁸/₁₆	9⁴/₁₆	M	Bella Coola, B. C.	Roger L. Adams	Roger L. Adams	1965	30
25¹²/₁₆	15¹³/₁₆	9¹⁵/₁₆	M	Alaska Range, Alaska	Elmer R. Schlachter	Elmer R. Schlachter	1971	32

119

GRIZZLY BEAR–*Continued*
Ursus arctos horribilis

Score	Greatest Length of Skull Without Lower Jaw	Greatest Width of Skull	Sex	Locality Killed	By Whom Killed	Owner	Date Killed	Rank
$25\frac{11}{16}$	$16\frac{3}{16}$	$9\frac{9}{16}$	M	Owikeno Lake, B. C.	W. W. Meeker	W. W. Meeker	1959	33
$25\frac{11}{16}$	$15\frac{11}{16}$	10	M	Tatshenshini River, B. C.	Robert E. Miller	Robert E. Miller	1974	33
$25\frac{11}{16}$	$16\frac{3}{16}$	$9\frac{9}{16}$	M	Kimsquit River, B.C.	Norman E. Kinsey	Norman E. Kinsey	1977	33
$25\frac{9}{16}$	$16\frac{1}{16}$	$9\frac{9}{16}$	M	Bralorne, B. C.	Bert Klineburger	Bert Klineburger	1956	36
$25\frac{9}{16}$	$16\frac{3}{16}$	$9\frac{7}{16}$	M	Dease River, B. C.	Herb Klein	Herb Klein	1960	36
$25\frac{9}{16}$	$16\frac{7}{16}$	$9\frac{8}{16}$	U	Eagle Creek, Wyo.	Picked Up	Loren L. Lutz & Harry Sanford	1961	36
$25\frac{9}{16}$	16	$9\frac{10}{16}$	M	Brooks Range, Alaska	John H. Epp	John H. Epp	1965	36
$25\frac{9}{16}$	$15\frac{5}{16}$	$10\frac{5}{16}$	M	Nabesna River, Alaska	Jack A. Shane, Sr.	Jack A. Shane, Sr.	1966	36
$25\frac{9}{16}$	$16\frac{2}{16}$	$9\frac{8}{16}$	M	Kuskokwim River, Alaska	George Panagos	George Panagos	1968	36
$25\frac{9}{16}$	$15\frac{15}{16}$	$9\frac{11}{16}$	M	Tok River, Alaska	Robert S. Thompson	Robert S. Thompson	1974	36
$25\frac{9}{16}$	16	$9\frac{10}{16}$	M	Machmell River, B. C.	Herbert J. Wenk	Herbert J. Wenk	1975	36
$25\frac{9}{16}$	16	$9\frac{8}{16}$	M	Missouri Breaks, Mont.	E. S. Cameron	U. S. Natl. Museum	1890	44
$25\frac{9}{16}$	$16\frac{4}{16}$	$9\frac{5}{16}$	M	Klinaklini River, B. C.	Grancel Fitz	Mrs. Grancel Fitz	1953	44
$25\frac{9}{16}$	16	$9\frac{9}{16}$	M	Kitseguecla Mts., B. C.	Jack Adams	Jack Adams	1975	44
$25\frac{8}{16}$	$16\frac{2}{16}$	$9\frac{9}{16}$	M	Owikeno Lake, B. C.	J. C. Russell	J. C. Russell	1957	47
$25\frac{8}{16}$	16	$9\frac{8}{16}$	M	Maxan Lake, B. C.	Alfred E. Matthew	Alfred E. Matthew	1967	47
$25\frac{8}{16}$	16	$9\frac{8}{16}$	M	Cassiar Mts., B. C.	Arlow Lothe	Arlow Lothe	1969	47
$25\frac{8}{16}$	$15\frac{15}{16}$	$9\frac{9}{16}$	M	Wakeman Sound, B. C.	Dennis King	Dennis King	1969	47
$25\frac{8}{16}$	$15\frac{12}{16}$	$9\frac{12}{16}$	M	McKinley River, Alaska	John R. Cardis	John R. Cardis	1970	47
$25\frac{8}{16}$	16	$9\frac{8}{16}$	M	Big River, Alaska	George Engel	George Engel	1976	47
$25\frac{7}{16}$	$15\frac{13}{16}$	$9\frac{10}{16}$	M	Clearwater River, Alta.	Jack Allen	Jack Allen	—	53
$25\frac{7}{16}$	$15\frac{12}{16}$	$9\frac{11}{16}$	M	Upper Boulder River, Mont.	Ted Johnston	E. C. Cates	1934	53
$25\frac{7}{16}$	16	$9\frac{7}{16}$	M	Tweedsmuir Park, B. C.	Lloyd B. Walker	Lloyd B. Walker	1950	53
$25\frac{7}{16}$	$15\frac{5}{16}$	$10\frac{4}{16}$	M	Zohini Creek, B. C.	Paul R. Beebe	Paul R. Beebe	1967	53
$25\frac{7}{16}$	$16\frac{10}{16}$	$8\frac{13}{16}$	M	Nordegg, Alta.	Charles W. Matter	Charles W. Matter	1974	53
$25\frac{5}{16}$	$16\frac{4}{16}$	9	M	Slave Lake, Alta.	R. W. H. Eben-Ebenau	R. W. H. Eben-Ebenau	1944	58
$25\frac{5}{16}$	$16\frac{1}{16}$	$9\frac{5}{16}$	M	Kleena Kleen, B. C.	A. W. Travis	A. W. Travis	1961	58
$25\frac{5}{16}$	$15\frac{5}{16}$	$9\frac{13}{16}$	M	Northway, Alaska	James A. Johnson	James A. Johnson	1964	58
$25\frac{5}{16}$	16	$9\frac{6}{16}$	M	Mussel Inlet, B. C.	Victor W. Budd	Victor W. Budd	1967	58
$25\frac{5}{16}$	$15\frac{10}{16}$	$9\frac{12}{16}$	M	Edson, Alta.	Jack Armstrong	Jack Armstrong	1967	58
$25\frac{5}{16}$	$15\frac{5}{16}$	$10\frac{3}{16}$	M	Brooks Range, Alaska	Rusty Pickus	Rusty Pickus	1979	58
$25\frac{5}{16}$	$15\frac{13}{16}$	$9\frac{8}{16}$	M	Anahim Lake, B. C.	Ace Demers	Ace Demers	1951	64

Score		M/U	Locality	Owner	By Whom Killed	Date	Rank
25 5/16	15 4/16	M	Kwatna River, B. C.	Walter W. Butcher	Walter W. Butcher	1954	64
25 5/16	15 1/16	M	Granite Lake, Yukon	Jim Papst	Jim Papst	1969	64
25 5/16	15 7/16	M	Kobuk River, Alaska	Hugh H. Chatham, Jr.	Hugh H. Chatham, Jr.	1971	64
25 5/16	15 8/16	M	Eutsuk Lake, B. C.	W. R. Macfarlane	W. R. Macfarlane	1974	64
25 5/16	15 12/16	M	Brooks Range, Alaska	Warren K. Parker	Warren K. Parker	1979	64
25 5/16	16	M	Prince Rupert, B.C.	Murray B. Wilson	Murray B. Wilson	1979	64
25 5/16	16	M	Anahim Lake, B. C.	Univ. Calif. Museum	C. D. Carrington	1957	64
25 4/16	16 3/16	M	Cascade Inlet, B. C.	Walter A. Frame	Walter A. Frame	1964	71
25 4/16	15 7/16	M	Salmon River, B. C.	Al Rand	Al Rand	1964	71
25 4/16	15 8/16	M	Yanert River, Alaska	Herbert A. Biss	Herbert A. Biss	1965	71
25 4/16	15 5/16	M	Anahim Lake, B. C	Bernard Nofziger	Bernard Nofziger	1970	71
25 4/16	15 13/16	M	Kynoch Inlet, B. C.	W. G. Hawes	P. J. Kennedy	1971	71
25 4/16	15 15/16	M	Berland River, Alta	Donald Brockman	Donald Brockman	1978	71
25 4/16	15 2/16	M	Alaska Range, Alaska	David L. Kulzer	David L. Kulzer	1979	71
25 3/16	15 8/16	M	Bella Coola, B. C.	Umberto Benedet	Umberto Benedet	1957	79
25 3/16	15 7/16	M	Wrangell Mts., Alaska	Peter W. Bading	Peter W. Bading	1963	79
25 3/16	15 3/16	M	Teller, Alaska	Harry Armitage	Harry Armitage	1965	79
25 3/16	16 4/16	U	Motase Lake, B. C.	Joel Franzoia	Joel Franzoia	1970	79
25 3/16	15 9/16	M	McClinchy River, B. C.	Bernie Gano	Picked Up	PR1974	79
25 3/16	15 7/16	M	Bella Coola, B. C.	Richard K. Miller	Richard K. Miller	1975	79
25 3/16	15 3/16	M	American River, Alaska	John M. Griffith, Jr.	John M. Griffith, Jr.	1977	79
25 3/16	15 9/16	M	Yellowstone River, Wyo.	Jack H. White	Bill Nymeyer	1960	86
25 2/16	16 7/16	M	Lignite, Alaska	Leonard Spencer	Leonard Spencer	1963	86
25 2/16	15 5/16	M	Mentasta Mts., Alaska	Basil C. Bradbury	Basil C. Bradbury	1965	86
25 2/16	15 11/16	M	Kotzebue, Alaska	F. W. Hatterscheidt	F. W. Hatterscheidt	1968	86
25 2/16	15 3/16	M	Bella Coola, B. C.	Howard Morrisey	Howard Morrisey	1971	86
25 2/16	15 3/16	M	McGrath, Alaska	Curtis C. Classen	Curtis C. Classen	1974	86
25 2/16	15 4/16	M	Butedale, B. C.	Walter R. Peters	Walter R. Peters	1974	86
25 2/16	15 7/16	M	Parsnip River, B.C.	Graham Markland	Graham Markland	1977	86
25 2/16	15 12/16	M	Teton Co., Wyo.	Jackson Hole Museum	C. C. Craven	1938	86
25 1/16	15 13/16	M	Knight Inlet, B. C.	Frederick N. Dodge	Frederick N. Dodge	1954	94
25 1/16	15 14/16	M	Bella Coola, B. C.	L. Rowe Davidson	L. Rowe Davidson	1958	94
25 1/16	15 9/16	M	Caribou Flats, B. C.	Edward Escott	Edward Escott	1962	94
25 1/16	15 11/16	M	Yanert River, Alaska	E. G. Brust, Jr.	E. G. Brust, Jr.	1964	94
25 1/16	16 3/16	M	Selby River, Alaska	Kenneth T. Alt	Kenneth T. Alt	1965	94
25 1/16	15 8/16	M	Bob Quinn Lake, B C	Dave Miscavish	Dave Miscavish	1971	94
25 1/16	16 3/16	M	Lewistown, Mont.	U. S. Natl. Museum	Mildred Connor	1888	94
25	16	M	Bella Coola, B. C.	H. J. Borden	David Maytag	1959	101
25	15 9/16	M	Nabesna River, Alaska	Marven Henriksen	Marven Henriksen	1964	101
25	10	M	Kotzebue, Alaska	Glen E. Park	Glen E. Park	1965	101
25	15 11/16	M	Yellowstone Natl. Park, Wyo.	John C. Kirk	Picked Up	PR1965	101
25	15 12/16	M	Hart Peaks, B. C.	T. T. Stroup	T. T. Stroup	1966	101
25	15 13/16	M	Mt. Hayes, Alaska	Benjamin H. Robson	Benjamin H. Robson	1968	101

121

GRIZZLY BEAR–*Continued*
Ursus arctos horribilis

Score	Greatest Length of Skull Without Lower Jaw	Greatest Width of Skull	Sex	Locality Killed	By Whom Killed	Owner	Date Killed	Rank
25	15⁵/₁₆	9¹²/₁₆	M	Noomst Creek, B.C.	James G. Shelton	James G. Shelton	1970	101
25	15⁸/₁₆	9⁸/₁₆	M	Stikine River, B.C.	Donald R. McClure, Sr.	Donald R. McClure, Sr.	1971	101
25	15¹⁰/₁₆	9⁶/₁₆	M	Tacu River, B.C.	W. N. Olson	W. N. Olson	1971	101
25	15¹³/₁₆	9³/₁₆	M	Hinton, Alta.	Oliver Hannula	Oliver Hannula	1972	101
25	15¹⁵/₁₆	9¹/₁₆	U	Whitecourt, Alta.	Sid Wheeler	Sid Wheeler	1974	101
25	15⁸/₁₆	9⁸/₁₆	M	Richland Co., Mont.	Picked Up	Jack Stewart	1976	101
24¹⁵/₁₆	15⁶/₁₆	9⁹/₁₆	M	Taseko Lake, B.C.	A. Cecil Henry	A. Cecil Henry	1956	114
24¹⁵/₁₆	15⁴/₁₆	9¹¹/₁₆	M	Ootsa Lake, B.C.	John Block & Doug Vantine	John Block	1965	114
24¹⁵/₁₆	15⁷/₁₆	9⁸/₁₆	M	Dudidontu River, B.C.	Bob Loewenstein	Bob Loewenstein	1965	114
24¹⁵/₁₆	15¹⁴/₁₆	9¹/₁₆	M	Teller, Alaska	Jack D. Putnam	Jack D. Putnam	1965	114
24¹⁵/₁₆	15¹⁰/₁₆	9⁵/₁₆	M	Lakelse River, B.C.	Victor Lepp	Victor Lepp	1968	114
24¹⁵/₁₆	15¹²/₁₆	9³/₁₆	M	Wrangell Mts., Alaska	James E. Saxton	James E. Saxton	1977	114
24¹⁴/₁₆	16¹/₁₆	8¹²/₁₆	M	Atnarko Region, B.C.	F. N. Bard	Chicago Nat. Hist. Museum	1938	120
24¹⁴/₁₆	15¹²/₁₆	9²/₁₆	M	Chilcotin, B.C.	R. J. Pop & J. Benan	R. J. Pop	1954	120
24¹⁴/₁₆	15⁷/₁₆	9⁷/₁₆	M	Chisana, Alaska	Larry Folger	Larry Folger	1957	120
24¹⁴/₁₆	15⁶/₁₆	9⁵/₁₆	M	Atnarko River, B.C.	Carl Molander	Carl Molander	1957	120
24¹⁴/₁₆	15¹¹/₁₆	9³/₁₆	M	Meziadin Lake, B.C.	Larry Spangler	Larry Spangler	1962	120
24¹⁴/₁₆	15¹³/₁₆	9¹/₁₆	M	Alaska Range, Alaska	Jack Williamson	Jack Williamson	1963	120
24¹⁴/₁₆	15⁷/₁₆	9¹⁰/₁₆	M	Brooks Range, Alaska	E. Wayne Gilley	E. Wayne Gilley	1963	120
24¹⁴/₁₆	15⁷/₁₆	9¹²/₁₆	M	Shishmiref, Alaska	James Harrower	James Harrower	1964	120
24¹⁴/₁₆	16¹/₁₆	8¹¹/₁₆	M	Taku River, B.C.	Robert J. Lacy	Robert J. Lacy	1964	120
24¹⁴/₁₆	16¹/₁₆	8¹¹/₁₆	M	Knights Inlet, B.C.	Levon Bender	Levon Bender	1965	120
24¹⁴/₁₆	15⁷/₁₆	9⁷/₁₆	M	Brooks Range, Alaska	W. F. Krebill	W. F. Krebill	1966	120
24¹⁴/₁₆	15⁶/₁₆	9⁸/₁₆	M	Cassiar Mts., B.C.	H. Kenneth Seiferd	H. Kenneth Seiferd	1966	120
24¹⁴/₁₆	15⁶/₁₆	9⁷/₁₆	M	McGregor Mts., B.C.	Edward Johnson	Edward Johnson	1967	120
24¹⁴/₁₆	15⁵/₁₆	9⁵/₁₆	M	McGregor River, B.C.	C. C. Carpenter	C. C. Carpenter	1968	120
24¹⁴/₁₆	15¹²/₁₆	9²/₁₆	M	Telkwa River, B.C.	Richard Pohlschneider	Richard Pohlschneider	1969	120
24¹⁴/₁₆	15⁷/₁₆	9⁸/₁₆	M	Seaskinnish Creek, B.C.	Thomas D. J. Fulkco	Thomas D. J. Fulkco	1977	120
24¹³/₁₆	15⁷/₁₆	9⁶/₁₆	M	Chisana River, Alaska	Larry Folger	Larry Folger	1957	136
24¹³/₁₆	15⁶/₁₆	9⁴/₁₆	M	Livengood, Alaska	Ada Holst	Ada Holst	1961	136
24¹³/₁₆	15³/₁₆	9¹⁰/₁₆	M	Tatla Lake, B.C.	R. D. Brooks	R. D. Brooks	1962	136
24¹³/₁₆	15⁶/₁₆	9⁹/₁₆	M	Clarence Lake, Alaska	E. A. Munroe	E. A. Munroe	1964	136

								Score
24 13/16	15 6/16	9 6/16	M	Tonzona River, Alaska	Francis Kernan	Francis Kernan	1964	136
24 13/16	15 12/16	9 1/16	M	Warden Creek, Alta.	Harvey R. Cook	Harvey R. Cook	1964	136
24 13/16	15 12/16	9 1/16	M	Chetwynd, B. C.	William E. Dugger	William E. Dugger	1964	136
24 13/16	15 6/16	9 7/16	M	Slim Lake, B. C.	Freda Stalder	Freda Stalder	1968	136
24 13/16	15 6/16	9 6/16	M	Noatak River, Alaska	John E. Batson	John E. Batson	1970	136
24 13/16	15 11/16	9 2/16	M	Telkwa Range, B.C.	Jack Adams	Jack Adams	1978	136
24 12/16	15 8/16	9 4/16	M	Spanish Lake, B. C.	Bill Niemi	Bill Niemi	1953	146
24 12/16	15 6/16	9 6/16	M	Sheep Creek, Alta.	R. V. Broadbent	R. V. Broadbent	1963	146
24 12/16	15	9 12/16	M	Brooks Range, Alaska	Lewis A. Meyers	Lewis A. Meyers	1964	146
24 11/16	15 10/16	9 2/16	M	Terminus Mtn., B. C.	Herb Klein	Herb Klein	1965	146
24 12/16	15 8/16	9 4/16	M	Kitimat, B. C.	Hans Lackner	Hans Lackner	1969	146
24 12/16	15 3/16	9 3/16	M	Burrage Creek, B. C.	Jack Worthy	Jack Worthy	1970	146
24 12/16	15 6/16	9 8/16	M	Bella Coola, B. C.	Joe M. Colvin	Joe M. Colvin	1973	146
24 12/16	15 6/16	9 4/16	M	Alaska Range, Alaska	Earl K. Edstrom	Earl K. Edstrom	1976	146
24 11/16	15 6/16	9 7/16	M	Wigwam River, B.C.	Ray S. Koontz	Ray S. Koontz	1977	146
24 11/16	15 6/16	9 9/16	M	Tok River, Alaska	Lewis B. Wyman	Lewis B. Wyman	1965	155
24 11/16	15 2/16	9 7/16	M	Stevens Lake, B. C.	R. L. Hambrick	R. L. Hambrick	1965	155
24 11/16	15 6/16	9 11/16	M	Alaska Range, Alaska	Tony Caputo	Tony Caputo	1967	155
24 11/16	15	8 13/16	M	MacMillan Plateau, Yukon	Paul Yeager	Paul Yeager	1967	155
24 11/16	15 14/16	9 3/16	U	Lesser Slave Lake, Alta.	Picked Up	James Erickson	1967	155
24 11/16	15 8/16	9 5/16	M	Butte Inlet, B. C.	Thomas M. Utigard	Thomas M. Utigard	1970	155
24 10/16	15 6/16	9 2/16	M	Kuzitrin River, Alaska	H. Doak Neal	H. Doak Neal	1976	162
24 10/16	15 8/16	9 6/16	M	Camp Island Lake, B. C.	Harold L. Jones	Harold L. Jones	1965	162
24 10/16	15 4/16	9 5/16	M	Point Hope, Alaska	Richard K. Siller	Richard K. Siller	1965	162
24 10/16	15 5/16	8 15/16	M	Brooks Range, Alaska	T. W. Bohannan	T. W. Bohannan	1968	162
24 9/16	15 11/16	9 6/16	M	Seymour Inlet, B. C.	Tim Fischer	Tim Fischer	1969	162
24 9/16	15 6/16	9 8/16	M	Wiseman, Alaska	David L. Howard	David L. Howard	1970	162
24 9/16	15 7/16	9 8/16	M	Toklat River, Alaska	Gary Miller	Gary Miller	1972	162
24 9/16	15 7/16	9 6/16	M	Mosley Creek, B. C.	Charles Harvey	Charles Harvey	1976	162
24 9/16	15 4/16	9 4/16	M	Alaska Range, Alaska	Victor Geibel	Victor Geibel	1978	162
24 10/16	15 6/16	9 5/16	M	Swan Lake, B. C.	A. C. Gilbert	A. C. Gilbert	1937	170
24 10/16	15 6/16	9 1/16	M	Tatla Lake, B. C.	D. McDermott	D. McDermott	1954	170
24 10/16	15 13/16	8 12/16	M	Bella Coola, B. C.	Wm. P. Mastrangel	Wm. P. Mastrangel	1956	170
24 10/16	15 6/16	9 5/16	U	Bella Coola, B. C.	Martin Anderson	Martin Anderson	1957	170
24 9/16	15 6/16	9 6/16	M	Bella Coola, B. C.	Norman W. Garwood	Norman W. Garwood	1960	170
24 9/16	15 7/16	9 2/16	M	Hulahula River, Alaska	Richard Sjoden	Richard Sjoden	1963	170
24 9/16	15 6/16	9 5/16	M	Ray Mts., Alaska	Mario Grassi	Mario Grassi	1965	170
24 9/16	16 1/16	8 8/16	M	Anahim Lake, B. C.	M. V. Nearing	M. V. Nearing	1966	170
24 9/16	15 6/16	9 3/16	M	Meziadin Lake, B. C.	Teuvo Pahti	Teuvo Pahti	1968	170
24 9/16	15 5/16	9 4/16	M	Tok River, Alaska	John W. Waller	John W. Waller	1968	170
24 9/16	15 1/16	9 8/16	M	Cape Lisburre, Alaska	Gerrit N. Vandenberg	Gerrit N. Vandenberg	1969	170
24 9/16	15 9/16	9	M	Kispiox River, B. C.	W. J. Love	W. J. Love	1971	170
24 9/16	16	8 9/16	M	Graham River, B. C.	Edward F. Lundberg	Edward F. Lundberg	1976	170

Grizzly Bear–Continued
Ursus arctos horribilis

Score	Greatest Length of Skull Without Lower Jaw	Greatest Width of Skull	Sex	Locality Killed	By Whom Killed	Owner	Date Killed	Rank
24 8/16	14 15/16	9 10/16	M	Yanert River, Alaska	Robert J. Barham	Robert J. Barham	1977	170
24 8/16	15	9 9/16	M	Quesnel Lake, B.C.	Thomas E. Phillippe, Sr.	Thomas E. Phillippe, Sr.	1978	170
24 8/16	15 2/16	9 9/16	M	Cassiar Mts., B. C.	Elgin T. Gates	Elgin T. Gates	1953	185
24 8/16	14 11/16	9 13/16	M	Mt. McKinley, Alaska	Howard W. Pollock	Howard W. Pollock	1953	185
24 8/16	15	9 8/16	M	Bella Coola, B. C.	James A. Perry	H. J. Borden	1959	185
24 8/16	15 4/16	9 4/16	M	Big Delta, Alaska	Harold E. Hogan	Harold E. Hogan	1961	185
24 8/16	14 15/16	9 9/16	M	Tatla Lake, B. C.	Harold A. Cowman	Harold A. Cowman	1964	185
24 8/16	15 13/16	8 11/16	M	Kleena Kleene River, B. C.	Martin J. Durkan	Martin J. Durkan	1966	185
24 8/16	15 2/16	9 6/16	M	Kotzebue, Alaska	C. J. McElroy	C. J. McElroy	1968	185
24 8/16	15 2/16	9 7/16	M	Brooks Range, Alaska	Jerry N. Martin	Jerry N. Martin	1968	185
24 8/16	15 2/16	9 6/16	M	Tweedsmuir Park, B. C.	Tom & Clara Ritter	Tom & Clara Ritter	1969	185
24 8/16	15 2/16	9 7/16	M	Brooks Range, Alaska	Rick Reakoff	Rick Reakoff	1969	185
24 8/16	14 11/16	9 13/16	M	Lakelse River, Skeena, B.C.	Kolbjorn Eide	Kolbjorn Eide	1970	185
24 8/16	14 14/16	9 10/16	M	Miner Lake, B. C.	Dwight E. Farr, Jr.	Dwight E. Farr, Jr.	1971	185
24 8/16	15 6/16	9 2/16	M	Coast Range, B. C.	Laverne D. Hirzel & Jay Petersen	Laverne D. Hirzel	1971	185
24 7/16	14 12/16	9 12/16	M	Stikine River, B. C.	Fred P. Grob	Fred P. Grob	1973	185
24 7/16	15 6/16	9 3/16	M	Tonzona River, B. C.	Jill L. Nunley	Jill L. Nunley	1974	185
24 7/16	15 6/16	9 3/16	M	Colville River, Alaska	Richard A. McClellan	Richard A. McClellan	1974	185
24 7/16	14 13/16	9 1/16	M	Ogilvie Mts., Yukon	Vearl Fowler	Vearl Fowler	1976	185
24 7/16	15 2/16	9 6/16	M	Brooks Range, Alaska	Calvin Danzig	Calvin Danzig	1977	185
24 7/16	15 4/16	9 4/16	M	Fraser River, B.C.	Paul F. Bays, Sr.	Paul F. Bays, Sr.	1978	185
24 7/16	15 7/16	9 1/16	M	Kugururok River, Alaska	Bruce A. Moe	Bruce A. Moe	1978	185
24 7/16	15 6/16	8 15/16	M	Table River, B.C.	George W. Morris	George W. Morris	1978	185
24 7/16	15	9 7/16	M	Cold Fish Lake, B. C.	Wm. E. Goudey	Wm. E. Goudey	1956	206
24 7/16	15 8/16	8 15/16	M	Dease River, B. C.	John Caputo	John Caputo	1958	206
24 7/16	15 6/16	9 1/16	M	Brooks Range, Alaska	Bobbie J. Cavnar	Bobbie J. Cavnar	1966	206
24 7/16	15 6/16	9 2/16	M	McClaren Glacier, Alaska	Gordon S. Pleiss	Gordon S. Pleiss	1967	206
24 7/16	15 7/16	9	M	Brooks Range, Alaska	Don Elder	Don Elder	1968	206
24 7/16	15 6/16	9 3/16	M	Ocena Falls, B. C.	Richard D. Dimick	Richard D. Dimick	1969	206
24 7/16	15 2/16	9 5/16	M	Coleville River, Alaska	Alfonso I. Casso	Alfonso I. Casso	1970	206
24 7/16	15 6/16	9 1/16	M	Grande Cache, Alta.	Laurier Adams	Laurier Adams	1976	206

				Locality	Owner	Owner	Date	Score
$24\frac{6}{16}$	15	$9\frac{6}{16}$	M	Alaska Hwy. Mile 175, B. C.	Selmer Torrison	Selmer Torrison	1958	214
$24\frac{6}{16}$	$15\frac{7}{16}$	$9\frac{4}{16}$	M	Alaska Range, Alaska	Hank Kramer	Hank Kramer	1964	214
$24\frac{6}{16}$	$14\frac{10}{16}$	$9\frac{12}{16}$	M	Yanert River, Alaska	P. W. LaHaye	P. W. LaHaye	1965	214
$24\frac{6}{16}$	$15\frac{5}{16}$	$9\frac{1}{16}$	M	Alaska Range, Alaska	Alberto Pipia	Alberto Pipia	1966	214
$24\frac{6}{16}$	$14\frac{15}{16}$	$9\frac{7}{16}$	M	Brooks Range, Alaska	Paul H. Magee	Paul H. Magee	1967	214
$24\frac{6}{16}$	$15\frac{6}{16}$	9	M	Atlin, B. C.	Jack E. Carpenter	Jack E. Carpenter	1967	214
$24\frac{6}{16}$	$14\frac{12}{16}$	$9\frac{10}{16}$	M	Prince George, B. C.	Wayne H. Laursen	Wayne H. Laursen	1969	214
$24\frac{6}{16}$	15	$9\frac{6}{16}$	M	Coleville Mts., Alaska	E. H. Borchers, Jr.	E. H. Borchers, Jr.	1970	214
$24\frac{6}{16}$	$15\frac{5}{16}$	$8\frac{14}{16}$	M	Wrangell Mts., Alaska	Victor W. Bullard	Victor W. Bullard	1971	214
$24\frac{6}{16}$	$14\frac{14}{16}$	$9\frac{8}{16}$	M	Ogilvie Mts., Yukon	Philip R. Murphy	Philip R. Murphy	1972	214
$24\frac{6}{16}$	$15\frac{5}{16}$	$9\frac{2}{16}$	M	Cassiar Mts., B. C.	Monte Hofstrand	Monte Hofstrand	1975	214
$24\frac{6}{16}$	$14\frac{11}{16}$	$9\frac{11}{16}$	M	Kelly River, Alaska	James B. Goodman	J. B. Goodman & Errol Remsing	1976	214
$24\frac{6}{16}$	15	$9\frac{6}{16}$	M	Alaska Range, Alaska	Larry W. Casey	Steve Casey	1977	214
$24\frac{5}{16}$	$15\frac{5}{16}$	$8\frac{12}{16}$	M	Kitimat, B. C.	Ewald Kirschner	Ewald Kirschner	1958	227
$24\frac{5}{16}$	$15\frac{5}{16}$	$8\frac{15}{16}$	M	Bear Berry Creek, Alta.	Phil Temple	Phil Temple	1958	227
$24\frac{5}{16}$	$14\frac{6}{16}$	$9\frac{15}{16}$	M	Blackstone River, Alta.	Wilhelm Eichenauer	Wilhelm Eichenauer	1963	227
$24\frac{5}{16}$	$15\frac{5}{16}$	$9\frac{1}{16}$	M	Nabesna River, Alaska	C. W. Houle	C. W. Houle	1965	227
$24\frac{5}{16}$	$15\frac{7}{16}$	$8\frac{14}{16}$	M	Cassiar Mountains, B. C.	Henry E. High	Henry E. High	1965	227
$24\frac{5}{16}$	$15\frac{5}{16}$	$9\frac{3}{16}$	M	Teller, Alaska	Bill Glunt	Bill Glunt	1965	227
$24\frac{5}{16}$	$15\frac{4}{16}$	$9\frac{11}{16}$	M	Tetachuck Lake, B. C.	Torben Dahl	Torben Dahl	1966	227
$24\frac{5}{16}$	$14\frac{10}{16}$	$8\frac{5}{16}$	M	Brooks Range, Alaska	Robert L. Cohen	Robert L. Cohen	1967	227
$24\frac{5}{16}$	16	$9\frac{7}{16}$	M	Edson, Alta.	Otto Braaz	Otto Braaz	1969	227
$24\frac{5}{16}$	$14\frac{14}{16}$	$8\frac{14}{16}$	M	Toba Inlet, B. C.	Jack C. Glover	Jack C. Glover	1970	227
$24\frac{5}{16}$	$15\frac{7}{16}$	$8\frac{14}{16}$	M	Chatscuot Creek, B.C.	Roger J. Ahern	Roger J. Ahern	1978	227
$24\frac{5}{16}$	$15\frac{7}{16}$	$8\frac{12}{16}$	M	Graham River, B. C.	William J. Fogarty, Jr.	William J. Fogarty, Jr.	1978	227
$24\frac{4}{16}$	$15\frac{5}{16}$	$8\frac{10}{16}$	M	Dease Lake, B. C.	G. C. F. Dalziel	G. C. F. Dalziel	1956	239
$24\frac{4}{16}$	$15\frac{10}{16}$	$9\frac{7}{16}$	M	S. Hay River, Alta.	Bert Shearer	Bert Shearer	1957	239
$24\frac{4}{16}$	$14\frac{13}{16}$	$9\frac{4}{16}$	M	Selkirk Mt., B. C.	Eli Paulson	Eli Paulson	1957	239
$24\frac{4}{16}$	$14\frac{9}{16}$	9	M	Kotzebue, Alaska	Don D. Giles	Don D. Giles	1965	239
$24\frac{4}{16}$	$15\frac{1}{16}$	$9\frac{9}{16}$	M	Kuskokwim River, Alaska	Edward W. Williams	Edward W. Williams	1967	239
$24\frac{4}{16}$	$14\frac{14}{16}$	$8\frac{9}{16}$	M	Brooks Range, Alaska	Stanley Blazovich	Stanley Blazovich	1970	239
$24\frac{4}{16}$	$15\frac{10}{16}$	$8\frac{13}{16}$	M	Bella Coola, B. C.	Howard Creason	Howard Creason	1971	239
$24\frac{4}{16}$	$15\frac{7}{16}$	$9\frac{10}{16}$	M	Sheep Creek, Alta.	Rolly Balzer	Rolly Balzer	1972	239
$24\frac{4}{16}$	$14\frac{10}{16}$	$9\frac{1}{16}$	M	Nilkitkwa River, B. C.	Roger Britton	Roger Britton	1976	239
$24\frac{3}{16}$	$15\frac{7}{16}$	$9\frac{5}{16}$	M	Nabesna, Alaska	Ernest B. Schur	Ernest B. Schur	1958	248
$24\frac{3}{16}$	$14\frac{11}{16}$	$8\frac{11}{16}$	M	Moose Creek, B. C.	R. Angell	R. Angell	1964	248
$24\frac{3}{16}$	$15\frac{8}{16}$	$9\frac{9}{16}$	M	Gardiner, Mont.	Marguerite McDonald	Marguerite McDonald	1964	248
$24\frac{3}{16}$	$15\frac{7}{16}$	$9\frac{5}{16}$	M	Toba Inlet, B. C.	Kenneth L. Wagner, Jr.	Kenneth L. Wagner, Jr.	1968	248
$24\frac{3}{16}$	$14\frac{14}{16}$	$9\frac{2}{16}$	M	Likely, B. C.	Louis Tremblay	Louis Tremblay	1970	248
$24\frac{3}{16}$	$15\frac{1}{16}$	$9\frac{7}{16}$	M	Alaska Range, Alaska	Gilbert L. Shelton	Gilbert L. Shelton	1975	248
$24\frac{3}{16}$	$15\frac{7}{16}$	$9\frac{5}{16}$	M	Parsnip River, B. C.	Richard O. A. Gunther	Richard O. A. Gunther	1976	248
$24\frac{3}{16}$	$14\frac{5}{16}$	$9\frac{14}{16}$	M	Tetlin Indian Res., Alaska	Robert Bruce Rhyne	Robert Bruce Rhyne	1976	248

GRIZZLY BEAR–Continued
Ursus arctos horribilis

Score	Greatest Length of Skull Without Lower Jaw	Greatest Width of Skull	Sex	Locality Killed	By Whom Killed	Owner	Date Killed	Rank
24³/₁₆	14¹³/₁₆	9⁶/₁₆	M	Kuskokwim River, Alaska	Roger J. Ahern	Roger J. Ahern	1977	248
24²/₁₆	15³/₁₆	8¹⁵/₁₆	M	Chisana River, Alaska	Larry Fogler	Larry Fogler	1961	257
24²/₁₆	14¹⁵/₁₆	9³/₁₆	M	McDonnell Lake, B.C.	W.C. Gardiner	W.C. Gardiner	1966	257
24²/₁₆	15²/₁₆	9	M	Dawson City, Yukon	Donald R. Hull	Ray C. Dillman	1971	257
24²/₁₆	15⁹/₁₆	8⁹/₁₆	M	Bella Coola, B. C.	Hugh M. Klein	Hugh M. Klein	1972	257
24²/₁₆	15	9²/₁₆	M	Sikanni Chief River, B.C.	Dale E. Mirr	Dale E. Mirr	1973	257
24²/₁₆	15⁵/₁₆	8¹⁴/₁₆	M	Quintette Mt., B.C.	Dennis J. Brady	Dennis J. Brady	1977	257
24¹/₁₆	15⁹/₁₆	8⁷/₁₆	M	Lake Owikeno, B. C.	R. C. Bentzen	R. C. Bentzen	1960	263
24¹/₁₆	15³/₁₆	8¹⁴/₁₆	M	Flathead Co., Mont.	T. H. Soldowski	T. H. Soldowski	1963	263
24¹/₁₆	14¹²/₁₆	9⁵/₁₆	M	Brooks Range, Alaska	Ted Schlaepfer	Ted Schlaepfer	1964	263
24¹/₁₆	14¹⁴/₁₆	9³/₁₆	M	Nabesna River, Alaska	F. C. Hibben	F. C. Hibben	1967	263
24¹/₁₆	14¹⁵/₁₆	9²/₁₆	M	Quesnel, B. C.	Larry Chaves	Larry Chaves	1968	263
24¹/₁₆	14⁹/₁₆	9⁸/₁₆	M	Toklat River, Alaska	Ronald Lauretti	Ronald Lauretti	1971	263
24¹/₁₆	14¹⁵/₁₆	9²/₁₆	M	Gataga River, B.C.	James E. Carson	James E. Carson	1977	263
24¹/₁₆	15²/₁₆	8¹⁵/₁₆	M	Tatlatui Lake, B.C.	Paul S. Burke, Jr.	Paul S. Burke, Jr.	1978	263
24¹/₁₆	14¹⁴/₁₆	9³/₁₆	M	Sukunka River, B.C.	Albert R. Heikel, Jr.	Albert R. Heikel, Jr.	1979	263
24	15⁵/₁₆	8¹¹/₁₆	M	Bella Coola, B. C.	Wynn Beebe	Wynn Beebe	1960	272
24	15⁴/₁₆	8¹⁴/₁₆	M	Wood River, Alaska	Gordon Studer	Gordon Studer	1963	272
24	15³/₁₆	8¹⁴/₁₆	M	Cantwell, Alaska	Donald R. Johnson	Donald R. Johnson	1964	272
24	14¹¹/₁₆	9⁵/₁₆	M	Little Tok River, Alaska	Herbert F. Fassler	Herbert F. Fassler	1966	272
24	15	9	M	Fernie, B. C.	James Sloan	James Sloan	1967	272
24	14¹⁴/₁₆	9⁷/₁₆	M	Fairbanks, Alaska	Rudolf von Strasser	Rudolf von Strasser	1968	272
24	14⁹/₁₆	9⁷/₁₆	M	Alaska Range, Alaska	R. A. Schriewer	R. A. Schriewer	1969	272
24	15¹²/₁₆	8⁴/₁₆	M	Bella Coola, B. C.	Alton Myhrvold	Alton A. Myhrvold	1969	272
24	14¹⁴/₁₆	9²/₁₆	M	Canyon Lake, B. C.	Luther E. Lilly	Luther E. Lilly	1970	272
24	14⁹/₁₆	9⁷/₁₆	M	Ayiyak River, Alaska	Tom Toscano	Tom Toscano	1971	272
24	14¹²/₁₆	9⁴/₁₆	M	Kuskokwim Mts., Alaska	James V. Travis	James V. Travis	1974	272

*Final Score subject to revision by additional verifying measurements.

ALASKA BROWN BEARS

A U.S. Fish & Wildlife Service photograph taken in McNeil Creek, Kamishak Bay, Alaska, by Dick Chace.

Alaska Brown Bear

Ursus arctos middendorffi and certain related subspecies

Minimum Score 28

Score	Greatest Length of Skull Without Lower Jaw	Greatest Width of Skull	Sex	Locality Killed	By Whom Killed	Owner	Date Killed	Rank
30 12/16	17 15/16	12 13/16	M	Kodiak Island, Alaska	Roy Lindsley	Los Angeles Co. Mus.	1952	1
30 11/16	18 10/16	12 1/16	M	Kodiak Island, Alaska	Erling Hansen	Erling Hansen	1961	2
30 6/16	18 7/16	12 6/16	M	Kodiak Island, Alaska	Fred A. Henton	Los Angeles Co. Museum	1938	3
30 6/16	18 12/16	11 12/16	M	Bear River, Alaska	Cap Wagner	Univ. Calif. Museum	PR1908	4
30 6/16	18	12 6/16	M	Kodiak Island, Alaska	Wm. S. Brophy, Jr. & Wm. E. McClure	Wm. S. Brophy, III	1966	4
30 7/16	19 13/16	10 10/16	M	Port Heiden, Alaska	Herschel A. Lamb	Herschel A. Lamb	1961	6
30 6/16	18	12 5/16	M	Deadman Bay, Alaska	Grancel Fitz	Mrs. Grancel Fitz	1955	7
30 6/16	18 12/16	11 9/16	M	Kodiak Island, Alaska	Donald S. Hopkins	National Collection	1940	8
30 6/16	18 12/16	11 9/16	M	Kodiak Island, Alaska	Jack Roach	Jack Roach	1947	8
30 6/16	18	12 6/16	M	Kodiak Island, Alaska	T. H. McGregor	T. H. McGregor	1960	8
30 6/16	18 5/16	12 1/16	M	Kodiak Island, Alaska	W. J. Fisher	U. S. Natl. Museum	PR1904	11
30 6/16	18	12 5/16	M	Kodiak Island, Alaska	Oliver L. Durbin	Oliver L. Durbin	1952	11
30 6/16	18 12/16	11 7/16	M	Kodiak Island, Alaska	A. L. Hooker	A. L. Hooker	1958	11
30 6/16	18 7/16	11 11/16	M	Kodiak Island, Alaska	Dave Connor	Dave Connor	1957	14
30 6/16	18 1/16	12	M	Kodiak Island, Alaska	Seymour P. Smith	U. S. Natl. Museum	1927	15
30 6/16	18 3/16	11 14/16	M	Kodiak Island, Alaska	John M. Tait	John M. Tait	1957	15
30 6/16	18 2/16	11 15/16	M	Alinchak Bay, Alaska	Clarence R. Scott	Clarence R. Scott	1961	15
29 15/16	18 6/16	11 9/16	M	Kodiak Island, Alaska	Donald S. Hopkins	National Collection	1939	18
29 15/16	18 6/16	11 9/16	M	Kodiak Island, Alaska	Samuel Atkinson	Samuel & Florence Atkinson	1953	18
29 14/16	18 2/16	11 12/16	M	Unimak Island, Alaska	Fred W. Shield	Fred W. Shield	1950	20
29 14/16	18	11 14/16	M	Kodiak Island, Alaska	Unknown	Kim Clark	1958	20
29 14/16	17 15/16	11 15/16	M	Kodiak Island, Alaska	H. F. Primosch	H. F. Primosch	1959	20
29 13/16	17 9/16	12 6/16	M	Nelson Lagoon, Alaska	Unknown	Harry H. Webb	1946	23
29 13/16	18 5/16	11 8/16	M	Cold Bay, Alaska	Robert C. Reeve	Am. Mus. Nat. History	1948	23
29 13/16	18 6/16	11 7/16	M	Alaska Pen., Alaska	Leed W. Rettig	Denver Mus. Nat. History	1955	23
29 13/16	18 5/16	11 9/16	M	Alaska Pen., Alaska	Don Johnson	Don Johnson	1962	23
29 12/16	17 13/16	11 15/16	M	Kodiak Island, Alaska	Wm. D. Holmes	Wm. D. Holmes	1957	27
29 12/16	18 11/16	11 1/16	M	Alaska Pen., Alaska	Russell J. Uhl	Russell J. Uhl	1963	27
29 11/16	17 13/16	11 14/16	M	Kodiak Island, Alaska	Herman Gibson	Herman Gibson	1951	29
29 11/16	17 9/16	12 7/16	M	Kodiak Island, Alaska	James H. Nash	James H. Nash	1954	29

$29\frac{11}{16}$	$17\frac{12}{16}$	$11\frac{15}{16}$	M	Kodiak Island, Alaska	A. J. Taylor & Edgar A. Chappell	Allen J. Taylor	1976	29
$29\frac{10}{16}$	$17\frac{13}{16}$	$11\frac{13}{16}$	M	Kodiak Island, Alaska	Eddie W. Stinnett	Eddie W. Stinnett	1974	32
$29\frac{9}{16}$	$19\frac{1}{16}$	$10\frac{8}{16}$	M	Unimak Island, Alaska	A. C. Gilbert	A. C. Gilbert	1950	33
$29\frac{9}{16}$	$17\frac{7}{16}$	$12\frac{2}{16}$	M	Kodiak, Alaska	Peter W. Bading	Peter W. Bading	1964	33
$29\frac{8}{16}$	$17\frac{14}{16}$	$11\frac{10}{16}$	M	Kodiak Island, Alaska	Helen & Elmer M. Rusten	Elmer M. Rusten	1941	35
$29\frac{8}{16}$	$18\frac{14}{16}$	$10\frac{10}{16}$	M	Mother Goose Lake, Alaska	Tom Moore	Chicago Nat. Hist. Mus.	1947	35
$29\frac{8}{16}$	$17\frac{13}{16}$	$11\frac{11}{16}$	M	Kodiak Island, Alaska	F. W. Crail	F. W. Crail	1950	35
$29\frac{8}{16}$	$17\frac{10}{16}$	$11\frac{14}{16}$	M	Kodiak Island, Alaska	W. H. Cothrum	W. H. Cothrum	1953	35
$29\frac{8}{16}$	$18\frac{6}{16}$	$11\frac{2}{16}$	M	Cold Bay, Alaska	W. P. Waltz	W. P. Waltz	1953	35
$29\frac{8}{16}$	$17\frac{12}{16}$	$11\frac{12}{16}$	M	Kodiak Island, Alaska	Carlos Alden	Carlos Alden	1956	35
$29\frac{8}{16}$	$18\frac{4}{16}$	$11\frac{4}{16}$	M	Alaska Pen., Alaska	Charles Gates	Charles Gates	1960	35
$29\frac{8}{16}$	18	$11\frac{8}{16}$	M	Alaska Pen., Alaska	Sam Pancotto	Sam Pancotto	1963	35
$29\frac{8}{16}$	$18\frac{2}{16}$	$11\frac{6}{16}$	M	Port Heiden, Alaska	Robert J. Miller	Robert J. Miller	1971	35
$29\frac{7}{16}$	$17\frac{10}{16}$	$11\frac{13}{16}$	M	Kodiak Island, Alaska	Robert R. Snodgrass	Robert R. Snodgrass	1949	44
$29\frac{7}{16}$	$17\frac{8}{16}$	$11\frac{15}{16}$	M	Deadman Bay, Alaska	Ira M. Piper	Ira M. Piper	1954	44
$29\frac{7}{16}$	$17\frac{11}{16}$	$11\frac{12}{16}$	M	Kodiak Island, Alaska	Keith Chisholm	Keith Chisholm	1956	44
$29\frac{7}{16}$	$17\frac{13}{16}$	$11\frac{10}{16}$	M	Kodiak Island, Alaska	Richard Van Dyke	Richard Van Dyke	1957	44
$29\frac{7}{16}$	$17\frac{13}{16}$	$11\frac{10}{16}$	M	Kodiak Island, Alaska	H. I. H. Prince Abdorreza Pahlavi	H. I. H. Prince Abdorreza Pahlavi	1967	44
$29\frac{6}{16}$	$18\frac{1}{16}$	$11\frac{4}{16}$	M	Pavlof Bay, Alaska	Willie Pavlof	U. S. Natl. Museum	1897	49
$29\frac{6}{16}$	$17\frac{13}{16}$	$11\frac{9}{16}$	M	Belkofski Bay, Alaska	Laurenti Kuzakin	U. S. Natl. Museum	1897	49
$29\frac{6}{16}$	$17\frac{15}{16}$	$11\frac{7}{16}$	M	Pavlof Bay, Alaska	H. Cutting	U. S. Natl. Museum	1917	49
$29\frac{6}{16}$	18	$11\frac{6}{16}$	M	Cold Bay, Alaska	Ira A. Minnick	U. S. Natl. Museum	1923	49
$29\frac{6}{16}$	$18\frac{5}{16}$	$11\frac{4}{16}$	M	Alaska Pen., Alaska	E. I. Garrett	Am. Mus. Nat. History	1926	49
$29\frac{6}{16}$	$17\frac{9}{16}$	$11\frac{13}{16}$	M	Kodiak Island, Alaska	John S. Day	John S. Day	1953	49
$29\frac{6}{16}$	$17\frac{6}{16}$	12	M	Amook Island, Alaska	Albert C. Bledsoe	Albert C. Bledsoe	1959	49
$29\frac{6}{16}$	$18\frac{3}{16}$	$11\frac{3}{16}$	M	Kodiak Island, Alaska	Herb Klein	Herb Klein	1965	49
$29\frac{6}{16}$	$18\frac{6}{16}$	11	M	Stepovak Bay, Alaska	Roy Fencl	Roy Fencl	1966	49
$29\frac{5}{16}$	$18\frac{1}{16}$	$10\frac{14}{16}$	M	Cold Bay, Alaska	Edwin Mallinkrodt, Jr	U. S. Natl. Museum	1920	58
$29\frac{5}{16}$	$17\frac{12}{16}$	$11\frac{9}{16}$	M	Sand Lake, Alaska	Wm. A. Fisher	Wm. A. Fisher	1953	58
$29\frac{5}{16}$	$17\frac{13}{16}$	$11\frac{8}{16}$	M	Kodiak Island, Alaska	Donated By Hal Waugh	Am. Mus. Nat. Hist.	PR1957	58
$29\frac{4}{16}$	$17\frac{14}{16}$	$11\frac{6}{16}$	M	Kodiak Island, Alaska	A. C. Skinner, Jr.	A. C. Skinner, Jr.	1951	61
$29\frac{4}{16}$	$17\frac{9}{16}$	$11\frac{14}{16}$	M	Kodiak Island, Alaska	Harry R. Eavey & Herb Wright	Harry R. Eavey	1960	61
$29\frac{4}{16}$	$17\frac{15}{16}$	$11\frac{5}{16}$	M	Alaska Pen., Alaska	Johnnie White	Horns Of Hunter Tr. Post	1962	61
$29\frac{4}{16}$	$18\frac{1}{16}$	$11\frac{7}{16}$	M	Alaska Pen., Alaska	H. S. Kamil	H. S. Kamil	1963	61
$29\frac{4}{16}$	$18\frac{4}{16}$	11	M	Port Heiden, Alaska	Ashley C. Sanders	Ashley C. Sanders	1965	61
$29\frac{3}{16}$	$18\frac{10}{16}$	$10\frac{9}{16}$	M	Alaska Pen., Alaska	J. A. Atkinson	Am. Mus. Nat. Hist.	1948	66
$29\frac{3}{16}$	$17\frac{15}{16}$	$11\frac{4}{16}$	M	Port Moller Bay, Alaska	A. M. Harper	A. M. Harper	1949	66
$29\frac{3}{16}$	$17\frac{10}{16}$	$11\frac{9}{16}$	M	Kodiak Island, Alaska	Fred B. Hawk	Fred B. Hawk	1959	66
$29\frac{3}{16}$	$17\frac{13}{16}$	$11\frac{6}{16}$	M	Kodiak Island, Alaska	William H. Sleith	Lutz Junior Museum	1966	66
$29\frac{3}{16}$	$17\frac{15}{16}$	$11\frac{11}{16}$	M	Port Heiden, Alaska	Ralph E. Smith	Ralph E. Smith	1966	66

ALASKA BROWN BEAR—*Continued*

Ursus arctos middendorffi and certain related subspecies

Score	Greatest Length of Skull Without Lower Jaw	Greatest Width of Skull	Sex	Locality Killed	By Whom Killed	Owner	Date Killed	Rank
$29^6/_{16}$	$18^6/_{16}$	$10^{10}/_{16}$	M	Mother Goose Lake, Alaska	Robert Denis	Robert Denis	1967	66
$29^6/_{16}$	$17^{10}/_{16}$	$11^6/_{16}$	M	Kodiak Island, Alaska	Mrs. J. Watson Webb	Mrs. J. Watson Webb	1948	72
$29^6/_{16}$	$17^{14}/_{16}$	$11^6/_{16}$	M	Alaska Pen., Alaska	Mrs. John J. Louis, Jr.	Mrs. John J. Louis, Jr.	1955	72
$29^6/_{16}$	$17^{15}/_{16}$	$11^3/_{16}$	M	Kodiak Island, Alaska	Alan O. Hickok	Alan O. Hickok	1957	72
$29^6/_{16}$	$17^{11}/_{16}$	$11^7/_{16}$	M	Port Moller, Alaska	Milton Knapp	Milton Knapp	1960	72
$29^6/_{16}$	$17^{10}/_{16}$	$11^8/_{16}$	M	Kodiak Island, Alaska	Edward F. Pedersen, Jr.	Edward F. Pedersen, Jr.	1961	72
$29^6/_{16}$	$18^3/_{16}$	$10^{15}/_{16}$	M	Alaska Pen., Alaska	Kenneth Richmond	Kenneth Richmond	1962	72
$29^6/_{16}$	$17^{10}/_{16}$	$11^8/_{16}$	M	Alaska Pen., Alaska	Wesley Pollock	Wesley Pollock	1964	72
$29^6/_{16}$	$18^2/_{16}$	11	M	Alaska Pen., Alaska	Richard Hodous	Richard Hodous	1966	72
$29^6/_{16}$	$18^3/_{16}$	$10^{15}/_{16}$	M	Ugashik, Alaska	Joseph K. Link	Joseph K. Link	1966	72
$29^6/_{16}$	$17^7/_{16}$	$11^{11}/_{16}$	M	Kodiak Island, Alaska	John F. Ries	John F. Ries	1967	72
$29^6/_{16}$	$17^8/_{16}$	$11^9/_{16}$	M	Kodiak Island, Alaska	John C. Ayres	Signa J. Byers	1934	82
$29^6/_{16}$	$17^{10}/_{16}$	$11^7/_{16}$	M	Kodiak Island, Alaska	H. H. Kissinger	H. H. Kissinger	1961	82
$29^6/_{16}$	$17^{11}/_{16}$	$11^9/_{16}$	M	Ugashik Lake, Alaska	George Purdie	George Purdie	1963	82
$29^6/_{16}$	$17^{11}/_{16}$	$11^8/_{16}$	M	Port Heiden, Alaska	Marshall Carr	Marshall Carr	1963	82
$29^6/_{16}$	$18^2/_{16}$	$10^{15}/_{16}$	M	Port Moller, Alaska	Russell H. Underdahl	Russell H. Underdahl	1967	82
29	$17^{10}/_{16}$	$11^8/_{16}$	M	Kodiak Island, Alaska	John Fox	John Fox	1959	87
29	$17^{14}/_{16}$	$11^2/_{16}$	M	Kodiak Island, Alaska	Raymond C. Boystel	Raymond C. Boystel	1963	87
29	$18^2/_{16}$	$10^4/_{16}$	M	Cold Bay, Alaska	J. S. Parker	J. S. Parker	1964	87
29	$17^{12}/_{16}$	$11^8/_{16}$	M	Cold Bay, Alaska	Fritz A. Nachant	Fritz A. Nachant	1965	87
29	$18^6/_{16}$	$10^{10}/_{16}$	M	Yakutat, Alaska	Jack DeWald	Jack DeWald	1973	87
29	$18^3/_{16}$	$10^{13}/_{16}$	M	Alaska Pen., Alaska	Johnnie R. Lowe	Johnnie R. Lowe	1979	87
$28^5/_{16}$	$17^{15}/_{16}$	$11^1/_{16}$	M	Kodiak Island, Alaska	Creig M. Sharp	Creig M. Sharp	1977	93
$28^5/_{16}$	$17^{11}/_{16}$	$11^8/_{16}$	M	Port Moller Bay, Alaska	C. A. Stenger	C. A. Stenger	1951	94
$28^5/_{16}$	$17^{13}/_{16}$	$11^2/_{16}$	M	Alaska Pen., Alaska	G. W. Folta	G. W. Folta	1954	94
$28^5/_{16}$	$17^6/_{16}$	$11^9/_{16}$	M	Kodiak Island, Alaska	Robert T. Leever	Robert T. Leever	1959	94
$28^5/_{16}$	$17^{12}/_{16}$	$11^3/_{16}$	M	Kodiak Island, Alaska	H. T. Hilderbrandt	H. T. Hilderbrandt	1961	94
$28^5/_{16}$	$17^{15}/_{16}$	11	M	Sand Lake, Alaska	J. J. Stallone	J. J. Stallone	1962	94
$28^5/_{16}$	$17^{14}/_{16}$	$11^1/_{16}$	M	Port Moller, Alaska	Andrew S. Allen	Andrew S. Allen	1963	94
$28^5/_{16}$	$17^8/_{16}$	$11^7/_{16}$	M	Kodiak Island, Alaska	Stephen A. Mihal	Stephen A. Mihal	1969	94
$28^5/_{16}$	$17^{11}/_{16}$	$11^4/_{16}$	M	Alaska Pen., Alaska	James A. Johnson	James A. Johnson	1970	94
$28^5/_{16}$	$17^4/_{16}$	$11^{11}/_{16}$	M	Kodiak Island, Alaska	Robert E. Pippen	Robert E. Pippen	1975	94

28⁵/₁₆	18¹/₁₆	10¹⁴/₁₆	M	Mother Goose Lake, Alaska	John H. Buckman	John H. Buckman	1976	94
28⁴/₁₆	17¹³/₁₆	11¹/₁₆	M	Yakataga Beach, Alaska	Melvin Grindel	Stanley P. Young	1933	104
28⁴/₁₆	16¹²/₁₆	12²/₁₆	M	Kodiak Island, Alaska	A. J. Casper	A. J. Casper	1936	104
28⁴/₁₆	17⁷/₁₆	11⁷/₁₆	M	Kodiak Island, Alaska	Jack Honhart	Jack Honhart	1952	104
28⁴/₁₆	18⁵/₁₆	10⁹/₁₆	M	Alaska Pen., Alaska	Herb Elliott	Herb Elliott	1960	104
28⁴/₁₆	17⁶/₁₆	11⁹/₁₆	M	Kodiak Island, Alaska	Maurice S. Ireland	Maurice S. Ireland	1961	104
28⁴/₁₆	18⁵/₁₆	10⁴/₁₆	M	Alaska Pen., Alaska	Ethel Prine	Ethel Prine	1964	104
28⁴/₁₆	18	10¹⁴/₁₆	M	Alaska Pen., Alaska	Richard Kilbane	Richard Kilbane	1965	104
28⁴/₁₆	17⁵/₁₆	11⁹/₁₆	M	Kodiak Island, Alaska	William B. Valen	William B. Valen	1965	104
28⁴/₁₆	17¹⁴/₁₆	11	M	Skwentna River, Alaska	Gerald N. Felando	Gerald N. Felando	1971	104
28⁴/₁₆	17¹²/₁₆	11²/₁₆	M	Alaska Pen., Alaska	Richard N. Von	Richard N. Von	1975	104
28⁴/₁₆	17⁶/₁₆	11⁸/₁₆	M	Kodiak Island, Alaska	Robert A. Wainscott	Robert A. Wainscott	1978	104
28³/₁₆	18²/₁₆	10¹¹/₁₆	M	Hoodco Lake, Alaska	A. C. Gilbert	A. C. Gilbert	1950	115
28³/₁₆	17⁴/₁₆	11⁹/₁₆	M	Port Heiden, Alaska	John Du Puy	John Du Puy	1951	115
28³/₁₆	17¹²/₁₆	11⁴/₁₆	M	Frazer Lake, Alaska	Rupert Chisholm	Rupert Chisholm	1956	115
28³/₁₆	17¹⁵/₁₆	10⁴/₁₆	M	Alaska Pen., Alaska	Elgin T. Gates	Elgin T. Gates	1960	115
28³/₁₆	17¹³/₁₆	11	M	Kodiak Island, Alaska	Charles Daniels	Charles Daniels	1962	115
28³/₁₆	17⁶/₁₆	11⁷/₁₆	M	Kodiak, Alaska	Hal Waugh	Hal Waugh	1964	115
28³/₁₆	17¹²/₁₆	11¹/₁₆	M	Alaska Pen., Alaska	Ernest Rush, Jr.	Ernest Rush, Jr.	1966	115
28²/₁₆	18²/₁₆	10⁹/₁₆	M	Sand Lake, Alaska	A. C. Gilbert	A. C. Gilbert	1939	122
28²/₁₆	18	10¹²/₁₆	M	Sand Lake, Alaska	A. C. Gilbert	A. C. Gilbert	1939	122
28²/₁₆	18⁴/₁₆	10⁹/₁₆	M	Pavlof Bay, Alaska	R. R. Stewart	R. R. Stewart	1949	122
28²/₁₆	18²/₁₆	10⁹/₁₆	M	Alaska Pen., Alaska	Harry H. Webb	Harry H. Webb	1952	122
28²/₁₆	17⁵/₁₆	11⁷/₁₆	M	Kodiak Island, Alaska	Robert D. Boone	Robert D. Boone	1960	122
28²/₁₆	17¹/₁₆	11¹¹/₁₆	M	Alaska Pen., Alaska	Bert Klineburger	Bert Klineburger	1961	122
28²/₁₆	17¹²/₁₆	11	M	Alaska Pen., Alaska	Hans Otto Meissner	Hans Otto Meissner	1961	122
28²/₁₆	17¹¹/₁₆	11¹/₁₆	M	Karluk Lake, Alaska	Alberto Fernandez Ruiloha	Alberto Fernandez Ruiloha	1962	122
28²/₁₆	16¹⁴/₁₆	11⁴/₁₆	M	Kodiak Island, Alaska	Vernon C. Jensen	Vernon C. Jensen	1963	122
28²/₁₆	17²/₁₆	11⁹/₁₆	M	Alaska Pen., Alaska	Bert Klineburger	Bert Klineburger	1964	122
28²/₁₆	17⁹/₁₆	11³/₁₆	M	Kodiak Island, Alaska	Joe M. Floyd, Jr.	Joe M. Floyd, Jr.	1966	122
28²/₁₆	17¹⁵/₁₆	10¹³/₁₆	M	Kodiak Island, Alaska	Clyde Ormond	Clyde Ormond	1968	122
28²/₁₆	18²/₁₆	10¹⁰/₁₆	M	Cold Bay, Alaska	Ted J. Forsi	Ted J. Forsi	1975	122
28¹/₁₆	17⁴/₁₆	11⁸/₁₆	M	Kodiak Island, Alaska	Roy Herman Tyler	Roy Herman Tyler	1977	122
28¹/₁₆	18⁴/₁₆	10⁷/₁₆	M	Cinder River, Alaska	Geo. W. Vaughn	Geo. W. Vaughn	1951	136
28¹/₁₆	17⁶/₁₆	11⁵/₁₆	M	Kodiak Island, Alaska	John Treillet	John Treillet	1953	136
28¹/₁₆	17⁶/₁₆	11⁵/₁₆	M	Kodiak Island, Alaska	Harold J. Ahrendt	Harold J. Ahrendt	1957	136
28¹/₁₆	18⁷/₁₆	10⁴/₁₆	M	Alaska Pen., Alaska	Edward R. Crooks	Edward R. Crooks	1958	136
28¹/₁₆	17³/₁₆	11⁸/₁₆	M	Kodiak Island, Alaska	Anthony A. Caldrone	Anthony A. Caldrone	1962	136
28¹/₁₆	18²/₁₆	10⁸/₁₆	M	Alaska Pen., Alaska	Basil C. Bradbury	Basil C. Bradbury	1963	136
28¹/₁₆	17¹⁵/₁₆	10¹²/₁₆	M	Afognak Island, Alaska	Clyde Gett	Clyde Gett	1969	136
28¹/₁₆	17⁷/₁₆	11⁴/₁₆	M	Afognak Island, Alaska	William A. Bardot	William A. Bardot	1972	136
28⁰/₁₆	18⁶/₁₆	10⁶/₁₆	M	Pavlof Bay, Alaska	R. H. Rockwell	U. S. Natl. Museum	1921	144
28⁰/₁₆	18²/₁₆	10⁸/₁₆	M	Alaska Pen., Alaska	Harry H. Webb	Harry H. Webb	1952	144

ALASKA BROWN BEAR—*Continued*

Ursus arctos middendorffi and certain related subspecies

Score	Greatest Length of Skull Without Lower Jaw	Greatest Width of Skull	Sex	Locality Killed	By Whom Killed	Owner	Date Killed	Rank
$28\frac{9}{16}$	$17\frac{11}{16}$	$10\frac{15}{16}$	M	Alaska Pen., Alaska	Arthur C. Popham, Jr.	Arthur C. Popham, Jr.	1953	144
$28\frac{9}{16}$	$17\frac{3}{16}$	$11\frac{7}{16}$	M	Kodiak Island, Alaska	Kenneth D. Landes	Kenneth D. Landes	1954	144
$28\frac{9}{16}$	$17\frac{9}{16}$	$11\frac{1}{16}$	M	Kodiak Island, Alaska	Pat Soderburg	Pat Soderburg	1959	144
$28\frac{9}{16}$	$17\frac{4}{16}$	$11\frac{5}{16}$	M	Alaska Pen., Alaska	Selmer Torrison	Selmer Torrison	1959	144
$28\frac{9}{16}$	$18\frac{1}{16}$	$10\frac{9}{16}$	M	Alaska Pen., Alaska	Win Condict	Win Condict	1960	144
$28\frac{9}{16}$	$17\frac{4}{16}$	$11\frac{5}{16}$	M	Cordova, Alaska	Wallace Fields	Wallace Fields	1962	144
$28\frac{9}{16}$	$17\frac{12}{16}$	$10\frac{4}{16}$	M	Kodiak Island, Alaska	Alfonso Pasquel	Alfonso Pasquel	1962	144
$28\frac{9}{16}$	$17\frac{8}{16}$	$11\frac{2}{16}$	M	Alaska Pen., Alaska	Frederick O. Kielmam	Frederick O. Kielmam	1963	144
$28\frac{9}{16}$	$17\frac{9}{16}$	$11\frac{1}{16}$	M	Alaska Pen., Alaska	Ed Shapiro	Ed Shapiro	1964	144
$28\frac{9}{16}$	$17\frac{3}{16}$	$11\frac{7}{16}$	M	Kodiak, Alaska	Michael Friedland	Michael Friedland	1964	144
$28\frac{9}{16}$	$17\frac{5}{16}$	$11\frac{5}{16}$	M	Kodiak Island, Alaska	John E. Crook	John E. Crook	1965	144
$28\frac{9}{16}$	$17\frac{8}{16}$	$11\frac{2}{16}$	M	Pavlof Bay, Alaska	William (Bill) Kessner	William (Bill) Kessner	1965	144
$28\frac{9}{16}$	$17\frac{8}{16}$	$11\frac{5}{16}$	M	Alaska Pen., Alaska	C. J. McElroy	C. J. McElroy	1965	144
$28\frac{9}{16}$	$17\frac{10}{16}$	11	M	Kodiak Island, Alaska	Alex W. McCoy, III	Alex W. McCoy, III	1965	144
$28\frac{9}{16}$	$17\frac{12}{16}$	$10\frac{4}{16}$	M	Port Gravina, Alaska	Norton T. Montague	Norton T. Montague	1967	144
$28\frac{9}{16}$	$17\frac{1}{16}$	$11\frac{9}{16}$	M	Kodiak Island, Alaska	Louis R. Kaminsky	Louis R. Kaminsky	1972	144
$28\frac{8}{16}$	$17\frac{8}{16}$	$11\frac{1}{16}$	M	Alaska Pen., Alaska	Charles E. King	Camp Fire Club	1922	162
$28\frac{8}{16}$	$17\frac{11}{16}$	$10\frac{4}{16}$	M	Kodiak Island, Alaska	Peggy Maxine Noles	Peggy Maxine Noles	1962	162
$28\frac{8}{16}$	$17\frac{2}{16}$	$11\frac{2}{16}$	M	Kodiak Island, Alaska	Charles Askins	Charles Askins	1963	162
$28\frac{8}{16}$	$17\frac{2}{16}$	$11\frac{2}{16}$	M	Becharof Lake, Alaska	Robert J. Brocker	Robert J. Brocker	1964	162
$28\frac{8}{16}$	$17\frac{9}{16}$	$11\frac{3}{16}$	M	Cordova, Alaska	Marvin Kocurek	Marvin Kocurek	1964	162
$28\frac{8}{16}$	$17\frac{12}{16}$	$10\frac{13}{16}$	M	Alaska Pen., Alaska	Robert L. Helms	Robert L. Helms	1966	162
$28\frac{8}{16}$	$17\frac{9}{16}$	$11\frac{5}{16}$	M	Alaska Pen., Alaska	George H. Landreth	George H. Landreth	1966	162
$28\frac{8}{16}$	18	$10\frac{9}{16}$	M	Chichagof Island, Alaska	Stewart N. Shaft	Stewart N. Shaft	1973	162
$28\frac{8}{16}$	$17\frac{9}{16}$	11	M	Alaska Pen., Alaska	James B. Lindahl	James B. Lindahl	1975	162
$28\frac{8}{16}$	$17\frac{8}{16}$	11	M	Kodiak Island, Alaska	Mrs. Donald S. Hopkins	National Collection	1939	171
$28\frac{8}{16}$	18	$10\frac{8}{16}$	M	Herendeen Bay, Alaska	Arthur Johnson	Univ. Of Alaska	1950	171
$28\frac{8}{16}$	$17\frac{2}{16}$	$11\frac{8}{16}$	M	Caribou Lake, Alaska	W. A. Heldt	W. A. Heldt	1956	171
$28\frac{8}{16}$	$16\frac{9}{16}$	$11\frac{14}{16}$	M	Kodiak Island, Alaska	Gloria Therese Zerega	Gloria Therese Zerega	1956	171
$28\frac{8}{16}$	$17\frac{4}{16}$	$11\frac{4}{16}$	M	Kodiak Island, Alaska	W. M. Hollinger	W. M. Hollinger	1958	171
$28\frac{8}{16}$	$17\frac{12}{16}$	$10\frac{12}{16}$	M	Port Heiden, Alaska	Chic Kawahara	Chic Kawahara	1963	171
$28\frac{8}{16}$	17	$11\frac{8}{16}$	M	Kodiak Island, Alaska	Ross Beach	Ross Beach	1963	171

			M	Locality	By Whom Killed	Owner	Date	Rank
$28\frac{8}{16}$	$17\frac{14}{16}$	$10\frac{10}{16}$	M	Alaska Pen., Alaska	W. H. Picher	W. H. Picher	1964	171
$28\frac{8}{16}$	$17\frac{4}{16}$	$11\frac{1}{16}$	M	Unimak Island, Alaska	Richard A. Guthrie	Richard A. Guthrie	1974	171
$28\frac{8}{16}$	$17\frac{6}{16}$	$11\frac{2}{16}$	M	Deadman Bay, Alaska	Frank Alabiso	Frank Alabiso	1976	171
$28\frac{8}{16}$	$17\frac{10}{16}$	$10\frac{14}{16}$	M	Pavlof Bay, Alaska	Melvin Gillis	Melvin Gillis	1976	171
$28\frac{8}{16}$	$17\frac{8}{16}$	$11\frac{1}{16}$	M	Alaska Pen., Alaska	William Broadwell	Lloyd Ronning	1958	182
$28\frac{8}{16}$	$16\frac{12}{16}$	$11\frac{11}{16}$	M	Kodiak Island, Alaska	Bill Polland	Bill Polland	1959	182
$28\frac{8}{16}$	$17\frac{15}{16}$	$10\frac{8}{16}$	M	Cold Bay, Alaska	Virgil Brill	Virgil Brill	1960	182
$28\frac{8}{16}$	$17\frac{10}{16}$	$10\frac{3}{16}$	M	Alaska Pen., Alaska	Milton L. Knapp	Milton L. Knapp	1961	182
$28\frac{8}{16}$	$17\frac{5}{16}$	$11\frac{2}{16}$	M	Kodiak Island, Alaska	Frank Rogers	Frank Rogers	1961	182
$28\frac{8}{16}$	$17\frac{2}{16}$	$11\frac{5}{16}$	M	Kodiak Island, Alaska	Edward F. Pedersen	Edward F. Pedersen	1961	182
$28\frac{8}{16}$	$17\frac{9}{16}$	$10\frac{14}{16}$	M	Alaska Pen., Alaska	Kenneth Golden	Kenneth Golden	1962	182
$28\frac{8}{16}$	$17\frac{7}{16}$	11	M	Afognak Island, Alaska	Robert Munger	Robert Munger	1962	182
$28\frac{8}{16}$	$17\frac{13}{16}$	$10\frac{9}{16}$	M	Alaska Pen., Alaska	Sam Pancotto	Sam Pancotto	1962	182
$28\frac{8}{16}$	$17\frac{13}{16}$	$10\frac{9}{16}$	M	Alaska Pen., Alaska	Dennis Burke	Dennis Burke	1964	182
$28\frac{8}{16}$	$17\frac{10}{16}$	$10\frac{3}{16}$	M	Ugashik Lake, Alaska	James E. Egger	James E. Egger	1966	182
$28\frac{8}{16}$	$17\frac{11}{16}$	$10\frac{12}{16}$	M	Kodiak Island, Alaska	William A. Ross, Jr.	William A. Ross, Jr.	1968	182
$28\frac{8}{16}$	$17\frac{2}{16}$	$11\frac{5}{16}$	M	Kodiak Island, Alaska	M. H. (Buddy) Brock	M. H. (Buddy) Brock	1971	182
$28\frac{8}{16}$	$17\frac{11}{16}$	$10\frac{12}{16}$	M	Alaska Pen., Alaska	James E. Otto	James E. Otto	1973	182
$28\frac{8}{16}$	$17\frac{4}{16}$	$11\frac{11}{16}$	M	Kodiak Island, Alaska	Virgil J. Sheppard	Virgil J. Sheppard	1978	182
$28\frac{8}{16}$	$17\frac{15}{16}$	$11\frac{3}{16}$	M	Moroski Bay, Alaska	Ivan Katchinof	U. S. Natl. Museum	1897	197
$28\frac{8}{16}$	$17\frac{14}{16}$	$10\frac{15}{16}$	M	Sand Lake, Alaska	Mrs. J. Watson Webb	Mrs. J. Watson Webb	1939	197
$28\frac{8}{16}$	$17\frac{9}{16}$	$10\frac{9}{16}$	M	Kodiak Island, Alaska	Martin J. Coyne	Martin J. Coyne	1960	197
$28\frac{8}{16}$	$17\frac{11}{16}$	$10\frac{13}{16}$	M	Alaska Pen., Alaska	Alberto Pipia	Alberto Pipia	1965	197
$28\frac{8}{16}$	$17\frac{8}{16}$	$10\frac{11}{16}$	M	Alaska Pen., Alaska	John F. Ault	John F. Ault	1967	197
$28\frac{8}{16}$	$17\frac{4}{16}$	$10\frac{14}{16}$	M	Prince William Sound, Alaska	Ron Kacsmaryk	Ron Kacsmaryk	1970	197
$28\frac{8}{16}$	$16\frac{12}{16}$	$11\frac{2}{16}$	M	Kodiak Island, Alaska	Darrel Williams	Earl Hahn	1976	197
$28\frac{8}{16}$	$17\frac{14}{16}$	$11\frac{10}{16}$	M	Port Heiden, Alaska	Jack Holland, Jr.	Jack Holland, Jr.	1976	197
$28\frac{8}{16}$	$17\frac{14}{16}$	$10\frac{8}{16}$	M	Pavlof Bay, Alaska	Peter Ruppi	U. S. Natl. Museum	1897	205
$28\frac{8}{16}$	$17\frac{4}{16}$	$10\frac{7}{16}$	M	Cold Bay, Alaska	L. S. Kuter	L. S. Kuter	1952	205
$28\frac{8}{16}$	$16\frac{14}{16}$	$11\frac{1}{16}$	M	Kodiak Island, Alaska	C. D. Fuller & F. C. Miller	C. D. Fuller & F. C. Miller	1959	205
$28\frac{8}{16}$	$16\frac{14}{16}$	$11\frac{7}{16}$	M	Kodiak Island, Alaska	J. D. Roebuck	J. D. Roebuck	1960	205
$28\frac{8}{16}$	$17\frac{9}{16}$	$11\frac{7}{16}$	M	Alaska Pen., Alaska	J. B. Kerley	J. B. Kerley	1964	205
$28\frac{8}{16}$	$17\frac{11}{16}$	$10\frac{12}{16}$	M	Port Heiden, Alaska	John S. Cochran, Jr.	John S. Cochran, Jr.	1964	205
$28\frac{8}{16}$	$17\frac{8}{16}$	$10\frac{8}{16}$	M	Mother Goose Lake, Alaska	H. T. Sliger	H. T. Sliger	1964	205
$28\frac{8}{16}$	18	$10\frac{13}{16}$	M	Kodiak Island, Alaska	Jerry Coon	Jerry Coon	1965	205
$28\frac{8}{16}$	17	$11\frac{2}{16}$	M	Port Heiden, Alaska	Leonard W. Bruns	Leonard W. Bruns	1967	205
$28\frac{8}{16}$	$16\frac{15}{16}$	$10\frac{6}{16}$	M	Kodiak Island, Alaska	Chris Klineburger	Chris Klineburger	1967	205
$28\frac{8}{16}$	$17\frac{6}{16}$	$11\frac{5}{16}$	M	Kodiak Island, Alaska	King Mahendra Of Nepal	King Mahendra Of Nepal	1967	205
$28\frac{8}{16}$	18	$11\frac{6}{16}$	M	Kodiak Island, Alaska	Theodore J. Schorsch, Sr.	Theodore J. Schorsch, Sr.	1968	205
$28\frac{8}{16}$	$17\frac{12}{16}$	$10\frac{15}{16}$	M	Alaska Pen., Alaska	Keith W. Bates	Keith W. Bates	1976	205
$28\frac{4}{16}$	17	$10\frac{8}{16}$	M	Port Moller Bay, Alaska	Harry H. Webb	Harry H. Webb	1953	218
$28\frac{4}{16}$	$17\frac{14}{16}$	$11\frac{4}{16}$	M	Kodiak Island, Alaska	T. E. Shillingburg	T. E. Shillingburg	1954	218
$28\frac{4}{16}$	$17\frac{4}{16}$	11	M	Afognak Island, Alaska	Edward M. Simko	Edward M. Simko	1957	218

Alaska Brown Bear—*Continued*

Ursus arctos middendorffi and certain related subspecies

Score	Greatest Length of Skull Without Lower Jaw	Greatest Width of Skull	Sex	Locality Killed	By Whom Killed	Owner	Date Killed	Rank
$28^6/_{16}$	$17^8/_{16}$	$10^5/_{16}$	M	Kodiak Island, Alaska	Willie Dene Payton	Willie Dene Payton	1959	218
$28^6/_{16}$	$17^9/_{16}$	$10^{11}/_{16}$	M	Alaska Pen., Alaska	Jeffrey G. Burmeister	Jeffrey G. Burmeister	1960	218
$28^6/_{16}$	$18^4/_{16}$	10	M	Alaska Pen., Alaska	Jean Branson	Jean Branson	1962	218
$28^6/_{16}$	17	$11^1/_{16}$	M	Uganik Bay, Alaska	Jerry Coker & John Meagher	Jerry Coker	1963	218
$28^6/_{16}$	$16^{13}/_{16}$	$11^8/_{16}$	M	Kodiak Island, Alaska	Keith Honhart	Keith Honhart	1965	218
$28^6/_{16}$	$17^3/_{16}$	$11^1/_{16}$	M	Kodiak Island, Alaska	Roy M. Champayne	Roy M. Champayne	1965	218
$28^6/_{16}$	$16^{15}/_{16}$	$11^5/_{16}$	M	Kodiak Island, Alaska	James E. Nelson	James E. Nelson	1979	218
$28^6/_{16}$	$17^4/_{16}$	$10^{15}/_{16}$	M	Aniakchak Bay, Alaska	Francis J. Fabick	Francis J. Fabick	1949	228
$28^6/_{16}$	$17^1/_{16}$	$11^3/_{16}$	M	Kodiak Island, Alaska	Raymond A. Du Four	Raymond A. Du Four	1959	228
$28^6/_{16}$	$17^{14}/_{16}$	$10^6/_{16}$	M	Alaska Pen., Alaska	Kenneth Holland	Kenneth Holland	1959	228
$28^6/_{16}$	$17^2/_{16}$	$11^1/_{16}$	M	Kodiak Island, Alaska	Wm. Offenheim	Wm. Offenheim	1960	228
$28^6/_{16}$	18	$10^6/_{16}$	M	Port Moller, Alaska	John D. Phillips	John D. Phillips	1961	228
$28^6/_{16}$	$17^7/_{16}$	$10^{12}/_{16}$	M	Alaska Pen., Alaska	Elmer Graham	Elmer Graham	1961	228
$28^6/_{16}$	$16^{15}/_{16}$	$11^8/_{16}$	M	Kodiak Island, Alaska	Frank Hollendonner	Frank Hollendonner	1961	228
$28^6/_{16}$	$17^4/_{16}$	$10^{15}/_{16}$	M	Port Heiden, Alaska	Michael Ferrell	Michael Ferrell	1964	228
$28^6/_{16}$	$17^6/_{16}$	$10^{13}/_{16}$	M	Talkeetna Mts., Alaska	Robert W. Holladay	Robert W. Holladay	1966	228
$28^6/_{16}$	$18^4/_{16}$	$9^5/_{16}$	U	Port Moller, Alaska	Ray Eyler	Ray Eyler	1966	228
$28^6/_{16}$	$16^{15}/_{16}$	$11^4/_{16}$	M	Kodiak Island, Alaska	T. Kimball Hill	T. Kimball Hill	1967	228
$28^6/_{16}$	$17^1/_{16}$	$11^1/_{16}$	U	Kodiak Island, Alaska	Picked Up	Jim Alexander	—	239
$28^6/_{16}$	$16^{11}/_{16}$	$11^7/_{16}$	M	Kodiak Island, Alaska	J. Watson Webb	J. Watson Webb	1948	239
$28^6/_{16}$	$17^{12}/_{16}$	$10^6/_{16}$	M	Alaska Pen., Alaska	J. D. Jones	J. D. Jones	1954	239
$28^6/_{16}$	$18^1/_{16}$	$10^6/_{16}$	M	Cold Bay, Alaska	Lewis E. Yearout	Lewis E. Yearout	1956	239
$28^6/_{16}$	17	$11^2/_{16}$	M	Kodiak Island, Alaska	Merril R. Reller	Merril R. Reller	1958	239
$28^6/_{16}$	$17^8/_{16}$	$10^{10}/_{16}$	M	Cinder River, Alaska	Russell Cutter	Russell Cutter	1960	239
$28^6/_{16}$	$17^{10}/_{16}$	$10^6/_{16}$	M	Port Heiden, Alaska	Herman Kuchanek	Herman Kuchanek	1961	239
$28^6/_{16}$	$17^{12}/_{16}$	$10^6/_{16}$	M	Alaska Pen., Alaska	Mrs. Sam Pancotto	Mrs. Sam Pancotto	1962	239
$28^6/_{16}$	$16^6/_{16}$	$11^8/_{16}$	M	Kodiak Island, Alaska	Gordon G. Maclean	Gordon G. Maclean	1964	239
$28^6/_{16}$	$17^8/_{16}$	$10^{10}/_{16}$	M	Alaska Pen., Alaska	Charles L. Ball, Jr.	Charles L. Ball, Jr.	1964	239
$28^6/_{16}$	$17^{12}/_{16}$	$10^6/_{16}$	M	Kodiak Island, Alaska	Robert Hansen	Robert Hansen	1966	239
$28^6/_{16}$	$17^{10}/_{16}$	$10^8/_{16}$	M	Cold Bay, Alaska	John D. Jones	John D. Jones	1966	239
$28^6/_{16}$	$17^8/_{16}$	$10^9/_{16}$	M	Unimak Island, Alaska	Don Burk	Don Burk	1966	239
$28^6/_{16}$	$16^4/_{16}$	$11^{10}/_{16}$	M	Eagle Harbor, Alaska	James T. Harrell	James T. Harrell	1966	239

28³/16	17¹⁰/16	10⁸/16	M	Alaska Pen., Alaska	Francis S. Levien	Francis S. Levien	1968	239
28³/16	17⁵/16	10¹³/16	M	Afognak Island, Alaska	Laszlo Lemhenyi-Hanko	Laszlo Lemhenyi-Hanko	1970	239
28³/16	17⁵/16	10¹³/16	M	Kodiak Island, Alaska	Dwight Hildebrandt	Dwight Hildebrandt	1971	239
28³/16	17¹/16	10¹⁵/16	M	Great Salmon Lake, Alaska	Siegfried Kube	Siegfried Kube	1974	239
28³/16	16⁹/16	11⁹/16	M	Kodiak Island, Alaska	Bart D'Averso	Bart D'Averso	1974	239
28³/16	17²/16	11	U	Afognak Island, Alaska	Picked Up	David L Lazer	PR1976	239
28³/16	17⁴/16	10¹⁴/16	M	Kodiak Island, Alaska	Charles A. Goldenberg	Charles A. Goldenberg	1978	239
28³/16	16¹⁵/16	11²/16	M	Port Moller Bay, Alaska	Enos A. Axtell	Enos A. Axtell	1950	260
28³/16	18	10⁸/16	M	Alaska Pen., Alaska	R. H. Blum	R. H. Blum	1954	260
28³/16	16¹²/16	11⁵/16	M	Kodiak Island, Alaska	Richard O. Daniels	Richard O. Daniels	1958	260
28³/16	17	11⁷/16	M	Kodiak Island, Alaska	Joe Maxwell	Joe Maxwell	1959	260
28³/16	17⁷/16	10¹³/16	M	Kodiak Island, Alaska	L. W. Zeug	L. W. Zeug	1959	260
28³/16	17⁷/16	10¹³/16	M	Alaska Pen., Alaska	Roscoe S. Mosiman	Roscoe S. Mosiman	1960	260
28³/16	17¹¹/16	10⁷/16	M	Cold Bay, Alaska	Keith C. Brown	Keith C. Brown	1962	260
28³/16	17¹¹/16	10⁹/16	M	Alaska Pen., Alaska	Bill Boone	Bill Boone	1964	260
28³/16	17	11¹/16	M	Kodiak Island, Alaska	Dan G. Brown	Dan G. Brown	1967	260
28³/16	16¹⁵/16	11²/16	M	Kodiak Island, Alaska	Cary E. Weldon	Cary E. Weldon	1968	260
28³/16	17⁸/16	10⁹/16	M	Kodiak Island, Alaska	Bill Ulich	Bill Ulich	1976	260
28	17⁷/16	10¹⁴/16	M	Alaska Pen., Alaska	Harold Dugdale	Harold Dugdale	1954	271
28	17¹⁰/16	10⁹/16	M	Alaska Pen., Alaska	Robert D. Jones, Jr.	Robert D. Jones, Jr.	1955	271
28	17	11	M	Kodiak Island, Alaska	Harry F. Weyher	Harry F. Weyher	1958	271
28	17¹⁵/16	10¹⁵/16	M	Alaska Pen., Alaska	Fred Bear	Fred Bear	1960	271
28	17¹²/16	10¹²/16	M	Alaska Pen., Alaska	Wendell S. Fletcher	Wendell S. Fletcher	1960	271
28	17⁷/16	10⁹/16	M	Alaska Pen., Alaska	W. T. Yoshimoto	W. T. Yoshimoto	1961	271
28	17³/16	10¹³/16	M	Alaska Pen., Alaska	Gilbert Elton	Gilbert Elton	1962	271
28	17¹²/16	10¹²/16	M	Port Moller, Alaska	Harry J. Armitage	Harry J. Armitage	1963	271
28	17³/16	10¹³/16	M	Kodiak Island, Alaska	Dean Herring	Dean Herring	1963	271
28	17⁷/16	10⁷/16	M	Alaska Pen., Alaska	James D. Smith	James D. Smith	1967	271
28	17¹⁴/16	10⁹/16	M	Alaska Pen., Alaska	Rudy Tuten	Rudy Tuten	1968	271
28	18	10	M	Alaska Pen., Alaska	Peter Santin	Peter Santin	1968	271
28	17	11	U	Alaska Pen., Alaska	James J. Fraioli	James J. Fraioli	1969	271
28	17¹²/16	10⁹/16	M	Alaska Pen., Alaska	Larry Lassley	Larry Lassley	1970	271
28	18	10	M	Chilkoot River, Alaska	Philip Nare	Philip Nare	1975	271

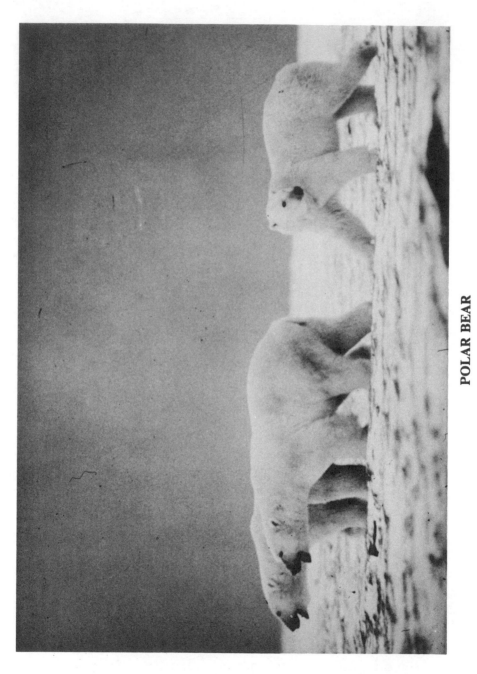

POLAR BEAR

A photograph taken in the Artic by Charles Jonkel.

Polar Bear

Ursus maritimus

Minimum Score 27

Score	Greatest Length of Skull Without Lower Jaw	Greatest Width of Skull	Sex	Locality Killed	By Whom Killed	Owner	Date Killed	Rank
29 15/16	18 5/16	11 7/16	M	Kotzebue, Alaska	Shelby Longoria	Shelby Longoria	1963	1
29 1/16	18 1/16	10 15/16	M	Kotzebue, Alaska	Louis Mussatto	Louis Mussatto	1965	2
28 12/16	17 13/16	10 15/16	M	Point Hope, Alaska	Tom F. Bolack	Tom F. Bolack	1958	3
28 12/16	17 11/16	11 1/16	M	Kotzebue, Alaska	Bill Nottley	Bill Nottley	1967	3
28 10/16	18	10 10/16	M	Little Diomede Is., Alaska	Richard G. Van Vorst	Richard G. Van Vorst	1963	5
28 10/16	17 2/16	11 2/16	M	Chukchi Sea, Alaska	Jack D. Putnam	Jack D. Putnam	1965	5
28 9/16	17 6/16	11 3/16	M	Kotzebue, Alaska	E. A. McCraken	E. A. McCraken	1966	7
28 8/16	17 6/16	11 2/16	M	Kotzebue, Alaska	Curtis S. Williams, Jr.	Curtis S. Williams, Jr.	1967	8
28 8/16	17 10/16	10 14/16	M	Kotzebue, Alaska	Winfred Lee English	Winfred Lee English	1968	8
28 7/16	17 5/16	11 7/16	M	Point Hope, Alaska	Rodney Lincoln	J. A. Columbus	1954	10
28 6/16	17 6/16	11	M	St. Lawrence Is., Alaska	H. B. Collins, Jr.	U. S. Natl. Museum	1929	11
28 6/16	17 8/16	10 14/16	M	Point Hope, Alaska	Clifford Thom	Clifford Thom	1964	11
28 6/16	17 3/16	11 3/16	M	Diomede Island, Alaska	Stephen Pyle, III	Stephen Pyle, III	1965	11
28 5/16	17 10/16	10 11/16	M	Teller, Alaska	Walter Simas	Walter Simas	1966	14
28 4/16	18 2/16	10 2/16	M	Kotzebue, Alaska	Peter W. Bading	Peter W. Bading	1960	15
28 4/16	17 9/16	10 11/16	M	Big Dicmede Is., Alaska	Vance A. Halverson	Vance A. Halverson	1963	15
28 4/16	17 1/16	10 13/16	M	Teller, Alaska	Jack C. Phillips	Jack C. Phillips	1964	15
28 3/16	17 9/16	10 10/16	M	Diomede Islands, Alaska	Louis F. Kincaid	Louis F. Kincaid	1955	18
28 3/16	17 15/16	10 4/16	M	Kotzebue, Alaska	Finis G. Cooper	Los Angeles Co. Museum	1959	18
28 3/16	17 9/16	10 13/16	M	Kotzebue, Alaska	Harold Trulin	Harold Trulin	1962	18
28 3/16	17 12/16	10 7/16	M	Kotzebue, Alaska	S. D. Slaughter	S. D. Slaughter	1962	18
28 3/16	17 6/16	10 13/16	M	Kotzebue, Alaska	C. J. McElroy	C. J. McElroy	1965	18
28 3/16	17 6/16	10 12/16	M	Point Hope, Alaska	Pete Kesselring	Pete Kesselring	1957	23
28 3/16	17 3/16	10 15/16	M	Big Diomede, Alaska	Francis Bogon	Francis Bogon	1957	23
28 3/16	17 1/16	11 1/16	M	Chukchi Sea, Alaska	Horace Steele	Horace Steele	1963	23
28 1/16	18 1/16	10	M	St. Paul Is., Alaska	C. H. Townsend	U. S. Natl. Museum	1875	26
28 1/16	17 6/16	10 11/16	M	Kotzebue, Alaska	Don Jahns	Don Jahns	1961	26
28	17 8/16	10 9/16	M	Point Hope, Alaska	Tommy Thompson	Pablo Bush Romero	1958	28
28	17 7/16	10 9/16	M	Kotzebue, Alaska	Rupert Chisholm	Rupert Chisholm	1959	28
28	17 9/16	10 10/16	M	Point Hope, Alaska	Wm. Stevenson	Wm. Stevenson	1959	28
28	17 10/16	10 6/16	M	Kotzebue, Alaska	W. H. Hagenmeyer	W. H. Hagenmeyer	1961	28
28	17 5/16	10 11/16	M	Kotzebue, Alaska	Alberto Pipia	Alberto Pipia	1964	28

POLAR BEAR–Continued
Ursus maritimus

Score	Greatest Length of Skull Without Lower Jaw	Greatest Width of Skull	Sex	Locality Killed	By Whom Killed	Owner	Date Killed	Rank
28	17 8/16	10 8/16	M	Kotzebue, Alaska	Leonard W. Bruns	Leonard W. Bruns	1966	28
27 15/16	17 8/16	10 7/16	M	Kotzebue, Alaska	Blair Truitt	Blair Truitt	1960	34
27 15/16	17 6/16	10 6/16	M	Diomede Is., Alaska	Russell C. Cutter	Russell C. Cutter	1960	34
27 15/16	17 4/16	10 11/16	M	Kotzebue, Alaska	Wm. Hill Smith, Jr.	Wm. Hill Smith, Jr.	1961	34
27 15/16	17 7/16	10 6/16	M	Kotzebue, Alaska	Jess L. Ferguson	Jess L. Ferguson	1961	34
27 15/16	17 7/16	10 6/16	M	Kotzebue, Alaska	James S. Martin	James S. Martin	1962	34
27 15/16	17 11/16	10 4/16	M	Teller, Alaska	R. Lynn Ross	R. Lynn Ross	1966	34
27 14/16	17 7/16	10 10/16	M	Point Barrow, Alaska	James W. Brooks	Univ. Of Alaska	1952	40
27 14/16	17 10/16	10 4/16	M	Kotzebue, Alaska	Roy E. Weatherby	Roy E. Weatherby	1959	40
27 14/16	17 3/16	10 12/16	M	Kotzebue, Alaska	Don R. Downey	Don R. Downey	1960	40
27 14/16	17 5/16	10 6/16	M	Kotzebue, Alaska	C. D. Dofflemyer	C. D. Dofflemyer	1961	40
27 14/16	17 5/16	10 12/16	M	Chukchi Sea, Alaska	Nikolaus Koenig	Nikolaus Koenig	1966	40
27 13/16	17 3/16	10	M	Kotzebue, Alaska	Hugh J. O'Dower	Hugh J. O'Dower	1959	45
27 13/16	17 7/16	10 6/16	M	Point Hope, Alaska	Wm. P. Boone	Wm. P. Boone	1960	45
27 13/16	17 8/16	10 5/16	M	Point Hope, Alaska	Helen Burnett	Helen Burnett	1962	45
27 13/16	16 15/16	10 14/16	M	Cape Lisburne, Alaska	Dale H. Wolff	Dale H. Wolff	1963	45
27 13/16	17 3/16	10 9/16	M	Kotzebue, Alaska	Charles Renaud	Charles Renaud	1963	45
27 13/16	17 4/16	10 9/16	U	Alaska Coast	Lowell M. Cooke	Lowell M. Cooke	1965	45
27 13/16	17 7/16	10 6/16	M	Chukchi Sea, Alaska	Robert M. Mallett	Robert M. Mallett	1967	45
27 12/16	17 5/16	10 7/16	M	Cape Lisburne, Alaska	Edward M. Simko	Edward M. Simko	1956	52
27 12/16	17 5/16	10 5/16	M	Kotzebue, Alaska	J. E. Ottoviano	J. E. Ottoviano	1958	52
27 12/16	17	10 12/16	M	Point Hope, Alaska	A. H. Woodward, Jr.	A. H. Woodward, Jr.	1959	52
27 12/16	17 8/16	10 4/16	M	Kotzebue, Alaska	Owen K. Murphy	Owen K. Murphy	1959	52
27 12/16	17 6/16	10 6/16	M	Little Diomede Is., Alaska	D. V. Merrick	D. V. Merrick	1959	52
27 12/16	17 5/16	10 7/16	M	Kotzebue, Alaska	Louis Menegas	Louis Menegas	1963	52
27 12/16	17 2/16	10 9/16	M	Kotzebue, Alaska	Arthur W. Clark	Arthur W. Clark	1963	52
27 12/16	17 4/16	10 8/16	M	Teller, Alaska	Earl Nystrom	Earl Nystrom	1965	52
27 12/16	16 4/16	10 8/16	M	Teller, Alaska	William M. Kessner	William M. Kessner	1966	52
27 11/16	17 6/16	11 7/16	M	Kotzebue, Alaska	Arthur W. Smith	Arthur W. Smith	1963	61
27 11/16	17 7/16	10 5/16	M	Kotzebue, Alaska	Andrew S. Allen	Andrew S. Allen	1965	61
27 11/16	17 11/16	10 4/16	M	Kotzebue, Alaska	Patricia Bergstrom	Patricia Bergstrom	1965	61
27 9/16	16 11/16	10 15/16	M	Kotzebue, Alaska	Joe Foss	Joe Foss	1960	64

			Sex	Locality	Hunter	Owner	Year	Score
27 9/16	17 4/16	10 9/16	M	Kotzebue, Alaska	Geo. P. Whittington	Geo. P. Whittington	1962	64
27 9/16	17 2/16	10 9/16	M	Kotzebue, Alaska	C. T. Kraftmeyer	C. T. Kraftmeyer	1962	64
27 9/16	16 15/16	10 11/16	M	Little Diomede, Alaska	Willard R. Skousen	Willard R. Skousen	1962	64
27 9/16	17 4/16	10 9/16	M	Kotzebue, Alaska	Kenneth W. Vaughn	Kenneth W. Vaughn	1963	64
27 9/16	17	10 10/16	M	Point Hope, Alaska	Norma Wahrer	Norma Wahrer	1963	64
27 9/16	17 9/16	10 4/16	M	Kotzebue, Alaska	Robert L. Cohen	Robert L. Cohen	1966	64
27 9/16	17 9/16	10 3/16	M	Point Hope, Alaska	T. E. Shillingburg	T. E. Shillingburg	1957	71
27 6/16	17 1/16	10 7/16	M	Cape Thompson, Alaska	Daniel H. Cuddy	Daniel H. Cuddy	1959	71
27 6/16	17 7/16	10 3/16	M	Chukchi Sea, Alaska	Angelo Alessio	Angelo Alessio	1963	71
27 6/16	17 9/16	10 3/16	M	Diomede Island, Alaska	Tony Oney	Tony Oney	1964	71
27 6/16	17 9/16	10 5/16	M	Point Hope, Alaska	Pat Auld	Pat Auld	1964	71
27 6/16	16 13/16	10 12/16	M	Kotzebue, Alaska	Harry D. Tousley	Harry D. Tousley	1961	76
27 6/16	17 3/16	10 5/16	M	Cape Lisburne, Alaska	Willard E. Flynn	Willard E. Flynn	1963	76
27 6/16	17 2/16	10 6/16	M	Point Hope, Alaska	Edward Frecker	Edward Frecker	1963	76
27 6/16	17 5/16	10 6/16	M	Kotzebue, Alaska	Russell J. Uhl	Russell J. Uhl	1965	76
27 6/16	17	10 8/16	M	Kotzebue, Alaska	Ted Lick	Ted Lick	1965	76
27 6/16	17 5/16	10 3/16	M	Kotzebue, Alaska	Mahlon T. Everhart	Mahlon T. Everhart	1959	81
27 7/16	16 9/16	10 4/16	M	Little Diomede Is., Alaska	Herb Klein	Herb Klein	1960	81
27 7/16	17 6/16	10 6/16	M	Kotzebue, Alaska	Gregory E. Koshell	Gregory E. Koshell	1961	81
27 7/16	17 5/16	10 7/16	M	Polar Circle, Alaska	Aurelio Caccomo	Aurelio Caccomo	1965	81
27 7/16	16 15/16	10 15/16	M	Kotzebue, Alaska	Andrew De Matteo	Andrew De Matteo	1965	81
27 7/16	17 1/16	10	M	Wales, Alaska	Univ. Of Alaska	Eskimo	1956	86
27 6/16	16 11/16	10 11/16	M	Cape Lisburne, Alaska	J. S. Lichtenfels	J. S. Lichtenfels	1957	86
27 6/16	17 5/16	10 7/16	M	Kotzebue, Alaska	W. H. Cato, Jr.	W. H. Cato, Jr.	1960	86
27 6/16	17	10 6/16	M	Kotzebue, Alaska	Gene Klineburger	Gene Klineburger	1963	86
27 6/16	17 5/16	10 7/16	M	Little Diomede Is., Alaska	Bob Payne	Bob Payne	1964	86
27 6/16	17	10 6/16	M	Teller, Alaska	James O. Campbell	James O. Campbell	1964	86
27 3/16	17 3/16	10 3/16	M	Kotzebue, Alaska	Glen E. Park	Glen E. Park	1965	86
27 5/16	16 10/16	10 13/16	M	Chukchi Sea, Alaska	Terry Kennedy	Terry Kennedy	1967	86
27 5/16	16 13/16	10 6/16	M	Kotzebue, Alaska	Harry Daum	Harry Daum	1971	95
27 5/16	17	10	M	Kotzebue, Alaska	W. L. Coleman	W. L. Coleman	1961	95
27 5/16	16 13/16	10 6/16	M	Point Hope, Alaska	Charles A. McKinsey	Charles A. McKinsey	1963	95
27 5/16	17 1/16	10 3/16	M	Point Barrow, Alaska	Bert Klineburger	Bert Klineburger	1963	95
27 5/16	16 15/16	10 7/16	M	Point Hope, Alaska	Sherman R. Whitmore	Sherman R. Whitmore	1963	95
27 5/16	17 1/16	10 6/16	M	Big Diomede Is., Alaska	Basil C. Bradbury	Basil C. Bradbury	1964	95
27 5/16	16 9/16	10 6/16	M	Kotzebue, Alaska	Lewis Figone	Lewis Figone	1965	95
27 5/16	16 12/16	10 13/16	M	Pt. Barrow, Alaska	James Senn	James Senn	1965	95
27 5/16	16 12/16	10 7/16	M	Bering Straits, Alaska	William D. Backman, Jr.	William D. Backman, Jr.	1965	95
27 5/16	17 1/16	10 7/16	M	Point Hope, Alaska	R. K. Siller	R. K. Siller	1966	95
27 5/16	17 1/16	10 7/16	M	Kotzebue, Alaska	Gene Barrow	Gene Barrow	1968	95
27 5/16	16 15/16	10 7/16	M	Point Hope, Alaska	E. F. Simon	E. F. Simon	1957	95
27 5/16	17 1/16	10 7/16	M	Wales, Alaska	Univ. Of Alaska	Eldon Brant	1960	105
27 5/16	17	10 7/16	M	Point Hope, Alaska	Charles Brauch	Charles Brauch		105

POLAR BEAR—*Continued*
Ursus maritimus

Score	Greatest Length of Skull Without Lower Jaw	Greatest Width of Skull	Sex	Locality Killed	By Whom Killed	Owner	Date Killed	Rank
27 4/16	16 12/16	10 8/16	M	Cape Lisburne, Alaska	Richard Hanks	Richard Hanks	1962	105
27 4/16	17 1/16	10 3/16	M	Point Hope, Alaska	C. Sam Sparks	C. Sam Sparks	1962	105
27 4/16	16 15/16	10 5/16	M	Kotzebue, Alaska	Bill Taylor	Bill Taylor	1964	105
27 4/16	16 14/16	10 6/16	M	Kotzebue, Alaska	Ralph Lenheim	Ralph Lenheim	1964	105
27 4/16	17	10 6/16	M	Kotzebue, Alaska	Russell Underdahl	Russell Underdahl	1965	105
27 4/16	16 14/16	10 6/16	M	Teller, Alaska	Joseph O. Porter, Sr.	Joseph O. Porter, Sr.	1965	105
27 3/16	17 5/16	9 14/16	M	Nome, Alaska	J. H. Rogers	J. H. Rogers	1956	114
27 3/16	16 11/16	10 6/16	M	Kotzebue, Alaska	Bud Lotstedt	Bud Lotstedt	1959	114
27 3/16	17 5/16	9 14/16	M	Bering Straits, Alaska	Henry S. Budney	Henry S. Budney	1959	114
27 3/16	16 13/16	10 6/16	M	Point Hope, Alaska	Kenneth Holland	Kenneth Holland	1960	114
27 3/16	17 4/16	9 15/16	M	Point Hope, Alaska	Bert Klineburger	Bert Klineburger	1961	114
27 3/16	16 12/16	10 7/16	M	Point Hope, Alaska	Richard Hanks	Richard Hanks	1962	114
27 3/16	16 13/16	10 6/16	M	Chukchi Sea, Alaska	Chas. P. Adkins	Chas. P. Adkins	1964	114
27 3/16	17 3/16	10	M	Kotzebue, Alaska	Barbara Sjoden	Barbara Sjoden	1966	114
27 3/16	17 1/16	10 3/16	M	Kotzebue, Alaska	Bernard Domries	Bernard Domries	1970	114
27 2/16	16 11/16	10 7/16	M	Point Hope, Alaska	Finis Gilbert	Finis Gilbert	1959	123
27 2/16	16 13/16	10 5/16	M	Kotzebue, Alaska	John F. Meyer	John F. Meyer	1960	123
27 2/16	17 4/16	9 14/16	M	Point Hope, Alaska	C. C. Irving	C. C. Irving	1960	123
27 2/16	16 15/16	10 3/16	M	Kotzebue, Alaska	W. T. Yoshimoto	W. T. Yoshimoto	1962	123
27 2/16	16 12/16	10 6/16	M	Point Barrow, Alaska	Frank Bydalek	Frank Bydalek	1963	123
27 2/16	17	10 6/16	M	Kotzebue, Alaska	E. B. Schur	E. B. Schur	1964	123
27 2/16	16 12/16	10 6/16	M	Shishmaref, Alaska	Richard V. Hoyt & W. H. Otis	Richard V. Hoyt & W. H. Otis	1965	123
27 2/16	16 14/16	10 4/16	M	Chukchi Sea, Alaska	R. G. Howlett	R. G. Howlett	1965	123
27 1/16	16 15/16	10 3/16	M	Cape Lisburne, Alaska	Howard W. Pollock	Howard W. Pollock	1957	131
27 1/16	16 13/16	10 4/16	M	Kotzebue, Alaska	Glenn B. Walker	Glenn B. Walker	1959	131
27 1/16	17 7/16	9 10/16	M	Point Hope, Alaska	True Davis	True Davis	1961	131
27 1/16	16 13/16	10 4/16	M	Kotzebue, Alaska	Bill Ellis	Bill Ellis	1962	131
27 1/16	16 10/16	10 3/16	M	Kotzebue, Alaska	Fritz Worster	Fritz Worster	1963	131
27 1/16	16 12/16	10 5/16	M	Diomede Is., Alaska	Flavy Davis	Flavy Davis	1963	131
27 1/16	16 11/16	10 6/16	M	Little Diomede Is., Alaska	Tony Oney	Tony Oney	1963	131
27 1/16	16 14/16	10 3/16	M	Kotzebue, Alaska	George W. Roberts	George W. Roberts	1965	131
27 1/16	16 11/16	10 6/16	M	Kotzebue, Alaska	Marshall Johnson	Marshall Johnson	1965	131

27	$16\frac{15}{16}$	$10\frac{1}{16}$	M	Point Barrow, Alaska	T. L. Richardson	U. S. Natl. Museum	1917	140
27	$17\frac{2}{16}$	$9\frac{14}{16}$	M	Kotzebue, Alaska	Unknown	Dick Drew	1959	140
27	$16\frac{7}{16}$	$10\frac{3}{16}$	M	Point Hope, Alaska	T. A. Warren	T. A. Warren	1959	140
27	$16\frac{14}{16}$	$10\frac{4}{16}$	M	Point Barrow, Alaska	Clifford H. Dietz	Clifford H. Dietz	1960	140
27	$16\frac{12}{16}$	$10\frac{4}{16}$	M	Kotzebue, Alaska	Henry Blackford	Henry Blackford	1961	140
27	$16\frac{12}{16}$	$10\frac{4}{16}$	M	Point Hope, Alaska	James T. Byrnes	Cin. Mus. Nat. History	1963	140
27	$16\frac{12}{16}$	$10\frac{4}{16}$	M	Kotzebue, Alaska	William A. Bond	William A. Bond	1964	140
27	$16\frac{14}{16}$	$10\frac{2}{16}$	M	Kotzebue, Alaska	Charles E. Shedd	Charles E. Shedd	1964	140
27	$16\frac{8}{16}$	$10\frac{8}{16}$	M	Kotzebue, Alaska	Norman W. Garwood	Norman W. Garwood	1964	140

A LOCALLY FAMED JAGUAR, OLD "ONE FANG"

Collected by John M. Phillips near Tampico, Mexico in 1910, as displayed in Carnegie Museum's Jaguar Group.

Jaguar

Felis onca hernandesii and related subspecies

Minimum Score 14½

Score	Greatest Length of Skull Without Lower Jaw	Greatest Width of Skull	Sex	Locality Killed	By Whom Killed	Owner	Date Killed	Rank
18 7/16	10 15/16	7 8/16	M	Sinaola, Mexico	C. J. McElroy	C. J. McElroy	1965	1
18 5/16	10 14/16	7 7/16	M	Cibecue, Ariz.	Jack Funk	U. S. Natl. Museum	1924	2
18 3/16	10 15/16	7 4/16	M	Nogales, Ariz.	Fred Ott	U. S. Natl. Museum	1926	3
18 2/16	11	7 2/16	M	Vera Cruz, Mexico	E. W. Nelson & E. A. Goldman	U. S. Natl. Museum	1894	4
18	10 5/16	7 11/16	M	Big Bend, Texas	Benjamin L. Bird	Benjamin L. Bird	1962	5
17 15/16	10 9/16	7 6/16	U	Tehuantepec, Mexico	Francis Sumuchrast	U. S. Natl. Museum	PR1869	6
17 13/16	10 9/16	7 4/16	M	Guadalajara, Mexico	Elgin T. Gates	Elgin T. Gates	1954	7
17 11/16	10 11/16	7	M	Campeche, Mexico	Jacinta S. Dorantes	Squire Haskins	1960	8
17 10/16	10 9/16	7 1/16	U	Chiapas, Mexico	E. W. Nelson & E. A. Goldman	U. S. Natl. Museum	1900	9
17 8/16	10 6/16	7 2/16	M	Tamaulipas, Mexico	Henderson Coquat	M. Nowotny	1940	10
17 8/16	10 8/16	7	M	Campeche, Mexico	Alex Hudson, III	Alex Hudson, III	1962	10
17 7/16	10 7/16	7	M	Tamaulipas, Mexico	Unknown	Bond Carroll	1959	12
17 6/16	10 7/16	6 15/16	M	Nayarit, Mexico	Aldegundo Garza de Leon	Aldegundo Garza de Leon	1969	13
17 2/16	10 6/16	6 13/16	M	Mills Co., Texas	H. D. Attwater	U. S. Natl. Museum	1903	14
17 2/16	10 5/16	6 13/16	M	Nayarit, Mexico	P. Mueller & D. O. Rudin	P. Mueller & D. O. Rudin	1959	14
17 2/16	10 4/16	6 12/16	M	Nayarit, Mexico	Kenneth Campbell	Kenneth Campbell	1971	14
17	10 4/16	6 12/16	M	Nayarit, Mexico	Graciano Guichard	Graciano Guichard	1969	17
16 15/16	10 4/16	6 11/16	M	Tamaulipas, Mexico	Squire Haskins	Dallas Mus. Nat. Hist.	1957	18
16 14/16	10 6/16	6 12/16	M	Helvetia, Ariz.	E. J. O'Doherty	U. S. Natl. Museum	1917	19
16 14/16	10 6/16	6 9/16	M	Sonora, Mexico	Frank C. Hibben	Frank C. Hibben	1934	19
16 14/16	10 5/16	6 9/16	M	Sonora, Mexico	Frank C. Hibben	Frank C. Hibben	1934	19
16 14/16	10 4/16	6 10/16	M	Nayarit. Mexico	J. F. Brinkley	J. E. Brinkley	1959	19
16 14/16	9 12/16	7 2/16	M	Tampico, Mexico	Hector Elizondao	Hector Elizondao	1962	19
16 13/16	10 5/16	6 8/16	M	Nayarit, Mexico	G. Hooker & Leonard Stephens	George Hooker	1957	24
16 12/16	10 4/16	6 11/16	M	Nayarit, Mexico	Herb Klein	Herb Klein	1955	25
16 2/16	10 4/16	6 9/16	M	Nayarit, Mexico	Picked Up	Lawson E. Miller, Jr.	1959	25
16 1/16	9 5/16	6 12/16	U	Chivela, Oaxaca, Mexico	Charles Oertel	U. S. Natl. Museum	1899	27
16 1/16	9 14/16	6 13/16	M	Sonora, Mexico	Dick Wooddell	Dick Wooddell	1955	27
16 1/16	10 4/16	6 9/16	M	Ft. Apache Res., Ariz.	Russell Culbreath	U. S. Natl. Museum	1964	27

143

JAGUAR–Continued
Felis onca hernandesii and related subspecies

Score	Greatest Length of Skull Without Lower Jaw	Greatest Width of Skull	Sex	Locality Killed	By Whom Killed	Owner	Date Killed	Rank
16 10/16	9 1/16	6 15/16	M	Nayarit, Mexico	John Ryan	John Ryan	1962	30
16 10/16	9 1/16	6 12/16	M	Nayarit, Mexico	Morton J. Greene	Morton J. Greene	1965	30
16 6/16	9 1/16	6 11/16	M	Vera Cruz, Mexico	A. Wetmore & Juan Canela	U. S. Natl. Museum	1939	32
16 6/16	9 5/16	6 10/16	M	Tamaulipas, Mexico	Juan Lebeira	Juan Lebeira	1965	32
16 6/16	9 4/16	6 8/16	M	Tamaulipas, Mexico	Alex Hudson	Alex Hudson	1964	34
16 6/16	9 4/16	6 8/16	M	Nayarit, Mexico	William J. Campbell	William J. Campbell	1970	34
16 5/16	9 4/16	6 7/16	M	Nayarit, Mexico	George H. Hodges, Jr.	George H. Hodges, Jr.	1960	36
16 5/16	9 2/16	6 9/16	M	Nayarit, Mexico	O. J. Fletcher	O. J. Fletcher	1964	36
16 4/16	9 1/16	6 9/16	M	Nayarit, Mexico	Charles Binney, II	443rd Hunting Club	1965	38
16 3/16	9 1/16	6 8/16	M	Nayarit, Mexico	Ventura Gonzalez Cosio	Ventura Gonzalez Cosio	1965	39
16 3/16	9 9/16	6 9/16	F	Ariz.	Arvid F. Benson	Arvid F. Benson	1961	40
16 3/16	9 1/16	6 7/16	M	Tamaulipas, Mexico	Juan A. Saenz, Jr.	Juan A. Saenz, Jr.	1970	40
16 1/16	9 9/16	6 8/16	M	Tamaulipas, Mexico	A. D. Stenger	A. D. Stenger	1957	42
16 1/16	9 10/16	6 9/16	M	Nayarit, Mexico	Kenneth Campbell	Kenneth Campbell	1970	42
16	9 2/16	6 14/16	M	Tamaulipas, Mexico	Frank R. Denman	Frank R. Denman	1966	44
15 13/16	9 10/16	6 9/16	M	Tamaulipas, Mexico	Winfred Lee English	Winfred Lee English	1966	45
15 5/16	9 5/16	6 9/16	M	Nayarit, Mexico	Roy E. Cooper	Roy E. Cooper	1960	46
15 5/16	9 5/16	6 9/16	M	Nayarit, Mexico	Gene Biddle	Gene Biddle	1961	46
15 5/16	8 14/16	6 10/16	M	Tamaulipas, Mexico	O. A. Washburn	O. A. Washburn	1964	46
15 5/16	9 1/16	6 9/16	M	Patagonia Mts., Ariz.	Laurence L. McGee	Univ. Of Ariz.	1965	49
15 5/16	9 1/16	6 9/16	M	Nayarit, Mexico	Jimmie Underwood	Steve M. Matthes	1963	50
15 3/16	9 2/16	6	M	Nayarit, Mexico	James G. Shirley, Jr.	James G. Shirley, Jr.	1959	51
15 1/16	9	6 1/16	M	Big Lake, Ariz.	Terry D. Penrod	Terry D. Penrod	1963	52
14 15/16	9	5 15/16	F	Nayarit, Mexico	E. W. Ennis, Jr.	E. W. Ennis, Jr.	1956	53
14 14/16	8 11/16	6 1/16	F	Nogales, Ariz.	John F. Nutt	John F. Nutt	1958	54
14 14/16	9	5 14/16	F	Nayarit, Mexico	Glenn W. Slade, Jr.	Glenn W. Slade, Jr.	1960	54
14 13/16	8 14/16	5 15/16	M	Nayarit, Mexico	Kenneth Campbell	Kenneth Campbell	1970	56
14 12/16	8 15/16	5 13/16	F	Nayarit, Mexico	Cecil M. Hopper	Cecil M. Hopper	1971	57
14 9/16	8 14/16	5 11/16	F	Santa Cruz Co., Ariz.	Ed Scarla	Ed Scarla	1959	58

COUGAR OR MOUNTAIN LION

A photograph taken in Idaho by Maurice Hornocker.

Cougar or Mountain Lion

Felis concolor hippolestes and related subspecies

Minimum Score 15

Score	Greatest Length of Skull Without Lower Jaw	Greatest Width of Skull	Sex	Locality Killed	By Whom Killed	Owner	Date Killed	Rank
16	9⁴/₁₆	6¹²/₁₆	M	Garfield Co., Utah	Garth Roberts	R. Scott Jarvie	1964	1
15¹⁵/₁₆	9¹/₁₆	6¹⁴/₁₆	M	Clearwater River, Alta.	Walter R. Weller	Walter R. Weller	1973	2
15¹²/₁₆	9⁵/₁₆	6⁷/₁₆	M	Meeker, Colo.	Theo. Roosevelt	U. S. Natl. Museum	1901	3
15¹²/₁₆	9²/₁₆	6¹⁰/₁₆	M	Dutch Creek, Alta.	Edward D. Burton	Edward D. Burton	1954	3
15¹²/₁₆	9¹/₁₆	6¹¹/₁₆	M	Okanagan Lake, B. C.	Ted Razook	Ted Razook	1973	3
15¹²/₁₆	9⁵/₁₆	6⁷/₁₆	M	Mesa Co., Colo.	Robert R. Meyer	Robert R. Meyer	1978	3
15¹¹/₁₆	9⁴/₁₆	6⁷/₁₆	M	Darby, Mont.	Lowell Hayes	Sherman L. Hayes	1953	7
15¹¹/₁₆	9³/₁₆	6⁸/₁₆	M	Selway River, Idaho	Gene R. Alford	Gene R. Alford	1961	7
15¹¹/₁₆	9	6¹¹/₁₆	M	Selway River, Idaho	Gene R. Alford	Gene R. Alford	1961	7
15¹¹/₁₆	9³/₁₆	6⁸/₁₆	M	Valley Co., Idaho	Louis Rebillet	Louis Rebillet	1961	7
15⁹/₁₆	9³/₁₆	6⁷/₁₆	M	Catherine Creek, Oreg.	Ron Lay	Ron Lay	1966	11
15⁹/₁₆*	9⁴/₁₆	6⁵/₁₆	M	Salmon River, Idaho	Art Ling	Art Ling	1971	11
15⁸/₁₆	9²/₁₆	6⁷/₁₆	M	Carbon Co., Utah	H. Alan Foster	H. Alan Foster	1959	13
15⁸/₁₆	9³/₁₆	6⁶/₁₆	M	Okanogan Co., Wash.	Mike Lynch	Mike Lynch	1964	13
15⁸/₁₆	9²/₁₆	6⁷/₁₆	M	Salmon River, Idaho	Doug Kittredge	Doug Kittredge	1971	13
15⁸/₁₆	9²/₁₆	6⁶/₁₆	M	Cottonwood, Nev.	Berkley Hunt	Berkley Hunt	1962	16
15⁸/₁₆	9	6⁸/₁₆	M	Porcupine Hills, Alta.	Ed Burton	Ed Burton	1965	16
15⁸/₁₆	9³/₁₆	6⁵/₁₆	M	Huerfano Co., Colo.	J. D. Dodge	J. D. Dodge	1971	16
15⁸/₁₆	9⁶/₁₆	6	M	Priest Lake, Idaho	Ron Book	Ron Book	1972	16
15⁸/₁₆	9¹/₁₆	6⁷/₁₆	M	Lincoln Co., Mont.	Robert Fleshman	Gary Grenfell	1975	16
15⁸/₁₆	9¹/₁₆	6⁷/₁₆	M	Loblaw Creek, Alta.	John A. Jorgensen	John A. Jorgensen	1977	16
15⁷/₁₆	8¹⁵/₁₆	6⁸/₁₆	M	Coleman, Alta.	Harry Freeman & Dick Girardi	Harry Freeman & Dick Girardi	1963	22
15⁷/₁₆	9	6⁷/₁₆	M	Kootenay, B. C.	Melvin E. Almas	Melvin E. Almas	1965	22
15⁷/₁₆	9¹/₁₆	6⁵/₁₆	M	Lewis And Clark Co., Mont.	Ron Jenkins	Ron Jenkens & Jim Lee	1967	22
15⁷/₁₆	9³/₁₆	6⁴/₁₆	M	Coal Canyon, Colo.	Larry Bamford	Larry Bamford	1967	22
15⁷/₁₆	9²/₁₆	6⁵/₁₆	M	Columbia Co., Wash.	William R. Randall	William R. Randall	1972	22
15⁶/₁₆	9¹/₁₆	6⁵/₁₆	M	Wind River Mts., Wyo.	M. Abbott Frazier	U. S. Natl. Museum	1892	27
15⁶/₁₆	8⁴/₁₆	6⁸/₁₆	M	Okanogan Co., Wash.	Merle Hooshagen	Merle Hooshagen	1957	27
15⁶/₁₆	8⁴/₁₆	6⁸/₁₆	M	Young, Ariz.	Ed Scarla	Ed Scarla	1958	27
15⁶/₁₆	9⁴/₁₆	6²/₁₆	M	Sedalia, Colo.	Walt Paulk	Walt Paulk	1961	27
15⁶/₁₆	8⁴/₁₆	6⁸/₁₆	M	Mineral Co., Mont.	Richard Ramberg	Richard Ramberg	1964	27
15⁶/₁₆	9²/₁₆	6¹/₁₆	M	West Salt Creek, Colo.	Hartle V. Morris	Hartle V. Morris	1964	27

15 5/16	8 13/16	6 5/16	M	Fernie, B. C.	Oscar Jansen	Oscar Jansen	27	1964
15 5/16	8 13/16	6 5/16	M	Natal, B. C.	Dick Ritco	Dick Ritco	27	1964
15 5/16	9	6 6/16	M	Missoula Co., Mont.	Jim Zeiler	William W Zeiler	27	1966
15 5/16	9	6 6/16	M	Sanders Co., Mont.	Lloyd F. Behling	Lloyd F. Behling	27	1969
15 5/16	9 1/16	6 5/16	M	Bull River, B.C.	Henry Fercho	Henry Fercho	27	1976
15 5/16	9 2/16	6 6/16	M	Colfax Co., N.M.	Marta Sue Burnside	Marta Sue Burnside	27	1977
15 5/16	8 14/16	6 7/16	M	Hamilton, Mont.	Lloyd Thompson	U. S. Natl. Museum	39	1922
15 5/16	8 12/16	6 8/16	M	Clearwater River, Alta.	Wm. A. Schutte	Wm. A. Schutte	39	1935
15 5/16	8 13/16	6 8/16	F	Missoula Co., Mont.	Ronald Thompson	U. S. Natl. Museum	39	1936
15 5/16	8 15/16	6 6/16	M	East Kootenay, B. C.	Martin Marigeau	C. Garrett	39	1940
15 5/16	8 13/16	6 6/16	M	Clearwater Co., Idaho	Andy Eatmon	H. H. Schnettler	39	1953
15 5/16	8 15/16	6 7/16	M	Spanish Fork Canyon, Utah	Ronald Jones & Guy Perce	Ronald Jones	39	1954
15 5/16	8 15/16	6 6/16	M	Granite Co., Mont.	Oscar E. Nelson	Oscar E. Nelson	39	1961
15 5/16	9 2/16	6 6/16	M	Idaho Co., Idaho	Wayne & Douglas England	Wayne England	39	1962
15 5/16	9 2/16	6 3/16	M	Eagle Nest, N. M.	Hal Vaught	Hal Vaught	39	1963
15 5/16	9 1/16	6 3/16	M	Lake Quinault, Wash.	C. A. Heppe	C. A. Heppe	39	1964
15 5/16	8 15/16	6 6/16	M	Lac La Hache, B. C.	Andy Hagberg	Andy Hagberg	39	1967
15 5/16	9 1/16	6 6/16	M	Grand Junction, Colo	John Lamicq, Jr.	John Lamicq, Jr.	39	1969
15 5/16	9 1/16	6 4/16	M	Elk City, Idaho	Wayne Goodwin & David Baldwin	David Baldwin	39	1969
15 5/16	9 1/16	6 1/16	M	Elko Co., Nev.	Kenneth A. Johnson	Kenneth A. Johnson	39	1974
15 5/16	8 15/16	6 6/16	M	Lemhi Co., Idaho	Larry L. Schweitzer	Larry L. Schweitzer	39	1975
15 5/16	8 13/16	6 8/16	M	Osoyoos, B. C.	Alvin L. Reiff	Alvin L. Reiff	39	1975
15 5/16	9	6 6/16	M	Okanogan Co., Wash.	Joel N. Hughes	Joel N. Hughes	39	1975
15 5/16	9	6 5/16	M	Hardesty Creek, Alta	John T. Shillingburg	John T. Shillingburg	39	1976
15 5/16	9	6 5/16	M	Custer Co., Idaho	Florence Buxton	Florence Buxton	39	1977
15 5/16	8 15/16	6 6/16	M	Jumpingpound Creek, Alta.	Max W. Good	Max W. Good	39	1978
15 5/16	8 15/16	6 6/16	M	Mineral Co., Mont.	Dennis E. Moos	Dennis E. Moos	39	1979
15 5/16	9	6 4/16	M	Okanogan Co., Wash.	Merle Hooshagen	Merle Hooshagen	60	1956
15 5/16	8 13/16	6 7/16	M	Wells Gray Park, B. C.	Colin Mann	Colin Mann	60	1960
15 5/16	8 13/16	6 7/16	M	Union Co., Oreg.	Dor. Haefer	W. H. Miller	60	1961
15 5/16	8 14/16	6 5/16	M	Motoqua, Utah	Basil C. Bradbury	Basil C. Bradbury	60	1963
15 5/16	9	6 6/16	M	Canim Lake, B. C.	H. C. Nickelsen	H. C. Nickelsen	60	1964
15 5/16	9	6 4/16	M	Missoula Co., Mont.	Richard Ramberg	Maurice Hornocker	60	1964
15 5/16	9	6 4/16	M	Missoula Co., Mont.	Bob Stanley & Clete Johnson	Bob Stanley	60	1967
15 5/16	8 15/16	6 4/16	M	Salmon River, Idaho	Aaron U. Jones	Aaron U. Jones	60	1967
15 5/16	8 13/16	6 4/16	M	Snake River, Idaho	Dee M. Cannon	Dee M. Cannon	60	1968
15 5/16	8 15/16	6 5/16	M	Okanogan Co., Wash.	Louis J. Ayers	Louis J. Ayers	60	1969
15 5/16	8 13/16	6 7/16	M	Sandpoint, Idaho	George C. Taft	George C. Taft	60	1969
15 5/16	8 15/16	6 5/16	U	Beaver Creek, Alta.	Oscar Markle	Oscar Markle	60	1970
15 5/16	9 3/16	6 1/16	F	Sanders Co., Mont.	Edna Hill	Edna Hill	60	1970
15 5/16	6 4/16	9	M	Vernal, Utah	Harold Schneider	Harold Schneider	60	1970
15 5/16	9 2/16	6 2/16	M	Ravalli Co., Mont.	Larry A. Rose	Larry A. Rose	60	1973

COUGAR OR MOUNTAIN LION—*Continued*

Felis concolor hippolestes and related subspecies

Score	Greatest Length of Skull Without Lower Jaw	Greatest Width of Skull	Sex	Locality Killed	By Whom Killed	Owner	Date Killed	Rank
15⁵/₁₆	8¹⁵/₁₆	6⁵/₁₆	M	Nakusp, B. C.	Glen Olson	Glen Olson	1974	60
15⁵/₁₆	8¹⁵/₁₆	6⁵/₁₆	M	Mineral Co., Mont.	Irving H. Ratnour	Irving H. Ratnour	1975	60
15⁵/₁₆	9	6⁴/₁₆	M	Lincoln Co., Mont.	Wayne B. Hunt	Wayne B. Hunt	1975	60
15⁵/₁₆	9	6⁴/₁₆	M	Meldrum Creek, B.C.	Walter A. Riemer	Walter A. Riemer	1977	60
15⁵/₁₆	8¹⁴/₁₆	6⁵/₁₆	M	Oliver, B.C.	Walter Snoke	Walter Snoke	1977	60
15⁵/₁₆	9	6⁴/₁₆	M	Threepoint Creek, Alta.	Robert C. Dickson	R.C. Dickson & R.J. Dickson, Jr.	1978	60
15³/₁₆	8¹⁵/₁₆	6⁴/₁₆	U	East Kootenay, B. C.	Martin Marigeau	C. Garrett	1940	81
15³/₁₆	8¹³/₁₆	6⁶/₁₆	M	Ventura Co., Calif.	Warren C. Johnston	Warren C. Johnston	1953	81
15³/₁₆	8¹⁴/₁₆	6⁵/₁₆	M	Churn Creek, B. C.	J. R. Aitchison	J. R. Aitchison	1956	81
15³/₁₆	9¹/₁₆	6³/₁₆	M	Nelson, B. C.	R. A. Rutherglen	Univ. Of B. C.	1956	81
15³/₁₆	8¹⁴/₁₆	6⁵/₁₆	M	Trout Creek, Alta.	Kenny McRae	Kenny McRae	1961	81
15³/₁₆	8¹⁴/₁₆	6⁵/₁₆	M	Pincher Creek, Alta.	Harry R. Freeman	Harry R. Freeman	1961	81
15³/₁₆	8¹⁴/₁₆	6⁵/₁₆	M	Saratoga, Wyo.	Win Condict	Win Condict	1961	81
15³/₁₆	8¹⁴/₁₆	6⁵/₁₆	M	McGregor Lake, Alta.	Gus Daley	A. C. Wilson	1962	81
15³/₁₆	8¹⁴/₁₆	6⁵/₁₆	M	Oliver, B. C.	Allan Nichol	Allan Nichol	1963	81
15³/₁₆	8¹⁴/₁₆	6⁴/₁₆	M	Okanogan Co., Wash.	Mike Lynch	Mike Lynch	1964	81
15³/₁₆	8¹⁵/₁₆	6⁸/₁₆	M	Oroville, Wash.	Leon Fleming & Joe Lemaster	Leon Fleming	1967	81
15³/₁₆	8¹¹/₁₆	6³/₁₆	M	Whitecourt, Alta.	K. J. Stanton	K. J. Stanton	1967	81
15³/₁₆	9	6	M	Tatlayoko Lake, B. C.	C. L. Anderson	C. L. Anderson	1967	81
15³/₁₆	9³/₁₆	6⁴/₁₆	F	Meeker, Colo.	Jack Cadario	Jack Cadario	1968	81
15³/₁₆	8¹⁵/₁₆	6⁵/₁₆	F	Orofino, Idaho	Fairly Bonner	Fairly Bonner	1969	81
15³/₁₆	8¹⁴/₁₆	6⁴/₁₆	M	Falkland, B. C.	Earl Carlson	Wildlife Tax. Studios	1974	81
15³/₁₆	8¹⁵/₁₆	6¹/₁₆	M	Prouton Lakes, B.C.	G. C. Ridley & Ross Gillespie	G. C. Ridley & Ross Gillespie	1976	81
15³/₁₆	9³/₁₆	6	M	Emery Co., Utah	Dan Scartezina	Dan Scartezina	1976	81
15²/₁₆	9²/₁₆	6¹/₁₆	M	Garfield Co., Utah	William A. Coats	William A. Coats	1978	81
15²/₁₆	8¹²/₁₆	6⁶/₁₆	U	East Kootenay, B. C.	Martin Marigeau	C. Garrett	1940	100
15²/₁₆	8¹⁴/₁₆	6⁴/₁₆	M	Benewak Co., Idaho	Karl Paulson	Karl Paulson	1945	100
15²/₁₆	9¹/₁₆	6¹/₁₆	M	Salmon River, Idaho	Bob Hagel	Bob Hagel	1950	100
15²/₁₆	8¹⁵/₁₆	6³/₁₆	M	Strawberry, Ariz.	Irene Morden	Irene Morden	1958	100
15²/₁₆	8¹⁴/₁₆	6⁴/₁₆	M	Pine, Ariz.	C. J. Prock	C. J. Prock	1958	100
15²/₁₆	9	6²/₁₆	M	Allison, Colo.	Georgianna Etheridge	Georgianna Etheridge	1962	100

				Location			Year	Score
15 2/16	9 1/16	6 2/16	M	New Harmony, Utah	Art Coates	Art Coates	1962	100
15 2/16	8 13/16	6 6/16	M	Coleman, Alta.	Ted & Connie Michalsky	Ted & Connie Michalsky	1962	100
15 2/16	8 11/16	6 4/16	M	Lendrum Creek, Alta.	Gary G. Giese	Gary G. Giese	1964	100
15 2/16	8 14/16	6 4/16	M	Parowan, Utah	William Mastrangel	William Mastrangel	1964	100
15 2/16	8 14/16	6 4/16	M	Reserve, N. M.	Wilmer C. Hansen	Wilmer C. Hansen	1966	100
15 2/16	8 15/16	6 3/16	M	Saratoga, Wyo.	Win Condict	Win Condict	1967	100
15 2/16	8 12/16	6 6/16	M	Little Fort, B. C.	Earl E. Hill	Earl E. Hill	1968	100
15 2/16	8 15/16	6 3/16	M	Duchesne Co., Utah	Clyde C. Edwards	Clyde C. Edwards	1969	100
15 2/16	8 12/16	6 6/16	M	Okaragan Valley, Wash.	Patrick M. Davis	Patrick M. Davis	1970	100
15 2/16	8 14/16	6 4/16	M	Manzano Mts., N. M.	C. J. McElroy	C. J. McElroy	1970	100
15 2/16	8 14/16	6 4/16	M	Duchesne Co., Utah	Richard B. Sydnor, Jr.	Richard B. Sydnor, Jr.	1972	100
15 2/16	8 12/16	6 2/16	M	Ferry Co., Wash.	Paul L. Watts	Paul L. Watts	1972	100
15 2/16	8 14/16	6 4/16	M	Stevens Co., Wash.	Leroy W. Kindsvogel	Leroy W. Kindsvogel	1972	100
15 2/16	8 13/16	6 5/16	M	Lincoln Co., Mont.	Katherine Kimberlin	Katherine Kimberlin	1973	100
15 2/16	9	6 2/16	M	Carbon Co., Utah	L. A. Grelling	L. A. Grelling	1974	100
15 2/16	9	6 2/16	M	Pend Oreille Co., Wash.	Robert J. Robertson	Robert J. Robertson	1974	100
15 2/16	8 11/16	6 7/16	M	Granby River, B.C.	Everett B. Pannkuk, Jr.	Everett B. Pannkuk, Jr.	1977	100
15 2/16	8 13/16	6 5/16	M	Cascade Range, B.C.	Dennis C. Roach	Dennis C. Roach	1978	100
15 2/16	8 15/16	6 3/16	M	Uintah Co., Utah	Dale Larson	Dale Larson	1978	100
15 2/16	8 14/16	6 4/16	M	Mt. Roderick, B.C.	Gail Holderman	Gail Holderman	1979	100
15 1/16	8 13/16	6 5/16	M	Okanogan Co., Wash.	Francis Randall	Francis Randall	1948	126
15 1/16	8 13/16	6 3/16	U	Princeton, B. C.	Alan Gill	C. F. Gigot	1948	126
15 1/16	8 15/16	6 5/16	M	Saratoga, Wyo.	Win Condict	Win Condict	1954	126
15 1/16	8 8/16	6 8/16	M	Ferris Mts., Wyo.	Win Condict & Ernie Levasseur	Win Condict	1959	126
15 1/16	8 14/16	6 3/16	M	Cat Creek, Alta.	Hyrum R. Baker	Hyrum R. Baker	1960	126
15 1/16	9	6 1/16	M	Wild Horse Basin, Wyo.	Win Condict	Win Condict	1961	126
15 1/16	8 13/16	6 4/16	M	Custer Co., Idaho	Joe Blackburn	Joe Blackburn	1962	126
15 1/16	8 14/16	6 3/16	M	Oliver, B. C.	Allan Nichol	Allan Nichol	1963	126
15 1/16	9	6 1/16	M	Clearwater River, Idaho	Ted Hall	Ted Hall	1964	126
15 1/16	8 14/16	6 3/16	M	Mineral Co., Mont.	Richard Ramberg	Neal & Richard Ramberg	1966	126
15 1/16	8 12/16	6 5/16	M	Missoula Co., Mcnt.	William Zeiler	William Zeiler	1966	126
15 1/16	8 14/16	6 3/16	M	Clearwater Co., Idaho	Robert W. Haskin	Robert W. Haskin	1967	126
15 1/16	8 13/16	6 6/16	M	Lincolr Co., Mont.	H. M. (Bert) Johnston	H. M. (Bert) Johnston	1967	126
15 1/16	8 13/16	6 4/16	M	S. Castle River, Alta.	James F. Simpson	James F. Simpson	1967	126
15 1/16	8 13/16	6 4/16	M	Little Fort, B. C.	Earl E. Hill	Earl E. Hill	1968	126
15 1/16	8 15/16	6 2/16	M	Oroville, Wash.	Dan Lynch	Dan Lynch	1968	126
15 1/16	9 1/16	6	M	Price, Utah	Robert H. Elder	Robert H. Elder	1968	126
15 1/16	9 1/16	6	M	Sunflower, Ariz.	John C. Shaw	John C. Shaw	1969	126
15 1/16	8 14/16	6 3/16	M	Douglas Co., Colo.	C. R. Anderson & E. H. Brown	Charles R. Anderson	1969	126
15 1/16	8 12/16	6 5/16	M	Mineral Co., Mont.	William E. Bullock	William E. Bullock	1971	126
15 1/16	9 1/16	6	M	Gunlock, Utah	L. Dean Taylor	L. Dean Taylor	1971	126

149

COUGAR OR MOUNTAIN LION–Continued
Felis concolor hippolestes and related subspecies

Score	Greatest Length of Skull Without Lower Jaw	Greatest Width of Skull	Sex	Locality Killed	By Whom Killed	Owner	Date Killed	Rank
15¹/₁₆	9	6¹/₁₆	M	Superior, Mont.	James L. Schaeffer	James L. Schaeffer	1972	126
15¹/₁₆	8¹³/₁₆	6¹/₁₆	M	Uintah Co., Utah	Brent L. Winchester	Brent L. Winchester	1972	126
15¹/₁₆	8¹⁴/₁₆	6³/₁₆	M	Pima Co., Ariz.	George W. Parker	George W. Parker	1972	126
15¹/₁₆	8¹³/₁₆	6⁴/₁₆	M	Emery Co., Utah	Sharon Ann Burkett	Sharon Ann Burkett	1973	126
15¹/₁₆	8¹⁵/₁₆	6²/₁₆	M	Granite Co., Mont.	James A. Raikos	James A. Raikos	1973	126
15¹/₁₆	8¹⁴/₁₆	6³/₁₆	M	Idaho Co., Idaho	Chester D. Haight	Chester D. Haight	1975	126
15¹/₁₆	8¹⁵/₁₆	6³/₁₆	M	Lake Co., Mont.	J. E. McCreedy & R. E. Seabaug	James McCreedy	1977	126
15¹/₁₆	8¹³/₁₆	6⁴/₁₆	M	Pend Oreille Co., Wash.	William M. Day	William M. Day	1978	126
15¹/₁₆	9¹/₁₆	6	M	Piute Co., Utah	Fred J. Markley	Fred J. Markley	1979	126
15	8¹³/₁₆	6³/₁₆	M	Grand Forks, B. C.	Clarence C. Bahr	Clarence C. Bahr	—	156
15	9	6	M	Columbia River, Wash.	J. K. Townsend	Acad. Nat. Sci., Phil.	1834	156
15	9	6	M	Dotsero, Colo.	J. T. Meirer	Univ. Kansas Museum	1887	156
15	8¹²/₁₆	6⁴/₁₆	M	Lincoln Co., Mont.	Frank Haacke	Univ. Of Montana	1950	156
15	8¹⁵/₁₆	6¹/₁₆	M	Salmon River, Idaho	Bob Hagel	Bob Hagel	1953	156
15	8¹³/₁₆	6³/₁₆	M	Iron Co., Utah	James A. Worthen	James A. Worthen	1958	156
15	8¹¹/₁₆	6⁵/₁₆	M	Elko Co., Nev.	Earl Dudley	Earl Dudley	1959	156
15	8¹⁴/₁₆	6¹/₁₆	M	Salmon River, Idaho	Roy Tumilsen	Roy Tumilsen	1959	156
15	8¹⁵/₁₆	6¹/₁₆	M	Invermere, B. C.	R. A. Merkner	R. A. Merkner	1959	156
15	8¹³/₁₆	6³/₁₆	M	Flat Creek, Alta.	Hyrum R. Baker	Hyrum R. Baker	1960	156
15	8⁸/₁₆	6⁸/₁₆	M	Magdalena Mts., N. M.	F. C. Hibben	F. C. Hibben	1960	156
15	8¹³/₁₆	6³/₁₆	M	Cranbrook, B. C.	Unknown	Aasland Taxidermy	1961	156
15	8¹²/₁₆	6⁴/₁₆	M	Powell Co., Mont.	Copenhaver Bros.	Norris Pratt	1961	156
15	8¹²/₁₆	6⁴/₁₆	M	Onyx, Calif.	Ray Mallory	Larry Mansfield	1961	156
15	8¹⁴/₁₆	6²/₁₆	M	Lumby, B. C.	Ronald Catt	Ronald Catt	1962	156
15	9	6	M	Jesmond, B. C.	Charlie Coldwell	Charlie Coldwell	1963	156
15	8¹⁰/₁₆	6⁶/₁₆	M	Socorro Co., N. M.	Hugh Olney	Hugh Olney	1964	156
15	9	6	U	Grass Valley, Oreg.	Danny Henderson	Danny Henderson	1965	156
15	8¹²/₁₆	6⁴/₁₆	M	Mesa Co., Colo.	John Adams	John Adams	1965	156
15	8¹²/₁₆	6⁴/₁₆	M	West Kootenay, B. C.	M. E. Goddard	M. E. Goddard	1966	156
15	8¹¹/₁₆	6⁵/₁₆	M	Darfield, B. C.	Ted Scott	Ted Scott	1966	156

15	8¹³/₁₆	M	Selway River, Idaho	Ken Wolfinbarger	Ken Wolfinbarger	1966	156
15	8¹²/₁₆	M	Idaho Co., Idaho	Jack D. Sheppard	Jack D. Sheppard	1966	156
15	8¹⁴/₁₆	M	Hanksville, Utah	Eddie D. Scheinost	Eddie D. Scheinost	1967	156
15	8¹²/₁₆	M	Fisher Creek, Alta.	Perry Jacobson	Ferry Jacobson	1967	156
15	8¹²/₁₆	M	Ferndale, Mont.	Loren R. Wittrock	Loren R. Wittrock	1967	156
15	8¹⁴/₁₆	M	Wolf Creek, Mont.	Gus R. Wolfe	Gus R. Wolfe & Jim Lee	1967	156
15	8¹³/₁₆	M	Spanish Fork Canyon, Utah	Richard C. Smith	Richard C. Smith	1968	156
15	8¹¹/₁₆	M	Alpine Co., Calif.	Jeffrey A. Brent	Jeffrey A. Brent	1968	156
15	8¹⁵/₁₆	M	Canon City, Colo.	Dale R. Leonard	Dale R. Leonard	1969	156
15	8¹⁴/₁₆	M	Lucile, Idaho	Carl P. Bentz	Mrs. W. H. Prescott, Jr.	1969	156
15	8¹¹/₁₆	M	Mizzezula Mts., B. C.	Bengt G. Bjalme	Bengt G. Bjalme	1969	156
15	8¹²/₁₆	M	Stevens Co., Wash.	Norman Willey & Lee Hedrick	Norman Willey & Lee Hedrick	1969	156
15	8¹⁰/₁₆	M	Ferry Co., Wash.	John D. Mercer	John D. Mercer	1969	156
15	8¹²/₁₆	M	Wells, Nev.	Marvin Johnson	Marvin Johnson	1970	156
15	8¹³/₁₆	M	Canon City, Colo.	Glen Rosengarten	Glen Rosengarten	1970	156
15	9	M	Antelope Pass, Colo.	Phil Nichols	Phil Nichols	1971	156
15	8¹³/₁₆	M	Kootenai Co., Idaho	George H. Daly	George H. Daly	1971	156
15	8¹⁴/₁₆	M	Millard Co., Utah	Picked Up	Utah Div. Wild.	1974	156
15	8¹⁴/₁₆	U	Las Animas Co., Colo.	Maricn M. Snyder	Mike Powell	1974	156
15	8¹²/₁₆	M	Stevens Co., Wash.	Roger Lofts	Roger Lofts	1974	156
15	8¹²/₁₆	M	Ashcroft, B. C.	Ken Kilback	Ken Kilback	1975	156
15	8¹²/₁₆	M	Union Co., Oregon	Brian Spencer	Brian Spencer	1977	156
15	8¹⁴/₁₆	M	Latah Co., Idaho	Earl Landrus	Earl Landrus	1977	156
15	8¹³/₁₆	M	Huerfano Co., Colo.	Sheila D. Bisgard	Sheila D. Bisgard	1977	156
15	8¹³/₁₆	M	Prouton Lakes, B.C.	G. C. Ridley	G. C. Ridley & Ross Gillespie	1977	156
15	8¹⁵/₁₆	M	Skookumchuck Creek, B.C.	Jack Walkley, Jr.	Jack Walkley, Jr.	1979	156

*Final Score subject to revision by additional verifying measurements.

WORLD'S RECORD ATLANTIC WALRUS TUSKS
SCORE: 118 6/8
Locality: Greenland. Date: before 1955
Hunter: unknown.
Donated by Roy Vail to the National Collection.

Atlantic Walrus

Minimum Score 95

Odobenus rosmarus rosmarus

Score	Entire Length of Loose Tusk R.	Entire Length of Loose Tusk L.	Circumference of Base R.	Circumference of Base L.	Circumference at Third Quarter R.	Circumference at Third Quarter L.	Sex	Locality Killed	By Whom Killed	Owner	Date Killed	Rank
118 6/8	30 5/8	30 3/8	8 3/8	8 4/8	5 3/8	5 3/8	U	Greenland	Gift Of Roy Vail	National Collection	PR1955	1
117 6/8	27 1/8	26 3/8	9 2/8	9 2/8	5 6/8	5 7/8	M	Greenland	Unknown	Zool. Mus., Copenhagen	—	2
116 6/8	29 3/8	29 3/8	7 3/8	7 4/8	6	5 7/8	M	Greenland	Unknown	Zool. Mus., Copenhagen	—	3
114	28 6/8	28	7 4/8	7 1/8	6	5 7/8	M	Greenland	Unknown	Zool. Mus., Copenhagen	—	4
105	25	25	7	7	5 4/8	5 4/8	M	Greenland	Unknown	Demarest Memorial Mus.	1909	5
103 4/8	24 6/8	25	7 4/8	7 7/8	5 2/8	5	M	Crockerland, Greenland	D. B. Macmillan	Am. Mus. Nat. History	PR1916	6
100 6/8	23 7/8	23 5/8	7 4/8	7 2/8	5 2/8	5 3/8	U	Unknown	Unknown	Zool. Mus., Copenhagen	—	7
98 4/8	22 3/8	20 7/8	8 2/8	8 3/8	4 7/8	4 5/8	M	Arctic Ocean	Gift Of Peary Arctic Club	Am. Mus. Nat. History	PR1899	8
98 4/8	24 4/8	24	6 7/8	6 7/8	5 2/8	5 1/8	M	Crockerland, Greenland	D. B. Macmillan	Am. Mus. Nat. History	PR1916	8

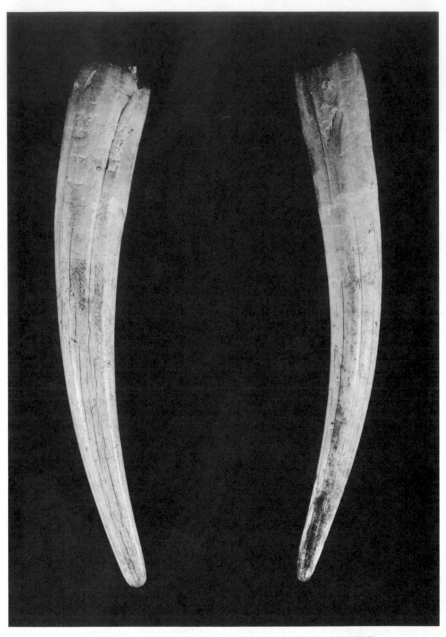

WORLD'S RECORD PACIFIC WALRUS TUSKS
SCORE: 145 6/8
Locality: Point Hope, Alaska. Date: 1957.
Hunter: an Eskimo. Owner: Jonas Brothers of Seattle.

Pacific Walrus

Odobenus rosmarus divergens

Minimum Score 100

Score	Entire Length of Loose Tusk R.	Entire Length of Loose Tusk L.	Circumference of Base R.	Circumference of Base L.	Circumference at Third Quarter R.	Circumference at Third Quarter L.	Sex	Locality Killed	By Whom Killed	Owner	Date Killed	Rank
145 6/8	32 2/8	32 1/8	12 2/8	13	7 2/8	7 1/8	M	Point Hope, Alaska	Eskimos	Jonas Bros. Of Seattle	1957	1
142 2/8	40 1/8	39 6/8	9 5/8	9 4/8	5 4/8	5 5/8	M	Bering Sea, Alaska	Bill Foster	Foster's Bighorn Rest.	1940	2
138 4/8*	35 2/8	35 1/8	9 3/8	9 2/8	6 6/8	6 2/8	M	St. Lawrence Island, Alaska	Valentin De Madariaga	Valentin De Madariaga	1976	3
137 2/8	36 2/8	36 2/8	9 7/8	10 2/8	6	6 1/8	M	Unknown	Gift Of N. A. Caesar	National Collection	PR1910	4
136 2/8	35 6/8	35	9 5/8	9 3/8	6 3/8	6	M	Bristol Bay, Alaska	Eskimo	James W. Brooks	1955	5
135	38	36 3/8	9	9 4/8	5 6/8	5 6/8	M	Unknown	Picked Up	Paul Umlauf	1970	6
134 6/8	34	34 2/8	9 3/8	9 4/8	6	6	M	Wainwright, Alaska	Helen Burnett	Helen Burnett	1964	7
133 6/8*	32 2/8	32 6/8	9 4/8	9 4/8	6 6/8	6 7/8	M	Diomede Island, Alaska	Eskimo	Univ. Iowa Museum	1893	8
133 6/8	34 4/8	36 3/8	8 7/8	8 5/8	6 7/8	6 4/8	M	Togiak Bay, Alaska	Picked Up	Bill Renfrew	1949	8
133 6/8*	32 5/8	33 1/8	9 7/8	10	6 4/8	6 6/8	M	Nunivak Island, Alaska	Ray Cyr	Ray Cyr	1978	8
133	35	35 2/8	8 4/8	8 4/8	6	6	M	St. Lawrence Island, Alaska	Eskimo	Eugene Saxton	1956	11
132 4/8	38 1/8	37 6/8	8 5/8	8 6/8	5 4/8	5 5/8	U	Alaska	Unknown	Harvard Univ. Museum	1870	12
132 4/8	37 6/8	35 3/8	8 6/8	8 6/8	6 2/8	5 5/8	M	St. Lawrence Island, Alaska	Eskimo	Adventurers Club Of N.Y.	1964	12
132 4/8	34 1/8	34	10 3/8	9 3/8	6 2/8	5 7/8	M	Hazen Bay, Alaska	Daniel B. Moore	Daniel B. Moore	1979	12
132 2/8	33 6/8	32 5/8	9 2/8	9	6 5/8	6 4/8	M	St. Lawrence Island, Alaska	Robert F. Hurford	Robert F. Hurford	1959	15
132	35 2/8	34	9 4/8	8 7/8	7 1/8	5 7/8	M	Savoonga, Alaska	Unknown	Victor Rovier	1967	16
132	29	28 6/8	10 4/8	10 5/8	7 3/8	6 7/8	M	Savoonga, Alaska	Gordon Iya	C. Vernon Humble	1977	16
131 4/8	36 3/8	35 2/8	8 4/8	8 4/8	5 5/8	5 5/8	M	Bering Sea, Alaska	Gift Of Wm. H. White	Am. Mus. Nat. History	1916	18
131 2/8	33 1/8	33 4/8	8 4/8	8 4/8	6 4/8	6 4/8	M	Wainwright, Alaska	Eskimo	Ken Armstrong	PR1946	19
131 2/8	31 5/8	31 6/8	9 1/8	9 4/8	6 6/8	6 4/8	M	Savoonga, Alaska	Robert M. Vinovich	Robert M. Vinovich	1976	19
131	33 5/8	34 2/8	8 5/8	8 5/8	6 2/8	6 2/8	M	Hagemeister Island, Alaska	Picked Up	Frank M. Thomason	1964	21
130 6/8	33 5/8	32 3/8	8 7/8	9 1/8	6 3/8	6 4/8	M	St. Lawrence Island, Alaska	Peter W. Bading	Peter W. Bading	1960	22
130 4/8	34 7/8	34 4/8	8 2/8	8	6 3/8	6 1/8	M	St. Lawrence Island, Alaska	Unknown	Univ. Of Alaska	PR1939	23
130 4/8	36 4/8	35 7/8	8 4/8	8	6 3/8	5 6/8	M	St. Lawrence Island, Alaska	George H. Landreth	George H. Landreth	1967	23
130 2/8	34 6/8	35	9	8 6/8	5 6/8	5 4/8	U	Point Barrow, Alaska	Eskimos	C. R. Gutermuth	1952	25
130 2/8	31 2/8	32	8 7/8	8 7/8	7 2/8	7 1/8	M	St. Lawrence Island, Alaska	Grancel Fitz	Mrs. Grancel Fitz	1957	25
129 4/8	34 6/8	33 4/8	8 3/8	8 3/8	6 4/8	6 1/8	M	Bering Sea, Alaska	Joseph J. Cafmeyer	Joseph J. Cafmeyer	1976	27
128	30 6/8	30 4/8	9 2/8	9 2/8	7 1/8	7	M	Savoonga, Alaska	W. M. Wheless, III	W. M. Wheless, III	1977	28
127 6/8	35 6/8	34 4/8	8 5/8	8 2/8	5 4/8	5 2/8	M	St. Lawrence Island, Alaska	Chris Klineburger	Chris Klineburger	1961	29
127 6/8	32 7/8	33	9	8 7/8	6	5 5/8	M	Nome, Alaska	Charles F. Kleptz	Charles F. Kleptz	1978	29
127 2/8	33 7/8	34 6/8	8 1/8	8 3/8	5 4/8	5 6/8	M	Wainwright, Alaska	J. Richard Reuter, III	J. Richard Reuter, III	1970	31
127	32 4/8	32 4/8	8 3/8	8 3/8	6 1/8	6	M	Pt. Barrow, Alaska	Karl W. Opryshek	Karl W. Opryshek	1965	32

Pacific Walrus–*Continued*

Odobenus rosmarus divergens

Score	Entire Length of Loose Tusk R.	L.	Circumference of Base R.	L.	Circumference at Third Quarter R.	L.	Sex	Locality Killed	By Whom Killed	Owner	Date Killed	Rank
127	33	32 7/8	8 5/8	9	5 6/8	6	M	St. Lawrence Island, Alaska	Norman W. Garwood	Norman W. Garwood	1976	32
127	32 4/8	32 5/8	8 4/8	9	6	6 2/8	M	St. Lawrence Island, Alaska	Dick Ullery	Dick Ullery	1976	32
126 2/8	32 3/8	32 7/8	8 5/8	8 4/8	6	5 6/8	M	St. Lawrence Island, Alaska	Martin J. Foerster	Martin J. Foerster	1958	35
126 2/8	31 6/8	31 1/8	9	8 6/8	6 2/8	6 2/8	M	Pt. Barrow, Alaska	Eskimos	Walter O. Sinn	1958	35
126 2/8	34 3/8	34 4/8	8	8 1/8	5 3/8	5 6/8	M	Savoonga, Alaska	Unknown	Wayne S. Weiler	1978	35
126	33 4/8	33	8	8	5 6/8	6 1/8	M	Alaska Pen., Alaska	Unknown	Sam Pancotto	1962	38
126	31 1/8	31 3/8	8 4/8	8 3/8	6 6/8	6 7/8	M	Bering Sea, Alaska	Wakon Iron Redbird	Wakon Iron Redbird	1977	38
125 6/8	34 2/8	34 5/8	7 6/8	7 6/8	5 6/8	5 7/8	M	St. Lawrence Island, Alaska	Eskimos	Sidney T. Shore	1950	40
125 6/8	30 4/8	30 4/8	9 5/8	9 3/8	6 1/8	6	M	St. Lawrence Island, Alaska	F. J. Bremer	F. J. Bremer	1971	40
125 4/8	35	34 4/8	8 6/8	8 5/8	4 7/8	4 7/8	M	Bering Sea, Alaska	Manfred O. Schroeder	Manfred O. Schroeder	1977	42
124 6/8	33 6/8	33 5/8	8 2/8	8 3/8	5 2/8	5	M	Bering Sea	Henry A. Snow	Snow Museum	1923	43
124 6/8	30 7/8	32	9 1/8	9 4/8	5 3/8	5 6/8	M	St. Lawrence Island, Alaska	Bert Klineburger	Bert Klineburger	1962	43
124 6/8	33 4/8	34 1/8	8 1/8	8	5 6/8	5 6/8	M	St. Lawrence Island, Alaska	Kenneth Campbell	Kenneth Campbell	1972	43
124 4/8	32 7/8	32 4/8	7 5/8	8 4/8	6 1/8	7 1/8	M	Pilot Point, Alaska	Picked Up	Dick Gunlogson	——	46
124 4/8	32 4/8	31 5/8	8 7/8	8 2/8	5 7/8	5 7/8	M	St. Lawrence Island, Alaska	Tim Gollorgeren	George H. Landreth	1966	46
124 4/8	36 2/8	35 6/8	7	7 1/8	5 1/8	5 3/8	M	Nunivak Island, Alaska	Terry Yager	Terry Yager	1977	46
124 2/8	32 6/8	33 1/8	8	8 4/8	5 6/8	6	M	Bering Sea, Alaska	F. E. Klinesmith	Am. Mus. Nat. History	——	49
124	35	33 6/8	7 3/8	7 5/8	5 6/8	6	M	St. Lawrence Island, Alaska	Bert Klineburger	Bert Klineburger	1969	50
123 6/8	34 7/8	33 4/8	7 6/8	7 3/8	5 5/8	5 6/8	M	Little Diomede Island, Alaska	Eskimo	James W. Brooks	1953	51
123 6/8	33 7/8	33 3/8	8 3/8	8	5 1/8	5 2/8	M	Bering Sea, Alaska	Dick Salemi	Dick Salemi	1978	51
123 4/8	29 3/8	29 1/8	9	8 6/8	6 2/8	6 3/8	M	St. Lawrence Island, Alaska	C. J. McElroy	C. J. McElroy	1968	53
123 4/8	31 5/8	32	9	8 1/8	5 5/8	5 7/8	M	Bering Sea, Alaska	Dan H. Brainard	Dan H. Brainard	1977	53
123 4/8	30	29 7/8	9 4/8	9 4/8	5 6/8	5 5/8	M	Bering Sea, Alaska	Arthur H. Bullerdick	Arthur H. Bullerdick	1978	53
123 2/8	34	31 7/8	8 4/8	8 4/8	5 5/8	5 3/8	M	Alaskan Arctic	Eskimo	Robert C. Reeve	PR1955	56
123 2/8	32 3/8	32 2/8	7 4/8	7 4/8	6 1/8	6 1/8	M	Nakuck, Alaska	Unknown	Leonard Schwah	1964	56
123 2/8	28 5/8	28 2/8	9 7/8	9 7/8	6 2/8	6 4/8	M	Teller, Alaska	Wm. J. Glunt	Wm. J. Glunt	1965	56
123	32 5/8	32 1/8	7 4/8	7 7/8	6 3/8	6 7/8	M	Cape Constantine, Alaska	Picked Up	Ray Tremblay	1960	59
123	31	31	8 2/8	8	6 2/8	6	M	St. Lawrence Island, Alaska	F. Phillips Williamson	F. Phillips Williamson	1961	59
123	33	32 5/8	7 5/8	7 5/8	6	5 5/8	M	Nunivak Island, Alaska	Arvid F. Benson	Arvid F. Benson	1970	59
122 6/8	32 3/8	31 2/8	8	7 6/8	6	6 4/8	M	Alaska	George Wright	Acad. Nat. Sci., Phil.	1960	62
122 6/8	32 5/8	31 6/8	8 1/8	8 1/8	5 6/8	5 6/8	M	Savoonga, Alaska	Lynn M. Castle	Lynn M. Castle	1971	62
122 4/8	32 1/8	31 4/8	8 4/8	8 3/8	5 7/8	5 6/8	M	St. Lawrence Island, Alaska	Herb Klein	Herb Klein	1959	64

122 4/8	32 2/8	32 5/8	8 2/8	8	5 4/8	5 5/8	M	Savoonga, Alaska	William W. Garrison	William W. Garrison	1971	64
122 2/8	30	32 2/8	8 2/8	8 2/8	6 3/8	6 2/8	M	Walrus Island, Alaska	Unknown	Robert C. Reeve	1962	66
122	27 2/8	28 6/8	10 2/8	10 2/8	5 7/8	6	M	Diomede Island, Alaska	Tony Oney	Tony Oney	1964	67
122	31 4/8	31 1/8	9 1/8	9 2/8	5 3/8	5 3/8	M	St. Lawrence Island, Alaska	Ted Lick	Ted Lick	1970	67
121 6/8	31 7/8	32 6/8	8 1/8	8 6/8	5 3/8	5 4/8	M	Diomede Island, Alaska	Jim Harrower	Tony Oney	1964	69
121 4/8	31 6/8	31	8 4/8	8 4/8	5 4/8	5 4/8	M	Savoonga, Alaska	Gerald G. Balciar	Gerald G. Balciar	1971	70
121 2/8	31 3/8	31 2/8	8 3/8	8 4/8	5 3/8	5 6/8	M	Savoonga, Alaska	Lowell C. Hansen, II	Lowell C. Hansen, II	1978	71
121	33 2/8	34 1/8	7 6/8	7 5/8	5 5/8	5 3/8	F	Bering Sea, Alaska	Eskimo	Elmer Keith	1956	72
121	28	28 5/8	11 2/8	9 6/8	5 6/8	5 7/8	M	Little Diomede Island, Alaska	William H. Picher	William H. Picher	1966	72
121	29 4/8	29 4/8	8 2/8	8 2/8	6 3/8	6	M	Nunivak Island, Alaska	C. Vernon Humble	C. Vernon Humble	1977	72
120 6/8	29 7/8	30 4/8	8 4/8	8 7/8	6	6	M	Cape Thompson, Alaska	Eskimo	Nick Petropolis	——	75
120 6/8	33 6/8	34	6 7/8	7	5 3/8	5 4/8	M	Point Hope, Alaska	Don Johnson	Don Johnson	1963	75
120 6/8	29	29 1/8	8 4/8	8 3/8	6 3/8	5 7/8	M	Little Diomede Island, Alaska	Robert Curtis	Robert Curtis	1963	75
120 6/8	29	30 1/8	9	9	5 7/8	5 6/8	M	Gambell, Alaska	L. Keith Mortensen	L. Keith Mortensen	1978	75
120 4/8	33 4/8	33 4/8	7	7 1/8	5 2/8	5 3/8	U	Alaska	S. R. Caldwell	Acad. Nat. Sci., Phil.	1902	79
120 2/8	28 7/8	29 1/8	9	9 1/8	5 4/8	5 4/8	M	Savoonga, Alaska	Werner-Rolf Muno	Werner-Rolf Muno	1971	80
120 2/8	30 2/8	29 4/8	8 4/8	8 3/8	5 7/8	5 7/8	M	Hazen Bay, Alaska	Richard D. Dimick	Richard D. Dimick	1979	80
120	33	30 6/8	8 4/8	8 4/8	5 2/8	6	M	St. Lawrence Island, Alaska	Sarkis Atamian	Sarkis Atamian	1968	82
120	31 6/8	29 2/8	8 7/8	8 4/8	5 6/8	6	M	Bering Sea, Alaska	George L. Hall	George L. Hall	1977	82
119 6/8	28	28 1/8	9 3/8	8 7/8	6 6/8	6 5/8	M	Savoonga, Alaska	Ed Cox, Jr.	Ed Cox, Jr.	1977	84
119 2/8	31 1/8	31 2/8	7 6/8	8	5 4/8	5 4/8	M	Bering Sea, Alaska	Unknown	Eugene M. Erwin	PR1975	85
119 2/8	31 5/8	30 3/8	8	8	5 7/8	5 7/8	M	Savoonga, Alaska	Douglas E. Miller	Douglas E. Miller	1976	85
119	31 4/8	30 2/8	9 1/8	8 4/8	5 5/8	5 1/8	U	Port Moller, Alaska	Picked Up	Bob Stokes	1961	87
118 6/8	29	27 5/8	9 1/8	9 3/8	6 1/8	6	U	Bristol Bay, Alaska	Eskimo	Foster H. Thompson	PR1959	88
118 4/8	28 3/8	28 6/8	8 2/8	8 4/8	6 2/8	5 7/8	M	Diomede Island, Alaska	Harry J. Armitage	Harry J. Armitage	1965	89
118 4/8	29 3/8	28 7/8	8 7/8	8 3/8	6 1/8	5 7/8	M	St. Lawrence Island, Alaska	Alice J. Landreth	Alice J. Landreth	1967	89
118 4/8	29 2/8	28 2/8	8 4/8	8 7/8	6 6/8	5 6/8	M	St. Lawrence Island, Alaska	Wilber L. Leworthy	Wilber L. Leworthy	1970	89
118 2/8	30 4/8	29 7/8	7 7/8	8	5 5/8	5 5/8	M	Savoonga, Alaska	Jack Schwabland	Jack Schwabland	1978	92
117 2/8	29	28 4/8	8	7 6/8	6	5 7/8	M	Little Diomede Island, Alaska	Robert Curtis	Robert Curtis	1963	93
117 2/8	28	30 1/8	8 5/8	8 2/8	6 4/8	5 7/8	M	St. Lawrence Island, Alaska	C. Pitt Sanders	C. Pitt Sanders	1978	93
116 6/8	28 6/8	26 7/8	8 6/8	9	6	5 6/8	M	Little Diomede Island, Alaska	Eskimos	Tony Oney	1962	95
116 4/8	28 6/8	27 2/8	8 7/8	8 5/8	6	6	M	Savoonga, Alaska	Arnold Carlson	Arnold Carlson	1971	96
116	28	28	8 3/8	8 3/8	5 6/8	5 5/8	M	Point Hope, Alaska	Picked Up	William C. Penttila	1965	97
116	30 3/8	29 6/8	8 6/8	8 2/8	5 1/8	5	M	Bering Sea, Alaska	Hugh L. Nichols, Jr.	Hugh L. Nichols, Jr.	1972	97
115 6/8	28 7/8	29	7 6/8	8 2/8	5 7/8	5 6/8	M	St. Lawrence Island, Alaska	Hugh H. Logan	U. S. Natl. Museum	1962	99
115 6/8	27 3/8	31 4/8	8 1/8	8	6 3/8	6	M	Savoonga, Alaska	Peter A. Bossart	Peter A. Bossart	1972	99
115 6/8	30 5/8	29 6/8	8	7 7/8	5 3/8	5 3/8	M	St. Lawrence Island, Alaska	Gerald L. Warnock	Gerald L. Warnock	1977	99
115 4/8	30 2/8	30 1/8	7 6/8	7 4/8	5 4/8	5 3/8	M	Diomede Island, Alaska	Unknown	Univ. Of Alaska	1953	102
115 4/8	27 2/8	25 2/8	9 2/8	9 2/8	6 1/8	6 1/8	M	St. Lawrence Island, Alaska	W. T. Yoshimoto	W. T. Yoshimoto	1962	102
115 4/8	28 1/8	28 2/8	7 6/8	7 6/8	6 2/8	6 2/8	M	Little Diomede Island, Alaska	Basil C. Bradbury	Basil C. Bradbury	1964	102
115 2/8	30 4/8	31	7 2/8	7 4/8	5 1/8	5 3/8	M	Little Diomede Island, Alaska	Jack D. Putnam	Jack D. Putnam	1965	105
115 2/8	27 6/8	31 6/8	8 6/8	8 7/8	5 5/8	5 2/8	M	Nunivak Island, Alaska	Lloyd Ward	Lloyd Ward	1971	105
115	31 1/8	30 7/8	6 7/8	7	5 4/8	5 6/8	M	Savoonga, Alaska	John Estes	John Estes	1978	107

PACIFIC WALRUS–*Continued*

Odobenus rosmarus divergens

Score	Entire Length of Loose Tusk R.	Entire Length of Loose Tusk L.	Circumference of Base R.	Circumference of Base L.	Circumference at Third Quarter R.	Circumference at Third Quarter L.	Sex	Locality Killed	By Whom Killed	Owner	Date Killed	Rank
114 6/8	29 6/8	29 4/8	7 6/8	7 6/8	5 3/8	5	U	Point Hope, Alaska	Eskimo	Jonas Bros. Of Alaska	1958	108
114 6/8	29	29 5/8	7 3/8	7 5/8	5 6/8	5 6/8	M	Kigluaik Mts., Alaska	Russell H. Underdahl	Russell H. Underdahl	1978	108
114 4/8	29 3/8	29 4/8	8 2/8	8 2/8	5 1/8	5 1/8	M	Savoonga, Alaska	Richard G. Van Vorst	Richard G. Van Vorst	1976	110
114	26 4/8	26 6/8	9 5/8	9 6/8	5 2/8	5 1/8	M	Kotzebue, Alaska	E. B. (Dusty) Rhodes	E. B. (Dusty) Rhodes	1964	111
113 6/8	26	26 1/8	8 2/8	8 1/8	6 1/8	6	M	Point Hope, Alaska	Glenn W. Slade	Glenn W. Slade	1961	112
113 6/8	29	29 5/8	7 5/8	7 6/8	5 2/8	5 3/8	M	Point Hope, Alaska	Eskimos	John W. Elmore	1966	112
113 6/8	29 4/8	28 2/8	7 3/8	7 3/8	5 6/8	5 5/8	M	St. Lawrence Island, Alaska	Denver D. Coleman	Denver D. Coleman	1968	112
113 6/8	28 4/8	28 5/8	7 5/8	7 5/8	5 6/8	5 4/8	M	St. Lawrence Island, Alaska	Dick Davis	Dick Davis	1976	112
113 6/8	31 3/8	30 5/8	7 3/8	7 2/8	5 1/8	5 1/8	M	Savoonga, Alaska	Warren K. Parker	Warren K. Parker	1979	112
113 4/8	28 7/8	28 5/8	7 5/8	7 4/8	5 4/8	5 4/8	M	Savoonga, Alaska	Tom Anderson	Tom Anderson	1978	117
113 2/8	27 5/8	27 2/8	8 6/8	8 3/8	5 3/8	5 3/8	M	St. Lawrence Island, Alaska	W. Brandon Macomber	W. Brandon Macomber	1965	118
113 2/8	28 1/8	28 3/8	8 2/8	8 3/8	5	5 3/8	M	Nunivak Island, Alaska	C. R. Feazell	C. R. Feazell	1972	118
113 2/8	27 5/8	27 5/8	7 5/8	7 5/8	6 2/8	5 7/8	M	Bering Sea, Alaska	Jack Holland	Jack Holland	1978	118
113	29 5/8	29 4/8	8 1/8	8	5	5	M	St. Lawrence Island, Alaska	Jim Roe	Jim Roe	1969	121
113	30 4/8	29 1/8	7 2/8	7 3/8	5 4/8	5 4/8	M	St. Lawrence Island, Alaska	I. D. Shapiro	I. D. Shapiro	1970	121
113	28	27	8 3/8	8	5 5/8	5 3/8	M	St. Lawrence Island, Alaska	Gail W. Holderman	Gail W. Holderman	1976	121
113	27 1/8	26	8 1/8	8	6	6 1/8	M	Bering Sea, Alaska	Jon Everis Holland	Jon Everis Holland	1978	121
113	31 7/8	31	6 6/8	6 6/8	4 7/8	4 6/8	M	St. Lawrence Island, Alaska	G. A. Treschow	G. A. Treschow	1979	121
112 6/8	28 7/8	26 5/8	9	9 1/8	5 1/8	5 2/8	M	St. Lawrence Island, Alaska	Maitland Armstrong	Maitland Armstrong	1961	126
112 6/8	27 7/8	27 6/8	8 2/8	8 1/8	5 3/8	5 1/8	M	St. Lawrence Island, Alaska	Alfred F. Corwin	Alfred F. Corwin	1964	126
112 4/8	27 7/8	27 6/8	8 2/8	8 2/8	5 4/8	5 4/8	U	Togiak Bay, Alaska	Picked Up	Lloyd Zeman	—	128
112 4/8	28 1/8	27 7/8	7 7/8	7 4/8	5 5/8	6 2/8	M	St. Lawrence Island, Alaska	Henry K. Leworthy	Henry K. Leworthy	1970	128
112 4/8	25	23 6/8	8 6/8	8 5/8	6 4/8	6 6/8	M	Nunivak Island, Alaska	W. K. Leech	W. K. Leech	1972	128
112 4/8	28 6/8	27 5/8	7 5/8	7 4/8	5 6/8	5 5/8	M	Savoonga, Alaska	Harm De Boer	Harm De Boer	1972	128
112 2/8	29 4/8	28 7/8	7 4/8	7 6/8	5 1/8	5	M	St. Lawrence Island, Alaska	Eskimo	George H. Landreth	1966	132
111 6/8	27 4/8	32 1/8	8 6/8	8 4/8	4 4/8	6	M	Point Hope, Alaska	Gary D'Agile	Gary D'Agile	1968	133
111 6/8	30 4/8	26 4/8	8 1/8	7 6/8	5 7/8	5 5/8	M	St. Lawrence Island, Alaska	Don L. Corley	Don L. Corley	1977	133
111	28 3/8	28 1/8	7	6 7/8	5 5/8	5 5/8	M	Savoonga, Alaska	Robert Edward Speegle	Robert Edward Speegle	1972	135
111	28 5/8	30	7 7/8	8	4 5/8	4 7/8	M	St. Lawrence Island, Alaska	Don Skidmore	Don Skidmore	1977	135
110 6/8	29 1/8	30 1/8	7 6/8	7 6/8	4 6/8	4 6/8	M	Savoonga, Alaska	John M. Blair	John M. Blair	1971	137
110 4/8	29 7/8	27 5/8	6 3/8	7 3/8	5 6/8	5 7/8	M	St. Lawrence Island, Alaska	Hugh H. Logan	Los Angeles Co. Museum	1962	138
110 2/8	27 6/8	27 4/8	8	7 4/8	5 4/8	5 1/9	M	St. Lawrence Island, Alaska	Robert Rood	Robert Rood	1966	139

110 2/8	27	26 4/8	8 1/8	8	5 4/8	5 3/8	U	Kuskokwin Bay, Alaska	James Lewis	Steve Bayless	1969	139
110 2/8	30 4/8	30 3/8	6 5/8	6 5/8	4 7/8	4 6/8	M	Nunivak Island, Alaska	Arthur LaCapria	Arthur LaCapria	1971	139
110 2/8	28 6/8	28 6/8	7 3/8	7 2/8	5 1/8	4 7/8	M	St. Lawrence Island, Alaska	Wayne S. Weiler	Wayne S. Weiler	1972	139
110 2/8	27 6/8	28	7 6/8	7 7/8	5	5	M	Point Barrow, Alaska	Cecil M. Hopper	Cecil M. Hopper	1972	139
110 2/8	29 7/8	29 1/8	7 3/8	7 3/8	4 7/8	4 6/8	M	St. Lawrence Island, Alaska	Eskimo	Val Tibbetts	1979	139
110 2/8	28 3/8	28 2/8	7 2/8	7 2/8	5 2/8	5 2/8	M	St. Lawrence Island, Alaska	James A. Bush, Jr.	James A. Bush, Jr.	1979	139
109 4/8	26 4/8	26 2/8	8 2/8	8 2/8	5	5 2/8	M	Savoonga, Alaska	Richard A. Furniss	Richard A. Furniss	1972	146
109 4/8	27 6/8	27 5/8	8	8	4 7/8	5 3/8	M	St. Lawrence Island, Alaska	Mahlon T. White	Mahlon T. White	1977	146
108 6/8	28 6/8	27 1/8	7 7/8	7 2/8	5 6/8	5 3/8	M	St. Lawrence Island, Alaska	T. E. Shillingburg	T. E. Shillingburg	1961	148
108 4/8	30 6/8	30 7/8	7	6 7/8	4 4/8	5 4/8	M	Wainwright, Alaska	Delano J. Lietzau	Delano J. Lietzau	1978	149
108 2/8	27	30	7 3/8	7 1/8	5 1/8	5 1/8	M	Little Diomede Island, Alaska	Barrie White	Barrie White	1963	150
107 2/8	26 5/8	28 4/8	7 6/8	7 6/8	4 6/8	4 7/8	M	Bering Sea, Alaska	Gary Boychuk	Gary Boychuk	1977	151
107	27 2/8	27 5/8	7 2/8	7 2/8	5 1/8	5 1/8	M	St. Lawrence Island, Alaska	Wm. A. Bond	Wm. A. Bond	1964	152
106	26 5/8	26	7 3/8	7 2/8	5 4/8	5 1/8	M	Savoonga, Alaska	Jon G. Koshell	Jon G. Koshell	1972	153
104 4/8	23 3/8	23 3/8	7 3/8	7 1/8	6 2/8	6 2/8	M	St. Lawrence Island, Alaska	L. M. Cole	L. M. Cole	1964	154
104 4/8	26 6/8	26 7/8	7 5/8	7 4/8	4 6/8	4 5/8	M	Bering Sea	Rudolf Sand	Rudolf Sand	1971	154
104	27 7/8	26 3/8	6 4/8	6 4/8	5 1/8	5 4/8	M	Wainwright, Alaska	Donald R. Theophilus	Donald R. Theophilus	1978	156
103 2/8	26	26 1/8	6 7/8	6 6/8	4 7/8	5	M	Point Barrow, Alaska	Glenn W. Slade	Glenn W. Slade	1968	157
103 2/8	27 3/8	27 4/8	6 3/8	6 2/8	5 1/8	4 5/8	M	St. Lawrence Island, Alaska	Gunther Matschke	Gunther Matschke	1972	157
102 6/8	28 2/8	25 4/8	6 5/8	6 3/8	5 5/8	5 4/8	M	Port Moller, Alaska	Picked Up	Dan Lynch	——	159
102	25 3/8	25 3/8	7 2/8	7 4/8	4 5/8	4 5/8	M	St. Lawrence Island, Alaska	Dalton Foster	Dalton Foster	1961	160
101 2/8	26 7/8	27 5/8	6 7/8	7	4 2/8	4 6/8	M	St. Lawrence Island, Alaska	Eskimo	Steve Fowler	1967	161

*Final Score subject to revision by additional verifying measurements.

WORLD'S RECORD WAPITI OR AMERICAN ELK
SCORE: 442 3/8
Locality: Dark Canyon, Colorado. Date: 1899.
Hunter: John Plute. Owner: Ed Rozman.

NUMBER TWO WAPITI OR AMERICAN ELK
SCORE: 441 6/8
Locality: Big Horn Mountains, Wyoming. Date: 1890.
Hunter: unknown.
Donated by Homer C. Richards to the Jackson Hole Museum and Pioneer Village Foundation, Inc.
Winner of the Sagamore Hill Medal, 1950.

Wapiti or American Elk

Minimum Score 375

Cervus elaphus nelsoni and related subspecies

Score	Length of Main Beam R.	Length of Main Beam L.	Inside Spread	Circumference at Smallest Place Between First and Second Points R.	Circumference at Smallest Place Between First and Second Points L.	Number of Points R.	Number of Points L.	Locality Killed	By Whom Killed	Owner	Date Killed	Rank
442 3/8	55 5/8	59 5/8	45 4/8	12 1/8	11 2/8	8	7	Dark Canyon, Colo.	John Plute	Ed Rozman	1899	1
441 6/8	61 6/8	61 2/8	47	10 2/8	9 7/8	8	7	Big Horn Mts., Wyo.	Unknown	Jackson Hole Museum	1890	2
419 6/8	62 3/8	62 2/8	49 2/8	10 3/8	10 3/8	6	8	Panther River, Alta.	Clarence Brown	Clarence Brown	1977	3
419 4/8	59 7/8	60 1/8	53	9 2/8	9 3/8	7	7	Madison Co., Mont.	Fred C. Mercer	Fred C. Mercer	1958	4
418	54 1/8	50 4/8	44 2/8	8 4/8	8 4/8	6	6	Muddywater River, Alta.	Bruce W. Hale	Bruce W. Hale	1971	5
414 4/8	51 6/8	51 1/8	42 5/8	10	9 1/8	9	8	Wieser River, Idaho	Elmer Bacus	Elmer Bacus	1954	6
410	56	53 4/8	44 2/8	8 6/8	8 1/8	7	7	Unknown	Picked Up	Neil R. Hinton	1943	7
407	56 7/8	56 6/8	43 4/8	9 4/8	8 4/8	8	7	Summit Co., Colo.	Robert G. Young	Robert G. Young	1967	8
405 7/8	53 4/8	55 5/8	44 6/8	8 5/8	8 5/8	6	8	Ft. Apache Res., Ariz.	Roy R. Blythe	Roy R. Blythe	1970	9
404 6/8	58 6/8	57	47 2/8	9 5/8	9 1/8	8	7	Mineral Co., Mont.	Carl B. Snyder	Carl B. Snyder	1959	10
403	59 1/8	60 1/8	42 6/8	9 3/8	10	7	7	Owyhee Co., Idaho	Cecil R. Coonts	Cecil R. Coonts	1965	11
402 5/8	59 1/8	59 6/8	44 1/8	9 1/8	8 5/8	7	7	Red Deer River, Alta.	Henry Folkman	Henry Folkman	1946	12
401 6/8	58 3/8	57 5/8	47 2/8	7 7/8	8	6	6	Teton Co., Wyo.	Douglas Spicer	Douglas Spicer	1972	13
401 4/8	53 1/8	55 1/8	44 4/8	7 7/8	8 1/8	7	7	Park Co., Mont.	Wayne A. Hertzler	Wayne A. Hertzler	1977	14
401 3/8	60 4/8	64 5/8	43 7/8	9 3/8	9	7	6	Grant Co., Oreg.	James T. Sproul	James T. Sproul	1972	15
400 7/8	59 3/8	59 3/8	47 5/8	8 4/8	8 2/8	7	7	Rock Lake, Alta.	Ray Hindmarsh	Ray Hindmarsh	1963	16
400 2/8	56	55 2/8	46	8 2/8	8 4/8	7	7	Jackson Hole, Wyo.	Cecil Atkins & Ott Maynard	Thomas Myers	1947	17
399 2/8	59 5/8	57 4/8	47 3/8	7 7/8	7 5/8	8	7	Ram River, Alta.	Ralph A. Fry	Ralph A. Fry	1952	18
398 5/8	57 2/8	53 4/8	40 5/8	9	9 2/8	8	8	Lewis & Clark Co., Mont.	Richard Mosher	J. A. Iverson	1953	19
398	50 5/8	50 7/8	39 4/8	10 5/8	11	7	7	Mora Co., N. M.	Bernabe Alcon	Bernabe Alcon	1963	20
397 6/8	53	53	44 2/8	8 7/8	9	8	7	Cascade Co., Mont.	John W. Campbell	John W. Campbell	1955	21
397 6/8	56 1/8	56 3/8	43 4/8	9 7/8	10 6/8	6	6	Volunteer Canyon, Ariz.	Lamar Haines	Lamar Haines	1960	21
397 2/8	50 2/8	50 6/8	45 2/8	9 6/8	9 5/8	8	7	Gunnison Co., Colo.	John R. Burritt	John R. Burritt	1970	23
397 1/8	54 4/8	55	61 1/8	9 6/8	10 3/8	7	7	Mont.	Robert Swan	National Collection	1912	24
396 2/8	48	50 4/8	32 4/8	10	9 4/8	7	7	Duck Mts., Man.	Paul Kirkowich	Paul Kirkowich	1960	25
396 1/8	51 5/8	50 2/8	49 7/8	7 4/8	7 4/8	7	8	Rock Lake, Alta.	Harold R. Vaughn	Harold R. Vaughn	1968	26
395 4/8	57 5/8	60 1/8	47	8 1/8	8 6/8	6	6	Fremont Co., Wyo.	Roger Linnell	Roger Linnell	1955	27
395 4/8	56 2/8	51 2/8	43 6/8	10 2/8	9 5/8	6	6	Silver Bow Co., Mont.	Wayne Estep	Wayne Estep	1966	27
395 1/8	56 4/8	57 2/8	46 5/8	10 2/8	9 3/8	7	8	Wallowa Co., Oreg.	Lawton McDaniel	Lawton McDaniel	1935	29
395	56 2/8	56 2/8	48 7/8	8 7/8	9	7	7	Salmon Natl. For., Idaho	Fred W. Thomson	Fred W. Thomson	1964	30
394 6/8	54 2/8	60 7/8	47 2/8	8 2/8	8 4/8	6	6	Jefferson Co., Mont.	John Willard	Mont. Hist. Museum	1953	31

Score						Pts. R	Pts. L	Locality	By whom killed	Owner	Date	Rank
394 4/8	55	57 5/8	52 5/8	10	9 4/8	7	6	Beaverhead Co., Mont.	Gwyn Brown	Gwyn Brown	1944	32
394 4/8	52 2/8	52 7/8	51 1/8	8 5/8	9	7	6	Big Horn Mts., Wyo.	Robert K. Hamilton	Robert K. Hamilton	1954	32
394 4/8	53 4/8	53 3/8	46 4/8	8 7/8	8 7/8	6	6	Idaho Co., Idaho	L. M. White	L. M. White	1977	32
394 3/8	56 3/8	57 3/8	42 3/8	9 2/8	7 5/8	7	6	Panther River, Alta.	Picked Up	George Browne	1938	35
394 2/8	53 3/8	56 3/8	41 3/8	9 2/8	9 2/8	6	6	Hoback Rim, Wyo.	Clyde Robbins	George Franz	1940	35
394 2/8	53 1/8	55 3/8	45 3/8	8 1/8	8 3/8	6	6	Elkwater, Alta.	Roy Crawford	Roy Crawford	1976	35
393 3/8	53 5/8	51 3/8	46 3/8	10 2/8	10	6	5	Big Horn, Wyo.	Edwin Shaffer	Edwin Shaffer	1946	38
393 3/8	55 2/8	54 3/8	51 1/8	8 3/8	8 3/8	6	5	Watertown Natl. Park, Alta.	Alan Foster	Alan Foster	1952	38
393 3/8	58 6/8	52 1/8	45 7/8	9 6/8	9 4/8	6	5	Winchester, Idaho	Doyle Shriver	Doyle Shriver	1954	38
393 2/8	63 1/8	64 3/8	44 3/8	9 5/8	9 5/8	6	5	Socorro Co., N.M.	Floyd R. Owens	Floyd R. Owens	1977	38
393 1/8	56 3/8	59 3/8	47 1/8	8 3/8	8 6/8	7	7	Kittitas Co., Wash.	Paul Anderson	Paul Anderson	1927	42
392 4/8	51 3/8	51 1/8	42 3/8	7 7/8	7 7/8	5	7	Buford, Colo.	Picked Up	Robert T. Fulton	—	43
392	58 7/8	58 6/8	48 5/8	9	8 7/8	7	7	Panther River, Alta.	Bill Brooks	Bill Brooks	1955	44
392	54 6/8	56 6/8	45 3/8	10	10	6	6	Jackson Co., Colo.	James A. Baller	North Park State Bank	1969	44
391 5/8	54 4/8	53	46	7 7/8	8 7/8	6	6	Thoroughfare Creek, Wyo.	Thomas A. Yawkey	Thomas A. Yawkey	1936	46
391 5/8	52 4/8	53 3/8	35 5/8	7 7/8	7 7/8	6	6	Slater, Colo.	W. J. Bracken	W. J. Bracken	1963	46
391 4/8	54 5/8	56 3/8	43 3/8	9 1/8	9	6	6	Mt. Evans, Colo.	Unknown	Frank Brady	1874	48
391 3/8	55 7/8	50 3/8	39 3/8	7 7/8	8 3/8	7	6	Grand Lake, Colo.	John Holzwarth	John Holzwarth	1949	49
390 6/8	53 6/8	54 3/8	49 6/8	8 7/8	9 5/8	7	6	Clearwater, Alta.	Bob Dial	Bob Dial	1955	50
390 6/8	49 4/8	51 3/8	42 3/8	12 2/8	12 2/8	7	7	Caribou Co., Idaho	Ken Homer	Ken Homer	1963	50
390 2/8	50 2/8	53	50 3/8	8	7 6/8	6	7	Nez Perce Co., Idaho	Picked Up	Michael Throckmorton	1949	52
389 5/8	56 5/8	52 5/8	52 5/8	9 2/8	9 2/8	7	7	Park Co., Mont.	Thomas B. Adams	Jack Adams	1932	53
389 5/8	55 4/8	56 5/8	45	10 5/8	10	7	7	Ft. A La Corne, Sask.	Jim Crozier	Jim Crozier	1955	53
389 4/8	57 3/8	55 4/8	42	8	8	6	6	Helena, Mont.	Picked Up	Robert L. Smith	1964	55
389 4/8	53 7/8	54 7/8	46	8 7/8	8 7/8	6	6	Bitterroot Area, Mont.	Unknown	John Le Blanc	1965	55
389 3/8	56 5/8	54 5/8	46	8 7/8	8 7/8	6	6	Big Horn Co., Wyo.	Floyd A. Clark	Floyd A. Clark	1976	55
389 2/8	49 7/8	60 5/8	43 7/8	8 3/8	8 3/8	6	6	Salmon River, Idaho	Unknown	John M. Anderson	1915	58
389	51	48 1/8	40	10 7/8	10 7/8	6	6	Sask.	Unknown	B. P. O. Elks Lodge	PR1956	59
388 7/8	56	48 3/8	41 1/8	8 2/8	8 5/8	6	6	Meacham, Oreg.	H. M. Bailey	H. M. Bailey	1963	60
388 2/8	62 4/8	63 5/8	49 2/8	9 6/8	9 3/8	6	6	Jackson Hole, Wyo.	Unknown	William Sonnenburg	PR1912	61
388	53 2/8	53 6/8	48 6/8	9	9 3/8	7	9	Unknown	Unknown	Carnegie Museum	—	62
388	57 1/8	55 5/8	48 6/8	8 6/8	8 1/8	6	6	Madison Co., Mont.	Terry Carlson	Christine Mullikin	1961	63
388	57 3/8	55	48 3/8	8 6/8	8 1/8	7	7	Medicine Lodge Creek, Idaho	D. W. Marshall & E. J. Stacy	D. W. Marshall & E. J. Stacy	1961	63
388	55 5/8	54	50 3/8	8 4/8	9	8	9	Converse, Wyo.	Jerry F. Cook	J. F. Cook & Mrs. Pete Muchmore	1965	63
387 7/8	54 5/8	55 5/8	44 5/8	9 5/8	9 5/8	7	6	Kelly, Wyo.	Roger Penney	Bernard Bronk	1963	66
387 7/8	55 3/8	57	37 5/8	10	9 5/8	7	6	Grant Co., Oreg.	Arnold Troph	Arnold Troph	1966	66
387 7/8	52 1/8	53	44 5/8	8	7 7/8	6	6	Lincoln, Wyo.	Dexter R. Gardner	Dexter R. Gardner	1967	66
387 7/8	57 5/8	56 5/8	51	7 7/8	7 7/8	6	6	Big Horn Mts., Wyo.	Elgin T. Gates	Elgin T. Gates	1954	69
387 7/8	50 2/8	51 7/8	43 3/8	9 5/8	10 2/8	6	6	Fremont, Idaho	Charles A. Preston	Charles A. Preston	1963	69
387 7/8	58 1/8	56	39 5/8	9 1/8	8 7/8	7	7	Yarrow Creek, Alta.	D. Belyea	D. Belyea	1970	71
387 7/8	49 1/8	49 7/8	41 7/8	8 7/8	8 7/8	7	7	Grant Co., Oreg.	Andy Chambers	Andy Chambers	1959	72

WAPITI OR AMERICAN ELK–*Continued*

Cervus elaphus nelsoni and related subspecies

Score	Length of Main Beam R.	Length of Main Beam L.	Inside Spread	Circumference at Smallest Place Between First and Second Points R.	Circumference at Smallest Place Between First and Second Points L.	Number of Points R.	Number of Points L.	Locality Killed	By Whom Killed	Owner	Date Killed	Rank
387 4/8	56 5/8	58 2/8	44 2/8	9	9	6	6	Sage Creek, Mont.	Joseph A. Vogel	Joseph A. Vogel	1970	72
387 3/8	52 2/8	52 3/8	47 3/8	8 1/8	8 1/8	6	6	Park Co., Mont.	Lawrence P. Deering	Lawrence P. Deering	1978	74
387 1/8	54 6/8	58 1/8	46	9 5/8	9 5/8	7	8	Meagher Co., Mont.	Harold Zehntner & Bud McLees	Bud McLees	1971	75
387	55	55 4/8	54 4/8	8 7/8	8 2/8	8	7	Chama, N. M.	Herb Klein	Herb Klein	1952	76
386 7/8	48 6/8	47 2/8	41 6/8	9 4/8	8 5/8	8	8	Powell Co., Mont.	Mildred Eder	Mildred Eder	1969	77
386 6/8	61 6/8	61 7/8	47 4/8	8 7/8	9 1/8	6	6	Flathead Co., Mont.	Floyd L. Jackson	Floyd L. Jackson	1976	78
386 4/8	49 2/8	50 3/8	39 6/8	8 6/8	9	7	7	Craig Mt., Idaho	H. H. Schnettler	H. H. Schnettler	1957	79
386 4/8	55 5/8	55 5/8	42	10	9 2/8	7	7	Smoky River, Alta.	Stephen Trulik	Stephen Trulik	1963	79
386 4/8	56 2/8	54 6/8	44	8 5/8	8 6/8	6	6	Coconino Co., Ariz.	Lee Clemson	Lee Clemson	1974	79
386 2/8	52 4/8	54 1/8	48	8 7/8	9 1/8	6	6	Delta Co., Colo.	Bert Johnson	Bert Johnson	1974	82
386 1/8	57 6/8	57 1/8	48 5/8	7 7/8	8 5/8	6	6	Forest Gatestore, Sask.	Edwin L. Roberts	Edwin L. Roberts	1962	83
386 1/8	59 1/8	58	36 5/8	10 3/8	9 4/8	6	6	Mescalero Apache Res., N. M.	Larry W. Bailey, Sr.	Larry W. Bailey, Sr.	1974	83
386	53 7/8	55 4/8	51	9 6/8	9 6/8	6	6	Valley Co., Idaho	Denny Young	Kenny Poe	1957	85
386	52 4/8	53	48 2/8	8 4/8	8 4/8	6	7	Big Horn Mt., Wyo.	Unknown	Fred Gray	1966	85
385 7/8	56 7/8	56 1/8	40 4/8	7 7/8	8	6	6	Big Smoky River, Alta.	Fred T. Huntington, Jr.	Fred T. Huntington, Jr.	1961	87
385 7/8	49 1/8	51 7/8	44 3/8	7 7/8	7 7/8	6	6	Shoshone Co., Idaho	Jerry Nearing	Jerry Nearing	1976	87
385 5/8	59 6/8	56 6/8	41 2/8	8 7/8	9 3/8	7	8	Ft. Apache Res., Ariz.	Glen Daly	Glen Daly	1957	89
385 5/8	53 2/8	53	40 3/8	8 4/8	8 1/8	6	6	Kootenai, Co., Idaho	Arth Day	Arth Day	1971	89
385 3/8	57 2/8	55 7/8	42 5/8	8	9	6	6	Sanders Co., Mont.	George R. Johnson	George R. Johnson	1977	91
385 1/8	48 5/8	49 3/8	34 7/8	8 3/8	8 6/8	6	6	Trappers Lake, Colo.	Byron W. Kneff	Byron W. Kneff	1954	92
385 1/8	56 7/8	56 4/8	46 5/8	8 3/8	10	6	7	Bozeman, Mont.	Robert B. McKnight	Robert B. McKnight	1966	92
385 1/8	51	52 4/8	48 4/8	11	11 4/8	8	6	Grande Cache Lake, Alta.	Kenneth A. Evans	Kenneth A. Evans	1966	92
384 6/8	55 3/8	54 3/8	36 4/8	9 2/8	9	6	6	Clearwater River, Alta.	William Lenz	William Lenz	1966	95
384 6/8	54	54	50	10 1/8	10	7	6	Hualapai Indian Res., Ariz.	Tod Reichert	Tod Reichert	1975	95
384 6/8	56 2/8	58 4/8	44	9 4/8	9 6/8	6	6	Ft. Apache Res., Ariz.	Jim P. Caires	Jim P. Caires	1978	95
384 5/8	55 3/8	54 6/8	47 1/8	8 4/8	8 7/8	6	6	Ram River, Alta.	Joe Kramer	Joe Kramer	1966	98
384 4/8	57	56 4/8	43 4/8	9 5/8	9 3/8	7	7	Bonneville Co., Idaho	David W. Anderson	David W. Anderson	1967	99
384 4/8	53 2/8	53 7/8	43	8 5/8	8 2/8	7	7	Bonneville Co., Idaho	Keith W. Hadley	Keith W. Hadley	1972	99
384 3/8	59 3/8	59 2/8	49 1/8	7 6/8	7 5/8	7	6	Jackson Hole, Wyo.	Francis X. Bouchard	Francis X. Bouchard	1956	101

Score						Pts.		Locality	Owner	Hunter	Year	Rank
384³/₈	59	58⁵/₈	46³/₈	10⁵/₈	9³/₈	6	6	Beaverhead Co., Mont.	Phil Matovich	Phil Matovich	1960	101
384³/₈	54⁵/₈	54⁵/₈	50⁷/₈	9⁷/₈	9²/₈	6	6	Clear Creek Co., Colo.	John Wallace	John Wallace	1973	101
384³/₈	61⁷/₈	64⁵/₈	40⁶/₈	11	10⁴/₈	8	6	Ft. Apache Res., Ariz.	Ralph C. Winkler, Jr.	Ralph C. Winkler, Jr.	1977	104
384	58⁷/₈	56⁴/₈	44	9⁶/₈	9¹/₈	7	6	Willow Creek, Mont.	Mike Miles	Mike Miles	1958	105
384	56⁶/₈	54	47	7⁷/₈	8¹/₈	7	7	Costilla Co., Colo.	William E. Carl	William E. Carl	1967	105
383⁷/₈	53⁴/₈	51⁴/₈	47⁷/₈	9⁷/₈	10²/₈	8	7	Blacktail Creek, Mont.	Floyd E. Winn	Floyd E. Winn	1959	107
383⁶/₈	53⁶/₈	54	43⁴/₈	9⁴/₈	9⁵/₈	6	6	Unknown	Unknown	S. Side Cody Elk Club	—	108
383⁴/₈	51³/₈	51³/₈	48⁴/₈	9⁵/₈	9⁵/₈	6	6	Unknown	Unknown	N. Side Cody Elk Club		109
383³/₈	53⁵/₈	55	50⁴/₈	8²/₈	8	7	6	Maycroft, Alta.	Steve Kubasek	Steve Kubasek	1957	110
383³/₈	52⁴/₈	52	41⁶/₈	9⁴/₈	9²/₈	6	7	Nez Perce Co., Idaho	Thenton L. Todd	Thenton L. Todd	1956	111
383²/₈	58¹/₈	54⁴/₈	53⁴/₈	9	9⁶/₈	8	6	Snowy Range, Wyo.	Kermit Platt	Kermit Platt	1961	112
383¹/₈	55	55	52²/₈	9³/₈	8⁶/₈	6	6	Coconino Co., Ariz.	Gene Bird	Gene Bird	1972	113
383	54³/₈	52⁷/₈	43⁵/₈	8⁶/₈	8⁵/₈	6	6	Castle River, Alta.	Albert Truant	Albert Truant	1970	114
382⁷/₈	56¹/₈	54⁵/₈	41⁵/₈	9⁷/₈	10²/₈	7	6	Rattlesnake Mt., Wyo.	Bob Edgar	Bob Edgar	1966	115
382⁶/₈	52³/₈	52³/₈	36⁵/₈	9²/₈	9	7	7	Kootenai Co., Idaho	Terry Cozad	Terry Cozad	1968	116
382⁵/₈	56⁶/₈	56⁷/₈	41⁶/₈	8⁷/₈	9²/₈	6	7	Summit Co., Colo.	Marshall Sherman	Marshall Sherman	1966	117
382⁴/₈	49	48⁵/₈	36⁴/₈	8⁵/₈	8⁶/₈	6	6	Teton Co., Wyo.	Randy Johnston	Randy Johnston	1970	117
382⁴/₈	53³/₈	54	50⁵/₈	8¹/₈	8⁴/₈	7	6	Sublette Co., Wyo.	Frank Dew	Frank Dew	1931	119
382³/₈	49⁴/₈	52¹/₈	35⁵/₈	11	10¹/₈	6	6	Morman Lake, Ariz.	Wayne A. Barry	John E. Rhea	1965	119
382³/₈	55⁵/₈	55	47⁴/₈	7⁴/₈	7⁷/₈	6	6	Sage Creek, Mont.	Henry Lambert	Charles F. Miller	1923	121
382²/₈	58⁴/₈	62⁵/₈	48	8	7⁴/₈	6	6	Williams, Ariz.	Oscar B. Skaggs	Oscar B. Skaggs	1954	121
382¹/₈	57³/₈	55⁷/₈	44³/₈	8¹/₈	8²/₈	7	7	Bob Marshall Wild., Mont.	Gene E. Trenary	Gene E. Trenary	1958	123
382¹/₈	54³/₈	54⁴/₈	45⁷/₈	8	8³/₈	6	6	Gallatin Co., Mont.	A. Francis Bailey	A. Francis Bailey	1966	123
382	52²/₈	51¹/₈	47⁴/₈	9²/₈	8⁶/₈	8	8	Missoula Co., Mont.	Fritz Frey	Clifford Frey	1943	125
382	53²/₈	51¹/₈	48	8⁷/₈	9¹/₈	6	6	Little Cimmaron, Colo.	Newell Beauchamp	Bud Lovato	1957	125
381⁷/₈	59⁵/₈	58	52³/₈	7⁶/₈	7⁵/₈	7	7	Gallatin Co., Mont.	H. K. Shields	H. K. Shields	1958	127
381⁶/₈	52²/₈	52	49⁷/₈	10²/₈	9³/₈	6	7	Beaverhead Co., Mont.	C. L. Jensen	C. L. Jensen	1960	128
381⁶/₈	49⁶/₈	48	32⁷/₈	14⁴/₈	13	9	6	Elbow River, Alta.	Harold F. Mailman	Harold F. Mailman	1964	128
381⁵/₈	56³/₈	56²/₈	41⁵/₈	10⁴/₈	10¹/₈	6	6	Granite Co., Mont.	Jeff Conn	Jeff Conn	1971	130
381⁴/₈	56⁶/₈	57²/₈	42⁴/₈	8⁷/₈	9²/₈	6	6	Fremont Co., Wyo.	John S. Maxson	John S. Maxson	1954	131
381³/₈	57²/₈	57⁷/₈	41¹/₈	9⁶/₈	9⁴/₈	7	7	Park Co., Mont.	Edward F. Skillman	Edward F. Skillman	1968	132
381³/₈	55⁴/₈	54⁴/₈	37⁴/₈	9⁶/₈	9¹/₈	7	7	Larimer Co., Colo.	Earl L. Erbes	Earl L. Erbes	1972	132
381¹/₈	57⁵/₈	56¹/₈	45¹/₈	8	7³/₈	6	6	Laramie Peak, Wyo.	Lawrence Prager	Lawrence Prager	1958	134
381¹/₈	49⁶/₈	51⁴/₈	39⁷/₈	8⁶/₈	9	7	6	Flathead Co., Mont.	Earl Weaver, Jr.	Earl Weaver, Jr.	1962	134
381	56³/₈	54⁴/₈	48⁴/₈	8²/₈	8³/₈	6	6	Gallatin Co., Mont.	Jack Bauer	Jack Bauer	1961	136
381	51¹/₈	50⁴/₈	43⁵/₈	8	7⁵/₈	7	7	Big Horn Co., Mont.	Jerry Barnes	Jerry Barnes	1962	136
381	48	54⁴/₈	40⁴/₈	8⁵/₈	8⁷/₈	7	7	Bonneville Co., Idaho	Mrs. E. LaRene Smith	Mrs. E. LaRene Smith	1966	136
381	54	53⁴/₈	48⁵/₈	8	7⁵/₈	6	6	Gallatin Co., Mont.	Gerald Schroeder	Gerald Schroeder	1977	136
380⁶/₈	51⁷/₈	51	43⁵/₈	10	9⁷/₈	7	7	Park Co., Mont.	John Caputo	John Caputo	1968	140

Wapiti or American Elk–*Continued*

Cervus elaphus nelsoni and related subspecies

Score	Length of Main Beam R.	Length of Main Beam L.	Inside Spread	Circumference at Smallest Place Between First and Second Points R.	Circumference at Smallest Place Between First and Second Points L.	Number of Points R.	Number of Points L.	Locality Killed	By Whom Killed	Owner	Date Killed	Rank
380 5/8	50 6/8	54 6/8	47 5/8	9 4/8	9 7/8	6	6	Medicine Bow Range, Colo.	Mike Holliday	Mike Holliday	1966	141
380 5/8	54 2/8	55	51 3/8	7 7/8	7 4/8	6	7	Chaffee Co., Colo.	Anton Purkat	Anton Purkat	1972	141
380 4/8	52 4/8	52 6/8	41	9	8 6/8	6	6	Payson, Ariz.	Harold Foard	Harold Foard	1947	143
380 3/8	62 7/8	63 2/8	47 1/8	8 6/8	8 6/8	7	8	Harney Co., Oregon	Pat L. Wheeler	Pat L. Wheeler	1967	144
380 2/8	56 1/8	57 2/8	49 4/8	8 1/8	8 6/8	7	7	Madison Co., Mont.	Phil Hensel	Phil Hensel	1959	145
380 2/8	57 4/8	57 3/8	46 4/8	8 4/8	8 3/8	7	7	Lewis Co., Wash.	Charles Rudolph	Charles Rudolph	1973	145
380 2/8	56 2/8	54 1/8	45	8 5/8	8 7/8	7	6	Coconino Co., Ariz.	Doug Kittredge	Doug Kittredge	1975	145
380 2/8	58 7/8	58 3/8	42 2/8	9 4/8	8 6/8	7	6	Granite Co., Mont.	Richard Shoner	Richard Shoner	1977	145
380	54	53 5/8	48 2/8	8 7/8	8 4/8	7	7	Spring Creek, Alta.	A. C. Bair	A. C. Bair	1948	149
380	53 2/8	56 2/8	50 3/8	10 3/8	9 7/8	7	6	Ft. Apache Res., Ariz.	George Ellis Crosby	George Ellis Crosby	1957	149
380	51 5/8	51 6/8	41 6/8	7 6/8	8 3/8	6	6	Duck Mt., Man.	G. N. Burton	G. N. Burton	1965	149
379 6/8	50 2/8	51 4/8	45 4/8	9 4/8	9 4/8	6	6	Rock Lake, Alta.	Jim Soneff	Jim Soneff	1961	152
379 6/8	57 2/8	57 2/8	40 4/8	7 6/8	7 6/8	6	6	Big Horn, Mont.	George F. Gamble	George F. Gamble	1968	152
379 6/8	54	54 6/8	45 6/8	7 7/8	8 1/8	6	6	Daisy Pass, Mont.	Larry R. Price	Larry R. Price	1971	152
379 6/8	52	51 6/8	36 2/8	10	10	9	8	Adams Co., Idaho	William V. Baker	William V. Baker	1976	152
379 5/8	57	53 1/8	48 1/8	9 2/8	9 2/8	6	6	Big Horn Mts., Wyo.	Unknown	L. M. Brownell	1956	156
379 5/8	58 3/8	58 4/8	45 2/8	9 2/8	9 6/8	6	6	Ruby Mts., Mont.	Jack Ballard	Jack Ballard	1960	156
379 4/8	51 7/8	52 3/8	39	9 7/8	9 7/8	6	6	Madison Co., Mont.	LeRoy Schweitzer	LeRoy Schweitzer	1964	158
379 3/8	54	52 6/8	42 3/8	8	7 4/8	6	6	Unknown	Gift Of Arch. Rogers	National Collection	——	159
379 2/8	58 3/8	57 2/8	41 6/8	9	9 4/8	6	6	Sierra Blanca Lake, Ariz.	Joseph A. Rozum	Joseph A. Rozum	1965	160
379 2/8	54 7/8	56 4/8	40 4/8	8 2/8	8 1/8	6	6	Sanders Co., Mont.	Robert L. Coates	Robert L. Coates	1974	160
379 1/8	56	57 4/8	33 7/8	8 6/8	9 1/8	6	6	Duvernay Bridge, Alta.	Alec Mitchell	Alec Mitchell	1917	162
379	50 4/8	51 1/8	40 6/8	9	8 6/8	6	6	Big Creek, Idaho	Picked Up	Geo. Dovel	1963	163
379	49	50 4/8	39	10 1/8	10 1/8	8	6	Teton Park, Wyo.	S. M. Vilven	S. M. Vilven	1964	163
378 7/8	55 7/8	56 1/8	44 4/8	9	8 7/8	6	6	Bozeman, Mont.	K. L. Berry	K. L. Berry	1959	165
378 7/8	57 5/8	58 6/8	47 1/8	8 2/8	8 2/8	6	6	Carbon Co., Wyo.	Donal F. Mueller	Donal F. Mueller	1964	165
378 7/8	56 6/8	56 1/8	46 5/8	8 4/8	8	6	6	Wildhay River, Alta.	Richard Clouthier	Richard Clouthier	1973	165
378 5/8	52	55 2/8	47 7/8	8 7/8	8 6/8	7	6	Dutch Creek, Alta.	Harold King	Harold King	1951	168
378 4/8	52 7/8	54 5/8	42 4/8	9 3/8	10	7	7	Park Co., Wyo.	Kenneth Smith	Kenneth Smith	1954	169
378 4/8	53 7/8	48 2/8	55	8 2/8	8 4/8	7	7	Valley Co., Idaho	Joe Gisler	Joe Gisler	1961	169
378 4/8	58 3/8	56 3/8	43 6/8	8 4/8	8 3/8	6	6	Beaverhead Co., Mont.	Milton F. Steele	Milton F. Steele	1963	169

378 4/8	54 3/8	55 3/8	45 2/8	8 6/8	8 6/8	6	6	Shoshone Co., Idaho	Edward L. Bradford	Edward L. Bradford	1963	169
378 3/8	55	54 1/8	45	8	7 4/8	6	6	Gallatin Co., Mont.	Ted Shook	Ted Shook	1966	173
378 2/8	51 4/8	52 5/8	50	9 2/8	10	6	7	White River, Colo.	Art Wright	Art Wright	1953	174
378 2/8	43 4/8	47 3/8	40	9 6/8	9 6/8	9	8	Duck Mt., Man.	John D. Harbarenko	John D. Harbarenko	1973	174
378	49 3/8	50 2/8	39 5/8	8 1/8	8 6/8	7	7	Richard's Peak, Mont.	Albert Sales	Richard Eastman	1931	176
378	56 1/8	56 7/8	44 2/8	7 6/8	7 6/8	7	6	Gunnison, Colo.	Ed Lattimore, Jr.	Ed Lattimore, Jr.	1966	176
377 6/8	51 3/8	52 3/8	45	8	8 3/8	7	7	Routt Co., Colo.	Tom Nidey	Tom Nidey	1959	178
377 6/8	56 6/8	55 6/8	41 6/8	8 2/8	8 2/8	7	10	Sanders Co., Mont.	Steve Barnes	Steve Barnes	1973	178
377 5/8	54 2/8	54 5/8	40 6/8	8 6/8	8 1/8	6	7	Apache Co., Ariz.	A. C. Goodell	A. C. Goodell	1963	180
377 4/8	54 3/8	51 5/8	45 5/8	8 6/8	8 6/8	7	7	Granite Co., Mont.	Tom Villeneue	Tom Villeneue	1966	181
377 4/8	52 2/8	53 1/8	42 2/8	8 1/8	8 6/8	6	6	Ft. Apache Res., Ariz.	Picked Up	Gary Marsh	1971	181
377 4/8	47 5/8	47 2/8	45	8 4/8	8 5/8	6	6	Gunnison Co., Colo.	Leo Welch	Leo Welch	1972	181
377 3/8	59	55	39 3/8	9 7/8	9 7/8	6	6	Teton Co., Wyo.	Walter V. Solinski	Walter V. Solinski	1962	184
377 3/8	60	58	41 7/8	8 5/8	8 4/8	6	6	Sanders Co., Mont.	Allen White	Allen White	1968	184
377 3/8	53 1/8	52	46 1/8	8 4/8	9 1/8	6	6	Missoula Co., Mont.	Tom Schenarts	Tom Schenarts	1970	184
377 2/8	53 2/8	51 6/8	45 4/8	9 2/8	8 6/8	8	8	Drummond, Mont.	Rex Sorenson	Univ. Mont. Museum	1952	187
377 2/8	53 5/8	53 6/8	49 2/8	8 2/8	8 2/8	6	7	Gallatin Range, Mont.	E. Dehart, Sr, P. Van Beek & H. Prestine	Earl Dehart, Sr.	1960	187
377 2/8	55 4/8	60 1/8	50 6/8	9 7/8	10 3/8	6	6	Show Low, Ariz.	Michael Pew	Michael Pew	1964	187
377 2/8	56	55 2/8	40 2/8	11 1/8	11	6	6	Park Co., Wyo.	Mary Jane Rickman	Mary Jane & Edward Rickman, Jr.	1965	187
377 1/8	53	51 6/8	45 4/8	9	8 5/8	6	8	Sublette, Wyo.	Ted Dew	Ted Dew	1928	191
377	54 6/8	54 1/8	47 2/8	9 2/8	8 5/8	7	6	Brazeau River, Alta.	Ted Loblaw	Ted Loblaw	1960	192
376 7/8	55	55 6/8	38 2/8	9 5/8	10 2/8	7	6	Jackson Hole, Wyo.	H. M. Hanna	Melville Hanna Haskell	——	193
376 7/8	56 4/8	57 2/8	52 7/8	7 3/8	7 7/8	6	6	Park Co., Wyo.	Warren C. Cubbage	Warren C. Cubbage	1957	193
376 6/8	56 2/8	54 4/8	44 6/8	9 4/8	9 3/8	7	7	Big Horn Mts., Wyo.	Unknown	A. W. Hendershot	1912	195
376 6/8	51 2/8	52 4/8	48 2/8	8 4/8	8 3/8	8	7	Lewis & Clark Co., Mont.	Cameron G. Mielke	Cameron G. Mielke	1964	195
376 6/8	61	58 7/8	51	8 3/8	7 3/8	8	7	Teton Co., Wyo.	Ward Keevert	Ward Keevert	1968	195
376 5/8	58 6/8	56 3/8	48 1/8	7 6/8	7 6/8	6	6	Granby, Colo.	Melvin Van Lewen	Colo. Game & Fish Dept.	1961	198
376 5/8	48	50 1/8	39 3/8	8 5/8	8 7/8	7	7	Teton Co., Idaho	Edwin E. Schiess	Tim Schiess	1966	198
376 4/8	55 1/8	53 4/8	49 6/8	8 2/8	8 5/8	8	7	Albany Co., Wyo.	Jerry F. Cook	Jerry F. Cook	1965	200
376 3/8	56 5/8	57	39 4/8	9 3/8	9 5/8	7	7	Highwood River, Alta.	L. Edwards	L. Edwards	1956	201
376 3/8	48 4/8	49 2/8	40 3/8	8	8 1/8	7	7	White River, Colo.	Ron Vance	Ron Vance	1957	201
376 3/8	49 3/8	49 7/8	41 5/8	7 7/8	7 4/8	6	6	Radium, Colo.	Bill Mercer	Bill Mercer	1964	201
376 3/8	54 2/8	55 5/8	43 3/8	9	9 1/8	6	6	Rocky Mt. House, Alta.	George Patrick Ebl	George Patrick Ebl	1966	201
376	60 4/8	59	44 4/8	7 5/8	8	6	6	Almont, Colo.	John Schwartz	John Schwartz	1961	205
376	55	54 1/8	42	9 3/8	9 1/8	6	6	Dormer River, Alta.	D. C. Thomas	D. C. Thomas	1978	205
375 7/8	54 6/8	54 4/8	43 5/8	8 4/8	8 5/8	8	8	Flathead Co., Mont.	Pat Roth	Pat Roth	1966	207
375 6/8	54 6/8	50 4/8	43	8 4/8	8 2/8	6	6	Big Horn Mts., Wyo.	Robert F. Retzlaff	Robert F. Retzlaff	1957	208
375 6/8	50 3/8	50 6/8	40 4/8	9 4/8	10 4/8	6	6	Crow Valley, Colo.	Dale R. Leonard	Dale R. Leonard	1961	208
375 5/8	58	59 6/8	40 3/8	10 2/8	10 4/8	7	7	Unknown	Unknown	Demarest Mem. Museum	——	210
375 5/8	57 2/8	57 7/8	43	7 2/8	7 3/8	6	6	Buck Creek, Wyo.	Andrew W. Heard, Jr.	Andrew W. Heard, Jr.	1958	210
375 5/8	53	51 3/8	40 3/8	9	9 1/8	6	7	Madison River, Mont.	Dale Alan Hancock	Dale Alan Hancock	1967	210

WAPITI OR AMERICAN ELK–*Continued*
Cervus elaphus nelsoni and related subspecies

Score	Length of Main Beam R.	L.	Inside Spread	Circumference at Smallest Place Between First and Second Points R.	L.	Number of Points R.	L.	Locality Killed	By Whom Killed	Owner	Date Killed	Rank
375⁵/₈	57⁵/₈	55²/₈	48⁴/₈	8⁷/₈	8⁷/₈	6	6	Jefferson Co., Mont.	Ralph J. Huckaba	Ralph J. Huckaba	1949	213
375⁵/₈	50	53²/₈	48⁴/₈	8⁴/₈	9¹/₈	6	6	Fremont Co., Wyo.	Edward J. Patik	Edward J. Patik	1962	213
375³/₈	52	52	43⁶/₈	9²/₈	10¹/₈	7	6	Jefferson Co., Mont.	Mrs. Lou Sweet	Mrs. Lou Sweet	1924	215
375³/₈	51¹/₈	52	44⁷/₈	7⁶/₈	8⁷/₈	6	7	Teton Co., Wyo.	Unknown	Nathan E. Hindman	PR1950	215
375³/₈	58⁷/₈	56⁵/₈	43¹/₈	8³/₈	9¹/₈	6	7	Snake River, Wyo.	W. H. Robinson	W. H. Robinson	1957	215
375³/₈	52⁶/₈	54⁴/₈	44⁴/₈	9	8³/₈	7	7	Park Co., Mont.	Bruce Brown	Bruce Brown	1967	215
375³/₈	49	50⁶/₈	39⁷/₈	7⁵/₈	7⁷/₈	6	6	Beaverhead Co., Mont.	Harold F. Krieger, Jr.	Harold F. Krieger, Jr.	1970	215
375³/₈	54⁴/₈	55³/₈	49	9³/₈	9⁷/₈	6	7	Jackson, Wyo.	Bill Blanchard	Bill Blanchard	1954	220
375³/₈	51¹/₈	53¹/₈	36³/₈	7⁷/₈	7⁷/₈	7	7	Ten Sleep, Wyo.	Kenneth Hadland	Kenneth Hadland	1959	220
375³/₈	55²/₈	52³/₈	47³/₈	8⁷/₈	8⁷/₈	8	8	Craig, Colo.	Kenneth W. Cramer	Kenneth W. Cramer	1960	220
375³/₈	53	52	41	10	10⁴/₈	7	8	Natrona Co., Wyo.	Victor R. Jackson	Victor R. Jackson	1976	220
375³/₈	52	53⁴/₈	39³/₈	9	10	6	7	Prince Albert, Sask.	Unknown	Lucky Lake Sask. Elks	1926	224
375³/₈	58⁴/₈	58⁵/₈	37³/₈	10⁴/₈	9⁷/₈	7	7	Tonto Lake, Ariz.	Louise Fay Campbell	Louise Fay Campbell	1967	224
375	57¹/₈	54	38	8	8	7	7	Denton Co., Texas	O. Z. Finley	Joe B. Finley, Jr.	1934	226
375	52⁶/₈	52⁵/₈	47⁴/₈	8⁶/₈	9	6	6	Fremont Co., Idaho	Eva Calonge	Eva Calonge	1960	226
375	57³/₈	54⁴/₈	41³/₈	9³/₈	9⁵/₈	7	7	Park Co., Mont.	Robert Michael Brogan	Robert Michael Brogan	1972	226

Photograph by Wm. H. Nesbitt

WORLD'S RECORD MULE DEER (TYPICAL ANTLERS)
SCORE: 225 6/8
Locality: Dolores County, Colorado. Date: 1972.
Hunter and owner: Doug Burris, Jr.
Winner of the Sagamore Hill Medal, 1974.

Photograph by Alex Rota

NUMBER TWO MULE DEER (TYPICAL ANTLERS)
SCORE: 217
Locality: Hoback Canyon, Wyoming. Date: unknown.
Hunter: unknown.
Donated by W.C. Lawrence to the Jackson Hole Museum and Pioneer Village Foundation, Inc.

Mule Deer *(Typical Antlers)*

Odocoileus hemionus hemionus and certain related subspecies

Minimum Score 195

Score	Length of Main Beam R.	Length of Main Beam L.	Inside Spread	Circumference at Smallest Place Between Burr and First Point R.	Circumference at Smallest Place Between Burr and First Point L.	Number of Points R.	Number of Points L.	Locality Killed	By Whom Killed	Owner	Date Killed	Rank
225 6/8	30 1/8	28 6/8	30 7/8	5 2/8	5 3/8	6	5	Dolores Co., Colo.	Doug Burris, Jr.	Doug Burris, Jr.	1972	1
217	28 4/8	28 2/8	26 6/8	5 5/8	5 6/8	6	6	Hoback Canyon, Wyo.	Unknown	Jackson Hole Museum	—	2
214 3/8	27 5/8	27 4/8	27 5/8	4 7/8	4 7/8	5	5	Gypsum Creek, Colo.	Paul A. Muehlbauer	Paul A. Muehlbauer	1967	3
214 2/8	26 7/8	28 1/8	29 4/8	5 3/8	5 3/8	5	7	Uinta Co., Wyo.	Gary L. Albertson	Gary L. Albertson	1960	4
214 2/8	27 3/8	27 1/8	28 6/8	5 4/8	5 4/8	5	6	Franklin Co., Idaho	Ray Talbot	Ray Talbot	1961	4
212 7/8	26 6/8	26 7/8	25 4/8	5 2/8	5 2/8	5	5	Gem Co., Idaho	Kirk Payne	Kirk Payne	1967	6
212 1/8*	26 3/8	26 6/8	26 4/8	6 1/8	6 1/8	8	6	San Juan Co., Utah	V. R. Rayburn	V. R. Rayburn	1973	7
212	28 6/8	28	27 6/8	6 5/8	6 5/8	5	6	Chama, N. M.	Jos. A. Garcia	Jos. A. Garcia	1965	8
211 7/8	30 3/8	30 1/8	25 3/8	5	5	5	6	Adams Co., Idaho	Boyd W. Dennis	Boyd W. Dennis	1970	9
211 2/8	29 7/8	29 6/8	30 3/8	4 5/8	4 5/8	7	8	Teton Co., Wyo.	Robert V. Parke	Robert V. Parke	1967	10
210 2/8	29 1/8	29 2/8	27	5 2/8	5 2/8	6	5	Southern Ute Res., Colo.	Jack D. Johnston	Jack D. Johnston	1963	11
210	26 2/8	26 4/8	25 4/8	5 2/8	5 1/8	6	6	Mamti-Lasal Mts., Utah	William Norton	William Norton	1970	12
209 5/8	29 7/8	29 2/8	29 2/8	5	5 2/8	5	7	Montrose Co., Colo.	Mike Thomas	Mike Thomas	1974	13
209 4/8	28 7/8	29 6/8	28	5 7/8	5 7/8	6	8	Wallowa Co., Oreg.	John Calvin Evans	Budd Gronquist	1920	14
209 2/8	27 6/8	27 1/8	27 4/8	5 6/8	5 6/8	5	5	Amherst Mt., Colo.	Herbert Graham	Herbert Graham	1963	15
209	24 4/8	25 4/8	24 1/8	6 1/8	6 2/8	5	7	Saquache Co., Colo.	William B. Pennington	William B. Pennington	1967	16
209	27 1/8	24 4/8	27 4/8	5 4/8	5 4/8	5	5	Rio Arriba Co., N. M.	Kirt I. Darner	B & B Outfitter Service	1968	16
208 6/8	27 6/8	26 7/8	26 2/8	5 1/8	5	6	5	North Kaibab, Ariz.	Horace T. Fowler	Horace T. Fowler	1938	18
208 6/8	24 4/8	24 6/8	17 4/8	5 3/8	5 3/8	6	6	Garfield Co., Colo.	George Shearer	Richard L. Baker	1952	18
208 6/8	26	27 3/8	26 4/8	5 2/8	5 2/8	4	5	Rio Arriba Co., N.M.	James R. Odiorne, Jr.	James R. Odiorne, Jr.	1978	18
208 4/8	26 7/8	27 1/8	27 2/8	5	5	5	5	Mesa Co., Colo.	Robert L. Zaina	Robert L. Zaina	1960	21
207 4/8	29 1/8	28 4/8	27 5/8	5 1/8	5 2/8	6	6	Carbondale, Colo.	Richard Cobb	Richard Cobb	1962	22
207 3/8	26 5/8	26 5/8	25 6/8	5 2/8	5 2/8	6	6	Jicarilla Apache Res., N. M.	Kenneth Campbell	Kenneth Campbell	1969	23
207 3/8	28 1/8	29 4/8	28 7/8	5 6/8	5 5/8	9	7	Mesa Co., Colo.	Wally Bruegman	Wally Bruegman	1972	23
207 2/8	28 5/8	27 1/8	28 1/8	6 5/8	6 4/8	6	6	Montrose Co., Colo.	Bill Crouch	Bill Crouch	1974	25
207 1/8	26 6/8	26 2/8	24 1/8	5 6/8	5 4/8	6	5	Golden, Colo.	Harold B. Moser	Harold B. Moser	1967	26
207	31 6/8	27 2/8	27 4/8	7	7	6	6	Split Rock, Wyo.	Herb Klein	Herb Klein	1960	27
207	26 7/8	28	26 5/8	5 3/8	5 3/8	5	6	Lincoln Co., Wyo.	Al Firenze, Sr.	Al Firenze, Sr.	1969	27
206 7/8	26 1/8	25 7/8	21 3/8	4 6/8	4 7/8	5	5	Montrose Co., Colo.	W. L. Boynton	W. L. Boynton	1973	29
206 5/8	27 7/8	27 4/8	31 4/8	5 1/8	5	5	6	Delta Co., Colo.	Tom Donaldson	Tom Donaldson	1972	30
206 3/8	27 4/8	26 3/8	26 7/8	5 2/8	5 3/8	5	5	Rio Arriba Co., N. M.	Jim Roddie	Jim Roddie	1971	31

Mule Deer (Typical Antlers)—Continued
Odocoileus hemionus hemionus and certain related subspecies

Score	Length of Main Beam R.	L.	Inside Spread	Circumference at Smallest Place Between Burr and First Point R.	L.	Number of Points R.	L.	Locality Killed	By Whom Killed	Owner	Date Killed	Rank
206 3/8	27 1/8	26 5/8	24 3/8	5 1/8	5 1/8	6	7	Coconino Co., Ariz.	Robert C. Kaufman	Robert C. Kaufman	1978	31
206 3/8	26	27 1/8	26 1/8	5 5/8	5 5/8	6	5	Rio Arriba Co., N. M.	Harley Hinds	Oran M. Roberts	1963	33
206 3/8	28	28 2/8	29	6	6	6	5	Montrose, Colo.	Warren S. Bachhofer	Warren S. Bachhofer	1966	33
206 1/8	27 2/8	27 7/8	28 1/8	5 1/8	5	5	4	Eagle Co., Colo.	Harold Taylor	Fred Palmer	1960	35
205 6/8	26 6/8	27 6/8	25 2/8	5 4/8	5 2/8	5	7	Kanab, Utah	Loyd A. Folkstad	Loyd A. Folkstad	1968	36
205 5/8	26 3/8	26 3/8	26 3/8	6	6	5	8	Peterson, Utah	Picked Up	Paul Crittenden	1979	37
205 5/8	26	24 7/8	25 5/8	4 7/8	5	6	5	Gunnison Co., Colo.	Picked Up	Kirt I. Darner	1979	37
205 5/8	25 3/8	27 3/8	22 7/8	5 5/8	5 4/8	6	5	Kremmling, Colo.	Larry Bell	Larry Bell	1962	39
205 5/8	26 6/8	25 7/8	24 6/8	5	5	5	5	Lincoln Co., Wyo.	John E. Myers	John E. Myers	1968	39
205 3/8	26 6/8	27	26 7/8	5 3/8	5 3/8	5	5	Starkey, Oreg.	H. M. Bailey	H. M. Bailey	1963	41
205	24	22 1/8	25	6	6 1/8	5	5	Eagle, Colo.	Harold L. Loesch	Harold L. Loesch	1967	42
204 7/8	27 2/8	27	23 5/8	5 5/8	5 4/8	6	5	Delta Co., Colo.	Frank Peterson	Frank Peterson	1956	43
204 7/8	26 3/8	25 6/8	28 2/8	5 1/8	4 7/8	5	4	Pagosa Springs, Colo.	Henry Trujillo, Jr.	Henry Trujillo, Jr.	1963	43
204 7/8	26 4/8	26 1/8	26 3/8	5 2/8	5 2/8	5	5	Ute Res., Colo.	Nolan Martins	Nolan Martins	1967	43
204 6/8	27	27 4/8	29 4/8	6 2/8	6 1/8	8	8	Pagosa Springs, Colo.	Richard V. Price	Richard V. Price	1962	46
204 2/8	26	26 2/8	22 2/8	5 5/8	5 4/8	4	4	Garfield Co., Utah	James D. Perkins	James D. Perkins	1969	47
204 1/8	28 6/8	30 4/8	24 1/8	4 5/8	4 7/8	6	4	Jicarilla Apache Res., N. M.	Juan Monarco	Juan Monarco	1960	48
204	27	27 3/8	24	5 5/8	5 3/8	5	5	Pitlin Co., Colo.	Jens O. Solberg	Jens O. Solberg	1950	49
203 7/8	24 5/8	26	24 4/8	5	5 2/8	6	6	North Park, Colo.	Edison A. Pillmore	Mrs. Edison A. Pillmore	1949	50
203 7/8	26 3/8	27 5/8	26 3/8	5 2/8	5 3/8	6	6	Mesa Creek, Colo.	Ed Craig	Jerome Craig	1951	50
203 7/8	29 3/8	29 4/8	25 5/8	5	5 5/8	5	5	Jicarilla, N. M.	Dick Wright	Dick Wright	1966	50
203 5/8	28 3/8	27 3/8	24 4/8	5 7/8	5 6/8	6	5	La Plata Co., Colo.	B. E. Gressett	B. E. Gressett	1950	53
203 4/8	25 7/8	29 5/8	27 6/8	5 4/8	5 2/8	5	5	Kaibab Forest, Ariz.	Herb Graham	Herb Graham	1939	54
203 4/8	27 5/8	24	24 4/8	5 5/8	5 3/8	5	5	Elko Co., Nev.	C. H. Wahl	C. H. Wahl	1953	54
203 4/8	24 5/8	25 5/8	25 5/8	4 5/8	4 5/8	5	5	Mesa Co., Colo.	William P. Burger	William P. Burger	1957	54
203 3/8	27	28 1/8	24 4/8	5 5/8	5 5/8	5	6	Rio Arriba Co., N. M.	Arnold Wendt	John Wm. Hughes	1965	54
203 3/8	26 1/8	26 4/8	20 5/8	5 5/8	5 5/8	5	5	Grand Junction, Colo.	Charles M. Bentley	Charles M. Bentley	1962	58
203 3/8	27 5/8	27 6/8	26 5/8	5	5	5	5	Bayfield, Colo.	Kirt Darner	Kirt Darner	1969	58
203 3/8	25 7/8	28	22 4/8	4 1/8	4 4/8	6	5	White River, Colo.	Ron Vance	Ron Vance	1943	60
203 3/8	26 5/8	26 6/8	27 1/8	5 5/8	5 6/8	6	6	North Kaibab, Ariz.	Monico Marquez	Monico Marquez	1957	60
203 3/8	25 3/8	25 7/8	24 6/8	4 5/8	4 5/8	6	7	Crook Co., Wyo.	Ora Mcgurn	Frances Sheperd	1957	60

Score	Main Beam R	Main Beam L	Inside Spread	Circ. R	Circ. L	Pts. R	Pts. L	Locality	By Whom Killed	Owner	Date	Rank
203 3/8	25 6/8	26 6/8	23 3/8	4 6/8	4 7/8	6	5	Dog Valley, Utah	James D. Perkins	Mrs. James D. Perkins	1965	60
203 3/8	27 1/8	26 6/8	22 2/8	4 7/8	4 6/8	5	5	Collbran, Colo.	Joe R. Colingo	Joe R. Colingo	1973	60
203	25	23 5/8	24	5 2/8	5 2/8	5	5	Mesa Co., Colo.	James K. Scott	James K. Scott	1966	65
203	26 3/8	26 3/8	31 5/8	5 3/8	5 3/8	6	5	Franklin Co., Idaho	Herb Voyler, Jr.	Herb Voyler, Jr.	1972	65
202 7/8	24 3/8	26 3/8	26 3/8	6	5 7/8	5	5	Adams Co., Idaho	James S. Denney	James S. Denney	1939	67
202 7/8	27 5/8	27 4/8	26 6/8	6	5 7/8	5	7	Jicarilla Apache Res., N. M.	Anthony Julian	Anthony Julian	1961	67
202 7/8	24 5/8	23	22 1/8	5 2/8	5 2/8	5	5	Lincoln Co., Wyo.	Monte J. Brough	Monte J. Brough	1968	67
202 7/8	26 5/8	26	23 7/8	4 7/8	4 7/8	6	7	Idaho Co., Idaho	Myron L. Gilbert	Myron L. Gilbert	1975	67
202 6/8	25 3/8	24 7/8	19 2/8	6 5/8	6 7/8	6	5	Ouray Co., Colo.	Jewel E. Schottel	Jewel E. Schottel	1966	71
202 5/8	27 1/8	25 5/8	21 5/8	5 1/8	5	5	5	Ouray Co., Colo.	Louis V. Schlosser	Louis V. Schlosser	1965	72
202 5/8	30 3/8	26 1/8	25 1/8	5	5 1/8	5	5	Adams Co., Idaho	David J. Couch	David J. Couch	1970	72
202 2/8	27 3/8	30	21 2/8	6	5 7/8	6	4	Collbran, Colo.	Jack Thompson	Jack Thompson	1968	74
202 2/8	24 5/8	27 4/8	27	5 3/8	5 3/8	6	6	Rio Arriba Co., N. M.	Gerald J. Weber	Gerald J. Weber	1970	74
202 1/8	26 3/8	26	27 6/8	4 7/8	4 7/8	5	5	Morgan Co., Utah	Kenneth R. Dickamore	Kenneth R. Dickamore	1967	76
202	30 3/8	25 5/8	27 1/8	5 5/8	5 5/8	8	8	Montrose Co., Colo.	Earl L. Markley	Earl L. Markley	1968	77
202	28	29 5/8	20 6/8	4 7/8	4 7/8	5	5	Archuleta Co., Colo.	Duane Yearwood	Duane Yearwood	1973	77
201 7/8	27 4/8	24 2/8	29 5/8	5 3/8	5 2/8	5	5	Debeque, Colo.	Francis A. Moore	Francis A. Moore	1962	79
201 6/8	26 5/8	26 3/8	24 2/8	5 1/8	5 1/8	5	6	Uncompahgre Forest, Colo.	Kenneth Klees	Kenneth Klees	1966	80
201 5/8	29 5/8	27 7/8	26 3/8	4 5/8	4 5/8	5	5	Dolores Co., Colo.	Leonard J. Ashcraft	Leonard J. Ashcraft	1958	81
201 5/8	26	26 5/8	21 2/8	5	5	6	5	Afton, Wyo.	Bernard Domries	Bernard Domries	1967	81
201 5/8	28 5/8	28 3/8	30 3/8	5 1/8	5 1/8	5	5	Jicarilla Apache Res., N. M.	Theodore Serafin	Theodore Serafin	1959	81
201 5/8	25 5/8	26	26	5	5	5	5	Pagosa Springs, Colo.	Allen R. Arnwine	Allen R. Arnwine	1960	81
201 5/8	26 3/8	26 5/8	23 3/8	5	5	5	5	Gunnison Natl. For., Colo.	Robert D. Rader	Robert D. Rader	1966	81
201 5/8	27 2/8	27 1/8	27 5/8	5 4/8	5 5/8	5	5	Chelan Co., Wash.	Unknown	Howard W. Hoskins	1970	81
201 4/8	26 3/8	25 3/8	24 3/8	5 3/8	5 3/8	5	5	Malheur Co., Oreg.	David L. Bauer	David L. Bauer	1971	87
201 4/8	28 3/8	28 3/8	22 7/8	5 5/8	5 5/8	7	7	Ravalli Co., Mont.	Sherman L. Williams	Sherman L. Williams	1973	87
201 3/8	27 5/8	27 7/8	26 5/8	5 5/8	5 5/8	7	7	Blaine Co., Idaho	Brent Jones	Brent Jones	1965	89
201 3/8	25 5/8	26 5/8	25 5/8	5 4/8	5 4/8	6	5	Grand Junction, Colo.	William C. Byrd	William C. Byrd	1967	89
201 3/8	26 3/8	25 5/8	25 5/8	5 5/8	5 5/8	6	5	Rio Arriba Co., N. M.	Donald W. Johnson	Donald W. Johnson	1970	89
201 3/8	30 4/8	28 3/8	28 7/8	4 5/8	4 6/8	5	5	Wasatch Co., Utah	Paul Probst	Paul Probst	1971	89
201 3/8	25 5/8	24 5/8	23 1/8	5 4/8	5 4/8	5	5	Montrose Co., Colo.	Grant Morlang	Grant Morlang	1972	89
201 2/8	28	29	28	5	4 6/8	6	6	Bayfield, Colo.	D. Rockwell	D. Rockwell	1956	94
201 2/8	26 5/8	26 5/8	26 5/8	6	6	5	5	Jicarilla Apache Res., N. M.	Anthony Julian	Anthony Julian	1961	94
201 2/8	28 3/8	24	24	5 3/8	5 1/8	5	5	Chama, N. M.	Emitt W. Mundy	Emitt W. Mundy	1961	94
201 1/8	26 3/8	26 5/8	26 5/8	6 5/8	6 3/8	4	6	Bayfield, Colo.	Les Patrick	Les Patrick	1966	97
201	29	26 3/8	22 5/8	6 1/8	6 1/8	5	8	Grand Junction, Colo.	Ernest Mancuso	Ernest Mancuso	1954	98
201	26 3/8	26 3/8	23 6/8	5 1/8	5 1/8	5	5	La Plata Co., Colo.	Larry Pennington	Larry Pennington	1978	98
201	25	25 1/8	24 4/8	4 7/8	5	5	5	Dolores Co., Colo.	Mark Loverin	Mark Loverin	1978	98
200 7/8	30 4/8	28 3/8	28 3/8	4 6/8	4 6/8	6	6	Elko Co., Nev.	Harry Irland	Mrs. Harry Irland	1919	101
200 7/8	28	25 5/8	25 5/8	5 3/8	5 3/8	5	5	Collbran, Colo.	Homer O. Hartley	Homer O. Hartley	1962	101
200 6/8	26 3/8	26 3/8	23	4 6/8	4 7/8	6	5	Provo Canyon, Utah	Karl D. Zaugg	Karl D. Zaugg	1948	103
200 6/8	26 3/8	28	25 5/8	5 5/8	5 5/8	5	5	Malheur Co., Oreg.	Raymond Duncan	Raymond Duncan	1949	103
200 6/8	27 1/8	25 5/8	22 2/8	5 7/8	5 5/8	5	5	Eagle Co., Colo.	John Robertson	John Robertson	1958	103

Mule Deer (*Typical Antlers*)–*Continued*

Odocoileus hemionus hemionus and certain related subspecies

Score	Length of Main Beam R.	Length of Main Beam L.	Inside Spread	Circumference at Smallest Place Between Burr and First Point R.	Circumference at Smallest Place Between Burr and First Point L.	Number of Points R.	Number of Points L.	Locality Killed	By Whom Killed	Owner	Date Killed	Rank
200 6/8	27	27 3/8	26	5	5 1/8	5	5	Southern Ute Res., Colo.	Jerry E. Morgan	Jerry E. Morgan	1965	103
200 6/8	26	26 6/8	23 4/8	5 6/8	5 4/8	6	7	Delta, Colo.	Emil Warber, Jr.	Emil Warber, Jr.	1966	103
200 6/8	25 6/8	26 1/8	26 4/8	5	5 4/8	5	6	Jicarilla Apache Res., N. M.	Arnold Cassador	Arnold Cassador	1967	103
200 5/8	27	26 4/8	26 4/8	4 6/8	5	7	9	Ogden, Utah	Carl F. Worden	Carl F. Worden	1948	109
200 5/8	26 2/8	26 2/8	25 3/8	5	4 7/8	5	5	Cameo, Colo.	Thomas C. Krauss	Thomas C. Krauss	1962	109
200 5/8	25 2/8	25 2/8	25 2/8	5	5 2/8	6	5	Lincoln Co., Wyo.	John Myers	John Myers	1973	109
200 4/8	26 1/8	26 2/8	28 2/8	4 7/8	4 7/8	5	6	Bear Lake Co., Idaho	Alan R. Crane	Alan R. Crane	1962	112
200 4/8	27	25 6/8	23 6/8	5 1/8	5	7	6	Bear Lake Co., Idaho	Lee Bridges	Lee Bridges	1966	112
200 4/8	26	26 2/8	23 2/8	5 2/8	5 1/8	5	6	Rio Arriba Co., N. M.	Jerry Longenbaugh	Jerry Longenbaugh	1969	112
200 4/8	26 4/8	26 6/8	23	5 3/8	5 3/8	5	5	Caribou Co., Idaho	Herb Voyler, Jr.	Herb Voyler, Jr.	1972	112
200 4/8	25	25 4/8	25	4 6/8	5	5	5	Eagle Co., Colo.	Jack Stevens	Jack Stevens	1975	112
200 4/8	26	24 6/8	27 4/8	5	4 7/8	5	5	Sweetwater Co., Wyo.	Arnold A. Bethke	Arnold A. Bethke	1976	112
200 3/8	27 5/8	27 4/8	27 1/8	5 4/8	5 2/8	4	4	Okanogan Co., Wash.	E. R. Crooks	E. R. Crooks	1939	117
200 3/8	27 4/8	27 4/8	26 1/8	5 4/8	5 3/8	7	7	Uncompahgre Natl. For., Colo.	Richard M. Holbrook	Richard M. Holbrook	1972	117
200 3/8	26 7/8	29 1/8	24 4/8	5 1/8	5 1/8	5	7	Gypsum, Colo.	Gene D. Lintz	Gene D. Lintz	1974	117
200 2/8	25	25 1/8	22 4/8	5 6/8	5 6/8	6	6	Battle Mt., Wyo.	Ron Vance	Ron Vance	1963	121
200 2/8	29 7/8	28 3/8	23 6/8	4 7/8	4 6/8	5	5	Southern Ute Res., Colo.	Arthur Burch	Steven Burch	1966	121
200 2/8	27 4/8	27	26 7/8	5	4 7/8	6	5	Ouray Co., Colo.	Joseph T. Hollingshead	Joseph T. Hollingshead	1967	121
200 2/8	27 5/8	28 5/8	26	4 7/8	5	4	4	Asotin Co., Wash.	Grant E. Holcomb	Grant E. Holcomb	1975	121
200 1/8	27 3/8	27 6/8	27 3/8	5 3/8	5 4/8	5	5	Cashmere, Wash.	John F. Schurle	Wm. H. Schott	1913	125
200 1/8	27 2/8	28 6/8	25 7/8	4 6/8	4 6/8	5	5	Uncompahgre Mesa, Colo.	John M. Domingos	John M Domingos	1965	125
200	26 2/8	27	27	5 5/8	5 5/8	5	6	Summit Co., Colo.	Picked Up	Bill Knorr	1959	127
200	24 2/8	25 4/8	25 2/8	4 7/8	4 6/8	5	5	Piedra River, Colo.	Glen A. Smith	Glen A. Smith	1960	127
200	27 4/8	28 7/8	28 7/8	6 3/8	6 3/8	6	5	Colo.	Unknown	John F. Frost	1963	127
200	29 6/8	29 7/8	24 4/8	5 3/8	5 2/8	6	6	Mouqi, Ariz.	Tom Corey	Tom Corey	1964	127
200	27 1/8	26	24 4/8	4 7/8	4 7/8	5	5	Eagle Co., Colo.	Dale R. Leonard	Dale R. Leonard	1976	127
199 7/8	22 6/8	23 2/8	22 6/8	5 1/8	5 1/8	7	6	Jackson Co., Colo.	G. B. Berger, Jr.	Denver Mus. Nat. Hist.	1934	132
199 7/8	24 1/8	24 7/8	23 1/8	5	5 1/8	5	5	Uncompahgre Natl. For., Colo.	H. E. Gerhart	H. E. Gerhart	1963	132
199 7/8	25 3/8	24 5/8	25 1/8	5 4/8	5 4/8	5	5	Stillwater Co., Mont.	Basil C. Bradbury	Basil C. Bradbury	1965	132

199 7/8	25 7/8	27 2/8	25 7/8	4 7/8	5	7	6	Coconino Co., Ariz.	John L. Johnson	John L. Johnson	1972	132
199 6/8	24 7/8	25 3/8	26	4 4/8	4 4/8	5	5	Mesa, Colo.	Robert W. Hill	Robert W. Hill	1963	136
199 6/8	26 4/8	26	27	5 6/8	5 6/8	5	6	Uncompahgre, Colo.	Mitchell J. Sacco	Mitchell J. Sacco	1966	136
199 6/8	26 6/8	24 7/8	28 4/8	6 3/8	6	5	5	Chama, N. M.	James W. Smith, II	James W. Smith, II	1969	136
199 6/8	24 1/8	24 1/8	25	5 4/8	5 4/8	5	6	Archuleta Co., Colo.	Kirt I. Darner	Kirt I. Darner	1973	136
199 4/8	28 2/8	27 3/8	28	6 1/8	6 2/8	7	8	Pagosa Springs, Colo.	Perry Dixon	Perry Dixon	1957	140
199 4/8	24 2/8	24 2/8	21 2/8	5 5/8	5 5/8	5	5	Bonneville Co., Idaho	Leonard J. Vella	Leonard J. Vella	1972	140
199 3/8	27 3/8	26	25 1/8	5 4/8	6	4	4	Silt, Colo.	V. M. Spiller	V. M. Spiller	1961	142
199 3/8	27	27 6/8	23 7/8	5 4/8	5 4/8	4	4	Rio Arriba Co., N. M.	John A. Farrell	John A. Farrell	1966	142
199 3/8	26 7/8	25 7/8	24 4/8	5 6/8	5 5/8	5	6	Rio Arriba Co., N. M.	Johnny L. Montgomery	Johnny L. Montgomery	1967	142
199 2/8	27 1/8	25 4/8	26	5	5 2/8	7	5	Beechy, Sask.	Marvin Taylor	Marvin Taylor	1961	145
199 2/8	27 5/8	28	25 4/8	5 2/8	5 2/8	5	5	Strawberry, Utah	Steve Payne	Steve Payne	1962	145
199 2/8	27 4/8	26 1/8	26 4/8	5 1/8	5 1/8	5	5	Eagle Co., Colo.	Howard Stoker	Howard Stoker	1965	145
199 2/8	26 1/8	25 1/8	24 1/8	5 6/8	5 5/8	6	6	Hidden Canyon, Ariz.	Milton Wyman	Milton Wyman	1972	145
199 2/8	25 2/8	25 1/8	25 1/8	5 2/8	5 2/8	7	6	Garfield Co., Colo.	Gary W. Hartley	Gary W. Hartley	1978	145
199 1/8	26 2/8	28 4/8	28 7/8	4 6/8	4 7/8	7	7	Salmon River, Idaho	C. A. Schwope	C. A. Schwope	1959	150
199 1/8	28 3/8	27 2/8	27 6/8	6	5 6/8	8	6	Jicarilla Apache Res., N. M.	David L. Chandler	David L. Chandler	1961	150
199 1/8	25 2/8	25 2/8	26 7/8	5 3/8	5 2/8	5	7	Boise County, Idaho	Delbert W. Crawford	Delbert W. Crawford	1969	150
199 1/8	25	24 3/8	24 3/8	5 6/8	5 5/8	6	5	San Juan Co., Utah	Phyllis O. Crookston	Phyllis O. Crookston	1971	150
199	26 6/8	27 1/8	26 2/8	4 7/8	5 1/8	5	5	Echo, Utah	Wilford Zaugg	Wilford Zaugg	1958	154
199	26 4/8	25 4/8	29 4/8	5 1/8	5 3/8	5	6	Gunnison Natl. For., Colo.	James M. Newsom	James M. Newsom	1963	154
199	25 1/8	26 3/8	23 4/8	5 4/8	5 1/8	5	5	Park Co., Wyo.	Lois M. Pelzel	Lois M. Pelzel	1965	154
199	24 2/8	24 2/8	21	5	5 2/8	5	6	Mohave Co., Ariz.	William M. Berger, Jr.	William M. Berger, Jr.	1973	154
199	25	25 4/8	26	4 6/8	5	5	5	Dolores Co., Colo.	Kenneth L. Peters	Kenneth L. Peters	1976	154
198 7/8	27	27 4/8	28 5/8	6 1/8	6 1/8	5	5	Silt, Colo.	George McCoy	George McCoy	1961	159
198 7/8	26 5/8	27 1/8	26 5/8	5 7/8	6	5	7	Jicarilla Apache Res., N. M.	Anthony Julian	Jicarilla Apache Tribe	1961	159
198 7/8	26 4/8	24 2/8	19 3/8	5 7/8	5 7/8	7	5	Burns, Colo.	Charles Douglas Rush	Charles Douglas Rush	1967	159
198 6/8	23 4/8	22 2/8	21 6/8	5 1/8	5 2/8	5	5	Hines Creek, Alta.	Charles Lundgard	Charles Lundgard	1960	162
198 6/8	32 7/8	32 4/8	25 3/8	6 3/8	7	7	6	Dulce, N. M.	Everett M. Vigil	Everett M. Vigil	1967	162
198 5/8	26 2/8	27 2/8	24 5/8	5	5	6	7	Carbondale, Colo.	Ralph Clock	Ralph Clock	1961	164
198 5/8	24 4/8	24 7/8	24 1/8	5 3/8	5 5/8	6	6	Swan Valley, Idaho	Harry G. Brinkley, Jr.	Harry G. Brinkley, Jr.	1966	164
198 5/8	25 1/8	25 2/8	23 1/8	4 7/8	5	5	7	Carbon Co., Wyo.	M. Gary Muske	M. Gary Muske	1968	164
198 4/8	29	27 2/8	32 7/8	5 5/8	5 4/8	6	9	Del Norte, Colo.	Esequiel Trujillo	Esequiel Trujillo	1947	167
198 4/8	25 4/8	25 6/8	20 4/8	5	5	5	5	Tabiona, Utah	Picked Up	H. A. Zumbrock	1957	167
198 4/8	29	28 7/8	22 4/8	5 1/8	5 1/8	4	5	Dark Canyon, Colo.	O. P. (Mick) McGuire	O. P. (Mick) McGuire	1966	167
198 4/8	26	25 4/8	21 4/8	5 3/8	5 2/8	5	4	Routt Co., Colo.	Lloyd D. Kindsfater	Lloyd D. Kindsfater	1966	167
198 4/8	28 5/8	28 4/8	24 5/8	5 3/8	5 3/8	5	6	Afton, Wyo.	Ray M. Vincent	Ray M. Vincent	1967	167
198 3/8	25	25 4/8	19 5/8	4 5/8	4 5/8	5	5	Bonneville Co., Idaho	Tony Dawson	Tony Dawson	1973	172
198 2/8	26 4/8	27 4/8	26 4/8	4 7/8	4 7/8	6	8	Summit Co., Colo.	Unknown	Louis Ceriani	—	173
198 2/8	25 2/8	25 5/8	22 4/8	6 1/8	6	8	5	Garfield Co., Colo.	Leroy Failor	Leroy Failor	1944	173
198 2/8	28	26 1/8	28 2/8	5	5	5	6	Kaibab Forest, Ariz.	W. O. Hart	W. O. Hart	1946	173
198 2/8	24 4/8	25 3/8	26 1/8	5 6/8	5 6/8	5	5	Disappointment Creek, Colo.	Clifford Le Neve	Clifford Le Neve	1954	173
198 2/8	22 5/8	22 7/8	27 6/8	5 3/8	6 3/8	6	6	Hayden, Colo.	M. W. Giboney	M. W. Giboney	1959	173

MULE DEER (Typical Antlers)—Continued

Odocoileus hemionus hemionus and certain related subspecies

Score	Length of Main Beam R.	L.	Inside Spread	Circumference at Smallest Place Between Burr and First Point R.	L.	Number of Points R.	L.	Locality Killed	By Whom Killed	Owner	Date Killed	Rank
198 2/8	25 5/8	25 5/8	24 3/8	5 1/8	5	5	6	Sonora, Mexico	Heinz G. Holdorf	Heinz G. Holdorf	1966	173
198 1/8	25 3/8	26 1/8	23 7/8	5 5/8	5 7/8	5	6	Bayfield, Colo.	C. Ben Boyd	C. Ben Boyd	1967	179
198 1/8	27 7/8	27 7/8	23 7/8	5	5	7	6	Montrose Co., Colo.	Robert A. Klatt	Robert A. Klatt	1975	179
198	26 7/8	25 7/8	22 1/8	5 3/8	5 3/8	5	7	Unknown	Unknown	Lunds Wildlife Exhibit	1931	181
198	25 3/8	26	25 3/8	5 5/8	5 4/8	5	4	Irwin, Idaho	Chet Warwick	Chet Warwick	1959	181
198	25	25 5/8	26	6	5 7/8	6	6	Mt. Trumbull, Ariz.	E. O. Brown	E. O. Brown	1960	181
198	25 3/8	24 7/8	25 1/8	5 5/8	5 3/8	6	5	Smithfield Canyon, Utah	Stanley Richardson	Stanley Richardson	1961	181
198	25	25	22 4/8	5 5/8	5 5/8	5	5	Montpelier, Idaho	Charles R. Mann	Charles R. Mann	1973	181
198	24	24 7/8	22 4/8	6 1/8	5 5/8	7	6	Eagle Co., Colo	Larry Schlasinger	Larry Schlasinger	1978	181
197 7/8	25 3/8	25 5/8	25	5 1/8	5 3/8	6	6	Sonora, Mexico	J. G. Cigarroa, Sr.	J. G. Cigarroa, Sr.	1957	187
197 7/8	25 3/8	25 1/8	24 5/8	4 5/8	4 7/8	5	6	Kaibab Forest, Ariz.	Eoans Pababla	Eoans Pababla	1957	187
197 7/8	26 1/8	27 7/8	24 1/8	4 7/8	5	5	5	Rio Blanco Co., Colo.	Gary L. Bicknell	Gary L. Bicknell	1967	187
197 7/8	28 3/8	27 7/8	24 5/8	5 3/8	5 3/8	5	5	Rossland, B. C.	Robert Simm	Robert Simm	1968	187
197 7/8	24 3/8	25	25 3/8	5 1/8	4 7/8	5	5	Coconino Co., Ariz.	Dale C. Morse	Dale C. Morse	1977	187
197 7/8	28 5/8	28 3/8	25 4/8	5	5	6	5	Eagle Co., Colo.	Lee Frudden	Lee Frudden	1978	187
197 6/8	27 7/8	28	25 3/8	4 5/8	4 4/8	5	5	Encampment, Wyo.	Ralph E. Platt, Jr.	Ralph E. Platt, Jr.	1936	193
197 6/8	25 5/8	25 7/8	23 6/8	5 5/8	5 3/8	6	5	Elk Ridge, Utah	Bill King	Joseph Fitting	1956	193
197 6/8	27 3/8	26 3/8	24 4/8	4 4/8	4 4/8	5	5	Jefferson Co., Mont.	James W. Rowe	James W. Rowe	1964	193
197 6/8	26 3/8	27 5/8	23 7/8	4 5/8	5	8	8	Teton Co., Wyo.	John W. Farlow, Jr.	John W. Farlow, Jr.	1971	193
197 6/8	26 7/8	26	26 3/8	5 3/8	5 5/8	5	5	Gunnison Co., Colo.	Bobby Joe Watson	Bobby Joe Watson	1975	193
197 6/8	22 7/8	22	22 2/8	4 5/8	4 4/8	5	5	Major, Sask.	Art Heintz	Art Heintz	1961	198
197 6/8	24	26	21 1/8	5 5/8	5 5/8	5	5	Moffat Co., Colo.	Russ H. Winslow	Russ H. Winslow	1967	199
197 6/8	26 3/8	25 7/8	24 7/8	4 6/8	4 7/8	5	6	Uinta Co., Wyo.	Ken Vernon	Ken Vernon	1968	199
197 6/8	26 7/8	26 3/8	24 5/8	5	5	6	5	White River Natl. For., Colo.	Picked Up	Jack Thompson	PR1957	201
197 5/8	26 7/8	25	22 3/8	5 5/8	5 3/8	5	5	Currant Creek, Utah	Morris Kidd	Morris Kidd	1960	201
197 5/8	27 1/8	27 3/8	24 2/8	5	5	5	7	Montrose, Colo.	H. R. Clark	H. R. Clark	1961	201
197 5/8	25	25 5/8	27 3/8	5 7/8	6	5	5	Chama, N. M.	Kirt I. Darner	Kirt I. Darner	1962	201
197 5/8	25 4/8	26 1/8	30 1/8	6 1/8	6	5	5	Archuleta Co., Colo.	Joe Moore	Joe Moore	1962	201
197 5/8	26 3/8	27 5/8	26 3/8	4 6/8	4 7/8	6	6	Fremont Co., Idaho	Stanley A. Gilgen	Stanley A. Gilgen	1964	201
197 5/8	26 3/8	26	25 4/8	5 3/8	5 3/8	5	6	Pagasa Springs, Colo.	John Damon Guess	John Damon Guess	1966	201

Score									Locality	Owner	By Whom Killed	Date	Rank
197 3/8	25 5/8	27 1/8	26 1/8	26 1/8	5	5	5 5/8	5 3/8	Apache Mesa, N. M.	Tom Martine	Tom Martine	1970	201
197 5/8	26 1/8	26 5/8	21 1/8	21 1/8	7	7	6 5/8	7	Beechy, Sask.	Pete Perrin	Pete Perrin	1947	209
197 3/8	27 1/8	27	26 7/8	26 7/8	5	8	5	5 3/8	Chaffee Co., Colo.	Marguerite Hill	Marguerite Hill	1956	209
197 3/8	27 3/8	27 3/8	26 7/8	27 1/8	6	5	5 5/8	5 3/8	Afton, Wyo.	Robert Williams	Robert Williams	1960	209
197 3/8	29 3/8	30 3/8	27 1/8	28 5/8	7	6	5 5/8	5 1/8	Harney Co., Oreg.	Guy Evan Osborne	Guy Evan Osborne	1963	209
197 3/8	26 3/8	26 1/8	21 1/8	21 1/8	5	5	4 5/8	4 3/8	Weber Co., Utah	Abe B. Murdock	Abe B. Murdock	1972	209
197 1/8	26 5/8	26 5/8	28	28	6	5	5 5/8	5 3/8	Craig, Colo.	Lucille Gooch	George Gooch	1951	214
197 1/8	24 3/8	24 1/8	24 7/8	24 7/8	5	5	5	4 7/8	Ashton, Idaho	Earl Johnson	O. M. Corbett	1959	214
197 1/8	26 5/8	27 7/8	26 3/8	26 3/8	5	5	5 1/8	5 3/8	Ashwood, Oreg.	Harvey Rhoads	Harvey Rhoads	1962	214
197 1/8	26 5/8	27 7/8	28 5/8	28 5/8	6	5	5 3/8	5 3/8	San Miguel Co., Colo.	Everett Stutler	Everett Stutler	1965	214
197 1/8	27 5/8	27 7/8	26	30 5/8	6	6	5 3/8	5	Adams Co., Idaho	Roy Eastlick	Roy Eastlick	1974	214
197	24 3/8	25 1/8	25 5/8	25 1/8	5	5	5 5/8	5 5/8	Grand Co., Colo.	Woodrow W. Dixon	Woodrow W. Dixon	1962	219
197	24 3/8	25 3/8	22	23 5/8	5	5	5 3/8	5 3/8	Franklin Co., Idaho	Robert C. Porter	Robert C. Porter	1972	219
196 7/8	26 5/8	26 1/8	24 5/8	24 7/8	5	5	4 5/8	4 3/8	Chama, N. M.	Kirt I. Darner	B & B Outfitter Service	1965	221
196 7/8	24 5/8	24 3/8	22 5/8	22 5/8	5	5	5 5/8	5 5/8	Boise Co., Idaho	Andrew T. Rogers	Andrew T. Rogers	1967	221
196 5/8	25 5/8	24	21 5/8	21 5/8	5	5	5 3/8	5 3/8	Lincoln Co., Mont.	Dennis J. Hauke	Dennis J. Hauke	1973	221
196 5/8	24 3/8	26 5/8	27 3/8	27 3/8	5	5	5 1/8	5 1/8	Bonneville Co., Idaho	Preston L. Winchell	Preston L. Winchell	1974	221
196 5/8	24 3/8	23 7/8	24 1/8	24 3/8	7	7	5 3/8	5 3/8	Bear Lake Co., Idaho	Nels H. Pehrson	Ralph V. Pehrson	1936	225
196 5/8	27	26 7/8	28 7/8	28 7/8	5	5	5	5	N. Kaibab, Ariz.	Simon C. Krevitsky	Simon C. Krevitsky	1963	225
196 5/8	25 1/8	25 5/8	24 7/8	24 7/8	5	5	5 5/8	5 5/8	Delta, Colo.	Howard G. Reed	Howard G. Reed	1968	225
196 5/8	23 3/8	24 1/8	22 5/8	22 1/8	5	5	5 3/8	5 1/8	Bonnieville Co., Idaho	William G. Pine	William G. Pine	1969	225
196 5/8	24 3/8	23 3/8	23 1/8	23 7/8	6	7	6 3/8	6 3/8	DeBeque, Colo.	Walter C. Friauf	Walter C. Friauf	1970	225
196 5/8	26 1/8	26	22 3/8	26	5	5	5	5	San Juan Natl. For., Colo.	Wilford E. Seymour, Jr.	Wilford E. Seymour, Jr.	1974	225
196 5/8	27 3/8	26 5/8	25 5/8	26 5/8	6	6	6	6	Chelan Co., Wash.	George Bolton	Welcome Sauer	1930	231
196 5/8	24 3/8	23 3/8	23 3/8	23 3/8	5	5	5 5/8	5 5/8	Ruby Mt., Nev.	Earl Frantzen	Earl Frantzen	1941	231
196 5/8	25 1/8	24 3/8	28 3/8	28 3/8	5	5	4 3/8	4 3/8	Morgan Co., Utah	Gayle Allen	Gayle Allen	1948	231
196 5/8	26	26 3/8	24 3/8	24 3/8	4	5	4 5/8	4 5/8	Slater, Colo.	W. J. Bracken	W. J. Bracken	1959	231
196 5/8	27 3/8	27 1/8	29 3/8	29 3/8	6	5	5 5/8	5 5/8	Cimarron, Colo.	Reynolds L. Vanstrom	Reynolds L. Vanstrom	1960	231
196 5/8	25 3/8	25 1/8	25 1/8	25 1/8	5	5	4 7/8	4 5/8	Weber River, Utah	Desmond Shields	Desmond Shields	1960	231
196 5/8	26	25 7/8	22 5/8	22 5/8	5	5	4 3/8	4 5/8	Dubois, Wyo.	P. C. Alfred Dorow	P. C. Alfred Dorow	1960	231
196 5/8	24 3/8	25 7/8	25 1/8	25 1/8	5	5	5 5/8	5 5/8	Grand Mesa, Colo.	Marvin L. Shepard	Marvin L. Shepard	1960	231
196 5/8	26	24 3/8	22 5/8	22 5/8	6	7	5 1/8	5 1/8	Rio Arriba Co., N. M.	Stanley Davis	Stanley Davis	1965	231
196 5/8	25 5/8	25 3/8	28	28	7	7	5 5/8	5 5/8	Summit Co., Utah	Jerry Lee Henriod	Jerry Lee Henriod	1967	231
196 5/8	22	22 5/8	24 1/2	24 1/2	7	5	4 7/8	5 3/8	Lemhi County, Idaho	Hubert M. Livingston	Hubert M. Livingston	1967	231
196 5/8	24 7/8	25	21 5/8	21 5/8	5	5	5	5 1/8	Maybell, Colo.	James W. Johnson	James W. Johnson	1968	231
196 5/8	23 7/8	24	23 5/8	23 5/8	5	5	4 5/8	4 5/8	Lincoln Co., Wyo.	Chester Michalski	Chester Michalski	1974	231
196 3/8	24 5/8	25 5/8	22 5/8	22 5/8	7	7	5 1/8	5 1/8	Flathead River, Mont.	Stanley Rauscher	Stanley Rauscher	1959	244
196 3/8	23 3/8	22 5/8	19 5/8	19 5/8	5	5	5	5	Garfield Co., Colo.	Elmer Nelson	Elmer Nelson	1962	244
196 3/8	24 3/8	25 1/8	21	21	5	5	6 1/8	6 1/8	Vernal, Utah	Selby G. Tanner	Selby G. Tanner	1966	244
196 3/8	25 3/8	24 5/8	23	23	5	5	5 7/8	5 5/8	Southern Ute Res., Colo.	William C. Forsyth	William C. Forsyth	1974	244
196 3/8	24 5/8	25 1/8	24 5/8	24 5/8	6	5	5 3/8	5 3/8	Powell Co., Mont.	Stanley F. Malcolm	Stanley F. Malcolm	1958	248
196 3/8	27 1/2	27 7/8	27	27	6	6	5 1/8	5 1/8	Chama, N. M.	Jerry Washburn	Jerry Washburn	1960	248
196 3/8	26 3/8	27 3/8	22 3/8	22 3/8	7	6	6 1/8	6	Jicarilla Apache Res., N. M.	Tim Vicenti	Tim Vicenti	1960	248

MULE DEER (*Typical Antlers*)—*Continued*

Odocoileus hemionus hemionus and certain related subspecies

Score	Length of Main Beam R.	L.	Inside Spread	Circumference at Smallest Place Between Burr and First Point R.	L.	Number of Points R.	L.	Locality Killed	By Whom Killed	Owner	Date Killed	Rank
196 3/8	23 7/8	25 5/8	27 1/8	4 7/8	4 7/8	7	7	Gunnison Co., Colo.	E. D. Palmer	E. D. Palmer	1962	248
196 3/8	25 4/8	24 5/8	24 5/8	5	5	5	4	Chama, N. M.	Robert W. Highfill	Robert W. Highfill	1964	248
196 3/8	26 4/8	26	24 4/8	5 3/8	5 3/8	6	5	Durango, Colo.	Ronald Chitwood	Ronald Chitwood	1964	248
196 3/8	28 1/8	28 3/8	26 1/8	4 7/8	5	4	4	Uncompahgre Plateau, Colo.	Earl L. Markley	Earl L. Markley	1969	248
196 3/8	26 3/8	27 1/8	25 1/8	5 5/8	5 5/8	6	6	Sublette Co., Wyo.	Kim Bonnett	Kim Bonnett	1978	248
196 2/8	27 4/8	27 1/8	25 1/8	4 5/8	5 1/8	7	5	Lincoln Co., Mont.	Tommy Boothman	Tommy Boothman	1960	256
196 2/8	26 1/8	23 7/8	23 5/8	6	5 7/8	5	6	Chama, N. M.	Laura Wilson	Laura Wilson	1967	256
196 2/8	22 5/8	22 5/8	21 5/8	5 3/8	5 3/8	6	6	Millard Co., Utah	Burnell Washburn	Burnell Washburn	1967	256
196 2/8	24	25	20 6/8	4 2/8	4 5/8	5	7	Big Horn Mts., Wyo.	Ruth Davis	Ruth Davis	1968	256
196 2/8	27	27 1/8	24 7/8	5 4/8	5 4/8	7	5	Rio Arriba Co., N. M.	B. D. Shipwash	B. D. Shipwash	1969	256
196 2/8	27 2/8	27 3/8	20 6/8	5 5/8	5 2/8	9	5	Meeker, Colo.	Mike Murphy	Mike Murphy	1971	256
196 2/8	25 4/8	25 6/8	22 4/8	5 2/8	5 3/8	8	6	Bingham Co., Idaho	Thomas D. Robison	Thomas D. Robison	1972	256
196 2/8	27	26 1/8	28 6/8	4 6/8	5 3/8	6	4	Hinsdale Co., Colo.	Alan L. VanDenBerg	Alan L. VanDenBerg	1978	256
196 1/8	26	27 7/8	24 6/8	5 7/8	5 6/8	5	5	Boise Co., Idaho	H. L. Rice	H. L. Rice	1966	264
196 1/8	25 7/8	25	23 5/8	5 5/8	5 3/8	7	4	Uncompahgre Natl. For., Colo.	Harry L. Whitlock	Harry L. Whitlock	1968	264
196 1/8	25 5/8	25 5/8	25 5/8	5	5 1/8	5	5	Meeker, Colo.	Max R. Zoeller	Max R. Zoeller	1972	264
196	27 3/8	26	21 1/8	5 3/8	5 3/8	5	7	N. Kaibab, Ariz.	John D. McNeley	John D. McNeley	1948	267
196	23 6/8	24 1/8	22 4/8	5	5 1/8	6	5	Kaibab Forest, Ariz.	Elgin T. Gates	Elgin T. Gates	1958	267
196	27 4/8	27 4/8	27 1/8	5 5/8	5 5/8	5	5	Huerfano Co., Colo.	F. C. Hibben	F. C. Hibben	1963	267
196	26 4/8	26 4/8	27 2/8	4 7/8	4 7/8	6	6	Uncompahgre Plateau, Colo.	Bill Styers	Bill Styers	1964	267
196	27 1/8	25 1/8	30 4/8	5 3/8	5 4/8	6	8	Delta, Colo.	Alvin T. Stivers	Alvin T. Stivers	1965	267
196	25	24 4/8	24	5 3/8	5	6	5	Corwin Spgs., Mont.	Donald Strazzabosco	Donald Strazzabosco	1966	267
196	29 4/8	29 2/8	25 4/8	5	5	5	5	Jicarilla Apache Res., N. M.	Collins F. Kellogg	Collins F. Kellogg	1973	267
196	25 4/8	28	23	5 5/8	5 5/8	6	6	Franklin Co., Idaho	Larry W. Cross	Larry W. Cross	1974	267
195 7/8	26 4/8	25 7/8	26 3/8	5 5/8	5 5/8	7	7	Bannock Co., Idaho	William J. Barry	William J. Barry	1956	275
195 7/8	26	26 7/8	26 6/8	5 4/8	5 4/8	6	6	Southern Ute Res., Colo.	Richard Schmidt	Southern Ute Tribe	1960	275
195 7/8	26 4/8	26 6/8	26 6/8	5 3/8	5 4/8	6	5	Rio Arriba Co., N. M.	Ross Lopez	Ross Lopez	1964	275
195 7/8	28	28	26 6/8	5 5/8	5 5/8	8	5	Cache Co., Utah	Richard E. Reeder	Richard E. Reeder	1968	275
195 7/8	27 4/8	26 5/8	24 7/8	5 5/8	5 5/8	5	5	San Miguel Co., Colo.	Jerry E. Albin	Jerry E. Albin	1972	275
195 6/8	26 4/8	26 4/8	24 7/8	5 3/8	5 2/8	5	5	Princeton, B. C.	Glen Stadler	Glen Stadler	1958	280

Score						R	L	Locality	By Whom Killed	Owner	Date	Final Score
195⁵/₈	27⁴/₈	29	26³/₈	5⁵/₈	5⁵/₈	7	9	Keating, Oreg.	Francis A. Delepierre	Francis A. Delepierre	1966	280
195⁵/₈	25⁵/₈	25⁵/₈	21³/₈	4⁶/₈	4⁶/₈	5	4	Pitkin Co., Idaho	William F. Kirby	William F. Kirby	1966	280
195⁵/₈	28⁷/₈	28⁴/₈	28⁴/₈	5¹/₈	4⁶/₈	5	5	Grant Co., Oreg	Larry Parlette	Larry Parlette	1967	280
195⁵/₈	25⁷/₈	26⁴/₈	24⁴/₈	4⁶/₈	4⁶/₈	5	5	Gunnison, Colo.	Randall R. Kieft	Randall R. Kieft	1967	280
195⁵/₈	24⁶/₈	25²/₈	22⁶/₈	5	5	5	7	Montrose Co., Colo.	Larry Della Bitta	Larry Della Bitta	1969	280
195⁵/₈	22⁷/₈	24⁶/₈	23⁵/₈	5³/₈	5²/₈	6	6	Gunnison Co., Colo.	George L. Hoffman, Jr.	George L. Hoffman, Jr.	1972	280
195⁵/₈	25⁴/₈	24⁴/₈	23¹/₈	4³/₈	4³/₈	5	5	Utah	Picked Up	Jarvie Taxidermy	1947	287
195⁵/₈	26⁵/₈	27¹/₈	26¹/₈	4⁷/₈	4⁶/₈	5	5	Ravalli Co., Mont.	William H. Cowan	William H. Cowan	1959	287
195⁵/₈	27⁴/₈	27⁶/₈	24¹/₈	6	5⁷/₈	7	7	Slocan Valley, B. C.	John Braun	John Braun	1962	287
195⁵/₈	30⁵/₈	29	26³/₈	6²/₈	6²/₈	6	8	Jicarilla Apache Res., N. M.	Eldrid Vigil	Eldrid Vigil	1962	287
195⁵/₈	27⁵/₈	25³/₈	20⁵/₈	4⁷/₈	4⁷/₈	5	5	Delta Co., Colo.	Royce J. Carville	Royce J. Carville	1974	287
195⁵/₈	25¹/₈	25⁴/₈	22⁴/₈	5²/₈	5²/₈	4	5	Grover, Utah	Vicki Davis	R. J. Davis	1959	292
195⁵/₈	26³/₈	25¹/₈	26³/₈	5³/₈	5³/₈	5	5	Raton, N. M.	Unknown	John H. Steinle, III	1963	292
195⁵/₈	24²/₈	25	20⁴/₈	5⁶/₈	5⁷/₈	5	5	Montrose, Colo.	Tony L. Hill	Tony L. Hill	1969	292
195⁵/₈	24²/₈	24⁷/₈	24²/₈	5²/₈	5⁷/₈	5	6	Garfield Co., Colo.	Billy R. Babb	Billy R. Babb	1969	292
195⁵/₈	28⁷/₈	28⁴/₈	25⁵/₈	5²/₈	5⁷/₈	7	5	Mohave Co., Ariz.	Bob B. Coker	Bob B. Coker	1972	296
195³/₈	27³/₈	26⁷/₈	26⁵/₈	4⁶/₈	4⁶/₈	5	5	Natrona Co., Wyo.	Richard Ullery	Richard Ullery	1977	296
195³/₈	26⁵/₈	25⁷/₈	26³/₈	5²/₈	5¹/₈	6	7	Moffat Co., Colo.	Frank J. Kubin	Frank J. Kubin	1978	296
195³/₈	26⁵/₈	27¹/₈	27	5⁵/₈	5⁷/₈	7	6	Montrose Co., Colo.	Edward A. Ipser	Edward A. Ipser	1965	299
195³/₈	26⁵/₈	27	25⁷/₈	5¹/₈	5¹/₈	7	5	Marble, Colo.	David R. Allen	David R. Allen	1968	299
195³/₈	26⁶/₈	26	28⁴/₈	5³/₈	5³/₈	6	5	Archuleta Co., Colo.	Hugh W. Gardner	Hugh W. Gardner	1971	299
195³/₈	25	26⁷/₈	24⁴/₈	5⁷/₈	5⁷/₈	5	5	Davis Co., Utah	Mitchell L. Cochran	Mitchell L. Cochran	1972	299
195³/₈	25	25³/₈	25³/₈	5¹/₈	5⁷/₈	5	6	Jarbidge Mt., Nev.	Donald G. Heidtman	Donald G. Heidtman	1954	303
195¹/₈	25¹/₈	25	27⁵/₈	5¹/₈	5⁵/₈	8	5	Summit Co., Utah	Wendell M. Smith	Nathan H. Smith	1954	303
195¹/₈	26³/₈	26¹/₈	24¹/₈	6	5⁴/₈	5	5	Montrose Co., Colo.	Eldon L. Webb	Eldon L. Webb	1965	303
195¹/₈	25⁴/₈	24³/₈	24¹/₈	5⁵/₈	6	5	6	Rio Arriba Co., N. M.	Eddie W. Brieno, Jr	Eddie W. Brieno, Jr.	1965	303
195¹/₈	22¹/₈	22³/₈	23⁵/₈	5³/₈	5⁵/₈	6	6	Heeney, Colo.	Steve Orecchio	Steve Orecchio	1967	303
195¹/₈	27	29⁵/₈	29⁵/₈	5⁷/₈	5⁴/₈	5	5	Fruitvale, B. C.	Allan Endersby	Allan Endersby	1968	303
195¹/₈	25	25⁵/₈	22⁴/₈	5	6	5	8	Salmon River, Idaho	Gary Bevan	Gary Bevan	1970	303
195¹/₈	26⁵/₈	26¹/₈	24⁷/₈	4⁷/₈	5	6	7	Coconino Co., Ariz.	Gary Ray Clark	Gary Ray Clark	1972	303
195	24⁴/₈	24³/₈	22²/₈	5⁵/₈	4⁷/₈	6	5	Utah	Picked Up	Jarvie Taxidermy	1959	311
195	24	24⁴/₈	26⁴/₈	5¹/₈	5¹/₈	5	6	N. Kaibab, Ariz.	Alex. J. Haas	Alex. J. Haas	1961	311
195	24⁴/₈	24³/₈	24⁴/₈	4⁵/₈	5⁵/₈	5	6	Moffat Co., Colo.	Orville R. Meineke	Craig Sports	1964	311
195	27¹/₈	26¹/₈	22²/₈	5⁶/₈	5³/₈	5	5	Sun River, Mont.	Dick Lyman	Dick Lyman	1966	311
195	25¹/₈	25¹/₈	25	4⁴/₈	5⁶/₈	5	5	Rio Arriba Co., N. M.	Pat Wilson	John Lind, Jr.	1967	311
195	26	25⁵/₈	23⁴/₈	4⁵/₈	4⁷/₈	5	5	Larimer Co., Colo.	Michael D. Blehm	Michael D. Blehm	1972	311
195	24⁴/₈	24⁷/₈	22²/₈	5	5	5	5	Rio Blanco Co., Colo.	Gene Lawrence	Gene Lawrence	1977	311
195	24⁴/₈	24⁴/₈	22³/₈	5¹/₈	6¹/₈	7	6	Sublette Co., Wyo.	Norm Busselle	Norm Busselle	1977	311

*Final Score subject to revision by additional verifying measurements.

WORLD'S RECORD MULE DEER (NON-TYPICAL ANTLERS)
SCORE: 355 2/8
Locality: Chip Lake, Alberta. Date: 1926.
Hunter and owner: Ed Broder.

NUMBER TWO MULE DEER (NON-TYPICAL ANTLERS)
SCORE: 330 1/8
Locality: Box Elder County, Utah. Date: 1943
Hunter: Alton Hunsacker. Owner: Andrew T. Johnson.

Mule Deer *(Non-Typical Antlers)*

Minimum Score 240 ***Odocoileus hemionus hemionus*** **and certain related subspecies**

Score	Length of Main Beam R.	Length of Main Beam L.	Inside Spread	Circumference at Smallest Place Between Burr and First Point R.	Circumference at Smallest Place Between Burr and First Point L.	Number of Points R.	Number of Points L.	Locality Killed	By Whom Killed	Owner	Date Killed	Rank
355 2/8	26 2/8	26 1/8	22 1/8	5	4 7/8	22	21	Chip Lake, Alta.	Ed Broder	Ed Broder	1926	1
330 1/8	23 2/8	22	9 4/8	8 2/8	8 3/8	21	28	Box Elder Co., Utah	Alton Hunsaker	Andrew T. Johnson	1943	2
319 4/8	24 2/8	24	23 5/8	7 7/8	7 1/8	27	23	Mariposa Co., Calif.	Harold Ray Laird	Harold Ray Laird	1972	3
316 7/8	25 5/8	25 1/8	32 7/8	6 5/8	6 5/8	16	17	N. Kaibab, Ariz.	William L. Murphy	Michael R. Karam	1943	4
306 2/8	28 6/8	27 4/8	22 6/8	5 6/8	5 4/8	14	23	Norwood Co., Colo.	Steve H. Herndon	Vernon D. & Dan. F. Holleman	1954	5
306 2/8	29	28 5/8	28 7/8	5 4/8	5 5/8	18	18	Chama, N. M.	Joseph A. Garcia	Joseph A. Garcia	1963	5
303 6/8	26 4/8	26 7/8	24 3/8	5 2/8	5	13	11	Minturn, Colo.	James Austill	James Austill	1962	7
302 4/8	25 1/8	26 2/8	25 2/8	5 7/8	6 3/8	18	17	Paonia, Colo.	Louis H. Huntington, Jr.	Louis H. Huntington, Jr.	1965	8
300	27	25 6/8	23 1/8	5 3/8	5 3/8	14	12	Uncompahgre Natl. For., Colo.	George Blackmon, Jr.	George Blackmon, Jr.	1961	9
299 1/8	27 7/8	28 3/8	24 4/8	5 6/8	5 4/8	13	16	Eureka Co., Nev.	Dan Avery, Jr.	Dan Avery, Jr.	1968	10
298 5/8	26 6/8	28 1/8	29 1/8	6 2/8	5 2/8	19	17	Rocky Mts.	Andrew Daum	National Collection	1886	11
292 5/8	26 4/8	24 6/8	27 6/8	5 6/8	5 4/8	18	16	Wyo.	J. B. Marvin, Jr.	National Collection	——	12
291 4/8	29 1/8	27 5/8	35 4/8	5 4/8	5 3/8	20	18	Malheur Co., Oreg.	Bradley Barclay	Bradley Barclay	1971	13
288 6/8	30 4/8	31 6/8	26 5/8	6 5/8	6 3/8	12	10	Chama, N. M.	Frank B. Maestas	W. H. Mundy, Jr.	1962	14
288 1/8	25	25 7/8	26	6	6	16	13	Hailey, Idaho	Robby Miller	Robby Miller	1969	15
287 5/8	24 4/8	25	26 4/8	5	5	12	13	Elko Co., Nev.	Joseph W. Dooley	Joseph W. Dooley	1954	16
286 1/8	21 2/8	22 7/8	20 6/8	4 5/8	4 4/8	14	21	Unknown	Walt Mednick	Ike Foster	——	17
284 3/8	27 4/8	24 3/8	26	5 1/8	5 2/8	15	15	Duchesne Co., Utah	Clyde Lambert	Lucy L. Back	1935	18
284	25 7/8	26 3/8	24 1/8	5 2/8	5 4/8	15	15	Provo River, Utah	Melvin T. Ashton	Melvin T. Ashton	1961	19
283	28	29 2/8	24 3/8	8	7 7/8	14	13	Rose Creek, Utah	Verl N. Creager	Verl N. Creager	1960	20
282 3/8	22 5/8	21 3/8	22 1/8	4 6/8	5 1/8	18	15	N. Kaibab, Ariz.	Robert C. Rantz	Robert C. Rantz	1969	21
282 2/8	25 3/8	25 6/8	24	7	6 2/8	17	13	Sask.	Herman Cox	Herman Cox	1947	22
280 5/8	29 4/8	29 6/8	35 4/8	5 1/8	5 1/8	13	13	Eagle Co., Colo.	Albert L. Mulnix	Leroy Martinez	1928	23
279 4/8	25 7/8	24 4/8	24 2/8	6	6	10	15	Otthon, Sask.	Unknown	W. G. Scholz	1940	24
278 7/8	24 4/8	26	18	4 7/8	5 1/8	8	11	Montrose Co., Colo.	Keith Thaute	Keith Thaute	1961	25
278 7/8	26 7/8	30	24 6/8	6 2/8	6 3/8	12	12	Eagle Co., Colo.	Dale L. Becker	Dale L. Becker	1978	25
278 3/8	27 2/8	28	26	5 2/8	5 3/8	11	13	Soda Springs, Idaho	Jack White	Jack White	1957	27
278 2/8	26 6/8	24 2/8	17 3/8	6 4/8	5 4/8	18	10	Kaibab Forest, Ariz.	Milroy Powell & Dan Auld, Jr.	Milroy Powell	1950	28

Score								Locality	Owner	By whom killed	Rank	Date
277 1/8	26 1/8	24 6/8	24 3/8	5 5/8	5 5/8	13	13	Bly, Oreg.	Alice C. O'Brien	David J. O'Brien	29	1949
277	25 5/8	24 7/8	25 3/8	5 7/8	5 5/8	12	10	Colo.	Indian	Charles Mcaden	30	1930
276 3/8	23 6/8	25 1/8	25 1/8	5 5/8	5 5/8	11	10	Morgan County, Utah	Jim Kilfoil	Gilbert Francis	31	1938
275 7/8	25 1/8	26 3/8	19 3/8	5 3/8	5 3/8	20	15	Dahlton, Sask.	Jim Hewitt	Jim Hewitt	32	1932
275 5/8	25	25	23	5	5	11	12	Glenwood Springs, Colo.	Larry Prehm	Larry Prehm	33	1967
275 3/8	26 3/8	26 3/8	25 5/8	5 3/8	5 3/8	11	13	Kaibab Forest, Ariz.	Picked Up	Cliff Cox	34	1950
275 1/8	27 1/8	22 4/8	20 7/8	5 7/8	6	14	15	Ruby Mts., Mont.	Peter Zemljak	Peter Zemljak	35	1960
274 7/8	23 6/8	28	23	5 4/8	5 7/8	10	15	Beaver, Utah	Murray Bonn	Parowen Rod & Gun Club	36	1920
274 1/8	28 2/8	23 2/8	22 2/8	4 7/8	5	11	11	North Fork, Idaho	James D. Edwards	Idaho Fish & Game Dept.	36	1967
273 7/8	21 7/8	24 2/8	23 3/8	5 4/8	5 5/8	15	11	Hayden, Colo.	Robert I. Roney	Colo. Div. Wild.	38	1930
273 7/8	23 3/8	26 1/8	26 1/8	5	5	15	18	Klamath Co., Oreg.	J. J. McDaniels	J. J. McDaniels	38	1952
273 7/8	26	25	26 5/8	5 3/8	5 5/8	15	9	San Miguel Co., Colo.	Kirt I. Darner	Kirt I. Darner	38	1977
273 5/8	25 1/8	28 2/8	23 7/8	6	6 1/8	9	16	Morgan Co., Utah	Harold B. Rollins	Harold B. Rollins	41	1944
273 3/8	28 5/8	25	23 2/8	6 1/8	6 1/8	15	13	Sublet, Idaho	Mrs. Jack Keen	Mrs. Jack Keen	42	1957
272 5/8	22 5/8	28	21 5/8	5 3/8	5 4/8	13	14	Glenwood Springs, Colo.	William L. Kurtz	William L. Kurtz	43	1967
272 3/8	29	28 2/8	28 5/8	5 1/8	5 5/8	16	12	Albany Co., Wyo.	S. A. Lawson	Acad. Nat. Sci., Phil.	44	1905
272	28 2/8	26 3/8	27 1/8	5 5/8	5 5/8	11	16	Caribou Co., Idaho	Picked Up	Newell Gilbert	45	1948
271 7/8	24 1/8	22 5/8	30 5/8	6 1/8	6 3/8	15	17	Cuprum, Idaho	Ed Martin	Ed Martin	46	1966
271 3/8	24 3/8	24 4/8	20	4 7/8	5 1/8	18	14	East Canyon, Utah	Joseph H. Greenig	Mrs. Joseph H. Greenig	47	1947
270 7/8	29 2/8	25 4/8	34 3/8	5 5/8	5 5/8	16	13	Highland Mts., Mont.	Peter Zemljak, Sr.	Peter Zemljak, Sr.	48	1962
270 5/8	28 2/8	28 2/8	27 5/8	5 7/8	5 7/8	15	15	Crook Co., Oreg.	C. F. Cheney	C. F. Cheney	48	1962
270 5/8	23 2/8	24 2/8	21 1/8	4 3/8	4 3/8	10	12	Bighorn Co., Mont.	R. Turnsback & J. Van Elsen	John Van Elsen	50	1961
270 3/8	24	25	27 4/8	5 5/8	6	10	10	Kaibab Forest, Ariz.	Dean Naylor	D. B. Sanford	51	1948
270 3/8	29 2/8	32 1/8	28	4 4/8	4 6/8	12	13	N. Kaibab, Ariz.	Thomas M Knoles, Jr	Thomas M. Knoles, Jr.	52	1944
269 3/8	25 4/8	27 5/8	23	6 1/8	6	17	11	Delta Co., Colo.	Shirley Smith	Shirley Smith	53	1962
268 7/8	28 3/8	28 4/8	24 6/8	5 5/8	5 5/8	12	13	Kaibab Forest, Ariz.	Milroy Powell	Milroy Powell	54	1952
268 5/8	27	27	25 1/8	5	5	14	16	Leader, Sask.	Cocks Brothers	Richard Jensen	55	1954
267 5/8	26 2/8	25 7/8	26 3/8	4 7/8	4 7/8	13	18	Jicarilla Apache Res., N. M.	Byrd L. Minter, Jr.	Byrd L. Minter, Jr.	56	1961
266 7/8	26	25 1/8	22 4/8	6 1/8	6 1/8	13	15	Wyo.	J. L. Kemmerer	Am. Mus. Nat. History	57	1905
266 7/8	22 5/8	22 7/8	18 5/8	5 1/8	5 1/8	8	8	Draper, Utah	Glenn W. Furrow	Glenn W. Furrow	57	1962
266 5/8	25 5/8	25 2/8	20 5/8	5	5	13	11	Philip, S. D.	Clifford Ramsey	Clifford Ramsey	59	1959
266 3/8	25 2/8	24 7/8	21	5 3/8	5 4/8	12	18	Park Co., Mont.	Delbert Chase	Delbert Chase	60	1945
266 1/8	24 4/8	22 7/8	16 4/8	5 5/8	5 1/8	16	13	Stevens Co., Wash.	Joe C. Mally	Joe C. Mally	61	1933
266	24 7/8	26 7/8	27 4/8	6 7/8	6 5/8	16	14	Chama, N. M.	Stephanie D. Tartaglia	Stephanie D. Tartaglia	62	1966
265 5/8	25 5/8	25 5/8	24 1/8	5 1/8	5 4/8	11	13	Cache Co., Utah	Jerry Steven Wuthrich	Jerry Steven Wuthrich	63	1966
265 3/8	25 3/8	25 1/8	21 5/8	5 3/8	5 3/8	13	14	Tyaughton River, B. C.	Terry E. Crawford	Terry E. Crawford	64	1970
265 3/8	25 4/8	24 7/8	18	5 5/8	5 5/8	22	13	Blue Mts., Wash.	Frank Henriksen	Frank Henriksen	65	1961
264 5/8	25 5/8	26 1/8	27 5/8	5 5/8	5 5/8	8	12	Sidney, Mont.	Buster Dodson	F. P. Murray	66	1954
264 5/8	26	26 5/8	22 4/8	5 5/8	5 5/8	18	13	Bannock Co., Idaho	Jarel Neeser	Jarel Neeser	66	1974
264 3/8	26	27 5/8	21 4/8	5 5/8	5 3/8	13	10	Gunnison Co., Colo.	Gordon E. Blay	Gordon E. Blay	68	1975
264	25 5/8	26 1/8	22 5/8	6 2/8	5 7/8	14	13	Elko Co., Nevada	Jim Stichter	Jim Stichter	69	1965
263 7/8	26 5/8	26 5/8	23 5/8	5	5	12	12	Montrose, Colo.	Robert L. Price	Robert L. Price	70	1963

MULE DEER *(Non-Typical Antlers)–Continued*

***Odocoileus hemionus hemionus* and certain related subspecies**

Score	Length of Main Beam R.	Length of Main Beam L.	Inside Spread	Circumference at Smallest Place Between Burr and First Point R.	Circumference at Smallest Place Between Burr and First Point L.	Number of Points R.	Number of Points L.	Locality Killed	By Whom Killed	Owner	Date Killed	Rank
263 1/8	27 4/8	26 1/8	26 4/8	6 2/8	6 1/8	20	13	Bigwood River, Idaho	Robert C. Young	Robert C. Young	1956	71
263	26 3/8	27 5/8	25 4/8	5	5	12	12	Kaibab Forest, Ariz.	Unknown	Bob Housholder	1940	72
262 5/8	26 2/8	24	23 7/8	4 6/8	4 6/8	14	13	Dawson Co., Mont.	Johnny Scheitlin	Bob Scheitlin	1949	73
262 4/8	28 2/8	29	28	5 4/8	5 4/8	14	12	Kaibab Forest, Ariz.	Jack Verner	Jack Verner	1947	74
262 3/8	30 2/8	27 6/8	28 2/8	6 2/8	6 4/8	10	15	Tierra Amarilla, N. M.	Pat Lovato, Jr.	Pat Lovato, Jr.	1966	75
262 3/8	30 7/8	29 3/8	29 4/8	5 3/8	5 6/8	10	11	Brush Creek, Colo.	Pete Taullie	Pete Taullie	1967	75
262	24 2/8	24 6/8	16 5/8	4 6/8	4 7/8	14	16	John Day River, Oreg.	Glen E. Park	Glen E. Park	1962	77
261 5/8	25	26 3/8	23 6/8	4 7/8	5	10	12	Heber Mountain, Utah	Duwayne C. Bailey	Duwayne C. Bailey	1963	78
261 3/8	25 4/8	24	27 2/8	5 2/8	5	10	10	Blaine Co., Idaho	Roger A. Crowder	Roger A. Crowder	1957	79
261 2/8	25 2/8	26 2/8	24 3/8	4 6/8	5 1/8	13	19	Iron Creek, Wash.	Win Coultas	Win Coultas	1924	80
261	25 2/8	26 2/8	25 6/8	5	5 1/8	12	12	Kaibab Forest, Ariz.	Unknown	Larry Arndt	1930	81
260 6/8	29 4/8	27 7/8	28 6/8	5 4/8	5 7/8	10	14	Rooks Co., Kan.	Lee Odle	Lee Odle	1965	82
260 6/8	26 5/8	26 3/8	22 3/8	4 7/8	4 7/8	10	13	Ada Co., Idaho	Howard R. Cromwell	Howard R. Cromwell	1975	82
260 4/8	25 5/8	27	26 6/8	5 7/8	5 7/8	13	14	Kaibab Forest, Ariz.	David Bevly	David Bevly	1949	84
260 2/8	26 7/8	25	21 2/8	4 6/8	4 5/8	12	13	Pinedale, Wyo.	James H. Straley	Monte W. Straley	1965	85
260 1/8	26	27 2/8	24 3/8	4 6/8	5 1/8	16	20	Newcastle, Utah	Unknown	Utah Fish & Game Dept.	1961	86
260	22 7/8	25	20	5	5	12	12	Caribou Co., Idaho	Arthur H. Summers	Arthur H. Summers	1966	87
259 7/8	25 7/8	24	24 6/8	4 7/8	4 6/8	11	13	Knab, Utah	Arthur Glover	Arthur Glover	1947	88
259 7/8	25 1/8	25 2/8	22 2/8	5	5	8	10	Caribou Co., Idaho	Jerry Hunt	Jerry Hunt	1966	88
259 6/8	24 2/8	25 4/8	21 3/8	5 3/8	5 3/8	13	13	Routt County, Colo.	R. V. Rhoads	Cecil R. Weston	1949	90
259 5/8	27 2/8	26 6/8	24 1/8	5 2/8	5 2/8	12	13	Glendo, Wyo.	Rudolph B. Johnson	Rudolph B. Johnson	1961	91
259 3/8	27 3/8	29 2/8	24 6/8	5 6/8	5 4/8	13	13	Iron Co., Utah	Mont Hunter	Mont Hunter	1939	92
259 1/8	23 1/8	24 3/8	25 4/8	5 7/8	6	15	17	Boise, Idaho	George M. Tweedy	George M. Tweedy	1946	93
258 7/8	28 5/8	27 7/8	28 2/8	4 6/8	4 7/8	13	13	N. Kaibab, Ariz.	Marvin Fridenmaker	Marvin Fridenmaker	1968	94
258 6/8	27 5/8	27 6/8	24 5/8	5	5	15	10	Valley Co., Idaho	Larry Dwonch	Larry Dwonch	1972	95
258 6/8	21	22	16 2/8	10	5	18	18	Sweetwater Co., Wyo.	John A. Fabian	John A. Fabian	1974	95
258 5/8	25 3/8	25 4/8	21	5 2/8	5 3/8	12	10	Elko Co., Nev.	Edward Giauque	Edward Giauque	1960	97
258 4/8	24 3/8	24	25 3/8	5	5 2/8	13	15	Boise Co., Idaho	Leroy Massey	Leroy Massey	1959	98
258 3/8	27	28 4/8	25 1/8	5 1/8	5 1/8	11	10	Monte Vista, Colo.	Geis Middlebeck	Phil Skinner	1956	99
258 2/8	29 5/8	30 5/8	29 3/8	6 6/8	6 7/8	15	14	Rock Creek, B. C.	George Whiting	B. C. Game Dept.	1909	100
258 1/8	27 3/8	26 4/8	23 6/8	5 1/8	5 1/8	13	14	Atlanta, Idaho	Kenneth E. Potts	Kenneth E. Potts	1968	101

258	20 4/8	22 1/8	19 3/8	4 2/8	4 5/8	13	13	Cimarron, N. M.	Ralph L. Smith	Ralph L. Smith	1957	102
257 7/8	24 2/8	26 7/8	20 6/8	5 3/8	5 4/8	11	13	Hell's Hole, Ariz.	D. L. Demente	D. L. Demente	1965	103
257 6/8	28 3/8	27 1/8	24 2/8	5 4/8	5 4/8	9	13	Leclerc Creek, Wash.	Ernest Fait	Ernest Fait	1960	104
257 6/8	27 1/8	26	26 7/8	5 7/8	5 6/8	14	14	Jicarilla Apache Res., N. M.	Henry Callado	Henry Callado	1961	104
257 4/8	24 5/8	23	19 2/8	5 4/8	5 4/8	11	11	Encampment, Wyo.	Sam Whitney	Mrs. Sam Whitney	1946	106
257 4/8	28 7/8	28 6/8	27 7/8	4 6/8	4 7/8	18	10	Utah Co., Utah	J. Clyde Burgess	Dave Burgess	1949	106
257 3/8	24 6/8	26 2/8	23 1/8	4 6/8	4 7/8	12	8	New Castle, Colo.	Unknown	A. E. Hudson	1952	108
257	26 7/8	26	24 2/8	5	4 7/8	12	12	Cache Co., Utah	Harold S. Shandrew	Harold S. Shandrew	1958	109
256 7/8	26 5/8	27 2/8	22 6/8	5 3/8	5 6/8	20	14	Chadron, Neb.	Art Thomsen	Art Thomsen	1960	110
256 7/8	23 7/8	22 4/8	21 4/8	4 1/8	4 6/8	12	13	Elmore Co., Idaho	Paul Vetter	Paul Vetter	1972	110
256 6/8	24 6/8	26 4/8	20 4/8	5	5 1/8	12	15	Hoback Basin, Wyo.	Buck Heide	Buck Heide	1968	112
256 5/8	25 7/8	27 2/8	25 6/8	5 3/8	5 3/8	14	13	Jicarilla Apache Res., N. M.	Picked Up	S. L. Canterbury, III	1967	113
256 5/8	25 7/8	24 7/8	29	6 3/8	5 7/8	15	14	Gooding Co., Idaho	Charles Hollingsworth	Charles Hollingsworth	1970	113
256 2/8	27 4/8	28 2/8	26 6/8	4 7/8	5 1/8	10	8	Trumbull, Ariz.	Ervin M. Schmutz	Ervin M. Schmutz	1965	115
256 1/8	22 7/8	22 4/8	20 1/8	4 5/8	5	14	12	Irwin, Idaho	Hale K. Charlton	Hale K. Charlton	1966	116
256	24 4/8	26 7/8	25 1/8	5	4 6/8	13	10	Garfield Co., Utah	James D. Perkins	James D. Perkins	1959	117
256	23 7/8	24 7/8	25	4 7/8	5 1/8	12	13	East Zion, Utah	Raymond Pocta	Raymond Pocta	1963	117
255 7/8	23	24 1/8	22 6/8	5 1/8	5	18	12	Unknown	Unknown	Lone Star Brewing Co.	—	119
255 7/8	24	24 5/8	25 2/8	6	6 1/8	12	11	Portreeve, Sask.	Mike Spies	Mike Spies	1947	119
255 2/8	26	26 5/8	25 1/8	4 7/8	4 5/8	9	9	Rio Arriba Co., N.M.	Gene Garcia	Gene Garcia	1964	121
255	28	27 3/8	28 2/8	5 7/8	5 5/8	14	12	Garfield Co., Colo.	Louis Lindauer	Louis Lindauer	1932	122
255	21 5/8	22 4/8	19 7/8	5 5/8	5 4/8	9	9	Dunkley Flat, Colo.	Richard A. Gorden	Richard A. Gorden	1966	122
254 4/8	25 1/8	24	18 5/8	5 4/8	5 2/8	13	15	Maloy, Alta.	Otto Schmalzbauer	Otto Schmalzbauer	1930	124
254 4/8	27 2/8	25 6/8	32 6/8	5 6/8	6 2/8	13	11	Mohave Co., Ariz.	John W. Sokatch	John W. Sokatch	1978	124
254 2/8	30	28 6/8	23 4/8	6 2/8	6 4/8	7	8	Columbine, Colo.	M. A. Story	M. A. Story	1955	126
253 6/8	25	26 1/8	25 6/8	6 1/8	6 1/8	9	12	Mohave Co., Ariz.	Manuel Machado	Manuel Machado	1973	127
253 3/8	27 6/8	26 6/8	21	5 2/8	5 3/8	11	13	Georgetown, Colo.	George Lappin	Doug Grubbe	1947	128
253 3/8	24 4/8	24 3/8	20 4/8	5 3/8	5 3/8	11	11	Rawlins, Wyo.	A. H. Henkel	A. H. Henkel	1952	128
253 2/8	24 3/8	25 2/8	20 5/8	5 2/8	5 5/8	15	17	Salmon, Idaho	Ben H. Quick	Ben H. Quick	1960	130
253 1/8	25 5/8	25 4/8	25 2/8	5 6/8	6	11	11	Paonia, Colo.	F. F. Parham	F. F. Parham	1961	131
252 5/8	25 3/8	23 4/8	26 1/8	5 4/8	5 4/8	13	17	Meeker, Colo.	George R. Howey	Robert L. Howey	1917	132
252 3/8	26 7/8	28 7/8	29 1/8	5 3/8	5 5/8	15	13	Kaibab Forest, Ariz.	Graves Peeler	Graves Peeler	1951	133
252 3/8	25 6/8	26 6/8	29 4/8	5 6/8	5 4/8	10	11	Hells Canyon, Idaho	Basil C. Bradbury	Basil C. Bradbury	1955	133
252 2/8	23 4/8	22	14 5/8	5 6/8	5 6/8	16	15	Glacier Co., Mont.	Bob Scriver	Philip Schlegel	1934	135
252 2/8	30	30	26 6/8	6	5 4/8	15	14	Garfield Co., Colo.	B. J. Slack	B. J. Slack	1973	135
252 1/8	25 1/8	24 1/8	21 5/8	4 6/8	4 7/8	11	10	Salina Canyon, Utah	James C. Larsen	James C. Larsen	1969	137
252	24 7/8	23	24 5/8	5	5	9	13	Eagle Co., Colo.	Richard G. Lundock	Richard G. Lundock	1945	138
251 7/8	24 6/8	25 1/8	25 6/8	5 2/8	5 1/8	11	10	Silt, Colo.	George McCoy	George McCoy	1961	139
251 6/8	24	25 4/8	20	5 1/8	5	13	14	Gem Co., Idaho	A. K. England	Roscoe E. Ferris	1969	140
251 5/8	27 4/8	25 2/8	23 6/8	5 2/8	5 2/8	9	14	Gunnison Co., Colo.	John M. Ringler	John M. Ringler	1956	141
251 5/8	24 1/8	26 1/8	21	5 1/8	5 4/8	10	14	Roan Creek, Colo.	Anthony Morabito	Anthony Morabito	1965	141
251 1/8	27 5/8	25 6/8	25 7/8	5 3/8	5 2/8	10	9	Meeker, Colo.	Henry Zietz, Jr.	Henry Zietz, Jr.	1955	143
251	25 1/8	26 1/8	26 1/8	5 1/8	5 1/8	13	14	Adams Co., Idaho	Clark Childers	Clark Childers	1955	144

Mule Deer *(Non-Typical Antlers)–Continued*

***Odocoileus hemionus hemionus* and certain related subspecies**

Score	Length of Main Beam R.	Length of Main Beam L.	Inside Spread	Circumference at Smallest Place Between Burr and First Point R.	Circumference at Smallest Place Between Burr and First Point L.	Number of Points R.	Number of Points L.	Locality Killed	By Whom Killed	Owner	Date Killed	Rank
250 7/8	26 4/8	27 2/8	24	5 4/8	6	19	13	Chelan Co., Wash.	Ben R. Williamson	Vera T. Williamson	1951	145
250 5/8	26 2/8	24 7/8	25 4/8	5	5	10	10	Cedaredge, Colo.	E. K. Plante	E. K. Plante	1963	146
250 4/8	29 7/8	26 7/8	22 4/8	6 2/8	8	7	13	Kunard Valley, Idaho	Ralph D. Hogan	Ralph D. Hogan	1966	147
250 3/8	29	28 4/8	27 4/8	5 1/8	4 6/8	10	12	Moffat Co., Colo.	Unknown	Carrol Grounds	1960	148
249 7/8	25 6/8	26 5/8	30 2/8	4 6/8	4 6/8	11	11	East End, Sask.	Henry Leroy	Henry Leroy	1960	149
249 6/8	22	24 1/8	17 1/8	4 6/8	4 5/8	10	10	Salem, Utah	John Vincent	John Vincent	1956	150
249 6/8	24 7/8	25 2/8	22	5	4 7/8	10	14	Merriun, Neb.	Delman H. Tuller	Delman H. Tuller	1965	150
249 6/8	23 3/8	21 6/8	23 3/8	6 2/8	5 7/8	12	12	Mt. Delenbaugh, Ariz.	Ted Riggs	Ted Riggs	1965	150
249 3/8	25	24 2/8	19 6/8	5 4/8	5 3/8	12	9	Routt Co., Colo.	Howard Stoker	Howard Stoker	1958	153
249 3/8	26 1/8	27 3/8	28 4/8	5 1/8	5	12	10	Wash.	Unknown	Pat Redding	PR1973	153
249 2/8	23 5/8	23 4/8	20 7/8	5	4 5/8	12	10	Mesa Co., Colo.	Gene Cavanagh	Gene Cavanagh	1967	155
249 1/8	30 4/8	30 3/8	28 3/8	6 1/8	6 2/8	11	11	Drummond, Mont.	Tom Brosovich	Tom Brosovich	1957	156
249 1/8	25 4/8	26	25 1/8	5 1/8	5 1/8	8	11	Kaibab, Ariz.	Robert G. McDonald	Robert G. McDonald	1969	156
249	25 1/8	23 4/8	23 1/8	5 1/8	5	14	10	Minturn, Colo.	John F. Baldauf	L. F. Nowotny	1941	158
249	27 7/8	29 7/8	25 6/8	5 3/8	5 1/8	11	8	Jemez Mts., N. M.	Max S. Jenson	Max S. Jenson	1962	158
249	26 7/8	26 7/8	26 7/8	5 1/8	5 1/8	8	10	Newcastle, Colo.	William Wiedenfeld	William Wiedenfeld	1969	158
248 3/8	26 3/8	26 6/8	23 4/8	5 4/8	5 2/8	10	16	Kaibab Forest, Ariz.	O. M. Corbett	O. M. Corbett	1953	161
248 1/8	25 7/8	24 7/8	22 6/8	5	5 1/8	11	10	Rio Blanco Co., Colo.	Claude E. Shults	Claude E. Shults	1956	162
248 1/8	25 4/8	25	23	5 2/8	5	15	18	San Juan Natl. For., Colo.	Leland R. Tate	Leland R. Tate	1973	162
248	25 4/8	25 1/8	26	5 6/8	5 5/8	13	11	Kaibab Forest, Ariz.	H. W. Meisch	H. W. Meisch	1942	164
248	23 3/8	22 4/8	23 2/8	5 6/8	5 6/8	12	14	Val Marie, Sask.	J. Milton Brown	J. Milton Brown	1958	164
248	26	27 1/8	22	5	5	12	9	Pinedale, Wyo.	Lyle Rosendahl	Lyle Rosendahl	1960	164
248	25 5/8	26 4/8	24 7/8	5 2/8	5	11	10	Colombine, Colo.	Bobby McLaughlin	Bobby McLaughlin	1962	164
247 7/8	26	25 3/8	25	5 6/8	6	16	11	Norwood, Colo.	Walter L. Reisbeck	Walter L. Reisbeck	1951	168
247 7/8	23 6/8	24	20 7/8	5	5	14	13	Asotin Co., Wash.	David G. Bennett	David G. Bennett	1971	168
247 5/8	28 4/8	26 7/8	24 4/8	6	5 7/8	10	13	Waterton Park, Alta.	Eric Westergreen	Eric Westergreen	1941	170
247 4/8	25 2/8	24 7/8	24 3/8	6 2/8	5 6/8	12	16	Bend, Oreg.	L. M. Martinson	L. M. Martinson	1949	171
247 4/8	28 3/8	28 5/8	28 3/8	5 1/8	5	9	10	Colo.	Vince Plaskett	Vince Plaskett	1970	171
247 1/8	23	23 1/8	21 3/8	5 4/8	5 2/8	12	13	Rio Blanco Co., Colo.	L. C. Denny, Jr.	L. C. Denny, Jr.	1961	173
247 1/8	26 2/8	25	27 2/8	4 6/8	4 5/8	12	9	Whitebird, Idaho	Harold Gustin	Wayne Demaray	1965	173
247 1/8	28 3/8	27 7/8	25	6 1/8	6	10	15	San Miguel Co., Colo.	W.F. (Bud) Grice	W.F. (Bud) Grice	1978	173

247	29 7/8	28 6/8	24 5/8	6	5 4/8	14	16	Elko Co., Nev.	Walter B. Hester	Walter B. Hester	1957	176
247	26	24 1/8	26 5/8	7 3/8	7 5/8	16	20	Hinsdale Co., Colo.	Fred Jardine	Fred Jardine	1966	176
247	23 4/8	24 2/8	21 1/8	4 7/8	4 7/8	11	8	Montrose Co., Colo.	Thomas M. Bost	Thomas M. Bost	1967	176
246 6/8	27	25 4/8	28	5 5/8	5 6/8	9	14	Okanogan Co., Wash.	Fred C. Heuer	Fred C. Heuer	1940	179
246 6/8	24 6/8	24 7/8	22 1/8	4 5/8	4 6/8	10	14	Lawrence Co., S. D.	Unknown	Old Style Saloon	1945	179
246 6/8	25	25 3/8	26 7/8	6 6/8	7	12	12	Kaibab Forest, Ariz.	Graves Peeler	Graves Peeler	1951	179
246 3/8	24 7/8	24 6/8	25 1/8	5 2/8	5 2/8	11	14	Kaibab Forest, Ariz.	Elgin T. Gates	Elgin T. Gates	1960	182
246 1/8	28 1/8	26 6/8	28 2/8	5 1/8	4 6/8	8	9	Eagle Co., Colo.	Charles H. Thornberg	Charles H. Thornberg	1949	183
246 1/8	26 6/8	25 4/8	25 4/8	5 3/8	5 4/8	12	10	Mesa Co., Colo.	Joseph J. Pitcherella	Joseph J. Pitcherella	1972	183
246	23 5/8	26 1/8	24 1/8	6 3/8	5 6/8	14	13	Mesa Co., Colo.	Harry A. Gay	Harry A. Gay	1962	185
245 7/8	24 2/8	23 3/8	25 1/8	5 2/8	5 2/8	13	11	Eagle Co., Colo.	William M. Nickels	William M. Nickels	1968	186
245 6/8	27 1/8	28 2/8	24 4/8	5 6/8	5 7/8	11	9	Rio Arriba Co., N. M.	Kenneth W. Lee	Kenneth W. Lee	1971	187
245 5/8	27 5/8	28	23 3/8	5 1/8	5 2/8	13	11	Rio Blanco Co., Colo.	Charlie Grove	Dorothy Shults	1934	188
245 5/8	25 2/8	25	26	5 4/8	5 2/8	9	11	Glenwood Springs, Colo.	Grady P. Lester	Grady P. Lester	1959	188
245 5/8	27 2/8	28 2/8	23 2/8	5 3/8	5 4/8	9	8	Eagle Co., Colo.	James Caraccioli	James Caraccioli	1978	188
245 2/8	23 6/8	24 6/8	24 3/8	5 1/8	5	18	12	Lac Lariche, Alta.	Julius Hagen	Olaf Hagen	1945	191
245 2/8	26 5/8	27 4/8	21 2/8	5 6/8	5 6/8	10	10	Jicarilla Apache Res., N. M.	Arthur Wanoskea	Arthur Wanoskea	1960	191
245	25 6/8	25 5/8	29 6/8	5 5/8	5 4/8	17	15	Bonner Co., Mont.	Dick Sherwood	Dick Sherwood	1963	193
244 7/8	21 2/8	21 6/8	24 6/8	5 4/8	5 7/8	9	10	Cabri, Sask.	Enos Mitchell, Jr.	Enos Mitchell, Jr.	1960	194
244 7/8	27 2/8	21 3/8	29 2/8	5 2/8	5 4/8	14	14	Needle Peak, Idaho	Michael G. Cameron	Michael G. Cameron	1966	194
244 6/8	29	29 1/8	35 1/8	5 4/8	5 3/8	11	13	Pagosa Springs, Colo.	Thomas Jarrett	Thomas Jarrett	1962	196
244 5/8	25 5/8	24 2/8	22 1/8	5 6/8	5 6/8	13	14	Teton Co., Wyo.	Vern Shinkle	Vern Shinkle	1968	197
244 5/8	25 5/8	25 4/8	20 3/8	5 1/8	5 1/8	13	10	Delta Co., Colo.	Neil A. Briscoe, Jr.	Neil A. Briscoe, Jr.	1969	197
244 5/8	26	25	18 6/8	5 5/8	5 4/8	15	20	Rossland, B. C.	Victor Mattiazzi	Victor Mattiazzi	1970	197
244 4/8	24 6/8	26 6/8	26	5	4 6/8	11	11	Kaibab Forest, Ariz.	C. M. Randal, Jr.	C. M. Randal, Jr.	1953	200
244 2/8	28 4/8	28 7/8	30 1/8	5 2/8	5 4/8	9	8	Oak Creek, Colo.	Scott C. Hinkle	Scott C. Hinkle	1961	201
244 2/8	22 6/8	21 6/8	19 4/8	4 4/8	4 7/8	9	13	Fremont City, Wyo.	Warren V. Spriggs	Warren V. Spriggs	1962	201
244 2/8	25 6/8	26 3/8	22 7/8	5 2/8	5 4/8	12	13	San Juan Co., Utah	Phil Acton	Phil Acton	1966	201
244 1/8	24 1/8	24 2/8	28	4 4/8	4 4/8	9	10	Bighorn Co., Wyo.	Picked Up	Hank Frey	1978	204
244	23 5/8	23	26 4/8	5 1/8	5 1/8	11	10	Craig, Colo.	Fred E. Trouth	Fred E. Trouth	1960	205
244	24 6/8	22 5/8	18 5/8	6 5/8	7	12	14	Mt. Trumbull, Ariz.	Tony Stromei	Tony Stromei	1960	205
244	26 4/8	27 1/8	24 6/8	4 6/8	4 6/8	9	10	East Canyon, Utah	Ronald E. Coburn	Ronald E. Coburn	1961	205
243 7/8	23 4/8	21	26 3/8	6 2/8	6 4/8	13	14	Modoc Co., Calif.	Bill Foster	Foster's Bighorn Rest.	1930	208
243 7/8	28 3/8	28 5/8	25	5 5/8	6 4/8	9	11	Eagle, Colo.	R. Rambo	R. Rambo	1963	208
243 7/8	23 4/8	24 1/8	26 4/8	5 1/8	5 1/8	12	11	Ravalli Co., Mont.	Lloyd G. Hunter	Lloyd G. Hunter	1963	208
243 6/8	26	24 5/8	22 4/8	6 2/8	6 4/8	10	12	North Mt., Colo.	Ben Crandell	Ben Crandell	1939	211
243 5/8	24 1/8	27 2/8	27 3/8	5 5/8	5 4/8	16	18	Slave Lake, Alta.	R. W. H. Eben-Ebenau	R. W. H. Eben-Ebenau	1930	212
243 1/8	29 2/8	28 2/8	28 6/8	4 6/8	5 2/8	8	9	Harrison Gulch, Colo.	George R. Mattern	George R. Mattern	1958	213
243 1/8	25 4/8	23 4/8	25 1/8	5 4/8	5 7/8	8	11	Fremont Co., Idaho	Larry D. Hawker	Larry D. Hawker	1970	213
243	25 7/8	25 6/8	20	5 2/8	5	15	12	Crook Co., Oreg.	Wes Mitts	Wes Mitts	1936	215
243	25	25 5/8	20 4/8	7 1/8	5 2/8	15	11	Winthrop, Wash.	Bruce Miller	Bruce Miller	1941	215
242 7/8	24 4/8	24 1/8	22 6/8	4 7/8	5	10	11	Sheridan, Wyo.	J. M. Blakeman	J. M. Blakeman	1952	217
242 6/8	23 2/8	23	20 2/8	5 3/8	5 6/8	12	17	Middle Park, Colo.	Picked Up	Karl H. Knorr	——	218

Mule Deer *(Non-Typical Antlers)–Continued*

Odocoileus hemionus hemionus and certain related subspecies

Score	Length of Main Beam R.	Length of Main Beam L.	Inside Spread	Circumference at Smallest Place Between Burr and First Point R.	Circumference at Smallest Place Between Burr and First Point L.	Number of Points R.	Number of Points L.	Locality Killed	By Whom Killed	Owner	Date Killed	Rank
242 5/8	25	26 3/8	18 3/8	6	5 6/8	11	10	Baison, Idaho	Daniel E. Osborne	Daniel E. Osborne	1959	219
242 5/8	27 3/8	26 7/8	25 5/8	5 7/8	5 6/8	12	9	Sanders Co., Mont.	Robert D. Frisk	Robert D. Frisk	1974	219
242 3/8	23 1/8	22 3/8	17 3/8	4 7/8	5	12	12	Arborfield, Sask.	Joseph Fournier	Joseph Fournier	1930	221
242 2/8	25 4/8	25 3/8	23 2/8	5	4 7/8	9	12	Rabbit Ears Pass, Colo.	Douglas Valentine	Douglas Valentine	1964	222
242 1/8	27 5/8	28 4/8	33 6/8	6 1/8	6 4/8	11	12	Missoula Co., Mont.	Harold Wample	Ralph Raymond	1949	223
242 1/8	20 7/8	23 2/8	17 4/8	6	5 7/8	12	11	Cabri, Sask.	Gordon Millward	Gordon Millward	1960	223
242 1/8	28	27 6/8	22 1/8	6 1/8	6 1/8	9	11	Bear Lake Co., Idaho	Robert N. Gale	Robert N. Gale	1970	223
242	24 4/8	26 2/8	28 4/8	5 6/8	5 5/8	9	8	Kaibab Forest, Ariz.	Ray Ramsey	Ray Ramsey	1952	226
242	25 1/8	25 5/8	19 2/8	5 3/8	5 2/8	14	13	Pondera Co., Mont.	Dan Mougeot	Dan Mougeot	1961	226
241 7/8	24 5/8	24 2/8	25	5 2/8	5 2/8	11	19	Jefferson Co., Oreg.	Spencer L. Darrar	Spencer L. Darrar	1953	228
241 7/8	28 2/8	24	31 6/8	5 1/8	5 1/8	10	7	Saquache Co., Colo.	Walter A. Larsen	Walter A. Larsen	1962	228
241 7/8	21	18	14 7/8	4 3/8	5 3/8	12	15	Sanders Co., Mont.	Buzz Faro	Buzz Faro	1963	228
241 5/8	26 6/8	25 6/8	33 6/8	6 2/8	5 2/8	14	10	Franklin Co., Idaho	Joan Butterworth	Quinten Butterworth	1961	231
241 4/8	28	28 2/8	25	5 4/8	5 4/8	7	10	Kamloops, B. C.	Ralph McLean	Ralph McLean	1960	232
241 4/8	26 4/8	27	27	5	5 3/8	8	7	Socorro Co., N. M.	James T. Everheart	James T. Everheart	1973	232
241 4/8	25 1/8	25 7/8	23 3/8	4 4/8	4 4/8	10	9	Summit Co., Colo.	Robert R. Ross	Robert R. Ross	1974	232
241 3/8	22 3/8	23 7/8	20 4/8	5 1/8	5 2/8	10	12	Adams Co., Idaho	Peter Renberg	Peter Renberg	1963	235
241 3/8	26 6/8	24 7/8	24 3/8	5	5 1/8	12	13	Salmon River, Idaho	Richard Shilling	Richard Shilling	1965	235
241 3/8	19	24 6/8	20	6 2/8	6 4/8	12	15	Nakusp, B. C.	Frank Vicen	Frank Vicen	1967	235
241 3/8	27 1/8	26 5/8	31 6/8	5 5/8	5 5/8	8	8	Mohave Co., Ariz.	Bernard E. Anderson	Bernard E. Anderson	1969	235
241 2/8	26 6/8	25 1/8	18 6/8	5	5	10	11	Oak Creek, Colo.	Richard J. Peltier	Richard J. Peltier	1967	239
241 2/8	25 6/8	27 2/8	29	5 3/8	5 3/8	11	10	Elko Co., Nev.	Paul Giuliani	Paul Giuliani	1971	239
241 1/8	25	26 2/8	29 2/8	5 5/8	5 6/8	11	12	Split Rock, Wyo.	Herb Klein	Herb Klein	1957	241
240 7/8	27	27 2/8	25 2/8	5 2/8	5 1/8	6	6	New Castle, Colo.	Harold F. Auld	Harold F. Auld	1960	242
240 5/8	26 4/8	27 6/8	23 2/8	6	5 7/8	10	13	Kaibab Forest, Ariz.	Bert Ellis George	Bert Ellis George	1949	243
240 5/8	22	23 2/8	21	4 7/8	4 7/8	10	9	Elko Co., Nev.	George M. Boman	George M. Boman	1956	243
240 4/8	26 4/8	27	21 4/8	6 2/8	5 6/8	10	9	Modoc Co., Calif.	Niilo Niemi	Niilo Niemi	1968	245
240 3/8	27 2/8	23 7/8	20 2/8	4 6/8	5 4/8	8	13	Hawley Creek, Idaho	Clifford Nealis	Clifford Nealis	1960	246
240 3/8	22 3/8	24 5/8	21 2/8	5 5/8	5 7/8	13	12	Missoula Co., Mont.	Richard A. Gendrow	Richard A. Gendrow	1973	246
240 2/8	27 2/8	25 3/8	29 4/8	5	5	10	11	Blaine Co., Idaho	Roger A. Crowder	Roger A. Crowder	1957	248
240 2/8	27 3/8	27 1/8	21 7/8	5 2/8	5 2/8	9	11	Mt. Dellenbaugh, Ariz.	Edwin R. (Ted) Riggs	Edwin R. (Ted) Riggs	1964	248

240 2/8	22 4/8	23 7/8	26 4/8	5 4/8	5 3/8	10	12	Gem Co., Idaho	Roland Bright	Roland Bright	1965	248
240 1/8	24 2/8	24	19 6/8	5 6/8	5 7/8	13	12	Harney Co., Oreg.	R. G. Creager	R. G. Creager	1957	251
240 1/8	23 4/8	23 1/8	23 2/8	5 6/8	5 5/8	12	12	Elmore Co., Idaho	Phillip K. Messer	Phillip K. Messer	1971	251
240	25 7/8	24 4/8	23 2/8	5 4/8	5 6/8	12	10	Grand Valley, Colo.	Ed Peters, Jr.	Ed Peters, Jr.	1962	253
240	26 1/8	28 5/8	27 1/8	4 6/8	4 7/8	9	8	San Juan Wild., Colo.	Tommie Cornelius	Tommie Cornelius	1967	253

WORLD'S RECORD COLUMBIA BLACKTAIL DEER
SCORE: 170 6/8
Locality: Elk City, Oregon. Date: 1962.
Hunter and owner: Clark D. Griffith.

NUMBER FOUR COLUMBIA BLACKTAIL DEER
SCORE: 170 1/8
Locality: Linn County, Oregon. Date: 1963.
Hunter and owner: Woodrow W. Gibbs.

Boundaries for Mule and Blacktail Deer

Since the beginning of the records keeping program, the boundary between the mule deer and the consistently smaller Columbia blacktail has been carefully studied, and periodically this boundary has been moved farther westward. The two types of deer belong to the same species and readily hybridize where their ranges meet. The Records Committee has always tried to place the boundary west of the known areas of intergradation in an effort to prevent the entry of hybrids or mule deer in the blacktail class.

In 1966 a detailed questionnaire was circulated to official measurers and game department officials familiar with the critical areas. Based on the information received, the boundary was readjusted westward in a number of places in 1977 and finalized in 1980. The present boundary is listed below:

British Columbia - Starting at the Washington-British Columbia border, blacktail deer range runs west of the height of land between the Skagit and the Chilliwack Ranges, intersecting the Fraser River opposite the mouth of Ruby Creek, then west to and up Harrison Lake to and up Tipella Creek to the height of land in Garibaldi Park and northwesterly along this divide past Alta Lake, Mt. Dalgleish and Mt. Waddington, thence north to Bella Coola. This boundary change excludes the area west of the Klesilkwa River and the west side of the Lillooet River.

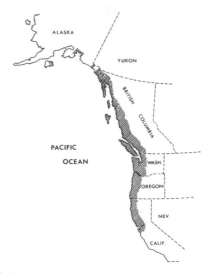

Shaded areas indicate ranges of the blacktail deer.

Washington - Beginning at the south boundary of North Cascades Park the new boundary line runs along the township line between R10E and R11E W.M. directly south to its intersection with the north border of Mt. Rainier National Park, then along the north, west, and south park boundaries until it intersects with the township line between R9E and R10E W.M., which is then followed directly south to the Columbia River near Cook.

Oregon - In Jackson and south Douglas Counties, the change begins at Tiller, with the new boundary following Highway 227 to Highway 62 at Trail, then south to Medford, from which the line follows the township line between R1W and R2W E.W.M. to the California border.

California - Beginning in Siskiyou County at the Oregon-California border, the new boundary lies between townships R8W and R9W M.D.M., extending south to and along the Klamath River to Hamburg, then south along the road to Scott Bar, continuing south and then east on the unimproved road from Scott Bar to its intersect with the paved road to Mugginsville, south through Mugginsville to State Highway 3, which is then followed to Douglas City in Trinity County, from which the line runs east on State Highway 299 to Interstate 5. The line follows Interstate 5 and the Sacramento River south to the area of Anderson, where the Sacramento River moves east of Interstate 5, following the Sacramento River until it joins with the San Joaquim River, which is followed to the south border of Stanislaus County. The line then runs west along this border to the east border of Santa Clara County. The east and south borders of Santa Clara County are then followed to the south border of Santa Cruz County, which is followed to the edge of Monterey Bay.

The Sitka blacktail ranges north of Bella Coola along the coast of British Columbia, on the Queen Charlotte Islands, and the islands and coast of southwestern Alaska. This deer has also been transplanted farther west along the Alaska coast and to islands such as Kodiak. Trophies of Sitka blacktails are eligible for entry in the Columbia blacktail class.

Columbia Blacktail Deer

Odocoileus hemionus columbianus and Odocoileus hemionus sitkensis

Minimum Score 130

Score	Length of Main Beam R.	L.	Inside Spread	Circumference at Smallest Place Between Burr and First Point R.	L.	Number of Points R.	L.	Locality Killed	By Whom Killed	Owner	Date Killed	Rank
172 2/8*	26 3/8	25 5/8	20 6/8	5 2/8	5 3/8	7	7	Marion Co., Oregon	B. G. Shurtleff	B. G. Shurtleff	1969	1
170 6/8	23 1/8	24	21 1/8	5 3/8	5 4/8	5	5	Elk City, Oreg.	Clark D. Griffith	Clark D. Griffith	1962	2
170 2/8*	25 5/8	25 5/8	20 2/8	4 5/8	4 6/8	5	5	Jackson Co., Oreg.	Dennis R. King	King Tax. Studios	1970	3
170 1/8	23	22 5/8	19 5/8	5	4 6/8	5	5	Linn Co., Oreg.	Woodrow W. Gibbs	Woodrow W. Gibbs	1963	4
165 4/8	23 6/8	24 5/8	21 6/8	5 1/8	5 1/8	4	4	Yamhill Co., Oreg.	Jim McKinley	Jim McKinley	1971	5
164	23 5/8	24 3/8	26 5/8	5 5/8	5 1/8	6	6	Glenn Co., Calif.	Peter Gerbo	Nordquist Tax. Studio II	1949	6
163 6/8	20 5/8	20 5/8	20 5/8	5 5/8	4 5/8	6	5	Cowlitz Co., Wash.	Harold Melland	Harold Melland	1962	7
163 4/8	21 3/8	22 5/8	19 5/8	5 1/8	5	5	5	Eugene, Oreg.	Russell Thomas	Russell Thomas	1964	8
162 3/8	22	22 1/8	18 1/8	4 1/8	4 4/8	5	5	Trinity Co., Calif.	Sidney A. Nystrom	Sidney A. Nystrom	1961	9
162 2/8	24 5/8	25 1/8	19 2/8	4 2/8	4 2/8	5	5	Glenn Co., Calif.	Roger L. Spencer	Roger L. Spencer	1956	10
162 2/8*	23 6/8	22 6/8	21	5 2/8	5 3/8	5	5	Jackson Co., Oreg.	Mickey Geary	Mickey Geary	1973	10
160 7/8	23 3/8	23 6/8	19 3/8	4 6/8	4 5/8	6	5	Jackson Co., Oreg.	G. Scott Jennings	G. Scott Jennings	1972	12
160 5/8	20 5/8	21 5/8	16 5/8	4 5/8	4 5/8	4	4	Camas Valley, Oreg.	Bernard L. Den	Bernard L. Den	1958	13
160 4/8	23 5/8	24 5/8	21	4 7/8	4 7/8	6	5	Siskiyou Co., Calif.	John L. Masters	John L. Masters	1967	14
159 7/8	22 2/8	21 7/8	16 3/8	4	4	5	5	Etna, Calif.	John C. Ley	E. R. Cummins	1937	15
159 7/8	22 5/8	22 2/8	21 7/8	4 5/8	4 4/8	5	5	Siskiyou Co., Calif.	Francis M. Sullivan	Francis M. Sullivan	1951	15
159 5/8	25 5/8	24 6/8	22 2/8	4 6/8	4 4/8	6	6	Jackson Co., Oreg.	Frank Chapman	Frank Chapman	1965	17
159 1/8	21 5/8	22 1/8	19 3/8	4 6/8	4 6/8	5	5	Trinity Co., Calif.	A. H. Hilbert	A. H. Hilbert	1939	18
158 6/8	22	22 1/8	17 3/8	4 3/8	4 4/8	5	5	Marion Co., Oreg.	Bradley M. Brenden	Bradley M. Brenden	1973	19
158 4/8	24	24 4/8	22 5/8	4 5/8	4 5/8	6	6	Trinity Co., Calif.	David Phillips	David Phillips	1974	20
158 3/8	23 5/8	21 5/8	20 5/8	5	4 7/8	7	6	Siskiyou Co., Calif.	Frank Barago	Frank Barago	1945	21
158	22 5/8	23 3/8	18 5/8	4 6/8	4 6/8	5	5	Camas Valley, Oreg.	Frank Kinnan	Frank Kinnan	1968	22
157 5/8	22 5/8	23 3/8	21 5/8	4 2/8	4 3/8	5	5	Shasta Co., Calif.	Richard L. Sobrato	Richard L. Sobrato	1969	23
157 4/8	21 3/8	19 3/8	17 3/8	4 7/8	5	5	5	Yamhill Co., Oreg.	Henry Davenport	Henry Davenport	1932	24
157 3/8	23 3/8	23 5/8	26 5/8	4	4	6	5	Trinity Co., Calif.	A. H. Hilbert	A. H. Hilbert	1929	25
157	24 7/8	26 4/8	24 4/8	5	5 1/8	5	7	Santa Clara Co., Calif.	Brud Eade	Brud Eade	1961	26
156 5/8	22 5/8	21 3/8	20 3/8	4 5/8	4 4/8	5	5	Pierce Co., Wash.	Horst A. Vierthaler	Horst A. Vierthaler	1963	27
156	24 5/8	24 3/8	23 3/8	5 5/8	5 5/8	5	3	Shasta Co., Calif.	Lorio Verzasconi	Lorio Verzasconi	1946	28
156	25	23 5/8	21	4 4/8	4 4/8	6	5	Polk Co., Oreg.	Wayne Bond	Wayne Bond	1965	28
155 5/8	21 5/8	20 5/8	17 5/8	4 2/8	4 3/8	5	5	King Co., Wash.	Horst Vierthaler	Horst Vierthaler	1960	30

COLUMBIA BLACKTAIL DEER—*Continued*

Odocoileus hemionus columbianus and *Odocoileus hemionus sitkensis*

Score	Length of Main Beam R.	Length of Main Beam L.	Inside Spread	Circumference at Smallest Place Between Burr and First Point R.	Circumference at Smallest Place Between Burr and First Point L.	Number of Points R.	Number of Points L.	Locality Killed	By Whom Killed	Owner	Date Killed	Rank
155 2/8	22 3/8	23 1/8	20 6/8	5 3/8	5	4	5	Jackson Co., Oreg.	L. M. Morgan & Lenny Miller	Lewis M. Morgan	1971	30
155 2/8	22 1/8	22 7/8	19 2/8	5 3/8	4 7/8	5	5	Mendocino Co., Calif.	Gary Land	Gary Land	1972	30
155 1/8	21	21 6/8	18 5/8	4 3/8	4 3/8	4	4	Shasta Co., Calif.	Vance Corrigan	Vance Corrigan	1956	33
154 6/8	22 4/8	23 4/8	18	4 5/8	4 6/8	5	6	Cowlitz Co., Wash.	Bud Whittle	Bud Whittle	1957	34
154 6/8	20 4/8	20 3/8	20 4/8	4 5/8	4 5/8	4	4	Mendicino Co., Calif.	William A. McAllister	William A. McAllister	1968	34
154 5/8	24	22 7/8	23 3/8	4 3/8	4 4/8	5	5	Humboldt Co., Calif.	Phillip Brown	Phillip Brown	1962	36
154 1/8	20 4/8	20 4/8	18 1/8	4 4/8	4 4/8	5	5	Lane Co., Oreg.	Eldon Lundy	Eldon Lundy	1943	37
154 1/8	21 6/8	22 2/8	18 6/8	4 6/8	4 7/8	6	7	Glenn Co., Calif.	Mitchell A. Thorson	Mitchell A. Thorson	1969	37
153 7/8	21 5/8	21 6/8	23 1/8	3 3/8	3 4/8	5	5	Trinity Co., Calif.	Fred Heider	Fred Heider	1927	39
153 3/8	21 5/8	20 5/8	19 1/8	5 2/8	5 2/8	6	7	Columbia Co., Oreg.	J. H. Roberts	Oregon Game Comm.	1946	40
153 3/8	21 2/8	21 5/8	17 4/8	5	5	6	5	Tehama Co., Calif.	James L. Carr	James L. Carr	1979	40
153 1/8	22 4/8	22	19 7/8	5 1/8	5 2/8	6	6	Canton Creek, Oreg.	Marell Abeene	Marell Abeene	1967	42
153	22 6/8	23 6/8	14 6/8	4 3/8	4 5/8	6	5	Siskiyou Co., Calif.	John Carmichael	J. A. Brose	1969	43
152 5/8	22 1/8	22	19 5/8	4	4 3/8	5	5	Mendocino Co., Calif.	Harold D. Schneider	Harold & Mary Jane Schneider	1979	44
152 1/8	22 4/8	21 4/8	17 7/8	4 2/8	4 1/8	5	5	Shell Mountain, Calif.	Robert V. Strickland	Robert V. Strickland	1966	45
152 1/8	20 4/8	21 1/8	17 4/8	5 5/8	5 7/8	7	6	Pemberton, B. C.	Jim Decker	Jim Decker	1968	45
152	23 3/8	22 7/8	21 6/8	4 4/8	4 4/8	5	5	Yolo Co., Calif.	Herman Darneille	E. L. Gallup	1943	47
151 7/8	25	24 3/8	20 3/8	4 3/8	4 5/8	5	5	Jackson Co., Oreg.	David Ellefson	David Ellefson	1972	48
151 6/8	26 4/8	25 7/8	28 6/8	4 4/8	4 6/8	6	6	Trinity Co., Calif.	A. H. Hilbert	A. H. Hilbert	1930	49
151 6/8	22 2/8	22 4/8	17 4/8	5 4/8	5 1/8	6	5	Glide, Oreg.	William Cellers	William Cellers	1947	49
151 4/8	20 3/8	19 1/8	16 4/8	4 5/8	4 7/8	5	5	Marion Co., Oreg.	John Davenport	John Davenport	1958	51
151 1/8	22 1/8	21 7/8	22 5/8	4 6/8	4 6/8	5	5	Siskiyou Co., Calif.	Jim A. Turnbow	Jim A. Turnbow	1973	52
151	20 4/8	21 6/8	17 2/8	4 6/8	4 6/8	6	6	Lewis Co., Wash.	Norman Henspeter	Norman Henspeter	1941	53
151	20 1/8	21	19 2/8	4 2/8	4 1/8	5	5	Humboldt Co., Calif.	Elgin T. Gates	Elgin T. Gates	1952	53
151	23 2/8	24	17 4/8	5 3/8	5 3/8	7	6	Lewis Co., Wash.	Harold Gossard	George V. Bagley	1967	53
150 7/8	21 7/8	22	19 5/8	4 4/8	4 5/8	5	5	Jackson Co., Oreg.	Darrell Leek	Darrell Leek	1974	56
150 5/8	21 4/8	20 7/8	16 5/8	5 4/8	5 6/8	5	5	Yamhill Co., Oreg.	Russell W. Byers	Russell W. Byers	1961	57
150 4/8	24 1/8	24 2/8	19 5/8	5 1/8	5	6	6	Trinity Co., Calif.	E. L. Brightenstine	E. L. Brightenstine	1978	58
150 1/8	20 3/8	21	14 1/8	5 2/8	5 2/8	5	5	Lewis Co., Wash.	Carroll H. Fenn	Carroll H. Fenn	1959	59

150 1/8	22 4/8	22	16 1/8	4 1/8	4 1/8	5	5	Napa Co., Calif.	Robert G. Wiley	Robert G. Wiley	1965	59
150 1/8	21	21	20 1/8	3 7/8	3 7/8	5	5	Trinity Co., Calif.	Thomas L. Hough	Thomas L. Hough	1969	59
150	24	25 1/8	24	4 5/8	4 4/8	4	4	Napa Co., Calif.	W. C. Lambert	W. C. Lambert	1957	62
150	22 5/8	22 7/8	19 4/8	5 6/8	5 5/8	5	5	Lester, Wash.	Roscoe Rainey	Roscoe Rainey	1963	62
150	20 5/8	21 5/8	16 6/8	5	4 7/8	5	5	Douglas Co., Oreg.	Norman Burnett	Norman Burnett	1967	62
150	20 7/8	20 2/8	20	5 3/8	5 3/8	4	4	Lake Co., Calif.	Bruce Strickler	Bruce Strickler	1970	62
149 6/8	22 7/8	22	18 7/8	5	5	5	6	Siskiyou Co., Calif.	Emit C. Jones	Emit C. Jones	1961	66
149 4/8	22 5/8	21	20 6/8	5 1/8	5 2/8	5	5	Glenn Co., Calif.	George Stewart, Jr.	George Stewart, Jr.	1957	67
149 4/8	20	21 3/8	17 7/8	4 4/8	4 4/8	5	5	Humboldt Co., Calif.	Robert Charles Stephens	Robert Charles Stephens	1961	67
149 2/8	24 3/8	24 3/8	17 6/8	5 4/8	5 4/8	8	8	Trinity Co., Calif.	Lauren A. Johnson	Lauren A. Johnson	1964	69
149 1/8	21 4/8	22 7/8	16 1/8	5	4 7/8	5	5	Callam Co., Wash.	Otis Dahman	E. A. Dahman	1943	70
148 6/8	24 5/8	24 2/8	20 2/8	5	5 1/8	5	5	Tillamook Co., Oreg.	Fred Dick	Fred Dick	1948	71
148 4/8	23 2/8	22 7/8	20 6/8	4 3/8	4 5/8	4	4	Mendocino Co., Calif.	N. D. Windbigler	N. D. Windbigler	1969	72
148 3/8	21 2/8	21	19 5/8	4 3/8	4 2/8	5	5	Douglas Co., Oreg.	Unknown	Bud Jackson	1929	73
148 3/8	21 7/8	21 1/8	18 6/8	4 2/8	4 1/8	5	10	Marion Co., Oreg.	Mike Fenimore	Mike Fenimore	1961	73
148 2/8	24	24 4/8	23 4/8	6 2/8	5 6/8	6	6	Shasta Co., Calif.	Jerry W. Sander	Jerry W. Sander	1977	74
147 7/8	22	22 3/8	18 5/8	4 1/8	4 2/8	5	5	Glenn Co., Calif.	Emmet T. Frye	Emmet T. Frye	1937	76
147 5/8	23	23 6/8	19 5/8	4 4/8	4 3/8	5	4	Santa Clara Co., Calif.	Maitland Armstrong	Maitland Armstrong	1944	77
147 4/8	19 7/8	21 7/8	22 1/8	4 6/8	4 7/8	5	4	Siskiyou Co., Calif.	James C. Elliott	James C. Elliott	1974	78
147 2/8	22 6/8	23 4/8	19 6/8	4 2/8	4 3/8	4	5	Jackson Co., Oreg.	Mike Taylor	Mike Taylor	1969	79
147	20 6/8	20 7/8	21 6/8	5	4 7/8	5	5	Shell Mt., Calif.	Chauncy Willburn	Chauncy Willburn	1955	80
147	18	18 2/8	17	4 3/8	4 2/8	5	5	Siskiyou Co., Calif.	Ray Whittaker	Ray Whittaker	1966	80
146 7/8	22 4/8	22 2/8	15 1/8	5 3/8	5 3/8	5	5	Clallam Co., Wash.	Charles W. Lockhart	Charles W. Lockhart	1946	82
146 6/8	20	20 4/8	18 4/8	4 3/8	4 3/8	5	5	Siskiyou Co., Calif.	Richard Silva	Richard Silva	1958	83
146 6/8	21 4/8	21 5/8	18 4/8	4 7/8	5	6	5	Camas Valley, Oreg.	Adam J. Hipp	Adam J. Hipp	1961	83
146 5/8	21 6/8	21	16 3/8	4 3/8	4 3/8	5	5	Meredian, Oreg.	Pete Serafin	Pete Serafin	1968	85
146 4/8	22 6/8	22 7/8	22	5 2/8	5 4/8	5	5	King Co., Wash.	Leo Klinkhammer	Leo Klinkhammer	1961	86
146 2/8	20 7/8	21 4/8	14 2/8	4 4/8	4 4/8	5	5	Reston Ridge, Oreg.	Bernard H. Schum	Bernard H. Schum	1966	87
146 2/8	21 6/8	22 3/8	13 6/8	5 6/8	5 6/8	5	5	Shasta Co., Calif.	William H. Taylor	William H. Taylor	1971	87
146 1/8	23 1/8	23 5/8	19 1/8	4 5/8	4	4	4	Trinity Co., Calif	Kenneth M. Brown	Kenneth M. Brown	1972	89
146	20	20 4/8	21 4/8	5	5	5	5	King Co., Wash.	Robert B. Gracey	Robert B. Gracey	1963	90
146	20 2/8	20 7/8	15 2/8	5	5	4	4	Little Fall Creek, Oreg.	Gene B. Johnson	Gene B. Johnson	1963	90
145 7/8	23 4/8	23 3/8	22	5 3/8	5 4/8	6	8	Lake Co., Calif.	Floyd Goodrich	Mrs. William Olson	1926	92
145 7/8	24 5/8	22 4/8	19	5 5/8	5 6/8	6	5	Linn Co., Oreg.	Harold Tonkin	C. Vernon Humble	1954	92
145 7/8	22 6/8	22 6/8	21 7/8	4 3/8	4 5/8	5	5	Shasta Co., Calif.	Gary J. Miller	Gary J. Miller	1968	92
145 6/8	19 4/8	20 2/8	14 6/8	5 3/8	6	5	6	Whatcom Co., Wash.	Dennis Miller	Dennis Miller	1970	95
145 5/8	22 4/8	23	18 7/8	4 1/8	4 1/8	6	5	Humboldt Co., Calif.	Joe Dickerson	Jay Grunert	1962	96
145 4/8	22	22 6/8	21 6/8	4 2/8	4 5/8	4	4	Mendocino Co., Calif.	Elmer H. Brown	Elmer H. Brown	1960	97
145 4/8	20 1/8	20 4/8	14 2/8	4 2/8	4 1/8	6	5	Jackson Co., Oreg.	Gary D. Kaiser	Gary D. Kaiser	1967	97
145 3/8	23 4/8	23 6/8	24 6/8	4 5/8	4 5/8	5	5	Covelo, Calif.	Carroll E. Dow	Carroll E. Dow	1962	99
145 2/8	22 5/8	17 5/8	17 2/8	4	4	4	4	Lake Harrison, B. C.	Lloyd L. Wood, Jr.	Lloyd L. Wood, Jr.	1947	100
145 2/8	22 4/8	21 2/8	16 2/8	4 4/8	4 7/8	5	5	Jackson Co., Oreg.	Bill Hays	Bill Hays	1968	100
144 7/8	22 1/8	23 1/8	22 7/8	4 1/8	4 1/8	5	5	Lane Co., Oreg.	Clair R. Thomas	Clair R. Thomas	1959	102

COLUMBIA BLACKTAIL DEER—Continued

Odocoileus hemionus columbianus and Odocoileus hemionus sitkensis

Score	Length of Main Beam R.	L.	In-side Spread	Circumference at Smallest Place Between Burr and First Point R.	L.	Number of Points R.	L.	Locality Killed	By Whom Killed	Owner	Date Killed	Rank
144 6/8	20	20 4/8	19 4/8	3 4/8	3 4/8	5	4	King Co., Wash.	R. Walter Williams	R. Walter Williams	1956	103
144 4/8	22 4/8	22 4/8	22 2/8	4 4/8	4 4/8	5	5	Mendocino Co., Calif.	Richard Vannelli	Richard Vannelli	1970	103
144 4/8	22 6/8	22 4/8	21 5/8	4 4/8	4 4/8	5	5	Lake Mt., Oreg.	Jerry C. Sparlin	Jerry C. Sparlin	1963	105
144 4/8	21 6/8	21 3/8	19 4/8	4 3/8	4 2/8	5	5	Shasta Co., Calif.	Ernie Young	Chet Young	1953	106
144 4/8	21 6/8	21 5/8	16 6/8	4 2/8	4 3/8	5	5	Clackamas Co., Oreg.	John R. Vollmer, Jr.	John R. Vollmer, Jr.	1960	106
144 4/8	21 7/8	20 5/8	17 7/8	4 2/8	4 2/8	5	5	Powers, Oreg.	Ray A. Davis	Ray A. Davis	1968	106
144 3/8	22 7/8	23 3/8	21 3/8	5	5 2/8	5	5	Santa Clara Co., Calif.	Maitland Armstrong	Maitland Armstrong	1946	109
144 2/8	20 5/8	21 5/8	17 2/8	4 4/8	4 4/8	5	5	Jackson Co., Oreg.	Warren Pestka	Warren Pestka	1974	110
144 2/8	22 3/8	21	22 3/8	4 5/8	4 4/8	5	5	Mendocino Co., Calif.	Paul M. Holleman, II	Paul M. Holleman, II	1976	110
144 1/8	21 7/8	21 3/8	17 7/8	4 5/8	4 4/8	5	5	Siskiyou Natl. For., Oreg.	Dennis E. Bourn	Dennis E. Bourn	1971	112
144	21 6/8	22 5/8	20 2/8	4 5/8	4 6/8	6	5	Mt. Sheazer, Wash.	Joseph B. Wilcox	Joseph B. Wilcox	1953	113
144	20 6/8	20 4/8	17 4/8	4 4/8	4 5/8	5	5	Skamania Co., Wash.	Wayne Crockford	Wayne Crockford	1960	113
143 7/8	21 7/8	23	20 6/8	5	4 5/8	6	6	Linn Co., Oreg.	Clarence Howe	Clarence Howe	1941	115
143 7/8	23 7/8	22 7/8	21 3/8	5	4 4/8	5	5	Clackamas Co., Oregon	Richard G. Mathis	Richard G. Mathis	1965	115
143 6/8	19 5/8	20 4/8	16	4 4/8	4 7/8	5	4	Squamish, B. C.	B. Miller	B. Miller	1962	117
143 6/8	21 4/8	21 4/8	21 4/8	4 4/8	4 4/8	5	5	Snoqualmie, Wash.	M. L. James	Milton L. James	1964	117
143 5/8	20 4/8	20 4/8	16 4/8	5	5	5	5	Lewis Co., Wash.	Bill W. Latimer	Bill W. Latimer	1974	117
143 5/8	21 7/8	21 7/8	17 7/8	5 5/8	5 7/8	6	6	Grays Harbor Co., Wash.	Eddie & Robert Dierick	Eddie & Robert Dierick	1958	120
143 5/8	20 4/8	20 4/8	18 5/8	4 4/8	4 4/8	4	4	Klamath Forest, Calif.	Emit C. Jones	Emit C. Jones	1960	120
143 4/8	21 4/8	22 5/8	16 2/8	4 1/8	4 3/8	5	5	Clark Co., Wash.	A. W. Gerber	Earl Gerber	1929	122
143 3/8	20	20 1/8	15 3/8	4 7/8	4 7/8	5	5	Chehalis River, B. C.	Clair A. Howard	Clair A. Howard	1971	123
143 3/8	21 5/8	21 5/8	19	4 3/8	4 5/8	5	5	Linn Co., Oreg.	Basil C. Bradbury	Basil C. Bradbury	1960	124
143 3/8	22 5/8	22 5/8	21 4/8	4 2/8	4 3/8	5	5	Lake Co., Calif.	Mario Sereni, Jr.	Mario Sereni, Jr.	1965	124
143 3/8	19 5/8	19 4/8	17 4/8	4	4	5	5	Eaton Rough, Calif.	Jack Stedman	Jack Stedman	1965	124
143 2/8	20 4/8	19 4/8	19	4 7/8	6 7/8	7	6	Jones Lake, B. C.	James Haslam	James Haslam	1967	124
143 1/8	26	26	25	4 4/8	4 4/8	6	6	Mendocino Co., Calif.	George W. Rogers	George W. Rogers	1977	124
143 1/8	21 4/8	20 7/8	17 3/8	4 1/8	4 4/8	6	5	Corvallis, Oreg.	A. C. Nelson	A. C. Nelson	1957	129
143 1/8	22	22 1/8	18 1/8	4	4	5	5	Humboldt Co., Calif.	Mitchell A. Thorson	Mitchell A. Thorson	1965	129
142 7/8	20 7/8	22	16 3/8	4	4	4	4	Logan, Oreg.	Larry Tracy	Larry Tracy	1965	131
142 6/8	20 7/8	20	16 5/8	4 1/8	4 1/8	5	5	Livermore Hills, Calif.	Picked Up	Ray & Neal Haera	—	132
142 6/8	22 5/8	22 3/8	19 7/8	4 3/8	4 3/8	5	5	Livermore Hills, Calif.	Picked Up	Russel Rasmussen	—	132

Score						Points	Locality			Date	Rank
142 5/8	22	22 3/8	17 1/8	4 3/8	4 1/8	5	Marion Co., Oreg.	Robert E. Bochsler	Robert E. Bochsler	1950	132
142 5/8	19 6/8	19 4/8	17 7/8	4 6/8	4 6/8	5	Browns Burrow, Oreg.	Leonard B. Sequeira	Nancy Sequeira	1959	132
142 4/8	22 2/8	22 6/8	13 3/8	4 6/8	4 6/8	4	South Fork Mt., Calif.	Jace Comfort	Jace Comfort	1965	136
142 4/8	18 3/8	18 3/8	15	4 5/8	4 6/8	5	Chilliwack, B.C.	Frank Rosenauer	Frank Rosenauer	1967	136
142 3/8	20 6/8	20 7/8	17 3/8	4 3/8	4 3/8	5	Laytonville, Calif.	Byron James Rowland, Jr.	Byron James Rowland, Jr.	1964	138
142 3/8	23	22	19 3/8	4	4	5	Humboldt Co., Calif.	Darol L. Damm	Darol L. Damm	1976	138
142 2/8	23 3/8	23 3/8	17	4 2/8	4 1/8	4	Mendocino Co., Calif.	James A. Shelton	James A. Shelton	1944	140
142 2/8	21 3/8	22 3/8	19 7/8	5 1/8	5 1/8	5	Shasta Co., Calif.	Richard R. Lowell	Richard R. Lowell	1953	141
142 1/8	20 1/8	20 6/8	17	4 3/8	4 2/8	5	Cowlitz Co., Wash.	Harold C. Johnson	Harold C. Johnson	1947	142
142	24	23 5/8	16 7/8	5 1/8	5 5/8	6	Marion Co., Oreg.	Hugh W. Gardner	Hugh W. Gardner	1966	142
142	24 6/8	24 6/8	17	5	5	5	Skamania Co., Wash.	Ted Howell	Ted Howell	1968	142
142	25 3/8	24	18 3/8	7	6 4/8	4	Doty, Wash.	Leslie A. Lusk	Leslie A. Lusk	1973	142
141 7/8	20 7/8	21 3/8	18 1/8	5 5/8	5 5/8	4	Bellingham, Wash.	Kjell A. Thompson	Kjell A. Thompson	1963	146
141 6/8	21 3/8	21 3/8	19 2/8	4 4/8	4 4/8	5	Lane Co., Oreg.	Jerry Shepard	Jerry Shepard	1954	147
141 6/8	22 7/8	22 3/8	17 5/8	4 5/8	4 6/8	7	Pierce Co., Wash.	Joseph Kominski	Joseph Kominski	1954	147
141 6/8	19 3/8	19 3/8	16 4/8	4 7/8	4 6/8	5	Hobart, Wash.	Donald R. Heinle	Donald R. Heinle	1958	147
141 4/8	20 2/8	20 6/8	17 6/8	4 7/8	5	5	Morton, Wash.	Ralph W. Cournyer	Ralph W. Cournyer	1962	150
141 3/8	19 6/8	19 6/8	17 7/8	4 7/8	4 6/8	6	Harrison Lake, B. C.	D. Harrison	D. Harrison	1963	151
141 3/8	25 6/8	25 5/8	21 5/8	5 5/8	5 5/8	6	Pierce Co., Wash.	John Streepy, Sr.	John Streepy, Sr.	1956	152
141 1/8	19 7/8	19 6/8	20 3/8	4	4 2/8	5	Trinity Co., Calif.	A. H. Hilbert	A. H. Hilbert	—	153
141	21 3/8	21 1/8	17	3 7/8	4 1/8	5	Humboldt Co., Calif.	Allen Pierce, Jr.	Allen Pierce, Jr.	1959	154
141	21	20 4/8	19 4/8	4 4/8	4	5	Mendocino Co., Calif.	Richard Vannelli	Richard Vannelli	1970	154
141	23	24 4/8	22	5 5/8	5 5/8	7	Mendocino Co., Calif.	Gerald Wayne Whitmire	Gerald Wayne Whitmire	1976	154
140 7/8	21 1/8	20 6/8	21 1/8	4 3/8	4 4/8	5	Shasta Co., Calif.	Dave Swenson	Dave Swenson	1968	157
140 6/8	21 1/8	21 1/8	18 6/8	5	4 6/8	5	Thurston Co., Wash.	Eric Anderson	Eric Anderson	1937	158
140 6/8	17 6/8	18 5/8	17 3/8	4 5/8	4 4/8	6	Mineral, Wash.	Nick Nilson	Nick Nilson	1944	158
140 6/8	23 6/8	23	18	4 6/8	4 5/8	4	Mendocino Co., Calif.	Robert Lynch	Robert Lynch	1971	158
140 5/8	23	21 7/8	18 3/8	4 6/8	4 6/8	5	Shasta Co., Calif.	Luther Clements	R. H. Bernhardy	1944	161
140 5/8	21	21	18 6/8	4	4	5	Glacier, Wash.	John J. A. Weatherby	John J. A. Weatherby	1965	161
140 3/8	22	21	17 7/8	4	4	5	Ditch Creek, Calif.	Rodney Irwin	Rodney Irwin	1966	163
140 2/8	20 6/8	21 3/8	16 7/8	4 7/8	4 5/8	5	Lewis Co., Wash.	Randy J. Brossard	Randy J. Brossard	1978	164
140 2/8	21 2/8	21 5/8	15 5/8	4 2/8	4 2/8	7	Potter Valley, Calif.	Clarence W. Nelson	Clarence W. Nelson	1948	165
140 2/8	23 7/8	22 7/8	18 1/8	5	5	6	Onalaska, Wash.	George Nichols	George Nichols	1964	165
140	20 4/8	19 4/8	16 3/8	4 3/8	4 3/8	4	Santa Clara Co., Calif.	Dick Sullivan	Dick Sullivan	1977	165
140	20 2/8	20 7/8	16	4 7/8	4 6/8	7	Laytonville, Calif.	Roy Bergstrom	Roy Bergstrom	1966	168
140	21	20 4/8	17	5	5	6	Polk Co., Oreg.	Harold E. Stepp	Harold E. Stepp	1970	168
139 6/8	20 4/8	22 2/8	16	4 1/8	4	8	Shasta Co., Calif.	Warren Hunter	Warren Hunter	1964	170
139 6/8	21 5/8	19 6/8	18 1/8	4 4/8	4 2/8	5	Josephine Co., Oreg.	Richard H. Caswell	Richard H. Caswell	1969	170
139 6/8	20 6/8	21 5/8	20 4/8	4 1/8	4 2/8	6	Lane Co., Oreg.	Gene Tinker	Gene Tinker	1955	172
139 6/8	21 7/8	21 4/8	17 7/8	3 7/8	3 7/8	5	Mt. Ashland, Oreg.	Arthur A. Ekerson	Arthur A. Ekerson	1966	172
139 3/8	22 4/8	21 5/8	16	4 6/8	4 6/8	7	Lewis Co., Wash.	Kevin Pointer	Kevin Pointer	1972	172
139 3/8	20 4/8	20 2/8	15 5/8	4 2/8	4 1/8	4	Whatcom Co., Wash.	Kim S. Scott	Kim S. Scott	1959	175
139 1/8	21 1/8	21 1/8	17 7/8	4 3/8	4 4/8	5	Monmouth, Oreg.	Roy W. Miller	Roy W. Miller	1967	175

COLUMBIA BLACKTAIL DEER—Continued
Odocoileus hemionus columbianus and Odocoileus hemionus sitkensis

Score	Length of Main Beam R.	L.	Inside Spread	Circumference at Smallest Place Between Burr and First Point R.	L.	Number of Points R.	L.	Locality Killed	By Whom Killed	Owner	Date Killed	Rank
139 7/8	21 3/8	21 1/8	20 1/8	4 1/8	4 1/8	5	4	Humboldt Co., Calif.	Jeff Bryant	Jeff Bryant	1964	177
139 7/8	21 7/8	21 7/8	18 5/8	3 7/8	4 1/8	4	5	Florence, Oreg.	Edwin C. Stevens	Warner Pinkney	1928	178
139 7/8	22 1/8	22	17 7/8	4	5 5/8	4	5	Mendocino Co., Calif.	John Winn, Jr.	John Winn, Jr.	1972	178
139	21 1/8	22 3/8	16 7/8	4 5/8	4 5/8	5	5	Jefferson Co., Wash.	Picked Up	Aubrey F. Taylor	1947	180
139	20	20 5/8	16 5/8	4 6/8	4 1/8	5	5	Morton, Wash.	Mike Cournyer	Mike Cournyer	1964	180
139	19 3/8	19 3/8	18 3/8	4 1/8	4	5	5	Douglas Co., Oreg.	Richard Wigle	Richard Wigle	1968	180
138 7/8	19 7/8	19 7/8	15 7/8	4 4/8	4 4/8	5	5	Greys River, Wash.	Russell Case	Russell Case	1956	183
138 7/8	21	22 2/8	20 5/8	4 5/8	4 2/8	4	4	Siskiyou Co., Calif.	Darrell Nowdesha	Darrell Nowdesha	1961	183
138 7/8	19 1/8	20 5/8	15 3/8	5	4 7/8	6	5	Trinity Co., Calif.	Wm. O. Louderback	Wm. O. Louderback	1963	183
138 7/8	23 7/8	24 4/8	18 7/8	4 4/8	4 1/8	5	5	Tiller, Oreg.	Ronald Elliott	Ronald Elliott	1963	183
138 7/8	20 2/8	21 3/8	15 5/8	5 1/8	5 2/8	6	7	Snohomish Co., Wash.	Walter J. Kau	Walter J. Kau	1950	187
138 7/8	23 3/8	23	15 3/8	4 7/8	4 5/8	5	6	Pierce Co., Wash.	James Latimer	James Latimer	1962	187
138 7/8	21 3/8	20 1/8	16	4	4 1/8	5	5	Humboldt Co., Calif.	Larry Bowermaster	Larry Bowermaster	1964	187
138 7/8	21	21	15 5/8	5 2/8	5	5	5	Clatsop Co., Oreg.	Russell L. Hemphill	Russell L. Hemphill	1972	190
138 7/8	22 4/8	22 7/8	18 7/8	4	4	4	4	Foster Mt., Calif.	Jess Jones	Jess Jones	1950	191
138 7/8	21 1/8	20	18 3/8	4 3/8	4	5	5	Siskiyou, Calif.	Bob Courts	Bob Courts	1965	191
138 7/8	19 7/8	19 4/8	17 7/8	4	4	5	6	Siskiyou Co., Calif.	John Carmichael	John Carmichael	1969	191
138 3/8	22 5/8	22	20 5/8	4 7/8	4 3/8	5	5	Clackamas Co., Oreg.	J. B. Mitts	Wes Mitts	1896	194
138 3/8	23 7/8	22 7/8	16 3/8	5 3/8	5 1/8	6	6	Pierce Co., Wash.	George W. Halcott	George W. Halcott	1966	194
138 3/8	22 4/8	22 2/8	18	4 4/8	4 1/8	5	5	Humboldt Co., Calif.	Garry Hughes	Garry Hughes	1968	194
138 2/8	19 4/8	19 5/8	20 6/8	4 2/8	4 2/8	6	5	Mendocino Co., Calif.	Walter R. Schubert	Walter R. Schubert	1952	197
138 2/8	19 7/8	21	16 2/8	5 2/8	4 4/8	5	5	Sauk River, Wash.	James McCarthy	James McCarthy	1961	197
138 2/8	21 3/8	21 3/8	15 4/8	4	3 7/8	5	5	Tehema Co., Calif.	Robt. L. Armanasco	Robt. L. Armanasco	1968	197
138 1/8	21 4/8	21 5/8	21 4/8	4 3/8	4 1/8	5	5	Siskiyou Co., Calif.	Loren L. Lutz	Loren L. Lutz	1964	200
138	19 6/8	19 6/8	16 6/8	4 6/8	4 5/8	5	6	Douglas Co., Oreg.	Will H. Brown	Will H. Brown	1948	201
137 7/8	20 3/8	20 3/8	17	4 4/8	4 5/8	6	6	Yamhill Co., Oreg.	Wallace Hill	Wallace Hill	1963	202
137 7/8	20 5/8	19 3/8	18 5/8	4	4 2/8	5	5	Shasta Co., Calif.	Paul G. Carter	Paul G. Carter	1964	202
137 7/8	18 5/8	17 5/8	17 3/8	4	4	5	5	Trinity Co., Calif.	Picked Up	North Coast Tax.	1965	202
137 7/8	18	18 5/8	18 5/8	5	4 5/8	4	4	Santa Clara Co., Calif.	Farber L. Johnston, Jr.	Farber L. Johnston, Jr.	1967	202
137 5/8	20 3/8	20 3/8	19 5/8	4 5/8	4 5/8	5	5	Mendocino Co., Calif.	P. R. Borton	John R. Borton	1965	206
137 5/8	20 5/8	20 5/8	16 5/8	4 5/8	4 5/8	6	5	Vancouver Island, B. C.	Gordie Simpson	Gordie Simpson	1966	206

137 4/8	19 3/8	19	17	4 1/8	4 1/8	5	5	Trinity Co., Calif.	Philip Grunert	Philip Grunert	1967	208
137 3/8	21 4/8	22 3/8	19	5 6/8	5 2/8	5	4	Arlington, Wash.	Ernest J. Kaesther	Ernest J. Kaesther	1959	209
137 3/8	23 6/8	23 6/8	17 3/8	4 1/8	4 2/8	4	4	Vancouver Island, B. C.	Herb Klein	Herb Klein	1964	209
137 2/8	19 3/8	20 7/8	18	4 2/8	4 1/8	5	5	Douglas Co., Oreg.	Bernard L. Den	Bernard L. Den	1934	211
137 2/8	19 6/8	20	15	4 3/8	4 1/8	5	5	Douglas Co., Oreg.	Francis R. Young	Francis R. Young	1972	211
137 1/8	21 3/8	19 2/8	15 7/8	4 2/8	4 2/8	4	4	Douglas Co., Oreg.	Peter Serafin	Peter Serafin	1932	213
137 1/8	23	22 4/8	22 7/8	5	4 6/8	5	4	Tehama Co., Calif.	Clint Heiber	Clint Heiber	1977	213
137	24	23 6/8	21 2/8	4 3/8	4 3/8	4	5	King Co., Wash.	Douglas F. Dammarell	Douglas F. Dammarell	1974	215
136 7/8	21 3/8	20 7/8	17 5/8	4 2/8	4 4/8	4	5	Lewis Co., Wash.	Allen J. Roehrick	Allen J. Roehrick	1968	216
136 6/8	21 3/8	21	14	5 2/8	5 2/8	5	5	King Co., Wash.	Ed Lochus	George B. Johnson	1930	217
136 6/8	21 6/8	23	18 2/8	4 7/8	4 6/8	4	4	Shasta Co., Calif.	Vance Corrigan	Vance Corrigan	1957	217
136 6/8	20 5/8	21 1/8	16	4 1/8	4 1/8	5	5	Pierce Co., Wash.	Patrick M. Blackwell	Patrick M. Blackwell	1971	217
136 5/8	21 5/8	22 1/8	19 5/8	4 5/8	4 6/8	5	5	Tillamook Co., Oreg.	J. A. Aaron	J. A. Aaron	1943	220
136 4/8	20 3/8	20 1/8	18	4 4/8	4 4/8	5	5	Ukiah, Calif.	Charles Tollini	Charles Tollini	1960	221
136 4/8	23 4/8	22 1/8	18 2/8	4 6/8	4 6/8	5	5	Lewis Co., Wash.	Larry F. Smith	Larry F. Smith	1964	221
136 3/8	20 2/8	20 1/8	19 1/8	4	4 1/8	4	5	Douglas Co., Oregon	Gerry F. Edwards	Gerry F. Edwards	1971	223
136 2/8	20 3/8	20 5/8	16	3 6/8	3 5/8	4	5	Jackson Co., Oreg.	Martin S. Durbin	Ellis A. Jones	1921	224
136 2/8	20 6/8	20 4/8	20 2/8	3 6/8	4 1/8	4	5	Covelo, Calif.	David G. Cox	David G. Cox	1967	224
136 2/8	30 3/8	21 3/8	17	4 7/8	5	5	5	Yamhill Co., Oreg.	Monty Dickey	Monty Dickey	1967	224
136	21 6/8	23	19	5 1/8	5 1/8	6	6	Santa Clara Co., Calif.	Mrs. Maitland Armstrong	Mrs. Maitland Armstrong	1956	227
136	21 4/8	21	17	4 4/8	4 3/8	5	5	Mendocino Natl. For., Calif.	Edward Q. Garayalde	Edward Q. Garayalde	1966	227
136	21 4/8	21	19 2/8	4 6/8	4 7/8	4	5	Tehema Co., Calif.	Robt. L. Armanasco	Robt. L. Armanasco	1968	227
136	23 1/8	23	21 6/8	4 7/8	4 6/8	3	4	San Mateo Co., Calif.	Dan Caughey, Sr.	Dan Caughey, Sr.	1973	227
136	20 4/8	19 2/8	19	4 1/8	4 1/8	6	6	Trinity Co., Calif.	Richard G. Shelton	Richard G. Shelton	1973	227
135 7/8	18 5/8	19 1/8	15 7/8	4 2/8	4 2/8	5	5	Langley, B. C.	Charles R. Yeomans	James G. Hill	1959	232
135 7/8	22 1/8	22 2/8	17 3/8	4 4/8	4 4/8	4	3	Jackson Co., Oreg.	Mrs. Ila B. Bethany	Mrs. Ila B. Bethany	1972	232
135 6/8	21 1/8	21 1/8	18 2/8	4 7/8	4 7/8	5	5	Powell River, B. C.	Paddy Price	Duncan Formby	1939	234
135 6/8	24 5/8	23 3/8	21 5/8	4 7/8	4 7/8	5	5	Trinity Co., Calif.	Andy Burgess	Andy Burgess	1964	234
135 6/8	20 2/8	20 1/8	19 4/8	3 4/8	3 3/8	4	4	Trinity Co., Calif.	Roy J. Renner	Roy J. Renner	1965	234
135 6/8	20 5/8	19 7/8	15	5 4/8	5 4/8	5	6	Whatcom Co., Wash.	Jack R Teeter	Jack R. Teeter	1969	234
135 5/8	19 6/8	19 3/8	17 5/8	4 3/8	4 1/8	4	4	Clallam Co., Wash.	Gary L. Smith	Gary L. Smith	1956	238
135 3/8	21 5/8	21 2/8	17 6/8	4 6/8	4 5/8	6	6	Clark Co., Wash.	Francis E. Gillette	Francis E. Gillette	1934	239
135 2/8	20 5/8	19 3/8	19 1/8	5 3/8	5 1/8	7	8	Benton Co., Oreg.	H. G. Slocum	H. G. Slocum	1953	240
135 2/8	19 6/8	20	15	3 4/8	3 3/8	4	4	Trinity Co., Calif.	Andy Burgess	Andy Burgess	1959	240
135	19	19 5/8	15 4/8	4 1/8	4 2/8	5	5	Humboldt Co., Calif.	Edward F. Burgess	Edward F. Burgess	1965	242
134 7/8	22 3/8	22 2/8	18 3/8	4	4 2/8	4	5	Tehama Co., Calif.	Mario Sereni, Jr.	Mario Sereni, Jr.	1964	243
134 7/8	21 1/8	21 5/8	14 4/8	4 1/8	4 2/8	5	6	San Bernadino Mts., Calif.	James Tacke	James Tacke	1966	243
134 7/8	21 2/8	21 4/8	16 1/8	3 4/8	3 6/8	4	4	Butte Falls, Oreg.	Bob Doan, Jr.	Bob Doan, Jr.	1973	243
134 6/8	21 5/8	23 2/8	19 2/8	4 3/8	4 2/8	5	5	Cowlitz Co., Wash.	Kenneth Dale Nicholson	Kenneth Dale Nicholson	1970	246
134 4/8	21 1/8	21 2/8	20 2/8	4 1/8	4 3/8	7	6	Trinity Co., Calif.	William M. Longhurst	William M. Longhurst	1951	247
134 4/8	22 2/8	23 2/8	18 2/8	4 5/8	4 6/8	4	4	Thurston Co., Wash.	Joseph Kominski	Joseph Kominski	1955	247
134 4/8	20	20 5/8	23 2/8	4 3/8	4 3/8	5	6	Shasta Co., Calif.	Jack Floyd	Jack Floyd	1957	247
134 4/8	20	17 5/8	14 4/8	3 7/8	4 7/8	4	5	Humboldt Co., Calif.	Stephen Walker	Stephen Walker	1961	247

Columbia Blacktail Deer–*Continued*

Odocoileus hemionus columbianus and *Odocoileus hemionus sitkensis*

Score	Length of Main Beam R.	Length of Main Beam L.	Inside Spread	Circumference at Smallest Place Between Burr and First Point R.	Circumference at Smallest Place Between Burr and First Point L.	Number of Points R.	Number of Points L.	Locality Killed	By Whom Killed	Owner	Date Killed	Rank
134 4/8	19 4/8	20	17	4 4/8	4 2/8	5	5	Humboldt Co., Calif.	J. A. Phelps	J. A. Phelps	1966	247
134 4/8	21 6/8	22 5/8	13	4 3/8	4 4/8	6	6	Johnson Creek, Wash.	Douglas G. McArthur	Douglas G. McArthur	1967	247
134 4/8	26	27 1/8	20 2/8	4 7/8	4 6/8	5	4	Lewis Co., Wash.	Daniel E. Longmire	Daniel E. Longmire	1974	247
134 3/8	21 3/8	21 2/8	19 7/8	4 5/8	4 7/8	5	5	Toba Inlet, B. C.	L. Mitchell	Peters Sport Shop	1962	254
134 3/8	21 3/8	21 6/8	19 5/8	4 2/8	4 2/8	5	5	Benton Co., Oreg.	John E. Peterson	John E. Peterson	1965	254
134 3/8	18	15	17 7/8	4 6/8	4 2/8	6	4	Lewis Co., Wash.	Melvin B. Henle	Melvin B. Henle	1973	254
134 2/8	20 3/8	19 6/8	16 4/8	4 2/8	4 3/8	5	5	Douglas Co., Oreg.	John R. Hughey	John R. Hughey	1965	257
134 2/8	21 7/8	22 1/8	16	4 4/8	4 4/8	4	5	Pierce Co., Wash.	James B. August	James B. August	1971	257
134 2/8	19 4/8	21	16	4	4 3/8	4	4	Humboldt Co., Calif.	G. L. Dorris	G. L. Dorris	1973	257
134 1/8	20 3/8	21 3/8	19 3/8	3 7/8	3 7/8	5	5	Coos Co., Oreg.	Dan Woolley	Dan Woolley	1971	260
134 1/8	19 5/8	20	16 5/8	4 4/8	4 4/8	5	5	Mendocino Co., Calif.	Danny Pardini	Danny Pardini	1976	260
134	19 6/8	19 2/8	16 2/8	3 6/8	3 4/8	7	5	Siskiyou Co., Calif.	Alicia Whittaker	Alicia Whittaker	1970	262
133 6/8	20 6/8	21 5/8	18 1/8	4 7/8	5 2/8	6	6	Pierce Co., Wash.	K. S. Sheets	K. S. Sheets	1966	263
133 5/8	22 2/8	21 1/8	18 1/8	5 5/8	5 1/8	6	4	Linn Co., Oregon	Richard L. Rounds	Richard L. Rounds	1978	264
133 4/8	20 4/8	19 6/8	15 2/8	5 6/8	4 4/8	5	5	Clackamas Co., Oreg.	C. A. Pond	C. A. Pond	1940	265
133 4/8	22	20 4/8	20 4/8	4 6/8	4 4/8	5	6	Trinity Co., Calif.	George M. Moxon	George M. Moxon	1977	265
133 3/8	18 6/8	19 3/8	17 6/8	4 2/8	4	6	5	Coos Co., Oreg.	Frank Neal	Foster M. Thompson	1924	267
133 3/8	19 3/8	19 6/8	18 5/8	4	3 7/8	5	5	Lane Co., Oreg.	John D. Woodmark	John D. Woodmark	1969	267
133 2/8	18 5/8	18 6/8	20 2/8	4 5/8	4 4/8	9	9	Mendocino Co., Calif.	O. E. Schubert	Walter R. Schubert	1917	269
133 2/8	21 1/8	21 1/8	13 6/8	4 6/8	4 5/8	5	5	Skagit Co., Wash.	L. A. Willoughby	L. A. Willoughby	1951	269
133 2/8	20	19 7/8	14 6/8	4 1/8	4 2/8	5	5	Linn Co., Oreg.	Leon Plueard	Leon Plueard	1965	269
133 2/8	20 5/8	20 4/8	14 6/8	4 5/8	4 6/8	5	5	Pierce Co., Wash.	Lowell Apple	Lowell Apple	1968	269
133 2/8	19	19 5/8	17	4 2/8	4	4	4	Clackamas Co., Oreg.	Mary A. Weseman	Mary A. Weseman	1971	269
133 1/8	22 7/8	22	21 1/8	4 5/8	5	5	5	Trinity Co., Calif.	Hugh A. Dow	Hugh A. Dow	1969	274
133	22 4/8	23 2/8	20 6/8	5 6/8	4 6/8	9	4	Lewis Co., Wash.	George Sevey	George Sevey	1941	275
133	20 4/8	20 4/8	19 4/8	4 4/8	5	4	4	Napa Co., Calif.	Fred C. Framsted	Fred C. Framsted	1966	275
132 6/8	19 5/8	21	18 6/8	4 4/8	4 4/8	5	5	Mendocino Co., Calif.	Mason Geisinger	Mason Geisinger	1967	277
132 5/8	19 1/8	17 6/8	16 4/8	3 6/8	3 7/8	5	5	Tehama Co., Calif.	Daniel E. Osborne	Daniel E. Osborne	1956	278
132 4/8	19	18 2/8	14	4 7/8	4 7/8	4	4	Lewis Co., Wash.	Robert L. Peck	Robert L. Peck	1964	279
132 3/8	19 6/8	19	15 5/8	5 2/8	5 1/8	5	5	Cowlitz Co., Wash.	James H. Wilson	James H. Wilson	1959	280
132 3/8	21 2/8	21 5/8	16 3/8	4	4	5	5	Aberdeen, Wash.	Jack A. Allen	Jack A. Allen	1963	280

132 2/8	21 6/8	21 1/8	12 4/8	5 2/8	4 6/8	4	4	Douglas Co., Oreg.	William McCaleb	William McCaleb	1963	282
132 2/8	20 3/8	20 2/8	16 2/8	5 1/8	5	5	4	Island Co., Wash.	Bert Klineburger	Bert Klineburger	1969	282
132 2/8	19 5/8	18 7/8	18 2/8	4 5/8	4 1/8	5	4	Mendocino Co., Calif.	P. R. Borton	William R. Borton	1971	282
132 1/8	20 6/8	20 4/8	15 1/8	5 2/8	5 1/8	4	4	Trinity Co., Calif.	R. C. Kauffman	R. C. Kauffman	1936	285
132 1/8	20 6/8	19 6/8	19 1/8	3 2/8	3 2/8	4	4	Mendocino Co., Calif.	Fred E. Borton, II	Matthew E. Borton	1971	285
131 6/8	19 1/8	19 3/8	14	4	3 7/8	5	5	Siskiyou Co., Calif.	Sid E. Ziegler	Sid E. Ziegler	1957	287
131 6/8	21	19 4/8	18	5	5	5	5	Trinity Co., Calif.	Carter B. Dow	Carter B. Dow	1961	287
131 5/8	19 1/8	19 6/8	14 7/8	4 6/8	4 6/8	5	5	Whatcom Co., Wash.	C. H. Head	C. H. Head	1972	289
131 4/8	19 5/8	20 4/8	16 4/8	4 3/8	4 3/8	5	5	Tillamook Co., Oreg.	Ted Wolcott	Ted Wolcott	1943	290
131 4/8	18 4/8	18 6/8	16 2/8	5 7/8	5 1/8	4	5	Mineral, Wash.	Ron N. Nilson	Ron N. Nilson	1963	290
131 4/8	18	18 3/8	14 2/8	4 3/8	4 4/8	5	5	Meridian, Oreg.	Helen Sanderlin	Helen Sanderlin	1966	290
131 2/8	24 4/8	24	19 7/8	4 1/8	4 2/8	5	4	Polk Co., Oreg.	Ray Burtis	Ray Burtis	1960	293
131 2/8	19 1/8	17 6/8	13 6/8	4 4/8	4 4/8	5	5	Estacada, Oreg.	Roy Tracy	Lamont Rumgay	1967	293
131	21 6/8	20 5/8	15 2/8	4 5/8	4 4/8	5	5	King Co., Wash.	J. A. Ryezek	George B. Johnson	1935	295
131	17 5/8	17 4/8	14 6/8	4 4/8	4 1/8	5	5	Jackson Co., Oreg.	Robert R. Maben	Robert R. Maben	1963	295
131	18 4/8	17 4/8	15 6/8	3 7/8	4	5	5	Siskiyou Co., Calif.	George Quigley	George Quigley	1971	295
130 6/8	21 6/8	21 4/8	19 4/8	4	4 2/8	8	6	Siskiyou Co., Calif.	Larry E. Richey	Larry E. Richey	1956	298
130 6/8	20 5/8	19	19	4 3/8	4	5	4	Mendocino Co., Calif.	Tom Enberg	Tom Enberg	1970	298
130 5/8	18	20	17 1/8	5	5	6	6	Lake Co., Calif.	Bernard Domries	Bernard Domries	1940	300
130 5/8	24 2/8	23 3/8	23 2/8	4 3/8	4 4/8	4	5	Siskiyou Co., Calif.	Vernon Sutherlin	Vernon Sutherlin	1961	300
130 4/8	21	20 6/8	17 3/8	4 6/8	4 6/8	6	5	Pierce Co., Wash.	Don Argo	Don Argo	1950	302
130 4/8	21 6/8	21 7/8	18 6/8	5 2/8	4 2/8	5	3	Mendicino Co., Calif.	Mitchell A. Thorson	Mitchell A. Thorson	1969	302
130 4/8	20 4/8	20 2/8	12 4/8	4 3/8	4 3/8	5	5	Cowlitz Co., Wash.	Michael A. Demery	Steven J. Hellem	1978	302
130 3/8	19	19	16 1/8	4 2/8	4 2/8	4	4	Lincoln Co., Oreg.	Bert Kessi	Bert Kessi	1942	305
130 3/8	19 1/8	18 3/8	15 3/8	4 2/8	4 2/8	5	5	Mt. Jupiter, Wash.	Jack Dustin	Jack Dustin	1946	305
130 3/8	20	20	16 3/8	4	4	5	5	Siskiyou Co., Calif.	John Carmichael	John Carmichael	1970	305
130 2/8	20 4/8	20	16 4/8	4 4/8	4 5/8	5	5	Clackamas Co., Oregon	Thomas A. Tremain	Thomas A. Tremain	1976	308
130	17 2/8	17 2/8	16	4 3/8	4 2/8	5	5	Longview, Wash.	Harold E. Koenig	Harold E. Koenig	1949	309

*Final Score subject to revision by additional verifying measurements.

WORLD'S RECORD WHITETAIL DEER (TYPICAL ANTLERS)
SCORE: 206 1/8
Locality: Burnett County, Wisconsin. Date: 1914.
Hunter: James Jordan. Owner: Charles T. Arnold.

Photograph by Wm. H. Nesbitt

NUMBER TWO WHITETAIL DEER (TYPICAL ANTLERS)
SCORE: 205
Locality: Randolph County, Missouri. Date: 1971.
Hunter and Owner: Larry W. Gibson.

Whitetail Deer *(Typical Antlers)*

Minimum Score 170

Odocoileus virginianus and certain related subspecies

Score	Length of Main Beam R.	Length of Main Beam L.	Inside Spread	Circumference at Smallest Place Between Burr and First Point R.	Circumference at Smallest Place Between Burr and First Point L.	Number of Points R.	Number of Points L.	Locality Killed	By Whom Killed	Owner	Date Killed	Rank
206 1/8	30	30	20 1/8	6 2/8	6 1/8	5	5	Burnett Co., Wisc.	James Jordan	Charles T. Arnold	1914	1
205	26 6/8	25 4/8	24 2/8	4 6/8	4 6/8	6	6	Randolf Co., Mo.	Larry Gibson	Larry Gibson	1971	2
204 4/8	27 5/8	26 6/8	23 5/8	6 1/8	6 2/8	7	6	Peoria Co., Ill.	M. J. Johnson	M. J. Johnson	1965	3
202	31 2/8	31	23 5/8	5 7/8	6	8	8	Funkley, Minn.	John A. Breen	Charles T. Arnold	1918	4
199 4/8	27 2/8	26 2/8	20	5 4/8	5 1/8	8	5	Clark Co., Mo.	Jeffrey Brunk	Jeffrey Brunk	1969	5
199 3/8	27 3/8	27 4/8	22 3/8	4 4/8	4 6/8	6	7	Missoula Co., Mont.	Thomas H. Dellwo	Thomas H. Dellwo	1974	6
198 3/8	29 5/8	29 4/8	18 1/8	4 6/8	4 6/8	6	8	Allegany Co., N. Y.	Roosevelt Luckey	N. Y. Cons. Dept.	1939	7
198 2/8	27 5/8	26 7/8	20 2/8	5	5	6	8	Nemaha Co., Kan.	Dennis P. Finger	Dennis P. Finger	1974	8
196 4/8	28 6/8	27 5/8	24 2/8	4 6/8	4 6/8	8	6	Maverick Co., Texas	Tom McCulloch	McLean Bowman	1963	9
194 7/8	27 5/8	26 7/8	18 4/8	4 4/8	4 5/8	8	7	Dimmitt Co., Texas	William Henry Pease	Jeff Vick Pease	1932	10
194 4/8	25 7/8	25 6/8	18 6/8	5 1/8	5 2/8	7	7	Monroe Co., Iowa	Lloyd Goad	Lloyd Goad	1962	11
194 4/8*	24 4/8	25	24	4 6/8	4 6/8	6	6	Kenedy Co., Texas	Alexander M. D. Guest	Alexander M. D. Guest	1973	11
193 6/8	24 5/8	24 4/8	18 1/8	5	5	7	7	Christopher Lake, Sask.	Jerry Thorson	Jerry Thorson	1959	13
192 2/8	27 2/8	27 3/8	22 6/8	4 2/8	4 4/8	8	7	Frio County, Texas	Basil Dailey	David M. Dailey	1903	14
192	27 4/8	28	19 2/8	4 6/8	4 6/8	8	9	Lyman Co., S. D.	Bob Weidner	E. N. Eichler	1957	15
191 6/8	27	26	19 6/8	4 5/8	4 6/8	5	6	Hudson Bay, Sask.	George Chalus	George Chalus	1973	16
191 5/8	26 7/8	26 2/8	19	5 1/8	5	6	7	Flathead Co., Mont.	Earl McMaster	McLean Bowman	1963	17
191 4/8	26 5/8	27 4/8	20	4 7/8	5	6	7	Chautauqua Co., Kan.	Michael A. Young	Michael A. Young	1973	18
191 3/8	31 6/8	31 1/8	27 5/8	6 1/8	6 1/8	5	6	Vilas Co., Wisc.	Robert Hunter	May Docken	1910	19
190 1/8	30	30 1/8	19 4/8	4 6/8	5	6	7	Dakota Co., Neb.	E. Keith Fahrenholz	E. Keith Fahrenholz	1966	20
190	24 2/8	25 2/8	20 6/8	5	5	7	6	Dimmitt Co., Texas	C. P. Howard	C. P. Howard	1950	21
189 5/8	29 2/8	29 2/8	21 4/8	4 7/8	4 6/8	5	6	Tabor, S. D.	Duane Graber	Sam Peterson	1954	22
189 3/8	25 7/8	24 1/8	23 1/8	6 2/8	6 2/8	6	7	Fillmore Co., Minn.	Tom Norby	Tom Norby	1975	23
189 1/8	27 5/8	26 6/8	25 7/8	5 1/8	5 2/8	6	6	Nuckolls Co., Neb.	Van Shotzman	Van Shotzman	1968	24
188 4/8	25	26 3/8	22 5/8	4 7/8	4 6/8	5	6	Burstall, Sask.	W. P. Rolick	W. P. Rolick	1957	25
188 4/8	27 2/8	24 5/8	22 2/8	5 6/8	5 5/8	5	5	Metiskow, Alta.	Norman T. Salminen	Norman T. Salminen	1977	25
187 5/8	28 2/8	27 6/8	19 6/8	5	5	6	8	Starr Co., Texas	Pickup	Jack F. Quist	1945	27
187 5/8	25	25 2/8	20 1/8	5 2/8	5 2/8	6	6	Linton, N. D.	Joseph F. Bosch	Joseph F. Bosch	1959	27
187 5/8	29 2/8	31 1/8	23 1/8	5 2/8	5 1/8	6	6	Cherokee Co., Iowa	Dennis R. Vaudt	Dennis R. Vaudt	1975	27
187 5/8	25 2/8	25 5/8	19 2/8	5 2/8	5 3/8	6	8	Winona Co., Minn.	Ken W. Koenig	Ken W. Koenig	1976	27
187 4/8	28 3/8	27	24 6/8	5 3/8	5 3/8	8	5	Winona Co., Minn.	Dan Groebner	Dan Groebner	1974	31

187 2/8	31 4/8	30 6/8	30 3/8	4 6/8	4 5/8	7	8	Warren Co., Iowa	Dwight E. Green	Dwight E. Green	1964	32
187 2/8	29	28 5/8	26 4/8	5 2/8	5 3/8	5	5	Lynd, Minn.	Lynn Jackson	Lynn Jackson	1967	32
187 2/8	26	26 2/8	19 4/8	4 6/8	4 6/8	6	8	Scotland Co., Mo.	Robin Berhorst	Robin Berhorst	1971	32
187 1/8	26 4/8	26 5/8	19 4/8	4 4/8	4 5/8	6	7	Cooper Co., Mo.	Joe Ditto	Joe Ditto	1974	35
186 7/8	25 3/8	25 5/8	20 1/8	4 7/8	5	5	5	Arkansas Co., Ark.	Walter Spears	Walter Spears	1952	36
186 3/8	27 5/8	27 1/8	20 4/8	6 1/8	5 6/8	7	6	Council Grove, Kan.	Garold D. Miller	Garold D. Miller	1969	37
186 2/8	25	25 4/8	22 4/8	5	5 2/8	6	7	Laclede Co., Mo.	Larry Ogle	Larry Ogle	1972	38
186 2/8	27 4/8	27 4/8	18	4 6/8	4 6/8	8	10	Kenedy Co., Texas	Jack Van Cleve, III	McGill Estate	1972	38
186 1/8	29 4/8	29 2/8	21	4 6/8	4 5/8	8	9	Zavala Co., Texas	Picked Up	Paul W. Sanders, Jr.	—	40
186 1/8	25 1/8	26 2/8	20 1/8	4 6/8	4 7/8	6	5	Roane Co., Tenn.	W. A. Foster	W. A. Foster	1959	40
186 1/8	28	26 2/8	21 4/8	6 1/8	6	8	5	Waupaca Co., Wisc.	Fred Penny	Dale Trinrud	1963	40
186	30 5/8	31 3/8	26 3/8	5 1/8	5	5	9	Erskin Lake, Minn.	Knud W. Jensen	Knud W. Jensen	1955	43
186	25 1/8	25 3/8	19	4 3/8	4 3/8	6	6	Flathead Co., Mont.	Douglas G. Mefford	Douglas G. Mefford	1966	43
185 5/8	24 3/8	25	19 5/8	4 6/8	4 5/8	6	8	Nenzel, Neb.	Richard Kehr	Richard Kehr	1965	45
185 4/8	26 6/8	27 1/8	22	4 5/8	4 5/8	6	6	Otter Tail Co., Minn.	Orris T. Neirby	Orris T. Neirby	1942	46
185 4/8	30	29 2/8	30 2/8	5 2/8	5 2/8	8	8	Elkton, Ky.	C. W. Shelton	Charles T. Arnold	1964	46
185 1/8	27 7/8	27 4/8	19 1/8	5 2/8	5	6	7	Harrison Co., Iowa	Marvin E. Tippery	Marvin E. Tippery	1971	48
185	29 1/8	28 5/8	18 6/8	4 4/8	4 3/8	5	5	Vernon Co., Wisc.	Harold Christianson	Harold Christianson	1968	49
184 6/8	26 7/8	27	24 4/8	5 3/8	5 3/8	8	9	Desha Co., Ark.	Lee Perry	Walter Brock	1961	50
184 6/8	24 1/8	26 1/8	21 2/8	5 3/8	5 4/8	6	6	Dore Lake, Sask.	Garvis C. Coker	Garvis C. Coker	1971	50
184 6/8	26 7/8	26 4/8	20 6/8	4 5/8	4 4/8	5	6	Greene Co., Pa.	Ivan Parry	Ivan Parry	1974	50
184 5/8	26 5/8	26 6/8	27	5 7/8	5 6/8	7	7	Lamont, Iowa	R. E. Stewart	R. E. Stewart	1953	53
184 3/8	28 4/8	29	25 5/8	5 6/8	5 7/8	5	7	Kingsbury Co., S. D.	Rudy F. Weigel	Rudy F. Weigel	1960	54
184 1/8	26 7/8	27 6/8	21	5	5	8	7	Marshall Co., Minn.	Alvin C. Westerlund	Alvin C. Westerlund	1953	55
184 1/8	29	31	20 5/8	5 5/8	4 4/8	6	5	Vinton Co., Ohio	Dan F. Allison	Dan F. Allison	1965	55
184	27 4/8	29 1/8	18 4/8	5	4 7/8	5	6	Newton Co., Ga.	Gene Almand	Gene Almand	1966	57
184	24 5/8	24 4/8	18 5/8	5 1/8	5 2/8	7	6	Menominee Co., Wisc.	Keith Miller	Charles Loberg	1969	57
183 7/8	27 7/8	28 3/8	20 1/8	6 2/8	6 5/8	6	7	Taylor Co., Iowa	Wayne Swartz	Wayne Swartz	1947	59
183 7/8	25 6/8	25 3/8	27	5	4 6/8	7	6	Webb Co., Texas	Henderson Coquat	Henderson Coquat	1949	59
183 6/8	26 7/8	25 1/8	18 6/8	5 4/8	5 4/8	7	7	Pepin Co., Wisc.	Laverne Anibas	Laverne Anibas	1965	61
183 6/8	26 6/8	27 6/8	19 2/8	4 3/8	4 4/8	6	6	Clinton Co., Indiana	Stuart C. Snodgrass	Stuart C. Snodgrass	1977	61
183 5/8	27 1/8	26	23 2/8	4 6/8	4 6/8	7	6	Buffalo Co., Wisc.	Lee F. Spittler	Mrs. Lee F. Spittler	1953	63
183 4/8	26 6/8	26 6/8	18 2/8	5 3/8	5 4/8	5	6	Sumner, Mo.	Marvin F. Lentz	Marvin F. Lentz	1968	64
183 3/8	21 5/8	23 3/8	19 3/8	5 4/8	5 2/8	7	9	Flathead Co., Mont.	Unknown	Edwin M. Sager	1957	65
183 3/8	27 1/8	26 4/8	18 5/8	4 3/8	4 4/8	8	9	Dorchester Co., Md.	John R. Seifert, Jr.	John R. Seifert, Jr.	1973	65
183 1/8	27 7/8	28 6/8	20 5/8	5	5	6	6	Duval Co., Texas	Charles Drennan	Bill Carter	1973	67
183	25 6/8	26	21	4 6/8	4 5/8	5	5	Red Deer River, Alta.	Unknown	Ovar Uggen	—	68
183	27 1/8	27 7/8	18 6/8	4 6/8	4 6/8	5	5	Desha Co., Ark.	R. J. Dierhoff	Franzen Bros.	1954	68
183	26 2/8	25	19 6/8	5	5	8	9	Piedmont Lake, Ohio	James Rumbaugh & John Ruyan	James Rumbaugh & John Ruyan	1958	68
182 7/8	28 5/8	28 5/8	19	5 6/8	6	6	6	Wayne Co., Ohio	Gary E. Landry	Gary E. Landry	1975	71
182 5/8	27 6/8	28 4/8	21 5/8	5 6/8	5 5/8	7	8	Virden, Man.	Darryl Gray	Darryl Gray	1957	72
182 5/8	23 6/8	24 3/8	19 4/8	5 5/8	5 7/8	6	8	Yuma Co., Colo.	Ivan W. Rhodes	Ivan W. Rhodes	1978	72

WHITETAIL DEER (*Typical Antlers*)–*Continued*

Odocoileus virginianus and certain related subspecies

Score	Length of Main Beam R.	Length of Main Beam L.	Inside Spread	Circumference at Smallest Place Between Burr and First Point R.	Circumference at Smallest Place Between Burr and First Point L.	Number of Points R.	Number of Points L.	Locality Killed	By Whom Killed	Owner	Date Killed	Rank
182 4/8	28 5/8	29	23 6/8	5 3/8	5 1/8	7	5	Carrot River, Sask.	Lori Lonson	Joel Andrews	1960	74
182 4/8	27	26 6/8	18 4/8	5 3/8	5 3/8	7	5	Warren Co., Mo.	Donald L. Tanner	Donald L. Tanner	1968	74
182 4/8	28 3/8	27 1/8	23 4/8	5 5/8	5 5/8	7	7	Kanabec Co., Minn.	Steven R. Berg	Steven R. Berg	1973	74
182 3/8	27	26 5/8	23 1/8	5 7/8	5 7/8	6	5	Waubausee Co., Kan.	Norman Anderson	Norman Anderson	1966	77
182 3/8	25 5/8	25 1/8	18 1/8	4 6/8	4 6/8	6	6	Marshall Co., Iowa	Barbara Daniel	Terry Daniel	1967	77
182 3/8	25 4/8	25 6/8	21 3/8	6	5 6/8	5	6	Freeborn Co., Minn.	Robert H. Dowd	Robert H. Dowd	1969	77
182 3/8	28 1/8	27 1/8	21 5/8	4 4/8	4 5/8	6	6	Braxton Co., W.Va.	William D. Given	William D. Given	1976	77
182	24 4/8	25	23	4 3/8	4	7	7	Zap, N. D.	Wally Duckwitz	Sioux Sporting Goods	1962	81
181 7/8	26 7/8	27 1/8	23 3/8	5 4/8	5 3/8	8	7	Mt. Lake, Minn.	Picked Up	Minn. Game & Fish Dept.	1963	82
181 7/8	24 4/8	24 4/8	15 5/8	4 3/8	4 4/8	6	6	McMullen Co., Texas	Oscar Hasette	Bill Carter	1971	82
181 6/8	23 6/8	23 3/8	20 6/8	5 3/8	5 2/8	5	5	Lyon Co., Kan.	Kenneth C. Haynes	Kenneth C. Haynes	1969	84
181 6/8	26 1/8	26 4/8	17 6/8	6	6 1/8	5	5	Wabasha Co., Minn.	Lee G. Partington	Lee G. Partington	1971	84
181 5/8	24 7/8	24 5/8	18 5/8	6 5/8	6 2/8	6	7	Pope Co., Ill.	Jack A. Higgs	Jack A. Higgs	1963	86
181 4/8	25 2/8	25 6/8	22 7/8	5 6/8	5 7/8	7	7	Licking Co., Ohio	Arlee McCullough	Arlee McCullough	1962	87
181 4/8	26	28 5/8	18 6/8	5 2/8	5 2/8	9	7	Canton, Ill.	Arnold C. Hegele	Arnold C. Hegele	1968	87
181 4/8	25 4/8	27	22 6/8	5 6/8	5 6/8	6	7	Pine Lake, Alta.	Robert Crosby	Robert Crosby	1977	87
181 3/8	27 4/8	27 5/8	20 6/8	4 4/8	4 4/8	7	6	Portage Co., Ohio	Robert M. Smith	Robert M. Smith	1953	90
181 3/8	25 2/8	24 3/8	21 2/8	5 6/8	5 6/8	7	6	Southey, Sask.	A. K. Flaman	Sam Peterson	1955	90
181 3/8	24 7/8	27 4/8	18 1/8	5	5	6	7	Orange Co., N. Y.	Roy Vail	Roy Vail	1960	90
181 1/8	27 3/8	27 6/8	20 7/8	6 2/8	5 6/8	10	7	Empress, Sask.	Don Leach	Don Leach	1960	93
181	25 7/8	24 6/8	22 3/8	4 7/8	5 3/8	6	8	Beltrami Co., Minn.	Robert C. Shaw	Robert C. Shaw	1910	94
181	27	26 5/8	20	5 7/8	5 7/8	5	6	Stettler, Alta.	Archie Smith	Archie Smith	1962	94
181	26 5/8	26 2/8	21 2/8	6 2/8	6 3/8	7	8	Lac Qui Parle, Minn.	Mary A. Barvels	Mary A. Barvels	1978	94
180 7/8	29	29 6/8	20 4/8	5 2/8	5 2/8	7	6	Jones Co., Ga.	James H. C. Kitchens	James H. C. Kitchens	1957	97
180 7/8	29 6/8	28 2/8	24 1/8	5 2/8	5	6	5	Keya Paha Co., Neb.	Steve R. Pecsenye	Steve R. Pecsenye	1966	97
180 6/8	31 6/8	31 2/8	19 4/8	6	5 5/8	6	8	N. B.	Unknown	Acad. Nat. Sci., Phil.	1937	99
180 6/8	26 6/8	26	25	5	4 4/8	6	9	Dimmitt Co., Texas	Edward Gardner	Edward Gardner	1937	99
180 5/8	24 7/8	25 1/8	18 3/8	4 7/8	4 6/8	6	7	Treasure Co., Mont.	Jack Welch	Jack Welch	1958	101
180 5/8	25	23 6/8	23 3/8	5 3/8	5 3/8	7	6	Cheat Mt., W. Va.	Jos. V. Volitis	Jos. V. Volitis	1969	101
180 5/8	25	28 3/8	18 7/8	4 7/8	5	8	5	St. Landry Parish, La.	Shawn P. Ortego	Shawn P. Ortego	1975	101
180 4/8	28	26 2/8	26 6/8	4 6/8	5 2/8	7	7	Jim Hogg Co., Texas	Roy Lee Henry	Roy Lee Henry	1958	104

180 4/8	23 5/8	24 4/8	17 2/8	5 2/8	5	6	5	Andrew Co., Mo.	Virgil M. Ashley	Virgil M. Ashley	1967	104
180 4/8	28	27	22 7/8	5 3/8	5 1/8	6	6	Leflore Co., Miss.	W. F. Smith	W. F. Smith	1968	104
180 4/8	26 7/8	25 5/8	19	5 1/8	5 1/8	6	6	Clay Co., S. D.	James E. Olson	James E. Olson	1975	104
180 3/8	30 2/8	30	23 1/8	5 1/8	5 2/8	8	6	Livingston Co., N. Y.	Edward Beare	Edward Beare	1943	108
180 3/8	26 4/8	27	20 2/8	4 3/8	4 6/8	7	8	Sheboygan Co., Wisc.	Unknown	James K. Lawton	1955	108
180 3/8	24 5/8	24 4/8	19 1/8	5 4/8	5 6/8	8	6	Orvando, Mont.	Clinton Berry	Clinton Berry	1957	108
180 3/8	25 6/8	26 3/8	21 5/8	5	5 1/8	7	6	Stoughton, Sask.	Joe Zbeetnoff	Joe Zbeetnoff	1961	108
180 3/8	27 5/8	26	21 5/8	4 5/8	4 5/8	5	5	Antler Lake, Alta.	German Wagenseil	German Wagenseil	1964	108
180 2/8	27 7/8	28	20	4 6/8	4 5/8	6	6	Lincoln Co., Wisc.	Alfred Thielig	Philip Schlegel	1928	113
180 2/8	26 4/8	25	22 5/8	5 4/8	5 2/8	7	7	Lumsden, Sask.	Mike Lukas	E. M. Gazda	1959	113
180 2/8	28 1/8	28 4/8	18 4/8	4 6/8	4 6/8	5	5	Newton Co., Ga.	David Moon	David Moon	1972	113
180 1/8	23 3/8	23 5/8	17 5/8	5 2/8	5 2/8	5	5	Maryfield, Sask.	Donald Cook	Richard Christoforo	1956	116
180 1/8	25 4/8	26 6/8	17 3/8	4 7/8	4 6/8	7	6	Ashland Co., Wisc.	Audrey Kundinger	Audrey Kundinger	1961	116
180 1/8	24	24 4/8	19 1/8	4 7/8	5	7	6	Vermillion, Alta.	Ralph M. McDonald	Ralph M. McDonald	1975	116
180	27 5/8	27 6/8	20	4 7/8	5	5	6	Oneida Co., Wisc.	Milo K. Fields	Milo K. Fields	1938	119
180	26 6/8	26 5/8	19 6/8	4 4/8	4 4/8	7	5	Desha Co., Ark.	Turner Neal	Turner Neal	1962	119
180	25 6/8	25 4/8	19 3/8	5	5 2/8	6	6	St. Peter, Minn.	T. J. Merkley	T. J. Merkley	1966	119
180	26	25 7/8	19	4 7/8	4 7/8	10	7	Zavala County, Texas	Mrs. Richard King, III	Mrs. Richard King, III	1966	119
180	25 7/8	25 5/8	19 4/8	6 1/8	6 1/8	6	8	Big Horn Co., Mont.	Clair W. Jensen	Clair W. Jensen	1967	119
180	26 7/8	26 1/8	20 4/8	5 7/8	5 7/8	5	7	Castor, Alta.	Kenneth Larson	Kenneth Larson	1969	119
179 6/8	28 1/8	26 4/8	22 2/8	4 6/8	4 6/8	6	5	Aitkin Co., Minn.	Harland Kern	Harland Kern	1973	125
179 6/8	29 1/8	28	21	5 6/8	5 5/8	7	6	Longview, Alta.	Eldred Umbach	Eldred Umbach	1977	125
179 5/8	25 4/8	25 7/8	19 5/8	6	6	5	6	Rumsey, Alta.	Arley Harder	Arley Harder	1969	127
179 4/8	23 4/8	23 5/8	19 2/8	4 6/8	4 5/8	6	6	Coronation, Alta.	Harold McKnight	Harold McKnight	1969	128
179 4/8	24 1/8	24 2/8	19 2/8	5 2/8	5 1/8	7	6	Spokane Co., Wash.	Bert E. Smith	Bert E. Smith	1972	128
179 4/8	27 5/8	27 3/8	19 7/8	5	5	6	6	Elk Co., Kan.	Lowell E. Howell	Lowell E. Howell	1973	128
179 4/8	24 1/8	25 3/8	19 5/8	5	4 7/8	7	8	Chouteau Co., Mont.	Richard L. Charlson	Richard L. Charlson	1977	128
179 3/8	29	29 2/8	19 7/8	4 6/8	4 5/8	10	8	Essex Co., N. Y.	Herbert Jaquish	Herbert Jaquish	1953	132
179 3/8	28 5/8	28	20 7/8	5 6/8	5 6/8	5	5	Parkman, Sask.	Harold Larsen	Sam Peterson	1958	132
179 3/8	26	26 2/8	17 3/8	6	5 5/8	6	6	Oberon, Man.	Arnold W. Poole	Arnold W. Poole	1968	132
179 2/8	27 2/8	27 1/8	23 3/8	5	5 2/8	9	11	Prairie Co., Ark.	Charles Newsom	Charles Newsom	1962	135
179 2/8	27 6/8	27	20	5 4/8	5 6/8	9	9	Cypress Hills, Sask.	Raymond McCrea	Raymond McCrea	1964	135
179 2/8	25 4/8	24 6/8	21 3/8	4 5/8	4 6/8	7	7	Lamar Co., Ga.	Gary Littlejohn	Gary Littlejohn	1968	135
179 2/8	26 5/8	25 5/8	17 7/8	5	4 6/8	7	7	Worth Co., Iowa	John Janssen	John Janssen	1976	135
179	27 1/8	25 5/8	19 4/8	5 5/8	5 4/8	6	7	Sherbourne Co., Minn.	Victor Nagel	Victor Nagel	1956	139
179	25 6/8	25 6/8	19 3/8	5	5 1/8	5	6	Waldersee, Man.	Wm. Wutke	Wm. Wutke	1959	139
178 7/8	24 3/8	28	21 7/8	5 3/8	5 3/8	6	6	Monroe Co., Ohio	Roger E. Schumacher	Roger E. Schumacher	1958	141
178 6/8	26	25	22 7/8	5 2/8	5 1/8	6	6	Elkhorn, Man.	Jerry May	Jerry May	1959	142
178 6/8	27 6/8	27 6/8	25 4/8	5 3/8	5 4/8	6	5	Windthorst, Sask.	Clarence E. Genest	Clarence E. Genest	1965	142
178 6/8	26	26 5/8	21 2/8	5 2/8	5 2/8	6	8	McPherson Co., Kan.	Larry D. Daniel	Larry D. Daniel	1967	142
178 5/8	28 7/8	27	24	5 1/8	5 1/8	7	7	Beechy, Sask.	Archie D. McRae	Archie D. McRae	1957	145
178 5/8	27	26 4/8	20 4/8	4 3/8	4 3/8	6	6	Harlan Co., Neb.	Don Tripe	Don Tripe	1961	145
178 5/8	27 7/8	29 2/8	26 3/8	5 2/8	5 2/8	6	7	Debden, Sask.	Henry Rydde	Henry Rydde	1966	145

WHITETAIL DEER *(Typical Antlers)–Continued*

Odocoileus virginianus and certain related subspecies

Score	Length of Main Beam R.	Length of Main Beam L.	Inside Spread	Circumference at Smallest Place Between Burr and First Point R.	Circumference at Smallest Place Between Burr and First Point L.	Number of Points R.	Number of Points L.	Locality Killed	By Whom Killed	Owner	Date Killed	Rank
178 5/8	27	26 4/8	21 1/8	5 3/8	5 3/8	5	5	Scott Co., Tenn.	Charles H. Smith	Charles H. Smith	1978	145
178 4/8	23 7/8	24 6/8	21 3/8	4 3/8	4 3/8	7	7	Addy, Wash.	Irving Naff	Irving Naff	1957	149
178 4/8	25 2/8	25	23 2/8	5 4/8	5 4/8	5	5	Tilden, Texas	D. H. Waldron	D. H. Waldron	1964	149
178 3/8	26 7/8	26 5/8	24 3/8	5 4/8	5 2/8	6	5	Aitkin, Minn.	George E. Jenks	George E. Jenks	1969	151
178 3/8	28 4/8	28 7/8	23 7/8	5 1/8	5 2/8	7	8	Lincoln Co., Minn.	Larry Lustfield	Larry Lustfield	1976	151
178 3/8	25 1/8	24 4/8	26 7/8	5 6/8	5 4/8	6	7	Hardisty, Alta.	George R. Walker	George R. Walker	1977	151
178 1/8	24 1/8	23 5/8	19 1/8	4 5/8	4 4/8	8	8	Dismal River, Neb.	Gift Of G. B. Grinnell	National Collection	PR1909	154
178 1/8	28 2/8	26 7/8	18 7/8	4 7/8	5	5	7	Concrete, N. D.	Lawrence E. Vandal	Lawrence E. Vandal	1947	154
178 1/8	35 1/8	35	15 6/8	5 3/8	5 2/8	6	6	Jasper Co., Ga.	M. C. Lennon, Jr.	M. C. Lennon, Jr.	1964	154
178 1/8	29 1/8	28 4/8	18 4/8	4 7/8	4 7/8	7	7	Harlan Co., Neb.	Duane E. Johnson	Duane E. Johnson	1967	154
178	26 7/8	27 2/8	21 6/8	4 3/8	4 3/8	6	6	Clark Co., Mo.	Allen L. Courtney	Allen L. Courtney	1966	158
178	25	24 6/8	17 2/8	4 6/8	4 5/8	6	7	Washington Co., Iowa	Brad Gardner	Vaughn Wilkins	1978	158
177 7/8	27	28 4/8	20	4 6/8	5	6	6	Chicot Co., Ark.	George Matthews	W. T. Haynes	1923	160
177 7/8	28	27 4/8	20 3/8	5 6/8	5 6/8	5	5	Iron Co., Mich.	Felix Brzoznowski	Joseph Brzoznowski	1939	160
177 7/8	24 2/8	23 7/8	19 3/8	4 6/8	4 4/8	7	7	Ymir, B. C.	Frank Gowing	Frank Gowing	1961	160
177 7/8	25 7/8	25 1/8	24 3/8	5	5 1/8	5	6	Wibaux Co., Mont.	Dan Amunrud	David Welliever	1967	160
177 7/8	26 3/8	26 6/8	22 1/8	5 2/8	5 2/8	6	6	Christian Co., Ill.	Rodney J. Gordon	Rodney J. Gordon	1974	160
177 6/8	24 5/8	24 7/8	19	4 5/8	4 6/8	6	6	Paxton, Neb.	Ole Herstedt	Ole Herstedt	1956	165
177 6/8	26 6/8	25 4/8	22 6/8	5	5	5	5	Atoka Co., Okla.	Skip Rowell	Skip Rowell	1972	165
177 6/8	24	24	22	4 4/8	4 4/8	6	6	Kleberg Co., Texas	Elaine A. O'Brien	Patrick O'Brien	1972	165
177 6/8	23 4/8	24	24	4 6/8	4 6/8	6	6	Duval Co., Texas	Harry Heimer	Harry Heimer	1974	165
177 6/8	26 5/8	27 4/8	23 4/8	4 5/8	4 4/8	6	5	Stearns Co., Minn.	Robert G. Schwarz	Robert G. Schwarz	1975	165
177 5/8	25 5/8	26 2/8	19 1/8	5 4/8	5 3/8	5	5	Endeavour, Sask.	Terry L. Halgrimson	Terry L. Halgrimson	1971	170
177 4/8	26	26 4/8	21 5/8	4 5/8	4 4/8	8	6	Oneida Co., Wisc.	Elmer Ahlborn	Gene Ahlborn	1926	171
177 4/8	27 6/8	27 4/8	23 4/8	5	5	6	5	Dimmit Co., Texas	Tom Brady	McLean Bowman	1926	171
177 4/8	25	24 4/8	21 1/8	5 2/8	5 4/8	5	6	Dundurn, Sask.	L. B. Galbraith	L. B. Galbraith	1956	171
177 4/8	26 1/8	26	21	4	4 1/8	5	5	Bedford Co., Pa.	Raymond Miller	Raymond Miller	1957	171
177 4/8	24 6/8	23 3/8	24 7/8	5 1/8	5 2/8	7	6	Dimmit Co., Texas	Carter Younts	Carter Younts	1963	171
177 4/8	28 2/8	28 3/8	22 4/8	5 6/8	5 6/8	5	6	Beltrami Co., Minn.	Sheldon M. Stockdale	Sheldon M. Stockdale	1968	171
177 3/8	25 4/8	25 4/8	18	6	6 2/8	5	6	Hall Co., Neb.	Charles R. Babel	Charles R. Babel	1969	177
177 2/8	26 6/8	25 3/8	26 2/8	5 1/8	5 1/8	7	7	Webb Co., Texas	Unknown	Eugene Roberts	1924	178

177 2/8	28 1/8	28	20 6/8	4 6/8	4 6/8	5	5	Augusta Co., Va.	Donald W. Houser	Donald W. Houser	1963	178
177 1/8	25 5/8	26 1/8	19	5 1/8	5 2/8	7	10	Newcastle, Wyo.	H. W. Julien	H. W. Julien	1954	180
177	25	26	19 1/8	6	5 7/8	6	5	Gage Co., Neb.	Art Wallmen	Art Wallmen	1968	181
177	26 2/8	27 6/8	18 4/8	4 4/8	4 6/8	5	5	Cass Co., Ind.	Herbert R. Frushour	Herbert R. Frushour	1974	181
176 7/8	29 2/8	28 3/8	23	5 7/8	5 4/8	5	6	Logan Co., Ohio	David Sutherly	David Sutherly	1975	183
176 6/8	27 1/8	26	20 7/8	5 2/8	5 2/8	5	6	Vilas Co., Wisc.	Porter Dean	Safari North Tax.	1938	184
176 6/8	25 5/8	27 3/8	20 6/8	5 7/8	5 1/8	12	11	Clinton Co., Mich.	Ray Sadler	Ray Sadler	1963	184
176 6/8	25 2/8	25	23 4/8	4 4/8	4 6/8	6	6	Frankfort, Kan.	Ray A. Mosher	Ray A. Mosher	1966	184
176 6/8	26 3/8	26 2/8	18 4/8	5	5 3/8	5	5	Knox Co., Neb.	Alvin Zimmerman	Alvin Zimmerman	1966	184
176 6/8	26 5/8	26 4/8	21 4/8	5 2/8	5 3/8	5	5	Pine Co., Minn.	Kim Shira	Kim Shira	1977	184
176 5/8	30	28	21 5/8	4 6/8	4 4/8	6	7	Mifflin Co., Pa.	John Zerba	Kenneth Zerba	1936	189
176 5/8	25 4/8	25 4/8	21 7/8	4 5/8	4 7/8	5	5	Bolivar Co., Miss.	Sidney D. Sessions	Sidney D. Sessions	1952	189
176 5/8	24 1/8	24 2/8	17 6/8	5	5 1/8	8	8	Wash.	Unknown	Jonas Bros. Of Seattle	PR1953	189
176 5/8	25 5/8	27 1/8	17 7/8	5 4/8	5 3/8	5	5	Montgomery Co., Iowa	Unknown	Chris Hein	1961	189
176 5/8	25	25	23 2/8	5	5	6	5	Rosholt, S. D.	Fred Kuehl	Fred Kuehl	1964	189
176 5/8	26 1/8	25 7/8	21 1/8	6 1/8	6 1/8	6	5	Buffalo, Alta.	Bob Fraleigh	Bob Fraleigh	1978	189
176 4/8	23 3/8	23 4/8	22	5 3/8	5 5/8	6	5	Esterhazy, Sask.	Albert Kristoff	Albert Kristoff	1960	195
176 4/8	25 2/8	24 2/8	19	3 7/8	4 1/8	6	6	Shackelford Co., Texas	H. V. Stroud	H. V. Stroud	1964	195
176 4/8	23	23	16 4/8	4 2/8	4 2/8	9	7	Carrizo Springs, Texas	Lin F. Nowotny	Lin F. Nowotny	1966	195
176 4/8	25	25	19 4/8	4 4/8	4 3/8	7	6	Crawford Co., Wisc.	Louis Franks	Louis Franks	1969	195
176 3/8	26	26 5/8	20 5/8	5 4/8	5 6/8	7	5	Baraga Co., Mich.	Paul Korhonen	Paul Korhonen	1945	198
176 2/8	25 6/8	28 6/8	25 3/8	4 6/8	5	5	5	Erie Co., N. Y.	Wesley Iulg	Wesley Iulg	1944	200
176 2/8	23	25 5/8	18 6/8	5	4 7/8	5	5	Swanson, Sask.	L. S. Wood	L. S. Wood	1959	200
176 2/8	24 4/8	26 4/8	17 1/8	5 4/8	5 4/8	8	7	Warren Co., N. Y.	Frank Dagles	Frank Dagles	1961	200
176 2/8	28 4/8	29 2/8	20 6/8	5 4/8	5 4/8	5	5	Richland Parish, La.	Willard Roberson	Willard Roberson	1968	200
176 2/8	30	28 2/8	23	6 1/8	6 1/8	7	6	Coshocton Co., Ohio	James R. Gardner	James R. Gardner	1976	200
176 1/8	28	27 4/8	21 2/8	5 4/8	5 4/8	6	5	Florence Co., Wisc.	Theron A. Meyer, Sr	Theron A. Meyer, Sr.	1943	205
176 1/8	25 3/8	24 5/8	19 7/8	6 6/8	6 7/8	7	7	Redwing, Minn.	David Anderson	David Anderson	1960	205
176	24 4/8	24 7/8	17 4/8	3 7/8	4	8	6	Bradford Co., Pa.	Clyde H. Rinehuls	Clyde H. Rinehuls	1944	207
176	27	25 2/8	20 4/8	5 2/8	5 6/8	5	5	Dawson Co., Neb.	Unknown	Spanky Greenville	1957	207
176	23 7/8	25 2/8	19 3/8	5 6/8	5 6/8	8	7	Klondike, Iowa	Duane K. Rohde	Duane K. Rohde	1964	207
176	26	26 3/8	20	5 3/8	5 4/8	5	5	Veblen, S. D.	John W. Cimburek	John W. Cimburek	1966	207
175 7/8	25 4/8	26	19 7/8	5 5/8	5 4/8	5	5	Pierson, Man.	Bud Smith	Bud Smith	1960	211
175 7/8	25 4/8	28 4/8	23 4/8	4 6/8	5	7	7	Whitehall, Mont.	Mrs. Louis Kis	Mrs. Louis Kis	1961	211
175 7/8	30 2/8	29	22 3/8	5 6/8	5 7/8	8	7	Hanover, Ill.	J. O. Engebretson	J. O. Engebretson	1963	211
175 7/8	23	23 1/8	16 7/8	5 1/8	5 1/8	5	5	Hanley, Sask.	Gavin Koyl & Wm. King	Gavin Koyl	1964	211
175 7/8	24 6/8	25 6/8	17 1/8	4 5/8	4 4/8	4	4	Logan Co., Colo.	Picked Up	Marvin Gardner	1971	211
175 6/8	25 6/8	26	20 2/8	4	4	6	6	Webb Co., Texas	William Bretthauer, Sr.	George H. Glass	1915	216
175 6/8	21 6/8	23 2/8	18	4 4/8	4 5/8	6	6	St. Onge, S. D.	Don Ridley	Don Ridley	1957	216
175 6/8	25 3/8	26 1/8	19 6/8	5 3/8	5 3/8	5	5	Southey, Sask.	J. A. Maier	J. A. Maier	1958	216
175 6/8	26 4/8	25 3/8	16 7/8	5 4/8	5 4/8	8	6	West Point, Neb.	Herman Blankenau	Herman Blankenau	1963	216
175 6/8	22 6/8	24 5/8	20	5	5	6	6	Bismarck, N. D.	Earl Haakenson	Earl Haakenson	1963	216
175 5/8	24 6/8	26 2/8	27 2/8	4 6/8	5	4	4	Hayes Co., Texas	Bill Kuykendall	Bill Kuykendall	1925	221

WHITETAIL DEER *(Typical Antlers)–Continued*

Odocoileus virginianus and certain related subspecies

Score	Length of Main Beam R.	Length of Main Beam L.	Inside Spread	Circumference at Smallest Place Between Burr and First Point R.	Circumference at Smallest Place Between Burr and First Point L.	Number of Points R.	Number of Points L.	Locality Killed	By Whom Killed	Owner	Date Killed	Rank
175 5/8	24 7/8	25 2/8	25 1/8	4 6/8	4 4/8	7	7	Missoula Co., Mont.	Kenneth D. Johnson	Kenneth D. Johnson	1974	221
175 4/8	25 5/8	25	21 2/8	5	5 2/8	6	6	McKean Co., Pa.	Arthur Young	C. R. Studholme	1830	223
175 4/8	25 6/8	27	21 2/8	5 1/8	5 1/8	6	5	Pepin Co., Wisc.	Carl E. Frick	Carl E. Frick	1954	223
175 4/8	25 6/8	25 4/8	21 2/8	5 5/8	6 1/8	5	5	Corning, Mo.	Orrie L. Schaeffer	Orrie L. Schaeffer	1962	223
175 4/8	25 5/8	27	20 4/8	4 4/8	4 4/8	5	5	Dodge Co., Neb.	Leroy W. Ahrndt	Leroy W. Ahrndt	1963	223
175 3/8	26 1/8	25 4/8	23 3/8	5 1/8	5 2/8	5	5	Bridgeford, Sask.	Elgin T. Gates	Elgin T. Gates	1958	227
175 3/8	25 2/8	25 4/8	20 1/8	5 2/8	5 2/8	5	5	Gallia Co., Ohio	Jack Auxier	Jack Auxier	1969	227
175 3/8	24 5/8	25 2/8	20 4/8	5 6/8	5 5/8	5	6	Williamson Co., Ill.	Lewis F. Simon	Lewis F. Simon	1973	227
175 3/8	24	22 2/8	19 4/8	4 7/8	4 7/8	6	8	Monroe Co., Ohio	David Mancano	David Mancano	1976	227
175 3/8	25	25	18 1/8	4 2/8	4 1/8	6	6	Dimmet Co., Texas	Betsy Campbell	Betsy Campbell	1978	227
175 2/8	22 7/8	22 7/8	19	4 4/8	4 5/8	6	6	Encinal, Texas	W. S. Benson, Sr.	W. S. Benson, III	1928	232
175 2/8	24	23 6/8	19 6/8	5 4/8	5 5/8	6	5	Qu'appelle, Sask.	Douglas Garden	Douglas Garden	1965	232
175 2/8	26 1/8	25 6/8	21 1/8	5 1/8	5 2/8	8	6	Wilkinson Co., Miss.	Johnnie J. Leake, Jr.	Johnnie J. Leake, Jr.	1978	232
175 1/8	25 5/8	26 5/8	22 1/8	4 5/8	4 5/8	5	5	Gerald, Sask.	Ken Cherewka	Ken Cherewka	1964	235
175 1/8	25 6/8	27	20 2/8	5	5	8	7	Menominee Co., Wisc.	Gerald Ponfil	Gerald Ponfil	1968	235
175 1/8	25 2/8	25 1/8	19	5 6/8	5 6/8	7	6	Knox Co., Neb.	Paul Klawitter	Paul Klawitter	1970	235
175 1/8	27 1/8	25 5/8	18 3/8	5	5	5	5	Houston Co., Minn.	Craig F. Swenson	Craig F. Swenson	1973	235
175 1/8	24 7/8	26 1/8	20 7/8	4 4/8	4 4/8	6	7	Lac Qui Parle, Minn.	Harold Kittleson	Harold Kittelson	1976	235
175	24 3/8	22 2/8	18 6/8	4 7/8	4 7/8	7	7	Lasalle Co., Texas	Leonard Wolf Bouldin	Leonard Wolf Bouldin	1972	240
174 7/8	26 5/8	25	22 6/8	5 3/8	5 4/8	6	9	Rivers, Man.	N. Manchur	N. Manchur	1954	241
174 7/8	28 1/8	28 1/8	21 3/8	5	5	4	4	Burnett Co., Wisc.	Myles Keller	Myles Keller	1977	241
174 6/8	26 2/8	27 4/8	21	5 6/8	5 6/8	8	6	Hayward, Wisc.	Bill Metcalf	John Metcalf	1924	243
174 6/8	23 6/8	24 4/8	17 5/8	6	5 6/8	6	7	Lancaster Co., Neb.	Vaughn Wright	Phillip Wright	1960	243
174 6/8	27 2/8	29 1/8	21 2/8	5 1/8	5	5	5	Coahoma Co., Miss.	O. P. Gilbert	O. P. Gilbert	1960	243
174 6/8	24 4/8	24 3/8	19 4/8	5 2/8	5 1/8	9	9	Unknown	Unknown	Gerald Hillman	PR1978	243
174 5/8	24 2/8	24 3/8	19 6/8	5 5/8	5 4/8	7	6	Man.	C. S. Browning	C. S. Browning	1960	247
174 5/8	25 2/8	26 1/8	18 3/8	5 1/8	4 7/8	5	6	Butler Co., Iowa	Vernon Simon	Vernon Simon	1972	247
174 5/8	24	22 5/8	18 3/8	4 5/8	4 4/8	5	5	Meeker Co., Minn.	James L. Mattson	James L. Mattson	1973	247
174 5/8	22 4/8	21 4/8	17 1/8	5	5	7	6	Jefferson Co., Kan.	Keith D. Hendrix	Keith D. Hendrix	1973	247
174 4/8	22 5/8	24 1/8	16 6/8	4 5/8	4 6/8	5	5	Ft. Steele, B. C.	John Lum	John Lum	1958	251
174 4/8	22 2/8	23 2/8	19 5/8	4 3/8	4 6/8	7	7	Powell Co., Mont.	Dave Rittenhouse	Dave Rittenhouse	1973	251

174 4/8	22 6/8	23 3/8	18	5	5 2/8	6	6	McKenzie Co., N.D.	Ben Dekker	Ben Dekker	1976	251
174 3/8	27	27 2/8	21 4/8	5 2/8	5 4/8	5	5	Lewis Co., Ky.	Darrell Tully	Darrell Tully	1968	254
174 3/8	28 1/8	26 7/8	23 5/8	5 3/8	5 4/8	6	5	Knox Co., Mo.	Jon Simmons	Jon Simmons	1972	254
174 2/8	28 2/8	27 3/8	25 2/8	5 2/8	5 4/8	4	4	Cerralvo, Mexico	Unknown	Antonio Garcia Gonzalez	1900	256
174 2/8	25 4/8	26	20	4 4/8	4 4/8	6	8	Zavala Co., Texas	Ernest Holdsworth	E. M. Holdsworth	1908	256
174 2/8	25 3/8	26 3/8	22	4 5/8	4 4/8	5	5	Livingston Co., N. Y.	Kenneth Bowen	Kenneth Bowen	1941	256
174 2/8	24 6/8	24 2/8	22	4 6/8	4 6/8	6	5	Dimmit Co., Texas	Red Tollet	McLean Bowman	1958	256
174 2/8	23 5/8	22 7/8	22 3/8	5 6/8	5 5/8	5	5	Chedderville, Alta.	Larry Trimble	Larry Trimble	1963	256
174 2/8	21 4/8	22	17	4 6/8	4 5/8	6	6	Cass Co., Texas	R. J. Perkins	John D. Small	1963	256
174 1/8	26 3/8	27 3/8	16 7/8	4 3/8	4 2/8	6	7	Essex Co., N. Y.	Denny Mitchell	Lewis P. Evans	1933	262
174 1/8	25	25	16 6/8	4 7/8	4 6/8	8	7	Calloway Co., Mo.	Jac LaFon	Jac LaFon	1968	262
174	25 6/8	25 1/8	21	4 4/8	3 7/8	5	5	New Salem, N. D.	John T. Cartwright	John T. Cartwright	1957	264
174	26 1/8	26 2/8	20 4/8	5	4 6/8	7	7	Bulyea, Sask.	W. H. Dodsworth	E. B. Shaw	1961	264
174	28 4/8	27 4/8	25	5 4/8	5 4/8	5	4	Washington Co., Neb.	Albert Ohrt	Albert Ohrt	1962	264
174	26 4/8	26	17 5/8	4 4/8	4 5/8	7	5	Jefferson Co., Wisc.	Gary A. Coates	Gary A. Coates	1970	264
173 7/8	24 5/8	23 7/8	23 3/8	5 1/8	4 7/8	8	7	Dundurn, Sask.	Herb Wilson	Herb Wilson	1960	268
173 7/8	25 4/8	26	19 3/8	5	5	6	6	Starr Co., Texas	Leonard Schwarz	Leonard Schwarz	1965	268
173 6/8	26 6/8	27 1/8	19 7/8	5 5/8	5 3/8	7	5	Mercer Co., Ill.	Floyd A. Clark	Floyd A. Clark	1961	270
173 6/8	26	26	18 6/8	5 7/8	6 1/8	6	5	Colfax Co., Neb.	Leonard Bowman	Leonard Bowman	1962	270
173 6/8	25	25 3/8	22 4/8	5 1/8	5	5	5	McAuley, Man.	Alex D. Vallance	Alex D. Vallance	1967	270
173 6/8	26 6/8	27 6/8	20 3/8	5 7/8	5 4/8	9	6	Bonner Co., Idaho	Robert L. Campbell	Robert L. Campbell	1967	270
173 6/8	23 2/8	24	19 6/8	4 6/8	4 6/8	6	6	Dimmit Co., Texas	Booth W. Petry	Booth W. Petry	1970	270
173 5/8	26 2/8	26 4/8	22 5/8	5 2/8	5 2/8	6	7	Alta.	Frank Lind	Frank Lind	1952	275
173 5/8	25 2/8	25 4/8	18 3/8	5	5	5	8	Gentry Co., Mo.	William F. Oberbeck	William F. Oberbeck	1969	275
173 5/8	22 6/8	21 7/8	20 5/8	4 7/8	4 7/8	6	6	Valley Co., Mont.	Scott Fossum	Scott Fossum	1978	275
173 4/8	26 4/8	27	20 6/8	4 4/8	4 6/8	7	8	Augusta Co., Va.	David H. Wolfe	David H. Wolfe	1957	278
173 4/8	24 7/8	23 6/8	17	5 6/8	5 7/8	7	6	Clover Leaf, Man.	Walter Lucko	Walter Lucko	1962	278
173 4/8	23 6/8	23 7/8	18 6/8	4 6/8	4 6/8	6	6	Shelby Co., Tenn.	John J. Heirigs	John J. Heirigs	1962	278
173 4/8	24 3/8	25	20 1/8	5 2/8	5 3/8	5	6	Tuffnell, Sask.	Ed Mattson	Ed Mattson	1964	278
173 4/8	28	27 4/8	21 6/8	4 7/8	5 1/8	5	5	Union Co., Iowa	Danny E. Abbott	Danny E. Abbott	1966	278
173 3/8	27 6/8	28 1/8	20 1/8	4 5/8	4 5/8	5	6	Clarion Co., Pa.	Meade Kiefer	Meade Kiefer	1947	283
173 3/8	25 6/8	26 2/8	17 5/8	4 4/8	4 4/8	5	5	Clarion Co., Pa.	Pick Up	Fred Gallagher	1954	283
173 3/8	23 3/8	23 3/8	23 3/8	5 1/8	5 1/8	5	5	Rosebud Co., Mont.	Ted Millhollin	Ted Millhollin	1975	283
173 3/8	24 4/8	25	16 7/8	5 1/8	5 1/8	5	5	Valley Co., Mont.	Steve K. Sukut	Steve K. Sukut	1978	283
173 2/8	30 3/8	29 6/8	21 1/8	5	5 7/8	6	8	Chicot Co., Ark.	Yan Sturdivant	Bruce Sturdivant	1951	287
173 2/8	25 6/8	24 2/8	25 2/8	5 4/8	5 1/8	7	6	Price Co., Wisc.	Clarence Parmelee	Clarence Parmelee	1959	287
173 2/8	24 3/8	25 3/8	20 6/8	4 5/8	4 6/8	5	5	Bemersyde, Sask.	R. L. McCullough	R. L. McCullough	1959	287
173 2/8	25 5/8	25 6/8	21	6	5 6/8	8	5	Whitewood, Sask.	L. Reichel	L. Reichel	1964	287
173 2/8	26 7/8	24 3/8	20 6/8	5 2/8	5	5	5	Antler, Sask.	Elmer Lowry	Elmer Lowry	1966	287
173 2/8	29	29 4/8	20	5 1/8	5 2/8	6	5	Furnas Co., Neb.	Marvin F. Wieland	Marvin F. Wieland	1969	287
173 2/8	25 3/8	25 3/8	21 6/8	4 3/8	4 4/8	5	5	Lyman Co., S. D.	William G. Psychos	William G. Psychos	1972	287
173 1/8	26 3/8	26 3/8	19 1/8	5 3/8	5 3/8	7	7	Arkansas Co., Ark.	Jimmy Hawson	Jimmy Hawson	1948	294
173 1/8	23 6/8	24 1/8	20 3/8	5	5	6	5	Marie, Sask.	King Trew	King Trew	1957	294

WHITETAIL DEER *(Typical Antlers)–Continued*

Odocoileus virginianus and certain related subspecies

Score	Length of Main Beam R.	Length of Main Beam L.	Inside Spread	Circumference at Smallest Place Between Burr and First Point R.	Circumference at Smallest Place Between Burr and First Point L.	Number of Points R.	Number of Points L.	Locality Killed	By Whom Killed	Owner	Date Killed	Rank
173 1/8	25 5/8	24 7/8	19 2/8	5	5	7	7	Estuary, Sask.	Melvin J. Anderson	Melvin J. Anderson	1962	294
173 1/8	23 3/8	23 6/8	18 3/8	4	4	6	6	Slope Co., N. D.	Robert L. Stroup	Robert L. Stroup	1967	294
173 1/8	28 5/8	28 6/8	22 2/8	5 4/8	5 7/8	6	6	Wabaunsee Co., Kan.	James D. Downey	James D. Downey	1970	294
173 1/8	26 1/8	24 6/8	21 1/8	4 7/8	4 6/8	5	5	Lake Co., Mont.	Darrell Brist	Darrell Brist	1971	294
173	25 5/8	27 2/8	25 3/8	5 7/8	5 6/8	6	5	Pawnee City, Neb.	Gary G. Habegger	Gary G. Habegger	1967	300
173	28	28 7/8	20 4/8	4 6/8	4 5/8	5	5	Sandusky Co., Ohio	Harold M. Chalfin	Harold M. Chalfin	1975	300
173	28	28 2/8	21 7/8	5 3/8	5 3/8	7	6	Howard Co., Mo.	Thomas R. Banning	Thomas R. Banning	1978	300
172 7/8	25 6/8	25 5/8	22 5/8	4 7/8	5	6	6	Windhorst, Sask.	Jack Glover	Jack Glover	1951	303
172 7/8	25 3/8	25	20 2/8	4 3/8	4 2/8	7	7	McHenry Co., N. D.	David Medalen	David Medalen	1959	303
172 7/8	26 1/8	27	18	5 3/8	5 3/8	6	7	Newton Co., Ga.	L. W. Shirley, Jr.	L. W. Shirley, Jr.	1967	303
172 7/8	27 1/8	26 2/8	21 7/8	4 6/8	4 7/8	6	5	Seneca Co., N. Y.	Martin J. Way	Martin J. Way	1968	303
172 7/8	24 3/8	25 1/8	21 1/8	4 5/8	4 4/8	6	8	Cascade Co., Mont.	Skip Halmes	Skip Halmes	1976	303
172 6/8	25 1/8	25 1/8	18 6/8	4 5/8	4 5/8	5	6	Woodruff, Wisc.	Unknown	Mac's Taxidermy	1918	308
172 6/8	28 6/8	29	22 4/8	4 4/8	4 4/8	5	6	Webb Co., Texas	B. A. Vineyard	B. A. Vineyard	1964	308
172 6/8	25 4/8	25 5/8	22 4/8	4 5/8	4 4/8	5	6	Spokane Co., Wash.	Maurice Robinette	Maurice Robinette	1968	308
172 6/8	24 1/8	24 2/8	20 3/8	6	6	6	5	Boone Co., Iowa	Lonne L. Tracy	Lonne L. Tracy	1975	308
172 5/8	24 2/8	24 4/8	21 1/8	5 2/8	5	6	6	Unknown	Unknown	Roy Hindes	PR1940	312
172 5/8	25 4/8	26	22 6/8	4 3/8	4 4/8	6	5	Esterhazy, Sask.	J. Weise	J. Weise	1960	312
172 5/8	25 1/8	24 5/8	19 1/8	5 7/8	5 6/8	7	5	Shoal Lake, Man.	Gary Phillips	Gary Phillips	1967	312
172 5/8	24 1/8	23	18 1/8	4 3/8	4 3/8	5	6	Tuscarawas Co., Ohio	Charles Kerns	Charles Kerns	1972	312
172 4/8	25 6/8	27	20 2/8	5 2/8	5	6	6	Cotulla, Texas	George E. Light, III	George E. Light, III	1959	316
172 4/8	24 4/8	24 4/8	18 4/8	4 4/8	4 4/8	6	7	Webb Co., Texas	A. M. Russell	A. M. Russell	1961	316
172 4/8	27 3/8	26 7/8	22 5/8	4 6/8	5 1/8	5	4	Laird, Sask.	A. E. Nikkel	A. E. Nikkel	1963	316
172 4/8	26 4/8	27 2/8	24	4 3/8	5 3/8	5	5	Fort Knox, Ky.	E. G. Christian	E. G. Christian	1966	316
172 4/8	24 4/8	24 3/8	20	5	5	6	6	Chauvin, Alta.	Ron D. Jakimchuk	Ron D. Jakimchuk	1971	316
172 3/8	28 5/8	29 3/8	23 2/8	6 3/8	6 2/8	7	8	Corfu, N. Y.	Martin Solway	N. Y. Cons. Dept.	1946	321
172 3/8	26	26 2/8	19 5/8	4 6/8	4 6/8	6	5	Monroe Co., Mo.	Clark Ernest Bray	Clark Ernest Bray	1967	321
172 3/8	27 4/8	27 2/8	20 4/8	6	6 1/8	5	6	Brookings, S. D.	Paul W. Back	Paul W. Back	1967	321
172 2/8	24 6/8	24 3/8	18	4 4/8	4 5/8	6	6	Vilas Co., Wisc.	Ray Hermanson	J. James Froelich	1936	324
172 2/8	28 6/8	26 4/8	21 5/8	4 1/8	4 3/8	6	6	Bedford Co., Pa.	John F. Sharpe	John F. Sharpe	1942	324
172 2/8	26 4/8	25 6/8	20	6	5 6/8	7	7	Weyburn, Sask.	Wilfred LaValley	Wilfred LaValley	1958	324

Score	Length R	Length L	Spread	Circ. R	Circ. L	Pts R	Pts L	Locality	Hunter	Owner	Year	Rank
172 2/8	27 7/8	26 5/8	19 5/8	4 5/8	4 5/8	6	8	Manor, Sask.	Albert McConnell	Albert McConnell	1962	324
172 2/8	25 5/8	25 7/8	23 5/8	5 1/8	5 1/8	6	6	Flathead Co., Mont.	Lonny Hanson	Lonny Hanson	1963	324
172 2/8	23	23	19	5	5	6	7	Adams Co., Wisc.	W. R. Ingraham	W. R. Ingraham	1965	324
172 2/8	25 3/8	22 4/8	23 3/8	4 7/8	5	7	6	Perry Co., Ill.	Ralph Przygoda, Jr.	Ralph Przygoda, Jr.	1978	324
172 1/8	25 5/8	25 5/8	19 5/8	5 5/8	5 5/8	6	5	Necedah, Wisc.	Clark G. Gallup	Unknown	1949	331
172 1/8	27	27 3/8	23 3/8	4 5/8	4 5/8	7	8	Hughes Co., S. D.	Mark Lilevjen	Mark Lilevjen	1971	331
172 1/8	28 5/8	28 3/8	19 2/8	5	4 7/8	6	7	Coshocton Co., Ohio	Virgil E. Carpenter	Virgil E. Carpenter	1972	331
172	26 5/8	25 7/8	19 1/8	5 3/8	5 3/8	5	6	Oconto Co., Wisc.	Henry J. Bredael	Henry J. Bredael	1939	334
172	24 4/8	23 5/8	17	5 3/8	5 2/8	5	5	Neepawa, Man.	Jim Sinclair	Jim Sinclair	1947	334
172	26 4/8	27 7/8	18 5/8	5 5/8	5 5/8	9	8	Wadena, Sask.	Edgar Smale	Edgar Smale	1959	334
172	26 4/8	23	21 1/8	4 7/8	4	5	6	Buffalo Co., Wisc.	Ralph Duellman	Ralph Duellman	1960	334
172	26 1/8	25	24 3/8	4 5/8	4 5/8	5	5	Bearden, Ark.	Buddy Wise	Buddy Wise	1962	334
172	24 3/8	24	17 7/8	5 5/8	5 5/8	6	5	N. Battleford, Sask.	Dick Napastuk	Dick Napastuk	1962	334
172	24 1/8	24 1/8	20 5/8	6 5/8	6 1/8	8	8	Butts Co., Ga.	Jack Hammond	Jack Hammond	1963	334
172	25	26 4/8	21 1/8	5 1/8	5 5/8	5	5	Parkman, Sask	A. T. Mair	A. T. Mair	1963	334
172	24 4/8	24 4/8	17 7/8	4 3/8	4 4/8	6	6	Joseph Plains, Idaho	Jim Felton	Jim Felton	1965	334
171 7/8	25	25 7/8	18 5/8	5 7/8	5 7/8	6	5	Adams Co., Miss.	Nan Foster New	Nan Foster New	1977	344
171 7/8	25 5/8	27	16 5/8	5 7/8	5 7/8	8	8	Scotch Bay, Man.	W. J. Harker	W. J. Harker	1951	344
171 7/8	24 4/8	24 4/8	19 4/8	5	5	9	10	Monton Co., N. D.	Sioux Sporting Goods	Dick Eastman	1955	344
171 7/8	26 1/8	27	20 5/8	4 5/8	4 7/8	5	5	Houston Co., Minn.	Donald R. Soboilk	Donald R. Soboilk	1958	344
171 7/8	26 1/8	25 5/8	20 1/8	5 1/8	5 5/8	7	6	Aroostook Co., Maine	Julian B. Perry	Julian B. Perry	1962	344
171 6/8	25 4/8	25 5/8	18 4/8	5	5	6	7	Union Co., Iowa	Darrell M. Gutz	Darrell M. Gutz	1973	349
171 6/8	26 5/8	26 1/8	18	4 7/8	4 5/8	5	6	Niagara, Wisc.	David Watson	Francis H. Van Ginkel	1945	349
171 6/8	26	27	18 5/8	6 7/8	6 7/8	5	5	St. Louis Co., Minn.	Paul S. Paulson	Paul S. Paulson	1946	349
171 5/8	27 5/8	26 5/8	21 5/8	4 5/8	4 7/8	9	5	Asquith, Sask.	M. S. Vanin	M. S. Vanin	1963	358
171 5/8	24 4/8	24 4/8	19	5 3/8	5 3/8	5	5	Turtle Mt., Man.	Roy Hainsworth	Roy Hainsworth	1963	358
171 5/8	25 5/8	25	18 2/8	4 4/8	4 4/8	5	5	Maple Creek, Sask.	G. J. Burch	G. J. Burch	1967	358
171 5/8	24 4/8	24 3/8	17 1/8	4 1/8	4 1/8	8	8	Muscatine Co., Iowa	Larry Dipple	Larry Dipple	1973	358
171 5/8	28 4/8	27 7/8	19 3/8	5 3/8	5 3/8	4	6	Buffalo Co., Wisc.	Richard Schultz	Richard Schultz	1974	358
171 5/8	25 1/8	24 4/8	18 4/8	4 7/8	4 7/8	5	5	Dawes Co., Neb.	Tim Morava	Tim Morava	1975	358
171 5/8	27 3/8	26 5/8	21	4 4/8	4 5/8	6	6	Adams Co., Ill.	R.C. Stephens	R.C. Stephens	1961	358
171 5/8	25 5/8	26 5/8	20 5/8	5 1/8	5 1/8	7	7	Hanley, Sask.	L. R. Libke	L. R. Libke	1962	358
171 5/8	25	24 4/8	22	4	6	7	7	Maverick Co., Texas	Harry Garner	Harry Garner	1968	358
171 5/8	28 5/8	28 6/8	22 7/8	5 7/8	6	5	5	Bonesteel, S. D.	Clifford Johnson	Clifford Johnson	1968	358
171 5/8	26	25 3/8	24 4/8	4 7/8	4 7/8	7	8	Langbank, Sask.	Thomas K. Grimm	Thomas K. Grimm	1977	358
171 4/8	27	25 5/8	18 2/8	5 2/8	5 2/8	6	6	Otter Tail Co., Minn.	Carl D. Hill	Carl D. Hill	1931	363
171 4/8	26 1/8	25 4/8	20 4/8	4 5/8	4 5/8	6	6	Beltrami Co., Minn.	Hank Sandland	Hank Sandland	1953	363
171 4/8	24 4/8	26 1/8	19 2/8	5 1/8	5 2/8	6	5	Hayter, Alta.	H. D. L. Loucks	H. D. L. Loucks	1961	363
171 4/8	26	26 3/8	21	5	4 7/8	11	11	Woodlands Dist., Man.	Bill Rutherford	Bill Rutherford	1965	363
171 4/8	26 3/8	27 7/8	23 5/8	5 5/8	5 7/8	7	9	Barnesville, Minn.	Clint Foslien	Clint Foslien	1968	363
171 3/8	26	26	23 2/8	4 7/8	4 7/8	5	7	Schroon Lake, N. Y.	Richard E. Johndrow	Richard E. Johndrow	1938	368
171 3/8	26 5/8	26 5/8	21 5/8	4 4/8	4 4/8	9	9	Juneau Co., Wisc.	Fay Hammersley	Fay Hammersley	1957	368
171 3/8	26	26 3/8	17 7/8	4 3/8	4 3/8	6	7	Herkimer Co., N. Y.	John Christie	John Christie		368

WHITETAIL DEER (Typical Antlers)—Continued
Odocoileus virginianus and certain related subspecies

Score	Length of Main Beam R.	L.	Inside Spread	Circumference at Smallest Place Between Burr and First Point R.	L.	Number of Points R.	L.	Locality Killed	By Whom Killed	Owner	Date Killed	Rank
171³⁄₈	22⁵⁄₈	22⁴⁄₈	18	5³⁄₈	5³⁄₈	7	6	Grenfell, Sask.	George DeMontigny	George DeMontigny	1965	368
171³⁄₈	25⁵⁄₈	25²⁄₈	19³⁄₈	4²⁄₈	4³⁄₈	6	7	Oceana Co., Mich.	Delos Highland	Delos Highland	1967	368
171³⁄₈	25³⁄₈	26⁶⁄₈	18⁵⁄₈	5³⁄₈	5²⁄₈	5	5	Forest Co., Wisc.	Chester Cox, Jr.	Chester Cox, Jr.	1969	368
171³⁄₈	22³⁄₈	23¹⁄₈	14⁵⁄₈	5	5	7	6	Metaline Falls, Wash.	Scott Hicks	Scott Hicks	1970	368
171³⁄₈	23⁴⁄₈	24²⁄₈	23¹⁄₈	4⁷⁄₈	4⁷⁄₈	5	5	Kandiyohi Co., Minn.	Werner B. Reining	Werner B. Reining	1974	368
171³⁄₈	25⁵⁄₈	24⁵⁄₈	22⁵⁄₈	5	5	7	6	Pope Co., Minn.	Corbin Corson	Corbin Corson	1975	368
171³⁄₈	24⁴⁄₈	23⁶⁄₈	21⁵⁄₈	4⁴⁄₈	4⁴⁄₈	5	5	Athabasca River, Alta.	Ron J. Holm	Ron J. Holm	1977	368
171²⁄₈	29²⁄₈	28⁶⁄₈	19²⁄₈	4⁴⁄₈	4⁴⁄₈	6	5	Arkansas Co., Ark.	Wilbur Stephens	Wilbur Stephens	1953	377
171²⁄₈	22⁶⁄₈	21	18⁵⁄₈	5¹⁄₈	5²⁄₈	6	6	Medicine Hat, Alta.	Frank Chevalier	Marcel Houle	1958	377
171²⁄₈	31¹⁄₈	29	16	5	5	7	9	Frio Co., Texas	Leonard Van Horn	Leonard Van Horn	1962	377
171²⁄₈	26²⁄₈	25	22⁴⁄₈	5⁵⁄₈	5⁵⁄₈	5	5	Macintosh, Ont.	Richard Kouhi	Richard Kouhi	1967	377
171²⁄₈	25⁴⁄₈	25³⁄₈	19⁴⁄₈	4⁶⁄₈	5	5	6	Webb Co., Texas	Ernie Pavlas	Ernie Pavlas	1970	377
171¹⁄₈	27⁴⁄₈	27⁴⁄₈	21¹⁄₈	4³⁄₈	4²⁄₈	5	5	Charlevoix Co., Mich.	Noel Thomson	Ivan Thomson	1957	382
171¹⁄₈	26	26⁷⁄₈	16⁷⁄₈	5⁵⁄₈	5⁵⁄₈	5	5	Douglas Co., Minn.	James M. Bircher	James M. Bircher	1962	382
171¹⁄₈	27⁴⁄₈	27¹⁄₈	18	4⁴⁄₈	4⁴⁄₈	8	7	Alger Co., Mich.	Shirley L. Robare	Shirley L. Robare	1963	382
171¹⁄₈	23¹⁄₈	23¹⁄₈	20⁶⁄₈	5	5⁴⁄₈	5	6	Whitewood, Sask.	Wm. Cook	Wm. Cook	1966	382
171	23⁵⁄₈	26	19³⁄₈	5¹⁄₈	5¹⁄₈	5	6	Windthorst, Sask.	Thomas Dovell	Thomas Dovell	1961	386
171	28⁵⁄₈	27⁷⁄₈	20⁴⁄₈	5¹⁄₈	5¹⁄₈	7	7	Perkins, S. D.	Ethel Schrader	Ethel Schrader	1963	386
171	22⁵⁄₈	20⁴⁄₈	19⁵⁄₈	5⁷⁄₈	5⁵⁄₈	7	8	Antelope Co., Neb.	Leo M. Beelart	Leo M. Beelart	1964	386
171	24⁴⁄₈	25²⁄₈	17⁷⁄₈	4²⁄₈	4¹⁄₈	6	5	Ray Co., Mo.	Darle R. Siegel	Darle R. Siegel	1966	386
171	24⁵⁄₈	23⁶⁄₈	21	5	5	5	5	Seven Persons, Alta.	Haven Lane	Haven Lane	1968	386
171	28⁴⁄₈	26⁷⁄₈	21	4⁴⁄₈	4⁴⁄₈	5	5	Speers, Sask.	Charles E. Strautman	Charles E. Strautman	1969	386
171	27	26⁵⁄₈	26²⁄₈	5³⁄₈	5²⁄₈	7	8	Otter Tail Co., Minn.	Lawrence J. Anderson	Lawrence J. Anderson	1974	386
170⁷⁄₈	26³⁄₈	25⁷⁄₈	19¹⁄₈	4⁶⁄₈	4⁷⁄₈	5	5	Bath Co., Va.	Maurice Smith	Maurice Smith	1953	393
170⁷⁄₈	27⁴⁄₈	26⁴⁄₈	18	5	5²⁄₈	6	7	Chicot Co., Ark.	Mrs. L. M. Hamilton	Mrs. L. M. Hamilton	1960	393
170⁷⁄₈	30	30	20⁴⁄₈	5	5	8	8	Des Moines Co., Iowa	Craig A. Field	Craig A. Field	1967	393
170⁷⁄₈	26⁵⁄₈	27¹⁄₈	21¹⁄₈	5⁵⁄₈	5⁵⁄₈	5	5	Kingman, Alta.	Robert D. Kozack	Robert D. Kozack	1971	393
170⁷⁄₈	26⁵⁄₈	27¹⁄₈	21²⁄₈	5⁵⁄₈	5⁵⁄₈	5	7	Holmes Co., Ohio	Ken Taylor	Ken Taylor	1975	393
170⁷⁄₈	25³⁄₈	24⁵⁄₈	18⁵⁄₈	5⁵⁄₈	5⁷⁄₈	7	6	Tippecanoe Co., Ind.	Harold A. Anthrop	Harold A. Anthrop	1976	393
170⁶⁄₈	25⁶⁄₈	26	21	5⁴⁄₈	5²⁄₈	5	5	Dimmit Co., Texas	J. H. Hixon	J. H. Hixon	1958	399
170⁶⁄₈	25⁵⁄₈	24⁴⁄₈	24²⁄₈	4⁴⁄₈	4⁴⁄₈	6	5	Elbow, Sask.	W. H. Crossman	W. H. Crossman	1959	399

Score	Length Main Beam R	Length Main Beam L	Inside Spread	Circ. R	Circ. L	Points R	Points L	Locality	Hunter	Owner	Rank	Date
170 6/8	25 3/8	25 5/8	19 4/8	5 3/8	5 3/8	7	7	Gerald, Sask.	Jerry Norek	Jerry Norek	399	1959
170 6/8	24	24	21 1/8	5 1/8	5	6	6	Arnes, Man.	T. Litwin	T. Litwin	399	1963
170 6/8	27 3/8	26 3/8	20	4 7/8	4 7/8	6	6	Howell Co., Mo.	Roy W. Woodson	Roy W. Woodson	399	1974
170 6/8	27	27 3/8	20 3/8	5 3/8	5 3/8	6	6	Desha Co., Ark.	Bob Norris	Bob Norris	404	1948
170 6/8	22 5/8	23 3/8	17 7/8	5	4 7/8	5	5	St. Charles Co., Mo.	Oscar Mallinckrodt	Oscar Mallinckrodt	404	1962
170 6/8	27 1/8	26 5/8	19 3/8	4 7/8	5 5/8	7	7	Hawthorne, Wisc.	George Pettingill	George Pettingill	404	1963
170 6/8	27 3/8	27 7/8	21 5/8	5 5/8	5 5/8	5	7	Sherburne Co., Minn.	Sylvester Zormeier	Sylvester Zormeier	404	1967
170 6/8	26 3/8	27 7/8	18 3/8	5 5/8	4 1/2	6	8	Price Co., Wisc.	Nyle H. Rodman	Nyle H. Rodman	404	1970
170 6/8	26 1/8	25 5/8	19 3/8	4 1/2	4 7/8	5	6	Boyd Co., Neb.	Leonard Reiser	Leonard Reiser	404	1973
170 6/8	25 7/8	24 5/8	18	4 7/8	5 3/8	6	6	Douglas Co., Minn.	August P. J. Nelson	Roger M. Holmes	410	1946
170 6/8	23 3/8	24 3/8	20 3/8	5 5/8	4 7/8	8	8	Day Co., S. D.	Gerald Bartell	Gerald Bartell	410	1960
170 6/8	25 3/8	24 5/8	19 1/4	4 7/8	5	8	8	Craven, Sask.	Ted Paterson	Ted Paterson	410	1960
170 6/8	24 3/8	24	20 7/8	5 1/8	4 7/8	7	7	Preeceville, Sask.	Vernon Hoffman	Vernon Hoffman	410	1965
170 6/8	24 3/8	25 3/8	19	4 7/8	3 7/8	5	5	La Salle Co., Texas	Jerome Knebel	Jerome Knebel	410	1974
170 6/8	25	25 3/8	22 1/4	3 7/8	5 1/8	6	6	Travis Co., Texas	W. A. (Will) Brown	W. A. (Will) Brown	415	1922
170 6/8	25 3/8	25 3/8	26 3/8	5 1/8	5 3/8	6	6	Whatshan Lake, B.C.	Ernest Roberts	Ernest Roberts	415	1957
170 6/8	26	26	19 1/2	5 3/8	5 5/8	6	6	Woodruff Co., Ark.	R. L. Taylor	R. L. Taylor	415	1960
170 6/8	27 3/8	26 3/8	25 5/8	5 5/8	4 7/8	5	5	Ft. Qu'Appelle, Sask.	L. A. Magnuson	L. A. Magnuson	415	1962
170 6/8	28 3/8	28 1/8	25 5/8	4 7/8	5 5/8	5	5	Hall Co., Neb.	Gust Bergman	Gust Bergman	415	1965
170 6/8	25 3/8	25 3/8	23 3/8	5 3/8	4 7/8	4	4	Grant Co., S. D.	James Boerger	James Boerger	415	1965
170 6/8	28 1/8	28 1/8	25 7/8	5	5	5	5	Saline Co., Ill.	Jack Crain	Jack Crain	415	1966
170 6/8	26 3/8	26	20 3/8	5 3/8	5	5	5	Portage La Prairie, Man.	Robert Boyachek	Robert Boyachek	415	1967
170 6/8	24 3/8	23 3/8	22	5 3/8	5	8	8	Duval Co., Texas	R. L. Kruger	R. L. Kruger	415	1968
170 6/8	28 5/8	28 3/8	23 4/8	5 1/8	5 1/8	8	8	Kingsbury Co., S. D.	Jerry Ellingson	Jerry Ellingson	415	1969
170 6/8	29 3/8	28 3/8	17 7/8	4 3/8	4 3/8	8	8	Muskingum Co., Ohio	John H. O'Flaherty	John H. O'Flaherty	415	1976
170 6/8	28 1/8	28 1/8	20	4 1/2	4 1/2	6	6	Clarion Co., Pa.	Meade R. Kifer	Meade R. Kifer	426	1945
170 6/8	25 3/8	25 5/8	20	5 1/8	5	5	5	Dafoe, Sask.	A. Linder	A. Linder	426	1959
170 6/8	27 5/8	26 5/8	19 3/8	5	4 7/8	6	6	McMullen Co., Texas	Earl Welch	Earl Welch	426	1964
170 6/8	24	24	21 1/8	4 7/8	4 3/8	6	6	Avonlea, Sask.	Doug English	Doug English	426	1965
170 6/8	24 3/8	24 3/8	22	4 3/8	5 3/8	7	7	Lestock, Sask.	Zolton Blaskovich	Zolton Blaskovich	426	1965
170 6/8	26 7/8	25 7/8	19 5/8	5 3/8	4 3/8	8	8	Jim Hogg Co., Texas	Tom P. Hayes	Tom P. Hayes	426	1968
170 6/8	24 5/8	24 3/8	15	4 1/2	4 7/8	8	7	Spokane Co., Wash.	Edward A. Floch	Edward A. Floch	426	1970
170 6/8	23 3/8	27 7/8	19 7/8	4 1/2	5 7/8	7	6	Jefferson Co., Ohio	James S. Pratt	James S. Pratt	426	1976
170 6/8	27 4/8	27	19 3/8	5 7/8	4 3/8	8	9	Massanutton Mts., Va.	Lloyd Lamm	Lloyd Lamm	434	1955
170 6/8	26 5/8	29 3/8	23 3/8	4 3/8	5 5/8	4	5	Winnebago, Minn.	Harlan Francis	Harlan Francis	434	1956
170 6/8	28 5/8	22 7/8	16 1/8	5 5/8	4 7/8	7	7	Swift Current, Sask.	Brian Baumann	Brian Baumann	434	1966
170 6/8	23 7/8	24 7/8	20 7/8	4 7/8	4 3/8	6	6	Jackson Co., Ohio	Theodore R. Yates	Theodore R. Yates	434	1967
170 6/8	27 7/8	25 5/8	20 5/8	4 3/8	4 3/8	5	5	Marinette Co., Wisc.	Leonard Schartner	Leonard Schartner	434	1968
170 6/8	23 5/8	24 3/8	18 1/8	4 3/8	4 1/8	5	5	Pincher Creek, Alta.	Dave Simpson	Dave Simpson	434	1971
170	24 3/8	24 3/8	18 5/8	4 1/8	4 1/8	6	7	Oiltown, Texas	L. D. Roberts	L. D. Roberts	440	1941
170	24 5/8	25 5/8	21 5/8	4 7/8	4 7/8	10	10	Blair Co., Pa.	Claude Feathers	Claude Feathers	440	1943
170	26 5/8	24 5/8	19 1/8	5	4 7/8	7	7	Sherwood, N. D.	Roy Foss	Roy Foss	440	1947
170	26 1/8	27	23	6 1/8	6 1/8	5	5	Virden, Man.	Jessie Byer	Jessie Byer	440	1951

WHITETAIL DEER *(Typical Antlers)–Continued*

Odocoileus virginianus and certain related subspecies

Score	Length of Main Beam		Inside Spread	Circumference at Smallest Place Between Burr and First Point		Number of Points		Locality Killed	By Whom Killed	Owner	Date Killed	Rank
	R.	L.		R.	L.	R.	L.					
170	27	28	22 4/8	4 4/8	4 4/8	6	5	Webb Co., Texas	Herbert Zieschang	Herbert Zieschang	1957	440
170	27 4/8	27 6/8	23 1/8	6 5/8	6 7/8	6	6	Fullerton, Neb.	Truman Lauterback	Truman Lauterback	1959	440
170	26 2/8	25 2/8	21	5 4/8	5 4/8	5	5	Cat Island, La.	Jerry Loper	Jerry Loper	1960	440
170	23 2/8	26	19 6/8	5 1/8	5 2/8	7	6	Henderson Co., Ill.	Donald R. Vaughn	Donald R. Vaughn	1960	440
170	27 5/8	26 5/8	24 1/8	4 1/8	4	6	8	Atascosa Co., Texas	Ben H. Moore, Jr.	Ben H. Moore, Jr.	1961	440
170	22 7/8	22 4/8	18 4/8	4 6/8	4 7/8	5	6	Stevens Co., Wash.	Clair Kelso	Clair Kelso	1966	440
170	26 1/8	24 5/8	17 7/8	4 4/8	4 4/8	6	6	Flathead Co., Mont.	Dave Delap	Dave Delap	1966	440
170	26 4/8	26 5/8	17 4/8	4 6/8	4 7/8	7	5	Bates Co., Mo.	Gary Rosier	Gary Rosier	1969	440
170	26 4/8	25 5/8	19 5/8	4 5/8	4 4/8	6	6	York Co., Maine	Aubin Huertas	Aubin Huertas	1973	440
170	28 3/8	25 6/8	21 1/8	5 2/8	5 3/8	6	7	Hancock Co., Ill.	Henry F. Collins	Henry F. Collins	1973	440
170	26 3/8	24 5/8	19 6/8	5 2/8	5 1/8	5	5	Shelby Co., Mo.	Rusty D. Gander	Rusty D. Gander	1973	440
170	24 3/8	23 2/8	20 6/8	4 7/8	4 6/8	5	5	Scotland Co., Mo.	Chester James Young	Chester James Young	1974	440
170	25 3/8	25 2/8	18	4 5/8	4 5/8	7	6	Ballard Co., Kent.	Rudolf Koranchan, Jr.	Rudolf Koranchan, Jr.	1977	440

*Final Score subject to revision by additional verifying measurements.

WORLD'S RECORD WHITETAIL DEER (NON-TYPICAL ANTLERS)
SCORE: 286
Locality: Brady, Texas. Date: 1892.
Hunter: Jeff Benson. Owner: Lone Star Brewing Company.

Photograph by Wm. H. Nesbitt

NUMBER TWO WHITETAIL DEER (NON-TYPICAL ANTLERS)
SCORE: 282
Locality: Clay County, Iowa. Date: 1973.
Hunter and owner: Larry Raveling

Whitetail Deer *(Non-Typical Antlers)*

Minimum Score 195

Odocoileus virginianus virginianus and certain related subspecies

Score	Length of Main Beam R.	Length of Main Beam L.	Inside Spread	Circumference at Smallest Place Between Burr and First Point R.	Circumference at Smallest Place Between Burr and First Point L.	Number of Points R.	Number of Points L.	Locality Killed	By Whom Killed	Owner	Date Killed	Rank
286	23 1/8	18 7/8	15 6/8	4 2/8	4 2/8	23	26	Brady, Texas	Jeff Benson	Lone Star Brewing Co.	1892	1
282	26 1/8	27	24 3/8	6 5/8	6 2/8	15	14	Clay Co., Iowa	Larry Raveling	Larry Raveling	1973	2
277 3/8	28 1/8	28 3/8	21 1/8	6 5/8	6 7/8	19	18	Hall Co., Neb.	Del Austin	Del Austin	1962	3
272	23 7/8	25	17 5/8	6 2/8	5 6/8	23	16	Junction, Texas	Picked Up	Fred Mudge	1925	4
268 5/8	20 6/8	24 6/8	14 2/8	6 4/8	5 3/8	20	21	Norman Co., Minn.	Mitchell A. Vakoch	Mitchell A. Vakoch	1974	5
261 6/8*	29	25 6/8	24 6/8	6 7/8	6 7/8	14	17	Holmes Co., Ohio	Picked Up	Ohio Dept. Nat. Res.	1975	6
261 4/8*	25	25 2/8	25 3/8	6	6	12	14	Pike Co., Ohio	Chester T. Veach	Chester T. Veach	1971	7
258 5/8	22 4/8	26 2/8	23 6/8	6 4/8	6	17	15	Republic Co., Kan.	John O. Band	John O. Band	1965	8
258 2/8*	27	26 6/8	19 5/8	4 7/8	4 6/8	17	17	Becker Co., Minn.	J. J. Matter	J. J. Matter	1973	9
257 3/8	25 5/8	23 5/8	16 2/8	4 6/8	4 4/8	21	17	Elkhorn, Man.	Harvey Olsen	Harvey Olsen	1973	10
256 2/8	28 7/8	28 1/8	20 4/8	6 5/8	6 4/8	11	16	Monona Co., Iowa	Carroll E. Johnson	Carroll E. Johnson	1968	11
253	28	28	21 4/8	5 5/8	5 6/8	14	26	Nova Scotia	Neil Macdonald	Charles T. Arnold	1945	12
252 1/8	25 6/8	28 3/8	19 5/8	5 3/8	5 6/8	9	9	Hill County, Mont.	Frank A. Pleskac	Frank A. Pleskac	1968	13
251 1/8	28 2/8	28	19	5 5/8	5 6/8	12	13	Mitchell Co., Kan.	Theron E. Wilson	Theron E. Wilson	1974	14
249 1/8	26 2/8	26 7/8	19 2/8	6 4/8	6 2/8	12	20	Lily, S. D.	Jerry Roitsch	Jerry Roitsch	1965	15
248 7/8	27 6/8	27 2/8	20 1/8	5 7/8	5 7/8	8	10	Greenwood Co., Kan.	Clifford G. Pickell	Clifford G. Pickell	1968	16
248 5/8	28 3/8	27	20 2/8	5 2/8	5	14	17	Stanley, N. D.	Roger Ritchie	Roger Ritchie	1968	17
248 4/8	22 6/8	24 3/8	22	5 7/8	5 7/8	13	11	Moose Mtn. Park, Sask.	Walter Bartko	George Hooey	1964	18
247 7/8	26 1/8	26	19 5/8	5 5/8	5 4/8	13	17	Frio Co., Texas	Raul Rodriquez, II	Raul Rodriquez, II	1966	19
247 2/8	25 4/8	25 3/8	24 6/8	5 5/8	6 1/8	16	14	Johnston Co., Okla.	Bill M. Foster	Bill M. Foster	1970	20
246 7/8	25	25	18 2/8	7 6/8	6 4/8	15	16	White Fox, Sask.	Elburn Kohler	Collin Bishop	1957	21
245 7/8	31 2/8	27 6/8	25 3/8	5 5/8	5 6/8	11	14	Elk River, B. C.	James I. Brewster	J. I. Brewster Est.	1905	22
245 4/8	24 6/8	21 5/8	16 5/8	5 3/8	5	18	12	Carrot River, Sask.	Picked Up	Ken. Halloway	1962	23
245	27 4/8	27	20 6/8	5 3/8	5 4/8	15	15	Buffalo Co., Wisc.	Elmer F. Gotz	Elmer F. Gotz	1973	24
244 2/8	27	27 2/8	16 5/8	5 6/8	5 5/8	13	13	Allegany Co., N. Y.	Homer Boylan	Harry Boylan	1939	25
243 7/8	26 7/8	26 3/8	16 2/8	8 2/8	8 2/8	18	15	Wirral, N. B.	H. Glenn Johnston	Charles T. Arnold	1962	26
243 5/8	24 1/8	24 1/8	22 2/8	5 1/8	5	11	15	Govan, Sask.	A. W. Davis	Sam Peterson	1951	27
242 5/8	27 2/8	26 1/8	17 2/8	6	5 4/8	13	16	Nance Co., Neb.	Robert E. Snyder	Robert E. Snyder	1961	28
242 2/8	24 3/8	21 5/8	20 5/8	6 1/8	6 5/8	18	14	Auburnville, N. B.	John L. Mackenzie	Charles T. Arnold	1958	29
241 7/8	26 1/8	25 2/8	20 1/8	4 5/8	5	14	19	Flathead Co., Mont.	George Wolstad	George Wolstad	1960	30
240 6/8	25 5/8	26 2/8	17 2/8	5 2/8	5 1/8	17	20	Central Lakes, Minn.	John Cesarek	John Cesarek	1964	31

WHITETAIL DEER *(Non-Typical Antlers)–Continued*

Odocoileus virginianus virginianus and certain related subspecies

Score	Length of Main Beam R.	Length of Main Beam L.	Inside Spread	Circumference at Smallest Place Between Burr and First Point R.	Circumference at Smallest Place Between Burr and First Point L.	Number of Points R.	Number of Points L.	Locality Killed	By Whom Killed	Owner	Date Killed	Rank
240 3/8	24 2/8	24 6/8	18 5/8	7 2/8	7 2/8	18	20	Monroe Co., Ga.	John L. Hatton, Jr.	John L. Hatton, Jr.	1973	32
240	26 4/8	26	21 5/8	5 4/8	5 4/8	15	11	Kerr Co., Texas	Walter R. Schreiner	Charles Schreiner, III	1905	33
238 7/8	22 4/8	21 6/8	18 1/8	5	5 2/8	17	15	Crook Co., Wyo.	Unknown	Pete Petera	1962	34
238 2/8	27 1/8	26 2/8	21 4/8	5 5/8	5 7/8	12	17	Bay Co., Mich.	Paul M. Mickey	Paul M. Mickey	1976	35
238 1/8	24 2/8	21 7/8	22	5 2/8	5 2/8	13	15	Whitewood, Sask.	Jack Davidge	Jack Davidge	1967	36
238	26 4/8	27 6/8	23 6/8	5 6/8	5 7/8	12	8	Valentine, Neb.	Donald B. Phipps	Donald B. Phipps	1969	37
237 3/8	24 2/8	23 7/8	20 2/8	5 4/8	5 4/8	12	16	Whiteshell, Man.	Angus McVicar	Angus McVicar	1925	38
236 4/8	24 6/8	25	20 5/8	5 4/8	5	17	12	Reserve, Sask.	Harry Nightingale	Charles T. Arnold	1959	39
235 4/8	29 2/8	27 1/8	22 7/8	5 7/8	5 6/8	11	13	Ashtabula Co., Ohio	James L. Clark	James L. Clark	1957	40
235 4/8	25 4/8	24 5/8	19 6/8	5 4/8	5 7/8	9	20	Pipestone Valley, Sask.	E. J. Marshall	E. J. Marshall	1958	40
234 4/8	29	28 2/8	20 7/8	5 3/8	5 6/8	14	16	Stevens Co., Wash.	Larry G. Gardner	Larry G. Gardner	1953	42
234 1/8	25 7/8	27 4/8	17 2/8	4 5/8	4 2/8	6	10	Glacier Co., Mont.	Unknown	Larry W. Lander	PR1968	43
233 7/8	27	26 7/8	21 4/8	5 5/8	5 3/8	16	15	Loraine, Wisc.	Homer Pearson	McLean Bowman	1937	44
233 7/8	23 6/8	22 4/8	16 5/8	6	5 7/8	9	14	Tompkins, Sask.	Don Stueck	McLean Bowman	1961	44
233 6/8	26 2/8	26	22	4 7/8	4 6/8	14	13	Thompson Creek, Wash.	George Sly, Jr.	George Sly, Jr.	1964	46
233	20 2/8	23 4/8	19 6/8	6 4/8	5 2/8	12	7	Punnichy, Sask.	Steve Kapay	McLean Bowman	1968	47
232 1/8	24 5/8	24 5/8	16 4/8	4 7/8	4 6/8	11	11	McLean Co., N.D.	Olaf P. Anderson	Burton L. Anderson	1886	48
231 7/8	24	22 2/8	18	5 5/8	5 4/8	10	20	Harris, Sask.	Herman Cox	R. M. Burnett	1954	49
231 4/8	29 3/8	27 4/8	23 1/8	4 3/8	4 3/8	9	10	Licking Co., Ohio	Norman L. Myers	Norman L. Myers	1964	50
231 3/8	28	28 4/8	26 1/8	6 6/8	6 3/8	9	9	Holland, Man.	Wm. Ireland	Wm. Ireland	1968	51
231 2/8	25 6/8	26 3/8	18 4/8	5	4 7/8	17	13	Forest Co., Wisc.	Robert Jacobson	Robert Jacobson	1958	52
231	26	25 7/8	18	5	5	12	12	Stevens Co., Wash.	Joe Bussano	Joe Bussano	1946	53
230 6/8	27 5/8	27 2/8	19 3/8	5 7/8	6	14	16	Red Deer, Alta.	Delmer E. Johnson	Delmer E. Johnson	1973	54
228 7/8	28 2/8	27 2/8	18 5/8	5 7/8	6	11	10	Cherryfield, Maine	Flora Campbell	Fred Goodwin	1953	55
228 2/8	26 6/8	29 2/8	21	5 2/8	5 2/8	13	10	Cable, Wisc.	Charles Berg	Eva Mae Fisher	1910	56
228 1/8	28 7/8	29	20 1/8	5 6/8	6	13	14	Maine	Henry A. Caesar	National Collection	PR1911	57
227 4/8	25 3/8	25 2/8	18 4/8	6 4/8	6 4/8	16	17	Bayfield Co., Wisc.	Earl Holt	Mrs. Earl Holt	1934	58
227 4/8	27 1/8	26 2/8	20 2/8	5 2/8	5 2/8	12	9	Pullman, Wash.	Glenn C. Paulson	Glenn C. Paulson	1965	58
227	25 7/8	26 6/8	24 1/8	7 2/8	7 4/8	12	10	Miami Co., Kan.	Gary A. Smith	Gary A. Smith	1970	60
226 6/8	25 5/8	27 4/8	15 5/8	4 7/8	5 2/8	22	25	Rusk Co., Wisc.	Joe Michalets	John R. Michalets	1911	61
226 6/8	28 4/8	28 2/8	22 1/8	5 4/8	5 5/8	10	12	Manor, Sask.	Stan Balkwill	McLean Bowman	1960	61

Score	Main Beam R	Main Beam L	Inside Spread	Circ. R	Circ. L	Pts. R	Pts. L	Locality	Hunter	Owner	Date	Rank
226 5/8	25 7/8	27 5/8	18 7/8	5 5/8	5 5/8	10	8	Lenore, Idaho	Mrs. Ralph Bond	Mrs. Ralph Bond	1964	63
226 1/8	25 5/8	26 5/8	20 7/8	4 7/8	4 7/8	10	10	Trumbull Co., Ohio	Paul E. Lehman	Paul E. Lehman	1948	64
225 5/8	29 5/8	29 5/8	20	6 7/8	5 5/8	15	13	Minn.	Unknown	Harvard Univ. Mus.	1890	65
224 3/8	26 7/8	27	21 1/2	5 1/8	5 3/8	8	7	Lac Qui Parle Co., Minn.	Mike Unzen	Mike Unzen	1969	66
224 2/8	26 7/8	27 5/8	20 5/8	5	5 1/8	11	11	Salmon River, N. B.	Ford Fulton	McLean Bowman	1966	67
224 1/8	25	24 7/8	19 7/8	4 5/8	4 3/8	12	13	Crook Co., Wyo.	John S. Mahoney	John S. Mahoney	1947	68
224	23 3/8	24	17 6/8	4 6/8	5	16	12	Lincoln Co., Mont.	Ray Baenen	Ed Boyes	1935	69
224	29 5/8	29 3/8	27	5 3/8	5 3/8	7	14	Hancock Co., Maine	Picked Up	Wesley B. Starn	PR1974	69
223 3/8	23 7/8	23 7/8	17	5 1/8	5 3/8	18	13	Richland Co., Mont.	Verner King	Verner King	1960	71
223 3/8	20 5/8	24 5/8	19	5 5/8	5 5/8	19	12	Cochin, Sask.	Vic Pearsall	Vic Pearsall	1960	72
223	25 7/8	23 7/8	17 5/8	5 5/8	5 5/8	16	12	Raymore, Sask.	S. L. Troskey	Fred Goodwin	1961	73
222 5/8	24 5/8	23 5/8	17 7/8	5 5/8	5 5/8	8	8	Rusk Co., Wisc.	Raymond Charlevois	Philip Schlegel	1936	74
222 2/8	24 5/8	25 5/8	20 6/8	5 5/8	5 5/8	16	10	Ostrea Lake, N. S.	Verden M. Baker	Charles T. Arnold	1949	75
221 1/8	30	29 3/8	23 3/8	6 3/8	6 3/8	12	12	Humbolt Co., Iowa	Donald Crossley	Donald Crossley	1971	76
221	22 5/8	25	22 5/8	4 5/8	4 4/8	16	11	Itasca Co., Minn.	Richard I. Goble	Richard I. Goble	1955	77
220 6/8	26 5/8	26 3/8	19 6/8	6 1/8	6 3/8	12	15	Anoka Co., Minn.	Donald Torgerson	Donald Torgerson	1946	78
220 3/8	30	25 5/8	18 6/8	4 7/8	4 4/8	14	9	Mercer Co., Ill.	Roger D. Hultgren	Roger D. Hultgren	1970	79
220 3/8	25 5/8	27 3/8	18 6/8	5	5	10	13	Olmsted Co., Minn.	E. E. Comartin, III	E. E. Comartin, Jr.	1963	80
219 6/8	27 3/8	25 5/8	19 7/8	6	6	6	10	Genesee Co., N. Y.	Robert Wood	Robert Wood	1944	81
219 3/8	25	27 5/8	20 6/8	4 5/8	4 5/8	10	12	Rockingham Co., Va.	Dorsey O. Breeden	Dorsey O. Breeden	1966	81
219 1/8	27 1/8	27	20	5 3/8	5 3/8	11	10	Webb Co., Texas	Richard Oliver Rivera	Richard Oliver Rivera	1972	83
218 7/8	28 5/8	27 7/8	18 6/8	5 5/8	5 5/8	9	15	Flathead Co., Mont.	R. C. Garrett	R. C. Garrett	1962	84
218 4/8	26 5/8	26 3/8	20	5 3/8	5 3/8	12	11	Florence Co., Wisc.	W. C. Gotstein	Elmer Foley	1914	85
218 3/8	27	24 5/8	17 7/8	5 5/8	5 5/8	8	8	St. Martin Parish, La.	Drew Ware	Gary S. Crnko	1941	86
218 3/8	20 5/8	27	17	5 7/8	5	9	11	La Crosse Co., Wisc.	Daniel P. Cavadini	Daniel P. Cavadini	1951	87
218	25	25 5/8	19 3/8	4 6/8	5 3/8	13	15	South Goodeve, Sask.	Fred Bohay	Fred Bohay	1958	87
218	25 5/8	27 3/8	19 3/8	5 5/8	5 5/8	11	12	Whatshan Lake, B. C.	Karl H. Kast	Karl H. Kast	1940	89
217 7/8	27 5/8	28 3/8	19	5 5/8	5 3/8	11	15	Otter Tail Co., Minn.	Dennis A. Pearson	Dennis A. Pearson	1977	89
217 5/8	26 5/8	28 5/8	21 3/8	5 5/8	5 7/8	10	16	Maries Co., Mo.	Gerald R. Dake	Gerald R. Dake	1974	91
217 5/8	25 5/8	25 3/8	18 5/8	5 1/8	5 3/8	12	12	Macoupin Co., Ill.	Albert Grichnik	Albert Grichnik	1966	92
217 2/8	23 5/8	23 3/8	19 4/8	6 3/8	6 5/8	11	12	Aitkin Co., Minn.	Fred C. Melichar	Fred C. Melichar	1973	93
217 2/8	22	20	20	5 5/8	5 1/8	11	11	Sprucehome, Sask.	Tom Pillar	Tom Pillar	1957	94
216 6/8	26 6/8	26 3/8	20 3/8	5 5/8	6 1/8	13	12	Talbot Co., Md.	Vincent Lee Jordan, Sr.	Vincent Lee Jordan, Sr.	1974	94
216 6/8	19 1/8	21 1/8	13 7/8	7	5 5/8	12	15	Sand Lake Nwr, S. D.	Francis Shattuck	Sand Lake N.W.R.	1960	96
216 6/8	26	24 5/8	22 3/8	6 3/8	5 5/8	11	13	Kathryn, N. D.	Gerald R. Elsner	Gerald R. Elsner	1963	97
216 3/8	25 1/8	25 3/8	18 3/8	5 1/8	5	10	13	Barber Co., Kan.	Robert L. Rose	Robert L. Rose	1972	97
216 3/8	26	24 5/8	18 6/8	6 3/8	5 3/8	14	17	Comanche Co., Okla.	Dwight O. Allen	Dwight O. Allen	1962	99
216 3/8	26	25 5/8	18 6/8	5 3/8	5 5/8	10	9	Clay Co., Iowa	Blaine Salzkorn	Blaine Salzkorn	1970	99
216 3/8	26 6/8	26 3/8	20 3/8	5 5/8	5	9	10	Powhatan Co., Va.	William E. Schaefer	William E. Schaefer	1970	99
216 3/8	27 3/8	24 5/8	23	4 7/8	5 3/8	14	14	Caroll Co., Miss.	Mark T. Hathcock	Mark T. Hathcock	1978	99
216 3/8	24	23	18 4/8	4 4/8	4 4/8	10	8	Buchanan, Sask.	Mike Spezrivka	Linda Christoforo	1961	103
216 3/8	26 5/8	27 5/8	20 3/8	5 1/8	5 7/8	10	14	Roosevelt Co., Mont.	Joseph P. Culbertson	Joseph P. Culbertson	1972	103

WHITETAIL DEER *(Non-Typical Antlers)–Continued*

Odocoileus virginianus virginianus and certain related subspecies

Score	Length of Main Beam R.	Length of Main Beam L.	Inside Spread	Circumference at Smallest Place Between Burr and First Point R.	Circumference at Smallest Place Between Burr and First Point L.	Number of Points R.	Number of Points L.	Locality Killed	By Whom Killed	Owner	Date Killed	Rank
216 1/8	23 1/8	19 4/8	15 2/8	5 3/8	6 1/8	15	16	Itasca Co., Minn.	Thomas Thurstin	Thomas Thurstin	1977	105
215 7/8	25	24 4/8	24 3/8	6 6/8	6	11	12	Long Pine, Neb.	Picked Up	Duane Lotspeich	1964	106
215 7/8	29 6/8	27 7/8	16 7/8	6 1/8	6 4/8	13	13	Putnam Co., Ga.	Thomas H. Cooper	Thomas H. Cooper	1974	106
215 6/8	24 4/8	24 4/8	23 3/8	6 2/8	7 4/8	10	12	Chippewa Co., Minn.	Micheal Allickson	Micheal Allickson	1974	108
215 5/8	26	25 6/8	20	5 5/8	5 6/8	16	12	Iron Co., Mich.	Chuck & Robert Lester	Chuck & Robert Lester	1970	109
215 5/8	28	28	20 2/8	5 2/8	5 1/8	10	9	Worth Co., Mo.	Burton Miller & Regan Nonneman	Burton Miller & Regan Nonneman	1974	109
215 3/8	29 4/8	28 6/8	23 7/8	5 6/8	5 6/8	8	8	Lafayette Co., Wisc.	Roger Vickers	Roger Vickers	1969	111
214 7/8	25 2/8	24 4/8	24 3/8	4 6/8	4 6/8	9	12	Aweme, Man.	Criddle Bros.	Criddle Bros.	1954	112
214 4/8	26 6/8	26 4/8	20 1/8	5 2/8	5	11	9	Swift Co., Minn.	Leonard N. Kanuit	Leonard M. Kanuit	1972	113
214 3/8	25	25 1/8	15 3/8	5 2/8	5 3/8	11	10	Price Co., Wisc.	Henry J. Copt	James A. Copt	1926	114
214 3/8	23 2/8	24	14 2/8	5 1/8	5 2/8	14	10	Missoula Co., Mont.	Lyle Pettit	Lyle Pettit	1962	114
214 3/8	27 3/8	26	17 5/8	5	5	11	11	Bayfield Co., Wisc.	Clarence Lauer	Mrs. Clarence Lauer	1963	114
214 2/8	24 6/8	25 3/8	20 4/8	6 4/8	6 2/8	8	8	Crook Co., Wyo.	Clinton Berry	Clinton Berry	1953	117
213 7/8	25	25 3/8	18	5 5/8	5 7/8	17	12	Sawyer Co., Wisc.	Charles Ross	Charles Ross	1949	118
213 7/8	27 3/8	25 3/8	16 5/8	5 3/8	5 3/8	12	8	Bresaylor, Sask.	Barry Braun	Barry Braun	1966	118
213 5/8	23	23 7/8	16 2/8	6	6 1/8	10	12	Buffalo Co., Wisc.	Norman C. Ratz	Ed Klink	1968	120
213 5/8	27 1/8	24 6/8	23 6/8	5 4/8	7	9	9	Bonner Co., Idaho	Rodney Thurlow	Rodney Thurlow	1968	120
213 4/8	26 3/8	23 2/8	18 6/8	6 1/8	6 4/8	12	11	Rochester, Alta.	Lamar A. Windberg	Lamar A. Windberg	1973	121
213 1/8	22	22	17	5 1/8	5 1/8	12	10	Havre, Mont.	Unknown	Frank English	1950	123
213	25 7/8	24 1/8	20 6/8	5 4/8	5 6/8	5	15	Rush Lake, Sask.	Jim Runzer	Murray Bromlay	1966	124
212 7/8	30	23 3/8	21 1/8	5 2/8	5	7	12	Waukesha Co., Wisc.	Max Mollgaard	Max Mollgaard	1976	125
212 6/8	27 1/8	26 7/8	18 1/8	5 2/8	5 2/8	14	16	Augusta, Mont.	Lefleur	L. S. Kuter	1952	126
212 5/8	25 3/8	25 4/8	23 6/8	4 2/8	4 4/8	11	11	Lincoln Co., Mont.	Charles F. Woods, Jr.	Charles F. Woods, Jr.	1973	127
212 5/8	29 6/8	28 2/8	23 7/8	5 7/8	5 7/8	10	9	Lake Co., Mont.	Dennis Courville	Dennis Courville	1975	127
212 3/8	29	28 4/8	24 3/8	5 5/8	5 6/8	11	10	Hershey, Neb.	Ray Liles	Ray Liles	1959	129
212 2/8	26 6/8	26 1/8	23 6/8	5 4/8	5 3/8	9	7	Houston Co., Minn.	Alfred C. Pieper	Alfred C. Pieper	1977	130
212 1/8	28 1/8	28 1/8	21 6/8	5 3/8	6	8	10	Woodbury Co., Iowa	Harold M. Leonard	Harold M. Leonard	1965	131
212 1/8	27	27 2/8	19 6/8	5 2/8	5 3/8	14	16	Meadowlands, Minn.	Robt. J. Lapine	Robt. J. Lapine	1968	131
212	29	27 4/8	23 6/8	6 7/8	6 5/8	8	9	Iron Co., Mich.	Ben Komblevicz	Ben Komblevicz	1942	133
211 7/8	25 6/8	26 3/8	24 1/8	6	5 7/8	14	11	Raymore, Sask.	Adolf Wulff	Adolf Wulff	1951	134

211 7/8	22	23 2/8	21 4/8	4 4/8	4 4/8	15	15	Crook Co., Wyo.	Curtis U. Nelson	Curtis U. Nelson	1971	134
211 5/8	23 1/8	22 5/8	13 4/8	7	5 4/8	18	11	Alda, Neb.	Donald Knuth	Donald Knuth	1964	136
211 4/8	25 3/8	25	18 3/8	5 1/8	4 7/8	14	17	St. Louis Co., Minn.	John E. Peterson, Jr.	John E. Peterson, Jr.	1963	137
211 3/8	24 7/8	25 2/8	16 6/8	5 6/8	5 6/8	11	10	Borden, Sask.	Leonard Verishine	Leonard Verishine	1972	138
211 2/8	23 2/8	24 4/8	16 6/8	5 7/8	5 7/8	10	9	Hughden, Alta.	Morris Sather	Morris Sather	1966	139
211	23 6/8	23 4/8	16 3/8	6	6	12	13	Zavala Co., Texas	Unknown	McLean Bowman	PR1973	140
210 7/8	24 2/8	24 1/8	18 1/8	5 2/8	5 2/8	11	9	Stevens Co., Wash.	Charles Tucker	Charles Tucker	1966	141
210 5/8	26 2/8	28 3/8	23 6/8	5	5	8	9	Lincoln Co., Mont.	Glen Savage	Patrick W. Savage	1934	142
210 5/8	24 7/8	25 7/8	18 6/8	5 6/8	5 5/8	14	10	Renville Co., N. D.	Glen P. Southam	Glen P. Southam	1978	142
210 4/8	26 7/8	25 6/8	20	5 1/8	5 1/8	12	11	Dane Co., Wisc.	Laverne W. Marten	Laverne W. Marten	1970	144
210 3/8	28 4/8	27 4/8	21 4/8	5	5 1/8	9	10	Marinette Co., Wisc.	George E. Bierstaker	Mrs. George E. Bierstaker	1947	145
210	26	26 1/8	18	5 5/8	5 4/8	10	9	Glenewen, Sask.	H. Frew	H. Frew	1955	146
209 7/8	25 2/8	24 1/8	22 4/8	4 4/8	4 5/8	9	9	Maryfield, Sask.	W. W. Nichol	W. W. Nichol	1967	147
209 3/8	26 1/8	26 1/8	21	5 1/8	5 1/8	13	9	Lasalle Co., Texas	Unknown	E. T. Reilly	1931	148
209 1/8	26	26 2/8	19 3/8	5	4 7/8	8	8	Clinton Co., Iowa	Gregory Stewart	Gregory Stewart	1963	149
208 7/8	25 1/8	26	21 6/8	5	4 7/8	8	11	Atchison Co., Mo.	Kenneth W. Lee	Kenneth W. Lee	1964	150
208 6/8	24	24 2/8	19 2/8	5	5 1/8	13	12	Daniel Boone Natl. For., Ky.	Richard G. Lohre	Richard G. Lohre	1968	151
208 5/8	19 6/8	23 4/8	18 4/8	5	5	11	10	Beaufort Co., S. C.	John Wood	John Wood	1971	152
208 4/8	28	27 1/8	23 5/8	6 2/8	6 1/8	11	10	Dixon Co., Neb.	Dan Greeny	Dan Greeny	1969	153
208 2/8	27	26 2/8	18 2/8	5 4/8	5 6/8	10	7	Unknown	Unknown	Roy Hindes	PR1950	154
208 1/8	25 7/8	24 5/8	19 6/8	4 6/8	4 4/8	8	8	Griswold, Man.	J. V. Parker	J. V. Parker	1946	155
208 1/8	24 1/8	25 2/8	20 2/8	4 7/8	4 7/8	13	8	Antelope Co., Neb.	Leon McCoy	Leon McCoy	1965	155
208 1/8	28 1/8	30 1/8	24 2/8	6 2/8	5	10	8	Atkinson Highway, Neb.	Russell Angus	Russell Angus	1966	155
208 1/8	21 6/8	23 7/8	24 1/8	5	4 7/8	8	8	Prairie Co., Mont.	Charles Danielson	Charles Danielson	1969	155
208	25 4/8	25	19 6/8	4 5/8	4 5/8	9	10	Chesaw, Wash.	Charles Eder	Charles Eder	1967	159
207 7/8	29 5/8	31 1/8	24 4/8	5 5/8	5 5/8	11	7	Port Royal, Pa.	C. Ralph Landis	C. Ralph Landis	1951	160
207 7/8	24 4/8	25 2/8	19	5 7/8	5 6/8	11	14	Minnehaha Co., S. D.	W. E. Brown	W. E. Brown	1957	160
207 5/8	25 4/8	25 4/8	21 2/8	6	6	11	7	Keephills, Alta.	Unknown	William J. Greenhough	——	162
207 5/8	24 2/8	23 6/8	17 5/8	5 6/8	5 4/8	7	8	Moosomin, Sask.	Leslie Hanson	Sam Peterson	1961	162
207 5/8	25	20 5/8	19 6/8	6	6	10	17	Seward Co., Neb.	Ladislav Dolezal	Ladislav Dolezal	1964	162
207 4/8	25 2/8	24 6/8	16 2/8	5 2/8	5 2/8	12	11	Burnett Co., Wisc.	Harold Miller	Harold Miller	1938	165
207 3/8	28 3/8	27 6/8	21 2/8	5 6/8	5 7/8	10	11	Roberts Co., S. D.	Delbert Lackey	Delbert Lackey	1975	166
207 2/8	26	25 6/8	26	5 6/8	5 6/8	11	13	Lycoming Co., Pa.	Al Prouty	Al Prouty	1949	167
207 2/8	24 4/8	19 5/8	11 7/8	5 6/8	5 5/8	11	17	Oroville, Wash.	Victor E. Moss	Victor E. Moss	1967	167
207 2/8	27 1/8	26 5/8	18 3/8	5 2/8	5 1/8	7	10	Drayton Valley, Alta.	Hassib Halabi	Hassib Halabi	1977	167
207 1/8	25 7/8	24 3/8	20 6/8	5 1/8	5 2/8	9	10	Provost, Alta.	Michael D. Kerley	Michael D. Kerley	1977	170
206 7/8	24 3/8	25	16 5/8	5 5/8	5 3/8	14	9	Oneida Co., Wisc.	Clarence Staudenmayer	Clarence Staudenmayer	1942	171
206 7/8	25	24 1/8	18	5 2/8	5 3/8	10	12	Loup Co., Neb.	T. A. Brandenburg	T. A. Brandenburg	1963	171
206 7/8	23 4/8	25 5/8	18 4/8	5 1/8	4 7/8	14	12	Horicon Marsh, Wisc.	Picked Up	Ronald A. Lillge	1966	171
206 7/8	28 6/8	30 3/8	23 4/8	6 1/8	5 6/8	11	10	Claiborne Parish, La.	J. H. Thurman	J. H. Thurmon	1970	171
206 6/8	25 4/8	25 4/8	24	5 4/8	5 4/8	7	11	Beechy, Sask.	Harold Penner	Harold Penner	1959	175
206 6/8	25 4/8	26 4/8	17 2/8	5 4/8	5 4/8	8	10	Grant Parish, La.	Richard D. Ellison	Richard D. Ellison	1969	175

WHITETAIL DEER *(Non-Typical Antlers)–Continued*

Odocoileus virginianus virginianus and certain related subspecies

Score	Length of Main Beam R.	Length of Main Beam L.	Inside Spread	Circumference at Smallest Place Between Burr and First Point R.	Circumference at Smallest Place Between Burr and First Point L.	Number of Points R.	Number of Points L.	Locality Killed	By Whom Killed	Owner	Date Killed	Rank
206 4/8	25 4/8	24 7/8	17 7/8	6 6/8	6 4/8	12	9	Yankton Co., S. D.	William Sees	William Sees	1973	177
206 4/8	26	26 1/8	19 2/8	6 3/8	6 1/8	11	6	Lac Qui Parle Co., Minn.	Steven J. Karels	Steven J. Karels	1974	177
206 4/8	28 4/8	26 7/8	20 5/8	5 1/8	5 3/8	10	9	Lawrence Co., Ill.	Shirley D. Lewis	Shirley D. Lewis	1976	177
206 2/8	25 4/8	25	16 6/8	5	5	7	9	Cotulla, Texas	George E. Light, III	George E. Light, III	1950	180
206 1/8	22 2/8	22 5/8	18 4/8	5 4/8	5 1/8	15	10	Kisbey, Sask.	J. Harrison	J. Harrison	1956	181
206 1/8	24 4/8	22 6/8	18	4 3/8	4 3/8	14	13	Boydel, Ark.	Picked Up	Clem Billgisher	1959	181
206 1/8	23 2/8	22 5/8	22	5 4/8	5 4/8	10	9	Lincoln Co., Wisc.	Picked Up	Lewis Pond	1974	181
205 7/8	28 6/8	27 4/8	17 1/8	5	5 4/8	8	17	Steuben Co., N. Y.	Fred J. Kelley	Fred J. Kelley	1938	184
205 7/8	22	20 6/8	20 7/8	4 5/8	4 6/8	10	10	Loon Lake, Wash.	Bill Quirt	Bill Quirt	1955	184
205 7/8	25 6/8	25 4/8	20 6/8	4 4/8	4 3/8	10	10	Houston Co., Texas	Gary Rogers	Gary Rogers	1969	184
205 5/8	26	25 2/8	21 2/8	5 4/8	5 7/8	14	9	Cottonwood Co., Minn.	Larry G. Gravley	Larry G. Gravley	1975	187
205 4/8	27 2/8	25 4/8	22 4/8	5 5/8	5 6/8	9	9	Swift, Minn.	Erwin Klaassen	Erwin Klaassen	1955	188
205 3/8	23 3/8	21 7/8	18 7/8	4 7/8	5	6	12	Kelvington, Sask.	D. Minor	D. Minor	1954	189
205 3/8	25 3/8	27 1/8	22 2/8	4 1/8	4 1/8	10	9	Trempealeau Co., Wisc.	Dennis L. Ulberg	Dennis L. Ulberg	1968	189
205 1/8	26 4/8	24 4/8	20 3/8	4 7/8	5	10	9	Leross, Sask.	R. Weger	R. Weger	1961	191
205 1/8	23 2/8	28 6/8	15	5	5 1/8	15	14	Washington Co., Maine	M. Chandler Stith	M. Chandler Stith	1963	191
205	28 4/8	26 5/8	21 7/8	5 7/8	5 7/8	10	12	Gilmer Co., W. Va.	Brooks Reed	Brooks Reed	1960	193
204 7/8	26 4/8	26 4/8	29 1/8	6	6	7	10	Portageville, N. Y.	Howard W. Smith	Howard W. Smith	1959	194
204 7/8	26 3/8	26 4/8	21 4/8	4 5/8	4 6/8	6	8	Trempeleau, Wisc.	Ralph Klimek	Ralph Klimek	1960	194
204 6/8	23 4/8	23 4/8	15 2/8	5 4/8	6 6/8	9	10	Moose Jaw, Sask.	Earl Sears	Earl Sears	1958	196
204 6/8	26 7/8	25 7/8	21 1/8	5 1/8	5	6	8	Innisfree, Alta.	Donald M. Baranec	Donald M. Baranec	1977	196
204 5/8	25 4/8	25 5/8	19 7/8	5 2/8	5 2/8	11	8	Unknown	Unknown	John A. Jarosz	—	198
204 4/8	30	28 6/8	21 1/8	4 7/8	5 2/8	10	12	Jackson Co., Ohio	Bernard Tennant	Bernard Tennant	1960	199
204 4/8	22 2/8	21 6/8	16 3/8	5 1/8	5	10	11	Love Co., Okla.	William B. Heller	William B. Heller	1970	199
204 3/8	26	24 4/8	18 3/8	4 7/8	5 2/8	11	12	Newport, Wash.	David R. Buchite	David R. Buchite	1960	201
204 2/8	23	23	17 2/8	4 6/8	4 4/8	11	15	Crook County, Wyo.	David Sipe	David Sipe	1956	202
204 1/8	22 3/8	22	18	5 6/8	5 1/8	7	8	Garrison, N. D.	Clarence Hummel	Clarence Hummel	1961	203
204	27 2/8	25 2/8	21 7/8	5 2/8	5 3/8	7	12	Sheep River, Alta.	Walter L. Brown	Walter L. Brown	1966	204
203 5/8	26 6/8	28	15 5/8	6 6/8	6	18	13	Chariton Co., Mo.	Vernon Sower	Vernon Sower	1953	205
203 5/8	23	30 6/8	15	6 6/8	6 6/8	8	14	Meigs Co., Ohio	Wesley Gilkey	Wesley Gilkey	1970	205
203 4/8	25	25 1/8	22	4 6/8	4 5/8	13	12	Live Oak Co., Texas	Alec Coker	Henderson Coquat	1916	207

203 4/8	23 4/8	22 1/8	18 5/8	5 3/8	5 2/8	9	10	Deadwood, S. D.	Ernest C. Larive	Ernest C. Larive	1957	207
203 3/8	25 2/8	25 2/8	21 5/8	5	5	10	8	Okanogan Co., Wash.	Michael A. Anderson	Michael A. Anderson	1961	209
203 3/8	22 4/8	23 2/8	19 2/8	6	6 1/8	8	8	S. Piapot, Sask.	Frank Kelly	Frank Kelly	1966	209
203 2/8	23 7/8	23 3/8	17 2/8	5 1/8	5 3/8	13	13	Esterhazy, Sask.	Walter Tucker	Walter Tucker	1966	211
203 1/8	28 1/8	27 5/8	21	4 7/8	4 6/8	9	7	Pawnee Co., Neb.	Virgil J. Fisher	Virgil J. Fisher	1970	212
203	26 2/8	26 1/8	15	5 2/8	5 1/8	9	11	Hancock Co., Ill.	S. E. Brockschmidt	S. E. Brockschmidt	1958	213
202 5/8	29	29 3/8	20 6/8	4 7/8	4 7/8	10	9	Dane Co., Wisc.	Ray S. Outhouse	Ray S. Outhouse	1964	214
202 3/8	26	24 5/8	21 2/8	5 4/8	5 4/8	11	12	Koochiching Co., Minn.	George Balaski	George Balaski	1955	215
202 3/8	23 5/8	25 3/8	16 5/8	4 5/8	4 5/8	11	6	Crook Co., Wyo.	Marshall Miller	Marshall Miller	1968	215
202 2/8	21 6/8	22 4/8	22	5	5 1/8	12	9	Fergus Co., Mont.	Harold K. Stewart	Harold K. Stewart	1948	217
202 2/8	24	23 5/8	27	5 4/8	5 4/8	11	8	Hungry Hollow, Sask.	K. W. Henderson	K. W. Henderson	1954	217
202 2/8	25 1/8	24 7/8	19 2/8	4 6/8	4 7/8	9	9	East Kooteney, B. C.	Andrew W. Rosicky	Andrew W. Rosicky	1956	217
202 1/8	25 1/8	25 2/8	22 6/8	4 7/8	5	9	9	Zehner, Sask.	Lee Danison	Lee Danison	1958	220
202 1/8	26 1/8	26 4/8	19 3/8	6 1/8	6 2/8	8	9	Gary, S.D.	Dennis Cole	Dennis Cole	1960	220
202	26 3/8	27	22 5/8	6 1/8	6 1/8	6	9	Bayfield Co., Wisc.	Indian	Richard Wanasek	1960	222
201 7/8	24 2/8	23 3/8	23 4/8	5 4/8	5 4/8	9	7	Burmis, Alta.	Joe Tapay	Joe Tapay	1964	223
201 5/8	27 6/8	22 2/8	20 5/8	5 6/8	5 5/8	8	12	Sisseton, S. D.	Truman M. Nelson	Truman M. Nelson	1967	224
201 5/8	27	26 6/8	18	5 6/8	5 6/8	15	6	Charlevoix Co., Mich.	Robert V. Doerr	Robert V. Doerr	1973	224
201 5/8	25	24 7/8	17 1/8	5 2/8	5 1/8	10	8	Ohaton, Alta.	Curtis Siegfried	Curtis Siegfried	1976	224
201 4/8	22 3/8	23 3/8	16 5/8	4 1/8	4 2/8	9	8	Campbell Co., S. D.	Edward J. Torigian	Edward J. Torigian	1957	227
201 4/8	25 2/8	23 1/8	16 5/8	4 5/8	5 2/8	14	13	Stevens Co., Wash.	Robert W. Newell	Robert W. Newell	1963	227
201 4/8	28 5/8	28 1/8	22 1/8	5 3/8	5 1/8	8	9	Brown County, Neb.	R. L. Tinkham	R. L. Tinkham	1965	227
201 4/8	29 7/8	28 5/8	19 7/8	5 2/8	5 4/8	10	10	Hubbard Co., Minn.	Duane G. Lorsung	Duane G. Lorsung	1973	227
201 4/8	22	29 2/8	23 6/8	6 7/8	6	9	8	Barber Co., Kan.	Joe Ash	Joe Ash	1975	227
201 4/8	28 5/8	25 6/8	18 3/8	6 7/8	6 7/8	7	7	Flathead Co., Mont.	Barry Wensel	Barry Wensel	1976	227
201 3/8	21 1/8	21 6/8	21 3/8	5 2/8	4 6/8	16	11	Bonner Co., Idaho	Leroy Coleman	Leroy Coleman	1960	233
201 3/8	26 4/8	27	18 5/8	4 6/8	4 7/8	9	10	Concordia Parish, La.	G. O. McGuffee	G. O. McGuffee	1963	233
201 1/8	28 2/8	27 3/8	16 5/8	5 1/8	5 2/8	8	9	Arkansas Co., Ark.	Daniel Boone Bullock	Daniel Boone Bullock	1953	235
201 1/8	21 6/8	22 3/8	16 3/8	5 2/8	5 2/8	9	11	Slope Co., N. D.	Arthur Hegge	Arthur Hegge	1961	235
201 1/8	23	22 5/8	14 5/8	4 6/8	5 1/8	13	16	Westmoreland Co., Pa.	Richard K. Mellon	Richard K. Mellon	1966	235
201 1/8	25	25 1/8	20 4/8	6 1/8	6 4/8	10	8	Freeborn Co., Minn.	Jim Palmer	Jim Palmer	1972	235
201 1/8	25 3/8	25 4/8	18 2/8	5	4 7/8	8	7	Butler Co., Neb.	James L. Sklenar	James L. Sklenar	1973	235
201	22 4/8	22 7/8	15 2/8	5 3/8	5 3/8	14	12	Delta Co., Mich.	Ernest B. Fosterling	Ernest B. Fosterling	1953	240
201	25 7/8	26 4/8	20 3/8	4 4/8	4 5/8	9	13	Cessford, Alta.	Russell C. Chapman	Russell C. Chapman	1966	240
201	27 1/8	27 6/8	21 4/8	5 4/8	5 5/8	11	8	Mercer Co., Ill.	Gerald Olson	Gerald Olson	1972	240
200 7/8	23 4/8	24 5/8	20 1/8	5 3/8	5 2/8	9	8	Mandan, N. D.	Virgil Chadwick	Peter Voigt	1957	243
200 7/8	23	23 7/8	19	4 7/8	4 6/8	11	9	Rusk Co., Wisc.	Gerald Cleven	Gerald Cleven	1963	243
200 5/8	28	27 6/8	22 1/8	5 3/8	5 2/8	8	7	Jackson Co., Ohio	Glenn McCall	Glenn McCall	1970	245
200 4/8	25 2/8	25 2/8	23	6 1/8	6 1/8	9	6	Brentford, S. D.	S. C. Mitchell	S. C. Mitchell	1948	246
200 4/8	25 1/8	22 4/8	19 6/8	6 1/8	6	10	10	Wainwright, Alta.	Paul Pryor	Paul Pryor	1968	246
200 4/8	24 5/8	24 7/8	19 7/8	5 4/8	5 4/8	12	10	Geauga Co., Ohio	Rudy C. Grecar	Rudy C. Grecar	1969	246
200 3/8	24 6/8	22 4/8	18	4 3/8	4 4/8	8	10	Crook Co., Wyo.	Paul L. Wolz	Paul L. Wolz	1967	249
200 1/8	26	24 2/8	23	6	6	11	12	Parrsboro, N. S.	Allison Smith	Edward B. Shaw	1960	250

WHITETAIL DEER (Non-Typical Antlers)—Continued

Odocoileus virginianus virginianus and certain related subspecies

Score	Length of Main Beam R.	L.	Inside Spread	Circumference at Smallest Place Between Burr and First Point R.	L.	Number of Points R.	L.	Locality Killed	By Whom Killed	Owner	Date Killed	Rank
200 1/8	27 3/8	26 3/8	21 3/8	4 7/8	5 5/8	12	12	Spicer, Minn.	Robert J. Custer	Robert J. Custer	1966	250
200	25 5/8	25 5/8	18 5/8	4 7/8	4 5/8	11	10	Outlook, Sask.	Earl B. Schmitt	Earl B. Schmitt	1966	252
197 5/8	20 3/8	20 7/8	14	5 5/8	5	7	14	Hickory Co., Mo.	Darwin Lee Stogsdill	Darwin Lee Stogsdill	1971	253
199 6/8	28 5/8	29 5/8	19 2/8	6 5/8	6	7	8	Meigs Co., Ohio	Cody R. Boothe	Cody R. Boothe	1970	254
199	29	27 7/8	19 4/8	6 6/8	6 1/8	8	6	Jefferson Co., Wisc.	Jerome Stockheimer	Jerome Stockheimer	1968	255
199 4/8	25 3/8	25 7/8	20 6/8	5 7/8	5 5/8	8	8	Aitkin Co., Minn.	Sanford Patrick	Sanford Patrick	1963	256
199 4/8	26 6/8	25 5/8	16 5/8	5 7/8	5 5/8	5	4	Centerville, S. D.	Ronald Merritt	Ronald Merritt	1964	256
199 3/8	28	26 4/8	21 6/8	5 6/8	5 5/8	10	8	Clark Co., Mo.	Bob Arnold	Bob Arnold	1973	258
199 2/8	21 4/8	21 5/8	20 6/8	5 6/8	5 5/8	8	8	Jasmin, Sask.	Richard Gill	Richard Gill	1958	259
198 7/8	24 4/8	28 3/8	24 7/8	6 4/8	7 3/8	7	9	Unknown	Unknown	Max E. Chittick	1900	260
198 7/8	23 5/8	26 3/8	20 3/8	5 3/8	5	10	8	Hunters, Wash.	Rachel Mally	Rachel Mally	1961	260
198 7/8	25	23 3/8	16 5/8	5 1/8	5 1/8	11	11	Weston Co., Wyo.	Gary E. Huls & Bruce L. Arfmann	Chester S. Jones	1973	260
198 5/8	24 4/8	24 3/8	17 7/8	5 5/8	6 4/8	9	15	Hayward, Wisc.	Unknown	Harold Burrows	PR 1920	263
198 5/8	26 6/8	26 1/8	18 3/8	5 5/8	5 5/8	11	13	Iron Co., Mich.	Eino Macki	Eino Macki	1930	263
198 5/8	26 4/8	27 5/8	22 2/8	6 7/8	5 5/8	6	11	Concordia Parish, La.	Raymond Cowan	Raymond Cowan	1961	263
198 5/8	26 6/8	26 6/8	17 4/8	5 3/8	5 4/8	9	6	Jackson Co., Ohio	Stanley Elam	Stanley Elam	1962	263
198 5/8	23 4/8	22 2/8	17 7/8	4 5/8	5	14	12	Will Co., Ill.	William H. Rutledge	William H. Rutledge	1977	263
198 5/8	25 3/8	25 2/8	23 2/8	5	5	10	10	Oconto Co., Wisc.	Paul M. Krueger	Paul M. Krueger	1977	263
198 4/8	24 4/8	23 1/8	18	5 3/8	5 4/8	13	12	Cow Creek, Wyo.	Thelma Martens	Thelma Martens	1951	269
198 4/8	23 7/8	23 5/8	17 7/8	4 4/8	4 7/8	8	9	Iroquois Co., Ill.	Charles E. Crow	Charles E. Crow	1974	269
198 3/8	23 3/8	22 5/8	21 6/8	5	5	9	12	Crow Wing Co., Minn.	Harold B. Stotts	Harold B. Stotts	1941	271
198 3/8	23 3/8	23 1/8	19 4/8	5 7/8	5 7/8	8	8	Rock Co., Neb.	Gerald M. Lewis	Gerald M. Lewis	1966	271
198 1/8	21 7/8	21 2/8	17	4 7/8	5	13	12	Nelway, B. C.	Edward John	Edward John	1935	273
198 1/8	27	26 3/8	20 2/8	5	5 1/8	10	7	Hocking Co., Ohio	Hugh Cox	Hugh Cox	1964	273
198 1/8	24 4/8	24 3/8	19 6/8	5 5/8	5 5/8	10	9	Kootenai Co., Idaho	Frank J. Cheney	Idaho Dept. Fish. & Game	1967	273
198	26 3/8	24 4/8	23	7 7/8	6 2/8	9	7	Valley, Neb.	Ivan Masher	Ivan Masher	1961	276
198	25 3/8	25 2/8	17 5/8	6 2/8	6 4/8	9	10	Osage Co., Kansas	Joe A. Rose, Jr.	Joe A. Rose, Jr.	1977	276
197 6/8	27 6/8	28 2/8	22 2/8	4 6/8	4 4/8	7	9	Harrison Co., Ohio	Roy Hines	Roy Hines	1959	278
197 6/8	21 4/8	21 4/8	18 4/8	4 4/8	4 3/8	10	8	Stevens Co., Wash.	Floyd Newell	Floyd Newell	1961	279
197 6/8	25 5/8	26 4/8	17	5 3/8	5	9	11	Riceville, Mont.	James R. Eastman	James R. Eastman	1965	279

197 6/8	24	24 4/8	18 4/8	5 1/8	5 4/8	10	7	Langham, Sask.	Leonard Waldner	Leonard Waldner	1967	279
197 5/8	24 4/8	24 1/8	20 3/8	6 2/8	5 1/8	7	11	Sawyer Co., Wisc.	James Borman	James Borman	1945	282
197 5/8	31 5/8	32 3/8	25 2/8	5 1/8	5 1/8	5	6	Welshfield, Ohio	Edward Dooner	Edward Dooner	1956	282
197 5/8	28	28 2/8	21	5 7/8	5 6/8	10	7	Jo Daviess Co., Ill.	David H. Carpenter	David H. Carpenter	1962	282
197 4/8	25 6/8	25 6/8	25	5 4/8	5 4/8	10	9	Pope Co., Ill.	Joe C. Schwegman	Joe C. Schwegman	1961	285
197 4/8	25 5/8	26 4/8	25 5/8	5	5	11	7	Wainwright, Alta.	George Bauman	George Bauman	1967	285
197 4/8	25	23 7/8	22 2/8	5 3/8	5 4/8	7	7	Johnson Co., Iowa	Dennis R. Ballard	Dennis R. Ballard	1971	285
197 3/8	24	26 5/8	16 4/8	5 6/8	5 6/8	9	10	Newton Co., Ga.	R. H. Bumbalough	R. H. Bumbalough	1969	288
197 2/8	23 2/8	26 1/8	17 1/8	5 4/8	6 1/8	10	9	Stanton, Neb.	Peter Bartman, III	Peter Bartman, III	1963	289
197	23 4/8	24 2/8	19 4/8	5	5	11	9	Oak River, Man.	Sam Henry	J. J. Henry	1946	290
197	28 2/8	26 5/8	22 1/8	5 5/8	6	6	9	Fayette Co., Iowa	Stanley E. Harrison	Stanley E. Harrison	1973	290
196 6/8	26 2/8	25 5/8	18 2/8	5 6/8	5 5/8	9	8	Perry Co., Pa.	Kenneth Reisinger	Kenneth Reisinger	1949	292
196 6/8	25	25	19 1/8	4 6/8	5	9	10	Unicoi Co., Tenn.	Elmer Payne	Elmer Payne	1972	292
196 4/8	26 6/8	28 5/8	19	5	4 7/8	8	8	Desha Co., Ark.	Turner Neal	Turner Neal	1955	294
196 4/8	25 4/8	25 4/8	17 7/8	4 7/8	5 1/8	9	12	Charlotte Co., N. B.	Clayton Tatton	Joel Andrews	1959	294
196 3/8	25 6/8	24 4/8	22 7/8	5	5 2/8	7	9	Prairie River, Sask.	Herb Kopperud	Herb Kopperud	1959	296
196	25 5/8	25 1/8	16 1/8	5 1/8	5 4/8	7	12	Westmoreland Co., Pa.	Edward G. Ligus	Edward G. Ligus	1956	297
196	26 4/8	25 6/8	18 7/8	5	5 2/8	6	7	Buffalo Co., Wisc.	William A. Gatzlaff	William A. Gatzlaff	1970	297
195 7/8	24 6/8	25	23 6/8	3 6/8	3 6/8	8	6	Webb Co., Texas	Chas. J. Schelper, Sr.	Vernon L. Watson	1930	299
195 7/8	27 1/8	25 2/8	20 2/8	5 2/8	5 2/8	11	10	Grant Co., Wisc.	Roger Derrickson	Roger Derrickson	1973	299
195 7/8	29 1/8	21 7/8	21 6/8	4 7/8	5	8	8	Perry Co., Ohio	Pearl R. Wiseman	Pearl R. Wiseman	1976	299
195 6/8	26 4/8	27 4/8	19 6/8	5 3/8	5 3/8	11	10	Moosomin, Sask.	Tom Ryan	Tom Ryan	1961	302
195 6/8	25 6/8	25	20 2/8	5 3/8	5 2/8	10	7	Briar Lake, Minn.	Mike Desanto	Mike Desanto	1963	302
195 6/8	24 2/8	24 6/8	18 3/8	5 1/8	5	7	7	Wetaskiwin, Alta.	Lewis D. Callies	Lewis D. Callies	1972	302
195 5/8	25 4/8	25 6/8	19	6	6 1/8	10	10	Parkman, Sask.	H. E. Kennett	H. E. Kennett	1949	305
195 4/8	24 5/8	24 1/8	17 6/8	4 4/8	4 2/8	9	9	Maverick Co., Texas	Ronald K. Hudson	Ronald K. Hudson	1971	306
195 3/8	26 2/8	26	19 4/8	5 2/8	5 5/8	7	10	Valley City, N. D.	William F. Cruff	William F. Cruff	1955	307
195 2/8	26	24 6/8	19 2/8	6 2/8	6 3/8	9	9	Rusk Co., Wisc.	Alexander King	Roger King	1890	308
195 2/8	28 4/8	27 2/8	20 5/8	4 7/8	4 6/8	11	8	Du Charme Coulee, Wisc.	Eugene E. Morovitz	Eugene E. Morovitz	1959	308
195 2/8	25	23 4/8	18 4/8	5 4/8	5 3/8	11	11	Pottawattamie Co., Iowa	Ted Houser	Ted Houser	1968	308
195 2/8	24 4/8	22	17 3/8	4 3/8	4 2/8	12	10	Kenedy Co., Texas	Don Harrison	Don Harrison	1974	308
195 1/8	26	25 7/8	21	4 4/8	4 6/8	9	9	Zapata Co., Texas	Corando Mirelez	Corando Mirelez	1966	312
195 1/8	24 2/8	23 4/8	23 2/8	5 2/8	5 2/8	10	9	Whitman Co., Wash.	Robert M. & Rodney M. Boyer	Robert M. & Rodney M. Boyer	1975	312

*Final Score subject to revision by additional verifying measurements.

WORLD'S RECORD COUES' WHITETAIL DEER (TYPICAL ANTLERS)
SCORE: 143
Locality: Pima County, Arizona. Date: 1953.
Hunter and owner: Ed. Stockwell.

Coues' Whitetail Deer *(Typical Antlers)*

Odocoileus virginianus couesi

Minimum Score 110

Score	Length of Main Beam R.	Length of Main Beam L.	Inside Spread	Circumference at Smallest Place Between Burr and First Point R.	Circumference at Smallest Place Between Burr and First Point L.	Number of Points R.	Number of Points L.	Locality Killed	By Whom Killed	Owner	Date Killed	Rank
143	20 2/8	20 5/8	15 3/8	5 4/8	5 6/8	5	6	Pima Co., Ariz.	Ed Stockwell	Ed Stockwell	1953	1
131 7/8	19 6/8	19 2/8	16 1/8	4 2/8	4 2/8	5	5	Huachuca Mts., Ariz.	George W. Kouts	George W. Kouts	1935	2
130 5/8	20 4/8	19 3/8	14 5/8	3 2/8	3 2/8	5	5	Chihuahua, Mexico	Wayne Kleinman	Wayne Kleinman	1958	3
126 5/8*	19 4/8	18 6/8	11 1/8	4 5/8	4 3/8	5	6	Pima Co., Ariz.	DeWayne M. Hanna	DeWayne M. Hanna	1977	4
125 4/8	18 6/8	19	16 2/8	3 7/8	3 6/8	5	5	Arivaca, Ariz.	Gerald Harris	Gerald Harris	1953	5
125	19 6/8	19 7/8	15 4/8	4 1/8	4 1/8	5	5	Ft. Apache Res., Ariz.	Picked Up	Jerry S. Pippen	——	6
124 5/8	19 6/8	19	14 1/8	4	4 1/8	6	6	Rincon Mts., Ariz.	James Pfersdorf	Mrs. J. E. Pfersdorf, Sr.	1936	7
124 5/8	18 2/8	18 7/8	13 5/8	3 6/8	3 6/8	5	5	Sonora, Mexico	Enrique Lares	Enrique Lares	1959	7
123 7/8	17 2/8	17 3/8	13 7/8	4 3/8	4 3/8	6	6	Gila Co., Ariz.	Stephen P. Hayes	Stephen P. Hayes	1965	9
122 4/8	22	20 4/8	15 2/8	3 1/8	3 2/8	5	5	Sonora, Mexico	Lloyd L. Ward, Jr.	Lloyd L. Ward, Jr.	1945	10
121 5/8	20 1/8	19 3/8	15 5/8	4 2/8	4	4	4	Pima Co., Ariz.	Joe Fanning	Joe Fanning	1964	11
121 4/8	19	17 6/8	14 1/8	4	3 6/8	6	6	Santa Rita Mts., Ariz.	Max E. Wilson	Max E. Wilson	1965	12
121 3/8	16 1/8	17	10 7/8	3 4/8	3 4/8	6	6	Santa Rita Mts., Ariz.	George Shaar	George Shaar	1964	13
121 1/8	19 5/8	19 2/8	15 7/8	3 7/8	3 7/8	5	5	Pima Co., Ariz.	T. Reed Scott	T. Reed Scott	1975	14
121	20 3/8	19 5/8	13	3 7/8	3 7/8	5	5	Sierra Madre Mts., Mexico	Herb Klein	Herb Klein	1965	15
120 7/8	20 7/8	19 4/8	16 3/8	4 3/8	4 1/8	5	6	Santa Rita Mts., Ariz.	Harold Lyons	Harold Lyons	1956	16
120 6/8	19 4/8	18 2/8	14 4/8	4	4	5	5	Sonora, Mexico	Manuel Alcaraz Caravantez	Manuel Alcaraz Caravantez	1960	17
120 5/8	19	19 2/8	12 1/8	4 2/8	4 4/8	4	5	Sonora, Mexico	Geo. W. Parker	Geo. W. Parker	1969	18
120 4/8	17 6/8	18 3/8	13	4 2/8	4	4	4	Sonora, Mexico	Diego G. Sada	Diego G. Sada	1969	19
120 1/8	18	18 5/8	13 5/8	4	4	5	6	Baboquivari Mts., Ariz.	Homer R. Edds	Homer R. Edds	1961	20
119 7/8	20 7/8	21 2/8	17 5/8	4 1/8	3 7/8	4	4	Gila Co., Ariz.	Tom Connolly	Tom Connolly	1960	21
119 7/8	20 2/8	20 4/8	15 1/8	4 4/8	4 6/8	4	5	Sonora, Mexico	Picked Up	George W. Parker	1960	21
119 6/8	20 1/8	19	12 2/8	4	4 1/8	5	4	Canelo Hills, Ariz.	George W. Parker	George W. Parker	1960	23
119 4/8	19 6/8	20 1/8	12	3 7/8	3 7/8	6	6	Canelo Hills, Ariz.	A. R. Anglen	A. R. Anglen	1967	24
119 2/8	16 7/8	18 6/8	15	3 7/8	4	7	6	Gila Co., Ariz.	Bert M. Pringle	Mrs. Bert M. Pringle	1952	25
119 1/8	18	19 2/8	10 5/8	5	5 3/8	6	4	Santa Rita Mts., Ariz.	Monte L. Colvin	Monte L. Colvin	1965	26
119	17 5/8	17 4/8	13 6/8	3 4/8	3 5/8	7	6	Hidalgo Co., N. M.	Jesse Williams	Jesse Williams	1971	27
118 5/8	19 5/8	19 7/8	14 5/8	4 4/8	4 3/8	4	4	Chiricahua Mts., Ariz.	Ward Becksted	Ward Becksted	1958	28
118 1/8	17 1/8	17 3/8	15 1/8	3 7/8	3 7/8	5	5	Santa Cruz Co., Ariz.	David W. Ahnell	David W. Ahnell	1977	29
118	16 6/8	16 5/8	14 1/8	4 1/8	4 2/8	8	7	Washington Mts., Ariz.	Ralph Vaga	Ralph Vaga	1962	30
117 7/8	19	18 1/8	16 5/8	4	4	4	4	Rincon Mts., Ariz.	Picked Up	H. L. Russell	1963	31

Coues' Whitetail Deer (*Typical Antlers*)–Continued

Odocoileus virginianus couesi

Score	Length of Main Beam R.	Length of Main Beam L.	Inside Spread	Circumference at Smallest Place Between Burr and First Point R.	Circumference at Smallest Place Between Burr and First Point L.	Number of Points R.	Number of Points L.	Locality Killed	By Whom Killed	Owner	Date Killed	Rank
117 7/8	19 5/8	19 4/8	12 3/8	4 1/8	3 7/8	6	5	Santa Rita Mts., Ariz.	George Shaar	George Shaar	1965	31
117 6/8	18 6/8	17 7/8	14	3 5/8	3 5/8	4	5	Canelo Hills, Ariz.	Raymond J. Kassler	Raymond J. Kassler	1958	33
117 5/8	20 3/8	20	18 5/8	4 2/8	4	4	4	Libertad, Mexico	Abe R. Hughes	Abe R. Hughes	1967	34
117 3/8	17 4/8	17 1/8	14 3/8	4 3/8	4 3/8	4	4	Atasco Mts., Ariz.	F. O. Haskell	F. O. Haskell	1939	35
117 3/8	17 2/8	17 2/8	12 5/8	3 6/8	3 6/8	5	6	Sicritta Mts., Ariz.	George S. Tsaguris	George S. Tsaguris	1958	35
117 3/8	19 2/8	19 3/8	16 3/8	3 6/8	3 6/8	4	4	Sonora, Mexico	Charles B. Leonard	Charles B. Leonard	1974	35
117 2/8	17 6/8	18 2/8	17 5/8	4 4/8	4 2/8	4	5	Chiricahua Mts., Ariz.	Picked Up	Warren A. Cartier	1963	38
117 2/8	18	18	12	3 5/8	3 4/8	5	5	Tumacacori Mts., Ariz.	Charles H. Pennington	Charles H. Pennington	1968	38
117	18 3/8	18 2/8	14 2/8	4 1/8	4 2/8	4	4	Cochise Co., Ariz.	W. R. Tanner	Fred Tanner	1941	40
117	18 7/8	19 1/8	16	3 6/8	3 6/8	7	6	Pima Co., Ariz.	Arthur L. Butler	Arthur L. Butler	1974	40
116 7/8	18 6/8	16 7/8	14 3/8	4 6/8	4 6/8	5	7	Sonora, Mexico	Berry B. Brooks	Berry B. Brooks	1954	42
116 7/8	18 1/8	17 3/8	13 1/8	3 6/8	3 6/8	5	5	Santa Cruz Co., Ariz.	Seymour H. Levy	Seymour H. Levy	1967	42
116 7/8	19	19 6/8	16 3/8	4	3 6/8	5	5	Pima Co., Ariz.	Arcenio G. Valdez	Arcenio G. Valdez	1971	42
116 5/8	17 5/8	19	14 3/8	4	4	5	5	Santa Rita Mts., Ariz.	Mike Holloran	Mike Holloran	1962	45
116 5/8	17 2/8	17 3/8	14 7/8	4 6/8	4 5/8	4	4	Gila Co., Ariz.	Richard A. Thom	Richard A. Thom	1978	45
116 4/8	19 5/8	20 2/8	14 5/8	3 7/8	3 6/8	5	6	Gila Co., Ariz.	Nathan Ellison	Nathan Ellison	1950	47
116 3/8	19 2/8	19	14 7/8	4 1/8	4 2/8	5	5	Blue River, Ariz.	Earl H. Harris	Earl H. Harris	1965	48
116 2/8	15 2/8	16 4/8	13 4/8	3 6/8	3 6/8	6	6	Chiricahua Mts., Ariz.	Freeman Neal	R. M. Woods	1947	49
116 2/8	19	19 3/8	11 6/8	4 7/8	4 4/8	8	6	Santa Rita Mts., Ariz.	George L. Garlitz	George L. Garlitz	1957	49
116	17 4/8	17 3/8	13 2/8	4 6/8	4 7/8	4	4	Santa Cruz Co., Ariz.	Ben Richardson	Ben Richardson	1978	51
115 5/8	18 5/8	18 4/8	14 3/8	3 6/8	3 7/8	4	5	Breadpan Mt., Ariz.	Mitchell R. Holder	Mitchell R. Holder	1966	52
115 2/8	18	20 1/8	15	4	4	5	4	Cerro Colo. Mts., Ariz.	Manuel V. Guillen	Manuel V. Guillen	1962	53
115 2/8	15 6/8	16 6/8	13	4	4 2/8	4	4	Santa Rita Mts., Ariz.	Unknown	James Bramhall	PR 1963	53
115 2/8	20 4/8	19 4/8	12 6/8	4 2/8	4 3/8	5	5	Santa Rita Mts., Ariz.	Bill J. Ford	Bill J. Ford	1965	53
115 2/8	20 1/8	19	16 4/8	4 2/8	4 3/8	5	5	Catalina Mts., Ariz.	Jim Stough	Jim Stough	1972	53
115	19 6/8	20 1/8	18 2/8	4	4	4	4	Coconino Co., Ariz.	Picked Up	Jerry C. Walters	—	57
115	17 2/8	17	13 4/8	5	4 7/8	5	4	Santa Rita Mts., Ariz.	Denis Wolstenholme	Denis Wolstenholme	1958	57
115	18 7/8	18 2/8	14 1/8	4 1/8	4	5	6	Chiricahua Mts., Ariz.	Roger Becksted	Roger Becksted	1960	57
115	19 5/8	19 5/8	17 6/8	4 2/8	4 1/8	4	4	Baboquivari Mts., Ariz.	Karl G. Ronstadt	Karl G. Ronstadt	1967	57
114 7/8	18 2/8	18 6/8	12 3/8	4 7/8	4 7/8	4	4	Ruby, Ariz.	Richard McDaniel	Richard McDaniel	1963	61
114 7/8	20	19 4/8	16 1/8	3 6/8	3 6/8	5	4	Santa Rita Mts., Ariz.	John H. Lake	John H. Lake	1965	61

114 6/8	16 6/8	16 6/8	13 6/8	4 1/8	4 1/8	5	5	Chihuahua, Mexico	Tom Jones	George B. Johnson	1932	63
114 6/8	19 5/8	19 3/8	14 5/8	4 4/8	4 5/8	6	8	Chiricahua Mts., Ariz.	John Miller	John Miller	1949	63
114 6/8	17 4/8	16	15 2/8	4 5/8	4 4/8	4	5	Santa Rita Mts., Ariz.	Art Pollard	Art Pollard	1951	63
114 6/8	18 3/8	18	15 1/8	4	3 7/8	6	5	Canelo Hills, Ariz.	Guy Perry	Guy Perry	1960	63
114 6/8	16 6/8	16 4/8	11	4 2/8	4 3/8	5	7	Santa Rita Mts., Ariz.	John Bessett	John Bessett	1965	63
114 6/8	17 5/8	17 5/8	14 4/8	4	4 1/8	5	5	Nogales, Ariz.	Arthur N. Lindsey	Arthur N. Lindsey	1967	63
114 4/8	19 3/8	20 4/8	15	4 2/8	4 4/8	4	4	Graham Mts., Ariz.	Robert Stonoff	Robert Stonoff	1962	69
114 4/8	15 6/8	16 1/8	12 4/8	3 7/8	4 1/8	6	4	Patagonia Mts., Ariz.	Verna Conlisk	Verna Conlisk	1964	69
114 4/8	17 5/8	17 1/8	13 7/8	3 5/8	3 5/8	6	5	Cherry Creek, Ariz.	Alan G. Adams	Alan G. Adams	1968	69
114 4/8	15 6/8	15 4/8	14 2/8	3 5/8	3 5/8	5	5	Chiricahua Mts., Mexico	Elgin T. Gates	Elgin T. Gates	1968	69
114 3/8	18	18 3/8	12 5/8	4	3 7/8	4	4	Atasco Mts., Ariz.	Antonio Lopez	Antonio Lopez	1961	73
114 3/8	18	17	14 3/8	4	4	4	4	Four Peaks Mt., Ariz.	Carl J. Slagel	Carl J. Slagel	1963	73
114 2/8	18 4/8	15 7/8	15 2/8	4 3/8	4 2/8	5	6	Catalina Mts., Ariz.	Wayne L. Heckler	Wayne L. Heckler	1958	75
114 2/8	16 2/8	17 1/8	11 5/8	4	4 2/8	5	6	Canelo, Ariz.	Earl Stillson	Earl Stillson	1967	75
114 1/8	18 7/8	16 3/8	14 1/8	4 4/8	4 2/8	4	4	Sonora, Mexico	Unknown	Bill Quimby	——	77
114	18 4/8	18 1/8	10 4/8	3 6/8	3 6/8	4	4	Animas Mts., N. M.	F. C. Hibben	F. C. Hibben	1955	78
113 7/8	18 4/8	17 6/8	14 2/8	3 5/8	3 4/8	4	5	Galiuro Mts., Ariz.	Clifford Kouts	Clifford Kouts	1964	79
113 7/8	20 1/8	19 7/8	12	4 5/8	4 5/8	5	5	Santa Rita Mts., Ariz.	Joe Moore	Joe Moore	1968	79
113 6/8	18 2/8	18 4/8	13 4/8	3 6/8	3 6/8	8	8	Chihuahua, Mexico	Herb Klein	Herb Klein	1957	81
113 6/8	15 4/8	16	13 6/8	4	4	5	5	Mt. Graham, Ariz.	Bill Sizer	Bill Sizer	1963	81
113 6/8	17 3/8	16	13 5/8	4 2/8	4 5/8	7	6	Galiuro Mts., Ariz.	Doran V. Porter	Doran V. Porter	1966	81
113 5/8	19	17 6/8	16 5/8	4 1/8	4	4	5	Graham Mts., Ariz.	J. H. Hunt	J. H. Hunt	1962	84
113 4/8	19 2/8	19 2/8	15	3 6/8	3 7/8	4	4	Sonora, Mexico	George W. Parker	George W. Parker	1947	85
113 4/8	19 6/8	19	14 2/8	4 4/8	4 5/8	4	6	Santa Rita Mts., Ariz.	George W. Parker	George W. Parker	1962	85
113 4/8	16 7/8	16 2/8	12 4/8	3 7/8	3 7/8	6	6	Santa Rita Mts., Ariz.	Jack Englet	Jack Englet	1962	85
113 3/8	16	16 3/8	12 5/8	4 5/8	4 4/8	5	5	Santa Teresa Mts., Ariz.	D. B. Sanford	D. B. Sanford	1950	88
113 3/8	17 3/8	16 7/8	13 3/8	4	4 2/8	4	4	Tumacacori Mts., Ariz.	Tom W. Caid	Tom W. Caid	1958	88
113 3/8	16 5/8	16 4/8	12 4/8	4 4/8	4 4/8	5	6	Pima Co., Ariz.	S. E. Harrison, Jr.	S. E. Harrison, Jr.	1969	88
113 2/8	16 7/8	17 6/8	15 4/8	3 6/8	3 6/8	5	5	Santa Rita Mts., Ariz.	Donna Greene	Donna Greene	1958	91
113 2/8	18 7/8	17 5/8	14 4/8	4	4	5	5	Tumacacori Mts., Ariz.	Carlos G. Touche	Carlos G. Touche	1961	91
113 1/8	20 1/8	19 6/8	19	4	4 1/8	5	6	Chiricahua Mts., Ariz.	Ralph Hopkins	Fred Tanner	1928	93
113	19	18 7/8	12 2/8	3 6/8	3 6/8	5	5	Tumacacori Mts., Ariz.	Basil C. Bradbury	Basil C. Bradbury	1968	94
112 7/8	17	17 1/8	14 6/8	4 2/8	4 2/8	4	4	Ruby, Ariz.	Roger Scott	Roger Scott	1962	95
112 6/8	17 5/8	18 4/8	14 4/8	5 1/8	4 6/8	5	6	Baboquivari Mts., Ariz.	Charles R. Whitfield	Charles R. Whitfield	1969	96
112 6/8	17 4/8	18 6/8	15 7/8	4 7/8	4 6/8	6	6	Cochise Co., Ariz.	Mike York	Mike York	1973	96
112 5/8	18 1/8	17 2/8	14 1/8	4	3 7/8	4	4	Sonora, Mexico	Henry Lares	Henry Lares	1959	98
112 4/8	17 3/8	17 3/8	15	4 2/8	4 3/8	5	4	Gila Co., Ariz.	R. T. Beach & L. H. Mossinger	Ronald T. Beach	1974	99
112 3/8	17 3/8	17	15 5/8	4 1/8	4 2/8	4	5	White Mts., Ariz.	Dennis E. Nolen	Dennis E. Nolen	1961	100
112 3/8	19	19 5/8	13 3/8	4 2/8	4 4/8	5	4	Santa Cruz Co., Ariz.	W. C. Grant	W. C. Grant	1973	100
112	18 1/8	18	15 4/8	4 2/8	4 2/8	4	4	Canelo Hills, Ariz.	Carlos Ochoa	Carlos Ochoa	1955	102
112	18 3/8	18 7/8	14 2/8	3 6/8	3 6/8	5	5	Bartlett Mts., Ariz.	Keith Robbins	Keith Robbins	1957	102
112	17 2/8	18	13 6/8	4	4	5	5	Baboquivari Mts., Ariz.	Jesse Genin	Jesse Genin	1961	102

COUES' WHITETAIL DEER *(Typical Antlers)–Continued*

Odocoileus virginianus couesi

Score	Length of Main Beam R.	Length of Main Beam L.	Inside Spread	Circumference at Smallest Place Between Burr and First Point R.	Circumference at Smallest Place Between Burr and First Point L.	Number of Points R.	Number of Points L.	Locality Killed	By Whom Killed	Owner	Date Killed	Rank
111 7/8	18 6/8	17 6/8	13 7/8	4	4	4	4	Canelo Hills, Ariz.	Walter G. Sheets	Walter G. Sheets	1959	105
111 7/8	19 6/8	19 1/8	11 6/8	3 4/8	3 5/8	5	4	Sonora, Mexico	George W. Parker	George W. Parker	1960	105
111 6/8	17 1/8	16 4/8	13 2/8	3 2/8	3 2/8	5	5	Gila Co., Ariz.	Karl J. Payne	Karl J. Payne	1955	107
111 6/8	17	17 1/8	11 6/8	3 5/8	3 5/8	5	5	Catron Co., N. M.	Charles Tapia	Charles Tapia	1959	107
111 6/8	18 6/8	19 5/8	14 1/8	4 5/8	3 7/8	6	5	Patagonia Mts., Ariz.	Norval L. Wesson	Norval L. Wesson	1967	107
111 6/8	18 2/8	18 5/8	14 4/8	3 5/8	3 4/8	5	5	Baboquivari Mts., Ariz.	Stanley W. Gaines	Stanley W. Gaines	1971	107
111 5/8	18 7/8	19	14 6/8	4 3/8	4 3/8	5	6	Santa Rita Mts., Ariz.	Rick Detwiler	Rick Detwiler	1968	111
111 4/8	20 1/8	19 5/8	14 2/8	4	3 7/8	5	5	Sonora, Mexico	George W. Parker	George W. Parker	1926	112
111 4/8	17 4/8	18	15	3 6/8	4	4	4	Santa Rita Mts., Ariz.	Tom L. Swanson	Tom L. Swanson	1965	112
111 3/8	20 6/8	21 2/8	12 3/8	3 6/8	3 4/8	4	4	Sierra Madre Mts., Mexico	Herb Klein	Herb Klein	1965	114
111 2/8	17 5/8	17 3/8	11 2/8	4	3 6/8	6	6	Santa Rita Mts., Ariz.	Lon E. Bothwell	Lon E. Bothwell	—	115
111 2/8	17 6/8	17	15 2/8	4	4	4	4	Graham Co., Ariz.	C. R. Hale	C. R. Hale	1958	115
111 2/8	19 2/8	19 4/8	16 6/8	4	4	4	6	Graham Mts., Ariz.	Bill Barney	Bill Barney	1962	115
111 2/8	19 1/8	19	15 6/8	4 2/8	4 3/8	4	4	Atascosa, Ariz.	Henry B. Carrillo	Henry B. Carrillo	1964	115
111 1/8	17 5/8	16 7/8	13 2/8	3 6/8	3 6/8	4	4	Herschel Mts., Ariz.	Carl Waldt	Carl Waldt	1959	119
111 1/8	17 5/8	17 6/8	16	4	3 7/8	5	6	Sonora, Mexico	Joe Daneker, Jr.	Joe Daneker, Jr.	1973	119
110 7/8	19 2/8	19 4/8	13 1/8	3 6/8	3 6/8	4	4	Chiricahua Mts., Ariz.	Wayne A. Dirst	Wayne A. Dirst	1954	121
110 7/8	17 2/8	18 6/8	11 2/8	4	4 1/8	5	7	Canelo Hills, Ariz.	Bill Fidelo	Bill Fidelo	1958	121
110 7/8	19 3/8	19	15 7/8	3 6/8	3 5/8	5	4	Rincon Mts., Ariz.	Ollie O. Barney, Jr.	Ollie O. Barney, Jr.	1961	121
110 6/8	18	18 2/8	13 4/8	3 6/8	3 6/8	4	5	Catalina Mts., Ariz.	H. C. Ruff	H. C. Ruff	1959	124
110 6/8	18 5/8	18 2/8	15 6/8	4	4	4	4	Santa Rita Mts., Ariz.	John S. McFarling	John S. McFarling	1965	124
110 4/8	16 7/8	17 6/8	14 2/8	4 4/8	4 4/8	4	4	Canelo Mts., Ariz.	Otto L. Fritz	Otto L. Fritz	1947	126
110 4/8	16 7/8	16 6/8	14 2/8	4 1/8	4	5	5	Tumacacori Mts., Ariz.	John Doyle	John Doyle	1966	126
110 3/8	17 7/8	17 7/8	13 7/8	4 1/8	4	4	4	Santa Rita Mts., Ariz.	Edward L. Blixt	Edward L. Blixt	1946	128
110 3/8	18 7/8	18 4/8	12 6/8	3 7/8	3 4/8	4	4	Santa Rita Mts., Ariz.	Lyle K. Sowls	Lyle K. Sowls	1956	128
110 2/8	18 7/8	19 5/8	11 6/8	3 4/8	3 4/8	4	5	Sonora, Mexico	George W. Parker	George W. Parker	1960	130
110 2/8	17	16 3/8	14	4 6/8	4 6/8	5	5	Gila Co., Ariz	William P. Hampton, Jr.	William P. Hampton, Jr.	1976	130
110 1/8	16 7/8	16 3/8	15 7/8	4 4/8	4 6/8	4	4	Payson, Ariz.	Picked Up	Richard Noonan	—	132
110	19 4/8	18 6/8	14 2/8	4 2/8	4 3/8	5	5	Sonora, Mexico	Enrique Cervera Cicero	Enrique Cervera Cicero	1966	133

*Final Score subject to revision by additional verifying measurements.

Photograph by Leo T. Sarnaki

WORLD'S RECORD COUES' WHITETAIL DEER (NON-TYPICAL ANTLERS)
SCORE: 151 4/8
Locality: Cochise County, Arizona. Date: 1929.
Hunter: Charles C. Mabry. Owner: Tom Mabry

Coues' Whitetail Deer (Non-Typical Antlers)

Odocoileus virginianus couesi

Minimum Score 120

Score	Length of Main Beam R	L	Inside Spread	Circumference at Smallest Place Between Burr and First Point R	L	Number of Points R	L	Locality Killed	By Whom Killed	Owner	Date Killed	Rank
151 1/8	18 5/8	18 5/8	15 5/8	5 4/8	5 4/8	9	8	Cochise Co., Ariz.	Charles C. Mabry	Tom Mabry	1929	1
150 5/8	18 1/8	19	12 5/8	4 3/8	4 4/8	8	8	Sasabe, Ariz.	Robert Rabb	Robert Rabb	1954	2
149 7/8	17 3/8	18 5/8	13 3/8	4 6/8	4 2/8	10	8	Chiricahua Range, Ariz.	Marvin R. Hardin	Marvin R. Hardin	1950	3
144 6/8*	20 4/8	21	16 6/8	5 2/8	4 6/8	7	5	Sonora, Mexico	Arturo Rodriguez Campoy	Arturo Rodriguez Campoy	1979	4
142 7/8	20 4/8	18 7/8	13 3/8	4 4/8	4 5/8	9	7	Apache Indian Res., Ariz.	Indian	Ariz. Dept. Fish & Game	1950	5
142 2/8	17 6/8	17 1/8	14 2/8	4 6/8	4 5/8	8	8	Pinal Mts., Ariz.	Phil Rothengatter	Phil Rothengatter	1967	6
139 7/8	18 3/8	18 3/8	15	4 7/8	4 7/8	8	6	Patagonia, Ariz.	Howard W. Drake	Howard W. Drake	1968	7
137 7/8	19 3/8	19 3/8	14 5/8	4 4/8	4 4/8	6	7	Patagonia Mts., Ariz.	Ivan J. Buttram	Ivan J. Buttram	1969	8
130 7/8	17 3/8	17 5/8	13 3/8	4 1/8	4 2/8	7	9	Canelo Hills, Ariz.	Jack Everhart	Fred Baker	1946	9
130 7/8	14 5/8	15 7/8	10 1/8	5	3 7/8	10	8	Ricon Mts., Ariz.	Velton Clark	Velton Clark	1962	10
130	17 3/8	16 6/8	13 7/8	4 3/8	5 5/8	6	11	Whetstone Range, Ariz.	Unknown	Roger Clyne	—	11
128	18 5/8	19 1/8	16 6/8	5 5/8	4 3/8	5	8	Santa Cruz Co., Ariz.	Carlos G. Touche	Carlos G. Touche	1968	12
125 3/8	15 3/8	16 6/8	13 6/8	4 4/8	4 3/8	9	6	Sonora, Mexico	Enrique C. Cicero	Enrique C. Cicero	1967	13
124 7/8	15 3/8	17 1/8	11 3/8	4 6/8	4 7/8	8	5	Las Guijas Mts., Ariz.	Aubrey F. Powell	Aubrey F. Powell	1966	14
124 1/8	17 1/8	19	15	4 3/8	4 4/8	6	6	Yavapai Co., Ariz.	James W. P. Roe	James W. P. Roe	1971	15
120 5/8	20 7/8	20	13 4/8	4	3 7/8	6	4	Santa Cruz Co., Ariz.	Jerry M. Myers	Jerry M. Myers	1970	16
120 2/8	14 4/8	17 5/8	11 5/8	4 3/8	4 3/8	8	8	Pima Co., Ariz.	Unknown	Mike Yeager	—	17

*Final Score subject to revision by additional verifying measurements.

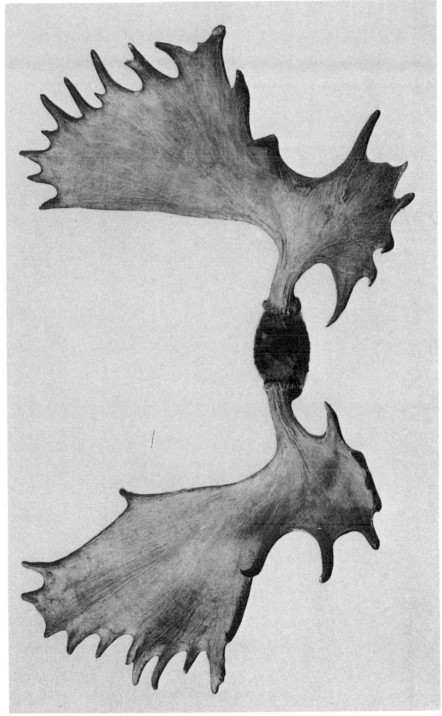

WORLD'S RECORD CANADA MOOSE
SCORE: 238 5/8
Locality: Bear Lake, Quebec. Date: 1914.
Hunter: Silas H. Witherbee
Donated by Mrs. John H. Boyle and Jack H Witherbee to the National Collection.

Photograph by Grancel Fitz

235

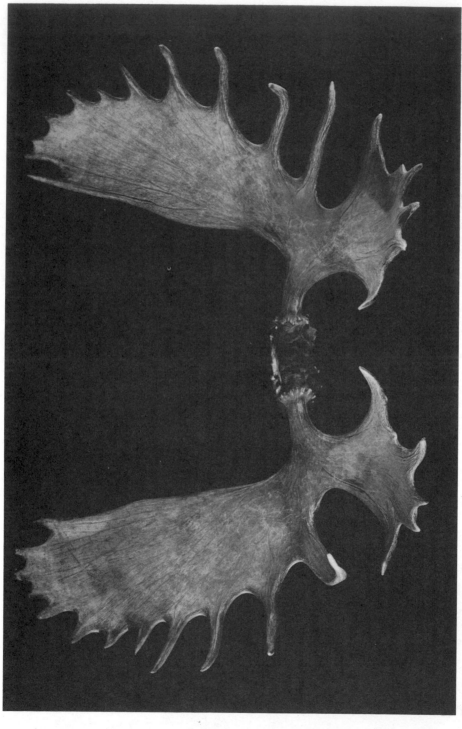

NUMBER FIVE CANADA MOOSE
SCORE: 225

Locality: Driftwood River, Alberta. Date: 1960.
Hunter and owner: Carl J. Buchanan.

236

Canada Moose

Alces alces americana and *Alces alces andersoni*

Minimum Score 195

Three categories of moose are recognized for records keeping, with boundaries based on geographic lines. Canada moose includes trophies from Newfoundland and Canada (except for the Yukon and Northwest Territories), Minnesota, and Maine.

Score	Greatest Spread	Length of Palm R.	Length of Palm L.	Width of Palm R.	Width of Palm L.	Circumference of Beam at Smallest Place R.	Circumference of Beam at Smallest Place L.	Number of Normal Points R.	Number of Normal Points L.	Locality Killed	By Whom Killed	Owner	Date Killed	Rank
238 5/8	65 5/8	44 6/8	43 1/8	21	18 6/8	7 5/8	7 7/8	18	19	Bear Lake, Que.	Silas H. Witherbee	National Collection	1914	1
229 1/8*	66 2/8	45 4/8	45 4/8	14 6/8	16	8 2/8	8 2/8	13	15	Muncho Lake, B.C.	Roger J. Ahern	Roger J. Ahern	1977	2
226 7/8*	63 1/8	48 5/8	47	16 4/8	16 4/8	8 4/8	8 3/8	11	10	Whitecourt, Alta.	Tim Harbridge	Tim Harbridge	1978	3
225 6/8*	62 6/8	44 7/8	42 1/8	18 2/8	17 5/8	7 2/8	7 2/8	15	16	Halfway River, B.C.	Richard Peterson	Richard Peterson	1977	4
225	60	45 7/8	46 1/8	14 6/8	14 3/8	7 4/8	7 2/8	17	15	Driftwood River, Alta.	Carl J. Buchanan	Carl J. Buchanan	1960	5
224 5/8*	65 5/8	45 1/8	48	13 6/8	13 4/8	7 3/8	7 4/8	15	14	Birch River, Sask.	Olaus R. Coffron	Olaus R. Coffron	1970	6
224 1/8	58 3/8	43 4/8	43	18 4/8	17 3/8	8 4/8	8 4/8	14	14	Nipawin, Sask.	Roy M. Hornseth	Roy M.Hornseth	1959	7
222	59	46	47 1/8	14 3/8	14	7 6/8	7 4/8	15	14	Clearwater River, Alta.	Manuel Dominguez	Manuel Dominguez	1947	8
222*	62	51 6/8	47 6/8	15 6/8	12 4/8	8	7 6/8	15	12	Duck Mtn. Prov. Park, Man.	Ray Wiebe	Ray Wiebe	1976	8
221 7/8*	63 5/8	47 7/8	45 6/8	13 2/8	13 7/8	8 1/8	8 2/8	13	12	Goat Creek, B. C.	Roland Wilz	Roland Wilz	1971	10
221 6/8	64 4/8	48 6/8	47 7/8	15 2/8	11	8 6/8	8 7/8	14	11	Arborfield, Sask.	Ed. Lutz	Ed. Lutz	1959	11
220 3/8	67 5/8	41 6/8	46 6/8	17 2/8	15 6/8	8 2/8	7 7/8	11	13	Cassiar, B. C.	Unknown	Luxton Museum	—	12
219 2/8	62 2/8	40 5/8	39 6/8	18 7/8	15 2/8	7 5/8	7 4/8	17	19	Canada	Gift Of W. B. O. Field	National Collection	—	13
219 2/8*	59 4/8	43 7/8	46 4/8	17 4/8	21	7 4/8	7 4/8	11	13	Muskwa River, B. C.	Sandra D. Vince	Sandra D. Vince	1978	13
219 1/8	64 1/8	45	43 1/8	15 5/8	13 7/8	7 6/8	7 4/8	14	13	Cold Fish Lake, B. C.	George & Phil Halvorson	George & Phil Halvorson	1974	15
218 1/8	61 7/8	44 3/8	42 5/8	15	15	7 4/8	7 5/8	13	13	Chuchinra River, B. C.	Friedbert Prill	Friedbert Prill	1973	16
217 6/8	64 4/8	44 1/8	47 2/8	15	15	7 6/8	7 4/8	10	12	Cassiar Mts., B.C.	J. Barry Dyar	J. Barry Dyar	1979	17
217 4/8	63 2/8	42 1/8	44	19 4/8	15 2/8	7 6/8	7 6/8	17	12	Hart Mt., B. C.	Donna Loewenstein	Donna Loewenstein	1966	18
217 2/8	63 6/8	42 2/8	39 5/8	17 5/8	15 3/8	7	6 6/8	15	15	Firebag River, Alta.	Frank Baldwin	Carlysle Baldwin	1977	19
216 7/8	59 3/8	41 6/8	44 2/8	17 2/8	15 4/8	7 4/8	7 4/8	17	14	Prophet River, B. C.	John G. Oltmanns	John G. Oltmanns	1971	20
216 3/8	58 5/8	43 6/8	46 2/8	14 6/8	15 3/8	8 3/8	8 4/8	16	12	Cassiar Mts., B.C.	Ross Ferguson	Ross Ferguson	1978	21
216 1/8	71 5/8	38 1/8	37	14 1/8	14 4/8	7 5/8	8	14	14	Maine	H. M. Boice	Everhart Museum	1900	22
215 4/8	64	41 4/8	42	13 4/8	13 4/8	6 7/8	6 6/8	14	15	Maine	Albert Bierstadt	National Collection	1880	23
215 3/8	54 7/8	39 4/8	38 6/8	17 3/8	17 3/8	7 1/8	7 1/8	17	20	Latornell River, Alta.	Artie G. Brown	Artie G. Brown	1971	24
215 2/8	60 4/8	44 2/8	45 2/8	12 7/8	13 1/8	7 6/8	7 6/8	13	13	Cassiar Mts., B.C.	Milton J. Duffin	Milton J. Duffin	1976	25
215 1/8	62 3/8	42 6/8	44 1/8	14 4/8	13 3/8	7 2/8	7 3/8	13	14	Dease Lake, B. C.	Bert Klineburger	Bert Klineburger	1960	26
214 6/8	53 6/8	44 2/8	44 2/8	16	13 4/8	7 6/8	7 5/8	16	15	Narraway River, Alta.	Karl Weber	Karl Weber	1956	27
214 6/8	68	39 5/8	39 3/8	16 4/8	15	8 4/8	8 4/8	13	13	Dease River, B. C.	Herb Klein	Herb Klein	1960	27

Canada Moose–*Continued*

Alces alces americana and *Alces alces andersoni*

Score	Greatest Spread	Length of Palm R.	Length of Palm L.	Width of Palm R.	Width of Palm L.	Circumference of Beam at Smallest Place R.	Circumference of Beam at Smallest Place L.	Number of Normal Points R.	Number of Normal Points L.	Locality Killed	By Whom Killed	Owner	Date Killed	Rank
214 1/8	60 7/8	44 5/8	42 5/8	17 3/8	14 5/8	7 3/8	7 5/8	12	12	Teslin River, B. C.	John P. Costello, II	John P. Costello, II	1976	29
214	62 6/8	43	43 5/8	13 2/8	13 1/8	7 1/8	7	13	14	Mile 100, Alaska Hwy., B. C.	Karl Fritzsche	Karl Fritzsche	1968	30
213 5/8	60 7/8	44 3/8	45 3/8	15 3/8	13 6/8	7 4/8	7 2/8	13	11	Prophet River, B. C.	Daniel T. Applebaker	Daniel T. Applebaker	1972	31
213 2/8	51 4/8	44	44	19	17 2/8	7 5/8	7 5/8	12	12	Atlin, B. C.	Ewald Krentz	Ewald Krentz	1971	32
213	62 2/8	45 1/8	42 4/8	14 3/8	11 5/8	8 3/8	8 2/8	14	13	Stikine River, B. C.	Sam Sanders, Jr.	Sam Sanders, Jr.	1975	33
213	63 2/8	41 4/8	39 6/8	15 4/8	15 2/8	7 7/8	7 7/8	12	12	Hines Creek, Alta.	Elwood Baird	Elwood Baird	1975	33
213	52	45	46 5/8	15	15 7/8	7 4/8	7 4/8	14	13	Liard River, B. C.	Hayden O. Woods, Sr.	Hayden O. Woods, Sr.	1976	33
212 6/8	61	42 5/8	42 6/8	13 1/8	14 4/8	7 5/8	7 6/8	14	13	Love, Sask.	Robert J. Rogers	Robert J. Rogers	1966	36
212 6/8	60 6/8	38 1/8	38	18	20	8	8 1/8	13	14	Sikanni Chief River, B.C.	David B. Willis	David B. Willis	1977	36
212 5/8	60 5/8	40 4/8	43 4/8	13 4/8	13 6/8	8	8	14	16	Slave Lake, Alta.	R. W. H. Eben-Ebenau	R. W. H. Eben-Ebenau	1937	38
212 5/8	55 7/8	39 4/8	41 4/8	16 7/8	18 3/8	7	7 2/8	15	16	Marion Lake, B. C.	J. Clifton Jensen	J. Clifton Jensen	1974	38
212 3/8	56 3/8	47 6/8	40 2/8	18 6/8	15 2/8	8 2/8	8	17	15	Cassiar Mts., B.C.	Dean A. Bloomfield	Dean A. Bloomfield	1979	40
211 7/8	65 3/8	38 2/8	44 2/8	13 3/8	12 7/8	7 2/8	7 1/8	15	15	Pasquia Hills, Sask.	William H. Schweitzer	William H. Schweitzer	1978	41
211 6/8	56 6/8	39 2/8	40	17 6/8	18	7	7 1/8	17	15	Fort St. John, B.C.	Jack Fries	Jack Fries	1977	42
211 5/8	61 7/8	46	42	14 4/8	18 7/8	8 3/8	8 6/8	12	10	Powell Lake, Ont.	Jerry R. Brocksmith	Jerry R. Brocksmith	1969	43
211 4/8	65	40 6/8	40 2/8	12 2/8	12 4/8	7 6/8	8 4/8	14	13	Pine Lake, Que.	Walter Geismar	Walter Geismar	1949	44
211 4/8	64 6/8	41 7/8	43	11 7/8	12 7/8	7 5/8	7 5/8	12	17	Atlin, B. C.	William L. Frederick	William L. Frederick	1969	44
211 3/8	54 1/8	40 1/8	40	18 1/8	15 4/8	7 2/8	7 1/8	17	16	Tochieka Range, B.C.	C. Thomas Manier	C. Thomas Manier	1978	46
211	49	43 6/8	43 4/8	16 2/8	14 4/8	8 1/8	8	15	15	Grande Prairie, Alta.	Lester C. Hearn	Lester C. Hearn	1972	47
210 7/8	70 1/8	40	40 2/8	14 4/8	11 3/8	8	8 1/8	11	12	Round Lake, Ont.	M. A. Kennedy	Royal Ontario Museum	1912	48
210 6/8	63 2/8	45 4/8	44 2/8	13 7/8	13 4/8	7	7 1/8	11	9	Sikanni Chief River, B. C.	Gerald Stecklein	Gerald Stecklein	1965	49
210 1/8	62 1/8	42 7/8	42 2/8	12 5/8	11 2/8	7 4/8	7 4/8	13	13	Sheep Creek, Alta.	R. V. D. Goltz	R. V. D. Goltz	1964	50
210	59 2/8	41 4/8	40 1/8	15 4/8	14 3/8	6 7/8	6 7/8	14	16	Sheep River, Alta.	Elton Boggs	Elton Boggs	1956	51
210	54 6/8	44 5/8	47 4/8	14 1/8	13 4/8	7 4/8	7 6/8	12	14	Cassiar Mts., B.C.	Richard J. Wristen	Richard J. Wristen	1978	51
209 7/8	53 3/8	43 1/8	43 5/8	12 7/8	12 6/8	7 4/8	7 3/8	15	15	Kakwa River, Alta.	Rolf Koelblinger	Rolf Koelblinger	1969	53
209 7/8	54 3/8	45 3/8	42 2/8	15 3/8	15 2/8	7 2/8	7 2/8	13	13	Turnagain River, B. C.	Gordon R. Cole	Gordon R. Cole	1974	53
209 7/8	58 5/8	42	40 4/8	14	14 6/8	7 2/8	7 1/8	14	14	Cassiar Mts., B.C.	William M. Silva	William M. Silva	1976	53
209 6/8	60 6/8	43 4/8	43 7/8	14	15 3/8	7	7 1/8	10	10	Jennings Lake, B. C.	Collins F. Kellogg	Collins F. Kellogg	1969	56
209 5/8	59 1/8	41 5/8	41 3/8	13 5/8	17 2/8	8 2/8	8 6/8	12	15	Malone Lake, Que.	Harvey A. Kipp	Harvey A. Kipp	1953	57
209 3/8	59 3/8	42 5/8	42 1/8	15 3/8	16 3/8	7 6/8	7 4/8	10	10	Cassiar Mts., B.C.	Hurnie H. Whitehead	Hurnie H. Whitehead	1978	58

209 5/8	59	44	50 4/8	12 5/8	12 5/8	7 4/8	7 7/8	12	11	Smoky River, Alta.	William R. Farmer	William R. Farmer	1970	59
209 1/8	55 5/8	40 6/8	41 6/8	13	13	7	7 7/8	16	16	Kenora, Ont.	David O. Moreton	David O. Moreton	1970	60
209	63	39 3/8	39	17 6/8	15	8	8	11	11	Manawaki, Que.	George A. Krikory	George A. Krikory	1953	61
208 7/8	56 5/8	39 3/8	43 4/8	15	15 7/8	6 7/8	7 5/8	15	15	Hudson Bay, Sask.	Don Hendricks	Don Hendricks	1961	62
208 7/8	60 7/8	39 7/8	41 7/8	13 4/8	15	7 5/8	7 7/8	13	14	Telegraph Creek, B. C.	T. T. Stroup	T. T. Stroup	1968	62
208 6/8	63 5/8	39 3/8	44 6/8	16 4/8	15 3/8	6 7/8	7 7/8	11	15	The Pas, Man.	Denver M. Wright	Denver M. Wright	1950	64
208 6/8	61	41 7/8	40 5/8	14	16 3/8	6 6/8	7	14	13	Ft. St. John, B. C.	Richard O. Vycital	Richard O. Vycital	1967	64
208 6/8	61 5/8	41	41 5/8	15 6/8	17 3/8	8	8	9	12	Hudson Bay, Sask.	Frank B. Miller	Frank B. Miller	1967	64
208 6/8	57 7/8	42 4/8	41 1/8	13 4/8	13 6/8	7 1/8	7 2/8	14	14	Catagua River, B. C	Dominic Arone	Dominic Arone	1969	64
208 6/8	56	43 5/8	47 6/8	14 2/8	12 5/8	7 6/8	7 4/8	13	16	Pepaw Lake, Sask.	Maurice R. LaRose	Maurice R. LaRose	1976	64
208 5/8	58 5/8	43 4/8	44 6/8	13 1/8	15 1/8	7 4/8	7 4/8	12	11	Muskwa River, B. C.	Gary D. Linsinbigler	Gary D. Linsinbigler	1969	69
208 5/8	52 3/8	46 4/8	45 5/8	13 1/8	16 4/8	8	7 3/8	14	12	Prophet River, B. C.	Vollrad J. von Berg	Vollrad J. von Berg	1967	70
208 4/8	61 3/8	40 5/8	40 7/8	12 4/8	11 6/8	7 5/8	8	14	14	Chetwynd, B.C.	Louis Carriere	Louis Carriere	1976	71
208 3/8	59 5/8	39 3/8	40 2/8	12	15 4/8	6 4/8	7 5/8	13	13	Halfway River, B. C.	Eugene F. Konopaski	Eugene F. Konopaski	1967	72
208 3/8	61 3/8	42 4/8	40	17 4/8	16 3/8	7	6 4/8	12	10	Cadomin, Alta.	Picked Up	E. F. Madole	1977	72
208	58 5/8	41 7/8	40 7/8	17 1/8	14 1/8	7 7/8	7	14	16	Muskwa River, B. C.	William D. Phifer	William D. Phifer	1969	74
207 7/8	56 5/8	43 3/8	43 4/8	12 3/8	13 2/8	7 5/8	7 7/8	14	12	Hudson Bay, Sask.	Harold Read	Philip Schlegel	1956	75
207 7/8	52 3/8	47 3/8	46 3/8	13 3/8	14 3/8	7 3/8	7 5/8	11	10	Neaves Creek, B. C.	Mrs. Geo. A. Strom, Jr.	Mrs. Geo. A. Strom, Jr.	1960	75
207 7/8	71 5/8	41 5/8	38 1/8	16	13 6/8	7 3/8	7 1/8	11	13	Moccasin Lake, Ont.	Charles W. Reiley	Charles W. Reiley	1961	77
207 7/8	56 6/8	42 4/8	42 4/8	12 5/8	12 4/8	7 7/8	7 5/8	14	15	Moose Call Lake, Alta.	Garry A. Debienne	Garry A. Debienne	1975	78
207 3/8	70 7/8	31	31	14	15	7 6/8	7 3/8	16	13	Alta.	Unknown	Acad. Nat. Sci., Phil.	1905	79
207 3/8	59 3/8	39 3/8	40 3/8	14	14 4/8	7 6/8	7 3/8	13	12	Smoky River, Alta.	Robert L. Carmichael, Jr.	Robert L. Carmichael, Jr.	1974	79
207 3/8	59 4/8	43	40 3/8	13 6/8	13 6/8	7 3/8	7 6/8	13	13	Hudson Bay, Sask.	A. L. Moore	A. L. Moore	1961	81
207 1/8	60 3/8	40 4/8	39 7/8	15	13 3/8	7 7/8	7 5/8	13	12	Manning, Alta.	Gary Cumming	Gary Cumming	1971	82
207	61 5/8	43 4/8	45 7/8	15	12 4/8	8	7 2/8	9	14	Goose River, Alta.	O. D. Evans	O. D. Evans	1960	83
207	58 5/8	42 2/8	42 2/8	14 3/8	13 4/8	7 5/8	7 7/8	12	13	Nipisi Lake, Alta.	J. M. Kirkpatrick	J. M. Kirkpatrick	1966	83
206 7/8	60 7/8	39 3/8	39 1/8	14	14	7 2/8	7 5/8	14	13	Smithers, B. C.	W. G. Reed	Louis Calder	1951	85
206 6/8	60 2/8	37 3/8	38 5/8	16 1/8	13 3/8	7 2/8	7 6/8	13	15	Black Sturgeon Lake, Ont.	Joseph John Casey	Joseph John Casey	1967	85
206 5/8	57 3/8	43 7/8	44 3/8	13	12 4/8	8 3/8	7 4/8	17	11	Assinboine River, Sask.	Francis Peecock	Francis Peecock	1976	87
206	60	40 2/8	35 5/8	17 7/8	16	7 3/8	9 2/8	11	14	White River, Ont.	Ronald L. Porter	Ronald L. Porter	1975	88
206 6/8	56 5/8	41 3/8	41 6/8	14 4/8	13 3/8	7 5/8	7 4/8	14	13	Horseranch Mts., B. C.	Bill McCoy	Bill McCoy	1976	88
206 3/8	56 3/8	46 3/8	49	12 5/8	15	8 1/8	7 6/8	15	9	Windfall Creek, Alta.	Brian Richardson	Brian Richardson	1978	90
206 5/8	55 5/8	41 2/8	42 4/8	13	13 4/8	6 5/8	8 2/8	9	13	Trutch, B.C.	Richard M. Wilkey	Richard M. Wilkey	1976	91
206 1/8	59 3/8	40 3/8	39 6/8	16 3/8	18 3/8	7 2/8	6 4/8	13	12	Brule, Alta.	Steven Rose	Steven Rose	1969	92
206	52 5/8	41 3/8	41 2/8	21 3/8	16 3/8	7 7/8	7 4/8	11	13	Trimble Lake, B. C.	Clifford E. Palmer	Clifford E. Palmer	1962	93
206	59 5/8	38 7/8	42 4/8	13 3/8	15 3/8	7 3/8	7 7/8	12	13	Moose Call Lake, B. C.	W. W. Harvie	W. W. Harvie	1965	93
206	54 4/8	40 3/8	40 6/8	15 3/8	16 3/8	6 7/8	7 3/8	13	14	Muskwa River, B. C.	C. Dale Hippensteel	C. Dale Hippensteel	1968	93
205 6/8	56	41 5/8	40 6/8	14 4/8	12 4/8	8 2/8	7 6/8	13	17	Sheep Creek, Alta.	Rudiger Schwarz	Rudiger Schwarz	1959	96
205	55	42	41 7/8	16 5/8	14 3/8	7 5/8	8 2/8	15	11	Kechika River, B. C.	Len Eklund	Len Eklund	1968	96
205 6/8	65 5/8	45	40	14 6/8	14 7/8	8 1/8	7 5/8	12	13	Vice Lake, Ont.	A. W. Winchester	A. W. Winchester	1959	98
205 6/8	55 5/8	43 4/8	43 6/8	12 5/8	13 7/8	7 6/8	7 2/8	13	12	Simonette River, Alta.	John G. Stelfox	John G. Stelfox	1965	98
205 4/8	54 4/8	41 4/8	41	17 6/8	12	8 1/8	8 1/8	15	15	Cassiar Mts., B. C.	Richard Trapp	Richard Trapp	1972	98
205 4/8	66 5/8	40 3/8	43 6/8	11 1/8	13 3/8	7 3/8	7 3/8	12	11	Bay Tree, Alta.	A. Iverson	Wally's Sporting Goods	1926	101

Canada Moose–*Continued*

Alces alces americana and *Alces alces andersoni*

Score	Greatest Spread	Length of Palm R.	Length of Palm L.	Width of Palm R.	Width of Palm L.	Circumference of Beam at Smallest Place R.	Circumference of Beam at Smallest Place L.	Number of Normal Points R.	Number of Normal Points L.	Locality Killed	By Whom Killed	Owner	Date Killed	Rank
205 4/8	61 6/8	39 6/8	40 6/8	16 7/8	17	7 6/8	7 6/8	9	8	Kedahda Lake, B. C.	Jack Perisits, Jr.	Jack Perisits, Jr.	1970	101
205 3/8	62 5/8	44 2/8	37 6/8	14 7/8	13 3/8	8 2/8	8 4/8	13	12	Kleena Kleene, B. C.	Roger Dane	Roger Dane	1965	103
205 3/8	59 7/8	38 5/8	44 2/8	15 5/8	16 3/8	7 4/8	7 5/8	11	15	Liard Plateau, B. C.	Charles W. Melton	Charles W. Melton	1971	103
205 2/8	57 2/8	39 4/8	39 7/8	13 2/8	14 3/8	7 3/8	7 2/8	17	14	Stikine Plateau, B.C.	Mike Papac	Mike Papac	1977	105
205 1/8	53 5/8	43 3/8	42	13 3/8	14 7/8	8 3/8	8 3/8	13	12	Cold Fish Lake, B. C.	A. Baltensweiler	A. Baltensweiler	1965	106
205	57 4/8	36 2/8	35 4/8	17 2/8	19 4/8	7 4/8	7 4/8	16	14	Prophet River, B. C.	John E. Hammett, Jr.	John E. Hammett, Jr.	1944	107
205	56	42 7/8	41 6/8	11 6/8	14	7 1/8	7	14	16	Moose Lake, Man.	Leif R. Langsjoen	Leif R. Langsjoen	1960	107
205	57 4/8	43 2/8	42 6/8	11 4/8	12	7 4/8	7 4/8	12	13	Cassiar, B. C.	James H. Bryant	James H. Bryant	1965	107
205	60 4/8	41	43	12	12	8 2/8	8 3/8	11	13	Cassiar Mts., B.C.	Earl I. Jones	Earl I. Jones	1978	107
204 7/8	62 3/8	38 7/8	40 2/8	14 4/8	14 3/8	7 2/8	7	15	11	Prophet River, B. C.	Lewis Morgan	Lewis Morgan	1970	111
204 6/8	56 2/8	46 6/8	43 6/8	15 1/8	15 7/8	7 3/8	7 4/8	8	8	Hudson Bay, Sask.	Fred Smorodin	Fred Smorodin	1957	112
204 4/8	54 4/8	40 3/8	40 2/8	13 5/8	12 2/8	6 5/8	6 4/8	16	16	Cassiar, B. C.	Unknown	B. C. Game Dept.	PR1918	113
204 4/8	51 6/8	45 3/8	44 2/8	15	14 3/8	7 2/8	7 4/8	13	11	Germansen Mts., B. C.	Edward A. McLarney	Edward A. McLarney	1978	113
204 3/8	57 7/8	40 6/8	39 7/8	14	13 7/8	7 7/8	7 4/8	12	13	Prophet River, B. C.	W. T. Yoshimoto	W. T. Yoshimoto	1966	115
204 3/8	55 7/8	42 3/8	41 6/8	16 6/8	14 4/8	8	8	12	10	Summit Lake, B. C.	R. A. Schweitzer	R. A. Schweitzer	1970	115
204 2/8	52 4/8	36 3/8	38 3/8	16 1/8	16 7/8	7 4/8	7 3/8	16	16	Buckinghorse, B. C.	John C. Belcher	John C. Belcher	1955	117
204 2/8	60	37 6/8	38 4/8	16 2/8	14 2/8	7 1/8	7 2/8	14	13	The Pas, Man.	Eddy Burkhartsmeir	Eddy Burkhartsmeir	1960	117
204 2/8	62 2/8	41 4/8	41 1/8	16 6/8	14 5/8	7 2/8	7 2/8	8	9	Ice Mt., B. C.	J. E. Mason	J. E. Mason	1966	117
204 2/8	62	37 4/8	38 2/8	15 3/8	16 6/8	8 2/8	8 2/8	10	10	Duty Lake, B. C.	John M. Haugen	John M. Haugen	1966	117
204 2/8	55 4/8	44 7/8	39 4/8	15 7/8	14 3/8	7 4/8	7 4/8	13	14	Muskwa River, B. C.	James C. Kolbe	James C. Kolbe	1969	117
204 2/8	58 6/8	36 2/8	41 7/8	19 1/8	18 4/8	7	7	11	16	Wawa, Ont.	Edward A. Hall	Edward A. Hall	1970	117
204 2/8	56 6/8	45	44 2/8	11 4/8	12 4/8	7	7 2/8	12	11	Tetsa River, B. C.	Alex Nesterenko	Alex Nesterenko	1973	117
204 1/8	55 1/8	41 3/8	46 2/8	15	13 5/8	7	7 2/8	13	16	Ft. St. James, B. C.	Ed Cornish	Ed Cornish	1964	124
204	68 4/8	35	33 6/8	15 2/8	13	8	8	13	13	Elderslay, Sask.	R. E. McKenzie	R. E. McKenzie	1930	125
204	55	40 7/8	41 2/8	13 4/8	13 5/8	7 1/8	7 1/8	15	13	Lake Nipigon, Ont.	Gary C. Jacobson	Gary C. Jacobson	1965	125
203 7/8	63 3/8	41 3/8	39 6/8	10 7/8	11 6/8	7 7/8	7 5/8	12	12	Lodge, Sask.	F. Foarie	F. Foarie	1962	127
203 6/8	55	38 1/8	39	15 2/8	15 3/8	7	7	14	15	Jackfish Lake, Alta.	A. Stopson	A. Stopson	1955	128
203 6/8	59 1/8	42 5/8	41 2/8	10 5/8	12 4/8	8 2/8	8 2/8	13	12	Hudson Bay, Sask.	Abraham Hassen	Abraham Hassen	1959	128
203 6/8	60	38 1/8	41 1/8	13	14	7 6/8	8	13	15	Rabbit River, B. C.	Bob V. Kelley	Bob V. Kelley	1969	128
203 6/8	58 4/8	39 1/8	39	12 2/8	12 5/8	8 3/8	8 3/8	13	14	Pink Mt., B. C.	Garth C. Hardy	Garth C. Hardy	1973	128
203 5/8	53 3/8	43 4/8	43 3/8	11 4/8	12 2/8	7 2/8	7 3/8	14	13	Overflowing River, Man.	Lester Ochsner	Lester Ochsner	1957	132

203 4/8	61	39 7/8	39 6/8	13 2/8	14 5/8	7 2/8	7 3/8	13	11	Graham River, B. C.	R. M. Frye	R. M. Frye	1970	133
203 3/8	64 7/8	41	36 3/8	15 4/8	14	7 7/8	8 2/8	11	11	Leaf Lake, Sask.	Tom Skoretz	Tom Skoretz	1959	134
203 3/8	55 3/8	42	48 6/8	12 6/8	14 2/8	7 2/8	7 3/8	12	13	Hudson Bay Junct., Sask.	Murray Griffin	Murray Griffin	1965	134
203 3/8	53 3/8	40 6/8	42	17 6/8	16 2/8	7 5/8	7 4/8	11	17	Big Smoky River, Alta.	Ross D. Carrick	Ross D. Carrick	1971	134
203 3/8	58 3/8	39 1/8	40	17 6/8	16 2/8	7 1/8	7 4/8	10	10	Muskwa River, B. C.	John A. Kolman	John A. Kolman	1975	134
203 2/8	69 2/8	32 7/8	32 6/8	17	16 1/8	7 1/8	7 1/8	11	11	Kvass Creek, Alta.	F. C. Hibben	F. C. Hibben	1958	138
203	55	39	40	15 2/8	14	7	9 2/8	14	15	Fawcett, Alta.	A. Juckli	Mrs. A. Juckli	PR1933	139
203	58 2/8	42	41 4/8	11	12 5/8	6 7/8	6 7/8	14	13	Cassiar, B. C.	Tom Lindahl	Tom Lindahl	1961	139
203	57 2/8	38 6/8	39 1/8	15 6/8	14	7 2/8	7 1/8	13	14	Cassiar Mts., B. C.	Arvid F. Benson	Arvid F. Benson	1965	139
203	58 2/8	41 1/8	38 5/8	12 5/8	13 1/8	7 1/8	7 2/8	16	14	Pink Mt., B. C.	T. C. Britt, Jr.	T. C. Britt, Jr.	1966	139
203	61 2/8	39 1/8	42	14 2/8	15 3/8	7 6/8	7 4/8	13	10	Manning, Alta.	James Harbick	James Harbick	1967	139
203	55	43 1/8	44 2/8	13 2/8	12 1/8	7 6/8	7 6/8	13	11	Robb Lake, B. C.	Jerome Metcalfe	Jerome Metcalfe	1967	139
203	62	39 2/8	44 7/8	11 7/8	12 5/8	7 3/8	7 3/8	12	12	Graham River, B. C.	Harold L. Sperfslage	Harold L. Sperfslage	1975	139
202 7/8	60 3/8	42	47 2/8	13 1/8	14 3/8	7 1/8	7 5/8	9	9	Prophet River, B. C.	Elbert Stiles	Elbert Stiles	1960	146
202 7/8	55 3/8	39 4/8	39 4/8	17 1/8	16	7 2/8	7 2/8	11	11	Atlin, B. C.	Robert H. Morgan	Robert H. Morgan	1973	146
202 5/8	59 7/8	43 1/8	43 7/8	12	14	7 2/8	7 2/8	9	13	Alder Flats, Alta.	Fred J. Simpson	Carnegie Museum	1966	148
202 5/8	56 1/8	39 3/8	40 5/8	13 7/8	13 5/8	7 2/8	7 4/8	13	14	Harmon Lake, Ont.	Dale C. Curtis	Dale C. Curtis	1969	148
202 5/8	55 1/8	40	40 6/8	14 5/8	13 5/8	7 4/8	7 1/8	13	13	High Prairie, Alta.	Dean L. Walker	Dean L. Walker	1973	148
202 4/8	57	39 5/8	38 7/8	14 7/8	15 7/8	8	8 1/8	11	13	Chelan, Sask.	Picked Up	Harold Bergman	1955	151
202 4/8	58 2/8	41 2/8	41 4/8	13 6/8	13 4/8	8	7 7/8	10	10	Watson Lake, B. C.	Lloyd Nosler	Lloyd Nosler	1964	151
202 4/8	61 6/8	41	40 2/8	14 3/8	15 6/8	7 6/8	7 7/8	8	10	Prophet River, B. C.	Lyle Nosler	Lyle Nosler	1964	151
202 3/8	59 1/8	39 2/8	40 4/8	13	15 1/8	7 3/8	7 3/8	12	14	Cassiar, B. C.	Unknown	B. C. Game Dept.	PR1918	154
202 3/8	53 5/8	43	39 4/8	19	16 2/8	7 6/8	7 5/8	13	12	Swan Hills, Alta.	Harold R. Wiese	Harold R. Wiese	1967	154
202 3/8	62 3/8	41	40 4/8	12 3/8	11 2/8	8 2/8	7 6/8	11	12	Grovedale, Alta.	Douglas R. Morris	Douglas R. Morris	1974	154
202 2/8	55 2/8	42	43 4/8	15	14	7 4/8	7 4/8	10	11	Cormorant, Man.	Howard J. Lang	Howard J. Lang	1950	157
202 2/8	60 6/8	42 3/8	41 3/8	12 7/8	16 2/8	7 6/8	7 4/8	12	9	Goose Mt., Alta.	Fred Bartel	Fred Bartel	1956	157
202 2/8	56 4/8	40 4/8	44 5/8	12 7/8	13 5/8	7 4/8	7 4/8	13	13	Hines Creek, Alta.	Ralph Jumago	Ralph Jumago	1960	157
202 2/8	59 2/8	36 6/8	38 3/8	16	17 6/8	6 6/8	6 6/8	12	13	Telegraph Creek, B. C.	George D. Young	George D. Young	1962	157
202 2/8	61 4/8	41	41	10 3/8	12 4/8	7 4/8	7 5/8	13	13	Turcotte Lake, Que.	Stanley B. Fredenburgh, Jr.	Stanley B. Fredenburgh, Jr.	1962	157
202 2/8	59	40 1/8	44 2/8	13 1/8	14 4/8	7 3/8	7 4/8	11	11	Atlin, B. C.	J. D. Kethley	J. D. Kethley	1966	157
202	58	37	37 2/8	14	16 4/8	7	7 2/8	14	15	St. Jovite, Que.	Ed. Schmeller	Ed. Schmeller	1942	163
202	61	39 2/8	42	14	15	7 3/8	7 2/8	10	10	Muskwa River, B. C.	Gordon C. Arndt	Gordon C. Arndt	1976	163
201 7/8	51 1/8	39 1/8	40 2/8	13 5/8	14 5/8	7 5/8	7 5/8	15	17	Sask.	Gordon Lund	Gordon Lund	PR1954	165
201 7/8	56 3/8	40 4/8	43 7/8	15	12 6/8	7 4/8	7 7/8	13	12	Cassiar Mt., B. C.	Clark A. Goetzmann	Clark A. Goetzmann	1968	165
201 7/8	56 5/8	38 3/8	41 2/8	15 2/8	12	7 2/8	7 2/8	15	16	Ft. St. John, B. C.	William J. Heiman	William J. Heiman	1969	165
201 6/8	60 2/8	37 5/8	40 3/8	15 4/8	16	7 5/8	7 5/8	10	14	Kechika Mts., B. C.	Norman Lougheed	Norman Lougheed	1964	168
201 6/8	57 2/8	39	39 6/8	14 5/8	14	7 2/8	7 4/8	17	12	Colt Lake, B. C.	James C. Wood	James C. Wood	1965	168
201 6/8	59 4/8	38 7/8	39 6/8	15	16 3/8	7 2/8	7 3/8	10	15	Pink Mt., B. C.	John P. Blanchard	John P. Blanchard	1970	168
201 6/8	55 2/8	41 2/8	42	13 4/8	13 2/8	8	7 6/8	11	12	Cabin Lake, B. C.	Donald F. Gould	Donald F. Gould	1974	168
201 5/8	53 5/8	37	39	18	20	7	7 2/8	12	12	Omineca Mt., B. C.	C. L. Burnette	C. L. Burnette	1973	172
201 4/8	49 2/8	42 7/8	42 3/8	15 2/8	13 3/8	7 3/8	7 3/8	15	13	Cold Fish Lake, B. C.	Charles E. Wilson, Jr.	Charles E. Wilson, Jr.	1957	173
201 4/8	56	36 6/8	34 5/8	18	19 2/8	7 1/8	7 2/8	17	13	Island Lake, Que.	Silvene Bracalente	Silvene Bracalente	1962	173

CANADA MOOSE–*Continued*

Alces alces americana and *Alces alces andersoni*

Score	Greatest Spread	Length of Palm R.	Length of Palm L.	Width of Palm R.	Width of Palm L.	Circumference of Beam at Smallest Place R.	Circumference of Beam at Smallest Place L.	Number of Normal Points R.	Number of Normal Points L.	Locality Killed	By Whom Killed	Owner	Date Killed	Rank
201 4/8	54 4/8	43 5/8	42 1/8	16 1/8	15 5/8	7 2/8	7 3/8	10	10	Ospika River, B. C.	Bill Goosman	Bill Goosman	1964	173
201 4/8	55 2/8	46 6/8	42 6/8	12 4/8	11 4/8	7 3/8	7 3/8	12	12	Mt. Lady Laurier, B. C.	Peter L. Halbig	Peter L. Halbig	1968	173
201 3/8	57 1/8	40	40 4/8	13 1/8	13 3/8	7	7	14	12	Swan Hills, Alta.	Earl C. Wood	Vale E. Wood	1967	177
201 2/8	56 2/8	41	40 6/8	13 2/8	14 4/8	7	7 2/8	12	13	Rocky Mt. House, Alta.	John B. Gibson	John B. Gibson	1955	178
201 2/8	62	40	43	11 2/8	13 2/8	7 3/8	7 6/8	11	12	Racing River, B. C.	Anthony Battaglia	Anthony Battaglia	1966	178
201 2/8	58	36 5/8	37 6/8	15	14 4/8	6 4/8	6 4/8	14	14	Upsala, Ont.	Daniel F. Volkmann	Daniel F. Volkmann	1969	178
201 2/8	63 6/8	34 6/8	34 1/8	15 3/8	15 1/8	7 7/8	7 4/8	13	12	Que.	Diana Baglino	Diana Baglino	1971	178
201 2/8	53	40 7/8	38 4/8	13 1/8	13 7/8	7 4/8	7 5/8	15	15	Lesser Slave Lake, Alta.	Bert Strain & Bill Baergen	Bert Strain	1976	178
201 1/8	53 5/8	39 6/8	42 4/8	15 7/8	15 7/8	7 5/8	8	11	11	Reserve, Sask.	O. A. Kjelshus	O. A. Kjelshus	1953	183
201 1/8	55 3/8	41 7/8	40	15 5/8	15	7 5/8	7 3/8	13	11	Big Sandy Lake, Sask.	John Longley	John Longley	1961	183
201 1/8	56 7/8	40 5/8	43	15 4/8	12 4/8	7 3/8	7	15	12	Slave Lake, Alta.	A. F. Harry	A. F. Harry	1967	183
201 1/8	61 3/8	41	45	16 6/8	13 1/8	7 5/8	7 2/8	11	13	Skeena Mts., B.C.	Wayne A. Tri	Wayne A. Tri	1978	183
201	55 4/8	38 2/8	42	14 4/8	15 1/8	8	8 2/8	13	12	Muskwa River, B. C.	J. H. Blu	J. H. Blu	1972	187
200 7/8	61 3/8	39 7/8	41 5/8	10 7/8	13 1/8	7 4/8	7 5/8	12	14	Grande Prairie, Alta.	John W. Benson	John W. Benson	1969	188
200 7/8	60 7/8	38 2/8	34 4/8	14 4/8	14 6/8	7 2/8	7	14	14	Spatsizi River, B. C.	G. C. Taylor	G. C. Taylor	1974	188
200 6/8	50 2/8	41 5/8	42	13 5/8	13 5/8	7	7	14	13	Goodwin Lake, B. C.	Bill R. Moomey	Bill R. Moomey	1974	190
200 5/8	63 1/8	38 3/8	39	11 4/8	12	7 7/8	7 7/8	11	13	Alta.	Ray Pierson	Ray Pierson	1967	191
200 5/8	61 1/8	39 1/8	39	11 2/8	11 5/8	6 4/8	6 4/8	13	15	Prophet River, B. C.	Chauncey Everard	Chauncey Everard	1967	191
200 5/8	58 1/8	37 6/8	39 2/8	13	12	7 4/8	7 6/8	14	14	Fort Nelson, B. C.	Everett L. Ashley	Everett L. Ashley	1975	191
200 5/8	59 1/8	39 1/8	41 1/8	16 3/8	13	7 7/8	7 5/8	15	11	Cassiar Mts., B.C.	G. L. Garrett	G. L. Garrett	1977	191
200 4/8	61	39 3/8	41 6/8	15 2/8	13 5/8	6 6/8	6 6/8	10	12	Deadmans Lake, B. C.	John Caputo	John Caputo	1950	195
200 4/8	61 4/8	38 2/8	39 2/8	14 2/8	16 2/8	7	7	10	12	Watson Lake, B. C.	Dan E. O'Neal, Jr.	Dan E. O'Neal, Jr.	1968	195
200 4/8	52	40	41 7/8	15	15 4/8	7 2/8	7 2/8	14	12	Muskwa River, B. C.	William W. Veigel	William W. Veigel	1971	195
200 4/8	59 2/8	42 3/8	40 1/8	15 3/8	15 1/8	6 7/8	7 1/8	9	10	Cassiar Mts., B. C.	Calvin D. Boatwright	Calvin D. Boatwright	1976	195
200 3/8	58 1/8	36 3/8	39	15	15	6 7/8	6 6/8	13	13	English River, Ont.	Jack Radke	Jack Radke	1966	199
200 3/8	59 3/8	43 6/8	41 1/8	11 3/8	11 5/8	8 1/8	8	10	11	Peace River, B. C.	Walter W. Kassner	Walter W. Kassner	1968	199
200 3/8	51 7/8	41 7/8	43	13 5/8	14	6 6/8	6 7/8	12	12	Cassiar Mts., B. C.	Don Stallings	Don Stallings	1971	199
200 2/8	62	42	40 2/8	13 4/8	11 5/8	7 5/8	7 2/8	10	10	Atlin, B. C.	John Vigna	John Vigna	1965	202
200 2/8	56 6/8	36 6/8	37 4/8	14 5/8	15 4/8	7 3/8	7 5/8	14	13	Pink Mt., B. C.	Danny Taylor	Danny Taylor	1970	202
200 1/8	56 7/8	39 7/8	41 2/8	12 7/8	12 2/8	8	8	12	13	Turcott Lake, Que.	George Clark, Jr.	George Clark, Jr.	1960	204
200 1/8	55 1/8	41 4/8	39 6/8	14 7/8	13 2/8	7 5/8	7 4/8	14	12	Whitebeech, Sask.	John J. Kuzma	John J. Kuzma	1966	204

200 1/8	52 7/8	46 2/8	46 6/8	11 6/8	10 2/8	7 1/8	7 2/8	12	10	Red Fern Lake, B. C.	M. Steven Weaver	M. Steven Weaver	1966	204
200	56 4/8	37 7/8	41 6/8	15 3/8	13 1/8	6 6/8	6 7/8	14	16	Lac Seul, Ont.	Robert B. Peregrine	Robert B. Peregrine	1966	207
200	59 2/8	40 3/8	41 1/8	14 1/8	12	7 4/8	7 5/8	11	12	Nass Lake, B. C.	Dan A. Pick	Dan A. Pick	1969	207
200	53	36 1/8	35 6/8	16	16 2/8	7 7/8	7 6/8	15	14	Muskwa River, B.C.	Roy V. Haskell	Roy V. Haskell	1978	207
199 7/8	62 3/8	32 6/8	33 2/8	16 6/8	13 4/8	7 6/8	7 4/8	15	15	Patapedia Lakes, Que.	William Darrow	Frederick K. Barbour	1911	210
199 7/8	46 5/8	41 6/8	40 3/8	17 5/8	15 7/8	7 3/8	7 3/8	13	13	Vanderhoof, B.C.	William Ilnisky	William Ilnisky	1978	210
199 6/8	61 4/8	36 6/8	36 1/8	12 7/8	13 7/8	8 3/8	8 1/8	12	12	Cutbank River, Alta.	Steve Kalischuk	Steve Kalischuk	1960	212
199 6/8	51 4/8	40 2/8	40 6/8	14 4/8	14 6/8	7 3/8	7 4/8	12	13	Halfway River, B. C.	Jack Taylor	Jack Taylor	1973	212
199 6/8	57	39 7/8	39 7/8	14	13 4/8	7 4/8	7 5/8	11	13	Kledo Creek, B. C.	Rick L. McGowan	Rick L. McGowan	1975	212
199 5/8	53 3/8	38 5/8	39 7/8	13 1/8	15 3/8	7 3/8	7 4/8	14	15	Greenbush, Sask.	Tom Flanagan	Tom Flanagan	1955	215
199 5/8	61 7/8	38 7/8	39 2/8	15 2/8	14	8	8	10	8	Prairie River, Sask.	Clarence Slater	Clarence Slater	1955	215
199 4/8	59	41	42	9 4/8	11 7/8	7 6/8	7 6/8	12	14	Drayton Valley, Alta.	Ollie Fedorus	Ollie Fedorus	1962	217
199 4/8	60	37 7/8	39 6/8	12 1/8	13	6 6/8	6 7/8	13	13	Dease Lake, B. C.	Peter Hohorst	Peter Hohorst	1968	217
199 3/8	49 7/8	43	45 1/8	13	12	7 6/8	7 6/8	12	14	Buckinghorse River, B. C.	Fain J. Little	Fain J. Little	1967	219
199 2/8	52 4/8	37 1/8	37 6/8	15 3/8	15 5/8	7 2/8	6 7/8	14	18	Glaslyn, Sask.	Allan Johnson	Allan Johnson	1956	220
199 2/8	63	38 7/8	37 1/8	14 1/8	15 1/8	7 3/8	7 3/8	10	14	English River, Ont.	Melvin Vetse	Melvin Vetse	1969	220
199 2/8	57 4/8	41 5/8	43 7/8	11 3/8	12 2/8	6 7/8	7 1/8	11	11	Pasco Hills, Sask.	Mac B. Ford	Mac B. Ford	1969	220
199 2/8	53 4/8	38 4/8	40	13 4/8	13	7 3/8	7 5/8	14	14	Kluayaz Lake, B.C.	William F. Jury	William F. Jury	1970	220
199 1/8	55 3/8	39 5/8	37	12 2/8	12 6/8	7 5/8	7 6/8	15	15	Mayerthorpe, Alta.	Unknown	Bennie Ziemmer	——	224
199 1/8	57 3/8	37 6/8	36 4/8	13	12 7/8	7 4/8	7 7/8	14	14	Dixonville, Alta.	Edward W. Filpula	Edward W. Filpula	1977	224
199	58 6/8	38	35 4/8	16	17	7 5/8	7 6/8	12	11	Hornepayne, Ont.	Harry T. Young	Harry T. Young	1967	226
199	57 4/8	38 4/8	37 4/8	14 3/8	14	7 2/8	7 4/8	12	16	Stikine River, B. C.	Francis O. N. Morris	Francis O. N. Morris	1968	226
199	61 6/8	36 6/8	35 5/8	12	13 2/8	8	8	14	13	Timmons, Ont.	Domenic Ripepiv	Domenic Ripepiv	1968	226
198 7/8	56 5/8	41 7/8	43	13 7/8	11 7/8	7 3/8	7 3/8	12	10	Hotchkiss, Alta.	R. A. Anderson	R. A. Anderson	1960	229
198 7/8	54 5/8	42 2/8	39 3/8	14 4/8	16 4/8	8 2/8	8 3/8	11	10	Monkman Pass, B. C.	A. E. Haddrell	A. E. Haddrell	1971	229
198 7/8	54 5/8	37 2/8	37 3/8	13	13 2/8	6 7/8	6 7/8	15	15	Manning, Alta.	Eugene G. McGee	Eugene G. McGee	1975	229
198 6/8	62 6/8	40 7/8	40 5/8	14 7/8	12 5/8	7 6/8	7 7/8	7	10	Prophet River, B. C.	Lyle Nosler	Douglas Nosler	1964	232
198 6/8	52	40 6/8	39 4/8	14	13 1/8	6 6/8	7	14	15	Prophet River, B. C.	T. D. Braden	T. D. Braden	1973	232
198 5/8	61 3/8	39 3/8	36	12 6/8	13 6/8	7 7/8	8	12	12	Stoney Lake, B. C.	George Kalischuk	George Kalischuk	1962	234
198 4/8	62 2/8	36 4/8	36 7/8	13 5/8	13	6 6/8	6 5/8	12	15	Serpentine Lake, B.C.	Randolph P. Wilson	Randolph P. Wilson	1976	235
198 3/8	53 5/8	43 3/8	39 6/8	17 4/8	18 5/8	7 1/8	7 2/8	8	11	Robb, B. C.	Bernholdt R. Nystrom	Bernholdt R. Nystrom	1973	236
198 3/8	60 3/8	40 3/8	43	10 5/8	12 7/8	7	7 2/8	11	12	Besa River, B.C.	Tommy D. Prance	Tommy D. Prance	1977	236
198 2/8	57 4/8	38	38 6/8	12 2/8	12	7 3/8	7 3/8	14	17	Whitecourt, Alta.	Glen Cox	Richard Jensen	1960	238
198 2/8	54 2/8	39 6/8	41 5/8	13 2/8	14	7	7	14	12	Beale Lake, B. C.	John O. Forster	John O. Forster	1963	238
198 2/8	53 4/8	43 6/8	42 2/8	12 2/8	12 6/8	6 7/8	7 1/8	11	11	Prairie River, B. C.	C. J. McElroy	C. J. McElroy	1967	238
198 2/8	59 4/8	36 5/8	41 5/8	17	15 6/8	7	7 1/8	11	14	Lake Co., Minn.	Dennis P. & Hugh Bradley	Dennis P. & Hugh Bradley	1973	238
198 1/8	56 5/8	42	43 2/8	12 1/8	13 2/8	7 7/8	7 5/8	10	9	Sask.	Neil Oliver	Neil Oliver	1954	242
198 1/8	56 3/8	40	40	12 7/8	11 6/8	7 1/8	7 2/8	13	12	Dore Lake, Sask.	O. Dore	O. Dore	1966	242
198 1/8	63 5/8	40 3/8	34	12 4/8	17	7 6/8	8 6/8	13	15	Chapleau, Ont.	Chester Anderegg	Chester Anderegg	1968	242
198 1/8	58 1/8	43 1/8	39	15	16 7/8	7	7 2/8	11	9	McCloud River, Alta.	Kenneth Campbell	Kenneth Campbell	1971	242
198	62 2/8	37 3/8	38 4/8	12 1/8	11 4/8	7	7	13	12	Cold Fish Lake, B. C.	Dan Edwards	Dan Edwards	1961	246

CANADA MOOSE–*Continued*

Alces alces americana and *Alces alces andersoni*

Score	Greatest Spread	Length of Palm R.	Length of Palm L.	Width of Palm R.	Width of Palm L.	Circumference of Beam at Smallest Place R.	Circumference of Beam at Smallest Place L.	Number of Normal Points R.	Number of Normal Points L.	Locality Killed	By Whom Killed	Owner	Date Killed	Rank
198	57	37	37 2/8	13	14 3/8	6 4/8	6 4/8	14	15	Hardwood Lake, Ont.	Weston Cook	Weston Cook	1963	246
198	56 4/8	38 3/8	36 3/8	15 7/8	14 6/8	7 5/8	7 6/8	12	14	Crooked Lake, B.C.	J. W. Cornwall	J. W. Cornwall	1977	246
198	63 2/8	37	36 2/8	14 2/8	15	7	6 7/8	10	11	Upper Besa River, B.C.	Lloyd Schoenauer	Lloyd Schoenauer	1977	246
197 7/8	55 7/8	44 1/8	40 6/8	11 5/8	13 3/8	7 6/8	7 5/8	11	11	Prophet River, B. C.	Paul W. Sharp	Paul W. Sharp	1963	250
197 7/8	59 7/8	39 6/8	40 1/8	11 4/8	12	7 6/8	7 6/8	10	11	Pink Mt., B. C.	Robert H. Ruth	Robert H. Ruth	1964	250
197 7/8	62 5/8	39	39	11 6/8	10 5/8	8	8 1/8	12	10	Swan Plain, Sask.	Gene Petryshyn	Gene Petryshyn	1971	250
197 7/8	56 3/8	40 2/8	40 7/8	14	15	7 5/8	7 4/8	9	9	Sikanni Chief River, B. C.	Nicholas M. Esposito	Nicholas M. Esposito	1974	250
197 6/8	63 6/8	38 7/8	41 7/8	10 4/8	10 3/8	6 7/8	6 6/8	12	11	Willow Creek, Alta.	Helmut Vollmer	Helmut Vollmer	1960	254
197 6/8	52	37 2/8	39 3/8	14 2/8	13 4/8	7 1/8	7 1/8	15	15	Marion Lake, B. C.	Virgil W. Binkley	Virgil W. Binkley	1964	254
197 6/8	59 6/8	34 5/8	36 6/8	14 4/8	12 4/8	7	6 7/8	15	16	Pipestone River, Ont.	Howard E. Bennett	Howard E. Bennett	1973	254
197 5/8	56 7/8	42 1/8	38 2/8	13 1/8	13 2/8	7 2/8	7	12	12	Glaslyn, Sask.	Ernest Noble	Ernest Noble	1960	257
197 4/8	57 2/8	42 5/8	41 5/8	10 4/8	14 1/8	7	7	11	15	Telegraph Creek, B. C.	Gordon Best	Gordon Best	1968	258
197 4/8	51 4/8	36 4/8	37 1/8	16 4/8	17 2/8	8	8	12	15	Cassiar Mts., B. C.	Russell H. Underdahl	Russell H. Underdahl	1968	258
197 4/8	56 2/8	39 3/8	39 4/8	13 6/8	13	7 2/8	7 3/8	14	11	Atlin, B. C.	John Konrad	John Konrad	1973	258
197 4/8	54 4/8	41	42 4/8	12 2/8	12	7 4/8	7 6/8	11	13	Dease River, B. C.	Terry Jackson	Terry Jackson	1975	258
197 3/8	58 1/8	40 1/8	41 7/8	13 7/8	13 4/8	8	8	11	8	Sikanni Chief River, B. C.	Leslie Bowling	Leslie Bowling	1962	262
197 3/8	48 3/8	43 4/8	47 4/8	13	11 2/8	7 6/8	7 6/8	12	12	Cabin Lake, B. C.	W. Harrison	W. Harrison	1964	262
197 3/8	57 5/8	41 3/8	38 3/8	13 2/8	16 1/8	7 2/8	7 2/8	11	15	Firth Lake, B. C.	Gordon J. Pengelly	Gordon J. Pengelly	1973	262
197 3/8	50 1/8	39 7/8	39 5/8	13	13 2/8	7 1/8	7	14	14	Fleming Lake, B.C.	Peter Holland	Peter Holland	1976	262
197 2/8	56 4/8	37 6/8	38 4/8	10 6/8	12 2/8	7 7/8	8 2/8	14	15	Jackfish Lake, Alta.	Unknown	Ovar Uggen	1955	266
197 2/8	50 4/8	40 5/8	43 4/8	13	16 2/8	7 6/8	7 6/8	12	15	Terminus Mt., B. C.	Basil C. Bradbury	Basil C. Bradbury	1962	266
197 2/8	50	44	43 5/8	14 4/8	17 4/8	7 4/8	7 4/8	8	8	Liard Plateau, B. C.	George Roberts	George Roberts	1970	266
197 1/8	56 5/8	40 4/8	38 1/8	13 4/8	13 3/8	7 6/8	7 7/8	11	13	Tisdale, Sask.	Bill Hrechka	Bill Hrechka	1960	269
197 1/8	54 7/8	38 4/8	43 2/8	12 7/8	15 4/8	6 6/8	6 6/8	13	14	Pink Mt., B. C.	Allison R. Smith	Allison R. Smith	1963	269
197	57 6/8	38	38 4/8	11 2/8	11 2/8	7 3/8	7 4/8	13	13	Cold Fish Lake, B. C.	George W. Hale	George W. Hale	1967	271
197	54 2/8	40	39 1/8	17 4/8	15 3/8	7 2/8	6 7/8	11	10	Brothers Lake, B. C.	William D. Phifer	William D. Phifer	1971	271
197	60 6/8	39 3/8	37 4/8	12 6/8	12 1/8	7 4/8	7 5/8	11	13	Swan Lake, B. C.	Carl E. Larson	Wild Kingdom Tax.	1975	271
196 7/8	58 7/8	36 3/8	38 5/8	13 5/8	12 5/8	7	7	13	14	Weeks, Sask.	Ken Holloway	Ken Holloway	1961	274
196 7/8	54 1/8	39 5/8	39 4/8	14 7/8	13 3/8	7 5/8	7 4/8	11	13	Slave Lake, Alta.	Kathleen Wickersham	Ernest Wickersham	1967	274
196 7/8	50 7/8	39 5/8	41 2/8	20 4/8	13 7/8	7 4/8	7	13	13	Cassiar Mts., B.C.	Larry Herwick	Larry Herwick	1979	274

The table below lists big-game records (Owner, locality, measurements, date, and rank).

Score										Locality	Owner	By whom killed	Date	Rank
196 5/8	49 5/8	43	44	14 5/8	12 5/8	6 7/8	6 5/8	15	11	Hines Creek, Alta.	Harry Kashuba	Harry Kashuba	1959	277
196 5/8	57	40 7/8	39 7/8	13 7/8	14 1/8	7 7/8	7 7/8	9	11	Atlin, B. C.	Dennis Downton	Dennis Downton	1969	277
196 5/8	58 5/8	41 1/8	40 1/8	11 7/8	15 7/8	7	7 3/8	13	10	Stoney Lake, B. C.	George Kalischuk	George Kalischuk	1963	279
196 5/8	53 3/8	42 3/8	43 7/8	12	12 3/8	7 7/8	7 7/8	10	11	Atlin, B. C.	Ernest Wilfong	Ernest Wilfong	1965	279
196 5/8	50 3/8	42 3/8	42 7/8	15 1/8	11 5/8	8 7/8	8 3/8	13	11	Cassiar, B. C.	Richard Pain	Richard Pain	1967	279
196 5/8	53 3/8	42 3/8	40 3/8	14 1/8	13 5/8	6 7/8	6 5/8	11	13	Medicine Lake, Alta.	Stan Reiser	Stan Reiser	1967	279
196 5/8	57 3/8	40 7/8	39 7/8	11 3/8	11 3/8	7 5/8	7 3/8	12	11	Telegraph Creek, B. C.	Paul Inzanti, Jr.	Paul Inzanti, Jr.	1969	279
196 5/8	46 5/8	37	37 7/8	18 1/8	18 1/8	8	7 5/8	12	13	Belcourt Lake, B. C.	Robert Agnello	Robert Agnello	1965	284
196 5/8	50 3/8	39 5/8	43 3/8	14	14	7 3/8	7 3/8	13	12	Perrault Falls, Ont.	A. H. Nettleship	A. H. Nettleship	1967	284
196 4/8	56 3/8	38 3/8	41 3/8	12	12 3/8	7 5/8	7 3/8	12	13	Sikanni Chief River, B. C.	W. C. Spencer	W. C. Spencer	1970	284
196 4/8	56 3/8	39 3/8	39 3/8	11 3/8	12 1/8	7 3/8	7 3/8	14	12	Kula Tan Tan River, B. C.	Arnold J. Kaslon	Arnold J. Kaslon	1972	284
196 4/8	53 3/8	43 3/8	38 7/8	14 3/8	14 7/8	7 7/8	7 1/8	11	13	Turnagain River, B. C.	George H. Biddle	George H. Biddle	1973	284
196 4/8	45 3/8	42 3/8	44 3/8	13 1/8	16 5/8	7 1/8	7 1/8	13	13	Pink Mt., B. C.	Gary Bloxham	Gary Bloxham	1973	284
196 4/8	60	36 7/8	36 7/8	16 3/8	17 3/8	7 5/8	7 5/8	9	8	Lake Co., Minn.	Roy H. Anderson	Roy H. Anderson	1977	284
196 3/8	59 3/8	38 3/8	41 3/8	10 3/8	11 3/8	8 3/8	8 3/8	12	12	Abitibi Co., Ont.	Pelham Glasier	Pelham Glasier	1951	291
196 3/8	52 3/8	41 3/8	43 3/8	12 3/8	12 7/8	7 3/8	7 3/8	11	11	Green Lake, Sask.	Mike Spies	Mike Spies	1959	291
196 3/8	58 1/8	38 3/8	37 7/8	15 3/8	14 1/8	7 3/8	7 3/8	10	11	Cassiar Mts., B. C.	E. David Slye	E. David Slye	1967	291
196 3/8	55 3/8	43	45 3/8	13 3/8	12 3/8	7	7	10	8	Anguille Mts., Nfld.	Robert D. Smith	Robert D. Smith	1963	294
196 2/8	59	39 3/8	39 3/8	12 3/8	16 3/8	6 7/8	6 7/8	10	10	Jack Pine, Ont.	William Picht	William Picht	1963	294
196 1/8	55 3/8	37 7/8	37 7/8	16 3/8	15 3/8	7	7 1/8	10	12	Cassiar Mts., B. C.	Bryan Upchurch	Bryan Upchurch	1975	294
196 1/8	55 3/8	36 5/8	37	15 7/8	16 5/8	7 5/8	7 3/8	11	13	Endeavor, Sask.	G. N. Galbraith	G. N. Galbraith	1955	297
196 1/8	55 7/8	42 3/8	39 3/8	13 7/8	13 7/8	7 3/8	7 3/8	10	16	Jack Pine River, Ont.	M. H. Brown	M. H. Brown	1962	297
196 1/8	56 1/8	38	38 3/8	13 3/8	12 3/8	6 5/8	6 5/8	13	14	Atlin, B. C.	Cliff Schmidt	Cliff Schmidt	1966	297
196 1/8	49 3/8	42 3/8	42 3/8	11 3/8	11 3/8	7	7	13	13	Atlin, B. C.	H. J. Schwegler	H. J. Schwegler	1967	297
196	52 3/8	41 5/8	40 3/8	15 5/8	14 3/8	7 3/8	7 3/8	10	12	Frog River, B. C.	Robert McMurray	Robert McMurray	1968	297
195 7/8	51 5/8	38 3/8	37 7/8	14 1/8	12 3/8	7 3/8	7 3/8	15	16	Ft. St. John, B. C.	Kanton R. Flemming	Kanton R. Flemming	1975	297
195 7/8	56 3/8	38 7/8	39 5/8	13 3/8	14 5/8	8	7 1/8	11	13	Pelican River, B. C.	Douglas A. Stoller	Douglas A. Stoller	1971	303
195 5/8	56 3/8	37 7/8	40 3/8	12 5/8	13 5/8	7 7/8	7 7/8	13	12	Cassiar Mts., B. C.	Donald F. Conway	Donald F. Conway	1965	304
195 5/8	54 1/8	39	38	14	13 5/8	7 1/8	7 1/8	13	13	Sheep Creek, Alta.	S. J. Blaupot Ten Cate	S. J. Blaupot Ten Cate	1966	304
195 5/8	56	38 3/8	39 1/8	11 3/8	13 3/8	8 1/8	8 1/4	15	12	Prophet River, B. C.	Earl Mumaw	Earl Mumaw	1957	306
195 5/8	53 3/8	37 5/8	39 3/8	12 7/8	13 5/8	7 3/8	7	13	14	Hudson Bay, Sask.	Charles Hamilton	Charles Hamilton	1964	306
195 5/8	59	44	43 3/8	13 3/8	13 3/8	7	7 3/8	10	14	Smoky River, Alta.	Ken G. Johnson	Ken G. Johnson	1966	306
195 4/8	56 3/8	42 3/8	39 3/8	13 3/8	13 5/8	7 3/8	7 3/8	11	14	Ft. St. John, B. C.	Louis M. Soetebeer	Louis M. Soetebeer	1969	306
195 4/8	58	37 3/8	37 7/8	15 1/8	15 3/8	7 7/8	7 3/8	9	12	Pasqua Hills, Sask.	Henry Dyck	Henry Dyck	1955	310
195 4/8	65 3/8	39	40 1/2	11 3/8	11 3/8	7 3/8	7 3/8	9	13	Sheep Creek, Alta.	H. C. Early	H. C. Early	1957	310
195 4/8	57 3/8	38 3/8	39 3/8	12 3/8	13 3/8	8	8	11	10	Blanchard River, B. C.	William E. Lauffer	William E. Lauffer	1969	310
195 3/8	61	37 5/8	36 7/8	13 3/8	13 3/8	7 7/8	7 7/8	10	13	Whitecourt, Alta.	John E. Esslinger	John E. Esslinger	1971	310
195 3/8	54 5/8	38 7/8	39 3/8	13 3/8	13 3/8	8	8 1/8	13	10	Stikine River, B. C.	Manfred Beier	Manfred Beier	1976	310
195 3/8	63 3/8	36 5/8	37 1/8	14 3/8	13 3/8	7 1/8	7 1/8	9	9	Trembleur Lake, B. C.	Harry McCarter	Harry McCarter	1965	315
195 3/8	57 3/8	38 5/8	39 5/8	12 3/8	12 5/8	7 5/8	7	10	10	Atlin, B. C.	Jerome A. Ree	Jerome A. Ree	1965	315
195 3/8	52 5/8	39 5/8	38 5/8	13	12 5/8	6 7/8	6 7/8	13	14	Prophet River, B. C.	Ronald B. Sorensen	Ronald B. Sorensen	1967	315
195 3/8	54 1/8	38 5/8	40 1/8	12 5/8	12 5/8	7 7/8	7 7/8	12	12	Ketchika Mts., B. C.	Frank S. Kohar	Frank S. Kohar	1968	315

CANADA MOOSE—Continued
Alces alces americana and Alces alces andersoni

Score	Greatest Spread	Length of Palm R.	Length of Palm L.	Width of Palm R.	Width of Palm L.	Circumference of Beam at Smallest Place R.	Circumference of Beam at Smallest Place L.	Number of Normal Points R.	Number of Normal Points L.	Locality Killed	By Whom Killed	Owner	Date Killed	Rank
195 3/8	60	39 2/8	39 7/8	12 7/8	11 1/8	7 3/8	7 7/8	13	10	Atlin, B. C.	Wilbert Hoffman	Wildlife Tax. Studios	1966	319
195 3/8	57 5/8	39 7/8	42 7/8	12 7/8	13 5/8	7 4/8	7 5/8	11	9	B. C.	Len Anderson	Len Anderson	1967	319
195 3/8	60	33 3/8	39 7/8	14 5/8	19 5/8	7 3/8	7 7/8	15	12	Ignace, Ont.	Ervey W. Smith	Ervey W. Smith	1969	319
195 3/8	56 2/8	41 5/8	40	10 3/8	13	7 1/8	7 7/8	14	12	Blanchard River, B. C.	Pat Archibald	Pat Archibald	1969	319
195 3/8	59 2/8	38 1/8	40	14 5/8	14 3/8	8 4/8	8 4/8	13	7	Lake Nipigon, B. C.	Danny E. Breivogel	Danny E. Breivogel	1974	319
195 3/8	50 2/8	39 6/8	41 5/8	13 3/4	13 5/8	7 3/8	7 3/8	15	11	Ospika River, B.C.	John L. Fullmer	John L. Fullmer	1977	319
195 1/8	55 1/8	40	42 6/8	13	12 2/8	7 7/8	7 5/8	14	10	Berland River, Alta.	W. C. Kadatz	W. C. Kadatz	1962	325
195 1/8	55 3/8	39 5/8	39 1/8	11 5/8	11 5/8	8 1/8	7 5/8	11	12	Hudson Bay, Sask.	Walter Sukkau	Walter Sukkau	1964	325
195 1/8	56 3/8	38 5/8	39 1/8	13 7/8	14 7/8	7	6 7/8	11	10	B. C.	Charles Waugaman	Charles Waugaman	1969	325
195	57 7/8	34 3/8	38 3/8	14 5/8	14	7 6/8	7 7/8	13	15	Little Codroy Pond, Nfld.	J. Russell Allison	J. Russell Allison	1957	327
195	57 5/8	37 1/8	38 3/8	11 5/8	12 5/8	6 3/8	6 5/8	13	14	Turner Valley, Alta.	Bart Rockwell	Bart Rockwell	1958	327
195	58	37 1/8	42 1/8	13 1/8	12 7/8	7 2/8	7 3/8	11	13	Pontiac Co., Que.	Roger Cashdollar	Roger Cashdollar	1966	327
195	52	41 1/8	40	14	15 7/8	7 7/8	8	10	13	Houston, B. C.	R. Starnes	R. Starnes	1966	327

*Final Score subject to revision by additional verifying measurements.

NEW WORLD'S RECORD ALASKA-YUKON MOOSE
SCORE: 255

Locality: McGrath, Alaska. Date: 1978.
Hunter and owner: Kenneth Best

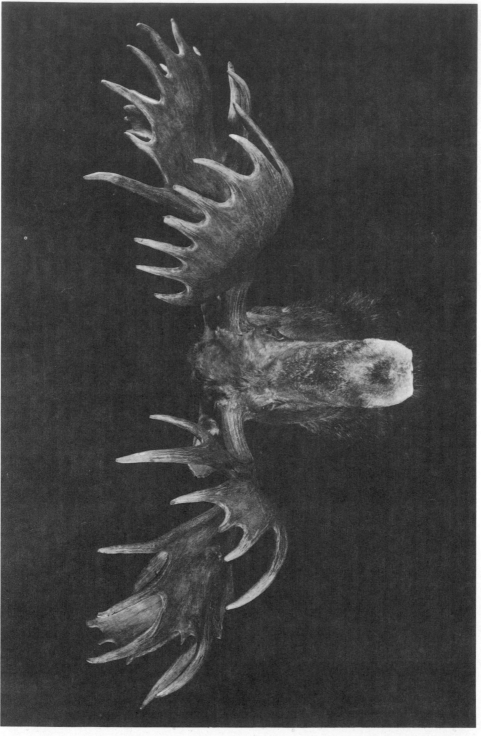

NUMBER TWO ALASKA-YUKON MOOSE
SCORE: 251
Locality: Mount Susitna, Alaska. Date: 1961.
Hunter and owner: Bert Klineburger.

Alaska-Yukon Moose

Alces alces gigas

Minimum Score 224

Alaska-Yukon moose includes trophies from Alaska, the Yukon Territory, and the Northwest Territories.

Score	Greatest Spread	Length of Palm R.	Length of Palm L.	Width of Palm R.	Width of Palm L.	Circumference of Beam at Smallest Place R.	Circumference of Beam at Smallest Place L.	Number of Normal Points R.	Number of Normal Points L.	Locality Killed	By Whom Killed	Owner	Date Killed	Rank
255	77	49 5/8	49 6/8	20 6/8	15 6/8	7 7/8	7 5/8	18	16	McGrath, Alaska	Kenneth Best	Kenneth Best	1978	1
251	77 4/8	46 3/8	51	17	29 6/8	7 7/8	8 1/8	18	17	Mt. Susitna, Alaska	Bert Klineburger	Bert Klineburger	1961	2
250 3/8	65 1/8	55 2/8	49 2/8	21 1/8	20	8 3/8	8 3/8	18	16	Kenai Pen., Alaska	Dyton A. Gilliland	National Collection	1947	3
249 6/8	67	47 7/8	48 2/8	22 1/8	21 1/8	7 3/8	7 5/8	15	15	Mother Goose Lake, Alaska	Josef Welle	Josef Welle	1967	4
249 2/8	72	48 4/8	49 6/8	19 2/8	17	8 1/8	8 5/8	15	16	Alaska Range, Alaska	Henry S. Budney	Henry S. Budney	1967	5
248 7/8	73 1/8	47 4/8	47 1/8	20	19 2/8	7 4/8	7 4/8	14	19	Farewell Lake, Alaska	Loren G. Hammer	Loren G. Hammer	1967	6
248 5/8	68 7/8	54 3/8	46 5/8	19 6/8	19 5/8	7 5/8	8	17	16	Kenai Pen., Alaska	Bill Foster	Foster's Bighorn Rest.	1912	7
248 1/8	77 5/8	47 5/8	48 5/8	18 3/8	18 6/8	8 2/8	8 3/8	13	16	Mulchatna River, Alaska	Bruce B. Hodson	Bruce B. Hodson	1970	8
247 4/8	79 6/8	45 7/8	46 1/8	22 1/8	22 6/8	9	8 7/8	10	7	Iliamna Lake, Alaska	Gale L. Galloway	Gale L. Galloway	1970	9
247 2/8	66 4/8	48	48	18 4/8	19	7 7/8	7 7/8	17	16	Mackenzie Mts., N.W.T.	Harry Rogers	Harry Rogers	1978	10
247	75	50	46 6/8	17 6/8	21 5/8	7 4/8	8 1/8	15	18	Kenai Pen., Alaska	A. S. Reed	National Collection	1900	11
246 5/8	77 5/8	48 7/8	48 4/8	16	17 6/8	7 5/8	7 4/8	13	15	Melozitna River, Alaska	Elmer Raphael	Elmer Raphael	1978	12
246 3/8	67 5/8	44 5/8	49 5/8	22 2/8	20 3/8	10 2/8	9 3/8	19	16	Kenai Pen., Alaska	Henry Hope	Henry Hope	1957	13
246 1/8	75 3/8	48	46 2/8	18 6/8	19 5/8	8 3/8	8 5/8	12	16	Alaska Range, Alaska	Ralph Davies	Ralph Davies	1970	14
245 6/8	72 2/8	46 3/8	46 3/8	17	17 4/8	7 3/8	7 4/8	16	17	Wrangell Mts., Alaska	Philip S. Davidson	Philip S. Davidson	1970	15
244 4/8	67 4/8	51 2/8	49 1/8	20	18 2/8	8 6/8	8 5/8	13	14	Talkeetna Mts., Alaska	Wm. H. Moore	Wm. H. Moore	1953	16
244 3/8	72 3/8	48 6/8	47 2/8	19 4/8	19 7/8	7 2/8	7 3/8	12	12	Long Lake, Alaska	William F. Rae, Jr.	William F. Rae, Jr.	1973	17
243 6/8	71 6/8	49 4/8	48 4/8	14 4/8	17 2/8	7 6/8	7 4/8	16	17	Mayo, Yukon	Carl Straub	Carl Straub	1971	18
243 6/8	69 4/8	49 6/8	50 6/8	15 6/8	21 1/8	8 1/8	7 5/8	17	14	Wrangell Mts., Alaska	John Ringstad	Loren St. Amand	1977	18
243	70	47 2/8	50 5/8	19 5/8	20 2/8	7 6/8	7 5/8	15	12	Kenai Pen., Alaska	Frank Walunga & Denny Thompson	Denny Thompson	1958	20
242 6/8	63 6/8	51 4/8	50 4/8	16 7/8	16 7/8	8	7 5/8	16	15	Alaska	Unknown	Jonas Bros. Of Seattle	1954	21
242 4/8	69 2/8	46 1/8	49 2/8	15 6/8	15 6/8	8 6/8	8 6/8	16	17	Upper Susitna, Alaska	Helen S. Rusten	Carnegie Museum	1948	22
242 1/8	78 7/8	44 4/8	44	19 4/8	21 7/8	8 4/8	8 1/8	11	11	Alaska Pen., Alaska	H. S. Kamil	H. S. Kamil	1963	23
242	73 6/8	48 5/8	45 5/8	19 6/8	19 6/8	8	7 6/8	15	11	Homer, Alaska	Dan Jones	Dan Jones	1957	24
241 5/8	72 5/8	49 6/8	48 3/8	16 7/8	16	8 5/8	9	12	16	Neresna, Alaska	Lorene Ellis	Lorene Ellis	1962	25
241 5/8	67 5/8	46 5/8	46 7/8	19 1/8	16 3/8	8 2/8	8	16	16	Dawson City, Yukon	Ray C. Dillman	Ray C. Dillman	1971	25

ALASKA-YUKON MOOSE–*Continued*

Alces alces gigas

Score	Greatest Spread	Length of Palm R.	Length of Palm L.	Width of Palm R.	Width of Palm L.	Circumference of Beam at Smallest Place R.	Circumference of Beam at Smallest Place L.	Number of Normal Points R.	Number of Normal Points L.	Locality Killed	By Whom Killed	Owner	Date Killed	Rank
241 4/8	76 6/8	47	47 2/8	16 4/8	15 3/8	8	8 2/8	14	12	King Salmon, Alaska	Orel O. Parker & Bill Bradley	Orel O. Parker & Bill Bradley	1960	27
240 5/8	80 5/8	43 4/8	43 2/8	18 6/8	16 2/8	8 5/8	8 4/8	13	12	Redout Bay, Alaska	Glenn B. Walker	Glenn B. Walker	1958	28
240 4/8	71 4/8	43 6/8	51 3/8	21 6/8	20 7/8	9	8 7/8	11	15	Ugashik Lake, Alaska	Gene Buckles	Gene Buckles	1973	29
240 2/8	64 6/8	48 4/8	42 5/8	17 4/8	20 5/8	8 5/8	9	21	21	Noatak River, Alaska	Jake & Mae Jacobson	Jake & Mae Jacobson	1974	30
240 1/8	66 3/8	49 6/8	47 5/8	15 4/8	18 4/8	7 6/8	7 6/8	16	17	Wrangell Mts., Alaska	Forest Bigelow	Forest Bigelow	1973	31
240	62 4/8	48 4/8	49 3/8	16 5/8	21	7 5/8	8 1/8	16	18	Beluga Mt., Alaska	Walter Renz	Walter Renz	1976	32
239 6/8	66 6/8	47 3/8	46 3/8	17 7/8	21 1/8	8 2/8	8 2/8	14	16	Rainy Pass, Alaska	Mrs. J. Watson Webb	Mrs. J. Watson Webb	1935	33
239 6/8	75 4/8	44 5/8	43 4/8	21 6/8	19 4/8	7 5/8	7 6/8	12	18	Mayo, Yukon	Dave Moses	Yukon Hist. Society	1950	33
239 6/8	70	52 7/8	47 6/8	14 7/8	21 5/8	8 2/8	8 2/8	15	14	Alaska Range, Alaska	James E. Egger	James E. Egger	1965	33
239 5/8	75 7/8	42	45 2/8	20 2/8	19	8	7 7/8	13	16	Gold King, Alaska	Billy Joe Morris	Billy Joe Morris	1971	36
239 4/8	62 4/8	53 4/8	56	16 1/8	20 4/8	8 7/8	8 7/8	11	10	Alaska Pen., Alaska	Lars Degefors	Lars Degefors	1967	37
239 4/8	74	44 7/8	45 2/8	17 3/8	15 1/8	9 2/8	8 6/8	14	14	Bonnet Plume Range, Yukon	Tafford E. Oltz	Tafford E. Oltz	1978	37
239 3/8	65 7/8	47 4/8	47 2/8	20 6/8	14 6/8	7 6/8	7 6/8	18	17	Alaska Pen., Alaska	J. Paul Dittrich	J. Paul Dittrich	1962	39
239 2/8	67	45 1/8	48 1/8	15	14 7/8	12 1/8	12 5/8	14	14	Baluga Lake, Alaska	Peter W. Bading	Peter W. Bading	1961	40
239 2/8	74	51 2/8	50 4/8	13 7/8	15	8 2/8	8 2/8	10	13	Alaska Pen., Alaska	George J. Markham	George J. Markham	1967	40
239 2/8	73 4/8	49 6/8	52 4/8	14 6/8	16 7/8	8 7/8	8 7/8	12	12	Ugashik, Alaska	Alois A. Mauracher	Alois A. Mauracher	1973	40
239	67	46 1/8	48 6/8	18 3/8	16 4/8	8 4/8	8 3/8	15	15	Mackenzie Mts., N. W. T.	Burl A. Jones	Burl A. Jones	1973	43
238 3/8	71 1/8	44	48	19 3/8	17 6/8	7 7/8	9 6/8	14	14	Lake Clark, Alaska	Frits Kielman	Frits Kielman	1973	44
238 2/8	72 4/8	46 3/8	45 6/8	18	22 1/8	8 1/8	8 4/8	11	13	Alaska Range, Alaska	Jeff Sievers	Jeff Sievers	1963	45
238 2/8	63 6/8	44	45 2/8	19 7/8	20 5/8	8 3/8	8 4/8	16	17	Anvil Range, Yukon	James F. Byers	James F. Byers	1977	45
238 1/8	74 5/8	43 5/8	43 2/8	21 4/8	25	8 5/8	8 4/8	9	16	Iliamna, Alaska	Joseph C. Anzalone	Joseph C. Anzalone	1972	47
238	69	48 4/8	47	17 6/8	17 5/8	9	8 7/8	11	15	Copper River, Alaska	Howard E. Thilenius, II	Howard E. Thilenius, II	1973	48
238	70 6/8	46 4/8	44 6/8	16	16 1/8	7 7/8	7 7/8	15	15	Mulchatna River, Alaska	Gary A. Smith	Gary A. Smith	1974	48
237 7/8	77 1/8	45 3/8	42 3/8	19 6/8	18 3/8	8 5/8	9	11	11	Dog Salmon River, Alaska	Peter Von Kap-Herr	Peter Von Kap-Herr	1971	50
237 3/8	67 1/8	46	48 2/8	18 3/8	18 1/8	8	8	17	13	Kenai Pen., Alaska	Leslie Maff	Temple Bros.	——	51
237	69 2/8	49 1/8	47 7/8	15 4/8	15 6/8	8 4/8	8 4/8	13	12	Talkeetna Mts., Alaska	Merle C. LaFortune	Merle C. LaFortune	1970	52
236 7/8	67 5/8	46 3/8	47 6/8	15 6/8	18 7/8	8 4/8	9	14	15	Talkeetna Mts., Alaska	Mario Pasquel	Mario Pasquel	1961	53
236 7/8	68 1/8	48 1/8	48 3/8	14 2/8	14 1/8	8 2/8	8 1/8	14	14	Baluga Mt., Alaska	Albert W. Erickson	Albert W. Erickson	1961	53
236 7/8	67 5/8	42 4/8	43	22	21 1/8	8	8 2/8	15	13	Koyukuk River, Alaska	Harry B. Markoskie	Harry B. Markoskie	1969	53

Score									Locality	By whom killed	Owner	Date killed	Rank
236 7/8	62 7/8	45 5/8	46 3/8	22 3/8	21 1/8	7 7/8	14	13	Kiana Lake, Alaska	Lane H. Drury	Lane H. Drury	1977	53
236 6/8	64 4/8	53 5/8	51	13 5/8	14	8 5/8	15	13	Susitna River, Alaska	T. A. Miller	T. A. Miller	1960	57
236 6/8	68 5/8	46 5/8	49 5/8	16 5/8	17 7/8	8 1/8	14	13	Wood River, Alaska	Ronald Long	Ronald Long	1963	58
236 3/8	70 5/8	44 5/8	45 5/8	16 5/8	17 1/8	7 6/8	14	18	Lake Clark, Alaska	Gordon F. Wentzel	Gordon F. Wentzel	1973	58
236 3/8	68 5/8	46 3/8	52 5/8	18 5/8	16 5/8	8 5/8	14	16	Brusha Kama River, Alaska	Robert Harnish	Robert Harnish	1953	60
236 3/8	72	47	41 5/8	16 5/8	18 1/8	8 1/8	16	17	Upper Kiana Lake, Alaska	Marvin Henriksen	Marvin Henriksen	1964	60
236 1/8	66 7/8	44 3/8	43 5/8	16 3/8	18 1/8	8 1/8	17	20	Birch Creek, Alaska	D. T. Sharp	D. T. Sharp	1962	62
236 1/8	70 7/8	47 5/8	48	14 5/8	15 5/8	7 5/8	14	13	Black Lake, Alaska	Robert B. Ryan	Robert B. Ryan	1969	62
235 7/8	73 5/8	50 5/8	46 5/8	16 5/8	17 5/8	3 3/8	10	10	Dog Salmon River, Alaska	Gary R. Swanson	Gary R. Swanson	1966	64
235 7/8	69 3/8	50	50 5/8	17 5/8	15 5/8	7 5/8	11	10	Farewell Lake, Alaska	Wilhelm Heinz Koehler	Wilhelm Heinz Koehler	1974	64
235 5/8	74	44 3/8	46 5/8	15 5/8	16 5/8	8 1/8	13	13	Alaska	Frank Alexander	Univ. Of Alaska	1952	66
235 5/8	65 5/8	46 5/8	51 5/8	20 5/8	21 5/8	8 3/8	13	10	Kenai Pen., Alaska	J. D. Rasmusson	J. D. Rasmusson	1959	66
235 3/8	71 5/8	50 5/8	50 5/8	14 1/8	14 5/8	8 4/8	9	10	Rainy Pass, Alaska	Ralph Vogel	Ralph Vogel	1956	68
235 3/8	66 5/8	51 5/8	49	17 5/8	16 5/8	7 7/8	12	12	Post Lake, Alaska	Charles Bradley	Charles Bradley	1978	68
235	71	47	45	14	15 5/8	8 3/8	15	16	Alaska Pen., Alaska	Otis Chandler	Otis Chandler	1964	70
235	74	45 5/8	45 5/8	15 5/8	14 5/8	8	15	13	Yellow River, Alaska	Peter Apokedak	Peter Apokedak	1966	70
235	71	47	46	16	17	8	12	14	Kateel River, Alaska	Ronald S. Peterson	Ronald S. Peterson	1976	70
234 7/8	74 5/8	50 7/8	49 5/8	16 5/8	16 5/8	7 5/8	12	8	Hewitt Lake, Alaska	Wm. L. Braun	Wm. L. Braun	1951	73
234 5/8	62 5/8	48 5/8	45 5/8	16 5/8	17 1/8	8 3/8	18	16	Mayo Landing, Yukon	Edwin Edger	J. H. McEvoy	1962	74
234 5/8	70 5/8	43	42 5/8	18 5/8	17 5/8	7 5/8	14	16	Alaska Pen., Alaska	Herb Klein	Herb Klein	1967	74
234 5/8	66 5/8	47 5/8	44 5/8	17 5/8	16 5/8	7 7/8	16	15	Alaska	L. M. Hanson	L. M. Hanson	1969	74
234 5/8	69	47 5/8	48	18 5/8	17 5/8	8 1/8	11	12	Alaska Pen., Alaska	Robert P. Bliss	Robert P. Bliss	1969	74
234 3/8	58	52 5/8	51 5/8	16 5/8	16 5/8	8 5/8	15	11	Alaska Range, Alaska	Wakon Iron Redbird	Wakon Iron Redbird	1969	78
234 3/8	71 5/8	45 5/8	44 5/8	16 5/8	15 5/8	7 5/8	14	15	Forty Mile River, Alaska	Orval R. Evans	Orval R. Evans	1973	78
234 3/8	70 5/8	45 5/8	46 5/8	17 5/8	17 5/8	8	12	11	Koyukuk River, Alaska	Oren Johnson	Oren Johnson	1975	78
234 1/8	71 3/8	41 5/8	43 5/8	19 5/8	18 1/8	7 5/8	16	14	Galena, Alaska	Michael J. Stowell	Michael J. Stowell	1977	81
234	68 5/8	46 5/8	43 5/8	18 5/8	17 5/8	8 1/8	14	14	Ugashik Lake, Alaska	Richard C. Rubin	Richard C. Rubin	1968	82
234	75 5/8	49 5/8	48 5/8	12 5/8	14 5/8	8	10	11	King Salmon, Alaska	Larry R. Price	Larry R. Price	1971	82
233 7/8	71 1/8	43 5/8	41	17 1/8	16 5/8	7 7/8	17	16	Kenai Pen., Alaska	A. S. Reed	National Collection	1900	84
233 5/8	76	42 5/8	50 5/8	20 5/8	19 5/8	8	10	12	Kenai Pen., Alaska	Otto Rohm	Otto Rohm	1964	84
233 5/8	63	50 5/8	49 5/8	15 5/8	20 5/8	7 3/8	13	14	Wrangell Mts., Alaska	Dan L. Quen	Dan L. Quen	1965	84
233 5/8	77 5/8	41	44 1/8	18 3/8	14 5/8	7 7/8	15	18	Kenai Pen., Alaska	Picked Up	Am. Mus. Nat. History	1938	87
233 5/8	65 7/8	46 5/8	45 5/8	20	18	7 6/8	15	13	Alaska Pen., Alaska	J. S. Parker	J. S. Parker	1968	87
233 5/8	71 3/8	45 5/8	50	15 5/8	16 5/8	8 5/8	14	17	Iliamna Lake, Alaska	Wayne Rattray	Wayne Rattray	1972	87
233 5/8	71 5/8	46 5/8	48 5/8	18 5/8	16 5/8	8	11	13	McGrath, Alaska	Art Beattie	Linda Beattie	1978	87
233 3/8	74 5/8	43 5/8	42 5/8	16 5/8	16 5/8	7 5/8	13	17	Kenai Pen., Alaska	Gift Of C. H. Mackay	National Collection	—	91
233	69	48 5/8	47 5/8	15 5/8	13 5/8	8 1/8	14	14	Merrill Pass, Alaska	Andrew F. Bjorge	Andrew F. Bjorge	1963	92
233	73 5/8	49 5/8	46 5/8	15 5/8	14 5/8	7 5/8	11	12	Dillinger River, Alaska	James N. McHolme	James N. McHolme	1976	92
232 5/8	65 5/8	46 5/8	42 5/8	15 5/8	18 5/8	7 7/8	17	17	Port Heiden, Alaska	Don C. Killom	Don C. Killom	1965	94
232 5/8	75	45 5/8	44 3/8	19 5/8	17 5/8	8 5/8	10	9	Port Heiden, Alaska	Gerald L. Lavenstein	Gerald L. Lavenstein	1967	94
232 5/8	65 5/8	43 5/8	45 5/8	18 5/8	18 5/8	8 3/8	15	14	Swede Lake, Alaska	Paul Bierdeman	Paul Bierdeman	1956	96
232 5/8	70 5/8	46 5/8	47 5/8	18 5/8	15 5/8	7 5/8	12	12	Ugashik Lake, Alaska	Jack A. Shane, Sr.	Jack A. Shane, Sr.	1967	96

ALASKA-YUKON MOOSE—Continued

Alces alces gigas

Score	Greatest Spread	Length of Palm R	Length of Palm L	Width of Palm R	Width of Palm L	Circ. of Beam R	Circ. of Beam L	Points R	Points L	Locality Killed	By Whom Killed	Owner	Date Killed	Rank
232 4/8	69 4/8	45	45	18 3/8	17 5/8	6 5/8	6 5/8	13	12	Talkeetna, Alaska	Ole Dahl	Boston Mus. Of Science	1950	98
232 4/8	67 4/8	47 7/8	48 3/8	15 4/8	17 1/8	7 4/8	8	12	15	Stewart River, Yukon	Patrick Seaman	Patrick Seaman	1968	98
232 4/8	68	45 7/8	46 7/8	17 4/8	17 1/8	7 7/8	8 1/8	12	12	Teklanika River, Alaska	Richard O. Cook	Richard O. Cook	1976	98
232 4/8	71	43	43 1/8	20 1/8	17	8 5/8	8 4/8	14	12	Alaska Pen., Alaska	Stewart G. Richards	Stewart G. Richards	1968	101
232	66 4/8	47 3/8	50 4/8	17 4/8	18 3/8	7 4/8	7 4/8	10	11	Alaska Pen., Alaska	A. R. Buckles	A. R. Buckles	1967	102
232	63	55	55 3/8	14	14 4/8	7 4/8	7 4/8	8	9	Alaska Pen., Alaska	L. W. Bailey, Jr.	L. W. Bailey, Jr.	1969	102
231 7/8	63 4/8	50 4/8	49 7/8	12	12 2/8	8 4/8	8 4/8	15	14	Talkeetna Mts., Alaska	T. A. Miller	T. A. Miller	1959	104
231 5/8	76	44 4/8	44 4/8	12 4/8	15 4/8	8 4/8	8 4/8	12	14	Kenai Pen., Alaska	Gift Of C. H. Mackay	National Collection	—	105
231 5/8	64 4/8	45 7/8	51 4/8	16 5/8	18	8 2/8	9	14	15	Lake Louise, Alaska	Paul Kunning	Paul Kunning	1966	105
231 5/8	73 3/8	48 4/8	44 4/8	17	15 4/8	7 7/8	7 7/8	12	16	Alaska Range, Alaska	Cecil M. Hopper	Cecil M. Hopper	1969	107
231 4/8	67 4/8	42 4/8	45 3/8	20 5/8	26 4/8	9 4/8	8 4/8	10	12	Alaska Pen., Alaska	George H. Landreth	George H. Landreth	1967	108
231 4/8	69 4/8	43 1/8	46 2/8	17	16 5/8	6 4/8	7 1/8	18	15	Steese Hwy., Alaska	Denver Perry	Denver Perry	1968	108
231 1/8	62 4/8	44	44 7/8	17 2/8	16 7/8	7 4/8	7 4/8	16	17	Brooks Range, Alaska	Peter J. Cassinelli	Peter J. Cassinelli	1977	108
231 1/8	67	47 1/8	47 3/8	16 2/8	16	8	8	13	11	Alaska Pen., Alaska	Lezlie D. Fickes	Lezlie D. Fickes	1972	111
231 1/8	66 5/8	49 3/8	49	15 4/8	14 1/8	7 4/8	7 6/8	12	11	Alaska Pen., Alaska	Frank N. Rome	Frank N. Rome	1976	112
231	67 7/8	42 7/8	45 4/8	18 1/8	17 4/8	7 4/8	7 3/8	14	17	Tazlina Glacier, Alaska	Stanley B. Hoagland	Stanley B. Hoagland	1963	113
231	67 4/8	45 3/8	46 3/8	17 3/8	19	7 4/8	8 1/8	11	12	Amber Bay, Alaska	Charles E. Guess	Charles E. Guess	1974	113
230 6/8	67 4/8	48 3/8	46	16 3/8	17 4/8	7 4/8	7 4/8	11	13	Petersville, Alaska	Johnny Lamb	Johnny Lamb	1969	115
230 5/8	68 4/8	54 4/8	53 4/8	15	14 4/8	9	8 4/8	6	6	Cordova, Alaska	John B. Pecel	John B. Pecel	1969	116
230 5/8	65 4/8	47	47	16 2/8	16 4/8	7 4/8	7 4/8	12	12	Port Heiden, Alaska	Brent Greenberg	Brent Greenberg	1972	116
230 5/8	71 5/8	43 3/8	44 2/8	17	14 4/8	7 4/8	7 4/8	22	14	Bonnet Plume Lake, Yukon	Walter P. Griffin	Walter P. Griffin	1978	116
230 3/8	69 3/8	49	47 1/8	15 1/8	18 1/8	8 3/8	8 4/8	10	15	Alaska Pen., Alaska	James H. Lieffers	James H. Lieffers	1963	119
230 3/8	66 4/8	45 1/8	47	15 5/8	16	8	8	14	15	Chelatna Lake, Alaska	G. O. Wiegner	G. O. Wiegner	1969	120
230 3/8	81 4/8	40 4/8	39 4/8	18 4/8	17	7 6/8	8	13	11	Iliamna Lake, Alaska	Peter Zipperle	Peter Zipperle	1972	120
230 3/8	70 3/8	46 5/8	46 2/8	17 1/8	17 2/8	8 1/8	8 3/8	9	11	Alaska Range, Alaska	Earl R. Hossman	Earl R. Hossman	1975	120
230 3/8	65 3/8	45 7/8	47 4/8	18 4/8	25	8	7 4/8	10	12	Alaska Pen., Alaska	Walter Pfisterer	Walter Pfisterer	1960	123
230	70 4/8	43 5/8	45	18 7/8	19 4/8	7 4/8	7 4/8	14	10	Port Heiden, Alaska	Norman Garwood	Norman Garwood	1964	124
229 7/8	66 7/8	42 4/8	41 5/8	17 4/8	17 1/8	7 4/8	7 4/8	17	15	Wood River, Alaska	Bert Klineburger	Bert Klineburger	1964	125
229 7/8	66 1/8	46	46 2/8	19 2/8	20 4/8	8 4/8	8 4/8	8	13	King Salmon River, Alaska	Wilfred von Brand	Wilfred von Brand	1966	125

229 6/8	60 4/8	48 4/8	51	17	18	8 1/8	8 3/8	11	11	Alaska Pen., Alaska	Robert H. Stewart	Robert H. Stewart	1963	127
229 6/8	67 2/8	47	45	17	19 6/8	8 2/8	8 2/8	12	11	Kenai Pen., Alaska	Barjona Meek	Barjona Meek	1973	127
229 6/8	64 6/8	45 6/8	45 6/8	17 2/8	17 2/8	7 4/8	7 4/8	12	12	Anvil Range, Yukon	Fritz Kemper	Fritz Kemper	1978	127
229 5/8	64 7/8	45	45 4/8	16 2/8	16 6/8	7 1/8	7 2/8	14	15	McGrath, Alaska	Fred M. Poorman	Fred M. Poorman	1958	130
229 5/8	68 7/8	47 4/8	48 1/8	15	18	7 7/8	8	12	10	Kuichack River, Alaska	C. J. McElroy	C. J. McElroy	1966	130
229 4/8	63 4/8	42	43	21	21	8 4/8	8 4/8	12	13	Alaska Pen., Alaska	Wm. M. Ellis	Wm. M. Ellis	1963	132
229 4/8	72 2/8	45 6/8	46 2/8	15 1/8	18 6/8	8	7 6/8	10	12	Alaska Pen., Alaska	Arnold H. Craine	Arnold H. Craine	1968	132
229	72 2/8	44 7/8	43 4/8	13 1/8	13 6/8	7 6/8	8	15	14	Wood River, Alaska	A. Knutson	A. Knutson	1957	134
229	62 4/8	47	45	19 3/8	20 1/8	7 4/8	6 7/8	12	13	Shaw Creek Flats, Alaska	William Bugh	William Bugh	1962	134
229	69	44	42 6/8	22 5/8	24	7 5/8	8	8	13	Mother Goose Lake, Alaska	Paul R. Sharick	Paul R. Sharick	1966	134
229	65 2/8	44 2/8	44 4/8	14	13 6/8	8	7 7/8	16	16	Wind River, Yukon	William G. Latimer	William G. Latimer	1973	134
228 7/8	65 7/8	47 3/8	44 4/8	17 4/8	16 5/8	8 6/8	8 3/8	15	13	Wood River, Alaska	Berry B. Brooks	Berry B. Brooks	1958	137
228 7/8	63 7/8	48 6/8	48 4/8	13 5/8	13 6/8	8 3/8	8 4/8	12	12	Talkeetna Mts., Alaska	David F. Bremner, Jr.	David F. Bremner, Jr.	1959	137
228 7/8	70 7/8	42 1/8	45 2/8	22 1/8	15 5/8	8 2/8	8 2/8	13	13	Cantwell, Alaska	Ray L. Aldridge	Ray L. Aldridge	1964	137
228 7/8	70 1/8	46 3/8	42 2/8	20 2/8	18 4/8	8 5/8	9 2/8	12	10	Ugashik Lake, Alaska	Russell Matthes	Russell Matthes	1969	137
228 6/8	65 6/8	47 5/8	44	17 4/8	18 1/8	8 1/8	8	12	13	Mulchatna River, Alaska	R. D. Eichenour	R. D. Eichenour	1968	142
228 6/8	72 6/8	43 6/8	48 6/8	14	16	8 2/8	8 4/8	13	12	Mulchatna River, Alaska	E. L. Dosdall	E. L. Dosdall	1975	142
228 5/8	78 3/8	42 4/8	40 2/8	22 2/8	20 1/8	8 2/8	8 2/8	11	15	Kenai Pen., Alaska	Dale R. Wood	Dale R. Wood	1960	144
228 5/8	54 3/8	48 4/8	48 4/8	16 4/8	18 4/8	8 1/8	9	15	14	Ugashik Bay, Alaska	Max Fugler	Max Fugler	1966	144
228 5/8	69 1/8	47 6/8	47 4/8	14	16	7 2/8	7 3/8	11	14	Kijik River, Alaska	Edward A. Kneeland	Edward A. Kneeland	1970	144
228 5/8	72 1/8	42	46 1/8	15 6/8	15 4/8	8	7 6/8	14	13	Wood River, Alaska	Larry B. Jamison	Larry B. Jamison	1979	144
228 4/8	58	47	45 4/8	16 2/8	21 2/8	8 4/8	8 5/8	19	15	Wrangell Mts., Alaska	G. W. Berry	G. W. Berry	1960	148
228 4/8	65 6/8	43 5/8	45 2/8	15 5/8	15 6/8	8 4/8	8 1/8	14	15	Bonnet Plume Lake, Yukon	Ted T. Debrowski	Ted T. Debrowski	1965	148
228 4/8	70	45 6/8	44 7/8	17 2/8	16 3/8	8	8 1/8	10	13	Alaska Pen., Alaska	Tom W. Degefors	Tom W. Degefors	1967	148
228 4/8	65 4/8	45 1/8	45 6/8	14 1/8	13 5/8	7 6/8	8 2/8	17	15	Wernecke Mts., Yukon	Hugh Beasley	Hugh Beasley	1968	148
228 3/8	70 7/8	47 5/8	46 3/8	15 4/8	15 3/8	7	7	13	11	Paxson Lake, Alaska	Vern Mahoney	Vern Mahoney	1953	152
228 2/8	66 6/8	44 1/8	44	16 3/8	15 4/8	8 5/8	8 2/8	15	14	Blair Lakes, Alaska	Jerry D. Redick	Jerry D. Redick	1979	153
228 1/8	71 7/8	40 5/8	41 4/8	18 1/8	19 3/8	8 3/8	8 4/8	12	11	Mother Goose Lake, Alaska	Bert Klineburger	Bert Klineburger	1967	154
228 1/8	65 5/8	46	45 6/8	15 2/8	15	8 1/8	8	13	15	Rainy Pass, Alaska	W. J. Brule	W. J. Brule	1968	154
228	69 6/8	45	44	17	18	7 2/8	7 1/8	17	15	Rainy Pass, Alaska	J. W. Dixon	J. W. Dixon	1949	156
228	69 4/8	42 2/8	44 2/8	14 6/8	15 2/8	8 2/8	8 3/8	16	14	Talkeetna Mts., Alaska	Wayne C. Eubank	Wayne C. Eubank	1957	156
228	62 2/8	46 5/8	45 7/8	15 2/8	15 7/8	7 6/8	7 5/8	14	14	Alaska Pen., Alaska	M. E. Davis, Jr.	M. E. Davis, Jr.	1958	156
228	69	41 2/8	43 1/8	16 4/8	16 1/8	8 3/8	8 1/8	17	14	Susitna Mt., Alaska	Peter W. Bading	Peter W. Bading	1963	156
228	67	47	45 4/8	15 6/8	20	7 6/8	8	12	12	Tonzona River, Alaska	Glen Miller	Glen Miller	1971	156
227 7/8	65 3/8	42 6/8	42 5/8	14 2/8	15	7 3/8	7 4/8	17	17	McKinley Park, Alaska	Jack V. Morkal	Thomas V. Scrivner	1966	161
227 6/8	62 2/8	44 2/8	44 3/8	14	13 4/8	7	7 3/8	18	21	Soslota Creek, Alaska	Alex Cox	Alex Cox	1957	162
227 6/8	72 4/8	42	43	17	16 4/8	8 5/8	8 1/8	11	12	Nikabuna Lake, Alaska	James E. Curley	James E. Curley	1968	162
227 6/8	73 2/8	50 2/8	42 5/8	16 1/8	17 1/8	7 4/8	8 4/8	12	16	Martin River, Alaska	Jim Goodfellow, Jr.	Jim Goodfellow, Jr.	1977	162
227 5/8	72 1/8	41 4/8	43 6/8	18 4/8	18 2/8	8 4/8	8	11	10	Livengood, Alaska	James W. Keasling	James W. Keasling	1973	165
227 5/8	67 3/8	47 3/8	47 5/8	15 1/8	19 2/8	7 5/8	7 3/8	10	12	Alaska Pen., Alaska	Floyd F. Marrs	Floyd F. Marrs	1977	165

ALASKA-YUKON MOOSE–*Continued*

Alces alces gigas

Score	Greatest Spread	Length of Palm R.	Length of Palm L.	Width of Palm R.	Width of Palm L.	Circumference of Beam at Smallest Place R.	Circumference of Beam at Smallest Place L.	Number of Normal Points R.	Number of Normal Points L.	Locality Killed	By Whom Killed	Owner	Date Killed	Rank
227 4/8	75 4/8	39 6/8	45 4/8	17 4/8	20 4/8	7 6/8	7 6/8	12	11	Cinder River, Alaska	John Humphreys	John Humphreys	1963	167
227 4/8	56 2/8	48 4/8	46 6/8	21 4/8	19 2/8	8 6/8	8 5/8	13	11	Alaska Pen., Alaska	R. H. Platt	R. H. Platt	1965	167
227 4/8	71 2/8	51 4/8	46 4/8	14 5/8	14 1/8	8 6/8	8 4/8	10	9	Iliamna Lake, Alaska	Robert L. Hammond	Robert L. Hammond	1968	167
227 4/8	63	46	46 5/8	17	16 4/8	9 2/8	8 6/8	11	12	Kluane Lake, Yukon	Richard C. Wolff	Richard C. Wolff	1971	167
227 3/8	69 1/8	44 2/8	44 6/8	15	15 5/8	8	7 7/8	12	14	Tok, Alaska	Walter W. Kellogg	Walter W. Kellogg	1967	171
227 2/8	69 6/8	44 6/8	44 1/8	16	15 1/8	8 4/8	8 5/8	11	12	Salana River, Alaska	Jules R. Ashlock	Jules R. Ashlock	1961	172
227 2/8	68 2/8	44 4/8	44 4/8	20	17 6/8	8 1/8	7 2/8	10	12	Port Heiden, Alaska	Pressley R. Rankin, Jr.	Pressley R. Rankin, Jr.	1966	172
227	69	47 2/8	45 3/8	15 2/8	14 1/8	8 5/8	8 4/8	11	12	Rainy Pass, Alaska	John A. Mueller	John A. Mueller	1966	174
227	68 2/8	48 4/8	46 6/8	15 6/8	18	8 1/8	7 7/8	9	12	Ugashik Lake, Alaska	Emil Underberg	Emil Underberg	1967	174
227	67 4/8	45 1/8	44 3/8	16 3/8	16 1/8	8 3/8	8 2/8	11	11	Ugashik Lake, Alaska	Robert Loch	Robert Loch	1967	174
227	64 4/8	52	46	15 4/8	14 7/8	7 3/8	7 4/8	13	13	Ketchumstuk, Alaska	C. O. Tweedy, J. Albright & W. Burnette, Sr.	C. O. Tweedy	1968	174
227	66 2/8	44 4/8	44 7/8	20 7/8	17	7 7/8	8	14	11	Farewell, Alaska	Duke Of Penaranda	Duke Of Penaranda	1969	174
227	69 2/8	48 4/8	43 1/8	14 5/8	14 6/8	8 1/8	8 1/8	13	15	Susitna River, Alaska	L. E. Wold & W. A. Vollendorf	L. E. Wold	1978	174
226 7/8	63 5/8	47 3/8	46 2/8	13 2/8	12	7 4/8	7 3/8	16	16	Wood River, Alaska	M. D. Gilchrist	M. D. Gilchrist	1958	180
226 7/8	63 7/8	41	43	17 7/8	17 2/8	8 2/8	8 7/8	16	15	Yakutat, Alaska	Ray E. Buckwalter	Ray E. Buckwalter	1963	180
226 7/8	61 7/8	47 3/8	44 7/8	16 2/8	16 4/8	7 3/8	7 3/8	16	14	Nessling Range, Yukon	Eric Pilkington	Eric Pilkington	1965	180
226 7/8	63 3/8	43 3/8	47	16 5/8	16 7/8	7 6/8	8	14	14	Eagle, Alaska	David G. Martini	David G. Martini	1969	180
226 7/8	67 7/8	48 4/8	43 2/8	12 2/8	16 6/8	7 5/8	7 4/8	18	17	Ray River, Alaska	William A. Galster	William A. Galster	1972	180
226 6/8	67	41 2/8	49	20 6/8	19 1/8	9	7 4/8	13	12	Alaska Pen., Alaska	George A. Waldriff	George A. Waldriff	1962	185
226 6/8	68	45 6/8	46 6/8	14	15 3/8	9 6/8	9 5/8	12	10	Nabesna River, Alaska	Ross L. Phillippi, Jr.	Ross L. Phillippi, Jr.	1968	185
226 4/8	70 6/8	44 2/8	44 6/8	15 4/8	14 4/8	7 1/8	7 3/8	12	12	Wood River, Alaska	Dan Auld, Jr.	Dan Auld, Jr.	1949	187
226 4/8	68	43 7/8	54 3/8	11 4/8	12 2/8	7 7/8	8	16	17	Charley River, Alaska	G. P. Nehrbas	Alaska Natl. Bank	1951	187
226 4/8	63	45 4/8	47	15	14 2/8	8	8	14	15	Rainy Pass, Alaska	W. B. Macomber	W. B. Macomber	1953	187
226 4/8	62 6/8	46	43 7/8	18 3/8	20	7 5/8	7 7/8	12	13	Paxson Lake, Alaska	L. M. Cole	L. M. Cole	1958	187
226 4/8	65 4/8	46	44 2/8	16 6/8	15 2/8	8	8	13	14	Chugach Mts., Alaska	R. E. Kelley	R. E. Kelley	1961	187
226 4/8	64 2/8	48 3/8	49	15 7/8	15	7 6/8	7 6/8	12	10	Talkeetna Mts., Alaska	Harold Froehle	Harold Froehle	1965	187
226 4/8	60 6/8	48	50 1/8	15 6/8	16	7 1/8	7 2/8	12	12	Dog Salmon River, Alaska	H. H. Ahlemann	H. H. Ahlemann	1968	187
226 3/8	69 5/8	46	41 2/8	21	19 4/8	7 6/8	7 5/8	10	14	Lake Louise, Alaska	H. C. Ragsdale, II	H. C. Ragsdale, II	1958	194
226 3/8	65 5/8	45 4/8	45 4/8	20 6/8	17 1/8	7 6/8	8 2/8	11	10	Alaska Pen., Alaska	Lit Ng	Lit Ng	1967	194

Score										Locality	Owner	By whom killed	Date Killed	Rank
226 4/8	65 4/8	42 4/8	47	16 4/8	18	8 3/8	8 4/8	13	14	Naknek, Alaska	Noel Thompson	Noel Thompson	1971	194
226 4/8	69	48 3/8	44 6/8	13 6/8	12 7/8	7 7/8	7 6/8	16	14	Talkeetna Mts., Alaska	T. L. Wynne, Jr.	T. L. Wynne, Jr.	1958	197
226 4/8	68	47 1/8	46 6/8	16 3/8	13	7 6/8	7 6/8	14	14	Kenai Pen., Alaska	Ottokar J. Skal	Ottokar J. Skal	1963	197
226 4/8	65 6/8	44	43	14 2/8	14 4/8	8	8	15	15	Bonnet Plume Lake, Yukon	Ted Dabrowski	Ted Dabrowski	1965	197
226 4/8	70 4/8	46 4/8	47	14 2/8	14 6/8	8	7 7/8	12	11	King Salmon Creek, Alaska	Tiney Mitchell	Tiney Mitchell	1971	200
226	65 6/8	40 7/8	41 3/8	15 5/8	17 5/8	8 1/8	8	16	20	Nelchina, Alaska	Denver Mus. Nat. Hist.	Jack D. Putnam	1961	201
226	66	46	48 6/8	17 6/8	16	7 7/8	8	10	11	Alaska Pen., Alaska	Robert L. Wesner	Robert L. Wesner	1963	201
226	67 6/8	46 4/8	46 6/8	18 6/8	20 7/8	8	7 6/8	11	14	Ft. Greeley, Alaska	Jerry L. Bailey	Jerry L. Bailey	1970	201
226	58 4/8	46 4/8	47	14 4/8	18 6/8	7 7/8	8	11	11	Black Lake, Alaska	John Mike Behan	John Mike Behan	1972	201
226	64 4/8	45 4/8	45 6/8	14 1/8	16 6/8	8 7/8	7 6/8	13	14	Dillinger River, Alaska	Jerry E. Romanowski	Jerry E. Romanowski	1976	201
225 7/8	68 5/8	43 1/8	43 6/8	13 6/8	13 2/8	8 3/8	8 4/8	14	14	Wrangell Mts., Alaska	Lee Chambers	Lee Chambers	1969	206
225 7/8	76 4/8	44 1/8	44 6/8	14 2/8	14 2/8	8 1/8	8 1/8	10	9	Alaska Pen., Alaska	Herman Kulhanek	Herman Kulhanek	1961	207
225 7/8	66 4/8	46 4/8	43 6/8	15	13 4/8	9 4/8	8 4/8	15	14	Alaska Pen., Alaska	Don Johnson	Don Johnson	1963	207
225 7/8	57 4/8	47 6/8	46 6/8	14 2/8	16 4/8	8 3/8	8 3/8	14	18	St. George Creek, Alaska	Joseph G. Gaillard	Joseph G. Gaillard	1968	207
225 7/8	63 4/8	45 6/8	46	18 7/8	18 5/8	7 3/8	8 4/8	12	10	Alaska Range, Alaska	J. B. Copeland, Jr.	J. B. Copeland, Jr.	1968	207
225 7/8	70 4/8	45	45	15 5/8	15 6/8	8 4/8	8 4/8	12	10	Farewell Station, Alaska	Daniel M. DiBenedetto, Sr.	Daniel M. DiBenedetto, Sr.	1973	207
225 7/8	75 4/8	38 4/8	43 6/8	14 3/8	15 2/8	8 4/8	8 4/8	14	14	Kenai Pen., Alaska	Willi Hilpert	Willi Hilpert	1973	207
225 7/8	66	46	46	13 4/8	13 4/8	8 3/8	8 3/8	12	12	Upper Mulchatna River, Alaska	O. B. Beard, III	O. B. Beard, III	1974	207
225 5/8	65 4/8	41	48 6/8	21 1/8	18 3/8	7 7/8	7 3/8	15	17	Spring Creek, Alaska	William David Phifer	William David Phifer	1975	207
225 5/8	71 4/8	42 4/8	42 6/8	14 6/8	15 3/8	9	9	12	14	Alaska Range, Alaska	Toby J. Johnson	Toby J. Johnson	1978	207
225 5/8	66 6/8	45	42 6/8	18 6/8	18 6/8	8 1/8	8 4/8	14	14	Unknown	National Collection	Gift Of C. H. Mackay	—	216
225 5/8	72 4/8	44	43 6/8	16	21 2/8	7 1/8	7 1/8	11	14	Port Heiden, Alaska	Harold Sill	Harold Sill	1964	216
225 5/8	65 4/8	45 4/8	46 6/8	16 2/8	14 2/8	7 5/8	7 4/8	13	11	High Lake, Alaska	Glen E. Park	Glen E. Park	1965	216
225 5/8	70 4/8	41 1/8	43	19 1/8	17 1/8	8	8	13	13	Alaska Range, Alaska	Robert Pinamont	R. Pinamont & J. Albright	1972	216
225 5/8	69 4/8	44 4/8	41 6/8	17 1/8	20 3/8	8 5/8	8 5/8	11	13	Farewell, Alaska	G. Jack Tankersley	G. Jack Tankersley	1975	216
225 5/8	68 4/8	41 1/8	41	20 3/8	18 4/8	8	8	14	11	Alaska Pen., Alaska	Dolores F. Jones	Dolores F. Jones	1958	221
225 5/8	66 4/8	47 4/8	48 6/8	18 4/8	16 6/8	8 3/8	8	10	14	Blackstone River, Yukon	Marc Korting	Marc Korting	1970	221
225 3/8	70 4/8	43 4/8	46 3/8	14 1/8	16 4/8	7 5/8	7 5/8	10	10	Clark Lake, Alaska	Geo. W. Robinson	Geo. W. Robinson	1965	223
225 1/8	64 4/8	48 4/8	44	16 3/8	17 5/8	7 5/8	8 3/8	10	10	Alaska Pen., Alaska	James Ford	James Ford	1970	224
225 1/8	69 6/8	40 4/8	43 6/8	16 1/8	13 6/8	8 2/8	7 5/8	15	16	Alaska Range, Alaska	Richard C. Beall	Richard C. Beall	1978	224
225	66 4/8	45 4/8	41 6/8	17 5/8	14 6/8	8 6/8	7 5/8	14	15	Kenai Pen., Alaska	Walter R. Peterson	Walter R. Peterson	1935	226
225	74	41	41 6/8	13 6/8	17	7 4/8	8 5/8	17	11	Livengood, Alaska	Univ. Of Alaska	Bill Thomas	1952	226
225	65 4/8	50	49	18 2/8	14 2/8	7 7/8	7 3/8	8	9	Alaska Range, Alaska	Basil C. Bradbury	Basil C. Bradbury	1963	226
225	72	45	47 6/8	15	16 1/8	7 6/8	7 5/8	10	15	Farewell Lake, Alaska	Lyman Strong	Lyman Strong	1965	226
225	58	47 4/8	45 6/8	14 2/8	17 5/8	8 5/8	7 4/8	14	17	Tok, Alaska	Bruce Dodson	Bruce Dodson	1974	226
224 7/8	71 4/8	48 1/8	42 2/8	16 1/8	17 2/8	7 3/8	7 6/8	12	11	Mt. Katmai, Alaska	Morris Roberts	Morris Roberts	1951	231
224 7/8	61 7/8	48 1/8	47 6/8	17 3/8	14 1/8	7 5/8	7 4/8	12	13	Ugashik Narrows, Alaska	Wayne Ewing	Wayne Ewing	1966	231
224 7/8	67 6/8	45 4/8	45 6/8	14 6/8	16 6/8	7 5/8	7 5/8	9	12	King Salmon, Alska	Albert B. Fay	Albert B. Fay	1969	231
224 7/8	67 6/8	45 4/8	46 6/8	16 6/8	14 6/8	8 3/8	8 2/8	11	13	Koyukuk River, Alaska	Dennis E. Reiner	Dennis E. Reiner	1973	231

ALASKA-YUKON MOOSE—*Continued*

Alces alces gigas

Score	Greatest Spread	Length of Palm R.	Length of Palm L.	Width of Palm R.	Width of Palm L.	Circumference of Beam at Smallest Place R.	Circumference of Beam at Smallest Place L.	Number of Normal Points R.	Number of Normal Points L.	Locality Killed	By Whom Killed	Owner	Date Killed	Rank
$224\frac{4}{8}$	$70\frac{4}{8}$	$41\frac{1}{8}$	$40\frac{2}{8}$	$19\frac{2}{8}$	$18\frac{4}{8}$	$7\frac{4}{8}$	$7\frac{4}{8}$	14	11	Farewell Lake, Alaska	Gust Pabst	Gust Pabst	1963	235
$224\frac{4}{8}$	$74\frac{4}{8}$	$41\frac{1}{8}$	$42\frac{2}{8}$	$14\frac{1}{8}$	$17\frac{3}{8}$	$7\frac{7}{8}$	$7\frac{5}{8}$	12	13	Alaska Pen., Alaska	Charles Bonnici	Charles Bonnici	1969	235
$224\frac{4}{8}$	$58\frac{4}{8}$	46	47	15	15	$8\frac{5}{8}$	$8\frac{4}{8}$	14	14	Cantwell, Alaska	Gene Sivell	Gene Sivell	1970	235
$224\frac{4}{8}$	$61\frac{4}{8}$	$46\frac{5}{8}$	$44\frac{4}{8}$	$20\frac{1}{8}$	$21\frac{2}{8}$	$9\frac{1}{8}$	$9\frac{5}{8}$	9	9	Lower Ugashik Lake, Alaska	Hugo Klinger	Hugo Klinger	1972	235
$224\frac{4}{8}$	$69\frac{4}{8}$	$44\frac{1}{8}$	$44\frac{1}{8}$	$16\frac{6}{8}$	14	$8\frac{4}{8}$	$8\frac{4}{8}$	12	11	Little Tok River, Alaska	Edward J. Janus	Edward J. Janus	1974	235
$224\frac{3}{8}$	$68\frac{1}{8}$	$45\frac{1}{8}$	$47\frac{2}{8}$	$16\frac{4}{8}$	$18\frac{7}{8}$	$8\frac{5}{8}$	$9\frac{1}{8}$	8	13	Port Heiden, Alaska	Jon G. Koshell	Jon G. Koshell	1964	240
$224\frac{2}{8}$	62	$44\frac{3}{8}$	$44\frac{3}{8}$	15	$15\frac{5}{8}$	$7\frac{7}{8}$	$7\frac{7}{8}$	14	16	Fog Lakes, Alaska	C. A. Schwope	C. A. Schwope	1960	241
$224\frac{2}{8}$	$68\frac{4}{8}$	$45\frac{1}{8}$	$43\frac{7}{8}$	18	$14\frac{2}{8}$	8	$8\frac{1}{8}$	14	12	Alaska Pen., Alaska	James E. McFarland	James E. McFarland	1967	241
$224\frac{2}{8}$	$71\frac{4}{8}$	$41\frac{6}{8}$	$46\frac{3}{8}$	$19\frac{5}{8}$	$18\frac{4}{8}$	$7\frac{2}{8}$	$7\frac{3}{8}$	9	9	Alaska Range, Alaska	William Mark Harrington	William Mark Harrington	1970	241
$224\frac{2}{8}$	$66\frac{4}{8}$	$46\frac{3}{8}$	$48\frac{5}{8}$	$16\frac{2}{8}$	$18\frac{4}{8}$	$7\frac{4}{8}$	$7\frac{4}{8}$	9	14	Koyukuk River, Alaska	Philip C. Wahlbom	Philip C. Wahlbom	1976	241
$224\frac{2}{8}$	$58\frac{4}{8}$	$44\frac{3}{8}$	$48\frac{7}{8}$	$19\frac{4}{8}$	$16\frac{5}{8}$	$8\frac{1}{8}$	$8\frac{2}{8}$	14	19	Kenai Pen., Alaska	Carole Colclasure	Carole Colclasure	1962	245
$224\frac{2}{8}$	$71\frac{4}{8}$	$47\frac{4}{8}$	$43\frac{3}{8}$	$18\frac{4}{8}$	$14\frac{4}{8}$	$8\frac{4}{8}$	$8\frac{2}{8}$	12	11	Alaska Pen., Alaska	Alice J. Landreth	Alice J. Landreth	1967	245
$224\frac{2}{8}$	$61\frac{5}{8}$	$47\frac{3}{8}$	$46\frac{1}{8}$	$13\frac{5}{8}$	$13\frac{3}{8}$	$7\frac{3}{8}$	$7\frac{4}{8}$	14	15	Kenai Pen., Alaska	Gloria Reiter	Gloria Reiter	1969	245
$224\frac{2}{8}$	$70\frac{4}{8}$	45	$46\frac{5}{8}$	$14\frac{5}{8}$	$15\frac{3}{8}$	$7\frac{1}{8}$	$8\frac{5}{8}$	11	10	Alligator Lake, Yukon	Arthur C. Popham. Jr.	Arthur C. Popham. Jr.	1950	248
$224\frac{2}{8}$	$63\frac{4}{8}$	$43\frac{5}{8}$	$43\frac{3}{8}$	$17\frac{4}{8}$	$14\frac{3}{8}$	$8\frac{5}{8}$	$8\frac{7}{8}$	14	16	Yukon	J. R. Gray	J. R. Gray	1951	248
$224\frac{2}{8}$	$61\frac{2}{8}$	$48\frac{1}{8}$	$48\frac{3}{8}$	$13\frac{3}{8}$	$13\frac{5}{8}$	$8\frac{1}{8}$	8	12	12	Susitna River, Alaska	Donald E. Wicks	Donald E. Wicks	1963	248
$224\frac{2}{8}$	$60\frac{4}{8}$	$42\frac{3}{8}$	$46\frac{2}{8}$	$16\frac{4}{8}$	$17\frac{3}{8}$	$7\frac{7}{8}$	$7\frac{6}{8}$	16	15	Post Lake, Alaska	Wulf Nosofsky	Wulf Nosofsky	1965	248
$224\frac{1}{8}$	$67\frac{3}{8}$	$44\frac{4}{8}$	$46\frac{3}{8}$	$18\frac{7}{8}$	$15\frac{6}{8}$	$8\frac{4}{8}$	$7\frac{7}{8}$	10	10	Lake Telaquana, Alaska	Paul G. Curren	Paul G. Curren	1960	252
$224\frac{1}{8}$	$68\frac{4}{8}$	$47\frac{2}{8}$	44	$14\frac{7}{8}$	$15\frac{2}{8}$	$7\frac{7}{8}$	$7\frac{6}{8}$	11	12	Port Salmon, Alaska	Graf Scheel-Plessen	Graf Scheel-Plessen	1965	252
224	$65\frac{4}{8}$	$43\frac{7}{8}$	$47\frac{1}{8}$	$18\frac{5}{8}$	$17\frac{1}{8}$	$7\frac{6}{8}$	$7\frac{6}{8}$	11	13	Alaska Range, Alaska	L. J. Pfeifer	L. J. Pfeifer	1977	254

WORLD'S RECORD WYOMING MOOSE
SCORE: 205 4/8
Locality: Green River Lake, Wyoming. Date: 1952.
Hunter: John M. Oakley.
Donated by W.C. Lawrence to the Jackson Hole Museum and Pioneer Village Foundation, Inc.

Wyoming or Shiras Moose

Minimum Score 155

Alces alces shirasi

Wyoming (Shiras) moose includes trophies taken in Utah, Idaho, Montana, Wyoming, and Washington.

Score	Greatest Spread	Length of Palm R.	Length of Palm L.	Width of Palm R.	Width of Palm L.	Circumference of Beam at Smallest Place R.	Circumference of Beam at Smallest Place L.	Number of Normal Points R.	Number of Normal Points L.	Locality Killed	By Whom Killed	Owner	Date Killed	Rank
205 4/8	53	38 6/8	38 5/8	16 7/8	15 6/8	6 7/8	6 7/8	15	15	Green River Lake, Wyo.	John M. Oakley	Jackson Hole Museum	1952	1
205 1/8	56 5/8	40	40	13 3/8	14 2/8	7 7/8	7 7/8	13	13	Fremont Co., Wyo.	Arthur E. Chandler	Arthur E. Chandler	1944	2
199 3/8	62 3/8	38 1/8	36 2/8	12 5/8	16 4/8	7 5/8	8 5/8	12	15	Elk City, Idaho	Reid T. Fisher	Reid T. Fisher	1957	3
195 5/8	52 1/8	41 4/8	40	13	11	7	6 6/8	14	15	Atlantic Creek, Wyo.	Alfred C. Berol	Alfred C. Berol	1933	4
195 1/8	55 7/8	43 1/8	35 6/8	15 1/8	14 5/8	7 3/8	7 2/8	14	14	Red Rock Lakes, Mont.	C. M. Schmauch	C. M. Schmauch	1952	5
189 3/8*	43 7/8	42 4/8	43 3/8	12 7/8	11 4/8	6 6/8	6 6/8	12	12	Jackson, Wyo.	Kenneth Booth	Kenneth Booth	1969	6
188 4/8	50 2/8	34 3/8	36 4/8	15	15 3/8	6 6/8	6 7/8	13	13	Madison Co., Idaho	Vicki Grover	Vicki Grover	1976	7
186 3/8	56 7/8	37 1/8	38 3/8	11 3/8	11 6/8	6 4/8	6 2/8	18	10	Sublette Co., Wyo.	Curt Mann	Curt Mann	1972	8
186 1/8	58 1/8	41 4/8	37 5/8	12 3/8	12 5/8	7 3/8	7	8	7	Hamilton, Mont.	Picked Up	Geo. Beechwood	1957	9
185 4/8	56 2/8	41 4/8	40	10 6/8	12 2/8	6 7/8	7	7	9	Sublette Co., Wyo.	Robert C. Neely	Robert C. Neely	1959	10
185	52 2/8	37 1/8	36 1/8	12 2/8	11	6 7/8	6 6/8	13	15	Teton Co., Wyo.	Isabelle Perry	Isabelle Perry	1961	11
184 7/8	56 3/8	33 7/8	33 6/8	13 1/8	14 1/8	7 7/8	7 3/8	11	10	Green River Lake, Wyo.	Vern A. Bapst	Vern A. Bapst	1961	12
184 4/8	49	42 4/8	40 4/8	10 2/8	11	7	7	10	10	Fremont Co., Wyo.	Jack C. Dow	Jack C. Dow	1948	13
183 2/8	45 6/8	37 5/8	38	13	13 6/8	6 1/8	6 2/8	12	15	Bear Lake Co., Idaho	Claudia R. Howell	Claudia R. Howell	1977	14
182 6/8	50	35 7/8	38	11 7/8	13	6 5/8	6 5/8	12	13	Spencer, Idaho	Charles A. Oswald	Charles A. Oswald	1957	15
182 2/8	55 6/8	35 6/8	36 4/8	11 6/8	12 1/8	6 6/8	6 7/8	10	9	Teton Co., Wyo.	Dick Gaudern	Dick Gaudern	1946	16
182	45 2/8	37 3/8	38 1/8	11 4/8	11 1/8	6 7/8	6 7/8	15	13	Sublett Co., Wyo.	James R. Brougham	James R. Brougham	1969	17
181 5/8	51 7/8	38 6/8	38 4/8	8 7/8	9 7/8	6 4/8	6 4/8	11	12	Bear River, Utah	John W. Way	Utah Fish & Game Dept.	1958	18
180 7/8	48 3/8	37 2/8	37 1/8	12 4/8	10 2/8	6 7/8	6 7/8	15	12	Sublette Co., Wyo.	Glen W. Beane	Glen W. Beane	1957	19
180 7/8	53 1/8	39 3/8	41	10 6/8	10 6/8	6 6/8	6 7/8	8	7	Sublette Co., Wyo.	Donald Irwin	Donald Irwin	1976	19
180	45 4/8	40 1/8	38 5/8	10 7/8	9 4/8	7 2/8	7 1/8	13	12	Green River, Wyo.	L. W. Isaacs	L. W. Isaacs	1948	21
180	47	33 5/8	34 6/8	11 2/8	12 4/8	6 6/8	6 5/8	15	16	Pinedale, Wyo.	Stuart W. Shepherd	Stuart W. Shepherd	1966	21
179 7/8	51 1/8	32 1/8	35 6/8	12 6/8	12 4/8	6 6/8	6 7/8	13	14	Gallatin Co., Mont.	John Williams	Powderhorn Sportsman Supply	1930	23
179 6/8	49 2/8	36 2/8	34 5/8	12 1/8	12 7/8	6 4/8	6 6/8	12	14	Greys River, Wyo.	Serena Malech	Serena Malech	1972	24
179 4/8	47 2/8	38 4/8	38 1/8	11 4/8	12 7/8	6 4/8	6 7/8	10	11	Teton Co., Wyo.	John D. Seifert	John D. Seifert	1976	25
179 1/8	45 1/8	35 5/8	34 6/8	14 6/8	11 4/8	6 6/8	6 6/8	14	14	Nalley, Wyo.	Stephen S. Fisher	Stephen S. Fisher	1964	26
178 7/8	52 5/8	38 5/8	37 1/8	9 7/8	10 1/8	6 1/8	6 2/8	11	10	Eagle Creek, Wyo.	Loren L. Lutz	Loren L. Lutz	1956	27

178 6/8	55 2/8	33 4/8	31 3/8	10 4/8	13 3/8	6	5 7/8	14	16	Upper Hoback River, Wyo.	Daniel T. Burch	Daniel T. Burch	1967	28
178 6/8	48 4/8	36 3/8	37 1/8	10 3/8	11 2/8	6 3/8	6 3/8	12	14	Sublette Co., Wyo.	Charles Thornton	Charles Thornton	1973	28
178 3/8	58 5/8	35 4/8	36 6/8	9 3/8	8 4/8	6 7/8	6 7/8	11	9	Sublette Co., Wyo.	Robert Dennis	Robert Dennis	1969	30
178 2/8	49 4/8	32 2/8	32 1/8	13 6/8	15 4/8	6 5/8	6 4/8	15	12	Sublette Co., Wyo.	Ross J. Berlin	Ross J. Berlin	1972	31
178 1/8	50 3/8	37	36 5/8	15 1/8	11 4/8	6 6/8	6 6/8	12	9	Buffalo Park, Wyo.	Walter Russell	Walter Russell	1956	32
178 1/8	49 7/8	36 7/8	38 4/8	10 6/8	12 6/8	6 4/8	6 4/8	10	12	Teton Co., Wyo.	Harold L. Roby	Garvice E. Roby	1961	32
177 6/8	50 2/8	37	33 1/8	13 3/8	12 5/8	7	7	11	13	Thoroughfare River, Wyo.	Earl Brahler	H. E. Wolfe	1959	34
177 6/8	49	35	34 3/8	14 7/8	14 7/8	6 1/8	6 2/8	9	14	Big Piney, Wyo.	George F. Stewart, Jr.	George F. Stewart, Jr.	1965	34
177 5/8	52 3/8	30 1/8	31 2/8	13 7/8	14	6 5/8	6 5/8	12	12	Green River, Wyo.	Walter C. Motta, Sr.	Walter C. Motta, Sr.	1956	36
177 1/8	50 3/8	35	34 2/8	11 2/8	11 4/8	6 1/8	5 7/8	13	12	Big Piney, Wyo.	Mrs. Robert R. Jamieson	Mrs. Robert R. Jamieson	1966	37
177	53	32 4/8	32	12 5/8	11 6/8	7 3/8	7 2/8	14	11	Teton Co., Wyo.	Elgin T. Gates	Elgin T. Gates	1947	38
176 7/8	50 5/8	36 4/8	37 6/8	11	11	6 2/8	6 1/8	10	10	Teton Co., Wyo.	Jack G. Binkley	Jack G. Binkley	1977	39
176 6/8	48 4/8	35	35 4/8	11 4/8	10 4/8	6 5/8	6 7/8	12	12	Teton Co., Wyo.	Charles L. Walters	Charles L. Walters	1966	40
176 4/8	50 6/8	35 4/8	33 5/8	11 2/8	10 7/8	7 3/8	7 3/8	11	12	Caribou Co., Idaho	Diggs Lewis	Diggs Lewis	1972	41
175 6/8	41 6/8	34 4/8	35 7/8	14 3/8	13 2/8	6 2/8	6 3/8	14	13	Weber Co., Utah	Robert A. Cox	Robert A. Cox	1973	42
175 2/8	50	31 6/8	34 6/8	12 5/8	11 6/8	7 1/8	7 2/8	12	13	Lincoln Co., Wyo.	Leon Gordon	Leon Gordon	1967	43
175 1/8	48 3/8	36 3/8	35 6/8	12 2/8	11 4/8	6 2/8	6 1/8	10	14	Hoback River, Wyo.	George Tolan	George Tolan	1964	44
175 1/8	46 7/8	33 7/8	37 4/8	12 1/8	11 7/8	6 3/8	6 4/8	12	15	Squaw Creek, Wyo.	Denton C. Barker	Triangle C Ranch	1969	44
175	54 4/8	34	34	11 2/8	10	6 2/8	6 2/8	10	11	Park Co., Mont.	Thomas J. Radoumis	Thomas J. Radoumis	1974	46
174 6/8	50 2/8	33 1/8	34 3/8	11 5/8	13	6 4/8	6 4/8	11	14	Livingston, Mont.	Bill Cutler	Bill Cutler	1964	47
174 4/8	45 4/8	37 2/8	36 3/8	10 1/8	11 5/8	7	7 1/8	11	13	Teton Co., Wyo.	John Fuller Cross	John Fuller Cross	1965	48
173 6/8	50 4/8	30 6/8	34 4/8	13 7/8	13 3/8	7 4/8	7 4/8	10	12	Atlantic Creek, Wyo.	Clyde Ormond	Clyde Ormond	1955	49
173 3/8	54 5/8	32 5/8	31 2/8	10 6/8	10 3/8	7 6/8	7 6/8	10	10	Flathead Co., Mont.	Tom Scheer	Tom Scheer	1976	50
173 1/8	48 3/8	34 6/8	38	8 4/8	10	7 1/8	7 1/8	12	12	Madison Co., Mont.	Thomas L. Carter	Thomas L. Carter	1955	51
173 1/8	52 1/8	32 6/8	34 4/8	11 6/8	11 6/8	6	6	10	12	Sublette Co., Wyo.	John C. Eklund	John C. Eklund	1970	51
173	49 4/8	33 1/8	35 3/8	11 2/8	12	6 4/8	6 3/8	11	13	Buffalo River, Wyo.	Robert L. Hitch	Robert L. Hitch	1951	53
172 6/8	41	35 1/8	35	11 3/8	11 3/8	6 4/8	6 4/8	13	13	Bridger Natl. For., Wyo.	J. D. Bradley	J. D. Bradley	1970	54
172 4/8	42	35 4/8	33 1/8	12 4/8	14 4/8	6 5/8	6 6/8	13	17	Lincoln Co., Mont.	Tom DeShazer	Tom DeShazer	1956	55
172 4/8	50	32 3/8	36 4/8	10 1/8	10 5/8	6 6/8	6 6/8	12	12	Kilgore Creek, Wyo.	Bill Jhun	Bill Jhun	1967	55
172 3/8	44 1/8	37 1/8	38 6/8	12	10 7/8	6 1/8	6 2/8	10	10	Pinedale, Wyo.	Basil C. Bradbury	Basil C. Bradbury	1969	57
172	51	36 6/8	38 4/8	8 7/8	9 6/8	6 7/8	6 7/8	8	10	Sublette Co., Wyo.	William D. Stewart	William D. Stewart	1954	58
171 5/8	49 1/8	32 1/8	31 6/8	12 5/8	12 2/8	7 2/8	8	10	11	Fremont Co., Idaho	Rodney Chandler	Rodney Chandler	1967	59
171	49 2/8	34 5/8	32	10 6/8	11 1/8	7 1/8	7 1/8	11	11	Teton Co., Wyo.	Keith H. Hanson	Keith H. Hanson	1972	60
170 6/8	50 2/8	35 6/8	34 2/8	8 7/8	11 7/8	6 1/8	6 1/8	12	11	Bridger Natl. For., Wyo.	Unknown	Neil Blair	1965	61
170 6/8	47 6/8	38 1/8	35 1/8	9 7/8	11 6/8	7 4/8	7 5/8	9	12	Sublette, Wyo.	Kenneth E. Myers	Kenneth E. Myers	1968	61
170 4/8	46 6/8	34 3/8	34 3/8	9 7/8	9 7/8	7 6/8	7 5/8	12	10	Warm Spring Creek, Wyo.	Herbert L. Palmer	Herbert L. Palmer	1951	63
170 3/8	39 7/8	34 7/8	35 5/8	10 7/8	12 2/8	6 4/8	6 5/8	13	13	Lincoln Co., Mont.	Picked Up	Wayne Lundberg	1974	64
169 7/8	47 1/8	34 6/8	33 2/8	10 6/8	10 3/8	7	6 6/8	11	12	Lincoln Co., Mont.	William A. Stevens	William A. Stevens	1967	65
169 7/8	50 1/8	33 1/8	32 2/8	10 7/8	11 2/8	7 2/8	6 6/8	10	10	Weber Co., Utah	Riley A. Bushman	Riley A. Bushman	1969	65
169 6/8	54 4/8	32 7/8	27 6/8	10 6/8	10 5/8	6 4/8	6 2/8	15	13	Wilson, Wyo.	Howard Bennage	Howard Bennage	1958	67
169 5/8	52 5/8	30 4/8	32 1/8	12 3/8	11 1/8	7	6 7/8	10	11	Merna, Wyo.	C. Von De Graaff	C. Von De Graaff	1959	68
169 4/8	40 6/8	35	35 2/8	12 1/8	11 3/8	7	7	11	11	Dubois, Wyo.	Albert Wagner, Jr.	Albert Wagner, Jr.	1962	69

WYOMING OR SHIRAS MOOSE–*Continued*

Alces alces shirasi

Score	Greatest Spread	Length of Palm R.	Length of Palm L.	Width of Palm R.	Width of Palm L.	Circumference of Beam at Smallest Place R.	Circumference of Beam at Smallest Place L.	Number of Normal Points R.	Number of Normal Points L.	Locality Killed	By Whom Killed	Owner	Date Killed	Rank
169 3/8	42 3/8	30 7/8	34	12	11 4/8	6 2/8	6 1/8	15	15	Lincoln Co., Wyo.	Vannetta Marshinsky	Vannetta Marshinsky	1968	70
169 1/8	54 5/8	31 4/8	31 4/8	9 4/8	9 4/8	6 2/8	6 2/8	10	12	Clark Co., Idaho	Carolyn Karvinen	Carolyn Karvinen	1966	71
169	52	33 3/8	33 4/8	8 6/8	8 7/8	7 3/8	7 3/8	9	9	Jackson Hole, Wyo.	Shirley Straley	Shirley Straley	1963	72
168 6/8	58	30 4/8	30	11 6/8	11 7/8	6 6/8	6 5/8	7	8	Park Co., Wyo.	John A. Mahoney, Jr.	John A. Mahoney, Jr.	1957	73
168 6/8	48 2/8	36 3/8	34 2/8	10 2/8	10 3/8	6 6/8	6 6/8	12	9	Sublette Co., Wyo.	Larry Petersen	Larry Petersen	1964	73
168 3/8	43 3/8	36 2/8	39 6/8	13 2/8	12 4/8	6 7/8	6 6/8	13	7	Park Co., Mont.	Victoria L. Miller	Victoria L. Miller	1977	75
167 7/8	43 5/8	39 4/8	33 2/8	10 5/8	11	6 2/8	6 4/8	13	12	Gros Ventre, Wyo.	Bonita Young	Bonita Young	1960	76
167 6/8	51	34 2/8	33 6/8	8 3/8	9 4/8	6 2/8	6 2/8	10	11	Teton Co., Wyo.	Roger Wilmot	Roger Wilmot	1972	77
167 4/8	47 4/8	34 6/8	32 4/8	11	11	6 4/8	6 4/8	10	10	Park County, Mont.	Leo C. Chapel	Leo C. Chapel	1967	78
167 3/8	43 7/8	37 5/8	33 7/8	12	10 1/8	6 6/8	6 6/8	12	11	Lincoln Co., Wyo.	Timothy Galen Coulson	Timothy Galen Coulson	1974	79
167 1/8	45 1/8	32 6/8	34	11 7/8	10 6/8	6 5/8	6 4/8	11	11	Teton Co., Wyo.	L. (Buck) Stanley	L. (Buck) Stanley	1964	80
167 1/8	48 1/8	32 7/8	30 7/8	10 7/8	11	6 6/8	6 7/8	11	11	Sublett Co., Wyo.	Bob Housholder	Bob Housholder	1968	80
167 1/8	48 3/8	32 7/8	36 1/8	10	9 6/8	7 2/8	6 6/8	11	10	Caribou Co., Idaho	Ernest Saxton	Ernest Saxton	1969	80
167	46 6/8	35 4/8	35 4/8	8 7/8	12 1/8	6 6/8	6 7/8	9	12	Sublette Co., Wyo.	Picked Up	Robert Dory	1976	83
167	46 2/8	38 6/8	34 2/8	9 5/8	10 5/8	6 5/8	6 4/8	13	10	Fremont Co., Wyo.	LeRoy Castagno	LeRoy Castagno	1977	83
166 5/8	48 7/8	34 4/8	36	7 5/8	10 3/8	7 2/8	7 4/8	10	11	Teton Co., Wyo.	R. G. De Graff	R. G. De Graff	1963	85
166 3/8	50 1/8	34 2/8	32 4/8	8 7/8	9 7/8	6 6/8	6 6/8	10	10	Teton Co., Wyo.	Terry Nilsen	Terry Nilsen	1970	86
166 3/8	48 5/8	37	35 2/8	11 6/8	9 6/8	6	5 7/8	8	11	Bonner Co., Idaho	Brian T. Farley	Brian T. Farley	1977	86
166	48 4/8	35 4/8	32 4/8	9 3/8	10	6 7/8	7	10	10	Tosi Creek, Wyo.	Roscoe O. McKeehan	Roscoe O. McKeehan	1960	88
166	47	30	31	12	11 4/8	7	7	11	13	Glade Creek, Wyo.	E. E. Hosafros	E. E. Hosafros	1961	88
166	48 4/8	34 1/8	33 5/8	14 7/8	9 7/8	6 2/8	6 3/8	10	9	Bonneville Co., Idaho	E. Ray Robinson	E. Ray Robinson	1977	88
165 7/8	52 5/8	29 4/8	29 4/8	11	11	7 2/8	7 1/8	11	9	Clark Co., Idaho	Elden L. Perry	Elden L. Perry	1975	91
165 6/8	48 4/8	33	33 5/8	11	11	6 5/8	6 6/8	8	9	Sublette Co., Wyo.	Ray Snow	Don Boyer	1959	92
165 6/8	48 4/8	32	30 2/8	13 2/8	13 3/8	7 2/8	7 1/8	8	9	Bridger Lake, Wyo.	Hugh W. Mildren	Larry Arndt	1959	92
165 4/8	46 2/8	32 4/8	36 2/8	9 3/8	11 2/8	6 6/8	7	11	13	Sublette Co., Wyo.	Paul A. Graham	Paul A. Graham	1970	94
165 2/8	43 6/8	32 2/8	32 6/8	10 4/8	12 6/8	6	6	12	13	Buffalo River, Wyo.	Jock H. White	Jock H. White	1953	95
165 2/8	47 6/8	32 4/8	32 2/8	12	12 4/8	6 4/8	6 5/8	8	10	Fremont Co., Idaho	Harvey W. Lewis	Harvey W. Lewis	1964	95
165 2/8	43 6/8	33 3/8	32 1/8	11 6/8	10	6 5/8	6 5/8	14	12	Dubois, Wyo.	Vernon Limbach	Vernon Limbach	1969	95
165 2/8	45 4/8	27 7/8	28 4/8	14 2/8	14 4/8	5 6/8	5 7/8	12	12	Lincoln Co., Wyo.	Ryley Z. Dawson	Ryley Z. Dawson	1969	95
165 1/8	47 1/8	34	35 4/8	9	9 2/8	7	7 2/8	9	12	Lincoln Moose, Wyo.	Bern Whittaker	Bern Whittaker	1964	99
165	51 2/8	35	32	9 7/8	9 3/8	7 5/8	7 4/8	9	8	Fremont Co., Wyo.	Charles A. Boyle	Charles A. Boyle	1965	100

164 7/8	52 1/8	30 2/8	34 1/8	9 7/8	9 5/8	6 4/8	6 4/3	10	10	Sublette Co., Wyo.	Edmund J. Giebel	Edmund J. Giebel	1971	101
164 5/8	50 3/8	34 1/8	32 7/8	8 6/8	9 1/8	6 7/8	6 4/3	9	9	Pinedale, Wyo.	Clifford G. McConnell	Clifford G. McConnell	1959	102
164 5/8	47 5/8	29 7/8	32 1/8	10 4/8	10 5/8	6 1/8	6 2/3	16	12	Teton Co., Wyo.	Ernest L. Cummings	Ernest L. Cummings	1960	102
164 5/8	50 7/8	33	33 4/8	9 6/8	8 4/8	6 3/8	6 4/3	10	9	Lincoln Co., Wyo.	Vernal J. Larsen	Vernal J. Larsen	1973	102
164 4/8	51 6/8	30 6/8	30 1/8	9 6/8	11 7/8	5 4/8	5 4/3	11	11	Flathead Co., Mont.	Picked Up	John Castles	——	105
164 4/8	51 4/8	32	30 4/8	10 4/8	10 1/8	6 4/8	6 3/8	11	10	Cache Co., Idaho	Bruce N. Moss	Bruce N. Moss	1977	105
164 2/8	48 4/8	34	34 2/8	8 3/8	11	6 4/8	6 7/8	9	10	Spread Creek, Wyo.	George Malouf	George Malouf	1966	107
164 1/8	52 5/8	31 1/8	28 5/8	10 1/8	8 6/8	6 4/8	6 3/8	12	12	Skull Crack, Utah	Blaine E. Worthen	Blaine E. Worthen	1975	108
164	55	26 3/8	29 3/8	10 6/8	11	6 7/8	6 7/8	11	11	Wilson, Wyo.	Avon Van Noye & Victor Tullis	Victor Tullis	1955	109
163 5/8	49 5/8	34	34 3/8	8 1/8	9 4/8	6 7/8	7	8	9	Bear Canyon, Mont.	John Olsen	John Olsen	1962	110
163 5/8	51 5/8	33 2/8	33 6/8	9 4/8	10 1/8	6 3/8	6 2/8	7	8	Teton Co., Wyo.	Gordon Hay	Gordon Hay	1970	110
163 5/8	47 3/8	33 2/8	36 1/8	11 7/8	12 2/8	6	6 1/8	7	12	Teton Co., Wyo.	Michael S. Greenwald	Micahel S. Greenwald	1978	110
163 4/8	50	34	32	10 4/8	11	6 2/8	6 2/8	10	8	West Yellowstone, Mont.	Pete Hansen	Forest B. Fenn	1948	113
163 4/8	43 6/8	35 4/8	37	9 1/8	10	6 2/8	6 4/8	9	9	Teton Co., Wyo.	Bruce C. Liddle	Bruce C. Liddle	1974	113
163 2/8	48 4/8	31 2/8	32 6/8	11 7/8	14 2/8	6 2/8	6 4/8	8	9	Lincoln Co., Wyo.	Russell J. Smuin	Russell J. Smuin	1976	115
163 1/8	44 3/8	31 3/8	32 4/8	10 2/8	10 2/8	6 6/8	6 6/8	11	11	Jackson, Wyo.	Richard Butts	Richard Butts	1968	116
163 1/8	49 7/8	31 3/8	29 7/8	13 2/8	11 2/8	6 4/8	6 6/8	9	9	Sublette Co., Wyo.	Gerald A. Hoefner	Gerald A. Hoefner	1974	116
162 3/8	46 7/8	30 6/8	31 1/8	13 2/8	11 3/8	6 5/8	6 5/8	9	11	Sublette Co., Wyo.	Donald K. Irvine	Donald K. Irvine	1969	118
162 1/8	44 5/8	31 4/8	31 4/8	10 4/8	9 6/8	6 7/8	6 4/8	12	11	Teton Co., Wyo.	Patrick L. Shanahan	Patrick L. Shanahan	1966	119
162	44 4/8	33 6/8	32 3/8	11 2/8	12 5/8	6 1/8	6 1/8	9	11	Upper Hoback, Wyo.	Walter L. Flint	Walter L. Flint	1951	120
161 6/8	51	30 6/8	32	9 6/8	10 4/8	5 7/8	6 1/8	10	9	Fremont Co., Wyo.	Robert E. Novotny	Ernest Novotny	1944	121
161 5/8	46 3/8	28 6/8	29 7/8	11 6/8	12 2/8	6 1/8	6 2/8	11	11	Flathead Co., Mont.	Sharon L. Chase	Sharon L. Chase	1979	121
161 4/8	51	32 4/8	28 3/8	10 1/8	10 6/8	6 6/8	6 6/8	10	10	Teton Co., Wyo.	Don M. Sheaffer	Don M. Sheaffer	1958	123
161 4/8	52 6/8	29	35 3/8	11 7/8	9 4/8	6 3/8	6 4/8	10	11	Jackson, Wyo.	Robert D. Lynn	Robert D. Lynn	1969	123
160 7/8	43 5/8	32 4/8	32 7/8	10 2/8	10 6/8	6 7/8	7 2/8	9	10	Park Co., Mont.	Wes Synness	Wes Synness	1970	125
160 6/8	49	32 1/8	34 4/8	8 6/8	9 4/8	6	6 2/8	9	12	Pend Oreille Co., Wash.	Archie D. Wyles	Archie D. Wyles	1977	126
160 4/8	48	29 2/8	30 4/8	11 4/8	11 1/8	6 7/8	7	10	9	Lincoln Co., Wyo.	Vic Dana	Fred's Taxidermy	1971	127
160 3/8	45 3/8	30 2/8	31 2/8	11 7/8	12 7/8	7 3/8	7 6/8	11	8	Madison Co., Mont.	Tom Bugni	Tom Bugni	1959	128
160 3/8	45 1/8	31 3/8	34 2/8	9 6/8	12 4/8	6 4/8	6 6/8	10	14	Jackson Hole, Wyo.	Jack Griset	Jack Griset	1967	128
160 3/8	49 3/8	29 6/8	31 4/8	9 4/8	11 6/8	6 2/8	6 3/8	10	12	Lincoln Co., Wyo.	Eugene Heap	Eugene Heap	1970	128
160 2/8	59 6/8	29	38	8 7/8	8 7/8	6 3/8	6 3/8	6	7	Lower Hoback, Wyo.	Obby Agins	Obby Agins	1966	131
159 4/8	49 2/8	31 4/8	31 6/8	9 4/8	8 6/8	7	6 7/8	8	10	Teton Co., Wyo.	Willis McAmis	Willis McAmis	1972	132
159 3/8	45 3/8	30 2/8	29 5/8	10 5/8	10 7/8	6 6/8	6 5/8	10	10	Pinedale, Wyo.	C. J. McElroy	C. J. McElroy	1969	133
159 2/8	53 4/8	34 1/8	30 2/8	11 4/8	10	7	6 5/8	6	9	Pine Creek, Wyo.	Bud Toliver	Bud Toliver	1971	134
159 1/8	51 1/8	33 3/8	29	8 7/8	8 6/8	7 2/8	7 2/8	9	9	Sublette Co., Wyo.	Robert W. Sievers	Mrs. R. B. McCullough	1967	135
159	48 4/8	33 4/8	27 4/8	13 2/8	11 6/8	6	6	10	12	Jackson, Wyo.	Earl F. Hayes	Earl F. Hayes	1953	136
159	41 2/8	36 4/8	35 4/8	9 4/8	10 6/8	6 7/8	6 7/8	8	7	Green River, Wyo.	W. M. Hightower	W. M. Hightower	1962	136
158 6/8	45 2/8	36 1/8	33 2/8	9 6/8	9 4/8	6	6	8	11	N. Hoback, Wyo.	Geo. W. Huncley	Geo. W. Hundley	1970	138
158 5/8	44 5/8	33	33	9 6/8	9 4/8	6 4/8	6 4/8	8	8	Trail Creek, Wyo.	John J. Huseas	John J. Huseas	1953	139
158 5/8	47 3/8	35 6/8	28 4/8	11 7/8	12 1/8	7 5/8	7 2/8	10	8	Teton Co., Wyo.	Albert Pantelis	Albert Pantelis	1967	139
158 4/8	47	32	34	11 2/8	9 6/8	6 1/8	6	8	8	Teton Co., Wyo.	Roy G. Hoover	Roy G. Hoover	1966	141
158 4/8	43 2/8	28 7/8	28 6/8	11 6/8	14 6/8	6 1/8	6 1/8	11	11	New Fork River, Wyo.	Oscar Boyd	Oscar Boyd	1966	141

WYOMING OR SHIRAS MOOSE—*Continued*

Alces alces shirasi

Score	Greatest Spread	Length of Palm R.	Length of Palm L.	Width of Palm R.	Width of Palm L.	Circumference of Beam at Smallest Place R.	Circumference of Beam at Smallest Place L.	Number of Normal Points R.	Number of Normal Points L.	Locality Killed	By Whom Killed	Owner	Date Killed	Rank
158 4/8	50 6/8	26	26 7/8	10 3/8	10 5/8	6 5/8	6 5/8	11	12	Pinedale, Wyo.	Donald C. Rehwaldt	Donald C. Rehwaldt	1966	143
158 4/8	51	30 5/8	26 3/8	11 1/8	11 1/8	7 7/8	7 1/8	10	9	Clark Co., Idaho	Harold Vietz	Harold Vietz	1968	143
158 1/8	42 5/8	33 4/8	35 6/8	11 6/8	11 6/8	6 5/8	6 4/8	9	6	Gravel Mt., Wyo.	W. A. Kalkofen	W. A. Kalkofen	1966	145
157 6/8	47 2/8	27	29	13 7/8	12 4/8	6 3/8	6	10	12	Cache Co., Idaho	David W. Jensen	David W. Jensen	1977	146
157 7/8	50 2/8	28 1/8	26 2/8	10 6/8	11 1/8	6 5/8	6 5/8	11	10	Greys River, Wyo.	Mary B. Mikalis	Mary B. Mikalis	1969	147
157 7/8	45 4/8	33	37 4/8	9 7/8	9 7/8	6	6	7	8	Lincoln Co., Mont.	Bob Stafford	Bob Stafford	1963	148
157	47 4/8	29 6/8	31 3/8	9 6/8	12 2/8	6 3/8	6 4/8	10	9	Fremont Co., Wyo.	Fred S. Finley	Fred S. Finley	1962	149
156 7/8	46 1/8	29 6/8	28	14 7/8	14 6/8	6 5/8	7 1/8	6	9	Ruby Mts., Mont.	Milton Burdick	Milton Burdick	1960	150
156 7/8	38 7/8	30 3/8	31	11 3/8	12 3/8	6 3/8	6 3/8	11	13	Deer Lodge Co., Mont.	Mike Munson	Mike Munson	1971	150
156 6/8	45 3/8	33 1/8	31 6/8	10 4/8	9	7 3/8	7	9	8	Teton Co., Wyo.	Palmer Hegge	Palmer Hegge	1952	152
156 6/8	37	34	36	11 2/8	13 3/8	6 5/8	6 5/8	8	9	Devil's Basin, Wyo.	Charlotte Bruce	Charlotte Bruce	1967	152
156 6/8	46 2/8	33 7/8	31 3/8	11	11 1/8	6 1/8	5 7/8	9	7	Sublette Co., Wyo.	Richard A. Bonander	Richard A. Bonander	1979	152
156 5/8	42 3/8	29 5/8	29 2/8	11 3/8	11 6/8	7 4/8	7 4/8	9	10	Teton Co., Wyo.	George A. Nevills	George A. Nevills	1977	155
156 5/8	42 6/8	32 3/8	34 5/8	12 2/8	12 4/8	6 3/8	6 3/8	6	6	Gallatin River, Mont.	Paul Mako	Paul Mako	1960	156
156 5/8	51 2/8	29	32	8 6/8	9	6 7/8	6 7/8	8	9	Buffalo Horn Lake, Mont.	Vincent De Stefano	Vincent De Stefano	1966	156
156 5/8	49 6/8	28	30	9	9	5 7/8	5 7/8	11	12	Thorofare River, Wyo.	Dean Johnson	Dean Johnson	1973	156
156 2/8	43	40 7/8	31 4/8	10 3/8	10 4/8	7	7	9	8	Teton Co., Wyo.	Gerda Prince	Gerda Prince	1970	159
156 2/8	47 3/8	31 5/8	34 4/8	9 6/8	7 4/8	6	6 1/8	10	9	Lewis Creek, Wyo.	Donald J. Krist	Donald J. Krist	1967	160
156 2/8	45 7/8	30 3/8	31 1/8	11	10 4/8	6 5/8	6 4/8	9	8	Glade Creek, Wyo.	Joseph A. Merrill, Jr.	Joseph A. Merrill, Jr.	1973	160
156	45 4/8	32 4/8	31 4/8	8 4/8	8	7	6 6/8	11	9	Missoula Co., Mont.	W. L. Rohrer	W. L. Rohrer	1957	162
155 7/8	52 3/8	29 4/8	30 4/8	7 2/8	9 1/8	7 1/8	7 2/8	9	9	Ashton, Idaho	Robert H. Thomas	Robert H. Thomas	1972	163
155 5/8	46	31 1/8	31 2/8	8 4/8	7 4/8	6 5/8	7	10	9	Jackson Hole, Wyo.	Don Phillips	Don Phillips	1956	164
155 5/8	48 4/8	27 6/8	27 5/8	10 4/8	11 6/8	6 3/8	6 4/8	9	10	Jackson Hole, Wyo.	Ralph Brumbaugh	Ralph Brumbaugh	1960	164
155 5/8	39 4/8	28	28 1/8	13	16 7/8	6 6/8	6 3/8	11	12	Upper Hoback, Wyo.	Stephen N. Bean	Stephen N. Bean	1969	164
155 5/8	51 2/8	30 7/8	31 2/8	11 1/8	8 7/8	6 3/8	6 3/8	9	7	Green River, Wyo.	H. S. Jackman	H. S. Jackman	1964	167
155 5/8	46	27 1/8	31	12 6/8	11 4/8	6	6	11	10	Jackson, Wyo.	Bud Weaver	Bud Weaver	1968	167
155 5/8	42 2/8	29	29	10 6/8	10 5/8	6 5/8	6 6/8	11	11	Lincoln Co., Wyo.	Ralph Wood	Ralph Wood	1977	167
155 3/8	52 3/8	28	27 4/8	9 7/8	9 2/8	6	6 1/8	8	8	Upper Yellowstone, Wyo.	Harold E. Anthony	Am. Mus. Nat. History	1934	170
155 3/8	49 5/8	30 5/8	30 2/8	8 5/8	9 5/8	6 1/8	6	8	10	Spread Creek, Wyo.	Marty Fiorello	Marty Fiorello	1963	170
155 3/8	43 3/8	31 1/8	30	10 2/8	10 6/8	7	7	9	9	Sublette Co., Wyo.	Tom J. Schwindt	Tom J. Schwindt	1973	170
155 2/8	51 2/8	28 2/8	25 2/8	10 1/8	10 3/8	6 5/8	6 5/8	11	10	Dubois, Wyo.	Clyde Thompson	Clyde Thompson	1954	173

155 2/8	46	29 2/8	30 2/8	9 4/8	8 6/8	6 5/8	6 5/8	10	11	Lolo Creek, Mont.	Edward Churchwell	Virgil Fite	1955	173
155 2/8	41 4/8	32 7/8	30 4/8	11 1/8	11 2/8	6 2/8	6 2/8	9	10	Teton Co., Wyo.	Thomas F. Smith	Thomas F. Smith	1973	173
155 1/8	40 3/8	33 4/8	30 7/8	11	11	5 4/8	5 5/8	10	14	Yellowstone River, Wyo.	T. Robert Johnson	T. Robert Johnson	1974	176
155	46 6/8	29 6/8	30	9	9 4/8	6 4/8	6 3/8	9	9	Jackson Hole, Wyo.	Vernon Williams, Jr.	Vernon Williams, Jr.	1969	177

*Final Score subject to revision by additional verifying measurements.

NEW WORLD'S RECORD MOUNTAIN CARIBOU
SCORE: 452
Locality: Turnagain River, British Columbia. Date: 1976.
Hunter and owner: Gary Beaubien.
Winner of the Sagamore Hill Medal, 1977.

NUMBER FIVE MOUNTAIN CARIBOU
SCORE: 446 2/8
Locality: Atlin, British Columbia. Date: 1955.
Hunter: Irvin Hardcastle. Owner: Mrs. Irvin Hardcastle.

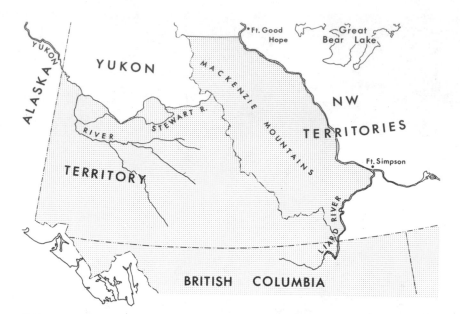

NEW NORTHERN BOUNDARY FOR MOUNTAIN CARIBOU

As explained in the chapter on the current records program, the boundary separating the barren ground caribou to the north and the mountain caribou to the south has been moved northward from the old boundary at the British Columbia-Yukon line. The new area from which caribou trophies may be entered as mountain caribou, rather than barren ground, is shown on the accompanying map and it includes the southern third of Yukon Territory and the boundary lies between Game Management Zones 1 and 2 to the north and Zones 3 and 5 to the south, as shown on the 1978 Yukon hunting map and described as follows.

Starting at the intersection of the Yukon River with the boundary between the Yukon Territory and the State of Alaska; thence southeasterly following upstream the center of the Yukon River to Dawson City; thence easterly and southerly along the center of the Klondike Highway to Stewart Crossing; thence northeasterly following the center of the road to Elsa; thence northeasterly following the center of the road to McQuesten Lake; thence easterly following the south shore of McQuesten Lake and upstream following the main drainage to the divide leading to Scougate Creek; thence southeasterly following downstream the center of Scougate Creek to its confluence with the Beaver River; thence southeasterly following downstream the center of the Beaver River to its confluence with the Rackla River; thence southeasterly following downstream the center of the Rackla River to its confluence with the Stewart River; thence northeasterly following upstream the center of the Stewart River to its confluence with the North Stewart River to the boundary between the Yukon and Northwest Territories.

In the Northwest Territories all of the Mackenzie Mountains are included. The boundary starts on the west where the head of the North Stewart River in the Yukon meets the Northwest Territories line, north along this divide to the 66th parallel; thence east to the Mackenzie River; thence southeasterly along the Mackenzie River to Fort Simpson; thence southwesterly up the Liard River to the British Columbia boundary; thence northwesterly along the divide between the Yukon and the Northwest Territories to the point of beginning.

Trophies listed in the 1977 book as barren ground caribou from within this area have been transferred to the mountain caribou list.

Barren ground caribou occur north of this boundary in the Yukon where the highly migratory Porcupine herd winters in the Ogilvie and the Wernecke Mountains. Also, sport hunting for non-residents has recently been instituted for barren ground caribou east of the Mackenzie River in Northwest Territories.

Mountain Caribou

Rangifer tarandus caribou

Minimum Score 390

Four categories of caribou are recognized for records keeping, with boundaries based on geographic lines. Mountain caribou includes trophies from British Columbia, Alberta, southern Yukon, and the McKenzie Mountains of the Northwest Territories.

Score	Length of Main Beam R.	Length of Main Beam L.	Inside Spread	Circumference at Smallest Place Between Brow and Bez Points R.	Circumference at Smallest Place Between Brow and Bez Points L.	Length of Brow Points R.	Length of Brow Points L.	Width of Brow Points R.	Width of Brow Points L.	Number of Points R.	Number of Points L.	Locality Killed	By Whom Killed	Owner	Date Killed	Rank
452	43 1/8	42 2/8	30 3/8	7 3/8	7 5/8	16 4/8	16 1/8	11 2/8	5	22	19	Turnagain River, B. C.	Garry Beaubien	Garry Beaubien	1976	1
448 6/8*	51 3/8	51 5/8	40 2/8	6 6/8	6 6/8	18	4	10 6/8	1	24	20	Great Salmon Lake, Yukon	John Tomko	John Tomko	1965	2
448 2/8*	47 6/8	50 4/8	39 4/8	6 4/8	6 5/8	19 3/8	18 4/8	15 1/8	1 6/8	18	18	Teena Lake, Yukon	Julian Gutierrez	Julian Gutierrez	1976	3
447 5/8*	47 6/8	45 6/8	45 3/8	7 4/8	7 4/8	14 1/8	15 2/8	9 4/8	10 5/8	18	15	Pelly Mts., Yukon	Emil Eichenberger	Emil Eichenberger	1960	4
446 2/8	55	53 5/8	40 2/8	7 5/8	7 2/8	14 7/8	13 2/8	9 3/8	5	20	14	Atlin, B. C.	Irvin Hardcastle	Irvin Hardcastle	1955	5
445 3/8	48 7/8	46 2/8	27 4/8	6 2/8	5 7/8	17 6/8	20 2/8	4 5/8	17 5/8	19	20	Cold Fish Lake, B. C.	John I. Moore	John I. Moore	1958	6
439 5/8	49 4/8	46 2/8	33 1/8	7	6 7/8	19 2/8	21	15 3/8	4 7/8	24	19	Cold Fish Lake, B. C	Drew W. Getgen	Carnegie Museum	1961	7
432 4/8*	47 1/8	46 1/8	41 5/8	6 4/8	6 6/8	17 3/8	17 1/8	12 4/8	14 1/8	21	22	Tay River, Yukon	Edmund D. Patterson, Jr.	Edmund D. Patterson, Jr.	1964	8
430 5/8*	46 6/8	47 3/8	43 5/8	7	7	15 3/8	20 6/8	3 3/8	15	15	19	Pelly Mts., Yukon	J. M. Conway	J. M. Conway	1960	9
428 5/8	42 5/8	47 2/8	35 2/8	7 4/8	7 1/8	17 1/8	16 1/8	12 3/8	10 4/8	21	22	Atlin, B. C.	Rafael Garcia Cano	Cascade Lodge	1968	10
428 4/8	56 6/8	55	37	7 4/8	7 4/8	15 4/8	15	17	15 6/8	19	19	Dease Lake, B. C.	Fred G. Kelly	Fred G. Kelly	1964	11
427 3/8	56 7/8	59	44 4/8	7 4/8	7 3/8	6	19 4/8	1/8	14 6/8	10	15	Atlin, B. C.	Anna Chabara	Anna Chabara	1960	12
424 3/8	47 7/8	49 5/8	43 5/8	6 7/8	7	16 6/8	16 2/8	10 7/8	8 5/8	22	22	Cold Fish Lake, B. C.	A. H. Clise	A. H. Clise	1968	13
424 2/8	47	46 4/8	37 3/8	6 1/8	6 2/8	15 2/8	15 2/8	9 7/8	7 2/8	20	19	Cold Fish Lake, B. C.	Howard Keeler	Howard Keeler	1954	14
423 7/8	46 2/8	45 3/8	34 6/8	7	6 5/8	14 5/8	14	10 3/8	4 3/8	19	16	Cold Fish Lake, B. C.	Edward E. Wilson	Edward E. Wilson	1963	15
423 6/8	42	40 5/8	33 1/8	6 3/8	6 4/8	17 6/8	16 3/8	13 4/8	6	21	23	Stikine Plateau, B. C.	Dwight Lewis	Dwight Lewis	1970	16
423 4/8	47 1/8	47 1/8	48 5/8	6 2/8	6 2/8	14 2/8	16	1 6/8	12 1/8	19	25	Cassiar, B. C.	Arvid F. Benson	Arvid F. Benson	1967	17
422 3/8	53 2/8	54 3/8	46	5 7/8	6 1/8	18 3/8	19 7/8	1/8	16 4/8	14	22	Keele Park, Yukon	Donald P. Smith, Jr.	Donald P. Smith, Jr.	1954	18
422 3/8	50 5/8	52	50	5 7/8	6	21 5/8	20 1/8	6 1/8	13 4/8	16	15	Little Dall Lake, N. W. T.	Dale L. Martin	Dale L. Martin	1976	18
422 2/8	65 1/8	62 2/8	50 5/8	7	7	15 4/8	–	8 3/8	–	22	14	Cassiar, B.C.	D. W. Bell	Acad. Nat. Sci., Phil.	1923	20
421 5/8	54	52 5/8	35 5/8	6 5/8	6 3/8	18 2/8	18	12 3/8	15 7/8	20	19	Aishihik Lake, Yukon	A. W. Fees, Jr.	A. W. Fees, Jr.	1971	21
421 1/8	49 3/8	43 4/8	41 4/8	7 5/8	7 2/8	18 2/8	3 3/8	16 1/8	1/8	27	20	Taku Lake, Yukon	Lloyd Walker	Lloyd Walker	1961	22
420 5/8	45 1/8	44 7/8	40 4/8	6 2/8	6	19 2/8	–	13 3/8	–	27	17	Cold Fish Lake, B. C.	Maurice C. Perkins	Maurice C. Perkins	1961	23

MOUNTAIN CARIBOU–Continued
Rangifer tarandus caribou

Score	Length of Main Beam R.	L.	Inside Spread	Circumference at Smallest Place Between Brow and Bez Points R.	L.	Length of Brow Points R.	L.	Width of Brow Points R.	L.	Number of Points R.	L.	Locality Killed	By Whom Killed	Owner	Date Killed	Rank
420	59⁶/₈	62³/₈	44³/₈	5⁷/₈	6	22⁷/₈	14⁷/₈	20²/₈	8⁴/₈	21	15	Mackenzie Mts., N.W.T.	Martin C. Ernest	Martin C. Ernest	1978	24
419⁶/₈	52²/₈	50²/₈	42²/₈	8³/₈	7⁴/₈	19⁵/₈	16¹/₈	13⁴/₈	11	21	18	Atlin Lake Area, B. C.	John Haefeli, Jr.	John Haefeli, Jr.	1964	25
419⁵/₈	50	50³/₈	37¹/₈	6⁷/₈	6⁵/₈	18⁴/₈	17⁶/₈	15¹/₈	¹/₈	20	16	Livingstone, Yukon	Charlie L. Bertani	Charlie L. Bertani	1977	26
417⁷/₈	43⁷/₈	43²/₈	30³/₈	6¹/₈	6	18⁷/₈	18⁵/₈	12⁵/₈	6	24	21	Cassiar, B. C.	Elgin T. Gates	Elgin T. Gates	1953	27
417⁷/₈	51⁵/₈	49⁴/₈	42⁴/₈	6⁴/₈	6⁴/₈	21¹/₈	10⁶/₈	¹/₈	14	15	16	Cold Fish Lake, B. C.	John E. Rhea	John E. Rhea	1959	27
417⁷/₈	47⁴/₈	50	36⁴/₈	6⁴/₈	6³/₈	6⁵/₈	17⁵/₈	¹/₈	12²/₈	13	21	Gladstone River, Yukon	Herman Peterson	Herman Peterson	1960	29
417¹/₈	49⁵/₈	49⁵/₈	40⁶/₈	7²/₈	7⁵/₈	11⁶/₈	17³/₈	1⁵/₈	14³/₈	15	19	Connally Lake, Yukon	Marlin P. Alt	Marlin P. Alt	1973	30
416⁶/₈	42²/₈	40²/₈	31⁵/₈	8³/₈	8²/₈	11¹/₈	15	3⁷/₈	11	24	26	Cold Fish Lake, B. C.	Charles E. Wilson, Jr.	Charles E. Wilson, Jr.	1970	31
416¹/₈	50²/₈	50	42	6¹/₈	6¹/₈	18³/₈	20¹/₈	8⁷/₈	9⁵/₈	13	13	Cold Fish Lake, B. C.	Clyde Williams	Clyde Williams	1966	32
415⁷/₈	57⁵/₈	53⁵/₈	45³/₈	7³/₈	7¹/₈	16⁵/₈	16	6	14³/₈	13	16	Atlin, B. C.	R. W. Johnson	R. W. Johnson	1956	33
415³/₈	51¹/₈	55	39³/₈	6⁷/₈	6⁵/₈	16	10⁶/₈	11¹/₈	¹/₈	15	10	Atlin, B. C.	Mrs. Ramon Somavia	Mrs. Ramon Somavia	1955	34
415³/₈	46⁴/₈	49	40²/₈	7²/₈	7²/₈	14⁶/₈	14⁵/₈	1⁵/₈	9²/₈	20	21	Cassiar, B. C.	James Keegan	James Keegan	1971	34
415³/₈	48²/₈	44⁷/₈	33⁴/₈	6⁵/₈	6⁷/₈	15	17¹/₈	1⁵/₈	13	18	23	Mackenzie Mts., N. W. T.	Gerald Schroeder	Gerald Schroeder	1974	34
415²/₈	48⁴/₈	47³/₈	34	7⁴/₈	7²/₈	16¹/₈	18⁴/₈	13³/₈	14	19	17	Arrowhead Lake, Yukon	Robert L. Pagel	Robert L. Pagel	1973	37
415	55³/₈	52³/₈	34	7³/₈	7⁷/₈	10	20²/₈	¹/₈	17⁶/₈	12	25	Dease Lake, B. C.	Unknown	National Collection	1917	38
414⁴/₈	50⁴/₈	51¹/₈	41⁴/₈	5⁵/₈	5⁵/₈	19³/₈	17⁵/₈	11	10⁶/₈	17	12	Watson Lake, B. C.	John H. Myaard	John H. Myaard	1971	39
414³/₈	54	53⁵/₈	28³/₈	7³/₈	7⁷/₈	15	15	11²/₈	5³/₈	15	19	Tweedsmuir Park, B. C.	Gary J. Deleenheer	Gary J. Deleenheer	1966	40
414¹/₈	49⁴/₈	51²/₈	26	6⁴/₈	6⁵/₈	15⁵/₈	17¹/₈	10	14³/₈	15	18	Cold Fish Lake, B. C.	D. W. Thiem	D. W. Thiem	1956	41
413³/₈	47⁴/₈	49	35⁴/₈	6⁷/₈	6⁶/₈	17⁴/₈	6³/₈	8¹/₈	1¹/₈	20	14	Dease Lake, B. C.	Bert Klineburger	Bert Klineburger	1960	42
413³/₈	49	49	36⁴/₈	6⁶/₈	6⁶/₈	20²/₈	19²/₈	11⁴/₈	2	17	15	Cassiar Mts., B. C.	Ira Jones	Ira Jones	1963	42

413 5/8	53 4/8	51 3/8	45 6/8	6 3/8	6 2/8	1	14 6/8	1/8	14 2/8	15	27	Atlin, B. C.	Mrs. Robert S. Marvin, Jr.	Mrs. Robert S. Marvin, Jr.	1956	44
413 2/8	44 4/8	49	31 6/8	7 1/8	7 1/8	18 4/8	7 2/8	13 6/8	1	16	14	Livingston, Yukon	Lawrence W. Dossman	Lawrence W. Dossman	1975	45
413	51 4/8	53 7/8	43	6 5/8	6 5/8	15 4/8	16 7/8	8 3/8	7 4/8	14	18	Drury Lake, Yukon	James H. Russell	James H. Russell	1971	46
412 6/8	50 3/8	53 6/8	47 3/8	6 2/8	6 3/8	18 1/8	2 6/8	12 3/8	1/8	18	15	Cassiar Mts., B. C.	John R. Rinkevich	John R. Rinkevich	1968	47
412 5/8	49 7/8	50 2/8	38 5/8	6 6/8	5	15 6/8	17 6/8	10 2/8	9 6/8	21	23	Cassiar Mts., B. C.	Nolan Martins	Nolan Martins	1967	48
412 4/8	55 6/8	57 4/8	26	6 6/8	6 2/8	12 4/8	12 2/8	6	11	20	22	Shesley, B. C.	James F. Clarke	James F. Clarke	1929	49
412 4/8	48 1/8	51 3/8	33 3/8	7 3/8	6 7/8	19 4/8	14 1/8	14 2/8	8 2/8	18	15	Cassiar Mts., B. C.	Leon Mazzeo	Leon Mazzeo	1971	49
412 3/8	49 2/8	48	36 3/8	6 2/8	6 3/8	18 2/8	12 2/8	14 5/8	3 7/8	16	16	Fort Nelson, B. C.	Elmer T. Newman	Elmer T. Newman	1970	51
412	47 2/8	47 4/8	33 2/8	6 1/8	6 1/8	14	14	11 2/8	7 2/8	26	25	Dease River, B. C.	Herb Klein	Herb Klein	1960	52
412	43	47	37 2/8	7 3/8	7 3/8	11 6/8	16 4/8	1/8	11 3/8	21	19	Livingston, Yukon	Arvo Walter Kannisto	Arvo Walter Kannisto	1974	52
411	39 5/8	40 5/8	31 6/8	7 6/8	7 5/8	20	17 2/8	14	10	17	17	Nisling Range, Yukon	Jack Odor	Jack Odor	1977	54
410 1/8	53	53 2/8	41 2/8	7 3/8	7 1/8	16 7/8	18 7/8	9	5 7/8	14	18	Atlin, B. C.	Dale L. McCord	Dale L. McCord	1966	55
410 1/8	55 4/8	54 2/8	30 7/8	7	7 1/8	17 6/8	17 5/8	9 2/8	5 4/8	15	12	Cassiar Mts., B. C.	Charles J. Woodruff	Charles J. Woodruff	1970	55
410	44 2/8	45 4/8	22 3/8	7 4/8	7 3/8	20 2/8	14 7/8	15 6/8	2 2/8	26	23	Level Mountain, B. C.	James W. Reilly	James W. Reilly	1968	57
409 7/8	46	45	44	7	7 5/8	20	18 5/8	9 3/8	15 6/8	17	20	Atlin, B. C.	Cliff Schmidt	Cliff Schmidt	1966	58
409 5/8	47 6/8	48	35	7	7	2 4/8	14 3/8	1	11 2/8	24	29	White River, Yukon	Perry Shankle	Perry Shankle	1955	59
409 3/8	41 4/8	42	36 4/8	7 7/8	7 1/8	20 4/8	7 2/8	15	3 1/8	17	13	Dease Lake, B. C.	Wilf W. Klingsat	Wilf W. Klingsat	1974	60
409 1/8	51 2/8	52 5/8	42 3/8	6 3/8	6 4/8	20	–	13 6/8	–	22	12	Ice Mountain, B. C.	David M. George	David M. George	1966	61
409 1/8	45 3/8	46	30 6/8	7 2/8	7 4/8	14 4/8	14 3/8	10 6/8	12 4/8	22	24	Johanson Lake, B. C.	George L. Seifert	George L. Seifert	1968	61
409	48 2/8	44	48 2/8	8 1/8	7 7/8	18 6/8	11 4/8	14 1/8	1/8	18	14	Level Mts., B.C.	Larry A. Zullo	Larry A. Zullo	1978	63
408 7/8	43	43 7/8	34 1/8	6 1/8	6	14	15 2/8	6	8 4/8	18	16	Duty Lake, B. C.	Gordon Baird	Gordon Baird	1966	64
408 4/8	48 6/8	47 6/8	35 6/8	6 7/8	6 6/8	14 7/8	16 4/8	1/8	6 2/8	16	16	Atlin, B. C.	Bradford O'Connor	Bradford O'Connor	1951	65
408 1/8	57 6/8	57	44 3/8	5 4/8	6	16 5/8	17 2/8	4 4/8	12 6/8	17	20	Canada	Unknown	Snow Museum	1890	66
407 6/8	49	48 2/8	33 5/8	6 7/8	6 5/8	17 1/8	19 4/8	15	16	18	20	Cassiar Mts., Yukon	H. R. Safford, III	H. R. Safford, III	1968	67
407 1/8	47 7/8	46 4/8	30	5 5/8	5 5/8	20 1/8	21	12 1/8	6 5/8	18	18	Lower Post, B. C.	Jack Jordon	Jack Jordon	1960	68
407	51 5/8	54 3/8	43 2/8	6 6/8	6 2/8	20 5/8	21 7/8	1 1/8	16 3/8	16	13	Watson Lake, B. C.	Len Anderson	Len Anderson	1967	69
406 7/8	45 6/8	48 1/8	39 3/8	6 6/8	6 6/8	18 4/8	18 [illegible]	10 6/8	10 3/8	17	14	Lake Tatlatui, B. C.	Winston P. Woodman	Winston P. Woodman	1966	70
406 3/8	54	52 6/8	37 5/8	6 6/8	6 3/8	17 4/8	–	11 4/8	–	27	20	Ketchika Mts., B. C.	Basil C. Bradbury	Basil C. Bradbury	1962	71
406 1/8	43 4/8	41 5/8	35 6/8	6 6/8	6 4/8	19	19 3/8	12 4/8	4 6/8	21	18	Cassiar Mts., B. C.	Arvid F. Benson	Arvid F. Benson	1965	72
406	48 6/8	43 5/8	37 4/8	6 2/8	6 7/8	16	16	10 4/8	12 4/8	19	18	Tweedsmuir Park, B. C.	Bob Stewart	Bob Stewart	1964	73
405 6/8	57 2/8	55 5/8	30	6 2/8	6 7/8	15	14 2/8	7 5/8	4 1/8	17	17	Watson Lake, B. C.	M. L. Walker	M. L. Walker	1968	74
405 4/8	52 5/8	51	38 3/8	6 2/8	6 7/8	17 2/8	19	13 3/8	7 4/8	14	14	Mackenzie Mts., N.W.T.	Robert J. Begeny	Robert J. Begeny	1976	75
404 5/8	44	40 5/8	36 4/8	6 3/8	6 4/8	16 4/8	16 5/8	5 6/8	9	14	15	Cold Fish Lake, B. C.	O. A. Campbell	O. A. Campbell	1959	76
404 2/8	48 2/8	48	40 2/8	5 4/8	5 4/8	16 2/8	18	8 6/8	7 4/8	15	17	Cassiar Mts., B. C.	Francis B. Wadelton	Francis B. Wadelton	1969	77
403 4/8	46 5/8	49	41 1/8	6	6 3/8	19 5/8	23 1/8	5 6/8	15 5/8	16	21	Keele River, N. W. T.	T. C. Britt, Jr.	T. C. Britt, Jr.	1968	78
403 4/8	49 7/8	50 7/8	36	6	5 6/8	23	7 7/8	1/8	19 6/8	16	23	Gem Lake, B. C.	Johann Gerdenits	Johann Gerdenits	1976	78

MOUNTAIN CARIBOU–*Continued*

Rangifer tarandus caribou

Score	Length of Main Beam R.	Length of Main Beam L.	Inside Spread	Circumference at Smallest Place Between Brow and Bez Points R.	Circumference at Smallest Place Between Brow and Bez Points L.	Length of Brow Points R.	Length of Brow Points L.	Width of Brow Points R.	Width of Brow Points L.	Number of Points R.	Number of Points L.	Locality Killed	By Whom Killed	Owner	Date Killed	Rank
403 3/8	44	46 1/8	32	6 3/8	6 1/8	17 1/8	10 3/8	12 1/8	1	26	14	Cassiar Mts., B. C.	Mrs. G. L. Rusty Gibbons	Mrs. G. L. Rusty Gibbons	1964	80
403 3/8	48 2/8	49 7/8	38 6/8	7 2/8	7	14	17	5 2/8	5 3/8	1	2	Gataga River, B. C.	Laurel E. Brown	Laurel E. Brown	1970	80
403 2/8	47 4/8	51 3/8	40 6/8	7	7	17 6/8	17 4/8	9 2/8	10 6/8	16	15	Pelly Mts., Yukon	B. F. Briggs	B. F. Briggs	1963	82
403 2/8	45 3/8	43 4/8	34 5/8	7 6/8	8 2/8	19 2/8	21 1/8	10 4/8	14	13	16	Drury Lake, Yukon	Henry Macagni	Henry Macagni	1963	82
403 2/8	52 3/8	50 6/8	31	9	8 5/8	13 5/8	16 6/8	7 7/8	8 4/8	18	24	Ketchum Lake, B.C.	Andy Proksch	Andy Proksch	1978	82
402 3/8	45 1/8	47	40 5/8	6 4/8	6 7/8	16 2/8	20 5/8	12	12 7/8	15	13	Dease Lake, B. C.	G. C. F. Dalziel	G. C. F. Dalziel	1958	85
402 1/8	41 6/8	47	39 4/8	7 1/8	7	13	7 5/8	8 1/8	1/8	19	15	Cottonwood Lake, B. C.	Collins F. Kellogg	Collins F. Kellogg	1969	86
401 7/8	50 4/8	51 4/8	39 6/8	5 4/8	5 4/8	20	16 7/8	17 1/8	1 3/8	19	13	Mackenzie Mts., N.W.T.	Thomas E. South	Thomas E. South	1976	87
401 4/8	43 7/8	46 6/8	32 1/8	6 2/8	5 7/8	8 1/8	10 4/8	8 7/8	10 3/8	19	19	Dease Lake, B. C.	Hugh Bennett	Hugh Bennett	1961	88
401 2/8	46 7/8	46 6/8	41 6/8	7	7 2/8	15 7/8	15 7/8	1/8	11 1/8	14	15	Cassiar, B. C.	Bernard W. McNamara	Bernard W. McNamara	1958	89
401 1/8	41 4/8	40	36 4/8	6 6/8	6 3/8	17	4 6/8	13 5/8	1 2/8	23	15	Cold Fish Lake, B. C.	P. Walsh	P. Walsh	1970	90
401	42	41 6/8	36 4/8	8 4/8	8 5/8	16 1/8	11 6/8	11 2/8	1/8	15	15	Ketchika Mts., B. C.	H. I. H. Prince Abdorreza Pahlavi	H. I. H. Prince Abdorreza Pahlavi	1960	91
400 5/8	54 7/8	54 5/8	36 1/8	7 2/8	7 4/8	16 4/8	2 3/8	10	7/8	19	22	Nascha Creek, B. C.	W. A. K. Seale	W. A. K. Seale	1968	92
400 3/8	47 2/8	47	39 4/8	7	8 6/8	19	3 1/8	14 4/8	4/8	21	17	Cold Fish Lake, B. C.	Juan Brittingham	Juan Brittingham	1961	93
400 3/8	44 6/8	44 6/8	34 4/8	6	6 3/8	17 3/8	19 3/8	11 6/8	13 1/8	14	18	Cassiar Mts., B. C.	Jack Fleishman, Jr.	Jack Fleishman, Jr.	1965	93
400 2/8	58 5/8	57 6/8	39 5/8	8	8 1/8	20 5/8	2 3/8	13 3/8	6/8	14	11	Dease Lake, B. C.	Stanley A. Chase	Stanley A. Chase	1973	95
400	37 1/8	39	31 1/8	6 5/8	6 4/8	13 7/8	13 2/8	9 6/8	7	19	22	Cold Fish Lake, B. C.	Charles P. Yarn, Jr.	Charles P. Yarn, Jr.	1965	96
399 7/8	49 5/8	50 2/8	32 4/8	6 1/8	6 1/8	3 3/8	17 4/8	5/8	8 7/8	16	22	Eagle Nest Mtns., B. C.	Robert J. Stevens	Robert J. Stevens	1967	97
399 4/8	46 5/8	48	34 1/8	6 7/8	6 6/8	17 1/8	17 6/8	4	12 2/8	21	17	Cassiar Mts., B. C.	William R. Franklin	William R. Franklin	1969	98
399	51 6/8	49	34 6/8	5 7/8	5 7/8	14 5/8	20	1 3/8	13 5/8	16	18	Cold Fish Lake, B. C.	George W. Hooker	George W. Hooker	1956	99
398 5/8	54 4/8	56	38 6/8	7 1/8	6 7/8	19	11 1/8	14 3/8	1	18	14	Spatsizi Plateau, B. C.	Warren Page	Warren Page	1970	100
397 6/8	46 4/8	47	29 4/8	5 7/8	5 7/8	4 7/8	16 7/8	6/8	14 2/8	17	23	Muncho Lake, B. C.	Bob Landis	Tom Mould	1960	101
397 4/8	48 3/8	50 2/8	41 2/8	6 7/8	6 5/8	11 3/8	19 2/8	1/8	14 2/8	34	44	Level Mts., B. C.	Phillip Neuweiler	Phillip Neuweiler	1956	102
397 2/8	47	49	39 6/8	8 3/8	7 7/8	17 4/8	18 1/8	10 1/8	12	11	13	Glacier Lake, B. C.	Helmuth Katz	Helmuth Katz	1967	103

397 2/8	52 7/8	51 2/8	42 4/8	7 3/8	7 6/8	16 4/8	15 6/8	4	10 4/8	11	14	Mackenzie Mts., N.W.T.	William J. Chronister	William J. Chronister	1978	103
396 4/8	46 2/8	44 4/8	29 4/8	7 1/8	7 1/8	19 5/8	20 4/8	2 4/8	14 3/8	14	15	Cold Fish Lake, B. C.	L. W. Zimmerman	L. W. Zimmerman	1960	105
396 2/8	54 2/8	58 4/8	44 7/8	7	6 5/8	18 4/8	15 4/8	13 1/8	1 4/8	19	12	Cassiar Mts., B. C.	Peter C. Jurs	Peter C. Jurs	1964	106
395 4/8	51 3/8	51 3/8	42 5/8	6 2/8	6 1/8	18 4/8	17 4/8	9	10 7/8	16	13	Atlin, B. C.	Ray Foerster	Ray Foerster	1960	107
395 2/8	48	48 2/8	29 6/8	7 1/8	7 1/8	2 2/8	14	1/8	10 4/8	15	21	Prophet River, B. C.	V. B. Seigel	V. B. Seigel	1961	108
395 2/8	47 4/8	47 3/8	36 4/8	6 5/8	6 2/8	20 7/8	20 7/8	17 3/8	3 3/8	20	14	Cold Fish Lake, B. C.	D. A. Boyd	D. A. Boyd	1963	108
395 2/8	43 4/8	42 1/8	34 2/8	6 6/8	6 6/8	14 7/8	13 1/8	9	2 5/8	17	15	Dease Lake, B. C.	George H. Glass	George H. Glass	1963	108
394 7/8	43 4/8	45 5/8	42 3/8	6 5/8	6 7/8	15 5/8	16 1/8	12	11	24	19	Cassiar, B. C.	Dorothy N. Benson	Dorothy N. Benson	1967	111
394 6/8	42 4/8	43	39 3/8	6 7/8	7 5/8	18 6/8	17 7/8	9	11 6/8	15	15	Cassiar, B. C.	Arcadio Guerra	Arcadio Guerra	1957	112
394 3/8	37 3/8	39 3/8	24 3/8	7 6/8	7 5/8	14 6/8	14 1/8	10 1/8	2 4/8	28	22	Muncho Lake, B. C.	H. W. Julien	H. W. Julien	1965	113
394 3/8	44	46 7/8	30 2/8	7 3/8	7 1/8	9 1/8	16 4/8	1 1/8	8 5/8	17	19	Cassiar Mts., B. C.	Raymond A. Schneider	Raymond A. Schneider	1968	113
394	56 6/8	56 7/8	51 4/8	6 4/8	7	–	19 3/8	–	13 7/8	11	18	Turnagain River, B. C.	Robert E. Miller	Robert E. Miller	1968	115
393 3/8	46 3/8	48 7/8	32	6 2/8	6 5/8	16 1/8	21	6	12	12	14	Ketchika Mts., B. C.	H. I. H. Prince Abdorreza Pahlavi	Game Council Of Iran	1960	116
393 2/8	38	37 6/8	30 2/8	8 1/8	8 4/8	14 3/8	13 6/8	12 3/8	2 4/8	18	21	Tweedsmuir Park, B. C.	Harold Daye	Harold Daye	1960	117
393 2/8	49 7/8	51 7/8	39 4/8	6 4/8	6 2/8	2 4/8	17 2/8	1/8	14 1/8	14	17	Cassiar Dist., B. C.	Robert E. Miller	Robert E. Miller	1966	117
393	52 4/8	50 5/8	39 2/8	5 4/8	5 6/8	18 7/8	16 7/8	4	12 2/8	13	17	Mt. Thule, B. C.	William L. Searle	William L. Searle	1963	119
392 7/8	47 6/8	49 6/8	37 6/8	6 6/8	6 7/8	6/8	15	4/8	11 1/8	16	16	Cassiar Mts., B. C.	Charles Haas	Charles Haas	1959	120
392 7/8	41 2/8	42 4/8	36	6 6/8	6 6/8	18	16 2/8	9 6/8	1 3/8	21	21	Atlin, B. C.	Earl H. Carlson	Wildlife Tax. Studios	1966	120
392 6/8	45 6/8	45 1/8	40 1/8	7 3/8	7 4/8	14 4/8	3 1/8	13 1/8	1/8	22	17	West Toad River, B. C.	Daniel Ray Bond	Daniel Ray Bond	1966	122
392 5/8	39 6/8	39 3/8	33 4/8	5 5/8	5 5/8	7 4/8	15 4/8	1/8	10 6/8	22	34	Cold Fish Lake, B. C.	Richard G. Van Vorst	Richard G. Van Vorst	1974	123
392 3/8	48 6/8	52 2/8	43 5/8	6 1/8	6 1/8	19 2/8	15 3/8	1/8	15 4/8	10	17	Ice Mountain, B. C.	J. E. Mason	J. E. Mason	1966	124
392 1/8	39 4/8	46 2/8	38	7 4/8	7 2/8	17 4/8	17	7 4/8	7 1/8	17	13	Rabbit River, B. C.	Bob C. Jones	Bob C. Jones	1969	125
391 7/8	53 3/8	53	40 3/8	6 2/8	6 1/8	17 5/8	15 7/8	5 2/8	5 4/8	11	11	Glacier Lake, B.C.	Lowell C. Hansen, II	Lowell C. Hansen, II	1970	126
391 5/8	46 3/8	43 7/8	34	5 7/8	6	18 3/8	21 3/8	19 4/8	17 6/8	18	21	Cassiar, B. C.	E. F. Ardourel	E. F. Ardourel	1960	127
391 1/8	46 5/8	43 2/8	38 4/8	6 7/8	6 6/8	3	18 4/8	1/8	15 4/8	13	16	Atlin, B. C.	Bob Reinhold	Bob Reinhold	1963	128
391	38 5/8	39 4/8	37 7/8	7	7	7 4/8	17 1/8	1/8	11 7/8	19	20	Tuya Range, B.C.	Robert L. Gilkey	Robert L. Gilkey	1978	129
390 7/8	40 3/8	39	34 1/8	6 2/8	6	15 6/8	2 7/8	10	1/8	23	17	Tuya Lake, B. C.	John H. Epstein	John E. Epstein	1953	130
390 7/8	46	46 6/8	34	5 7/8	5 4/8	2 4/8	16 3/8	1/8	11 5/8	18	23	Snake River, B. C.	J. W. L. Monaghan	J. W. L. Monaghan	1963	130
390 5/8	51 7/8	48 7/8	45 1/8	7 3/8	7 1/8	6 6/8	18 3/8	3 6/8	13 3/8	12	12	Atlin, B. C.	Vern Cox	Vern Cox	1962	132
390 4/8	39 2/8	39 3/8	36	5 6/8	6 2/8	16	18 2/8	11 5/8	7 5/8	20	18	Muncho Lake, B. C.	Dennis Dean	Dennis Dean	1963	133
390 4/8	37 4/8	38 5/8	37 5/8	7 4/8	7 5/8	18 2/8	17 4/8	11 7/8	13 4/8	17	19	Cassiar Mts., B. C.	Milo L. Blickenstaff	Milo L. Blickenstaff	1965	133
390 4/8	36 1/8	37 2/8	29 4/8	7 2/8	7 4/8	17 4/8	15 1/8	12 6/8	11 3/8	20	17	Halfway River, B. C.	Steven L. Rose	R. Lynn Ross	1965	133
390 3/8	54 2/8	54 6/8	37 2/8	7	6 6/8	17	1	11 5/8	2/8	15	14	Level Mts., B. C.	Donald S. Hopkins	National Collection	1928	136
390 3/8	55	56 6/8	47 2/8	7 4/8	8 1/8	18 2/8	16 5/8	8 7/8	1/8	12	12	Cassiar, B. C.	Orlando Bodeau	Orlando Bodeau	1953	136
390 1/8	47 1/8	50	40 4/8	6 7/8	6 3/8	17 1/8	6	14 3/8	1/8	21	16	Dease Lake, B. C.	W. A. Tharp	W. A. Tharp	1962	138
390 1/8	55 2/8	51 6/8	34 1/8	6 3/8	6 2/8	17 6/8	18 4/8	12 5/8	2 3/8	15	11	Firesteel Lake, B. C.	Melvin K. Wolf	Melvin K. Wolf	1970	138

*Final Score subject to revision by additional verifying measurements.

WORLD'S RECORD WOODLAND CARIBOU
SCORE: 419 5/8
Locality: Newfoundland. Date: before 1910.
Donated by Casimir de Rham to the National Collection.

NUMBER TWO WOODLAND CARIBOU
SCORE: 405 4/8
Locality: Gander River, Newfoundland. Date: 1951.
Hunter and owner: George H. Lesser.
Winner of the Sagamore Hill Medal, 1951.

Woodland Caribou

Minimum Score 295

Rangifer tarandus caribou

Woodland caribou includes trophies from Nova Scotia, New Brunswick, and Newfoundland.

Score	Length of Main Beam R.	Length of Main Beam L.	Inside Spread	Circumference at Smallest Place Between Brow and Bez Points R.	Circumference at Smallest Place Between Brow and Bez Points L.	Length of Brow Points R.	Length of Brow Points L.	Width of Brow Points R.	Width of Brow Points L.	Number of Points R.	Number of Points L.	Locality Killed	By Whom Killed	Owner	Date Killed	Rank
419 5/8	50 1/8	47 3/8	43 2/8	6 1/8	6 5/8	20	17 7/8	17 6/8	12 2/8	19	18	Nfld.	Gift Of Casimir DeRham	National Collection	PR1910	1
405 4/8	45	44	30 3/8	5 6/8	5 6/8	20 1/8	20 1/8	19 4/8	19 5/8	22	21	Gander River, Nfld.	George H. Lesser	George H. Lesser	1951	2
405 1/8	38	39 6/8	34	5 4/8	6 1/8	21 7/8	20 3/8	18 7/8	18 4/8	22	25	Millertown, Nfld.	Robert V. Knutson	Robert V. Knutson	1966	3
373 6/8	39 7/8	43 3/8	22 1/8	5 2/8	5 4/8	24 4/8	22 3/8	20	21	21	22	Nfld.	Gift Of J. B. Marvin, Jr.	National Collection	PR1924	4
373 1/8*	42 1/8	43 2/8	36 2/8	7 4/8	7 4/8	19	18 3/8	13 1/8	15 1/8	16	16	Grey Islands, Nfld.	Percy G. Gilbert	Percy G. Gilbert	1975	5
370 1/8*	47 4/8	48 6/8	34 2/8	6	6	17 4/8	16 4/8	13	14 3/8	20	16	Avalon Pen., Nfld.	John T. MacIsaac	John T. MacIsaac	1970	6
368 1/8*	49 3/8	46 3/8	35 7/8	6	6	15 3/8	15	17 5/8	16 6/8	22	18	Bonavista Bay, Nfld.	Unknown	Crow's Nest Officers Club	1935	7
359 7/8	42 5/8	43 3/8	32	5 2/8	5 4/8	19 2/8	22 7/8	17 4/8	16 2/8	16	18	Serpentine Lake, N. B.	F. W. Ayer	Carnegie Museum	1899	8
358 6/8*	46 2/8	50 5/8	30 5/8	6 2/8	6	13 4/8	14	8 1/8	8	17	16	Avalon Pen., Nfld.	Gerald R. Bourgoin	Gerald R. Bourgoin	1976	9
357 5/8*	49 2/8	48 7/8	39 5/8	5 6/8	6 1/8	15 5/8	18 2/8	8	7 5/8	12	14	Avalon Pen., Nfld.	Barrett Greening	Barrett Greening	1972	10
357 1/8	43	43 4/8	31 6/8	5 2/8	5 4/8	19 4/8	19 3/8	17 3/8	16 5/8	15	18	Serpentine Lake, N. B.	Frederick K. Barbour	Carnegie Museum	1929	11
350 3/8	44 4/8	41 7/8	45 2/8	5 5/8	5 4/8	17 2/8	17 1/8	14 4/8	7 4/8	14	16	Louse Lake, Nfld.	William J. Chasko	William J. Chasko	1963	12
350 1/8	39 3/8	44	30 5/8	5 6/8	6 3/8	21 5/8	19 5/8	22	17 2/8	21	18	Gander, Nfld.	Robert M. Lee	Robert M. Lee	1951	13
347 7/8	41 3/8	39 7/8	39 4/8	6 2/8	5 7/8	15 2/8	14 6/8	14	5 5/8	20	20	Gander River, Nfld.	E. B. Warner	E. B. Warner	1951	14
345 5/8	42 3/8	43	35 2/8	7 1/8	6 5/8	14	14 7/8	15 4/8	1 2/8	23	14	Lake Kaegudeck, Nfld.	J. J. Veteto	J. J. Veteto	1968	15
345 2/8	39 7/8	39 7/8	23 2/8	6 6/8	6 7/8	17 3/8	16 5/8	15 7/8	16 3/8	18	19	Nfld.	Wilson Potter	National Collection	1909	16
340 7/8	38 6/8	40 3/8	31	5 4/8	5 6/8	15 2/8	16 4/8	12 3/8	10 2/8	19	17	Shenadithit River, Nfld.	Gene Manion	Gene Manion	1964	17
340 2/8	46	44 6/8	27 2/8	5 6/8	6 1/8	17 2/8	17 5/8	15 1/8	10 6/8	15	16	Victorian River, Nfld.	Dempsey Cape	Dempsey Cape	1966	18
340 2/8	40 2/8	41 1/8	35 3/8	5 1/8	4 7/8	16 1/8	17	13 4/8	10 2/8	17	17	Wall's Pond, Nfld.	Jeff Lawton	Jeff Lawton	1971	18
339 2/8	50 6/8	50	30 5/8	8 6/8	8 6/8	1 3/8	16 3/8	1/8	13 2/8	10	20	New Gander, Nfld.	Elgin T. Gates	Elgin T. Gates	1962	20
339 1/8	40 4/8	41	42 7/8	6 3/8	6 1/8	17	18	8 3/8	12 3/8	11	10	Gander, Nfld.	Michael Savino	Michael Savino	1969	21

Score												Locality			Date	Rank
334	34 4/8	37 5/8	29 6/8	5 6/8	5 6/8	14 1/8	14 5/8	10 6/8	12 6/8	25	16	Red Indian Lake, Nfld.	Grancel Fitz	Mrs. Grancel Fitz	1960	22
332 7/8	46 6/8	43 5/8	28 6/8	5 1/8	5	15 3/8	15 5/8	14 3/8	11 3/8	20	19	La Poile, Nfld.	Donald A. Piombo	Donald A. Piombo	1979	23
332 2/8	35 5/8	36	27 6/8	6 6/8	6 6/8	16 3/8	17 5/8	16 2/8	13 3/8	23	18	Nfld.	Gift Of J. B. Marvin, Jr.	National Collection	PR1924	24
332 2/8	35 5/8	36 7/8	28	6 2/8	6	15	16 1/8	13 5/8	13 3/8	25	21	Nfld.	Gift Of Grover Asmus	National Collection	1932	24
330 5/8	31 2/8	34 5/8	26 6/8	5 6/8	5 6/8	15 3/8	15 5/8	13 4/8	1	22	23	N. B.	R. W. Gelbach	M. C. McQueen	1900	26
330 5/8	41 2/8	42 5/8	33 6/8	5 6/8	5 6/8	16 2/8	14 1/8	13 4/8	14 3/8	18	19	Meelpaeg, Nfld.	Alex Kariotakis	Alex Kariotakis	1969	26
328 3/8	35 5/8	38	31 1/8	5 1/8	5 4/8	17	15 5/8	12 5/8	13 3/8	18	17	Gulp Pond, Nfld.	Michael E. Lombardo	Michael E. Lombardo	1968	28
327 7/8	44 4/8	44 5/8	32 1/8	5 6/8	5 6/8	12 7/8	14 5/8	13 5/8	11 3/8	18	17	Princess Lake, Nfld.	Dermod O. Sullivan	Dermod O. Sullivan	1967	29
327 3/8	39 6/8	39 5/8	27	4 6/8	4 6/8	17 5/8	16 1/8	5 4/8	14 3/8	18	18	Caribou Lakes, Nfld.	Conrad R. Bragg	Conrad R. Bragg	1962	30
326 3/8	41 6/8	40 6/8	31 1/8	5 7/8	6	15 7/8	14 1/8	11 3/8	9 7/8	21	23	Avalon Pen., Nfld.	Harrold Clarke	Harrold Clarke	1971	31
326 3/8	39 5/8	41 1/8	31 7/8	5 6/8	5 6/8	12 4/8	15 5/8	9	8 3/8	13	17	Rocky Pond, Nfld.	Thomas E. Phillippe, Jr.	Thomas E. Phillippe, Jr.	1975	32
326 1/8	46 6/8	48	40 6/8	5 6/8	5 6/8	18 4/8	17 2/8	11	14	11	11	Nfld.	Frederick Brooks	Harvard Univ. Museum	1881	33
325	45 7/8	44 5/8	42 6/8	6 6/8	6 2/8	2	12 5/8	16 5/8	1/8	17	14	Bear Pond, Nfld.	Stanley T. Beers	Stanley T. Beers	1970	34
322 5/8	37 5/8	36 7/8	37 1/8	6 1/8	5 7/8	15 1/8	14 7/8	14 3/8	10 7/8	14	14	Avalon Pen., Nfld.	Richard F. Lewis	Richard F. Lewis	1977	35
322 3/8	40 6/8	38 1/8	35 1/8	5	4 5/8	15 3/8	13 2/8	8 3/8	9 6/8	12	20	Avalon Pen., Nfld.	Angus J. Chafe	Angus J. Chafe	1969	36
321 6/8	42 6/8	43 5/8	35 6/8	6 1/8	6 1/8	17 2/8	13 2/8	6 5/8	15 1/8	11	16	Princess Lake, Nfld.	Henry Bondesen	Henry Bondesen	1966	37
320 7/8	37 7/8	40 5/8	34 6/8	6	5 5/8	16 4/8	15 3/8	8 5/8	11 7/8	15	17	La Poile, Nfld.	David J. Coleman	David J. Coleman	1974	38
319 5/8	40 6/8	39	38 6/8	5 4/8	5 2/8	15 5/8	15	11 5/8	3 1/8	17	15	Conne River, Nfld.	Lloyd W. McClelland	Lloyd W. McClelland	1970	39
318 7/8	37 7/8	38 5/8	29 6/8	5 1/8	4 7/8	15 7/8	15 2/8	12 5/8	9 3/8	20	20	Deer Lake, Nfld.	Alexander Thane	Alexander Thane	1951	40
318 7/8	38 7/8	39 5/8	27	4 7/8	5	14 5/8	13 4/8	11 2/8	13 3/8	16	17	Lake Margaret, Nfld.	Edward J. Bugden	Edward J. Bugden	1973	40
318 4/8	38 7/8	38 5/8	34 1/8	5 4/8	5 4/8	17	18 5/8	15 5/8	4 5/8	12	9	Great Rattling Brook, Nfld.	Henry D. Frey	Henry D. Frey	1970	42
318 3/8	40	41 5/8	26 6/8	5 4/8	5 3/8	12 7/8	13 6/8	11 5/8	6 3/8	22	16	La Poile, Nfld.	Van R. Johnson	Van R. Johnson	1977	43
318 3/8	40 7/8	37	38 6/8	5	5 5/8	16	12 1/8	3 4/8	2 2/8	20	18	Gander River, Nfld.	Wm. H. Wilson	Wm. H. Wilson	1955	44
317 7/8	32	34 5/8	31 6/8	5	5 1/8	13 4/8	13	11 4/8	10	18	18	Walls Pond, Nfld.	Laurence Brown	Laurence Brown	1967	45
317 6/8	45 7/8	45 5/8	30 7/8	5 4/8	5 4/8	18 3/8	17	1/8	15 2/8	9	15	Doyles, Nfld.	Franklin H. Burns	Franklin H. Burns	1956	46
317 1/8	43 5/8	42 5/8	50 6/8	5 4/8	5 1/8	16 3/8	16 4/8	11 7/8	10 3/8	13	10	Hynes Lake, Nfld.	Martin W. Nasadowski	Martin W. Nasadowski	1969	47
316 3/8	40 7/8	42	33 1/8	5 6/8	5 6/8	18	16 4/8	1 5/8	16 5/8	16	21	Sandy Pond Barrens, Nfld.	Geo. L Harrison	Acad. Nat. Sci., Phl.	1897	48
315 7/8	43 7/8	46 1/8	33 5/8	5 2/8	4 7/8	16 4/8	14 2/8	1 3/8	11 1/8	9	16	Newton Lake, Nfld.	Wm. H. Wilson	Wm. H. Wilson	1957	49
315 5/8	43 7/8	42 1/8	33 6/8	5 7/8	6 1/8	12	12 4/8	7 3/8	6 1/8	10	14	Sitdown Pond, Nfld.	H. R. (Dutch) Wambold	H. R. (Dutch) Wambold	1966	50
314	36 7/8	35	34 1/8	6	6 1/8	14 5/8	14	11 6/8	12 5/8	14	16	Rainy Lake, Nfld.	Arnold H. Craine	Arnold H. Craine	1967	51
312 5/8	39 3/8	40 5/8	40 5/8	5 2/8	5 3/8	16 6/8	16 1/8	11 7/8	15 3/8	13	14	Crooked Lake, Nfld.	Vernon L. Hanlin	Vernon L. Hanlin	1967	52
312 2/8	36 7/8	36 4/8	29 6/8	6 4/8	6 6/8	14 5/8	12 7/8	9 7/8	6 6/8	20	15	Stag Pond, Nfld.	Max Meister	Max Meister	1976	53

Woodland Caribou–*Continued*

Rangifer tarandus caribou

Score	Length of Main Beam R.	Length of Main Beam L.	Inside Spread	Circumference at Smallest Place Between Brow and Bez Points R.	Circumference at Smallest Place Between Brow and Bez Points L.	Length of Brow Points R.	Length of Brow Points L.	Width of Brow Points R.	Width of Brow Points L.	Number of Points R.	Number of Points L.	Locality Killed	By Whom Killed	Owner	Date Killed	Rank
311 6/8	40 5/8	43 6/8	40 4/8	5 1/8	5 2/8	13 3/8	15 7/8	4 6/8	14	17	14	Buchans Plateau, Nfld.	Basil C. Bradbury	Basil C. Bradbury	1971	54
309 4/8	38	36	34 2/8	5 5/8	5 5/8	16 2/8	15 2/8	5 6/8	13 6/8	15	12	Noela Paul Brook, Nfld.	Ted Dreimans	Ted Dreimans	1962	55
309 3/8	43	43 3/8	33	5 3/8	5 2/8	16	15	13 3/8	13 6/8	15	15	Rainy Lake, Nfld.	A. L. Levenseler	A. L. Levenseler	1967	56
309	42 3/8	44	33	5 1/8	5 3/8	15 3/8	2 1/8	17 5/8	1/8	16	15	Corner Brook, Nfld.	Gilbert J. Heuer	Gilbert J. Heuer	1970	57
308	39 6/8	40 6/8	34 5/8	5 5/8	5 2/8	15 2/8	13 7/8	2 2/8	11 6/8	12	16	Eastern Meelpaeg, Nfld.	Richard M. Moorehead	Richard M. Moorehead	1969	58
308	38 2/8	41 2/8	35 2/8	5 2/8	5 2/8	13 6/8	11 7/8	10 2/8	5 7/8	14	15	Shenadithit River, Nfld.	L. Ben Hull	L. Ben Hull	1969	58
307 5/8	38 3/8	39 5/8	34 5/8	5 6/8	5 4/8	16 4/8	16	15	2 2/8	19	13	White Bear Bay, Nfld.	John K. Howard	John K. Howard	1938	60
306 3/8	39	39 3/8	29 1/8	4 7/8	4 7/8	16 3/8	13 1/8	12 5/8	1/8	13	13	Millertown, Nfld.	Gerhart H. Huber	Gerhart H. Huber	1966	61
306 2/8	41 3/8	39 3/8	37 3/8	5	4 7/8	13 1/8	12 5/8	10 2/8	9 5/8	17	20	Portage Lake, Nfld.	Arnold Tonn	Arnold Tonn	1967	62
304 6/8	44 6/8	48 2/8	26 5/8	5 4/8	5 3/8	18 7/8	20 7/8	1 2/8	18 1/8	9	15	Middle Ridge, Nfld.	Nat Levenson	Nat Levenson	1950	63
302 7/8	51 4/8	50 5/8	29 1/8	5 7/8	6	18 4/8	11 3/8	16 4/8	1/8	14	10	Nfld.	Gift Of Casmir DeRham	National Collection	—	64
301 1/8	38	39 6/8	27 4/8	5 2/8	5	15 2/8	13 6/8	12 2/8	9 3/8	15	13	Eastern Pond, Nfld.	H. W. Doyle	H. W. Doyle	1953	65
299 4/8	37 5/8	35 5/8	28 5/8	5 3/8	5 3/8	13 6/8	13 4/8	6 3/8	9 6/8	14	17	La Poile, Nfld.	W. T. Yoshimoto	W. T. Yoshimoto	1973	66
298 5/8	40 2/8	41 5/8	31 6/8	5 4/8	6	15	16 3/8	16 3/8	12 3/8	14	11	Pasadena, Nfld.	C. J. McElroy	C. J. McElroy	1968	67
295 4/8	40 4/8	38 1/8	26 7/8	5	5	14 4/8	15 6/8	9 5/8	14	16	17	Top Pond, Nfld.	Robert L. Rex	Robert L. Rex	1966	68
295 4/8	41 5/8	41 1/8	28	5 2/8	5	16 5/8	14 5/8	12 2/8	9 6/8	18	14	South Branch, Nfld.	Victor Pelletier	Victor Pelletier	1967	68

*Final Score subject to revision by additional verifying measurements.

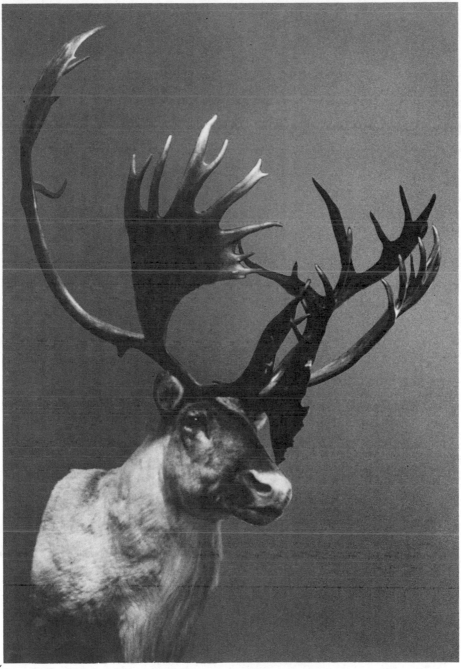

WORLD'S RECORD BARREN GROUND CARIBOU
SCORE: 463 6/8
Locality: Ugashik Lake, Alaska. Date: 1967.
Hunter and owner: Ray Loesche.

Photograph by Dale Schmeling

NUMBER TWO BARREN GROUND CARIBOU
SCORE: 461 6/8
Locality: Post River, Alaska. Date: 1976.
Hunter and owner: John V. Potter, Jr.

Barren Ground Caribou

Minimum Score 400 ***Rangifer tarandus granti* and *Rangifer tarandus groenlandicus***

Barren ground caribou includes trophies from Alaska, northern Yukon Territory, the Northwest Territories (except the McKenzie Mountains), Saskatchewan, Manitoba, and Ontario.

Score	Length of Main Beam R.	Length of Main Beam L.	Inside Spread	Circumference at Smallest Place Between Brow and Bez Points R.	Circumference at Smallest Place Between Brow and Bez Points L.	Length of Brow Points R.	Length of Brow Points L.	Width of Brow Points R.	Width of Brow Points L.	Number of Points R.	Number of Points L.	Locality Killed	By Whom Killed	Owner	Date Killed	Rank
463 6/8	51 2/8	51 5/8	46 7/8	5 7/8	6 1/8	18 2/8	24 6/8	12 7/8	21 4/8	22	23	Ugashik Lake, Alaska	Ray Loesche	Ray Loesche	1967	1
461 6/8	53 2/8	55 3/8	35	8 6/8	8 4/8	20	18 2/8	16 4/8	12 4/8	29	21	Post River, Alaska	John V. Potter, Jr.	John V. Potter, Jr.	1976	2
459 6/8	58	59 3/8	40 6/8	7 1/8	7	19 4/8	18 3/8	16 5/8	4	30	17	Slana, Alaska	Floyd A. Blick	Floyd A. Blick	1954	3
458 6/8	68 2/8	68 6/8	41 6/8	6 1/8	5 6/8	18 6/8	15 7/8	9	2 3/8	21	17	Alaska Pen., Alaska	Joseph Shoaf	Joseph Shoaf	1968	4
458 2/8	55 2/8	54 4/8	45 3/8	5 4/8	5 6/8	20 6/8	21 3/8	10 6/8	15 2/8	15	21	Cinder Creek, Alaska	Josef Meran	Josef Meran	1967	5
458 1/8	54 1/8	56	38 6/8	6 6/8	7 2/8	15 1/8	20 5/8	1/8	20 6/8	21	29	Gulkana River, Alaska	W. J. Krause	W. J. Krause	1953	6
457 7/8	49 7/8	50	31 2/8	7 3/8	7 3/8	17 6/8	15 2/8	13 2/8	8 7/8	18	17	Alaska Range, Alaska	Bobbie E. Robinson	Bobbie E. Robinson	1963	7
456 3/8	53 1/8	55	43 5/8	7	7	9 4/8	19 3/8	1/8	16 6/8	27	31	Mulchatna River, Alaska	Dan Bottrell	Dan Bottrell	1965	8
456 1/8	63 3/8	59 7/8	48	6 7/8	6 7/8	23 1/8	25 6/8	8 3/8	13 1/8	22	21	Alaska Pen., Alaska	Kenneth R. Best	Bavarian Builders, Inc.	1978	9
455 6/8	49 6/8	48 6/8	41 1/8	7 3/8	7 3/8	21 1/8	19	10 5/8	15 3/8	22	26	Alaska Pen., Alaska	Fred H. Blatt, Jr.	Fred H. Blatt, Jr.	1979	10
454 3/8	57 3/8	58 1/8	44 6/8	9 4/8	7 4/8	22 6/8	21 4/8	19 2/8	2 3/8	19	17	Wrangell Mts., Alaska	Mary Brisbin	Mary Brisbin	1959	11
453 1/8	46 5/8	46 6/8	38 2/8	6 7/8	6	17	18 4/8	10 4/8	5 7/8	23	21	Tangle Lakes, Alaska	Mrs. Robert Dosdall	Mrs. Robert Dosdall	1955	12
451 6/8	54 7/8	54 1/8	31 2/8	7 3/8	7 5/8	19 4/8	18 6/8	13 4/8	9 4/8	23	22	Alaska Range, Alaska	Leah Clemmons	Leah Clemmons	1956	13
450 4/8	64 7/8	61	44 3/8	6 5/8	6 1/8	22 2/8	20 7/8	7 4/8	10 4/8	16	18	Alaska Pen., Alaska	Phillip D. Wagner	Phillip D. Wagner	1977	14
450	47 7/8	48 5/8	36 6/8	7 3/8	6 5/8	17	16 2/8	13 5/8	4 3/8	20	24	Talkeetna Mts., Alaska	George L. Clark	George L. Clark	1960	15
449 4/8	50	47 5/8	46	6 3/8	6 3/8	17 1/8	19 1/8	11 5/8	12 7/8	19	23	Lake Ugashik, Alaska	Frank Knies	Frank Knies	1965	16
448 6/8	50 5/8	51 1/8	40 5/8	8 4/8	7 3/8	20	13 3/8	15 1/8	7 5/8	22	24	Little Mulchatna Lake, Alaska	Morton P. Donohue	Morton P. Donohue	1968	17
447 7/8	59 4/8	58 5/8	49	7 5/8	6 5/8	20	23 4/8	4 6/8	14 3/8	18	19	Alaska Pen., Alaska	A. D. Heetderks	A. D. Heetderks	1966	18
447 5/8	54 1/8	57 1/8	48 5/8	6 1/8	6	17 2/8	20	13	14 4/8	24	22	Denali Highway, Alaska	K. K. Anton	K. K. Anton	1957	19
447 5/8	52 3/8	50 3/8	42 5/8	6 6/8	7	19	18 5/8	15 6/8	16 7/8	26	21	Ugashik Lake, Alaska	Neil C. McLaughlin	Neil C. McLaughlin	1971	19
447 5/8	52 4/8	52 4/8	48 5/8	7 4/8	6 7/8	17 1/8	17 1/8	14 4/8	13 6/8	26	22	Alaska Range, Alaska	Richard K. Tollison	Sandra L. Tollison	1978	19
447 4/8	58 3/8	59 5/8	52 7/8	5	5	17 1/8	19 5/8	11 6/8	12 1/8	20	24	Nelchina, Alaska	Bert Klineburger	Bert Klineburger	1964	22
446 6/8	58 2/8	55 5/8	48 5/8	5 7/8	6	20 5/8	23 6/8	1/8	17 5/8	15	19	Cinder River, Alaska	Cliff Thom	Cliff Thom	1966	23

Barren Ground Caribou–*Continued*

Rangifer tarandus granti and *Rangifer tarandus groenlandicus*

Score	Length of Main Beam R.	Length of Main Beam L.	Inside Spread	Circumference at Smallest Place Between Brow and Bez Points R.	Circumference at Smallest Place Between Brow and Bez Points L.	Length of Brow Points R.	Length of Brow Points L.	Width of Brow Points R.	Width of Brow Points L.	Number of Points R.	Number of Points L.	Locality Killed	By Whom Killed	Owner	Date Killed	Rank
446 1/8	60	54 5/8	43 3/8	7 3/8	8 1/8	21	18 4/8	15 2/8	12 2/8	19	21	Alaska Range, Alaska	Toby J. Johnson	Toby J. Johnson	1978	24
444 4/8	60 6/8	57 6/8	59	6	6 3/8	24 2/8	21 5/8	17 6/8	1/8	18	13	Mother Goose Lake, Alaska	S. W. Terry	S. W. Terry	1967	25
444 1/8	47 4/8	51	41 4/8	6 5/8	6	21 3/8	20 1/8	19 2/8	16 7/8	21	22	King Salmon River, Alaska	John C. Belcher	John C. Belcher	1967	26
443 7/8	51 6/8	50 3/8	45 1/8	5 7/8	6	22	19 4/8	3 1/8	15 7/8	19	21	Wrangell Mts., Alaska	A. E. Bruggeman	A. E. Bruggeman	1962	27
443 2/8	45	50	38 2/8	7 4/8	7 1/8	1 3/8	21 6/8	1/8	17 5/8	17	26	Talkeetna Mts., Alaska	Jack C. Robb	Jack C. Robb	1958	28
443 1/8	46 6/8	49 6/8	39 7/8	6	5 7/8	15 6/8	19 1/8	9 3/8	15 2/8	16	22	Denali Highway, Alaska	Stephen Vacula	Stephen Vacula	1967	29
443	57 1/8	57 6/8	51 7/8	6 3/8	6 2/8	10	21	1	16 1/8	12	18	Denali Hwy. Mile 80, Alaska	C. W. Hilbish	C. W. Hilbish	1958	30
443	50 7/8	50 5/8	37	8	6 7/8	17 4/8	19 6/8	12	14 4/8	22	23	Lime Village, Alaska	Billy Ellis, III	Billy Ellis, III	1978	30
441 6/8	51 5/8	53 7/8	47	6 3/8	6	22 3/8	5 3/8	16 7/8	1 1/8	20	13	Alaska Pen., Alaska	George Waldriff	George Waldriff	1962	32
441 4/8	62 6/8	62 7/8	41 4/8	7	7 1/8	24 2/8	7 2/8	20 1/8	1/8	21	14	Wood River, Alaska	Charles M. Bentley	Charles M. Bentley	1960	33
441 4/8	55 6/8	53 3/8	37 2/8	5 7/8	6 2/8	20	15 1/8	14 4/8	1/8	17	15	Healy, Alaska	G. H. Gunn	G. H. Gunn	1968	33
440 7/8	59 6/8	56 4/8	44 2/8	6 4/8	6 2/8	13 6/8	22 2/8	1/8	17 2/8	11	16	Snow Shoe Lake, Alaska	Ray Al Winchester	Demarest Mem. Museum	1953	35
440 2/8	54 2/8	58 1/8	44 2/8	7	6 2/8	9 1/8	20 7/8	1/8	16 5/8	19	28	Blue Berry Creek, Alaska	Ed Shapiro	Ed Shapiro	1964	36
439 6/8	44 6/8	46 4/8	51 2/8	6 6/8	7	18 2/8	3 3/8	14 7/8	5/8	25	17	Port Heiden, Alaska	Marshall Carr	Marshall Carr	1963	37
439 5/8	60 5/8	61 3/8	40 6/8	6 5/8	6 6/8	7 2/8	7 3/8	11 5/8	1/8	16	12	Talkeetna Mts., Alaska	Chris Klineburger	Chris Klineburger	1961	38
439 2/8	45 7/8	36 1/8	38 4/8	5 5/8	6 5/8	23 4/8	19 1/8	16	13 1/8	25	33	Egegik River, Alaska	Norman Tibbetts	Norman Tibbetts	1959	39
439 1/8	59 4/8	59	46	7	5 6/8	2 4/8	18 4/8	1 1/8	10 4/8	12	15	Twin Lakes, Alaska	Thomas H. Lutsey	Thomas H. Lutsey	1955	40
439 1/8	53 4/8	53 4/8	45 6/8	5 6/8	5 5/8	22 5/8	21 4/8	16 5/8	3 3/8	23	15	Iliamna Lake, Alaska	Edward L. Fuchs	Edward L. Fuchs	1955	40
439 /8	62 5/8	60 2/8	53 4/8	5 7/8	5 5/8	21 1/8	15 3/8	16 6/8	9 6/8	19	22	Alaska Pen., Alaska	Joseph H. Johnson	Joseph H. Johnson	1976	42
438	60 6/8	55 4/8	40 7/8	8 6/8	7 5/8	21 4/8	6 2/8	15	1/8	16	12	Ugashik Lake, Alaska	Norman W. Gilmore	Norman W. Gilmore	1967	43
437 7/8	46 2/8	51	38 2/8	6 2/8	6 3/8	21 4/8	16 7/8	15 2/8	9 4/8	20	14	Alaska Pen., Alaska	Herb Klein	Herb Klein	1967	44
437 6/8	61 6/8	61 3/8	37 2/8	6 2/8	6 1/8	5 1/8	23 3/8	1/8	9 1/8	15	25	Nelchina River, Alaska	Don Flynn	Don Flynn	1959	45

437 4/8	48 1/8	48 1/8	38 6/8	7 2/8	6	21 4/8	20 3/8	14 4/8	18 5/8	21	22	Tangle Lake, Alaska	Dennis Weston	Dennis Weston	1964	46
437 3/8	60	61 2/8	50 5/8	6 7/8	7 2/8	13 6/8	19 5/8	1 4/8	12 3/8	15	19	Naknek, Alaska	C. J. McElroy	C. J. McElroy	1966	47
437 2/8	59 3/8	57 2/8	43 5/8	6 3/8	5 5/8	20 1/8	19 4/8	5	12 6/8	19	23	Mulchatna River, Alaska	Lyle W. Bentzen	Lyle W. Bentzen	1974	48
436 5/8	52 2/8	53	48	6 2/8	6	16 6/8	19 5/8	12 6/8	10 6/8	15	16	Chisana River, Alaska	Terry Overly	Terry Overly	1976	49
436 2/8	54 6/8	53 1/8	41 6/8	6	5 4/8	19 1/8	20 2/8	15 4/8	15 7/8	22	18	Nabesna, Alaska	Bill Ellis	Bill Ellis	1964	50
436 2/8	55 4/8	58 7/8	42 1/8	7 3/8	6	20 6/8	24 3/8	1 7/8	19 3/8	19	23	Alaska Pen., Alaska	A. R. Buckles	A. R. Buckles	1967	50
436 1/8	54 4/8	55	47 5/8	5 7/8	5 6/8	9 6/8	24 2/8	1 1/8	21 5/8	15	27	Port Muller, Alaska	Marvin L. Fergastad	Marvin L. Fergastad	1962	52
435 7/8	56 2/8	54	44 3/8	6 3/8	7	18 1/8	3	16	1/8	23	16	McClaren Ridge, Alaska	Peter W. Bading	Peter W. Bading	1959	53
435 7/8	55 2/8	51 5/8	39 4/8	6 7/8	8 3/8	10 3/8	17 4/8	10	5 2/8	23	33	Wrangell Mtns., Alaska	Fred Williams	Fred Williams	1964	53
435 6/8	48 2/8	52 2/8	43	8 1/8	8 6/8	14 1/8	13 6/8	11 3/8	10	22	19	Farewell, Alaska	Henry Budny	Henry Budny	1960	55
435 5/8	53 6/8	54 3/8	37	6 7/8	6 7/8	18 4/8	20 6/8	11 1/8	14 4/8	22	19	Talkeetna Mts., Alaska	Mrs. Arnt Antonsen	Mrs. Arnt Antonsen	1960	56
435 3/8	51 2/8	50 3/8	41 7/8	7 7/8	7	23 7/8	12 1/8	18 1/8	2 7/8	19	13	Ugashik Lake, Alaska	Robert E. Sass	Robert E. Sass	1963	57
435 2/8	52 2/8	49 6/8	32 2/8	9 2/8	9 5/8	19 7/8	22 2/8	9 5/8	6 5/8	19	19	Naknek River, Alaska	Chris M. Kendrick	Chris M. Kendrick	1977	58
435 1/8	53 1/8	55 4/8	30 2/8	5 6/8	5 3/8	22 2/8	18 7/8	11 5/8	12 3/8	25	19	Alaska Range, Alaska	Kermit G. Johnson	Kermit G. Johnson	1970	59
434 4/8	53 1/8	53	41	6 2/8	5 7/8	4 3/8	17 4/8	1/8	11 4/8	17	24	Talkeetna Mts., Alaska	John M. Killian	John M. Killian	1960	60
434 3/8	58 4/8	57 5/8	42 4/8	6 2/8	6	17 7/8	17 3/8	11 4/8	9	22	22	Tangle Lakes, Alaska	Bryant Flynn	Bryant Flynn	1953	61
434 1/8	42 3/8	45 4/8	35 2/8	6 4/8	6 5/8	16	17 4/8	7 5/8	12 4/8	21	22	Tazlina, Alaska	Chuck Sutter	Chuck Sutter	1958	62
434	61 3/8	60	40 4/8	6 4/8	6 2/8	19 3/8	19 7/8	11 4/8	6 4/8	14	18	Little Nelchina River, Alaska	Joseph Brisco, Jr.	Joseph Brisco, Jr.	1955	63
434	51 6/8	48 6/8	44 3/8	6 1/8	6 1/8	20 1/8	19 4/8	15 4/8	14 2/8	21	16	King Salmon, Alaska	Roger W. Seiler	Roger W. Seiler	1959	63
433 6/8	59 2/8	56 7/8	41 2/8	6 4/8	6 2/8	15 5/8	20 4/8	10 1/8	15	25	21	Port Moller, Alaska	Paul M. Sweezey	Paul M. Sweezey	1968	65
433 4/8	59 4/8	59 7/8	57 2/8	6 3/8	6 2/8	23	8 4/8	18 2/8	1	22	13	Alaska Pen., Alaska	Herb Klein	Herb Klein	1964	66
433 3/8	59 3/8	56	55 5/8	5 6/8	6	3 6/8	19 7/8	5/8	14 6/8	16	22	Port Heiden, Alaska	D. R. Klein	D. R. Klein	1966	67
432 7/8	52 1/8	52 6/8	48 4/8	6 5/8	6 1/8	5 5/8	23 7/8	4	16 5/8	16	19	Black Lake, Alaska	John Tyler Swiss	John Tyler Swiss	1967	68
432 4/8	58 3/8	50 3/8	50	7 1/8	6 1/8	5 4/8	22	1	16 2/8	15	19	King Salmon, Alaska	Dan E. McCarty	Dan E. McCarty	1967	69
432	52 1/8	51 5/8	42 4/8	7	7	10 1/8	15	4 6/8	12 1/8	21	22	Lake Louise, Alaska	Mike Walganski	Mike Walganski	1961	70
431 6/8	49 2/8	49 4/8	37 6/8	6	5 5/8	18 3/8	15 5/8	11 7/8	1/8	18	19	Upper Susitna River, Alaska	Theodore A. Warren	Theodore A. Warren	1955	71
431 6/8	49 2/8	45 6/8	33 3/8	7 1/8	7	–	19 2/8	–	16 5/8	20	29	Clarence Lake, Alaska	Jack Hill	Jack Hill	1964	71
431 5/8	54 3/8	54 7/8	41 6/8	6 3/8	6 6/8	17	18 7/8	1 3/8	10 7/8	15	17	Talkeetna Mts., Alaska	Joseph R. Good	Joseph R. Good	1956	73
431 3/8	49	52 4/8	36 4/8	6 7/8	6 5/8	15 6/8	13 3/8	14	5 6/8	28	24	Cold Bay, Alaska	Gary D'Aigle	Gary D'Aigle	1973	74
431 3/8	54 1/8	51 7/8	35 4/8	6 7/8	7 3/8	18 4/8	18 7/8	14 1/8	10 7/8	20	20	Lake Clark, Alaska	William R. Lykken	William R. Lykken	1976	74
431	50 6/8	54 2/8	39	6 6/8	6 5/8	21	21	13 3/8	14 5/8	20	21	Port Heiden, Alaska	Ray B. Nienhaus	Ray B. Nienhaus	1966	76
430 6/8	50 2/8	49 6/8	32 3/8	5 6/8	6	17 4/8	16 6/8	10 6/8	10 5/8	20	26	Talkeetna Mts., Alaska	Nelson Spencer	Nelson Spencer	1962	77
430 3/8	47	49 6/8	35 6/8	6 6/8	7	22	13 4/8	8 4/8	14 1/8	24	24	Gulkana River, Alaska	Troy Bogard	Troy Bogard	1954	78

Barren Ground Caribou–*Continued*

Rangifer tarandus granti and *Rangifer tarandus groenlandicus*

Score	Length of Main Beam R.	Length of Main Beam L.	Inside Spread	Circumference at Smallest Place Between Brow and Bez Points R.	Circumference at Smallest Place Between Brow and Bez Points L.	Length of Brow Points R.	Length of Brow Points L.	Width of Brow Points R.	Width of Brow Points L.	Number of Points R.	Number of Points L.	Locality Killed	By Whom Killed	Owner	Date Killed	Rank
430 3/8	57	54 1/8	46 4/8	8	8 5/8	17 3/8	6 1/8	9 5/8	6/8	22	17	Alaska Pen., Alaska	Michaux Nash, Jr.	Michaux Nash, Jr.	1968	78
430 2/8	57 7/8	53 6/8	44 5/8	6 2/8	6 4/8	18 3/8	16 6/8	15 2/8	10 6/8	23	16	Mother Goose Lake, Alaska	R. C. Parker	R. C. Parker	1959	80
430 2/8	53 1/8	54 3/8	44 1/8	6 1/8	5 6/8	22 4/8	22 4/8	2 6/8	17 3/8	15	20	Alaska Pen., Alaska	Ernest Milani	Ernest Milani	1961	80
429 4/8	50 6/8	51 5/8	30 7/8	5 3/8	5 7/8	18 6/8	19 2/8	15 7/8	12 6/8	21	24	Bonnet Plume, Yukon	R. G. Studemann	R. G. Studemann	1963	82
429 3/8	53 6/8	59	42 6/8	7 6/8	7	15 6/8	–	11 3/8	–	24	17	Mulchatna River, Alaska	Lem Crofton	Lem Crofton	1978	83
429 1/8	58	58	35	6 6/8	6	26	15	19	1/8	22	15	Alaska Range, Alaska	J. C. Phillips	Harvard Univ. Museum	1928	84
429 1/8	49	48 3/8	43 6/8	9 3/8	7	16 6/8	17 3/8	8 7/8	8 7/8	21	20	Tyone Lake, Alaska	Ralph Marshall	Ralph Marshall	1960	84
427 5/8	56 3/8	59 2/8	44 1/8	5 2/8	5 4/8	19 6/8	18 4/8	13 7/8	1/8	19	11	Talkeetna Mts., Alaska	Donald Parker	Donald Parker	1969	86
426 7/8	49	46	40 5/8	6 1/8	5 7/8	16	21 7/8	9 2/8	11 1/8	22	25	Cinder River, Alaska	John G. Merry, Jr.	John G. Merry, Jr.	1968	87
426 6/8	52 4/8	53 1/8	45 1/8	6 1/8	7 2/8	15 2/8	6 1/8	17 3/8	1/8	25	17	Anchorage, Alaska	Peter W. Bading	Peter W. Bading	1963	88
426 6/8	52 6/8	52 6/8	49 1/8	7 2/8	5 6/8	11 4/8	20	1/8	15 2/8	17	20	Alaska Range, Alaska	Dan Parker	Dan Parker	1971	88
426 3/8	52 6/8	54 6/8	37 6/8	6 5/8	6 3/8	18 1/8	18 7/8	3 2/8	15 5/8	15	22	Eureka, Alaska	C. C. Grey	C. C. Grey	1953	90
426 3/8	52 3/8	48 7/8	40 5/8	8 2/8	8	3 2/8	17	1/8	11 3/8	17	22	Wrangell Mts., Alaska	Richard Conroy	Richard Conroy	1961	90
426 3/8	53 2/8	54 4/8	44 3/8	8 3/8	8	24	–	13 6/8	–	19	18	Black Lake, Alaska	Lester W. Miller, Jr.	Lester W. Miller, Jr.	1963	90
426 2/8	86 2/8	60 3/8	41 6/8	6 1/8	6 1/8	19 6/8	13	15 3/8	1/8	17	15	White River, Yukon	F. C. Havemeyer	National Collection	1912	93
425 6/8	45 4/8	49 2/8	32 2/8	6	6	17 7/8	19 3/8	11 4/8	18 6/8	18	18	Denali Highway, Alaska	Sam Pancotto	Sam Pancotto	1960	94
425 6/8	53 2/8	55 2/8	39 4/8	7 4/8	7 4/8	3 2/8	14	1/8	10 1/8	15	19	Nabesna, Alaska	Frank Martin, Jr.	Frank Martin, Jr.	1965	94
425 5/8	52 6/8	48	31	7 2/8	7 2/8	13	19	1/8	13 4/8	14	19	Iliamna Lake, Alaska	Donald R. Barnes	Donald R. Barnes	1973	96
425 2/8	46 7/8	48 2/8	35 2/8	6 4/8	6 5/8	16	17 2/8	7 5/8	12 3/8	20	21	McClaren Ridge, Alaska	Peter W. Bading	Peter W. Bading	1959	97
425	52 2/8	52 6/8	40 5/8	6 1/8	6 3/8	17 5/8	9 3/8	12 2/8	1/8	23	17	Susitna Area, Alaska	Elmer M. Rusten	Elmer M. Rusten	1952	98
425	45 1/8	45 2/8	36 7/8	5 6/8	5 3/8	20 3/8	21 6/8	15 1/8	7 7/8	22	22	Talkeetna Mts., Alaska	Thorne Donnelley	Thorne Donnelley	1959	98
425	47 1/8	52 4/8	36	7	6 3/8	8	23	1 3/8	18 5/8	18	32	Lake Louise, Alaska	H. E. O'Neal	H. E. O'Neal	1964	98
424 7/8	57 1/8	54	49 5/8	6 2/8	6 5/8	20 5/8	14 4/8	14 7/8	1 4/8	18	16	La Pas, Manitoba	Unknown	Luxton Museum	——	101

Score												Locality	By whom killed	Owner	Date	Rank
424 7/8	52 5/8	58 5/8	43 3/8	7 6/8	8 1/8	15 5/8	14 4/8	5 4/8	9	19	16	Denali Highway, Alaska	Moyer Johnstone	Moyer Johnstone	1958	101
424 4/8	51 1/8	47 1/8	43 6/8	6 5/8	6 4/8	17	17	11 3/8	8 1/8	18	20	Talkeetna Mts., Alaska	Wayne C. Eubank	Wayne C. Eubank	1959	103
424 4/8	55	52 5/8	47 5/8	7 1/8	7 6/8	19 6/8	15 5/8	14 6/8	1 6/8	18	13	Talkeetna Mts., Alaska	Karl Weber	Karl Weber	1959	103
424 3/8	51 7/8	52 1/8	48	5 5/8	5 5/8	19 6/8	14 5/8	13	4 5/8	23	14	Post River, Alaska	Guntran Rhomberg	Guntran Rhomberg	1966	105
424 4/8	51 1/8	49	43 3/8	6 3/8	6 3/8	12 2/8	22 4/8	1	17 7/8	16	23	Talkeetna Mts., Alaska	Morris Spencer	Morris Spencer	1962	106
424 4/8	50	46 1/8	38 4/8	6 5/8	6 5/8	20 1/8	19 6/8	7 4/8	16	18	26	Summit, Alaska	Myron Bethel	Myron Bethel	1976	106
424 4/8	61	59	46	7 7/8	6 3/8	16 4/8	12 6/8	8 3/8	4/8	17	13	Lake Louise, Alaska	Dick Luckow	Dick Luckow	1959	108
424 4/8	52 5/8	52 4/8	46 6/8	6 3/8	6 3/8	17 6/8	19 6/8	9 1/8	4 6/8	16	17	Talkeetna Mts., Alaska	Lyle E. Reynolds	Lyle E. Reynolds	1960	108
423 3/8	43 3/8	43 4/8	32 7/8	6 3/8	6 7/8	16	1 7/8	13 4/8	5/8	37	24	Wrangell Mts., Alaska	Dan G. Best	Dan G. Best	1961	110
423 3/8	56 5/8	55 1/8	40 7/8	6 4/8	6 6/8	18 4/8	14 4/8	12 5/8	1 4/8	16	12	Alaska Pen., Alaska	Rex Hancock	Rex Hancock	1961	110
423 3/8	52 7/8	50 5/8	40 3/8	5 3/8	5 7/8	1 7/8	1 5/8	1/8	10 4/8	19	23	King Salmon River, Alaska	Henry N. Warren	Henry N. Warren	1978	110
423 3/8	44 6/8	44	32 4/8	7 1/8	6 7/8	19 3/8	20 3/8	9 1/8	17	18	24	Tyone River, Alaska	Alva H. Rich	Alva H. Rich	1961	113
423 3/8	59 3/8	59 4/8	41 1/8	5 5/8	5 5/8	19	19 2/8	8	16 2/8	17	21	Ferry, Alaska	Roy Maxwell	Roy Maxwell	1965	113
423	53 1/8	55 5/8	44 1/8	6 7/8	6 7/8	16	15 3/8	6 5/8	9 6/8	13	25	Gulkana River, Alaska	Lewis E. Yearout	Lewis E. Yearout	1956	115
422 7/8	50 6/8	51 5/8	37	6 3/8	6 3/8	21 1/8	20 3/8	9 4/8	15 4/8	20	21	Rainy Pass, Alaska	L. Arthur Cushman, Jr.	L. Arthur Cushman, Jr.	1961	116
422 6/8	49 3/8	48 6/8	47 3/8	6 3/8	6 3/8	16 5/8	14 5/8	11 5/8	6 6/8	19	13	Slana River, Alaska	Kirby Kiltz	Kirby Kiltz	1959	117
422 6/8	46 6/8	51 7/8	40	5 7/8	6 1/8	19 6/8	17	12 6/8	3 6/8	18	17	Matanuska River, Alaska	Stephen E. Skaggs	Stephen E. Skaggs	1978	117
422 2/8	52 1/8	47 7/8	45 4/8	5 5/8	5 5/8	20 7/8	13	4 7/8	11 7/8	22	20	Iliamna Lake, Alaska	Bill Sims	Bill Sims	1973	119
422 2/8	49 2/8	49 3/8	37 4/8	6 3/8	6 3/8	21 4/8	19 3/8	13 3/8	11 4/8	22	20	Tangle Lakes, Alaska	Leroy G. Bohuslor	Leroy G. Bohuslor	1952	120
422 1/8	42 3/8	45 7/8	37	7 6/8	7 6/8	16 5/8	13	15 5/8	11	27	21	Susitna River, Alaska	Warren Jones	Warren Jones	1961	121
421 7/8	55 6/8	48	33 6/8	7 3/8	7 2/8	17 5/8	20	16 3/8	10 7/8	22	21	Farewell Lake, Alaska	Richard K. Siller	Richard K. Siller	1958	122
421 5/8	64 5/8	59 3/8	57	7 3/8	7 1/8	22 3/8	2 6/8	16 5/8	1	18	12	King Salmon, Alaska	Edwin W. Seiler	Edwin W. Seiler	1958	123
421 5/8	51 4/8	50	36 3/8	7 4/8	8 7/8	18 3/8	17 7/8	9	14	17	23	Port Mohler, Alaska	John S. Clark	John S. Clark	1966	124
421 5/8	56 7/8	55 5/8	56	5 5/8	5 7/8	18 3/8	1/8	12 5/8	-	10	9	Upper Ugashik Lake, Alaska	Barry Barbour	Barry Barbour	1969	124
421 4/8	55 3/8	54 6/8	42 6/8	7 3/8	7 1/8	20 3/8	19 6/8	12 7/8	15 5/8	17	16	Denali Highway, Alaska	D. G. Skagerberg	D. G. Skagerberg	1956	126
421 1/8	55	53 6/8	43	5 7/8	5 7/8	16 3/8	15 5/8	10	9 7/8	18	18	Denali Highway, Alaska	John Schmidel	John Schmidel	1961	126
421 1/8	55 1/8	54 2/8	45 5/8	5 5/8	5 5/8	15 5/8	20 4/8	4 5/8	17	17	26	Twin Lakes, Alaska	Paul O'Hollaren	Paul O'Hollaren	1964	126
421 1/8	58 1/8	58 1/8	44 6/8	7 1/8	7 1/8	19	2 4/8	12 3/8	1/8	17	12	Kuskokwim River, Alaska	Dennis Harms	Dennis Harms	1967	126
421 1/8	48 7/8	49 7/8	37 1/8	6 3/8	6 3/8	21 2/8	19 2/8	12 7/8	11 6/8	22	19	Alaska	Jonas Bros. Of Seattle	Unknown	1953	130

Barren Ground Caribou–*Continued*

Rangifer tarandus granti and *Rangifer tarandus groenlandicus*

Score	Length of Main Beam R.	Length of Main Beam L.	Inside Spread	Circumference at Smallest Place Between Brow and Bez Points R.	Circumference at Smallest Place Between Brow and Bez Points L.	Length of Brow Points R.	Length of Brow Points L.	Width of Brow Points R.	Width of Brow Points L.	Number of Points R.	Number of Points L.	Locality Killed	By Whom Killed	Owner	Date Killed	Rank
421 1/8	47	51 4/8	37 3/8	7 4/8	7 3/8	18 2/8	19	10 5/8	10 5/8	24	21	Lake Louise, Alaska	Orel O. Parker	Orel O. Parker	1959	131
421 1/8	58 7/8	57 3/8	45 6/8	5 7/8	5 6/8	19 2/8	–	10 5/8	–	19	12	Ugashik Lake, Alaska	Jack A. Shane, Sr.	Jack A. Shane, Sr.	1967	131
421 1/8	47 2/8	48 6/8	43 6/8	6	6	–	19 6/8	–	14 1/8	17	21	Alaska Pen., Alaska	Alice J. Landreth	Alice J. Landreth	1968	131
421	56 4/8	58 4/8	49 1/8	5 4/8	6 1/8	20 3/8	20 4/8	15 5/8	14 1/8	13	19	Alaska Pen., Alaska	Lloyd W. Birdwell	Lloyd W. Birdwell	1970	134
420 7/8	56 2/8	55 2/8	45 3/8	5 6/8	5 5/8	23 6/8	2 4/8	21 4/8	4/8	16	14	Port Heiden, Alaska	Otis Chandler	Otis Chandler	1964	135
420 7/8	54 1/8	54 7/8	38 4/8	8	7 7/8	20 1/8	9 1/8	14 6/8	1/8	22	15	Farewell, Alaska	Vern G. Smith	Vern G. Smith	1967	135
420 4/8	59 4/8	57 4/8	42 4/8	8 6/8	8 5/8	12	18 2/8	1	17 2/8	11	16	Tangle Lake, Alaska	J. W. Latham	J. W. Latham	1961	137
420 4/8	46 4/8	48	39 5/8	6 1/8	6 2/8	18 1/8	18 3/8	3 3/8	13 2/8	19	24	Dog Salmon River, Alaska	Gary R. Swanson	Gary R. Swanson	1966	137
420 3/8	55	52 4/8	40 4/8	5 4/8	5 4/8	23	15 3/8	17 4/8	3	19	12	Alaska Pen., Alaska	Wm. M. Ellis	Wm. M. Ellis	1963	139
420 1/8	59 2/8	57 2/8	40 4/8	6 2/8	6 3/8	22 7/8	22 6/8	5 4/8	17 4/8	15	19	Iliamna Lake, Alaska	A. E. Wilson	A. E. Wilson	1955	140
419 6/8	54 6/8	50 5/8	47 3/8	7 4/8	6 5/8	17 1/8	16 4/8	9 2/8	10 2/8	15	16	Dog Salmon River, Alaska	Ralph H. Eisaman	Ralph H. Eisaman	1971	141
419 6/8	44	46 1/8	46 2/8	6 7/8	7 7/8	14 4/8	15 5/8	1/8	12 2/8	15	22	Aleutian Range, Alaska	Fred Dykema	Fred Dykema	1973	141
419 5/8	43 6/8	45 3/8	29 7/8	7 2/8	7 5/8	14	15 4/8	8 7/8	10 7/8	22	22	Chisana, Alaska	Thomas F. Esper	Thomas F. Esper	1965	143
419 5/8	51 1/8	50 1/8	35 6/8	6 2/8	6 1/8	16 5/8	15 7/8	9 5/8	12 4/8	22	23	Mt. Drum, Alaska	Jerald T. Waite	Jerald T. Waite	1966	143
419 5/8	53 3/8	53 5/8	39 4/8	6 6/8	6 5/8	16 4/8	20 4/8	14 7/8	10 2/8	16	16	Nabesna, Alaska	Bernard Kendall	Bernard Kendall	1969	143
419 4/8	50	51 7/8	45 3/8	7 2/8	7 2/8	6 4/8	19 3/8	1/8	12 3/8	13	21	Rainy Pass, Alaska	Warren Page	Warren Page	1956	146
419 4/8	46 2/8	47 2/8	32	7	7 2/8	16 5/8	15 2/8	8 1/8	8 4/8	20	20	Talkeetna, Alaska	Dale Westenbarger	Dale Westenbarger	1965	146
419 3/8	45	45 4/8	35 5/8	7 4/8	8 1/8	13 1/8	1 2/8	15 3/8	18	26	21	Fairbanks, Alaska	Unknown	Ladd Air Force Base PR	1953	148
419 2/8	50 2/8	50 5/8	42	7 1/8	7 3/8	17 2/8	13	13 1/8	1/8	20	17	Chisana, Alaska	John S. Newkam, Jr.	John S. Newkam, Jr.	1960	149
419	45 2/8	44 2/8	35 5/8	7 4/8	7 4/8	15 7/8	14 1/8	8 2/8	9 1/8	18	19	Becharos Lake, Alaska	Ron L. Lerch	Ron L. Lerch	1966	150
418 7/8	49 5/8	50	43	6	5 6/8	18	1 4/8	12	1/8	28	20	Nabesna River Valley, Alaska	Wayne Platt	Wayne Platt	1958	151
418 7/8	52 6/8	51 5/8	50 4/8	6 2/8	5 6/8	18 7/8	19	5 2/8	8 2/8	12	13	Chistochina, Alaska	James H. Lahey	James H. Lahey	1961	151
418 7/8	52 6/8	53 1/8	40 1/8	5 5/8	5 6/8	19 2/8	22 6/8	9	8 4/8	10	15	Mother Goose Lake, Alaska	Robert A. Epperson	Robert A. Epperson	1963	151
418 7/8	54 1/8	50 5/8	40 6/8	7	6 2/8	15 3/8	17	10 6/8	11 4/8	18	17	Hoholitna River, Alaska	O. B. Beard, III	O. B. Beard, III	1974	151

418 7/8	49 4/8	49 3/8	44	5 6/8	5 6/8	17 2/8	18 2/8	12 4/8	11 1/8	20	19	Cold Bay, Alaska	James E. Carson	James E. Carson	1974	151
418 6/8	59	55 5/8	34 4/8	6 4/8	6 1/8	14	22 3/8	1 2/8	6 1/8	17	21	Alaska Pen., Alaska	Otis Chandler	Otis Chandler	1964	156
418 5/8	59 6/8	60	53 1/8	6 6/8	6 7/8	19 7/8	17 2/8	12 5/8	3 3/8	12	15	Eureka, Alaska	William Curtis	F. A. Harrington	1949	157
418 5/8	50 4/8	49 1/8	32 7/8	5 6/8	5 3/8	19 5/8	–	12 7/8	–	27	17	Hicks Creek, Alaska	Charles Brumbelow	Charles Brumbelow	1956	157
418 5/8	54 2/8	52 3/8	37	7	6 4/8	20 2/8	19 3/8	7 7/8	11 7/8	14	17	Alaska Pen., Alaska	C. Driskell	C. Driskell	1965	157
418 3/8	52 7/8	52 5/8	45 5/8	5 6/8	6	12 1/8	19 1/8	1 3/8	15 7/8	15	17	Rainy Pass, Alaska	Aaron Saenz, Jr.	Aaron Saenz, Jr.	1964	160
418 3/8	47 1/8	46 5/8	39 6/8	7	7 3/8	19 3/8	–	11 4/8	–	21	12	High Lake, Alaska	Glen E. Park	Glen E. Park	1965	160
418 3/8	53	56	38 7/8	6 6/8	6 5/8	8	18 1/8	1	14 1/8	19	23	Aleutian Range, Alaska	Wayne Patton	Wayne Patton	1968	160
418 1/8	61 3/8	61 4/8	40 1/8	6 2/8	6 3/8	11 1/8	20 2/8	1	14 7/8	13	22	Clarence Lake, Alaska	James K. Harrower	James K. Harrower	1961	163
418 1/8	50 5/8	48 4/8	34 7/8	6	6	18 2/8	16 5/8	16 1/8	8	24	19	Denali Highway, Alaska	Jerry Shepard	Jerry Shepard	1961	163
418 1/8	53 3/8	50 7/8	39 7/8	7	6 4/8	20	10 5/8	18 6/8	1/8	23	13	Caribou Creek, Alaska	Gary Joll	Gary Joll	1963	163
418 1/8	50 2/8	53 2/8	45 3/8	6 2/8	6 3/8	13 6/8	17	2 6/8	14 6/8	22	23	Chistochina, Alaska	Delbert H. Bullock	Delbert H. Bullock	1964	163
418	54 2/8	54	42 7/8	6 3/8	6 1/8	19 7/8	14 1/8	15 2/8	1/8	18	15	Alaska Range, Alaska	Richard L. McClellan	Richard L. McClellan	1978	167
417 6/8	52 2/8	54 5/8	43 1/8	6 4/8	6	20 5/8	21 2/8	4	15 4/8	14	20	Big Susitna, Alaska	Forrest Boyce	Jack Dustin	1957	168
417 6/8	51 7/8	50 1/8	42 1/8	6 5/8	6 1/8	–	16 5/8	–	12 4/8	13	19	Talkeetna Mts., Alaska	Mrs. R. S. Mosiman	Mrs. R. S. Mosiman	1958	168
417 6/8	55 2/8	60 4/8	46 2/8	5 5/8	5 6/8	15 7/8	21 7/8	9	13 6/8	15	19	Alaska Pen., Alaska	William J. Miller	William J. Miller	1967	168
417 5/8	52 6/8	51 2/8	38 4/8	6 7/8	6 7/8	15 6/8	12 5/8	1/8	11 7/8	15	26	Wrangell Mts., Alaska	Fred Packer	Fred Packer	1955	171
417 5/8	50	49 2/8	27 3/8	6 4/8	6	21 7/8	13 2/8	17 7/8	17	25	16	Alaska Range, Alaska	Richard K. Mellon	Richard K. Mellon	1959	171
417 4/8	52 3/8	55 7/8	38 1/8	6 4/8	7 1/8	17 6/8	18 1/8	12 7/8	13 1/8	19	21	Mulchatna River, Alaska	R. D. Eichenour	R. D. Eichenour	1968	173
417 3/8	51 3/8	53	35 2/8	7 6/8	6 6/8	14 6/8	19	7 7/8	15	17	17	Twin Lakes, Alaska	Samuel B. Webb, Jr.	Samuel B. Webb, Jr.	1960	174
417 3/8	48 7/8	49 4/8	45 4/8	6	6 3/8	24 5/8	18 6/8	12 7/8	11 1/8	14	16	Alaska Pen., Alaska	Herb Klein	Herb Klein	1964	174
417 3/8	48 4/8	48 2/8	41 7/8	5 3/8	5 5/8	18 4/8	17	12 1/8	3 1/8	26	17	Alaska Pen., Alaska	Tyson Nichols	Tyson Nichols	1979	174
417 1/8	50 5/8	52	25 3/8	6	6 2/8	19 5/8	17 1/8	5	11	16	19	Rainy Pass, Alaska	Sigurd Jensen	Sigurd Jensen	1956	177
417	50 5/8	52 3/8	33 6/8	8 3/8	9 1/8	15 1/8	15 4/8	10 2/8	9 5/8	13	17	Little Delta River, Alaska	Fred Bear	Fred Bear	1959	178
416 6/8	54 3/8	51 7/8	43	8	8	7 5/8	18 5/8	1/8	15 1/8	17	20	Wood River, Alaska	A. Knutson	A. Knutson	1957	179
416 5/8	56 4/8	58 4/8	41	7	6 6/8	12 2/8	19 3/8	1	14 6/8	15	16	Mulchatna River, Alaska	R. D. Eichenour	R. D. Eichenour	1968	180
416 5/8	51 2/8	51 4/8	36 4/8	6 4/8	6 5/8	17 7/8	4 5/8	12 3/8	1 4/8	31	21	Alaska Pen., Alaska	Jim Ford	Jim Ford	1970	180
416 4/8	56	54	37 5/8	7 4/8	7 4/8	13 6/8	16 2/8	7 3/8	13 2/8	15	21	Rainy Pass, Alaska	J. Watson Webb, Jr.	J. Watson Webb, Jr.	1934	182
416 4/8	45 1/8	45 7/8	41 4/8	8 4/8	7 6/8	20 7/8	18 6/8	5 1/8	14 4/8	17	20	Upper Ugashik Lake, Alaska	Russell Matthes	Russell Matthes	1969	182
416 3/8	52 1/8	51 3/8	44 2/8	7 5/8	7 4/8	15 4/8	17 4/8	9	8 3/8	13	17	Talkeetna Mts., Alaska	Karris Keirn	Karris Keirn	1958	184
416 3/8	53 4/8	52 7/8	38 3/8	6 2/8	5 6/8	18 6/8	19	16 1/8	14 5/8	24	18	Post Lake, Alaska	Gerald Scheuerman	Gerald Scheuerman	1961	184
416 3/8	58 1/8	59 7/8	46	7 5/8	8 2/8	20 7/8	10 1/8	13 2/8	1/8	13	11	Iliamna Lake, Alaska	Michael J. Ryan, Sr.	Michael J. Ryan, Sr.	1973	184
416 1/8	52 6/8	52 7/8	37 5/8	6 2/8	6 2/8	15 3/8	19 1/8	1 2/8	15 2/8	11	20	Wrangell Mts., Alaska	William H. Warrick	William H. Warrick	1961	187

Barren Ground Caribou–*Continued*

Rangifer tarandus granti and *Rangifer tarandus groenlandicus*

Score	Length of Main Beam R.	Length of Main Beam L.	Inside Spread	Circumference at Smallest Place Between Brow and Bez Points R.	Circumference at Smallest Place Between Brow and Bez Points L.	Length of Brow Points R.	Length of Brow Points L.	Width of Brow Points R.	Width of Brow Points L.	Number of Points R.	Number of Points L.	Locality Killed	By Whom Killed	Owner	Date Killed	Rank
416 1/8	54 2/8	56 6/8	46 1/8	7	7	–	20 2/8	–	16	11	20	Farewell Lake, Alaska	K. T. Miller	K. T. Miller	1962	187
416 1/8	49 2/8	49 2/8	38 2/8	6 3/8	6 5/8	24	17 7/8	17 4/8	4 4/8	16	14	Crooked Creek, Alaska	Bill E. Slone	Bill E. Slone	1964	187
416 1/8	51 2/8	50 4/8	35	5 7/8	5 6/8	19	18 5/8	15	12 2/8	20	22	Little Mulchatna River, Alaska	M. E. Kulik	M. E. Kulik	1967	187
416	57 3/8	56 7/8	39 6/8	6 1/8	6 2/8	21 2/8	3 1/8	17 3/8	6/8	17	14	Ugashik, Alaska	Richard S. Farr	Richard S. Farr	1966	191
416	50 2/8	51 5/8	48	5 5/8	5 4/8	18 1/8	17 6/8	13 5/8	10	19	22	Alaska Pen., Alaska	Bill E. Hodson	Bill E. Hodson	1978	191
415 7/8	55 2/8	53 5/8	45 3/8	6	6 3/8	16	16 7/8	10 5/8	10 2/8	25	25	Steese Highway, Alaska	Howard Hill	Howard Hill	1958	193
415 5/8	49 2/8	52 6/8	39 2/8	5 7/8	6 1/8	17 6/8	17 4/8	6 6/8	11 7/8	19	20	King Salmon River, Alaska	Robert G. Barta	Robert G. Barta	1978	194
415 4/8	56 3/8	56 7/8	35 7/8	6 5/8	6 5/8	19 1/8	7 7/8	12 3/8	5 4/8	20	16	Tyone Creek, Alaska	E. H. Miller	E. H. Miller	1956	195
415 4/8	54 7/8	53	39 2/8	5 5/8	5 4/8	20 3/8	22 3/8	15 7/8	9 7/8	22	18	Egegik River, Alaska	George J. Markham	George J. Markham	1967	195
415	56 4/8	57	44 5/8	6 1/8	6 6/8	16 4/8	19 5/8	8 2/8	9 6/8	14	15	Alaska Pen., Alaska	Picked Up	William P. Bredesen, Jr.	1974	197
414 7/8	54 2/8	53 1/8	46 1/8	5 4/8	5 3/8	20 3/8	23 2/8	9 6/8	8 1/8	16	17	Alaska Pen., Alaska	Herb Klein	Herb Klein	1967	198
414 6/8	56	55 1/8	42 1/8	6	6 1/8	21 3/8	16 7/8	16 5/8	1 2/8	15	10	Denali Highway, Alaska	Paul Patz	Paul Patz	1965	199
414 5/8	57 3/8	54 3/8	42 4/8	7	6 2/8	19 2/8	–	15 7/8	–	20	16	Rainy Pass, Alaska	Mahlon T. White	Mahlon T. White	1969	200
414 4/8	53 6/8	52 4/8	50 3/8	5 6/8	5 5/8	2 4/8	19 5/8	4/8	15 2/8	15	22	Naknek, Alaska	C. J. McElroy	C. J. McElroy	1966	201
414 4/8	46 3/8	54 5/8	40 1/8	6	6	5 2/8	21 1/8	6/8	17 1/8	16	24	Alaska Pen., Alaska	George H. Landreth	George H. Landreth	1967	201
414 3/8	54	55 6/8	39 4/8	7 1/8	7	16 3/8	16	10 5/8	9 1/8	15	17	Denali Highway, Alaska	C. W. Hilbish	C. W. Hilbish	1958	203
414 3/8	54 2/8	54 4/8	49	6 2/8	6 4/8	14 4/8	16 4/8	1/8	14 4/8	14	15	Talkeetna Mts., Alaska	G. W. Berry	G. W. Berry	1960	203
414 3/8	57	49 3/8	47 2/8	6 3/8	6 4/8	20 7/8	17 2/8	12 1/8	9 7/8	17	17	Alaska Pen., Alaska	Robert Wessner	Robert Wessner	1969	203
414 1/8	45 1/8	46 4/8	35 7/8	11 6/8	11 2/8	14 4/8	17 7/8	3 4/8	11 5/8	15	20	Clarence Lake, Alaska	Jack Hill	Jack Hill	1964	206
414	53 4/8	54 3/8	38 6/8	6 7/8	8	4 7/8	20 4/8	1/8	15 6/8	17	22	Upper Susitna, Alaska	Harold Gould	Harold Gould	1953	207
414	38 7/8	40 3/8	36 3/8	5 7/8	6	17 4/8	15 1/8	7 7/8	10 1/8	23	24	Little Nelchina River, Alaska	Picked Up	Temple Bros. Tax.	1954	207
413 6/8	57 4/8	59 2/8	44 5/8	7	6 4/8	19 5/8	–	12 6/8	–	19	14	Alaska Pen., Alaska	Ira Swartz	Ira Swartz	1967	209

413 6/8	51 2/8	39 3/8	6 1/8	6 1/8	6 6/8	12	18 1/8	1/8	13 3/8	20	Wrangell Mts., Alaska	Robert Reed	Robert Reed	1968	209
413 5/8	47 6/8	44 6/8	7 1/8	6 6/8	6 6/8	22 6/8	2 7/8	6/8	17 7/8	20	King Salmon River, Alaska	Basil C. Bradbury	Basil C. Bradbury	1967	211
413 5/8	52	33 5/8	5 7/8	5 7/8	5 7/8	16 5/8	17 7/8	13 1/8	15 5/8	18	Kuskokwim River, Alaska	Walther Schmitz	Walther Schmitz	1969	211
413 4/8	50 4/8	38	7	7	7	8	18	1	16 4/8	29	Talkeetna Mts., Alaska	Louis Mussatto	Louis Mussatto	1964	213
413 3/8	52 3/8	44	6	6	5 6/8	20 4/8	19 3/8	13	1/8	12	Denali Highway, Alaska	Albert E. Greer	Albert E. Greer	1963	214
413 1/8	59 3/8	40 5/8	5 5/8	5 5/8	5 7/8	20 5/8	16 5/8	8 7/8	7 5/8	14	Tyone River, Alaska	Walter Elam	Walter Elam	1959	215
413	38 5/8	40 2/8	7	7	6 1/8	16 1/8	17 3/8	12 5/8	8 5/8	18	Tangle Lakes, Alaska	David J. Morlock	David J. Morlock	1956	216
413	61 4/8	45 5/8	6 3/8	6	6	17 5/8	20 5/8	7 7/8	11 5/8	25	Aniakchak Crater, Alaska	M. G. Johnson	M. G. Johnson	1964	216
412 7/8	48 7/8	31 5/8	8 5/8	8 7/8	7 5/8	11 5/8	14 5/8	2 5/8	9 5/8	28	Rainy Pass, Alaska	Ernst Von Hake	Ernst Von Hake	1963	218
412 7/8	56 5/8	41	5 5/8	5 5/8	6 3/8	16 5/8	14 5/8	10	7 5/8	16	Lake Clark, Alaska	William F. Rae, Jr.	William F. Rae, Jr.	1968	218
412 5/8	56 5/8	58	6	6	6 3/8	17	21 3/8	4 2/8	14 5/8	16	Alaska Pen., Alaska	John Prewitt Nelson, Jr.	John Prewitt Nelson, Jr.	1961	220
412 3/8	61 3/8	47	6	6	6	–	20 5/8	–	15 3/8	16	Alaska Pen., Alaska	H. Sagesser	Mus. Nat. History, Berne	1962	221
412 3/8	50 5/8	41 3/8	6 1/8	6 1/8	6	20 5/8	14 6/8	15 5/8	8 6/8	18	Twin Lakes, Alaska	Inge Hill, Jr.	Inge Hill, Jr.	1965	221
412 2/8	48	34 2/8	5 3/8	5 3/8	5 3/8	15 2/8	19 5/8	3 5/8	12 7/8	17	Upper Susitna, Alaska	Elmer M. Rusten	Elmer M. Rusten	1950	223
412 2/8	58 5/8	24 7/8	8 5/8	8 7/8	8 7/8	19	13 3/8	13 4/8	7	15	Slana, Alaska	William Kiltz	William Kiltz	1959	223
412 1/8	46 4/8	25 3/8	7 1/8	7 1/8	6 5/8	17 3/8	17 3/8	5 7/8	13 3/8	18	Tay Lake, Yukon	Dan Newlon	Dan Newlon	1963	224
412	43 6/8	33 3/8	8	8	7	19 5/8	20	13	13 4/8	27	Alaska Pen., Alaska	Paul T. Hartman	Paul T. Hartman	1966	226
411 7/8	57	46 5/8	7 3/8	8 3/8	7	3 3/8	23 3/8	1/8	20	12	Talkeetna Range, Alaska	Walter J. Wojciuk	Walter J. Wojciuk	1960	227
411 7/8	59 7/8	49 1/8	5 7/8	5 5/8	5 7/8	20 5/8	4 4/8	18 3/8	1 1/8	10	Jimmy Lake, Alaska	Jack M. Matthews	Jack M. Matthews	1966	227
411 4/8	45 3/8	45 5/8	6 6/8	6 1/8	6 4/8	20 3/8	18 4/8	8 3/8	7 1/8	13	Lake Louise, Alaska	John Trautner	John Trautner	1960	229
411 4/8	52 5/8	40 5/8	6 5/8	6 5/8	6	12 5/8	18 5/8	1	15 5/8	25	Susitna River, Alaska	Richard G. Drew	Richard G. Drew	1961	229
411 3/8	49	34 1/8	6 5/8	6 5/8	6	17 5/8	18 1/8	7 3/8	13 7/8	17	Twin Lakes, Alaska	Richard R. Oberle	Richard R. Oberle	1973	229
411 3/8	51 7/8	33 5/8	6 4/8	6 1/8	6 1/8	15	18 5/8	14 3/8	15 3/8	21	Tanana Valley, Alaska	Bob Hagel	Bob Hagel	1961	232
411	43	32 5/8	8 1/8	8	8	18 3/8	17	15	9 5/8	21	Healy, Alaska	Michael A. Couch	Michael A. Couch	1969	233
411	55 5/8	35 5/8	5 4/8	5 5/8	5 4/8	21 1/8	16	11	9 1/8	17	Wood River, Alaska	James C. Midcap	James C. Midcap	1970	233
410 7/8	53 5/8	32 7/8	6 1/8	6 3/8	6 1/8	21	16 5/8	15 5/8	6 2/8	24	Wrangell Mts., Alaska	John Belcher	John Belcher	1956	235
410 7/8	49 5/8	47 1/8	6 5/8	6 5/8	7	19	20 3/8	10 7/8	12 4/8	20	Talkeetna Mts., Alaska	Clifford F. Hood	Clifford F. Hood	1958	235
410 5/8	58 5/8	47 3/8	5 1/8	5 1/8	5 1/8	16 7/8	17 5/8	11 1/8	12 3/8	14	Lake Chandalar, Alaska	L. A. Miller	L. A. Miller	1953	237
410 5/8	64 5/8	53	5 3/8	5 5/8	5 5/8	19 3/8	1 5/8	16 7/8	7/8	31	Talkeetna Mts., Alaska	Elgin T. Gates	Elgin T. Gates	1960	237
410 5/8	54 7/8	40 7/8	6 7/8	6 4/8	6 4/8	18 7/8	12 4/8	14 7/8	1 1/8	11	Denali Highway, Alaska	Ray W. Holler	Ray W. Holler	1965	237
410 5/8	57 5/8	41 5/8	6 5/8	6 5/8	6 5/8	3 5/8	17 3/8	1	14 1/8	28	Alaska Pen., Alaska	Jim Keeler	Jim Keeler	1966	237

BARREN GROUND CARIBOU–*Continued*

Rangifer tarandus granti and *Rangifer tarandus groenlandicus*

Score	Length of Main Beam R.	Length of Main Beam L.	Inside Spread	Circumference at Smallest Place Between Brow and Bez Points R.	Circumference at Smallest Place Between Brow and Bez Points L.	Length of Brow Points R.	Length of Brow Points L.	Width of Brow Points R.	Width of Brow Points L.	Number of Points R.	Number of Points L.	Locality Killed	By Whom Killed	Owner	Date Killed	Rank
410 5/8	54 3/8	55 3/8	45 1/8	7 3/8	7 2/8	16 7/8	17 2/8	8	9 7/8	15	13	Denali Highway, Alaska	J. W. Jett	J. W. Jett	1960	241
410 5/8	51 4/8	51 4/8	31 3/8	7 5/8	8 2/8	–	21 3/8	–	4 7/8	19	20	McKinley Natl. Park, Alaska	Joseph M. Messana	Joseph M. Messana	1968	241
410 5/8	58 3/8	56 7/8	33 7/8	6 6/8	6 5/8	16 5/8	21 4/8	1	16 5/8	12	16	Wrangell Mts., Alaska	Lee Chambers	Lee Chambers	1969	241
410 2/8	57 6/8	56	41 4/8	6	6 1/8	18 3/8	17 7/8	7 7/8	12 3/8	14	18	Rainy Pass, Alaska	Mrs. J. Watson Webb	Mrs. J. Watson Webb	1934	244
410	50 7/8	51	43 3/8	6 5/8	6 5/8	15 3/8	19 1/8	10 4/8	10 5/8	16	15	Fog Lakes, Alaska	Squee Shore	Squee Shore	1958	245
410	53 6/8	54 7/8	40	6 6/8	6 6/8	16 7/8	21	1/8	17 2/8	12	13	Nenana River, Alaska	Tom Grady	Tom Grady	1961	245
410	47 5/8	51 7/8	43 6/8	9 7/8	9	28 6/8	–	13 4/8	–	20	18	Alaska Pen., Alaska	C. G. Suits	C. G. Suits	1965	245
410	54 2/8	59	44 3/8	5 6/8	6 3/8	16 1/8	18 6/8	7 1/8	14 3/8	14	17	White River, Alaska	Dirk E. Brinkman	Dirk E. Brinkman	1974	245
409 7/8	59 5/8	59 7/8	42 4/8	7 6/8	6 6/8	20 6/8	4 5/8	13	1	15	16	Post Lake, Alaska	Werner Frey	Werner Frey	1963	249
409 5/8	54 7/8	55 5/8	33 2/8	6 7/8	7 6/8	22 5/8	16	16 7/8	1/8	17	14	Tyone Lake, Alaska	Ralph Marshall	Ralph Marshall	1960	250
409 5/8	46 2/8	48 7/8	47 1/8	6 1/8	5 7/8	21	11	15 6/8	4/8	19	13	Point Moller, Alaska	John S. Clark	John S. Clark	1966	250
409 4/8	54 6/8	53 6/8	42 4/8	6 3/8	6 6/8	18 2/8	18 3/8	10 3/8	2/8	17	14	Paxton Lake, Alaska	Gary J. Lundgren	James Lundgren	1950	252
409 4/8	57 3/8	58 2/8	41 1/8	6	5 7/8	16 2/8	15 7/8	10 3/8	7 7/8	17	17	Port Heiden, Alaska	Frank W. Ussery, Jr.	Frank W. Ussery, Jr.	1963	252
409 3/8	54 5/8	54 7/8	38 3/8	6 3/8	6 2/8	24 7/8	12 5/8	18 6/8	1	20	13	King Salmon River, Alaska	Lit Ng	Lit Ng	1967	254
409 3/8	47 2/8	46 6/8	48	6 2/8	6 2/8	16	17 4/8	12 4/8	12 6/8	20	24	Alaska Pen., Alaska	L. W. Bailey	L. W. Bailey	1969	254
409 3/8	55 5/8	53 5/8	35 2/8	6 4/8	6 2/8	20 3/8	21 4/8	15 3/8	1/8	19	13	Alaska Range, Alaska	James W. Rehm	James W. Rehm	1978	254
409 2/8	53 2/8	53	40 6/8	5 5/8	6	21 3/8	19 7/8	7	12	15	20	Alaska Pen., Alaska	Herb Klein	Herb Klein	1967	257
409 2/8	45 6/8	47 2/8	28 7/8	9	8	22	13 2/8	15 5/8	5 2/8	28	20	Chisana, Alaska	James B. Higgins	James B. Higgins	1967	257
409 1/8	46 2/8	51 5/8	36 1/8	8	7 7/8	16 1/8	18 1/8	9 5/8	13 3/8	21	19	Alaska Pen., Alaska	Herb Klein	Herb Klein	1968	259
409	48 6/8	46 3/8	35 2/8	11	6 6/8	17 7/8	16 7/8	8 4/8	12 4/8	19	21	Chisana Valley, Alaska	William Burns	William Burns	1963	260
409	55 2/8	54 3/8	41 1/8	6 2/8	6	23	9 7/8	18 1/8	1/8	23	11	Port Heiden, Alaska	D. J. Lehman	D. J. Lehman	1967	260
408 7/8	55	53 7/8	45	6 6/8	6	15 6/8	16 1/8	6 5/8	9 7/8	19	19	Deadman Lake, Alaska	R. J. Brocker	R. J. Brocker	1950	262
408 7/8	41 6/8	42 7/8	37 5/8	8 6/8	8 5/8	16 5/8	12 2/8	11	1 1/8	18	16	Talkeetna Mts., Alaska	H. I. H. Prince Abdorreza Pahlavi	H. I. H. Prince Abdorreza Pahlavi	1960	262

408 6/8	54 4/8	54 7/8	39 6/8	6 4/8	7 1/8	18 1/8	10 7/8	9 7/8	3 3/8	14	13	Ingersol Lake, Alaska	John A. Du Puis	John A. Du Puis	1973	264
408 5/8	46 4/8	46 5/8	40 1/8	7	7 4/8	5 6/8	19 4/8	7/8	19 7/8	20	23	Talkeetna Mts., Alaska	Bill Lachenmaier	Bill Lachenmaier	1961	265
408 5/8	55 5/8	56 2/8	37 3/8	6 2/8	6 4/8	18 4/8	12 6/8	13 5/8	1 3/8	18	14	Lake Clark, Alaska	J. G Blow	J. G. Blow	1968	265
408 4/8	54 3/8	56 2/8	38 5/8	7	6 1/8	17 4/8	19 4/8	8 3/8	10 6/8	18	22	Sandy River, Alaska	Mrs. Ken McConnell	Mrs. Ken McConnell	1966	267
408 4/8	56	49 2/8	40 3/8	6 1/8	5 6/8	17 5/8	17 7/8	6 7/8	9	13	15	Alaska Pen., Alaska	Robert E. L. Wright	Robert E.L. Wright	1978	267
408 2/8	47	49	35 4/8	8 5/8	6 6/8	19	16 6/8	15 3/8	5 1/8	22	15	Snowshoe Lake, Alaska	John P. Hale	John P. Hale	1962	269
408 2/8	50 6/8	51 6/8	35 4/8	6 3/8	6 1/8	20 7/8	20 1/8	7 5/8	13 7/8	13	13	Rainy Pass, Alaska	John S. Howell	John S. Howell	1966	269
408 2/8	52 6/8	52 6/8	50	5 6/8	6	13	14 5/8	11 3/8	4	17	18	Alaska Pen., Alaska	Robert J. Nellett	Robert J. Nellett	1966	269
408 1/8	52 6/8	54	36 4/8	7	7 1/8	21 4/8	16	15	1/8	17	13	Wood River, Alaska	Max Lukin	Max Lukin	1964	272
407 7/8	46 1/8	48	41 3/8	7 1/8	9	15 4/8	15 1/8	2 2/8	9 3/8	16	19	Caribou Creek, Alaska	Donald Kettlekamp	Donald Kettlekamp	1957	273
407 7/8	54 3/8	51	36 1/8	7 1/8	6 6/8	20 4/8	17 5/8	4 7/8	10 4/8	15	15	Alaska Pen., Alaska	Frank R. Fowler	Frank R. Fowler	1976	273
407 5/8	45	49 5/8	46 1/8	6 2/8	7	19 2/8	19	1 5/8	13 7/8	15	18	Butte Creek, Alaska	J. H. Doolittle	J. H. Doolittle	1956	275
407 4/8	45 2/8	44 6/8	32 2/8	6 7/8	6 5/8	15 6/8	16 7/8	11 2/8	9 5/8	16	16	Little Nelchina, Alaska	Simon Jensen	Simon Jensen	1960	276
407 4/8	58 1/8	56 6/8	45 1/8	6 5/8	7 1/8	19	5	12 2/8	3/8	13	11	Alaska Pen., Alaska	Pete Serafin	Pete Serafin	1966	276
407 3/8	57	55 5/8	44 4/8	5 6/8	6	16 6/8	2 6/8	12 2/8	1/8	20	14	Tetelin River, Alaska	O. F. Goeke	O. F. Goeke	1954	278
407 3/8	50	47 3/8	37 2/8	6 2/8	6 2/8	14	14 4/8	3 3/8	10 2/8	20	18	Chisana, Alaska	Lewis S. Kunkel, Jr.	Lewis S. Kunkle, Jr.	1964	278
407 2/8	47 6/8	50	31 4/8	7	6 2/8	8 1/8	17	7/8	13 2/8	22	24	Chandler Lake, Alaska	Steve Scheidness	Steve Scheidness	1974	280
407 1/8	53 4/8	51 4/8	38 1/8	6 1/8	5 6/8	20 4/8	16 3/8	14 5/8	1	22	18	Mt. Watana, Alaska	James A. Jana	James A. Jana	1966	281
407	52	54 2/8	35 4/8	6 4/8	6 1/8	21 4/8	19 1/8	13 5/8	5 6/8	18	16	Farewell Lake, Alaska	Ken Golden	Ken Golden	1962	282
406 7/8	52	52 6/8	44 3/8	8 2/8	8	16 3/8	18 4/8	6 4/8	10 3/8	15	14	Cantwell, Alaska	Wm. Files Shoemaker	Wm. Files Shoemaker	1958	283
406 4/8	46 2/8	47 1/8	41 3/8	7	7	16 1/8	14 4/8	4	8 2/8	21	20	Denali Highway, Alaska	D. L. Lucas	D. L. Lucas	1957	284
406 3/8	53 6/8	55 4/8	41 6/8	6	6	18	1	1/8	12 6/8	16	18	Kuskokwin River, Alaska	Dennis Harms & Cheryl Harms	Cheryl Harms	1967	285
406 2/8	51 7/8	53	28 6/8	6	6 2/8	24 4/8	18 6/8	10 1/8	8 5/8	14	13	Talkeetna Mts., Alaska	Herb Klein	Herb Klein	1960	286
406 2/8	48	50	35 6/8	7 4/8	8	20 2/8	19 6/8	5 6/8	13	13	16	Lake Louise, Alaska	Eugene Fetzer	Eugene Fetzer	1961	286
406 1/8	52 2/8	50	44 3/8	7 6/8	6 3/8	16 4/8	4 1/8	13 4/8	1/8	20	18	Moller Bay, Alaska	Harry H. Webb	Herry H. Webb	1953	288
406 1/8	50 6/8	52 2/8	42 2/8	6 4/8	6 6/8	18	9 1/8	11 7/8	7/8	20	18	Talkeetna Mts., Alaska	Digvijay Sinh	Digvijay Sinh	1963	288
406	50 4/8	47 3/8	36 1/8	7 4/8	7 2/8	23	11	18 3/8	1	17	12	Lake Louise, Alaska	C. J. Sullivan	C. J. Sullivan	1960	290
406	50	49 7/8	30 5/8	7 7/8	7 5/8	6 4/8	19 5/8	1	15 2/8	14	19	Squaw Creek, Alaska	Elmo Strickland	Elmo Strickland	1960	290
406	51 2/8	51 6/8	47 1/8	6 5/8	6 4/8	14	15 5/8	10 6/8	8	16	16	Fairbanks, Alaska	H. A. Cox, Jr.	H. A. Cox, Jr.	1968	290
405 7/8	54 3/8	53 4/8	42	6 4/8	6 4/8	14	15 5/8	7 4/8	10 4/8	14	13	Rainy Pass, Alaska	Wm. D. Vogel	Wm. D. Vogel	1958	293
405 5/8	47 4/8	51 2/8	45 2/8	6 3/8	6 2/8	6 1/8	17 1/8	11 1/8	2/8	20	16	Paxton, Alaska	Maurice A. Stafford	Maurice A. Stafford	1956	294
405 5/8	47 7/8	48 7/8	36 4/8	5 6/8	5 6/8	17 3/8	19 6/8	2	16 6/8	17	24	Port Heiden, Alaska	James V. Pepa	James V. Pepa	1968	294

BARREN GROUND CARIBOU–*Continued*

Rangifer tarandus granti and *Rangifer tarandus groenlandicus*

Score	Length of Main Beam R.	Length of Main Beam L.	Inside Spread	Circumference at Smallest Place Between Brow and Bez Points R.	Circumference at Smallest Place Between Brow and Bez Points L.	Length of Brow Points R.	Length of Brow Points L.	Width of Brow Points R.	Width of Brow Points L.	Number of Points R.	Number of Points L.	Locality Killed	By Whom Killed	Owner	Date Killed	Rank
405 4/8	54 7/8	52 5/8	44 2/8	5 6/8	5 7/8	20 4/8	3	13	1	17	14	Denali Highway, Alaska	Edna Conegys	Edna Conegys	1958	296
405 2/8	46 6/8	46 4/8	43 4/8	6 5/8	6 6/8	6 2/8	17 4/8	1 1/8	13 5/8	17	22	Ochetna River, Alaska	Elbert E. Husted	Elbert E. Husted	1962	297
405 2/8	58 2/8	57 6/8	52 1/8	6 2/8	5 7/8	18	17 7/8	9 7/8	1/8	12	9	Alaska Pen., Alaska	Jose Garcia	Jose Garcia	1971	297
405 1/8	45 6/8	46 7/8	35	9	7 4/8	12 4/8	17	1/8	9 6/8	20	23	Wood River, Alaska	Herb Klein	Herb Klein	1955	299
405 1/8	55	52 4/8	41	5 4/8	5 4/8	18	17 1/8	13 2/8	11 6/8	19	22	Nabesna, Alaska	B. C. Varner	B. C. Varner	1955	299
405 1/8	49 4/8	50 6/8	35 4/8	6 2/8	6	16 2/8	15	8 6/8	6 1/8	22	17	Denali Highway, Alaska	Wm. Auckland	Wm. Auckland	1958	299
405	55 4/8	60 4/8	33 1/8	6 4/8	6 7/8	9 4/8	19 4/8	1/8	17 4/8	15	27	Susitna Valley, Alaska	E. Michael Rusten	E. Michael Rusten	1948	302
405	56 4/8	60 2/8	55 2/8	5 3/8	5 3/8	7/8	15 6/8	6/8	9 5/8	16	20	Port Heiden, Alaska	Lee W. Richie	Lee W. Richie	1963	302
405	45 4/8	43 6/8	31 6/8	7 5/8	8	8	16	1/8	9 1/8	15	20	Wrangell Mts., Alaska	Roger H. Belke	Roger H. Belke	1974	302
404 7/8	49 2/8	49 4/8	35	6 4/8	6 4/8	7 5/8	17	1	11 6/8	16	15	Wrangell Mts., Alaska	J. D. Waring	J. D. Waring	1959	305
404 7/8	48 7/8	47 2/8	42 5/8	6 2/8	6 1/8	19	7 2/8	14 1/8	1	19	14	Alaska Pen., Alaska	M. C. Worster	M. C. Worster	1963	305
404 6/8	56 6/8	54 6/8	36 5/8	6 4/8	6 5/8	7	23 4/8	1 1/8	19	14	21	King Salmon, Alaska	Henry A. Elias	Henry A. Elias	1965	307
404 6/8	49 5/8	50	43 5/8	6	5 6/8	16 3/8	–	7 4/8	–	20	17	King Salmon, Alaska	Paul (Buzz) Hopkins	Paul (Buzz) Hopkins	1973	307
404 5/8	50 4/8	48 7/8	44 4/8	7 2/8	7 1/8	16 6/8	16 2/8	9 6/8	10 3/8	15	15	Eureka, Alaska	Charles C. Parsons	Charles C. Parsons	1950	309
404 5/8	45 4/8	47	32 4/8	6 7/8	6 4/8	16 4/8	17 2/8	15 1/8	20	18	24	Taylor Highway, Alaska	John C. Howard	John C. Howard	1960	309
404 5/8	54 5/8	55	33 7/8	6 2/8	6	16 2/8	17 4/8	11	11 2/8	18	17	Talkeetna Mts., Alaska	J. W. Lawson	J. W. Lawson	1965	309
404 4/8	53 4/8	53 4/8	35 1/8	6 5/8	7 3/8	17 6/8	7 7/8	11 5/8	1/8	16	13	Wrangell Mts., Alaska	William B. Henley Jr.	William B. Henley, Jr.	1962	312
404 4/8	53	54 6/8	40	5 7/8	5 6/8	16 6/8	18 7/8	10 2/8	7 5/8	16	14	Alaska Pen., Alaska	Peter Roemer	Peter Roemer	1970	312
404 3/8	52 1/8	52 3/8	46 4/8	6 3/8	6 3/8	19	6/8	13 6/8	5/8	20	15	Wood River, Alaska	C. A. Stenger	C. A. Stenger	1968	314
404 2/8	58 6/8	58 5/8	59 4/8	5 4/8	5 5/8	18 7/8	4 6/8	16 2/8	1/8	20	12	Port Heiden, Alaska	Jon B. Chaney	Jon B. Chaney	1962	315
404 1/8	45 2/8	48	41	7	6 4/8	18 7/8	18 4/8	14 7/8	14 3/8	18	16	Wood River, Alaska	Berry B. Brooks	Berry B. Brooks	1958	316
404	52	55 2/8	36 2/8	8	8 1/8	19 5/8	17	9 4/8	13 1/8	17	15	Salmon Mts., Yukon	Earl Faas	Earl Faas	1960	317
403 7/8	52 1/8	52 4/8	32	5 5/8	6 7/8	3 5/8	16 6/8	1 1/8	11 7/8	17	22	Butte Creek, Alaska	John R. Copenhaver	John R. Copenhaver	1956	318
403 7/8	38 4/8	37	36 4/8	6	6 3/8	16 3/8	16 2/8	14 3/8	14 2/8	21	22	Talkeetna Mts., Alaska	Ken Oldhem	Ken Oldhem	1959	318
403 7/8	50 2/8	50 6/8	43 5/8	5 7/8	5 4/8	22 5/8	21 3/8	18	1 6/8	21	15	Port Moller, Alaska	Melvin Hetland	Melvin Hetland	1962	318

403 7/8	57 6/8	52 6/8	30	11 2/8	6 7/8	21 3/8	21	12	8	13	14	Cantwell, Alaska	Ben Bearse	Ben Bearse	1968	318
403 7/8	47 5/8	44 2/8	44	6	5 6/8	2 4/8	14 4/8	1/8	11 4/8	16	18	Halfway Mt., Alaska	Richard S. Hembroff	Richard S. Hembroff	1974	318
403 6/8	41 2/8	43 6/8	27 1/8	6 2/8	6 5/8	16 6/8	17 2/8	9 7/8	14 2/8	21	25	Talkeetna Mts., Alaska	Joe Nevins	Joe Nevins	1958	323
403 6/8	52 6/8	51 5/8	29 3/8	6 4/8	6 5/8	19 5/8	15 1/8	14 3/8	1	20	14	Denali Highway, Alaska	Robert R. Opland	Robert R. Opland	1959	323
403 6/8	48 5/8	47 2/8	44 5/8	6 6/8	6 2/8	2 4/8	18	1	13 5/8	15	19	Denali Highway, Alaska	Jim Carpenter	Jim Carpenter	1960	323
403 6/8	53 1/8	52 6/8	49 6/8	7	7	19 7/8	19 3/8	13 4/8	9 2/8	12	12	Alaska Pen., Alaska	W. T. Yoshimoto	W. T. Yoshimoto	1961	323
403 6/8	47 7/8	47 4/8	44 2/8	6	5 7/8	18 2/8	2 2/8	13 2/8	6/8	23	16	Port Heiden, Alaska	Gene Gall	Gene Gall	1967	323
403 5/8	51 5/8	50 6/8	34 6/8	6 1/8	6 4/8	15	14	8 6/8	6 7/8	21	21	Lake Louise, Alaska	Marvin Kocurek	Marvin Kocurek	1961	328
403 4/8	43 5/8	42 7/8	29 6/8	7 4/8	7 4/8	21	20 4/8	15 4/8	5 2/8	18	14	Tazlina, Alaska	Harry L. Swank, Jr.	Harry L. Swank, Jr.	1959	329
403 4/8	49 1/8	48 4/8	38 5/8	6 3/8	6 2/8	16 4/8	19 7/8	5 3/8	14 7/8	17	19	Eureka, Alaska	James S. Evans	James S. Evans	1960	329
403 4/8	50 1/8	50 5/8	39 7/8	6 2/8	6 3/8	13	21	1/8	17 2/8	14	19	Port Heiden, Alaska	Mrs. Jon B. Chaney	Mrs. Jon B. Chaney	1962	329
403 4/8	53 5/8	55 3/8	49 6/8	5 7/8	6	15 5/8	17 1/8	11 6/8	11 4/8	14	17	Alaska Pen., Alaska	Gerald R. Gold	Gerald R. Gold	1977	329
403 2/8	56 6/8	50	42 2/8	6 2/8	6	16 1/8	18 5/8	8	12 4/8	19	21	Deadman Lake, Alaska	Chas. R. Green	Chas. R. Green	1959	333
403 2/8	52 1/8	52 6/8	38 6/8	7 2/8	7 3/8	22 5/8	16 4/8	7 3/8	10	15	16	Oshetna River, Alaska	Marvern A. Henriksen	Marvern A. Henriksen	1962	333
403	53 2/8	50 2/8	43 6/8	6 1/8	6 1/8	16 3/8	14 5/8	1 7/8	8 1/8	13	16	Deadman Lake, Alaska	E. C. Lentz	E. C. Lentz	1955	335
402 7/8	48	46 4/8	28 6/8	6 7/8	8	11 7/8	19 6/8	1/8	17 1/8	17	25	Ogilvie Range, Yukon	E. J. Miller	E. J. Miller	1956	336
402 6/8	49	54	33	7 1/8	7	14 6/8	15 6/8	8	9	15	18	Rainy Pass, Alaska	William Sleith	William Sleith	1961	337
402 5/8	46 2/8	47 1/8	34 4/8	5 4/8	5 4/8	16 3/8	15 4/8	1 5/8	13 5/8	19	26	Old Crow, Yukon	J. M. Mouchet	Otto Wm. Geist	1958	338
402 4/8	46 3/8	47 2/8	39 4/8	7 4/8	7 4/8	15 3/8	16 2/8	6 3/8	7 4/8	14	15	Clarence Lake, Alaska	John C. Heck	John C. Heck	1951	339
402 4/8	58	54 4/8	34 6/8	6 5/8	6 2/8	16 1/8	19 3/8	6 1/8	10 5/8	13	16	Rainy Pass, Alaska	Mahlon White	Mahlon White	1954	339
402 4/8	49 2/8	49 3/8	30 2/8	6	7 3/8	16 2/8	15 5/8	13 4/8	1/8	23	17	Talkeetna Mts., Alaska	Arvid F. Benson	Arvid F. Benson	1956	339
402 4/8	45	48	34 7/8	11 6/8	8 3/8	18 3/8	17	10	12 4/8	20	21	Talkeetna Mts., Alaska	A. Sweat	A. Sweat	1959	339
402 4/8	53 4/8	53 3/8	36 2/8	7	7	22 2/8	21 5/8	18 1/8	2 1/8	14	11	Glen Highway, Alaska	Walter Pfisterer	Walter Pfisterer	1959	339
402 4/8	52 4/8	51 2/8	41 2/8	7	7 2/8	8 4/8	16 5/8	1 3/8	13 1/8	13	24	Nelchina, Alaska	Joseph Caputo	Joseph Caputo	1964	339
402 4/8	59 4/8	59 6/8	37 5/8	6 1/8	5 6/8	19 2/8	23 1/8	1 7/8	17 1/8	13	12	Port Heiden, Alaska	Walter Schubert	Walter Schubert	1965	339
402 3/8	49 7/8	46 6/8	33 4/8	7 6/8	7 7/8	16 7/8	15 3/8	8 2/8	6	19	18	Tyone Lake, Alaska	Ralph E. Marshall	Ralph E. Marshall	1957	346
402 3/8	55 3/8	55	59 4/8	5 6/8	5 4/8	18 4/8	–	11 5/8	–	17	10	Alaska Pen., Alaska	Gilbert Elton	Gilbert Elton	1961	346
402 3/8	51 2/8	55 7/8	44	6 3/8	6 2/8	7 1/8	17 2/8	3 6/8	14 4/8	15	20	Denali Highway, Alaska	Jerry Shepard	Jerry Shepard	1961	346
402 2/8	54 4/8	53 1/8	49 1/8	6 1/8	6 3/8	19 6/8	2 7/8	15 3/8	1/8	20	18	Ugashik Lake, Alaska	John Elmore	John Elmore	1964	349
402 2/8	46	46	39	5 6/8	5 6/8	17	16	12 4/8	12 2/8	17	16	Alaska Pen., Alaska	William K. Leech	William K. Leech	1977	349
402 1/8	55 3/8	54	42 5/8	6 3/8	7	21 1/8	4 1/8	17 5/8	1/8	19	11	Twin Lakes, Alaska	Cecil Glessner	Cecil Glessner	1966	351
402 1/8	52 1/8	47	32 4/8	7	7	1 1/8	17 7/8	4/8	14 3/8	16	24	Rainy Pass, Alaska	George V. Lenher	George V. Lenher	1967	351

BARREN GROUND CARIBOU—Continued

Rangifer tarandus granti and *Rangifer tarandus groenlandicus*

Score	Length of Main Beam R.	L.	Inside Spread	Circumference at Smallest Place Between Brow and Bez Points R.	L.	Length of Brow Points R.	L.	Width of Brow Points R.	L.	Number of Points R.	L.	Locality Killed	By Whom Killed	Owner	Date Killed	Rank
402 1/8	48	49 3/8	43 6/8	8 3/8	6 4/8	23 4/8	–	13 1/8	–	19	16	Susitna River, Alaska	Frederick W. Thornton	Frederick W. Thornton	1969	351
402	48 4/8	55 4/8	41 5/8	7 3/8	7 3/8	19 6/8	23 3/8	11 3/8	11 3/8	12	12	Mulchatna River, Alaska	Phillip Miller	Phillip Miller	1972	354
401 7/8	59 3/8	56 2/8	35 1/8	6 6/8	7 3/8	19	18 1/8	5 7/8	16 5/8	18	24	Nabesna, Alaska	Bill Copeland	Bill Copeland	1969	355
401 7/8	54 4/8	54 2/8	44 6/8	5 1/8	4 7/8	17 7/8	20 4/8	14	4 4/8	15	13	Alaska Range, Alaska	Glenn E. Allen	Glenn E. Allen	1979	355
401 6/8	45 4/8	49 7/8	39 4/8	6 6/8	6 6/8	17 7/8	15 4/8	5 5/8	7 7/8	18	14	Talkeetna Mts., Alaska	David Maroney	David Maroney	1961	357
401 6/8	50 4/8	50 2/8	37 4/8	6 5/8	6 3/8	19	17 7/8	10 2/8	11 1/8	18	10	Totatlanika River, Alaska	Heinrich K. Springer	Heinrich K. Springer	1969	357
401 5/8	45 4/8	44 6/8	36 5/8	6 7/8	7 3/8	16 4/8	18 5/8	13	9 4/8	19	21	Lake Louise, Alaska	Dale A. Hillmer	Dale A. Hillmer	1961	359
401 5/8	50 2/8	51 1/8	30 2/8	7	7	13 3/8	20 4/8	7 3/8	15 2/8	17	24	Rainy Pass, Alaska	Reed Sandvig	Reed Sandvig	1964	359
401 5/8	50	54 2/8	35 2/8	7 1/8	7 4/8	17 3/8	18 4/8	7	11 1/8	13	18	Talkeetna River, Alaska	J. Donald Neill	J. Donald Neill	1961	361
401 4/8	53 4/8	54 4/8	40 5/8	6 4/8	6 3/8	6 4/8	19 4/8	1/8	17 2/8	11	21	Rainy Pass, Alaska	John Weirdsma	John Weirdsma	1961	361
401 4/8	52	53	32 5/8	5 3/8	5 3/8	14 4/8	14 4/8	9 4/8	8	20	18	Wrangell Mts., Alaska	Gerald F. McNamara	Gerald F. McNamara	1968	361
401 3/8	51 2/8	51 2/8	35 5/8	6 1/8	6 1/8	16 4/8	15 4/8	9 5/8	9 5/8	18	21	Denali Highway, Alaska	Norman Smith	Norman Smith	1959	364
401 3/8	43 6/8	44 7/8	33 7/8	8 7/8	7 6/8	15 7/8	14 7/8	7	13 7/8	18	20	Tyone Lake, Alaska	Leon J. Brochu	Leon J. Brochu	1959	364
401 3/8	57 5/8	56 5/8	42 7/8	6 3/8	6	9 3/8	16 5/8	1/8	13	14	18	Wrangell Mtns., Alaska	Ronald Bergstrom	Ronald Bergstrom	1965	364
401 2/8	48 6/8	43 5/8	34 4/8	6 5/8	8	16 5/8	13 6/8	13 1/8	9 2/8	18	17	Alaska Range, Alaska	Robert Boone	Robert Boone	1959	367
401 1/8	52	52 6/8	45 5/8	7 1/8	7 3/8	15 1/8	18	8 4/8	13 5/8	15	16	Nicholson Lake, Alaska	John P. Scribner	John P. Scribner	1956	368
401 1/8	54 5/8	56 6/8	41 1/8	5 3/8	5 5/8	19 4/8	19 1/8	14 2/8	11 7/8	18	17	Nelchina, Alaska	Chris Klineburger	Chris Klineburger	1957	368
401 1/8	49 6/8	48 2/8	52 2/8	6 6/8	6 6/8	19	2 1/8	13	7/8	22	20	Talkeetna Mts., Alaska	Joe Van Daalwyk	Joe Van Daalwyk	1957	368
401 1/8	41 1/8	40 4/8	40 5/8	6 3/8	5 7/8	13 7/8	13 7/8	11 2/8	9 2/8	29	27	Tazlina, Alaska	Lloyd Ronning	Lloyd Ronning	1958	368
401 1/8	51 3/8	50 4/8	42	6 3/8	6 7/8	13 7/8	14 1/8	6/8	10 1/8	15	19	Denali Highway, Alaska	Wilbur T. Gamble	Wilbur T. Gamble	1963	368

												Locality	Name	Owner	Year	Rank
401 1/8	61 5/8	57 7/8	47 3/8	5 5/8	6 2/8	22 4/8	18 7/8	9 4/8	1/8	13	10	Little Nelchina River, Alaska	Elton Aarestad	Elton Aarestad	1964	368
401 1/8	54 3/8	51	44	6 4/8	7 4/8	17	19 5/8	7 4/8	14 5/8	14	17	Nondalton, Alaska	Anton L. Cerro	Anton L. Cerro	1973	368
401	55 5/8	55 5/8	35 5/8	7 3/8	9 3/8	17 6/8	18 5/8	11 3/8	15 5/8	16	15	Tyone Lake, Alaska	Eileen Marshall	Eileen Marshall	1961	375
401	61 1/8	58	46	7	8	20	14 4/8	8	8	16	19	Talkeetna Mts., Alaska	Louis Mussatto	Louis Mussatto	1964	375
400 6/8	51 1/8	50 7/8	38	6 5/8	7 4/8	11 7/8	13 7/8	6 7/8	9 6/8	14	19	Chisana, Alaska	Harry L. Thompson	Harry L. Thompson	1966	377
400 5/8	57 6/8	57 7/8	38 1/8	7 5/8	7 2/8	8 2/8	21 4/8	1	13	12	22	Alaska Pen., Alaska	E. J. Hansen	E. J. Hansen	1964	378
400 4/8	56 5/8	56	43 4/8	6 5/8	6 2/8	19 3/8	19 7/8	10 4/8	7	11	10	Talkeetna Mts., Alaska	W. L. Miers	W. L. Miers	1959	379
400 3/8	57 3/8	58 3/8	40	7 5/8	7 4/8	17 3/8	4	12	4/8	20	13	Wood River, Alaska	Berry B. Brooks	Berry B. Brooks	1958	380
400 3/8	42 1/8	41 7/8	33 5/8	5 5/8	5 7/8	3 4/8	18 1/8	1/8	13 6/8	15	19	Talkeetna, Alaska	S. H. Sampson	S. H. Sampson	1959	380
400 3/8	52	35	45 5/8	7 5/8	7 4/8	8 5/8	23 5/8	1	16	12	11	Ingersoll Lake, Alaska	Peter H. Merlin	Peter H. Merlin	1970	380
400 3/8	49 2/8	49	42	5 7/8	5 5/8	17 2/8	16 6/8	9 2/8	9 7/8	19	14	Cinder River, Alaska	Mervin Bergstrom	Mervin Bergstrom	1975	380
400 3/8	49 5/8	47 6/8	39 4/8	6 2/8	6 5/8	-	19	-	15 3/8	19	26	Alaska Pen., Alaska	James Swartout	James Swartout	1978	380
400 1/8	59 3/8	59 5/8	43	5 5/8	5 5/8	18	15 5/8	10 5/8	1	17	16	Monahan Flats, Alaska	C. H. Dana, Jr.	C. H. Dana, Jr.	1965	385
400 1/8	48 5/8	48 5/8	31 1/8	5 7/8	5 7/8	16	16 5/8	6 5/8	7	13	18	Alaska Pen., Alaska	Lillie E. Kriss	Lillie E. Kriss	1972	385
400	47 7/8	50 5/8	30 5/8	8 1/8	5 5/8	3	17	4/8	10 5/8	13	19	Anchorage, Alaska	C. C. Irving	C. C. Irving	1959	387
400	57 4/8	56 5/8	37 4/8	7 4/8	6	18 7/8	19	12 5/8	11 5/8	14	16	Alaska Pen., Alaska	Bert Klineburger	Bert Klineburger	1961	387
400	53 5/8	53 5/8	37	5 5/8	5 5/8	20 5/8	21 3/8	1	14 4/8	9	19	Lake Louise, Alaska	George Moerlein	George Moerlein	1962	387
400	45	46 5/8	44 1/8	5	5	16 5/8	5 7/8	12 5/8	7/8	24	16	Nelchina, Alaska	Webb Hilgar	Webb Hilgar	1962	387
400	54 3/8	56 5/8	35 1/8	7 1/8	7 1/8	19 3/8	16 5/8	17 5/8	1/8	17	8	King Salmon, Alaska	G. O. Wiegner	G. O. Wiegner	1970	387

Photograph by Grancel Fitz

WORLD'S RECORD QUEBEC-LABRADOR CARIBOU
SCORE: 474 6/8
Locality: Nain, Labrador. Date: 1931.
Hunter: Zack Elbow, an Eskimo.
Donated by Charles R. Peck to the National Collection

Photograph by Wm. H. Nesbitt

NUMBER TWO QUEBEC-LABRADOR CARIBOU
SCORE: 439 2/8
Locality: Schefferville, Quebec. Date: 1975.
Hunter and owner: Ron Ragan.

Quebec-Labrador Caribou

Rangifer tarandus from Quebec and Labrador

Minimum Score 375

Score	Length of Main Beam R.	L.	Inside Spread	Circumference at Smallest Place Between Brow and Bez Points R.	L.	Length of Brow Points R.	L.	Width of Brow Points R.	L.	Number of Points R.	L.	Locality Killed	By Whom Killed	Owner	Date Killed	Rank
474 6/8*	60 4/8	61 1/8	58 2/8	6 6/8	6 1/8	14 4/8	21 1/8	9	14 6/8	22	30	Nain, Lab.	Zack Elbow	National Collection	1931	1
438 6/8	59 3/8	55 4/8	52 7/8	5 3/8	5 3/8	8	21 1/8	1/8	19 1/8	17	25	Beach Camp, Que.	Ron Ragan	Ron Ragan	1975	2
433 4/8	50 6/8	53 7/8	54	5 5/8	5 5/8	16 6/8	20 4/8	9 7/8	16 6/8	22	28	George River, Que.	Dewey Mark	Dewey Mark	1973	3
429 6/8	55 1/8	59 1/8	50 1/8	5 5/8	5 5/8	21 1/8	2 1/8	19 1/8	1/8	15	12	Ford Lake, Que.	George Shultz	George Shultz	1972	4
428 5/8	51 5/8	52 2/8	38 5/8	6	6	14 7/8	15 3/8	9 2/8	12	26	30	George River, Que.	Cayetano G. Arriola, Jr.	Cayetano G. Arriola, Jr.	1975	5
427 5/8*	51	54 4/8	47	6 2/8	6 6/8	11	20 4/8	1 2/8	17 4/8	22	33	George River, Que.	Larry Barnett	Larry Barnett	1978	6
426 4/8*	50 4/8	51 3/8	52 7/8	5 3/8	5 5/8	15 2/8	15 1/8	10 1/8	7 3/8	14	19	Tunulic River, Que.	Kenneth J. Gerstung	Kenneth J. Gerstung	1978	7
423 3/8*	53 7/8	54	53 3/8	6 4/8	6 5/8	12	20 4/8	2 2/8	17 3/8	19	28	George River, Que.	Claude E. Genet	Claude E. Genet	1967	8
419 4/8*	44 5/8	48 1/8	47 1/8	5	5	13 4/8	16 5/8	6 4/8	11	28	28	George River, Que.	Collins F. Kellogg	Collins F. Kellogg	1978	9
417 5/8*	52 7/8	49 6/8	46 5/8	6 4/8	6	18 7/8	17 3/8	14 2/8	13 6/8	23	20	George River, Que.	Edgar Brochu	Edgar Brochu	1976	10
416 1/8*	59 4/8	59 5/8	52 5/8	5 1/8	5	18 4/8	18 7/8	13 4/8	8 3/8	16	14	Ungava Region, Que.	Richard S. Neeley	Richard S. Neeley	1977	11
416*	51 7/8	49 4/8	54 7/8	4 7/8	5 3/8	27 7/8	26 4/8	23 3/8	23 4/8	25	25	Slippery Creek, Que.	Picked Up	Claude E. Genet	—	12
415 5/8*	55 2/8	55 3/8	55 5/8	5 3/8	5 3/8	23	19 1/8	13 6/8	14 4/8	16	20	Ungava Pen., Que.	Gerald R. Warnock	Gerald R. Warnock	1978	13
415	42 7/8	43 5/8	41	5 5/8	6	15 1/8	13 7/8	8 3/8	8 7/8	22	23	George River Lodge, Que.	James E. McCarthy	James E. McCarthy	1974	14
413 4/8*	51 7/8	51 3/8	50 1/8	6 4/8	6 6/8	16 7/8	17 7/8	2 7/8	11 2/8	21	14	George River, Que.	Picked Up	Claude E. Genet	—	15
412 4/8	53 6/8	52 2/8	45 5/8	6	6 4/8	17 7/8	16	13 1/8	11 1/8	16	22	Whale River, Que.	Daniel E. Merrell	Daniel E. Merrell	1972	16
411 1/8	51	51 7/8	52 5/8	7	8 7/8	13 4/8	14	5 4/8	4 4/8	9	14	Mistinibi Lake, Lab.	Rudolf Sand	Rudolf Sand	1973	17
410 4/8	59 3/8	60 4/8	40 6/8	5 7/8	5 5/8	17 5/8	17 2/8	14	8 7/8	26	22	George River, Que.	Kenneth E. Goslant	Kenneth E. Goslant	1974	18
405 1/8*	50 3/8	48 7/8	45 3/8	5 3/8	5 3/8	20	15 5/8	17 3/8	1/8	23	19	George River, Que.	Howard Shelley	Howard Shelley	1971	19
405	53 1/8	54 4/8	51 1/8	5	5 3/8	20	20 3/8	17 4/8	9 5/8	15	15	Knob Lake, Que.	Chester Gluck	Chester Gluck	1964	20
403 4/8	58 6/8	61	44 2/8	5 3/8	5 5/8	19 5/8	18 4/8	10 4/8	12 1/8	18	21	Ungava Bay, Que.	John A. Gulius	John A. Gulius	1975	21
401 4/8*	49 7/8	51	49 2/8	5 7/8	6 1/8	16 1/8	18 4/8	1 5/8	13 7/8	15	16	George River, Que.	Claude E. Genet	Claude E. Genet	1966	22
401	51 2/8	52 6/8	44 4/8	5 5/8	5 5/8	15 4/8	19 4/8	10 4/8	16	20	24	George River, Que.	Robert A. Krizek	Robert A. Krizek	1979	23
400 6/8	52 6/8	52 7/8	37 7/8	5 5/8	5 5/8	13	13	15 4/8	8 2/8	24	22	Tunulic River, Que.	M. Farrel Gosman	M. Farrel Gosman	1978	24
400 4/8	54 5/8	56 2/8	52 5/8	5 5/8	5 4/8	23	23 4/8	17 7/8	8 7/8	15	11	George River, Que.	Dale D. Wieand	Dale D. Wieand	1977	25
400	56 4/8	58 2/8	51 4/8	5 1/8	5 5/8	6/8	16 3/8	17 2/8	9 2/8	15	19	George River, Que.	John C. Sullivan, Jr.	John C. Sullivan, Jr.	1978	26
398 1/8	54 3/8	55 7/8	52 4/8	4 7/8	4 7/8	10 4/8	20 3/8	1/8	15 5/8	15	21	Ford Lake, Que.	George H. Fearons	George H. Fearons	1977	27
397 7/8	55	56	58	5	4 7/8	7 7/8	18 5/8	2 7/8	12 2/8	13	14	George River, Que.	David L. George	David L. George	1968	28

Score											Pts. R	Pts. L	Locality	Owner	By whom killed	Date	Rank
397 7/8	43 5/8	47 7/8	46 7/8	6	5 7/8	21	17 7/8	2 1/8	1/8	12 7/8	21	18	Twin River Lodge, Que.	Fred W. Sheaman, Jr.	Fred W. Sheaman, Jr.	1969	29
396 5/8	46 7/8	47 7/8	39 3/8	5 7/8	5 7/8	21	19 5/8	15 5/8	1/8	15 5/8	21	23	Tunulic River, Que.	Charles W. Dixon	Charles W. Dixon	1979	30
396 3/8	59 7/8	59 7/8	46 4/8	6	5 7/8	16	20 5/8	20 5/8	17 1/8	8 5/8	16	17	George River Lodge, Que.	Robert S. Carroll	Robert S. Carroll	1974	31
394 2/8*	58 5/8	55 5/8	54 5/8	5 5/8	6	14	7 5/8	20 4/8	1/8	13 7/8	14	13	Fiddle Lake, Que.	Robert Hammond	Robert Hammond	1967	32
394 1/8	52 5/8	52 5/8	46 5/8	4 7/8	4 7/8	16	19 2/8	19 3/8	4 4/8	13	16	19	Ungava Region, Que.	James F. Tappan	James F. Tappan	1967	33
393 6/8	50 7/8	54 7/8	40 5/8	4 7/8	5	22	9 5/8	16 5/8	12 5/8	1/8	22	16	George River, Que.	Rick Ullery	Rick Ullery	1975	34
393 5/8	55 5/8	50 5/8	52 5/8	5 1/8	5 3/8	12	15 4/8	17 4/8	4 3/8	9 7/8	12	14	Ungava Bay, Que.	Arthur Bashore	Arthur Bashore	1971	35
393 3/8	59 3/8	57 7/8	53 5/8	6 1/8	6 2/8	17	17 4/8	—	11 3/8	1/8	17	13	George River, Que.	Michael J. Merritt	Michael J. Merritt	1978	35
392 6/8	56 5/8	56 5/8	53 5/8	5 5/8	5 5/8	19	2	18 1/8	8 5/8	1/8	19	17	George River, Que.	Morris Weinstein	Morris Weinstein	1972	37
392 3/8	57 3/8	57 7/8	43 4/8	5 5/8	5 7/8	15	18 1/8	16 7/8	2 4/8	13	15	20	Ungava Area, Que.	Frank J. Blaha, Jr.	Frank J. Blaha, Jr.	1978	38
391 7/8	56 3/8	56	51 7/8	6 1/8	6 1/8	14	19 5/8	16 5/8	3/8	13 4/8	14	11	George River, Que.	Alex Kariotakis	Alex Kariotakis	1974	39
390 3/8	54	52 5/8	47 7/8	6 5/8	6 5/8	12	14 4/8	—	1 2/8	12 5/8	12	17	George River, Que.	John Daniels	John Daniels	1972	40
390	53	55	46 5/8	5 5/8	5 2/8	21	18 4/8	15 4/8	1 2/8	14	12	17	Schefferville, Que.	Samuel March, Jr.	Samuel March, Jr.	1972	41
389 4/8	48 3/8	51 5/8	39 6/8	5 3/8	5 3/8	21	19 6/8	2	17 6/8	17 7/8	21	25	Ungava Region, Que.	Eugene M. Decker	Eugene M. Decker	1973	42
386 7/8	54 3/8	54 7/8	47 3/8	6 5/8	6 5/8	17	7	14 5/8	1/8	14 5/8	17	14	George River, Que.	Arthur C. Sadowski	Arthur C. Sadowski	1979	43
383 7/8	52 5/8	51 7/8	45 3/8	5 5/8	5	15	18 1/8	18 1/8	4 3/8	14	15	14	George River Lodge, Que.	Clayton C. Dovey, Jr.	Clayton C. Dovey, Jr.	1969	44
382 7/8	51 6/8	53 5/8	42 5/8	6 5/8	6 3/8	14	6 7/8	17 3/8	14 7/8	1 7/8	14	14	George River, Que.	Ralph Zampella	Ralph Zampella	1972	45
381 7/8	59 3/8	59 5/8	54 5/8	5 5/8	6 5/8	14	15	18 3/8	10 3/8	5 7/8	19	14	Ungava Region, Que.	John R. Oakes	John R. Oakes	1971	46
381 1/8	53 5/8	53 5/8	46	7	7	16	20 6/8	1 5/8	14 7/8	14 7/8	15	16	Kogaluk, Lab.	Basil C. Bradbury	Basil C. Bradbury	1949	47
380 5/8	52 7/8	55 5/8	53 3/8	6 2/8	6	16	15 4/8	17 3/8	10 3/8	5 1/8	15	16	Fiddle Lake, Que.	Herb Dittmar	Herb Dittmar	1966	48
380 2/8	53 4/8	51	48 5/8	7 2/8	7	15	15 4/8	8 7/8	6 7/8	16 2/8	11	15	Fort Chimo, Que.	B. N. McCrum	B. N. McCrum	1967	49
379 5/8	52 1/8	54 4/8	52 7/8	5 4/8	5 4/8	12	19	15 5/8	6 7/8	10	12	13	George River, Que.	Frank R. Heller	Frank R. Heller	1978	50
378 4/8	56	56 5/8	56 5/8	5 5/8	5 4/8	18	5 5/8	15 4/8	10 4/8	1/8	18	15	Ford River, Que.	Vivian Sleight	Vivian Sleight	1973	51
378	53	51 2/8	49 5/8	5 2/8	4 7/8	15	18 1/8	2 1/8	1/8	13 3/8	15	17	George River, Que.	Dick Ullery	Dick Ullery	1975	52
377 7/8	45 7/8	45	41 5/8	6 1/8	6 1/8	16	19	6 7/8	1/8	14 3/8	16	20	George River, Que.	Normand Poulin	Normand Poulin	1976	53
377	53 5/8	55	49 5/8	5 5/8	5 5/8	12	18	19	4	16 4/8	12	11	George River, Que.	Stanley R. Smith	Stanley R. Smith	1975	54
376 6/8	51 5/8	53 5/8	52 5/8	5 2/8	5 5/8	21	14 5/8	18 5/8	1 7/8	17 7/8	21	24	George River, Que.	C. J. McElroy	C. J. McElroy	1969	55
376 3/8	45 4/8	48 7/8	52 5/8	5 3/8	5 3/8	15	16 3/8	19 3/8	3/8	14 5/8	15	19	George River, Que.	Carl J. Los	Carl J. Los	1970	56
376 2/8	40 4/8	42 5/8	28	4 4/8	4 7/8	27	11 3/8	20 4/8	1 2/8	18	21	27	Schefferville, Que.	Norman Clausen	Norman Clausen	1973	57
376 1/8	53	53	46 4/8	6 1/8	6 1/8	20	2 6/8	17 2/8	1/8	13 3/8	18	20	George River, Que.	Don Peters	Don Peters	1969	58
375 5/8	55 7/8	54 4/8	55 3/8	5 1/8	5 5/8	12	19 5/8	10 3/8	12 2/8	2 7/8	15	12	North Tudor Lake, Que.	Collins F. Kellogg	Collins F. Kellogg	1970	59
375 7/8	50 4/8	52 3/8	37 7/8	7 2/8	7	16	19 1/8	14 2/8	1/8	19 1/8	16	13	George River, Que.	Norma J. Laros	Norma J. Laros	1975	60
375	52 3/8	53 3/8	46 3/8	5 7/8	5 1/8	17	19	1/8	14 6/8	9 6/8	17	19	Fritz Lake, Que.	Donald A. Boyer	Donald A. Boyer	1978	61

*Final Score subject to revision by additional verifying measurements.

Photograph by Wm. H. Nesbitt

NEW WORLD'S RECORD PRONGHORN
SCORE: 93
Locality: Yavapai County, Arizona. Date: 1975.
Hunter and owner: Edwin L. Wetzler.

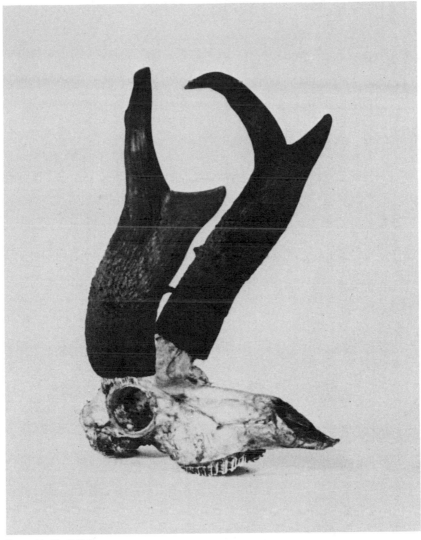

Photograph by Wm. H. Nesbitt

NUMBER TWO PRONGHORN (TIE)
SCORE: 91 4/8
Locality: Garfield County, Montana. Date: 1977
Hunter and owner: Donald W. Yates

Pronghorn

Minimum Score 82

Antilocapra americana americana and related subspecies

Score	Length of Horn R.	Length of Horn L.	Circumference of Base R.	Circumference of Base L.	Circumference at Third Quarter R.	Circumference at Third Quarter L.	Inside Spread	Tip to Tip Spread	Length of Prong R.	Length of Prong L.	Locality Killed	By Whom Killed	Owner	Date Killed	Rank
93	18 1/8	18 2/8	7 2/8	7	2 5/8	2 6/8	10 1/8	6 5/8	7 6/8	7 2/8	Yavapai Co., Ariz.	Edwin L. Wetzler	Edwin L. Wetzler	1975	1
91 4/8	20 1/8	20	7 4/8	7	2 6/8	2 6/8	12	11 3/8	4 5/8	5 3/8	Ariz.	Wilson Potter	National Collection	1899	2
91 4/8	15 1/8	15 2/8	7 7/8	7 7/8	3 2/8	3 4/8	10 4/8	9 4/8	7	7	Weld Co., Colo.	Bob Schneidmiller	Bob Schneidmiller	1965	2
91 4/8	17 1/8	17	7 3/8	7 1/8	3 3/8	3 2/8	13 5/8	10 1/8	4 4/8	4 7/8	Garfield Co., Mont.	Donald W. Yates	Donald W. Yates	1977	2
91	16 6/8	16 4/8	7 6/8	7 7/8	2 5/8	2 6/8	10 3/8	3	7 2/8	7 4/8	Carbon Co., Wyo.	J. Ivan Kitch	J. Ivan Kitch	1964	5
91	16 2/8	15 6/8	7 1/8	7 1/8	3	3 1/8	14 1/8	11 7/8	5 6/8	5 5/8	Rawlins, Wyo.	Fred Starling	Fred Starling	1967	5
90 6/8	16 2/8	16 4/8	7 4/8	7 4/8	2 5/8	2 5/8	17 2/8	15 2/8	7 5/8	7 5/8	Weston Co., Wyo.	Allen Douglas	J. E. Macy	1943	7
90	19 4/8	19 5/8	7	6 6/8	2 7/8	3	10 1/8	8	4 7/8	4 6/8	Guano Creek, Oreg.	E. C. Starr	E. C. Starr	1942	8
89 6/8	18 3/8	18	6 5/8	6 4/8	2 6/8	2 7/8	9 4/8	4	7 1/8	7 3/8	Seligman, Ariz.	J. W. Johnson	J. W. Johnson	1959	9
89 6/8	17 5/8	17 6/8	7 3/8	7 3/8	2 6/8	2 6/8	11 1/8	6 5/8	6 1/8	6 2/8	Rawlins, Wyo.	Mary Carol Kircher	Mary Carol Kircher	1961	9
89 6/8	17 2/8	17 4/8	7	6 7/8	2 6/8	2 5/8	12 5/8	11 1/8	7 4/8	7 2/8	Rosebud Co., Mont.	Jim Ollom	Jim Ollom	1973	9
89 4/8	17 6/8	17 4/8	7 2/8	7 1/8	2 5/8	2	10	3 2/8	6 3/8	6	Ferris, Wyo.	John T. Peddy	John T. Peddy	1957	12
89 4/8	17 2/8	17 4/8	7	7 1/8	3 2/8	3 2/8	13 5/8	9 7/8	6 1/8	6 1/8	Laramie Co., Wyo.	Roy Vail	Roy Vail	1958	12
89 4/8	16	15 4/8	7 4/8	7 4/8	2 7/8	2 6/8	12	8 5/8	6 5/8	5 6/8	Sierra Co., N. M.	P. K. Colquitt, Jr.	Thomas V. Schrivner	1961	12
89 4/8	17 2/8	17 5/8	6 7/8	7	3	3	9 4/8	3 2/8	6 6/8	6 3/8	Humboldt Co., Nev.	Richard Steinmetz	Richard Steinmetz	1977	12
89 2/8	18 6/8	18 4/8	7 7/8	7 5/8	2 6/8	2 6/8	11 1/8	3 6/8	5 1/8	5 2/8	Grant Co., N. M.	Jerry Saint	N. M. Dept. Game & Fish	1975	16
88 6/8	18 7/8	18 6/8	7 2/8	7	3	3	11 7/8	10 1/8	6 2/8	5 1/8	Socorro Co., N.M.	J. Lyn Perry	J. Lyn Perry	1976	17
88 4/8	16 6/8	17 1/8	7	7	2 5/8	2 6/8	10	5 4/8	5 7/8	6 2/8	Fremont Co., Wyo.	Terry N. TenBoer	Terry N. TenBoer	1974	18
88	17 3/8	17	7 4/8	7 6/8	2 5/8	2 5/8	12 7/8	7 5/8	6	6	Sweet Grass Co., Mont.	William S. Amos	William S. Amos	1971	19
88	16 6/8	17 1/8	7	7	2 7/8	2 7/8	9 4/8	5 1/8	5 5/8	5 6/8	Coconino Co., Ariz.	Richard J. Hallock	Richard J. Hallock	1973	19
87 6/8	17	16 7/8	7 4/8	7 4/8	2 6/8	2 6/8	15 2/8	12 1/8	5 3/8	5 2/8	Fremont Co., Wyo.	William I. Crump	William I. Crump	1963	21
87 6/8	15	15 2/8	7 2/8	7 2/8	3 1/8	3 1/8	10 4/8	6 3/8	7 2/8	7 1/8	Fremont Co., Wyo.	Frank Schuele	Frank Schuele	1975	21
87 4/8	17 5/8	17 3/8	6 4/8	6 3/8	2 5/8	2 6/8	11 5/8	6 3/8	6 4/8	6 3/8	Gillette, Wyo.	Stanley Scott	Stanley Scott	1961	23
87 4/8	16	17 4/8	7 1/8	7	4 7/8	3 4/8	11 2/8	12	6	6 4/8	Modoc Co., Calif.	Lynn M. Greene	Lynn M. Greene	1971	23
87 4/8	17 2/8	17 2/8	6 3/8	6 3/8	2 6/8	2 6/8	9 4/8	2 4/8	6 5/8	6 5/8	Modoc Co., Calif.	Ron L. Reasor	Ron L. Reasor	1979	23
87 2/8	16 4/8	17	7	6 7/8	2 4/8	2 4/8	13 3/8	11 4/8	7 4/8	7 2/8	Lake Co., Oreg.	Ronald E. Hills	Ronald E. Hills	1966	26
87 2/8	16 3/8	16 1/8	6 5/8	6 4/8	2 5/8	2 4/8	13 5/8	11	7 4/8	7 5/8	Fremont Co., Wyo.	Scott A. Trabing	Scott A. Trabing	1973	26
87 2/8	16 2/8	16 2/8	6 7/8	6 7/8	2 5/8	2 4/8	12 2/8	10 4/8	7	6 7/8	Humboldt Co., Nev.	Steve Young	Steve Young	1975	26
87 2/8	17 5/8	17 4/8	6 7/8	6 6/8	2 5/8	2 4/8	10 7/8	4 2/8	6 7/8	6 4/8	Sweetwater Co., Wyo.	Jay R. Anderson	Jay R. Anderson	1975	26
87 2/8	16 5/8	16 5/8	7 4/8	7 2/8	2 6/8	2 7/8	14 2/8	10 2/8	6	5 7/8	Carbon Co., Wyo.	Lee Miller	Lee Miller	1976	26
87 2/8	16	16 1/8	7 2/8	7 1/8	2 7/8	2 7/8	12 1/8	9	6 3/8	6 4/8	Niobrara Co., Wyo.	Stephen M. Cameron	Stephen M. Cameron	1976	26

87	16 2/8	15 6/8	7 3/8	7 4/8	2 7/8	2 3/8	16	12 2/8	6 3/8	7	Hudspeth Co., Texas	E. R. Rinehart	E. R. Rinehart	1959	32
87	16 2/8	16 1/8	6 3/8	6 3/8	2 7/8	2 7/8	10 6/8	4 7/8	6 4/8	6 5/8	Washoe Co., Nev.	William E. Walker	William E. Walker	1970	32
87	17 6/8	17 4/8	6 3/8	6 3/8	3 2/8	3 1/8	15 4/8	10 4/8	5 2/8	5 3/8	Magdalena, N. M.	Picked Up	Jim Riggs	1970	32
87	17 2/8	17 2/8	6 4/8	6 6/8	2 5/8	2 7/8	10 7/8	6 4/8	6 2/8	5 7/8	Lake Co., Oreg.	JoAnn Hathaway	JoAnn Hathaway	1976	32
87	15 7/8	15 7/8	7 1/8	7	2 4/8	2 4/8	10 5/8	5	6 1/8	6 4/8	Sweetwater Co., Wyo.	Dell J. Barnes	Dell J. Barnes	1976	32
86 6/8	18 7/8	18 6/8	6 3/8	6 3/8	2 7/8	2 6/8	12 4/8	7 1/8	4 6/8	5	Anderson Mesa, Ariz.	Gene Tolle	Gene Tolle	1941	37
86 6/8	17 4/8	17 3/8	6 4/8	6 6/8	2 4/8	2 4/8	15 5/8	13 4/8	7 4/8	6	Rock Springs, Wyo.	Stanley Sinclair	Stanley Sinclair	1952	37
86 6/8	16 2/8	17	7	7	2 4/8	2 6/8	8 1/8	3 4/8	6 5/8	6 1/8	Jefferson Co., Idaho	Dale Nealis	Dale Nealis	1961	37
86 6/8	17 4/8	17 5/8	6 3/8	6 3/8	2 6/8	2 6/8	9 6/8	6 1/8	5 5/8	5 2/8	Yavapai Co., Ariz.	Louis R. Dees	Louis R. Dees	1963	37
86 6/8	16 3/8	16 3/8	7	7	2 7/8	3	11 6/8	9 4/8	6	6 1/8	Carbon Co., Wyo.	Chuck Sanger	Chuck Sanger	1968	37
86 6/8	16 5/8	16 5/8	7	7	2 6/8	2 6/8	8 4/8	2 5/8	6 4/8	7	Fremont Co., Wyo.	Richard A. Fruchey	Richard A. Fruchey	1973	37
86 6/8	15 3/8	15 6/8	6 3/8	6 2/8	2 6/8	2 6/8	9 3/8	6	7 5/8	8 2/8	Sublette Co., Wyo.	Mrs. Arvid J. Siegel	Mrs. Arvid J. Siegel	1974	37
86 4/8	16 7/8	16 7/8	6 5/8	6 5/8	2 7/8	2 7/8	10 5/8	10 5/8	6	5 4/8	Moffat Co., Colo.	Joseph R. Maynard	Joseph R. Maynard	1972	44
86 4/8	15 7/8	15 7/8	6 5/8	6 5/8	2 7/8	2 7/8	10 4/8	5 2/8	6 7/8	7	Lake Co., Oreg.	James W. Greer	James W. Greer	1976	44
86 3/8	16 4/8	16 5/8	7 2/8	7 2/8	2 4/8	2 4/8	9 7/8	6 5/8	6 2/8	6 1/8	Rawlins, Wyo.	C. M. Chandler	C. M. Chandler	1963	46
86 2/8	16 7/8	16 6/8	6 7/8	6 5/8	3 1/8	3	13 5/8	10	5 4/8	5 7/8	Brooks, Alta.	S. Prescott Fay	Boston Mus. Science	1913	47
86 2/8	16 6/8	16 2/8	6 4/8	6 3/8	3	3	11 4/8	10	7	6 1/8	Manville, Wyo.	J. J. Hartnett	Roy Vail	1952	47
86 2/8	16	16 2/8	7 1/8	7 2/8	2 3/8	2 4/8	9 7/8	5 4/8	6 5/8	6 5/8	Coconino Co., Ariz.	Eugene Anderson	Eugene Anderson	1961	47
86 2/8	16 7/8	16 6/8	6 6/8	6 4/8	3	2 7/8	11 7/8	4 7/8	5 4/8	5	Du Gas, Ariz.	Rex Earl	Rex Earl	1962	47
86 2/8	15	15 2/8	7 6/8	7 6/8	2 7/8	2 7/8	9	5 6/8	6	5 6/8	Casper, Wyo.	William W. Brummet	William W. Brummet	1963	47
86 2/8	17 6/8	17 6/8	6 3/8	6 3/8	2 7/8	3	10 6/8	7 4/8	5 3/8	5 3/8	Coconino Co., Ariz.	Jon Hugo Bryan	Jon Hugo Bryan	1970	47
86 2/8	16 7/8	16 1/8	6 5/8	6 6/8	2 6/8	2 6/8	12 1/8	7 2/8	6 6/8	6 4/8	Carbon Co., Wyo.	Mike Davich	Mike Davich	1974	47
86 2/8	17 7/8	17 6/8	6 4/8	6 4/8	3	3	14 2/8	9 1/8	4 5/8	4 4/8	Ft. Apache Res., Ariz.	Jack Pierce	Jack Pierce	1974	47
86 2/8	16 6/8	16 2/8	6 4/8	6 4/8	3 2/8	3 1/8	12 3/8	9 4/8	6	6	Big Horn Co., Wyo.	Robert Temme	Robert Temme	1974	47
86 2/8	17 2/8	17	7	7	2 7/8	2 6/8	12 6/8	10 7/8	5 6/8	5 7/8	Carbon Co., Wyo.	Harold Jack Rollison	Harold Jack Rollison	1975	47
86 2/8	16 4/8	16 5/8	7 7/8	7 7/8	2 5/8	2 5/8	14 3/8	9 6/8	5	5 1/8	Fremont Co., Wyo.	Douglas B. Stromberg	Douglas B. Stromberg	1976	47
86 2/8	17 3/8	17 3/8	6 7/8	7	2 6/8	2 6/8	13 7/8	13 7/8	5	5	Carbon Co., Wyo.	James Poydack	James Poydack	1977	47
86	15 4/8	15 1/8	7	7 2/8	3 4/8	3 4/8	6 6/8	4 2/8	6	6	Medicine Bow, Wyo.	Jack R. Campbell	Jack R. Campbell	1959	59
86	17 3/8	18	6 6/8	6 7/8	2 3/8	2 5/8	12 6/8	8	6 4/8	6 3/8	Coconino Co., Ariz.	Richard R. Barney	Richard R. Barney	1969	59
86	16 2/8	16 3/8	7 3/8	7	3 3/8	3 2/8	9 7/8	4 1/8	4 4/8	4 4/8	Carter Co., Mont.	Jamie Byrne	Jamie Byrne	1972	59
86	15	15	7 2/8	7 1/8	3	2 7/8	13 6/8	11 6/8	6 7/8	6 6/8	Fremont Co., Wyo.	Robert Hall	Robert Hall	1973	59
86	17 1/8	16 4/8	6 7/8	7	3	2 7/8	11 3/8	7 6/8	5 6/8	6 7/8	Yavapai Co., Ariz.	Ruth McCasland	Ruth McCasland	1975	59
85 6/8	17 2/8	17 4/8	6 7/8	6 7/8	3 5/8	3 1/8	12 4/8	10 4/8	4 5/8	4 6/8	Fergus Co., Mont.	H. H. Applegate	H. H. Applegate	1951	64
85 6/8	16 5/8	16 4/8	6 4/8	6 4/8	2 7/8	2 7/8	13 6/8	10 6/8	6	6	Carbon Co., Wyo.	B. L. Holman	B. L. Holman	1953	64
85 6/8	18	17 5/8	6 4/8	6 4/8	2 6/8	2 7/8	7 7/8	3 4/8	5 3/8	5 6/8	Chugwater, Wyo.	Louis C. Morrison	Louis C. Morrison	1955	64
85 6/8	15 1/8	16 3/8	6 6/8	7	3 2/8	3 4/8	12 5/8	7 3/8	6	5 3/8	Chihuahua, Mexico	Juan A. Saenz	Juan A. Saenz	1955	64
85 6/8	15	15 4/8	7 4/8	7 1/8	3 1/8	2 7/8	6	2 2/8	6 4/8	6 2/8	Sioux Co., Neb.	Gerald R. Larson	Gerald R. Larson	1962	64
85 6/8	16 2/8	16 1/8	6 5/8	6 6/8	2 6/8	2 6/8	12 5/8	9 6/8	6 2/8	6 1/8	Brooks, Alta.	Oliver Ost	Oliver Ost	1964	64
85 6/8	18 4/8	18 1/8	6	6 1/8	2 4/8	2 6/8	6 5/8	–	6 1/8	6	Socorro Co., N. M.	V. F. Tannich	V. F. Tannich	1965	64
85 6/8	16	15 6/8	7	6 5/8	2 7/8	3	10 6/8	6 1/8	6 3/8	6 1/8	Boise City, Okla.	R. L. Williams	R. L. Williams	1966	64
85 6/8	16 4/8	16 5/8	6 6/8	6 5/8	3	3	9 1/8	5 1/8	6 1/8	6	Beaverhead Co., Mont.	Vern Hensley	Vern Hensley	1968	64
85 6/8	15 2/8	15 2/8	7 2/8	7 2/8	2 7/8	3	13 4/8	10 6/8	7	6 7/8	Rock Springs, Wyo.	C. J. McElroy	C. J. McElroy	1969	64
85 6/8	16 3/8	15 7/8	6 2/8	6 2/8	3	3	10	9	4 4/8	4 4/8	Sweetwater Co., Wyo.	E. Tom Thorne	E. Tom Thorne	1969	64

PRONGHORN–*Continued*

Antilocapra americana americana and related subspecies

Score	Length of Horn R.	Length of Horn L.	Circumference of Base R.	Circumference of Base L.	Circumference at Third Quarter R.	Circumference at Third Quarter L.	Inside Spread	Tip to Tip Spread	Length of Prong R.	Length of Prong L.	Locality Killed	By Whom Killed	Owner	Date Killed	Rank
85 6/8	16 5/8	16 5/8	6 2/8	6 2/8	3	3	9 7/8	5 6/8	5 2/8	5 3/8	Sweetwater Co., Wyo.	Roger A. Perkins	Roger A. Perkins	1971	64
85 6/8	16	16	6 5/8	6 5/8	2 5/8	2 5/8	13 1/8	8	6 2/8	6 2/8	Humbolt Co., Nev.	Thomas R. Pitts	Thomas R. Pitts	1973	64
85 6/8	18 3/8	18 2/8	6 6/8	6 4/8	2 6/8	2 6/8	7 7/8	4 7/8	5 2/8	4 3/8	Carbon Co., Wyo.	Robert F. Johnston	Robert F. Johnston	1977	64
85 4/8	16 6/8	16 5/8	7 5/8	7 4/8	2 2/8	2 3/8	11 6/8	8 4/8	7 3/8	6 5/8	Rawlins, Wyo.	Paul C. Himelright	Paul C. Himelright	1960	78
85 4/8	17 2/8	16 5/8	6 1/8	6 2/8	2 5/8	2 6/8	10 7/8	6 2/8	6 2/8	6 2/8	Campbell Co., Wyo.	Eugene D. Springen	Eugene D. Springen	1962	78
85 4/8	15 4/8	15 3/8	7 2/8	7 2/8	2 7/8	2 6/8	7 6/8	4 1/8	6 2/8	6 3/8	Saratoga, Wyo.	Carlyn J. Ourada	Carlyn J. Ourada	1969	78
85 4/8	16	16 6/8	6 7/8	6 7/8	3	2 7/8	11 1/8	10 2/8	6 4/8	6 2/8	Rosebud Co., Mont.	Calvin F. Mayes	Calvin F. Mayes	1973	78
85 4/8	16 6/8	16 6/8	7 6/8	7 4/8	2 5/8	2 5/8	10 2/8	2 2/8	6 2/8	5 5/8	Washoe Co., Nev.	Mario E. Gildone	Mario E. Gildone	1977	78
85 2/8	16 3/8	16 4/8	7 1/8	7 1/8	2 6/8	2 6/8	12 4/8	8 6/8	5 6/8	5 4/8	Saratoga, Wyo.	Russell Cutter	Russell Cutter	1957	83
85 2/8	16 4/8	17 1/8	6 4/8	6 3/8	2 5/8	3 2/8	10 2/8	6 1/8	4 6/8	4 4/8	Sage Creek Basin, Wyo.	Aydeen Auld	Aydeen Auld	1959	83
85 2/8	17 4/8	17 6/8	7 2/8	7 2/8	2 6/8	2 6/8	7 2/8	2	5 4/8	5 4/8	Yavapai Co., Ariz.	Robert C. Bogart	Robert C. Bogart	1963	83
85 2/8	15 4/8	15 4/8	7 1/8	7 1/8	2 6/8	2 7/8	12 2/8	11 1/8	6	6	Lower Sweetwater, Wyo.	John Kereszturi	John Kereszturi	1963	83
85 2/8	16 3/8	16 2/8	6 5/8	6 3/8	2 6/8	2 4/8	12 1/8	8	6 1/8	6 1/8	Maple Creek, Sask.	Glen A. Lewis	George Hooey	1964	83
85 2/8	17	17	6 6/8	6 4/8	2 7/8	2 7/8	10 6/8	8	5 1/8	5 3/8	Bow City, Alta.	H. M. Stephens	H. M. Stephens	1964	83
85 2/8	14 4/8	14 3/8	6 6/8	6 6/8	2 4/8	2 4/8	14	11 5/8	6 4/8	6 3/8	Sublette, Wyo.	Mike Wilson	Mike Wilson	1966	83
85 2/8	17 1/8	16 6/8	6 2/8	6 3/8	2 6/8	2 6/8	11 1/8	5 6/8	6 3/8	6 1/8	Sweetwater Co., Wyo.	Mario Shassetz	Mario Shassetz	1968	83
85 2/8	15 6/8	16	6 3/8	6 3/8	2 6/8	2 5/8	10 3/8	7 4/8	7 4/8	7 4/8	Johnson Co., Wyo.	Robert P. Murphy	Robert P. Murphy	1968	83
85 2/8	14 4/8	14 4/8	7 6/8	7 2/8	2 6/8	2 6/8	11 7/8	9 7/8	4 6/8	4 6/8	S. Wamustter, Wyo.	William G. Hepworth	William G. Hepworth	1970	83
85 2/8	15 7/8	15 6/8	7 2/8	7 1/8	2 6/8	2 6/8	8 3/8	3 6/8	6 4/8	6 4/8	Carbon Co., Wyo.	Daryl L. Frank	Daryl L. Frank	1973	83
85 2/8	15 6/8	15 6/8	6 6/8	6 6/8	2 5/8	2 7/8	12 5/8	8 2/8	7 1/8	6 7/8	Lincoln Co., Wyo.	James R. Gunter	James R. Gunter	1976	83
85 2/8	15 2/8	15 1/8	7 5/8	7 3/8	2 5/8	2 4/8	10 6/8	6 3/8	4	4 1/8	Baker Co., Oregon	Robert Spears	Robert Spears	1977	83
85 2/8	17 7/8	18 1/8	6 7/8	6 4/8	3	3 1/8	11 1/8	4 7/8	5	4 3/8	Colfax Co., N.M.	John D. Pearson	John D. Pearson	1977	83
85 2/8	17 4/8	17 5/8	7	7	2 7/8	3	9 4/8	6 1/8	4 6/8	5 2/8	Colfax Co., N. M.	Rick H. Jackson	Rick H. Jackson	1977	83
85 2/8	16 4/8	16 3/8	7	7 1/8	3	3	8 5/8	4 3/8	5 6/8	5 2/8	Carbon Co., Wyo.	Paul M. Ostrander	Paul M. Ostrander	1977	83
85 2/8	14 4/8	14 4/8	5 7/8	5 7/8	2 7/8	2 7/8	9 7/8	6 7/8	6	5 7/8	Carbon Co., Wyo.	Roland W. Anthony	Roland W. Anthony	1978	83
85 2/8	16 1/8	16 1/8	6 7/8	7	2 5/8	2 5/8	13 4/8	11 7/8	6 5/8	6 3/8	Lake Co. Oregon	James H. Hastings	James H. Hastings	1979	83
85	15 3/8	14 7/8	7 4/8	7 4/8	2 7/8	2 7/8	11 1/8	6 1/8	6	5 6/8	Douglas, Wyo.	Floyd Bishop	Floyd Bishop	1937	101
85	15 3/8	15 2/8	7 4/8	7 4/8	2 5/8	2 5/8	11	10 1/8	6 4/8	6	Henderson, N. M.	Ron Vance	Ron Vance	1943	101
85	17 5/8	17 4/8	5 5/8	5 5/8	2 5/8	2 5/8	9 7/8	7 2/8	6 2/8	6 3/8	Washoe Co., Nev.	Walter Craig Bell	Walter Craig Bell	1949	101
85	14 7/8	15 1/8	6 4/8	6 4/8	3	3	14 4/8	12 2/8	5 3/8	5 6/8	Brothers, Oreg.	Orlo Flock	Orlo Flock	1955	101
85	15	15	6 6/8	6 5/8	3 1/8	3 1/8	14 1/8	10 7/8	5 7/8	6	Raleigh, N. D.	Archie Malm	Archie Malm	1958	101
85	19 3/8	18 7/8	6 4/8	6 2/8	3 2/8	2 4/8	14 1/8	8 5/8	5 3/8	4 7/8	Williams, Ariz.	Donovan E. Smith	Donovan E. Smith	1959	101

85	15 5/8	15 6/8	6	6	3	3	9 6/8	8 1/8	4 5/8	5 3/8	Sage Creek Basin, Wyo.	Robert A. Hill	Robert A. Hill	1959	101
85	17 5/8	17 5/8	6 6/8	6 6/8	2 7/8	2 7/8	17 3/8	14 4/8	5	5 1/8	Forsyth, Mont.	John M. Broadwell	John M. Broadwell	1961	101
85	15 4/8	15 4/8	6 6/8	6 4/8	3 2/8	3 2/8	10	5 4/8	5	4 6/8	Brusett, Mont.	Unknown	Frank Mc Keever	PR1962	101
85	16 1/8	15 6/8	6 7/8	7	2 7/8	2 7/8	10 4/8	7 4/8	6 7/8	6 2/8	Garfield Co., Mont.	W. A. Delaney	W. A. Delaney	1965	101
85	16	15 7/8	7 1/8	7	2 5/8	2 5/8	8 6/8	4 6/8	5 6/8	5 7/8	Rawlins, Wyo	Clarence J. Becker	Clarence J. Becker	1965	101
85	14 5/8	14 4/8	8 1/8	7 6/8	2 7/8	2 7/8	11 5/8	10 2/8	5 7/8	5 6/8	Saratoga, Wyo.	Benny E. Bechtol	Benny E. Bechtol	1968	101
85	16 2/8	16 2/8	6 6/8	6 6/8	3	3	14 1/8	9 1/8	5 7/8	6	Rawlins, Wyo.	H. H. Eighmy	H. H. Eighmy	1969	101
85	15 4/8	15 6/8	7 2/8	7	2 4/8	2 4/8	13 2/8	8 7/8	6 5/8	6 1/8	Uinta Co., Wyo.	Joan Beachler	Joan Beachler	1974	101
85	16 3/8	16 1/8	6 3/8	6 4/8	3	3	9 2/8	3 5/8	5 5/8	5 5/8	Torrance Co., N. M.	Stephen A. Nisbet	Stephen A. Nisbet	1975	101
85	17 3/8	17 7/8	6 2/8	6 4/8	3 2/8	3 2/8	13 5/8	8 5/8	4 7/8	4 7/8	Yavapai Co., Ariz.	David M. Sanders	David M. Sanders	1976	101
85	18 2/8	18 5/8	6 4/8	6 5/8	2 5/8	2 6/8	13 1/8	9	5	5 3/8	Sierra Co., N. M.	Charles R. Bowen	Charles R. Bowen	1977	101
85	16 5/8	16 5/8	6 6/8	6 6/8	2 5/8	2 5/8	10 6/8	7 2/8	6	5 7/8	Lake Co., Oregon	Frank R. Biggs	Frank R. Biggs	1978	101
84 7/8	18	18 1/8	6 5/8	6 4/8	2 6/8	2 5/8	18 2/8	14 4/8	5 1/8	5 1/8	Plush, Oreg.	Ernest E. Puddy	Ernest E. Puddy	1949	119
84 6/8	15 7/8	16 1/8	7 3/8	7 3/8	2 3/8	2 4/8	7	1	6 2/8	5 6/8	Modoc Co., Calif.	William A. Shaw	William A. Shaw	1942	120
84 6/8	16 5/8	16 6/8	6 7/8	6 6/8	2 6/8	2 5/8	14 6/8	11 2/8	6 7/8	5 5/8	Anderson Mesa, Ariz.	Elgin T. Gates	Elgin T. Gates	1955	120
84 6/8	16 4/8	16 4/8	6 5/8	6 5/8	2 4/8	2 4/8	8 3/8	3 4/8	6 1/8	5 5/8	Laramie, Wyo.	Roger D. Ramsay	Roger D. Ramsay	1958	120
84 6/8	16 3/8	16 4/8	6 1/8	6	2 7/8	2 7/8	11 3/8	7 4/8	4 5/8	4 7/8	Laramie Peak, Wyo.	Elmer Rupert	Elmer Rupert	1961	120
84 6/8	16	16 1/8	7 2/8	7 1/8	3	3	12 1/8	6 6/8	5	4 6/8	Alliance, Neb.	Joseph Nelson	Joseph Nelson	1962	120
84 6/8	17 3/8	16 7/8	7 1/8	7 1/8	3	2 7/8	14 6/8	12 4/8	5 4/8	4 4/8	Fremont Co., Wyo.	Dick Cone	Dick Cone	1963	120
84 6/8	15 4/8	15 4/8	6 4/8	6 6/8	3 6/8	3 5/8	7 4/8	1 7/8	5 4/8	5 5/8	Harney Co., Oreg.	D. R. Knoll	D. R. Knoll	1963	120
84 6/8	16 3/8	16 4/8	6 5/8	6 6/8	3	3	11 1/8	7	5	5	Sinclair, Wyo.	John Kastner	John Kastner	1963	120
84 6/8	17	17 4/8	6 6/8	6 6/8	2 4/8	2 5/8	14 6/8	11 1/8	6 1/8	5 3/8	Jenner, Alta.	J. E. Edwards	J. E. Edwards	1964	120
84 6/8	16 6/8	16 5/8	6 7/8	7	3	2 7/8	12	11	5 2/8	4 7/8	Johnson Co., Wyo.	John G. Carroll	John G. Carroll	1965	120
84 6/8	15 7/8	15 7/8	6 2/8	6 2/8	2 5/8	2 5/8	10 6/8	6 2/8	7	7	Rock Springs, Wyo.	W. Daniel English	W. Daniel English	1966	120
84 6/8	16 2/8	16 3/8	6	6 1/8	2 4/8	2 3/8	8 5/8	3 5/8	7	6 7/8	Navajo Co., Ariz.	George M. Owen	George M. Owen	1966	120
84 6/8	17	16 6/8	6 5/8	6 5/8	2 4/8	2 4/8	17	16	5 3/8	5 1/8	Custer County, Idaho	Claus Karlson	Claus Karlson	1966	120
84 6/8	15 5/8	15 7/8	7 7/8	7 6/8	2 5/8	2 7/8	10 2/8	5 7/8	5 6/8	5 5/8	Poison Spider Creek, Wyo.	Robert Ziker	Robert Ziker	1966	120
84 6/8	16	16	6 6/8	6 4/8	2 6/8	2 6/8	11 2/8	5 4/8	6 4/8	6 4/8	Casper, Wyo.	John E. Mohritz	John E. Mohritz	1966	120
84 6/8	16 5/8	17	6 2/8	6 2/8	2 3/8	2 3/8	10 4/8	5 1/8	6 5/8	6 5/8	Modoc Co., Calif.	Leland C. Lehman	Leland C. Lehman	1969	120
84 6/8	19 7/8	19 4/8	6 1/8	5 7/8	2 5/8	2 5/8	18	13 6/8	5 2/8	4 5/8	Boquillas Ranch, Ariz.	Bob Dixon	Bob Dixon	1970	120
84 6/8	15 7/8	15 6/8	6 5/8	6 5/8	3 6/8	3 5/8	13 5/8	8 6/8	5 4/8	5 2/8	Ft. Apache Res., Ariz.	Donald Smith	Donald Smith	1972	120
84 6/8	16 3/8	16 3/8	7	7 1/8	2 6/8	2 5/8	11	5 1/8	5 6/8	5 7/8	Moffat Co., Colo.	James C. MacLachlan	James C. MacLachlan	1975	120
84 6/8	15 6/8	15 5/8	7 1/8	7 1/8	2 6/8	2 7/8	10 2/8	7 1/8	6 3/8	5 7/8	Garden Co., Neb.	Richard Mosley	Richard Mosley	1978	120
84 4/8	16 3/8	16 3/8	7 1/8	7 1/8	2 5/8	2 5/8	9 6/8	6	5 3/8	5 3/8	Rawlins, Wyo.	A. A. Carrey	A. A. Carrey	1944	140
84 4/8	16 4/8	16 2/8	6 2/8	6 2/8	2 6/8	2 6/8	12 7/8	9 2/8	7 6/8	7 5/8	Chihuahua, Mexico	Julio Estrada	Julio Estrada	1945	140
84 4/8	16	16	5 5/8	5 5/8	2 7/8	2 7/8	14 4/8	13 7/8	5 1/8	5	Fremont Co., Wyo.	Ernest R. Novotny	Ernest R. Novotny	1954	140
84 4/8	15 6/8	15 7/8	7 5/8	7 5/8	2 4/8	2 4/8	14 2/8	10 3/8	5 6/8	5 7/8	Rawlins, Wyo.	Eloise Kees	Eloise Kees	1962	140
84 4/8	16 6/8	16 5/8	6 1/8	6 1/8	2 6/8	2 6/8	10 3/8	4 2/8	6 3/8	6 2/8	Tripp Co., S. D.	Roy Hazuka	Roy Hazuka	1962	140
84 4/8	18 4/8	18	7	7	3	3	13	8 4/8	5	3 4/8	Seligman, Ariz.	Garth A. Brown	Garth A. Brown	1964	140
84 4/8	14 7/8	14 6/8	7 4/8	7 4/8	2 6/8	2 6/8	9 1/8	5 7/8	5 7/8	6 2/8	Baggs, Wyo.	Tom Elberson	Tom Elberson	1966	140
84 4/8	17	17 1/8	6 4/8	6 5/8	2 4/8	2 4/8	11 1/8	5 1/8	5 6/8	5 6/8	Sweetwater Co., Wyo.	Harvey B. Bartley	Harvey B. Bartley	1970	140
84 4/8	16 2/8	16 2/8	6	6	2 3/8	2 3/8	13	8	7 1/8	7	Carbon Co., Wyo.	William G. Mackey	William G. Mackey	1972	140

PRONGHORN–Continued
Antilocapra americana americana and related subspecies

Score	Length of Horn R.	L.	Circumference of Base R.	L.	Circumference at Third Quarter R.	L.	Inside Spread	Tip to Tip Spread	Length of Prong R.	L.	Locality Killed	By Whom Killed	Owner	Date Killed	Rank
84 5/8	14 5/8	14 7/8	6 7/8	7 1/8	2 5/8	2 5/8	12 5/8	8 5/8	6 1/8	6 5/8	Lake Co., Oreg.	Gene Cormie	Gene Cormie	1973	140
84 5/8	16	16	6 7/8	6 7/8	2 5/8	2 5/8	12 3/8	7 3/8	6 5/8	6 5/8	Lincoln Co., Wyo.	George Kirkman	George Kirkman	1973	140
84 5/8	17	16 5/8	7 3/8	7 3/8	2 3/8	2 3/8	9 5/8	7 3/8	6	6 1/8	Fields, Oreg.	John H. Johnson	John H. Johnson	1974	140
84 5/8	16 3/8	16 3/8	7 1/8	7 1/8	2 5/8	2 5/8	13 3/8	7 3/8	5 5/8	5 5/8	Washoe Co., Nev.	Frances M. Hansell	Frances M. Hansell	1974	140
84 5/8	15 5/8	16	7 7/8	7 7/8	3	3 1/8	10 1/8	6 5/8	5 1/8	5 5/8	Carbon Co., Wyo.	John C. Sjogren	John C. Sjogren	1976	140
84 5/8	17 5/8	16 5/8	6 7/8	6 3/8	2 5/8	2 5/8	15 5/8	13 7/8	6 3/8	6 7/8	Modoc Co., Calif.	J. Bob Johnson	J. Bob Johnson	1978	140
84 5/8	16 3/8	16 3/8	7	6 7/8	3	3	14 3/8	12 5/8	6	5 5/8	Sweetwater Co., Wyo.	Frankie Miller	Frankie Miller	1979	140
84 3/8	16 5/8	16 5/8	6 7/8	6 7/8	2 5/8	2 5/8	10 7/8	5 7/8	5 5/8	5 5/8	Sweetwater River, Wyo.	Kermit Platt	Kermit Platt	1952	156
84 3/8	17 3/8	16 5/8	6 1/8	6 3/8	2 5/8	2 5/8	12 3/8	10 5/8	6 7/8	6 7/8	Slate Creek, Wyo.	Jim Calkins	Jim Calkins	1956	156
84 3/8	15 7/8	15	6 3/8	6 3/8	3 3/8	3 3/8	11 3/8	11	4 3/8	4 3/8	Pumpkin Buttes, Wyo.	John B. Miller	John B. Miller	1957	156
84 3/8	17 3/8	16 1/8	6 5/8	6 3/8	2 5/8	2 5/8	13	6 7/8	5 1/8	5 1/2	Anderson Mesa, Ariz.	Bill Gray	Bill Gray	1960	156
84 3/8	16 7/8	16 1/2	7	7	2 3/8	2 3/8	7 5/8	1 7/8	6	6	Natrona, Wyo.	William Fisher	William Fisher	1960	156
84 3/8	16	16 3/8	7	7	2 5/8	2 5/8	11 5/8	7 5/8	6 1/8	6 3/8	Unita Co., Wyo.	Ross Lukenbill	Ross Lukenbill	1965	156
84 3/8	15 7/8	17 1/2	6 1/8	6 1/8	3	2 7/8	10 3/8	5 1/8	4 5/8	4 1/8	Rawlins, Wyo.	Armin O. Baltensweiler	Armin O. Baltensweiler	1966	156
84 3/8	17 5/8	17 3/8	6 5/8	6 5/8	3	3	12 1/8	7 7/8	6 5/8	7 1/8	Ft. Apache Res., Ariz.	Frank E. White	Frank E. White	1967	156
84 3/8	14 5/8	14 7/8	7 1/8	7 1/8	2 3/8	2 3/8	9 3/8	7 1/8	5 5/8	5 5/8	Big Piney, Wyo.	Lawrence M. Kick	Lawrence M. Kick	1967	156
84 3/8	16 7/8	16 1/2	7 5/8	7 5/8	2 5/8	2 5/8	12 3/8	8 5/8	8	8	Fremont Co., Wyo.	Edward S. Friend	Edward S. Friend	1967	156
84 3/8	15	15	7 3/8	7 3/8	2 5/8	2 5/8	13 3/8	11 7/8	8	8	Fremont Co., Wyo.	Lee Arce	Lee Arce	1968	156
84 3/8	17 1/8	17 7/8	7 3/8	7 3/8	2 5/8	2 5/8	8 3/8	5 5/8	4 1/2	6	Humboldt Co., Nev.	Gerald A. Lent	Gerald A. Lent	1970	156
84 3/8	15 5/8	15	6	6	2 7/8	2 7/8	11 5/8	8 7/8	4 7/8	4 7/8	Natrona Co., Wyo.	Donald F. Mahnke	Donald F. Mahnke	1971	156
84 3/8	16 1/8	16 1/2	7	7	2 5/8	2 5/8	15 1/8	11 5/8	5 3/8	5 3/8	Albany Co., Wyo.	George Panagos, Jr.	George Panagos, Jr.	1972	156
84 3/8	16 3/8	16 5/8	6 5/8	6 5/8	2 5/8	2 5/8	8 3/8	3 7/8	5 3/8	5 3/8	Apache Co., Ariz.	Alaine D. Neal	Alaine D. Neal	1973	156
84 3/8	17 1/8	17 3/8	5 5/8	5 5/8	2 5/8	2 5/8	8 7/8	1 7/8	7	6 7/8	Abbott, N. M.	George H. Ray, III	George H. Ray, III	1974	156
84 3/8	16	16 5/8	6 7/8	6 7/8	3	3	9 7/8	7	4 5/8	4 3/8	Carbon Co., Wyo.	William O. Queen	William O. Queen	1975	156
84 3/8	16 5/8	17 1/8	6 5/8	6 5/8	2 5/8	2 5/8	16	11 5/8	5 3/8	5 3/8	Meade Co., S. D.	John Hostetter	John Hostetter	1975	156
84 3/8	16 5/8	16 3/8	6 3/8	6 3/8	3	3	8 3/8	5 5/8	5 5/8	5 5/8	Humboldt Co., Nev.	David Perondi	David Perondi	1976	156
84 3/8	15 5/8	15 7/8	7 1/8	7 1/8	2 5/8	2 5/8	13	12 5/8	5 5/8	5 5/8	Carbon Co., Wyo.	Kenneth Mellin	Kenneth Mellin	1976	156
84 3/8	17 3/8	17 1/4	6 5/8	6 5/8	2 5/8	2 5/8	11 3/8	8 1/8	4 5/8	4 3/8	Sweetwater Co., Wyo.	Bill Jordan	Bill Jordan	1976	156
84 3/8	15 5/8	15 7/8	7 3/8	7 3/8	2 5/8	2 5/8	14 1/8	13	5 5/8	5 7/8	Carbon Co., Wyo.	Glenn F. Galbraith	Glenn F. Galbraith	1977	156
84	16	15 5/8	7 7/8	7 7/8	3 7/8	3 7/8	14 1/8	10 5/8	3 3/8	3 3/8	Lost Cabin, Wyo.	Jack Henrey	Jack Henrey	1955	178
84	17 1/8	17 1/8	6 5/8	6 5/8	2 5/8	2 5/8	14 3/8	11 1/8	5	5 5/8	Meadowdale, Wyo.	Mrs. Lodisa Pipher	Mrs. Lodisa Pipher	1956	178
84	16 1/4	17 3/4	6	6	2 7/8	2 7/8	10 3/8	5 5/8	6	5 3/8	Yavapai Co., Ariz.	Walter Tibbs	Walter Tibbs	1959	178

84	15 6/8	16	6 6/8	6 6/8	2 6/8	2 6/8	11 2/8	8	6 4/8	6 4/8	Campbell Co., Wyo.	Fred J. Brogle	Fred J. Brogle	1960	178
84	14 6/8	14 4/8	7 5/8	7 5/8	3 1/8	3 1/8	14 4/8	13 6/8	6	5 7/8	Pinedale, Wyo.	Edward Sturla	Edward Sturla	1960	178
84	16	16 1/8	6 6/8	6 5/8	2 5/8	2 6/8	8 6/8	5 2/8	5 7/8	6 2/8	Rawlins, Wyo.	John M. Sell	John M. Sell	1964	178
84	17 1/8	17 4/8	6 4/8	6 5/8	3 1/8	3	13 4/8	12 5/8	5 3/8	5 1/8	Carbon Co., Wyo.	Mrs. Thom. H. Green	Mrs. Thom. H. Green	1964	178
84	16 5/8	16 5/8	6 3/8	6 2/8	3	3	11 2/8	6	6 2/8	6 1/8	Fremont Co., Wyo.	Robert E. Novotny	Robert E. Novotny	1964	178
84	17	17 2/8	7 1/8	7 1/8	2 6/8	2 5/8	12 2/8	6 7/8	4 7/8	4 7/8	Milk River, Alta.	George Vandervalk	George Vandervalk	1966	178
84	16 4/8	16 3/8	6 6/8	6 4/8	3	3	8	3	5 3/8	5 2/8	Washington Co., Colo.	Christian Heyden	Christian Heyden	1967	178
84	15 5/8	15 5/8	6 7/8	6 7/8	2 5/8	2 4/8	14 7/8	12 2/8	6 4/8	6 4/8	Leola, S. D.	Leonard Lahr	Leonard Lahr	1967	178
84	15 4/8	15 4/8	6 5/8	6 5/8	2 5/8	2 6/8	11 6/8	8 7/8	7 1/8	6 7/8	Choteau Co., Mont.	W. E. Cherry	W. E. Cherry	1968	178
84	14 4/8	14 4/8	7	6 6/8	2 7/8	2 7/8	11 5/8	11 5/8	6	6 2/8	Red Desert, Wyo.	Fred Morgan	Fred Morgan	1969	178
84	15 6/8	16 2/8	6 6/8	6 7/8	2 3/8	2 4/8	14 2/8	9	6 4/8	6 5/8	Washoe Co., Nev.	Robert L. Mallory	Robert L. Mallory	1969	178
84	16 6/8	16 1/8	6 7/8	6 7/8	2 6/8	2 6/8	7 3/8	3 5/8	4 6/8	4 6/8	Carbon Co., Wyo.	Russ Allen	Russ Allen	1970	178
84	16 5/8	16 3/8	6 7/8	6 6/8	2 4/8	2 4/8	8 6/8	2 3/8	6 1/8	6 3/8	Humbolt Co., Nev.	Gary D. Bader	Gary D. Bader	1970	178
84	15	15 2/8	7	7	2 5/8	2 6/8	14 1/8	11 4/8	6	6	Albany Co., Wyo.	Andy Pfaff	Andy Pfaff	1972	178
84	18 6/8	18 2/8	6 4/8	6 4/8	2 4/8	2 3/8	17 6/8	15 7/8	5	4 5/8	Sublette Co., Wyo.	Dick Reilly	Dick Reilly	1974	178
84	16 3/8	16 3/8	6 6/8	6 6/8	2 5/8	2 5/8	11 6/8	8 3/8	5 4/8	5 5/8	Presidio Co., Texas	W. Wayne Roye	W. Wayne Roye	1977	178
84	15 1/8	14 7/8	6 4/8	6 5/8	3 3/8	3 1/8	11 1/8	9 6/8	6 6/8	5 7/8	Sioux Co., Neb.	Harvey Y. Suetsugu	Harvey Y. Suetsugu	1977	178
84	16 7/8	16 7/8	6 5/8	6 5/8	3	2 6/8	10 6/8	4 7/8	5 4/8	5 2/8	Coconino Co., Ariz.	Robert F. Veazey	Robert F. Veazey	1979	178
83 6/8	16 4/8	17	6 6/8	6 6/8	2 5/8	2 5/8	12 4/8	6	5 4/8	5 4/8	Coconino Co., Ariz.	Marvin Redburn	Marvin Redburn	1950	199
83 6/8	16 3/8	16	7	7 1/8	2 7/8	3	12 7/8	11	5 2/8	4 6/8	Saratoga, Wyo.	Bob Herbison	Bob Herbison	1955	199
83 6/8	16 1/8	16 1/8	6 7/8	7	2 5/8	2 5/8	10 2/8	8 3/8	5 7/8	6 3/8	Plainview, S. D.	Bernie Wanhanen	Bernie Wanhanen	1960	199
83 6/8	16 4/8	15 7/8	6 6/8	6 6/8	2 7/8	2 6/8	12 6/8	8 6/8	5 3/8	5 1/8	Chino Valley, Ariz.	Max Durfee	Max Durfee	1960	199
83 6/8	15 4/8	15 3/8	7 1/8	7	2 7/8	2 5/8	10 4/8	6 3/8	5 7/8	5 7/8	Poison Spider, Wyo.	Robert Ziker	Robert Ziker	1960	199
83 6/8	17 4/8	16 6/8	6	6	3	3	10 6/8	6 7/8	5 6/8	3 6/8	Williams, Ariz.	Dave Blair	Dave Blair	1961	199
83 6/8	16 5/8	16 7/8	6 4/8	6 4/8	3 2/8	3 1/8	15 6/8	10 6/8	4 4/8	4 5/8	Yavapai Co., Ariz.	C. J. Adair	C. J. Adair	1961	199
83 6/8	17 5/8	17 3/8	6 3/8	6 3/8	3	2 5/8	8 6/8	10 7/8	5 2/8	5	Hudspeth City, Texas	Jim Perry	Jim Perry	1963	199
83 6/8	15 7/8	15 7/8	7	7 2/8	2 4/8	2 5/8	8 3/8	5 6/8	5 7/8	5 7/8	Alcova, Wyo.	Donald G. Gebers	Donald G. Gebers	1964	199
83 6/8	15 2/8	15 1/8	6 6/8	6 5/8	2 7/8	2 6/8	11 7/8	6 7/8	6 7/8	7 1/8	Meridian, Oreg.	Dale E. Beattie	Dale E. Beattie	1964	199
83 6/8	15 6/8	15 5/8	7 2/8	7	3	2 6/8	10 3/8	6 1/8	6 2/8	6 2/8	Hudspeth Co., Texas	Basil C. Bradbury	Basil C. Bradbury	1966	199
83 6/8	18 4/8	19 1/8	6 1/8	6 2/8	2 6/8	2 6/8	7 7/8	8 3/8	4 5/8	4 4/8	Motley Co., Texas	Ronald Vandiver	Ronald Vandiver	1967	199
83 6/8	16 6/8	16 4/8	6 3/8	6 3/8	3 2/8	3	10	5 6/8	4 7/8	5	Black Tank, Ariz.	George Malin Lewis	George Malin Lewis	1968	199
83 6/8	15	15	6 5/8	6 5/8	3	3	13 4/8	10 4/8	5 4/8	6 3/8	Sweetwater Co., Wyo.	R. L. Brown, Jr.	R. L. Brown, Jr.	1970	199
83 6/8	15 6/8	15 7/8	7 4/8	7 2/8	2 5/8	2 5/8	9 3/8	4 1/8	5 1/8	5 2/8	Lake Co., Oreg.	Dennis E. Carter	Dennis E. Carter	1972	199
83 6/8	15	15 1/8	7 2/8	7 2/8	2 5/8	2 7/8	14 2/8	11 3/8	5 6/8	5 7/8	Sweetwater Co., Wyo.	Betty J. Oliver	Betty J. Oliver	1974	199
83 6/8	14 4/8	14 3/8	6 5/8	6 6/8	2 6/8	2 6/8	10 6/8	7 4/8	6 2/8	6 2/8	Divide, Sask.	Leslie Banford	Leslie Banford	1975	199
83 6/8	15 6/8	16 2/8	6 4/8	6 4/8	2 2/8	2 1/8	10 4/8	10	6 7/8	6 6/8	Park Co., Wyo.	Don F. & Tim Holt	Don F. Holt	1975	199
83 6/8	16 6/8	16 6/8	6 4/8	6 1/8	2 6/8	2 6/8	7 1/8	2	6 4/8	6 4/8	Modoc Co., Calif.	William B. Steig	William B. Steig	1977	199
83 5/8	16 6/8	16 4/8	6 6/8	6 4/8	2 4/8	2 4/8	11 4/8	9	5 5/8	5 2/8	Sage Creek, Wyo.	Pat Swarts	Pat Swarts	1960	218
83 4/8	16 1/8	15 7/8	6 2/8	6 2/8	2 7/8	2 7/8	10 4/8	6 5/8	6 1/8	6 1/8	Park Co., Mont.	William E. Randall	William E. Randall	1947	219
83 4/8	17	16 2/8	6 4/8	6 2/8	2 6/8	2 6/8	14 1/8	11 1/8	6 4/8	6 1/8	Farson, Wyo.	Geo. E. MacGillivray	Geo. E. MacGillivray	1951	219
83 4/8	16 7/8	17	7	7	2 7/8	2 5/8	10 4/8	6 7/8	5 2/8	5 2/8	Miles City, Mont.	J. Louis Mann	J. Louis Mann	1954	219
83 4/8	18 1/8	17 6/8	6 4/8	6 3/8	2 4/8	2 2/8	16	14 2/8	5 6/8	5 2/8	Ariz.	O. Patton	William N. Henry	1956	219
83 4/8	15 5/8	16 1/8	6 3/8	6 2/8	2 3/8	2 5/8	9 5/8	5	6 4/8	6 5/8	Atlantic City, Wyo.	James S. Kleinhammer	James S. Kleinhammer	1958	219

Pronghorn–*Continued*

Antilocapra americana americana and related subspecies

Score	Length of Horn R.	Length of Horn L.	Circumference of Base R.	Circumference of Base L.	Circumference at Third Quarter R.	Circumference at Third Quarter L.	Inside Spread	Tip to Tip Spread	Length of Prong R.	Length of Prong L.	Locality Killed	By Whom Killed	Owner	Date Killed	Rank
83 4/8	17	17	6 4/8	6 4/8	2 6/8	2 4/8	10 2/8	5 6/8	5	4 5/8	Navajo Co., Ariz.	Mrs. Don Lambert	Mrs. Don Lambert	1961	219
83 4/8	14	14 4/8	6 7/8	6 4/8	3 5/8	3 4/8	12 5/8	10 1/8	6 4/8	6 2/8	Watford City, N. D.	Dean Etl	Dean Etl	1964	219
83 4/8	15 6/8	15 6/8	6 1/8	6 1/8	3 2/8	3 1/8	11 3/8	6 3/8	4 6/8	4 6/8	Shoshoni, Wyo.	Collins F. Kellogg	Collins F. Kellogg	1965	219
83 4/8	16	15 7/8	6 4/8	6 4/8	2 4/8	2 4/8	10 5/8	5 7/8	7	6 6/8	Boone, Colo.	Mahlon T. White	Mahlon T. White	1966	219
83 4/8	15 6/8	15 5/8	7	7 1/8	2 4/8	2 6/8	9 6/8	6 7/8	5 4/8	5 3/8	Wamsutter, Wyo.	Kenneth L. Swanson	Kenneth L. Swanson	1967	219
83 4/8	15 5/8	15 7/8	7 2/8	7 1/8	2 4/8	2 5/8	11 1/8	7 1/8	5 2/8	5 4/8	Craig, Colo.	Albert Johnson	Albert Johnson	1969	219
83 4/8	16 2/8	16 2/8	6 3/8	6 4/8	2 6/8	2 5/8	15 4/8	12 2/8	5 5/8	5 7/8	Red Desert, Wyo.	David W. Knowles	David W. Knowles	1970	219
83 4/8	16 2/8	16 2/8	6 6/8	6 6/8	2 4/8	2 5/8	12	10 1/8	5	5 1/8	Carbon Co., Wyo.	Billy C. Randall	Billy C. Randall	1970	219
83 4/8	17 1/8	17	6 6/8	6 6/8	2 6/8	2 6/8	15 5/8	10 6/8	5	5	Hoback Rim, Wyo.	F. Larry Storey	F. Larry Storey	1973	219
83 4/8	17 2/8	17 1/8	6 2/8	6 3/8	2 5/8	2 5/8	14 6/8	9 5/8	5 5/8	5 6/8	Coconino Co., Ariz.	Thomas A. Dunlap	Thomas A. Dunlap	1974	219
83 4/8	17	17 1/8	6 5/8	6 6/8	2 7/8	2 6/8	6 2/8	1 3/8	4 5/8	4 6/8	Coconino Co., Ariz.	Cheryl Alderman	Cheryl Alderman	1974	219
83 4/8	16	16	7 4/8	7 4/8	2 7/8	2 7/8	9	3 2/8	5 3/8	4 6/8	Fremont Co., Wyo.	Ruth Muller	Ruth Muller	1974	219
83 4/8	15 3/8	15 6/8	7 2/8	7	2 4/8	2 4/8	8 1/8	2 2/8	5 3/8	5 1/8	Fremont Co., Wyo.	James G. Allard	James G. Allard	1974	219
83 4/8	17 3/8	17 2/8	6 3/8	6 4/8	2 5/8	2 6/8	9 5/8	5 3/8	5 5/8	5 1/8	Fremont Co., Wyo.	Robert B. Cragoe, Sr.	Robert B. Cragoe, Sr.	1975	219
83 4/8	16 3/8	16 2/8	7 2/8	7 2/8	2 5/8	2 5/8	9 4/8	3 6/8	8 3/8	4 3/8	Harney Co., Oregon	Craig Foster	Craig Foster	1977	219
83 4/8	17	17	6 5/8	6 3/8	2 7/8	2 6/8	10 6/8	6 6/8	5 1/8	5 1/8	De Baca Co., N.M.	Glenn C. Conner	Glenn C. Conner	1977	219
83 4/8	16 4/8	16 4/8	6 6/8	6 5/8	3	2 6/8	10 4/8	5 3/8	4 7/8	5 2/8	Box Butte Co., Neb.	Derald E. Morgan	Derald E. Morgan	1977	219
83 4/8	15 3/8	15 3/8	6 3/8	6 3/8	3	3	10 3/8	6 4/8	6	6 1/8	Washoe Co., Nevada	James R. Cobb	James R. Cobb	1978	219
83 4/8	15 2/8	16 1/8	6 6/8	6 5/8	2 5/8	2 6/8	10 2/8	6	6 2/8	6 3/8	Uinta Co., Wyo.	Velma B. O'Neil	Velma B. O'Neil	1978	219
83 4/8	16 6/8	16 7/8	6 6/8	6 5/8	2 5/8	2 5/8	8 6/8	2 4/8	5 2/8	5 2/8	Sweetwater Co., Wyo.	Otis T. Page	Otis T. Page	1978	219
83 2/8	16 6/8	17 1/8	6 2/8	6 1/8	2 4/8	2 5/8	16 5/8	15 3/8	6	6	Arminto, Wyo.	Edward H. Bohlin	Edward H. Bohlin	1951	244
83 2/8	16 1/8	16	7	6 7/8	2 5/8	2 6/8	12 3/8	10 4/8	5 2/8	4 7/8	Newcastle, Wyo.	Rupert Chisholm	Rupert Chisholm	1953	244
83 2/8	15 3/8	14 7/8	8 2/8	8 2/8	2 4/8	2 1/8	8 5/8	6 3/8	6 3/8	6 7/8	Campbell Co., Wyo.	Phillip M. Hodge	Phillip M. Hodge	1955	244
83 2/8	16 5/8	16 3/8	6 5/8	6 5/8	2 7/8	2 7/8	8 1/8	7 6/8	5 2/8	5	Kaycee, Wyo.	R. B. Nienhaus	R. B. Nienhaus	1961	244
83 2/8	15 2/8	15 5/8	6 2/8	6 2/8	2 4/8	2 6/8	9 6/8	6 5/8	6 6/8	7 1/8	Jeffrey City, Wyo.	Harry G M Jopson	Harry G M Jopson	1961	244
83 2/8	14 7/8	14 7/8	6 2/8	6 2/8	2 5/8	2 5/8	9 7/8	6	4 6/8	4 5/8	Fergus Co., Mont.	Steven G. Ard	Steven G. Ard	1962	244
83 2/8	16 3/8	16	6 4/8	6 4/8	3	2 7/8	9 3/8	4 3/8	6	6	Ferris Mt., Wyo.	Ron Vance	Ron Vance	1962	244
83 2/8	16 7/8	16 7/8	6 2/8	6 1/8	2 5/8	2 4/8	11 2/8	7 6/8	5 4/8	5 4/8	Capitan, N. M.	Lee H. Ingalls	Lee H. Ingalls	1969	244
83 2/8	18 2/8	18 2/8	6 2/8	6 3/8	2 5/8	2 5/8	12 5/8	8 3/8	4 4/8	4 2/8	Navajo Co., Ariz.	Joseph R. Rencher	Joseph R. Rencher	1970	244
83 2/8	16 7/8	16 7/8	7 1/8	7	2 2/8	2 4/8	14 3/8	12 4/8	5 2/8	5	Sweetwater Co., Wyo.	Allen Tanner	Allen Tanner	1970	244
83 2/8	17 1/8	17 1/8	6 5/8	6 6/8	2 4/8	2 3/8	8	2 4/8	5 1/8	5	Washoe Co., Nev.	David Pohl	David Pohl	1972	244
83 2/8	17	17	6 2/8	6 3/8	2 5/8	2 5/8	13 1/8	9 2/8	5 3/8	5 3/8	Culberson Co., Texas	Jim Smith	Jim Smith	1972	244

83 2/8	16 7/8	15 2/8	6 4/8	6 4/8	2 7/8	2 6/8	12	7 4/8	6 2/8	6 4/8	Coconino Co., Ariz.	Vernon E. North	Vernon E. North	1972	244
83 2/8	17 2/8	17 7/8	6 4/8	6 2/8	2 4/8	2 5/8	9 4/8	6 2/8	5	5 4/8	Coconino Co., Ariz.	Russell Fischer	Russell Fischer	1973	244
83 2/8	16	16 2/8	6 1/8	6 2/8	2 4/8	2 6/8	11	8 4/8	7 1/8	7 2/8	Carbon Co., Wyo.	Ray Freitas	Ray Freitas	1973	244
83 2/8	16	15 6/8	6 1/8	6 1/8	3	3	8 3/8	5 5/8	5 2/8	5 2/8	Park Co., Wyo.	Dwight Brunsvold	Dwight Brunsvold	1974	244
83 2/8	14 5/8	14 5/8	7	6 6/8	3 2/8	3 2/8	9 5/8	7 7/8	5 1/8	5 1/8	Jackson Co., Colo.	James R. Mosman	James R. Mosman	1975	244
83 2/8	17 5/8	17 4/8	6 2/8	6 3/8	3 2/8	3 1/8	12 6/8	6 3/8	4 1/8	4 4/8	Yavapai Co., Ariz.	J. Mike Foley	J. Mike Foley	1975	244
83 2/8	16 3/8	17	6 7/8	7	2 4/8	2 5/8	15 4/8	12 6/8	6 5/8	5 1/8	Yavapai Co., Ariz.	Ralph Koepke	Ralph Koepke	1975	244
83 2/8	17	17	6 2/8	6 2/8	2 6/8	2 5/8	15	11 3/8	5 2/8	5 4/8	Coconino Co., Ariz.	Edmond C. Morton	Edmond C. Morton	1975	244
83 2/8	16	16	7	6 7/8	2 5/8	2 5/8	11 6/8	7 5/8	5 5/8	6	Harding Co., S. D.	Kathleen Prestjohn	Kathleen Prestjohn	1975	244
83 2/8	16 4/8	16 2/8	6	6 1/8	2 7/8	2 6/8	10 6/8	4 1/8	6 3/8	6 5/8	Rolling Hills, Alta.	Dennis A. Andrews	Dennis A. Andrews	1975	244
83 2/8	15 6/8	15 2/8	6	6 1/8	2 5/8	2 6/8	11	4 1/8	7 2/8	7 5/8	Medicine Hat, Alta.	Roger H. Stone	Roger H. Stone	1975	244
83 2/8	14 5/8	14 5/8	6 5/8	6 6/8	2 6/8	2 6/8	12 4/8	10	7 2/8	7 6/8	Carter Co., Mont.	Joseph Henderson	Joseph Henderson	1975	244
83 2/8	15 6/8	15 6/8	6 4/8	6 4/8	2 7/8	2 7/8	9	2 6/8	5 2/8	5	Cochise Co., Ariz.	Keith Lee Miller	Keith Lee Miller	1976	244
83 2/8	14 6/8	14 6/8	7 1/8	7 1/8	3	3 2/8	13	10 6/8	4 2/8	5 1/8	Goshen Co., Wyo.	William E. Patterson	William E. Patterson	1976	244
83 2/8	15 6/8	16	6 5/8	6 6/8	2 4/8	2 5/8	9 6/8	4 4/8	6 3/8	6	Sweet Grass Co., Mont.	Dennis E. Moos	Dennis E. Moos	1977	244
83 2/8	15 2/8	15 2/8	7 1/8	6 6/8	2 7/8	2 7/8	14	10 5/8	6 1/8	6 1/8	Natrona Co., Wyo.	Dean L. Johnson	Dean L. Johnson	1977	244
83	16 2/8	16 5/8	6 4/8	6 3/8	3 6/8	3	16 2/8	16 4/8	4 1/8	5 1/8	Shirley Basin, Wyo.	Duncan G. Weibel	Duncan G. Weibel	1946	272
83	15 7/8	15 4/8	7 1/8	7	2 5/8	2 5/8	9 1/8	3 1/8	5 5/8	5 4/8	Rawlins, Wyo.	Richard Eisner	Richard Eisner	1951	272
83	14 4/8	15 2/8	7 6/8	7 2/8	2 2/8	2 4/8	10 4/8	8 7/8	6 2/8	6 4/8	Casper, Wyo.	Tom R. Frye	Tom R. Frye	1954	272
83	15 2/8	14 7/8	6 5/8	6 4/8	3	3 1/8	12 2/8	9 1/8	6	5 5/8	Heber, Ariz.	Grady L. Beard	Grady L. Beard	1954	272
83	15 2/8	15 1/8	6 5/8	6 4/8	2 5/8	2 5/8	14 6/8	13 4/8	6 5/8	6 2/8	Saratoga, Wyo.	Dave Erickson	Dave Erickson	1957	272
83	16 4/8	16 1/8	6 7/8	6 4/8	3	2 6/8	13 7/8	11 4/8	5 2/8	5 2/8	Rawlins, Wyo.	Melvin Birks	Melvin Birks	1960	272
83	16	16 1/8	6 4/8	6 4/8	2 7/8	2 7/8	11	5 1/8	5 7/8	5 7/8	Lame Deer, Mont.	G. E. Badgley	G. E. Badgley	1961	272
83	16 3/8	16 7/8	6 2/8	6 2/8	2 3/8	2 3/8	11	5 7/8	5 6/8	6 1/8	Lake Co., Oreg.	Ken Smith	Ken Smith	1962	272
83	15 4/8	15 2/8	7 1/8	7 2/8	2 6/8	3	13 4/8	9 3/8	5 3/8	6 1/8	Plevna, Mont.	Joseph P. Burger	Joseph P. Burger	1963	272
83	16 2/8	16 5/8	6 7/8	6 6/8	2 5/8	2 5/8	8 7/8	3 7/8	5 5/8	5 5/8	Boyero, Colo.	Henry H. Zietz	Henry H. Zietz	1965	272
83	16 6/8	17 1/8	6 5/8	6 5/8	3	3	14 4/8	13 7/8	5 4/8	4 3/8	Thatcher, Colo.	M. A. May	M. A. May	1965	272
83	16 3/8	16 2/8	7	6 6/8	3 1/8	3	11	8 5/8	4 6/8	4 4/8	Wamsutter, Wyo.	Marlene Simons	Marlene Simons	1970	272
83	16 1/8	16 2/8	6 4/8	6 2/8	2 5/8	2 4/8	8 7/8	8	6 4/8	6 5/8	Moffat Co., Colo.	Michael Coleman	Michael Coleman	1971	272
83	16	16	6 6/8	6 6/8	2 6/8	2 6/8	13 6/8	10 4/8	5	5	Springer, N. M.	Ronald E. McKinney	Ronald E. McKinney	1973	272
83	16	15 5/8	7	7	2 5/8	2 4/8	9	4 2/8	5 7/8	6	Fremont Co., Wyo.	Robert Cragoe, Jr.	Robert Cragoe, Jr.	1974	272
83	16 2/8	16 3/8	6 4/8	6 3/8	3	3	10 2/8	4 1/8	5 6/8	4 6/8	Colfax Co., N. M.	Jim Hoots	Jim Hoots	1975	272
83	16 5/8	17	6 4/8	6 3/8	2 5/8	2 5/8	11	6 4/8	5 7/8	6	Yavapai Co., Ariz.	Artie L. Thrower	Artie L. Thrower	1975	272
83	16 2/8	16 2/8	6 3/8	6 2/8	3 2/8	3 3/8	15	12 5/8	5 2/8	5 2/8	Valley Co., Mont.	Timothy R. Logan	Timothy R. Logan	1976	272
83	17	16 6/8	6 1/8	6 1/8	2 7/8	3	13 5/8	9 6/8	4 6/8	5 2/8	Wagon Mound, N. M.	Dale R. Leonard	Dale R. Leonard	1976	272
83	16 5/8	16 4/8	6 2/8	6 2/8	2 2/8	2 2/8	11 2/8	7 1/8	6 4/8	6 3/8	Lake Co., Oregon	Francis G. Dalrymple	Francis G. Dalrymple	1978	272
83	16	16 1/8	6 4/8	6 4/8	2 6/8	2 6/8	9 5/8	4 2/8	6 1/8	6 4/8	Sweetwater Co., Wyo.	Douglas Grantham	Douglas Grantham	1978	272
83	17 1/8	17 1/8	6 2/8	6 2/8	2 6/8	2 6/8	8 3/8	2 2/8	5 3/8	5 3/8	Sublette Co., Wyo.	Thomas A. Scott	Thomas A. Scott	1978	272
83	16 2/8	16 2/8	7	7 1/8	2 4/8	2 2/8	9 5/8	5	6 1/8	6 2/8	Sublette Co., Wyo.	Kenneth D. Knight	Kenneth D. Knight	1978	272
82 6/8	17 2/8	17	7	6 4/8	2 5/8	2 4/8	12 1/8	5 6/8	5 7/8	5 1/8	Natrona Co., Wyo.	Unknown	G. S. Peterson	1948	295
82 6/8	16	16 2/8	6 4/8	6 4/8	3 2/8	3 2/8	12 1/8	11 5/8	5	5	Angora, Neb.	Harold C. Rusk	Neb. Game Dept.	1954	295
82 6/8	16 6/8	17	6 4/8	6 4/8	2 6/8	2 6/8	14 3/8	14	5	5 1/8	Prairie Co., Mont.	Gordon Spears	Gordon Spears	1954	295
82 6/8	15 4/8	15 4/8	6 7/8	6 7/8	2 4/8	2 6/8	14 2/8	11	6	5 6/8	Jelm Mt., Wyo.	Guy Murdock	Guy Murdock	1955	295

PRONGHORN—Continued

Antilocapra americana americana and related subspecies

Score	Length of Horn R.	L.	Circumference of Base R.	L.	Circumference at Third Quarter R.	L.	Inside Spread	Tip to Tip Spread	Length of Prong R.	L.	Locality Killed	By Whom Killed	Owner	Date Killed	Rank
82 6/8	15 7/8	15 3/8	7 1/8	7 2/8	2 6/8	2 6/8	11 7/8	9 1/8	5	5	Glad Valley, S. D.	D. M. Davis	D. M. Davis	1958	295
82 6/8	17 3/8	17 3/8	5 7/8	6	3	3 1/8	10 7/8	3 5/8	5 5/8	5 5/8	Butte Co., S. D.	P. T. Theodore	P. T. Theodore	1958	295
82 6/8	17 5/8	17 4/8	6 4/8	6 4/8	2 5/8	2 7/8	13 3/8	9 4/8	4 7/8	5 2/8	Yavapai Co., Ariz.	Vaughan Rock	Vaughan Rock	1959	295
82 6/8	14 7/8	14 4/8	7	6 7/8	2 7/8	2 7/8	8 3/8	2 6/8	5 3/8	5 2/8	Gillette, Wyo.	R. R. Kirchner	R. R. Kirchner	1961	295
82 6/8	15 5/8	15 4/8	6 7/8	6 7/8	2 3/8	2 3/8	8 3/8	5 3/8	6 2/8	6 2/8	Sweetwater Co., Wyo.	A. L. Bruner	A. L. Bruner	1962	295
82 6/8	16 5/8	16 4/8	6 2/8	6 4/8	2 3/8	2 3/8	11	5 7/8	5 4/8	5 7/8	Lake Co., Oreg.	Kenneth Smith	Kenneth Smith	1963	295
82 6/8	15 5/8	15 7/8	7	7	2 7/8	2 6/8	11 3/8	8 1/8	6 2/8	6 3/8	Natrona Co., Wyo.	William S. Martin	William S. Martin	1964	295
82 6/8	17 5/8	17 4/8	6	6	2 7/8	2 5/8	14 2/8	9 1/8	4 6/8	4 7/8	Ft. Apache Res., Ariz.	Robert L. Martin	Robert L. Martin	1965	295
82 6/8	15 3/8	15 3/8	6 6/8	6 6/8	2 4/8	2 4/8	15 3/8	11 7/8	6 5/8	6 2/8	Sweetwater Co., Wyo.	James C. Klum	James C. Klum	1965	295
82 6/8	14 2/8	14 1/8	7 4/8	7 6/8	2 6/8	2 6/8	12 5/8	10 4/8	5 5/8	5 7/8	Alcova, Wyo.	June & Vaughn Johnson	New Park Hotel	1965	295
82 6/8	15 5/8	15 4/8	7 7/8	7 5/8	2 6/8	3	8 6/8	8 3/8	5	6	Converse Co., Wyo.	Paul W. Tomlin	Paul W. Tomlin	1965	295
82 6/8	16 3/8	16 4/8	6 4/8	6 4/8	2 4/8	2 4/8	10	4 7/8	5 5/8	5 5/8	Farson, Wyo.	Ronald O. West	Ronald O. West	1967	295
82 6/8	17 3/8	17 3/8	6 2/8	6 2/8	2 7/8	2 6/8	14 4/8	10 2/8	4 2/8	4 4/8	Mora Co., N. M.	R. L. Wakefield	R. L. Wakefield	1967	295
82 6/8	17 3/8	17 3/8	6 5/8	6 4/8	3	2 7/8	8 4/8	1 4/8	4	4 2/8	Round Mt., Ariz.	Dennis L. Fife	Dennis L. Fife	1967	295
82 6/8	15 7/8	15 4/8	7	6 7/8	2 6/8	2 5/8	10 5/8	8 1/8	6 1/8	5 5/8	Fremont Co., Wyo.	Terry N. Tenboer	Terry N. Tenboer	1967	295
82 6/8	15 1/8	15 3/8	6 5/8	6 6/8	2 6/8	2 5/8	10 5/8	8 6/8	6 1/8	5 5/8	Rocky Ford, Colo.	Henry A. Helmke	Henry A. Helmke	1967	295
82 6/8	15 3/8	15 4/8	6 2/8	6 5/8	2 5/8	2 4/8	8 6/8	5 2/8	6 3/8	6 3/8	Carbon Co., Wyo.	John M. Sell	John M. Sell	1969	295
82 6/8	16 5/8	16 5/8	6 3/8	6 3/8	2 3/8	2 3/8	15 4/8	13 2/8	5 4/8	5 1/8	Socorro Co., N. M.	Lawrence D. Vigil	Lawrence D. Vigil	1970	295
82 6/8	14 4/8	14	7 5/8	7 5/8	2 6/8	2 5/8	9	7 4/8	5 4/8	5 4/8	Sweetwater Co., Wyo.	Keith F. Dunbar	Keith F. Dunbar	1970	295
82 6/8	15 3/8	15 3/8	6 6/8	6 6/8	3 1/8	3 1/8	8 5/8	5 1/8	6 1/8	6	Custer Co., Mont.	George E. Sanquist	George E. Sanquist	1970	295
82 6/8	16 3/8	16 3/8	6 3/8	6 3/8	2 5/8	2 3/8	8 4/8	2 7/8	6 3/8	5 5/8	Natrona Co., Wyo.	Kenneth Niedan	Kenneth Niedan	1971	295
82 6/8	16 1/8	15 5/8	6 4/8	6 4/8	2 5/8	2 7/8	10 7/8	8 5/8	6 6/8	6 7/8	Medicine Bow, Wyo.	Raymond Freitas	Raymond Freitas	1973	295
82 6/8	16 3/8	16	6 2/8	6 2/8	2 7/8	3 3/8	13	7 7/8	6	5 4/8	Modoc Co., Calif.	Dennis McClelland	Dennis McClelland	1977	295
82 6/8	16 6/8	17 2/8	6 6/8	6 6/8	2 3/8	2 2/8	10 6/8	6	5 1/8	5 2/8	Catron Co., N.M.	David Chavez	David Chavez	1978	295
82 6/8	15 5/8	16 3/8	6 3/8	6 3/8	2 5/8	2 6/8	10 6/8	5 5/8	6 4/8	6 5/8	Weld Co., Colo.	Chester N. Erwin	Ronald G. Erwin	1978	295
82 4/8	15 7/8	15 5/8	7 3/8	7 4/8	3	2 6/8	10 6/8	5 5/8	5 2/8	6 3/8	N. D.	Dale Linderman	Dale Linderman	—	324
82 4/8	17 1/8	17	6 1/8	6	2 3/8	2 3/8	8	3 1/8	6	6	Calif.	Bill Foster	Foster's Bighorn Rest.	1930	324
82 4/8	16 1/8	16 4/8	6 5/8	6 5/8	2 5/8	2 6/8	9 3/8	4 4/8	5 3/8	5 3/8	Saratoga Co., Wyo.	Helen R. Peterson	Helen R. Peterson	1945	324
82 4/8	16 1/8	16 5/8	6 6/8	6 4/8	2 4/8	2 3/8	11 2/8	5 5/8	5 3/8	5 4/8	Catron Co., N. M.	Chas. J. Boyd	Chas. J. Boyd	1952	324
82 4/8	14 2/8	14 2/8	7 6/8	7 6/8	2 5/8	2 5/8	12 3/8	11 2/8	6	5 6/8	Ferris Mt., Wyo.	Donald Anderson	Donald Anderson	1959	324
82 4/8	16 7/8	16 6/8	6 1/8	6 1/8	2 6/8	2 7/8	10	6 7/8	5 4/8	5 4/8	Seligman, Ariz.	Cleo E. Wallace	Cleo E. Wallace	1959	324
82 4/8	16 2/8	16	6 6/8	6 5/8	2 4/8	2 3/8	10 7/8	7 1/8	4 7/8	5 1/8	Shirley Basin, Wyo.	Walter B. Hester	Walter B. Hester	1960	324

82 4/8	16 1/8	15 7/8	6 5/8	6 6/8	3	3	11 1/8	8	5 3/8	5 3/8	Campbell Co., Wyo.	Fred J. Brogle	Fred J. Brogle	1960	324
82 4/8	16 2/8	16 4/8	6 5/8	6 4/8	3	2 6/8	13 1/8	8 7/8	3 5/8	3 5/8	Poison Spider, Wyo.	Clarence Meddock	Clarence Meddock	1961	324
82 4/8	17	17	6 2/8	6 2/8	2 4/8	2 6/8	10 4/8	6 3/8	5 4/8	5	Springerville, Ariz.	Malcolm Silvia	Malcolm Silvia	1962	324
82 4/8	15 2/8	15 2/8	6 7/8	6 7/8	2 4/8	2 5/8	11 1/8	7 2/8	6 1/8	5 7/8	Medicine Hat, Alta.	Nick Mandryk	Nick Mandryk	1963	324
82 4/8	16 3/8	16 6/8	7 5/8	7 5/8	2 5/8	2 3/8	10 2/8	4 1/8	4 6/8	5	Park Co., Colo.	Mrs. Cotton Gordon	Mrs. Cotton Gordon	1964	324
82 4/8	16 6/8	16 6/8	6 1/8	6 2/8	2 4/8	2 4/8	16 1/8	11 4/8	5	5 7/8	Ingomar, Mont.	L. P. Treaster	L. P. Treaster	1965	324
82 4/8	16 5/8	16 6/8	6 2/8	6 2/8	2 6/8	2 7/8	10 5/8	7 3/8	5 4/8	5 4/8	Seligman, Ariz.	Glenn Olson	Glenn Olson	1965	324
82 4/8	15 1/8	16	6 5/8	6 3/8	2 5/8	3	6 3/8	4 5/8	6 1/8	6 4/8	Butte, N. D.	E. J. Weigel	E. J. Weigel	1966	324
82 4/8	15 6/8	15 7/8	6 7/8	7 1/8	2 6/8	2 5/8	11	7 1/8	5 5/8	6	Laramie, Wyo.	Noel Weidner	Noel Weidner	1966	324
82 4/8	13 6/8	13 6/8	9 2/8	9 1/8	3	3	9 4/8	6 4/8	5 1/8	5 1/8	Pecos Co., Texas	Ben H. Moore, Jr.	Ben H. Moore, Jr.	1967	324
82 4/8	16 1/8	16 1/8	6 5/8	6 6/8	2 4/8	2 4/8	12 1/8	6 3/8	5 6/8	5 6/8	Lake Co., Oreg.	Charles R. Waite	Charles R. Waite	1969	324
82 4/8	15 6/8	15 5/8	6 5/8	6 5/8	2 5/8	2 4/8	14	10 7/8	5 3/8	5 4/8	Washoe Co., Nev.	James R. Stoner, Jr.	James R. Stoner, Jr.	1969	324
82 4/8	16	15 7/8	6 7/8	6 7/8	3	3 1/8	10 2/8	5 1/8	5 4/8	5 5/8	Uinta Area, Wyo.	Barry Hyken	Barry Hyken	1969	324
82 4/8	15 6/8	15 3/8	6 6/8	6 5/8	2 6/8	2 4/8	8 7/8	6 4/8	5 4/8	5 4/8	Humboldt Co., Nev.	Robert C. Lawson	Robert C. Lawson	1970	324
82 4/8	15 1/8	15 3/8	6 6/8	6 7/8	3	3 1/8	8 5/8	4	3 6/8	3 6/8	Brewster Co., Texas	Joseph W. Burkett, III	Joseph W. Burkett, III	1971	324
82 4/8	16 1/8	16	6 5/8	6 5/8	2 7/8	2 7/8	9 7/8	6 3/8	5 2/8	5 6/8	Platte Co., Wyo.	Dwight E. Farr	William R. Brewer	1972	324
82 4/8	17 2/8	17 1/8	6 4/8	6 4/8	2 7/8	2 7/8	10 2/8	5	5	4 6/8	Coconino Co., Ariz.	Robert J. Hallock	Robert J. Hallock	1973	324
82 4/8	16 4/8	16 5/8	6 2/8	6	2 4/8	2 5/8	11 7/8	10 6/8	5 5/8	5 4/8	Converse Co., Wyo.	J. A. Merrill, Jr. & C. Davis	J. A. Merrill, Jr.	1973	324
82 4/8	14 4/8	14 6/8	7 1/8	7	3 1/8	3	11	9 3/8	6	5 6/8	Cimarron, N. M.	Ronald E. McKinney	Ronald E. McKinney	1974	324
82 4/8	14 5/8	14 3/8	7	6 7/8	3	3 1/8	9 5/8	5 5/8	5 5/8	5 5/8	Rosebud Co., Mont.	Norman G. Kern	Norman G. Kern	1974	324
82 4/8	16	16 3/8	6 3/8	6 2/8	2 4/8	2 4/8	11 1/8	6 6/8	5 6/8	5 7/8	Custer Co., Mont.	Harry Zirwas	Harry Zirwas	1974	324
82 4/8	16 7/8	17	6 2/8	6 1/8	2 6/8	2 7/8	10 2/8	6 1/8	5 2/8	5 5/8	Slope Co., N. D.	Marlin J. Kapp	Marlin J. Kapp	1975	324
82 4/8	17	17 2/8	6 2/8	6 2/8	2 4/8	2 5/8	11 6/8	7 6/8	5 3/8	5	Coconino Co., Ariz.	David S. Hibbert	David S. Hibbert	1976	324
82 4/8	15 3/8	15 3/8	6 4/8	6 3/8	2 5/8	2 4/8	13 5/8	10 4/8	6 3/8	7	Lassen Co., Calif.	Brad L. Ayotte	Brad L. Ayotte	1977	324
82 4/8	14 7/8	14 7/8	7	7	3	2 7/8	11 7/8	8 7/8	5 2/8	5 4/8	Richland Co., Mont.	Lloyd Holland	Lloyd Holland	1977	324
82 4/8	16	16 1/8	6 6/8	6 6/8	2 5/8	2 5/8	12 3/8	8 1/8	5 2/8	5	Carter Co., Mont.	James A. White	James A. White	1977	324
82 4/8	16	15 5/8	6 4/8	6 6/8	2 2/8	2 6/8	14 1/8	14 2/8	5 7/8	5 7/8	Washakie Co., Wyo.	Greg Warner	Greg Warner	1977	324
82 4/8	16 3/8	16 4/8	6 6/8	7	2 5/8	2 5/8	11 1/8	5 4/8	5 6/8	5 4/8	Fremont Co., Wyo.	Wayne D. Kleinman	Wayne D. Kleinman	1977	324
82 4/8	15	15	6 4/8	6 4/8	2 6/8	2 6/8	9 4/8	4	6 4/8	6 4/8	Sublette Co., Wyo.	Larry W. Cross	Larry W. Cross	1977	324
82 4/8	15 4/8	15 2/8	6 6/8	6 5/8	2 5/8	2 4/8	12 2/8	7 1/8	5 5/8	5 6/8	Modoc Co., Calif.	Mark Hansen	Mark Hansen	1978	324
82 4/8	16 5/8	16 3/8	6 4/8	6 3/8	2 6/8	2 7/8	9 1/8	5 3/8	5 2/8	5 1/8	Sweetwater Co., Wyo.	Fred B. Keyes	Fred B. Keyes	1978	324
82 4/8	16 2/8	16 3/8	7	6 7/8	2 3/8	2 4/8	8 1/8	6 2/8	5 5/8	5 3/8	Siskiyou Co., Calif.	Rodney F. Royer	Rodney F. Royer	1979	324
82 4/8	14 6/8	14 7/8	6 6/8	6 5/8	2 7/8	2 7/8	13 7/8	11 7/8	6 4/8	6 4/8	Carbon Co., Wyo.	Michael Boender	Michael Boender	1979	324
82 3/8	16 4/8	16 7/8	6 1/8	6	2 2/8	2 4/8	14 2/8	10	5 3/8	5 6/8	Green Mt., Wyo.	Forrest H. Burnett	Forrest H. Burnett	1962	364
82 2/8	16 7/8	16 7/8	5 7/8	6	2 4/8	2 4/8	14 5/8	13 4/8	6 2/8	6 3/8	Chaves Co., N. M.	Harvey Pirtle	Glenn Marshall	1939	365
82 2/8	14 5/8	14 4/8	7 1/8	7 1/8	3 1/8	2 7/8	8 2/8	4 4/8	5 4/8	5 5/8	Henderson, N. M.	Ron Vance	Ron Vance	1947	365
82 2/8	16 6/8	16 5/8	6 4/8	6 4/8	2 4/8	2 4/8	15 7/8	11 1/8	5 5/8	5 7/8	Split Rock, Wyo.	Herb Klein	Herb Klein	1952	365
82 2/8	17 4/8	17 3/8	6 4/8	6 3/8	2 5/8	2 6/8	14 1/8	10	4 2/8	4 4/8	Anderson Mesa, Ariz.	Roy Stevens	Roy Stevens	1953	365
82 2/8	16	16 4/8	6 4/8	6 2/8	2 4/8	2 6/8	8 6/8	5 5/8	6 3/8	5 7/8	Rawlins, Wyo.	Thomas B. McNeill	Thomas B. McNeill	1955	365
82 2/8	15 4/8	15 4/8	6 4/8	6 4/8	3 1/8	3 1/8	8 6/8	4 4/8	5	5	Saratoga, Wyo.	J. E. Prothroe	J. E. Prothroe	1955	365
82 2/8	16 5/8	16 6/8	6 4/8	6 3/8	3	3	10 5/8	4 5/8	4 5/8	4 4/8	Hettinger, N. D.	Art Score	Art Score	1957	365
82 2/8	15 2/8	15 7/8	7	7 1/8	2 4/8	2 7/8	13 2/8	8 6/8	6	6 1/8	Sage Creek, Wyo.	Glenn P. Anderson	Glenn P. Anderson	1959	365

PRONGHORN—Continued
Antilocapra americana americana and related subspecies

Score	Length of Horn R.	L.	Circumference of Base R.	L.	Circumference at Third Quarter R.	L.	Inside Spread	Tip to Tip Spread	Length of Prong R.	L.	Locality Killed	By Whom Killed	Owner	Date Killed	Rank
82 2/8	16 2/8	16 2/8	6 1/8	6	2 6/8	2 6/8	13 5/8	10 5/8	5 5/8	5 5/8	Williams, Ariz.	Fred Udine	Fred Udine	1959	365
82 2/8	16 2/8	16 2/8	6 6/8	6 6/8	2 7/8	2 7/8	13 3/8	10 5/8	4 4/8	4 4/8	Sierra Blanca, Texas	Charles Nichols	Charles Nichols	1960	365
82 2/8	16 1/8	16 1/8	6 5/8	6 4/8	2 4/8	2 4/8	6 4/8	4 4/8	5 3/8	5 2/8	Park Co., Wyo.	Don A. Johnson	Don A. Johnson	1960	365
82 2/8	16 1/8	16 1/8	6 3/8	6 3/8	2 4/8	2 3/8	10 4/8	6	6 4/8	6 6/8	Crook Co., Wyo.	John P. Wood	John P. Wood	1960	365
82 2/8	16 1/8	16	6 6/8	6 6/8	3	3 1/8	14	9	5	5	Shirley Basin, Wyo.	T. C. Gonya	T. C. Gonya	1961	365
82 2/8	16 2/8	16 2/8	6 4/8	6 3/8	3	2 7/8	11 1/8	7 1/8	5 5/8	5 5/8	Poison Spider, Wyo.	Unknown	Robert F. Ziker	1961	365
82 2/8	17 2/8	16 6/8	6	6	2 4/8	2 4/8	7 5/8	12 5/8	6 3/8	6 3/8	N. M.	Joan V. Gordon	Joan V. Gordon	1961	365
82 2/8	15 5/8	15 5/8	6 5/8	6 5/8	2 5/8	2 5/8	10 4/8	5	5 5/8	6	Lewis & Clark Co., Mont.	Leo M. Bergthold	Leo M. Bergthold	1963	365
82 2/8	15 7/8	15 5/8	7 1/8	7 2/8	2 6/8	2 6/8	11 4/8	6 4/8	5 3/8	5 3/8	Casper, Wyo.	Frank Gardner	Frank Gardner	1963	365
82 2/8	15 6/8	16	6 4/8	6 4/8	2 5/8	2 5/8	13 3/8	9	6 3/8	6 3/8	Lavina, Mont.	W. J. Morrelle	W. J. Morrelle	1963	365
82 2/8	15 7/8	16	7	7	3	2 6/8	11 7/8	7 7/8	5 5/8	5 1/8	Hanna, Alta.	Rita Shumka	C. W. Edwards	1964	365
82 2/8	16 1/8	16 1/8	6 4/8	6 3/8	2 4/8	2 4/8	12	9 3/8	5	5	Laramie, Wyo.	Susan W. Tupper	Susan W. Tupper	1964	365
82 2/8	16 1/8	16 1/8	6 3/8	6 3/8	2 4/8	2 4/8	13 3/8	9 1/8	5 5/8	5 3/8	Knappen, Alta.	Ken Bosch	Ken Bosch	1965	365
82 2/8	16 3/8	16 3/8	6 3/8	6 4/8	2 5/8	2 4/8	11	11 1/8	5	5	Bowen, N. D.	Lee Atkinson	Sioux Sport Goods	1966	365
82 2/8	16 2/8	16 2/8	6 3/8	6 3/8	2 4/8	2 4/8	10 4/8	4 1/8	5 5/8	5 3/8	Foremost, Alta.	Les Gordon	Les Gordon	1966	365
82 2/8	14 7/8	15	6 5/8	6 5/8	2 4/8	2 4/8	9 1/8	5 5/8	6 5/8	6 3/8	Weld Co., Colo.	Mrs. Paul Goodwin	Mrs. Paul Goodwin	1967	365
82 2/8	15	15 4/8	6 6/8	6 7/8	2 4/8	2 4/8	11 4/8	7 3/8	6 4/8	6 4/8	Vivian, S. D.	Larry K. Lantz	Larry K. Lantz	1969	365
82 2/8	15 7/8	15 7/8	6 4/8	6 5/8	2 5/8	2 4/8	9 6/8	4 5/8	6	6	Powderville, Mont.	Morrell W. Ivie	Morrell W. Ivie	1969	365
82 2/8	16 4/8	16 3/8	6 5/8	6 5/8	2 5/8	2 7/8	10 4/8	8 1/8	5 3/8	6 2/8	Natrona Co., Wyo.	R. O. Marshall, Jr.	R. O. Marshall, Jr.	1970	365
82 2/8	17 3/8	17 2/8	7 2/8	7 2/8	1 7/8	1 5/8	7 1/8	3 1/8	4 7/8	4 7/8	Wild Horse, Alta.	Adam Schmick	Adam Schmick	1970	365
82 2/8	15 6/8	15 7/8	6 5/8	6 5/8	2 6/8	2 6/8	10 7/8	4 4/8	5 7/8	5 5/8	Fergus Co., Mont.	Carl Aus	Carl Aus	1971	365
82 2/8	16 4/8	16 2/8	6 4/8	6 3/8	2 4/8	2 4/8	13	8 3/8	5 4/8	5 4/8	Coconino Co., Ariz.	William Lee Butler	William Lee Butler	1973	365
82 2/8	15	15 3/8	6 6/8	6	2 5/8	2 5/8	10 6/8	9 3/8	5 4/8	5 3/8	Fremont Co., Wyo.	Collins F. Kellogg	Collins F. Kellogg	1974	365
82 2/8	15 5/8	15 5/8	6 3/8	6 4/8	2 7/8	2 6/8	9 6/8	5 7/8	5 5/8	5 5/8	Treasure Co., Mont.	Joseph A. Balmelli	Joseph A. Balmelli	1974	365
82 2/8	15 7/8	15 7/8	6 3/8	6 3/8	2 7/8	2 7/8	7 7/8	3 3/8	5	5	Gillette, Wyo.	Gary Simonson	Gary Simonson	1975	365
82 2/8	15 7/8	15 5/8	7 2/8	7 1/8	2 6/8	2 5/8	8 7/8	5 7/8	6 1/8	6 3/8	Duchesne Co., Utah	David L. Peterson	David L. Peterson	1976	365
82 2/8	15 3/8	14 7/8	6 6/8	6 6/8	2 5/8	2 5/8	13 3/8	9 5/8	6 3/8	6 3/8	Harney Co., Oregon	Dean Dunson	Dean Dunson	1977	365
82 2/8	15 5/8	16	6 1/8	6 2/8	2 4/8	2 4/8	12 2/8	9	6 4/8	7	Lassen Co., Calif.	Del S. Oliver	Del S. Oliver	1978	365
82 2/8	16 3/8	16 3/8	6 4/8	6 4/8	2 3/8	2 3/8	15	11	6 1/8	6 1/8	Otero Co., N. M.	Heber Simmons, Jr.	Heber Simmons, Jr.	1978	365
82 2/8	16 3/8	16 3/8	6 5/8	6 5/8	2 3/8	2 3/8	12 3/8	8	5 5/8	5 5/8	Apache Co., Ariz.	Richard L. Simmons, Sr.	Richard L. Simmons, Sr.	1978	365

82	16	16	6 5/8	6 6/8	2 6/8	2 7/8	12 3/8	8 6/8	5 5/8	5 3/8	Carbon Co., Wyo.	Martin J. Stuart	Martin J. Stuart	——	403
82	17 4/8	17 4/8	6 4/8	6 2/8	3 2/8	3 2/8	14 6/8	11 6/8	3 4/8	4	Pahsimeroi Valley, Idaho	Elmer Keith	Elmer Keith	1936	403
82	15 4/8	15 5/8	6 7/8	6 7/8	2 4/8	2 5/8	12 4/8	6 3/8	5 4/8	5 4/8	Catron Co., N. M.	Floyd Todd	Floyd Todd	1947	403
82	16 2/8	15 6/8	6 4/8	6 4/8	3	3	11	7 2/8	5	5 2/8	Mormon Lake, Ariz.	Bob Housholder	Bob Housholder	1949	403
82	16 2/8	16 2/8	6 2/8	6 4/8	2 4/8	2 6/8	13 1/8	10 4/8	5 6/8	6	Shirley Basin, Wyo.	Earl Fisher	Earl Fisher	1951	403
82	17 7/8	17 4/8	6 5/8	6 5/8	3	3	16	11 7/8	3 5/8	3 4/8	Williams, Ariz.	Paul D. Hosman	Paul D. Hosman	1951	403
82	15 4/8	15 5/8	6 5/8	6 4/8	2 6/8	3 3/8	16 3/8	14 2/8	6 2/8	5 6/8	Navajo Co., Ariz.	Joe D. Sutton	Joe D. Sutton	1951	403
82	16 1/8	15 6/8	6 7/8	6 7/8	2 6/8	2 5/8	11 4/8	5	5 2/8	4 7/8	Anderson Mesa, Ariz.	Mrs. C. C. Cooper	Mrs. C. C. Cooper	1953	403
82	17 4/8	17 5/8	6 1/8	6	2 7/8	2 7/8	12 3/8	5 6/8	4 5/8	4 6/8	Santa Rosa, N. M.	F. C. Hibben	F. C. Hibben	1955	403
82	15	14 6/8	6 7/8	6 7/8	2 7/8	2 7/8	10 3/8	7 6/8	5 6/8	5 5/8	Bow Island, Alta.	R. F. Dunmire	R. F. Dunmire	1957	403
82	15 2/8	15 2/8	7	7	3	3	14 6/8	12 3/8	5 6/8	5 3/8	Limon, Colo.	Walt Paulk	Walt Paulk	1958	403
82	16 7/8	16 5/8	6	6	2 5/8	2 6/8	11 1/8	5	6	5 4/8	Arpan, S. D.	Dell Shanks	Dell Shanks	1960	403
82	14 7/8	14 6/8	6 6/8	6 7/8	2 5/8	2 5/8	9 4/8	8 1/8	6 3/8	5 7/8	Sage Creek, Wyo.	Mrs. Ramon Somavia	Mrs. Ramon Somavia	1960	403
82	16	16 4/8	6 5/8	6 2/8	2 4/8	2 5/8	12 2/8	8 2/8	6	5 7/8	Encampment, Wyo.	G. A. Surface	G. A. Surface	1960	403
82	15 4/8	15 4/8	6 1/8	6 1/8	2 3/8	2 4/8	11 1/8	6 4/8	6 4/8	6 6/8	Shirley Basin, Wyo.	Norman Miller	Norman Miller	1961	403
82	15 5/8	15 6/8	6 7/8	6 7/8	2 7/8	2 7/8	10 3/8	6 1/8	5 2/8	5	Natrona Co., Wyo.	Fred Deiss	Fred Deiss	1961	403
82	16 1/8	16	6 4/8	6 3/8	2 6/8	2 6/8	9 5/8	7 6/8	5 2/8	5	Shirley Basin, Wyo.	Henry Macagni	Henry Macagni	1962	403
82	15 4/8	15 4/8	7 2/8	7 1/8	2 6/8	2 6/8	14 2/8	12 7/8	5 2/8	5 1/8	Shirley Basin, Wyo.	Norma H. Yeatman	Norma H. Yeatman	1962	403
82	16	16 1/8	6 6/8	6 6/8	2 4/8	2 4/8	16 5/8	14 2/8	5 6/8	5 6/8	Shirley Basin, Wyo.	G. C. Cunningham	G. C. Cunningham	1962	403
82	15 4/8	15 4/8	6 5/8	6 5/8	2 6/8	2 6/8	12 4/8	7 7/8	5 2/8	6	Yavapai Co., Ariz.	Noel Scott	Noel Scott	1963	403
82	14 6/8	14 6/8	6 5/8	6 6/8	2 6/8	2 6/8	11	6 3/8	6 5/8	6 2/8	Hartley Co., Texas	Walter O. Ford, Jr.	Walter O. Ford, Jr.	1964	403
82	17	17	6 2/8	6 1/8	2 7/8	2 6/8	12 1/8	6 4/8	4 3/8	3 2/8	McKinley Co., N. M.	W. R. Phillips	W. R. Phillips	1965	403
82	16 1/8	16	6 6/8	6 6/8	2 6/8	2 7/8	12 7/8	11 4/8	5 2/8	5 3/8	Navajo Co., Ariz.	John Welch, III	John Welch, III	1965	403
82	15 3/8	15 3/8	5 6/8	5 6/8	2 4/8	2 4/8	11	9	6	5 7/8	Arco, Idaho	Ernest L. Ellis, Jr.	Ernest L. Ellis, Jr.	1965	403
82	15 2/8	15	6	6	2 5/8	2 4/8	8 4/8	7	6 7/8	7	Eston, Sask.	Dennis Crowe	Dennis Crowe	1966	403
82	16 5/8	16 3/8	6 1/8	6 1/8	2 5/8	2 4/8	9 3/8	8 4/8	5 7/8	5 6/8	Lake Co., Oreg.	Eldon Hayes	Eldon Hayes	1966	403
82	15 2/8	15	6 5/8	6 5/8	3	3	10 1/8	8 2/8	5 7/8	5 5/8	Carbon Co., Wyo.	C. W. Hermanson	C. W. Hermanson	1968	403
82	14 6/8	14 6/8	6 4/8	6 3/8	3	3	8 7/8	3 6/8	7	6	Garfield Co., Mont.	Dean V. Ashton	Dean V. Ashton	1968	403
82	15 5/8	15 2/8	7 1/8	7 1/8	2 6/8	2 6/8	8	7	5	5 4/8	Farson, Wyo.	Larry Nolan Garner	Larry Nolan Garner	1969	403
82	15 3/8	15 3/8	7 2/8	6 7/8	2 6/8	2 5/8	15	13	5 5/8	5 2/8	Wamsutter, Wyo.	Frank Simons	Frank Simons	1969	403
82	15 3/8	15 3/8	6 2/8	6 2/8	2 4/8	2 4/8	14 3/8	13 1/8	6	6	Albany Co., Wyo.	Edwin J. Keppner	Edwin J. Keppner	1969	403
82	15 3/8	15	7	7	2 4/8	2 3/8	10 1/8	5	6 2/8	5 3/8	Washoe Co., Nev.	Oliver V. Iveson	Oliver V. Iveson	1970	403
82	15 2/8	15 2/8	5 7/8	6	3 2/8	3 4/8	11 2/8	7 1/8	4 1/8	4 3/8	Brewster Co., Texas	Joseph W. Burkett, III	Joseph W. Burkett, III	1972	403
82	14 3/8	14	7 4/8	7 3/8	2 3/8	2 2/8	13	9 4/8	6 6/8	7	Garfield Co., Mont.	Don E. Traughber	Don E. Traughber	1973	403
82	14 5/8	14 3/8	7 3/8	7 3/8	3 4/8	3 4/8	9 3/8	7 3/8	5 2/8	5 2/8	Sweet Rock, Wyo.	Alphonse Cuomo, Jr.	Alphonse Cuomo, Jr.	1973	403
82	17	17 2/8	6 2/8	6 1/8	2 3/8	2 5/8	11 2/8	5 4/8	5 6/8	5 7/8	Coconino Co., Ariz.	Jerry Ray Killman	Jerry Ray Killman	1973	403
82	15 5/8	15 4/8	7	6 5/8	2 4/8	2 4/8	10 1/8	8	6 4/8	6	Sublette Co., Wyo.	Gary D. Jorgensen	Gary D. Jorgensen	1973	403
82	16 2/8	16 1/8	6 4/8	6 4/8	2 5/8	2 5/8	12	7 3/8	5 6/8	5 6/8	Carbon Co., Wyo.	Reg. R. Smith	Reg. R. Smith	1974	403
82	16 1/8	16 4/8	6 7/8	6 5/8	3 2/8	3 2/8	11	7 2/8	2 6/8	3 4/8	Wolf Point, Mont.	Raymond A. Gould	Raymond A. Gould	1974	403
82	15	15	7 3/8	7 1/8	2 5/8	2 5/8	12 4/8	10 3/8	5 6/8	5	Carbon Co., Wyo.	Peck Rollison	Peck Rollison	1975	403
82	15 2/8	15 3/8	6 6/8	6 4/8	3 2/8	3 2/8	9	2 7/8	5 6/8	5 6/8	Wallace Co., Kansas	Curtis R. Penner	Curtis R. Penner	1976	403
82	14 1/8	13 6/8	7	6 6/8	3	3	11 4/8	9 6/8	4 4/8	4 4/8	Sweetwater Co., Wyo.	Starla L. Cairns	Starla L. Cairns	1976	403

Pronghorn–*Continued*

Antilocapra americana americana and related subspecies

Score	Length of Horn R.	Length of Horn L.	Circumference of Base R.	Circumference of Base L.	Circumference at Third Quarter R.	Circumference at Third Quarter L.	Inside Spread	Tip to Tip Spread	Length of Prong R.	Length of Prong L.	Locality Killed	By Whom Killed	Owner	Date Killed	Rank
82	14 5/8	14 6/8	6 4/8	6 4/8	3	3	10 3/8	5 6/8	5 7/8	5 7/8	Campbell Co., Wyo.	Gilbert Steinen, Jr.	Gilbert Steinen, Jr.	1977	403
82	16	16	6	6	3	3 2/8	9	6 2/8	5 4/8	5 4/8	Hartley Co., Texas	John A. Wright	John A. Wright	1977	403
82	16 4/8	16 4/8	6 6/8	6 6/8	2 3/8	2 2/8	11 4/8	8 2/8	5 4/8	5 4/8	Fremont Co., Wyo.	Daniel R. Hahn	Daniel R. Hahn	1977	403
82	17 7/8	17 6/8	5 5/8	5 4/8	2 4/8	2 2/8	12 7/8	6 7/8	5 4/8	5 3/8	Otero Co., N. M.	Robert E. Anton	Robert E. Anton	1978	403
82	16 4/8	16 4/8	6 2/8	6 2/8	2 6/8	2 5/8	8 7/8	4	5 1/8	5 2/8	Hudspeth Co., Texas	Luther V. Oliver	Luther V. Oliver	1978	403
82	16 4/8	16 3/8	7 5/8	7	2 5/8	2 7/8	12 6/8	10 3/8	5 4/8	5	Fremont Co., Wyo.	John J. Eichhorn	John J. Eichhorn	1978	403
82	14 5/8	15 1/8	6 7/8	6 7/8	2 4/8	2 4/8	10 7/8	6 7/8	6 3/8	6 5/8	Sweetwater Co., Wyo.	Dan B. Artery	Dan B. Artery	1979	403

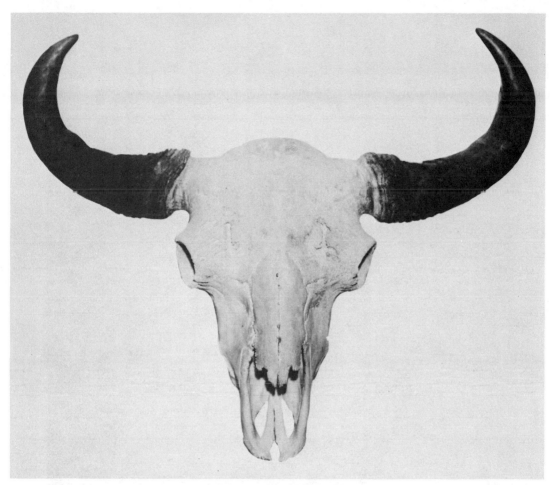

WORLD'S RECORD BISON
SCORE: 136 4/8
Locality: Yellowstone National Park, Wyoming. Date: 1925.
Hunter: S. Woodring. Owner: Fishing Bridge Museum, Yellowstone National Park.

NUMBER TWO BISON
SCORE: 136 2/8
Locality: Northwest Territories. Date: 1961.
Hunter and owner: Samuel Israel.

Bison

Bison bison bison and Bison bison athabascae

Minimum Score 115

Beginning in 1977, hunter taken trophies from the lower 48 states are acceptable only for records, not awards, and only from states that recognize bison as wild and free-ranging and for which a hunting license and/or big game tag is required for hunting.

Score	Length of Horn R.	L.	Circumference of Base R.	L.	Circumference at Third Quarter R.	L.	Greatest Spread	Tip to Tip Spread	Sex	Locality Killed	By Whom Killed	Owner	Date Killed	Rank
136 4/8	21 7/8	23 3/8	16	15	8 7/8	8	35 5/8	27	M	Yellowstone Natl. Park, Wyo.	S. Woodring	Fishing Bridge Museum	1925	1
136 2/8	19	18 6/8	18 4/8	14 7/8	6 5/8	6 7/8	30 1/8	22 3/8	M	N. W. T.	Samuel Israel	Samuel Israel	1961	2
134 2/8	21 2/8	20 6/8	14 6/8	17	8 6/8	7 6/8	33 7/8	26 6/8	M	Park Co., Wyo.	Picked Up	H. A. Moore	1977	3
133 4/8	19 2/8	18 6/8	17	17	7	7	29 2/8	21 3/8	M	Great Slave Lake, Alta.	Mike Dempsey	Natl. Mus. Of Canada	1935	4
132 4/8	21 2/8	22 2/8	16 4/8	16 7/8	7 5/8	6	35 2/8	26 6/8	M	Unknown	James H. Lockhart	Carnegie Museum	PR1939	5
132 2/8	22 7/8	21 7/8	14 1/8	14 4/8	6 6/8	6 5/8	32 6/8	24 3/8	M	Sweet Grass, Alta.	Ken Cooper	Univ. Of Sask.	1961	6
131 6/8	20 5/8	20 5/8	15	15	7	7	30	20 7/8	M	Hell Roaring Creek, Mont.	Picked Up	Univ. Of Mont.	1945	7
129 6/8*	20 4/8	20 4/8	16	16	7	6 7/8	30 2/8	21 2/8	M	Fort Smith, N. W. T.	Lloyd L. Ward, Jr.	Lloyd L. Ward, Jr.	1971	8
129	21 1/8	20 4/8	14 4/8	14 4/8	7 5/8	7 5/8	29 4/8	18 6/8	M	Big Horn Mts., Wyo.	Picked Up	George S. Burnap, Jr	1953	9
128 6/8*	21 1/8	20 7/8	16 1/8	15 7/8	5 5/8	5 5/8	32 2/8	24	M	Fort Smith, N. W. T.	Billy Day	Billy Day	1960	10
128 6/8*	19 1/8	18 7/8	17 1/8	16 7/8	6 4/8	6 4/8	33 4/8	18 7/8	M	N. W. T.	Bert Klineburger	Bert Klineburger	1960	10
128 4/8	18 4/8	18 5/8	14 4/8	14 4/8	8 7/8	8 4/8	28 6/8	20 6/8	M	Yellowstone Natl. Park, Wyo.	Unknown	U. S. Natl. Museum	1913	12
127 6/8	19 5/8	20 4/8	15 6/8	15 5/8	5 5/8	5 5/8	31 2/8	22 6/8	M	N. W. T.	Leslie Bowling	Leslie Bowling	1961	13
127 6/8	19 5/8	19 6/8	15 5/8	15 3/8	6 3/8	6 4/8	32 2/8	25 3/8	M	N. W. T.	Wilbur Hilgar	Wilbur Hilgar	1961	13
127	21 7/8	22 3/8	13 6/8	13 6/8	6 6/8	7 7/8	29	18 6/8	M	Canada	Unknown	Raymond Brown	1899	15
126 6/8	19 6/8	19 4/8	15 3/8	15 1/8	7 3/8	7 3/8	27 6/8	18 5/8	M	Gillette, Wyo.	D. C. Basolo, Jr.	D. C. Basolo, Jr.	1963	16
126 2/8	17 5/8	18 3/8	15 5/8	15 5/8	7 5/8	7	30 2/8	24 3/8	M	Yellowstone River, Mont.	Picked Up	Edward J. Melby	1935	17
126 2/8	18 1/8	18 1/8	16	16	6 2/8	6 4/8	29 2/8	21 6/8	M	Fort Smith, N. W. T.	V. N. Holderman	V. N. Holderman	1961	17
126	20 5/8	20 4/8	15	15 4/8	5 7/8	5 4/8	27 2/8	13 3/8	M	Slave River, N. W. T.	Edward A. Feser	Edward A. Feser	1975	19
126	18 3/8	21	15	15 2/8	6	7 7/8	31 2/8	24 6/8	M	Wrangell Mts., Alaska	Walter H. Hammer	Walter H. Hammer	1977	19
125 6/8	19 4/8	19 4/8	15	15 4/8	6	6	30 2/8	24	M	Yellowstone Natl. Park, Wyo.	Lee L. Coleman	Jackson Hole Museum	1958	21
125 4/8	17 7/8	17 4/8	14	14	8	8	26 7/8	21 6/8	M	Park Co., Wyo.	Unknown	James Patterson	PR1970	22
125 2/8	19 5/8	20	17 4/8	14 3/8	6 7/8	7 1/8	28 4/8	19 5/8	M	Mont.	Unknown	O. P. Chisholm	PR1891	23
125	18 6/8	18 7/8	15	14 5/8	6 6/8	6 7/8	28 3/8	18 5/8	M	Fort Smith, N. W. T.	Leonard J. Ostrom	Leonard J. Ostrom	1959	24
124 6/8	20 5/8	20 3/8	15 1/8	15 1/8	6 1/8	5 5/8	30 1/8	21 6/8	M	Wyo.	Lord Rerdlesham	National Collection	1892	25

315

BISON–Continued
Bison bison bison and *Bison bison athabascae*

Score	Length of Horn R.	L.	Circumference of Base R.	L.	Circumference at Third Quarter R.	L.	Greatest Spread	Tip to Tip Spread	Sex	Locality Killed	By Whom Killed	Owner	Date Killed	Rank
124 4/8	20 4/8	20 1/8	15 4/8	15 1/8	6 1/8	6 4/8	31 1/8	24	M	Copper River, Alaska	Earl E. Knutson	Earl E. Knutson	1965	26
124 4/8	19 6/8	20	15 3/8	15 1/8	5 7/8	5 5/8	29 3/8	20 4/8	M	Delta Junction, Alaska	Mike Stagno	Mike Stagno	1975	26
124 3/8	17 6/8	17 5/8	16 3/8	16 7/8	6 3/8	5 5/8	32 4/8	28 4/8	M	Fort Smith, N. W. T.	Margaret Buckner	Margaret Buckner	1960	28
124 3/8	17 1/8	17 7/8	14 6/8	14 7/8	7 4/8	7 7/8	31 3/8	27 3/8	M	Custer State Park, S. D.	Stuart Godin	Stuart Godin	1975	28
124 3/8	19 1/8	19 2/8	15 5/8	15 5/8	6 4/8	5 5/8	31	25 2/8	M	Chitina River, Alaska	Robert E. Day	Robert E. Day	1976	28
124	21 2/8	20 3/8	14	13 3/8	6 5/8	5 7/8	29 5/8	20 4/8	U	Jardine, Mont.	Unknown	Kerry Constan	1962	31
124	16 5/8	16 3/8	15 3/8	15 4/8	7 7/8	7 7/8	25 5/8	18 5/8	M	Slave River, N. W. T.	Rudolf Sand	Rudolf Sand	1972	31
124	19 5/8	19 2/8	14	14 2/8	6 1/8	5 7/8	30 6/8	22 5/8	M	Hook Lake, N.W.T.	Manfred Kurtz	Manfred Kurtz	1973	31
123 5/8	20 2/8	20 4/8	16	16	5 1/8	5 4/8	31	20 7/8	M	N. W. T.	J. S. Sanders	J. S. Sanders	1961	34
123 5/8	17 1/8	18	15	15	7 5/8	7 4/8	25	15 5/8	M	Gillette, Wyo.	D. C. Basolo, Jr.	D. C. Basolo, Jr.	1963	34
123 4/8	19 5/8	19 5/8	14 2/8	14 4/8	5 7/8	6 3/8	28 4/8	21 4/8	M	Yellowstone Natl. Park, Wyo.	Harry Trishman	Roger J. Contor	1924	36
123 4/8	18	18	16	15 6/8	6 2/8	6 4/8	29 4/8	21 4/8	U	Yellowstone Natl. Park, Wyo.	Picked Up	C. Watters & D. Moore	1956	36
123 4/8	20	20 4/8	15 3/8	15 4/8	5 2/8	6	32 5/8	22 5/8	M	Delta Junction, Alaska	Donald A. Prescott	Donald A. Prescott	1963	36
123 4/8	20 2/8	20 2/8	15 5/8	15 4/8	5 5/8	5 4/8	29 2/8	19	M	Gillette, Wyo.	H. I. H. Prince Abdorreza Pahlavi	H. I. H. Prince Abdorreza Pahlavi	1967	36
123 2/8	18 6/8	19 1/8	15	14 6/8	7 5/8	7 3/8	26	21 1/8	M	Fort Smith, N. W. T.	Earl H. Harris	Earl H. Harris	1969	36
122 6/8	20 1/8	19 3/8	15 3/8	15 2/8	5 5/8	5 1/8	31 4/8	24 7/8	M	Big Delta, Alaska	Unknown	Chuck Sutter	1950	41
122 4/8	20 4/8	20 4/8	14 4/8	14 4/8	5	5	26 4/8	16 4/8	M	Henry Mountains, Utah	Greg Harper	Greg Harper	1978	42
122 2/8	20 5/8	20 4/8	13 7/8	13 4/8	6 4/8	6 4/8	32 7/8	26 4/8	M	Absarokee Wild., Mont.	H. E. Lillis	H. E. Lillis	1953	43
122 2/8	18	18 4/8	14 2/8	14 1/8	7 2/8	7 3/8	29 4/8	23 7/8	M	Ft. Greely, Alaska	Picked Up	McClaren Johnson, Jr.	PR1961	43
122 2/8	19 2/8	19 1/8	15	15 1/8	6 2/8	6 3/8	28 4/8	19 1/8	M	N. W. T.	A. Sanford	A. Sanford	1961	43
122 2/8	18 2/8	18 2/8	14 4/8	14 3/8	7 4/8	7 4/8	28 5/8	20 5/8	M	Gillette, Wyo.	Tom R. Bowles	Tom R. Bowles	1963	43
122	18 5/8	18 3/8	16 1/8	16	5 3/8	5 4/8	29 1/8	22 5/8	M	Hook Lake, N.W.T.	Picked Up	Robert C. Jones	1974	47
121 6/8	19 4/8	20 3/8	14 6/8	14 4/8	5 5/8	5 7/8	29 3/8	21 3/8	M	Wayne Co., Utah	Ardell K. Woolsey	Ardell K. Woolsey	1974	48
121 4/8	21 1/8	22 1/8	13 5/8	14	5 3/8	5 5/8	29 7/8	18 7/8	M	Custer, Mont.	Picked Up	Martin Sorensen, Jr.	1962	49
121 2/8	18	18 6/8	14	14 3/8	6 3/8	7	28 3/8	17 7/8	M	Fort Smith, N. W. T.	W. C. Whitt	W. C. Whitt	1972	50
121 2/8	16	14 7/8	16 3/8	16 3/8	8 7/8	8	29 4/8	25 7/8	M	Ogalala Sioux G. R., S. D.	Robert B. Peregrine	Robert B. Peregrine	1972	50
121	16 7/8	17 7/8	14 3/8	14 2/8	7 1/8	7 1/8	29 2/8	21 5/8	M	Slave River, N. W. T.	Franz M. Wilhelmsen	Franz M. Wilhelmsen	1959	52
121	17 7/8	18 2/8	14 7/8	15 2/8	6 6/8	7 7/8	28	21 7/8	M	House Rock, Ariz.	Larry R. French	Larry R. French	1965	52

Rank	Owner	Date	By whom killed	Locality	Sex									Score
52	Larry Edgar	1972	Picked Up	Shoshone Natl. For., Wyo.	M	20	28⅜	6⅛	6⅛	14⅛	14⅛	18⅜	20⅛	121
52	Dave Ramey	1978	Dave Ramey	Big Horn Co., Mont.	M	18⅞	27⅞	6⅝	6⅝	14⅛	14⅜	18	18⅞	121
52	James Patterson	—	Picked Up	Custer Co., S.D.	M	19⅛	30⅜	5⅞	5⅜	14⅞	14⅞	18⅜	19⅛	121
57	George R Horner	1950	George R Horner	Park Co., Wyo.	M	16⅝	28⅞	7⅛	7⅛	14⅞	13⅞	16⅜	16⅝	120⅞
57	George W. Parker	1961	George W. Parker	Delta Junction, Alaska	M	17	31⅞	5⅜	5⅜	15⅝	15⅜	17⅞	17	120⅞
57	Bernard Domries	1968	Bernard Domries	Hook Lake, N. W. T.	M	18⅜	29⅞	5⅞	5⅜	15⅜	15⅜	18⅜	18⅜	120⅞
57	Louis Vaughn	1968	Louis Vaughn	Afton, Wyo.	M	17⅝	29	5⅜	5⅜	15⅞	15⅝	17⅝	17⅝	120⅞
57	C. J. McElroy	1970	C. J. McElroy	Custer Co., S. D.	M	17	29⅛	7	7⅜	14⅛	14⅜	17	17	120⅞
57	Greg V. Parker	1975	Greg V. Parker	Gillette, Wyo.	M	20⅞	31⅛	5⅜	5⅛	16⅛	15⅜	20⅞	20⅞	120⅞
57	Charles H. Stoll	1961	Charles H. Stoll	Coconino Co., Ariz.	M	17⅛	29⅛	6⅜	6⅜	15⅜	15⅛	17⅛	17⅛	120⅞
64	Philip L. Nare	1974	Philip L. Nare	N. W. T.	M	20⅛	29⅜	5⅜	5⅜	14⅜	14	18	20⅛	120⅞
64	Mrs. Malcom McKenzie	1960	Unknown	Custer State Park, S. D.	M	17	28⅞	7⅛	7	14⅝	14⅝	20⅜	17	120⅞
66	James M. Hill	1978	James M. Hill	Slave River, N. W. T.	M	17⅞	27⅞	6⅝	6⅜	14⅛	14⅛	17	17⅞	120⅞
66	National Park Service	1939	Frank Oberhansley	Delta Junction, Alaska	M	19⅞	31⅛	5	5	15⅜	15⅜	20	19⅞	120⅞
68	Robert C. Reeve	1950	Unknown	Lamar River, Wyo.	U	21	27⅞	4⅝	4⅝	16	16	20⅜	21	120
68	Patrick Britell	1961	Patrick Britell	Big Delta, Alaska	M	15⅛	28⅛	7⅛	7⅛	14⅞	14⅞	15⅛	15⅛	120
70	Pitt Sanders	1961	Pitt Sanders	N. W. T.	M	17⅝	25⅞	6⅜	6⅜	14⅞	15⅜	17⅝	17⅝	119⅞
70	Ann Denardo	1961	Ann Denardo	N. W. T.	M	18	28⅛	6⅜	6⅜	15⅜	15⅛	18	18	119⅞
70	Sheldon H. Weinstein	1975	Sheldon H. Weinstein	Big Delta, Alaska	M	19⅞	30⅜	5	5	14⅞	14⅝	20	19⅞	119⅞
70	Walt Paulk	1962	Walt Paulk	Ft. Smith, N. W. T.	M	17⅛	28⅛	5⅜	5⅜	14⅝	14⅜	17⅛	17⅛	119⅞
74	Jim Ford	1972	Picked Up	Gillette, Wyo.	M	17⅛	29	5⅝	5⅝	15⅝	15⅜	17⅛	17⅛	119⅜
74	Glenn Ellingson	1961	Glenn Ellingson	Yellowstone Natl. Park, Wyo.	M	17	25⅝	6	6⅝	13⅞	13⅜	17	17	119⅜
76	Harold G. Arnold	1975	Unknown	Gillette, Wyo.	M	19⅞	32	5⅜	5⅜	14⅞	14⅝	19⅞	19⅞	119½
76	John H. Epp	1960	John H. Epp	Ravalli, Mont.	M	20	27⅜	5⅜	5⅜	15⅜	15⅜	20	20	119½
78	John G. Zelenka	1971	John G. Zelenka	Fort Smith, N. W. T.	M	18⅛	25⅜	6⅞	6⅞	13⅝	13⅜	18⅛	18⅛	119
78	D. N. Rowe	1960	D. N. Rowe	Hook Lake, N. W. T.	M	17⅞	25⅜	6	6	15⅜	15⅜	17⅞	17⅞	119
80	W. J. Nixon	1960	W. J. Nixon	Ft. Smith, N. W. T.	M	18⅛	27⅜	5⅜	5⅜	15⅝	15⅝	18⅛	18⅛	118⅞
80	Charles Sides	1960	Charles Sides	Fort Smith, N. W. T.	M	15⅝	29	6	6	15⅜	16	15⅝	15⅝	118⅞
80	Herb Klein	1960	Herb Klein	N. W. T.	M	17⅞	28⅞	7⅛	7⅛	14⅛	14⅛	17⅞	17⅞	118⅞
80	Richard P. Platz	1961	Richard P. Platz	Big Delta, Alaska	M	18	28⅞	7	7⅛	14⅜	14⅜	18	18	118⅞
80	Jack A. Shane, Sr.	1968	Jack A. Shane, Sr.	Arlee, Mont.	M	16⅞	29⅞	4⅝	4⅛	14⅞	14⅞	16⅞	16⅞	118⅞
80	Basil C. Bradbury	1968	Basil C. Bradbury	Big Horn Co., Mont.	M	19⅛	31½	7⅛	7⅛	14⅜	14⅜	20⅜	19⅛	118⅞
80	G. A. Treschow	1972	G. A. Treschow	Hook Lake, N. W. T.	M	15⅜	23¾	6⅜	6⅜	15⅜	15⅜	15⅜	15⅜	118⅞
80	David G. Hansen	1975	David G. Hansen	Garfield Co., Utah	M	15⅜	31½	5	5	15⅛	16	20⅜	15⅜	118⅞
89	Jim Harrower	1964	Jim Harrower	Copper River, Alaska	M	17⅝	29	5⅞	5⅞	16	16	17⅝	17⅝	118⅜
89	Mary L. Pipp	1972	Mary L. Pipp	Pine Ridge Indian Res., S. D.	M	20⅜	28¾	6	6	14⅛	14⅜	18⅛	20⅜	118⅜
91	Snow Museum	—	Sidney Snow	Wyo.	M	18⅛	31	4⅝	5⅜	15⅜	14⅛	18⅜	18⅛	118⅜
91	Earl Murnaw	1962	Earl Murnaw	Pierre, S. D.	M	20⅜	28¾	5⅜	5⅜	14⅛	14⅜	20⅜	20⅜	118⅜

BISON—Continued

Bison bison bison and Bison bison athabascae

Score	Length of Horn R.	L.	Circumference of Base R.	L.	Circumference at Third Quarter R.	L.	Greatest Spread	Tip to Tip Spread	Sex	Locality Killed	By Whom Killed	Owner	Date Killed	Rank
118 2/8	19 1/8	19 6/8	14 7/8	14 7/8	5 7/8	5 4/8	29	18 5/8	M	Houserock Valley, Ariz.	Fred Shook	Fred Shook	1967	91
118	17 7/8	18 6/8	15	15 5/8	6 4/8	6 4/8	29 4/8	21	M	Yellowstone Natl. Park, Wyo.	Unknown	Alfred C. Berol	1927	94
118	17 2/8	17 3/8	14 2/8	14 2/8	6 7/8	7	30	26 4/8	M	Crow Indian Res., Mont.	Pete Laird	Curt Laird	1956	94
118	17 4/8	16 7/8	14 1/8	16	6	6	25 5/8	19	M	Henry Mts., Utah	John Goldenstein	John Goldenstein	1962	94
118	16	16	16	16	5 7/8	5 7/8	27 4/8	20 4/8	M	Gillette, Wyo.	D. C. Basolo, Jr.	D. C. Basolo, Jr.	1962	94
117 4/8	18 3/8	17 6/8	14 2/8	14 1/8	5 5/8	6 4/8	30 6/8	25 4/8	M	Farewell, Alaska	Thomas R. Keele	Thomas R. Keele	1975	98
117 4/8	17 4/8	17 4/8	13 5/8	13 5/8	5 5/8	5 5/8	26	20 4/8	M	Garfield Co., Utah	Sheldon D. Worthen	Sheldon D. Worthen	1977	98
117 4/8	16 5/8	16 5/8	15 5/8	15 5/8	6	6 7/8	29	23	M	Custer State Park, S. D.	Thomas J. Radoumis	Thomas J. Radoumis	1973	100
117 4/8	17 7/8	17 3/8	14	14 3/8	6 5/8	6 5/8	30	25	M	Henry Mts., Utah	Don Genessy	Don Genessy	1960	101
117 4/8	18 7/8	18 7/8	14 4/8	14 4/8	4 7/8	4 5/8	27	16	M	Gillette, Wyo.	D. C. Basolo, Jr.	D. C. Basolo, Jr.	1963	101
117 4/8	19	19 4/8	14 2/8	14 4/8	5	5	31	27	M	Campbell Co., Wyo.	Leroy Van Buggenum	Leroy Van Buggenum	1968	101
117	18 3/8	18	14 4/8	14 1/8	6 3/8	5 4/8	30 6/8	25	M	Fort Smith, N. W. T.	Fred Burke	Fred Burke	1960	104
117	17 6/8	17 6/8	15 1/8	15 2/8	5 4/8	5	28 4/8	22 7/8	M	Gillette, Wyo.	D. C. Basolo, Jr.	D. C. Basolo, Jr	1963	104
117	18 5/8	18 5/8	15	15 3/8	4 4/8	5 4/8	29 5/8	26	M	Dadina River, Alaska	Joe Van Conia	Joe Van Conia	1965	104
117	19	19 3/8	14 6/8	14 3/8	4 4/8	5	29 4/8	29 4/8	M	Delta Junction, Alaska	William T. Warren	William T. Warren	1978	104
116 4/8	16 5/8	15 5/8	14 7/8	14 6/8	6 5/8	6 3/8	32 7/8	28 4/8	M	Raymond Ranch, Ariz.	Unknown	Jack Brooks	1954	108
116 4/8	16 5/8	15 7/8	13 6/8	13 7/8	7	7 7/8	28	24	M	Custer State Park, S. D.	Merle G. Smith	Merle G. Smith	1974	108
116 4/8	21	20 5/8	12 3/8	13 1/8	5 5/8	5 7/8	29 4/8	17 5/8	M	Donnelly Dome, Alaska	Frank Glaser & Ray Tremblay	Univ. Of Alaska	1954	110
116 4/8	16 7/8	16 3/8	15	14 6/8	7	5 7/8	28	22	M	Gillette, Wyo.	D. C. Basolo, Jr	D. C. Basolo, Jr.	1963	110
116 4/8	18	18 2/8	15	14 6/8	4 4/8	4 4/8	30 4/8	26 4/8	M	Alta.	Casper Whitney	National Collection	1907	112
116 4/8	20 4/8	20 5/8	13 4/8	14 1/8	4 4/8	4 4/8	30 4/8	23 4/8	M	Osage Co., Okla.	Harold A. Yocum	Harold A. Yocum	1943	112
116 4/8	17 1/8	17 3/8	17	16 4/8	4 7/8	5	25 4/8	18 1/8	M	Slave River, N. W. T.	Jim Wellman	Jim Wellman	1960	112
116 4/8	18 4/8	20	14 3/8	14 3/8	5	5 3/8	23 2/8	23 3/8	M	Delta Junction, Alaska	Alma Eades	Alma Eades	1963	112
116 4/8	17 4/8	17 3/8	14 4/8	14 4/8	5 3/8	6 4/8	33	28 4/8	M	Hook Lake, N. W. T.	Jerry Bick	Jerry Bick	1970	112
116 4/8	16 5/8	16 4/8	14 4/8	14 3/8	6 4/8	6 7/8	25 3/8	17	M	Hook Lake, N. W. T.	Jens K. Touborg	Jens K. Touborg	1972	112
116	19 4/8	18 4/8	14 4/8	14 3/8	5 5/8	4 4/8	28 7/8	20 4/8	M	Custer Co., S.D.	James B. Wade	James B. Wade	1976	112
116	15	15 1/8	14 7/8	15 4/8	6 4/8	6 4/8	27 4/8	22 4/8	M	Gillette, Wyo.	D. C. Basolo, Jr.	D. C. Basolo, Jr.	1962	119
116	17 4/8	18	14 7/8	15 1/8	5 4/8	5 5/8	30 4/8	24 4/8	M	Copper River, Alaska	Tony Oney	Tony Oney	1964	119
116	17 5/8	18 1/8	14 6/8	14 6/8	5 4/8	5 3/8	30 1/8	23 7/8	M	Coconino Co., Ariz.	John Renkema, Jr.	John Renkema, Jr.	1977	119
115 5/8	18 5/8	18 2/8	14	14	5 5/8	6	33	25	M	Big Delta, Alaska	Barbara A. Nagengast	Barbara A. Nagengast	1963	122

115 4/8	17 4/8	18	14 3/8	14 6/8	4 7/8	5 1/8	28 3/8	20 4/8	M	Sanders Co., Mont.	Glenn W. Slade, Jr.	Glenn W. Slade, Jr.	1961	123
115 4/8	19 4/8	19 7/8	14	14	4 6/8	5 1/8	–	–	M	Delta Junction, Alaska	Wm. S. Jarusiewicz	Wm. S. Jarusiewicz	1963	123
115 4/8	19 1/8	19	13 7/8	14	5	5	27 1/8	15 4/8	M	Hook Lake, N. W. T.	Robert C. Jones	Robert C. Jones	1974	123
115 2/8	16 2/8	17 2/8	13 6/8	13 6/8	6 7/8	7 2/8	28 2/8	23 2/8	M	Black Hills, S. D.	Unknown	John H. Brandt	1969	126
115	19 2/8	18 3/8	14	13 6/8	5 3/8	4 7/8	28 2/8	18 1/8	M	Ft. Smith, N. W. T.	Jules R. Ashlock	Jules R. Ashlock	1973	127

*Final Score subject to revision by additional verifying measurements.

WORLD'S RECORD ROCKY MOUNTAIN GOAT
SCORE: 56 6/8
Locality: Babine Mountains, British Columbia. Date: 1949.
Hunter and owner: E.C. Haase.
Winner of the Sagamore Hill Medal, 1949.

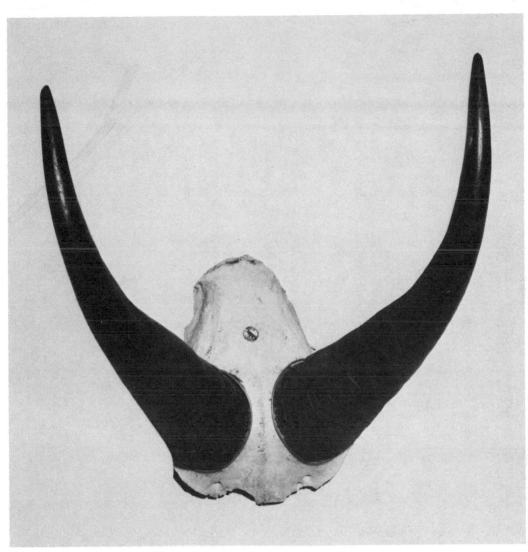

NUMBER TWO ROCKY MOUNTAIN GOAT (TIE)
SCORE: 56 2/8
Locality: Hedley, British Columbia. Picked up in 1969.
Donated by Robert Kitto to the National Collection.

Rocky Mountain Goat

Minimum Score 50 — ***Oreamnos americanus americanus* and related subspecies**

Score	Length of Horn R.	Length of Horn L.	Circumference of Base R.	Circumference of Base L.	Circumference at Third Quarter R.	Circumference at Third Quarter L.	Greatest Spread	Tip to Tip Spread	Sex	Locality Killed	By Whom Killed	Owner	Date Killed	Rank
56 6/8	12	12	6 4/8	6 4/8	2	2	9 2/8	9	M	Babine Mts., B. C.	E. C. Haase	E. C. Haase	1949	1
56 2/8	11 5/8	11 5/8	5 6/8	5 5/8	2 1/8	2 1/8	7 2/8	6 4/8	M	Helm Bay, Alaska	W. H. Jackson	W. H. Jackson	1933	2
56 2/8	11 3/8	11 3/8	6 3/8	6 4/8	2 1/8	2	8 6/8	8 3/8	M	Hedley, B. C.	Gift Of Robert Kitto	National Collection	1969	2
56 1/8	10 4/8	10 6/8	6 1/8	6	2 5/8	2 6/8	6 7/8	6 4/8	M	Kenai Pen., Alaska	Peter W. Bading	Peter W. Bading	1963	4
55 6/8*	10 5/8	10 4/8	6 1/8	6 1/8	2 2/8	2 2/8	7 6/8	6 3/8	M	Blunt Mt., B. C.	Picked Up	Jack Adams	1970	5
55	11 7/8	11 7/8	5 4/8	5 3/8	2	2	8 3/8	6 4/8	M	Cleveland Pen., Alaska	Elmer W. Copstead	Jonas Bros. Of Seattle	1939	6
55	12 1/8	12 1/8	5 2/8	5 1/8	2	2 2/8	7 7/8	5 6/8	M	Alex. Archipelago, Alaska	James Wilson	James Wilson	1969	6
54 6/8	10 5/8	11 3/8	6 2/8	6 2/8	2	1 7/8	8 3/8	7 5/8	M	Coquihalla Mts., B. C.	Fred D. Fouty	Fred D. Fouty	1959	8
54 6/8	10 7/8	11 2/8	6	6	2 3/8	2 3/8	7 5/8	6 5/8	M	Telkwa Mts., B. C.	Mrs. V. Goudie	Mrs. V. Goudie	1964	8
54 6/8	11 3/8	11 3/8	5 6/8	5 5/8	2	2	7 6/8	5 5/8	M	Reflection Lake, Alaska	Lue Wilson, Jr.	Lue Wilson, Jr.	1979	8
54 2/8	11	11	6 3/8	6 3/8	1 6/8	1 7/8	10 1/8	10	M	Fairmont Range, B. C.	Ira McLemore	Ira McLemore	1947	11
54 2/8	11 2/8	11 4/8	6	5 7/8	1 7/8	1 7/8	10	9 3/8	M	Hastings Arm, B. C.	Rupert Maier	Rupert Maier	1963	11
54 2/8	10 3/8	10 4/8	6	5 7/8	2 2/8	2 2/8	8 2/8	7 4/8	M	Cassiar Mts., B.C.	Richard J. Wristen	Richard J. Wristen	1978	11
54 2/8	11	10 6/8	6 2/8	6 2/8	2	2	9 6/8	9 4/8	M	Cassiar Mts., B.C.	Raymond M. Stenger	Raymond M. Stenger	1979	11
54	11 2/8	11 1/8	6 2/8	6 2/8	2	2	9 2/8	9 2/8	M	Bow Summit, Alta.	Indian	N. K. Luxton	1907	15
54	11	11	6 1/8	6 1/8	2	2	8 1/8	8 1/8	M	Terminus Mountain, B. C.	Herb Klein	Herb Klein	1965	15
53 6/8	11 1/8	11 2/8	5 7/8	5 7/8	2	1 7/8	9 4/8	8 4/8	M	Telegraph Creek, B. C.	V. D. E. Smith	V. D. E. Smith	1954	17
53 6/8	10 7/8	10 7/8	6	6	1 7/8	1 7/8	7 6/8	6 6/8	M	Tumeka Lake, B. C.	Robert Hunter Edwards	Robert Hunter Edwards	1972	17
53 6/8	10 3/8	10 3/8	5 7/8	6	2 1/8	2 1/8	7 7/8	7 5/8	M	Elko Co., Nevada	Robert D. Kennedy	Robert D. Kennedy	1978	17
53 4/8	11 4/8	11 2/8	5 7/8	5 7/8	2	2	7 4/8	6 7/8	M	Stikine River, B. C.	John Creyke	John Creyke	1926	20
53 4/8	10 6/8	11	6	6	1 7/8	1 7/8	9 2/8	8 7/8	M	Coldstream Creek, B. C.	R. J. Pop	H. W. Klein	1952	20
53 4/8	10 7/8	9 5/8	6 5/8	6 6/8	2	2 3/8	7	6	M	Bella Coola, B. C.	Darryl Hodson	Darryl Hodson	1966	20
53 4/8	11 4/8	11 4/8	5 6/8	5 7/8	1 7/8	1 7/8	8 1/8	7 4/8	M	Kitimat, B. C.	Fred Hahn	Fred Hahn	1966	20
53 4/8	11 4/8	11 3/8	5 5/8	5 5/8	2	2	9 2/8	8 7/8	M	Cassiar Mts., B. C.	William Rohlfs	William Rohlfs	1971	20
53 2/8	11 1/8	11 1/8	5 6/8	5 6/8	2	2	8 7/8	7 7/8	M	Cassiar Mts., B. C.	W. Reuen Fisher	W. Reuen Fisher	1945	25
53 2/8	10 6/8	11	5 7/8	5 7/8	2	2	6 6/8	5 6/8	M	Ketchikan, Alaska	Charles E. Slajer	Charles E. Slajer	1966	25
53 2/8	10 7/8	11 1/8	6 3/8	6 3/8	1 6/8	1 7/8	7 7/8	7 2/8	M	Mt. Findlay, B. C.	Glenn Welsh	Glenn Welsh	1971	25
53	10 1/8	10	5 6/8	5 5/8	2 1/8	2	8 4/8	8	M	Skagway, Alaska	Charles R. Heath	Charles R. Heath	1965	28

53	10 7/8	11	5 7/8	6	1 7/8	1 7/8	6 5/8	6 2/8	M	Skeena-Copper Rivers, B. C.	John A. Paetkau	John W. Kroeker	1967	28
53	9 7/8	10	6 2/8	6 2/8	2	2	8 7/8	8 7/8	M	Cassiar Mts., B. C.	Jack Thorndike	Jack Thorndike	1970	28
53	11 2/8	10 5/8	6	6 1/8	2	2	6 5/8	4 7/8	M	Aaron Mtn., Alaska	John Sturgeon	John Sturgeon	1973	28
53	10 4/8	10 4/8	6	6	2	2	8 2/8	8 1/8	M	Homer, Alaska	Robert W. Hertz, Jr.	Robert W. Hertz, Jr.	1974	28
52 6/8	11 4/8	11 4/8	5 5/8	5 5/8	1 7/8	1 7/8	7 4/8	7 3/8	M	Idaho Co., Idaho	Farrell M. Trenary	Farrell M. Trenary	1933	33
52 6/8	11	11	5 7/8	5 7/8	1 7/8	1 7/8	8 5/8	8 2/8	M	Kootenay, B. C.	A. C. Gilbert	Jules V. Lane	1935	33
52 6/8	11 4/8	11 4/8	5 1/8	5 1/8	1 6/8	1 6/8	7 5/8	7 4/8	M	Whatcom Co., Wash.	Arie Vander Hoek, Jr.	Arie Vander Hoek, Jr.	1966	33
52 6/8	10 1/8	10 1/8	6	5 7/8	2 3/8	2 3/8	6 5/8	5 6/8	M	Cold Fish Lake, B. C.	Stanley W. Glasscock	Stanley W. Glasscock	1967	33
52 6/8	11 1/8	11 1/8	5 6/8	5 6/8	2	2	6 3/8	5 5/8	M	Vernon, B. C.	Robert B. Procter	Robert B. Procter	1968	33
52 6/8	10 2/8	10 5/8	5 7/8	6	2 1/8	2 1/8	8 3/8	8 1/8	M	Ashnola Valley, B. C.	Brian Chipperfield	Brian Chipperfield	1968	33
52 6/8	10 3/8	10 3/8	6	6	2	2	7 5/8	7	M	Terrace, B. C.	R. P. Kolterman	R. P. Kolterman	1971	33
52 4/8	10 4/8	10 2/8	5 7/8	5 7/8	2	2	7 6/8	7 2/8	M	Okanagon Co., Wash.	Richard Shatto	Richard Shatto	1962	40
52 4/8	10 6/8	11	6	5 7/8	1 7/8	1 6/8	9 1/8	8 6/8	M	Terminus Mt., B. C.	Herb Klein	Herb Klein	1965	40
52 4/8	11 1/8	11 3/8	5 5/8	5 4/8	1 7/8	1 7/8	7 1/8	6	M	Whatcom Co., Wash.	John W. Bullene	John W. Bullene	1965	40
52 4/8	10 1/8	10 1/8	5 7/8	5 7/8	2	2	6 7/8	6 6/8	M	Colt Lake, B. C.	George P. Jackson, Jr.	George P. Jackson, Jr.	1965	40
52 4/8	10 1/8	10	6	6	2	2	7 6/8	7 2/8	M	Sheep Creek, Wash.	R. C. Dukart	R. C. Dukart	1967	40
52 4/8	10 7/8	10 7/8	5 5/8	5 6/8	2	2	10 2/8	10	M	Cassiar, B. C.	Otto Machek	Otto Machek	1968	40
52 4/8	10 1/8	10 4/8	5 7/8	5 7/8	2 1/8	2 1/8	7 7/8	7 7/8	M	Spectrum Range, B. C.	Kelly Good	Kelly Good	1973	40
52 4/8	10 1/8	10 2/8	6	6	2	2	8 2/8	7 3/8	M	Rock Island Lake, B. C.	Joe E. Coleman	Joe E. Coleman	1976	40
52 4/8	10	10 6/8	5 7/8	5 6/8	2 1/8	2 1/8	8 2/8	7 5/8	M	Skeena Mts., B.C.	Hardy Murr	Hardy Murr	1977	40
52 2/8	11	11 1/8	5 6/8	5 6/8	1 7/8	2	8 3/8	8	M	Swan Lake, B. C.	A. C. Gilbert	A. C. Gilbert	1938	49
52 2/8	10 3/8	10 3/8	6	6	2	2	7 1/8	6	M	Cassiar, B. C.	Frank H. Schramm	Frank H. Schramm	1947	49
52 2/8	10 1/8	10 1/8	5 6/8	5 6/8	2	2	7 3/8	6 6/8	M	Hastings Arm, B. C.	Ernest Dietschi	Ernest Dietschi	1963	49
52 2/8	10 4/8	10 2/8	5 7/8	5 7/8	2	2	8 2/8	7 6/8	M	Copper River, Alaska	Fritz Maier	Fritz Maier	1964	49
52 2/8	10 3/8	10 3/8	5 7/8	5 7/8	1 7/8	1 7/8	6 5/8	5 3/8	M	Bella Bella, B. C.	William B. Chivers	William B. Chivers	1965	49
52 2/8	11	10 7/8	5 4/8	5 5/8	2	1 7/8	7 6/8	7 1/8	M	Boca De Quadra, Alaska	Doug Vann	Doug Vann	1968	49
52 2/8	10 7/8	10 7/8	5 2/8	5 2/8	1 7/8	1 7/8	8	7 5/8	M	Boca De Quadra, Alaska	Dan Hook	Dan Hook	1968	49
52 2/8	10 6/8	10 6/8	5 6/8	5 6/8	2	1 7/8	8 5/8	8	M	Whatcom Co., Wash.	Al Hershey	Al Hershey	1969	49
52 2/8	10 5/8	10 5/8	5 7/8	5 7/8	2	2	8 2/8	7 7/8	M	Seward, Alaska	Donald R. Platt, Sr.	Donald R. Platt, Sr.	1969	49
52 2/8	11	11 1/8	6 1/8	6	1 6/8	1 6/8	9 3/8	8 3/8	M	Cassiar Mts., B. C.	Peter Fenchak	Peter Fenchak	1970	49
52 2/8	10 6/8	10 4/8	6 1/8	6	1 7/8	1 6/8	6 7/8	5 2/8	M	Mt. Cronin, B. C.	Vinko Strgar	Vinko Strgar	1972	49
52 2/8	10 6/8	10 5/8	5 6/8	5 6/8	1 7/8	1 7/8	8 2/8	7 5/8	M	Chelan Co., Wash.	John W. Lane	John W. Lane	1973	49
52 2/8	10	10	5 7/8	6	1 7/8	1 7/8	9 4/8	8 6/8	M	Cold Fish Lake, B. C.	Larry Bonetti	Larry Bonetti	1975	49
52 2/8	10 1/8	10 2/8	5 4/8	5 4/8	1 5/8	1 6/8	8 4/8	8 3/8	M	Kutcho Creek, B. C.	J. C. Page	J. C. Page	1975	49
52 2/8	10 1/8	10 1/8	5 6/8	5 6/8	2	2	6 7/8	6 4/8	M	Chelan Co., Washington	Thomas A. Lovas	Thomas A. Lovas	1976	49
52	10 1/8	10 4/8	6 1/8	6 1/8	2	2	8 6/8	8 4/8	M	Cassiar, B. C.	Walter R. Peterson	Walter R. Peterson	1937	64
52	10 4/8	10	5 6/8	5 6/8	2	2	9	9	M	Tweedsmuir Park, B C.	Chester G. Moore	Chester G. Moore	1946	64
52	10 3/8	10 3/8	5 4/8	5 5/8	2	2 1/8	6 7/8	4 5/8	M	Jumbo Mt., Wash.	Clyde Lewis	Clyde Lewis	1948	64
52	10 7/8	11 1/8	5 4/8	5 4/8	1 7/8	1 7/8	7 4/8	6 7/8	M	Watson Peak, Alaska	Harold M. Wright	Harold M. Wright	1957	64
52	10 6/8	10 3/8	5 6/8	5 6/8	2	2	6 7/8	6 2/8	M	Idaho Co., Idaho	Charlie T. Knox	Charlie T. Knox	1959	64
52	10 4/8	11	5 7/8	6	2 1/8	2 1/8	8 7/8	8 2/8	M	Bulkley Range, B. C.	Ingvar Wickstrom	Ingvar Wickstrom	1960	64
52	10 2/8	10 3/8	5 7/8	6	2	1 7/8	7 6/8	7 5/8	M	Mission Ridge, B. C.	B. Naimark	B. Naimark	1960	64

Rocky Mountain Goat–*Continued*

Oreamnos americanus americanus and related subspecies

Score	Length of Horn R.	Length of Horn L.	Circumference of Base R.	Circumference of Base L.	Circumference at Third Quarter R.	Circumference at Third Quarter L.	Greatest Spread	Tip to Tip Spread	Sex	Locality Killed	By Whom Killed	Owner	Date Killed	Rank
52	10 1/8	10 2/8	5 7/8	5 7/8	1 7/8	1 7/8	7 2/8	6 1/8	M	Kootenay River, B. C.	Howard Paish	Howard Paish	1961	64
52	10	10	6	6	2	2	7 3/8	7	M	Sundial Lake, Alaska	Arnold W. Johnson	Arnold W. Johnson	1962	64
52	10 3/8	10 2/8	5 7/8	5 7/8	2 1/8	2	7 4/8	7 1/8	M	Coquihalla, B. C.	Fred D. Fouty	Fred D. Fouty	1962	64
52	11 4/8	11 3/8	5 3/8	5 3/8	2	2	7	4 5/8	M	Boca De Quadra, Alaska	James Todahl	James Todahl	1962	64
52	10 1/8	10 2/8	5 7/8	5 7/8	2	2	9 1/8	7 6/8	M	Skeena River, B. C.	R. H. Simonds	R. H. Simonds	1963	64
52	10 5/8	10 6/8	6	6 1/8	1 7/8	1 7/8	7 7/8	6	M	Kitsumgallum Lake, B. C.	Manfred Beier	Manfred Beier	1965	64
52	9 7/8	10	5 6/8	5 6/8	2 1/8	2 1/8	8	7 5/8	M	Hart Mt., B. C.	Donna Loewenstein	Donna Loewenstein	1965	64
52	10 1/8	10 2/8	5 5/8	5 4/8	2	2	6 3/8	5 4/8	M	Southgate River, B. C.	R. T. Ostby	R. T. Ostby	1966	64
52	10 2/8	10 1/8	6 1/8	6 1/8	2	2	6 1/8	5 3/8	M	Okanogan Co., Wash.	E. W. Butler	E. W. Butler	1967	64
52	10 7/8	10 2/8	5 4/8	5 4/8	1 7/8	1 7/8	9 6/8	9 2/8	M	Auke Bay, Alaska	Kenneth L. Klawunder	Kenneth L. Klawunder	1968	64
52	9 7/8	9 6/8	5 6/8	5 6/8	2	2	7 5/8	7	M	Skagit Co., Wash.	John C. Casebeer	John C. Casebeer	1970	64
52	9 4/8	9 5/8	5 7/8	5 7/8	2 1/8	2 2/8	7	5 7/8	M	Skeena Mts., B. C.	William F. Jury	William F. Jury	1971	64
52	10 1/8	10 2/8	6	6 1/8	1 7/8	2	7	6 3/8	M	Chelan Co., Wash.	Robert A. Beckton	Robert A. Beckton	1971	64
52	11	10 6/8	6 1/8	6	1 6/8	1 6/8	8 4/8	7 7/8	M	Kispiox Range, B. C.	John W. Allen	John W. Allen	1974	64
52	10 1/8	10 3/8	5 6/8	5 6/8	2 2/8	2 2/8	8 5/8	8	M	Camp Island Lk., B. C.	C. N. Hoffman	C. N. Hoffman	1974	64
52	10 2/8	10 1/8	6	6	2 1/8	2	7	5 3/8	M	Whatcom Co., Wash.	George W. Bowen	George W. Bowen	1978	64
52	10 1/8	10 1/8	5 6/8	5 6/8	2 1/8	2	7	6 3/8	M	Elko Co., Nevada	Les Boni	Les Boni	1978	64
51 6/8	10 3/8	10 3/8	5 5/8	5 5/8	2	2	8 7/8	8 3/8	M	Telegraph Creek, B. C.	John S. McCormick, Jr.	John S. McCormick, Jr.	1936	88
51 6/8	10 6/8	10 6/8	5 4/8	5 5/8	1 7/8	2	7 5/8	7 4/8	M	Mile 402, Alaska Hwy., Alaska	E. J. Blumenshine	E. J. Blumenshine	1948	88
51 6/8	10 3/8	10 2/8	6 1/8	6 1/8	1 7/8	1 7/8	6 3/8	6 2/8	M	Lake Co., Mont.	Glenn Conklin	Glenn Conklin	1958	88
51 6/8	10 4/8	10 4/8	5 6/8	5 6/8	2	2	8 4/8	8 2/8	M	Wolf Creek, Mont.	Jim B. Beard	Jim B. Beard	1963	88
51 6/8	10 2/8	10	5 7/8	5 7/8	2	2	7 7/8	7	M	Telegraph Creek, B. C.	John Caputo, Sr.	John Caputo, Sr.	1965	88
51 6/8	11 2/8	11	5 6/8	5 6/8	1 6/8	1 6/8	7 4/8	6 7/8	M	Flathead Co., Mont.	John J. Allmaras	John J. Allmaras	1965	88
51 6/8	10 6/8	10 5/8	5 6/8	5 7/8	1 7/8	1 7/8	9 3/8	9 1/8	U	Atlin, B. C.	Bill Slikker	Bill Slikker	1965	88
51 6/8	11 5/8	12	5 1/8	5 1/8	1 6/8	1 6/8	1 3/8	1 3/8	F	Cassiar Mts., B. C.	Bruce N. Spencer	Bruce N. Spencer	1966	88
51 6/8	10 4/8	10 3/8	5 6/8	5 6/8	1 7/8	1 7/8	7 4/8	5 7/8	M	Copper-Skeena Rivers, B. C.	Henry Dyck	Henry Dyck	1967	88
51 6/8	10 1/8	10	5 7/8	5 7/8	2	2	6 6/8	5 7/8	M	Ecstall River, B. C.	William A. Kristmanson	William A. Kristmanson	1967	88
51 6/8	10 3/8	10 4/8	6 1/8	6 1/8	1 6/8	1 7/8	9 2/8	8 7/8	M	Hobo Creek, B. C.	Roy K. Pysher	Roy K. Pysher	1968	88

51 6/8	11 2/8	11 3/8	5 6/8	5 6/8	1 5/8	1 5/8	10	9 7/8	M	Clearwater Creek, B. C.	Stephen W. Cook	Stephen W. Cook	1968	88
51 6/8	10 2/8	10 3/8	5 6/8	5 6/8	1 6/8	1 6/8	7	6 2/8	M	Turnagain River, B. C.	John R. Braun	John R. Braun	1968	88
51 6/8	10 1/8	10 2/8	5 7/8	5 6/8	1 7/8	1 7/8	8 4/8	8 4/8	M	Wrangell Mts., Alaska	Basil C. Bradbury	Basil C. Bradbury	1968	88
51 6/8	10 5/8	10 4/8	5 4/8	5 4/8	1 7/8	1 7/8	7 7/8	7 5/8	M	Skeena-Exstew Rivers, B. C.	Frans Fait	Frans Fait	1968	88
51 6/8	10 5/8	10 7/8	5 5/8	5 5/8	2	2	6 2/8	5 1/8	M	The Pinnacles Mt., B. C.	Michael Bigford	Michael Bigford	1968	88
51 6/8	10 3/8	10 2/8	6	6	2	2	7 6/8	7 1/8	M	Burns Lake, B. C.	Ellis Dee Skidmore	Ellis Dee Skidmore	1969	88
51 6/8	10 6/8	10 7/8	5 5/8	5 5/8	1 7/8	1 7/8	6 3/8	5	M	Tongass Natl. For., Alaska	Roderick Martin	Roderick Martin	1970	88
51 6/8	10	10	5 7/8	5 7/8	2	2	6 6/8	5 1/8	M	Bradfield River, Alaska	James M. Remza	James M. Remza	1970	88
51 6/8	10 3/8	10 4/8	6 1/8	6 1/8	1 7/8	1 7/8	8 7/8	8 6/8	M	Cassiar Mts., B. C.	Kenneth Campbell	Kenneth Campbell	1971	88
51 6/8	10 7/8	10 6/8	5 5/8	5 5/8	2	1 7/8	7 2/8	6 3/8	M	Cleveland Pen., Alaska	H. D. Costello	H. D. Costello	1973	88
51 6/8	10 5/8	10 6/8	5 4/8	5 7/8	1 7/8	2	6	5 2/8	M	Snohomish Co., Wash.	Des F. Hinds	Des F. Hinds	1974	88
51 6/8	10 2/8	10 3/8	6	6	1 7/8	2	6	4 5/8	M	Mt. Allard, B. C.	David Brousseau	David Brousseau	1975	88
51 6/8	11	10 6/8	5 6/8	5 6/8	2	1 7/8	7 3/8	7	M	Ketchikan, Alaska	Donald K. Oldenberg	Donald K. Oldenberg	1977	88
51 6/8	10 5/8	10 3/8	5 4/8	5 6/8	1 7/8	1 7/8	8 5/8	7 6/8	M	Zymoetz River, B.C.	William I. Bond	William I. Bond	1978	88
51 4/8	11	11 2/8	5 6/8	5 6/8	1 6/8	1 6/8	8 4/8	7 6/8	M	Kootenay, B. C.	Herb Klein	Herb Klein	1946	113
51 4/8	11 3/8	11 5/8	5 4/8	5 5/8	1 6/8	1 6/8	7 4/8	7 3/8	M	Ella River, B. C.	Lee G. Smith	Lee G. Smith	1950	113
51 4/8	10 2/8	10 1/8	5 6/8	5 6/8	2	2	6 6/8	5 7/8	M	Cold Fish Lake, B. C.	Geo. W. Hooker	Geo. W. Hooker	1956	113
51 4/8	10	10	5 6/8	5 6/8	1 7/8	1 7/8	6 7/8	6 3/8	M	Jarvis Lake, B. C.	G. F. Juhl	G. F. Juhl	1960	113
51 4/8	10 4/8	10 3/8	5 6/8	5 6/8	1 7/8	1 6/8	9 3/8	9 3/8	M	Cold Fish Lake, B. C.	Dan Edwards	Dan Edwards	1961	113
51 4/8	10 3/8	10 3/8	5 6/8	5 6/8	2	1 7/8	6 3/8	5 7/8	M	Cleveland Pen., Alaska	Allen E. Linn	Allen E. Linn	1961	113
51 4/8	10	10	5 7/8	5 7/8	2	2	7	6 2/8	M	Cassiar, B. C.	Adolf Doerre	Adolf Doerre	1961	113
51 4/8	10 2/8	10 2/8	5 5/8	5 4/8	1 7/8	1 7/8	6 8/8	6	M	Boca De Quadra, Alaska	Charles E. Simmons	Charles E. Simmons	1961	113
51 4/8	10 5/8	10 7/8	5 6/8	5 6/8	1 6/8	1 7/8	7 1/8	6 6/8	M	Kenai Pen., Alaska	Alan Olson	Alan Olson	1962	113
51 4/8	9 5/8	9 5/8	5 6/8	5 6/8	1 6/8	1 6/8	7 4/8	6 7/8	M	Chugach Mts., Alaska	Donald A. Turcke	Donald A. Turcke	1964	113
51 4/8	11 1/8	11 3/8	5 3/8	5 3/8	1 7/8	1 7/8	6 3/8	4 1/8	M	Boca De Quadra, Alaska	Arthur N. Wilson, Jr.	Arthur N. Wilson, Jr.	1965	113
51 4/8	10 6/8	10 5/8	5 7/8	5 7/8	1 6/8	1 6/8	6 6/8	5 4/8	M	Clearwater Creek, B. C.	Richard H. Leedy	Richard H. Leedy	1967	113
51 4/8	10 1/8	9 7/8	5 7/8	6 1/8	1 7/8	1 7/8	7 4/8	7 2/8	M	Sheep Creek, Alta.	Russell A. Fischer	Russell A. Fischer	1967	113
51 4/8	10 1/8	10 2/8	6	6	2	1 7/8	7 4/8	6 5/8	M	Coast Range, B. C.	Siegfried Lantenhammer	Siegfried Lantenhammer	1967	113
51 4/8	9 5/8	9 6/8	6	6	2	2	7 1/8	6 2/8	M	Toads River, B. C.	Bill Goosman	Bill Goosman	1970	113
51 4/8	10 3/8	10 3/8	5 6/8	5 6/8	2	2	8	7 4/8	M	Bowen Lake, Alaska	Ted A. Dedmon	Ted A. Dedmon	1971	113
51 4/8	10 2/8	10 4/8	5 7/8	5 6/8	1 7/8	2	8 4/8	8	M	Terrace, B. C.	George A. Shaw	George A. Shaw	1972	113
51 4/8	10 4/8	10 2/8	5 7/8	5 7/8	1 7/8	1 7/8	7 2/8	6 4/8	M	Ketchikan, Alaska	Kevin Downey	Kevin Downey	1973	113
51 4/8	11	10 3/8	5 6/8	5 6/8	1 7/8	1 7/8	6 2/8	5 5/8	M	Stikine River, Alaska	Donald E. Fossen	Donald E. Fossen	1973	113
51 4/8	10 2/8	10 1/8	5 4/8	5 4/8	1 7/8	1 7/8	6 7/8	5 5/8	M	Chelan Co., Wash.	Virgil N. Carpenter	Virgil N. Carpenter	1973	113
51 4/8	10 2/8	10 3/8	5 7/8	6	2	2 1/8	7 4/8	7 1/8	M	Stikine Range, B. C.	L. A. Candelaria	L. A. Candelaria	1974	113
51 4/8	10 4/8	10 5/8	5 6/8	5 6/8	1 7/8	2	8 5/8	8 1/8	M	Mt. Edziza, B. C.	A. Coe Frankhauser	A. Coe Frankhauser	1974	113
51 4/8	9 4/8	9 7/8	5 7/8	5 7/8	1 7/8	1 7/8	9 3/8	8 6/8	M	Pine Lake, B. C.	Charles H. Duke, Jr.	Charles H. Duke, Jr.	1975	113
51 4/8	10 2/8	10 5/8	5 6/8	5 5/8	2 1/8	2 1/8	8 1/8	7 4/8	M	Bulkley Mts., B.C.	Gordon Hannas	Gordon Hannas	1976	113
51 4/8	10 4/8	10 4/8	5 4/8	5 6/8	1 6/8	1 6/8	8 6/8	8 6/8	M	Kodiak Island, Alaska	Ron Eller	Ron Eller	1978	113
51 3/8	10 6/8	10 7/8	5 4/8	5 4/8	1 6/8	1 7/8	8 1/8	7 6/8	M	Kechika Range, B. C.	W. C. Dabney, Jr.	W. C. Dabney, Jr.	1965	138

ROCKY MOUNTAIN GOAT–*Continued*

Oreamnos americanus americanus and related subspecies

Score	Length of Horn R.	Length of Horn L.	Circumference of Base R.	Circumference of Base L.	Circumference at Third Quarter R.	Circumference at Third Quarter L.	Greatest Spread	Tip to Tip Spread	Sex	Locality Killed	By Whom Killed	Owner	Date Killed	Rank
51 2/8	10 7/8	10 7/8	5 6/8	6	1 6/8	1 6/8	8 1/8	7 7/8	M	Kootenay, B. C.	Teddy MacLachlan	W. K. Porter	1925	139
51 2/8	10 2/8	10 4/8	6 1/8	6 1/8	1 6/8	1 6/8	7 7/8	7 5/8	M	Hard Scrabble Pass, Alta.	Justus von Lengerke	Justus von Lengerke	1937	139
51 2/8	10 1/8	10 1/8	5 4/8	5 4/8	2	2	8 1/8	8 1/8	M	Katalla, Alaska	John Goeres	John Goeres	1943	139
51 2/8	10	10	6 1/8	6 1/8	2	2	6 6/8	6	M	Mt. Robson, B. C.	E. T. Reilly	E. T. Reilly	1948	139
51 2/8	10 6/8	10 6/8	5 6/8	5 6/8	1 5/8	1 6/8	8 7/8	8 5/8	M	Cassiar, B. C.	Elmer E. Rasmuson	Elmer E. Rasmuson	1952	139
51 2/8	10 4/8	10 6/8	5 5/8	5 6/8	1 6/8	1 7/8	7 2/8	6 7/8	M	Bulkley Range, B. C.	Mrs. Billie Gardiner	Mrs. Billie Gardiner	1959	139
51 2/8	10	10 4/8	6	6	1 7/8	2 1/8	7 7/8	7 5/8	M	Kechika Range, B. C.	Paul A. Bagalio	Paul A. Bagalio	1965	139
51 2/8	9 6/8	9 6/8	5 7/8	5 7/8	2	2 1/8	7 5/8	7	M	Gataga River, B. C.	Robert C. McAtee	Robert C. McAtee	1965	139
51 2/8	9 3/8	9 2/8	6 1/8	6 1/8	2 2/8	2 1/8	7 7/8	7 5/8	U	Anchorage, Alaska	Wade Charles	Wade Charles	1966	139
51 2/8	10 3/8	10 3/8	5 6/8	5 5/8	2	2	8 4/8	7 5/8	M	Atlin Lake, B. C.	Nolan Martins	Nolan Martins	1967	139
51 2/8	9 6/8	10	5 6/8	5 6/8	2	2	7 4/8	6 7/8	M	Atlin, B. C.	Walter O. Johnston	Walter O. Johnston	1968	139
51 2/8	10 3/8	10 3/8	5 6/8	5 7/8	1 7/8	1 7/8	7 4/8	6 6/8	M	Vetter Peak, B. C.	Tracy Skead	Tracy Skead	1969	139
51 2/8	10 1/8	10 1/8	5 6/8	5 6/8	2	2	6 4/8	5 6/8	M	Kechika Mts., B. C.	W. A. McKay	W. A. McKay	1970	139
51 2/8	10 1/8	10 4/8	5 3/8	5 2/8	2 2/8	2 1/8	8 2/8	7 6/8	M	Wrangell Mts., Alaska	John E. Meyers	John E. Meyers	1971	139
51 2/8	10 5/8	10 7/8	5 6/8	5 6/8	1 7/8	1 7/8	8 4/8	8 2/8	M	Skeena Mts., B. C.	Michael A. Wright	Michael A. Wright	1972	139
51 2/8	10 3/8	10 3/8	5 6/8	5 5/8	1 7/8	1 7/8	7 3/8	6 3/8	M	Tsetia Creek, B. C.	Douglas V. Turner	Douglas V. Turner	1973	139
51 2/8	10 4/8	10 2/8	6	5 7/8	2	1 7/8	6 4/8	5 3/8	M	Pend Oreille Co., Wash.	William R. Stevens	William R. Stevens	1975	139
51 2/8	10 5/8	10 6/8	5 4/8	5 5/8	1 7/8	1 7/8	10 4/8	10 3/8	M	Marker Lake, Yukon	James K. Montgomery	James K. Montgomery	1978	139
51 2/8	10 2/8	10	5 7/8	5 7/8	2	2	7 2/8	6 3/8	M	Morice Lake, B.C.	George Fitchett & Larry Austin	George Fitchett	1978	139
51 2/8	10 4/8	10 3/8	5 5/8	5 5/8	1 7/8	1 7/8	7 2/8	6 4/8	M	Idaho Co., Idaho	Lorraine Ravary	Lorraine Ravary	1978	139
51	9 6/8	10	5 7/8	5 7/8	2	2	8 2/8	7 7/8	M	Morice River, B. C.	Warren Bodeker	Warren Bodeker	1958	159
51	9 6/8	9 5/8	5 7/8	5 6/8	2 2/8	2 1/8	6 6/8	6 1/8	M	Resurrection Bay, Alaska	Peter W. Bading	Peter W. Bading	1961	159
51	11	10 6/8	5 7/8	5 7/8	1 7/8	1 6/8	7 2/8	6 4/8	M	Smithers, B. C.	John Strban	John Strban	1962	159
51	10 2/8	10 6/8	5 4/8	5 4/8	2	2	7 5/8	6 1/8	M	Butte Inlet, B. C.	Reuben C. Carlson	Reuben C. Carlson	1963	159
51	10 7/8	11	5 7/8	5 7/8	1 6/8	1 6/8	7 1/8	6 6/8	M	Kootenay Range, B. C.	Norbert M. Welch	Norbert M. Welch	1963	159
51	10	10	5 6/8	5 6/8	2	2	7 6/8	7	M	Dease Lake, B. C.	W. M. Rudd	W. M. Rudd	1964	159
51	10 2/8	10 2/8	5 5/8	5 5/8	1 7/8	1 7/8	7 4/8	7 3/8	M	Telegraph Creek, B. C.	John Caputo, Jr.	John Caputo, Jr.	1965	159
51	10 3/8	10 5/8	5 2/8	5 2/8	1 6/8	1 6/8	7 2/8	6 2/8	M	Flathead Co., Mont.	Johnny Powell	Johnny Powell	1965	159
51	10 6/8	10 4/8	5 6/8	5 3/8	1 7/8	1 7/8	7 1/8	5 5/8	M	Alaska Panhandle, Alaska	Donald W. Moody	Donald W. Moody	1966	159

Score	L. Horn R	L. Horn L	Circ. Base R	Circ. Base L	Circ. 3rd Qtr R	Circ. 3rd Qtr L	Greatest Spread	Tip to Tip	Cat.	Locality	Owner	Hunter	Date	Rank
51	10 1/8	10 1/8	5 5/8	5 5/8	2	2	9 2/8	9	M	Terrace, B. C.	Gary Townsend	Gary Townsend	1967	159
51	9 7/8	9 5/8	5 7/8	5 5/8	2	2	7 7/8	7 7/8	M	Hart Mountain, B. C.	Marvin F. Lawrence	Marvin F. Lawrence	1967	159
51	10 1/8	10	6	6	1 7/8	1 7/8	7 7/8	6 5/8	M	Tete Jaune, B. C.	George Hanschen	George Hanschen	1967	159
51	10 2/8	10 2/8	5 5/8	5 5/8	2	2	8 3/8	7 7/8	M	Okanagan, B. C.	Earl Dawson	Earl Dawson	1967	159
51	10 2/8	10 2/8	5 5/8	5 5/8	2	1 7/8	8	7 3/8	M	Telegraph Creek, B. C.	George McCullough	George McCullough	1967	159
51	9 5/8	9 5/8	5 7/8	5 7/8	1 7/8	1 7/8	5 5/8	5 5/8	M	McBride, B. C.	Ervin Voelk	Ervin Voelk	1968	159
51	10 1/8	10 1/8	5 5/8	5 5/8	1 6/8	1 6/8	7 7/8	7 3/8	M	Nuka Bay, Alaska	Curt Henning	Curt Henning	1968	159
51	10 1/8	10 1/8	5 5/8	5 5/8	1 6/8	1 6/8	8 3/8	8 3/8	M	Lillocet, B. C.	Helmut Krieger	Helmut Krieger	1969	159
51	10	10	5 5/8	5 5/8	2	2 1/8	6 7/8	6	M	Yakutat, Alaska	Robert Sinko	Robert Sinko	1971	159
51	9 6/8	9 6/8	5 5/8	5 5/8	2 1/8	2 2/8	6 6/8	5 7/8	M	Snohomish Co., Wash.	David T. Lewis	David T. Lewis	1972	159
51	10 1/8	10 1/8	5 3/8	5 3/8	2	1 7/8	6 6/8	7 5/8	M	Findlay Creek, B.C.	Sharon Robey	Sharon Robey	1978	159
50 6/8	10 1/8	10 1/8	5 7/8	5 7/8	1 7/8	1 7/8	8	6 4/8	M	Cassiar, B. C.	Wm. N. Beach	Wm. N. Beach	1918	179
50 6/8	10 1/8	10 1/8	5 7/8	5 7/8	1 7/8	1 7/8	7 1/8	8 5/8	M	Cassiar, B. C.	Clement B. Newbold	Clement B. Newbold	1926	179
50 6/8	11	11 1/8	5 5/8	5 4/8	1 5/8	1 5/8	9	4 3/8	U	Flathead Co., Mont.	Charlie Shaw	Picked Up	1936	179
50 6/8	9 4/8	9 4/8	5 7/8	5 4/8	1 6/8	1 6/8	5 4/8	7 6/8	M	Similkameen, B. C.	John D. Rempel	John D. Rempel	1939	179
50 6/8	10 4/8	10 2/8	5 5/8	5 5/8	2 1/8	2 1/8	7 7/8	6 7/8	M	Cassiar, B. C.	Peter Schramm	Peter Schramm	1950	179
50 6/8	10 2/8	10 2/8	5 4/8	5 4/8	2	2	8 3/8	8	M	Cordova, Alaska	Ralph E. Renner	Ralph E. Renner	1950	179
50 6/8	10 7/8	11 2/8	5 5/8	5 5/8	1 7/8	1 6/8	6 7/8	7 2/8	M	Telegraph Creek, B. C.	Wayne C. Eubank	Wayne C. Eubank	1953	179
50 6/8	9 6/8	9 6/8	5 7/8	5 7/8	1 7/8	1 7/8	9 2/8	7 3/8	M	Telegraph Creek, B. C.	A. J. Duany	A. J. Duany	1954	179
50 6/8	9 4/8	9 6/8	5 7/8	5 7/8	2 1/8	2 1/8	7 7/8	7 3/8	M	Knik River, Alaska	C. M. Van Meter	C. M. Van Meter	1956	179
50 6/8	10 1/8	10 2/8	5 6/8	5 6/8	2	2	8	5 7/8	M	Boca De Quadra Inlet, Alaska	Lyman Reynoldson	Lyman Reynoldson	1957	179
50 6/8	9 6/8	9 6/8	6	6	2	2	7 1/8	5 5/8	M	Maxan Lake, B. C.	K. J. Nysven	K. J. Nysven	1961	179
50 6/8	10 4/8	10 4/8	5 5/8	5 5/8	2	2	8 2/8	7 5/8	M	Kenai Pen., Alaska	Elgin T. Gates	Elgin T. Gates	1961	179
50 6/8	10 2/8	10 2/8	6	6	1 7/8	1 7/8	7 4/8	6 6/8	M	Cold Fish Lake, B. C.	Howard Boazman	Howard Boazman	1962	179
50 6/8	10 4/8	10 2/8	5 5/8	5 5/8	1 7/8	1 7/8	9 4/8	8 3/8	M	Gataga River, B. C.	Herb Klein	Herb Klein	1963	179
50 6/8	9 6/8	9 6/8	6 1/8	6 1/8	1 6/8	1 6/8	6 1/8	5 5/8	M	Keremeos, B. C.	Bill Postill	Bill Postill	1963	179
50 6/8	10	9 4/8	6	6	2 1/8	2 1/8	9 2/8	8 6/8	M	Atlin, B. C.	G. Vernon Boggs	G. Vernon Boggs	1964	179
50 6/8	9 4/8	9 4/8	6 1/8	6 1/8	1 7/8	1 7/8	6 7/8	6 7/8	M	Hedley, B. C.	Donald J. Robb	Donald J. Robb	1965	179
50 6/8	9 6/8	9 6/8	5 7/8	5 7/8	1 7/8	1 7/8	6 4/8	6	M	Ketchika Mts., B. C.	Basil C. Bradbury	Basil C. Bradbury	1965	179
50 6/8	9 4/8	9 6/8	6 1/8	6 1/8	2	2	7 7/8	7 7/8	M	Cassiar Mts., B. C.	Ernest Granum	Ernest Granum	1965	179
50 6/8	10 2/8	10 1/8	5 7/8	5 7/8	1 5/8	1 5/8	6	5 7/8	M	Mt. Antero, Colo.	Leroy C. Wood	Leroy C. Wood	1965	179
50 6/8	9 6/8	9 6/8	5 3/8	5 3/8	2 1/8	2 1/8	3 7/8	3 1/8	M	Klappan Range, B. C.	Larry P. Miller	Larry P. Miller	1965	179
50 6/8	10 1/8	10 1/8	5 5/8	5 5/8	2 1/8	2 1/8	3	3	M	Cold Fish Lake, B. C.	Armin Baltensweiler	Armin Baltensweiler	1965	179
50 6/8	10 4/8	10 4/8	5 5/8	5 5/8	2	2	8 3/8	8 3/8	U	Horsethief Creek, B. C.	Bill Pitt	Bill Pitt	1966	179
50 6/8	10 4/8	10 4/8	5 5/8	5 5/8	1 7/8	1 7/8	6 4/8	6 6/8	M	Skeena River, B. C.	G. Best	G. Best	1966	179
50 6/8	10 4/8	9 6/8	5 3/8	5 3/8	1 7/8	1 7/8	7 5/8	5 5/8	M	Ashnola River, B. C.	Robert C. Bateson	Robert C. Bateson	1966	179
50 6/8	9 6/8	10	5 7/8	5 7/8	2 1/8	2 1/8	8 3/8	7 3/8	M	Toad River, B. C.	Walt Paulk	Walt Paulk	1966	179
50 6/8	10 4/8	9 6/8	5 5/8	5 5/8	1 7/8	1 7/8	6 6/8	5 7/8	M	Black Hills, S. D.	Lloyd Weaver	Lloyd Weaver	1967	179
50 6/8	9 7/8	9 7/8	5 7/8	5 7/8	2	2	7 3/8	7 3/8	M	Kenai Mts., Alaska	Stephen D. LaBelle	Stephen D. LaBelle	1971	179
50 6/8	9 4/8	9 4/8	5 5/8	5 5/8	2 2/8	2 2/8	7 3/8	7 3/8	M	Dease Lake, B. C.	John H. Epp	John H. Epp	1972	179
50 6/8	10 1/8	10 1/8	5 7/8	5 7/8	2	2	8 5/8	8 5/8	M	Kechika River, B. C.	Dennis Laabs	Dennis Laabs	1973	179
50 6/8	10 1/8	10 1/8	5 5/8	5 5/8	1 6/8	1 6/8	8 3/8	8 1/8	M	Chelan Co., Wash.	Raymond J. Hammer	Raymond J. Hammer	1973	179

ROCKY MOUNTAIN GOAT–*Continued*

Oreamnos americanus americanus and related subspecies

Score	Length of Horn R.	Length of Horn L.	Circumference of Base R.	Circumference of Base L.	Circumference at Third Quarter R.	Circumference at Third Quarter L.	Greatest Spread	Tip to Tip Spread	Sex	Locality Killed	By Whom Killed	Owner	Date Killed	Rank
50 6/8	10 1/8	10	5 7/8	5 7/8	1 7/8	1 7/8	7 7/8	7 2/8	M	Kenai Pen., Alaska	Jack Allen	Jack Allen	1974	179
50 6/8	10	8 7/8	6 1/8	6	2 1/8	2 1/8	7 2/8	6 5/8	M	Cassiar Mts., B.C.	Kenneth E. Bishop	Kenneth E. Bishop	1979	179
50 4/8	12 1/8	12 4/8	4 6/8	4 6/8	1 6/8	1 7/8	7 1/8	6 4/8	F	Cassiar, B. C.	A. Bryan Williams	Mrs. N. S. Gooch	PR1916	212
50 4/8	10 2/8	10 3/8	5 4/8	5 4/8	2	2	7 4/8	7	M	Cassiar, B. C.	George E. Burghard	George E. Burghard	1925	212
50 4/8	10 1/8	10 2/8	5 5/8	5 5/8	1 7/8	1 7/8	7 2/8	6 5/8	M	Telegraph Creek, B. C.	John S. McCormick, Jr.	John S. McCormick, Jr.	1936	212
50 4/8	10 2/8	10 4/8	5 2/8	5 3/8	2	2	7	5 5/8	M	Brazeau River, Alta.	Walter B. McClurkan	Walter B. McClurkan	1942	212
50 4/8	11 1/8	11 1/8	5	5	2	2	7	5 2/8	M	Stikine River, Alaska	W. F. Littleton	W. F. Littleton	1953	212
50 4/8	10 4/8	10 5/8	5 6/8	5 5/8	2	1 7/8	7 1/8	6	M	Bull River, B. C.	Albert Markstein	Albert Markstein	1954	212
50 4/8	10 1/8	9 7/8	5 4/8	5 4/8	1 7/8	2 1/8	8 2/8	7 1/8	M	Cold Fish Lake, B. C.	Joseph Smith	Joseph Smith	1955	212
50 4/8	10	10	5 6/8	5 6/8	1 7/8	1 6/8	6 5/8	6 4/8	M	Okanogan Mts., Wash.	Neil Castner	Neil Castner	1956	212
50 4/8	10 1/8	10	5 5/8	5 6/8	1 6/8	1 6/8	8	7 1/8	M	Cold Fish Lake, B. C.	Patrick Britell	Patrick Britell	1957	212
50 4/8	10 2/8	10 4/8	5 1/8	5 1/8	1 7/8	1 7/8	–	–	U	Seward, Alaska	Picked Up	A. D. Stenger	PR1957	212
50 4/8	9 6/8	9 6/8	5 6/8	5 6/8	1 7/8	1 7/8	8 1/8	7 5/8	M	Chugach Mts., Alaska	Elmer A. Patson	Elmer A. Patson	1958	212
50 4/8	10 4/8	10 4/8	5 4/8	5 4/8	2	2	7 4/8	6 7/8	M	Cold Fish Lake, B. C.	L. A. Wunsch	L. A. Wunsch	1958	212
50 4/8	10 2/8	10 1/8	5 5/8	5 5/8	2	2	7 2/8	6 3/8	M	Lake Bennet, Yukon	H. Kennedy	H. Kennedy	1958	212
50 4/8	10 3/8	10 2/8	5 6/8	5 6/8	2	2	6 6/8	5 1/8	M	Okanogan, Wash.	Bob Hazelbrook	Bob Hazelbrook	1960	212
50 4/8	10 1/8	10 2/8	5 6/8	5 6/8	1 6/8	1 6/8	7 7/8	6 7/8	M	Smithers, B. C.	A. S. Langan	A. S. Langan	1960	212
50 4/8	10 2/8	10 3/8	5 1/8	5 1/8	2 1/8	2	7	7	F	Chilco Lake, B. C.	C. Marc Miller	C. Marc Miller	1960	212
50 4/8	9 4/8	9 4/8	5 5/8	5 6/8	2 1/8	2 1/8	5 6/8	4 4/8	M	Terrace, B. C.	Gerald Prosser	Gerald Prosser	1962	212
50 4/8	10	10 2/8	5 6/8	5 6/8	1 7/8	1 7/8	8 1/8	7 6/8	M	Kenai Pen., Alaska	Gordon Best & Ronald Reed	Gordon Best	1962	212
50 4/8	9 3/8	9 3/8	5 5/8	5 5/8	2 1/8	2 1/8	6 3/8	5 4/8	M	Mt. Stoyoma, B. C.	Frank S. T. Bradley	Frank S. T. Bradley	1962	212
50 4/8	9 3/8	9 7/8	6	6	2	2	6 7/8	6 6/8	M	Lake Chelan, Wash.	Ed Pariseu	Ed Pariseu	1962	212
50 4/8	10 1/8	9 7/8	5 6/8	5 6/8	1 7/8	2	7	6 2/8	M	White Sales Mt., B. C.	Robert McDonald	Robert McDonald	1962	212
50 4/8	9 7/8	10	5 7/8	5 7/8	1 7/8	2	7 2/8	7 2/8	M	Ketchika Range, B. C.	G. W. Hawkins	G. W. Hawkins	1963	212
50 4/8	10 5/8	10 6/8	5 4/8	5 4/8	1 6/8	1 6/8	7 2/8	6 7/8	M	Cape Yakataga, Alaska	Lynn M. Castle	Lynn M. Castle	1964	212
50 4/8	10	10	5 7/8	5 7/8	1 6/8	1 5/8	7 1/8	5 4/8	M	Wrangell Mts., Alaska	Charles S. Moses	Charles S. Moses	1965	212
50 4/8	10 3/8	10 4/8	5 5/8	5 5/8	1 7/8	1 7/8	7 6/8	6 6/8	M	Lake Kinniskan, B. C.	Michel Boel	Michel Boel	1965	212
50 4/8	9 4/8	9 4/8	5 6/8	5 6/8	2 1/8	2 1/8	8	8	M	Smoky River, Alta.	Terry Thrift, Jr.	Terry Thrift, Jr.	1965	212
50 4/8	10 1/8	10 2/8	5 4/8	5 6/8	2	1 7/8	7 3/8	6 2/8	U	McDonald Lake, B. C.	Henry P. Foradora	Henry P. Foradora	1966	212
50 4/8	10 4/8	10 3/8	5 5/8	5 5/8	1 7/8	1 6/8	7 3/8	7 7/8	U	Seward, Alaska	Frank W. Pinkerton	Frank W. Pinkerton	1966	212

50 4/8	10 5/8	10 3/8	5 4/8	5 3/8	1 7/8	1 7/8	7 3/8	5 4/8	M	Winstanley Lakes, Alaska	James R. Simms	James R. Simms	1966	212
50 4/8	9 6/8	9 7/8	5 5/8	5 6/8	2	2	8	7 5/8	M	Sloko Lake, B. C.	John Haefeli	John Haefeli	1966	212
50 4/8	10 2/8	10 3/8	5 4/8	5 4/8	1 7/8	1 7/8	6	5 1/8	M	Revelstoke, B. C.	Picked Up	George Lines	1966	212
50 4/8	9 6/8	9 4/8	5 5/8	5 6/8	2	2	8 1/8	7 6/8	M	Atlin, B. C.	Raymond Bartram	Raymond Bartram	1966	212
50 4/8	10 5/8	10 5/8	5 3/8	5 3/8	1 6/8	1 6/8	7 2/8	6 3/8	M	Black Hills, S. D.	Robert M. Aalseth	Robert M. Aalseth	1967	212
50 4/8	10 1/8	10 1/8	5 6/8	5 6/8	1 7/8	1 7/8	9 2/8	9 2/8	M	Cassiar Mts., B. C.	Donovon N. Branch	Donovon N. Branch	1967	212
50 4/8	10 2/8	10 2/8	5 4/8	5 4/8	1 7/8	1 7/8	8 4/8	7 6/8	M	Telegraph Creek, B. C.	T. T. Stroup	T. T. Stroup	1968	212
50 4/8	10 1/8	9 7/8	5 7/8	6	2	1 7/8	6 5/8	5 4/8	M	Turnagain River, B. C.	Howard S. Duffield	Howard S. Duffield	1969	212
50 4/8	11	11	5 4/8	5 5/8	1 7/8	1 6/8	7 1/8	5 1/8	M	Stikine River, Alaska	Donald E. Fossen	Donald E. Fossen	1973	212
50 4/8	10 3/8	10 4/8	5 6/8	6	1 6/8	1 6/8	7 7/8	7 7/8	M	Lewis And Clark Co., Mont.	Robert F. Thelen	Donald C. Thelen	1974	212
50 4/8	10	10 2/8	5 6/8	5 6/8	1 7/8	2	7 7/8	7 5/8	M	Dease Lake, B. C.	James T. Knutson	James T. Knutson	1975	212
50 4/8	10	10	5 7/8	5 7/8	1 7/8	1 7/8	7 1/8	6 6/8	M	Pennington Co., S.D.	Floyd J. Campbell	Floyd J. Campbell	1978	212
50 4/8	9 7/8	9 6/8	5 6/8	5 6/8	1 7/8	1 7/8	7	6 4/8	M	Wrangell Mts., Alaska	Leonard O. Farlow	Leonard O. Farlow	1978	212
50 3/8	10	10 1/8	5 4/8	5 4/8	2	2	7 5/8	7	M	Atlin Lake, B. C.	Wendell Bever	Wendell Bever	1962	253
50 2/8	10 4/8	10 4/8	5 6/8	5 6/8	1 6/8	1 6/8	8 5/8	8 4/8	M	Swan Lake, B. C.	A. C. Gilbert	A. C. Gilbert	1938	254
50 2/8	10 1/8	9 6/8	5 6/8	5 6/8	2	2	7 7/8	7 1/8	M	Cassiar Mts., B. C.	James King	James King	1947	254
50 2/8	9 5/8	9 7/8	5 6/8	5 6/8	2	2	7 4/8	6 7/8	M	Taseko Lake, B. C.	L. W. Howell	L. W. Howell	1952	254
50 2/8	10	10	5 5/8	5 5/8	2	2	7 4/8	7 1/8	M	Cold Fish Lake, B. C.	T. A. Walker	Univ. Of B. C.	1952	254
50 2/8	10	10	5 6/8	5 6/8	1 6/8	1 7/8	7	6 4/8	M	Blue Goat Mt., Wash.	Picked Up	Chas. F. Martinsen	1956	254
50 2/8	10 4/8	10 3/8	5 4/8	5 4/8	1 6/8	1 6/8	7 2/8	7 2/8	M	Turnagain River, B. C.	John La Rocca	John La Rocca	1957	254
50 2/8	10 4/8	10 3/8	5 4/8	5 5/8	1 6/8	1 6/8	6 6/8	6 6/8	M	Pentagon Mt., Mont.	Guy Brash	Guy Brash	1957	254
50 2/8	10	10	5 4/8	5 5/8	2	2	8	7 5/8	M	Okanogan Co., Wash.	Victor E. Moss	Victor E. Moss	1957	254
50 2/8	10 1/8	10 3/8	5 5/8	5 6/8	1 7/8	1 7/8	8	7 4/8	M	Shuswap Creek, B. C.	Nolan Rad	Nolan Rad	1958	254
50 2/8	10 2/8	10 2/8	5 5/8	5 6/8	1 6/8	1 6/8	7 2/8	6	M	Sheridan Glacier, Alaska	Leslie B. Maxwell	Leslie B. Maxwell	1959	254
50 2/8	10 2/8	10 2/8	5 5/8	5 5/8	1 7/8	1 6/8	6 3/8	5 2/8	M	Smithers, B. C.	William Stallone	William Stallone	1960	254
50 2/8	9 4/8	9 1/8	5 6/8	5 6/8	2 1/8	2	7 4/8	7 2/8	M	Ft. St. John, B. C.	Billy Ross	Billy Ross	1962	254
50 2/8	10 2/8	10 1/8	5 6/8	5 6/8	1 6/8	1 6/8	8 4/8	8 2/8	M	Sukunka River, B. C.	Robert C. Sutton	Robert C. Sutton	1962	254
50 2/8	10	10 2/8	5 7/8	5 7/8	1 6/8	1 6/8	7	6 4/8	M	Oroville, Wash.	G. Pickering	G. Pickering	1963	254
50 2/8	9 6/8	9 4/8	5 5/8	5 6/8	2 2/8	2 1/8	6 7/8	6 7/8	M	Telegraph Creek, B. C.	Anthony Bechik	Anthony Bechik	1963	254
50 2/8	10 5/8	9 5/8	6	6	2	1 7/8	7 3/8	7 3/8	M	Cassiar, B. C	James E. Kelley	James E. Kelley	1963	254
50 2/8	9 5/8	9 5/8	5 6/8	5 6/8	1 7/8	2	5 2/8	6 3/8	M	Dease Lake, B. C.	John T. Blackwell	John T. Blackwell	1963	254
50 2/8	11 2/8	10 6/8	5 5/8	5 4/8	1 6/8	1 6/8	8 4/8	7 7/8	M	Elk Valley, B. C.	Emile Gele	Emile Gele	1964	254
50 2/8	10 7/8	11	5 4/8	5 3/8	1 7/8	1 7/8	8 4/8	8 1/8	M	Atlin, B. C.	Walter F. Ramage	Walter F. Ramage	1965	254
50 2/8	10 2/8	10 1/8	5 4/8	5 4/8	1 7/8	1 7/8	6 4/8	5 5/8	M	Chehalis Lake, B. C.	Fred E. Harper	Fred E. Harper	1965	254
50 2/8	10 5/8	10 3/8	5 4/8	5 4/8	1 6/8	1 6/8	6 6/8	5 2/8	M	Invermere, B. C.	Laszlo Molnar	Laszlo Molnar	1965	254
50 2/8	10 4/8	10 3/8	5 5/8	5 6/8	1 6/8	1 6/8	8	7 2/8	M	Ravalli Co., Mont.	Mark J. Jakobson	Mark J. Jakobson	1965	254
50 2/8	10 2/8	10 2/8	5 6/8	5 6/8	1 6/8	1 6/8	7 5/8	7 3/8	M	Koch Creek, B. C.	Pat Archibald	Pat Archibald	1965	254
50 2/8	10	10	5 7/8	5 5/8	1 6/8	1 6/8	7 4/8	6 5/8	M	Chelan Co., Wash.	Ned Shiflett	Ned Shiflett	1966	254
50 2/8	10 6/8	10 7/8	5 5/8	5 4/8	1 6/8	1 6/8	6 5/8	5 6/8	M	Skeena River, B. C.	Jack E. Monet	Jack E. Monet	1966	254
50 2/8	10 2/8	10 3/8	5 6/8	5 6/8	1 4/8	1 5/8	6 3/8	5 1/8	M	Telkwa, B. C.	A. W. (Mike) Phillips	A. W. (Mike) Phillips	1967	254
50 2/8	9 4/8	9 4/8	5 6/8	5 6/8	2	2	7 4/8	7	M	Cassiar, B. C.	John A. Mueller	John A. Mueller	1968	254

Rocky Mountain Goat–*Continued*

Oreamnos americanus americanus and related subspecies

Score	Length of Horn R.	Length of Horn L.	Circumference of Base R.	Circumference of Base L.	Circumference at Third Quarter R.	Circumference at Third Quarter L.	Greatest Spread	Tip to Tip Spread	Sex	Locality Killed	By Whom Killed	Owner	Date Killed	Rank
50 2/8	10 1/8	10 1/8	5 3/8	5 4/8	2	2	7 5/8	7 5/8	M	Lynn Canal, Alaska	Jacques M. Norvell, Sr.	Jacques M. Norvell, Sr.	1968	254
50 2/8	10	9 6/8	6	5 7/8	1 7/8	1 7/8	6 4/8	6	M	Lake Chelan, Wash.	Gary L. Aichlmayr	Gary L. Aichlmayr	1969	254
50 2/8	10 5/8	10 2/8	5 3/8	5 4/8	1 7/8	2	6 5/8	5	M	Esctall River, B. C.	Thomas J. Perry	Thomas J. Perry	1970	254
50 2/8	9 7/8	9 5/8	5 5/8	5 5/8	2	2	6 7/8	6 2/8	M	Juneau, Alaska	Jerry Kressin	Jerry Kressin	1971	254
50 2/8	10 1/8	10 2/8	5 6/8	5 6/8	1 7/8	1 7/8	7 1/8	6 2/8	M	Tumeka Lake, B. C.	Dan M. Edwards, Jr.	Dan M. Edwards, Jr.	1972	254
50 2/8	10 1/8	10 1/8	5 3/8	5 3/8	1 7/8	1 7/8	7 7/8	7 5/8	M	Dease Lake, B. C.	Carl K. Beaudry	Carl K. Beaudry	1975	254
50 2/8	10 6/8	10 6/8	5 4/8	5 5/8	1 6/8	1 7/8	8 7/8	8 2/8	M	Stikine River, B. C.	R. H. (Dick) Weaver	R. H. (Dick) Weaver	1976	254
50 2/8	9 7/8	9 6/8	5 7/8	5 7/8	2	1 7/8	7 5/8	7 5/8	M	Ice Mt., B.C.	J. S. Van Alsburg	J. S. Van Alsburg	1978	254
50 2/8	9 7/8	9 7/8	5 6/8	5 6/8	1 7/8	1 7/8	7 3/8	6 1/8	M	Cassiar Mts., B.C.	Ron Ragan	Ron Ragan	1978	254
50	10 2/8	10 6/8	5 5/8	5 5/8	1 7/8	1 6/8	7 3/8	7	M	Klinaklini River, B. C.	Powhatan Robinson	Camp Fire Club	1916	290
50	10 1/8	10 1/8	5 4/8	5 4/8	2	1 7/8	7 6/8	7 6/8	M	Okanogan Co., Wash.	John Hutchinson	Ralph Hutchinson	1950	290
50	9 3/8	9 4/8	6	6	2	1 7/8	7 3/8	6 4/8	M	Kenai Pen., Alaska	Coke Elms	Coke Elms	1956	290
50	9 6/8	10	5 6/8	5 6/8	2	1 7/8	6	5 5/8	M	Keremeos Mt., B. C.	Robert Quaedvlieg	Robert Quaedvlieg	1956	290
50	10 1/8	10 1/8	5 6/8	5 6/8	1 7/8	2 1/8	7 6/8	6 7/8	M	Prophet River, B. C.	F. C. Hibben	F. C. Hibben	1956	290
50	10 4/8	10 2/8	5 4/8	5 4/8	2	1 6/8	7 2/8	6 6/8	M	Flathead River, Mont.	Gene Biddle	Gene Biddle	1957	290
50	10 7/8	10 6/8	5 5/8	5 6/8	1 6/8	1 5/8	6 5/8	5 6/8	M	Squaw Creek, Idaho	William A. Callaway	William H. Lockhart	1959	290
50	9 3/8	10	5 7/8	5 7/8	1 7/8	2	7 1/8	6 4/8	M	Cape Yakataga, Alaska	Edward I. Worst	Edward I. Worst	1960	290
50	9 6/8	9 4/8	5 7/8	5 7/8	1 7/8	1 7/8	6	5 2/8	M	K-Mountain, B. C.	Fred D. Fouty	Fred D. Fouty	1961	290
50	9 7/8	9 4/8	5 6/8	5 6/8	1 7/8	1 7/8	7 5/8	7 3/8	M	Girdwood, Alaska	Franklin Maus	Franklin Maus	1961	290
50	10	10	5 6/8	5 6/8	1 6/8	1 6/8	6 2/8	5 4/8	M	Bear Point, Idaho	Aaron U. Jones	Aaron U. Jones	1961	290
50	9 6/8	10 2/8	6	6	1 6/8	1 6/8	7	6 6/8	M	Grand Forks, B. C.	Norman Dawson, Jr.	Norman Dawson, Jr.	1962	290
50	9 4/8	9 4/8	5 4/8	5 4/8	2 1/8	2 2/8	7 5/8	7 5/8	M	Halfway River, B. C.	Victor Tullis	Victor Tullis	1963	290
50	10 1/8	10 1/8	5 4/8	5 4/8	2	2	6 7/8	6 1/8	M	Lincoln, Mont.	James A. Gunn, III	James A. Gunn, III	1963	290
50	10 3/8	10 2/8	5 4/8	5 4/8	1 7/8	1 7/8	6 7/8	6 4/8	M	Spatsizi, B. C.	William L. Searle	William L. Searle	1963	290
50	10 3/8	10 2/8	5 3/8	5 3/8	1 6/8	1 7/8	9 2/8	8 2/8	M	Gataga River, B. C.	Herb Klein	Herb Klein	1963	290
50	10 3/8	10 3/8	5 5/8	5 5/8	1 6/8	1 6/8	7 6/8	6 6/8	M	Smithers, B. C.	John Rienhart	John Rienhart	1964	290
50	10 1/8	10	5 6/8	5 7/8	1 6/8	1 5/8	4 5/8	6 4/8	M	Rudyerd Bay, Alaska	Joseph H. Keeney	Joseph H. Keeney	1964	290
50	9 6/8	9 5/8	5 6/8	5 7/8	1 7/8	1 7/8	6	5 1/8	M	Blue Sheep Lake, B. C.	O. A. McClintock	O. A. McClintock	1964	290
50	9 7/8	10 1/8	5 4/8	5 5/8	2	2 1/8	7 7/8	6 2/8	M	Heart Peak, B. C.	Bob Loewenstein	Bob Loewenstein	1965	290
50	9 6/8	9 6/8	5 4/8	5 4/8	2	2	6	6 7/8	M	Keremeos, B. C.	Picked Up	Bob Kitto	1965	290
50	10 1/8	10	5 6/8	5 6/8	1 6/8	1 6/8	8 2/8	8	M	Chilkat Range, Alaska	Jacques M. Norvell	Jacques M. Norvell	1965	290
50	10 7/8	10 7/8	5 4/8	5 4/8	1 5/8	1 5/8	7	6	M	Missoula Co., Mont.	Charles Barry	Charles Barry	1965	290

50								M	Location	Name	Name	Year	290
50	10 3/8	10 3/8	5 3/8	1 7/8	1 7/8	6 5/8	5 3/8	M	Hope, B. C.	Peter Konrad	Peter Konrad	1965	290
50	10	10 3/8	5 5/8	2	2	7 7/8	7 7/8	M	Morice River, B. C.	Dennis A. Sperling	Dennis A. Sperling	1965	290
50	9 7/8	9 7/8	5 5/8	1 7/8	1 7/8	6 3/8	5 5/8	M	Nass River, B. C.	Vernon Rydde	Vernon Rydde	1966	290
50	10 3/8	10 3/8	5 7/8	1 7/8	1 7/8	8 3/8	8 3/8	M	Seward, Alaska	John Lee	John Lee	1966	290
50	11 7/8	11 7/8	5	1 7/8	1 7/8	8 1/8	7 7/8	M	Petersburg, Alaska	James (Pat) Briggs	James (Pat) Briggs	1966	290
50	9 3/8	9 5/8	5 7/8	1 7/8	1 7/8	6 3/8	5 5/8	M	Lake Chelan, Wash.	Don Francis	Don Francis	1966	290
50	10	10	5 5/8	2	2	8 7/8	8 7/8	M	Cassiar Mts., B. C.	E. David Slye	E. David Slye	1967	290
50	10 3/8	10 3/8	5 5/8	1 7/8	1 7/8	7 7/8	7 3/8	M	Kenai Pen., Alaska	A. P. Funk	A. P. Funk	1967	290
50	10 3/8	10 3/8	5 5/8	1 7/8	1 7/8	7 3/8	6 7/8	M	Cassiar Mt., B. C.	Arthur M. Scully, Jr.	Arthur M. Scully, Jr.	1967	290
50	9 7/8	9 7/8	5 5/8	2	2	7 7/8	7 3/8	M	Nass River, B. C.	D. E. O'Shea	D. E. O'Shea	1967	290
50	9 7/8	9 7/8	5 5/8	1 7/8	1 7/8	6 5/8	5 5/8	M	Tatla Lake, B. C.	Jack Close	Jack Close	1967	290
50	10 3/8	10 3/8	5 5/8	1 7/8	1 7/8	6	4 5/8	M	Chelan Co., Wash.	Carl Lewis	Carl Lewis	1968	290
50	9 7/8	9 7/8	5 3/8	2	2	7 3/8	6 5/8	M	Hastings Arm, B. C.	Walter J. Eisele	Walter J. Eisele	1968	290
50	10 3/8	10 3/8	5 3/8	1 5/8	1 5/8	7 1/8	6 5/8	M	Skagway, Alaska	Don Sather	Don Sather	1968	290
50	9 7/8	9 7/8	5 5/8	1 7/8	1 7/8	7 5/8	7 5/8	M	Whittier, Alaska	Myron Dean Cowell	Myron Dean Cowell	1968	290
50	10 3/8	10 3/8	5 5/8	1 7/8	1 7/8	6 5/8	6	M	St. Mary's River, B. C.	Frederick Brahniuk	Frederick Brahniuk	1969	290
50	9 7/8	9 7/8	5 7/8	2	2	5	4 3/8	M	Chelan Co., Wash.	William R. Hooper	John F. Hooper	1970	290
50	9 7/8	9 7/8	5 5/8	2	2	6 5/8	5 7/8	M	Lake Kitchener, B. C.	Aubrey W. Minshall	Aubrey W. Minshall	1971	290
50	10 3/8	10 3/8	5 3/8	2	2	8 5/8	8 5/8	M	Port Dick, Alaska	Neil Smith	Neil Smith	1972	290
50	9 7/8	9 7/8	5 5/8	1 7/8	1 7/8	6 5/8	6	M	Hendon River, B. C.	R. A. Wiseman	R. A. Wiseman	1973	290
50	10 3/8	10 3/8	5 5/8	1 7/8	1 7/8	8 3/8	8	M	Goodwin Lake, B. C.	Bill Moomey	Bill Moomey	1974	290
50	10 3/8	10 3/8	5 3/8	2	2	7 7/8	6 5/8	M	Gataga River, B. C.	Jerald T. Waite	Jerald T. Waite	1975	290
50	10 3/8	10 3/8	5 5/8	1 7/8	1 7/8	7 5/8	7 5/8	M	Terrace, B.C.	Joe Zucchiatti	Joe Zucchiatti	1976	290
50	9 7/8	9 7/8	5 3/8	1 7/8	1 7/8	8 3/8	7 7/8	M	Cassiar Mts., B.C.	Gordon A. Read	Gordon A. Read	1976	290
50	10 3/8	10 3/8	5 5/8	1 5/8	1 5/8	8 3/8	7 3/8	M	Cassiar Mts., B. C.	Murray B. Wilson	Murray B. Wilson	1977	290
50	10 3/8	10 3/8	5 3/8	1 7/8	1 7/8	8 3/8	7 1/8	M	Prince William Sound, Alaska	Ernest H. Youngs	Ernest H. Youngs	1978	290

*Final Score subject to revision by additional verifying measurements.

Photograph by Wm. H. Nesbitt

NEW WORLD'S RECORD MUSKOX
SCORE: 122
Locality: Perry River, Northwest Territories. Date: picked up in 1979.
Owner: Robert J. Decker.

NUMBER THREE MUSKOX
SCORE: 115 2/8
Locality: Ellesmere Island, Northwest Territories. Date: 1900.
Hunter: I.S. Wombath Owner: Harvard Museum of Comparative Zoology.

Muskox

Minimum Score 90

Ovibos moschatus moschatus and certain related subspecies

Score	Length of Horn R.	Length of Horn L.	Width of Boss R.	Width of Boss L.	Circumference at Third Quarter R.	Circumference at Third Quarter L.	Tip to Tip Spread	Greatest Spread	Sex	Locality Killed	By Whom Killed	Owner	Date Killed	Rank
123 6/8*	28 1/8	28 3/8	10 4/8	10 5/8	6 2/8	6 5/8	31	31 2/8	M	N. W. T.	Unknown	Sam Pancotto	PR1976	1
122	29	28 1/8	10	9 7/8	6 5/8	5 7/8	30 3/8	30 5/8	M	Perry River, N. W. T.	Picked Up	Robert J. Decker	1979	2
115 2/8	26	27	10 6/8	10 2/8	5 4/8	5 4/8	27	27	M	Ellesmere Is., N. W. T.	I. S. Wombath	Harvard Univ. Mus.	1900	3
114 2/8	29 6/8	29 4/8	9 5/8	9 7/8	5 2/8	5	25 5/8	26	U	Hudson Bay, N. W. T.	Monjo	Carnegie Mus.	1910	4
113 4/8*	25 2/8	25 7/8	9 6/8	10	6 1/8	6 1/8	29 5/8	30	M	Cambridge Bay, N.W.T.	Unknown	Edmonton Tannery & Taxidermy	1979	5
113 2/8	28	29	8 5/8	8 6/8	4 7/8	4 7/8	28 5/8	29 5/8	M	Barren Grounds, N. W. T.	Gift Of Casmir DeRham	National Collection	—	6
111 4/8	24 3/8	24 4/8	10 1/8	10 2/8	5 6/8	5 1/8	25 3/8	26 4/8	U	Pr. Whales Is., N. W. T.	Picked Up	J. William Kerr	1970	7
109*	26 6/8	26 4/8	8 7/8	8 7/8	5 2/8	5 2/8	26 1/8	26 7/8	M	Nunivak Island, Alaska	Douglas E. Miller	Douglas E. Miller	1976	8
108 4/8*	25	23	9 1/8	9 3/8	6 6/8	6 7/8	23 1/8	25 3/8	U	Hornaday River, N. W. T.	Picked Up	Dan Murphy	PR1976	9
108	24 5/8	25 2/8	9 4/8	9 5/8	5 2/8	5 4/8	26	26 5/8	M	Barren Grounds, N. W. T.	Gift Of J. B. Marvin	National Collection	—	10
108*	24 6/8	26 5/8	9	8 7/8	5 6/8	6 2/8	26 6/8	27	M	Nunivak Island, Alaska	Helga Schroeder	Helga Schroeder	1977	10
107 6/8	25 6/8	25 1/8	9 3/8	9 5/8	5 5/8	5	24 6/8	25 5/8	M	Melville Island, N.W.T.	Picked Up	D. C. Thomas	1974	12
107 6/8	26 3/8	26 2/8	8 3/8	8 3/8	5	4 7/8	27 1/8	27 3/8	M	Nunivak Island, Alaska	John H. Taucher, II	John H. Taucher, II	1976	12
107 4/8	26 5/8	27 7/8	8	8 2/8	5 3/8	5 4/8	25 2/8	25 6/8	M	Canada	George Vaux	Acad. Nat. Sci., Phil.	—	14
107 2/8	26 2/8	24 7/8	8 6/8	9 1/8	5 1/8	5	29 2/8	29 4/8	M	Greenland	Bill Foster	Foster's Bighorn Rest.	PR1945	15
107 2/8	27 3/8	26 6/8	9	8 7/8	5 6/8	5	26 2/8	27 6/8	M	Nunivak Island, Alaska	William A. Keller	William A. Keller	1977	15
107 2/8	26 2/8	26 2/8	8 1/8	8 1/8	5	4 6/8	27 3/8	28	M	Nunivak Island, Alaska	Normand Poulin	Normand Poulin	1977	15
107 2/8	26 3/8	26 3/8	8 4/8	8 4/8	5 2/8	5 4/8	27 4/8	27 6/8	M	Nunivak Island, Alaska	Jacob Metzger	Jacob Metzger	1978	15
107 2/8	25	25 2/8	9 1/8	9	5 2/8	5 4/8	23	24 4/8	M	Cambridge Bay, N.W.T.	Picked Up	Manfred Huellbusch	1979	15
107	24 5/8	25 6/8	9 6/8	10 1/8	4 6/8	4 7/8	24	26 6/8	M	Hudson Bay, N. W. T.	Indian	N. K. Luxton	1890	20
107	26 3/8	26 6/8	8 5/8	8 4/8	4 6/8	5	26 1/8	27 3/8	M	Nunivak Island, Alaska	Russell Reed	Russell Reed	1978	20
106 6/8	27 3/8	28 1/8	8 6/8	8 3/8	4 5/8	5 3/8	26 4/8	26 7/8	U	Greenland	Unknown	Rudolph Sand	1930	22
106 6/8	25	27 3/8	8 5/8	8 2/8	5 3/8	6	25 5/8	26 3/8	M	Greenland	Alvin Pedersen	Zool. Mus., Copenhagen	1935	22
106 6/8	25 1/8	25 1/8	8 3/8	8 4/8	5	5	27 6/8	28	M	Nunivak Island, Alaska	Bert Klineburger	Bert Klineburger	1959	22
106 6/8	26 1/8	27 1/8	8 6/8	8 6/8	4 7/8	4 7/8	27 2/8	27 5/8	M	Nunivak Island, Alaska	Ethel D. Leedy	Ethel D. Leedy	1975	22
106 2/8	26	25 6/8	8 4/8	8 2/8	4 7/8	4 4/8	29 4/8	29 6/8	M	Nunivak Island, Alaska	L. G. Sullivan	L. G. Sullivan	1977	26
106	26 3/8	25 1/8	10 4/8	10 5/8	4 4/8	4 5/8	27	27	M	Nunivak Island, Alaska	Gail W. Holderman	Gail W. Holderman	1976	27

105 6/8	25 6/8	27 2/8	9 4/8	9 6/8	4 4/8	5 2/8	24 6/8	27	M	Barren Grounds, N. W. T.	Unknown	Snow Museum	1890	28
105 6/8	25 2/8	25 1/8	8 5/8	8 7/8	5 5/8	5	24 4/8	25 2/8	M	Nunivak Island, Alaska	Lynn Castle	Lynn Castle	1977	28
105 6/8	25 6/8	25 2/8	8 4/8	8 4/8	5	4 6/8	26 4/8	27 2/8	M	Nunivak Island, Alaska	William K. Leech	William K. Leech	1977	28
105 6/8	26	25 2/8	9 2/8	9 1/8	4 5/8	4 5/8	23 6/8	25 7/8	M	Nunivak Island, Alaska	Gary E. Brown	Gary E. Brown	1978	28
105 4/8	26	26	8 2/8	8 2/8	4 7/8	4 6/8	26 2/8	27	M	Nunivak Island, Alaska	Sam C. Arnett, III	Sam C. Arnett, III	1976	32
105 4/8	25 7/8	25 7/8	8 2/8	8 3/8	5	4 6/8	26 6/8	27	M	Nunivak Island, Alaska	Robert E. Speegle	Robert E. Speegle	1976	32
105 4/8	26	25 7/8	8 1/8	8 1/8	5 2/8	5	25 1/8	26 3/8	M	Nunivak Island, Alaska	Jean Louis L'Ecuyer	Jean Louis L'Ecuyer	1978	32
105 4/8	25 4/8	25 4/8	8 1/8	8 2/8	5 2/8	5 1/8	24 4/8	25 6/8	M	Nunivak Island, Alaska	Curtis S. Williams	Curtis S. Williams	1978	32
105 4/8	25 4/8	25 3/8	8 7/8	9 1/8	4 6/8	4 6/8	27	28	M	Nunivak Island, Alaska	Roland Stickney	Roland Stickney	1979	32
105 2/8	25 5/8	26	7 5/8	7 4/8	5 3/8	5 3/8	26 7/8	27 5/8	M	Nunivak Island, Alaska	G. A. Treschow	G. A. Treschow	1978	37
105 2/8	26 1/8	25 3/8	8 2/8	8 1/8	6	5 4/8	24	25 6/8	M	Nunivak Island, Alaska	F. Phillips Williamson	F. Phillips Williamson	1978	37
105	26 5/8	25 3/8	8 3/8	8 7/8	4 7/8	4 7/8	23 4/8	24 4/8	M	Hudson Bay, N. W. T.	Indian	N. K. Luxton	1905	39
105	26	26 6/8	8 7/8	8 2/8	4 7/8	-4 7/8	26 1/8	26 7/8	M	Nunivak Island, Alaska	Carlo Bonomi	Carlo Bonomi	1976	39
105	26 2/8	27 5/8	8 5/8	8 3/8	4 3/8	4 5/8	26	27 5/8	M	Bering Sea, Alaska	Jack M. Holland, Jr.	Jack M. Holland, Jr.	1977	39
105	25 7/8	25 4/8	8 4/8	9	4 6/8	4 6/8	27	27 7/8	M	Nunivak Island, Alaska	Dan H. Brainard	Dan H. Brainard	1977	39
105	24 7/8	25 6/8	9 1/8	8 4/8	5 1/8	5 4/8	24	24 6/8	M	Cambridge Bay, N.W.T.	Unknown	Manfred Huellbusch	PR1979	39
104 6/8	24 7/8	24 4/8	9	8 5/8	5 3/8	5 6/8	24 7/8	26	M	Ellsmere Is., N. W. T.	Hugh H. Logan	Los Angeles Co. Mus.	1960	44
104 6/8	31 1/8	29 4/8	8 4/8	8 2/8	4 2/8	3 7/8	25 2/8	25 2/8	M	Nunivak Island, Alaska	Jerry D. Mercer	Jerry D. Mercer	1975	44
104 6/8	28 3/8	26 3/8	8 3/8	8 2/8	5 6/8	4 6/8	25 1/8	25 6/8	M	Nunivak Island, Alaska	Wilson W. Crook Jr.	Wilson W. Crook, Jr.	1976	44
104 6/8	24 1/8	24 6/8	8 4/8	8 2/8	5 5/8	6 2/8	25 3/8	25 6/8	M	Nunivak Island, Alaska	Milton N. Stevens	Milton N. Stevens	1977	44
104 6/8	23 2/8	24 1/8	8	7 6/8	6 4/8	6 4/8	26 3/8	26 3/8	M	Nunivak Island, Alaska	Joseph J. Cafmeyer	Joseph J. Cafmeyer	1977	44
104 2/8	26	26 5/8	8 5/8	8 3/8	4 3/8	4 6/8	26 5/8	27 5/8	M	Nunivak Island, Alaska	Donald A. Stone	Donald A. Stone	1976	49
103 6/8	25 2/8	25 1/8	8 2/8	8 3/8	5 1/8	5 1/8	25 4/8	26 1/8	M	Nunivak Island, Alaska	Richard F. Davis	Richard F. Davis	1976	50
103 6/8	25 7/8	25 4/8	8 4/8	8 3/8	4 6/8	4 6/8	26 2/8	27 6/8	M	Nunivak Island, Alaska	Donald K. Kremer	Donald K. Kremer	1976	50
103 6/8	25 4/8	26 1/8	9 5/8	9 4/8	4 2/8	5 1/8	24 5/8	26 6/8	M	Pr. Wales Is., N.W.T.	Picked Up	Alan Kennedy	1977	50
103 6/8	25	25 4/8	8 3/8	8 4/8	4 6/8	5 1/8	24 7/8	25 5/8	M	Nunivak Island, Alaska	Maurice Ireland	Maurice Ireland	1979	50
103 4/8	24 6/8	24	9	9 1/8	5 7/8	5 2/8	27	27	M	Nunivak Island, Alaska	Dick Ullery	Dick Ullery	1976	54
103 4/8	25	24 6/8	8 4/8	8 4/8	5 2/8	4 4/8	23 4/8	24 5/8	M	Nunivak Island, Alaska	Beverly Stevens	Beverly Stevens	1977	54
103 4/8	24 4/8	24	8 6/8	8 6/8	5	5 1/8	27	27 4/8	M	Nunivak Island, Alaska	Ricardo Medem	Ricardo Medem	1977	54
103 2/8	24 1/8	23 4/8	9 7/8	9 6/8	5 1/8	5 1/8	24 6/8	25 5/8	M	Unknown	Unknown	Samuel B. Webb	—	57
103	26 6/8	26 2/8	8 4/8	8 5/8	5	4 6/8	22 2/8	23 7/8	M	Greenland	R. E. Peary	Am. Mus. Nat. History	1909	58
103	25 2/8	25 6/8	7 6/8	7 6/8	4 5/8	5	24 3/8	26 3/8	M	Nunivak Island, Alaska	G.L. Rusty Gibbons	G.L. Rusty Gibbons	1977	58
102 6/8	25 7/8	25 3/8	7 7/8	8 2/8	5 2/8	5	26 4/8	26 7/8	M	Grant Land, Greenland	R. E. Peary	Am. Mus. Nat. History	1909	60
102 6/8	25 4/8	25 2/8	9 1/8	10	5 2/8	5 4/8	29 6/8	31 1/8	M	Bathhurst Inlet, N. W. T.	David E. Wheeler	Everett P. Wheeler	1913	60
102 6/8	26 5/8	25 2/8	8	8 1/8	6	5	27 2/8	27 5/8	M	Nunivak Island, Alaska	Mitch Wagner	Mitch Wagner	1976	60
102 6/8	23	25	9 1/8	8 5/8	6 1/8	5 7/8	25 5/8	26 4/8	M	Nunivak Island, Alaska	Rudolf Sand	Rudolf Sand	1976	60
102 6/8	25 6/8	25 2/8	8	8 2/8	5	4 5/8	28 7/8	29 1/8	M	Nunivak Island, Alaska	C. J. McElroy	C. J. McElroy	1977	60
102 2/8	24 3/8	24 5/8	9 2/8	9 3/8	4 6/8	5	26 1/8	26 3/8	M	Hudson Bay, N. W. T.	George E. Comer	Am. Mus. Nat. History	1902	65
102	25 3/8	27 5/8	9 2/8	8 6/8	3 7/8	5 5/8	26 1/8	26 3/8	M	Ellsemere Is., N. W. T.	Elijah Nutara	Archie Knill	1971	66
102	24 2/8	25 6/8	8 4/8	8 4/8	5 3/8	5 3/8	26 3/8	27 3/8	U	Unknown	Unknown	Larry W. Lander	PR1972	66
102	28 3/8	27 3/8	8	7 7/8	4 2/8	4	24 2/8	25 7/8	M	Nunivak Island, Alaska	Gerald L. Warnock	Gerald L. Warnock	1976	66

MUSKOX–*Continued*

Ovibos moschatus moschatus and certain related subspecies

Score	Length of Horn R.	Length of Horn L.	Width of Boss R.	Width of Boss L.	Circumference at Third Quarter R.	Circumference at Third Quarter L.	Tip to Tip Spread	Greatest Spread	Sex	Locality Killed	By Whom Killed	Owner	Date Killed	Rank
102	23 5/8	25 2/8	8 6/8	8 3/8	5 3/8	5 1/8	24 3/8	25	M	Nunivak Island, Alaska	Manfred O. Schroeder	Manfred O. Schroeder	1977	66
102	28 5/8	28 1/8	7 5/8	7 2/8	4 3/8	4 5/8	24 2/8	26	M	Nunivak Island, Alaska	A. A. Samuels, Jr.	A. A. Samuels, Jr.	1979	66
101 4/8	25 6/8	24 5/8	8 5/8	8 6/8	5 5/8	4 3/8	26 4/8	27 4/8	M	Nunivak Island, Alaska	Robert Chisholm	Robert Chisholm	1977	71
101 4/8	24 7/8	24 5/8	8 2/8	8 5/8	4 6/8	4 4/8	25	26 7/8	M	Nunivak Island, Alaska	Daniel B. Moore	Daniel B. Moore	1977	71
101 4/8	24 5/8	25 5/8	8 4/8	8 1/8	4 5/8	4 7/8	25 1/8	26 6/8	M	Nunivak Island, Alaska	Denny Pilling	Denny Pilling	1978	71
101 2/8	26 6/8	27 1/8	6 3/8	6 7/8	5 5/8	4 7/8	25 4/8	27 4/8	M	Barren Grounds, N. W. T.	Warburton Pike	National Collection	1889	74
101 2/8	24 4/8	24 7/8	9 1/8	9 1/8	4 5/8	4 7/8	27 4/8	27 7/8	M	Hudson Bay, N. W. T.	George Comer	Am. Mus. Nat. History	1902	74
101 2/8	25 1/8	25 5/8	8 2/8	7 6/8	4 4/8	4 6/8	25 6/8	27 1/8	M	Nunivak Island, Alaska	Cecil M. Hopper	Cecil M. Hopper	1977	74
101 2/8	25 1/8	23 1/8	8	8	5 4/8	5 2/8	26 2/8	26 5/8	M	Nunivak Island, Alaska	William Koller	William Koller	1977	74
101 2/8	25	25 6/8	8 2/8	7 7/8	4 3/8	4 5/8	28 5/8	29	M	Nunivak Island, Alaska	James A. Bush, Jr.	James A. Bush, Jr.	1978	74
101	22 1/8	23 1/8	8 2/8	8 2/8	5 7/8	5 7/8	25 2/8	25 6/8	M	Nunivak Island, Alaska	Gene D. Klineburger	Gene D. Klineburger	1975	79
100 7/8	24 2/8	24 1/8	9 2/8	8 7/8	4 6/8	4 2/8	28	28 4/8	M	Nunivak Island, Alaska	Unknown	Univ. Calif. Mus.	1952	80
100 6/8	25 1/8	25 6/8	8 3/8	8	4 2/8	4 5/8	26	27 1/8	M	Nunivak Island, Alaska	Kenneth Campbell	Kenneth Campbell	1975	80
100 6/8	23 2/8	25 4/8	9 1/8	9 1/8	5	5 1/8	26 6/8	26 6/8	M	Nunivak Island, Alaska	Henry Brockhouse	Henry Brockhouse	1976	80
100 6/8	23 5/8	23 5/8	8 1/8	8 1/8	5 1/8	5 2/8	25	25 6/8	M	Nunivak Island, Alaska	Arthur LaCapria	Arthur LaCapria	1976	80
100 4/8	22 6/8	24 1/8	8 2/8	8 3/8	5 1/8	5 6/8	26 5/8	27 1/8	M	Nunivak Island, Alaska	Unknown	Iran Game & Fish Dept.	1967	84
100 4/8	23 7/8	24	7 7/8	8	5	5 1/8	24 3/8	26 2/8	M	Nunivak Island, Alaska	W. T. Yoshimoto	W. T. Yoshimoto	1976	84
100 4/8	24 1/8	24 5/8	8 3/8	8 2/8	4 4/8	4 4/8	22 6/8	25 7/8	M	Nunivak Island, Alaska	William A. Bond	William A. Bond	1976	84
100 2/8	22 6/8	23 6/8	8 5/8	8 4/8	5 1/8	5	23 7/8	25 1/8	U	Pr. Patrick Is., N. W. T.	Picked Up	William P. Hampton	——	87
100	23 2/8	25 3/8	10 5/8	9 4/8	4	4 7/8	26	26 2/8	M	Nunivak Island, Alaska	Marion L. Connerly	Marion L. Connerly	1976	88
99 6/8	26 4/8	27 1/8	8 1/8	7 7/8	4 5/8	5	24 1/8	25	U	Greenland	Eskimo	Charles T. Arnold	1959	89
99 6/8	24 5/8	26 2/8	7 7/8	8	4 2/8	5 1/8	25 6/8	26 4/8	M	Nunivak Island, Alaska	J. W. Lawson	J. W. Lawson	1977	89
99 6/8	24 4/8	25 1/8	8 2/8	8	4 4/8	4 5/8	25 3/8	27 1/8	M	Nunivak Island, Alaska	Ronald H. Stover	Ronald H. Stover	1977	89
99 4/8	24 4/8	23 4/8	8 1/8	8 1/8	6	4 6/8	27	27	M	Nunivak Island, Alaska	Ray Tremblay	Univ. Alaska Mus.	1959	92
99	27 2/8	26	7	7	4 6/8	5	23 2/8	25	U	Greenland	Unknown	Harvard Univ. Mus.	——	93
99	24 7/8	25 5/8	7 4/8	7 4/8	4 4/8	4 5/8	28	28 3/8	M	Nunivak Island, Alaska	Richard H. Leedy	Richard H. Leedy	1976	93
99	25 1/8	24	8 4/8	8 5/8	4 7/8	4 1/8	24 7/8	25 6/8	M	Nunivak Island, Alaska	Lowell Hansen, II	Lowell Hansen, II	1978	93
99	24 5/8	25 2/8	8	8	4 2/8	4 3/8	25 1/8	26 6/8	M	Nunivak Island, Alaska	R. W. Howe	R. W. Howe	1979	93
98 6/8	24 2/8	24 3/8	7 6/8	7 6/8	4 6/8	4 7/8	24 4/8	22 6/8	M	Hudson Land, Greenland	Arthur D. Norcross	Arthur D. Norcross	1931	97

98 6/8	24 3/8	24	7 5/8	7 4/8	4 7/8	5 1/8	25 5/8	26 3/8	M	Greenland	U. M. Hansen	Zool. Mus., Copenhagen	1947	97
98 6/8	23 1/8	22 2/8	8 1/8	8 1/8	5 3/8	5	26	26 3/8	M	Nunivak Island, Alaska	Warren K. Parker	Warren K. Parker	1978	97
98 6/8	24 5/8	23 6/8	8	8 1/8	5 6/8	4 6/8	26 7/8	27 6/8	M	Nunivak Island, Alaska	Ronald Cunningham	Ronald Cunningham	1978	97
98 4/8	24 2/8	24 2/8	7 1/8	7 3/8	4 6/8	5	26 4/8	27 1/8	M	Ellsemere Is., N. W. T.	Harry Whitney	National Collection	1909	101
98 4/8	22 6/8	23 3/8	7 6/8	7 4/8	5 3/8	5 3/8	24 7/8	25 1/8	M	Nunivak Island, Alaska	Valentin Madariaga	Valentin Madariaga	1976	101
98 4/8	21 6/8	24 1/8	8 7/8	8 6/8	5 1/8	6	27 3/8	27 7/8	M	Nunivak Island, Alaska	John L. Estes	John L. Estes	1976	101
98 4/8	25 3/8	24 1/8	8 5/8	8 5/8	4 5/8	4	26 2/8	27 2/8	M	Nunivak Island, Alaska	H. I. H. Prince Abdorreza Pahlavi	H. I. H. Prince Abdorreza Pahlavi	1976	101
98 4/8	23 5/8	25 4/8	8 1/8	8 1/8	4 7/8	4 7/8	26 1/8	26 2/8	M	Nunivak Island, Alaska	Lawrence B. Harbison	Lawrence B. Harbison	1976	101
98 2/8	24	26	8	7 6/8	4 7/8	5 7/8	26	26 6/8	M	Greenland	Unknown	Zool. Mus., Copenhagen	1926	106
98 2/8	24 4/8	23 6/8	7 6/8	8	5 1/8	4 5/8	22 7/8	24 2/8	M	Hudson Land, Greenland	Arthur D. Norcross	Arthur D. Norcross	1931	106
98	24 6/8	24 1/8	7 5/8	7 5/8	4 5/8	4 5/8	22 7/8	24 7/8	M	Greenland	Harry Whitney	Acad. Nat. Sci., Phil.	1930	108
98	25	27 1/8	7 5/8	7 4/8	5	4 4/8	24 1/8	25 3/8	U	Greenland	Finn Kristoffersen	Finn Kristoffersen	1940	108
98	24 1/8	26 1/8	8 1/8	8	4 5/8	5 4/8	24 4/8	25 4/8	M	Axel Heiberg Is., N. W. T.	Picked Up	Bryan Robertson	1961	108
98	22 2/8	23 5/8	8 2/8	8 1/8	4 7/8	5 5/8	25 4/8	25 7/8	M	Nunivak Island, Alaska	Picked Up	Steve C. Leirer	1977	108
97 6/8	23 5/8	25 6/8	8 3/8	7 7/8	4 6/8	4 4/8	26 1/8	26 2/8	U	Black Fox Creek, Yukon	Picked Up	David M. Twamley	1973	112
97 6/8	23	24 1/8	8 3/8	8	4 5/8	5 3/8	25 4/8	25 7/8	M	Nunivak Island, Alaska	Steve C. Leirer	Steve C. Leirer	1977	112
97 4/8	23 6/8	25 1/8	8 1/8	7 6/8	4 4/8	5	23 5/8	24 2/8	M	Unknown	Unknown	Camp Fire Club	—	114
97 4/8	25 2/8	25 6/8	7 5/8	7 4/8	4 1/8	4 6/8	25 6/8	26 7/8	M	Grant Land, Greenland	R. E. Peary	Am. Mus. Nat. History	1906	114
97 2/8	25 5/8	24 5/8	7 3/8	7 4/8	5 1/8	4 3/8	28 6/8	28 6/8	M	Greenland	Unknown	Zool. Mus., Copenhagen	—	116
97	22 7/8	24 7/8	9	9 2/8	4 3/8	4 6/8	23 7/8	24 3/8	U	Nunivak Island, Alaska	Picked Up	Darrell D. McCullaugh	1962	117
97	26 1/8	24 1/8	8 2/8	8 4/8	4 7/8	4 1/8	27 3/8	28 3/8	M	Nunivak Island, Alaska	Norman W. Garwood	Norman W. Garwood	1977	117
96 4/8	23 6/8	22 4/8	8 4/8	8 6/8	5 4/8	4 2/8	25 4/8	25 5/8	M	Barren Grounds, N. W. T.	Picked Up	James P. Borman	—	119
96 4/8	25	23 4/8	7 7/8	8	4 7/8	4 7/8	23 5/8	24 7/8	M	Clavering Is., Greenland	Harry Whitney	Acad. Nat. Sci., Phil.	1930	119
96 4/8	24 3/8	25 3/8	8 1/8	8	4	4 6/8	25 6/8	25 6/8	M	Shannon Island, Greenland	Arthur D. Norcross	Arthur D. Norcross	1931	119
96 2/8	24 5/8	24 5/8	7	6 6/8	4 7/8	5 4/8	26 3/8	27	M	Greenland	Ryder	Zool. Mus., Copenhagen	1892	122
96 2/8	24 6/8	22 7/8	9 5/8	9 5/8	4 5/8	3 6/8	25 5/8	22 7/8	M	Melville Island, N.W.T.	Picked Up	M. G. Sullivan	1977	122
96	23 6/8	24 2/8	7 6/8	7 7/8	4 6/8	5	26 5/8	27	M	Axel Heiberg Is., N. W. T.	Brian F. Glenister	Brian F. Glenister	1955	124
96	25	25 6/8	7 1/8	7 3/8	4	4 2/8	24 5/8	25 4/8	M	Nunivak Island, Alaska	Larry G. Dunn	Larry G. Dunn	1977	124
95 6/8	23 6/8	25 3/8	8 6/8	9 1/8	4	4 3/8	27 4/8	27 7/8	M	Hudson Bay, N. W. T.	George Comer	National Collection	1909	126
95 6/8	23 1/8	23 4/8	7 6/8	7 6/8	4 4/8	4 6/8	25	26 4/8	M	Nunivak Island, Alaska	Herman A. Lawrence	Herman A. Lawrence	1976	126
95 4/8	23 7/8	26	8 2/8	8	3 6/8	4 7/8	25	26 1/8	M	Nunivak Island, Alaska	James E. Conklin	James E. Conklin	1979	128
95	23 3/8	24 4/8	8 6/8	8 4/8	4 2/8	5 7/8	24 3/8	24 6/8	U	Unknown	Unknown	Loren Lutz	—	129
94 4/8	23 2/8	24	7 5/8	7 4/8	4 3/8	5	25 2/8	26 5/8	M	Hudson Land, Greenland	Arthur D. Norcross	Arthur D. Norcross	1931	130
94 4/8	23	23 6/8	8	7 5/8	4 3/8	5 4/8	24 3/8	25	M	Greenland	W. S. Webb, Jr.	J. Watson Webb	1932	130

MUSKOX—Continued
Ovibos moschatus moschatus and certain related subspecies

Score	Length of Horn R.	L.	Width of Boss R.	L.	Circumference at Third Quarter R.	L.	Tip to Tip Spread	Greatest Spread	Sex	Locality Killed	By Whom Killed	Owner	Date Killed	Rank
94⁴/₈	23⁵/₈	24⁴/₈	6⁴/₈	6⁴/₈	4³/₈	4³/₈	25⁵/₈	26⁴/₈	M	Nunivak Island, Alaska	C. Vernon Humble	C. Vernon Humble	1976	130
93³/₈	23⁷/₈	24⁵/₈	7⁵/₈	7⁷/₈	3⁷/₈	4⁶/₈	22⁴/₈	24⁴/₈	M	Greenland	Unknown	Jules V. Lane	—	133
93³/₈	23³/₈	23¹/₈	6⁶/₈	7¹/₈	4⁶/₈	4⁵/₈	20⁷/₈	22⁶/₈	U	Greenland	Joern Ladegaard	Joern Ladegaard	1975	133
92⁶/₈	24²/₈	25	7⁵/₈	7²/₈	4	5	22⁴/₈	24²/₈	M	Greenland	Harry Whitney	Acad. Nat. Sci., Phil.	1930	135
92⁴/₈	23³/₈	22⁷/₈	7⁴/₈	7⁵/₈	4⁵/₈	4⁴/₈	22²/₈	23⁵/₈	M	Unknown	A. Brock	Acad. Nat. Sci., Phil.	—	136
92	23¹/₈	24⁴/₈	7⁷/₈	7²/₈	4¹/₈	4⁶/₈	25⁴/₈	26	M	Nunivak Island, Alaska	Terry Yager	Terry Yager	1976	137
91⁶/₈	23⁴/₈	24⁴/₈	7⁷/₈	7⁵/₈	4⁴/₈	4⁴/₈	21³/₈	22⁵/₈	M	Greenland	W. T. Hornaday	E. H. Herrick	—	138
90	21⁷/₈	21⁷/₈	6⁷/₈	7¹/₈	4⁴/₈	4⁴/₈	24	24²/₈	M	Greenland	Herb Klein	Herb Klein	1947	139

*Final Score subject to revision by additional verifying measurements.

WORLD'S RECORD BIGHORN SHEEP
SCORE: 208 1/8
Locality: Blind Canyon, Alberta. Date: 1911.
Hunter: Fred Weiller. Owner: Clarence Baird

NUMBER TWO BIGHORN SHEEP
SCORE: 207 2/8
Locality: Oyster Creek, Alberta. Date: 1924.
Hunter and owner: Martin Bovey.

Bighorn Sheep

Minimum Score 180

Ovis canadensis canadensis and certain related subspecies

Score	Length of Horn R.	Length of Horn L.	Circumference of Base R.	Circumference of Base L.	Circumference at Third Quarter R.	Circumference at Third Quarter L.	Greatest Spread	Tip to Tip Spread	Locality Killed	By Whom Killed	Owner	Date Killed	Rank
208 1/8	44 7/8	45	16 5/8	16 5/8	11 2/8	11 7/8	22 6/8	19 3/8	Blind Canyon, Alta.	Fred Weiller	Clarence Baird	1911	1
207 2/8	45	45 2/8	15 6/8	16	11 6/8	11 7/8	23 1/8	19 3/8	Oyster Creek, Alta.	Martin Bovey	Martin Bovey	1924	2
206 3/8	44 4/8	44 3/8	15 7/8	15 7/8	12 1/8	12 1/8	21 4/8	21 4/8	Burnt Timber Creek, Alta.	Picked Up	Roy C. Stahl	1955	3
204	49 4/8	48 2/8	15 2/8	15 3/8	10 5/8	10 2/8	23 7/8	23 7/8	Sheep Creek, B. C.	James Simpson	Am. Mus. Nat. History	1920	4
202 2/8	46 7/8	44 5/8	15 5/8	15 2/8	11	10 6/8	23 2/8	23 2/8	Panther River, Alta.	Tom Kerquits	National Collection	1918	5
201 1/8	44	43 7/8	15 5/8	15 5/8	11 3/8	11 4/8	25	25	Jasper, Alta.	Picked Up	A. H. Hilbert	1932	6
200 7/8	43 6/8	43 3/8	16 5/8	16 7/8	9	9 2/8	22 5/8	20 3/8	Fernie, B. C.	H. J. Johnson	Royal Ont. Mus.	1902	7
200 1/8	44 3/8	44	15 1/8	15 2/8	11 6/8	11 3/8	23	23	Brazeau River, Alta.	Unknown	Norman L. Lougheed	1937	8
200 1/8	40 4/8	41 3/8	16 3/8	16 3/8	11 3/8	11 3/8	22 2/8	18 5/8	Alta.	Picked Up	Otis Chandler	1955	8
200	40 6/8	41 6/8	16 4/8	16 3/8	11 2/8	11 2/8	22	19 6/8	Wind River Range, Wyo.	Crawford	Duncan Weibel	1883	10
199	45	45 4/8	15 1/8	15	10 3/8	10 6/8	22 5/8	22 5/8	Spence's Bridge, B. C.	Picked Up	Parliament Bldg., B. C	1969	11
198 6/8	43 4/8	43 6/8	15 4/8	15 4/8	10 7/8	11 3/8	24 6/8	24 6/8	Alta.	Bill Foster	Foster's Bighorn Rest.	——	12
198 1/8	42 4/8	41 3/8	15 6/8	15 6/8	12	11 3/8	23 3/8	23 3/8	Sask. Lake, Alta.	Herb Klein	Herb Klein	1965	13
197 5/8	44 7/8	43 4/8	14 6/8	14 6/8	10 6/8	11 1/8	23 4/8	18 3/8	Alta.	Bill Foster	Foster's Bighorn Rest.	——	14
197 2/8	39 1/8	42 3/8	17	17	9 5/8	9 6/8	23 4/8	20	E. Kootenay, B. C.	Picked Up	Victoria Fish & Game Assn.	PR1930	15
196 7/8	41 1/8	40 4/8	17 4/8	17 3/8	10	9 7/8	23 2/8	18 1/8	Yarrow Creek, Alta.	George W. Biron	George W. Biron	1968	16
196 6/8	41 2/8	40 4/8	16 4/8	16 4/8	9 7/8	10 1/8	22 6/8	19 4/8	Badlands, N. D.	Howard Eaton	Richard K. Mellon	1880	17
196 6/8	45 2/8	44 2/8	16 1/8	15 7/8	9 3/8	8 7/8	23	23	Wardner, B. C.	Jim Buss	Jim Buss	1961	17
196 5/8	41 5/8	42	16 2/8	16 1/8	10 6/8	10 7/8	22 2/8	20	Brazeau River, Alta.	Donald S. Hopkins	Donald S. Hopkins	1924	19
196 5/8	39 5/8	41 6/8	16	16	10 5/8	11 4/8	21 2/8	19 1/8	Alta.	Bill Foster	Foster's Bighorn Rest.	1938	19
196 5/8	45 2/8	44 3/8	14 5/8	14 6/8	10 4/8	10 4/8	24 5/8	24 4/8	Sun River, Mont.	Don Anderson	Don Anderson	1961	19
196 2/8	42 4/8	42 4/8	16 2/8	16 2/8	10	9 5/8	21 6/8	16 5/8	Highwood, Alta.	Joseph F. Kubasek	Joseph F. Kubasek	1953	22
196	44 7/8	44 3/8	15	15	10 3/8	10 1/8	24 5/8	24 5/8	Cadomin, Alta.	Al Leary	Al Leary	1962	23
195 7/8	45 4/8	44 3/8	15 5/8	15 6/8	9 2/8	8 6/8	24	24	Mont.	Unknown	Dole & Bailey, Inc.	1890	24
195 5/8	41 5/8	40 2/8	16 3/8	16 5/8	11 3/8	10 4/8	22 2/8	18 6/8	Castle River, Alta.	R. E. Woodward	R. E. Woodward	1965	24
195 4/8	43	43 6/8	14 5/8	14 7/8	11 1/8	11	23	19 4/8	Bow River, Alta.	Indian	N. K. Luxton	1890	26
195 3/8	42 3/8	42 4/8	15 7/8	15 6/8	10 1/8	10 4/8	22 2/8	20 7/8	West Sundre, Alta.	Jim Neeser	Jim Neeser	1961	27
195	44 2/8	38 4/8	15 5/8	16	11	11 6/8	26 7/8	26 7/8	Sun River, Mont.	Gold White	Lee M. Ford	1911	28
194 7/8	42 4/8	42 5/8	15 4/8	15	11 1/8	11 2/8	23 5/8	19 6/8	Ram River, Alta.	G. M. De Witt	G. M. De Witt	1944	29
194 6/8	42	41 6/8	15 1/8	15 3/8	10 5/8	10 7/8	20 3/8	20	Storm Mt., Alta.	Bryan M. Watts	Bryan M. Watts	1957	30
194 3/8	40 4/8	41 3/8	15 7/8	15 7/8	10 6/8	10 4/8	22 2/8	17 4/8	Sheep River, Alta.	Picked Up	Harry McElroy	1966	31

Bighorn Sheep–*Continued*

Ovis canadensis canadensis and certain related subspecies

Score	Length of Horn R.	Length of Horn L.	Circumference of Base R.	Circumference of Base L.	Circumference at Third Quarter R.	Circumference at Third Quarter L.	Greatest Spread	Tip to Tip Spread	Locality Killed	By Whom Killed	Owner	Date Killed	Rank
194 2/8	45 2/8	44	15	14 7/8	9 7/8	9 4/8	21 4/8	21 4/8	Panther River, Alta.	Picked Up	N. K. Luxton	1930	32
194	44	42 6/8	14 4/8	14 4/8	10 6/8	10 6/8	22 3/8	21 2/8	Alta.	Bill Foster	Foster's Bighorn Rest.	——	33
193 6/8	39 4/8	42 4/8	16 2/8	16 3/8	9 3/8	9 4/8	22 1/8	16 7/8	Yarrow Creek, Alta.	F. H. Riggall	F. H. Riggall	1906	34
193 6/8	41	42	16	16	10 5/8	10 2/8	24	18 1/8	Cameron Pass, Colo.	F. Cotter	Herbert J. Havemann	1954	34
193 6/8	40 5/8	40 5/8	15 4/8	15 4/8	10 6/8	10 6/8	22 1/8	17 4/8	Tornado Pass, B. C.	John Stuber	John Stuber	1956	34
193 4/8	44 5/8	42 4/8	15 1/8	15 2/8	9 7/8	10 1/8	21 7/8	21 7/8	Spence's Bridge, B. C.	M. Da Rosa	M. Da Rosa	1961	37
193 3/8	42 1/8	40 4/8	15 5/8	15 7/8	10 2/8	10	22 3/8	17 1/8	Coleman, Alta.	George Hagglund	George Hagglund	1952	38
193	43 1/8	43 5/8	14 6/8	14 6/8	10 1/8	9 7/8	22 1/8	22 1/8	Spence's Bridge, B. C.	Norman Holland	Norman Holland	1971	39
192 6/8	44 6/8	43 2/8	14 2/8	14 2/8	10 7/8	11 1/8	22 1/8	22 1/8	Clearwater, Alta.	Edward L. Fuchs	Edward L. Fuchs	1943	40
192 5/8	42 7/8	44 2/8	14 3/8	14 2/8	10 6/8	10 3/8	24	24	Sun River, Mont.	Unknown	Robert E. Gabbert	——	41
192 5/8	39 5/8	40 2/8	15 4/8	15 6/8	11 4/8	11 4/8	21 2/8	17 4/8	Clearwater River, Alta.	James Allan	James Allan	1977	41
192 3/8	40 7/8	40 2/8	15 6/8	15 4/8	10 5/8	11 3/8	22 7/8	18 4/8	Alta.	Henry Graves, Jr.	National Collection	PR1931	43
192 2/8	45 2/8	43	16	15 6/8	8 3/8	8 3/8	21	21	Sanders Co., Mont.	Richard W. Browne	Richard W. Browne	1968	44
192 2/8	40 5/8	40 5/8	16 7/8	16 7/8	8 6/8	9 2/8	22	17 6/8	Sanders Co., Mont.	Michael A. Jorgenson	Michael A. Jorgenson	1978	44
192	41 6/8	42 4/8	15 1/8	15	10	10 3/8	21 5/8	20 1/8	Narrow Creek, Alta.	Henry Mitchell	Henry Mitchell	1910	46
191 7/8	40 4/8	41 1/8	15	15	11 1/8	11 6/8	23 3/8	21 4/8	Colo.	Emory Whilton	Kern Co. (Calif.) Mus.	1901	47
191 7/8	44	41 7/8	15 3/8	15 3/8	9 6/8	8 7/8	24 4/8	22 2/8	Wild Horse Is., Mont.	Picked Up	Univ. Mont. Mus.	1961	47
191 6/8	40	42 2/8	15 6/8	15 5/8	9 7/8	10 3/8	23 3/8	22 6/8	Smoky River, Alta.	Picked Up	Carl M. Borgh	1944	49
191 5/8	40 2/8	40 3/8	15 6/8	15 6/8	10 2/8	10 1/8	22 1/8	15	Dinwoody Creek, Wyo.	Oris Miller	Oris Miller	1954	50
191 4/8	42 4/8	41 4/8	14 6/8	15	10 2/8	9 7/8	22 6/8	22 3/8	Lincoln Co., Mont.	Picked Up	Ed Boyes	——	51
191 3/8	40 7/8	42 4/8	15	14 7/8	10 5/8	10 5/8	22 1/8	20 7/8	Canada	Unknown	A. H. Hilbert	PR1930	52
191 3/8	42 3/8	40	14 6/8	14 7/8	10 4/8	10 7/8	21 4/8	15 2/8	Natal, B. C.	John A. Morais	John A. Morais	1960	52
191 2/8	45 6/8	44 2/8	15 2/8	15 2/8	7 7/8	8 4/8	24 5/8	24 5/8	Grassmere, B. C.	Donald F. Letcher	Donald F. Letcher	1965	54
191 1/8	39 3/8	39 2/8	15 1/8	15 4/8	11 1/8	10 7/8	22	18 3/8	Castle River, Alta.	Picked Up	E. B. Cunningham	——	55
191 1/8	40 1/8	42	15 2/8	15 3/8	10	9 6/8	19 6/8	19 6/8	Cadomin, Alta.	Frank Nuspel	Frank Nuspel	1962	55
191	40 4/8	39	15 3/8	15 4/8	11	11	22 5/8	18	Kvass Creek, Alta.	Joseph W. Dent	Joseph W. Dent	1962	57
191	39 6/8	38 1/8	16 1/8	16 1/8	11 1/8	10 5/8	20	18 3/8	Cadomin, Alta.	Tony Oney	Tony Oney	1966	57
191	42 1/8	43 1/8	14 2/8	14 4/8	10 5/8	11	22 5/8	19 1/8	Prospect Creek, Alta.	Kenneth Campbell	Kenneth Campbell	1971	57
190 6/8	42 4/8	44 4/8	14 7/8	15	9 1/8	9 2/8	23 3/8	23 3/8	Fernie, B. C.	J. J. Osman	J. J. Osman	1950	60
190 6/8	37 1/8	37 5/8	16 7/8	16 7/8	11 1/8	11	22	15 4/8	Elko, B. C.	Charles Weikert	Charles Weikert	1970	60
190 5/8	41 5/8	39 4/8	17	16 7/8	8 6/8	9	23 4/8	16 7/8	Brazeau River, Alta.	Julio Estrada	Julio Estrada	1936	62
190 3/8	46 3/8	40	15 1/8	15 1/8	8 4/8	8 3/8	22 6/8	22 6/8	Highwood, Alta.	Nick Sekella	Nick Sekella	1953	63

Score							Locality	By whom killed	Owner	Date	Rank
190 3/8	39 7/8	39 7/8	16	16	10 6/8	10 6/8	21 7/8	Sun River, Mont.	F. P. Murray	F. P. Murray	1957	63
190	39 6/8	39 6/8	15 7/8	15 7/8	10 5/8	10 5/8	22 1/8	Alta.	Stony Indian	Acad. Nat. Sci., Phil.	1901	65
190	40 7/8	39 7/8	15 1/8	15 2/8	10 5/8	10 5/8	19 1/8	Brazeau River, Alta.	Donald S. Hopkins	Acad. Nat. Sci., Phil.	1927	65
189 7/8	39 7/8	39 1/8	16	16 2/8	10 3/8	10 3/8	21 5/8	Clearwater Forest, Alta.	George Bugbee	Sally Bugbee	1928	67
189 7/8	41 1/8	40 4/8	15 5/8	15 5/8	9	9 1/8	17 7/8	Ribbon Lake, Alta.	Ovar Uggen	Ovar Uggen	1957	67
189 7/8	40 7/8	40 3/8	15 3/8	15 3/8	9 5/8	9 5/8	20 1/8	Highwood Range, Alta.	Unknown	Earl Johnson	1928	69
189 7/8	40 7/8	40 6/8	15 5/8	15 5/8	9 1/8	9 4/8	14 1/8	Swan Lake, B. C.	Billy Stork	A. C. Gilbert	1936	69
189 7/8	40 1/8	40 1/8	16	16	9 4/8	9 4/8	20 5/8	Yarrow Creek, Alta.	Allan Foster	Allan Foster	1963	71
189 7/8	40 7/8	40 4/8	14 5/8	14 7/8	9 3/8	9 3/8	21	Park Co., Wyo.	Picked Up	Dale McWilliams	1975	72
189 7/8	39 7/8	39 3/8	16	16	11 5/8	11 5/8	19 3/8	Nikanassin Range, Alta.	Colleen Bodenchuk	Colleen Bodenchuk	1976	72
189 7/8	41 7/8	41 3/8	14 4/8	14 4/8	9 6/8	9 7/8	17 5/8	Panther River, Alta.	Picked Up	George Browne	1928	74
189 3/8	40 3/8	41 3/8	14 2/8	14 4/8	11 1/8	11 3/8	22 3/8	Spence's Bridge, B. C.	Bert Walkem	Bert Walkem	1964	74
189 1/8	43	43	14 2/8	14 4/8	9 4/8	10 2/8	20 5/8	Brazeau River, Alta.	Donald S. Hopkins	Donald S. Hopkins	1937	76
189 1/8	42 1/8	42 1/8	15 3/8	15 2/8	10 5/8	10 4/8	22	Canal Flat, B. C.	Robert Lemaster	Robert Lemaster	1962	76
189	39	39	15 5/8	15 5/8	9 7/8	9 7/8	24	Alta.	Bill Foster	Foster's Bighorn Rest.	—	78
189	42	40 5/8	14 7/8	14 7/8	9 6/8	9 7/8	20 6/8	Highwood River, Alta.	Hanson Bearspaw	W. S Armstrong	1917	79
188 7/8	41	41	15 5/8	15 5/8	10 5/8	10 5/8	17 7/8	Alta.	Clarence Hardy	Russel Vanslett	—	80
188 7/8	42 3/8	42 3/8	15 3/8	15 3/8	9 4/8	9 6/8	19 5/8	Bow Valley, Alta.	Picked Up	Joseph Kovach	1928	80
188 7/8	41 1/8	41 1/8	14 6/8	14 6/8	9 6/8	9 6/8	22 4/8	Ram Creek, Alta.	Wm. N Beach	Wm. N. Beach	1962	80
188 7/8	40 1/8	40 1/8	14 6/8	14 5/8	9 7/8	10	25 5/8	Gannet Peak, Wyo.	James Huffman	James Huffman	1965	80
188 5/8	41	41	14 6/8	14 6/8	10 6/8	10 6/8	18	Gallatin Range, Mont.	Alden B. Walrath	Alden B. Walrath	1953	80
188 5/8	41 7/8	44 5/8	15 1/8	15	8 7/8	9	17	Highwood, Alta.	Steve Kubasek	Steve Kubasek	1955	85
188 5/8	38 1/8	38 1/8	17 1/8	17 1/8	8 4/8	8 4/8	23 3/8	Alta.	Bill Foster	Foster's Bighorn Rest.	1936	86
188 3/8	40 1/8	40 1/8	15 5/8	15 5/8	9 4/8	9 6/8	20 5/8	Sun River, Mont.	Bruce McCracken	Bruce McCracken	1977	86
188 1/8	41 1/8	41 1/8	15 5/8	15 5/8	10 5/8	10 5/8	21 3/8	Opal Range, Alta.	Unknown	Norman Lougheed	1978	88
188 1/8	39 1/8	39 3/8	14 5/8	14 5/8	9 1/8	9 1/8	19 6/8	Clearwater, Alta.	Robert Zebedee	Robert Zebedee	1950	88
188 1/8	45 1/8	45 5/8	14 5/8	14 5/8	11	11	27	Rivalli Creek, Mont.	Sandy Rose	Sandy Rose	1950	88
188 1/8	40	40	16 2/8	16 2/8	8 5/8	9 5/8	19 4/8	Surprise Lake, B. C.	Herb Klein	Herb Klein	1959	91
188	40 5/8	40 5/8	15 7/8	15 7/8	9 5/8	10	22 4/8	White Swan Lake, B. C.	A. C. Gilbert	James V. Bosco	1966	91
188	40 5/8	40 5/8	15 5/8	15 4/8	9 2/8	9 2/8	21	Alta.	Arthur Smith	Arthur Smith	1912	91
187 7/8	38	37 7/8	16	16	9 7/8	9 7/8	20 5/8	Burnt Timber Creek, Alta.	Walter O. Ford, Jr.	Walter O. Ford, Jr.	1958	91
187 7/8	39 5/8	39 5/8	15 5/8	15 5/8	9 5/8	9 5/8	15 5/8	Sun River, Mont.	Bruce Neal	Bruce Neal	1961	95
187 7/8	40	40 5/8	15 1/8	15 1/8	9 3/8	9 3/8	19	Sun River, Mont.	J. R. Pfeifer	J. R. Pfeifer	1958	95
187 7/8	40 5/8	40 5/8	15	15	10	10 7/8	21 3/8	Kananaskis, Alta.	Terry Webber	Terry Webber	1963	95
187 7/8	37 5/8	37 7/8	15 5/8	15 7/8	10 6/8	10 7/8	15	Kananaskis River, Alta	C. Allenhof	C. Allenhof	1958	98
187 7/8	40 5/8	40 5/8	14 7/8	15 3/8	10 6/8	10	16 6/8	Kananaskis Summit, Alta.	Ted Howell	Ted Howell	1963	98
187 7/8	39 1/8	39 1/8	15 5/8	15 5/8	10	10	13 5/8	Salmon River, Idaho	Picked Up	Dwight Smith	1951	100
187 7/8	44 5/8	44 2/8	14 7/8	14 7/8	8 5/8	9 2/8	24 2/8	Chase, B. C.	Lloyd McNary & J. Langer	Lloyd McNary	1956	100
187 7/8	38 1/8	42 3/8	14 5/8	14 5/8	9 2/8	8 4/8	21 4/8	Ram River, Alta.	Geo. W. Parker	Geo. W. Parker	1961	100
187 7/8	40 5/8	43 3/8	15 1/8	15 2/8	8 5/8	11 3/8	24 3/8	Wild Hay River, Alta.	Jim Papst	Jim Papst	1967	100
187 7/8	43 5/8	38 7/8	14 5/8	14 7/8	11 3/8	9 6/8	15	Glacier Natl. Park, Mont.	Olmstead, Dow, & Hawley	Mont. Dept. Fish & Game	1956	104
187 7/8	40 3/8	40 3/8	15 2/8	15 5/8	9 6/8	10 5/8	21 3/8	Butcher Creek, Alta.	Vince Bruder	Vince Bruder	1958	104
187 7/8	39 5/8	39 5/8	16 1/8	16	8 7/8	8	25 3/8	Teton Co., Wyo.	William R. Flagg	William R. Flagg	1967	104

BIGHORN SHEEP–*Continued*

Ovis canadensis canadensis and certain related subspecies

Score	Length of Horn R.	Length of Horn L.	Circumference of Base R.	Circumference of Base L.	Circumference at Third Quarter R.	Circumference at Third Quarter L.	Greatest Spread	Tip to Tip Spread	Locality Killed	By Whom Killed	Owner	Date Killed	Rank
187 5/8	45 7/8	42	14 7/8	14 4/8	8 6/8	8 7/8	23	22 2/8	Spence's Bridge, B. C.	J. David Smith	J. David Smith	1969	104
187 4/8	39 5/8	43 1/8	15 5/8	15 4/8	9	8 4/8	26 4/8	19	Crystal Creek, Wyo.	Picked Up	Melvin R. Fowlkes	1970	108
187 4/8	40 5/8	39 7/8	15 3/8	15 3/8	9 4/8	9 3/8	20 4/8	19 2/8	Ram Range, Alta.	John F. Snyder	John F. Snyder	1978	108
187 3/8	39 2/8	39 3/8	15 4/8	15 4/8	9 6/8	9 7/8	21 4/8	20	Sundre, Alta.	Stan Burrell	Stan Burrell	1953	110
187 3/8	40 4/8	40 3/8	16 2/8	16 1/8	8 3/8	8 4/8	22 7/8	22 7/8	Elbow River, Alta.	Sam Ross Sloan	Sam Ross Sloan	1962	110
187 3/8	42	41 7/8	15 3/8	15 4/8	8 4/8	8 4/8	21 4/8	21 4/8	Lytton, B. C.	R. G. Jones & Pat B. Wilmot	R. George Jones	1973	110
187 2/8	40 3/8	43 1/8	14 7/8	15 1/8	9 1/8	9 3/8	22 4/8	19 7/8	McDonald Creek, Alta.	Ernest F. Greenwood	Ernest F. Greenwood	1965	113
187 1/8	41 3/8	41 4/8	15 5/8	15 4/8	9 1/8	9 1/8	21	21	White Swan Lake, B. C.	Lucius A. Chase	Lucius A. Chase	1961	114
187 1/8	41 5/8	43 4/8	15	15	9 1/8	8 5/8	23 4/8	23	Fallen Timber Creek, Alta.	Picked Up	Joe Blakemore	1968	114
187	36 6/8	38	15 6/8	15 7/8	10 3/8	10 6/8	23 4/8	22 7/8	Colo.	Picked Up	E. H. Brown	——	116
187	37 7/8	38 1/8	16	16 1/8	10	10 2/8	17 6/8	22 5/8	Unknown	Unknown	Dale Selby	——	116
187	39	39 4/8	15	15	10 5/8	10 4/8	22 6/8	17 4/8	Wind River Mts., Wyo.	Ralph E. Platt	Ralph E. Platt	1963	116
187	40 6/8	40 6/8	15 5/8	15 5/8	8 4/8	8 6/8	22 2/8	20 7/8	Sanders Co., Mont.	Bruce L. Hartford	Bruce L. Hartford	1978	116
186 7/8	34 3/8	40 2/8	15 6/8	15 6/8	10 5/8	10 5/8	22 4/8	18 6/8	Burnt Timber, Alta.	C. J. McElroy	C. J. McElroy	1965	120
186 6/8	39 4/8	38 4/8	16 2/8	16 3/8	10	9 2/8	23 6/8	18 7/8	E. Kootenay, B. C.	Jerry Mortimer	Jerry Mortimer	1959	121
186 6/8	39 1/8	39 7/8	15 1/8	15 2/8	10 2/8	10 4/8	22	17 4/8	Whitehorse Creek, Alta.	Philip H. R. Stepney	Prov. Mus. Alta.	1978	121
186 5/8	42 4/8	41 3/8	14 5/8	14 6/8	9 4/8	9 4/8	24 4/8	21 6/8	Panther River, Alta.	Picked Up	Belmore Browne	1936	123
186 5/8	42 6/8	42 1/8	15	15	8 3/8	8 2/8	25 6/8	25 6/8	Shell Rock, Idaho	Lea J. Bacos	Lea J. Bacos	1953	123
186 4/8	40 5/8	39 1/8	15 6/8	15 7/8	9 3/8	8 7/8	19	22 6/8	Fording River, B. C.	M. C. Baher	M. C. Baher	1942	125
186 4/8	41 4/8	43	14 7/8	14 6/8	9	8 6/8	22 6/8	19 3/8	Lincoln Co., Mont.	Marge M. Kis	Marge M. Kis	1965	125
186 3/8	41 7/8	40 4/8	14 1/8	14 1/8	10 4/8	10 4/8	20	18	Tyrrell Creek, Alta.	Picked Up	John H. Batten	1949	127
186 3/8	41	41 7/8	14 1/8	14	10 6/8	11 1/8	22 1/8	17 6/8	Ventre-Flat, Wyo.	John Evasco	John Evasco	1953	127
186 3/8	38 1/8	36	16	16 1/8	10	10	22 4/8	18 2/8	Castle River, Alta.	Ed Burton	Ed Burton	1954	127
186 3/8	42	41 1/8	15 3/8	15 3/8	8 6/8	8 3/8	21 6/8	16 6/8	Fernie, B. C.	Thomas Krall	Thomas Krall	1963	127
186 2/8	41 7/8	42 1/8	14	14	9 7/8	9 7/8	22 4/8	21 4/8	Cadomin, Alta.	R. A. Craig	R. A. Craig	1936	131
186 2/8	42 3/8	41 3/8	14 5/8	14 6/8	9 4/8	9 4/8	24 2/8	20 6/8	Clearwater River, Alta.	Picked Up	John H. Batten	1954	131
186 2/8	40 3/8	40 1/8	15 1/8	15 3/8	9 7/8	9 5/8	21 4/8	19 5/8	Sheep Creek, Alta.	G. A. Reiche	G. A. Reiche	1960	131
186 2/8	37	38 4/8	15 7/8	15 7/8	10	9 4/8	20 1/8	17	Junction Mtn., Alta.	Robert R. Willis	Robert R. Willis	1978	131
186 1/8	39 5/8	40 2/8	15 6/8	15 4/8	8 3/8	8 2/8	22	17 4/8	Waterton Natl. Park, Alta.	Picked Up	Robert Thompson	——	135
186 1/8	43 2/8	44 5/8	16 4/8	16 5/8	6 5/8	6 7/8	24 5/8	24 5/8	Yellowstone Park, Mont.	William H. Dirrett	James K. Weatherford	1913	135
186 1/8	39 4/8	38 3/8	15 2/8	15 3/8	10 4/8	10	22 3/8	15 6/8	Highwood, Alta.	Terry J. Webber	Terry J. Webber	1959	135

Score								Locality	Owner	By whom killed	Date	Rank
186 2/8	41 5/8	15 3/8	15 4/8	8 3/8	8 5/8	20 5/8	19 5/8	Sun River Canyon, Mont.	Glen Roberts	Glen Roberts	1961	135
186	40 4/8	16	16	8 4/8	8 7/8	19 5/8	19 3/8	Clear Water, Alta.	Herb Hamilton	Herb Hamilton	1964	139
185 7/8	40 3/8	15	15	9 5/8	9 5/8	21	21	Panther River, Alta.	J. F. Blakemore	J. F. Blakemore	1961	140
185 7/8	35	14 4/8	14 4/8	13	13	20 3/8	20 3/8	Ural, Mont.	Curtis Gatson	Curtis Gatson	1962	140
185 7/8	38 7/8	15 5/8	15 5/8	10	10 1/8	21 5/8	20 3/8	Burnt Timber Creek, Alta.	John T. Blackwell	John T. Blackwell	1967	140
185 5/8	40 2/8	15	14 7/8	10 1/8	10 1/8	21	20 7/8	Ghost River, Alta.	William D. Cox	William D. Cox	1959	143
185 5/8	41 3/8	14	14 2/8	10 6/8	10 6/8	22 5/8	21	Mystery Lake, Alta.	Jim Babala	Jim Babala	1962	143
185 5/8	41 3/8	14 5/8	14 4/8	9 3/8	9 6/8	22 7/8	21 7/8	Dubois, Wyo.	B. N. Lively	B. N. Lively	1953	145
185 5/8	40 6/8	17 3/8	17 3/8	8 1/8	8 4/8	20 3/8	20 2/8	Rocky Mt. House, Alta.	Robert B. Johnson	Robert B. Johnson	1960	145
185 5/8	38 4/8	17 3/8	17 3/8	8 7/8	9	22 3/8	21 3/8	Lemhi Co., Idaho	W. R. Franklin	W. R. Franklin	1963	145
185 4/8	40	15 3/8	15 2/8	9	9	23 4/8	23 2/8	Wind River Mts., Wyo.	Elgin T. Gates	Elgin T. Gates	1954	148
185 4/8	41	13 6/8	14	9 7/8	9 7/8	21 7/8	21 2/8	Sask. River, Alta.	Herb Klein	Herb Klein	1963	148
185 4/8	40	14 5/8	14 6/8	10	10	22 4/8	22 4/8	Highwood River, Alta.	M. R. Wagner	W. Erdman	1964	148
185 3/8	38 5/8	15 4/8	15 4/8	10	10	24	24	Natal, B. C.	Myles Travis	H. Beard	1921	151
185 3/8	39 6/8	16 3/8	16 3/8	8	8 1/8	21 5/8	21 1/8	Fremont Co., Colo.	Leonard L. Kiser	Leonard L. Kiser	1955	151
185 3/8	39 5/8	16	16	9 6/8	9 1/8	21	21	Lillooet, B. C.	Glen E. Park	Glen E. Park	1964	151
185 3/8	40 3/8	14 6/8	14 6/8	10 1/8	10 1/8	23 6/8	23 4/8	Banff, Alta.	E. Kent. Univ.	Unknown	PR1974	151
185 2/8	39 6/8	15 5/8	15 5/8	10 5/8	10 5/8	21 4/8	21 1/8	Unknown	Art Esslinger	Unknown	1930	155
185 2/8	40 3/8	16	15 5/8	8 5/8	8 5/8	21	21	Big Creek, Idaho	Edson Piers	Edson Piers	1962	155
185 2/8	40 1/8	16	15 3/8	9 7/8	9 7/8	20 5/8	20 1/8	Spence's Bridge, B. C.	J. C. Atkinson	J. C. Atkinson	1965	155
185 1/8	39 1/8	16 5/8	16 5/8	8 6/8	8 7/8	23 3/8	23 2/8	Fremont Co., Colo.	Robert W. Wallace	Robert W. Wallace	1978	155
185 1/8	38 6/8	15 3/8	15 3/8	9 1/8	9 2/8	22 2/8	21	Tornado Mt., B. C.	Vincent A. Kehm	Vincent A. Kehm	1958	159
185 1/8	40 2/8	15 7/8	15 3/8	9 2/8	9 4/8	23	15 2/8	Big Horn River, Alta.	Chris Klineburger	Chris Klineburger	1962	159
185	39 5/8	16 3/8	15 7/8	9 4/8	9	23 3/8	18 3/8	Alta.	Acad. Nat. Sci., Phil.	Gift Of Lynford Biddle	1901	161
185	39 1/8	14 7/8	16 3/8	8 4/8	8 2/8	22	19 4/8	Green River, Wyo.	Elsie Stalnaker	Floyd J. Stalnaker	1913	161
185	41 1/8	15 1/8	14 7/8	10 4/8	10 6/8	23	17 7/8	Mitchell River, B. C.	Mr. & Mrs. N. A. Meckstrot	Mr. & Mrs. N. A. Meckstrot	1963	161
184 7/8	40 1/8	14 6/8	15 1/8	9 4/8	9 4/8	18 4/8	17 7/8	Westhorse Mts., Idaho	Cecil Dodge	Cecil Dodge	1953	164
184 7/8	37 5/8	15	15	10 4/8	10 4/8	23 5/8	22 3/8	Glenwood Springs, Colo.	Mark E. Cook	Picked Up	1960	164
184 7/8	40 4/8	15 1/8	15 1/8	8 5/8	9 3/8	20 7/8	17 7/8	Cadomin, Alta.	Rita Oney	Rita Oney	1966	164
184 6/8	38 7/8	15 1/8	15 1/8	10 7/8	10 2/8	21 3/8	21 3/8	Unknown	George Ostashek	Unknown	PR1920	167
184 6/8	40 1/8	15 2/8	15 2/8	9 6/8	9 7/8	21 5/8	19 3/8	Brazeau River, Alta.	Mrs. Grancel Fitz	Grancel Fitz	1931	167
184 6/8	41 3/8	14 4/8	14 4/8	9 4/8	9 4/8	21 3/8	21	Castle Mt., Mont.	E. L. Anderson	E. L. Anderson	1954	167
184 6/8	40	14 3/8	14 3/8	10 5/8	10 5/8	23 2/8	21 2/8	Jackson Hole, Wyo.	Johnny Kretschman	Johnny Kretschman	1962	167
184 5/8	40 4/8	16 3/8	16 3/8	8 1/8	7 7/8	21 1/8	21 1/8	Little Elbow River, Alta.	Alex Cornett	Alex Cornett	1976	167
184 5/8	39 2/8	15 7/8	15 7/8	9 4/8	9 4/8	22 3/8	22 3/8	Salmon River, Idaho	Ted Biladeau	Ted Biladeau	1939	172
184 5/8	38 5/8	14 7/8	14 7/8	9 4/8	9 6/8	20 5/8	20 5/8	Clearwater, Alta.	G. C. Matthews	G. C. Matthews	1942	172
184 5/8	39 2/8	14 7/8	14 7/8	10 6/8	10 6/8	22 5/8	22 5/8	Rock Lake, Alta.	Clifford Wolfe	Bill Bodenchuk	1960	172
184 5/8	39 2/8	14 3/8	14 3/8	9 7/8	9 6/8	22 5/8	22 5/8	Burnt Timber Creek, Alta.	Berry B. Brooks	Berry B. Brooks	1960	172
184 5/8	41 1/8	15	15	10	9 6/8	22	22	Luscar Creek, Alta.	Doug W. Whiteside	Doug W. Whiteside	1976	172
184 4/8	39	16	16	8 1/8	8 4/8	22 6/8	22 2/8	Smoky River, Alta.	Wm. C. Barthman	Wm. C. Barthman	1946	177
184 4/8	39 2/8	14 4/8	14 4/8	10 6/8	10 6/8	21 5/8	21 5/8	Sun River, Mont.	W. H. Stecker	Picked Up	1948	177
184 3/8	37 3/8	15 3/8	15 3/8	11	11	21 5/8	13 7/8	Gunnison Co., Colo.	Daniel C. Harrington	Billy Prior	1915	179

BIGHORN SHEEP–*Continued*

Ovis canadensis canadensis and certain related subspecies

Score	Length of Horn R.	Length of Horn L.	Circumference of Base R.	Circumference of Base L.	Circumference at Third Quarter R.	Circumference at Third Quarter L.	Greatest Spread	Tip to Tip Spread	Locality Killed	By Whom Killed	Owner	Date Killed	Rank
184 3/8	38 7/8	40 3/8	15	15	10 7/8	9 4/8	20 1/8	18 4/8	Drinnan Creek, Alta.	John H. Epstein	John H. Epstein	1963	179
184 3/8	37 3/8	41 2/8	15 6/8	15 2/8	8 7/8	9	22 1/8	17 6/8	Cadomin, Alta.	John H. Marcum	John H. Marcum	1969	179
184 2/8	37 6/8	37 6/8	15 4/8	15 4/8	10 1/8	10 7/8	24	24	Middle Mts., Wyo.	Wm. Underwood	Wm. Underwood	1959	182
184 1/8	39 5/8	42	15 2/8	15 1/8	8 5/8	8 1/8	22 5/8	22 5/8	Alta.	Bob Wood	N. Am. Wildl. Mus.	1964	183
184 1/8	38 7/8	39	17	17	7 7/8	7 6/8	23 1/8	23 1/8	Castle River, Alta.	E. B. Cunningham	E. B. Cunningham	1965	183
184 1/8	39 7/8	39 4/8	15 2/8	15 4/8	9 1/8	9 3/8	24	21 7/8	Panther River, Alta.	Picked Up	Paul Ujfalusi	1966	183
184	40 5/8	37 7/8	14 6/8	14 7/8	9 2/8	9 4/8	22 4/8	22 3/8	Valley Co., Idaho	Picked Up	LaVarr Jacklin	1949	186
184	41 1/8	41 1/8	14 2/8	14 1/8	10	10	20 5/8	19	Ghost River, Alta.	W. D. Norwood	W. D. Norwood	1955	186
184	39 1/8	39 1/8	14 7/8	14 7/8	10 1/8	10 3/8	21 6/8	21 6/8	Sun River, Mont.	Carl Mehmke	Carl Mehmke	1957	186
184	35	36 4/8	16 2/8	16 1/8	10 6/8	11	21	20	Cardston, Alta.	August Glander	August Glander	1969	186
183 7/8	41 1/8	40	14 4/8	14 4/8	9 6/8	9 4/8	23	20 5/8	Sask. River, Alta.	Basil C. Bradbury	Basil C. Bradbury	1968	190
183 6/8	37 2/8	37 2/8	15 5/8	15 5/8	9 2/8	9 6/8	20 4/8	17 4/8	Fernie, B. C.	Unknown	Fred Braatz	1930	191
183 6/8	39 7/8	39 3/8	14 6/8	14 6/8	9 7/8	10	21 4/8	15 7/8	Natal, B. C.	Mrs. A. L. Musser	A. L. Musser	1947	191
183 6/8	40 1/8	39 5/8	14 3/8	14 4/8	10 2/8	10 2/8	19 5/8	18 1/8	Castle River, Alta.	George Hagglund	George Hagglund	1959	191
183 6/8	37 2/8	38	15 4/8	15 4/8	10	10	21 4/8	18 2/8	Highwood Range, Alta.	K. Fred Coleman	K. Fred Coleman	1977	191
183 5/8	37 4/8	37 3/8	16 2/8	16 3/8	9 2/8	9 3/8	21 6/8	17 2/8	Mystery Lake, Alta.	Paul Inzanti	Paul Inzanti	1960	195
183 5/8	38 2/8	39 3/8	15 6/8	15 5/8	9 2/8	9 2/8	19 4/8	18 7/8	Marble Creek, Idaho	Joseph T. Pelton	Joseph T. Pelton	1961	195
183 5/8	37 7/8	39	15 2/8	15 3/8	9 5/8	10 1/8	22	16 1/8	Burnt Timber Area, Alta.	Jay H. Giese	Jay H. Giese	1966	195
183 4/8	36 7/8	37 7/8	16 1/8	16 3/8	8 5/8	8 7/8	23 5/8	17 6/8	S. Castle River, Alta.	Leon Atwood	Leon Atwood	1962	198
183 4/8	33 4/8	39	15 6/8	16	10 4/8	10 4/8	22 3/8	18 2/8	Sweetgrass Co., Mont.	Basil C. Bradbury	Basil C. Bradbury	1965	198
183 4/8	42	36 6/8	14 5/8	14 7/8	9 7/8	9 4/8	21 2/8	21 1/8	Mystery Lake, Alta.	Armando Tomasso	Armando Tomasso	1967	198
183 4/8	38 4/8	37 6/8	15 4/8	15 6/8	9 5/8	9 4/8	20 4/8	20 4/8	C. M. R. Game Range, Mont.	Mrs. Gordon Pagenkopf	Mrs. Gordon Pagenkopf	1970	198
183 3/8	41	38 1/8	16	15 6/8	8	8 3/8	24 1/8	23 5/8	Lewis & Clark Co., Mont.	John Coston	John Coston	1961	202
183 3/8	37 3/8	38 4/8	15 3/8	15 3/8	10 1/8	10 7/8	22	16 2/8	Clearwater, Alta.	C. J. McElroy	C. J. McElroy	1969	202
183 2/8	39 4/8	39 2/8	14 2/8	14 3/8	11 1/8	11 5/8	20	17 6/8	Snake-Indian River, Alta.	Oswald Fowler & Jack Brewster	Fred Brewster	1919	204
183 2/8	39 4/8	38 4/8	14 6/8	14 7/8	9 7/8	9 6/8	23 2/8	23 2/8	Sun River, Mont.	Earl Hofland	Earl Hofland	1957	204
183 2/8	39 4/8	38	15 7/8	15 7/8	9 4/8	9 7/8	19 6/8	19 6/8	Smoky River, Alta.	F. C. Hibben	F. C. Hibben	1957	204
183 1/8	40	37 1/8	16	16	9	8 6/8	22 4/8	20	Unknown	Unknown	Jonas Bros. Of Seattle	PR1939	207
183 1/8	34 7/8	36	16 2/8	16 2/8	9 7/8	10 1/8	24 5/8	20	S. Platte Canyon, Colo.	Harold C. Eastwood	Harold C. Eastwood	1957	207
183 1/8	38 4/8	38 5/8	15 5/8	15 5/8	9	9 1/8	22 2/8	16 7/8	Kootenay River, B. C.	W. Vernon Walsh	W. Vernon Walsh	1962	207

183 1/8	36 7/8	37 2/8	15 3/8	15 3/8	10 3/8	10	22	18 4/8	Fraser River, B. C.	Karl P. Willms	Karl P. Willms	1977	207
183	39 4/8	38	16 2/8	16 2/8	8 2/8	8 4/8	21 4/8	17 6/8	Teton Basin, Wyo.	William A. Baillie-Grohman	John H. Batten	1876	211
183	37 5/8	39 1/8	15 1/8	15 5/8	10 5/8	10 5/8	19 4/8	15 6/8	Clearwater River, Alta.	John H. Batten	John H. Batten	1931	211
183	39 2/8	40	15 5/8	15 4/8	8 3/8	8 5/8	21 5/8	21 5/8	Cadomin, Alta.	Otis Chandler	Otis Chandler	1969	211
183	38	38 6/8	15 1/8	15 1/8	9	9 2/8	21 1/8	21 1/8	Solomon Creek, Alta.	Picked Up	William Gosney	1977	211
182 7/8	40 5/8	38 6/8	15	15 1/8	9 4/8	9 4/8	22	17 4/8	Alta.	G. L. (Rusty) Gibbons	G. L. (Rusty) Gibbons	1963	215
182 6/8	37 5/8	37 5/8	15 2/8	15 2/8	10	9 7/8	23 7/8	20 4/8	Lake Louise, Alta.	Picked Up	Howard Bronsdon	1952	216
182 6/8	39 6/8	38	14 3/8	14 4/8	10 2/8	10	22 4/8	18	Salmon River, Idaho	Picked Up	Wayne Demaray	1963	216
182 6/8	38 4/8	37 4/8	14 6/8	15	10 5/8	10 3/8	21 7/8	15 5/8	Burnt Timber, Alta.	Mrs. W. E. Anderson	Mrs. W. E. Anderson	1964	216
182 6/8	39 2/8	39	15	15	9 7/8	9 4/8	22	18 6/8	Wild Hay River Valley, Alta.	Jim Papst	Jim Papst	1968	216
182 6/8	40 4/8	40 4/8	14 6/8	14 5/8	9	9 1/8	22 5/8	22 6/8	Lower Salmon River, Idaho	Glenn H. Schubert	Glenn H. Schubert	1970	216
182 6/8	40 6/8	39 2/8	16 1/8	16	7 6/8	7 7/8	22 5/8	19 6/8	Sanders Co., Mont.	Terrence Pond	Terrence Pond	1978	216
182 5/8	44 1/8	42 4/8	13 7/8	14	9 3/8	8 4/8	23 1/8	23 1/8	Alta.	John D. Hazen	National Collection	1918	222
182 5/8	37 7/8	38 6/8	16 6/8	16 6/8	8 2/8	7 3/8	19 4/8	16	Brazeau Forest, Alta.	H. A. Yocum	H. A. Yocum	1941	222
182 5/8	40 3/8	39 4/8	15	15 2/8	8 6/8	8 4/8	22 7/8	13 4/8	Bull River, B. C.	Ralph W. Sterns	Ralph W. Sterns	1950	222
182 5/8	42 1/8	40 4/8	15 2/8	15 2/8	7 5/8	7 3/8	20 2/8	20	Sun River, Mont.	Martin Alzheimer	Martin Alzheimer	1955	222
182 5/8	39 1/8	36 4/8	15 5/8	15 4/8	9 4/8	9 4/8	21 4/8	20 6/8	Narraway River, Alta.	John C. Seidensticker	John C. Seidensticker	1959	222
182 5/8	38 1/8	38 4/8	15	14 7/8	9 6/8	10 2/8	21 2/8	15 6/8	Storm Mt., Alta.	W. Glaser	W. Glaser	1961	222
182 5/8	38 4/8	37 3/8	16	16	9 2/8	8 7/8	19 2/8	13 1/8	Junction Creek, Alta.	Robert F. Brooks	Robert F. Brooks	1978	222
182 4/8	40 3/8	40 1/8	14 5/8	14 5/8	9 7/8	9 6/8	21 4/8	21	Shoshone N. Fork, Wyo.	Herb Klein	Herb Klein	1934	229
182 4/8	37	35 4/8	15 4/8	15 3/8	11 2/8	10 4/8	23	21	Wind River, Wyo.	Hubert Weibel	Hubert Weibel	1956	229
182 4/8	35 4/8	35 2/8	16 4/8	16 4/8	10	9 4/8	24	22 5/8	Waterton, Colo.	Wm. D. Jenkins	Wm. D. Jenkins	1956	229
182 4/8	38 4/8	39 2/8	15 5/8	15 5/8	8 4/8	8 2/8	22 1/8	19 1/8	Kananaskis Summit, Alta.	Ted Howell	Ted Howell	1964	229
182 4/8	38 3/8	37 5/8	15	14 6/8	10 6/8	10 5/8	22 1/8	18 2/8	Turtle Creek, Wyo.	Russell C. Cutter	Russell C. Cutter	1968	229
182 4/8	41 1/8	40 5/8	15	15	8 1/8	8 2/8	22	18 4/8	Edgewater, B. C.	William N. Ward	William N. Ward	1969	229
182 4/8	40 2/8	40	15 3/8	15 3/8	8 2/8	8 1/8	23 1/8	20	Spence's Bridge, B. C.	Don Ticehurst	Don Ticehurst	1973	229
182 3/8	38 3/8	37 4/8	14 5/8	14 6/8	10 2/8	10 4/8	22	16 2/8	Banff, Alta.	Gift Of Madison Grant	National Collection	—	236
182 3/8	37 2/8	37 3/8	15 3/8	15 2/8	10 4/8	10 4/8	21 7/8	17	Teton River, Mont.	Geoffrey A. Morrison	Geoffrey A. Morrison	1969	236
182 2/8	40 7/8	40 1/8	15	15	8 7/8	8 6/8	23 4/8	20 4/8	Dubois, Wyo.	George Pate	Larry Pate	1960	238
182 2/8	39 5/8	39 7/8	15	15 2/8	9 1/8	9 4/8	21 4/8	17 4/8	Ram River, Alta.	Louise McConnell	Louise McConnell	1961	238
182 2/8	36	36 6/8	15 4/8	15 4/8	10	10	21 3/8	16	Sulphur River, Alta.	Unknown	Roy Everest	1963	238
182 2/8	40 1/8	39 7/8	15	14 5/8	9 4/8	10 2/8	21 2/8	21 2/8	Wild Hay River, Alta.	James H. Duke, Jr.	James H. Duke, Jr.	1967	238
182 1/8	41 5/8	39	12 7/8	13 1/8	11 6/8	11 5/8	22 6/8	22 6/8	Salmon River, Idaho	Picked Up	Arson Eddy	PR1959	242
182 1/8	35 4/8	39 3/8	15 2/8	15 2/8	11 2/8	9 2/8	24 6/8	24 6/8	Lemhi Co., Idaho	Leonard C. Miller, Sr.	Leonard C. Miller, Sr.	1963	242
182 1/8	38 3/8	37 4/8	15 2/8	15 1/8	9 4/8	9 4/8	22 1/8	17 3/8	Panther River, Alta.	W. H. Slikker	W. H. Slikker	1966	242
182 1/8	37 7/8	37 4/8	16	16 2/8	8 5/8	8 5/8	20 1/8	18 2/8	Crowsnest Lake, Alta.	John Truant	John Truant	1970	242
182	40	41	14 5/8	14 7/8	8 5/8	8 7/8	24	24	Salmon River, Idaho	Picked Up	Elmer Keith	1957	246
182	37 5/8	36 7/8	15 6/8	15 7/8	9 7/8	10	21	16 4/8	Pincher Creek, Alta.	Delton Smith	Delton Smith	1958	246
182	41	37 6/8	15	14 7/8	9 2/8	9 1/8	21 5/8	17 4/8	Canal Flat, B. C.	Allen Cudworth	Allen Cudworth	1958	246
181 7/8	39 2/8	39 1/8	14 3/8	14 2/8	10 5/8	10 1/8	20 7/8	20 4/8	Coal Branch, Alta.	John Caputo	John Caputo	1962	249
181 7/8	36 5/8	36 2/8	16 5/8	16 4/8	8 4/8	8 5/8	20 7/8	20	Elko, B. C.	Percy McGregor	Percy McGregor	1974	249

BIGHORN SHEEP—*Continued*

Ovis canadensis canadensis and certain related subspecies

Score	Length of Horn R.	Length of Horn L.	Circumference of Base R.	Circumference of Base L.	Circumference at Third Quarter R.	Circumference at Third Quarter L.	Greatest Spread	Tip to Tip Spread	Locality Killed	By Whom Killed	Owner	Date Killed	Rank
181 6/8	37	37 2/8	15 4/8	15 2/8	9 5/8	9 5/8	18	14 4/8	Ghost River, Alta.	L. C. Nowlin	L. C. Nowlin	PR1940	251
181 5/8	35	34 2/8	15 2/8	15 2/8	11 2/8	10 6/8	22 5/8	17	Texas Creek, Colo.	Picked Up	Jack Putnam	—	252
181 5/8	42	40 1/8	15 2/8	15 1/8	8	7 6/8	21	20 2/8	Ghost River, Alta.	J. S. Parker	J. S. Parker	1954	252
181 5/8	39 1/8	37	15 6/8	15 6/8	8 4/8	9 3/8	23 2/8	21 2/8	Custer Co., Mont.	Picked Up	W. S. Maloit	1959	252
181 5/8	36 7/8	39 2/8	15 4/8	15 3/8	9	8 7/8	23 4/8	23 4/8	Elbow River, Alta.	Ernest F. Dill	Ernest F. Dill	1961	252
181 5/8	39 6/8	40 1/8	15 5/8	15 3/8	8 4/8	7 6/8	22 7/8	22 7/8	Sun River, Mont.	Walter L. Bodie	Walter L. Bodie	1965	252
181 5/8	41 5/8	37 6/8	14 2/8	14 4/8	10	10 2/8	21 4/8	20 4/8	Burnt Timber Creek, Alta.	George H. Glass	George H. Glass	1967	252
181 5/8	38 4/8	39 3/8	14 4/8	14 6/8	9 2/8	9 6/8	23 5/8	19	Park Co., Wyo.	Keith Frick	Keith Frick	1972	252
181 4/8	40	40 5/8	15 1/8	15 2/8	8 2/8	8 4/8	22	21 1/8	Sulphur River, Alta.	John E. Hammett	John E. Hammett	1938	259
181 4/8	38 6/8	41 2/8	14 6/8	14 4/8	8 5/8	8 5/8	22 2/8	22 2/8	Castle River, Alta.	Cliff Johnson	Cliff Johnson	1957	259
181 4/8	36	36 2/8	15 1/8	15 1/8	11 1/8	11 1/8	23	21	Dubois, Wyo.	Jack Adams	Jack Adams	1959	259
181 4/8	38 5/8	39 1/8	15 1/8	15 3/8	8 6/8	9	23 1/8	19 6/8	Cadomin, Alta.	John Caputo	John Caputo	1961	259
181 4/8	40 3/8	43 4/8	16	16	6 7/8	6 2/8	23	29 4/8	Gallatin Co., Mont.	Richard D. Gilman	Richard D. Gilman	1967	259
181 4/8	41 3/8	39 7/8	15 2/8	15 2/8	8	7 7/8	22 5/8	22 5/8	Lewis And Clark Co., Mont.	Picked Up	William L. Wesland	1973	259
181 4/8	39	37 6/8	15 1/8	15 1/8	9	9 1/8	22	18 6/8	Spray Lake, Alta.	George R. Willows	George R. Willows	1974	259
181 4/8	41	41 2/8	16 1/8	16	6 5/8	6 6/8	21 4/8	21 4/8	Deer Lodge Co., Mont.	Gerald P. Wendt	Gerald P. Wendt	1978	259
181 3/8	38 2/8	39 3/8	15 1/8	15 2/8	9 2/8	9 4/8	20 4/8	14 4/8	Big Horn Creek, Alta.	Earl Foss	Earl Foss	1960	267
181 3/8	37 2/8	36 7/8	17	17	8	8 1/8	20 4/8	15 4/8	Park Co., Colo.	Richard L. Rudeen	Richard L. Rudeen	1963	267
181 3/8	38 6/8	37 7/8	14 7/8	14 7/8	9 3/8	9 3/8	20 4/8	19 6/8	Clearwater River, Alta.	Joseph T. Pelton	Joseph T. Pelton	1966	267
181 3/8	38 3/8	38 4/8	15	14 7/8	9 5/8	9 5/8	21 4/8	15	Beartooth Plateau, Mont.	Olav E. Nelson	Olav E. Nelson	1970	267
181 3/8	39	39 5/8	15 4/8	15 5/8	8 3/8	8 2/8	22 3/8	19 4/8	Lincoln Co., Mont.	Lowell Olin	Lowell Olin	1977	267
181 2/8	42	41 4/8	14	14	8 5/8	8 2/8	24 6/8	24 6/8	Teton Basin, Wyo.	Michael Huppuch	Philip Schlegel	1901	272
181 2/8	40 3/8	40 7/8	15 4/8	15 4/8	7 2/8	7 5/8	22 4/8	22 4/8	McBride, B. C.	Alfred Saulnier	Alfred Saulnier	1966	272
181 1/8	39 3/8	39 6/8	15 1/8	14 6/8	9 4/8	9 1/8	25	21	Clearwater River, Alta.	Phil Temple	Phil Temple	1951	274
181 1/8	38 2/8	38 5/8	14	14 2/8	11	10 3/8	20 2/8	15 1/8	Cooke City, Mont.	Larry L. Altimus	Larry L. Altimus	1969	274
181	40 5/8	45 7/8	14 1/8	13 7/8	7 6/8	7 7/8	26 2/8	26 2/8	Kootenay, B. C.	A. E. Matthew	A. E. Matthew	1950	276
181	39 4/8	39 6/8	14 7/8	14 6/8	8 3/8	8 3/8	23 5/8	17 6/8	Lincoln Co., Mont.	Hal Kanzler	Hal Kanzler	1960	276
181	39 2/8	39 2/8	15 2/8	15 2/8	8 6/8	8 6/8	21	17	Brule, Alta.	Picked Up	G. W. Warner	1963	276
181	37 6/8	37	15 5/8	15 5/8	9	9	23	15	Mystery Lake, Alta.	Peter Lazio	Peter Lazio	1967	276
181	38 7/8	37 5/8	14 2/8	14 3/8	11 1/8	11	19 1/8	19 1/8	Simpson Creek, B. C.	Walt Failor	Walt Failor	1968	276
180 6/8	38 2/8	42	15	15	8 1/8	8 3/8	22 7/8	22 1/8	Seebe, Alta.	Ted Trueblood	Ted Trueblood	1956	281

180 6/8	37	38 4/8	15 7/8	15 7/8	8 5/8	8 5/8	22 5/8	15	Bull River, B. C.	Walter J. Ruehle	Walter J. Ruehle	1962	281
180 6/8	37 4/8	35 6/8	16 2/8	16	8 6/8	8 4/8	21	15 3/8	Flat Creek, Alta.	G. I. Franklin	G. I. Franklin	1964	281
180 6/8	37 5/8	38 3/8	15 1/8	15	9 6/8	9 7/8	21 3/8	16 4/8	Panther Creek, Alta.	C. D. Sharp	C. D. Sharp	1966	281
180 5/8	39 4/8	39 5/8	13 6/8	13 5/8	10 7/8	11	22	17 6/8	Wind River Mts., Wyo.	Alfred Hume	Alfred Hume	1960	285
180 5/8	38 1/8	38 2/8	14 6/8	14 6/8	10 1/8	10	21 1/8	21 1/8	Sun River, Mont.	Robert W. Boucher	Robert W. Boucher	1966	285
180 5/8	38	39 3/8	14 3/8	14 3/8	9 6/8	10 3/8	19 4/8	19 4/8	Salmon River, Idaho	Emerson Hall	Emerson Hall	1968	285
180 5/8	37 1/8	35	15 4/8	15 5/8	9 4/8	9 4/8	22 4/8	15 4/8	Waterton Lake, B. C.	Victor T. Zarnock, Jr.	Victor T. Zarnock, Jr.	1972	285
180 4/8	39	41 4/8	14 5/8	14 5/8	8	8 2/8	22 5/8	22	Smoky River, Alta.	H. P. Brandenburg	H. P. Brandenburg	1924	289
180 4/8	40 2/8	38 2/8	15 5/8	15 4/8	8 3/8	8	21 2/8	20	White Swan Lake, B. C.	John Barton	John Barton	1936	289
180 4/8	38	39	14 2/8	14 2/8	10 6/8	10 6/8	22 3/8	18 2/8	Coal Branch, Alta.	R. G. F. Brown	R. G. F. Brown	1962	289
180 4/8	38	38 4/8	15	15	8 7/8	9	19 7/8	18 6/8	Moosehorn Lake, Alta.	Maynard Mathews	Maynard Mathews	1964	289
180 4/8	38 6/8	39 2/8	13 6/8	13 6/8	10 3/8	10 5/8	20 6/8	20 6/8	Park Co., Wyo.	Picked Up	Sam L. Beasom	1974	289
180 4/8	34 7/8	35 5/8	15 4/8	15 5/8	10 1/8	10 2/8	21 2/8	13 1/8	Thistle Creek, Alta.	Paul H. Chance	Paul H. Chance	1975	289
180 3/8	39 6/8	39 7/8	16 2/8	16	7 1/8	7 1/8	22 1/8	22 1/8	Sulphur River, Alta.	W. D. Parker	W. D. Parker	1955	295
180 3/8	41	36 7/8	15 4/8	15 5/8	8	8 1/8	19 7/8	19 7/8	Ghost River, Alta.	Art Brewster	Art Brewster	1960	295
180 3/8	36 1/8	37 2/8	15 4/8	15 2/8	9 6/8	10	22	19 4/8	Jakey's Fork, Wyo.	Eugene Schilling	Eugene Schilling	1962	295
180 3/8	37 5/8	38 6/8	14 6/8	14 4/8	9 4/8	10 1/8	22 6/8	19	Sheep Creek, Wyo.	Picked Up	Loren L. Lutz	1962	295
180 3/8	38 1/8	39 4/8	15	14 7/8	9 4/8	9	21 4/8	17	Ghost River, Alta.	J. E. Edwards	J. E. Edwards	1964	295
180 3/8	39 5/8	39 4/8	14 6/8	15	8 7/8	9	23 2/8	23 2/8	Wallowa Co., Oregon	Kirk W. Jones	Kirk W. Jones	1979	295
180 2/8	36 4/8	38 6/8	15	15 1/8	9	9	20 4/8	20 4/8	Cecelia Lake, B. C.	Dan Auld	Dan Auld	1950	301
180 2/8	39 3/8	38 1/8	14 1/8	14 1/8	10 6/8	10	20 7/8	20 3/8	Salmon River, Idaho	Ralph Puckett	Ralph Puckett	1958	301
180 2/8	38 6/8	37 2/8	14 6/8	14 6/8	10 3/8	9 6/8	21 1/8	15	Burnt Timber Creek, Alta.	Ruth Mahoney	Ruth Mahoney	1963	301
180 1/8	36 4/8	34 5/8	15 2/8	15 1/8	10 3/8	10 7/8	22 1/8	18 4/8	Sugarloaf Mt., Colo.	Picked Up	Henry Zietz	1947	304
180 1/8	36 5/8	37 2/8	15 4/8	15 3/8	9 1/8	9 1/8	23 3/8	20 5/8	Green River, Wyo.	John N. Leonard	John N. Leonard	1953	304
180 1/8	36 1/8	40 6/8	15 4/8	15 2/8	8 5/8	8 3/8	20 4/8	18	Sun River, Mont.	Dennis Reichelt	Dennis Reichelt	1958	304
180 1/8	39 5/8	40 2/8	14 7/8	15	8 3/8	8 5/8	23	23	Salmon River, Idaho	C. A. Schwope	C. A. Schwope	1959	304
180 1/8	37 2/8	34 5/8	15 4/8	15 3/8	10 4/8	9 6/8	22 1/8	16 5/8	Gannet Peak, Wyo.	Wilbur Rickett	Wilbur Rickett	1964	304
180 1/8	37 3/8	37 6/8	14 4/8	14 6/8	10	10	22 4/8	19 1/8	Ghost River, Alta.	Lloyd E. Zeman	Lloyd E. Zeman	1968	304
180 1/8	36 4/8	34 3/8	15 6/8	15 7/8	9 7/8	9 5/8	22 5/8	18 2/8	Castle River, Alta.	Don W. Caldwell	Don W. Caldwell	1969	304
180 1/8	37 6/8	38 1/8	15 7/8	15 7/8	8 1/8	8	18 6/8	18 6/8	Nye, Mont.	Ira H. Kent	Ira H. Kent	1974	304
180 1/8	37 5/8	37 4/8	16 4/8	16 4/8	8 1/8	8	20	20	Sanders Co., Mont.	Gene N. Meyer	Gene N. Meyer	1976	304
180	37 1/8	38 7/8	15	15	9 4/8	10	22	18 2/8	Seebe, Alta.	Anson Brooks	Anson Brooks	1956	313
180	39 1/8	37 1/8	15	15 2/8	9 4/8	9 6/8	21	19 4/8	Forbidden Creek, Alta.	James Haugland	James Haugland	1958	313
180	38 1/8	38 3/8	15 2/8	15 2/8	9	9	21 5/8	18 2/8	Kootenay, B. C.	Walter L. Bjorkman	Walter L. Bjorkman	1963	313
180	37 6/8	37 2/8	14 4/8	14 4/8	10 4/8	10 4/8	22 3/8	22 3/8	Panther Creek, Alta.	Walter R. Schubert	Walter R. Schubert	1966	313
180	38 5/8	37 3/8	15 4/8	15 4/8	9	8 4/8	20 4/8	16 3/8	Whitehorse Creek, Alta.	Philip H. R. Stepney	Prov. Mus. Alta.	1978	313
180	38 5/8	41 1/8	14 5/8	14 5/8	8 3/8	8 4/8	24	23 4/8	Lewis And Clark Co., Mont.	James G. Braddee, Jr.	James G. Braddee, Jr.	1978	313
180	39 6/8	39 2/8	15 3/8	15 3/8	8	8	22 4/8	20 6/8	Wallowa Co., Oregon	F. Carter Kerns	F. Carter Kerns	1978	313

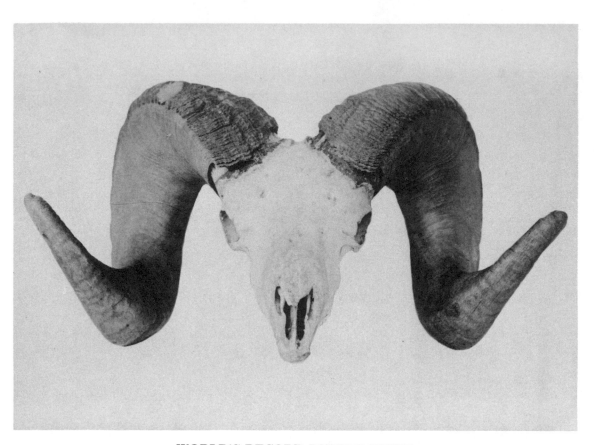

WORLD'S RECORD DESERT SHEEP
SCORE: 205 1/8
Locality: Lower California, Mexico. Date: 1940.
Hunter: an Indian. Owner: Carl M. Scrivens.

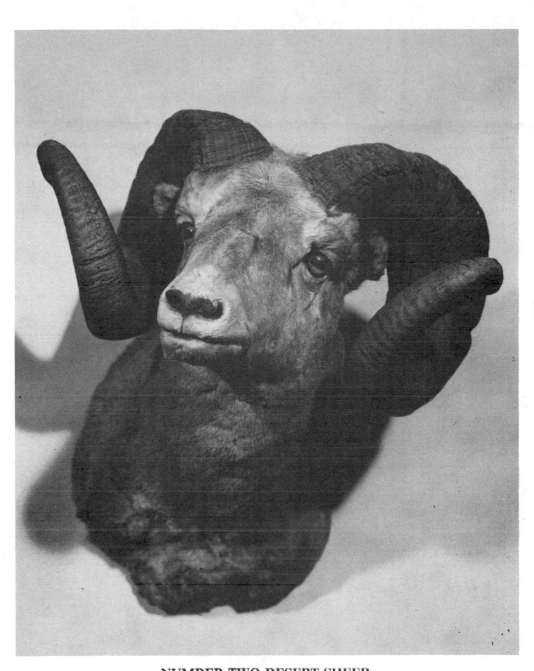

NUMBER TWO DESERT SHEEP
SCORE: 197 4/8
Locality: Lower California, Mexico. Date: 1892.
Hunter: unknown.
Donated by Dr. H.M. Beck to the Academy of Natural Sciences, Philadelphia.

Desert Sheep

Minimum Score 168

Ovis canadensis nelsoni and certain related subspecies

Score	Length of Horn R.	Length of Horn L.	Circumference of Base R.	Circumference of Base L.	Circumference at Third Quarter R.	Circumference at Third Quarter L.	Greatest Spread	Tip to Tip Spread	Locality Killed	By Whom Killed	Owner	Date Killed	Rank
205 1/8	43 5/8	43 6/8	16 6/8	17	10 5/8	10 6/8	25 5/8	25 5/8	Lower Calif., Mexico	Indian	Carl M. Scrivens	1940	1
197 4/8	44	43 4/8	15 7/8	15 7/8	10 5/8	10	23 7/8	23 7/8	Lower Calif., Mexico	Gift Of H. M. Beck	Acad. Nat. Sci., Phil.	1892	2
191 6/8	42	43 4/8	15 4/8	15 3/8	9 6/8	9 3/8	23 4/8	23 4/8	Baja Calif., Mexico	Lit Ng	Lit Ng	1968	3
191 3/8	40	41 3/8	16 5/8	16 5/8	9 1/8	9 6/8	24 1/8	24 1/8	Mexico	Picked Up	Snow Museum	——	4
189 4/8	39 5/8	39 4/8	15 4/8	15 4/8	10 3/8	11	21 3/8	21 3/8	Lower Calif., Mexico	M. B. Silva	M. B. Silva	1939	5
188 2/8	43	43	14 4/8	14 5/8	9 5/8	9 4/8	27 3/8	27 3/8	Baja Calif., Mexico	A. Cal Rossi, Jr.	A. Cal Rossi, Jr.	1974	6
187 6/8	42	40	15 2/8	15 2/8	10 1/8	10 1/8	23 5/8	23 5/8	Baja Calif., Mexico	Ed Stedman, Jr.	Ed Stedman, Jr.	1976	7
187 5/8	38 4/8	40 5/8	16 2/8	16 2/8	9	9 4/8	21 4/8	20 6/8	Baja Calif., Mexico	Romulo Sanchez Mireles	Romulo Sanchez Mireles	1969	8
187 3/8	39 2/8	39 7/8	15 1/8	15 2/8	10 2/8	10 5/8	21	21	Sonora, Mexico	Herb Klein	Herb Klein	1952	9
187 3/8	39 1/8	39 2/8	16	16	10 2/8	10 3/8	17 6/8	17 6/8	Sonora, Mexico	Oscar J. Brooks	Oscar J. Brooks	1955	9
187	39 1/8	39 5/8	16	16	9 3/8	9 5/8	24 5/8	24 5/8	Lower Calif., Mexico	Unknown	Snow Museum	——	11
187	40 4/8	40 2/8	15 4/8	15 2/8	9 6/8	10	26	26	Kofa Mts., Ariz.	Louis R. Dees	Louis R. Dees	1965	11
186 5/8	38 3/8	38 4/8	14 7/8	14 7/8	11 3/8	11 3/8	22	20 1/8	Sonora, Mexico	F. B. Heider	O. M. Corbett	1927	13
186 2/8	40 5/8	38 3/8	16	16	9	9 1/8	21 1/8	20 7/8	Maricopa Co., Ariz.	Ralph Grossman	Ralph Grossman	1961	14
185 3/8	39 5/8	40	16	16	10 2/8	9 2/8	22 3/8	19 7/8	Baja Calif., Mexico	Graciano Guichard	Graciano Guichard	1970	15
185 2/8	39 7/8	38 7/8	15 5/8	15 6/8	9	9 3/8	19 4/8	16 3/8	Baja Calif., Mexico	Wilmer C. Hansen	Wilmer C. Hansen	1972	16
185 2/8	39 2/8	39 2/8	15 3/8	15 4/8	10 4/8	9 7/8	25 2/8	25 2/8	Baja Calif., Mexico	Albert Pellizzari	Albert Pellizzari	1978	16
185	39 4/8	39 2/8	15 7/8	15 7/8	8 7/8	9	20 3/8	18 6/8	San Borja Mts., Mexico	Alice J. Landreth	Alice J. Landreth	1969	18
184 6/8	42	40 6/8	14 6/8	15	9 4/8	9 2/8	29 4/8	29 4/8	Kofa Mts., Ariz.	W. A. Rudd	W. A. Rudd	1965	19
184 6/8	39 4/8	38 4/8	16 2/8	16 3/8	8 5/8	8 7/8	22 5/8	21 1/8	Baja Calif., Mexico	Burton L. Smith, Sr.	Burton L. Smith, Sr.	1973	19
184 5/8	40 1/8	37 4/8	15 1/8	15 1/8	10	10 3/8	22 4/8	21 2/8	Baja Calif., Mexico	Steven L. Rose	Steven L. Rose	1967	21
184 4/8	38 6/8	39	15 5/8	16	9 2/8	9 4/8	20 6/8	21	Baja, Mexico	H. Clayton Poole	H. Clayton Poole	1966	22
184 4/8	43 1/8	45 3/8	13 7/8	13 5/8	8 6/8	8 6/8	26 4/8	26 4/8	Santa Teresa Mts., Ariz.	Picked Up	Ariz. Game & Fish Dept.	1967	22
184 4/8	40 4/8	40	15 2/8	15 2/8	9 2/8	9	22	22	Baja Calif., Mexico	Clint Heiber	Clint Heiber	1978	22
184 1/8	38 5/8	40	15 2/8	15 2/8	9 3/8	9 4/8	22	20 1/8	Papago Indian Res., Ariz.	Ralph J. Murrietta	Ollie O. Barney, Jr.	1965	25
184	40 1/8	38 7/8	14 6/8	14 6/8	10 1/8	9 7/8	25 4/8	25 4/8	Santa Rosa Mts., Calif.	Picked Up	Fred L. Jones	1955	26
183 7/8	39 3/8	38 4/8	16	16	9 5/8	9 3/8	23 5/8	23 5/8	Gonzaga, Mexico	Glenn Napierskie	Glenn Napierskie	1970	27
183 3/8	40	40 3/8	14	13 7/8	10 4/8	9 6/8	24 7/8	24 1/8	Pinkley, Ariz.	Picked Up	Organ Pipe Cactus Natl. Mon.	1957	28
183 2/8	39 4/8	41 6/8	15 2/8	15 2/8	9	9	25 3/8	25 3/8	Lower Calif., Mexico	George H. Gould	National Collection	1894	29
183 2/8	39 7/8	38 1/8	15 2/8	15 2/8	9 7/8	9 6/8	23	23	Clark Co., Nevada	Gerald A. Lent	Gerald A. Lent	1976	29
182 6/8	39 2/8	37 6/8	14 6/8	14 4/8	11	10 7/8	22	20 6/8	Colo. River, Ariz.	Picked Up	Phil Schlegel	1956	31

182 6/8	41 6/8	38 6/8	15 4/8	15 4/8	8 2/8	8 4/8	23 4/8	23 4/8	Baja Calif., Mexico	Rita Oney	Rita Oney	1976	31
182 5/8	39	39 1/8	15 5/8	15 6/8	8 6/8	9 2/8	22 5/8	22 6/8	Baja Calif., Mexico	Duane H. Loomis	Duane H. Loomis	1972	33
182 5/8	36	35 5/8	16 4/8	16 3/8	9 4/8	9 6/8	22 2/8	19 5/8	Pima Co., Ariz.	Charles W. Fisher	Charles W. Fisher	1972	33
182 4/8	39 7/8	39 3/8	14 6/8	14 5/8	9 6/8	9 7/8	21 1/8	21 1/8	Lower Calif., Mexico	Picked Up	C. G. Clare	1958	35
182 4/8	37	37 4/8	14 7/8	15 2/8	10	10 2/8	22 3/8	21 3/8	Riverside Co., Calif.	Picked Up	Orson Morgan	1963	35
182 3/8	38 5/8	37 6/8	14 6/8	15	10 5/8	10 1/8	22 1/8	22 1/8	Lower Calif., Mexico	Elgin T. Gates	Elgin T. Gates	1940	37
182 3/8	39 3/8	40	14 7/8	15	9 3/8	9 5/8	22	22	Baja Calif., Mexico	Robert Zachrich	Robert Zachrich	1978	37
182	38	36 6/8	15 6/8	15 6/8	9 2/8	9 2/8	22 1/8	19 4/8	Baja Calif., Mexico	John M. Griffith, Jr.	John M. Griffith, Jr.	1974	39
181 5/8	39 2/8	41 3/8	15 2/8	15 1/8	8 7/8	8 7/8	24 1/8	24 1/8	Sheep Mt. Range, Nev.	David Ingram	David Ingram	1962	40
181 5/8	36 2/8	36 3/8	16 1/8	16 1/8	10 3/8	10 3/8	22	20 1/8	Baja Calif., Mexico	Elvin Hawkins	Elvin Hawkins	1978	40
181 4/8	42 2/8	40	14 3/8	14 6/8	8 5/8	9	24	24	Sonora, Mexico	George W. Parker	George W. Parker	1939	42
181 3/8	38 6/8	38 7/8	15 1/8	15 4/8	9 6/8	9 6/8	25 6/8	25 1/8	Maricopa Co., Ariz.	Kirt I. Darner	Kirt I. Darner	1971	43
181 2/8	37	37	15	15	10 3/8	10 6/8	21 7/8	21 1/8	Sonora, Mexico	Ira C. Green	Ira C. Green	1939	44
180 7/8	40	38 1/8	15 4/8	15 4/8	8 7/8	9 1/8	22 5/8	22 5/8	Baja Calif., Mexico	Geo. H. Landreth	Geo. H. Landreth	1969	45
180 7/8	37 7/8	34 4/8	15 6/8	15 6/8	9 6/8	9 6/8	20 6/8	20 5/8	Baja Calif., Mexico	Jack Atcheson, Jr.	Jack Atcheson, Jr.	1978	45
180 4/8	35 7/8	37 3/8	16 1/8	16 3/8	9	8 6/8	19 [illegible]/8	18 4/8	Dragon Teeth Mt., Ariz.	Raymond White	Raymond White	1966	47
180 3/8	38 1/8	40 2/8	15 1/8	15 1/8	9	9 1/8	20 3/8	20 3/8	Baja, Mexico	Arthur R. Dubs	Arthur R. Dubs	1966	48
180 3/8	39 2/8	39 5/8	14 5/8	14 6/8	9 3/8	9 6/8	22 4/8	22 4/8	Baja Calif., Mexico	Fritz A. Nachant	Fritz A. Nachant	1970	48
180 3/8	38	37 5/8	14 7/8	15	10 2/8	9 4/8	21 7/8	17	Yuma Co., Ariz.	James K. McCasland	James K. McCasland	1978	48
180 1/8	37 4/8	39 1/8	14 3/8	14 2/8	9 3/8	9 6/8	22 5/8	22 2/8	Tank Mts., Ariz.	Picked Up	Calvin C. Wallerich	1960	51
180	36 1/8	36 1/8	15 6/8	15 6/8	9 4/8	10 1/8	21 3/8	17 3/8	Pima Co., Ariz.	Clifford W. Saylor	Clifford W. Saylor	1976	52
179 7/8	38 7/8	36 4/8	15 3/8	15 2/8	10 2/8	9 4/8	25 4/8	23 5/8	Clark Co., Nevada	Sal Quilici	Nevada State Museum	1978	53
179 7/8	37 5/8	37 2/8	15 2/8	15 2/8	8 7/8	9 2/8	19 5/8	–	Baja Calif., Mexico	George W. Vogt	George W. Vogt	1978	53
179 6/8	39 1/8	39 1/8	16	16	7 5/8	7 4/8	24	24	Baja Calif., Mexico	Don L. Corley	Don L. Corley	1978	55
179 4/8	38 1/8	37 3/8	15 3/8	15 4/8	9 4/8	9 7/8	21	19 6/8	Baja Calif., Mexico	Mrs. Carroll Pistell	Mrs. Carroll Pistell	1969	56
179 2/8	36 5/8	35 7/8	16 2/8	16 2/8	9 1/8	9 1/8	20 5/8	19 3/8	Baja, Mexico	Jim Buss	Jim Buss	1966	57
179 2/8	38 2/8	37	15 2/8	15 2/8	9 6/8	9 4/8	21 2/8	21 2/8	Baja Calif., Mexico	Francisco Salido	Francisco Salido	1968	57
179 1/8	36 1/8	38 2/8	15 4/8	15 5/8	8 4/8	8 6/8	21 4/8	18 4/8	Baja Calif., Mexico	W. J. Boynton, Jr.	W. J. Boynton, Jr.	1974	59
179	37 3/8	36 1/8	16 2/8	16 1/8	8 5/8	8 6/8	19 4/8	18 7/8	Baja Calif., Mexico	Graciano G. Michel	Graciano G. Michel	1970	60
178 7/8	39 1/8	36	16 2/8	16 2/8	8	7 5/8	20 5/8	20	Hidalgo Co., N. M.	L. P. McKinney	Frank McKinney	1921	61
178 7/8	36 7/8	37	15 3/8	15 4/8	9 7/8	10 1/8	23	22 6/8	Sauceda Mts., Ariz.	Picked Up	Edward Hunt	1962	61
178 6/8	39 6/8	39 4/8	14 3/8	14 4/8	9 1/8	9	27	27	Colo. River, Nev.	E. A. Goldman	U. S. Natl. Mus.	1913	63
178 6/8	37 2/8	37	14 6/8	14 6/8	10 2/8	10 2/8	22 3/8	18 5/8	Sonora, Mexico	Oscar J. Brooks	Oscar J. Brooks	1950	63
178 4/8	38 3/8	35 3/8	15 5/8	15 5/8	9 5/8	9 1/8	22 3/8	20	Pima Co., Ariz.	Ken Broyles	Ken Broyles	1971	65
178 4/8	36 4/8	36 2/8	15 6/8	15 6/8	9	9 2/8	20 4/8	19 2/8	Baja Calif., Mexico	Henry Culp	Henry Culp	1978	65
178 2/8	38 4/8	38 3/8	14 3/8	14 2/8	10 4/8	9 5/8	21	21	Lower Calif., Mexico	F. Stephens	U. S. Natl. Mus.	1902	67
178 1/8	34	40 1/8	15	14 6/8	9 5/8	10 2/8	19 7/8	18	Maricopa Co., Ariz.	Michael Holt	Michael Holt	1970	68
178	36	37	16	16	8 6/8	9	15 4/8	22	Sonora, Mexico	Aaron Saenz, Jr.	Aaron Saenz, Jr.	1969	69
178	38 3/8	37 3/8	15	14 6/8	9 3/8	9 6/8	21 4/8	19 4/8	Baja Calif., Mexico	Basil C. Bradbury	Basil C. Bradbury	1969	69
177 7/8	39 7/8	38 6/8	15 1/8	15 3/8	8 3/8	8	25 5/8	26 5/8	San Boros Mts., Mexico	Jerald T. Waite	Jerald T. Waite	1972	71
177 7/8	38 1/8	37 4/8	15	15 1/8	9 2/8	9 2/8	20 5/8	19 2/8	Baja Calif., Mexico	Richard C. Hansen	Richard C. Hansen	1973	71
177 4/8	38	42	14 4/8	14 4/8	8 1/8	8 3/8	27 6/8	27 6/8	Lower Calif., Mexico	Earl A. Garrettson	William Foster	1912	73
177 4/8	38	37	14 5/8	14 6/8	9 4/8	9 3/8	25 5/8	24	Baja, Mexico	Herb Klein	Herb Klein	1966	73

Desert Sheep–*Continued*

Ovis canadensis nelsoni and certain related subspecies

Score	Length of Horn R.	Length of Horn L.	Circumference of Base R.	Circumference of Base L.	Circumference at Third Quarter R.	Circumference at Third Quarter L.	Greatest Spread	Tip to Tip Spread	Locality Killed	By Whom Killed	Owner	Date Killed	Rank
177 4/8	36 7/8	35 7/8	14 7/8	15 1/8	9 4/8	9 5/8	15 7/8	18 7/8	Baja Calif., Mexico	Joe Osterbauer	Joe Osterbauer	1978	73
177 3/8	36 6/8	37 5/8	14 3/8	14 5/8	9 6/8	9 6/8	22 6/8	22	Yuma Co., Ariz.	George I. Parker	George I. Parker	1968	76
177 3/8	37 3/8	38	15 4/8	15 2/8	8 7/8	8 7/8	21 7/8	21 7/8	Baja Calif., Mexico	Arthur W. Carlsberg	Arthur W. Carlsberg	1970	76
177 2/8	37 1/8	37 1/8	15 3/8	15 3/8	9	9 3/8	20 2/8	20 2/8	San Borjas Mts., Mexico	Lloyd Zeman	Lloyd Zeman	1970	78
177 2/8	37	36	15 2/8	15 3/8	9 1/8	9 1/8	23	20 6/8	Yuma Co., Ariz.	Robert Fritzinger	Robert Fritzinger	1976	78
177 1/8	36 1/8	36 2/8	15 6/8	15 6/8	8 6/8	8 6/8	21 4/8	20 6/8	Pima Co., Ariz.	Michael A. Jensen	Michael A. Jensen	1978	80
177	36 4/8	36 2/8	15 3/8	15 4/8	9	9 2/8	19	18	Baja, Mexico	Alain Ferraris	Alain Ferraris	1966	81
177	36 4/8	37	15 1/8	14 6/8	9 1/8	9 2/8	21 3/8	20	Sonora Desert, Mexico	Herb Klein	Herb Klein	1969	81
177	35 4/8	36 6/8	15 7/8	15 7/8	9 2/8	9 1/8	19 6/8	17 3/8	Baja Calif., Mexico	Roy A. Woodward	Roy A. Woodward	1969	81
176 7/8	38 1/8	42	14 2/8	14 2/8	8 2/8	8 3/8	27 6/8	27 6/8	Mexico	Bill Foster	Foster's Bighorn Rest.	1950	84
176 7/8	38 7/8	36 2/8	14 5/8	14 6/8	9	8 6/8	23 7/8	23 2/8	Muddy Mts., Nev.	Arthur Alles	Lauren A. Johnson	1956	84
176 6/8	38	39 2/8	14 6/8	14 6/8	8 6/8	7 6/8	21 3/8	20 2/8	Kofa Range, Ariz.	Picked Up	Duard B. Sanford	1957	86
176 6/8	36 3/8	36 1/8	14 1/8	13 6/8	10 5/8	10 7/8	23 3/8	23 3/8	Santa Rosa Mts., Calif.	Picked Up	John C. Belcher	PR1958	86
176 5/8	36 3/8	38	15 6/8	15 6/8	8 4/8	8 7/8	20	20	Baja Calif., Mexico	Fernando Garcia	Fernando Garcia	1968	88
176 4/8	38 6/8	37 2/8	15 2/8	15 1/8	8 3/8	8 4/8	23 2/8	23 2/8	Lower Calif., Mexico	E. W. Funcke	U. S. Natl. Mus.	1905	89
176 4/8	38	38 2/8	13 6/8	14	10 1/8	9 7/8	21 6/8	21 6/8	Baja Calif., Mexico	Picked Up	Leland Brand	1973	89
176 3/8	34 5/8	34 6/8	16 4/8	16 5/8	8 5/8	9	19 7/8	18 1/8	Baja Calif., Mexico	William L. Baker, Jr.	William L. Baker, Jr.	1974	91
176 3/8	35 2/8	37 1/8	15 3/8	16	9	9 2/8	21 1/8	15 6/8	Baja Calif., Mexico	Joe E. Coleman	Joe E. Coleman	1976	91
176 3/8	37 5/8	36	15 3/8	15 2/8	8 2/8	8 5/8	29 1/8	29 1/8	Baja Calif., Mexico	C. J. McElroy	C. J. McElroy	1978	91
176 3/8	36 5/8	36 6/8	15 7/8	15 7/8	8 4/8	8 4/8	19 7/8	14 7/8	Baja Calif., Mexico	Richard Wehling	Richard Wehling	1978	91
176 2/8	35 6/8	36 6/8	14 3/8	14 3/8	9 6/8	10	23 1/8	22 4/8	Clark Co., Nev.	F. Lorin Ronnow	F. Lorin Ronnow	1957	95
176 2/8	39 2/8	34 4/8	15 2/8	15 3/8	8 7/8	8 4/8	28 5/8	28 5/8	Clark Co., Nev.	Robert M. Bransford	Robert M. Bransford	1966	95
176 1/8	37 2/8	36 5/8	15	15 1/8	9 2/8	9 2/8	25 3/8	25 3/8	Baja Calif., Mexico	N. J. Segal, Jr.	N. J. Segal, Jr.	1972	97
176	38 3/8	39 7/8	15 1/8	15 1/8	7 4/8	8 1/8	22 1/8	20 5/8	Sonora, Mexico	Fritz Katz	Fritz Katz	1941	98
176	37 2/8	38 2/8	14 4/8	15	9	9 4/8	25	25	Black Mts., Ariz.	Picked Up	R. A. (Dick) Wagner	1954	98
176	37 4/8	34 2/8	15 4/8	15 5/8	9 2/8	9 2/8	21 4/8	18 4/8	Kofa Mts., Ariz.	Robin Underdown	Robin Underdown	1966	98
176	34 6/8	34 2/8	17 1/8	17 1/8	8 3/8	8 3/8	19 6/8	17	Sonora, Mexico	Ollie O. Barney	Ollie O. Barney	1968	98
175 7/8	35 7/8	35 4/8	15	15 1/8	9 7/8	9 3/8	22 4/8	22	Yuma Co., Ariz.	J. Don McGaffee	J. Don McGaffee	1978	102
175 6/8	39	38 4/8	14 6/8	15 2/8	9 5/8	8 7/8	22 1/8	–	Barstow, Calif.	Picked Up	Thomas Hodges	1941	103
175 6/8	35 5/8	36 1/8	14 1/8	14	10 2/8	10 4/8	21 2/8	17 5/8	San Diego Co., Calif.	Picked Up	Anza-Borrego Desert State Park	1951	103
175 6/8	35 3/8	35 3/8	16 1/8	16 3/8	8 5/8	8 3/8	18 6/8	18 6/8	Baja Calif., Mexico	Jack Leeds	Jack Leeds	1976	103

175 6/8	33 3/8	35 5/8	16	16	9 4/8	9 1/8	22	20 6/8	Pima Co., Ariz.	Robert F. Lebo	Robert F. Lebo	1977	103
175 6/8	36 6/8	36 4/8	14 3/8	14 3/8	9 6/8	9 6/8	21	21	Lincoln Co., Nevada	Denny L. Frook	Denny L. Frook	1977	103
175 4/8	36	36 4/8	15 4/8	15 4/8	8 4/8	8 4/8	20 6/8	19 3/8	Yuma, Ariz.	Unknown	Tom D. Moore	——	108
175 4/8	37 2/8	36	15	14 4/8	9 4/8	10	21 4/8	21 4/8	Maricopa Co., Ariz.	Picked Up	Robert B. Thompson	1963	108
175 4/8	37 3/8	36 5/8	14 4/8	14 6/8	9 3/8	9 4/8	21 6/8	19	Baja Calif., Mexico	Tony Oney	Tony Oney	1968	108
175 4/8	36 4/8	37 4/8	14 7/8	14 7/8	8 7/8	9 7/8	22 3/8	21 6/8	Plomosa Mts., Ariz.	J. James Froelich	J. James Froelich	1969	108
175 3/8	37	37 3/8	14 5/8	14 5/8	8 6/8	9 2/8	21 2/8	21 2/8	Lincoln Co., Nev.	Robert Fagan	Robert Fagan	1968	112
175 3/8	35 6/8	35 3/8	15 4/8	15 3/8	9 4/8	9 2/8	21 6/8	18 4/8	Plomosa Mts., Ariz.	M. S. MacCollum	M. S. MacCollum	1968	112
175 2/8	37 4/8	37 4/8	14 2/8	14 3/8	9 1/8	9 1/8	21 5/8	21 3/8	Baja Calif., Mexico	K. C. Brown	K. C. Brown	1966	114
175 1/8	37 1/8	40	13 7/8	13 7/8	8 6/8	9 3/8	20 5/8	22 6/8	Riverside Co., Calif.	Picked Up	George F. Stewart, Jr.	——	115
175 1/8	36 4/8	37 3/8	15 2/8	15 1/8	8 2/8	8 5/8	19 3/8	19 3/8	Mexico	Bill Foster	Foster's Bighorn Rest.	1950	115
175 1/8	36 5/8	37 2/8	14 7/8	15	9 4/8	8 7/8	19 4/8	17 4/8	Sonora, Mexico	Unknown	Paul W. Hughes	1952	115
175 1/8	37 2/8	38 3/8	14 2/8	14 2/8	9 2/8	8 5/8	20 1/8	20 1/8	Lamb Springs, Nev.	D. B. Walkington	D. B. Walkington	1965	115
175 1/8	37 1/8	37	14 6/8	14 6/8	9 5/8	9 2/8	25 7/8	25 7/8	Clark Co., Nev.	Wayne C. Matley	Wayne C. Matley	1966	115
175 1/8	36 5/8	35 5/8	15 2/8	15 2/8	8 7/8	8 7/8	31 1/8	18 6/8	Baja Calif., Mexico	C. J. Wimer	C. J. Wimer	1977	115
175	35	36	15	15 2/8	10	9 2/8	16	22 4/8	Sonora, Mexico	Juan A. Saenz, Jr.	Juan A. Saenz, Jr.	1969	121
174 7/8	37	35 1/8	15	15	9 3/8	8 6/8	20 3/8	19 6/8	Pima, Ariz.	Picked Up	Robert J. Kirkpatrick	——	122
174 7/8	37 1/8	38 4/8	13 5/8	13 5/8	9 3/8	9 4/8	23 3/8	21	Ariz.	Picked Up	Nathan Frisby	1974	122
174 5/8	34 7/8	34 6/8	15 7/8	15 5/8	9 1/8	9 2/8	18 7/8	16 4/8	Baja Calif., Mexico	Stanley S. Gray	Stanley S. Gray	1972	124
174 4/8	36 4/8	36	14	14 2/8	9 6/8	9 4/8	19 4/8	19 4/8	Maricopa Co., Ariz.	Picked Up	Robert B. Thompson	1963	125
174 4/8	37	36 6/8	15 1/8	15 2/8	8 2/8	8 3/8	20 6/8	20 6/8	Baja, Mexico	Jack Walters	Jack Walters	1966	125
174 2/8	37	36	15 7/8	15 7/8	7 7/8	7 5/8	20 4/8	18 3/8	Baja Calif., Mexico	Basil C. Bradbury	Basil C. Bradbury	1968	127
174 2/8	37	38 2/8	14	14 1/8	10 1/8	10 1/8	21 7/8	21 7/8	Las Vegas, Nev.	Thos. R. McElhenney	Thos. R. McElhenney	1969	127
174	40	38 4/8	15 2/8	15 4/8	7 4/8	7 6/8	25 2/8	25 2/8	Lower Calif., Mexico	E. W. Funcke	Harvard Univ. Mus.	1911	129
174	36 4/8	37 4/8	15 4/8	15 3/8	9	8	21 5/8	21	Yuma Co., Ariz.	Wynn Robestal	U. S. Fish & Wild. Ser.	1913	129
174	37 2/8	36 2/8	14 4/8	14 4/8	9 2/8	9	19 4/8	18	Sonora, Mexico	F. C. Hibben	F. C. Hibben	1940	129
174	36 6/8	37 4/8	13 4/8	13 5/8	10	10	24 4/8	24 4/8	McCullough Mts., Nev	Picked Up	William H. Pogue	PR1958	129
173 7/8	37 2/8	37 1/8	14 3/8	14 5/8	8 4/8	8 7/8	24 5/8	24 5/8	Kofa Mts., Ariz.	William L. Snider	William L. Snider	1965	133
173 7/8	36 5/8	37	13 1/8	13 4/8	10 2/8	10 4/8	22 2/8	19 3/8	Anza-Borrego Desert, Calif.	Picked Up	Anza-Borrego Desert State Park	1971	133
173 7/8	34 6/8	34 7/8	15 6/8	15 4/8	9 1/8	9 1/8	22 5/8	22 2/8	Baja Calif., Mexico	Erwin Dykstra	Erwin Dykstra	1978	133
173 6/8	34 6/8	34 4/8	14 2/8	14 4/8	9 6/8	10 2/8	22 4/8	21 6/8	Yuma Co., Ariz.	Picked Up	Bob Housholder	1953	136
173 6/8	35 7/8	36 1/8	16 2/8	16 2/8	8 4/8	8	20 5/8	20 5/8	Baja Calif., Mexico	Fritz A. Nachant	Fritz A. Nachant	1969	136
173 5/8	37	37 1/8	15 1/8	15 3/8	8 4/8	8 6/8	20 7/8	20 4/8	Baja Calif., Mexico	James H. Duke, Jr.	James H. Duke, Jr.	1969	138
173 5/8	35 4/8	34 5/8	15 1/8	15 1/8	9	8 7/8	22 2/8	22 2/8	Baja Calif., Mexico	John H. Batten	John H. Batten	1975	138
173 4/8	35 6/8	36 6/8	15 5/8	15 6/8	8 1/8	8	21 3/8	21 3/8	Muleje Baja, Mexico	Victor M. Ruiza	Victor M. Ruiza	1966	140
173 4/8	35 6/8	35 6/8	15 1/8	15 4/8	8 7/8	8 3/8	20 7/8	20 1/8	Baja Calif., Mexico	James H. Russell	James H. Russell	1970	140
173 4/8	34 6/8	33 6/8	16 2/8	16 2/8	8 2/8	9	19 7/8	15	Sonora, Mexico	Walter Snoke	Walter Snoke	1978	140
173 4/8	35	33 4/8	16	16	8 4/8	8 2/8	23 1/8	23 1/8	Clark Co., Nevada	Ira H. Kent	Ira H. Kent	1978	140
173 3/8	36 6/8	36 1/8	14 5/8	14 5/8	8 6/8	8 5/8	21 1/8	17 7/8	Baja Calif., Mexico	M. Alessio Robles	M. Alessio Robles	1956	144
173 3/8	36 2/8	36 3/8	15 5/8	15 5/8	8 1/8	8 2/8	21 3/8	20 3/8	Sonora, Mexico	Gaston Cano	Gaston Cano	1968	144
173 3/8	36 6/8	37 3/8	14 6/8	14 7/8	8 6/8	8 4/8	22 3/8	22 3/8	Baja Calif., Mexico	Roy A. Schultz	Roy A. Schultz	1971	144
173 3/8	37	37 7/8	15	15 1/8	8 4/8	8 6/8	22	22	Baja Calif., Mexico	Dale R. Leonard	Dale R. Leonard	1972	144

Desert Sheep–*Continued*

Ovis canadensis nelsoni and certain related subspecies

Score	Length of Horn R.	Length of Horn L.	Circumference of Base R.	Circumference of Base L.	Circumference at Third Quarter R.	Circumference at Third Quarter L.	Greatest Spread	Tip to Tip Spread	Locality Killed	By Whom Killed	Owner	Date Killed	Rank
173 2/8	34 7/8	35 3/8	15 4/8	15 4/8	8 6/8	8 5/8	25 3/8	25 3/8	Little Horn Mts., Ariz.	Joseph J. Sobotka	Joseph J. Sobotka	1969	148
173 2/8	36 3/8	36 1/8	15 5/8	15 2/8	8 4/8	8 2/8	21 1/8	19 3/8	Baja Calif., Mexico	Ernest Righetti	Ernest Righetti	1974	148
173 2/8	35 2/8	34 6/8	15 4/8	15 3/8	8 6/8	8 6/8	21 5/8	21 5/8	Baja Calif., Mexico	Marion H. Scott	Marion H. Scott	1978	148
173 1/8	37 1/8	35 2/8	14 1/8	14 5/8	9 4/8	9	21	21	Little Horn Mts., Ariz.	Picked Up	Duane J. Hall	1960	151
173 1/8	32 6/8	30 7/8	15 4/8	15 3/8	11	11 6/8	24 4/8	23	Tulelake, Calif.	Einar Johnson	Natl. Park Service	1968	151
173 1/8	37 4/8	40 1/8	14	13 1/8	7 7/8	9 7/8	21 3/8	18	Sonora Desert, Mexico	Picked Up	Herb Klein	1969	151
173 1/8	37 1/8	37	14 3/8	14 4/8	9 1/8	8 3/8	27 5/8	27 5/8	Clark Co., Nev.	Chris Hurtado	Chris Hurtado	1975	151
173	36	38	15	15	8 2/8	8 4/8	24 4/8	21 4/8	Lower Calif., Mexico	Henry H. Blagden	Henry H. Blagden	1914	155
173	36 1/8	38 3/8	14 6/8	14 6/8	8 4/8	9 1/8	19 1/8	19 1/8	Sheep Mt. Range, Nev.	Gilbert A. Helsel	Gilbert A. Helsel	1960	155
173	36	35 2/8	14 3/8	14 3/8	9 4/8	9	21 6/8	16 6/8	Aguila Mts., Ariz.	Picked Up	C. G. Clare	1961	155
173	37 1/8	37 1/8	13 6/8	14	10 3/8	10 5/8	20	17 5/8	Maricopa Co., Ariz.	Stephen K. Weisser	Stephen K. Weisser	1973	155
173	39	35	15	15	8 3/8	8 3/8	24	24	Baja Calif., Mexico	Charles Oyer	Charles Oyer	1975	155
173	34 4/8	35	15 5/8	15 6/8	8 2/8	8 6/8	20 4/8	17 2/8	Baja Calif., Mexico	P. Franklin Bays, Jr.	P. Franklin Bays, Jr.	1976	155
172 7/8	34	34 1/8	15 2/8	15 2/8	9 3/8	9 3/8	20 5/8	19 4/8	Baja Calif., Mexico	Mahlon T. White	Mahlon T. White	1969	161
172 6/8	37 1/8	38 5/8	13 4/8	13 5/8	9	9	23 7/8	23 7/8	Baja Calif., Mexico	Otis Chandler	Otis Chandler	1966	162
172 6/8	37 2/8	35 4/8	15 7/8	15 5/8	8 7/8	8 4/8	21 2/8	21 2/8	Baja Calif., Mexico	Graciano Guichard	Graciano Guichard	1969	162
172 6/8	36 3/8	36 3/8	14 3/8	14 3/8	8 4/8	8 5/8	20 3/8	19	Yuma Co., Ariz.	Norman F. Mathews	Norman F. Mathews	1977	162
172 5/8	34 1/8	36 4/8	15 3/8	15 3/8	8 1/8	9 2/8	20 6/8	18 2/8	Sonora, Mexico	Lloyd O. Barrow	Lloyd O. Barrow	1969	165
172 5/8	35 7/8	35 2/8	14 4/8	14 4/8	9 6/8	10	19 6/8	19 6/8	Baja Calif., Mexico	G. David Edwards	G. David Edwards	1973	165
172 5/8	37 3/8	36	15 5/8	15 4/8	8	8	21 3/8	21 3/8	Baja Calif., Mexico	Daniel Smith	Daniel Smith	1975	165
172 5/8	32 3/8	35 4/8	15 2/8	15 4/8	8 3/8	9	19 2/8	18 6/8	Clark Co., Nevada	Charles W. Knittle	Charles W. Knittle	1976	165
172 5/8	40 3/8	38 6/8	13 3/8	12 6/8	8 6/8	8 2/8	26 5/8	26 5/8	White Mts., Calif.	Picked Up	Danny Lowe	1978	165
172 4/8	36 2/8	34 6/8	15 3/8	15 5/8	8 3/8	8 2/8	22 1/8	19 6/8	Yuma Co., Ariz.	Margaret Wood	Margaret Wood	1958	170
172 4/8	36	34 4/8	15	15	8 4/8	8 4/8	23	23	Yuma Co., Ariz.	Picked Up	Donald Ogan	1964	170
172 3/8	34 6/8	32 5/8	15	15 1/8	9 6/8	9 2/8	21 5/8	21 1/8	Sauceda Mts., Ariz.	Wayne Grippin	Wayne Grippin	1962	172
172 2/8	38	37 4/8	15	15 4/8	7 3/8	7 4/8	27 1/8	27 1/8	Lower Calif., Mexico	Wm. E. Humphrey	Wash. State Mus.	1909	173
172 2/8	36 5/8	35 3/8	15 1/8	15 1/8	8 5/8	8 4/8	20 2/8	20 2/8	Baja Calif., Mexico	Herb Klein	Herb Klein	1966	173
172 2/8	35 2/8	35 2/8	15 6/8	15 4/8	9	8 6/8	19 1/8	16 6/8	Baja Calif., Mexico	Armando de la Parra	Armando de la Parra	1966	173
172 1/8	36	35 7/8	15	15 2/8	8 4/8	8 4/8	23	14	Kofa Range, Ariz.	Picked Up	Ariz. Game & Fish Dept.	1953	176
172	33	36	15	15 4/8	9	8 4/8	30 2/8	30 2/8	Tulelake, Calif.	Picked Up	Natl. Park Service	1963	177
172	34 6/8	35	15	15	8 7/8	8 7/8	20 6/8	20 6/8	Baja Calif., Mexico	Robert O. Cromwell	Robert O. Cromwell	1974	177
172	34 5/8	34 5/8	16 4/8	16 1/8	8 3/8	8 5/8	21 3/8	20 3/8	Baja Calif., Mexico	Bill Silveira	Bill Silveira	1974	177

171 7/8	33 1/8	32 6/8	16 1/8	15 7/8	8 6/8	8 6/8	19 7/8	17 7/8	Baja Calif., Mexico	Joan Leeds	Joan Leeds	1976	180
171 7/8	33 7/8	35 2/8	15 2/8	15 4/8	9 7/8	9 7/8	22 1/8	21 4/8	Baja Calif., Mexico	Don L. Corley	Don L. Corley	1978	180
171 6/8	37 2/8	36 4/8	14	13 4/8	9 5/8	9 4/8	20 1/8	20 1/8	Kofa Range, Ariz.	Harvey Davison	Harvey Davison	1953	182
171 6/8	36 4/8	36	15 6/8	15 6/8	7 6/8	8 3/8	21	18 2/8	Baja Calif., Mexico	Earl H. Harris	Earl H. Harris	1968	182
171 6/8	35 6/8	35 2/8	14	14	10	10 1/8	23	20 7/8	Lincoln Co., Nevada	William A. Molini	William A. Molini	1977	182
171 5/8	36 4/8	36 3/8	14 3/8	14 5/8	8 7/8	8 5/8	21 4/8	21 4/8	Sonora, Mexico	Picked Up	Bob C. Jones	—	185
171 5/8	38 6/8	38 1/8	15 5/8	15 4/8	7	7	23	23	Sonora, Mexico	Julio Estrada	Julio Estrada	1931	185
171 5/8	33 3/8	35	15 4/8	15 5/8	8 6/8	8 7/8	20	18 4/8	Baja Calif., Mexico	Dan L. Quen	Dan L. Quen	1968	185
171 5/8	35 6/8	35 3/8	14 7/8	15	9 1/8	8 7/8	19 3/8	19 3/8	Baja Calif., Mexico	C. J. McElroy	C. J. McElroy	1969	185
171 5/8	35 3/8	35 4/8	15 2/8	15 4/8	8 7/8	8 7/8	21 4/8	20	Baja Calif., Mexico	Roberto Martin del Campo	Roberto Martin del Campo	1969	185
171 5/8	34 3/8	32 2/8	15 3/8	15 4/8	9 3/8	9 6/8	21 7/8	20 4/8	Clark Co., Nevada	Edward M. Evans	Edward M. Evans	1977	185
171 5/8	35 3/8	35 4/8	14 5/8	14 6/8	9 3/8	9	20 5/8	20 5/8	Clark Co., Nevada	George Hueftle	George Hueftle	1977	185
171 4/8	35 1/8	34 7/8	14	14	10 2/8	10	19 4/8	19 4/8	Bullion Mts., Calif.	Picked Up	Fred L. Jones	1950	192
171 4/8	37 4/8	37 6/8	13 6/8	13 6/8	8 3/8	8 3/8	23	22 6/8	Clark Co., Nev.	Jerry P. Devin	Jerry P. Devin	1976	192
171 3/8	36 7/8	36 4/8	14 3/8	14 3/8	8 5/8	8 4/8	22 2/8	22 2/8	Anvil Mt., Ariz.	George Stewart, Jr.	George Stewart, Jr.	1961	194
171 3/8	34 2/8	34 3/8	15 5/8	15 6/8	8 2/8	8 5/8	19 7/8	16 1/8	Crater Mts., Ariz.	Raymond I. Skipper, Jr.	Raymond I. Skipper, Jr.	1971	194
171 2/8	35 2/8	35 6/8	14 2/8	14 3/8	8 6/8	9 2/8	21 2/8	18 3/8	Growler Mts., Ariz.	David E. Brown	David E. Brown	1967	196
171 1/8	35 4/8	35 1/8	16 4/8	16 4/8	7 6/8	7 2/8	19 1/8	19 1/8	Yuma Co., Ariz.	Elizabeth Barganski	Elizabeth Barganski	1959	197
171 1/8	36 4/8	36 7/8	14 3/8	14 4/8	8 2/8	8 3/8	22 2/8	19 7/8	Palomas Mts., Ariz.	James F. Pierce	James F. Pierce	1967	197
171	36	36 2/8	14 3/8	14 4/8	8 4/8	8 7/8	20 3/8	19 4/8	Sauceda Mts., Ariz.	Kelly S. Neal, Jr.	Kelly S. Neal, Jr.	1969	199
171	36 4/8	35 4/8	14 4/8	14 4/8	8 7/8	8 6/8	22 1/8	22 1/8	Baja Calif., Mexico	George S. Gayle, III	George S. Gayle, III	1975	199
170 7/8	34 7/8	34 7/8	15 2/8	15 1/8	9	9	19 3/8	19 3/8	Mohave Co., Ariz.	John H. Houzenga, Jr.	John H. Houzenga, Jr.	1961	201
170 7/8	35 5/8	35 4/8	16	16	8	8 1/8	22 5/8	22 5/8	Sonora Desert, Mexico	Herb Klein	Herb Klein	1962	201
170 7/8	38 1/8	37 4/8	14	14 2/8	9 3/8	8 2/8	21 5/8	21 5/8	Baja Calif., Mexico	Michaux Nash, Jr.	Michaux Nash, Jr.	1964	201
170 7/8	32 7/8	36 4/8	14 4/8	14 4/8	9 7/8	9 5/8	19 2/8	17 6/8	Baja Calif., Mexico	John T. Blackwell	John T. Blackwell	1966	201
170 6/8	33 3/8	35 1/8	14	14	9 5/8	10 2/8	23 1/8	23 1/8	San Bernadino Co., Calif.	Picked Up	John M. Parrish	1960	205
170 6/8	36 7/8	36 3/8	15 6/8	15 3/8	7 6/8	7 5/8	21 6/8	20 7/8	Little Horn Mts., Ariz.	Dale Wagner	Dale Wagner	1963	205
170 6/8	36 1/8	36 7/8	16 3/8	16 3/8	7 2/8	7 3/8	21 4/8	21 4/8	Baja Calif., Mexico	Gino Perfetto	Gino Perfetto	1968	205
170 6/8	35 2/8	34 6/8	15 6/8	15 6/8	7 7/8	7 7/8	20 5/8	20 5/8	Baja Calif., Mexico	Enrique Cervera Cicero	Enrique Cervera Cicero	1968	205
170 6/8	39 4/8	37 4/8	13 1/8	13 7/8	9 4/8	8 4/8	22 6/8	22 6/8	Clark Co., Nevada	Roy Gamblin	Roy Gamblin	1977	205
170 5/8	34	38 5/8	13 6/8	13 5/8	9 2/8	9 1/8	24 4/8	24 4/8	Death Valley, Calif.	Picked Up	Fred L. Jones	PR1955	210
170 5/8	34 2/8	35 3/8	15	15 2/8	8 4/8	8 2/8	19 3/8	17 6/8	Baja Calif., Mexico	Bill Lewis	Bill Lewis	1969	210
170 5/8	32 6/8	35 7/8	16 1/8	16 1/8	8 6/8	8 6/8	23 1/8	23 1/8	Pima Co., Ariz.	David Chavez	David Chavez	1972	210
170 4/8	36	35	14 1/8	14 3/8	10 1/8	9 1/8	20 2/8	20 2/8	Clark Co., Nev.	Robert E. Coons	Robert E. Coons	1971	213
170 3/8	32	34 3/8	16 2/8	16 2/8	7 6/8	8 7/8	19 2/8	19 2/8	Sonora, Mexico	F. C. Hibben	F. C. Hibben	1935	214
170 3/8	35 3/8	36 2/8	15	15	7 5/8	7 7/8	19 7/8	18	Chemehuevi Mts., Ariz.	James B. Lingo	James B. Lingo	1970	214
170 2/8	35 2/8	36 4/8	15	15 2/8	8	8 4/8	20 1/8	20 1/8	Baja Calif., Mexico	Richard Buffington	Richard Buffington	1966	216
170 2/8	37 7/8	34 7/8	14 7/8	14 4/8	8 2/8	8 4/8	24 1/8	24 1/8	Clark Co., Nevada	Landon D. Mack	Landon D. Mack	1977	216
170 2/8	37 2/8	35	15 4/8	15 4/8	8	7 5/8	21 3/8	20 4/8	Baja Calif., Mexico	James W. Owens	James W. Owens	1978	216
170 1/8	34 6/8	34 7/8	14 6/8	15	8 6/8	9	19 1/8	18 2/8	Baja Calif., Mexico	Fred T. LaBean	Fred T. LaBean	1969	219
170 1/8	40 3/8	34 2/8	13 6/8	13 6/8	8 5/8	8 3/8	25 4/8	25 4/8	Mineral Co., Nev.	Picked Up	Nev. Dept. Fish & Game	1969	219
170 1/8	37 1/8	37	15 3/8	15 5/8	7 1/8	7 1/8	22 4/8	22 4/8	Baja Calif., Mexico	Arthur E. Davis	Arthur E. Davis	1972	219

Desert Sheep–*Continued*

Ovis canadensis nelsoni and certain related subspecies

Score	Length of Horn R.	Length of Horn L.	Circumference of Base R.	Circumference of Base L.	Circumference at Third Quarter R.	Circumference at Third Quarter L.	Greatest Spread	Tip to Tip Spread	Locality Killed	By Whom Killed	Owner	Date Killed	Rank
170 1/8	36	36 3/8	15 3/8	15 3/8	7 7/8	7 7/8	19 2/8	16 5/8	Baja Calif., Mexico	Edward V. Wilson	Edward V. Wilson	1974	219
170	33	33	15 5/8	15 3/8	9 1/8	9 1/8	21 4/8	19 5/8	Little Horn Mts., Ariz.	Ivan L. Shiflet	Ivan L. Shiflet	1966	223
170	37 4/8	33 4/8	15 2/8	15 1/8	7 7/8	7 6/8	22 2/8	21 7/8	Baja Calif., Mexico	Warren K. Parker	Warren K. Parker	1970	223
170	33	34 6/8	14 2/8	14 2/8	9 6/8	10 2/8	20 7/8	18 5/8	Clark Co., Nev.	Lee R. Williamson	Lee R. Williamson	1972	223
170	35 2/8	35 2/8	14 5/8	14 6/8	8 5/8	8 6/8	19 5/8	19 5/8	Baja Calif., Mexico	Rudolf Sand	Rudolf Sand	1973	223
170	34 7/8	34 1/8	14 5/8	14 4/8	10 1/8	9 5/8	21 2/8	21 2/8	Clark Co., Nevada	Jim Lathrop, Jr.	Jim Lathrop, Jr.	1976	223
169 7/8	35 3/8	35 2/8	14 6/8	14 6/8	8 3/8	8 4/8	20 4/8	19 5/8	Baja Calif., Mexico	Harold Hallick	Harold Hallick	1971	228
169 6/8	35 2/8	35 6/8	14 1/8	14	9 3/8	9 5/8	21 2/8	21 2/8	Baja Calif., Mexico	W. M. Wheless, III	W. M. Wheless, III	1974	229
169 5/8	34 5/8	36 4/8	14 3/8	14 4/8	9 1/8	9 1/8	23	19	Muddy Mts., Nev.	Peter Dietrick	Peter Dietrick	1962	230
169 5/8	35 1/8	36 2/8	15	15	8	8 1/8	20	18 7/8	Baja Calif., Mexico	Leonard W. Gilman	Leonard W. Gilman	1969	230
169 5/8	35 3/8	34	15 4/8	15 4/8	8 2/8	8 2/8	20 4/8	20 4/8	San Borjas Mts., Mexico	John T. Blackwell	John T. Blackwell	1970	230
169 5/8	35 5/8	34	15	15	9	8 7/8	18 2/8	16 3/8	Baja Calif., Mexico	Gunter M. Paefgen	Gunter M. Paefgen	1975	230
169 5/8	33 6/8	34 5/8	15 7/8	16	7 6/8	8 3/8	21 6/8	21 6/8	Baja Calif., Mexico	Emerson Hall	Emerson Hall	1978	230
169 4/8	34 4/8	34 6/8	14 1/8	14 3/8	9 6/8	10 5/8	21	18 5/8	Hart Tank, Ariz.	Picked Up	Greg Diley	——	235
169 4/8	33	36	15 4/8	15 4/8	8 4/8	8 4/8	25 4/8	25 4/8	Lower Calif., Mexico	Henry H. Blagden	Henry H. Blagden	1914	235
169 4/8	35 6/8	35 6/8	14 5/8	14 4/8	8 4/8	8 5/8	18	18	Baja Calif., Mexico	Lowell C. Hansen, II	Lowell C. Hansen, II	1974	235
169 4/8	33 6/8	36	14 6/8	14 7/8	9 2/8	8 5/8	22 7/8	22 5/8	Quartzsite, Ariz.	Maurice D. Mathews	Maurice D. Mathews	1975	235
169 3/8	35 3/8	35	15 7/8	16	7 2/8	7 2/8	20 4/8	20 4/8	Sonora, Mexico	Unknown	National Collection	——	239
169 3/8	34 4/8	34 3/8	14 5/8	14 5/8	9 3/8	9	20 1/8	20 1/8	Baja Calif., Mexico	Kenneth Campbell	Kenneth Campbell	1973	239
169 2/8	34 5/8	34 7/8	14	13 7/8	9 6/8	9 7/8	21 2/8	21 2/8	White Mts., Calif.	Picked Up	Fred L. Jones	PR1951	241
169 2/8	33 7/8	34 7/8	15 2/8	15 2/8	8 4/8	9 1/8	18 3/8	18 3/8	Baja Calif., Mexico	Joe Osterbauer	Joe Osterbauer	1977	241
169 1/8	33 4/8	33 7/8	14 4/8	14 4/8	10	10	20 6/8	15 5/8	Lower Calif., Mexico	Picked Up	William W. Renfrew	1953	243
169 1/8	35	34 1/8	14 2/8	14 2/8	9 1/8	9	22 4/8	22 4/8	Chocolate Mts., Ariz.	Dan Oliver	Dan Oliver	1966	243
169 1/8	35 6/8	38 7/8	15	15	7 1/8	7 3/8	25 4/8	25 4/8	Baja Calif., Mexico	James W. Owens	James W. Owens	1977	243
169	36 1/8	36 3/8	15 6/8	15 4/8	6 6/8	6 5/8	22 3/8	22 2/8	Lower Calif., Mexico	William E. Humphrey	Wash. State Mus.	1909	246
169	37	36	13 4/8	14	8	8 4/8	27	27	Yuma Co., Ariz.	Picked Up	Dean Bowdoin	1964	246
168 7/8	34 1/8	35	14 6/8	14 4/8	8 6/8	8 6/8	22 2/8	16 3/8	Aquila Mts., Ariz.	John Carr	John Carr	1969	248
168 7/8	35	33 7/8	16	16	8 1/8	7 7/8	21 1/8	21 1/8	Baja Calif., Mexico	Larry R. Price	Larry R. Price	1973	248
168 7/8	36 2/8	36 7/8	14 6/8	14 7/8	7 5/8	7 6/8	20 1/8	18 4/8	Baja Calif., Mexico	Gary Davis	Gary Davis	1975	248
168 7/8	36 5/8	33 2/8	14 6/8	14 7/8	8 2/8	8 7/8	22	22	Clark Co., Nevada	Robert Darakjy	Robert Darakjy	1978	248
168 6/8	35 2/8	33 4/8	14	14 2/8	10 1/8	9 6/8	19 7/8	16 4/8	Sonora, Mexico	Jack O'Connor	Jack O'Connor	1946	252
168 6/8	35 2/8	36 6/8	13 5/8	13 3/8	9	9 2/8	22 4/8	22 4/8	Lincoln Co., Nev.	Von A. Mitton	Von A. Mitton	1966	252

Score									Locality	Owner	Hunter	Date	Total
168 6/8	36 6/8	36 2/8	14 2/8	14 3/8	7 7/8	7 6/8	22 5/8	21 5/8	Little Horn Mts., Ariz.	Dean Bowdoin	Dean Bowdoin	1966	252
168 6/8	34 7/8	35 5/8	15 2/8	15 3/8	7 7/8	8 1/8	19	16 5/8	Sierra De Jaraguay, Mexico	Jack A. Shane, Sr.	Jack A. Shane, Sr.	1972	252
168 5/8	36 6/8	34 4/8	13 6/8	13 7/8	9 1/8	9 4/8	23 5/8	23 5/8	Ariz.	D. B. Sanford	Picked Up	PR1961	256
168 5/8	36 1/8	33 5/8	14	14	9 3/8	10	20 7/8	18	Castle Dome Peak, Ariz.	Tommy G. Moore	Tommy G. Moore	1966	256
168 5/8	34 4/8	34 4/8	14 5/8	14 5/8	8 7/8	8 4/8	21 1/8	17 3/8	Aquila Mts., Ariz.	David C. Thornburg	David C. Thornburg	1969	256
168 4/8	33 6/8	34 4/8	15 4/8	15 4/8	8 4/8	8 7/8	18 5/8	17 7/8	Baja Calif., Mexico	Russell C. Cutter	Russell C. Cutter	1964	259
168 4/8	35 3/8	35 5/8	15	15	9 1/8	8 4/8	25 5/8	25	Kofa Game Range, Ariz.	Judy Franks	Judy Franks	1965	259
168 4/8	36 2/8	36 2/8	14 1/8	13 5/8	9 1/8	9 3/8	23 7/8	21 1/2	Clark Co., Nev.	Kenneth K. Reuter	Kenneth K. Reuter	1969	259
168 4/8	35	35	16 3/8	16 3/8	7 7/8	7	21 1/4	20 3/4	Pima Co., Ariz.	Jerald S. Wager	Jerald S. Wager	1977	259
168 4/8	35 5/8	36 3/8	13 5/8	13 5/8	9	9 4/8	18 5/8	18 5/8	Baja Calif., Mexico	W. T. Yoshimoto	W. T. Yoshimoto	1978	259
168 4/8	34 7/8	34 2/8	15 5/8	15 5/8	8	7 6/8	17 7/8	17 7/8	Sand Tank Mts., Ariz.	Homer Coppinger	Homer Coppinger	1960	264
168 3/8	35	34 3/8	14 5/8	14 5/8	9 2/8	9 2/8	19 1/8	17 5/8	Yuma Co., Ariz.	Leanna G. Mendenhall	Leanna G. Mendenhall	1975	264
168 3/8	34 3/8	35 5/8	14 6/8	14 6/8	8	8 4/8	21	21 5/8	Baja Calif., Mexico	George H. Glass	George H. Glass	1964	266
168 2/8	34 7/8	34 4/8	15 5/8	15 6/8	7 7/8	7 5/8	20 7/8	14	Sonora, Mexico	Sergio Rios Aguilera	Sergio Rios Aguilera	1968	266
168 2/8	34 4/8	34 7/8	14 4/8	14 4/8	9	8 5/8	21 4/8	19 7/8	Clark Co., Nev.	Marie F. Reuter	Marie F. Reuter	1969	266
168 2/8	33 5/8	33 6/8	15 3/8	15 3/8	8 1/8	8 5/8	22 7/8	19 1/2	Clark Co., Nev.	Charles J. Lindberg	Charles J. Lindberg	1971	266
168 2/8	34 1/8	35 5/8	14 7/8	14 7/8	8 3/8	8 1/8	22	22	Yuma Co., Ariz.	Ervin Black	Ervin Black	1972	266
168 2/8	33 5/8	33 5/8	14	14	9 3/8	9 5/8	23 3/8	23 1/4	Lincoln Co., Nevada	Dale Deming	Dale Deming	1977	266
168 1/8	34 3/8	37 6/8	15	15	8	7 7/8	24 5/8	24 1/4	Lower Calif., Mexico	Acad. Nat. Sci., Phil.	G. L. Harrison	1903	272
168 1/8	34 7/8	34 5/8	14 1/8	14	8 6/8	9 2/8	20 7/8	18 5/8	Baja Calif., Mexico	James C. Nystrom	James C. Nystrom	1969	272
168 1/8	32 3/8	31 5/8	16 1/8	16 1/8	8 6/8	8 4/8	19 4/8	18 5/8	Pima Co., Ariz.	Jeff R. Snodgrass	Jeff R. Snodgrass	1970	272
168	35	35	14	14	10	9	25	25	Lamb Springs, Nev.	Leslie H. Farr	Leslie H. Farr	1966	275
168	34 7/8	34 7/8	15	14 6/8	8 3/8	8 6/8	21 1/8	21	Clark Co., Nev.	Edward Friel	Edward Friel	1969	275
168	34 7/8	35 6/8	15 1/8	15 5/8	8	8 6/8	21 1/8	21 1/2	Baja Calif., Mexico	Lee Frudden	Lee Frudden	1972	275
168	35	35 5/8	14 3/8	14 3/8	9 1/8	9	23	23	Clark Co., Nev.	Leonard M. Faike	Leonard M. Faike	1973	275
168	33 1/8	34 6/8	14 6/8	14 6/8	8 3/8	9 3/8	13 5/8	17 7/8	Mohave Co., Ariz.	Robert L. Fletcher	Robert L. Fletcher	1974	275

Photograph by Alex Rota

WORLD'S RECORD DALL'S SHEEP
SCORE: 189 6/8
Locality: Wrangell Mountains, Alaska. Date: 1961.
Hunter and owner: Harry L. Swank, Jr.
Winner of the Sagamore Hill Medal in 1961.

NUMBER TWO DALL'S SHEEP
SCORE: 185 6/8
Locality: Chugach Mountains, Alaska. Date: 1956.
Hunter and owner: Frank Cook.
Winner of the Sagamore Hill Medal in 1957.

Dall's Sheep

Ovis dalli dalli and Ovis dalli kenaiensis

Minimum Score 170

Score	Length of Horn R.	L.	Circumference of Base R.	L.	Circumference at Third Quarter R.	L.	Greatest Spread	Tip to Tip Spread	Locality Killed	By Whom Killed	Owner	Date Killed	Rank
189 6/8	48 5/8	47 7/8	14 5/8	14 6/8	6 5/8	6 7/8	34 3/8	34 3/8	Wrangell Mts., Alaska	Harry L. Swank, Jr.	Harry L. Swank, Jr.	1961	1
185 5/8	49 2/8	44 2/8	14	13 7/8	6 6/8	7 3/8	24 2/8	24 2/8	Chugach Mts., Alaska	Frank Cook	Frank Cook	1956	2
185 4/8	43 6/8	40 6/8	14 7/8	14 7/8	9 6/8	9 3/8	20 7/8	20 7/8	Chugach Mts., Alaska	Jack W. Lentfer	Jack W. Lentfer	1964	3
185 3/8*	46	45 7/8	15 2/8	15 2/8	6 3/8	6 4/8	29 3/8	29 3/8	Coast Mts., Yukon	David W. Young	David W. Young	1972	4
184 6/8	43 6/8	46	14 1/8	14 3/8	9	7 6/8	21 6/8	21 6/8	Wrangell Mts., Alaska	B. L. Burkholder	B. L. Burkholder	1958	5
184	44 6/8	44 4/8	14 2/8	14 2/8	7 1/8	7 2/8	24 5/8	24 5/8	Chugach Mts., Alaska	Thomas C. Sheets	Thomas C. Sheets	1962	6
183 7/8	46 5/8	47 4/8	13 6/8	13 6/8	6 6/8	6 5/8	31	31	Wrangell Mts., Alaska	Tony Oney	Tony Oney	1963	7
183 6/8	48	47 4/8	14	13 6/8	6 2/8	6 5/8	33 4/8	33 4/8	Alaska Range, Alaska	Jonathan T. Summar, Jr.	Jonathan T. Summar, Jr.	1965	8
183 4/8	45 7/8	45 1/8	13 7/8	14	7 1/8	7 6/8	27 7/8	27 7/8	Whitehorse, Yukon	W. Newhall	Robert E. Barnes	1924	9
183 3/8	44 6/8	43 6/8	14 7/8	14 5/8	7 3/8	7 1/8	23 6/8	23 6/8	Champagne, Yukon	Earl J. Thee	Earl J. Thee	1948	10
183	42 3/8	39 3/8	14 6/8	14 6/8	9 5/8	9 5/8	22 5/8	19 4/8	Wrangell Mts., Alaska	Gene M. Effler	Gene M. Effler	1959	11
182	38 5/8	39	15 2/8	15 5/8	10 1/8	10 1/8	–	–	Kenai Pen., Alaska	Picked Up	C. E. (Red) Lyons	—	12
181 6/8	44 4/8	44 4/8	14 5/8	14 5/8	6 6/8	6 6/8	27 7/8	27 7/8	Knik River, Alaska	Matthew Lahti	National Collection	1930	13
181 6/8	47 7/8	47 5/8	14 6/8	14 4/8	5 7/8	6 3/8	28 7/8	28 7/8	Atlin, B. C.	Robert Landis	Ralph & Pearl Landis	1969	13
181 5/8	46 7/8	46 5/8	14	14 1/8	6	6 2/8	32 6/8	32 6/8	McCarthy, Alaska	Bud Nelson	Bud Nelson	1953	15
181 3/8	42 5/8	42 5/8	15 1/8	15 1/8	7 4/8	7 6/8	24 6/8	24 6/8	Wrangell Mts., Alaska	James K. Harrower	James K. Harrower	1961	16
181	46 3/8	46 3/8	13 6/8	13 6/8	6 2/8	6 2/8	28 6/8	28 6/8	Mt. Selous, Yukon	George C. Morris, Sr.	George C. Morris, Sr.	1962	17
180 7/8	44 2/8	44 1/8	14 7/8	14 5/8	6 5/8	6 4/8	30 6/8	30 6/8	Wrangell Mts., Alaska	Robert W. Engstrom	Robert W. Engstrom	1973	18
180 6/8	43 3/8	43 7/8	14 1/8	14 1/8	7 2/8	7 2/8	27	25 3/8	Kluane Lake, Yukon	Indian	Joe Jacquot	1953	19
180 6/8	42 5/8	44 2/8	15	15	6 3/8	7	26 5/8	26 5/8	Yukon	Billy Jack	Yukon Govt.	1966	19
180 6/8	45 7/8	46 3/8	13 5/8	13 5/8	6 6/8	6 5/8	29 3/8	29 1/8	Johnson River, Alaska	P. A. Johnson & J. N. Brennan	P. A. Johnson & J. N. Brennan	1950	21
180 1/8	39 2/8	46 1/8	14 6/8	15 3/8	7 7/8	7 3/8	27 1/8	27 1/8	Wrangell Mts., Alaska	Harry H. Wilson	Harry H. Wilson	1961	22
180	39 2/8	40 6/8	14 6/8	14 4/8	8 3/8	8 1/8	23	21	Grand View, Alaska	Nellie Neal	Nellie Neal	1917	23
179 7/8	45 4/8	45 5/8	13	13	6 4/8	7 4/8	27 7/8	27 7/8	Kenai Pen., Alaska	A. B. Learned	A. B. Learned	1936	24
179 6/8	41 5/8	41 5/8	14 5/8	14 5/8	7	7	28 3/8	28 3/8	Chugach Mts., Alaska	J. H. Esslinger	J. H. Esslinger	1959	25
179 5/8	40 7/8	41 1/8	14 5/8	14 4/8	8	8	26 2/8	26 2/8	Kluane Lake, Yukon	George E. Thompson	George E. Thompson	1956	26
179 1/8	44 5/8	44 2/8	14 2/8	14 2/8	6 5/8	6 4/8	27	27	Chugach Mts., Alaska	Boyd Howard	Boyd Howard	1957	27
178 7/8	40 7/8	40 4/8	14 6/8	14 7/8	7 5/8	7 3/8	23 7/8	24	Chugach Mts., Alaska	Daniel A. Story	Daniel A. Story	1954	28
178 6/8	42 4/8	42 2/8	13 6/8	13 4/8	8 5/8	8 2/8	25 5/8	25 5/8	Knik River, Alaska	V. A. Morgan	V. A. Morgan	1934	29
178 5/8	40 2/8	40 1/8	15 5/8	15 4/8	7	7	30 2/8	30 2/8	Champagne, Yukon	B. V. Seigel	B. V. Seigel	1964	29
178 3/8	45 3/8	43 6/8	13 5/8	13 5/8	6 1/8	6 4/8	23 6/8	23 6/8	Alaska Hwy., Yukon	William H. Miller	William H. Miller	1947	31

178 3/8	43 2/8	42 5/8	13 7/8	14	6 7/8	6 6/8	27 1/8	27 1/8	Chugach Mts., Alaska	Sam Jaksick, Jr	Sam Jaksick, Jr.	1966	31
178 2/8	45 6/8	46 4/8	13	13	6 5/8	6 3/8	26 3/8	26 3/8	Pelly Mts., Yukon	Eric W. French	Eric W. French	1958	33
178 2/8	45 4/8	42 2/8	14 6/8	14 6/8	6 3/8	6	31 5/8	31 5/8	Wrangell Mts., Alaska	Wilbur Ternyik	Wilbur Ternyik	1958	33
178 1/8	45 7/8	43 6/8	13 4/8	13 5/8	7 1/8	6 2/8	23 5/8	23 5/8	Wrangell Mts., Alaska	Unknown	Jeff Sievers	PR1950	35
178 1/8	45 7/8	44	14	13 7/8	7 4/8	7 3/8	28	28	Chugach Mts., Alaska	J. S. Lichtenfels	J. S. Lichtenfels	1956	35
178	43 4/8	43	15	15	6 4/8	6 4/8	30 2/8	30 2/8	Chitina River, Alaska	F. C. Hibben	F. C. Hibben	1963	37
177 7/8	44 5/8	45	14 3/8	14	6 3/8	6 2/8	28 3/8	28 3/8	Chugach Mts., Alaska	William R. Champlain	William R. Champlain	1965	38
177 6/8	43 3/8	44 3/8	14 4/8	14 2/8	6 2/8	6 1/8	27 4/8	27 4/8	Chugach Mts., Alaska	Chris Klineburger	Chris Klineburger	1957	39
177 5/8	41 7/8	43 2/8	13 2/8	13 2/8	8 7/8	9 1/8	22	22	Rainy Pass, Alaska	F. Edmond Blanc	F. Edmond Blanc	1937	40
177 5/8	44	43 5/8	14 4/8	14 4/8	6	6	27 5/8	27 6/8	Kenai Pen., Alaska	John Swiss	John Swiss	1959	40
177 5/8	44 1/8	44 4/8	14 1/8	14	6 4/8	6 6/8	26 5/8	26 5/8	Wrangell Mts., Alaska	Elgin T. Gates	Elgin T. Gates	1961	40
177 4/8	42 5/8	42 5/8	14 6/8	14 5/8	6 7/8	6 7/8	26 3/8	26 3/8	Matanuska River, Alaska	Gordon Madole	Gordon Madole	1955	43
177 4/8	44	43 6/8	14 3/8	14 2/8	6 2/8	6 2/8	28 7/8	28 7/8	Wrangell Mts., Alaska	Rita Oney	Rita Oney	1963	43
177 4/8	43 2/8	44	14 2/8	14 1/8	6 3/8	6 4/8	25 5/8	25 6/8	Aishihik Lake, Yukon	Eleanor O'Connor	Eleanor O'Connor	1963	43
177 4/8	40 1/8	42 7/8	13 7/8	13 7/8	7 4/8	7 4/8	23 1/8	23	Ruby Mt. Range, Yukon	Kenneth Campbell	Kenneth Campbell	1971	43
177 4/8	45 4/8	44 4/8	13 6/8	14	6 1/8	6	28 5/8	28 3/8	Chugach Mts., Alaska	Robert Kraai	Robert Kraai	1977	43
177 2/8	42 4/8	43 4/8	13 6/8	13 6/8	7	7	23 6/8	23 6/8	Kenai Pen., Alaska	Luke Elwell	Luke Elwell	1936	48
177 2/8	38	40 6/8	15 2/8	15 2/8	7 3/8	7 2/8	22 7/8	20 1/8	Chugach Mts., Alaska	Harry H. Wilson	Harry H. Wilson	1960	48
177 1/8	43 4/8	43 3/8	14	13 6/8	6 6/8	6 6/8	27 2/8	27 2/8	Kenai Pen., Alaska	C. R. Cross, Jr.	Harvard Club Of Boston	1907	50
177 1/8	43 5/8	42 2/8	14 6/8	14 7/8	6 3/8	6 1/8	23 4/8	23 4/8	Sifton Range, Yukon	Jack O'Connor	Jack O'Connor	1950	50
177 1/8	45 3/8	44 6/8	14	14	6	5 7/8	30 7/8	30 7/8	Chugach Mts., Alaska	Jim Milito	Jim Milito	1971	50
177 1/8	44 3/8	45 4/8	13 5/8	13 5/8	6 2/8	6 1/8	25 3/8	25 3/8	Mackenzie River, N. W. T.	Joseph Scott	Joseph Scott	1973	50
177	44 6/8	44 6/8	13 7/8	13 6/8	6	6	27 1/8	27 1/8	Chugach Mts., Alaska	Paul E. Huling	Paul E. Huling	1959	54
176 7/8	41 3/8	42	14 7/8	14 7/8	6 4/8	6 6/8	28	28	Wrangell Mts., Alaska	Vic S. Sears	Vic S. Sears	1960	55
176 6/8	43	43	15	15	6 2/8	5 7/8	23 3/8	23 3/8	Wrangell Mts., Alaska	Ed Bilderback	Ed Bilderback	1959	56
176 5/8	44 4/8	44 7/8	13 1/8	13 1/8	6 5/8	6 6/8	26 1/8	26 1/8	Mayo, Yukon	C. L. Bestoule	C. L. Bestoule	1960	57
176 4/8	45	45 6/8	13	13 3/8	7 2/8	7	32	32	Donjek, Yukon	Olof Erickson	Mrs. Jacquot	1933	58
176 4/8	46 2/8	40 6/8	13 7/8	13 6/8	6 4/8	6 4/8	22 7/8	22 7/8	Knik River, Alaska	Philip English	Philip English	1955	58
176 4/8	43 5/8	43 5/8	14	14	6 7/8	6 6/8	25 6/8	25 6/8	Mt. River, N. W. T.	Daniel E. Yaeger	Daniel E. Yaeger	1973	58
176 3/8	41 2/8	41 7/8	14	14	8	7 6/8	24 2/8	24 2/8	Chugach Mts., Alaska	Lloyd Ronning	Lloyd Ronning	1953	61
176 2/8	40 4/8	42 2/8	14 4/8	14 4/8	6 4/8	7	24	24	Champagne, Yukon	H. W. Meisch	H. W. Meisch	1957	62
176 2/8	40 7/8	41 3/8	13 4/8	13 4/8	8 4/8	8 2/8	21 2/8	18 2/8	Ruby Range, Yukon	J. Martin Benchoff	J. Martin Benchoff	1963	62
176 2/8	41 6/8	42	14 4/8	14 3/8	7	7 1/8	27 5/8	27 5/8	Chugach Mts., Alaska	Donald P. Chase	Donald P. Chase	1978	62
176 1/8	43 7/8	44	13	13 1/8	7	7 1/8	22 1/8	22 1/8	Ship Creek, Alaska	Oliver Tovsen	Oliver Tovsen	1940	65
176	40 4/8	42	14 2/8	14 2/8	7	7	23	22	Knik River, Alaska	John S. Lahti	John S. Lahti	1930	66
176	39	38 4/8	14 7/8	15	9 6/8	7 6/8	26	26	Tonsina Lake, Alaska	Horace E. Groff	Horace E. Groff	1960	66
176	42	41 6/8	14 7/8	15	6 5/8	6 4/8	28 7/8	28 7/8	Chugach Mts., Alaska	William D. Backman, Jr.	William D. Backman, Jr.	1960	66
176	42	43	14 3/8	14 3/8	6 4/8	6 4/8	22 6/8	22 6/8	Alaska	Picked Up	T. H. Rowe	PR1960	66
176	46 4/8	45 4/8	13 2/8	13 2/8	6	6	31 4/8	31 4/8	Wrangell Mts., Alaska	Harold Meeker	Harold Meeker	1965	66
176	41 2/8	41 4/8	15	15	6	6	25	25	Wrangell Mts., Alaska	Paul D. Weingart	Paul D. Weingart	1974	66
175 6/8	40 4/8	46 6/8	13 4/8	13 4/8	6 6/8	6 7/8	23 4/8	23 4/8	Ruby Range, Yukon	John K. Hansen	John K. Hansen	1960	72
175 6/8	42 3/8	42 7/8	15	14 7/8	6 2/8	6 2/8	23 5/8	22 7/8	Yukon	William E. Portman	William E. Portman	1966	72
175 6/8	43 7/8	43 7/8	13 5/8	13 5/8	6 4/8	6 4/8	30 3/8	30 3/8	Wrangell Mts., Alaska	Ben C. Boynton	Ben C. Boynton	1971	72

Dall's Sheep–*Continued*

Ovis dalli dalli and *Ovis dalli kenaiensis*

Score	Length of Horn R.	Length of Horn L.	Circumference of Base R.	Circumference of Base L.	Circumference at Third Quarter R.	Circumference at Third Quarter L.	Greatest Spread	Tip to Tip Spread	Locality Killed	By Whom Killed	Owner	Date Killed	Rank
175 5/8	41 4/8	42 3/8	13 4/8	13 4/8	7 4/8	7 5/8	24	24	Chugach Mts., Alaska	Harry Anderson	Harry Anderson	1955	75
175 4/8	42	42	14	14	7	6 7/8	28 6/8	28 6/8	Wrangell Mts., Alaska	Swen Honkola	Swen Honkola	1958	76
175 3/8	37 6/8	40 3/8	14 4/8	14 4/8	8 2/8	8 3/8	23 5/8	23 5/8	Wrangell Mts., Alaska	Burt Ahlstrom	Burt Ahlstrom	1959	77
175 2/8	40 4/8	46 6/8	14 6/8	14 4/8	6 2/8	6 3/8	26 4/8	26 4/8	Chitina River, Alaska	Henry Boyden	Am. Mus. Nat. History	1936	78
175 2/8	41 4/8	42	14 3/8	14 5/8	6 4/8	6 6/8	26 2/8	26 2/8	Wrangell Mts., Alaska	Grant Smith	Grant Smith	1963	78
175 2/8	41 7/8	43 3/8	14 2/8	14 4/8	6 7/8	6 6/8	30 3/8	30 3/8	Chugach Mts., Alaska	Miles Hajny	Miles Hajny	1969	78
175 1/8	42 3/8	44 2/8	14 2/8	14	6 4/8	6 4/8	29	29	Talkeetna Mts., Alaska	Dale Caldwell	Dale Caldwell	1957	81
175 1/8	42 1/8	37	14 3/8	14 2/8	8	8 2/8	20 2/8	19 2/8	Wrangell Mts., Alaska	Herman F. Wyman	Herman F. Wyman	1964	81
175 1/8	41	40 7/8	14 3/8	14 3/8	6 7/8	6 7/8	23	23	Chugach Mts., Alaska	Edward A. Champlain	Edward A. Champlain	1965	81
175 1/8	41 3/8	39	15	15	7 4/8	6 4/8	26 6/8	26 6/8	Wrangell Mts., Alaska	John M. Griffith, Jr.	John M. Griffith, Jr.	1976	81
175	42 4/8	42 2/8	14 2/8	14 2/8	6 4/8	6 3/8	23 2/8	23 2/8	Kenai Pen., Alaska	Russel Gainer	Russel Gainer	1959	85
175	42 7/8	42 7/8	13 7/8	14	6 6/8	6 4/8	23 4/8	23 4/8	Chugach Mts., Alaska	Arthur R. Dubs	Arthur R. Dubs	1961	85
174 7/8	44 5/8	44	13 3/8	13 3/8	6 6/8	6 5/8	26 5/8	26 5/8	Lake Arkell, Yukon	J. J. Elliott	J. J. Elliott	1924	87
174 7/8	41 3/8	40 4/8	13 7/8	13 7/8	8 2/8	8	19 7/8	19 7/8	Chugach Mts., Alaska	Leroy Holen	Leroy Holen	1957	87
174 7/8	43 1/8	43	13 5/8	13 7/8	6 6/8	6 6/8	29	29	Wrangell Mts., Alaska	R. W. Ulman	R. W. Ulman	1962	87
174 7/8	44 6/8	42 1/8	13 6/8	13 4/8	7	6 5/8	29	29	Chitina River, Alaska	Ray B. Nienhaus	Ray B. Nienhaus	1966	87
174 6/8	47 4/8	47	13	12 6/8	5 6/8	5 6/8	26	26	Carcross, Yukon	Billy Smith	Acad. Nat. Sci., Phil.	1927	91
174 6/8	46 6/8	43	13	13	7 1/8	6 1/8	25 4/8	25 4/8	Sifton Mts., Yukon	Herb Klein	Herb Klein	1950	91
174 6/8	45 2/8	45	13 1/8	13 1/8	6 4/8	6 2/8	28 5/8	28 5/8	Wrangell Mts., Alaska	Watten W. Wilbur	Warren W. Wilbur	1952	91
174 6/8	42 2/8	40 3/8	13 7/8	14	7 4/8	7 7/8	28 2/8	28 2/8	Aishihik Lake, Yukon	Abe Goldberg	Abe Goldberg	1962	91
174 6/8	41 3/8	43 5/8	14 4/8	14 5/8	6 4/8	6 1/8	28 2/8	28 2/8	Wheaton, Yukon	Herbert Carlson	Herbert Carlson	1963	91
174 6/8	40 5/8	40 3/8	14 4/8	14 2/8	6 6/8	6 7/8	26 3/8	26 3/8	Wrangell Mts., Alaska	Peter W. Bading	Peter W. Bading	1963	91
174 6/8	42	42 4/8	14	13 6/8	6 7/8	7	23 7/8	24 1/8	Chugach Mts., Alaska	Bill Silveira	Bill Silveira	1969	91
174 6/8	40 1/8	40 7/8	15 3/8	15 4/8	6 4/8	6 4/8	20 4/8	20 4/8	Mt. Wrangell, Alaska	Tod Reichert	Tod Reichert	1976	91
174 6/8	41 2/8	41 2/8	14	14	6 7/8	7 3/8	27 3/8	27 2/8	Wrangell Mts., Alaska	Don L. Corley	Don L. Corley	1978	91
174 5/8	40 4/8	43 5/8	14 2/8	14 2/8	6 4/8	6 4/8	22 3/8	22 3/8	Kenai Mts., Alaska	C. A. Brauch	C. A. Brauch	1959	100
174 5/8	40 5/8	42 2/8	14 5/8	14 5/8	7 2/8	6 4/8	27 1/8	27 1/8	Raft Creek, Yukon	Marvin Wood	Marvin Wood	1961	100
174 5/8	43 4/8	42 3/8	13 7/8	14 1/8	6 5/8	6 6/8	26 1/8	26 1/8	Kusawa Lake, Yukon	Lawrence J. Kolar	Lawrence J. Kolar	1973	100
174 4/8	41	41 4/8	13 5/8	13 6/8	8 1/8	8 5/8	22	21 3/8	Wrangell Mts., Alaska	Lloyd Walker	Lloyd Walker	1959	103
174 4/8	42 2/8	41 6/8	13 7/8	13 7/8	8	7 4/8	20 1/8	20 1/8	Wrangell Mts., Alaska	Robert L. Jenkins	Robert L. Jenkins	1963	103
174 4/8	40 3/8	40 5/8	15 1/8	14 7/8	6 4/8	6 7/8	23 7/8	23 5/8	Chugach Mts., Alaska	Lawrence T. Keenan	Lawrence T. Keenan	1976	103
174 3/8	43 2/8	43 1/8	14 3/8	14 3/8	6 2/8	6 2/8	24	24	Wrangell Mts., Alaska	John J. Liska	John J. Liska	1963	106

174 3/8	42 1/8	42 4/8	14 1/8	14 2/8	6 4/8	6 5/8	25 6/8	25 6/8	Nahannie Range, N.W.T.	Nick Trenke	Nick Trenke	1979	106
174 2/8	41 5/8	41 5/8	14 2/8	14 2/8	6 4/8	6 3/8	26 4/8	26 4/8	Talkeetna Mts., Alaska	William J. Konesky	William J. Konesky	1958	108
174 2/8	40 2/8	41 5/8	14 4/8	14 4/8	7 4/8	7	22	22	Wrangell Mts., Alaska	Jerry L. Beason	Jerry L. Beason	1961	108
174 2/8	41 4/8	43 4/8	13 7/8	14	6 3/8	6 3/8	31 1/8	31 1/8	Coast Mts., Yukon	Clarence Hinkle	Clarence Hinkle	1963	108
174 1/8	40	42 7/8	14 5/8	14 4/8	6 4/8	6 4/8	25	25	Ruby Range, Yukon	Lawrence S. Kellogg	Lawrence S. Kellogg	1958	111
174 1/8	43 6/8	43 3/8	14 1/8	14 1/8	5 7/8	6	30 7/8	30 7/8	Wrangell Mts., Alaska	Sven Johanson	Sven Johanson	1960	111
174	40 7/8	42 3/8	13 5/8	13 7/8	7 4/8	7 6/8	21 7/8	21 7/8	Kenai Pen., Alaska	Basil C. Bradbury	Basil C. Bradbury	1960	113
174	42 4/8	45	14	14	6 1/8	6 1/8	27	27	Wrangell Mts., Alaska	Howard Gilmore, Jr.	Howard Gilmore, Jr.	1969	113
174	43 3/8	44 7/8	14	14	5 5/8	5 7/8	32 1/8	31 6/8	Wrangell Mts., Alaska	Dan Parker	Dan Parker	1972	113
174	43 5/8	42 1/8	14 3/8	14 4/8	5 7/8	5 4/8	29	29 2/8	Alaska Range, Alaska	Harry Robert Hannon	Harry Robert Hannon	1976	113
173 7/8	40 1/8	40 4/8	14 2/8	14 4/8	6 2/8	6 3/8	25 1/8	25 1/8	Chugach Mts., Alaska	Peter W. Bading	Peter W. Bading	1961	117
173 7/8	44 1/8	42 4/8	13 7/8	13 7/8	6 2/8	6 5/8	26	26	Twitya River, N. W. T.	Lewis W. Lindemer	Lewis W. Lindemer	1970	117
173 6/8	42 6/8	43 2/8	14 2/8	14 5/8	6 1/8	6 4/8	29 3/8	29 3/8	Talkeetna Mts., Alaska	Frank Cook	Frank Cook	1961	119
173 6/8	36 2/8	41 6/8	15 1/8	15	7 2/8	7 2/8	24 6/8	24 6/8	Wrangell Mts., Alaska	Gene Effler	Gene Effler	1964	119
173 6/8	40 2/8	40 2/8	14 7/8	14 6/8	5 4/8	5 4/8	30 4/8	30 4/8	Keele River, N. W. T.	John M. Azevedo	John M. Azevedo	1975	119
173 5/8	41 6/8	45 3/8	12 7/8	13	7	6 7/8	24 6/8	24 6/8	Ruby Range, Yukon	John E. Hammett	John E. Hammett	1949	122
173 5/8	45 2/8	45 1/8	13 1/8	13 2/8	5 7/8	5 6/8	30 6/8	30 7/8	Chitina, Alaska	Dene Leonard, Jr.	Dene Leonard, Jr.	1959	122
173 5/8	38 5/8	38 2/8	13 7/8	13 7/8	9 3/8	9 3/8	21 1/8	19 6/8	Wrangell Mts., Alaska	B. L. Burkholder	B. L. Burkholder	1960	122
173 5/8	42 1/8	42 6/8	14 3/8	14 6/8	5 4/8	5 4/8	28	28	Chugach Mts., Alaska	Richard T. Kopsack	Richard T. Kopsack	1961	122
173 5/8	43 4/8	41 3/8	13 2/8	13 4/8	7 2/8	7 2/8	23 3/8	22 2/8	Champagne, Yukon	Edmund D. Patterson, Jr.	Edmund D. Patterson, Jr.	1963	122
173 5/8	41 4/8	41 7/8	14 2/8	14 2/8	6 7/8	6 7/8	24 2/8	24 2/8	Lake Clark, Alaska	Melvin C. Paxton	Melvin C. Paxton	1968	122
173 4/8	43 5/8	43 5/8	13 6/8	14	5 7/8	5 7/8	29 7/8	29 7/8	Primrose River, Yukon	W. R. Collier	W. R. Collier	1962	128
173 4/8	42	44 4/8	13 7/8	13 7/8	6 3/8	6 4/8	29 7/8	29 7/8	Wrangell Mts., Alaska	James Harrower	James Harrower	1963	128
173 4/8	41 1/8	40 7/8	14 6/8	14 7/8	6 4/8	6 4/8	31 1/8	30 6/8	Chitina Glacier, Alaska	Robert W. Kubick	Robert W. Kubick	1967	128
173 3/8	43 5/8	43	13 5/8	13 5/8	6 5/8	6 4/8	28 4/8	28 4/8	Tonseno Lake, Alaska	James St. Amour	James St. Amour	1957	131
173 3/8	44 6/8	44 7/8	13 3/8	13 3/8	5 6/8	5 6/8	28 5/8	28 6/8	Chugach Mts., Alaska	Howard Haney	Howard Haney	1961	131
173 3/8	40 1/8	40 4/8	15	15	6 1/8	6 2/8	27 5/8	27 5/8	Whitehorse, Yukon	Francis Bouchard	Francis Bouchard	1961	131
173 3/8	42 2/8	43 3/8	13 2/8	13 1/8	6 2/8	6 4/8	19 4/8	19 4/8	Kenai Pen., Alaska	Spud Dillon	Spud Dillon	1966	131
173 3/8	39 7/8	44 4/8	13 7/8	13 5/8	6 4/8	6 2/8	25 3/8	24 4/8	Wrangell Mts., Alaska	Basil C. Bradbury	Basil C. Bradbury	1968	131
173 3/8	42	42 7/8	13 3/8	13 4/8	7	7 4/8	22 3/8	22 3/8	Alaska Range, Alaska	Arthur L. Spicer	Arthur L. Spicer	1970	131
173 2/8	35 2/8	45	14 3/8	14 4/8	6 2/8	6 7/8	25 2/8	23 3/8	Wrangell Mts., Alaska	J. H. Shelton	J. H. Shelton	1958	137
173 1/8	46 4/8	41 5/8	13 3/8	13 2/8	6	6	20 1/8	26 7/8	Kenai Pen., Alaska	W. R. Shellhorn	D. Shellhorn	1936	138
173 1/8	41 2/8	39 7/8	14 3/8	14 2/8	7 4/8	7 3/8	18 4/8	21 7/8	Dawson Mts., Yukon	Bill Goosman	Bill Goosman	1972	138
173	42	42 4/8	13 4/8	13 5/8	6 4/8	6 4/8	28 1/8	28 1/8	Wrangell Mts., Alaska	Ken Knudson	Ken Knudson	1961	139
173	40 3/8	40 3/8	15	15	6 3/8	6 4/8	28 6/8	28 6/8	Whitehorse, Yukon	Earl DuBois	Earl DuBois	1961	139
173	45 6/8	45 2/8	13 3/8	13 4/8	5 5/8	5 4/8	33	33	Wrangell Mts., Alaska	Bob Merz	Bob Merz	1966	139
173	40 5/8	41 5/8	13 5/8	13 3/8	7 2/8	7 2/8	20 5/8	20 5/8	Chugach Mts., Alaska	J. C. Hemming	J. C. Hemming	1970	139
173	40 6/8	43	14 7/8	14 5/8	5 7/8	5 7/8	28 3/8	27 7/8	Wrangell Mts., Alaska	Charles A. Pohland	Charles A. Pohland	1971	139
173	43 6/8	44	13 5/8	13 5/8	6	6	28	28	Chugach Mts., Alaska	Thomas Clark	Thomas Clark	1975	139
172 7/8	39 1/8	39	14 2/8	14 2/8	7 7/8	7 5/8	25 1/8	25 1/8	Wrangell Mts., Alaska	Ralph Cox	Ralph Cox	1971	146
172 7/8	43 7/8	42 6/8	14 4/8	14 4/8	6 1/8	5 7/8	24 2/8	24	Alaska Range, Alaska	George Faerber	George Faerber	1976	146
172 6/8	40 3/8	40 3/8	13 4/8	13 4/8	7 7/8	7 6/8	22	20 6/8	Kusawa Lake, Yukon	John I. Moore	John I. Moore	1955	148
172 6/8	38 7/8	43 5/8	14 2/8	14 2/8	8	6 4/8	27 7/8	27 7/8	Nabesna River, Alaska	J. C. Phillips	J. C. Phillips	1956	148

DALL'S SHEEP–*Continued*

Ovis dalli dalli and *Ovis dalli kenaiensis*

Score	Length of Horn R.	Length of Horn L.	Circumference of Base R.	Circumference of Base L.	Circumference at Third Quarter R.	Circumference at Third Quarter L.	Greatest Spread	Tip to Tip Spread	Locality Killed	By Whom Killed	Owner	Date Killed	Rank
172 6/8	41 2/8	41 2/8	13 5/8	13 5/8	6 6/8	6 6/8	25 6/8	25 6/8	Chugach Mts., Alaska	Ruby Wyatt	Ruby Wyatt	1960	148
172 6/8	43 5/8	43 3/8	13 5/8	13 5/8	6 4/8	6 4/8	33	33	Chugach Mts., Alaska	Richard Kopsack	Richard Kopsack	1963	148
172 6/8	41 2/8	42 2/8	14 2/8	14 1/8	6 4/8	6 3/8	28 5/8	28 5/8	Wrangell Mts., Alaska	Alvin W. Huba, Jr.	Alvin W. Huba, Jr.	1968	148
172 6/8	40	40 4/8	14 4/8	15	7	6 5/8	30 3/8	30 3/8	Gerstle River, Alaska	John A. Shilling	John A. Shilling	1968	148
172 6/8	41 7/8	41 7/8	14 1/8	14 1/8	6 3/8	6 2/8	29	29	Radelet Creek, B. C.	Norman W. Dougan	Norman W. Dougan	1972	148
172 6/8	43 2/8	43	13 6/8	13 5/8	5 7/8	6 1/8	28 5/8	28 5/8	Chandalar River, Alaska	Robert M. Welch	Robert M. Welch	1974	148
172 6/8	43 1/8	43 7/8	14	14	5 5/8	5 6/8	30 3/8	30 1/8	Wrangell Mts., Alaska	Robert J. Wykel	Robert J. Wykel	1976	148
172 5/8	43 4/8	42 3/8	12 7/8	13 2/8	7	7	29 4/8	29 4/8	Knik Glacier, Alaska	Picked Up	Howard G. Romig	1932	157
172 5/8	42 1/8	42 4/8	13 4/8	13 6/8	6 6/8	6 4/8	26 3/8	26 3/8	Mt. Arkell, Yukon	Stuart Hall	Stuart Hall	1957	157
172 5/8	42	41 3/8	14 5/8	14 6/8	5 7/8	5 6/8	32	32	Wrangell Mts., Alaska	William T. Ellis	William T. Ellis	1960	157
172 5/8	38 7/8	39 2/8	14 7/8	15 3/8	6 5/8	6 7/8	33 7/8	33 1/8	Caribou Creek, Yukon	Harold J. Lund	Harold J. Lund	1963	157
172 5/8	41 5/8	42	14 4/8	14 2/8	8 6/8	6 2/8	27 1/8	27 1/8	Yukon	S. P. Viezner	S. P. Viezner	1964	157
172 5/8	41 1/8	41 6/8	14 1/8	14 1/8	6 3/8	6 3/8	29 7/8	29 7/8	Knik River, Alaska	Miles G. France	Miles G. France	1969	157
172 5/8	42	41 3/8	13	13	7 6/8	7 3/8	21 6/8	21 6/8	Talbot Creek, Yukon	Lloyd E. Zeman	Lloyd E. Zeman	1969	157
172 4/8	42 4/8	41 4/8	14 2/8	14 2/8	6 4/8	6 6/8	26 1/8	26 1/8	Wrangell Mts., Alaska	W. A. Bailey, Jr.	W. A. Bailey, Jr.	1959	164
172 4/8	43 4/8	42 6/8	13 1/8	13 1/8	7 2/8	6 7/8	24 3/8	24 3/8	Wrangell Mts., Alaska	H. E. Eldred	H. E. Eldred	1960	164
172 4/8	39 5/8	45 1/8	14 1/8	14	5 6/8	5 6/8	27 5/8	27 5/8	Chugach Mts., Alaska	Raymond Capossela	Raymond Capossela	1963	164
172 4/8	41 1/8	42 1/8	14 2/8	14 2/8	6 1/8	6	31 3/8	31 3/8	Primrose Lake, Yukon	Walter Sutton	Walter Sutton	1968	164
172 3/8	41 5/8	41 2/8	13 5/8	13 6/8	6 6/8	6 6/8	25 1/8	25	Chugach Mts., Alaska	Chuck Moe	Chuck Moe	1979	168
172 2/8	41 7/8	41 6/8	14 3/8	14 1/8	5 7/8	6 1/8	26 5/8	26 5/8	Chugach Mts., Alaska	Justin L. Smith	Justin L. Smith	1963	169
172 1/8	40	39 7/8	14 2/8	14 2/8	6 4/8	6 6/8	24 3/8	24 3/8	Wrangell Mts., Alaska	Kirk Gay	Kirk Gay	1958	170
172 1/8	39 7/8	39	15 4/8	15 3/8	7	6 5/8	26	26	Wrangell Mts., Alaska	Horace Groff	Horace Groff	1961	170
172 1/8	38 5/8	42	14 1/8	14 1/8	7	7	21 7/8	21 3/8	Chugach Mts., Alaska	E. F. Craig	E. F. Craig	1963	170
172 1/8	42	41 7/8	14 5/8	14 6/8	6	6 2/8	25 6/8	25 6/8	Wrangell Mts., Alaska	Walter E. Cox	Walter E. Cox	1966	170
172 1/8	43	38 7/8	14 4/8	14 4/8	5 7/8	5 7/8	29 2/8	29 2/8	Kuskokwim River, Alaska	Ken M. Wilson	Ken M. Wilson	1973	170
172	41 3/8	41 7/8	14 5/8	14 6/8	6 2/8	5 7/8	26 2/8	26 2/8	Wrangell Mts., Alaska	Carroll W. Gibbs	Carroll W. Gibbs	1957	175
172	43 6/8	44 6/8	13 6/8	13 6/8	5 6/8	6	26 1/8	26 1/8	Chugach Mts., Alaska	M. L. Magnusson	M. L. Magnusson	1957	175
172	41 6/8	42	13 5/8	13 6/8	6 4/8	7	25 3/8	25 3/8	Sheep Mt, Yukon	Ray Hoffmann, III	Ray Hoffmann, III	1961	175
172	36	39	15	15 1/8	8	8	22 6/8	20	Chugach Mts., Alaska	Ward Gay, Jr.	Ward Gay, Jr.	1961	175
172	41 4/8	41 4/8	14 4/8	14 2/8	6 2/8	6 2/8	22 3/8	22 3/8	Sekwi Mt., N.W.T.	J. D. Martin, Jr.	J. D. Martin, Jr.	1978	175
171 7/8	45 2/8	42 7/8	13 1/8	13 1/8	6	6 7/8	27 6/8	27 6/8	McCarthy, Alaska	Eugene E. Saxton	Eugene E. Saxton	1953	180
171 7/8	43 2/8	41 3/8	13 5/8	13 4/8	6 2/8	6 1/8	25 4/8	25 4/8	Talkeetna Mts., Alaska	Paul S. Lawrence	Paul S. Lawrence	1960	180

171 7/8	39 5/8	38	15 6/8	15 7/8	6	6 2/8	25 6/8	25 6/8	Wrangell Mts., Alaska	Kenneth Knudson	Kenneth Knudson	1963	180
171 7/8	41 4/8	40 1/8	13 3/8	13 3/8	7 6/8	7 3/8	44 4/8	44 4/8	Chugach Mts., Alaska	Herb Klein	Herb Klein	1964	180
171 7/8	41 5/8	40 2/8	14 6/8	14 4/8	6 1/8	6 3/8	22 2/8	22 2/8	Chugach Range, Alaska	Frank Cook	Frank Cook	1965	180
171 6/8	38 7/8	42 5/8	14	13 7/8	6 5/8	6 4/8	28 4/8	28 4/8	Wrangell Mts., Alaska	Charles C. Parsons	Charles C. Parsons	1955	185
171 6/8	42 7/8	42 3/8	13 7/8	14	6 3/8	6 2/8	30 7/8	30 7/8	Wrangell Mts., Alaska	Ross Jardine	Ross Jardine	1960	185
171 6/8	35 4/8	42	14 7/8	14 7/8	6 5/8	6 7/8	24 3/8	24 3/8	Chugach Mts., Alaska	C. J. McElroy	C. J. McElroy	1969	185
171 4/8	40 5/8	40 5/8	13 6/8	13 6/8	6 7/8	6 7/8	23 4/8	23 4/8	Kenai Pen., Alaska	C. R. Wright	C. R. Wright	1936	188
171 4/8	40 6/8	39 4/8	14 6/8	15	6 2/8	5 7/8	28	28	Whitehorse, Yukon	Howard Creason	Howard Creason	1969	188
171 4/8	41 5/8	42 5/8	13 5/8	13 5/8	6 3/8	6 6/8	26	26	Wrangell Mts., Alaska	Robert V. Walker	Robert V. Walker	1971	188
171 3/8	44 3/8	45 2/8	12 7/8	13	6 7/8	5 6/8	34 2/8	34 2/8	Wood River, Alaska	R. R. M. Carpenter	Acad. Nat. Sci., Phil.	1940	191
171 3/8	39 4/8	40 1/8	13 5/8	13 6/8	7 5/8	7 7/8	27 2/8	27 2/8	Coal Creek, Alaska	W. W. Fultz	W. W. Fultz	1955	191
171 3/8	41 1/8	41 2/8	14	14	6 3/8	6 2/8	30 3/8	30 3/8	Chugach Mts., Alaska	Perley Colbeth	Perley Colbeth	1958	191
171 3/8	36 7/8	39 3/8	14	14	8	8 3/8	20 6/8	19 3/8	Chugach Mts., Alaska	Raymond Capossela	Raymond Capossela	1961	191
171 3/8	42	42 3/8	13 3/8	13 3/8	7 2/8	7 3/8	29 2/8	29 2/8	Wrangell Mts., Alaska	Arthur R. Dubs	Arthur R. Dubs	1962	191
171 3/8	36 3/8	44	14 6/8	14 5/8	6 3/8	6 7/8	26 4/8	25 6/8	Wrangell Mts., Alaska	Doug McRae, Sr.	Doug McCrae, Sr.	1972	191
171 3/8	41 1/8	42 2/8	14	14	6	6 7/8	26 6/8	26 4/8	Chugach Mts., Alaska	Michael J. Ebner	Michael J. Ebner	1977	191
171 2/8	36 3/8	38 1/8	14 7/8	14 7/8	7 6/8	7 6/8	24 3/8	24 1/8	Wrangell Mts., Alaska	Gordon Madole	Gordon Madole	1956	198
171 2/8	39 4/8	40	12 4/8	12 3/8	9 3/8	9 4/8	21 6/8	21 6/8	Ruby Range, Yukon	Picked Up	William J. Joslin	1960	198
171 2/8	39 6/8	41 2/8	14 7/8	14 6/8	6 5/8	6	24 1/8	23 7/8	Wrangell Mts., Alaska	Rudolpho Valladolid	Rudolpho Valladolid	1974	198
171 1/8	45	44 1/8	12 1/8	12 1/8	6 2/8	6 2/8	26 4/8	26 4/8	Wrangell Mts., Alaska	Picked Up	Dick Gunlogson	1968	201
171 1/8	42	42 5/8	13 7/8	14	6 1/8	6 6/8	24	24	Kusawa Lake, Yukon	Maurice G. Katz	Maurice G. Katz	1970	201
171 1/8	40 7/8	40 6/8	13 6/8	14	6 5/8	6 5/8	22 2/8	22 2/8	Robertson River, Alaska	Beuron A. McKenzie	Beuron A. McKenzie	1971	201
171	42 7/8	43 1/8	13 5/8	13 5/8	5 6/8	5 7/8	30 4/8	30 4/8	Carcross, Yukon	Henry Brockhouse	Henry Brockhouse	1955	204
171	42 1/8	41 1/8	14	13 7/8	6 1/8	6 2/8	21 [illegible]/8	26 7/8	Alligator Lake, Yukon	D. Graham	D. Graham	1968	204
171	40 6/8	41 2/8	13 6/8	14	6 4/8	6 3/8	26 3/8	26 3/8	Ruby Range, Yukon	Harry T. Scharfenberg	Harry T. Scharfenberg	1977	204
170 7/8	41 5/8	41 4/8	14 6/8	14 6/8	5 3/8	5 4/8	26 3/8	26 3/8	Kenai Pen., Alaska	David Jones	David Jones	1963	207
170 7/8	35 3/8	39 6/8	15 2/8	15 2/8	7 1/8	7 2/8	25 7/8	25 7/8	Wrangell Mts., Alaska	Richard Stingley	Richard Stingley	1965	207
170 7/8	42	41 5/8	14 1/8	14 4/8	6 5/8	6 3/8	29 5/8	29 2/8	Wrangell, Alaska	Thomas Sperstad	Thomas Sperstad	1969	207
170 7/8	36	36 5/8	14	14 2/8	9 1/8	9 1/8	25 4/8	24 5/8	Chugach Mts., Alaska	Gerald L. Warnock	Gerald L. Warnock	1970	207
170 7/8	40 6/8	40 7/8	14 2/8	14 2/8	6	6	25 7/8	25 7/8	Trench Lake, N. W. T.	Wayne G. Myers	Wayne G. Myers	1974	207
170 6/8	41 5/8	41 7/8	14 1/8	14 1/8	5 6/8	5 6/8	26 4/8	26 4/8	Wrangell Mts., Alaska	Joseph A. Tedesco	Joseph A. Tedesco	1959	212
170 6/8	39 2/8	39 2/8	14 6/8	14 7/8	6 6/8	6 6/8	28 2/8	28 2/8	Wrangell Mts., Alaska	George Stelious	George Stelious	1962	212
170 6/8	42 2/8	42 4/8	13 6/8	13 6/8	6	6 1/8	26 4/8	26 4/8	Wrangell Mts., Alaska	Robert V. Broadbent	Robert V. Broadbent	1965	212
170 5/8	41 4/8	41 7/8	14	14	6 2/8	6 2/8	30 1/8	30 1/8	Nabesna River, Alaska	J. S. Rutherford	J. S. Rutherford	1956	215
170 5/8	42 1/8	40 6/8	12 7/8	12 7/8	7 4/8	7 6/8	21 3/8	21 3/8	Wrangell Mts., Alaska	W. A. Fisher	W. A. Fisher	1959	215
170 5/8	41 3/8	42 2/8	13 7/8	13 7/8	6 3/8	6 4/8	25 1/8	25 1/8	Wrangell Mts., Alaska	Gene Sperstad	Gene Sperstad	1961	215
170 5/8	43 2/8	40 7/8	14 1/8	14 1/8	5 5/8	5 6/8	25 5/8	25 6/8	Nutzotin Mts., Alaska	Dorothy Andersen	Larry Folger	1965	215
170 5/8	41 2/8	42 1/8	15	14 6/8	5 2/8	5 3/8	28	28	Chugach Mts., Alaska	Harry C. Heckendorn	Harry C. Heckendorn	1972	215
170 4/8	44 2/8	38	13 5/8	13 6/8	6 4/8	6 4/8	29 3/8	29 3/8	Wrangell Mts., Alaska	Harry L. Swank, Jr.	Harry L. Swank, Jr.	1962	220
170 4/8	40 2/8	40 6/8	14 4/8	14 4/8	6 2/8	6 4/8	21 3/8	21 3/8	Ruby Range, Yukon	Harold C. Casey	Harold C. Casey	1964	220
170 4/8	41 2/8	41 2/8	14 2/8	14 2/8	6 3/8	6 4/8	23 6/8	23 6/8	Brooks Range, Alaska	Donald E. Harrell	Donald E. Harrell	1979	220
170 3/8	40	40 3/8	14 2/8	14 2/8	6 2/8	6 2/8	22	22	Kenai Pen., Alaska	Vance Corrigan	Vance Corrigan	1957	223
170 3/8	39 7/8	43	14 2/8	14 2/8	6 2/8	6 2/8	23	28	Wrangell Mts., Alaska	Joseph A. Tadesco	Joseph A. Tadesco	1960	223

Dall's Sheep–*Continued*

Ovis dalli dalli and *Ovis dalli kenaiensis*

Score	Length of Horn R.	Length of Horn L.	Circumference of Base R.	Circumference of Base L.	Circumference at Third Quarter R.	Circumference at Third Quarter L.	Greatest Spread	Tip to Tip Spread	Locality Killed	By Whom Killed	Owner	Date Killed	Rank
170 3/8	42 4/8	43 5/8	13 2/8	13 2/8	5 7/8	6 4/8	31 2/8	31 2/8	Chugach Mts., Alaska	William H. Smith	William H. Smith	1961	223
170 3/8	41 5/8	42 4/8	14 2/8	14 2/8	5 6/8	5 7/8	27 7/8	27 7/8	Wrangell Mts., Alaska	Willie Bogner, Sr.	Willie Bogner, Sr.	1961	223
170 2/8	40 5/8	41 3/8	14 1/8	14 2/8	5 6/8	6 1/8	22 2/8	22 2/8	Kenai Pen., Alaska	C. R. Wright	C. R. Wright	1935	227
170 2/8	39 7/8	39 7/8	14 5/8	14 5/8	6 2/8	6 4/8	25 3/8	25 3/8	Champagne, Yukon	Walter Butcher	Walter Butcher	1956	227
170 2/8	39 5/8	41 7/8	15 3/8	15 3/8	5 6/8	5 6/8	23 3/8	23 3/8	Tonsina River, Alaska	R. J. Uhl	R. J. Uhl	1959	227
170 2/8	38 7/8	39 7/8	13 6/8	13 6/8	7 6/8	7 6/8	19 6/8	19 6/8	Chugach Mts., Alaska	Donald Stroble	Donald Stroble	1961	227
170 2/8	37 2/8	38	14 7/8	14 7/8	7	6 7/8	20 6/8	19 4/8	Kenai Pen., Alaska	Lee Miller	Lee Miller	1963	227
170 2/8	40 3/8	40 3/8	14 6/8	14 7/8	6 2/8	6 2/8	27 2/8	27 2/8	Wrangell Mts., Alaska	C. Driskell	C. Driskell	1965	227
170 2/8	41	40	14 5/8	14 5/8	6 5/8	5 7/8	28 3/8	28 3/8	Wrangell Mts., Alaska	Jim Babala	Jim Babala	1967	227
170 2/8	41 2/8	41 4/8	13 6/8	13 7/8	6 4/8	6 4/8	25 7/8	25 7/8	Talkeetna Mts., Alaska	H. Albertas Hall	H. Albertas Hall	1971	227
170 2/8	40	40	14 4/8	14 4/8	6 4/8	7	26 6/8	23 6/8	Wrangell Mts., Alaska	Bernard J. Meinerz	Bernard J. Meinerz	1972	227
170 1/8	42	42 7/8	13 5/8	13 5/8	6 5/8	6 7/8	28	28	Donjek, Yukon	Unknown	Acad. Nat. Sci., Phil.	1921	236
170 1/8	40 1/8	41	14 5/8	14 5/8	6 3/8	6 2/8	25 4/8	25 4/8	Mt. Arkell, Yukon	Ed. Steiner	Ed. Steiner	1955	236
170 1/8	40 2/8	40 3/8	13 2/8	13 4/8	7 6/8	7 5/8	22	22	Wrangell Mts., Alaska	Chester Beer	Chester Beer	1959	236
170 1/8	41 4/8	41 1/8	14	14	5 5/8	5 5/8	24 5/8	24 5/8	Chugach Mts., Alaska	James A. Kirsch	James A. Kirsch	1961	236
170 1/8	38	37 3/8	14	14 2/8	8 3/8	8 2/8	20 3/8	20 3/8	Wrangell Mts., Alaska	W. T. Yoshimoto	W. T. Yoshimoto	1967	236
170	42	42 2/8	13 1/8	13 1/8	6 1/8	6 2/8	30 1/8	30 1/8	Wrangell Mts., Alaska	Ralph Morava, Jr.	Ralph Morava, Jr.	1954	241
170	40 6/8	42 2/8	14 3/8	14 1/8	6 1/8	6 1/8	27 3/8	27 3/8	Nabesna River, Alaska	Raymond A. Talbott	Raymond A. Talbott	1958	241
170	40 2/8	39 4/8	13 4/8	13 1/8	7 5/8	8 2/8	23 3/8	23 3/8	Kluane Lake, Yukon	Herb Graham	Herb Graham	1959	241
170	41 5/8	42 5/8	13 5/8	13 6/8	6 1/8	6	23 4/8	23 4/8	Wrangell Mts., Alaska	Mrs. Melvin Soder	Mrs. Melvin Soder	1961	241

*Final Score subject to revision by additional verifying measurements.

Photograph by Grancel Fitz

WORLD'S RECORD STONE'S SHEEP
SCORE: 196 6/8
Locality: Muskwa River, British Columbia. Date: 1936.
Hunter: L.S. Chadwick. Owner: The National Collection.
Many sportsmen consider this head to be the finest known North American big game trophy.

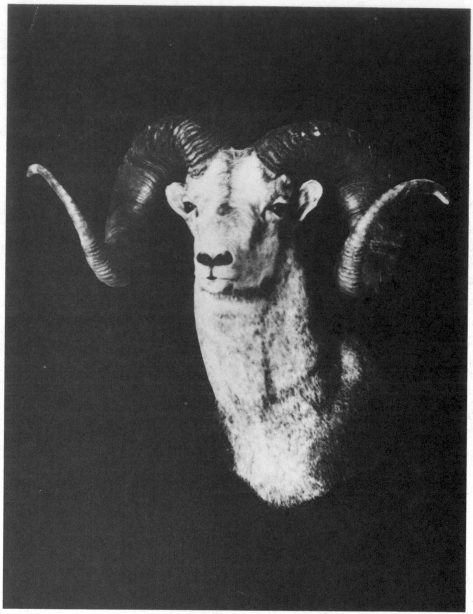

Photograph by Ray Todd

NUMBER TWO STONE'S SHEEP
SCORE: 190
Locality: Sikanni Chief River, British Columbia. Date: 1962.
Hunter and owner: Norman Blank.
Winner of the Sagamore Hill Medal in 1963.

Stone's Sheep

Ovis dalli stonei

Minimum Score 170

Score	Length of Horn R.	Length of Horn L.	Circumference of Base R.	Circumference of Base L.	Circumference at Third Quarter R.	Circumference at Third Quarter L.	Greatest Spread	Tip to Tip Spread	Locality Killed	By Whom Killed	Owner	Date Killed	Rank
196 6/8	50 1/8	51 5/8	14 6/8	14 6/8	6 6/8	7	31	31	Muskwa River, B. C	L. S. Chadwick	National Collection	1936	1
190	46 6/8	46 6/8	15 2/8	15 1/8	6 5/8	6 6/8	30 6/8	30 6/8	Sikanni Chief River, B. C.	Norman Blank	Norman Blank	1962	2
189 6/8	48 2/8	46 2/8	14 7/8	14 7/8	7 2/8	7 4/8	28	28	Blue Sheep Lake, B. C.	G. C. F. Dalziel	G. C. F. Dalziel	1965	3
187 4/8	43	44	14 6/8	14 6/8	8 4/8	8 4/8	22	22	Ospika River, B. C.	Paul D. Weingart	Paul D. Weingart	1970	4
186 3/8*	44 1/8	44	16	16 1/8	6 1/8	6 2/8	26 3/8	26 3/8	Watson Lake, B. C.		Keith Brown	1971	5
185 5/8*	47 5/8	49 2/8	13 4/8	13 3/8	6 4/8	7 4/8	29	29	Ice Mt., B.C.	Picked Up	Bruce Creyke	1977	6
185 3/8*	45 6/8	44 3/8	15 7/8	15 7/8	6 1/8	5 7/8	29 3/8	29 3/8	Prophet River, B. C.	Felipe Palau	Felipe Palau	1970	7
184 6/8	43	43 4/8	15 6/8	15 6/8	7	7 1/8	28 4/8	28 4/8	Prophet River, B. C.	Joseph H. Shirk	Mrs. C. Barnaby	1948	8
184 4/8	44 4/8	45	15 4/8	15 3/8	6 3/8	6 4/8	26 3/8	26 3/8	Hudson Hope, B. C.	John W. Pitney	Am. Mus. Nat. History	1936	9
184 3/8	44 3/8	46	14 1/8	14 2/8	8	7	28 6/8	28 6/8	Colt Lake, B. C.	Lloyd E. Hall	Lloyd E. Hall	1963	10
184 2/8	42 1/8	42 3/8	16 2/8	16 2/8	7 1/8	7 1/8	24 4/8	24 4/8	Blue Sheep Lake, B. C.	G. C. F. Dalziel	G. C. F. Dalziel	1964	11
184 2/8	47 5/8	45 3/8	14 2/8	14 4/8	6 6/8	6 3/8	31 3/8	31 3/8	Colt Lake, B. C.	Herb Klein	Herb Klein	1965	11
184 2/8	45 7/8	42 7/8	14 7/8	15	7 3/8	7 3/8	22 5/8	22 3/8	Ketchika Mts., B. C.	Arthur R. Dubs	Arthur R. Dubs	1966	11
183 7/8	44 4/8	45 5/8	13 7/8	13 7/8	7	7 5/8	23 7/8	23 7/8	Hudson Hope, B. C.	Picked Up	Bill Beattie	1961	14
183 6/8	44 3/8	44 5/8	14 6/8	14 6/8	7	6 7/8	20 5/8	19	Dease Lake, B. C.	Otis Chandler	Otis Chandler	1966	15
183 5/8	43 3/8	43 2/8	14 7/8	14 7/8	7 1/8	7	25 7/8	25 7/8	Sikanni Chief River, B. C.	Picked Up	Bob & Don Beattie	1962	16
183 3/8	44 6/8	44 1/8	15	15	6 6/8	6 4/8	26 3/8	26 1/8	Ketchika Range, B. C.	John Caputo, Jr.	John Caputo, Jr.	1961	17
183 3/8	49 2/8	44 7/8	13 4/8	13 4/8	6 6/8	6 5/8	25	25	Terminus Mt., B. C.	Picked Up	Herb Klein	1969	17
183 1/8	44 7/8	46 4/8	14 1/8	14 1/8	6 7/8	7	29 6/8	29 5/8	Cassiar Mts., B. C.	Robert S. Jackson	Robert S. Jackson	1968	19
183	45 4/8	44 4/8	14	14	7 6/8	7 6/8	25 3/8	25 3/8	Muskwa River, B. C.	T. E. Shillingburg	T. E. Shillingburg	1937	20
183	44	44 6/8	14 5/8	14 5/8	7	7 3/8	25 7/8	25 7/8	Ketchika Range, B. C.	John Caputo, Sr.	John Caputo, Sr.	1966	20
183	45 6/8	44 6/8	14 6/8	14 6/8	6 5/8	6 4/8	27 6/8	27 6/8	Cassiar Mts., B. C.	Gordon Studer	Gordon Studer	1967	20
182 6/8	46 1/8	45 7/8	14 4/8	14 2/8	6 6/8	6 5/8	26 3/8	26 3/8	Cassiar Mts., B. C.	Alex Cox	Alex Cox	1959	23
182 6/8	43	42 2/8	15 1/8	15 1/8	7 1/8	7 3/8	24 7/8	24 7/8	Redfern Lake, B. C.	James P. Winters	James P. Winters	1970	23
182 3/8	45 1/8	45 6/8	14 5/8	14 6/8	6 3/8	6 4/8	31 4/8	31 3/8	Telegraph Creek, B. C.	Mrs. John Crowe	Mrs. John Crowe	1967	25
182 3/8	43	44 7/8	14 5/8	14 6/8	7	7	26 6/8	26 5/8	Kechika Range, B. C.	Hallett Ward, Jr.	Hallett Ward, Jr.	1967	25
182	41	42	15 4/8	15 4/8	8	8 2/8	27	27	Prophet River, B. C.	John E. Hammett, Jr.	John E. Hammett, Jr.	1944	27
182	45 6/8	45 4/8	14 2/8	14 2/8	6 7/8	7 1/8	26 4/8	26 4/8	Sand Pile Lake, B. C.	Al Robbins	Al Robbins	1963	27
182	45 1/8	44 5/8	14 3/8	14 4/8	6 5/8	6 5/8	26	26	Gataga River, B. C.	Gary Moore	Gary Moore	1965	27
181 7/8	43 3/8	43 4/8	15	15 1/8	6 4/8	6 5/8	26 5/8	26 5/8	Cassiar Mts., B. C.	Norman Lougheed	Norman Lougheed	1965	30
181 4/8	39	45 2/8	14 3/8	14 4/8	7 6/8	7 6/8	23 6/8	23 6/8	Burnt Rose Lake, B. C.	Lloyd Zeman	Lloyd Zeman	1970	31
181 3/8	44 3/8	44 6/8	15	14 7/8	6 4/8	6 6/8	27 2/8	27 2/8	Toad River, B. C.	Jerry E. Dahl	Jerry E. Dahl	1971	32

STONE'S SHEEP–*Continued*
Ovis dalli stonei

Score	Length of Horn R.	Length of Horn L.	Circumference of Base R.	Circumference of Base L.	Circumference at Third Quarter R.	Circumference at Third Quarter L.	Greatest Spread	Tip to Tip Spread	Locality Killed	By Whom Killed	Owner	Date Killed	Rank
181	44 3/8	44 7/8	14 3/8	14 4/8	6 2/8	6 4/8	30 5/8	30 5/8	Watson Lake, B. C.	C. W. Houle	C. W. Houle	1967	33
180 7/8	41 1/8	42 3/8	15	14 7/8	7 2/8	7 7/8	26 5/8	26 5/8	Hudson Hope, B. C.	Don Beattie	Don Beattie	1945	34
180 7/8	44	43 1/8	14 7/8	14 6/8	6 5/8	6 7/8	26 7/8	26 7/8	Sand Pile Lake, B. C.	David S. Loos	David S. Loos	1967	34
180 5/8	40 5/8	43	14 1/8	14 2/8	7 7/8	8	22 5/8	22 5/8	Hudson Hope, B. C.	David Slutker	David Slutker	1966	36
180 5/8	38 5/8	38 2/8	15 1/8	15 2/8	9 1/8	9 2/8	23 7/8	19	Prophet River, B. C.	Joseph Madonia	Joseph Madonia	1970	36
180 3/8	45	44 5/8	14 5/8	14 3/8	6	6 3/8	29	29	Telegraph Creek, B. C.	John B. Winsor	John B. Winsor	1966	38
180 2/8	44	44	14 5/8	14 2/8	7	6 5/8	26 5/8	26 5/8	Burnt Rose Lake, B. C.	E. L. Cook	E. L. Cook	1970	39
179 7/8	42 5/8	42 2/8	14 5/8	14 2/8	8	7 7/8	24 7/8	24 7/8	Prophet River, B. C.	Bill Thomas	Bill Thomas	1963	40
179 7/8	44	43 3/8	14 2/8	14 1/8	7 1/8	7 5/8	—	28	Ice Mt., B. C.	J. E. Mason	J. E. Mason	1966	40
179 5/8	39 5/8	44 5/8	13 5/8	13 7/8	9	8 5/8	21 3/8	21 3/8	Cassiar Mts., B. C.	Ralph W. Hull	Ralph W. Hull	1963	42
179 3/8	43 5/8	39 3/8	14 5/8	14 5/8	7 3/8	7 5/8	21 3/8	21 3/8	Pink Mt., B. C.	Gerald E. Howe	Gerald E. Howe	1970	43
179 3/8	45 5/8	44 7/8	14 3/8	14 2/8	6 5/8	6 3/8	24	24	Gathto Creek, B. C.	Gary J. Powell	Gary J. Powell	1970	43
179 2/8	43 5/8	44 5/8	13 7/8	13 5/8	7 2/8	6 5/8	26 3/8	26 3/8	Toad River, B. C.	Dennis Callison	Dennis Callison	1957	45
179 1/8	41 5/8	40 5/8	14 2/8	14 5/8	8 2/8	8 5/8	22 5/8	19 5/8	Eydee Creek, B. C.	Jack McNeill	Jack McNeill	1967	46
178 7/8	43	45 5/8	13 5/8	14	6 7/8	6 4/8	28 5/8	28 5/8	Frog & Kechika Rivers, B. C.	W. C. Waldron	W. C. Waldron	1967	47
178 7/8	39 5/8	48	13 5/8	13 5/8	7	7 3/8	26	24 7/8	Moody Lake, B. C.	J. Martin Benchoff	J. Martin Benchoff	1966	48
178 7/8	43 5/8	44 2/8	14 2/8	14 2/8	6 5/8	6 4/8	24 5/8	24 7/8	Tuchodi Lakes, B. C.	Ross Peck	Ross Peck	1963	49
178 2/8	40 5/8	41 1/8	14 5/8	14 7/8	7 1/8	7 4/8	24	24	Moody Lake, B. C.	Raymond G. Speer	Raymond G. Speer	1966	49
178 1/8	43 5/8	45	13 7/8	14	6 5/8	6 7/8	26 5/8	26 5/8	Gatago Mt., B. C.	Dan Auld	Dan Auld	1960	51
177 7/8	44 3/8	43 2/8	15	15	5 7/8	6	31	31	Skookum Mt., Yukon	Ira H. Kent	Ira H. Kent	1968	52
177 7/8	41 5/8	40 2/8	14 2/8	14 2/8	8 5/8	8 7/8	24 5/8	24 5/8	Frog River, B. C.	Don Palmer	Don Palmer	1968	52
177 6/8	43	42 5/8	14 2/8	14 5/8	6 3/8	6 4/8	27 5/8	27 5/8	Muskwa River, B. C.	Donald S. Hopkins	Donald S. Hopkins	1948	54
177 6/8	43 5/8	44 5/8	13 5/8	13 5/8	6 5/8	6 5/8	27 1/8	27 1/8	Ketchika Range, B. C.	John Caputo	John Caputo	1961	54
177 6/8	44 5/8	44	13 7/8	13 7/8	6 3/8	6 3/8	28 1/8	28 1/8	Sikanni Chief River, B. C.	Steven L. Rose	Steven L. Rose	1961	54
177 6/8	39 5/8	39 3/8	14 5/8	14 5/8	9	9	22 5/8	22 5/8	Turnagain River, B. C.	Byron Dalziel	Byron Dalziel	1970	54
177 5/8	43 5/8	44	14 3/8	14 2/8	6 2/8	6 7/8	26 5/8	26 5/8	Telegraph Creek, B. C.	Paul O'Hollaren	Paul O'Hollaren	1967	58
177 5/8	45 2/8	44 3/8	13 2/8	13	7	6 5/8	27 5/8	27 5/8	Toad River, B. C.	Dewey Rawlings	Dewey Rawlings	1969	58
177 4/8	44 5/8	44 5/8	14 2/8	14 3/8	6 5/8	6 5/8	23 5/8	23 5/8	Kechika Mts., B. C.	Tucker Davis	Tucker Davis	1965	60
177 4/8	44 2/8	42 5/8	14 5/8	14 5/8	6 5/8	6 3/8	24 5/8	24 1/8	Watson Lake, Yukon	Edgar A. Robertson	Edgar A. Robertson	1968	60
177 3/8	42 1/8	42	13 5/8	13 5/8	8	8 1/8	23 5/8	23 5/8	Toad River, B. C.	John Huml	John Huml	1969	62
177 2/8	42 2/8	42	14 5/8	13 7/8	7 2/8	7 5/8	22 5/8	22 5/8	Racing River, B. C.	Robert H. Kunzli	Robert H. Kunzli	1959	63

177 2/8	44 5/8	44 3/8	13 6/8	13 6/8	6 4/8	6 2/8	24 5/8	24 6/8	Atlin, B. C.	Delmar Aldrich	Delmar Aldrich	1964	63
177 2/8	40 4/8	42 4/8	15 1/8	15 1/8	6 5/8	6 6/8	29 2/8	29 2/8	Ft. St. John, B. C.	Ted T. Dabrowski	Ted T. Dabrowski	1967	63
177 2/8	38 1/8	38 1/8	14 5/8	14 5/8	9	8 7/8	20 7/8	20 7/8	Watson Lake, Yukon	Keith Thompson	Keith Thompson	1969	63
177 2/8	43 1/8	42 3/8	14 5/8	14 6/8	6 1/8	6 1/8	29 4/8	29 4/8	Cassiar Mts., B. C.	H. H. Kissinger	H. H. Kissinger	1970	63
177 1/8	44	42 3/8	14 6/8	15	6 1/8	6	27 7/8	27 7/8	Red Fern Lake, B. C.	W. H. Kirk	National Collection	1923	68
177 1/8	40 7/8	40 6/8	14 2/8	14 2/8	7 1/8	7 2/8	23 5/8	23 5/8	Mt. Lady Laurier, B. C.	Chet Gifford	Chet Gifford	1963	68
177	42 1/8	40 3/8	14 4/8	14 5/8	6 6/8	6 6/8	25 6/8	25 4/8	Prophet River, B. C.	Wade Martin	Wade Martin	1960	70
176 7/8	44 5/8	45 4/8	13 1/8	13 3/8	6 6/8	6 6/8	29	29	Dease Lake, B. C.	Thomas M. Dye	Thomas M. Dye	1966	71
176 7/8	41 6/8	39 1/8	15 2/8	15	7 1/8	7	25 3/8	25 3/8	Rabbit River, B. C.	George H. Rhoads	George H. Rhoads	1971	71
176 6/8	44 2/8	43 4/8	14	14	6	6	24 3/8	24 3/8	Cassiar Mts., B. C.	Donald J. Robb	Donald J. Robb	1969	73
176 5/8	40	43 7/8	14 6/8	14 4/8	6 7/8	7 4/8	23	23	Muskwa River, B. C.	T. E. Shillingburg	T. E. Shillingburg	1947	74
176 4/8	42 7/8	39 7/8	13 6/8	13 2/8	8 3/8	8 4/8	21 5/8	21	Prophet River, B. C.	Jim Caves	Jim Caves	1959	75
176 3/8	44	44 7/8	14 2/8	14 2/8	6 3/8	6 3/8	28 3/8	28 3/8	Cassiar Mts., B. C.	Gene Klineburger	Gene Klineburger	1965	76
176 3/8	40 7/8	40 2/8	15 4/8	15 4/8	6 7/8	6 4/8	23 6/8	23 6/8	Prophet River, B. C.	O. B. Kahn	O. B. Kahn	1965	76
176 3/8	42 7/8	43 4/8	15	15	5 6/8	5 5/8	29 4/8	29 2/8	Nabesche River, B. C.	Kenneth W. Kleiman	Kenneth W. Kleiman	1973	76
176 2/8	41 6/8	44	14 4/8	14 4/8	6 1/8	6 1/8	26 7/8	26 7/8	Prophet River, B. C.	W. A. Newmiller	W. A. Newmiller	1958	79
176 1/8	42 4/8	43 7/8	14 4/8	14 2/8	7 1/8	7	27 4/8	27 4/8	Watson Lake, B. C.	James C. Maly	James C. Maly	1963	80
176 1/8	36 3/8	39 2/8	15	15	8 7/8	7 7/8	22 6/8	18 6/8	Richard Creek, B. C.	James Milito	James Milito	1967	80
176 1/8	40 7/8	36	15	15	7 4/8	7 6/8	21 7/8	19 7/8	Pink Mt., B. C.	Roland Schroeder	Roland Schroeder	1968	80
176 1/8	43 3/8	43 2/8	14 1/8	14 1/8	6 5/8	6 5/8	25 4/8	25 4/8	Watson Lake, B. C.	Elgin T. Gates	Elgin T. Gates	1969	80
176	45 7/8	41 1/8	13 7/8	13 6/8	6 6/8	7	25 4/8	25 4/8	Cassiar Mts., B. C.	Walter O. Ford, Jr.	Walter O. Ford, Jr.	1967	84
176	39 2/8	39 4/8	15	14 7/8	7 2/8	7 5/8	20 2/8	19 1/8	Gataga River, B.C.	William A. S. Heuer	William A. S. Heuer	1979	84
175 6/8	41 4/8	39 6/8	14 7/8	14 7/8	7 2/8	7 2/8	22 4/8	22 4/8	Prophet River, B. C.	Jack O'Connor	Jack O'Connor	1946	86
175 6/8	40 4/8	40 6/8	13 3/8	13 3/8	8 7/8	9	23 1/8	23 1/8	Terminus Mt., B. C.	Irvin Hart	Irvin Hart	1964	86
175 6/8	42 1/8	37 1/8	15 5/8	15 5/8	7	7 1/8	21 1/8	20 7/8	Tutnagain River, B. C.	Lester C. Brewick	Lester C. Brewick	1967	86
175 6/8	43 2/8	43 4/8	14 1/8	13 7/8	6 6/8	6 7/8	29 2/8	29 2/8	Blue Sheep Lake, B. C.	John M. Griffith, Jr.	John M. Griffith, Jr.	1971	86
175 5/8	42 5/8	42 6/8	14 4/8	14 2/8	6 2/8	6 3/8	22	22	Pelly Mts., Yukon	John Caputo	John Caputo	1953	90
175 5/8	42 4/8	41 5/8	14	14	6 6/8	6 7/8	21 6/8	21 6/8	Top Lake, B. C.	Richard Buffington	Richard Buffington	1964	90
175 5/8	46 3/8	43 4/8	13 5/8	13 5/8	5 5/8	5 4/8	23	27 7/8	Hudson Hope, B. C.	Jim Papst	Jim Papst	1966	90
175 4/8	46 6/8	48	12 6/8	12 5/8	5 5/8	5 5/8	30 6/8	30 6/8	Kiniskan Lake, B. C.	Richard Stough	Richard Stough	1961	93
175 4/8	41 2/8	41 2/8	14	14 2/8	7 3/8	7 5/8	23 6/8	23 6/8	Frog River, B. C.	Robert McMurray	Robert McMurray	1968	93
175 4/8	42 2/8	42	14 7/8	14 6/8	6 3/8	6 2/8	28 1/8	28 1/8	Colt Lake, B. C.	Marsh Dear	Marsh Dear	1970	93
175 4/8	40 1/8	36 3/8	14 4/8	14 4/8	8	7 7/8	22 2/8	19 4/8	Prophet River, B. C.	Sam C. Arnett, III	Sam C. Arnett, III	1972	93
175 3/8	43	42 5/8	14 2/8	14 4/8	6 4/8	6 4/8	26	26	Pelly Mts., Yukon	Pat S. McInturff	Pat S. McInturff	1962	97
175	42 2/8	41 6/8	14 2/8	14 2/8	6 5/8	6 5/8	26 5/8	26 5/8	Hudson Hope, B. C.	Harry M. Haywood	Harry M. Haywood	1949	98
175	40 5/8	41 3/8	14 1/8	14 2/8	7	7 1/8	22	21 5/8	Cassiar, B. C.	John Sochor	John Sochor	1962	98
175	42 6/8	42 6/8	13 7/8	13 7/8	6 3/8	6 5/8	28 5/8	28 5/8	Cold Fish Lake, B. C.	Chris Reynolds	Chris Reynolds	1963	98
175	42 4/8	43 2/8	14 2/8	14 2/8	6 1/8	6 2/8	24	24	Colt Lake, B. C.	Warren Page	Warren Page	1965	98
174 7/8	41 6/8	42 3/8	14 6/8	14 5/8	6 7/8	6 4/8	21 7/8	21 7/8	Cassiar, B C.	John W. Hull	John W. Hull	1962	102
174 6/8	38 6/8	38 2/8	14 5/8	14 5/8	7 7/8	8	21 4/8	19 7/8	Watson Lake, B. C.	Philip English	Philip English	1965	103
174 5/8	42 1/8	41 4/8	14 6/8	14 4/8	6 1/8	6	30 2/8	30 2/8	Stikine River, B. C.	Hugh J. O'Dower	Hugh J. O'Dower	1952	104
174 5/8	41 4/8	41 5/8	14 1/8	14 1/8	7 3/8	6 5/8	24 7/8	24 7/8	Sikanni Chief River, B. C.	Joseph W. Quarto	Joseph W. Quarto	1965	104
174 4/8	40 6/8	41 2/8	15	14 6/8	8	8 2/8	27 4/8	27 4/8	Dease Lake, B. C.	Alice J. Landreth	Alice J. Landreth	1964	106

STONE'S SHEEP—Continued
Ovis dalli stonei

Score	Length of Horn R.	L.	Circumference of Base R.	L.	Circumference at Third Quarter R.	L.	Greatest Spread	Tip to Tip Spread	Locality Killed	By Whom Killed	Owner	Date Killed	Rank
174 4/8	42 5/8	42	14 5/8	14 4/8	5 5/8	6	24 4/8	24 4/8	Ram Lake, B. C.	Walter Smetaniuk	Walter Smetaniuk	1966	106
174 3/8	41 7/8	40 4/8	13 3/8	13 5/8	7 5/8	8	20 5/8	20 5/8	Racing River, B. C.	Lash Callison	Lash Callison	1959	108
174 3/8	39 4/8	41 5/8	14 4/8	14 4/8	7 3/8	6 4/8	21 5/8	21 5/8	Top Lake, B. C.	W. E. Fisher	W. E. Fisher	1964	108
174 3/8	37	38 5/8	14 4/8	14 3/8	8 7/8	8 5/8	21 5/8	21	Cassiar Mts., B. C.	Gordon Studer	Gordon Studer	1966	108
174 2/8	42 2/8	46 2/8	12 5/8	12 4/8	6 5/8	6 5/8	26 3/8	26 3/8	W. Toad River, B. C.	Unknown	N. B. (Red) Sorenson	—	111
174 2/8	46 4/8	46 2/8	13 3/8	13 3/8	5 5/8	5 3/8	33	33	Watson Lake, B. C.	G. C. F. Dalziel	G. C. F. Dalziel	1962	111
174 1/8	42 2/8	40 7/8	14	14	7	7 5/8	23	23	Cold Fish Lake, B. C.	Roberto De La Garza	Roberto De La Garza	1961	113
174 1/8	42 2/8	41 3/8	14 7/8	15 2/8	5 2/8	5 3/8	25	25	Gold Bar, B. C.	Henry O. Carlson	Henry O. Carlson	1962	113
174 1/8	39 2/8	43 3/8	14 4/8	14 4/8	6 4/8	6 3/8	25 3/8	25 3/8	Mt. Winston, B.C.	Norman A. Hill	Norman A. Hill	1967	113
174 1/8	41 1/8	41 1/8	14 1/8	14 3/8	6 5/8	6 7/8	23 5/8	23 5/8	Muskwa River, B.C.	Gary Powell	Gary Powell	1974	113
174	44 5/8	41	14	13 5/8	6 7/8	6 7/8	22 7/8	22 7/8	Muskwa River, B. C.	Wade Martin	Wade Martin	1961	117
174	40 5/8	41 2/8	14	14	7	6 7/8	24 5/8	24 4/8	Halfway River, B. C.	Frank H. Rogers	Frank H. Rogers	1962	117
174	44 4/8	40	14 1/8	14 1/8	6 4/8	6 5/8	27	27	Cassiar Mts., B. C.	Russell Castner	Russell Castner	1966	117
174	41 5/8	38 5/8	14 1/8	14 1/8	6 7/8	6 7/8	26 3/8	26 3/8	Cassiar Mts., B. C.	George H. Glass	George H. Glass	1966	117
174	40	41	14 5/8	14 4/8	6 5/8	6 4/8	19 4/8	19 4/8	Muskwa Area, B. C.	W. R. Collie	W. R. Collie	1972	117
173 7/8	44 3/8	43 5/8	13 4/8	13 3/8	7	6 4/8	27 7/8	27 7/8	Stikine River, B. C.	Vernon D. E. Smith	Vernon D. E. Smith	1960	122
173 7/8	44 3/8	44 4/8	13 2/8	13 3/8	5 7/8	6	29 7/8	29 7/8	Cassiar, B. C.	Fred F. Wells	Fred F. Wells	1961	122
173 7/8	42 5/8	42	14 3/8	14 3/8	6 3/8	5 7/8	23 7/8	23 7/8	Hudson Hope, B. C.	G. F. Moore	G. F. Moore	1963	122
173 7/8	39 5/8	38 1/8	14 4/8	14 3/8	8 7/8	9	25	25	Gataga River, B. C.	H. L. Hale	H. L. Hale	1968	122
173 7/8	40 1/8	38 5/8	13 4/8	13 6/8	8 3/8	8 7/8	20 3/8	16	Testa River, B. C.	Eugene P. LaSota	Eugene P. LaSota	1973	122
173 5/8	47 3/8	43 3/8	13 5/8	13 6/8	6 4/8	5 5/8	25 4/8	25 4/8	Halfway River, B. C.	Lynn Ross	Lynn Ross	1957	127
173 5/8	43 4/8	43 4/8	13 5/8	14	6 6/8	6 3/8	28 4/8	28 4/8	Terminus Mt., B. C.	Chester A. Crago	Chester A. Crago	1962	127
173 5/8	41 5/8	40 7/8	14 4/8	14 4/8	6 5/8	7 7/8	25 5/8	25 5/8	Muskwa River, B. C.	Wm. Michalsky	Wm. Michalsky	1965	127
173 5/8	41 1/8	43	14	14	6 6/8	6 5/8	30 4/8	30	Ketchika River, B. C.	Russell C. Cutter	Russell C. Cutter	1965	127
173 4/8	45 4/8	40 1/8	13 5/8	13 3/8	6 5/8	6 5/8	26 6/8	26 6/8	Peace River, B. C.	Melvin Shearer	National Collection	1933	131
173 4/8	42 3/8	42	14 3/8	14 2/8	6 6/8	6 6/8	22 6/8	22 6/8	Rose Mt., Yukon	Karl Fritzsche	Karl Fritzsche	1972	131
173 4/8	40 2/8	41 2/8	13 5/8	13 3/8	8 1/8	7 7/8	20 5/8	20 5/8	Cassiar, B. C.	Charles F. Haas	Charles F. Haas	1960	133
173 4/8	41 4/8	41 6/8	14 1/8	14 1/8	6 3/8	6 4/8	28 5/8	28 5/8	Telegraph Creek, B. C.	L. Iverson	L. Iverson	1961	133
173 4/8	39	42	15	15	7 4/8	6 6/8	22 4/8	22 4/8	Dease Lake, B. C.	George I. Parker	George I. Parker	1963	133
173 4/8	41	41 4/8	14	14	9 4/8	9	27	27	Dease Lake, B. C.	John Thomas Blackwell	John Thomas Blackwell	1964	133
173 3/8	39 4/8	41	14	14 2/8	8 1/8	8	23	23	Watson Lake, Yukon	Harry S. Rinker	Harry S. Rinker	1964	133
173 3/8	43 3/8	44	13 3/8	13 3/8	6	6 5/8	28	28	Toad River, B. C.	H. L. Vidricksen	H. L. Vidricksen	1960	138

									Location	Owner	Hunter	Date	Rank
173 3/8	38 3/8	38 3/8	14 3/8	14 3/8	8 3/8	8	20 5/8	19 3/8	Tuchodi Lakes, B. C.	George S. Gayle, III	George S. Gayle, III	1972	138
173 3/8	41 1/8	41 7/8	14 3/8	14 7/8	6 7/8	6 7/8	24 5/8	24 5/8	Cassiar Mts., B. C.	John Caputo	John Caputo	1962	140
173 3/8	44 7/8	45	13 7/8	13 7/8	5 7/8	5 7/8	26 5/8	26 5/8	Cassiar Mts., B. C.	William Warrick	William Warrick	1963	140
173 3/8	40 7/8	41 3/8	14 7/8	14 7/8	6	6 3/8	27 1/8	27 1/8	Cassiar Mts., B.C.	Charles F. Nadler	Charles F. Nadler	1967	142
173 1/8	41 3/8	40	14 3/8	14 3/8	7 3/8	7 3/8	21 1/8	21 1/8	Summit Lake, B.C.	Henry L. Baddley	Henry L. Baddley	1979	142
173	39 1/8	38	14 3/8	14 3/8	8	8	26	26	Muskwa River, B. C.	Elmer Keith	Elmer Keith	1937	144
173	34	45	15	15	7 1/8	7 1/8	24 7/8	24 7/8	Gataga River, B. C.	Wilson Southwell	Wilson Southwell	1958	144
173	40 7/8	41 3/8	13 7/8	13 5/8	7 7/8	7 5/8	23 3/8	23 3/8	Prophet River, B. C.	Merrimen M. Watkins	Merrimen M. Watkins	1965	144
173	42	42 3/8	14 3/8	14 5/8	5 5/8	5 5/8	22 5/8	22 5/8	Watson Lake, Yukon	E. P. (Al) Gray	E. P. (Al) Gray	1968	144
173	42	42 3/8	13 5/8	13 3/8	6 5/8	6 5/8	23 7/8	23 7/8	Prophet River, B. C.	Robert E. Hammond	Robert E. Hammond	1969	144
173	42 5/8	42 5/8	14	14	5 5/8	5 5/8	27 1/8	27 1/8	Cold Fish Lake, B. C.	A. H. Clise	A. H. Clise	1970	144
173	41 5/8	42 5/8	14 3/8	14 3/8	5 7/8	5 7/8	24 3/8	24 3/8	Mile 422, Alaska Hwy., B. C.	Garland N. Teich	Garland N. Teich	1971	144
172 7/8	40 1/8	39 5/8	14 3/8	14 3/8	6 7/8	6 5/8	24 7/8	24 1/8	Prophet River, B. C.	Harry M. Haywood	Harry M. Haywood	1956	151
172 7/8	40 7/8	42 7/8	14 7/8	14 7/8	5 5/8	6	25 3/8	25 3/8	Summit Lake, B. C.	A. Tony Mathisen	A. Tony Mathisen	1958	151
172 7/8	42 7/8	42 7/8	13 7/8	13 7/8	6 3/8	6 3/8	25 1/8	25 1/8	Cassiar Mts., B. C.	Wayne C. Eubank	Wayne C. Eubank	1963	151
172 7/8	46 3/8	35	14	14	6 1/8	6 1/8	21 7/8	21 7/8	Cassiar Mts., B. C.	Orval H. Ause	Orval H. Ause	1968	151
172 7/8	37 7/8	37	14 5/8	15	7 5/8	7 7/8	23	23	Cassiar Mts., B.C.	Greg Williams	Greg Williams	1976	151
172 6/8	40 5/8	40 1/8	14 3/8	14 3/8	7 1/8	7 1/8	24 5/8	24 5/8	Liard River, B. C.	Jack N. Allen	Jack N. Allen	1959	156
172 6/8	36 5/8	37	14 5/8	15	8 3/8	8 3/8	19 5/8	19 5/8	Sikanni Chief River, B. C.	Mrs. Maitland Armstrong	Mrs. Maitland Armstrong	1962	156
172 6/8	40 5/8	41 5/8	14 3/8	14 3/8	6 5/8	7	22	22	Gataga River, B. C.	Basil C. Bradbury	Basil C. Bradbury	1968	156
172 6/8	36 5/8	36 7/8	14 5/8	15	8 5/8	8 5/8	15 5/8	15 3/8	Muskwa River, B. C.	Andrew A. Samuels, Jr.	Andrew A. Samuels, Jr.	1969	156
172 6/8	42	41 5/8	14 5/8	14 5/8	6 1/8	6 1/8	27 5/8	27 5/8	Dall Lake, B. C.	Robert J. Rood	Robert J. Rood	1971	156
172 5/8	43 5/8	43 5/8	13 7/8	13 7/8	6 7/8	6 7/8	28 3/8	28 3/8	Cassiar Mts., B. C.	Kenneth Campbell	Kenneth Campbell	1976	156
172 5/8	39 5/8	40 7/8	15	15	6 5/8	6 5/8	23 3/8	23 3/8	Hudson Hope, B. C.	Don Stewart	Don Stewart	1961	162
172 4/8	42 5/8	42	13 7/8	13 7/8	5 7/8	5 7/8	29 4/8	29 4/8	Halfway River, B. C.	Cecil V. Mumbert	Cecil V. Mumbert	1958	163
172 4/8	40 5/8	41 5/8	14 4/8	14 4/8	6 7/8	6 5/8	25	25	Dease Lake, B. C.	John T. Blackwell	John T. Blackwell	1963	163
172 4/8	37 7/8	38	15 5/8	15 7/8	6 5/8	6 5/8	27 5/8	27 5/8	Prophet River, B. C.	William A. Miller	William A. Miller	1969	163
172 4/8	39 5/8	42	14 1/8	14 1/8	6 6/8	7	25 5/8	25 5/8	Watson Lake, B. C.	Julian Gutierrez	Julian Gutierrez	1970	163
172 3/8	37 5/8	41 5/8	14 3/8	14 3/8	6 5/8	7	23 3/8	23 3/8	Muskwa River, B. C.	L. A. Denson	L. A. Denson	1971	163
172 3/8	37 1/8	38 5/8	14 5/8	14 5/8	8 5/8	8 3/8	23 4/8	23 4/8	Sandbar Creek, B. C.	John La Rocca	John La Rocca	1957	168
172 3/8	41 5/8	42 5/8	14 5/8	14 5/8	5 7/8	5 7/8	27 7/8	27 7/8	Pelly Mts., Yukon	Walter R. Michael	Walter R. Michael	1960	168
172 3/8	45 1/8	45 7/8	13	13	5 7/8	5 7/8	28	28	Cold Fish Lake, B. C.	Juan Brittingham	Juan Brittingham	1961	168
172 3/8	39 6/8	39 5/8	15 5/8	15 5/8	6	6	20 5/8	20 5/8	Ospika Drainage, B. C.	Mark Swenson	Mark Swenson	1964	168
172 3/8	41 5/8	41 1/8	14 5/8	14 5/8	6 5/8	6 1/8	23 5/8	23 5/8	Dall Lake, B. C.	Paul M. Rothermel, Jr.	Paul M. Rothermel, Jr.	1965	168
172 2/8	41 1/8	41 1/8	14 5/8	14 5/8	6	6	21 5/8	21 5/8	Prophet River, B.C.	George F. Crain	George F. Crain	1961	173
172 2/8	40 5/8	38 7/8	14 5/8	14 5/8	6 7/8	6 7/8	21 4/8	21 4/8	Muskwa River, B. C.	Arvid F. Benson	Arvid F. Benson	1963	173
172 2/8	39 5/8	42 5/8	14	14	7 7/8	7 7/8	26 5/8	26 5/8	Cassiar Mts.. B. C.	Michaux Nash, Jr.	Michaux Nash, Jr.	1967	173
172 2/8	41 5/8	36 5/8	14 5/8	14 5/8	7 7/8	8	23 5/8	23 5/8	Sikanni Chief River, B. C.	John B. Collier, IV	John B. Collier, IV	1967	173
172 2/8	42 5/8	42 5/8	14 5/8	14 5/8	5 5/8	5 5/8	29	29	Prophet River, B. C.	S. E. Burrell	S. E. Burrell	1967	173
172 2/8	41 5/8	41 5/8	14 5/8	14 5/8	6 1/8	6 1/8	28 4/8	28 1/8	Akie River, B. C.	O. J. Baggenstoss	O. J. Baggenstoss	1968	173
172 1/8	39	38 5/8	14 5/8	14 5/8	7 5/8	7 5/8	20 4/8	18 5/8	Prophet River, B.C.	Larry Ciejka	Larry Ciejka	1977	173
172 1/8	41 5/8	41	13	13	9 5/8	9 5/8	30	30	Dease Lake, B. C.	W. M. Rudd	W. M. Rudd	1964	180

Stone's Sheep–*Continued*

Ovis dalli stonei

Score	Length of Horn R.	Length of Horn L.	Circumference of Base R.	Circumference of Base L.	Circumference at Third Quarter R.	Circumference at Third Quarter L.	Greatest Spread	Tip to Tip Spread	Locality Killed	By Whom Killed	Owner	Date Killed	Rank
172 1/8	37 6/8	34 5/8	14	14 2/8	9 1/8	9 1/8	23 2/8	19	Cassiar Mts., B. C.	Keith M. Kissinger	Keith M. Kissinger	1968	180
172 1/8	39	40 5/8	14 4/8	14 2/8	7 1/8	6 7/8	23 2/8	23 2/8	Alaska Hwy., B. C.	Robert Murdock	Robert Murdock	1968	180
172 1/8	40 2/8	38 1/8	14 2/8	14 2/8	7 3/8	7 2/8	23 2/8	21 2/8	Burnt Rose Lake, B. C.	John K. De Broux	John K. De Broux	1970	180
172	45 5/8	43 3/8	12 7/8	13	6 2/8	6 2/8	25 7/8	25 7/8	Atlin, B. C.	Thomas E. Francis	Thomas E. Francis	1964	184
172	40 2/8	41 6/8	14 2/8	14 2/8	6 1/8	6	25 2/8	25 2/8	Ingenika Wild., B. C.	Robert A. Lubeck	Robert A. Lubeck	1968	184
172	41 2/8	41 4/8	14 3/8	14 2/8	6 2/8	6 1/8	26 6/8	26 6/8	Denetiah Lake, B. C.	Michael G. Meeker	Michael G. Meeker	1969	184
172	40 2/8	40	14 5/8	14 5/8	6 2/8	6 1/8	29	29	Prairie River, B. C.	C. J. McElroy	C. J. McElory	1969	184
172	42 1/8	42 1/8	14	14	6 2/8	6 2/8	25 1/8	25 1/8	Toad River, B. C.	David G. Kidder	David G. Kidder	1975	184
171 7/8	38 6/8	38 1/8	14 2/8	14 1/8	7 3/8	7 5/8	23 6/8	20 2/8	Akie River, B. C.	Henry K. Leworthy	Henry K. Leworthy	1966	189
171 7/8	38 3/8	39	13 7/8	13 7/8	8 5/8	8 7/8	20 4/8	20 4/8	Island Lake, B. C.	Martin Frank Wood	Martin Frank Wood	1970	189
171 7/8	43 2/8	41 3/8	14 1/8	14 1/8	5 6/8	5 6/8	30 2/8	30 2/8	Cache Creek, B. C.	Kenneth A. Jeronimus	Kenneth A. Jeronimus	1974	189
171 6/8	39 2/8	41	13 4/8	13 4/8	8	8	27 4/8	27 4/8	Gataga River, B. C.	Dan Auld	Dan Auld	1958	192
171 6/8	43 2/8	43	14 4/8	14 2/8	5 3/8	5 4/8	27 1/8	27 1/8	Cassiar Mts., B. C.	John Caputo, Sr.	John Caputo, Sr.	1960	192
171 6/8	40 4/8	42 6/8	14	14 1/8	6 4/8	7 2/8	24 6/8	24 6/8	Trimble Lake, B. C.	Roy E. Stare	Roy E. Stare	1962	192
171 6/8	36 2/8	37	14 4/8	14 5/8	10 2/8	8 3/8	21 6/8	13 4/8	Muskwa River, B. C.	W. I. Spencer	W. I. Spencer	1963	192
171 6/8	37 6/8	39 6/8	16	16	6 7/8	6 3/8	21 3/8	21 3/8	Gataga River, B. C.	D. R. Seabaugh	D. R. Seabaugh	1971	192
171 6/8	38 4/8	38 4/8	15 5/8	15 5/8	6 3/8	6 7/8	23 5/8	24 2/8	Profit River, B.C.	Don Haemmerlein	Don Haemmerlein	1977	192
171 5/8	37 2/8	37 1/8	14	14	8 6/8	8 6/8	20 3/8	20 3/8	Tuchodi Lakes, B. C.	Win Condict	Win Condict	1951	198
171 5/8	42 4/8	42 3/8	13 4/8	13 4/8	6 1/8	6 2/8	26 1/8	26	Dease Lake, B. C.	C. E. Krieger	C. E. Krieger	1962	198
171 5/8	44 1/8	40	13 5/8	13 4/8	6 3/8	6 2/8	25 6/8	25 6/8	Muncho Lake, B. C.	H. W. Julien	H. W. Julien	1966	198
171 5/8	38 6/8	36 3/8	14 2/8	14 2/8	8 5/8	8 5/8	20 1/8	20 1/8	Toad River, B. C.	H. W. Julien	H. W. Julien	1969	198
171 4/8	40 4/8	40 4/8	14 2/8	14 2/8	6 2/8	6 2/8	23 3/8	23 3/8	Prophet River, B. C.	L. A. Denson	L. A. Denson	1963	202
171 4/8	37	38 4/8	14 4/8	14 4/8	7 4/8	7 6/8	22 2/8	17	Trutch, B. C.	Charles F. Waterman	Charles F. Waterman	1964	202
171 4/8	45 4/8	45	13 5/8	13 6/8	5 6/8	5 4/8	29 7/8	29 7/8	Turnagain River, B. C.	George H. Landreth	George H. Landreth	1966	202
171 4/8	42 5/8	43 5/8	13 6/8	13 6/8	5 7/8	6 1/8	29 7/8	29 7/8	Turnagain River, B. C.	Lewis M. Mull	Lewis M. Mull	1966	202
171 4/8	39	38 4/8	14 6/8	14 6/8	7	7	23	23	Cassiar Mts., B. C.	Robert R. Bridges	Robert R. Bridges	1966	202
171 4/8	45	43 6/8	13 2/8	13 1/8	5 4/8	5 4/8	28 4/8	28 4/8	Cassiar Mts., B. C.	William A. Kelly	William A. Kelly	1969	202
171 4/8	39	34 4/8	15 6/8	15 5/8	7	7 2/8	25 6/8	23	Lower Besa River, B.C.	Peter Hochleitner	Peter Hochleitner	1977	202
171 3/8	43	42 7/8	13 6/8	14	6	6	30 4/8	30 4/8	Ketchika Mts., B. C.	H. I. H. Prince Abdorreza Pahlavi	H. I. H. Prince Abdorreza Pahlavi	1960	209
171 3/8	37 7/8	37	14	14 1/8	8 4/8	8 7/8	21 7/8	18 3/8	Horseshoe Lake, Yukon	Jack G. Giannola	Jack G. Giannola	1973	209
171 2/8	38	45 4/8	13	13 3/8	6 2/8	7 2/8	20 4/8	20 4/8	Telegraph Creek, B. C.	Picked Up	John Crowe	——	211

171 2/8	42 5/8	42 5/8	13 5/8	13 6/8	6 4/8	6 4/8	24 3/8	24 3/8	Muskwa River, B. C.	Bernard J. Brown	Bernard J. Brown	1953	211
171 2/8	41 2/8	41	13 7/8	13 7/8	6 3/8	6	26 2/8	26 2/8	Pelly Mts., Yukon	Jack Tillotson	Jack Tillotson	1955	211
171 2/8	41 6/8	43	13 6/8	13 6/8	5 7/8	6 2/8	27 2/8	27 2/8	Cold Fish Lake, B. C.	Robert Brittingham	Robert Brittingham	1961	211
171 2/8	44 1/8	43 1/8	12 7/8	12 7/8	5 7/8	5 6/8	27 3/8	27 3/8	Pelly Lake, B. C.	Robert M. Mallett	Robert M. Mallett	1966	211
171 2/8	41	39 6/8	14 3/8	14 4/8	6 7/8	6 6/8	21 6/8	20 6/8	Cassiar Mts., B. C.	G. A. Treschow	G. A. Treschow	1966	211
171 2/8	39 1/8	40 3/8	15 2/8	15 3/8	5 7/8	6	25 1/8	25 1/8	Colt Lake, B. C.	Roscoe Hurd	Roscoe Hurd	1967	211
171 2/8	42	42 2/8	13 5/8	13 5/8	6 3/8	6	26 3/8	26 3/8	Cassiar, B. C.	Herb Parsons	Herb Parsons	1969	211
171	41	42	14	14 2/8	6	6	30	30	Cassiar, B. C.	Wilson Potter	Harvard Univ. Mus.	1906	219
171	40 3/8	39 7/8	15	15	5 5/8	5 5/8	28 7/8	28 7/8	Sandbar Creek, B. C.	John La Rocca	John La Rocca	1958	219
171	40	40	14 2/8	14 2/8	6 4/8	6 4/8	25 5/8	25 5/8	Halfway River, B. C.	S. J. Seidensticker	S. J. Seidensticker	1962	219
171	41 7/8	41 3/8	14	14 2/8	5 7/8	5 7/8	24 7/8	24 7/8	Cassiar Mts., B. C.	Sam Jaksick, Jr.	Sam Jaksick, Jr.	1967	219
171	35 6/8	40 6/8	14 4/8	14 4/8	6 7/8	6 7/8	22 3/8	22 3/8	Wrede Creek, B. C.	Jack Feightner	Jack Feightner	1972	219
171	41	44 4/8	13 4/8	13 5/8	5 7/8	6	27 1/8	27 1/8	Cassiar Mts., B. C.	Ed Stedman, Jr.	Ed Stedman, Jr.	1974	219
171	38 5/8	38 7/8	14 7/8	15	6 1/8	6 1/8	24 5/8	24 5/8	Ice Mt., B. C.	David P. Jacobson	David P. Jacobson	1974	219
171	39 5/8	40 1/8	14 7/8	14 7/8	6 2/8	6 4/8	21 3/8	18 6/8	Burnt Rose Lake, B.C.	John Drift	John Drift	1977	219
170 7/8	41 2/8	41 5/8	13 3/8	13 3/8	7	7 1/8	26 5/8	26 5/8	Watson Lake, B. C.	Ed Ball	Ed Ball	1960	227
170 7/8	44 5/8	41 4/8	13 2/8	13 3/8	6 1/8	6 1/8	28	28	Watson Lake, Yukon	Richard G. Peters	Richard G. Peters	1962	227
170 7/8	39 6/8	39 5/8	14 4/8	15	6 3/8	6 1/8	19 6/8	19 6/8	Prophet River, B. C.	John J. Lo Monaco	John J. Lo Monaco	1963	227
170 7/8	38	38 1/8	14 2/8	14	7 7/8	8	19 7/8	19	Prophet River, B. C.	Ted Howell	Ted Howell	1964	227
170 7/8	37 5/8	38 4/8	14 5/8	14 5/8	7 3/8	7 4/8	24 6/8	18 1/8	Tuchodi Lakes, B. C.	Robert C. Ries	Robert C. Ries	1965	227
170 7/8	39 2/8	41 1/8	14 4/8	14 4/8	6 3/8	6 2/8	28 1/8	28 1/8	Telegraph Creek, B. C.	R. B. England	R. B. England	1966	227
170 7/8	37 3/8	38 6/8	14 6/8	14 6/8	7 2/8	7 2/8	23	22 3/8	Cassiar Mts., B. C.	W. G. Rathmann	W. G. Rathmann	1971	227
170 6/8	42	41	13 7/8	14	6 5/8	6 3/8	24 4/8	24 4/8	Peace River, B. C.	C. A. Freese	C. A. Freese	1960	234
170 6/8	41	41	14	14	6	6	27 4/8	27 4/8	Gataga River, B. C.	Herb Klein	Herb Klein	1963	234
170 6/8	43	42 2/8	13 4/8	13 5/8	5 6/8	5 7/8	22 2/8	22 2/8	Pelly Creek, B. C.	Jon A. Jourdonnais	Jon A. Jourdonnais	1968	234
170 6/8	40 6/8	41	14 1/8	14 2/8	6 3/8	6 3/8	25 3/8	25 3/8	Ketchika Range, B. C.	Ferdinand Stemann	Ferdinand Stemann	1970	234
170 5/8	43 2/8	43 3/8	13 5/8	13 4/8	5 5/8	6 1/8	29 6/8	29 6/8	Cassiar, B. C.	John W. Beban	John W. Beban	1956	238
170 5/8	40 4/8	40 1/8	14 4/8	14 4/8	6	6	29 5/8	29 5/8	Prophet River, B. C.	E. R. Wells	E. R. Wells	1967	238
170 5/8	41 3/8	39	14	14 2/8	6 4/8	6 7/8	21 2/8	21 2/8	Toad River, B. C.	Jay Stewart	Jay Stewart	1969	238
170 4/8	42 7/8	42 5/8	13 4/8	13 4/8	6	5 7/8	33 1/8	33 1/8	Pelly Mts., Yukon	William Fisher	William Fisher	1957	241
170 4/8	39 4/8	40	14	14	7	6 4/8	22	20 4/8	Toad River, B. C.	Fred Sothmann	Fred Sothmann	1963	241
170 4/8	42	42	13 4/8	13 4/8	6 1/8	6 1/8	26 4/8	26 4/8	Telegraph Creek, B. C.	Joseph T. Pelton	Joseph T. Pelton	1963	241
170 4/8	40 7/8	39 3/8	14 2/8	14 2/8	6 7/8	6 3/8	21 6/8	21 6/8	Dease Lake, B. C.	Melvin A. Hetland	Melvin A. Hetland	1965	241
170 4/8	41 2/8	40	14 4/8	14 4/8	6 2/8	6 2/8	26 1/8	26 1/8	Pink Mt., B. C.	Rita Oney	Rita Oney	1966	241
170 4/8	40	40 4/8	14 2/8	14 3/8	6 7/8	6 4/8	21 2/8	22 4/8	Watson Lake, B. C.	W. Brandon Macomber	W. Brandon Macomber	1966	241
170 4/8	32	41 4/8	14 4/8	14 6/8	8	8 4/8	22	24	Muskwa River, B. C.	Donald P. Eickhoff	E. C. Eickhoff	1968	241
170 4/8	42 2/8	40 2/8	13 4/8	13 5/8	6 4/8	6 4/8	25 4/8	25 2/8	Mt. Edziza, B. C.	William J. Pollard	William J. Pollard	1974	241
170 3/8	41 3/8	40 2/8	13 7/8	13 7/8	6 2/8	6 2/8	22 3/8	22 3/8	Sikanni, B. C.	W. A. K. Seale	W. A. K. Seale	1961	249
170 3/8	39 6/8	40 7/8	14	14 2/8	6 1/8	6 3/8	28	28	Ketchika Mt., B. C.	Basil C. Bradbury	Basil C. Bradbury	1965	249
170 3/8	37 5/8	38 2/8	14 6/8	14 6/8	6 5/8	6 5/8	22 4/8	22 4/8	Ospika Area, B. C.	Ray E. Bigler	Ray E. Bigler	1972	249
170 2/8	40	43 2/8	13 3/8	13 4/8	6 4/8	6 5/8	25 6/8	25 6/8	Beale Lake, B. C.	John Forester	John Forester	1963	252
170 2/8	35	35 2/8	14 6/8	14 5/8	8	8 2/8	21 6/8	19 2/8	Richards Creek, B. C.	Herbert A. Leupold	Herbert A. Leupold	1965	252
170 2/8	38 4/8	39	15	14 7/8	6 7/8	6 5/8	22 6/8	22 6/8	Halfway River, B. C.	Steven L. Rose	Steven L. Rose	1967	252

STONE'S SHEEP–*Continued*

Ovis dalli stonei

Score	Length of Horn R.	Length of Horn L.	Circumference of Base R.	Circumference of Base L.	Circumference at Third Quarter R.	Circumference at Third Quarter L.	Greatest Spread	Tip to Tip Spread	Locality Killed	By Whom Killed	Owner	Date Killed	Rank
170 2/8	41	41	14 2/8	14 2/8	6 1/8	6 2/8	26	26	Keohka River, B. C.	Fritz A. Nachant	Fritz A. Nachant	1970	252
170 2/8	39 4/8	39 6/8	14 6/8	14 7/8	6 1/8	6	21 7/8	21 2/8	Muskwa River, B. C.	James S. Griffin	James S. Griffin	1972	252
170 2/8	38 4/8	43 2/8	14 1/8	14 1/8	6 3/8	6 3/8	23 6/8	23 6/8	Turnagain River, B. C.	Jerald T. Waite	Jerald T. Waite	1976	252
170 1/8	43 1/8	42 6/8	13 3/8	13 3/8	6	6 2/8	30 7/8	30 7/8	Rabbit River, B. C.	George W. Young	George W. Young	1965	258
170 1/8	39 4/8	38 1/8	14 7/8	14 7/8	6	6 2/8	24 6/8	24 6/8	Ram Creek, B. C.	Kim Cox	Kim Cox	1966	258
170 1/8	39 2/8	43 7/8	13 4/8	13 4/8	6	6 1/8	21 5/8	21 5/8	Needham Creek, B. C.	Roy Fukunaga	Roy Fukunaga	1974	258
170 1/8	43 2/8	42 3/8	12 5/8	12 5/8	6 4/8	6 2/8	27 5/8	27 5/8	Cassiar Mts., B.C.	James H. Duke, Jr.	James H. Duke, Jr.	1976	258
170	42 4/8	38 6/8	14 1/8	14 2/8	6	6	24 3/8	24 3/8	Prophet River, B. C.	Walter B. McClurkan	Walter B. McClurkan	1945	262
170	39 2/8	43 4/8	13 7/8	13 5/8	6 3/8	6	25	25	Cold Fish Lake, B. C.	Howard Boazman	Howard Boazman	1962	262
170	42	37	14 1/8	14 1/8	6 4/8	6 5/8	22 4/8	22 4/8	Alaska Hwy., B. C.	Arthur Gordon	Arthur Gordon	1965	262
170	39 4/8	39 2/8	14 5/8	14 6/8	6 4/8	6 3/8	27 3/8	27 3/8	Cassiar Mts., B. C.	Neil Castner	Neil Castner	1966	262
170	38 4/8	39 4/8	13 6/8	13 7/8	7 2/8	7 3/8	21	17 5/8	Tetsa River, B. C.	Owen R. Walker	Owen R. Walker	1967	262
170	39 5/8	40 1/8	14 2/8	14 4/8	6 4/8	6 4/8	21 5/8	16 5/8	Cassiar Mts., B. C.	Glen E. Park	Glen E. Park	1967	262
170	41	41	14	14	6 2/8	6 4/8	20 6/8	20 6/8	Prophet River, B. C.	Jim Nystrom	Jim Nystrom	1968	262
170	40	39 2/8	15 4/8	15 4/8	5 2/8	5 2/8	22 6/8	22 6/8	Muskwa River, B. C.	W. J. Boynton, III	W. J. Boynton, III	1970	262
170	42 3/8	43 7/8	13 2/8	13 2/8	6	6 1/8	29 2/8	29 2/8	Gataga River, B. C.	Paul L. C. Snider	Paul L. C. Snider	1970	262

*Final Score subject to revision by additional verifying measurements.

Score Charts
of the
Offical Scoring System
for
North American
Big Game Trophies

Records of North American
Big Game

BOONE AND CROCKETT CLUB

205 South Patrick Street
Alexandria, Virginia 22314

BEAR

Kind of Bear black

Sex unknown

Minimum Score:
Alaska brown 28
black 21
grizzly 24
polar 27

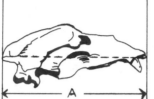

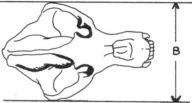

SEE OTHER SIDE FOR INSTRUCTIONS	Measurements
A. Greatest Length without Lower Jaw	14 12/16
B. Greatest Width	8 14/16
TOTAL AND FINAL SCORE	23 10/16

Exact locality where killed 7 miles east of Ephraim, San Pete Co., Utah

Date killed 1 July 1975   By whom killed Picked up

Present owner Alma R. Lund and Merrill Daniels

Address

Guide's Name and Address

Remarks: (Mention any abnormalities or unique qualities)

I certify that I have measured the above trophy on 9 Jan.   1976
at (address) 1596 W. N. Temple   City Salt Lake City   State Utah
and that these measurements and data are, to the best of my knowledge and belief, made in
accordance with the instructions given.

Witness: Harold Boyack   Signature: Rudy Drobnick
                                                        Official Measurer

<u>INSTRUCTIONS FOR MEASURING BEAR</u>

Measurements are taken with calipers or by using parallel perpendiculars, to the nearest <u>one-sixteenth</u> of an inch, without reduction of fractions. Official measurements cannot be taken for at least sixty days after the animal was killed. All adhering flesh, membrane and cartilage must be completely removed <u>before</u> official measurements are taken.

A. Greatest Length is measured between perpendiculars parallel to the long axis of the skull, without the lower jaw and excluding malformations.

B. Greatest Width is measured between perpendiculars at right angles to the long axis.

* * * * * * * * * * * *

FAIR CHASE STATEMENT FOR ALL HUNTER-TAKEN TROPHIES

To make use of the following methods shall be deemed as UNFAIR CHASE and unsportmanlike, and any trophy obtained by use of such means is disqualified from entry for Awards.
  I.   Spotting or herding game from the air, followed by landing in its vicinity for pursuit;
  II. Herding or pursuing game with motor-powered vehicles;
  III. Use of electronic communications for attracting, locating or observing game, or guiding the hunter to such game;
  IV. Hunting game confined by artificial barriers, including escape-proof fencing; or hunting game transplanted solely for the purpose of commercial shooting.

I certify that the trophy scored on this chart was not taken in UNFAIR CHASE as defined above by the Boone and Crockett Club. I further certify that it was taken in full compliance with local game laws of the state, province, or territory.
Date_____Signature of Hunter_____
(Have signature notarized by a Notary Public)

Records of North American
    Big Game

BOONE AND CROCKETT CLUB

205 South Patrick Street
Alexandria, Virginia 22314

Minimum Score:
  cougar 15
  jaguar 14½

COUGAR and JAGUAR

Kind of Cat _cougar_

Sex _male_

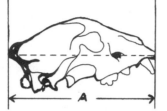

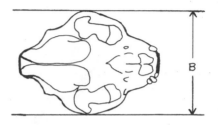

SEE OTHER SIDE FOR INSTRUCTIONS	Measurements
A. Greatest Length without Lower Jaw	9 4/16
B. Greatest Width	6 12/16
TOTAL AND FINAL SCORE	16

Exact locality where killed Garfield Co., Utah

Date killed January 1964   By whom killed Garth Roberts

Present owner R. Scott Jarvie

Address

Guide's Name and Address

Remarks: (Mention any abnormalities or unique qualities)

I certify that I have measured the above trophy on 28 Feb.   19 66
at (address) Carnegie Museum   City Pittsburgh   State Pennsylvania
and that these measurements and data are, to the best of my knowledge and belief, made in
accordance with the instructions given.

Witness:__John H. Batten_____ ___ Signature: __John E. Hammett_____
                                                        Official Measurer

INSTRUCTIONS FOR MEASURING COUGAR AND JAGUAR

Measurements are taken with calipers or by using parallel perpendiculars, to the nearest one-sixteenth of an inch, without reduction of fractions. Official measurements cannot be taken for at least sixty days after the animal was killed. All adhering flesh, membrane and cartilage must be completely removed before official measurements are taken.

A. Greatest Length is measured between perpendiculars parallel to the long axis of the skull, without the lower jaw and excluding malformations.

B. Greatest Width is measured between perpendiculars at a right angle to the long axis.

* * * * * * * * * * * * *

FAIR CHASE STATEMENT FOR ALL HUNTER-TAKEN TROPHIES

To make use of the following methods shall be deemed as UNFAIR CHASE and unsportmanlike, and any trophy obtained by use of such means is disqualified from entry for Awards.
    I.   Spotting or herding game from the air, followed by landing in its vicinity for pursuit;
    II. Herding or pursuing game with motor-powered vehicles;
    III. Use of electronic communications for attracting, locating or observing game, or guiding the hunter to such game;
    IV. Hunting game confined by artificial barriers, including escape-proof fencing; or hunting game transplanted solely for the purpose of commercial shooting.

I certify that the trophy scored on this chart was not taken in UNFAIR CHASE as defined above by the Boone and Crockett Club. I further certify that it was taken in full compliance with local game laws of the state, province, or territory.
Date_____ Signature of Hunter_____
(Have signature notarized by a Notary Public)

Copyright 1981 by Boone and Crockett Club
(Reproduction strictly forbidden without express, written consent)

Records of North American
Big Game

BOONE AND CROCKETT CLUB

205 South Patrick Street
Alexandria, Virginia 22314

Minimum Score:
Atlantic 95
Pacific 100

WALRUS

Kind of Walrus __Pacific__

Sex __male__

SEE OTHER SIDE FOR INSTRUCTIONS		Column 1	Column 2	Column 3
A. Greatest Spread	unknown	Right Tusk	Left Tusk	Difference
B. Tip to Tip Spread	unknown			
C. Entire Length of Loose Tusk		32 2/8	32 1/8	1/8
D-1. Circumference of Base		12 2/8	13	6/8
D-2. Circumference at First Quarter		11 6/8	12 2/8	4/8
D-3. Circumference at Second Quarter		9 5/8	9 5/8	
D-4. Circumference at Third Quarter		7 2/8	7 1/8	1/8
TOTALS		73 1/8	74 1/8	1 4/8

ADD	Column 1	73 1/8	Exact locality where killed Chukchi Sea off Point Hope, Alaska
	Column 2	74 1/8	Date killed Spring1957 By whom killed Eskimo
	Total	147 2/8	Present owner Jonas Brothers of Seattle
SUBTRACT Column 3		1 4/8	Address
FINAL SCORE		145 6/8	Guide's Name and Address
			Remarks: (Mention any abnormalities or unique qualities) Skull missing - both tusks slightly chipped at tips

I certify that I have measured the above trophy on 18 Feb. 1958
at (address) Am. Museum of Nat. History   City New York   State New York
and that these measurements and data are, to the best of my knowledge and belief, made in
accordance with the instructions given.

Witness: _____   Signature: __Grancel Fitz__
                                                      Official Measurer

INSTRUCTIONS FOR MEASURING WALRUS

All measurements must be made with a ¼-inch flexible steel tape to the nearest one-eighth of an inch. Enter fractional figures in <u>eighths</u>, without reduction. Tusks <u>must</u> be removed from mounted specimens for measuring. Official measurements cannot be taken for at least sixty days after the animal was killed.

A. Greatest Spread is measured between perpendiculars at a right angle to the center line of the skull.

B. Tip to Tip Spread is measured between tips of tusks.

C. Entire Length of Loose Tusk is measured over outer curve from base to a point in line with tip.

D-1. Circumference of Base is measured at a right angle to axis of tusk. Do not follow edge of contact between tusk and skull.

D-2-3-4. Divide measurement C of LONGER tusk by four. Starting at base, mark <u>both</u> tusks at these quarters (even though other tusk is shorter) and measure circumferences at these marks.

* * * * * * * * * * * * *

FAIR CHASE STATEMENT FOR ALL HUNTER-TAKEN TROPHIES

To make use of the following methods shall be deemed as UNFAIR CHASE and unsportmanlike, and any trophy obtained by use of such means is disqualified from entry for Awards.
I. Spotting or herding game from the air, followed by landing in its vicinity for pursuit;
II. Herding or pursuing game with motor-powered vehicles;
III. Use of electronic communications for attracting, locating or observing game, or guiding the hunter to such game;
IV. Hunting game confined by artificial barriers, including escape-proof fencing; or hunting game transplanted solely for the purpose of commercial shooting.

I certify that the trophy scored on this chart was not taken in UNFAIR CHASE as defined above by the Boone and Crockett Club. I further certify that it was taken in full compliance with local game laws of the state, province, or territory.
Date_____ Signature of Hunter_____
(Have signature notarized by a Notary Public)

Records of North American
Big Game

BOONE AND CROCKETT CLUB

205 South Patrick Street
Alexandria, Virginia 22314

Minimum Score:
Roosevelt 290
American 375

WAPITI

Kind of Wapiti __American__

DETAIL OF POINT MEASUREMENT

	Abnormal Points	
	Right	Left
Total to E	2 5/8	

	SEE OTHER SIDE FOR INSTRUCTIONS		Column 1 Spread Credit	Column 2 Right Antler	Column 3 Left Antler	Column 4 Difference
A.	Number of Points on Each Antler	R. 8 L. 7				
B.	Tip to Tip Spread	39 6/8				
C.	Greatest Spread	51 6/8				
D.	Inside Spread of Main Beams 45 4/8 Credit may equal but not exceed length of longer antler		45 4/8			
	IF Spread exceeds longer antler, enter difference.					
E.	Total of Lengths of all Abnormal Points					2 5/8
F.	Length of Main Beam			55 5/8	59 5/8	4
G-1.	Length of First Point			20 5/8	20 5/8	
G-2.	Length of Second Point			27 3/8	25 5/8	1 6/8
G-3.	Length of Third Point			20	18 5/8	1 3/8
G-4.	Length of Fourth (Royal) Point			22 4/8	21 5/8	7/8
G-5.	Length of Fifth Point			15 7/8	15 4/8	3/8
G-6.	Length of Sixth Point, if present			11 7/8	7 3/8	4 4/8
G-7.	Length of Seventh Point, if present					
H-1.	Circumference at Smallest Place Between First and Second Points			12 1/8	11 2/8	7/8
H-2.	Circumference at Smallest Place Between Second and Third Points			7 5/8	7 5/8	
H-3.	Circumference at Smallest Place Between Third and Fourth Points			7 7/8	8	1/8
H-4.	Circumference at Smallest Place Between Fourth and Fifth Points			8	9	1
	TOTALS		45 4/8	209 4/8	204 7/8	17 4/8

ADD	Column 1	45 4/8	Exact locality where killed Dark Canyon, Colorado
	Column 2	209 4/8	Date killed 1899 By whom killed John Plute
	Column 3	204 7/8	Present owner Ed Rozman
	Total	459 7/8	Address
SUBTRACT Column 4		17 4/8	Guide's Name and Address
FINAL SCORE		442 3/8	Remarks: (Mention any abnormalities or unique qualities)

I certify that I have measured the above trophy on ___*8 February*___ 19 *1962*
at (address) *Am. Museum of Nat. History* City *New York* State *New York*
and that these measurements and data are, to the best of my knowledge and belief, made in accordance
with the instructions given.

Witness: _____ Signature: ___*Elmer M. Rusten*___
                                                        OFFICIAL MEASURER

INSTRUCTIONS FOR MEASURING WAPITI

All measurements must be made with a ¼-inch flexible steel tape to the nearest one-eighth of an inch.
Wherever it is necessary to change direction of measurement, mark a control point and swing tape at
this point. Enter fractional figures in eighths, without reduction. Official measurements cannot
be taken for at least sixty days after the animal was killed.

A. Number of Points on Each Antler. To be counted a point, a projection must be at least one inch
long and its length must exceed the width of its base. All points are measured from tip of point to
nearest edge of beam as illustrated. Beam tip is counted as a point but not measured as a point.

B. Tip to Tip Spread is measured between tips of main beams.

C. Greatest Spread is measured between perpendiculars at a right angle to the center line of the
skull at widest part whether across main beams or points.

D. Inside Spread of Main Beams is measured at a right angle to the center line of the skull at widest point between main beams. Enter this measurement again in Spread Credit column if it is less
than or equal to the length of longer antler; if longer, enter longer antler length for Spread Credit.

E. Total of lengths of all Abnormal Points. Abnormal points are those nontypical in location (such
as points originating from a point or from bottom or sides of main beam) or pattern (extra points,
not generally paired). Measure in usual manner and enter in appropriate blanks.

F. Length of Main Beam is measured from lowest outside edge of burr over outer curve to the most distant point of what is, or appears to be, the main beam. The point of beginning is that point on the
burr where the center line along the outer curve of the beam intersects the burr, then following generally the line of the illustration.

G-1-2-3-4-5-6-7. Length of Normal Points. Normal points project from the top or front of the main
beam in the general pattern illustrated. They are measured from nearest edge of main beam over outer
curve to tip. Lay the tape along the outer curve of the beam so that the top edge of the tape coincides with the top edge of the beam on both sides of the point to determine the baseline for point
measurement. Record point length in appropriate blanks.

H-1-2-3-4. Circumferences are taken as detailed for each measurement.
* * * * * * * * * * * *

FAIR CHASE STATEMENT FOR ALL HUNTER-TAKEN TROPHIES

To make use of the following methods shall be deemed as UNFAIR CHASE and unsportsmanlike, and any
trophy obtained by use of such means is disqualified from entry for Awards.

   I. Spotting or herding game from the air, followed by landing in its vicinity
      for pursuit;
  II. Herding or pursuing game with motor-powered vehicles;
 III. Use of electronic communications for attracting, locating or observing
      game, or guiding the hunter to such game;
  IV. Hunting game confined by artificial barriers, including escape-proof fencing;
      or hunting game transplanted solely for the purpose of commercial shooting.
    ****

I certify that the trophy scored on this chart was not taken in UNFAIR CHASE as defined above by the
Boone and Crockett Club. I further certify that it was taken in full compliance with local game laws
of the state, province, or territory.

Date_____ Signature of Hunter_____
(Have signature notarized by a Notary Public)

Records of North American
Big Game

BOONE AND CROCKETT CLUB

205 South Patrick Street
Alexandria, Virginia 22314

Minimum Score:
mule   195
blacktail 130

TYPICAL
MULE AND BLACKTAIL DEER

Kind of Deer __mule__

DETAIL OF POINT
MEASUREMENT

Abnormal Points	
Right	Left
Total to E	2 5/8

SEE OTHER SIDE FOR INSTRUCTIONS			Column 1	Column 2	Column 3	Column 4
A. Number of points on Each Antler	R. 6	L. 5	Spread Credit	Right Antler	Left Antler	Difference
B. Tip to Tip Spread	28 5/8					
C. Greatest Spread	33 2/8					
D. Inside Spread of Main Beams 30 7/8	Credit may equal but not exceed length of longer antler		30 1/8			
IF Spread exceeds longer antler, enter difference						6/8
E. Total of Lengths of Abnormal Points						2 5/8
F. Length of Main Beam				30 1/8	28 6/8	1 3/8
G-1. Length of First Point, if present				2 3/8	2 6/8	3/8
G-2. Length of Second Point				22 4/8	22 3/8	1/8
G-3. Length of Third Point, if present				14 2/8	14 3/8	1/8
G-4. Length of Fourth Point, if present				14 6/8	13 6/8	1
H-1. Circumference at Smallest Place Between Burr and First Point				5 2/8	5 3/8	1/8
H-2. Circumference at Smallest Place Between First and Second Points				4 4/8	4 4/8	
H-3. Circumference at Smallest Place Between Main Beam and Third Point				4	4 1/8	1/8
H-4. Circumference at Smallest Place Between Second and Fourth Points				4 2/8	4 4/8	2/8
TOTALS			30 1/8	102	100 4/8	6 7/8

ADD	Column 1	30 1/8	Exact locality where killed Cortez, Colorado
	Column 2	102	Date killed 19Oct72 By whom killed Doug Burris, Jr.
	Column 3	100 4/8	Present owner Doug Burris, Jr.
TOTAL		232 5/8	Address
SUBTRACT Column 4		6 7/8	Guide's Name and Address
FINAL SCORE		225 6/8	Remarks: (Mention any abnormalities or unique qualities)

I certify that I have measured the above trophy on _27 February_ 19 _74_
at (address) _Grosh-Tucker,Inc._ City _Atlanta_ State _Georgia_
and that these measurements and data are, to the best of my knowledge and belief, made in accordance
with the instructions given.

Witness: _B.A.Fashingbauer_   Signature: _Arnold O. Haugen_
OFFICIAL MEASURER

INSTRUCTIONS FOR MEASURING MULE AND BLACKTAIL DEER

All measurements must be made with a ¼-inch flexible steel tape to the nearest one-eighth of an inch.
Wherever it is necessary to change direction of measurement, mark a control point and swing tape at
this point. Enter fractional figures in eighths, without reduction. Official measurements cannot
be taken for at least sixty days after the animal was killed.

A. Number of Points on Each Antler. To be counted a point, a projection must be at least one inch
long and its length must exceed the width of its base. All points are measured from tip of point to
nearest edge of beam as illustrated. Beam tip is counted as a point but not measured as a point.

B. Tip to Tip Spread is measured between tips of main beams.

C. Greatest Spread is measured between perpendiculars at a right angle to the center line of the
skull at widest part whether across main beams or points.

D. Inside Spread of Main Beams is measured at a right angle to the center line of the skull at widest point between main beams. Enter this measurement again in Spread Credit column if it is less
than or equal to the length of longer antler; if longer, enter longer antler length for Spread Credit.

E. Total Lengths of all Abnormal Points. Abnormal points are those nontypical in location such as
points originating from a point (exception: G-3 originates from G-2 in perfectly normal fashion) or
from sides or bottom of main beam or any points beyond the normal pattern of five (including beam
tip) per antler. Measure each abnormal point in usual manner and enter in appropriate blanks.

F. Length of Main Beam is measured from lowest outside edge of burr over outer curve to the tip of
the main beam. The point of beginning is that point on the burr where the center line along the
outer curve of the beam intersects the burr, then following generally the line of the illustration.

G-1-2-3-4. Length of Normal Points. Normal points are the brow and the upper and lower forks as
shown in the illustration. They are measured from nearest edge of beam over outer curve to tip.
Lay the tape along the outer curve of the beam so that the top edge of the tape coincides with the
top edge of the beam on both sides of the point to determine baseline for point measurement. Record
point lengths in appropriate blanks.

H-1-2-3-4. Circumferences are taken as detailed for each measurement. If brow point is missing,
take H-1 and H-2 at smallest place between burr and G-2. If G-3 is missing, take H-3 halfway between
the base and tip of second point. If G-4 is missing, take H-4 halfway between the second point and
tip of main beam. * * * * * * * * * * * *

FAIR CHASE STATEMENT FOR ALL HUNTER-TAKEN TROPHIES

To make use of the following methods shall be deemed as UNFAIR CHASE and unsportsmanlike, and any
trophy obtained by use of such means is disqualified from entry for Awards.

  I.   Spotting or herding game from the air, followed by landing in its vicinity
       for pursuit;
 II.   Herding or pursuing game with motor-powered vehicles;
III.   Use of electronic communications for attracting, locating or observing
       game, or guiding the hunter to such game;
 IV.   Hunting game confined by artificial barriers, including escape-proof fencing;
       or hunting game transplanted solely for the purpose of commercial shooting.
       ****

I certify that the trophy scored on this chart was not taken in UNFAIR CHASE as defined above by the
Boone and Crockett Club. I further certify that it was taken in full compliance with local game laws
of the state, province, or territory.

Date_____ Signature of Hunter_____
(Have signature notarized by a Notary Public)

OFFICIAL SCORING SYSTEM FOR NORTH AMERICAN BIG GAME TROPHIES

Records of North American
Big Game

BOONE AND CROCKETT CLUB

205 South Patrick Street
Alexandria, Virginia 22314

Minimum Score: 240

**NON-TYPICAL
MULE DEER**

DETAIL OF POINT
MEASUREMENT

Abnormal Points			
Right		Left	
5 1/8	2 3/8	1 3/8	1 4/8
8 3/8	6 7/8	5 1/8	1 7/8
2	1 7/8	3 4/8	2 7/8
1 3/8	2 4/8	2 3/8	1 3/8
3 3/8	8 1/8	2 7/8	1 7/8
2 7/8	8 7/8	8	
10		7 7/8	
5 3/8		5 3/8	
8 1/8		4 5/8	
6 7/8		8 5/8	
5 4/8		1 4/8	
Total to E	147 7/8		

		Column 1	Column 2	Column 3	Column 4
SEE OTHER SIDE FOR INSTRUCTIONS					
A. Number of Points on Each Antler R.22 L.21		Spread Credit	Right Antler	Left Antler	Difference
B. Tip to Tip Spread	16				
C. Greatest Spread	38 5/8				
D. Inside Spread of Main Beams 22 1/8 Credit may equal but not exceed length of longer antler		22 1/8			
IF Spread exceeds longer antler, enter difference					
E. Total of Lengths of Abnormal Points	147 7/8				
F. Length of Main Beams			26 2/8	26 1/8	1/8
G-1. Length of First Point, if present			4 4/8	3 5/8	7/8
G-2. Length of Second Point			18 2/8	19 5/8	1 3/8
G-3. Length of Third Point, if present			13 3/8	14	5/8
G-4. Length of Fourth Point, if present			12 6/8	10 3/8	2 3/8
H-1. Circumference at Smallest Place Between Burr and First Point			5	4 7/8	1/8
H-2. Circumference at Smallest Place Between First and Second Points			4 6/8	5	2/8
H-3. Circumference at Smallest Place Between Main Beam and Third Point			5 7/8	6 4/8	5/8
H-4. Circumference at Smallest Place Between Second and Fourth Points			5 3/8	5 4/8	1/8
TOTALS		147 7/8	22 1/8 96 1/8	95 5/8	6 4/8

ADD	Column 1	22 1/8	Exact locality where killed Chip Lake, Alberta, Canada
	Column 2	96 1/8	Date killed 26Nov26 By whom killed Ed Broder
	Column 3	95 5/8	Present Owner Ed Broder
	TOTAL	213 7/8	Address
SUBTRACT	Column 4	6 4/8	
	Result	207 3/8	Guide's Name and Address
Add Line E Total		147 7/8	Remarks: (Mention any abnormalities or unique qualities)
FINAL SCORE		355 2/8	

I certify that I have measured the above trophy on ___24 February___ 19_62_
at (address) _Am. Museum of Nat. History_ City _New York_ State _New York_
and that these measurements and data are, to the best of my knowledge and belief, made in accordance
with the instructions given.

Witness: ___Grancel Fitz___   Signature: ___John E. Hammett___
                                                    OFFICIAL MEASURER

Records of North American
Big Game

BOONE AND CROCKETT CLUB

205 South Patrick Street
Alexandria, Virginia 22314

Minimum Score:
whitetail 170
Coues' 110

TYPICAL
WHITETAIL AND COUES' DEER

Kind of Deer __whitetail__

DETAIL OF POINT
MEASUREMENT

	Abnormal Points	
	Right	Left
Total to E		

SEE OTHER SIDE FOR INSTRUCTIONS			Column 1 Spread Credit	Column 2 Right Antler	Column 3 Left Antler	Column 4 Difference
A. Number of Points on Each Antler	R. 5	L. 5				
B. Tip to Tip Spread		7 5/8				
C. Greatest Spread		23 6/8				
D. Inside Spread of Main Beams 20 1/8 Credit may equal but not exceed length of longer antler. IF Spread exceeds longer antler, enter difference.			20 1/8			
E. Total of Lengths of all Abnormal Points						
F. Length of Main Beam				30	30	
G-1. Length of First Point, if present				7 6/8	7 3/8	3/8
G-2. Length of Second Point				13	13 1/8	1/8
G-3. Length of Third Point				10	10 4/8	4/8
G-4. Length of Fourth Point, if present				6	7 5/8	1 5/8
G-5. Length of Fifth Point, if present						
G-6. Length of Sixth Point, if present						
G-7. Length of Seventh Point, if present						
H-1. Circumference at Smallest Place Between Burr and First Point				6 2/8	6 1/8	1/8
H-2. Circumference at Smallest Place Between First and Second Points				6 2/8	6 4/8	2/8
H-3. Circumference at Smallest Place Between Second and Third Points				7 3/8	7 4/8	1/8
H-4. Circumference at Smallest Place between Third and Fourth Points (see back if G-4 is missing)				7	6 7/8	1/8
TOTALS			20 1/8	93 5/8	95 5/8	3 2/8

ADD	Column 1	20 1/8	Exact locality where killed Burnett Co., Wisconsin
	Column 2	93 5/8	Date killed __1914__ By whom killed James Jordan
	Column 3	95 5/8	Present owner Charles T. Arnold
	Total	209 3/8	Address
SUBTRACT Column 4		3 2/8	Guide's Name and Address
FINAL SCORE		206 1/8	Remarks: (Mention any abnormalities or unique qualities)

I certify that I have measured the above trophy on **28 February** 19 **66**
at (address) **Carnegie Museum** City **Pittsburgh** State **Pa.**
and that these measurements and data are, to the best of my knowledge and belief, made in accordance
with the instructions given.

Witness: **George P. Norris**   Signature: **George T. Church, Jr.**
                                                              OFFICIAL MEASURER

INSTRUCTIONS FOR MEASURING WHITETAIL AND COUES' DEER

All measurements must be made with a ¼-inch flexible steel tape to the nearest one-eighth of an inch.
Wherever it is necessary to change direction of measurement, mark a control point and swing tape at
this point. Enter fractional figures in eighths, without reduction. Official measurements cannot
be taken for at least sixty days after the animal was killed.

A. Number of Points on Each Antler. To be counted a point, a projection must be at least one inch
long and its length must exceed the width of its base. All points are measured from tip of point to
nearest edge of beam as illustrated. Beam tip is counted as a point but not measured as a point.

B. Tip to Tip Spread is measured between tips of main beams.

C. Greatest Spread is measured between perpendiculars at a right angle to the center line of the
skull at widest part whether across main beams or points.

D. Inside Spread of Main Beams is measured at a right angle to the center line of the skull at widest point between main beams. Enter this measurement again in Spread Credit column if it is less
than or equal to the length of longer antler; if longer, enter longer antler length for Spread Credit.

E. Total of lengths of all Abnormal Points. Abnormal points are those nontypical in location (points
originating from points or from sides or bottom of main beam) or extra points beyond the normal pattern
of up to eight normal points, including beam tip, per antler. Measure in usual manner and enter in
appropriate blanks.

F. Length of Main Beam is measured from lowest outside edge of burr over outer curve to the most
distant point of what is, or appears to be, the main beam. The point of beginning is that point on
the burr where the center line along the outer curve of the beam intersects the burr, then following
generally the line of the illustration.

G-1-2-3-4-5-6-7. Length of Normal Points. Normal points project from the top of the main beam. They
are measured from nearest edge of main beam over outer curve to tip. Lay the tape along the outer
curve of the beam so that the top edge of the tape coincides with the top edge of the beam on both
sides of the point to determine baseline for point measurements. Record point lengths in appropriate
blanks.

H-1-2-3-4. Circumferences are taken as detailed for each measurement. If brow point is missing,
Take H-1 and H-2 at smallest place between burr and second point.

* * * * * * * * * * * *

FAIR CHASE STATEMENT FOR ALL HUNTER-TAKEN TROPHIES

To make use of the following methods shall be deemed as UNFAIR CHASE and unsportsmanlike, and any
trophy obtained by use of such means is disqualified from entry for Awards.

I. Spotting or herding game from the air, followed by landing in its vicinity
for pursuit;
II. Herding or pursuing game with motor-powered vehicles;
III. Use of electronic communications for attracting, locating or observing
game, or guiding the hunter to such game;
IV. Hunting game confined by artificial barriers, including escape-proof fencing;
or hunting game transplanted solely for the purpose of commercial shooting.
****

I certify that the trophy scored on this chart was not taken in UNFAIR CHASE as defined above by the
Boone and Crockett Club. I further certify that it was taken in full compliance with local game laws
of the state, province, or territory.

Date_____Signature of Hunter_____
(Have signature notarized by a Notary Public)

Records of North American
Big Game

BOONE AND CROCKETT CLUB

205 South Patrick Street
Alexandria, Virginia 22314

Minimum Score:
whitetail 195
Coues' 120

NON-TYPICAL
WHITETAIL AND COUES' DEER

Kind of Deer __whitetail__

Abnormal Points			
Right		Left	
2 4/8	1 5/8	5 5/8	5 3/8
7	4 1/8	1	1 7/8
1 4/8	4 5/8	2 4/8	2
2 4/8	1 3/8	1 1/8	7 4/8
1 3/8	8 1/8	6 5/8	3 1/8
2 4/8	1 6/8	1 2/8	3
4 7/8		1 3/8	3 3/8
6 7/8		8 3/8	6 3/8
2 6/8		2 1/8	4
1 4/8		7 1/8	
4 4/8		3 4/8	

Total to E   137

SEE OTHER SIDE FOR INSTRUCTIONS		Column 1	Column 2	Column 3	Column 4
A. Number of Points on Each Antler R. 23 L. 26		Spread Credit	Right Antler	Left Antler	Difference
B. Tip to Tip Spread		11 1/8			
C. Greatest Spread		27 3/8			
D. Inside Spread of Main Beams 15 6/8 Credit may equal but not exceed length of longer antler		15 6/8			
IF Spread exceeds longer antler, enter difference.					
E. Total of Lengths of Abnormal Points		137			
F. Length of Main Beam			23 1/8	18 7/8	4 2/8
G-1. Length of First Point, if present			7 3/8	6 7/8	4/8
G-2. Length of Second Point			10 6/8	11 1/8	3/8
G-3. Length of Third Point			9	8 5/8	3/8
G-4. Length of Fourth Point, if present			6 6/8	3 3/8	3 3/8
G-5. Length of Fifth Point, if present			3 5/8	1	2 5/8
G-6. Length of Sixth Point, if present					
G-7. Length of Seventh Point, if present					
H-1. Circumference at Smallest Place Between Burr and First Point			4 2/8	4 2/8	
H-2. Circumference at Smallest Place Between First and Second Points			4	3 7/8	1/8
H-3. Circumference at Smallest Place Between Second and Third Points			4 3/8	4 3/8	
H-4. Circumference at Smallest Place Between Third and Fourth Points			4 6/8	4 5/8	1/8
TOTALS		137	15 6/8	78	67	11 6/8

ADD	Column 1	15 6/8	Exact locality where killed Brady, Texas
	Column 2	78	Date killed 1892 By whom killed Jeff Benson
	Column 3	67	Present owner Lone Star Brewing Company
	Total	160 6/8	Address
SUBTRACT	Column 4	11 6/8	
	Result	149	Guide's Name and Address
Add line E Total		137	Remarks: (Mention any abnormalities or unique qualities)
FINAL SCORE		286	

I certify that I have measured the above trophy on ___*1 January*___ 19 *55*
at (address) _____ City *San Antonio* State *Texas*
and that these measurements and data are, to the best of my knowledge and belief, made in accordance
with the instructions given.

Witness: ___*Betty Fitz*___   Signature: ___*Grancel Fitz*___
                                                    OFFICIAL MEASURER

INSTRUCTIONS FOR MEASURING NON-TYPICAL WHITETAIL AND COUES' DEER

All measurements must be made with a ¼-inch flexible steel tape to the nearest one-eighth of an inch.
Wherever it is necessary to change direction of measurement, mark a control point and swing tape at
this point. Enter fractional figures in eighths, without reduction. Official measurements cannot
be taken for at least sixty days after the animal was killed.

A. Number of Points on Each Antler. To be counted a point, a projection must be at least one inch
long and its length must exceed the width of its base. All points are measured from tip of point to
nearest edge of beam as illustrated. Beam tip is counted as a point but not measured as a point.

B. Tip to Tip Spread is measured between tips of main beams.

C. Greatest Spread is measured between perpendiculars at a right angle to the center line of the
skull at widest part whether across main beams or points.

D. Inside Spread of Main Beams is measured at a right angle to the center line of the skull at widest point between main beams. Enter this measurement again in Spread Credit column if it is less
than or equal to the length of longer antler; if longer, enter longer antler length for Spread Credit.

E. Total of Lengths of all Abnormal Points. Abnormal points are those nontypical in location (points
originating from points or from sides or bottom of main beam) or extra points beyond the normal pattern
of up to eight normal points, including beam tip, per antler. Measure in usual manner and enter in
appropriate blanks.

F. Length of Main Beam is measured from lowest outside edge of burr over outer curve to the most distant point of what is, or appears to be, the main beam. The point of beginning is that point on the
burr where the center line along the outer curve of the beam intersects the burr, then following generally the line of the illustration.

G-1-2-3-4-5-6-7. Length of Normal Points. Normal points project from the top of the main beam.
They are measured from nearest edge of main beam over outer curve to tip. Lay the tape along the
outer curve of the beam so that the top edge of the tape coincides with the beam on both sides of
the point to determine baseline for point measurement. Record point lengths in appropriate blanks.

H-1-2-3-4. Circumferences are taken as detailed for each measurement. If brow point is missing,
take H-1 and H-2 at smallest place between burr and G-2. If G-3 is missing, take H-3 halfway between
the base and tip of second point. If G-4 is missing, take H-4 halfway between the second point and
tip of main beam.   * * * * * * * * * * * *

FAIR CHASE STATEMENT FOR ALL HUNTER-TAKEN TROPHIES
To make use of the following methods shall be deemed as UNFAIR CHASE and unsportsmanlike, and any
trophy obtained by use of such means is disqualified from entry for Awards.
   I.   Spotting or herding game from the air, followed by landing in its vicinity
        for pursuit;
   II. Herding or pursuing game with motor-powered vehicles;
   III. Use of electronic communications for attracting, locating or observing
        game, or guiding the hunter to such game;
   IV. Hunting game confined by artificial barriers, including escape-proof fencing;
        or hunting game transplanted solely for the purpose of commercial shooting.
        ****
I certify that the trophy scored on this chart was not taken in UNFAIR CHASE as defined above by the
Boone and Crockett Club. I further certify that it was taken in full compliance with local game laws
of the state, province, or territory.

Date_____Signature of Hunter_____
(Have signature notarized by a Notary Public)

Records of North American
Big Game

BOONE AND CROCKETT CLUB

205 South Patrick Street
Alexandria, Virginia 22314

Minimum Score:
Alaska-Yukon 224
Canada 195
Wyoming 155

MOOSE

Kind of Moose Alaska-Yukon

DETAIL OF POINT
MEASUREMENT

SEE OTHER SIDE FOR INSTRUCTIONS	Column 1	Column 2	Column 3	Column 4
A. Greatest Spread	77	Right Antler	Left Antler	Difference
B. Number of Abnormal Points on Both Antlers				
C. Number of Normal Points		18	16	2
D. Width of Palm		20 6/8	15 6/8	5
E. Length of Palm including Brow Palm		49 5/8	49 6/8	1/8
F. Circumference of Beam at Smallest Place		7 7/8	7 5/8	2/8
TOTALS	77	96 2/8	89 1/8	7 3/8

ADD	Column 1	77	Exact locality where killed McGrath, Alaska
	Column 2	96 2/8	Date killed 9 Sep 78 By whom killed Kenneth Best
	Column 3	89 1/8	Present owner Kenneth Best
Total		262 3/8	Address
SUBTRACT Column 4		7 3/8	Guide's Name and Address
FINAL SCORE		255	Remarks: (Mention any abnormalities or unique qualities)

I certify that I have measured the above trophy on 13 March 19 80
at (address) Missouri Dept. of Cons.   City Jefferson City State Missouri
and that these measurements and data are, to the best of my knowledge and belief, made in
accordance with the instructions given.

Witness: B. A. Fashingbauer _____ Signature: Glen C. Sanderson
                                                      Official Measurer

INSTRUCTIONS FOR MEASURING MOOSE

All measurements must be made with a ¼-inch flexible steel tape to the nearest one-eighth of an inch. Wherever it is necessary to change direction of measurement, mark a control point and swing tape at this point. Enter fractional figures in eighths, without reduction. Official measurements cannot be taken for at least sixty days after the animal was killed.

A. Greatest Spread is measured between perpendiculars in a straight line at a right angle to the center line of the skull.

B. Number of Abnormal Points on Both Antlers - Abnormal points are those originating from normal points or from the upper or lower palm surface, or from the inner edge of palm (see illustration). Abnormal points must be at least one inch long, with length exceeding width at one inch or more of length.

C. Number of Normal Points - Normal points originate from the outer edge of palm. To be counted a point, a projection must be at least one inch long, with the length exceeding width at one inch or more of length.

D. Width of Palm is taken in contact with the under surface of palm, at a right angle to the length of palm measurement line. The line of measurement should begin and end at the midpoint of the palm edge, which gives credit for the desirable character of palm thickness.

E. Length of Palm including Brow Palm is taken in contact with the surface along the under side of the palm, parallel to the inner edge, from dips between points at the top to dips between points (if present) at the bottom. If a bay is present, measure across the open bay if the proper line of measurement parallel to inner edge, follows this path. The line of measurement should begin and end at the midpoint of the palm edge, which gives credit for the desirable character of palm thickness.

F. Circumference of Beam at Smallest Place is taken as illustrated.

* * * * * * * * * * * *

FAIR CHASE STATEMENT FOR ALL HUNTER-TAKEN TROPHIES

To make use of the following methods shall be deemed as UNFAIR CHASE and unsportsmanlike, and any trophy obtained by use of such means is disqualified from entry for Awards.

    I. Spotting or herding game from the air, followed by landing in its vicinity for pursuit;

    II. Herding or pursuing game with motor-powered vehicles;

    III. Use of electronic communications for attracting, locating or observing game, or guiding the hunter to such game;

    IV. Hunting game confined by artificial barriers, including escape-proof fencing; or hunting game transplanted solely for the purpose of commercial shooting.

I certify that the trophy scored on this chart was not taken in UNFAIR CHASE as defined above by the Boone and Crockett Club. I further certify that it was taken in full compliance with local game laws of the state, province, or territory.

Date_____ Signature of Hunter_____

(Have signature notarized by a Notary Public)

OFFICIAL SCORING SYSTEM FOR NORTH AMERICAN BIG GAME TROPHIES

Records of North American
Big Game

BOONE AND CROCKETT CLUB

205 South Patrick Street
Alexandria, Virginia 22314

Minimum Score:
  barren ground   400
  mountain   390
  Quebec-Labrador 375
  woodland   295

CARIBOU   Kind of Caribou   mountain

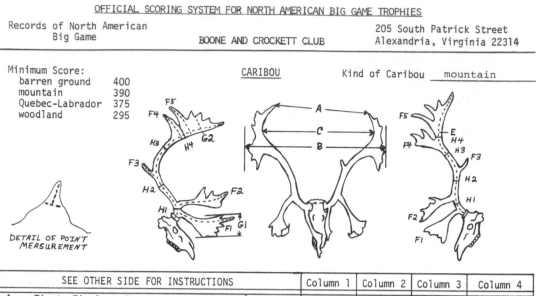

DETAIL OF POINT
MEASUREMENT

SEE OTHER SIDE FOR INSTRUCTIONS		Column 1	Column 2	Column 3	Column 4
A. Tip to Tip Spread	27 1/8	Spread Credit	Right Antler	Left Antler	Difference
B. Greatest Spread	33 3/8				
C. Inside Spread of Main Beams 30 3/8 Credit may equal but not exceed length of longer antler		30 3/8			
IF Spread exceeds longer antler, enter difference.					
D. Number of Points on Each Antler excluding brows			18	15	3
Number of Points on Each Brow			4	4	
E. Length of Main Beam			43 1/8	42 2/8	7/8
F-1. Length of Brow Palm or First Point			16 4/8	16 1/8	
F-2. Length of Bez or Second Point			20 4/8	20 5/8	1/8
F-3. Length of Rear Point, if present			6 4/8	8	1 4/8
F-4. Length of Second Longest Top Point			22	23 2/8	1 2/8
F-5. Length of Longest Top Point			22 5/8	23 4/8	7/8
G-1. Width of Brow Palm			11 2/8	5	
G-2. Width of Top Palm			16 4/8	15 6/8	6/8
H-1. Circumference at Smallest Place Between Brow and Bez Points			7 3/8	7 5/8	2/8
H-2. Circumference at Smallest Place Between Bez and Rear Point, if present			6 6/8	6 4/8	2/8
H-3. Circumference at Smallest Place Before First Top Point			6 1/8	6 1/8	
H-4. Circumference at Smallest Place Between Two Longest Top Palm Points			17 6/8	26 4/8	8 6/8
TOTALS		30 3/8	219	220 2/8	17 5/8

ADD	Column 1	30 3/8	Exact locality where killed Turnagain River, B. C.
	Column 2	219	Date killed 15Sep76 By whom killed Gary Beaubien
	Column 3	220 2/8	Present owner Gary Beaubien
	TOTAL	469 5/8	Address
SUBTRACT Column 4		17 5/8	Guide's Name and Address
FINAL SCORE		452	Remarks: (Mention any abnormalities or unique qualities)

I certify that I have measured the above trophy on _____7 June_____ 19 77
at (address) 6060 Broadway   City Denver   State Colorado
and that these measurements and data are, to the best of my knowledge and belief, made in accordance
with the instructions given.
Witness: John G. Stelfox_____   Signature: Frank Cook
                                                            OFFICIAL MEASURER

INSTRUCTIONS FOR MEASURING CARIBOU

All measurements must be made with a ¼-inch flexible steel tape to the nearest one-eighth of an inch.
Wherever it is necessary to change direction of measurement, mark a control point and swing tape at
this point. Enter fractional figures in eighths, without reduction. Official measurements cannot
be taken for at least sixty days after the animal was killed.

A. Tip to Tip Spread is measured between tips of main beams.

B. Greatest Spread is measured between perpendiculars at a right angle to the center line of the
skull at widest part, whether across main beams or points.

C. Inside Spread of Main Beams is measured at a right angle to the center line of the skull at widest point between main beams. Enter this measurement again in Spread Credit colum if it is less
than or equal to the length of longer antler; if longer, enter longer antler length for Spread Credit.

D. Number of points on each antler. To be counted a point, a projection must be at least one-half
inch long, with length exceeding width at the point of measurement. Beam tip is counted as a point
but not measured as a point. There are no "abnormal" points in caribou.

E. Length of Main Beam is measured from lowest outside edge of burr over outer curve to the most distant point of what is, or appears to be, the main beam. The point of beginning is that point on the
burr where the center line along the outer curve of the beam intersects the burr.

F-1-2-3. Length of Points are measured from nearest edge of beam on the shortest line over outer
curve to tip. Lay the tape along the outer curve of the beam so that the top edge of the tape coincides with the top edge of the beam on both sides of the points to determine baseline for point
measurement. Record point lengths in appropriate blanks.

F-4-5. Length of points are measured from the tip of the point to the top of the beam, then at a
right angle to the lower edge of beam. The Second Longest Top Point cannot be a point branch of the
Longest Top Point.

G-1. Width of Brow is measured in a straight line from top edge to lower edge, as illustrated, with
measurement line at a right angle to main axis of brow.

G-2. Width of Top Palm is measured from midpoint of lower rear edge of main beam to midpoint of a
dip between points, at widest part of palm. The line of measurement begins and ends at mid-points of
palm edges, which gives credit for palm thickness.

H-1-2-3-4. Circumferences are taken as described for measurements. If rear point is missing, take
H-2 and H-3 measurements at smallest place between bez and first top point.
* * * * * * * * * * *

FAIR CHASE STATEMENT FOR ALL HUNTER-TAKEN TROPHIES

To make use of the following methods shall be deemed as UNFAIR CHASE and unsportsmanlike, and any
trophy obtained by use of such means is disqualified from entry for Awards.

    I.   Spotting or herding game from the air, followed by landing in its vicinity
         for pursuit;
    II. Herding or pursuing game with motor-powered vehicles;
    III. Use of electronic communications for attracting, locating or observing
         game, or guiding the hunter to such game;
    IV. Hunting game confined by artificial barriers, including escape-proof fencing;
         or hunting game transplanted solely for the purpose of commercial shooting.
    ****

I certify that the trophy scored on this chart was not taken in UNFAIR CHASE as defined above by the
Boone and Crockett Club. I further certify that it was taken in full compliance with local game laws
of the state, province, or territory.
Date_____Signature of Hunter_____
(Have signature notarized by a Notary Public)

OFFICIAL SCORING SYSTEM FOR NORTH AMERICAN BIG GAME TROPHIES

Records of North American
Big Game

BOONE AND CROCKETT CLUB

205 South Patrick Street
Alexandria, Virginia 22314

Minimum Score: 82

PRONGHORN

SEE OTHER SIDE FOR INSTRUCTIONS		Column 1	Column 2	Column 3
A. Tip to Tip Spread	6 5/8	Right Horn	Left Horn	Difference
B. Inside Spread of Main Beams	10 1/8			
IF inside Spread exceeds longer horn, enter difference.				
C. Length of Horn		18 1/8	18 2/8	1/8
D-1. Circumference of Base		7 2/8	7	2/8
D-2. Circumference at First Quarter		7 5/8	7 4/8	1/8
D-3. Circumference at Second Quarter		4 1/8	4	1/8
D-4. Circumference at Third Quarter		2 5/8	2 6/8	1/8
E. Length of Prong		7 6/8	7 2/8	4/8
TOTALS		47 4/8	46 6/8	1 2/8

ADD	Column 1	47 4/8	Exact locality where killed Williamson Valley, Arizona
	Column 2	46 6/8	Date killed 21Sep75 By whom killed Edwin L. Wetzler
	Total	94 2/8	Present owner Edwin L. Wetzler
SUBTRACT Column 3		1 2/8	Address
FINAL SCORE		93	Guide's Name and Address
			Remarks: (Mention any abnormalities or unique qualities)

I certify that I have measured the above trophy on 8 June   19 77
at (address) 6060 Broadway   City Denver   State Colorado
and that these measurements and data are, to the best of my knowledge and belief, made in
accordance with the instructions given.

Witness: __B. A. Fashingbauer_____ Signature: __Scott M. Showalter__
                                                    Official Measurer

All measurements must be made with a ¼-inch flexible steel tape to the nearest one-eighth of an inch. Wherever it is necessary to change direction of measurement, make a control point and swing tape at this point. Enter fractional figures in eighths, without reduction. Official measurements cannot be taken for at least sixty days after the animal was killed.

A. Tip to Tip Spread is measured between tips of horns.

B. Inside Spread of Main Beams is measured at a right angle to the center line of the skull, at widest point between main beams.

C. Length of horn is measured on the outside curve on the general line illustrated. The line taken will vary with different heads, depending on the direction of their curvature. Measure along the center of the outer curve from tip of horn to a point in line with the lowest edge of the base, using a straight edge to establish the line end.

D-1. Measure around base of horn at a right angle to long axis. Tape must be in contact with the lowest circumference of the horn in which there are no serrations.

D-2-3-4. Divide measurement of longer horn by four. Starting at base, mark both horns at these quarters (even though other horn is shorter) and measure circumferences at these marks. If the prong interferes with D-2, move the measurement down to just below the swelling of the prong. If the prong interferes with D-3, move the measurement up to just above the swelling of the prong.

E. Length of Prong- Measure from the tip of the prong along the upper edge of the outer curve to the horn; then continue around the horn to a point at the rear of the horn where a straight edge across the back of both horns touches the horn, with the latter part being at a right angle to the long axis of horn.

* * * * * * * * * * * * *

FAIR CHASE STATEMENT FOR ALL HUNTER-TAKEN TROPHIES

To make use of the following methods shall be deemed as UNFAIR CHASE and unsportmanlike, and any trophy obtained by use of such means is disqualified from entry for Awards.
   I.   Spotting or herding game from the air, followed by landing in its vicinity for pursuit;
   II. Herding or pursuing game with motor-powered vehicles;
   III. Use of electronic communications for attracting, locating or observing game, or guiding the hunter to such game;
   IV. Hunting game confined by artificial barriers, including escape-proof fencing; or hunting game transplanted solely for the purpose of commercial shooting.

I certify that the trophy scored on this chart was not taken in UNFAIR CHASE as defined above by the Boone and Crockett Club. I further certify that it was taken in full compliance with local game laws of the state, province, or territory.
Date_____   Signature of Hunter _____
(Have signature notarized by a Notary Public)

Records of North American
Big Game

BOONE AND CROCKETT CLUB

205 South Patrick Street
Alexandria, Virginia 22314

Minimum Score: 115

BISON

Sex male

SEE OTHER SIDE FOR INSTRUCTIONS		Column 1	Column 2	Column 3
A. Greatest Spread	35 3/8	Right	Left	
B. Tip to Tip Spread	27	Horn	Horn	Difference
C. Length of Horn		21 2/8	23 2/8	2
D-1. Circumference of Base		16	15	1
D-2. Circumference at First Quarter		13 4/8	13	4/8
D-3. Circumference at Second Quarter		11 4/8	11	4/8
D-4. Circumference at Third Quarter		8 2/8	8	2/8
TOTALS		70 4/8	70 2/8	4 2/8

ADD	Column 1	70 4/8	Exact locality where killed Yellowstone Natl. Park, WY
	Column 2	70 2/8	Date killed 1925 By whom killed S. Woodring
	Total	140 6/8	Present owner Fishing Bridge Museum
SUBTRACT Column 3		4 2/8	Address
FINAL SCORE		136 4/8	Guide's Name and Address
			Remarks: (Mention any abnormalities or unique qualities)

I certify that I have measured the above trophy on 24 Sept. 19 51
at (address) Yellowstone National Park   City   State WY
and that these measurements and data are, to the best of my knowledge and belief, made in
accordance with the instructions given.

Witness: _____   Signature: Grancel Fitz
                                                          Official Measurer

INSTRUCTIONS FOR MEASURING BISON

All measurements must be made with a ¼-inch flexible steel tape to the nearest one-eighth of an inch. Wherever it is necessary to change direction of measurement, mark a control point and swing tape at this point. Enter fractional figures in eighths, without reduction. Official measurements cannot be taken for at least sixty days after the animal was killed.

A. Greatest Spread is measured between perpendicular at a right angle to the center line of the skull.

B. Tip to Tip Spread is measured between tips of horns.

C. Length of Horn is measured from lowest point on under side over outer curve to a point in line with tip. Use a straight edge, perpendicular to horn axis, to end the measurement, if necessary.

D-1. Circumference of Base is measured at a right angle to axis of horn. Do not follow the irregular edge of horn; the line of measurement must be entirely on horn material, not the jagged edge often noted.

D-2-3-4. Divide measurement C of longer horn by four. Starting at base, mark both horns at these quarters (even though the other horn is shorter) and measure circumferences at these marks, with measurements taken at right angles to horn axis.

* * * * * * * * * * * * *

FAIR CHASE STATEMENT FOR ALL HUNTER-TAKEN TROPHIES

To make use of the following methods shall be deemed as UNFAIR CHASE and unsportmanlike, and any trophy obtained by use of such means is disqualified from entry for Awards.
   I.   Spotting or herding game from the air, followed by landing in its vicinity for pursuit;
   II. Herding or pursuing game with motor-powered vehicles;
   III. Use of electronic communications for attracting, locating or observing game, or guiding the hunter to such game;
   IV. Hunting game confined by artificial barriers, including escape-proof fencing; or hunting game transplanted solely for the purpose of commercial shooting.

I certify that the trophy scored on this chart was not taken in UNFAIR CHASE as defined above by the Boone and Crockett Club. I further certify that it was taken in full compliance with local game laws of the state, province, or territory.
Date_____   Signature of Hunter_____
(Have signature notarized by a Notary Public)

Records of North American
Big Game

BOONE AND CROCKETT CLUB

205 South Patrick Street
Alexandria, Virginia 22314

Minimum Score: 50   ROCKY MOUNTAIN GOAT   Sex ___male___

SEE OTHER SIDE FOR INSTRUCTIONS			Column 1	Column 2	Column 3
A. Greatest Spread		9 2/8	Right Horn	Left Horn	
B. Tip to Tip Spread		9			Difference
C. Length of Horn			12	12	
D-1. Circumference of Base			6 4/8	6 4/8	
D-2. Circumference at First Quarter			4 7/8	4 6/8	1/8
D-3. Circumference at Second Quarter			3 2/8	3 1/8	1/8
D-4. Circumference at Third Quarter			2	2	
TOTALS			28 5/8	28 3/8	2/8

	Column 1	28 5/8	Exact locality where killed Babine Mountains, B.C.
ADD	Column 2	28 3/8	Date killed 1949 By whom killed E. C. Haase
	Total	57	Present owner E. C. Haase
SUBTRACT	Column 3	2/8	Address
FINAL SCORE		56 6/8	Guide's Name and Address Allen Fletchers
			Remarks: (Mention any abnormalities or unique qualities)

I certify that I have measured the above trophy on 28 Jan. ɪ9 50
at (address) Am. Museum Nat. History   City New York   State New York
and that these measurements and data are, to the best of my knowledge and belief, made in
accordance with the instructions given.

Witness: ___Samuel B. Webb___ ___ Signature: ___Grancel Fitz___
                                                      Official Measurer

404

INSTRUCTIONS FOR MEASURING ROCKY MOUNTAIN GOAT

All measurements must be made with a ¼-inch flexible steel tape to the nearest one-eighth of an inch. Wherever it is necessary to change direction of measurement, mark a control point and swing tape at this point. Enter fractional figures in <u>eighths</u>, without reductions. Measurements are most accurately taken <u>before</u> mounting of the trophy. Official measurements cannot be taken for at least sixty days after the animal was killed.

A. Greatest Spread is measured between perpendiculars at a right angle to the center line of the skull.

B. Tip to Tip Spread is measured between tips of horns.

C. Length of Horn is measured from lowest point in front over outer curve to a point in line with tip.

D-1. Circumference of Base is measured at a right angle to axis of horn. DO NOT follow irregular edge of horn.

D-2-3-4. Divide measurement C of longer horn by four. Starting at base, mark <u>both</u> horns at these quarters (even though other horn is shorter) and measure circumferences at these marks.

* * * * * * * * * * * * *

FAIR CHASE STATEMENT FOR ALL HUNTER-TAKEN TROPHIES

To make use of the following methods shall be deemed as UNFAIR CHASE and unsportmanlike, and any trophy obtained by use of such means is disqualified from entry for Awards.
   I.   Spotting or herding game from the air, followed by landing in its vicinity for pursuit;
   II.   Herding or pursuing game with motor-powered vehicles;
   III. Use of electronic communications for attracting, locating or observing game, or guiding the hunter to such game;
   IV.   Hunting game confined by artificial barriers, including escape-proof fencing; or hunting game transplanted solely for the purpose of commercial shooting.

I certify that the trophy scored on this chart was not taken in UNFAIR CHASE as defined above by the Boone and Crockett Club. I further certify that it was taken in full compliance with local game laws of the state, province, or territory.
Date_____   Signature of Hunter_____
(Have signature notarized by a Notary Public)

Records of North American
Big Game

BOONE AND CROCKETT CLUB

205 South Patrick Street
Alexandria, Virginia 22314

Minimum Score: 90

<u>MUSKOX</u>

Sex __male__

SEE OTHER SIDE FOR INSTRUCTIONS		Column 1	Column 2	Column 3
A. Greatest Spread	30 5/8	Right	Left	
B. Tip to Tip Spread	30 3/8	Horn	Horn	Difference
C. Length of Horn		29	28 1/8	7/8
D-1. Width of Boss		10	9 7/8	1/8
D-2. Width at First Quarter		7	6 3/8	5/8
D-3. Circumference at Second Quarter		12 1/8	10 6/8	1 3/8
D-4. Circumference at Third Quarter		6 5/8	5 7/8	6/8
TOTALS		64 6/8	61	3 6/8

ADD	Column 1	64 6/8	Exact locality where killed Perry River, N.W.T., Canada
	Column 2	61	Date killed 1979 By whom killed Picked up
	Total	125 6/8	Present owner Robert J. Decker
SUBTRACT Column 3		3 6/8	Address
FINAL SCORE		122	Guide's Name and Address
			Remarks: (Mention any abnormalities or unique qualities)

I certify that I have measured the above trophy on 12 March 19 80
at (address) Missouri Dept. of Cons.   City Jefferson City State Missouri
and that these measurements and data are, to the best of my knowledge and belief, made in
accordance with the instructions given.

Witness: __Philip L. Wright_____ Signature: __Frank Cook_____

Official Measurer

INSTRUCTIONS FOR MEASURING MUSKOX

All measurements must be made with a ¼-inch flexible steel tape and adjustable calipers to the nearest one-eighth of an inch. Whenever it is necessary to change direction of measurement, mark a control point and swing tape at this point. Enter fractional figures in eighths, without reduction. Official measurements cannot be taken for at least sixty days after the animal was killed.

A. Greatest Spread is measured between perpendiculars at a right angle to the center line of the skull.

B. Tip to Tip Spread is measured between tips of horns by using large calipers, which are then read against a yardstick.

C. Length of Horn is measured along center of upper horn surface, staying within curve of horn as illustrated, to a point in line with tip. Attempt to free the connective tissue between the horns at the center of the boss to determine the lowest point of horn material on each side, near the top center of the skull. Hook the tape under the lowest point of the horn and measure the length of horn, with the measurement line maintained in the center of the upper surface of horn following the converging lines to the horn tip.

D-1. Width of Boss is measured with calipers at greatest width of base, with measurement line forming a right angle with horn axis. It is often helpful to measure D-1 before C, marking the midpoint of the boss as the correct path of C.

D-2-3-4. Divide measurement C of longer horn by four. Starting at base, mark both horns at these quarters (even though other horn is shorter). Then, using calipers, measure width of boss at D-2, making sure the measurement is at a right angle to horn axis and in line with the D-2 mark. Circumferences are then measured at D-3 and D-4, with measurements being taken at right angles to horn axis.

* * * * * * * * * * * * *

FAIR CHASE STATEMENT FOR ALL HUNTER-TAKEN TROPHIES

To make use of the following methods shall be deemed as UNFAIR CHASE and unsportsmanlike, and any trophy obtained by use of such means is disqualified from entry for Awards.
  I. Spotting or herding game from the air, followed by landing in its vicinity for pursuit;
  II. Herding or pursuing game with motor-powered vehicles;
  III. Use of electronic communications for attracting, locating or observing game, or guiding the hunter to such game;
  IV. Hunting game confined by artificial barriers, including escape-proof fencing; or hunting game transplanted solely for the purpose of commercial shooting.

I certify that the trophy scored on this chart was not taken in UNFAIR CHASE as defined above by the Boone and Crockett Club. I further certify that it was taken in full compliance with local game laws of the state, province, or territory.
Date_____ Signature of Hunter_____
(Have signature notarized by a Notary Public)

OFFICIAL SCORING SYSTEM FOR NORTH AMERICAN BIG GAME TROPHIES

Records of North American
Big Game

BOONE AND CROCKETT CLUB

205 South Patrick Street
Alexandria, Virginia 22314

Minimum Score:
bighorn   180
desert   168
Stone   170
white or Dall 170

SHEEP

Kind of Sheep Stone

MEASURE TO
A POINT IN
LINE WITH
HORN TIP

SEE OTHER SIDE FOR INSTRUCTIONS		Column 1	Column 2	Column 3
A. Greatest Spread (Is often Tip to Tip Spread)	31	Right	Left	
B. Tip to Tip Spread	31	Horn	Horn	Difference
C. Length of Horn		50 1/8	51 5/8	
D-1. Circumference of Base		14 6/8	14 6/8	
D-2. Circumference at First Quarter		14 1/8	14 2/8	1/8
D-3. Circumference at Second Quarter		11 7/8	12 1/8	2/8
D-4. Circumference at Third Quarter		6 6/8	7	2/8
TOTALS		97 5/8	99 6/8	5/8

	Column 1	97 5/8	Exact locality where killed Muskwa River, B. C.
ADD	Column 2	99 6/8	Date killed 1936 By whom killed L. S. Chadwick
	TOTAL	197 3/8	Present owner National Collection
SUBTRACT Column 3		5/8	Address
FINAL SCORE		196 6/8	Guide's Name and Address
			Remarks: (Mention any abnormalities or unique qualities)

I certify that I have measured the above trophy on 10 April 1951
at (address) Am. Museum Nat. History   City New York   State New York
and that these measurements and data are, to the best of my knowledge and belief, made in
accordance with the instructions given.

Witness: Samuel B. Webb   Signature: Grancel Fitz
                                                          Official Measurer

INSTRUCTIONS FOR MEASURING SHEEP

All measurements must be made with a ¼-inch flexible steel tape to the nearest one-eighth of an inch. Wherever it is necessary to change direction of measurement, mark a control point and swing tape at this point. Enter fractional figures in eighths, without reduction. Official measurements cannot be taken for at least sixty days after the animal was killed.

A. Greatest Spread is measured between perpendiculars at a right angle to the center line of the skull.

B. Tip to Tip Spread is measured between tips of horns.

C. Length of Horn is measured from the lowest point in front on outer curve to a point in line with tip. Do not press tape into depressions. The low point of the outer curve of the horn is considered to be the low point of the frontal portion of the horn, situated above and slightly medial to the eye socket, (not the outside edge). Use a straight edge, perpendicular to horn axis, to end measurement on "broomed" horns.

D-1. Circumference of Base is measured at a right angle to axis of horn. Do not follow irregular edge of horn; the line of measurement must be entirely on horn material, not the jagged edge often noted.

D-2-3-4. Divide measurement C of longer horn by four. Starting at base, mark both horns at these quarters (even though the other horn is shorter) and measure circumferences at these marks, with measurements taken at right angles to horn axis.

* * * * * * * * * * * * *

FAIR CHASE STATEMENT FOR ALL HUNTER-TAKEN TROPHIES

To make use of the following methods shall be deemed as UNFAIR CHASE and unsportmanlike, and any trophy obtained by use of such means is disqualified from entry for Awards.
  I. Spotting or herding game from the air, followed by landing in its vicinity for pursuit;
  II. Herding or pursuing game with motor-powered vehicles;
  III. Use of electronic communications for attracting, locating or observing game, or guiding the hunter to such game;
  IV. Hunting game confined by artificial barriers, including escape-proof fencing; or hunting game transplanted solely for the purpose of commercial shooting.

I certify that the trophy scored on this chart was not taken in UNFAIR CHASE as defined above by the Boone and Crockett Club. I further certify that it was taken in full compliance with local game laws of the state, province, or territory.
Date_____ Signature of Hunter_____
(Have signature notarized by a Notary Public)